The Cabling Handbook

Second Edition

John R. Vacca

Prentice Hall PTR
Upper Saddle River, NJ 07458
www.phptr.com

ISBN 0-1
D1365581
883179

Library of Congress Cataloging-in-Publication Data

Vacca, John R.
 The cabling handbook / John Vacca.--2nd ed.
  p. cm.
 Includes bibliographical references and index.
 ISBN 0-13-088317-4
 1. Telecommunication wiring--Handbooks, manuals, etc. 2. Telecommunication
cables--Handbooks, manuals, etc. 3. Computer networks--Handbooks, manuals, etc. I. Title

TK5103.12.V33 2000
621.382--dc21   00-065276

Editorial/Production Supervision: *MetroVoice Publishing Services*
Acquisitions Editor: *Mary Franz*
Editorial Assistant: *Noreen Regina*
Marketing Manager: *Dan DePasquale*
Cover Design: *Nina Scuderi*
Cover Design Direction: *Jerry Votta*
Manufacturing Manager: *Alexis R. Heydt*
Buyer: *Maura Zaldivar*

© 2001 Prentice Hall PTR
Prentice-Hall, Inc.
Upper Saddle River, NJ 07458

Prentice Hall books are widely used by corporations and government agencies for training, marketing, and resale.

The publisher offers discounts on this book when ordered in bulk quantities.
For more information, contact Corporate Sales Department, phone: 800-382-3419;
fax: 201-236-7141; e-mail: corpsales@prenhall.com
Or write: Prentice Hall PTR
    Corporate Sales Department
    One Lake Street
    Upper Saddle River, NJ 07458

Printed in the United States of America
10 9 8 7 6 5 4 3 2 1

ISBN 0-13-088317-4

Prentice-Hall International (UK) Limited, *London*
Prentice-Hall of Australia Pty. Limited, *Sydney*
Prentice-Hall Canada Inc., *Toronto*
Prentice-Hall Hispanoamericana, S.A., *Mexico*
Prentice-Hall of India Private Limited, *New Delhi*
Prentice-Hall of Japan, Inc., *Tokyo*
Pearson Education Asia Pte. Ltd.
Editora Prentice-Hall do Brasil, Ltda., *Rio de Janeiro*

*To David Lee for his invaluable support and friendship
and for changing my life by introducing me to Bee.*

Contents

2 Types of Networks   53

5 Types of Vendor and Third-Party Cabling Systems 227

PART II   *Designing Cabling Systems*

6   **Network Design Issues   303**

13   Specifying Fibers   555

17 OTDR: Optical Time Domain Reflectometer   663

18 Selecting Connectors and Splices   677

22 Implementation Plan Development 785

PART V   *Installation of the Cabling System*

23 Testing Techniques 807

25 Certification of System Performance 935

PART VI *Maintaining Cabling Systems*

26 **Ongoing Maintenance   967**

27 **Standards Development   985**

PART VII *Future Directions*

28   Cableless Connectivity: The Wireless Future   1019

29 The Networked House: A Brave New Home 1055

30 Summary, Conclusions, and Recommendations 1089

PART VIII   *Appendices*

E   EENET Interconnect Directory   1175

F   List of Top Cable Labeling Companies   1177

G   List of Top SCSI Companies   1179

H   List of Wireless LAN Products and Sites   1181

I   List of CCITT/ISO Standards   1189

Glossary   1193
Index   1281

Foreword

It is an incredibly exciting time for information technology (IT) professionals as well as for people that use computers for both business and pleasure. This excitement is driven through an increase in connectivity and a maturing of computer networks that enable access to a world of information resources and online entertainment. But too many people take for granted the veins of the computer network: the cabling that ties computer systems together and facilitates connectivity. Cabling is the last thing most IT staff want to think about and the thing that most computer users probably understand the least. Cabling, however, is an absolutely necessary element for successful connectivity.

Computer network cabling is not just wires. It is a properly designed, installed, and maintained system of many types of wires, connectors, and terminations that must be matched to their tasks, locations, and load requirements. Without good cabling even the best of computers will limp along and underperform. Without good cabling much of the money that is spent for connecting to high-speed networks is wasted. Without good cabling the interconnected computing resources of an organization can never be utilized to their maximum capabilities.

The complexities of cabling technology and the myriad of cabling standards frustrates IT people and the shear volume of what must be understood to achieve a good cabling system can be intimidating. The second edition of *The Cabling Handbook* is the essential guide to computer network cabling. The handbook provides an explanation to the ins and outs of cabling as well as the standards by which cabling must be installed in order to achieve maximum network performance—all in one easy-to-read volume. The handbook is useful for all types of IT professionals in all types and sizes of organizations.

Cabling systems must also grow and change. Technology will continue to change at a rapid pace, placing greater demands on cabling systems. Those organizations that already have cabling in place will likely face an upgrade during the next few years in order to take advantage of new broadband applications. Organizations that are moving into new facilities and those that are expanding their existing facilities also face evolving cabling requirements. *The Cabling Handbook* should be on the buy, read, and use lists of all of the IT professionals that are planning for system upgrades, network expansions, or business relocation. The handbook will quickly bring IT professionals up to speed on cabling technology and techniques and will serve as an incredible reference tool as new and expanded networks are planned, designed, and installed.

Technology, organization size, and physical locations are not the only things that change in the life of IT professionals—careers also change. To move through an IT career and especially to move into management positions, IT professionals need a well-rounded knowledge of computing and communications technology. *The Cabling Handbook* can give the fast-moving IT professional an incredible competitive edge. Cabling is the last thing most IT staff want to think about, but to manage a data center or IT operation IT professionals must understand cabling requirements, systems, and standards.

It is also advisable for the young IT professional or IT student to get a good grasp on cabling early in their career. *The Cabling Handbook* can help young professionals achieve a necessary understanding of cabling because it is well organized, easy to read, and comprehensive in its coverage of cabling technologies. It is also not likely that students will find a good cabling course at a university or technical school, which makes *The Cabling Handbook* even more important to a well-rounded education.

Education requirements for IT careers are also changing rapidly. Higher education institutions are retooling curriculums to meet the demands of the information age. However, too few university programs have strong computer networking courses in their curriculum and most totally overlook the science of cabling. *The Cabling Handbook* is an off-the-shelf cabling course for colleges or technical schools. This means two things. First, *The Cabling Handbook* makes it incredibly easy for schools to offer courses because the handbook is comprehensive, easy to read, and makes cabling principles easy to learn. Second, *The Cabling Handbook* takes away the excuse that a university or college can't offer a course because there isn't an adequate textbook.

John Vacca has done an excellent job on the second edition of *The Cabling Handbook,* just as he did on the first edition. The second edition is expanded and provides coverage of new and emerging technologies and it addresses high-speed network and WAN connectivity issues and methods in greater depth. *The Cabling Handbook* has evolved from a book into a valuable professional and learning asset. *The Cabling Handbook* will benefit all who use it to learn or to teach.

—Michael Erbschloe
Vice President of Research, Computer Economics
Carlsbad, CA

Introduction

The cabling industry is becoming a full-service provider as it evolves its infrastructure into an all-digital superhighway. Both the telephone and computer industries are suggesting that their networking models—traditional point-to-point and extended distributed local area network (LAN) and wide area network (WAN) technology—become part of the cable industry solution. Cable is creating the multimedia networking model solution for the next millennium as a full-service provider through its migration to higher speed bandwidths.

MIGRATING TO HIGH-BANDWIDTH CABLING SOLUTIONS

Network cabling may not always be the first thing mentioned in the marketing literature for high-speed LAN technologies, but it certainly is the first thing considered by experts contemplating a migration to high-speed bandwidth solutions. That's why, according to recent cable industry research studies and cabling professionals, many large companies are turning to wiring such as category 5e copper cable and multimode fiber. Furthermore, such cabling is becoming more prevalent for desktop connections.

The push to upgrade both backbone and desktop wiring is indicative of the fear IT managers have that older cabling will not be able to handle next-generation technologies such as ATM and fast Ethernet. This migration is calling into question the value of 25 Mbps ATM and fast-Ethernet technology designed to run over the old category 3 cable.

Category 5e is now the most dominant form of cabling for large installations, and multimode fiber is the most popular medium for vertical connections between floors and buildings in those organizations. Experts in the cabling industry say that massive category 5e upgrades are indeed under way to prepare for future technologies. Most cabling experts agree that when faced with a choice between category 3 and category 5e copper, most people find category 5e worth the extra cost, mostly because the cost of the cable itself is trivial in comparison with installation costs, so one might as well go to category 5e. Cable industry experts have also found that many of the companies that are planning cable changes are also putting fiber in at the desktop level. A lot of people are installing category 5e and fiber to prepare for the future.

The primary application driving the desire for greater bandwidth, cable industry analysts found, was desktop video conferencing. Sixty-five percent of the large organizations surveyed said they planned to implement desktop video conferencing. In the long run, video conferencing is much cheaper than travel. Nevertheless, although big companies are bulking up on category 5e, technology vendors continue to tout the potential to run high-speed bandwidth applications over category 5e's older sibling, category 3. Naturally, that's because of the huge installed base of category 3.

Members of the ATM25 Alliance claim that 25 Mbps ATM can run over category 3 cabling, but implementations of such technology are hard to find. Concerns such as these are driving IT managers to update their cable plants. But as long as copper remains the predominant cable source, testing problems will continue to occur. Because of the difficulty in testing category 5e (caused mostly by the connections between cable segments), networks will still experience cable-related problems—although technology is minimizing cable-related problems. In other words, testing category 5e is a real problem and there is virtually no way to certify a cable installation.

Furthermore, despite the number of industry standard tests (TIA Cat 5, 5E, 6, 7; ISO/IEC Class C, D, E, F; etc.), other groups and organizations have needs for test limits that differ from the standards. This includes vendors that tailor test limits to a particular connection system or organizations that require performance that exceeds standards.

Eventually we're all going to go to fiber optic, optical systems, or wireless anyway. So, can widening the fiber highway or optical systems through wave division multiplexing deliver the bandwidth promise?

WIDENING THE OPTICAL SYSTEMS HIGHWAY

Recent advances in wave division multiplexing (WDM) technology have offered the potential for the deployment of cost-effective, highly reliable, high-capacity fiber optic network solutions. This is particularly important since the sustained growth of increasingly bandwidth-hungry applications requires an unprecedented rate of fiber optic network expansion, and places increasing demands on network design and planning. Development of time division multiplexing (TDM) transport systems has reached a plateau and operators can no longer wait for technology, such as managed Synchronous Transfer Mode-64 (STM-64) transmission, to mature. As a result, operators are increasingly pursuing WDM solutions to address evolving capacity issues. Cost-benefit analysis, however, reveals that the deployment of currently available small-scale (four wavelength) stand-alone systems only makes sense in long-distance carrier networks—of the kind found in North America, for example. For European intraoperator networks, efficiencies only begin to be realized with 16 wavelength systems.

As a longer-term strategy, the creation of a high-capacity managed WDM network layer using optical add–drop multiplexers or wavelength routers is gaining acceptance in the formulation of future network architectures. The biggest challenge in implementing an all-optical fiber network will be in the delivery of an optical layer network management platform and the successful integration with existing synchronous digital hierarchy (SDH) network management systems. Most modern fiber optic networks today use time division multiplexing techniques to send data down the Physical layer. But, experts say, most TDM equipment utilizes only about 2 percent of the intrinsic capacity of fiber. Dense wavelength division multiplexing is a technology that allows multiple data streams to be simultaneously transmitted over a single fiber at data rates as high as the fiber plant will allow—typically 3.5 Gbps. The WDM approach multiplies the simple 3.5 Gbps system by up to 16 times. So a 16-channel system (with ITU-recommended channel-spacing) will support 50 Gbps in each direction over a fiber pair. Also under development are 50-channel systems that will support 200 Gbps—the equivalent of over 20 STM-64 transmitters.

Current WDM technology utilizes a composite optical signal carrying 4, 8, or 16 data streams, each transmitted on a distinct optical wavelength. Although WDM has been a known technology for years, its early application was restricted to providing two widely separated wavelengths. Only recently has the technology evolved to the point where parallel wavelengths can be densely packed and integrated into a transmission system with multiple, simultaneous, extremely high frequency signals in the 192 to 200 Terahertz (Thz) range. The 16-channel system in essence provides a virtual 16-fiber cable, with each frequency channel serving as a unique STM-16 carrier. The most common form of WDM uses a fiber pair—one for transmission and one for reception. The availability of precise demultiplexers and erbium-doped fiber amplifiers has allowed WDM with 8 and 16 channel counts to be commercially delivered. Incoming optic streams are split into individual wavelengths using a newly developed technique of embedding a component (known as a fiber Bragg grating) so that the refractive index of the core is permanently modified to allow only a specific wavelength to pass through. A series of such gratings are used to split the carrier into a required composite wave. The fiber gating creates a highly selective, narrow bandwidth filter that functions somewhat like a mirror and provides significantly greater wavelength selectivity than any other optical technology.

So, would wireless technology be any better?

WIRELESS WANs AND LANs

As school districts struggle with how to interconnect local area networks that they have in operation at various campuses to form a wide area network, one viable solution that is not well known is the use of wireless technology. Wireless network bridges to transmit data within or between buildings, using spread spectrum radio waves or infrared technologies or microwaves, can be used to connect LANs that are separated by as much as 50 miles. Many of the less powerful bridges, however, may be limited to a range of five to eight miles. These wireless links can provide data transfer rates from less than 1 Mbps to more than 10 Mbps. As one might expect, the greater the link distance capability, and the higher the data transfer rate, the more expensive the equipment. For example, a pair of bridges operating at a radio frequency of 900 MHz may cost over $9,000, provide a link distance of two to three miles, and transfer data at 1 Mbps. A 2.4 Ghz bridge might cost over $8,000, provide a reliable link over a distance of six to nine miles, and transfer data at 2 Mbps. On the other hand, a microwave link at 31 Ghz may provide a connection over 10 to 13 miles at 10 Mbps (full duplex) for an equipment cost of less than $60,000.

One really attractive feature of wireless connections, and their major advantage, is that there is a one-time cost for the equipment and installation. There are no recurring, ongoing monthly costs! Thus, when compared to connection options that have continuing monthly fees associated, the wireless solution quickly pays for itself.

The potential drawbacks to a wireless solution include environmental factors. Terrain may eliminate wireless as an option; intervening hills and tall buildings or trees can block the radio frequency (RF) signals. Terrestrial wireless RF technology (non-satellite-based) is referred to as line-of-sight. This means that the antennas on the wireless bridge units must be able to see each other. There must be no obstacles in the way to block or reflect the transmitted signals. Severe weather, such as torrential rains, can adversely affect signal transmission and temporarily down the link. Similarly, the link might be susceptible to other radio frequency interference. Dense fog could possibly be a problem for microwave links.

On the other hand, wireless broadband networks can solve the terrain problem via fixed satellite orbital patterns. Wireless broadband networks are *defined* as communication without wires over distance by the use of arbitrary codes. Modern examples include hand-held devices like pagers, smart phones, personal digital assistants (PDAs) and personal communication services (PCS) using wireless modems or satellites to enable wireless data communications.

The bottom line: Wireless connectivity must be seriously considered if the terrain allows its use or satellites are capable of receiving (uplink) and sending (downlink) high-speed data. Some reports indicate that microwave links can be more reliable than leased data lines. Furthermore, there are some major potential benefits to wireless solutions. For example, school district administrators could enter a conference room, turn on their laptop computers, and achieve high-speed connectivity to the district network. Teachers could sit down in the cafeteria with their notebooks and instantly update class schedules, grades, and attendance records in a centralized database. Students can take hand-held devices outside of the classroom, collect scientific data, and share their findings in real time with peers via the Internet.

Finally, as the price of technology drops and demand for next-generation applications rises, home cable networking is moving into a new phase of convenience and functionality. The reasons have everything to do with the phenomenal success of the Internet and the advent of the integrated digital home.

It's an exciting time for home networks. Multicomputer households are definitely on the rise as the power of the Web grows daily and new Internet-based applications and appliances are introduced. High-speed Internet access via DSL, cable, or satellite service is imminent if not already available in your area, unlocking the full capabilities of the Internet for home-based communications, education, commerce, entertainment, and more.

The integrated digital home will merge with what we now think of as separate application dimensions (security, music and video entertainment, telephone and fax, and computing devices) into one seamless environment. The key to that future is the development of the home gateway (a network device that translates between different types of networks or computer systems) with its ability to bridge these different systems so that they can communicate with one another.

Sound like a vision for the middle part of this century? Actually, all of these scenarios are taking place today thanks to recent advances in mobile computing and wireless technology. Already, wireless local area networks (WLANs) have extended, or replaced, traditional LANs in hundreds of educational sites, and many more IT managers are carefully examining the benefits of wireless solutions. Actually, the bottom line to all of this is that although the initial investment for WLAN hardware might be higher, long-term cost savings can be realized because technicians never need to pull wire through walls or ceilings to expand the network.

WHO THIS BOOK IS FOR

This book can be used by domestic and international system administrators, government computer security officials, network administrators, senior managers, engineers, sales engineers, marketing staff, Web developers, military senior top brass, network designers and technicians, cabling project managers, cable installers, LAN and PBX administrators, and other satellite communications personnel. In short, the book is targeted for all types of people and organizations around the globe who have responsibility for cabling decisions and/or project implementation, network cabling installation, cost justification and investments, and standards. Others who may find it useful are scientists, engineers, educators, top-level executives, information technology and department managers, technical staff, and the more than 800 million Internet, intranet, and extranet users around the world. Some previous experience with cabling installation is required.

WHAT'S SO SPECIAL ABOUT THIS BOOK?

The Cabling Handbook, Second Edition, is unique in its comprehensive coverage of network cabling installation, cost justification and investments, and the latest standards. The book is a thorough, up-to-the-minute professional's guide to every aspect of LAN and telecommunications cabling, from planning through installation and management. From category 5e twisted pair and fiber to the latest wireless LAN solutions, it's all here: standards, product comparisons, topology and architecture design, electrical and safety considerations, and more—including invaluable information for anyone preparing for CompTIA Network+ certification. This brand-new second edition has been updated with extensive new coverage of fiber technologies, home networking, cable modems, and much more. Key features include:

- Intermediate- to advanced-level instruction to help you install the latest copper, fiber, and wireless network cabling systems.
- Practical tips on cost-justifying your cabling investments.
- Tips on how to manage contractor/client relationships.
- Extensive coverage of how to certify cabling system requirements performance to 100 Mbit/second and beyond.
- Discussion of the latest LAN design issues: optimal use in structured cabling systems; how to drive a project from design to certification; and how to ensure today's cable design supports emerging workgroup technologies.
- A thorough discussion of all of the latest national and international cabling standards.
- An installation section covering testing techniques, installation, and certification of system performance.
- Estimating the cost of cable plant upgrades.
- Choosing the right installer and supervising installation.
- Selecting the optimal cabling system and products.
- Deploying wireless LANs with maximum reliability, coverage, throughput, and security.
- Managing cable systems to minimize long-term costs and maximize long-term reliability.
- Troubleshooting cable system problems rapidly and effectively.

The book is organized into eight parts and includes appendices as well as an extensive glossary of network cabling terms and acronyms at the back. It provides a step-by-step approach to everything you need to know about network cabling as well as information about many topics relevant to the planning, design, and implementation of high-speed performance network cabling systems. The book gives an indepth overview of the latest structured cabling technology and emerging global standards. It discusses what background work needs to be done, such as developing a cabling technology plan, and shows how to develop network cabling plans for organizations and educational institutions. More importantly, this book shows how to install a network cabling system, along with the techniques used to test the system, as well as the certification of system performance. It covers many of the common pieces of network cabling equipment used in the maintenance of the system, as well as the ongoing maintenance issues. The book concludes with a discussion about future planning, standards development, and the cabling industry.

Part I: Overview of Cabling Technology

In this part of the book, the three cabling media (copper, fiber, and wireless) are discussed, followed by a discussion about the six major types of networks: local area network (LAN), wide area network (WAN), virtual area network (VAN), virtual private network (VPN), intranet, extranet, and Internet. Some companies are fortunate to have all six types connecting their systems. Next, we'll examine how all three cabling media can be used with one or all six of the network types to allow your organization to soar beyond the traditional constraints of network cabling. You'll be shown how and when to expand, contract, or redeploy your network type(s) virtually anywhere, anytime, as quickly as today's accelerating pace of change demands. Next, an indepth discussion of the various cabling standards (TIA/EIA568A, ISO/IEC 11801, IEEE 802.x, FDDI, ISDN, LATM, etc.) is presented. Part I reaches its climax with an indepth presentation of the current state of cable modem access versus DSL. It also examines how prevalent cable modem and DSL services are in major U.S. markets. A comparison of the two technologies with regard to speed, cost, and so on, are presented. It also covers the planning implications or considerations for the enterprise network manager (for example, to support telecommuting employees, etc.) and the N+ certification audience. In addition, Part I will take a close look at DSL; cable modems; ADSL; CDSL; G.Lite; HDSL; IDSL; RADSL; SDSL; VDSL; POTS; DSL and cable modem rollouts; high-speed data entry; buying DSL service; installing DSL; security problems, residential users, telecommuters, DSL system components; DSL networks; and DSL hubs. Finally, Part I discusses future directions for cable modems and DSL and concludes by taking a close look at some third-party vendor cabling systems: AT&T (Lucent) Systimax and Powersum, IBM Cabling System, DECconnect, Northern Telecom IBDN, AMP Connect, KRONE, Mod-Tap, BCS, ITT, IBCS, and so on.

Part II: Designing Cabling Systems

Part II begins by giving an overview of network design issues and how they can help you design and install a better cabling system. Next, it discusses the various category 5 structured wiring components and how they all fit together. Part II also discusses a more proactive approach to cost justification issues, with regard to how fiber's higher cost is compensated or countered by UTP's more troubled implementations and downtime. It provides an overview of the various aspects of cabling system standards design issues and of cabling system architectural design considerations (structured cabling system, wiring closet design, cabling facilities, and user-to-outlet ratios). Additionally, Part II discusses copper design considerations (layout, components, connectors, and shielding and maintenance). It concludes with a discussion of wireless design considerations (spread spectrum, microwave, infrared, wireless WANs and LANs, etc.).

Part III: Fiber-Optic Systems: A Hands-On Approach

Part III opens up by taking a thorough look at fiber optic types and materials, with an emphasis in how fibers guide light; and how single-mode (SMF) and multimode fiber (MMF) are different. Next, it examines how to specify fibers by covering loss and attenuation of fibers; bandwidth, the capacity for information; and physical sizes of fiber. Part III also shows you how to use fiber optic transmitters and receivers by taking a close look at light sources and how to detect light with photodiodes. Next, it shows you how to design cable plants by examining indoor cable, outdoor cable, and how you would benefit from structured cabling options. In addition, Part III also discusses how to verify cable installations and provides you with testing tips and techniques to make verification seem less painful. It also shows you how to conduct acceptance testing and help you troubleshoot your fiber systems. Next, Part III examines optical time domain reflectometer (OTDR), and shows you how to test fiber paths with OTDR and interpret OTDR traces. It also shows you how to select connectors and splices by examining the quality factors, mechanical and fusion splices, and identify different types of connectors. Additionally, it shows you how to build connectors and splices by taking a look at practical fiber termination. Finally, Part III comes to a close with a look at the latest fiber optic cutting-edge technologies. It focuses on advanced fiber optic components such as fiber couplers, optical amplifiers, wavelength division multiplexers (WDM), and the advantages of specialty fibers.

Part IV: Planning for High-Speed Cabling Systems

Part IV covers high-speed real-time data compression and how to plan for higher-speed cabling systems. It also describes the development of the high-speed cabling system implementation plan (scheduling, analyzing site surveys, connectivity requirements, equipment, security, and performance).

Part V: Installing the Cabling System

This part begins by taking a look at the installation of the cabling system, starting with a presentation on testing techniques as part of preinstallation activities, including the preparation of cable facilities, testing the cable and components, and code compliance and safety considerations. Next, it describes in detail the installation of the cabling system and covers specific areas such as core drilling considerations; conduit installation and fill guidelines; grounding, shielding, and safety; pulling the cable without damage; splicing and patching; blown fiber; labeling schemes; and quality control and installation standards. Part V concludes by taking a close look at the following post-installation activities: cable fault detection with OTDR; cabling system troubleshooting and testing; copper and fiber optic loss testing; documenting the cabling system; cabling system performance certification; and accuracy levels testing as defined in Telecommunications System Bulletin (TSB) 67.

Part VI: Maintaining Cabling Systems

Opening up with a discussion on how to maintain your cabling system, this part examines the facilitation of ongoing cabling system maintenance by covering the building of the Cable Plant Management (CPM) database, vendor CPM products, and the EIA/TIA 606 standard. Part VI also examines future standards development (ATM, 300–600 Mhz cable systems [Category 6], zone wiring, TIA/EIA-T568-B, EN50174, 100BaseT2, 1000BaseT [Gigabit Ethernet, etc.]).

Part VII: Future Directions

Part VII opens up by taking a look at the future of wireless communications—cable-less connectivity. It also takes a look at home networking and how to connect to your home in the future. Finally, Part VII concludes by making recommendations and taking a peek at the cabling industry as it continues on its way to becoming a full information service provider in the beginning of this millennium via the ever changing cable specification process.

You'll find a glossary of network cabling-related terms at the end of the text.

Part VIII: Appendices

Nine appendices provide direction to additional resources available for cabling. Appendix A is a list of fiber channel products, organizations, vendors, and high-energy projects and applications. Appendix B is a list of top cable installation companies. Appendix C is a list of top fiber optic cable companies, and Appendix D is a Cabling Directory—an interactive buyer's guide for cabling products as well as for all cabling-related topics with direct links to each company's website. Appendix E is an EENET Interconnect Directory—a comprehensive listing of interconnect companies in different categories. Appendix F is a list of top cable labeling companies, Appendix G is a list of top SCSI companies, Appendix H is a list of wireless LAN products and sites, and Appendix I is a list of CCITT/ISO standards.

CONVENTIONS

This book has several conventions to help your way around and to help you find important facts, notes, cautions, and warnings:

- **Sidebars:** We use sidebars to highlight related information, give an example, discuss an item in greater detail, or help you make sense of the swirl of terms, acronyms, and abbreviations so abundant to this subject. The sidebars are meant to supplement each chapter's topic. If you're in a hurry on the a cover-to-cover read, skip the sidebars. If you're quickly flipping through the book looking for juicy information, read only the sidebars.
- **Notes:** A note highlights a special point of interest about the cabling topic.
- **Caution:** A caution tells you to watch your step to avoid any cabling-related problems (safety or security, etc.).
- **Warning:** A warning alerts you to the fact that a cabling-related problem is imminent or will probably occur (safety, security, etc.).

Acknowledgments

There are many people whose efforts on this book have contributed to its successful completion. I owe each a debt of gratitude and want to take this opportunity to offer my sincere thanks.

A very special thanks to my editor Mary Franz, without whose continued interest and support would not have made this book possible. Thanks also go to editorial assistant Noreen Regina, who provided staunch support and encouragement when it was most needed. Special thanks to my technical editor, Jorge Martinez, who ensured the technical accuracy of the book and whose expertise in cabling and telecommunications system technology was indispensable. Thanks to my production coordinator, Anne Trowbridge; project manager, Scott Suckling (MetroVoice); and copy editor, Laura Specht Patchkofsky, whose fine editorial work has been invaluable. Thanks also to my marketing manager, Dan DePasquale, whose efforts on this book have been greatly appreciated. Finally, thanks to all the other people at Prentice Hall whose many talents and skills are essential to a finished book.

Thanks to my wife, Bee Vacca, for her love, her help, and her understanding of my long work hours.

I wish to thank the organizations and individuals who granted me permission to use the research material and information necessary for the completion of this book.

Finally, a very special thanks to my publisher, Jeff Pepper, without whose initial interest and support would not have made this book possible and whose guidance and encouragement was over and above the business of being a publisher.

Overview of Cabling Technology

CHAPTER 1

Types of Cable and Hardware

As the demand for high-speed telecommunications increases across the globe, copper, fiber optic, and wireless systems are being deployed to fulfill the needs of telephone companies, cable TV companies, and businesses with high-speed LANs. The battle for supremacy between copper, fiber, and wireless systems in telecommunications and data communications continues to increase in complexity rather than becoming more clear. This has put serious pressure on the copper wire and cable industry, which has seen its market share decline steadily over the past decade as fiber and wireless systems take hold. A number of major copper cable suppliers have either pulled out of the copper cable business and embraced fiber optics or redesigned their organizations around adding value to traditional copper wire and cable products. This has provided market opportunities for some nimble market-oriented firms with lower manufacturing costs to enter niche markets.

The copper-based network equipment manufacturers continue to fight back, using recent developments in digital signal processing technology to extend the bandwidth and usefulness of copper cabling, in order to preserve both the embedded base of copper cabling and to retain market share for present and future installations. In the telephone network, asymmetric digital subscriber line (ADSL), high-bit-rate digital subscriber line (HDSL), and very-high-data-rate digital subscriber line (VDSL) technologies are delivering megabit speeds over the local loop, allowing for the delivery of high-speed Internet access, telecommuting, and eventually video services. For premises networks,100 Mbps (megabits per second) Ethernet equipment has quickly eclipsed fiber distributed data interface (FDDI) technology, and standards are underway for gigabit Ethernet and copper-based asynchronous transfer mode (ATM) LANs.

3

This chapter provides detailed assessments of competing cable types and hardware technologies and discusses cabling solutions for telecommunications and data networks with an emphasis on Network+ (N+) certification, which sets the stage for the rest of this book. Network+ is a new testing program from the Computing Technology Industry Association (CompTIA) [1]. Attaining Network+ certification indicates that the individual knows how to configure and install the TCP/IP client. In other words, N+ is substantially more than how to configure and install the TCP/IP client, it covers network topologies, technology, cable section, WANs, and so on.

Network+ is a new testing program intended to certify networking technicians with 18 to 24 months of experience. This certification is the logical next step for those who have already attained A+ certification. The point here is that this book is not an A+ or N+ specific certification study guide, but it does target N+ students and graduates. For further information on A+ and N+ certification, see the Introduction.

This chapter also describes the global copper cable market and briefly analyzes the effect of sweeping regulatory reforms standards. Finally, this chapter also provides major players in the fiber optics, copper cable, and wireless industry (copper wire manufacturers, copper wire companies seeking joint ventures or acquisitions, copper producers, telecommunications suppliers, telecommunications systems vendors, fiber optics manufacturers, networking equipment vendors, investors, consultants, long-range planners, strategic planners, and executives like presidents and CEOs) with a brief look at the range of strategies that can be pursued in order for them to remain competitive in this changing marketplace.

COPPER, FIBER, OR WIRELESS MEDIA: CHOOSE ONE

Perhaps your company thrives on copper cabling. Perhaps you're considering fiber optic alternatives. Or maybe you have problems that only a wireless LAN can solve.

Private network providers are often involved with providing systems to support future applications, while at the same time they're confronted with the seemingly contradictory objectives of lowering costs. Today, network providers are often faced with the question of whether to install an unshielded twisted pair (UTP) copper or multimode fiber cabling system or a wireless local area network (LAN) when searching for an answer to these objectives.

Unfortunately, this question does not have a clearly defined answer. In order to create the most cost-effective networks for voice, video, and data, most private networks require a mixture of all three media. UTP is unquestionably the right choice for traditional telephone and fax services. However, the answer is not as clear for data services. With rates from 100 to 155 Mbps, high performance Category 5 UTP provides the lowest initial cost for LANs. Nevertheless, recurring operational costs can be reduced by fiber-based networks. Furthermore, with wireless systems, you can bring 21st-century technology to older buildings without disturbing a single historic brick, go mobile for on-the-spot presentations, and even create instant extensions to an existing LAN anywhere in the building. These savings can, over time, far exceed the higher initial costs.

By definition, cable is the medium through which information usually moves from one network device to another. As previously mentioned, there are several types of cable media that are commonly used with LANs. In some cases, other networks will use a variety of cable media, while a network will utilize only one type of cable media. The type of cable media chosen for a network is related to the network's size, topology, and protocol. Therefore, what is necessary for the development of a successful network is an understanding of the characteristics of different types of cable media and how they relate to other aspects of a network.

The choice of media depends largely on the customer's present and future applications and business situations. A selection made without considering these fundamentals has little chance of providing the best solution. That is why it is important to understand not only the capabilities of each media, but also specific customer needs.

Overall, this chapter briefly examines the situation surrounding each of the cable media today and when and how to use them. The following sections discuss the types of cable media and hardware used in networks and other related topics.

COPPER MEDIA

If cost concerns are more critical than high bandwidth, you should consider a copper media cabling solution. There are two main reasons for the broad acceptance and rapid growth of copper media: low initial cost and the ability to deliver high data rate LAN services.

Copper media encompasses basically two major types of cable: unshielded twisted pair (UTP) and shielded twisted pair (STP). There is also a third type, coaxial cabling, which will also be discussed.

Unshielded Twisted Pair Cabling

Twisted pair cabling comes in two varieties: unshielded and shielded. Unshielded twisted pair (UTP) is the most popular and is generally the best option for school networks, as shown in Figure 1–1 [2].

UTP can support telephone, 4- and 16-megabyte per second (Mbps) token ring, Ethernet, 100 Mbps Ethernet, copper fiber distributed data interface (CFDDI), 155 Mbps asynchronous transfer mode (ATM), and is generally deployed as the cable of choice for many installations. UTP cable is rated by the Electronic Industry Association/Telecommunication Industry Association (EIA/TIA) standards into categories, which are shown in Table 1–1.

Currently the best value on pricing is Category 3 and Category 5. Category 3 is the low price choice for today's cable plant, and there are plans to support 100 Mbps over Category 3 cable by using all 4 pair (100BASE-T4, for example). The price gap between Category 4 and Category 5 is so small that most people are going right to Category 5.

You may hear of Level 5 cable. Underwriters Laboratories (UL) rates cable from Levels 1 to 5. Levels 3–5 correspond to Categories 3–5. UL Levels 1 and 2 are voice grade cable, not normally deployed with data transmission requirements.

UTP cable is generally wired in a star topology, with the troubleshooting advantages associated with stars. Although most of the topologies require only 2 pair (4 wires), the specific 2 pair used varies by network type (see Chapter 6, " Network Design Issues," for more information on topologies). Telephone requires only 1 pair for a single-line phone. Normal data network deployments are done with 4 pair cabling so that it will support any possible combination without requiring you to put new connectors or reterminate each connection if you change network types.

UTP quality may also vary from extremely high-speed cable to telephone-grade wire. Four pairs of cable wires exist inside the jacket. In order to help eliminate interference from adjacent pairs and other electrical devices,

Figure 1–1   Unshielded twisted pair.

each pair is twisted with a different number of twists per inch. As previously stated, the Electronic Industry Association/Telecommunication Industry Association (EIA/TIA) has also established standards of UTP and rated five categories of wire, as shown in Table 1–1. For further information on these UTP standards, see Chapter 3, "Standards."

Table 1–1   Categories of Unshielded Twisted Pair

Category	Use
1	Alarm systems, voice only (telephone wire), characteristics specified up to 0 (MHz) and other noncritical applications.
2	Voice, EIA-232, data to 4 Mbps (LocalTalk), characteristics specified up to 0 (MHz) and other low speed data.
3	10BaseT Ethernet, 4-Mbits/s token ring, 100BaseT4, 100VG-AnyLAN, basic rate ISDN, data to 10 Mbps (suitable for Ethernet) and characteristics specified (rated) up to 16 (MHz). Generally the minimum standard for new installations.
4	16-Mbits/s token ring. Not widely used, data to 20 Mbps (16 Mbps suitable for token ring) and characteristics specified up to 20 (MHz).
5	TP-PMD, SONet, OC-3 (ATM), 100BaseTX. The most popular for new data installations, data to 100 Mbps (suitable for Fast Ethernet) and characteristics specified up to 100 (MHz) and ATM (155 Mbps).

The tightness of the twisting of the copper pairs is one difference among the different categories of UTP shown in Table 1–1. The higher the supported transmission rate and greater cost per foot, the tighter the twisting. Buy the best cable you can afford. Most schools purchase Category 5 or Category 3. Category 5 cable comes highly recommended.

Remember, the Category 5 cable will provide more room to grow as transmission technologies increase—especially if you are designing a 10 Mbps Ethernet network and are considering the cost savings of buying Category 3 wire instead of Category 5. A maximum segment length of 100 meters exists in both Category 3 and Category 5 UTP. In most schools, Category 5 cable is required for retrofit grants. Also, the specifications for unshielded twisted pair cable (Category 3, 4, or 5) carrying Ethernet signals is referred to as 10BaseT, as shown in Table 1–2.

Unshielded Twisted Pair Connector

An RJ45 connector is the standard connector for unshielded twisted pair cabling. This is a large, plastic, telephone-style connector (Figure 1–2) [3]. The placement of a slot allows the RJ45 connector to be inserted only one way. RJ stands for registered jack. The implication here is that the connector follows a

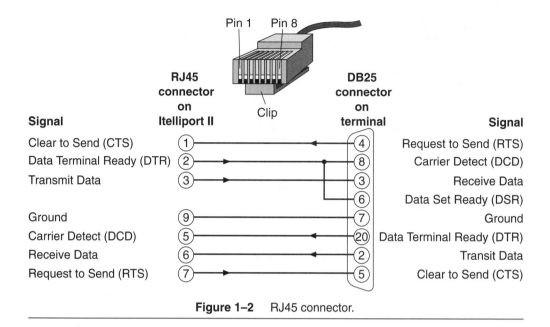

Figure 1–2   RJ45 connector.

standard borrowed from the telephone industry. Thus, which wire goes with each pin inside the connector is designated by this borrowed standard.

Shielded Twisted Pair

STP has come to mean two entirely different types of cable. The original STP cabling was proposed by IBM and was used for token ring networks. It sported a universal data connector (UDC), which was large and neither male nor female (the connectors could always plug into each other). The cable was bulky, and had a shield around each pair, plus a shield around all of the pairs. It was rated to 16 MHz. IBM called this Type 1 cable.

Type 1 STP cable really doesn't have much of a future except in IBM's token-ring shops, due to its low speed, bulkiness, connector size, and one-network support.

Recently, a new version of STP cable has been introduced. Instead of shielding around each pair, it has only one shield around the entire cable. This type of STP cabling uses an RJ45 connector with some metal on it so that the system can be grounded. It's not bulky, and it's easy to work with and terminate.

The jury is still out on whether or not this shielding is needed, but proponents say it will become critical as 155 Mbps signals are transmitted for ATM usage. Electromagnetic interference (EMI) tests show that STP cable radiates less signal than UTP cable. Overall, though, the new STP has all the advantages of UTP, and perhaps better signal carrying capability. While most technicians choose UTP for their installation, STP warrants a close watch.

In other words, a disadvantage of UTP is that it may be susceptible to radio and electrical frequency interference. Shielded twisted pair (STP), on the other hand, is suitable for environments with electrical interference. However, the extra shielding can make the cables quite bulky. Shielded twisted pair is often used on networks using token ring topology, the industry standard (Project 802.5 of the IEEE) that specifies protocols for connection and transmission in local area networks. As a media access method, it operates at layers 1 and 2 in the OSI (Open System Interconnection) model. Token ring transmits at 4 or 16 Mb/s.

A Comparison: STP Versus UTP

This section continues the debate of UTP versus STP, presenting an indepth comparison of the advantages and disadvantages of how and when to use cables and systems.

A debate has recently arisen on the advantages and disadvantages of unshielded twisted-pair (UTP) cable and shielded twisted-pair (STP) cable. Without adequately presenting both sides of the story, advocates of STP cable (a category that includes screened twisted-pair cable and foil twisted-pair cable) have attempted to claim that their product is superior to UTP cable. In order to provide reliable connectivity of electronic equipment, STP and UTP's purpose should still be the same, even though it is true that they are inherently different in design and manufacture. The true test comes when you look at the performance of each of these cable types within its respective end-to-end system, although, in theory, both types of cable should perform this task successfully.

In order to form a twisted pair, two copper wires, each encased in its own color-coded insulation, are twisted together. But, to form twisted-pair cable, multiple twisted pairs are packaged in an outer sheath, or jacket. The possibility of interference between pairs in the same cable sheath can be minimized by varying the length of the twists in nearby pairs.

Twisted-pair cable has been around for quite a while. In fact, early telephone signals were sent over a type of twisted-pair cable. Just about every building today still uses twisted-pair cable to carry telephone and other signals. Evolving from 1200 bps to over 100 Mbps, signals have become more complex over the years. Today, there are many more sources of interference that might disrupt those signals than there were at the turn of the century. Coaxial cable and fiber optic cable were developed to support emerging technologies and handle higher bandwidth applications. Now, high-data-rate signals can be carried because of the evolution of twisted-pair cable.

To reduce the potential for electromagnetic interference (EMI), some twisted-pair cables contain a metal shield. Signals from other sources such as electric motors, power lines, high-power radio, and radar signals cause EMI. If these signals are in the vicinity, they may cause disruptions or interference, called noise. Thus, STP cable encases the signal-carrying wires in a conducting shield. At first glance, it may appear that because STP cable is physically encased in a shield, all outside interference is automatically blocked. However, this is not true.

The shield acts as an antenna (just like a wire) when it has been properly grounded, converting received noise into current flowing in the shield. In turn, this current induces an opposite and equal current flowing in the twisted pairs. The two currents cancel each other out and deliver no net noise to the receiver as long as they are symmetrical. However, the current in the twisted pairs is interpreted as noise if any discontinuity in the shield or other asymmetry in the current in the shield exists. As long as the entire end-to-end link is shielded and properly grounded, STP cable is effective at preventing radiation or blocking interference. Every component of a shielded cabling system must be just that—fully shielded—in order to work properly.

STP cable also has drawbacks. For instance, STP cable's attenuation may increase at high frequencies. Also, STP cable's balance (or longitudinal conversion loss) may decrease if the effects of the shield are not compensated for (which leads to cross talk and signal noise). The shielding effectiveness depends on the material of the shield, its thickness, the type of EMI noise field, its frequency, the distance from the noise source to the shield, the grounding structure used, and any shield discontinuity. There's also no guarantee that the shield itself will contain no imperfections.

A thick, braided shield is used by some STP cables. Harder to install than their UTP counterparts, these cables are heavier and thicker. A relatively thin overall outer foil shield is also used by some STP cables. Thinner and less expensive than braided STP cable, these cables are also known as screened twisted-pair (ScTP) cables or foil twisted-pair (FTP) cables. However, they are not any easier to install. When these cables are installed, the minimum bending radius and maximum pulling tension force must be rigidly observed; otherwise, the shield may experience a tear.

On the other hand, UTP cable does not rely on physical shielding to block interference. But UTP does rely on balancing and filtering techniques through media filters and/or baluns. Noise is induced equally on two conductors. The noise then cancels out at the receiver. This technique is easier to maintain than the shielding continuity and grounding of an STP cable if the UTP cable has been properly designed and manufactured.

UTP cable has evolved over the years, with the result that there are different varieties of UTP cable available for different needs. Basic telephone cable (also known as direct-inside wire, or DIW) is still available. Improvements over the years (such as variations in the twists or in individual wire sheaths or overall cable jackets), have led to the development of EIA/TIA-568 standard-compliant Category 5 (for specifications on signal bandwidth up to 100 MHz and greater) UTP cable, Category 4 (for specifications on signal bandwidth up to 20 MHz), and Category 3 (for specifications on signal bandwidth up to 16 MHz). Millions of nodes have been and continue to be wired with UTP cable (even for high-data-rate applications), because UTP cable is lightweight, thin, and flexible, as well as versatile, reliable, and inexpensive. UTP cable should be used as part of a well-engineered structured cabling system for best performance.

STP Cabling Systems Versus UTP Cabling Systems

Overall signal quality will be degraded if STP cable is combined with improperly shielded connectors (connecting hardware or outlets, or if the foil shield itself is damaged). Also, degradation of emission and immunity performance can often result if the connectors are improperly shielded. Therefore, every component within the cabling system must be fully and seamlessly shielded, as well as properly installed and maintained for it to succeed totally in interference reduction.

An STP cabling system, likewise, requires good earthing and grounding practices. A primary source of emissions and interference can result if a system is improperly grounded. The frequency of the application dictates whether this ground is at one end or both ends of the cable run. At a minimum (for high-frequency signals), an STP cabling system must be grounded at both ends of the cable run, and, it must be continuous. There is no effect against magnetic field interference if a shield is grounded at one end. A source of problems can also be the length of the ground conductor itself. It no longer acts as a ground if it is too long. Therefore, since it depends on the application, optimum grounding for an STP cabling system is not possible. This problem does not exist with UTP cabling systems.

A UTP cabling system inherently has fewer points for potential failure and is easier to install. Moreover, an STP cabling system is dependent on such factors as physical continuity of the cable shield itself or installation with adequately shielded and grounded components.

EMC and STP Versus UTP Cabling Systems

Another factor to consider when choosing a cabling system relates to the recent adoption of the electromagnetic compatibility (EMC) directive. This directive is in addition to requirements for precision design and manufacture, as well as end-to-end integrity. EMC refers to the ability of an electronic system to function properly in its environment. This would be an environment where several pieces of equipment are located in the same workspace, each radiating electromagnetic emissions. EMC becomes increasingly more important here (with the existence of an increased amount of electronic equipment in the average workspace) as excess radiation from one piece of equipment can adversely affect performance of another piece of equipment. This means that every electronic system (which includes either an STP or UTP cabling system) must meet this directive.

EMC regulations have existed for years in some countries, such as the U.S. and Germany. However, attention on EMC has refocused since the implementation of the European EMC Directive in 1989. The European EMC Directive 89/336/EEC states that all electronic equipment and apparatus must comply with the directive. These systems must pass the essential requirements of the directive before they can be sold anywhere in the European Economic Area (EEA). Some national regulations (such as Amtsblatt Verfugung 243/91 of Germany) exempted STP-based systems from immunity testing. However, as of January 1, 1996, these national regulations no longer apply, and all systems must be tested. Those that do not pass will not be able to be sold in the EEA.

How well do STP- and UTP-based systems stand up to rigorous EMC testing? Not all STP based systems can automatically pass EMC tests (contrary to some popular assumptions), while a well-designed UTP cabling system can. Further discussions on this topic will be addressed in Chapter 5, "Types of Vendor and Third-Party Cabling Systems."

Coaxial Cable

Now let's briefly look at the third type of copper media: coaxial cabling. This is the copper media type most frequently used in cable television systems, the transmission line for television and radio signals.

Coaxial can be a good solution for small networks. Because it is generally wired in a bus topology, it requires less cable than other solutions and doesn't require a hub. Generally it is easy to install the connections. Coaxial

Figure 1–3
Coaxial cable.

also offers relatively high immunity to interference from noise sources, so it is often used in manufacturing environments.

Coaxial cabling has a single copper conductor at its center. A plastic layer provides insulation between the center conductor and a braided metal shield, as shown in Figure 1–3 [4]. As previously mentioned, the metal shield also helps to block any outside interference from fluorescent lights, motors, and other computers.

Coaxial cabling is highly resistant to signal interference, despite the fact that it is difficult to install. Also, it can support greater cable lengths between network devices than twisted pair cable. The two types of coaxial cabling are thin coaxial and thick coaxial.

Thin coaxial cable is also referred to as thinnet. 10Base2 refers to the specifications for thin coaxial cable carrying Ethernet signals, as shown in Table 1–2 [5]. The 2 refers to the approximate maximum segment length of 200 meters. In actual fact, the maximum segment length is 185 meters. Thin coaxial cable is popular in school networks, especially linear bus networks.

Table 1–2   Ethernet Cable Comparison Summary

Cable Type	10BaseF	10Base5	10Base2	10BaseT	Single-Mode Fiber	Multi-mode Fiber*	Standard AUI	Office AUI
Maximum length	2000 m	500 m	185 m	100 m	5 Km	1 Km	50 m	16.5 m
Number of taps	n/a	100	30	n/a	n/a	n/a	n/a	n/a
Tap spacing	n/a	2.5 m	5 m	n/a	n/a	n/a	n/a	n/a
Propagation delay	n/a	≤ .00433	≤ .00514	≤ .0057	≤ .005	≤ .005	≤ .00514	≤ .0156
Maximum segment delay	n/a	2.165 micro-seconds	.95 micro-seconds	1.0 micro-seconds	25 micro-seconds	5.0 micro-seconds	.257 micro-seconds	.257 micro-seconds
Velocity of propagation	n/a	≥ .77 c	≥ .65 c	≥ .585 c	≥ .66 c	≥ .66 c	≥ .65 c	≥ .65 c

* The IEEE 802.3 Fiber Optic Inter-Repeater Link (FOIRL) standard specifies 1 kilometer, while the 802.3j standard allows for 2 kilometers.

Thick coaxial cable is also referred to as thicknet. 10Base5 refers to the specifications for thick coaxial cable carrying Ethernet signals, as shown in Table 1–2. The 5 refers to the maximum segment length of 500 meters. Thick coaxial cable has an extra protective plastic cover that helps keep moisture away from the center conductor. This makes thick coaxial a great choice when running longer lengths in a linear bus network. One disadvantage of thick coaxial is that it is difficult to install and does not bend easily.

However, there are some disadvantages to coaxial. The same bus topology that makes it less expensive makes it more difficult to isolate problems. Currently its LAN use is pretty much confined to 10BASE2 Ethernet. The new high-speed networks are not supporting coaxial, so this cabling may be a dead end.

Coaxial used for Ethernet networks is 50 ohms. Coax for cable television (CATV) is 75 ohms. Using the wrong cable for your network will cause network problems.

Ohms is defined as a measure of resistance. One ohm allows one ampere of current to flow across a one-volt potential.

Coaxial Cable Connectors

The most common type of connector used with coaxial cables is the Bayone-Neill-Concelman (BNC) connector, shown in Figure 1–4 [6]. Different types of adapters are available for BNC connectors, including a T-connector, terminator, and barrel connector. The weakest points in any network are the connectors on the cable. Always use the BNC connectors that crimp, rather than screw onto the cable, to help avoid problems with your network. For further information on copper media, please see Chapter 10, "Copper Design Considerations."

Figure 1–4   BNC connector.

FIBER OPTIC MEDIA

Let's look at the next type of cabling media: fiber optic cable. With the relentless pursuit of bandwidth, fiber optic cabling is being deployed at an ever increasing rate. This cable, which uses glass to carry light pulses, poses both advantages and challenges. Fiber optic cabling has much to offer, and in most cases, its use will provide benefits that warrant the implementation. We will get into an indepth discussion of fiber optic cabling in Part III, "Fiber Optic Systems: A Hands-On Approach" (Chapters 12–20).

Furthermore, fiber optic cable offers the possibility of near infinite bandwidth and perfect immunity to noise. The trade-off is simply cost and difficulty in installation. It costs significantly more to purchase fiber optic cable, connectors, patch panels, jumper cables, tools, and network interface cards (NICs).

Since the invention of the telegraph by Samuel Morse in 1838, there has been a constant push to provide data at higher and higher rates. Today, the push continues. Just as RS-232 attached terminals gave way to 10 Mbps Ethernet and 4 and 16 Mbps token ring. These are giving way to Fast Ethernet (100 Mbps), FDDI (100 Mbps), ATM (155 Mbps), Fiber Channel (1062 Mbps), and Gigabit Ethernet (1000 Mbps). With each of these increases in speed, the physical layer of the infrastructure is placed under more stress and more limitations. The cabling installed in many environments today cannot support the demands of Fast Ethernet, let alone ATM, Fiber Channel, or Gigabit Ethernet.

Fiber optic cabling thus provides a viable alternative to copper. Unlike its metallic counterpart, fiber cabling does not have the astringent speed and distance limitations that plague network administrators wishing to upgrade their networks. Because it is transmitting light, the limitations are on the devices driving it more than on the cable itself. By installing fiber optic cabling, the high cost of labor and the time associated with the cabling plant can be expected to provide service for the foreseeable future.

Plastic optical fiber (POF) technology is making fiber even more affordable and easier to install. Because the core is plastic instead of glass (more on cores and fiber construction follows), terminating the cable is easier. The trade-off for this lower cost and ease of installation is shorter distance capabilities and bandwidth limitations.

This section is intended to give you an understanding of fiber optic cable technology and its applications as well as presenting this light-speed technology through fiber optic systems, where 10BaseF (as shown in Table 1–2) refers to the specifications for fiber optic cable carrying Ethernet signals. It's one of the most sophisticated cabling media solutions available today, with a range of more than 70 miles (120 kilometers) and certified performance up to gigabit speeds.

Fiber Optic Components

Fiber optic cabling consists of a center glass core surrounded by several layers of protective materials, as shown in Figure 1–5 [7]. It has the following components (starting in the center and working out): core, cladding, coating, strength member, and jacket (Figure 1–6) [Advanced Cable Connection Inc., 1]. The design and function of each of these will be defined later.

The core is in the very center of the cable and is the medium of propagation for the signal. The core is made of silica glass or plastic (in the case of POF) with a high refractive index (discussed in detail later). The actual core is very small (compared to the wire gauges that most of us are used to). Typical core sizes range from 8 microns (millionth of a meter) for single-mode silica glass cores and up to 1,000 microns for multimode POF.

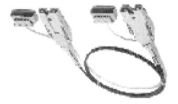

Figure 1–5   Fiber optic cable.

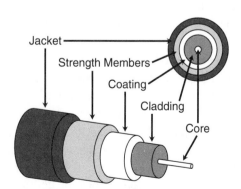

Figure 1–6   Fiber optic cable construction.

The cladding is a material with a lower index of refraction that surrounds the core. This difference in index forms a mirror at the boundary of the core and cladding. Because of the lower index, it reflects the light back into the center of the core, forming an optical wave guide. This is the same effect as looking out over a calm lake and noting the reflection, while looking straight down you see through the water. It is this interaction of core and cladding that is at the heart of how optical fiber works.

The coating (also referred to as buffer or buffer coating) is a protective layer around the outside of the cladding. It is typically made of a thermoplastic material for tight buffer construction and a gel material for loose buffer construction. As the name implies, in tight buffer construction, the buffer is extruded directly onto the fiber, tightly surrounding it. Loose buffer construction uses a gel-filled tube that is larger than the fiber itself. Loose buffer construction offers a high degree of isolation from external mechanical forces such as vibration. Tight buffer construction, on the other hand, provides for a smaller bend radius, smaller overall diameter, and crush resistance.

To further protect the fiber from stretching during installation, and to protect it from expansion and contraction due to temperature changes, strength members are added to the cable construction. These members are made from various materials from steel (used in some multistrand cables) to Kevlar. In single- and double-fiber cables, the strength members are wrapped around the coating. In some multistrand cables, the strength member is in the center of the bundle.

The jacket is the last item in the construction, and provides the final protection from the environment in which the cable is installed. Of concern here is the intended placement of the cable. Different jackets provide different solutions for indoor, outdoor, aerial, and buried installations.

So, how would you know which is the right fiber cable type for your network? The next section addresses this question.

The Right Fiber Optic Cable

One of the design considerations is the type of fiber to use when deciding to install optical fiber in buildings or across a campus. What should you install: single-mode (SMF), multimode (MMF), or both types of fiber? The choice is usually guided by a few key issues. For example, the primary considerations are: intended applications support, distance, data (baud) rate, and the difficulty and expense of retrofitting at a later time. Table 1–3 addresses the first three considerations for LANs and video applications.

Single-mode and/or multimode are fiber cable that use light pulses instead of electricity to carry data. In multimode cable, the light bounces off the cable's walls as it travels down, which causes the signal to weaken sooner and therefore data cannot travel as much distance as with single mode fiber. In SMF cables, the light travels straight down the cable. The size of the cable/cladding is 62.5/125 micron for MMF, and 8/125 micron for SMF.

Table 1–3   Standardized Distances for LANs over Single Mode and Multimode

Application	Data rate	Fiber distance (meters) and type	
		Single Mode (9/125 micron)	Multimode (62.5/125 micron)
10BaseF (Ethernet)	20 Mbaud	nonstandard	2,000
100BaseFX	125 Mbaud	nonstandard	2,000
100VG-AnyLAN	120 Mbaud	nonstandard	2,000
1000BaseX	1250 Mbaud	3,000	440 (draft)
ATM and SONET	155 Mbaud	40,000	2,000
	622 Mbaud	40,000	500
Baseband Video	6 MHz	65,000	10,000
Broadband Video	500 MHz	20,000	n/a
FDDI	125 Mbaud	60,000	2,000
Fiber Channel	133 Mbaud	nonstandard	1,500
	266 Mbaud	10,000	1,500
	531 Mbaud	10,000	350
	1062 Mbaud	10,000	300
Token Ring	32 Mbaud	2,000	nonstandard

As previously mentioned, the most common size of multimode fiber used in networking is 62.5/125 fiber. This fiber has a core of 62.5 microns and a cladding of 125 microns. This is ideally suited for use with 850 nm and 1300 nm wavelength drivers and receivers. For single-mode networking applications, 8.3/125 is the most common size. Its smaller core is the key to single mode operation (defined later).

Numerical aperture and acceptance angle are two different ways of expressing the same thing. For the core/cladding boundary to work as a mirror, the light needs to strike at a small/shallow angle (referred to as the angle of incidence). This angle is specified as the acceptance angle and is the maximum angle at which light can be accepted by the core, as shown in Figure 1–7 [Advanced Cable Connection Inc., 1]. Acceptance angle can also be specified as Numerical Aperture, which is the SIN of the acceptance angle (Numerical Aperture = SIN [acceptance angle]).

To date, all LAN standards specify 62.5/125 micron multimode fiber and some also specify single-mode fiber. Table 1–3 lists the standardized distances for LANs over both media. All LANs operating up to 266 megabaud have sufficient distance capability on multimode fiber to span most campuses. Above that rate, the distance capabilities of multimode fiber LANs are sufficient to cable most buildings using single-point administration (centralized cabling) architecture. For longer distances, single-mode fiber provides the LAN solution at these higher rates. Multimode-to-single-mode converters are available to convert multimode signals to single mode, even for those LANs where single-mode fiber is non-standard. Converters typically have 20- to 50-kilometer single-mode capability.

For video, multimode fiber is capable of delivering baseband (single channel) video over distances exceeding the span of most campuses. Multimode fiber is also capable of providing several channels of video (multichannel), but not capable of cost-effective broadband (20–80 channel) video delivery today. However, single-mode fiber is quite capable of providing broadband video services.

As Table 1–3 indicates, multimode fiber has the capability to meet both the distance and data rate demands of most LAN networks. Generally, multimode systems cost far less than single-mode systems, since the optoelectronics that can be used with multimode fiber are much less costly than those used with single-mode fiber. This cost advantage explains the popularity of multimode fiber over single-mode fiber in premises networks.

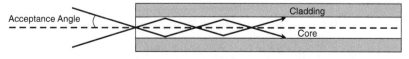

Figure 1–7   Fiber optic specifications.

Optoelectronics has a rapidly growing range of applications that includes optical communications, optical data storage, and optical sensing. It is fundamentally concerned with the interaction of light and matter and with devices that interface between electronics and optics.

However, single-mode fiber is practically the only fiber used by telephone and cable television companies. These industries require the very long distance capability and high information carrying capacity of single-mode fiber. In these longer distance applications, single-mode systems are cost-effective because fewer optoelectronic devices are needed overall.

Today, most premises networks are being installed with multimode fiber in the building backbone and campus backbone segments. Some forward-thinking companies are also installing single-mode fiber in backbones along with the multimode fiber.

"Backbone" is a fairly nebulous term for a part of the network that interconnects other parts of the network. For example, a campus might have an FDDI ring that interconnects a number of Ethernets. The FDDI ring could be called the network's backbone.

Multimode fiber is also growing in the horizontal cabling scheme, bringing the benefits of fiber all the way to the desktop. A few companies are even installing single-mode fiber to these work areas. Most of these companies are not using the single-mode fiber at this time, but are installing it in the event that they will need its higher information-carrying capacity in the future. Also, because of its popularity with telephone and cable television companies, single-mode fiber is capable of extending telephony and cable services throughout a campus. For information regarding cost-related issues with installing both single-mode and multimode fiber at the same time, see Chapter 24, "Installation."

Horizontal cabling extends from the telecommunications outlet/connector to the horizontal cross-connect. All horizontal wiring must be placed in a physical star topology with the floor wiring closet (FWC) as the center. Physical topology is a star (each telecommunications outlet/connector has its own mechanical termination position at the horizontal cross-connect in the telecommunications closet).

The published building cabling standards, ANSI/TIA/EIA-568-A, ISO/IEC 11801, and EN-50173, recognize both multimode and single-mode fiber for building and campus backbones. However, these standards do not recognize single-mode fiber for horizontal segments to the work area or desktop. This position reflects the present view of fiber-based services within premises networks, taking into consideration practical issues of active equipment availability, relative cost, and the remote likelihood of needing at the desktop the type of information-carrying capacity that single-mode fiber can provide. Looking into the future from a fiber distribution perspective, the most likely scenario (for data that may be delivered to a building or campus on single-mode fiber) is that the single-mode fiber will terminate at an electronic multiplexing device. This multiplexer then extracts lower-speed signals for delivery to the desktop over multimode fiber.

Looking into the future from a technology perspective, several technologies exist for extending the capability of multimode fiber. For example, no LAN standards have yet to use multilevel coding on multimode fiber to increase transmission capacity using less bandwidth, a technique very popular in copper-based LANs. Nor have any LANs used wavelength division multiplexing (WDM), which provides additional channels over the same fiber by using different colors of light. However, some multichannel video links on multimode fiber and long-distance telephony on single-mode fiber use WDM today. Also, new devices, such as short wavelength lasers and vertical cavity surface emitting lasers (VCSELs), are emerging as the transmitter technology capable of providing cost-effective gigabit-rate data links over multimode fiber.

Considering these largely untapped technologies, it appears that multimode fiber has the capability to provide desktop LAN services far into the future. In the backbone however, where speeds and distances are generally 10 times greater than to the desktop, the clear trend is toward single-mode solutions.

The remaining consideration is the cost of retrofitting a network with single-mode fiber at a later time. This issue depends on many variables that are customer-specific and often complex. For example, items such as the cable placement method (directly buried, in conduits, or aerial), obstacles (streets, lakes, rivers, fire stops), right-of-way passage, and work disruption all affect this decision. For these reasons it is often prudent, particularly in campus backbones, to place both multimode and single-mode cables at the same time. Again, for information regarding cost-related issues with installing both single-mode and multimode fiber at the same time, see Chapter 24, "Installation."

It is important to install enough fiber to support the present and future applications that will simultaneously share the cable segment. Take into account the type and number of fibers that each application requires and add in spare capacity for future proofing. Generally, LAN applications will each require two fibers, while video applications will require one or two fibers depending on whether they are unidirectional or bidirectional. Video links that use bidirectional communications include those that return video, audio, camera control, or data signals. Add in at least 50 percent spare capacity and round the fiber count upward to the next standard cable size.

If you decide to place both multimode and single-mode fibers along the same route, the general recommendation is that you run separate cables for each type. Composite cable, with both multimode and single-mode fibers in one sheath, are specifically not recommended in outside plant (OSP) applications. Initially, these cable types may appear attractive. However, in practice, OSP composite cable can prove problematic because of increased difficulty in fiber-type identification. This can lead to inappropriate use of splice and connector hardware; and, unintended interconnection of multimode to single-mode fibers at splice points. Using separate OSP cables helps to identify and segregate the two fiber types, reducing confusion during installation, maintenance, and administration. Furthermore, composite cables have more limited availability and higher cost than noncomposite cable. However, for applications inside buildings, the issues of fiber-type identification and resulting mix-ups at splice and termination points have been mitigated by the design of composite building cables. The tight-buffer construction of the composite building cable uses a color-coded plastic coating over each individual fiber within the cable. This buffer carries special markings that easily identify the single-mode fibers within the cable. Therefore, the general recommendation would be to use the composite cable (see Figures 1–8 and 1–9) in buildings where both single-mode and multimode fibers are required along the same route [8].

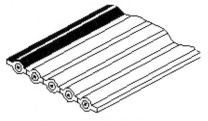

Figure 1–8   Composite cable.

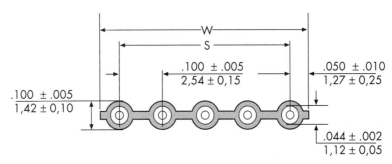

Figure 1–9 Composite cable circuit dimensions.

To improve the management of the fiber system for administration and record keeping, route the two fiber types to separate patch panels in closets or equipment rooms. The fiber type should be identified by distinctive labeling. Color coding the connectors and couplings (adapters) is recommended. The use of blue for single-mode and beige for multimode connections is consistent with ANSI/TIA/EIA-568-A, ISO/IEC 11801, and EN-50173.

Fiber Optic Transmitter

As previously mentioned, fiber optic cabling transmits light rather than electronic signals. This eliminates the problem of electrical interference. Fiber optic is ideal for certain environments that are subject to a large amount of electrical interference. Its immunity to the effects of moisture and lighting has also made fiber optic cabling the standard for connecting networks between buildings.

Fiber optic cable has the ability to transmit signals over much greater distances than twisted pair and coaxial. It also has the capability to carry information at vastly greater speeds. This capacity broadens communication possibilities to include services such as interactive services and video conferencing. The cost of fiber optic cabling is comparable to copper cabling. Nevertheless, it is more difficult to install and modify. A comparison between the two media is given later in the chapter.

There does appear to be an inconsistency as to the cost of fiber. On the one hand, the cost of fiber is substantially more than any other form of cabling. Some industry analysts suggest that it is comparable to copper. Though an argument could be made that fiber is reaching less expensive levels, and may very well be comparable to copper today, it is suggested that the industry analysts take one position or the other, not both.

Specifications

With a basic understanding of fiber construction, explanation of transmitters (the devices that put the pulses of light into the fiber) is in order. From a general level, there are three aspects of transmitters to discuss:

- Type of transmitter.
- Wavelength of transmitter.
- Power of the transmitter.

Transmitters can be divided into two groups: lasers and light emitting diodes (LEDs). LEDs are by far the most common, as they provide low-cost and very efficient solutions. Most multimode transmitters are of the LED variety. When high power is required for extended distances, lasers are used. Lasers provide coherent light and the ability to produce a lot of light energy. The drawbacks to lasers are their cost and electrical power consumption. Equipment using high-power lasers must provide cooling and access to a primary power source such as 120V AC.

Type of Transmitter. Transmitter types can also be broken down into single-mode versus multimode transmitters. Multimode transmitters are used with larger cable (typically 62.5/125 microns for most data networking applications) and emit multiple rays or *modes* of light into the fiber. Each one of these rays enters at a different angle and as such has a slightly different path through the cable. This results in the light reaching the far end at slightly different times. This difference in arrival times is termed "modal dispersion" and causes signal degradation. Single-mode transmitters are used with very small cable (typically 8/125 microns) and emit light in a single ray. Because there is only one mode, all light gets to the far end at the same time, eliminating modal dispersion.

The preceding explains what modal dispersion (MD) is, but does not explain how the system copes or facilitates the communication. Being that this is an introductory chapter, an explanation of how the system copes with MD will be reserved for later chapters.

Wavelength of Transmitter. The wavelength of the transmitter is the *color* of the light. The visible light spectrum starts around 750 nanometer (nm) and goes to 390 nm. The 850 nm transmitters common in multimode Ethernet can be seen because 850 nm is the center of their bandwidth and they emit some visible light in the 750 nm range, giving them their red color.

The 1300 nm and 1550 nm transmitters emit light only in the infrared spectrum. The difference in performance of the various wavelengths is beyond the scope of this section. What is important is an awareness of the wavelengths and that the equipment on both ends of the fiber needs to be matched.

Power of The Transmitter. The final characteristic of transmitters is the output power. This is a measure of the optical energy (intensity) launched into the fiber. It is measured in decibel milliwatt (dBm). A typical value for multimode transmitters used in Ethernet is –15 dBm. Single-mode transmitters have a wide range in power, depending on the application.

Fiber Optic Receiver Specifications

With a knowledge of transmitters, what happens at the other end of the cable is important. The light pulses are terminated and detected with a receiver. Receivers have three basic considerations. These are:

- Wavelength (discussed in the preceding).
- Mode (single vs. multi discussed in the preceding).
- Sensitivity.

Sensitivity is the counterpart to power for transmitters. It is a measurement of how much light is required to accurately detect and decode the data in the light stream. It is expressed in dBm and is a negative number. The smaller the number (remember –40 is smaller than –30), the better the receiver. Typical values range from –30 dBm to –40 dBm.

dB refers to decibel (dB); a unit of relative change of power (for example, –10 dB).

Receive sensitivity and transmitter power are used to calculate the optical power budget available for the cable. This calculation is:

```
Power Budget = Transmitter Power - Receiver Sensitivity
```

Using the typical values given for multimode Ethernet in the preceding, the power budget would be:

```
15 dBm = -15 dBm - (-30 dBm)
```

Therefore, the optical power budget must be greater than all of the cable plant losses (such as attenuation, losses due to splices and connectors, etc.) for the installation to work properly.

Fiber Optic Cable Connectors

Many different connector styles have found their way into fiber optic networking. The most common connector used with fiber optic cable is a straight tip (ST) connector. It is barrel-shaped, similar to a BNC connector. A newer connector, the subscriber connector (SC) is becoming more popular. It has a squared face and is easier to connect in a confined space. The SC connector has recently been standardized by ANSI TIA/EIA-568A for use in structured wiring installations. Many single-mode applications are now only available in the SC style.

FDDI, on the other hand, uses the medium interface connector (MIC), which is a duplex connector. It is physically larger then the SC connector, and the SC connector is gaining acceptance in the FDDI marketplace.

COPPER VERSUS FIBER CABLE

At this point in the chapter, it's appropriate to make a quick comparison of copper versus fiber media before going on to wireless media.

There are two main reasons for the broad acceptance and rapid growth of Category 5 UTP as a horizontal media: low initial cost and the ability to deliver high-data-rate LAN services. A standard media for LAN applications up to 155 Mbps is Category 5 UTP. However, copper-based LANs require more complex and expensive electronics as speeds increase. This trend, combined with continuing decreases in fiber media and optoelectronics prices, causes the initial price of the two solutions to converge as data rates increase. Today, for example, the price differential between copper and fiber (fiber being more expensive) for 155 Mbps ATM electronics is as small as 12 percent—with the 12 percent differential gap closing rapidly.

A third reason for the popularity of Category 5 UTP is that it allows customers to use only one media for both voice and data. In some instances, though, customers select lower performance Category 3 UTP to support voice services, leaving the choice between Category 5 UTP and fiber for data services.

Fiber Advantages: Ethernet Networks

Fiber provides several advantages to Ethernet and Fast Ethernet networks. The most common advantage and therefore use of fiber is to overcome the distance limitations of coaxial and twisted-pair copper topologies. Ethernet being run on coax (10Base2) has a maximum distance limitation of 185 m, and Ethernet being run on twisted-pair (10BaseT and 100BaseTX) has a limitation of 100 m. Fiber can greatly extend these distances with multimode fiber providing 2000 m and single-mode fiber supporting 5 km in half-duplex environments, and much more (depending on transmitter strength and receiver sensitivity) in full-duplex installations. Ethernet running at 10 Mbps has a limitation of 4 repeaters, providing some leniency in the solutions available for distance. However, Fast Ethernet only allows for two repeaters and only 5 m of cable between them. As Fast Ethernet becomes more ubiquitous, the need for fiber optic cabling will grow as well. When distance is an issue, fiber provides what may be the only solution.

Even when using coaxial cable or twisted pair (shielded or unshielded), some electrical noise may be emitted by the cable. This is especially true as connectors and ground connections age or weaken. In some environments (medical, for example), the potential risk associated with this is just not acceptable, and costs of alternative cable routings too high. Because fiber optic cabling uses light pulses to send the signal, there is no radiated noise. This makes it perfectly safe to install this cabling in any sensitive environment. Optical fiber adds additional security protection as well. There are no emissions to pick up and decode, and it is not feasible to *tap* into it for the purposes of *eavesdropping*. This makes fiber optic cabling ideal for secure network installations.

Another problem that is common when using copper cabling is other electrical noise getting into the desired electrical networking signal. This can be a problem in noisy manufacturing environments or other heavy industrial applications. The use of optical fiber provides a signal that will be completely unaffected by this noise.

In some instances, fiber provides the advantage that it can withstand more tension during the cable pulling. It is also smaller in size then twisted-pair cables and therefore takes up less room. Compared to Category 5 UTP, most duplex fiber optical cable can also endure a tighter bend radius while maintaining specified performance.

Nevertheless, 62.5/125 micron multimode fiber is already popular as a backbone media and its popularity is growing as a horizontal media. Although fiber is presently deployed in less than 9 percent of horizontal cabling systems, analysts project it will triple or quadruple in some vertical markets over the next four years. The main reasons for this growth are the need for high-bandwidth services and the desire to never need to install cabling again over the life of the building. In addition, fiber eliminates potential problems of radio frequency interference, cross talk, and lightning, thereby increasing the reliability of the network.

However, many customers may not realize one of fiber's greatest strengths. Fiber's longer distance capability permits cabling architectures that reduce recurring network operational costs. Fiber allows a centralized cabling design with a single point of administration. By collecting all hubs, switches, routers, and gateways into one location, the network requires less active equipment, maintenance, and administration effort. This generates substantial savings in initial and recurring operating costs. For example, the simplicity and flexibility of centralized electronics facilitates rapid rearrangements of distributed workgroup networks, and avoids expensive protocol conversions and switching that are often deployed between traditional horizontal and backbone cabling. In addition, centralization increases electronic equipment efficiencies, resulting in reduced equipment costs due to higher port usage. These savings multiply when supporting more than one LAN technology simultaneously, as is almost always the case when migrating to higher speed networks. All of these advantages can make fiber very cost-effective, even for lower-speed applications.

As mentioned earlier, it is critical to consider the customer's needs and business situation in order to make the best choice of horizontal media. Important issues include present and future data speed requirements, upgrade migration strategy, workgroup rearrangement frequency, building ownership and tenancy, remaining building occupancy, work area environment, horizontal distances, suitability of telecommunications closets, and long-term and short-term cost sensitivity. With these issues in mind, some conditions that indicate a centralized fiber architecture as the best choice for desktop connectivity include:

- A need to migrate efficiently to speeds above 155 Mbps at the desktop.
- A need to configure special workgroup networks quickly and easily.
- A need to support multiple LAN technologies efficiently.
- Long-term single-tenant occupancy.
- High security, high electromagnetic field, high lightning strike, or corrosive environments.
- Extreme intolerance to data errors or radiated emissions.

- Horizontal distances exceeding 100 meters (325 feet).
- Small, overcrowded, or insufficient numbers of telecommunications closets.
- A need to increase control over network operations.
- A need to reduce recurring operational costs.

If the customer's situation matches a number of these conditions, then fiber is probably the best choice. If the match is minimal, or if addressing the condition is not critical, then copper is probably the best choice. For some conditions, such as the need to exceed the standardized rates of UTP or support horizontal distances longer than 100 meters, fiber may be the only solution.

Challenges

However, fiber optical cabling is not a panacea; there are some challenges to be resolved. The first (and probably the best known), is the cost of termination. Because of the need for *perfect* connections, splices and connections must be carefully cut and then polished to preserve the optical characteristics. The connectors must also maintain a very high level of precision to guarantee alignment of the fibers.

The second problem that is encountered when installing fiber cabling is that legacy equipment does not support fiber connections. Very few desktop computers have a fiber network interface, and some critical network equipment does not offer a fiber interface.

In Ethernet, the size of the collision domain can affect the use of fiber. In a half-duplex (shared media) environment, no two devices can be separated by more then 512 bit times. While the propagation of a signal is faster through fiber than copper, it is only about 11% faster and not enough to make a significant difference. This limitation means that there are times when the signal quality and fiber are sufficient to carry the signal but the distance and network design preclude its use.

Solutions

Fortunately, the problems are not without solutions. As fiber deployment increases, the economy of scale for the manufacturers is driving costs down. Also, much work is being done to further reduce these costs. Plastic optical fiber is an example of one such development.

The need to connect to legacy equipment and infrastructure also has a solution. By using copper to fiber media converters, fiber can be connected to almost any legacy environment. Equipment equipped with an attachment unit interface (AUI) port can also make use of fiber transceivers as well. Media converters are small devices that take signals from one media type and retransmit it onto another media type. These converters are usually small enough to fit in the palm of your hand.

For those instances when collision domain restrictions preclude the use of fiber, a two port bridging device (such as a transition networks bridging media converter) with a 10/100-Base-T(X) on one port and fiber on the other can be used. Bridges by definition break collision domains, and when connected to a server, workstation, or another bridge can operate in full-duplex mode. In this mode, there are no limitations imposed by collision domains, and the distance attainable is solely a function of the fiber cable.

ATM/FDDI

As networks move to even faster protocol speeds, such as FDDI and ATM, fiber plays an increasingly important role. FDDI and ATM pose all the same problems and advantages as Ethernet. The copper version of FDDI (CFDDI) has a cable distance limitation of 100 m. Because these topologies are typically used in a campus backbone application, the distance limitations of multimode fiber can present a problem (2 km). By using single-mode fiber, distances of up to 60 km are possible. Since typically only one or two segments need that kind of distance, single-mode to multimode fiber mode converters can be used to convert just those segments to single-mode without incurring that cost for every segment in the network.

The WAN Backbones

Wide area networks (WAN) provide an inherent distance problem, and as a result, fiber has found widespread deployment. Carriers are migrating large portions of their networks to fiber to take advantage of its superior bandwidth and compact size. As more WAN services are provisioned to the customer premises via fiber, the need to convert from single mode (used almost exclusively in the WAN venue) to multimode will grow. Some of the services that are being provided directly on fiber are ATM and synchronous optical network (SONET).

WIRELESS MEDIA

Finally, let's take a look at the last cabling media type: wireless networks. Again, the intent of this final section is not to take away from the very detailed and indepth discussion of wireless media in Chapter 11, "Wireless Design Considerations." But, it is the intent of this section to discuss the basics of how, through wireless media technology, you can create an instant standalone network (that can even link the local area networks of several buildings) with a complete, integrated system of hardware and software. Not all networks are connected with cabling; some networks are wireless. Wireless LANs use high frequency radio signals or infrared light beams to communicate between the workstations and the file server. Each workstation and file server on a wireless network has some sort of transceiver/antenna to send and receive the data. Information is relayed between transceivers as if they were physically connected. For longer distances, wireless communications can also take place through cellular telephone technology or by satellite, as shown in Figure 1–10.

Wireless media is great for allowing laptop computers or remote computers to connect to the LAN. Wireless networks are also beneficial in older buildings, where it may be difficult or impossible to install cables.

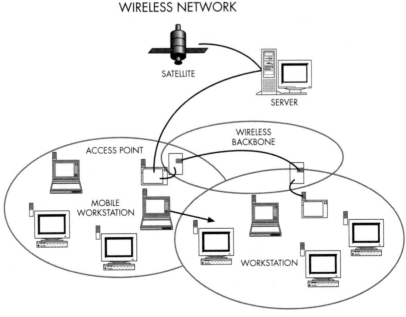

Figure 1–10   Wireless network.

So What Really is a Wireless LAN?

Today, many personal computers are interconnected with local area networks. Individuals are able to access and share data, applications, and services via the LAN. Most of these individuals use their computers in a fixed location where wired networking is possible, as shown in Figure 1–11 [9]. In a wireless LAN, the connection between the client and user is accomplished by the use of a wireless medium such as Radio Frequency (RF) or Infra Red (IR) communications instead of a cable. This allows the remote user to stay connected to the network while mobile or not physically attached to the network. The wireless connection is most usually accomplished by the user having a handheld terminal or laptop that has an RF interface card installed inside the terminal or through the PC card slot of the laptop. The client connection from the wired LAN to the user is made through an access point (AP) that can support multiple users simultaneously, as shown in Figure 1–10. The AP can reside at any node on the wired network and acts as a gateway for wireless users' data to be routed onto the wired network.

However, a growing number of applications require mobility and simultaneous access to a network. Until recently, if an application required information from a central database, it had to be connected to a wired network using a docking station. A wireless LAN enables mobile computers to be in constant contact with servers and each other. Healthcare, warehousing, and education are examples of some of the industries that utilize wireless LANs, as shown in Figure 1–10.

The computers in Figure 1–10 must all be in range of each other to maintain the wireless connection. However, most computers require greater range and flexibility since servers are often located on a wired Ethernet LAN somewhere else in the facility or at another site on an enterprise network. A wireless access point solves this problem by connecting wireless clients to Ethernet, as shown in Figure 1–12 [AMP, 1–2].

STANDARD WIRED ETHERNET

Figure 1–11   Clients communicate with server over standard wired Ethernet LANs.

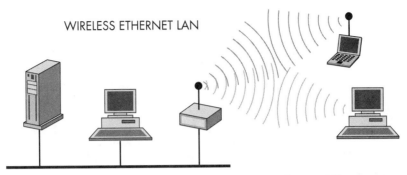

WIRELESS ETHERNET LAN

Figure 1–12   Access points connect wireless clients to Ethernet.

The range of these systems is very dependent on the actual usage and environment of the system, but varies from 100 feet inside a solid walled building to over 1,000 feet outdoors, in direct line of sight. This is a similar order of magnitude as the distance that can be covered by the wired LAN in a building. However, much like a cellular phone system, the wireless LAN is capable of roaming from the AP and reconnecting to the network through other APs residing at other points on the wired network. This can allow the wired LAN to be extended to cover a much larger area than the existing coverage by the use of multiple APs such as in a campus environment. In other words, an access point will usually provide 50,000 to 250,000 square feet of coverage depending on your building structure. Numerous access points will allow wireless clients to roam and function in all the necessary areas. Roaming occurs seamlessly and transparently to the wireless client. Figure 1–13 shows roaming conceptualized [AMP, 2]. Implementing mobile or wireless applications in an existing environment consists of two simple steps:

- Step 1: Replace the PCMCIA (PC card) wired network interface card (NIC) or the industry-standard architecture broadcast and unknown server (ISABUS) wired NIC with a wireless NIC.
- Step 2: Replace the Ethernet driver with a wireless Ethernet driver [AMP, 1]

Wireless drivers exist for all versions of Windows and DOS. ND&Is, ODI, and packet drivers are also offered. These drivers support a wide range of network operating systems, protocol stacks (Netware, Vines, TCP/IP, Lantastic, LAN server, etc.), and applications.

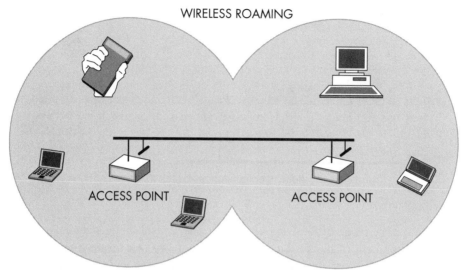

Figure 1–13   Wireless clients roam seamlessly throughout a facility.

Another important feature of the wireless LAN is that it can be used independently of a wired network. It may be used as a standalone network anywhere to link multiple computers together without having to build or extend a wired network. A useful example that is in use today is an outside auditing group inside a client company. If each of the auditors has a laptop equipped with a wireless client adapter, then a peer-to-peer workgroup can immediately be established for transfer or access of data. A member of the workgroup may be established as the server or the network can act in a peer-to-peer mode.

A wireless LAN is also capable of operating at speeds in the range of 1–2 Mbps, depending on the actual system. Both of these speeds are supported by the standard for wireless LAN networks defined by the international body, IEEE. At first approach, this suggests that the wireless network will have throughput that is 5 to 10 times less than the wired network. In practice, however, the real user of wireless networks will see a reduction in throughput compared to a wired network but not as great as the raw numbers suggest. The actual usage of the network is a much better indication of the throughput that can be expected. This is not dissimilar to the model of highway traffic when a surface street is compared to a highway to get from point A to point B. While travel is significantly faster on the highway at the optimum time or at offpeak hours when maximum speeds are possible, during peak usage, the highway can often be slower than the surface streets due to the load of traffic that the highway has to deal with.

Wireless LANs are billed on the basis of installed equipment cost; once in place there are no charges for use of the network. The network communications take place in a part of the radio spectrum that is designated as *license free*. In this band, 2.4-2.5 GHz, users can operate without a license so long as they use equipment that has been type-approved for use in the license-free bands. In the United States, these licenses are granted by the FCC for operation under part 15 regulations. The 2.4 GHz band has been designated as license free by the International Telecommunications Union (ITU) and is available for use license free in most countries in the world. Unfortunately, the rules of operation are different in almost every country, but they are similar enough that the products can be programmed for use in every country without changing the hardware component.

The Wireless Technology

It is not the intent of this section to detail the technology that makes it possible for a wireless LAN to operate; however, as with many new technologies, it is better for the potential user to understand some of the technical details that will affect the way that the product operates. Without some background, it is very hard to differentiate between the attributes of competing systems. The necessary new specifications that are needed to understand the system are not as obvious as one might think. In a wired world, the connection is a given. It is assumed that if it is designated as there, then it will be. In a wireless network of any kind, it must be assumed that the connection will be a tradeoff between data rate and robustness of the network connection.

Specifications

On first approach, the only issues that a user of a new data communications network usually asks are: *What is the range? What is the data rate?* However, there are other considerations that are even more critical, which are based on the radio portion of the technology, not simply the data protocol, such as: *How robust and interference-resistant is this network?* This is especially important when a wireless network is used in a license-free part of the spectrum where the range of potential interference is very broad. In an unlicensed band, there are many and varied users of the band that can strongly interfere with the high speed data user unless the system has been designed to work in that environment.

The ability to build a dynamically scaleable network is critical to the viability of a wireless LAN as it will inevitably be used in this mode. The interference rejection of each node will be the limiting factor to the expandability of the network and its user density in a given environment.

Radio Frequency Systems

There are two main technologies that are used for wireless communications today: radio frequency (RF) and infra red (IR). In general, they are good for different applications and have been designed into products that optimize particular features of advantage.

RF is very capable of being used for applications where communications are not in the *line of sight* and over longer distances. The RF signals will travel through walls and communicate where there is no direct path between the terminals. In order to operate in the license free portion of the spectrum called the ISM band (industrial, scientific, and medical), the radio system must use a modulation technique called Spread Spectrum (SS). In this mode, a radio is required to distribute the signal across the entire spectrum and cannot remain stable on a single frequency, as shown in Figure 1–14 [10]. This is done so that no single user can dominate the band and that all users collectively look like noise.

Security.   Spread spectrum communications were developed during World War II by the military for secure communications links. The fact that such signals appear to be noise in the band means that they are difficult to

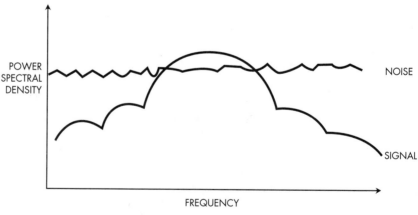

Figure 1–14   Spread spectrum signals.

find and to jam. This technique lends itself well to the expected conditions of operation of a wireless LAN application in this band and is by its very nature difficult to intercept, thus increasing security against unauthorized listeners.

Also, because wireless technology has roots in military applications, security has long been a design criterion for wireless devices. Security provisions are typically built into wireless LANs, making them more secure than most wired LANs. It is extremely difficult for unintended receivers (eavesdroppers) to listen in on wireless LAN traffic. Complex encryption techniques make it impossible for all but the most sophisticated to gain unauthorized access to network traffic. Individual nodes must be security-enabled before they are allowed to participate in network traffic.

Coverage and Range.   The distance over which radio frequency (RF) waves can communicate is dependent on the building or environment in which the wireless LAN is installed. Interactions with typical building objects, including walls, metal, and even people, can affect how energy propagates and thus what range and coverage a particular system achieves. A wireless LAN system uses RF because radio waves can penetrate many indoor walls and surfaces. The range of a wireless LAN is up to 500 feet in normal office environments and up to 1,000 feet in open space. Coverage can be extended, and true freedom of mobility via roaming is provided through microcells.

In view of this, the use of spread spectrum is considered to be especially important, as it allows many more users to occupy the band at any given time and place than if they were all static on separate frequencies. As with any radio system, one of the greatest limitations is available bandwidth; and so, the ability to have many users operate simultaneously in a given environment is critical for the successful deployment of a wireless LAN.

There are several bands available for use by license-free transmitters. The most commonly used bands are at 902-928 MHz, 2.4–2.5 GHz, and 5.7–5.8 GHz. Of these, the most useful is probably the 2.4 GHz band, as it is available for use throughout most of the world. In recent years, nearly all of the commercial development and the basis for the new IEEE standard has been in the 2.4 GHz band. While the 900 MHz band is widely used for other systems, it is only available in the United States and has greatly limited available bandwidth. In the license-free bands, there is a strict limit on the broadcast power of any transmitter, so that the spectrum can be reused at a short distance away without interference from a distant transmitter. This is similar to the operation of a cellular telephone system.

Safety.   The output power of wireless LAN systems is very low, much less than that of a handheld cellular phone. Since radio waves fade rapidly over distance, very little exposure to RF energy is provided to those in the area of a wireless LAN system. Wireless LANs must meet stringent government and industry regulations for safety. No adverse health effects have ever been attributed to wireless LANs.

Infra Red Systems

The second technology that is used for wireless LAN systems is infra red— where the communication is carried by light in the invisible part of the spectrum. This system has much to recommend in some circumstances. It is primarily of use for very short distance communications—less than 3 feet where there is a line of sight connection. It is not possible for the infra red light to penetrate any solid material. It is even attenuated greatly by window glass, so it is really not a useful technology in comparison to radio frequency for use in a wireless LAN system.

The application where infra red comes into its element is as a docking function and in applications where the power available is extremely limited (such as a pager or personal digital assistant [PDA]). There is a standard for such products by the Infrared Data Association (IrDA) that has been championed by Hewlett Packard, IBM, and many others. This is now found in many notebook and laptop PCs, and allows a connectionless docking facility at up to 1 Mbps to a desktop machine at up to 2 feet line of sight.

The Infrared Data Association is a group of device manufacturers that developed a standard for transmitting data via infrared light waves. Increasingly, computers and other devices (such as printers) come with IrDA ports. This enables you to transfer data from one device to another without any cables. For example, if both your laptop computer and printer have IrDA ports, you can simply put your computer in front of the printer and output a document, without needing to connect the two with a cable. IrDA ports support roughly the same transmission rates as traditional parallel ports. The only restrictions on their use is that the two devices must be within a few feet of each other and there must be a clear line of sight between them.

Such products are point-to-point communications and not networks, which makes them very difficult to operate as a network, but does offer increased security, as only the user to whom the beam is directed can pick it up. Attempts to provide wider network capability by using a diffused IR system where the light is distributed in all directions have been developed and marketed, but they are limited to 30–50 feet and cannot go through any solid material. There are now very few companies pursuing this implementation.

The main advantage of the point-to-point IR system—increased security—is undermined by the distributing of the light source as it can now be received by any body within range, not just the intended recipient.

Implementation of Spread Spectrum

There are two methods of spread spectrum modulation that are used to comply with the regulations for use in the industrial, scientific, and medical (ISM) band: frequency hopping spread spectrum (FHSS) and direct sequence spread spectrum (DSSS). Let's take a close look at both.

Direct Sequence Spread Spectrum. Historically many of the original systems available used DSSS as the required spread spectrum modulation because components and systems were available from the direct broadcast satellite industry, in which DSSS is the modulation scheme used. However, the majority of commercial investment in wireless LAN systems is now in FHSS and the user base of FHSS products have now exceeded that of DSSS. Most new wireless LAN applications are now FHSS.

The term *direct sequence spread spectrum* is a complicated (and unrelated) way of describing a system that takes a signal at a given frequency and spreads it across a band of frequencies where the center frequency is the original signal, as shown in Figure 1–15 [10]. The spreading algorithm, which is the key to the relationship of the spread range of frequencies, changes with time in a pseudorandom sequence that appears to make the spread signal a

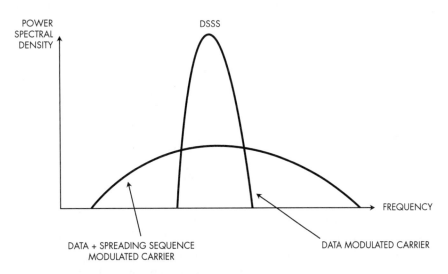

Figure 1–15   Direct sequence spread spectrum.

random noise source. The strength of this system is that when the ratio between the original signal bandwidth and the spread signal bandwidth is very large, the system offers great immunity to interference. For instance, if a 1 Kbps signal is spread across 1 GHz of spectrum, the spreading ratio is one million times, or 60 dB. This is the type of system developed for strategic military communications systems, as it is very difficult to find and even more difficult to jam.

However, in an environment such as wireless LAN in the license-free, ISM band (where the available bandwidth critically limits the ratio of spreading), the advantages that the DSSS method provides against interference become greatly limited. A realistic example in use today is a 2 Mbps data signal that is spread across 20 MHz of spectrum and offering a spreading ratio of 10 times. This is only just enough to meet the lower limit of *processing gain* (a measure of this spreading ratio, as set by the Federal Communications Corporation [FCC], the United States government body that determines the rule of operation of radio transmitters). This limitation significantly undermines the value of DSSS as a method to resist interference in real wireless LAN applications.

Frequency Hopping Spread Spectrum.   In simple terms, an FHSS system is not dissimilar to the radio in a car, where the preset buttons are pushed one after another in an apparent random sequence. The time on each channel is very short, but at a data rate of 1 Mbps or higher. Even a fraction of a second provides significant overall throughput for the communications system. On the other hand, with wired LAN systems, actual throughput in wireless LANs is dependent on your set-up. Factors that affect throughput include airwave congestion (number of users), propagation factors such as range and multipath, as well as the latency and bottlenecks on the wired portions of the wireless LAN. Typical data rates range from 1 to 10 Mbps.

The term "multipath" describes a situation in which a transmitted signal follows several propagation paths from a transmitter to a receiver. This may result from the signal reflecting off several objects to arrive at the receiver.

Users of traditional Ethernet LANs generally experience little difference in performance when using a wireless LAN and can expect similar latency behavior. Wireless LANs provide throughput sufficient for the most common LAN-based office applications, including electronic mail exchange, access to shared peripherals, and access to multiuser databases and applications.

Nevertheless, FHSS is an altogether much simpler system to understand than DSSS. It is based on the use of a signal at a given frequency that is constant for a small amount of time and then moves to a new frequency. The sequence of different channels determined for the hopping pattern (where will the next frequency be to engage with this signal source), is pseudorandom. "Pseudo" means that a very long sequence code is used before it is repeated, over 65,000 hops, making it appear to be random. This makes it very difficult to predict the next frequency, at which such a system will stop and transmit or receive data as the system appears to be a random noise source to an unauthorized listener. This makes the FHSS system very secure against interference and interception, as shown in Figure 1–16 [10].

This system is a very robust method of communicating, as it is statistically close to impossible to block all of the frequencies that can be used and as there is no *spreading ratio* requirement that is so critical for DSSS systems. The resistance to interference is actually determined by the capability of the hardware filters that are used to reject signals other than the frequency of interest, and not by mathematical-spreading algorithms. In the case of a standard FHSS wireless LAN system (with a two-stage receive section), the filtering will be provided in excess of 100,000 times rejection of unwanted signals, or over 50 dB for the engineers, as shown in Figure 1–17 [10].

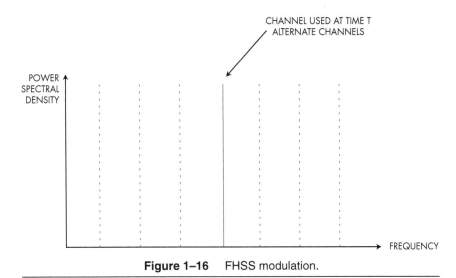

Figure 1–16   FHSS modulation.

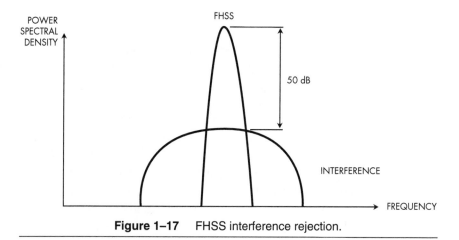

Figure 1–17   FHSS interference rejection.

Comparison DSSS And FHSS

DSSS technology is basically a mathematically derived solution. Therefore, it is useful to use math to analyze the comparative value of such a system. There are some very compelling arguments against DSSS in a constrained bandwidth system that are clearly demonstrated by such an analysis.

The ability to resist interference of a radio system is called the *jamming margin* and can be approximated to the ratio of the interfering signal to the intended signal that can be endured by the system while still functioning. In a standard fixed frequency radio system (the instantaneous equivalent of an FHSS system), this has been designed to be around 100,000 times, or 50 dB. In a DSSS system, it has been shown for the wireless LAN model that the spreading ratio is at best 10 times. This shows that a DSSS system has 10,000 times less interference rejection than is provided by an FHSS system as used in a practical wireless LAN implementation (see Figure 1–18) [10].

Working this backward, it is clear that for a DSSS product to offer the same interference rejection as an FHSS system (100,000 times and that in the license-free ISM bands the maximum practical spread bandwidth is 20 MHz for a DSSS system), the maximum data rate would have to be 20 MHz divided by 100,000. That means that the maximum data rate for a practical DSSS system with good interference rejection is 200 bps!

As a point of reference in other real systems, the global positioning system (GPS) is the largest commercially implemented application of DSSS sys-

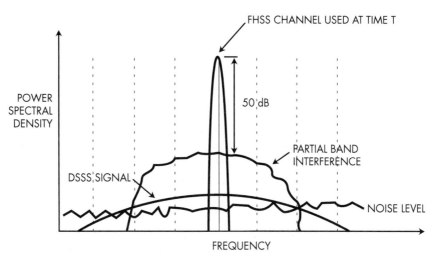

Figure 1–18 DS versus FH interference rejection.

tems. In that system, in order to reject interference, 50 bps are spread across 5 MHz of bandwidth. That is approximately the spreading ratio that was derived for a DSSS wireless LAN for use in the ISM bands—with data rate limited to 200 bps to provide interference rejection. This confirms the value of DSSS for a well-designed application; however, it is not exactly a compelling model for a multimegabit-per-second wireless LAN implementation in a constrained bandwidth spectrum with interference present!

Finally, with regard to the issue of interference rejection, this is actually the controlling specification that will determine if a system will work or not. For wireless LAN products to be successful for users, they need to be available in some quantity to reduce the costs and then become a ubiquitous network. FHSS is clearly the technology of choice to implement wireless LAN systems in unlicensed bands; and most of the commercial development supports this position.

Key Specifications

In looking at the value of the two competing technologies, there are a number of other key specifications that should be reviewed. However, it must be remembered that the DSSS implementation does not meet the minimum acceptable criteria for successful operation, unless very few people buy these systems. Therefore, exceeding a single FHSS specification is somewhat meaningless.

Variations in Data Rate

The most significant variation in data rate can usually be attributed to how well the underlying data transfer protocol is designed and implemented by the specific manufacturer and the quality of the overall systems architecture they have developed, not the spread spectrum implementation used.

Because of the spreading ratio, it is possible for existing DSSS implementations to marginally exceed the performance of FHSS systems (but, they will both nominally be rated at 1–2 Mbps over the air data rate). In effective throughput, the DSSS system has an advantage because the data packets are transmitted continuously—whereas in FHSS, a percentage of the operational time is spent hopping between frequencies and resynchronizing. This time is minimized by design and should not reduce throughput by more than 20 percent.

Some systems are now including data compression that provide 50–100 percent increases in effective data rate under some conditions. However, compression is algorithmic in nature and is very dependent on what sort of data is being transmitted. The algorithm for text compression is capable of around 2–3 times reduction, and is very different from the algorithm used for, say, video compression, where an optimized algorithm can provide 50–100 times reduction. Therefore, compression is most useful when it can be tailored to a known type of data source.

Range Capabilities

In the analysis of range, there is a marginal theoretical difference in the range capabilities of FHSS and DSSS systems. The largest range difference will be caused by two sources: the type and placement of the antenna system, not the spread spectrum modulation used, and the environment that the system is operating in.

Antenna diversity is one of the most significant influences on the range and performance of systems—especially near the edge of the range profile (the marginal area). Antenna diversity is the use of multiple antennas that are physically separated. This is done because the radio waves will reflect off all objects, walls, buildings, bridges, cars, and so on—and cause nulls and peaks randomly distributed in the air. This is much the same as the peaks and troughs that are seen on the surface of water when separate waves encounter each other. This is called *multipath* in the radio environment. With two antennas separated by a quarter of a wavelength (a few inches for 2.4 GHz systems), it is statistically very unlikely that both antennas will be in a null or wave trough at the same time—whereas a single antenna will likely be in a null in a highly reflective environment such as an office building.

Large antennas placed high above the ground will always provide better range than small antennas that extend marginally from a PC card and are low down on the side of a notebook computer. The range of the different system components is therefore different. Single-piece PC cards have the shortest range: 100–500 feet, depending on the environment. Access points with elevated, efficient antennas will achieve 500–3,000 feet. Luckily, in most systems, the client card will communicate with an access point. The overall link will benefit from the better antenna on the access point, though it will still have a shorter range than two access points communicating with each other.

The environment that the system is used in has a very significant influence on the range and performance. This should be of little surprise to anybody that has used a cordless phone—as they suffer from similar range and performance problems as wireless LANs (except that voice quality can be substituted for data rate). When the environment is outside (in line of sight, with little to reflect off and cause multipath), the range is at its best. When the environment is in a solid-walled building (such as an old stone house), the range is greatly reduced. This is the same for a wireless LAN; however, the multipath problem can significantly degrade megabit communications where it will not significantly affect voice quality.

Most office environments and modern homes are constructed of materials that are relatively *translucent* to radio waves at 2.4 GHz. So that the range will not be greatly limited, however, they do tend to present very reflective and refractive environments; and the ultimate limitation will probably be caused by severe multipath problems.

Power, Cost, and Size

Although these are three different and critical specifications, they are very closely linked in the wireless LAN environment. They also align with each other closely in a comparative review of DSSS and FHSS technology. The reason for this is because these specifications are all driven by implementation, which is limited by the required components to implement the spread spectrum and the level of integration of those components.

DSSS is driven by digital signal processing (DSP) multiplication. Therefore, it has a heavy requirement for large, expensive, and power-hungry digital circuitry in its implementation. The spreading can be achieved by multiplying the data signal by the spreading code, which is very DSP-intensive. This is in addition to the baseband processing requirements for the communications protocol being used. While further integration and increases in the capability of DSP processors will reduce the vulnerability of DSSS technology in these specifications, it will probably always lag the simplicity of FHSS systems.

In terms of the radio technology, all practical DSSS systems use phase modulation (PM) as the basic data modulation prior to spreading, whereas all practical FHSS systems use frequency modulation (FM) as the basic data modulation prior to spreading. This is important for several reasons.

FM is a method of modulation in which the frequency represents the value of a digital 1 or 0 as an offset above or below the nominal channel frequency. In this technique, the only information that needs to be recovered from the received signal is the frequency. This requires no linearity of the receive path. It is very cheap and low in power consumption to implement. PM is essentially a version of amplitude modulation (AM), in which the amplitude or size of a signal at a given frequency is measured. The size of this signal represents a digital 1 or 0. In this technique, it is not only necessary to know at which frequency the signal is, but it is also necessary to know the amplitude of the signal (two pieces of information instead of just one for FM). The limitation of such a system is that a change in range from the receiver has a similar effect on amplitude as a change in amplitude that represents a 1 or a 0. Therefore, the system needs to resolve whether an amplitude change is caused by a change in the range of the transmitted signal or a different bit. This requires a linear system, so that the measurement of amplitude has accurate and automatic gain control circuitry (AGC). The requirement to have a linear system costs money and more importantly uses power to implement.

FHSS implementation is effectively the same system that is found in a consumer radio with the addition of a system to hop the frequency through the band. This is a simple and very well understood technique that is simple and cheap to implement. There is no requirement for any DSP to implement FHSS, so the power requirements are significantly reduced from that needed for DSSS with no additional cost for components or extra size for the product.

The Wireless LAN Industry Standard Based System

Industry standards are absolutely critical in the computer business and its related industries. They are the vehicle that provides a large enough target market to be realistically defined and targeted with a single, compatible technological solution that many manufacturers can develop. This process reduces the cost of the products to implement the standard, which further expands the market. The result is not dissimilar to a nuclear chain reaction in terms of the user explosion (see Figure 1–19) [10].

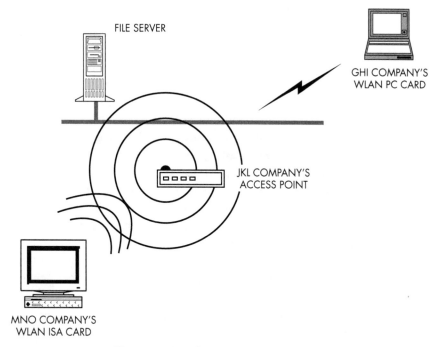

FILE SERVER

GHI COMPANY'S
WLAN PC CARD

JKL COMPANY'S
ACCESS POINT

MNO COMPANY'S
WLAN ISA CARD

Figure 1–19   Standards-based system.

IEEE 802.11

In 1990, the IEEE 802 standards groups for networking setup a specific group to develop a wireless LAN standard similar to the Ethernet standard. On June 26, 1997, the IEEE 802.11 Wireless LAN Standard Committee approved the IEEE 802.11 specification. This is critical for the industry, as it now provides a solid specification for the vendors to target, both for systems products and components. While there are three sections of the specification representing FHSS, DSSS, and IR physical layers, almost all of the industry and associated commercial development money is now being expended in the FHSS marketplace.

The standard is a detailed software, hardware, and protocol specification with regard to the physical and data link layer of the open system interconnection (OSI) reference model that integrates with existing wired LAN standards for a seamless roaming environment. It is specific to the 2.4 GHz band and defines two levels of modulation that provide a basic 1 Mbps and enhanced 2 Mbps system.

Implications of Standards

The implications of an agreed standard are very significant, and is really the starting point for the wireless LAN industry in terms of a broader horizontal market. To this point, the market has been dominated by vertical implementations that are custom developments—using a specific manufacturer's proprietary protocol and system. The next generation of these products for both vertical and horizontal office systems will be based on the final recitified standard.

At two levels, this standard has already had a strong effect on the market. At the system level, almost everybody is claiming broad *compatibility* with what the standard will be. Most of these different proprietary systems will not communicate with each other. However, they do all have hardware that is capable of meeting the specification without significant change. At a lower level, component companies are starting to release products that are aimed at becoming standard components in winning wireless LAN designs. Especially important is the integrated circuit (IC) integration efforts that are under development, as this has the most significant chance of reducing greatly the cost of these solutions.

All of this effort is starting to reduce the cost of the systems and making the whole concept more appealing to the user community. Many of the market watchers and information companies that have been cold on this market are now starting to warm up and predict lower-cost products and large markets.

Products that are Noncompliant

There are some products available or promised to be available soon that do not intend to meet the IEEE specification. These are aimed at higher performance, more in line with the data rate of a wired Ethernet card (10 Mbps). These systems will probably operate under different regulations for the RF performance, which will limit the range to less than 100 feet due to power output. The method used to achieve the 10 Mbps data rate is somewhat dubious and remains to be proven as viable.

While these systems will be useful in certain circumstances, they will not benefit from the cost reductions that will be achieved through the IEEE standard. It is currently not clear how such systems could offer dual capability to operate as 802.11 wireless LANs. Also, the 10 Mbps systems (both digital and RF hardware) would be significantly different. It will be unlikely that an advanced system will survive on its own without being able to also work as an IEEE-compatible terminal.

Regulatory Compliance of Wireless LAN Systems

The wireless LAN systems discussed in this section and those specified by the IEEE 802.11 standard all operate in the unlicensed spectrum (as detailed earlier). The unlicensed spectrum rules allow a manufacturer to develop a piece of equipment that operates to meet predefined rules and for any user to operate the equipment without a requirement for a specific user license. This requires the manufacturer to make products that conform to the regulations for each country of operation. And, they should also conform with the IEEE 802.11 standard.

While the 2.4 GHz band is available in most countries, each countries' regulatory bodies usually have set requirements that are different in detail. There are three major specification groups that set the trend which most other countries follow. The U.S. FCC sets a standard covered by the Part 15 regulations that are copied in much of the rest of the Americas and the world. The Japanese Nippon Telegraph and Telephone Corporation (NTT) has its own standard. The European countries have set a specification through the European Telecommunications Standards Institute (ETSI) covered by RES 02.

While all of these differ in detail, it is possible to make a single hardware product that is capable of meeting all three specifications with only changes to the operating software. Although the software could be downloaded from a host such as a notebook PC, the changes are required to be set by the manufacturer, not the user, in order to meet the rules of operation.

Flexible and Growing

Finally, the increasing demand for network access while mobile will continue to drive the demand for wireless LAN systems. Because it's wireless, this type of media or network can go where no other network has gone before. It can plug right into your existing network.

But what can a wireless network do for you? You might be surprised. Imagine the gains in productivity you'll achieve when everyone on the factory floor has instant access to your parts database, on the spot, without traveling to a distant terminal for information. Think about how much you'll save in labor costs with a network that requires virtually none of the planning, installation, or reconfiguration traditional LANs require to keep pace with rapidly changing business conditions.

Now, imagine the improvements in both retail sales and customer service you'll achieve when point-of-sale terminals can be moved to areas of peak demand overnight, or even over a lunch break. Next, imagine six notebook computers hastily opened on a conference table and sharing data minutes later. Imagine being able to do the same thing an hour after that—in a client's office, on a factory floor, or at a trade show.

Also, imagine linking the networks of two buildings a mile apart virtually overnight, without the expense of a leased telephone line. And, think about having an instant LAN set up and ready to cope—anywhere, anytime—when sudden business opportunities beckon or when a midnight phone call brings unthinkable news.

Now, take an empty room, add half a dozen workstations and link them all in a fast, partially secure local area network—within a few minutes. Impossible? Well, the security part may be.

Installing a wireless network actually can be just that simple. There's no wiring or conduit pathways to consider. All you need to create a fully functioning standalone network comes packed in a small box. Plug a card into each computer, install the software and your LAN is ready to go.

Could this unprecedented freedom help solve a few problems for you? Consider the possibilities. Cabling can be difficult or impossible to install in some situations. Asbestos makes older buildings problematic, hospitals can't accommodate new conduit pathways, warehouses can be simply too vast to rewire. But in each case a wireless network can be up and running virtually overnight.

Construction costs of recabling can overwhelm companies that change the workplace frequently. Retailers alter floor plans, manufacturers retool, banks redeploy branches. A wireless network effortlessly glides into place anywhere—and immediately becomes a versatile asset rather than a burdensome construction expense.

Finally, with the arrival of an industry standard, the concentration of manufacturers upon frequency hopping spread spectrum solutions will lower the cost and drive the market growth. The frequency hopping technology has the ability to support significant user density successfully, so there is no limitation to the penetration of such products in the user community. Wireless LAN solutions will be especially viable in new markets such as the small office/home office (SOHO) market, where there is rarely a wired LAN, due to the complexity and cost of wiring. Wireless LAN offers a solution that will connect a generation to *wired* access, but without the wires.

FROM HERE

Today's businesses require constant communication and instant access to information—both in and away from the office. The three cabling media (copper, fiber, and wireless) discussed in this chapter provide you with the mobility and flexibility you need—but you also have to manage the network that provides your communication requirements.

With that in mind, fiber optic cabling is rapidly becoming the most viable choice for data networking infrastructure. With the cost of cable, connectors, installation, and equipment becoming competitive with traditional copper solutions, fiber should be given serious consideration.

Finally, wireless LANs have some disadvantages. They are presently very expensive, provide poor security, and are susceptible to electrical interference from lights and radios. They are also slower than LANs using cabling. But they do have many advantages over traditional LANs. It's the way we're going to be doing business in this century.

The next chapter discusses the seven major types of networks: local area network (LAN), wide area network (WAN), virtual area network (VAN), virtual private network (VPN), intranet, extranet, and Internet. Some companies are fortunate to have all seven types connecting their systems. This chapter will cover how all three cabling media can be used with one or all seven of the network types to allow your organization to soar beyond the traditional constraints of network cabling. The next chapter will show you how and when to expand, contract, or redeploy your network type(s) virtually anywhere, anytime, as quickly as today's accelerating pace of change demands.

NOTES

[1]   CompTIA Headquarters, 450 East 22nd St., Suite 230, Lombard, IL 60148-6158, 2000.

[2]   "Local Area Network Cables," Remee Products Corp., P. O. Box 488, 186 North Main Street, Florida, NY 10921, USA, 2000, p. 1.

[3]   "Connecting Terminals and PCs with DB25 Connectors," Computone Corporation, 1100 Northmeadow Parkway, Suite 150 Roswell, GA 30076, 1997, p. 1.

[4]   "CATV, CCTV & Communication Coaxial Cable," Remee Products Corp., P. O. Box 488, 186 North Main Street, Florida, NY 10921, USA2000, p. 2.

[5]   "Ethernet Cable Comparison Chart," Cabletron Systems, 35 Industrial Way, Rochester, NH 03866 U.S.A., 2000, p. 1.

[6]   Scientific Instrument Services, 1027 Old York Rd., Ringoes, NJ 08551, 1999, p. 1.

[7]   "Fiber Optic Cabling Installations," Advanced Cable Connection Inc., 922A E. 124 Avenue, Tampa, FL 33612, 2000, p. 1.

[8]   Molex Incorporated, 2222 Wellington Court, Lisle, Illinois 60532 U.S.A., 2000, p. 1.

[9]   "What is a Wireless LAN?," Reprinted with the permission of AMP Incorporated, Investor Relations, 176-42, PO Box 3608, Harrisburg, PA USA 17105-3608, 1999, p. 1.

[10]   "Wireless LAN Systems—Technology and Specifications," SOHOware, Inc., NDC Communications, Inc., 265 Santa Ana Court, Sunnyvale, CA 94086, USA, 2000

CHAPTER 2

Types of Networks

We are in the middle of another information revolution that is reaching out and touching every aspect of our professional and personal lives. This time, the revolution has less to do with creating new information and more to do with resistance to change—that tension between centrifugal and centripetal forces. In cabling, the tension lies between the effects of different types of networking technologies that pull computing power out to the fringes of the network, and the effects that tend to centralize it. Finding and maintaining the dynamic balance between these forces is what makes the job of information technology (IT) professionals so hard.

A network consists of two or more computers that are linked in order to share resources (such as printers and CD-ROMs), exchange files, or allow electronic communications. The computers on a network may be linked through cables, telephone lines, radio waves, satellites, or infrared light beams. This chapter discusses seven major types of networks: local area network (LAN), wide area network (WAN), virtual area network (VAN), Internet, intranet, extranet, and virtual private network (VPN), which are available to organizations. The chapter also addresses ways in which the three cabling media (copper, fiber, and wireless) can be used with the various network types to allow your organization to be able to add and integrate new capabilities into their existing cabling infrastructure.

LOCAL AREA NETWORK

Let's begin our journey by looking at the first of these major types of networks: the local area network (LAN).

A LAN or local area network is a computer network (or data communications network) that is confined to a room, a building, or a group of adjacent buildings, as shown in Figure 2–1 [1]. Rarely are LAN computers more than a mile apart.

A similar network on a larger scale is sometimes referred to as a WAN (wide area network), or in some cases more specifically, a VAN (virtual area network) or MAN (metropolitan area network), if it is confined to a single metropolitan area. VANs are discussed later in this chapter.

The term LAN is most often used to refer to networks created using a certain class of networking equipment. This equipment is tailored to communication over a short distance and is in contrast to networks that happen to span long distances. These networks are constructed using WAN equipment (equipment capable of transmitting long distances). LAN-style networking equipment typically transmits data at a higher rate than WAN-style equipment. The equipment's design takes advantage of the short distance to supply a high transmission rate at a relatively low cost.

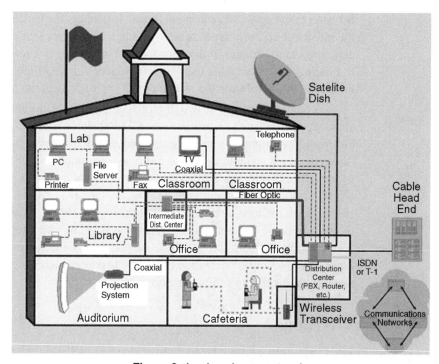

Figure 2–1   Local area network.

Both LAN and WAN equipment typically offers faster data transfer than even the fastest ordinary modem/phone-line access (LAN transfers being on the order of a million times faster).

If you are familiar with network access using a modem and an ordinary telephone line, the graphics that are loaded through a LAN network can be displayed significantly faster. In other words, there are things that are practical to do on a LAN that you would never do with a modem. For example, rather than setting up your computer to load your word processing application through your hard disk, you should load it from the LAN. In either case, the time you have to wait while it loads would be similar (a few seconds). In contrast, loading such an application through a modem would require minutes or hours.

A typical use of a LAN is to tie together personal computers in an office in such a way that they can all use a file server and a single printer. A file server is a computer set up so that other computers can access its hard disk as if it were their own.

LANs are also used to transmit e-mail between personal computers in an office. Additionally, they are also used to attach all the personal computers in an office to a WAN or to the Internet.

However, there is some variation in the way the term LAN is used. As previously stated, for example, it is used to refer to a file server and printer and often to the personal computers that are tied to them. People refer to saving their files on a PC LAN, or on a LAN. But the term LAN is also used more specifically to refer to the equipment and data communications wiring that ties the personal computers to the printer and file server.

In a typical LAN configuration, one computer is designated as the file server. It stores all of the software that can be shared by the computers attached to the network, as well as the software that controls the network. Thus, computers connected to the file server are called workstations. The workstations can be less powerful than the file server. They may even have additional software on their hard drives. Furthermore, cables are used to connect the network interface cards in each computer on most LANs.

Some other types of LANs (or in the jargon, other LAN technologies) are token ring, FDDI (fiber distributed data interface), and fast Ethernet. Ethernet is the most common type in use today. It's an example of what is called LAN technology; or, in the more specific sense of the word LAN—one of several types of LANs.

Equipment of two different technologies cannot be plugged together without a special device such as a bridge or router. These devices essentially translate between one technology and the other. In other words, network equipment cannot be interconnected by a piece of wire if the equipment being connected has dissimilar technology (such as the network server having an Ethernet adapter and your PC having a token ring adapter). However, if each adapter were attached to the same bridge—specifically, one that translates between Ethernet and token ring—then they could communicate.

Today, organizations are lured by the many benefits of distributed computing over LANs and WANs. They are faced with the daunting task of bringing workability to the diversity and complexity of today's data communications landscape. The need to interconnect dissimilar LANs and diverse equipment becomes even more urgent as enterprise networks continue to grow and expand to include telecommuters, small branch offices, and far-flung international locations. Among the key challenges facing network managers today is how to meld legacy systems and LANs, consolidate multiprotocol traffic over a single WAN backbone, and tie together incompatible LANs. Furthermore, without inflicting performance penalties on end users, all of this must be done at minimum cost.

WIDE AREA NETWORK

With that in mind, let's continue our journey and take a look at the next network type: the wide area network.

Sometimes referred to as "long haul networks," wide area networks (WANs) can cover large distances. Multiple buildings, cities, or even continents can be connected by WANs. Dedicated transoceanic cabling or satellite uplinks may be used to connect the type of network shown in Figure 2–2 [2].

Now (without having to pay enormous phone bills), schools in the United States can communicate with places like Tokyo in a matter of minutes using a WAN. A WAN is complicated. It uses multiplexers (a device that allows multiple logical signals to be transmitted simultaneously across a single physical channel) to connect local and metropolitan networks to global communications networks like the Internet. To users, however, a WAN will not appear to be much different from a LAN or a VAN. WANs operate at bandwidths ranging from 9.6 Kbps (thousand bits per second) up to and beyond 655 Mbps (million bits per second), as shown in Figure 2–3 [3]. Delays are usually large. They range from 10 milliseconds up to several hundred milliseconds across a satellite network.

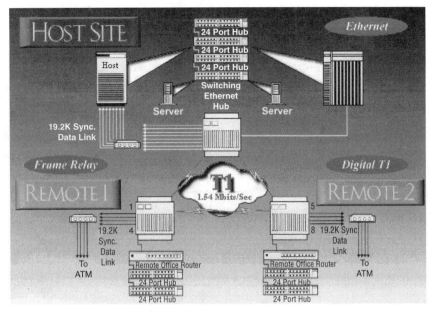

Figure 2–2   Wide area network.

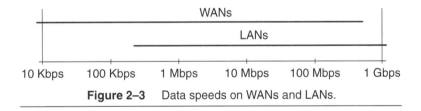

Figure 2–3   Data speeds on WANs and LANs.

Even though it is not shown in Figure 2–3, several of the Internet backbone providers are currently running or planning to run OC-24/OC-48 (1.2/2.4 Gbps) on their backbones.

Virtual Area Networks

Now, let's take a look at one of the most obvious and significant industries that will rise out of bandwidth abundance and our next type of network: virtual area networks (VANs).

Virtual area networks (VANs) or metropolitan area networks (MANs) have been around for several years, but the development of MANs has been limited due to the lack of bandwidth.

Initially, MANs were designed to cover larger geographic areas, such as cities or school districts, as shown in Figure 2–4 [4]. Information is easily disseminated throughout the network by interconnecting smaller networks within a large geographic area. A MAN is often used by local libraries and government agencies to connect citizens and private industries. The Fife and Tayside Metropolitan Area Network (FaTMAN) located at the University of Dundee, in Scotland, is one example of a MAN. The links (University of Dundee to University of Abertay Dundee: 1.5 km; University of Dundee to University of St. Andrews: 23 km; and University of St. Andrews to University of Abertay Dundee: 23.3 km), totaling 47.8 km (28 miles), are very long for directly driven fiber optic connections and use special purpose drivers to cover these distances. A high speed ATM network is used to support teaching and research activities in Fife and Tayside.

In the near future, VANs will become the gathering place for communities, both geographical and special interest. VANs may return some sense of community, which has been eroded by the automobile and urban sprawl. Additionally, VANs will create opportunities for special interest communities to form over widely dispersed geographical areas. They will empower telecommuting for company employees, individuals, government, and independent business.

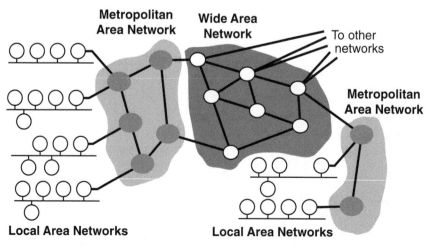

Figure 2–4   Virtual area network (VAN) or metropolitan area network (MAN).

The Telecommuting Factor

One of the goals of telecommuting is to allow a worker to accomplish from home the same things he or she would accomplish by traveling to the office. The virtual trip to the office can closely simulate the actual trip by utilizing interactive video and audio technology. You will be able to say hello to your secretary and coworkers once you are at your computer. You will pass the coffee lounge (virtual or real) and notice who is there. You will see that Diane the secretary is already on the phone and that the boss's office door is closed. You can discuss a new idea with a visitor you run into in a room or in the hall. Also, when someone new arrives in the area, computer-generated sounds of footsteps will alert you. Thus, telecommuting from your home or office will take on new meaning.

Through the creation of a new social context for communities, the benefits of a virtual office will be offered to the public at large. The interactive technology that was developed for multiuser computer games will be incorporated by VANs. VANs serve a number of community and social functions, as well as businesses. A virtual site will be created through chance encounters, social interaction, and multiple public sites that will closely resemble being together.

VAN Example

Residents in the town of Bozeman, Montana, have the opportunity to see each other on a university campus, meet for coffee, travel to each others' offices, and conduct business. A growing number of citizens work at home. The lack of social barriers is a distinguishing characteristic of Bozeman and the surrounding area. With a minimum amount of distraction or attracting attention, movie stars and business moguls are common in the shops and coffeehouses and are free to interact in the community. This type of interaction will be possible in virtual communities anywhere in the world. People can limit their exposure to selected groups, interact anonymously and electronically, and still allow for chance encounters and random visits.

In a virtually connected community, citizens can address the school board or the city commission without leaving home. Customers can talk to their accountants and bankers. Homebound students can talk to teachers. Merchants can market their products. And home office workers can look into connected coffeehouses, see who is there, and decide whether or not to take a break.

VAN technology will be limited to perhaps several hundred participants per system. Numerous VANs will develop in larger cities. A directory of

VANs and access codes will also evolve. Each viewer will be able to display numerous participants on the computer screen at one time among the potential participants of a VAN. Clicking on one participant will bring it to full screen view.

The legal and medical communities may initially receive the greatest benefits from VANs. Prisoners can be arraigned virtually, eliminating the need for expensive and dangerous transportation. They could receive routine health care virtually. Medical specialists can consult without leaving their offices and clinics. Lawyers can telecommute to the courthouse and their clients. Private rooms on the VAN will provide confidentiality for business in general, attorney–client privilege, and medical confidences. A quick return on investment for the VAN will result from savings in time and travel, with an estimated payback period of usually less than a few months. Additional benefits will be less stress, reduced traffic, and increased efficiency. More professions, businesses, and individuals will benefit directly from the virtual connection to their community as the VAN develops.

The question of privacy must be addressed by this technology. Access to certain individuals or groups can be limited by participants. Members of a private group can go to a virtual private room where only other group members and their guests are granted access. Control of access and exposure on the VAN will be given to each participant. VANs may shift our cities back toward the communal nature of small towns (with their benefits and drawbacks). Standards for privacy can be agreed upon and implemented to fit individual values and the community.

Connectivity Factor

Hardware and software to implement VANs can be developed with existing technology. Bandwidth has been the limiting factor to date. Some major steps in bandwidth are listed in Table 2–1 [5].

Table 2–1   Major Bandwidth Steps

Home/Small Office Use	Year	Faster than Previous	Improvement Factor
0.3 Kbps modem	1990		
1.2 Kbps modem	1991	4.0	4
14.4 Kbps modem	1992	12.0	48
28.8 Kbps modem	1994	2.0	96
128 Kbps BRI-ISDN	1996	4.5	428
768 K–2.0 Mbps HDSL with PairGain	1997	6.0	2560
6 Mbps ADSL on AT&T GlobeSpan	1998	7.8	20,000
10 Mbps to 36 Mbps Cable Modem	1999	6.0	120,000
10 Gbps wave multiplexed fiber	2001	278.8	33,333,333
1,700 Gbps wave multiplexed fiber	2006	170.0	5,666,666,610

Each step in Table 2–1 represents a dramatic improvement over the previous. Cable modems have already been deployed in northern California, and the BRI-ISDN (basic rate interface-integrated services digital network) has begun to spread in much of the country. PairGain Technologies has shipped 768 Kbps mega modems, which now operate over copper lines. AT&T Paradyne claims their 6.0 Mbps GlobeSpan asymmetric digital subscriber line (ADSL) service is now available in most parts of the country. With the significant benefits of increased bandwidth, the question for anyone looking into VANs becomes which connectivity technology should be implemented. In most parts of the country, the highest step currently available economically is BRI-ISDN. But everything short of cable modems could soon be obsolete. Processing and storing data at this flow rate will push the limits of the fastest and most memory-endowed computers.

Among connected office computers, the high speed of local area networks (LAN) connections allows for high quality audio and video (10 Mbps for Ethernet, 4 or 16 Mbps for token ring). But quality and speed for inter-LAN multimedia connections is greatly limited by bandwidth of publicly switched telephone lines. High-bit-rate digital subscriber line (HDSL) connection devices operating at 768 Kbps are available for connections over unconditioned dry copper pairs. The HDSL connection devices can be rented from the local exchange carrier (LEC), usually a Bell operating company. This speed is adequate for high quality audio and video connection between remote LANs and over the Internet. AT&T Paradyne has unveiled an application of ADSL that is capable of providing 6 Mbps over copper wires. This is reportedly on the market now in most parts of the country. AT&T claims that rates are comparable to standard phone service.

Cable Modem Technology

Cable modem technology, which has spread, is making all the other connection schemes obsolete. Cable modem technology provides access to VANs and the Internet at speeds in the 30–56 Mbps range downstream (network to computer). Computer connections are usually based on Ethernet 10BaseT. Early cable modems are operating asymmetrically, with downstream bandwidths considerably wider than upstream bandwidths (computer to network). @Home, a venture of the Silicon Valley venture capital group of Kleiner, Perkins, Caufield, and Beyer, reportedly has a cable modem Internet access trial currently underway in Fremont, California. Continental Cablevision is planning to use LANCity cable modems to provide high-bit-rate service in New England. Bozeman, Montana, the birthplace of TCI Cable, is leveraging existing connections for a VAN in anticipation of cable modems.

Computer and interface limitations have lowered these bandwidths. Downstream bandwidths are 5 to 12 Mbps and upstream bandwidths are usually between 400 Kbps to 4 Mbps. Cable modems do MOdulate and DEModulate, but they are actually a combination modem, tuner, bridge, encrypter, router, Network Interface Card (NIC), Simple Network Management Protocol (SNMP), and hub in one.

Cable modem is a descriptive but inaccurate term.

Even cable operators with older one-way delivery systems are now able to provide bidirectional Internet access. The availability of bandwidth at this magnitude leads to the next limiting factor of the digital age: the global telecommunication backbone. The backbone is presently undergoing a radical upgrade. Phone companies installed an estimated 10 million kilometers of fiber in the 1980s, and only a fraction of the potential bandwidth has been utilized. Wave division multiplexing is a method of sending different wavelengths or colors down the fiber and filtering them at the other end. Four colors increases the 2.4 Gbps capacity of a single fiber to 9.6 Gbps. This is the equivalent of sending 1,000 novels per second. By the year 2002, that is expected to rise to 700 Gbps. This would relatively permit the transmission of a medium-sized bookstore in less than a second. Theoretically, approximately 700 separate wavelength streams could be sent and filtered, resulting in a capacity of 1,700 Gbps over a single fiber.

In addition to being radically faster than other forms of digital connectivity, cable modems offer much simpler installation. ISDN installation and connection is notoriously complicated, requiring the customer to act as his or her own systems integrator. Cable companies are now able to offer a turnkey ready-to-operate system commonly referred to as a "managed system" (see Chapter 4, "Digital Subscriber Line (DSL) Versus Cable," for more information on cable modems).

INTERNET

Web pages today are mainly for disseminating information, not receiving it (beyond vital statistics). The proliferation of video conferencing equipment combined with increasing bandwidth will create more Internet users looking for virtual places to go. That brings us to the next type of network: the Internet.

The Internet, also known as the first wave of the World Wide Web (WWW) evolution, is the largest network in existence. It can be defined as the physical network that connects many different computer systems in a loosely associated network that spans the globe. The Internet carries most of the information shared on a worldwide scale. It currently connects 80 to 140 million machines located throughout 92 percent of the world, as shown in Figure 2–5, and is growing at an astounding rate [6].

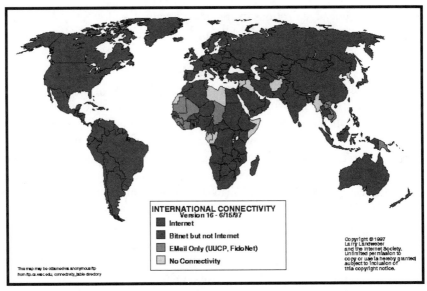

Figure 2–5   Internet connectivity to different parts of the world.

Current estimates indicate that there were 380 million Internet users at the end of 1999, up from 91 million Internet users in 1998, an annual growth of nearly 51.8 percent. Estimates by independent research organizations indicate that another 1.6 billion users (mostly from China) will join the Internet by 2003. With this many users, the Internet has grown far beyond the expectations of its designers when it was created 31 years ago [10].

Wave One: The Public Domain Internet

The Internet and WWW have provided unprecedented ways of linking people with information. With the Web's ubiquitous software and technology, global access to data, text, documents, pictures, sound, animation, video, and other information from any Web-enabled computer or workstation is now a reality. The recent awareness and popularity of this medium has been fueled primarily by the fundamental simplicity and adaptability of the Internet's open and standard protocols. More than simply a vehicle for information dissemination, the Internet is leading networking computing shifts away from fat clients, closed proprietary systems, and costly network operating system (NOS) environments.

Internet Use

With billions of interconnected systems and users, the Internet offers a way for organizations to compete globally. The low cost of entry and global reach associated with establishing a website level the playing field among organizations with respect to size or technology investment. However, the quality of that presence plays a much bigger role in terms of its technical and communicative function.

The World Wide Web is by far the most popular choice for a public presence on the Internet. It can provide a single platform for developing a corporate identity, advertising, and marketing products and services. In a recent study by an independent research organization, 68 percent of the companies surveyed felt that using Internet technology resulted in an improvement in their respective business environments [7]. An increasing number of organizations are using Internet technologies for useful business applications such as Federal Express's computerized cargo tracking system. But is Internet technology the right choice for you? Remember, the answer depends on the goals and objectives of your organization and how they match up against criteria such as the types of communications and the nature of transactions.

For example, the objective of *The New York Times* was to develop an interactive version of its daily newspaper. Internet technology was a good choice because the information in its publication is public and freely available. Security is not a major issue. The Internet also provides a convenient way to offer timely coverage of major news stories to readers at their desktops anywhere around the world.

Although the well-known Ben & Jerry's ice cream Internet site started out as a private business system for its employees and franchisers, the focus of the site was soon shifted to the consumer. To satisfy the universal desire for its product, the company developed an Internet website that offers information such as ice cream flavors and products, scoop shop locations, company-sponsored film and music festivals, factory tours, and Ben & Jerry's business philosophy.

In some cases, a public website on the Internet is needed to provide the easiest and most wide-ranging access, while still ensuring a high degree of security for sensitive transactions. The Chicago Board of Trade (CBOT) implemented its integrated website to allow the exchange to conduct secure electronic commerce and communications on a global basis. Visitors seeking recent quotes, educational material, or other information can get it all online 24 hours a day.

From just a brief look at these few business cases, it's clear that successful networking choices begin with well-defined goals and objectives based on an organization's needs and capabilities. Only then are the objectives matched to available network technologies. Specific networking strategies and tactics are negotiated from this match-up. For some objectives, intranets (which will be discussed next) are the clear choice, especially when internal communications must be kept secure or when the bandwidth and throughput must be optimized for multimedia and real-time communications.

For other objectives, the Internet offers an unprecedented opportunity to reach a global base of users in a manner that is convenient and has a low cost of entry and maintenance. Ultimately, the real question is not Internet versus intranet, but rather when and how each networking strategy should be used to serve the many and changing needs of an organization.

INTRANETS

Intranets, also known as the second wave of the Internet evolution, are secured areas that utilize the Internet and WWW to conduct internal communication and collaboration activities. When the Internet and the World Wide Web architecture are brought inside of a company and used to distribute a company's private information, you have an intranet. Adopted by companies at an increasingly phenomenal rate, intranets have produced efficiencies for businesses that allow users to manage their organizations more efficiently and effectively behind the firewall. To date, three-quarters of Fortune 500 corporations and thousands of other companies have already established intranets, the majority of which are being used to manage tasks, information, and groupwork within individual organizations [8].

Whether network managers are considering Internet access or intranet implementation, they need to understand that both are important new approaches to networking technology. As such, they must be in every network manager's bag of tricks. More important, intranets are a technology, or more accurately a collection of technologies, that dramatically change how companies do business internally and with their customers and suppliers. As a telecommunications technology, intranet technology truly re-engineers communications, which is its real value.

A Cost-Effective and Timely Solution

Increasingly, forward-thinking organizations are taking advantage of the *intranet* as a more cost-effective and efficient approach. As previously mentioned, the intranet refers to the use of Internet WWW technology within the organization or the *intraprise* rather than for external connection to the Internet.

At the foundation of the intranet is the World Wide Web server. Organizations with internal WWW sites store and update information electronically on a WWW server configured on a local area network. As information changes, the server content can be easily updated with the new or revised data. This approach enables organizations to deliver timely, consistent, and accurate information to their employees worldwide—without expensive typesetting, printing, distribution, and mailing charges.

Depending on LAN configuration, an organization may have one or more internal WWW servers used as a central, internal clearinghouse to manage and disseminate information within the intraprise. For example, a corporate WWW server accessible to every company employee may contain key information such as employee handbooks, internal newsletters, and stock plan descriptions. Multinational companies may choose to set up a WWW site at each geographical location. And, depending on their size and specific needs, organizations may implement a combination of the preceding, with a corporate WWW server accessible to all employees, plus dedicated web servers for individual departments.

A secure WWW site offers numerous advantages for the internal exchange of highly confidential material. For example, a WWW can be set up to restrict information to certain departments (such as finance and human resources [HR] or for geographically distributed departments to share information securely) by using the Internet as the backbone. In such a scenario, the corporate HR department of a multinational company based in Columbus, Ohio, can share salary planning information with its European HR department in Milan, Italy. Additionally, the Intranet, since configured to operate on the LAN, is well-suited for multimedia applications with video and audio integration.

A Good Fit?

The intranet is an ideal solution for any organization with many users, and/or with remote locations distributed over wide geographical areas. It's an appropriate fit for any business that needs a cost-effective way to disseminate constantly fluctuating information on demand to its employees. Among some of the functional areas that can benefit from this technology are Human Resources, Training, Sales and Marketing, MIS, Finance, Corporate Communications, Telesales, Research & Development, and Technical Documentation departments.

Human resources departments will find the intranet a highly effective way to enhance communications and increase staff productivity, while reducing costs. The use of an internal WWW server provides employees worldwide with easy and convenient access to standard HR material, including information about benefits, stock purchase plans, policies and procedures, job postings, and more. The intranet website can virtually eliminate the corporate overhead associated with printing employee handbooks.

The training departments can benefit from intranet technologies by having an easy way to provide staff members with up-to-the minute materials including video and audio aids without going through the expense of reproducing expensive materials that would otherwise be impossible to fathom. Another benefit is that the internal intranet can provide employees with a "self-paced" method of training. For example, a new sales hire may want to simply review the *solutions selling* portion of the new hire training class. At the touch of a button and at his or her convenience, the new hire simply clicks on the right spot without pouring through reams of paper.

Marketing departments must support sales with a wide variety of material—customer presentations, pricing, special promotions, incentives, and much more. With the intranet, marketing can be confident that their worldwide sales force can always have access to the latest information—wherever and whenever they need it. For example, by storing PowerPoint presentations on your internal WWW server, you can be sure that the same information is being presented consistently worldwide. Instant access to the intranet from any network location saves the marketing department time and money.

For example, employees can check the intranet for information ranging from:

- Dental coverage before making a dental appointment on the HR information section;
- allowable business trip expenses on the business travel reimbursement section;
- up-to-the minute cost figures on cost or sales prices on the marketing/manufacturing section;
- product specification literature on the marketing section; and
- distribution information on product suppliers and availability on the inventory section.

All of the information from the preceding listing is made up from the convenience of the desktop of any computer in the office, at home or abroad. This is all made possible with a good information technology (IT) department that can develop an integrated intranet site that interconnects the accounting databases with the marketing databases, the inventory information with the distributor/product supplier information, and so on.

Intranet Architectural Design:
Integrating Information Design with Business Planning

The corporate intranet has been hailed as the most important business tool since the typewriter, but the track record so far has been mixed. Despite many successes, particularly in cost and time savings, many sponsors of corporate intranets are dissatisfied. They have spent time and money on development, Net-enabled desktops, even intranet training, but still aren't enjoying significant enough productivity or cost savings. Why? While critics often point to technological glitches, the real problems may lie in information design.

Intranets can help employees collaborate on business processes such as product development or order fulfillment, which create value for a company and its customers. Specifically, intranets centralize the business process in an easily accessible, platform-independent virtual space. Successful intranets allow employees from a variety of departments to contribute the different skills necessary to carry out a particular process. While each department of a company may have its own virtual space, intranets should be organized primarily around the business processes they help employees carry out, rather than the organizational chart of the company.

Focusing on processes rather than departments is a widely hailed business trend. Recent shifts in corporate structure point to the emergence of *communities of process*. Management gurus are helping companies move away from vertical, hierarchical organizational lines toward horizontal, process-oriented groups that link cross-functional teams focused on the same set of business tasks. The trouble is that this requires significant interaction between departments, functions, even countries. Enter the intranet, the ideal vehicle for creating and empowering process-based corporate communities.

Successful process-oriented intranets look and work as differently as the processes they enable, but they share several common characteristics. First they are built on smart information design. Second, they focus on tasks, not documents, and aim to integrate those tasks into distinct processes. Finally, the best intranets encourage collaboration by creating shared and familiar spaces that reflect the personality of the company and create a common ground for all employees.

Careful Design

Just as physical work spaces rely on architectural plans to optimize efficiency, an intranet needs to be carefully designed to help employees access information and collaborate effectively. Because the public doesn't see the intranet, information design for intranets often receives scant attention. Unlike customers, employees are assumed to be insiders, able to easily locate company information. Therefore, while the company web site usually has the input of the marketing department, the design and structure of the intranet is often relegated to the IT department.

By default, an organizational chart of the company is often used to organize information on the intranet. While seemingly the obvious candidate for the structure of the intranet, an organizational chart actually works against the collaboration the intranet is meant to foster. An organizational chart can't help employees from the marketing and legal departments collaborate on bringing a document through the approval process. It won't allow employees from marketing and R & D to work together to create a new product.

A Task-Oriented Design

Thinking of the intranet as a tool means understanding the intranet as more than a collection of documents. While important, documents are usually a means to an end. People use documents to complete tasks. Tasks include fulfilling orders, looking up a customer's billing history, or collaborating on a research document. To complete these tasks, people need to have related documents and tools close at hand.

The principal of organizing by task can be demonstrated by the example of working at a desk. When you sit down to begin a task (creating a budget), you have a variety of information and tools at hand. While a spreadsheet is a *calculation* tool and last year's budget is an *internal document,* both need to be next to each other in order to develop a new budget. Similarly, on the corporate intranet, the tasks of the users, rather than the classification of documents or tools, should dictate the organization of the intranet.

Designed effectively around dynamic tasks rather than static documents, intranets can contribute to dramatic increases in efficiency (as much as a 50 percent improvement in time spent processing documents, according to the GIGA Group)[9]. Organizing documents within the context of tasks also focuses employees on the function of the documents on which they are working. For example, to save employee time while signing up for various retirement plans, information on various retirement plans (including links to financial web sites) should be placed near the forms actually used to register for those plans.

Organizational Processes for Larger Tasks

Isolated tasks are usually part of a larger process. Intranets should group together all the tasks that make up a business process. Processes can be relatively discrete, such as tracking deliveries or getting approval for documents. Or, they can be more complex, such as developing or selling products. The most important processes in a company are those that create value for a customer. These are the central processes that every intranet should help employees accomplish.

Even simple processes can become more efficient when incorporated into an intranet. For example, when the Ford Motor Company implemented an intranet, the company included an application to help geographically dispersed engineers to get authorization for new projects. What would previously be a time-consuming, expensive process, involving the potential for lost documents and delays, is now centralized in an efficient electronic process. Naturally, more complex processes can also be effectively integrated into an intranet with proper planning.

Creating and Organizing Virtual Workgroups Around Processes

Intranets can break though departmental walls to help accomplish business processes more efficiently. For example, a customer complaint might involve people and information from the accounting, sales, and marketing departments. Even though the employees necessary to resolve the complaint work in different departments, they are all involved in the process of customer service. By creating spaces for cross-departmental collaboration, the intranet can help employees collaborate to efficiently carry out the central processes of the company, and cut costs by avoiding in-person conferences and employee reallocations.

Intranets (and private extranets, which will be discussed later) can also bring together employees and partners who are geographically dispersed to work on common problems. Travel costs are eliminated, and employees can increase their productivity by sharing knowledge. One simple example of leveraging an intranet might involve a pharmaceutical company that uses its intranet to allow scientists from all over the world to collaborate on the research and development of drugs.

The Company and Intranet are a Reflection of Each Other

The corporate intranet can help a company organize around *communities of process* both on- and offline. When Texas Instruments (in Dallas, Texas) initiated a process-centered organization, oriented around collaborative work groups, average software development time fell from 20 to 6 months. The Texas Instruments intranet was established after this shift, and was designed to reflect and enhance the new organization. Whether it precedes or follows the organizational shift, an intranet that encourages this type of collaborative work environment can provide a significant return-on-investment.

Using an intranet to shift the way work is done in an organization may require a cultural change within the organization. Unless there is a clear commitment from senior management to have employees collaborate across departments to more efficiently accomplish key business processes, the intranet may have only limited application and benefit. Even after the intranet is designed to encourage collaboration, marketing the intranet to employees remains essential. As the intranet creates new forms of collaboration, it will challenge traditional ways of doing work and obtaining information. For the intranet to be successful, it must provide ways of empowering all employees, offering concrete incentives for employees to use, and encourage the use of the intranet.

The process-oriented intranet is then *in sync* with the company for which it works. This is where graphic design, tone, and standards emerge as vital to the intranet's success. Like it or not, intranets have personalities, which are amalgams of visual style, tone, and content. An intranet that reflects the culture of its company will make employees feel more at home, will help dispersed employees feel that they share the same space, and will encourage collaboration and communication around the processes they support. The Turner Entertainment Group (in Atlanta, Georgia), for example, created a distinctive, casual feel for its intranet with a home page that uses a refrigerator with magnates to represent the various divisions. The unique imagery created a friendly, shared, familiar space for all employees.

Good Business is a Good Design

Good intranets should be machines for doing business. Just as design is integral to a good building, it is key to creating an effective intranet. The organization and design of information on an intranet should map out the key business processes of a company, and provide employees with access to the information and people necessary to carry out those processes.

The truly effective intranet creates new channels of communication that overcome inefficient organizational structures and foster new forms of efficient collaboration. It serves as a model for a company centered around processes rather than departments, and collaboration rather than closed doors.

Building an effective intranet means thinking about how documents can be used to accomplish tasks, how tasks can be organized into processes, and how those processes can be carried out collaboratively by virtual work groups. The effective intranet is not only a tool, it is also a model for an efficient process-centered enterprise—a machine for doing business.

Getting Started in Creating a WWW Intranet Site

Now that you have built and designed the intranet, it is now time to create the WWW intranet site. Creating an internal web site is a low-cost, minimal-risk investment. It is relatively easy to implement, with very little training or equipment required. The basic system configuration consists of a server hardware platform/operating system and WWW server software. Assuming that your organization already has client PCs in place, the client investment should be minimal.

As a server platform, the rule of thumb is server hardware with sufficient memory and disk space to run Windows NT, Windows 2000, and/or a UNIX system platform, depending on your preference and in-house expertise. You will also need to configure the hardware with LAN cards for TCP/IP connection over the network to the clients. Today, an increasing number of organizations are opting for Windows NT or Windows 2000 because of their open architecture and ease of use.

TCP/IP is an abbreviation for Transmission Control Protocol/Internet Protocol, which are two interrelated protocols that are part of the Internet protocol suite. TCP operates on the OSI Transport Layer and breaks data into packets. IP operates on the OSI Network Layer and routes packets. TCP/IP was originally developed by the U.S. Department of Defense.

Web server software enables you to manage your internal WWW presence on the Intranet. The right WWW server software solution will give you the functionality required to set up and manage home pages, develop WWW content based on the Hypertext Markup Language (HTML), perform text searches, and integrate with internal corporate databases or BackOffice applications.

BackOffice refers to a suite of network server software from Microsoft that includes Windows NT Server; BackOffice Server, for the integrated development, deployment, and management of BackOffice applications in departments, branch offices, and medium-sized businesses; Exchange Server; Proxy Server; Site Server for intranet publishing, management, and search; Site Server Commerce Edition, for comprehensive Internet commerce transactions; Small Business Server, for business operations, resource management, and customer relations; SNA Server, for the integration of existing and new systems and data; SQL Server, for scalable, reliable database and data warehousing; and Systems Management Server (SMS), for centralized change and configuration management.

On the client side, each user who plans to access the internal WWW site will need at least a 486 or Pentium-PC (or notebook) with a minimum of 16 MB memory, sufficient hardware to accommodate an industry standard browser application. Typically, a commercial client browser costs less than $50, although freeware versions that provide much the same functionality are also available. The client browser can launch a variety of applications, access disparate databases, retrieve information from across the Internet, and so on.

WWW content software is also required to generate HTML code so that you can add HTML tags to convert your current MS Word documents into WWW documents. It's very easy to develop content for the Web using one of the many inexpensive, third-party HTML authoring tools and editors, such as Microsoft's Internet Assistant or Front Page Express, which are typically available free of charge. Depending on your organization's requirements, you can also take advantage of numerous other commercial tools that are also available, including graphics software and packages to convert documents to HTML code, as well as text retrieval/indexing software, linking database management systems, and server configuration or management tools.

Key Considerations in Choosing a WWW Server

Since the WWW server serves as the cornerstone for managing the WWW site, it's important to determine the type of functionality you require. Use the following questions as guidelines in making the right choice:

- Are HTML tools supported for application development?
- Are there special resource or configuration requirements?
- Do you plan to use WWW browsers such as Netscape Communicator? If so, what Internet proxy support (HTTP, GOPHER, FTP) will you need?
- Does the WWW server support these protocols?
- Must your employees have access to corporate databases? If so, what type of database support is required, such as Microsoft's Open Database Connectivity (ODBC) standard or SQL for database integration?
- Should Linux, UNIX, Windows NT, or Windows 2000 serve as the WWW server platform?
- What addressing schemes are supported?
- What are your security requirements? For example, will it be necessary to protect highly confidential information and restrict access to certain workgroups? If so, what types of access controls can the WWW server define?
- What type of interface does the WWW server use? Is it intuitive, Windows-like, and easy to use?
- What type of search engine and text retrieval is supported?
- What type of training, documentation, and ongoing support is available?
- Who will be installing the WWW server? How important is easy installation?
- Who will be responsible for managing the content? Will this be someone technical or nontechnical?
- Who will set up the home page? What type of training is required?
- Will multiple home pages be installed on the same server? If so, how easy is it to manage and administer? Is remote administration a requirement [13]?

Groupware versus Intranet: The Key Differences

The bottom line difference between a WWW server and *collaborative* computing solutions such as Lotus Notes is design philosophy. Designed as a proprietary system in an era lacking widespread connectivity, Lotus Notes uses a proprietary database structure, which replicates data and, without some customization, does not provide quick access to remote databases. A WWW server, however, should be designed to take advantage of the Internet's worldwide computer network. It eliminates the need to replicate databases by providing users with easy access to source data using a nonproprietary system allowing open connectivity.

Another important difference is that a single WWW server platform can support internal and external applications for both internal information-sharing and external marketing on the Internet. Notes, on the other hand, is primarily an internal application.

Since the Intranet takes advantage of WWW open-standard technology, it offers a great starting point for corporations to disseminate information within the company efficiently and cost-effectively. Initial WWW startup costs and commitment are very low, with a minimal upfront investment or training. For example, an investment of less than $2,000 is estimated for site development, a dedicated infrastructure or staff is not required, and it is extremely easy to migrate existing content to HTML.

According to a recent research study, the average corporate investment in a Lotus Notes implementation is $356,000, with an average payback period of more than three years. Eighty percent of the respondents to this study targeted a single application. WWW applications can be fully developed and deployed for $20,000 or less [10].

The WWW enables users to centralize their information resources in a single point-and-click environment (the browser), which is available for a variety of client platforms (PC, Mac, Unix, etc.).

The use of client browsers with one standard Window interface offers easy integration with other applications, such as electronic mail, faxes, calendaring, video conferencing, and hot links within messages. As a single interface to a variety of information sources, the browser is cost-effective, highly efficient, and very easy to use.

In a traditional sense, it is less expensive to develop content for the open browser operable Web than for a proprietary product such as Notes. A wide variety of third-party content tools are available for the WWW server development, while the content development tools are available for Notes. Since familiar tools, such as Microsoft Word or other general user word processors, can generate HTML code, less technical support staff can easily create WWW content.

The WWW can be adapted easily to multimedia applications. For example, video is an easy extension to the basic WWW platform. By using readily available free or inexpensive utilities (CU SEE ME, Internet Phone, etc.), a corporation can deploy bidirectional desktop video conferencing relatively inexpensively.

Most organizations do not specifically require *collaborative* groupware applications, but instead need an easy, effective, fast, and inexpensive way to share information for a competitive business advantage. Thus the introduction of the WWW applications. These broaden the reach of team applications to more than an enlightened and highly technical few.

As mentioned previously, the benefits offered by the Intranet include and incorporate cost savings, minimal training, single source of data, links to outside data sources, and easy management and delivery of information. When you weigh these advantages, you will see that, for most organizations, they far outweigh the benefits of the information-handling capabilities of collaborative-groupware tools.

Applying WWW Technology to Internal Communications

More and more companies are realizing the efficiencies of applying WWW technology to internal communications. A WWW server enables organizations to apply the power and cost efficiency of the WWW to an internal communication program(s). By using a WWW on a LAN, organizations can easily disseminate and update a variety of corporate information sources, improve productivity, and significantly reduce costs.

Effective implementation of an internal communication system such as the intranet requires some good advance planning, a clear understanding of the internal communication needs, and familiarity with the appropriate tools. It addition, it requires an intact infrastructure.

Intranet Infrastructure

The Internet and intranets comprise not only the physical connection of the systems, but also the wide range of software that allows the creation, organization, and distribution of information, including the World Wide Web. These technologies are revolutionizing the way information is produced, gathered, distributed, and used.

Most businesses agree that the availability of cheap, organized information is a benefit and a requirement to staying competitive. However, most businesses are unsure of exactly how to take advantage of the Internet/intranet information pipeline and how to integrate this pipeline into their existing mission-critical networks, which were built as the result of a decade of expensive investments.

The problems of building and integrating a network infrastructure suitable to support mission-critical intranets are manifold. They include:

- The question of whether intranets are a practical investment;
- the consideration of today's LAN infrastructure, which may not be suitable for hosting a high-speed intranet; and
- the requirements for hosting a mission-critical intranet. [11]

A number of challenges have arisen because of the growing importance of intranets and the World Wide Web. Two of the most important are how to enable the widespread exchange of information and how to deal with the type and structure of this new information. IT and network managers are facing the challenge of enabling the exchange of information on a scale that is broader than the LAN. This requires implementing a technology gateway between an organization's existing infrastructure and the infrastructure improvements needed to support intranets.

How practical is it to build the client/server infrastructure necessary to support an intranet? The client/server concept and its associated issues are well understood; so are its benefits and pitfalls. Not only are there issues in building client/server applications, but there are also issues related to building the physical cabling infrastructure to support the wide-scale deployment of these applications.

Building the Physical Cabling Infrastructure

Fortunately, building a cabling infrastructure that can support an intranet is a logical step in moving a network toward the support of client/server applications. Today an intranet, with its client-side browser and its service-side servers, is the best low-cost, widely available implementation of a client/server architecture. In addition, an intranet can be built to incorporate and support many different computing platforms. Furthermore, most of the software needed to implement intranets is available at a relatively low cost.

Intranets, therefore, can benefit an organization by providing information on an organizational or worldwide scale, and also serve as a low-cost proving ground for the implementation of additional client/server applications.

If a cabling infrastructure can support an intranet, it is well on the way toward supporting other client/server applications. Many CIOs now are asking: Can my current cabling architecture support the new high-speed intranet software?

Supporting the Intranet

Can your cabling architecture support an intranet? The answer to this question is most likely "no" if your network has the following characteristics:

- congested network backbones with poor server-to-workstation or inter-network response time;
- microsegmentation to control excess broadcast traffic; and
- lack of available bandwidth caused by a large number of end-stations trying to access a smaller number of servers (Gluck, 3).

When evaluating the potential return on investment of an intranet, cabling architects must decide on the type of technology that will be used to build the intranet backbone. Today's technologies offer ATM (asynchronous transfer mode), FDDI (fiber distributed data interface), or fast Ethernet as solutions that will meet the bandwidth requirements of servers and backbones in the campus or metropolitan network. It is important to understand the differences among these technologies, especially where scalability is concerned.

When delivery of the right amount of bandwidth to where it is needed is important, ATM is a better solution than FDDI or fast Ethernet. One key difference between ATM and FDDI is that FDDI is a shared-media, token-passing technology similar to a token ring. ATM, on the other hand, is a switched-technology media.

Because an FDDI backbone is built as a token ring, the total available 300 Mbps is shared among all attached users. For example, connecting 32 users (or devices) to an FDDI ring means that these devices will be competing for a maximum available bandwidth of 300 Mbps, thereby giving each device an average bandwidth of only 9 Mbps. With this shared architecture, there is no way to allocate a specific amount of bandwidth to any one of the connections, and no way to scale available bandwidth.

Connectivity

Connect the same 32 devices to an ATM network, and each of the 32 devices can be allotted a dedicated 465 Mbps of bandwidth or, in fact, any amount of bandwidth from 76.8 Mbps to over 3 Gbps. This bandwidth is available because the architecture of ATM allows direct connections or circuits to be established between two end points over a meshed network where each of the circuits can be allocated a fixed amount of bandwidth.

Why is this an advantage? First, scalability allows each section of the network to be given bandwidth according to its particular needs. While desktop applications might find 76.8 Mbps more than adequate, work groups or corporate servers might require 300 Mbps or 465 Mbps, and corporate backbones might need even more. With ATM networks, the cabling architect can scale the available bandwidth to provide exactly the amount needed using a single network topology from the desktop through the backbone.

Second, meshed networks allow scalability and can be built as a collapsed backbone either inside a chassis or over a wide area. This allows available scalable bandwidth to be allocated exactly where it is needed.

Finally, bandwidth within a meshed network is additive. This characteristic allows the construction of large multigigabit networks that can provide high throughput at the top of a bandwidth hierarchy.

Switching and Scalability

ATM and fast Ethernet are best when combined in a single solution that supports cost-efficient operation of the data center—each technology doing what it does best. Why? ATM and fast Ethernet are both switched and scalable technologies. As a bandwidth hierarchy is built, both Ethernet and ATM can scale to support the needs of users, LANs, and data centers. Fast Ethernet also is considered to be simpler in sites where Ethernet is the only topology. In pure Ethernet sites, there is no packet-to-cell conversion or heterogeneous bridging necessary to move data from one point to another. Fast Ethernet does not scale well over large geographical areas. It is limited to five miles, so problems may arise when installing backbones across a campus. Also, fast Ethernet cannot provide WAN solutions; ATM addresses this issue.

Fast Ethernet cannot support the connection of token ring networks if it is used as a backbone. It also cannot be meshed because of the requirement that spanning tree algorithms should be implemented to prevent loops in a network. However, ATM can be used to build meshed networks or backbones for redundancy and efficiency.

One other fact to consider: Connecting servers directly to ATM is technologically feasible and rapidly dropping in price. It can be implemented today with almost no network changes other than the addition of an ATM network interface card to the server. Based on these considerations, it is best to consider ATM as the technology for high-speed backbones and fast Ethernet as the technology for the LAN section of the network.

Finally, many technologies cross our desks each year in the never-ending march to deliver information where it is needed. The second and first Internet technology wave, intranets, and the World Wide Web have already proven themselves as highly useful paradigms that can improve information availability in the business and even the home environment. Always keep in mind that the benefits that intranets can bring may be lost in an overwhelming avalanche of network overload and uncompleted projects if not implemented correctly. Learn, plan, start slowly, and factor in growth from the beginning. Intranets can then deliver all that they promise.

EXTRANET

Now that you know all about intranets, the next logical step in your thought processes might involve an *extranet*—the third wave of the Internet evolution. Let's look at how organizations are intelligently joining their intranets to create extranets.

The extranet represents the bridge between the public Internet and the private corporate Intranet. It connects multiple and diverse organizations online behind virtual firewalls, where those who share in trusted circles can network in order to achieve commerce-oriented objectives. The extranet defines and supports this extended business enterprise, including partners, suppliers, distributors, contractors, and others that operate outside the physical walls of an organization but are nonetheless critical to the success of business operations. With the Internet providing for public outreach or communication, and the Intranet serving internal business interests, the extranet serves the business-critical domain between these extremes where the majority of business activity occurs.

Nailing It Down

The exact definition of an extranet still is shaking out, but the most universally accepted one defines an extranet as a network that links business partners to one another over the Internet by tying together their corporate intranets. Put simply, an extranet means expanding your intranet to include perhaps customers, clients, suppliers, and almost anyone else who has contact with your business on a daily basis. You actually give people outside your company (who somehow relate to your business) access to your intranet using Internet technology. Extranets can help businesses improve customer service, increase revenue, and save time, money, and resources.

An extranet, or *corporate intranet*, can also be defined as a Web-centric network application that allows the customers, partners, and vendors of an enterprise to communicate and share data across its firewall in an interactive, secure, and individualized basis.

The unification of robust-enabling technologies and ubiquitous access through the Web is resulting in unique and interesting market dynamics that are changing the way many companies are doing business. Interactive communities are beginning to emerge that exist solely in cyberspace, where information travels faster, more cost-effectively, and with greater accuracy when compared to other forms of communication and information exchange. These interactive communities are the driving and sustaining force behind the extranet concept, and their insatiable collective need to access content when, where, and how they want to see it will continue to push the limits of what is technologically possible.

Extranet solutions built to engage and support these interactive communities are designed to emphasize and foster the customer relationship. As successful businesses know, the cost of obtaining a new customer far outweighs the cost of maintaining a current one. With commerce-enabled extranets, companies are now able to establish and maintain one-on-one relationships with each of their customers, members, staff, or others at very low cost through the Web, offering a customized and individualized experience that can be dynamically generated or modified based upon a user's privileges, preferences, or usage patterns. Information entered by the user (registration form, online surveys, etc.) can be compiled with statistics and other information that is captured automatically by the system (searches performed, products purchased, time spent in each site area, etc.) to provide the company a complete picture for each and every visitor to the system. This comprehensive user profile offers unprecedented opportunity to present relevant information, advertising, product and service offerings, and other content to a qualified, targeted interactive user community on a one-on-one basis.

A company that supplies tools to other companies, for example, might allow its customers to browse its catalog and place orders online, eliminating the need for customer service representatives. Or a hospital could link up with health maintenance organizations and others in the healthcare field. Other user profiles for an extranet include newsgroups to share experiences and ideas among colleagues, suppliers, clients, and so on; collaboration to develop a new application all interested parties could use; and providing training programs or other educational material.

With the preceding in mind, how do you develop an extranet?

Extranet Development

Let's say you think an extranet would be the right approach for your business. How do you proceed? The following discussion focuses on some of the things that you need to know with regard to developing an extranet.

Objectives Formalization

First of all, who should be involved with extranet planning? It is important to realize that an extranet can have a significant impact on the relationship between a company and its customers and suppliers and can profoundly alter the company's competitive position. Because of this, it is critical that senior management be directly involved in setting the strategic objectives and upper-level requirements for the extranet. In most cases, this means the CEO or vice president of marketing will set the objectives, or at least the preliminary objectives.

How do you specify the strategic objectives of your extranet? These are usually high-level statements of purpose that will guide your requirements specifications. A typical strategic objective could be to significantly simplify and/or automate the customer service experience.

It may be difficult to evaluate the success of a strategic objective such as significantly simplifying the customer service experience. A statement of high-level requirements will provide a quantifiable definition of your strategic objectives (and may actually help in refining those objectives). For example, a high-level requirement for your extranet may be stated like the following:

> First, you will contract with a market research firm to survey customer service satisfaction for your business and its major competitors—before and after extranet deployment. The second survey must show statistically significant improvement in your customer satisfaction, and must show your company as having the highest satisfaction rate among your major competitors.

When you formalize your extranet strategic objectives and high-level requirements, you should do so with an understanding of extranet capabilities and constraints. Let's look at some of these constraints or obstacles.

Obstacles.   Building an extranet is hard work—even harder than building an intranet! Many issues (such as compatibility, access, and culture) must be worked out ahead of time. An extranet will require more planning than an intranet. And, it will normally cost a lot more, too; funding needs to be built in for training, security, additional firewalls, and ID/password controls.

While the benefits of an extranet greatly outweigh the drawbacks in the long run, various obstacles must be overcome. They include:

- A system that runs over the Internet is not fully secure and could be vulnerable to attack. Certain data (for instance, financial) is sensitive and must be kept completely secure.
- When something on your extranet isn't working, who is responsible? Is it broken on your end or theirs? Support for applications, hardware, and so on (especially when developed jointly) may fall through the cracks.
- Your site is only as fast as its slowest link and many applications that may be used on an extranet (for instance, video conferencing) are still very slow.
- Having an extranet may require that employees become familiar with new technologies they currently know nothing about. This can lead to frustration among staff.

Running through the right planning process can help alleviate or eliminate many of these problems. Those companies developing an extranet can learn from those companies who have been there. Good planning processes include:

- Meeting with key employees to determine your goals.
- Meeting with key customers, suppliers, and so on (those who will be using your extranet), to determine what kind of information they expect to be able to find.
- Developing processes to keep your information up to date.
- Building in time and money for training. In addition to your employees, clients, suppliers, and so on will need to use your site. Training is an integral part of keeping everyone on the same page.

Requirements Formalization

High-level requirements will help to define your strategic objectives, but they may not help much in the *how do we do it* department. Let's say, for instance, that you want to significantly simplify the customer service experience and you think you have a high-level requirement that quantifies that objective. What's next?

You must develop a model of where you are and where you need to go. For example, your customer service manager should be familiar with customer inquiries and complaints, and will know how resources are currently allocated and where bottlenecks are. Your marketing group (or an extranet specialist) may be familiar with your competitors' solutions to customer service issues. It is experts like these who will be brought in to compose the requirements for your extranet.

Of course this process must be moderated. Each participant may have his or her own model for what needs to be done, so each posited requirement must pass the gauntlet:

- How does it complement, supplement, or support other requirements?
- How effectively does it contribute to your strategic objectives and high-level requirements?
- How is it supported by current and future technologies?
- What are its risks and costs [14]?

While the first two points in the preceding are germane to any business effort, the latter two are particularly critical for extranet development.

For example, an extranet can expose internal business information to external customers and partners. Typical IT information structures are not designed for such exposure. Will an extranet requirement force you to redesign IT facilities, or will it suffice to place protective barriers around these facilities?

Extranet technologies are evolving rapidly, and it may be difficult to draw a balance between the cutting edge and the obsolete. Is an extranet requirement dependent on untried technology? If so, can you restate the requirement to enable a staged approach from a more established foundation? Examples of extranet requirements for a customer service simplification strategic objective that illustrate such issues are as follows: First, the extranet must provide controlled real-time access to internal order-status and product-options databases; and, second, the extranet must provide an automated tool that enables the customer to identify and resolve the most commonly encountered product problems. In a subsequent release of this automated problem resolution tool, the customer must be able to alert and communicate with a customer service representative via plain old telephone service (POTS) or Internet phone.

POTS refers to the standard telephone service that most homes use. In contrast, telephone services based on high-speed, digital communications lines, such as ISDN and FDDI, are not POTS. The main distinctions between POTS and non-POTS services are speed and bandwidth. POTS is generally restricted to about 52 Kbps (52,000 bits per second). The POTS network is also called the public switched telephone network (PSTN).

Design Formalization

Now you have a set of requirements that addresses your strategic objectives and reflects your model of where you are and where you need to go. How do you translate these requirements into a design for your extranet? This is basically done through systems analysis and design.

Systems Analysis.   Systems analysis dovetails with requirements specification. You need to define the boundaries between your extranet and other business entities. You also need to analyze the ways your extranet will be used by external and internal users, and the ways in which extranet information will flow through your business. Next, you must evaluate the scale behind operational requirements, such as anticipated communication traffic rates. Systems analysis provides the necessary parameters for a well-planned design. Your corporate IT personnel should have some experience in systems analysis—use them!

For example, a systems analysis of the requirement for controlled real-time access to internal order-status and product-options databases might indicate that the databases are currently on an AS/400 machine. It could also indicate that an SQL/SNA gateway will be involved, and that the maximum traffic rate will be 5 transactions per second. All of this is technical information that a company's existing IT personnel can and should provide.

Systems Design.   Systems design takes the insights derived from system analysis and uses them to detail your extranet design. The objective is to provide all the structure needed to direct an implementation. You need to design and prototype interfaces such as specific Web forms. You also need to storyboard the flow of control among extranet components. Next, you need to define programmatic interfaces. Finally, you need to design and prototype databases and database interfaces.

For example, as part of the systems design for the requirement-controlled real-time access to internal order-status and product-options databases, you should prototype the SQL/SNA interface and demonstrate a scalable multithreading programmatic interface. Therefore, at the conclusion of systems design, you should have a prototype for your extranet's human interfaces and functionality. This will help to illustrate and validate the design, and will stimulate critical feedback. At the completion of systems design, you will have a better grasp of the implementation costs and development schedule.

Extranet Implementation

In an ideal world, extranet implementation would simply be a translation of a design into program components. You may have to make accommodations for availability of software and hardware; and you certainly should stage the implementation so that some functionality can be demonstrated at a moment's notice.

You will probably discover that extranet implementation requires resources that are difficult to find. Extranet experts can also help to assure that your requirements, system analysis, and system design actually reflect your strategic objectives. If you bring such expertise on board early in the process, your extranet will be more robust and more cost-effective.

Extranet Testing

Your company's IT group may be authorized to enforce constraints on internal data access control, software suites, and hardware configurations; however, an extranet extends your IT environment to external customers and business partners. This complicates the testing process that is essential to ensure seamless implementation.

In other words, you should identify possible security issues and test your extranet to protect against accidental or malicious damage. You should also test your extranet with a range of client software (for instance, different browser applications and/or versions) and hardware configurations.

An Extranet is always evolving to provide new services, to meet new competitive demands, and to accommodate new tools and technologies. A testing methodology should be an up-front component of your extranet plan.

Extranet Deployment

Your extranet will provide a primary interface for your customers and business partners around the world. This usually implies total availability, and the extranet site should be chosen to this end. You may also choose to outsource your extranet deployment to a specialist.

If your Extranet connects to internal company IT services that do not have full-time availability, you should design referral mechanisms such as transaction queues in order to minimize the impact on your extranet activity. Again, extranet specialists can assist in this design.

System Maintenance

To make the system maintenance process more cohesive, some organizations have instituted extranet web committees or councils to promote and facilitate the use of the extranet as a knowledge and information dissemination vehicle. In addition to designating cross-organizational standards such as a document and style guides and providing user training and support, the cross-organizational and cross-functional collaborative nature of the council fosters and promotes the best practices while avoiding structural or bureaucratic hurdles.

Industry Standards

Proprietary elements that exist within an extranet's architecture can severely hamper the flexibility to interface with new applications, the portability for the system to be moved to a larger HTTP or database server, and the scalability to incorporate new objects, users, or features. Organizations within an extranet cannot afford to be held hostage by any single vendor due to lock-in strategies instituted by software companies. Extranets are best built upon industry cabling standards (such as TIA/EIA-established UTP standards) to allow for maximum flexibility in system growth and sustainability—the subject of Chapter 3, "Standards."

Tying It All Together

All of the steps outlined previously require close collaboration between people who understand your business and people who understand extranet technologies, development methodologies, and tools. It is considerably more difficult to undertake the development of an extranet.

Any development process should anticipate change. Nowhere is this more true than in the extranet arena. Competitive pressures and new business opportunities demand a quick response, and the playing field provided by extranet technologies and tools changes daily.

Extranets represent a new frontier for many companies. An extranet is both a competitive opportunity and a competitive necessity; however, extranet development will require methodologies that may be unfamiliar to your business.

Finally, communication among all interested parties is the key to a successful extranet. Take your time and develop your site at a pace everyone can handle.

Now that you know all about extranets, the next logical step in your thought processes might involve a VPN—the fourth wave of the Internet evolution, and the last of the network types.

Virtual Private Networks

A virtual private network (VPN) is a network that uses the Internet or other public network service as its wide area network backbone (see Figure 2–6) [12]. In a VPN, dial-up connections to remote users and leased line or frame relay connections to remote sites are replaced with local connections to an

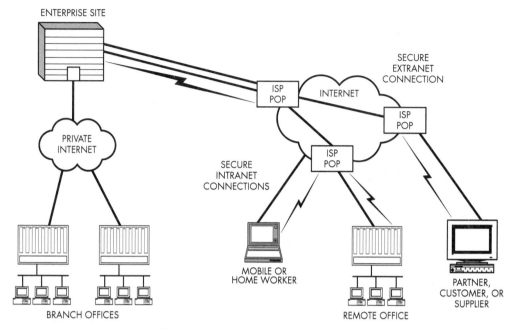

Figure 2–6   A virtual private network.

Internet service provider (ISP) or other service provider point of presence (POP). There are three main types of VPNs:

- *Intranet VPNs* allow private networks to be extended across the Internet or other public network service in a secure way. Intranet VPNs are sometimes referred to as site-to-site or LAN-to-LAN VPNs.
- *Remote access VPNs* allow individual dial-up users to connect to a central site across the Internet or other public network service in a secure way. Remote access VPNs are sometimes referred to as dial VPNs.
- *Extranet VPNs* allow secure connections with business partners, suppliers, and customers for the purpose of e-commerce. Extranet VPNs are an extension of intranet VPNs with the addition of firewalls to protect the internal network [12].

The term VPN is used for many different services, including remote access, data, fax, and voice-over-IP (VoIP). The following sections in this discussion are concerned with just two types of VPN service: remote access and intranet. However, much of the discussion on intranet Quality of Service (QoS) requirements is relevant to multimedia, including VoIP.

Intranet VPNs

Intranet, or site-to-site, VPNs apply to several categories of sites, from small-office home-office (SOHO) sites to branch sites to central and enterprise sites. SOHO sites could be considered sites where remote access user dial services are used; but, as SOHO sites often have more than one PC, they are really small LAN sites.

Intranet VPNs can be used to provide cost-effective, site-to-site, branch office networking and offer significant cost savings over traditional leased-line solutions.

In an intranet or site-to-site VPN, expensive long-distance leased lines are replaced with local ISP connection to the Internet, or secure frame relay or ATM connections, as shown in Figure 2-7 [12]. Local ISP connections can be provisioned using many technologies, from dial-up POTS and ISDN for small sites, to leased lines or frame relay for larger sites. With new emerging *last mile* technologies such as digital subscriber lines (DSL), cable and wireless provide both low-cost and high-speed access (see Chapter 4, "Digital Line Subscriber Versus Cable," for more information on this technology). Many ISPs and service providers are now starting to support these emerging technologies for Internet access, particularly for home users and SOHO sites.

The intranet VPN market is one where traditional WAN carriers are likely to compete heavily with ISPs. Traditional WAN carriers can offer a VPN service similar to a frame relay service with Quality of Service (QoS) based on committed information rate. Traditional WAN carriers are well placed to push their advantage in providing secure, *private*, reliable, low-latency, site-to-site links by adopting their current services to support routed VPN links (see Sidebar, "Intranet VPN Solutions: Advantages and Disadvantages").

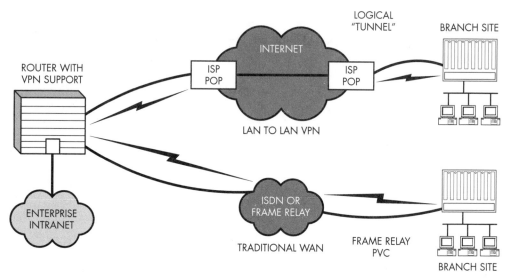

Figure 2–7   Site-to-site VPN versus traditional WAN.

INTRANET VPN SOLUTIONS: ADVANTAGES AND DISADVANTAGES

Intranet VPN Solutions Advantages

Possible advantages of an Intranet VPN include the following.

Cheaper Line Rental

Typically, VPN carriers provide a leased-line feed by contracting to a traditional carrier company. Since leased lines often have a distance-related cost structure, connecting to a local point of presence (POP) will provide savings compared to a direct long-distance or international link.

Scalable

Unlike leased lines and frame relay permanent virtual circuits (PVCs), there is no additional cost for new peer-to-peer links. However, in order to offer frame relay-style quality of service, VPN carriers may well need to introduce a per virtual-link factor to cover costs.

Cheaper Backup

If a company uses traditional carrier end-to-end data services for primary site-to-site links, the VPN carrier service may offer cheap *get what you can, when you can* bandwidth, backup, or low-priority data routing. To do this effectively, the tunnels (a technique for connecting two networks via a third, while totally isolating the connected traffic from other traffic in the third network) need the support of dynamic tunnel monitoring. For example, how does a customer premises equipment (CPE) router know the effective throughput of a tunnel without an end-to-end reliable data link or intimate knowledge of the higher-layer protocol sessions carried over the link? Without a solution to this problem, path sharing between a VPN tunnel and a private leased line may give worse throughput than using just the private leased line. If the VPN tunnel is used in partnership with a private data service that had a use-based tariff, for example frame relay, then this solution could offer considerable savings.

Cheaper High Bandwidth over Last Mile
Renting high-bandwidth leased lines (for example, T1/E1 or T3/E3) is expensive, and cheaper options exist for last-mile connections in some areas such as cable, xDSL, wireless, and satellite.

Cheap Global Virtual Backbone
For companies that do not already have a national/international backbone, there is no cheaper option than setting up a virtual backbone using VPN carrier services.

Intranet VPN Solutions Disadvantages
Possible disadvantages of an Intranet VPN include the following.

Denial-of-Service Attacks
Unlike a private leased line, traffic that is not from the peer remote site (tunnel end point) can flood down the receive path of a VPN tunnel from anywhere on the public network. This unsolicited traffic may reach such a level (as it did in the massive denial of service attacks against CNN, Amazon, AOL, etc., earlier in 2000) that solicited data can no longer be retrieved. To combat this, the VPN carrier could offer to filter non-VPN traffic, or perhaps provide a bandwidth reservation or quality of service (QoS) service.

No End-To-End Data Link in Some Cases
For some tunnel technologies, there is no end-to-end data link, so detection of reachability will need to be supported at the routing layer with protocols capable of rapid failure detection and instant reroute.

Packet Loss
A VPN tunnel can sometimes suffer high packet loss and can reorder packets. Reordering can cause problems for some bridged protocols, and high packet loss may have an impact on the optimal configuration of higher-layer protocols.

Increased Down Time
Decreased mean time between failures, longer lasting outages, painful problem solving, and down-time compensation claims.

Aggregation of Functions
Doing business with partners is clearly easier to implement using the VPN model, but aggregating private tunnels, customer tunnels, and web publishing access in a single system is difficult without combined VPN and firewall capability. Separating VPN and non-VPN traffic is a sensible precaution [12].

Remote Access VPNs

Remote access refers to the ability to connect to a network from a distant, "nonlocal" location. A remote access client system connects to a network access device, such as a network server or access concentrator. When logged in, the client system becomes a host on the network. Typical remote access clients might be:

- Laptop computers on a shared LAN. For example, some hotel chains are now offering LAN connection points in hotel rooms so that Ethernet cards can be used, with no need for a modem card.
- Laptop computers with modems used by mobile workers.
- PCs with modems or ISDN connections used at home by telecommuters [12].

Remote access VPNs are rapidly replacing traditional remote access solutions (RAS), as they provide a more flexible and lower-cost solution, as shown in Figure 2–8 [12]. Remote access connections are divided into two groups: local dial and long-distance dial.

For traditional, private remote access networks, local area users connect using a variety of telecommunication data services. Remote access long-distance users rarely have a choice other than modem access over telephone networks. The aggregation devices that the clients connect to typically use channelized leased line and primary-rate ISDN, offering dedicated circuit switched access.

With VPNs, local area users typically have a wider range of data services to choose from, regardless of the support at the enterprise or central site VPN equipment. However, long-distance connections are currently made via modem access. What VPN carriers currently offer corporations are *Work Globally, Dial Locally* services. The VPN equipment will use high-speed leased lines to the nearest POP of the chosen VPN carrier, and all remote access traffic can be aggregated or routed as IP datagrams over this single link (see Sidebar, "Advantages and Disadvantages of Dial VPNs over Traditional Direct-Dial Remote Access").

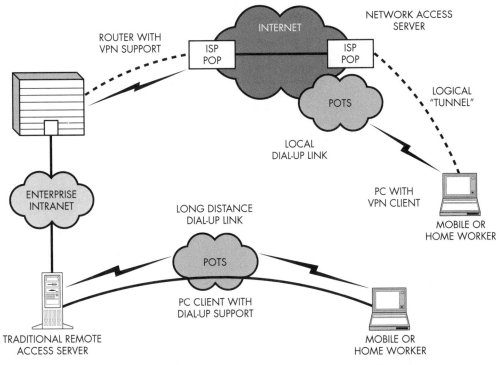

Figure 2–8   Remote access VPN versus traditional RAS.

ADVANTAGES AND DISADVANTAGES OF DIAL VPNS OVER TRADITIONAL DIRECT-DIAL REMOTE ACCESS

Advantages of Dial VPNs over Traditional Direct-Dial Remote Access

Most of the advantages listed here refer to Internet-based VPNs and the solutions that will be available on VPN-focused carriers. Possible advantages of VPN remote access include the following.

Cheaper Dial-Service Costs for Long-Distance Users

When a company partners with a VPN carrier to provide global remote access, the employees are issued information on local telephone number access points in each country they have support for. Since local calls are significantly cheaper than national and international calls, this would appear to offer sizable savings.

This *savings* of course depends on the throughput achieved and the relative cost of local, national, and international calls. In most regions of the world, local calls are not free, and this may mean that real savings are not achieved. For example, if local calls offer a 60 percent savings over national calls, but the VPN throughput means that it takes twice as long to copy mail from a central office than it would have done using a direct-dial call, no telecommunication savings would have occurred and company resources have been wasted. For local users with telephone lines (or ISDN), a VPN offers no dial-in cost savings and may even be worse service for the user.

Better Data Rates for Modems

Because long-distance VPN users can dial a local modem at the VPN carrier's office, the data rate achieved by the modem should be better than for a long-distance or international direct call. Again, partnering with a VPN carrier to provide a service is important. For example, international VPN throughput can deteriorate badly when using the Internet as a carrier.

Scalability

Adding 200 users to a modem pool typically presents more problems to the network manager than adding 200 users to an enterprise Security Gateway that only deals with IP datagrams over a high-speed leased line.

Less Equipment Upgrading Needed

As modem technology improves, and new local loop services become available, new hardware would be required at a *modem pool* site. With VPNs, this problem is handled (and normally paid for) by the VPN carriers.

Improved Local Access Services

With a traditional direct-dial remote access network, the data services that can be used by the remote users are dictated by the data services supported by the aggregation device. With a VPN, the user can choose the best local loop service available, for example, cable modems or xDSL. This advantage is currently only a reality for home users, but may eventually apply to all nonlocal users.

Better Utilization of Bandwidth

With the traditional approach, each user is typically allocated a fixed bandwidth, for example, an ISDN B-channel or a 56 Kb channel on a T1 circuit. Most remote working sessions have very low overall utilization of the reserved bandwidth allocated. Also, with a circuit-switched approach, there is also a fixed number of users that can be supported before new users are completely blocked. With a VPN approach, it is possible to fully utilize the available bandwidth. As the number of connected users increases, the service to each user gradually decreases, but is not completely blocked. Users equipped with high-speed local access services may also take advantage of any spare capacity much easier.

Disadvantages of VPN Remote Access

Most of the disadvantages listed here refer to Internet-based VPNs and solutions will be available on VPN-focused carriers. Possible disadvantages of VPN remote access include the following.

Quality of Service

Unlike circuit-switched or leased-line data services, VPN links (or tunnels) over public routed networks do not typically offer any end-to-end throughput guarantees. In addition, packet loss is variable and can be very high, and packets can be delivered out-of-order and fragmented. Because of these QoS issues, data compression performance over a tunnel can be less efficient than normal network traffic.

Security

VPN connections are made by first connecting to a POP of the public network, and then using that network to reach a remote peer to form a private tunnel. Once the connection has been made to the POP, unsolicited data from other users, or attacks, of the public network can be received. The protection from these *attacks* requires comprehensive and complex security measures.

Accounting and Billing

If dial-in costs are being incurred on a link that is not directly connected to the company that will pick up the bill, it becomes difficult to monitor the usage (although this seems achievable with VPN carrier-based Layer Two Tunneling Protocol (L2TP)).

Bandwidth Reservation or Quality of Service

Bandwidth reservation refers to the ability to *reserve* transmission bandwidth on a network connection for particular classes or types of traffic. It is much harder to achieve this with VPNs than traditional networks. Some reservation can be done on outbound traffic, but for the inbound reservation to be achieved, the VPN carrier would need to help. Some inbound flow control is available with L2TP. However, controlling incoming data from power users is a problem that requires some way to flow-control input from each remote client. As a result, bandwidth reservation issues arise at the enterprise or central site.

Two-Way Calling

Small office/home office sites that use ISDN to access a central site directly enjoy the capabilities of two-way calling. If the link is idle (the inactivity timer has fired and disconnected the call), the traffic needs to flow from the central site to the remote site, then the central site can initiate the call. Offering to pick up the dial-in costs incurred by partners and customers is also difficult. Again, L2TP does include support for these features in its current implementation.

Overhead

VPN tunnels impose overhead for dial-in users: encryption algorithms may impact the performance of the user's system; there will be an increased protocol header overhead; authentication latency will increase; and point-to-point protocol (PPP) and IP compression will perform somewhat poorer than a direct link.

Support Issues

Replacing direct-dial links with VPN tunnels may produce some very painful fault-finding missions. Due to the complexity of VPN carrier networks, the opportunities for *hand-washing*, or transferring the blame, are enormous.

Reconnection Time

Using tunneling may increase the reconnection time for dial users. With the VPN carrier L2TP model, the client has to go through two authentication phases—one contacting the VPN carrier POP, and another to contact the enterprise Security Gateway. Although the authentication exchange with the POP may well be trivial, the VPN database look-up can take time. ISDN SOHO sites that wish to use cost-saving techniques may need to implement special features to cache these look-ups in order to allow rapid reconnects.

Multimedia

Applications such as video conferencing only work acceptably over low-latency links that can offer the required minimum throughput. Currently on the Internet, latency and throughput can vary. Multichannel data services, such as ISDN and xDSL, solve this problem in the short term, allowing the *data* channel to be used for VPN tunneling, while a separate *voice* channel can be used for business telephone calls or video conferencing.

Encryption

When using encryption to protect a tunnel, data compression is no longer achievable as encrypted data is not compressible. This means that hardware compression over a modem connection is not possible given today's implementations [12].

All of the preceding types of VPNs aim to provide the reliability, performance, quality of service, and security of traditional WAN environments using lower-cost connection methods and more flexible ISP or other service provider connections. VPN technology can also be used within an intranet to provide security or control access to sensitive information, systems, and resources. For example, to restrict access to financial systems to certain users, or to ensure confidentiality of sensitive information, it may be sent in a secure way.

There are many ways of implementing a VPN. Below are some of the more common.

- IP tunnels between a remote user and a corporate firewall with tunnel creation and deletion controlled by the user's computer and the firewall.
- IP tunnels between an ISP and a corporate firewall with tunnel creation and deletion controlled by the ISP.
- IP tunnels between sites over the public Internet, or over a service provider's IP network that is separate from the public Internet.

- ISDN, frame relay, or ATM connections between sites with integrated services digital network-broadband (ISDN B) channels, permanent virtual circuits (PVCs), or switched virtual circuits (SVCs) used to separate traffic from other users.

VPNs Based on IP Tunnels

VPNs based on IP tunnels encapsulate a data packet within a normal IP packet for forwarding over an IP-based network. The encapsulated packet does not need to be IP and could be any protocol such as IPX, AppleTalk, SNA, or DECnet. The encapsulated packet does not need to be encrypted and authenticated. However, with most IP-based VPNs, especially those running over the public Internet, encryption is used to ensure privacy and authentication to ensure the data's integrity.

VPNs based on IP tunnels are mainly self-deployed; users buy connections from an ISP and install VPN equipment, which they configure and manage themselves, relying on the ISP only for the physical connections. VPN services based on IP tunnels are also provided by ISPs, service providers, and other carriers. These are usually fully managed services with options such as service level agreements (SLAs) to ensure Quality of Service (QoS). Figure 2–9 shows an Internet-based VPN that uses secure IP tunnels to connect remote clients and devices [12]. VPNs based on IP tunnels provide the following benefits:

- Easier e-commerce and extranet connections with business partners, suppliers, and customers.
- External Internet access, internal intranet access, and extranet access can be provided using a single secure connection.
- Greater flexibility in deploying mobile computing, teleworking, and branch-office networking.
- Reduced telecom costs, as dedicated and long distance connections are replaced with local connections [12].

The main disadvantage of VPNs based on IP tunnels is that QoS levels may be erratic and are not yet as good as alternative solutions. Also, for VPNs based on the public Internet, higher levels of security such as authentication and data encryption are essential to ensure integrity and security of data.

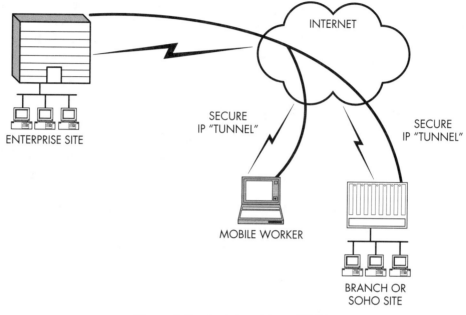

Figure 2–9   An Internet-based VPN.

ISP connections used for Intranet and remote access VPNs do not necessarily need to be protected by a firewall as data is protected by using tunneling, encryption, and so on. You can use separate ISP connections for general Internet access and VPN access or you can use a single connection with a common router with a VPN device and firewall in parallel. In some cases, you can use devices that integrate one or more of these functions. When using extranet VPNs to provide e-commerce connections to business partners, suppliers, or customers, it is advisable to use a firewall to protect your internal network (see Sidebar, "Firewalls and VPNs," for more details).

FIREWALLS AND VPNs

Firewalls are security devices whose primary function is to protect an enterprise's internal network from unintended access by users on the Internet. VPNs are designed to provide secure paths known as tunnels across the Internet between two devices in an enterprise network. VPN technology is inherently secure, provided that the connections to the Internet are only used for VPN access. In this case, most VPN products provide sufficient security to protect an enterprise's internal network from unauthorized access by users on the Internet.

As soon as these VPN connections are shared to allow general Internet access to internal users, or to provide extranet access for e-commerce with business partners, suppliers, and customers, potential security problems arise. In most situations, it is preferable to have a separate connection, one for intranet and remote access VPN for internal users, and one for general Internet access and extranet access protected by a firewall. In other situations it is acceptable to include firewall capabilities in the VPN device, or to place the VPN device on a firewall demilitarized zone (DMZ). It is also common to put the VPN device in parallel with a firewall and router on a LAN.

In all situations, choosing whether to use VPN products with integrated firewall capability or to use an external firewall depends not only on the cost of separate connections and the level of security required, but also on the degree of manageability needed. Configuring and managing a single network device with multiple functions can be difficult. Separating the VPN and firewall capabilities means that the configuration and management is easier, but there are now two devices to manage instead of one!

The level of protection provided by VPN products with integrated firewall capability depends on the type of firewall technology included. For example, low-end VPN products for the SOHO market may have a firewall capability that provides adequate protection for this type of site. Some high-end products have complex firewall capabilities that provide a high level of protection more appropriate for a central site. In all cases, it is important to understand the different types of firewalls so that the appropriate level of protection can be implemented for the particular circumstances.

Firewall Types

Comparing different types of firewalls is difficult since every product uses a different means to achieve different objectives. Firewalls generally fall into one of two categories: packet-filtering firewalls and application-level firewalls. A third category that utilizes a combination of the two different methodologies also exists. This common type of mixed solution is a stateful-inspection firewall.

Packet-Filtering

Packet-filtering firewalls are sometimes referred to as network-level firewalls, or a firewall in which traffic is examined at the network protocol level. Many routers implement packet filtering that is often described as a firewall capability. Access control is based mainly on source and destination address or type of application. Packet-filtering firewalls are typically the fastest because they don't offer the complex data analysis, reporting, and general functionality of other types of firewalls.

Packet-filtering firewalls are suitable where a reasonably high level of trust exists between parties, such as in applications where external partners, customers, and business suppliers need access to your VPN. In such circumstances, it is appropriate to use VPN products with packet-filtering firewall capabilities on connections that are used only for VPN access. Connections for general Internet access should be secured with a separate application-level or stateful-inspection firewall.

Application-Level

Commonly referred to as proxy-level firewalls, application-level firewalls often readdress traffic so that outgoing traffic appears to have originated from the firewall, rather than the internal host. These firewalls serve as a proxy for the external servers, instead of providing a direct connection between internal and external devices, as packet filters do. Application-level firewalls traditionally offer more functionality, such as auditing, time-of-day control, and user-level access control. Application-level firewalls are typically used to secure general Internet access and are commonly used in conjunction with one or more routers running Border Gateway Protocol (BGP) and packet filtering.

Stateful-Inspection

A stateful-inspection firewall uses a combination of Packet-filtering and application-layer processing to determine whether a packet should be accepted or rejected. This is accomplished by examining the contents of the incoming packet. Stateful inspection firewalls are configured by layering different filters that conform to an organization's security policy. Stateful inspection firewalls also offer more functionality, such as auditing, time-of-day control, and user-level access control.

Stateful-inspection firewalls are typically used to secure general Internet access. They are typically used in conjunction with routers running Border Gateway Protocol (BGP) and packet filtering [12].

Now that we have an understanding of how to deploy VPNs based on IP tunnels, how do we deploy an Internet-based VPN? The following 10-point plan for building a VPN shows some of the steps to take when deploying an Internet-based VPN.

Building an Internet-Based VPN: A 10-Point Plan

Implementing a VPN requires a good deal of preparation. Unless you have investigated the options, compared the costs, and have written an implementation plan, you may not reap the full benefits of your VPN. The design of the VPN doesn't have to be difficult or complex. You may believe you have unique remote access and branch office connectivity requirements, but in fact most organizations have similar design and implementation needs. Here are

10 points to help you build a VPN that will better meet the needs of your organization now and down the road:

1. Assess your connectivity requirements.
2. Implement or update the corporate security policy.
3. Implement a backup plan.
4. Determine the best product or service solution.
5. Test the proposed solution.
6. Size the system.
7. Pick the location for the VPN equipment.
8. Reconfigure other network devices.
9. Install and configure the VPN.
10. Monitor and manage the VPN [12].

As previously stated, building a VPN requires considerable planning. This 10-point plan outlines steps to help you successfully build a VPN.

Assess Your Connectivity Requirements.   The first step is to look at your current network and determine which remote access and branch-office connections could be replaced with a VPN. Remember that uptime, performance, and latency requirements all help determine whether an Internet VPN or a public network VPN is more suitable (see Sidebar, "Public Network VPNs"). You may decide that replacing your current remote access connections with a remote access VPN service makes technical and economic sense, but the potential impact on performance and latency does not justify the cost savings of replacing dedicated leased lines between branch offices with an Intranet VPN service.

PUBLIC NETWORK VPNs

Public networks such as ISDN, frame relay, and ATM networks can carry mixed data types, including voice, video, and data. They can also be used to provide VPN services by using broadband channels (B channels), permanent virtual circuits (PVCs), or switched virtual circuits (SVCs) to separate traffic from other users. Optionally, authentication and encryption can be used where the identity of users and the integrity of data needs to be guaranteed. Using

PVCs, SVCs, or B channels means that it is easier to provide additional bandwidth or backup when needed. The traffic-shaping capabilities of frame relay and ATM can be used to provide different levels of QoS; and, because these services are based on usage, there is significant opportunity to reduce telecom costs even further by using bandwidth optimization features.

VPNs Based on ATM, ISDN, or Frame Relay

VPNs based on ISDN, frame relay, or ATM connections are very different than VPNs based on IP tunnels. This type of VPN uses public-switched data network services and uses ISDN B channels, PVCs, or SVCs to separate traffic from other users. Single or multiple B channels, PVCs, or SVCs may be used between sites with additional features such as backup and bandwidth on demand. Data packets do not need to be IP and do not need to be encrypted. However, due to more widespread awareness about security issues, many users now choose to encrypt their data. Figure 2–10 shows a carrier-based VPN that uses ISDN B channels and frame relay PVCs to connect remote clients and devices [12].

VPNs based on public-switched data networks are usually provided by service providers and other carriers, and may or may not provide fully managed services. In most cases, additional services such as QoS options are available. This type of VPN is likely to become popular in Europe, where public-switched data networks are widely available and where business use of the Internet is less developed. The main benefits of VPNs based on ISDN, frame relay, or ATM connections are:

- connections can be used for any type of communication, from PBX connections and video conferences to private data;
- extensive billing and accounting information is available since these services are well established;
- international connections are relatively easy to obtain, especially for frame relay, although they can be expensive; and
- security is less of a concern since data is usually carried over the service provider's or carrier's private network.

Frame Relay

Frame relay, on the other hand, has become a popular, widespread, and relatively low cost networking technology that is also suitable for VPNs. Running VPNs over a frame relay network allows expensive dedicated leased lines to be replaced and makes use of frame relay's acknowledged strengths, including bandwidth-on-demand, support for variable data rates to support bursty traffic, and switched as well as permanent virtual circuits for any-to-any connectivity on a per-call basis.

Frame relay's ability to handle bursty traffic and built-in buffering means that it makes optimum use of available bandwidth, something that is important in a VPN environment where latency and performance are chief concerns. Frame relay can be used to create a VPN in two ways: by creating a mesh of frame relay connections between sites and by using IP tunnels over frame relay connections between sites.

Creating a Mesh of Frame Relay Connections between Sites

These connections are essentially point-to-point links and are similar in concept to dedicated leased lines. Data is kept separate from other frame relay users as each connection uses a separate virtual circuit.

Using IP Tunnels over Frame Relay Connections between Sites

As noted previously, these connections are essentially point-to-point links similar in concept to dedicated leased lines and each connection uses a separate virtual circuit. However, several separate IP tunnels can be run over each connection and each tunnel can be encrypted and authenticated to provide additional security.

End-To-End Protocol

Frame relay is an end-to-end protocol that can be run over a variety of access technologies—for example, ISDN, Digital Subscriber Loop (DSL), and even POTS dial-up lines. New access methods such as switched virtual circuits (SVCs), ISDN access, and backup mean that frame relay is now a much more reliable and cost-effective solution. Frame relay can also run over and interoperate with ATM backbones, making it one of the most widely available and implemented public data-networking services worldwide. As a result, major service providers and carriers have created global frame relay networks that are cost-effective and offer high availability. When coupled with tunneling, encryption, and authentication, these attributes make frame relay an ideal candidate for global VPN services.

Nevertheless, the main disadvantages of public network VPNs are that ISDN, frame relay, and ATM services may be expensive, are not as widely available as ISP services, and it is often harder to provide extranet and e-commerce connections to business partners, suppliers, and customers [12].

Once you have determined your connectivity requirements, you need to decide what kind of WAN technology is most appropriate. Do remote users reach the corporate network over LAN/WAN or dial-up links? Are remote users part of the same organization? Do branch-office connections use dedicated leased lines or switched services such as ISDN or frame relay? WAN connections for VPNs fall into two categories: intranet links and extranet links.

Intranets typically connect trusted users and locations within the same organization, such as links between headquarters, branch offices, and remote users. For intranet links, the VPN should provide the same level of service to branch offices and remote users as if they were physically connected to the corporate network. An intranet VPN should also provide the same security policies as the standard corporate security policy once users have been authenticated. The standard corporate security policy might restrict remote access users to certain parts of the corporate network; in this case, the VPN design might require stronger authentication, or it might limit access to isolated subnets on the head-

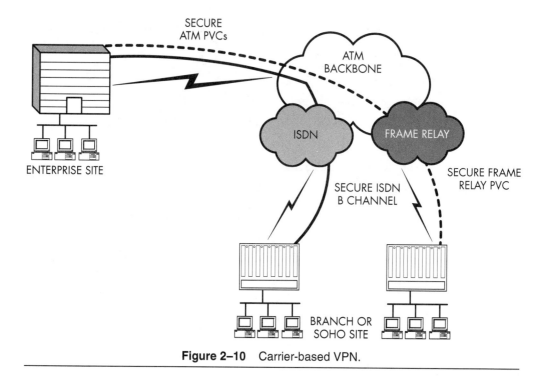

Figure 2–10 Carrier-based VPN.

quarters network. For branch office connections, little or no restrictions might apply. In such a case, an *open pipe* VPN with no user authentication between headquarters and branch offices could replace traditional site-to-site connections.

Extranets typically connect outside users such as business partners, suppliers, and customers. For extranet links, security requirements are more stringent. Access to information is restricted or granted only under certain conditions, and, access to sensitive network resources is restricted or even blocked. Since extranet connections may involve personnel outside an organization, you will need to implement additional security measures when granting access to these users. This is more of a political than a technical issue, but it needs to be addressed when designing the extranet.

If you plan to extend your VPN to customers, partners, and suppliers, you also need to consider what authentication scheme you will use to authenticate users. Typically, when third parties are involved, a higher level of authentication is required.

Implement or Update the Corporate Security Policy. VPNs offer considerable cost savings over traditional remote access and branch-office solutions. Corporate networks are ordinary and preferred targets for hackers. As a result, most corporate systems make attempts to protect against intruders such that management can be assured that the data is secure.

An organization's security policy should define what forms of remote access are or are not allowed, and what types of authentication and authorization are used. The security policy needs to be thoroughly revised when implementing VPNs. In particular, it needs to address whether digital certificates, certification authorities, and public key infrastructure have a role to play in the VPN. If there is no security policy, implementing a VPN is an ideal and critical reason for creating one.

In addition to security issues, the policy should address eligibility for remote access, executive accountability, responsibility for connections, and monitoring of VPN usage. It also should cover procedures for giving Internet access to traveling and remote employees. The policy might also cover such technical details as the lengths of encryption keys used in relation to time sensitivity of the data handled. Legal assistance will be needed if export authorization is required for the encryption algorithms.

For extranets, the policy should specify a procedure for rapid notification of changes in the remote user population. Those who are no longer with the organization must be removed from the authentication database as quickly as possible. This requires coordination between the external user's organization and the VPN administrator. Human resources departments may already have procedures for managing consultant access and these may be appropriate for VPN users.

Implement a Backup Plan. Once users become familiar with VPNs, they are likely to start using the VPN to run more mission-critical applications. Also, as VPN technology is expanded to include business partners, suppliers, and customers through extranet connections, the need for a backup plan becomes even more important. Besides having redundant equipment and links, sites with high traffic loads will need to support load balancing across multiple devices and paths. Most VPN service providers support these features as part of their VPN solutions. Determining the backup plan early is key to long-term success and also ensures the right solution is finalized before equipment is purchased or an outsourced service is negotiated.

Having a combination of traditional remote access and remote access VPN (especially in one remote access product) means that the migration from one technology to the other is less painful. As users move over to remote access VPN, traditional remote access servers can be used to provide backup in the event that the VPN fails and can be used for those users where a traditional remote access solution makes more economic sense. ISDN tariffs in Europe are low, and extensive use of time cutting, protocol spoofing, and filtering can dramatically reduce costs. Using traditional remote access may also be better for local users from a performance perspective, as a local direct-dial connection will probably offer superior performance over an Internet connection.

For intranet VPNs, having a combination of traditional WAN access and VPN capability is essential. Today, most VPN solutions are unable to provide the same level of performance and low latency as dedicated leased lines or frame relay services. The opportunity to reduce costs by using VPNs to connect branch offices is always attractive, but ensuring 100 percent connectivity is probably more important. An ISDN or frame relay SVC backup connection, especially in one branch-office product, means that connectivity is always maintained even when the VPN connection fails. It may be advantageous to prioritize time-critical data by sending it over the leased-line, ISDN, or frame relay connection, and using the VPN connection for lower priority, less time-critical data. However, in some cases, it may be advantageous to use the VPN service for backup or top up. In this case, data is only sent over the VPN if the leased-line, ISDN, or frame relay connection fails or becomes fully utilized.

Determine the Best Product or Service Solution. There are many different VPN products and services available and choosing the solution most appropriate for your environment is not an easy task. Fortunately, all VPN solutions fall into one of three categories: firewall-based systems, software-based systems, and hardware-based systems.

All of these support remote access and some support intranets as well. For all solutions, you need to check five key areas of VPN technology: protocol support, encryption support, authentication methods, export of encryption technology, and management of encryption keys.

Protocol support includes both the type of end-user protocols that the VPN can handle and the method by which they are encapsulated or tunneled across the VPN. While most VPN solutions focus on IP only, some can handle other protocols such as IPX or SNA either natively or by encapsulation within IP. Both methods rely on tunneling to transport the information across the VPN. Tunnel protocols include level 2 protocols such as point-to-point tunnel protocol (PPTP), level 2 tunnel protocol (L2TP), and level 3 tunneling protocols such as IP Security (IPSec).

IPSec is an effort by the IETF (Internet Engineering Task Force) to add standards-based authentication and encryption to TCP/IP. Most vendors support IPSec; however, since the standards have only just been agreed upon, only a few vendors have been able to demonstrate that their solutions interoperate with other vendors' products. As the IPSec standard becomes more widely established, interoperability will become less of an issue. In order to prevent any immediate issues, you may want to use products from the same vendor to build your VPN.

Some VPN solutions use their own authentication servers, while others may use an established authentication method such as Remote Authentication Dial-In User Server (Radius) or Terminal Access Controller Access System (TACACS). The advantage of established authentication methods is that they can be centralized and scaled to a large number of users.

Export of encryption technology from the United States and the management of encryption keys are two areas that require considerable thought. U.S. law forbids the export of strong encryption, although legislation is under way to ease the current restrictions. Multinational organizations may need to consider two strengths of encryption: strong encryption for the U.S. market and weaker encryption for international connections. Key management is another area that requires attention. U.S. law maintains that all encrypted data must use key recovery techniques, which could allow the data to be deencrypted if required—for example, in the case of unlawful or criminal activity. This raises the issue of who should own the key recovery system and who should maintain it. Should key generation and recovery be managed in-house using an approved mechanism, or should this be outsourced to an approved third party?

Firewall-Based VPNs. Firewall-based VPNs offer the advantage of a robust built-in security mechanism to restrict access to the internal network. Firewalls perform a number of other functions required to implement VPNs such as address translation, user authentication, and authorization. Also, many firewalls harden the host operating system by disabling or stripping out unnecessary services. As previously mentioned, most firewalls support a third interface known as a demilitarized zone (DMZ) with its own access controls. The DMZ allows controlled access to web servers, proxies, and other services in an environment that can be compromised without affecting the security of the internal network.

Other advantages of firewalls are that they offer comprehensive, real-time alarms and extensive logging capabilities, making it easier to monitor what is happening. As most firewalls run on host's operating systems, they tend to have user-friendly interfaces, which make the security features easier to set up and use.

Firewall-based VPNs are the best choice for intranet-based VPNs requiring limited remote access. They can also be used to provide extranet connections to business partners, suppliers, and customers. However, they are generally not suitable for large-scale remote access or intranet VPNs due to the potential throughput and performance issues related to the underlying host-based operating system. Firewall-based VPNs may also require an external router to provide the physical Internet connection.

Software-Based VPNs.   VPN software running on a server, for example an NT server, is another alternative. These software-based VPNs are simpler to implement than firewall-based VPNs and may offer more flexibility when setting up VPN services. Many VPN software products allow tunneling according to address or protocol—something that is useful when there is a mix of traffic at remote sites, including both VPN (database inquiries to a central server) and non-VPN (Web surfing) traffic. Where performance requirements are low, such as remote users connecting over dial-up links, software-based VPNs may provide the best and most cost-effective solution.

The disadvantage of software-based VPN systems is that they are unlikely to be as integrated as a firewall-based solution and may be harder to manage as they require familiarity with the host operating system, the application, and the appropriate security mechanisms. Some software-based VPN solutions may also require changes to routing tables and network addressing.

Hardware-Based Solutions.   Hardware-based VPN solutions are typically routers that support encryption and other security capabilities. More recently, hybrid hardware solutions that include elements of routing, encryption, authentication, firewall, and so on have become available. As these solutions have been designed from the ground up, they offer a more integrated approach to VPNs both from the functionality and management points of view. These solutions tend to offer higher performance and throughput than other VPN solutions. In general, as hardware-based solutions use hardware-based encryption and a proprietary real-time operating system, they are harder to crack or hack through than software-based solutions.

The main disadvantage is that by their nature, hardware-based VPN solutions require custom hardware such as encryption modules or WAN interface cards to be purchased from the vendor. Also, as all the elements required to implement the VPN are integrated into one product, it is harder to separate the different functions for management purposes. For example, unless there is a mechanism to separate security management from routing table management, all functions need to be managed via the same interface. This is especially a problem if you want a managed VPN service, whereby the ISP or carrier provides the management of the WAN links and routing, but you maintain control over user authentication and security. Fortunately, some hardware-based VPN solutions implement split management horizons, which allow these aspects to be managed separately. Many hardware-based VPN solutions use an external server for authentication, authorization, and auditing. This provides a more manageable solution and may also allow VPN access to be integrated into existing authentication, authorization, and auditing services.

Test the Proposed Solution.   The fifth step in building a VPN is to test the proposed solution by carrying out a pilot project and testing it extensively. One of the best ways to help ensure adequate testing is to enlist the help of users who will use the VPN solution. Choose a small group of mobile users or a few remote sites and ask them to participate in the testing. It is essential to include a good cross-section of users so that you can assess the problems that real users are likely to encounter.

You should aim to cover the following assessment criteria during your pilot VPN test:

- *Authentication and authorization.* The VPN should support all of the access control mechanisms currently used in your network.
- *Configuration.* You should check that the VPN can be configured according to your corporate security policy.
- *Key production and distribution.* You must show that keys can be produced and distributed efficiently and securely.
- *Performance.* The VPN must allow remote users and branch sites to continue working as before with minor degradation in performance and latency.
- *Troubleshooting.* Check to see what problem-solving tools are provided and whether they will meet your needs.
- *Usability.* The VPN should be easy to set up and use, by both technical and nontechnical users [12].

Only when you are satisfied that the proposed VPN solution passes the above assessment criteria should you move on to the next step.

Size the System.   When sizing the system, make sure you estimate the total number of users, the typical number of concurrent sessions, and the time sensitivity of critical data. Make sure you take into account the connectivity requirements determined during Step 1 of the 10-point plan just discussed.

If using a software-based VPN solution, a 300-MHz Pentium processor should be able to handle a single T1/E1 network connection, assuming there is triple Data Encryption Standard (DES) encryption using 128-bit keys, data compression, and message authentication. You should ensure that there is as much memory as possible since additional memory allows more simultaneous connections. Finally, you should check to see whether any options are available to provide hardware assistance for encryption or WAN connectivity.

Network connections faster than T1/E1, or multiple T1/E1 connections, will probably require hardware-based VPNs. In this case, determine whether the vendor has different models for varying numbers of users or types of sites. Often, a T1/E1 hardware device may be able to handle a T1/E1 line, but may not be able to handle the required number of simultaneous sessions. This is especially true for devices designed for intranet VPNs where T1/E1 throughput is typically required, but only over a limited number of tunnels. Similarly, T3/E3 devices may be designed to handle many simultaneous tunnels for remote access users, but throughput may be significantly less than a T3/E3 line allows.

A T1 line is a dedicated phone connection supporting data rates of 1.544 Mbits per second. A T3 line is a dedicated phone connection supporting data rates of 44.736 Mbits per second.

Similar to the North American T1, E1 is the European format for digital transmission. E1 carries signals at 2.048 Mbps (30 channels at 64 Kbps), versus the T1, which carries signals at 1.544 Mbps (24 channels at 64 Kbps). E1 and T1 lines may be interconnected for international use. E3 lines carry signals at 34.368 Mb/s (480 channels).

Check vendors' performance information carefully and if possible obtain detailed test information. The network press and magazines often provide detailed comparisons of VPN products, including simulated tests and test reports. However, make sure that you are making *like for like* comparisons. For example, make sure that performance is using the same frame lengths, that encryption algorithms are using the same key lengths, that you are using similar compression algorithms, and that there's a presence or absence of message authentication algorithms.

Finally, bear in mind any backup and redundancy requirements you may have when choosing VPN products or services. You may also want to ensure that the VPN solution used at central or HQ sites can provide load balancing across multiple lines for additional redundancy. See Step 10 for further details.

Pick the Location for the VPN Equipment.   When choosing the site of the VPN equipment, the number and type of remote users and the proximity of branch offices to each other are important considerations. Mobile and remote employees will expect to have access to corporate intranet resources as before. In this case, the VPN equipment and authentication servers can be placed on the intranet, since most VPN products provide sufficient security to protect an enterprise's internal network from unintended or unauthorized access by users on the Internet.

However, if the majority of users are from outside organizations, it may make sense to put the VPN equipment on a firewall DMZ. This is safer than placing the VPN equipment completely outside the security perimeter, as the firewall provides additional screening and protects systems on the intranet. If a separate authentication server is used, it should also be placed on the firewall DMZ so that it can be managed and protected from both internal and external threats. Mobile or remote users from inside the organization will still be able to use the VPN via authentication requests to the authentication server, which checks their identity and authorizes access.

Extranet connections solely for external users such as customers, business partners, or suppliers need more thought. Here, separate connections for extranet access and internal VPN access may offer the best protection. Alternatively, if a single connection is used for both, then the VPN server and authentication server should be located on separate firewall DMZs. In this case, connection requests go to the VPN server on the first DMZ, and are then passed to the authentication server on the second DMZ. Requests that are accepted are then passed through the firewall and finally to the requested resource.

It is easier to set up intranet VPN links between branch offices since traffic is always sent over a point-to-point encrypted tunnel between sites. Also, most VPN products, if properly deployed, provide sufficient security to protect an enterprise's internal network. For larger sites, the VPN equipment can be located on a parallel with the firewall, which should be set up to allow a generic proxy or pass-through rule for the encapsulated VPN traffic. However, there are other factors to keep in mind such as the cost of providing VPN services to all branch sites versus aggregating several sites into one site using traditional WAN services such as ISDN, and then providing a VPN link from this site into the corporate backbone. Hopefully, you will have determined the approach you want to take as part of Step 1, *Assess your connectivity requirements*.

Reconfigure Other Network Devices.   Installing a VPN will impact other network devices. This may mean reconfiguring these other network devices, especially when it comes to IP address management and firewalls. VPNs may make use of network address translation (NAT), which maps private addresses from a block of reserved addresses to one or more public addresses visible on the Internet.

Most likely, you will need to configure VPN equipment to understand which addresses are reserved for internal use. Also, since some VPN equipment supports the dynamic host configuration protocol (DHCP), which is used to assign IP addresses to client systems automatically, you may need to change DHCP parameters to ensure that client systems do not end up with routes only to the Internet and not the private network, or vice versa.

Some VPN equipment uses virtual network adapters, which require the assignment of valid IP addresses on the private network. Make sure you assign these addresses from an unused address range. And also remember to make the required changes to routers and other network equipment.

Firewalls may also need reconfiguration if the VPN server is inside the firewall. Most VPNs take all traffic and encapsulate it into a stream that uses a single TCP port number. The firewall will need a generic proxy or pass-through rule for the encapsulated VPN traffic, as well as an *allow* rule to transport the traffic to the VPN equipment.

For extranets, where the VPN device is on a DMZ segment, the firewall will need one rule for allowing encrypted traffic to travel from the Internet to the DMZ, and additional rules for application traffic from the DMZ to the internal network. If the authentication server is located on the internal network, make sure you configure the firewall to allow authentication requests between the DMZ and the private network.

One place you should not need to make changes is on your domain name system (DNS) server, which is responsible for resolving the host names of private network machines to IP addresses. You should also make sure that the DNS server is not visible on the public Internet, otherwise attackers could learn the layout of your private network; otherwise, no one will be authenticated.

Install and Configure the VPN.   For software-based VPNs and those built around firewalls, it is essential to begin with a secure system. Remove all unnecessary services, applications, and user accounts from the server. Make sure the latest patches and security releases are installed. This should all be done prior to installing your VPN software.

When configuring the VPN itself, network managers will need to set parameters for key length, primary and secondary authentication servers (with associated shared secrets), connection and idle timeouts, certificate generation, and key generation and distribution mechanisms. Digital certificates verify the identity of VPN users and are implemented by most VPN products. Some vendors use a model where all this information is entered once at a headquarters device, and then remote devices download the information as they are brought online. For remote users, it also will be necessary to set up passwords, prepare connection scripts, and establish authentication procedures.

Net managers also need to sync up authentication and authorization routines. These sound similar, but there are subtle and important differences. Authentication involves proving that a remote user is who she or he claims to be (and in extranet settings, proving the opposite so that the server is trusted). Authorization determines which network resources the remote user has rights to utilize. If the authentication server also controls authorization by groups (for example, for marketing or engineering), be sure to verify that it communicates group information correctly to the VPN devices.

Monitor and Manage the VPN. Finally, you need to set up the appropriate procedures to monitor and manage the VPN, ideally before users start to really use the VPN service. You need to do this so you can measure how well the VPN is performing in terms of network utilization and throughput. You also need to ensure that the support staff has been trained to operate the VPN devices, including how to add new users, as well as how to set up and manage authentication and firewall services. You should also brief network managers on how the VPN works and on basic troubleshooting to ensure that someone knowledgeable about the system is always available if something goes wrong. You will also need to train users on how to use the VPN and how the VPN works so that they can do some basic troubleshooting themselves before having to call the support staff.

If you have a managed VPN service offered through a service provider or carrier, you will need to monitor the performance of the VPN to ensure that the agreed QoS metrics are maintained as specified in your service-level agreement (SLA). Your service provider may provide you with a Web-based application that allows you to monitor the VPN, or you may need to investigate and implement a management system that provides you with the necessary monitoring capability. This may be essential if your service provider implements a split management horizon in their VPN equipment, whereby they manage and monitor the WAN side of the equipment (WAN connections, routing, etc.) to provide the appropriate QoS, while you manage and monitor the security side (authorization, firewall, etc.). Remember, unless you can monitor the VPN, you cannot determine whether you are receiving the QoS for which you are paying.

FROM HERE

This chapter discussed the seven major types of networks: local area network (LAN), wide area network (WAN), virtual area network (VAN), Internet, intranet, extranet, and VPN. The next chapter presents an indepth overview of the various cabling standards (TIA/EIA568A, ISO/IEC 11801, IEEE 802.x, FDDI, ISDN, LATM, etc.) that are associated with the cabling technologies discussed in Chapter 1. Further discussions of cabling standards are presented in Chapter 8, "Standards Design Issues" and Chapter 27, "Standards Development."

NOTES

[1] "Networking in the School," AT&T, 32 Avenue of the Americas, New York, NY 10013-2412 1999, p. 1.

[2] "LAN/WAN Services," PM Systems Corporation, 115 Clark Street, Chapin, S.C., 2000, p. 1.

[3] Bradley H. Lamont, "A Guide to Networking a K-12 School District," University of Illinois at Urbana-Champaign, Urbana, Illinois, 1998, p. 18.

[4] Godred Fairhurst, "Metropolitan Area Networks (MANs)," Electronics Research Group, Department of Engineering at the University of Aberdeen, Fraser Noble Building, King's College, Old Aberdeen, Abereden, United Kingdom, AB24 3UE UK, 2000, p. 1.

[5] Claud E. Matney, P.E., "Virtual Area Networks (VANs)," Digital Horizon, Telephony Newsletter, Broadband Guide, PennWell Media Online L.L.C., 2875 South Congress Avenue, Delray Beach, Florida, 33445, 1999, p. 5.

[6] Internet Society, Post: 12020, Sunrise Valley Drive, Reston, VA 20191-3429, USA, 1999.

[7] Paul David Henry and Gene De Libero, "Intranet or Internet," Telecommunications® Online, Horizon House Publications, Inc., 685 Canton Street, Norwood, MA 02062, (January, 1999), p. 8.

[8] "The Extranet Solution: The Business Software Application for the 21st Century," OneSoft Corporation, 7010 Little River Turnpike, Suite 410, Annandale, VA 22003-3241, 1999, p. 2.

[9] Giga Information Group, 139 Main Street, 5th Floor, Cambridge, MA 02138 USA, 2000.

[10] International Data Corporation, 5 Speen St. Framingham, MA 01701, 2000.

[11] Fredric B. Gluck, "The Basics of Building Intranet Infrastructure," Telecommunications® Online, Horizon House Publications, Inc., 685 Canton Street, Norwood, MA 02062, (January, 1999), p. 1.

[12] "What is a Virtual Private Network," Enterasys Networks, 35 Industrial Way, Rochester, NH 03867, 2000.

[13] "Intranet—A Guide To 'Intraprise-Wide' Computing," IPWORKS.COM, Process Software, 959 Concord St., Framingham, MA 01701, 2000.

[14] "Developing an Extranet," Harrison & Troxell, Inc., 2 Faneuil Hall, Boston, MA 02109, 2000.

CHAPTER 3

Standards

Remember the good old days when network cabling requirements consisted of telephone connections and precious little else? If you were moving into a new building, you had one telephone number to remember—that of the Bell Telephone Company. Computer cabling was proprietary and complicated. Eventually coaxial and shielded cabling systems became the norm. Then, with the advent of LANs and the breakup of the Bell system, our world changed. By the late 1980s, proprietary network cabling systems were being phased out. Even then, knowledgeable observers were predicting the future—increasing dependency on network cabling.

Those predictions were accurate. Manufacturers have developed cabling systems that accommodate both voice and data transmission. Open systems have become universal, and proprietary systems are hard to find. Standard media and connecting components such as jacks and patch panels are UTP (unshielded twisted pair) or STP (shielded twisted pair). In the United States, UTP cabling systems have become dominant; shielded cabling systems are more common in Europe.

As we move toward higher data rates—100 Mbps and beyond—we are once again on the precipice of a major change. That shift is reflected in the new cabling standards being developed by the major network cabling standards institutes around the world.

NETWORK CABLING STANDARDS ORGANIZATIONS

Cabling standards are documented agreements containing technical specifications or other precise criteria to be used consistently as rules, guidelines, or definitions of characteristics to ensure that cabling materials, products, processes, and services are fit for their purpose. Standards thus contribute to making life simpler and to increasing the reliability and effectiveness of the goods and services we use. Before delving into an indepth discussion of cabling standards, it's appropriate to briefly identify the major international, regional, and national standards institutes found on the WWW, since they will be mentioned periodically from time to time in later chapters. All of these organizations are involved in one form or another in the development of network cabling standards around the world.

International

The growth of the international cabling industry has been well documented over the last 13 years. The major reason for this growth has been due to the following major international standards organizations that have been instrumental in developing new cabling standards.

International Organization for Standardization

The International Organization for Standardization (ISO) is a worldwide federation of national standards bodies from some 120 countries, one from each country. ISO is a nongovernmental organization established in 1947. The mission of ISO is to promote the development of standardization and related activities in the world with a view to facilitating the international exchange of goods and services, and to developing cooperation in the spheres of intellectual, scientific, technological, and economic activity.

Structure.   The ISO consists of some 180 technical committees, 750 subcommittees, 1,900 working groups, and 20 ad hoc study groups. These represent the viewpoints of manufacturers, vendors and users, engineering professions, testing laboratories, public services, governments, consumer groups, and research organizations in each of the 120 member countries.

International Standards.   Some 9,000 International Standards and technical reports have been published by ISO since 1980, representing over 76,000 pages of technical text in one language. They include information processing, graphic industry and photography (19,000 pages), mechanical engineering (17,700 pages), basic chemicals (6,300 pages), and nonmetallic materials (5,700 pages). Some 560 international organizations are in liaison with ISO technical committees and subcommittees.

ISO's work results in international agreements that are published as International Standards. For a list of some ISO/CCITT (International Organization for Standardization/Consultative Committee for International Telegraph and Telephone) standards, see Appendix I, "List of CCITT/ISO Standards."

International Electrotechnical Commission

The object of the International Electrotechnical Commission (IEC) is to promote international cooperation on all questions of standardization and related matters in the fields of electrical and electronic engineering and thus to promote international understanding. The IEC is composed of national committees, of which there are 70 at present, representing all the industrial countries in the world.

Video Electronics Standards Association

The Video Electronics Standards Association (VESA) is the international organization that sets and supports industry-wide interface standards for the PC, workstation, and other computing environments. VESA promotes and develops timely, relevant, and open standards for the electronics industry, ensuring interoperability and encouraging innovation and market growth.

International Telecommunication Union

The International Telecommunication Union (ITU) is an intergovernmental organization within which the public and private sectors cooperate for the development of telecommunications. The ITU adopts international regulations and treaties governing all terrestrial and space uses of the frequency spectrum as well as the use of the geostationary-satellite orbit within which countries adopt their national legislation. It also develops standards to facilitate the interconnection of telecommunication systems on a worldwide scale regardless of the type of technology used.

The Internet Engineering Task Force

The Internet Engineering Task Force (IETF) is the protocol engineering and development arm of the Internet. The IETF is a large, open international community of network designers, operators, vendors, and researchers concerned with the evolution of the Internet architecture and the smooth operation of the Internet. It is open to any interested individual. The actual technical work of the IETF is done in its working groups, which are organized by topic into several areas (routing, network management, security, etc.). Much of the work is handled via mailing lists. However, the IETF also holds meetings three times per year. Chairs and presenters might find it helpful to read the instructions for sessions and plenaries and first-time attendees might find it helpful to read "The Tao of IETF."

United National Educational, Scientific, and Cultural Organization

The main objective of the United National Educational, Scientific, and Cultural Organization (UNESCO) is to contribute to peace and security in the world by promoting collaboration among nations through education, science, culture, and communication in order to further universal respect for justice, for the rule of law, and for the human rights and fundamental freedoms that are affirmed for the peoples of the world, without distinction of race, sex, language, or religion, by the Charter of the United Nations. Its constitution was adopted by the London Conference in November 1945, and entered into effect on November 4, 1946, when 20 states had deposited instruments of acceptance. It currently has 188 member states.

The Internet Society

The Internet Society is a nongovernmental international organization for global cooperation and coordination for the Internet and its internetworking technologies and applications. The Society's individual and organizational members are bound by a common stake in maintaining the viability and global scaling of the Internet. The Society comprises the companies, government agencies, and foundations that have created the Internet and its technologies, as well as innovative new entrepreneurial organizations contributing to maintain the dynamic global scaling of the Internet. The Society is governed by its board of trustees elected by its membership around the world.

The World Wide Web Consortium

The World Wide Web Consortium (W3C) exists to realize the full potential of the Web. W3C is an industry consortium that develops common standards for the evolution of the Web by producing specifications and reference software. Although W3C is funded by industrial members, its products are freely available to all. The Consortium is run in the United States by the MIT Laboratory for Computer Science and in Europe by the National Institute for Research in Computer Science and Control, in collaboration with CERN (European Laboratory for Particle Physics), where the Web originated.

The Institute of Electrical and Electronics Engineers

The Institute of Electrical and Electronics Engineers (IEEE) is the world's largest technical professional society. Founded in 1884 by a handful of practitioners of the new electrical engineering discipline, today's Institute comprises more than 540,000 members who conduct and participate in its activities in 160 countries. The men and women of the IEEE are the technical and scientific professionals making the revolutionary engineering advances that are reshaping our world today. The technical objectives of the IEEE focus on advancing the theory and practice of electrical, electronics, and computer engineering and computer science. To realize these objectives, the IEEE sponsors technical conferences, symposia, and local meetings worldwide and publishes nearly 38 percent of the world's technical papers in electrical, electronics, and computer engineering. It provides educational programs to keep its members' knowledge and expertise state-of-the-art. The purpose of all these activities is two-fold: 1) to enhance the quality of life for all peoples through improved public awareness of the influences and applications of its technologies; and 2) to advance the standing of the engineering profession and its members.

The IEEE Standards Association (IEEE-SA) is the 21st century organization under which all IEEE Standards activities and programs are carried out. The IEEE-SA was formed to provide a major entity that would offer increased responsiveness to the standards interests of IEEE societies and their representative industries.

While the cornerstone of the IEEE-SA continues to be the traditional standards-setting process and the IEEE Standards Board activities, the IEEE-SA is opening up new program opportunities to those society activities and industry initiatives requiring changed methods and reduced time to market for their standards-related documents and resulting products.

IEEE-SA membership is open to both individuals and corporations, as well as to government agencies and trade associations. A board of governors is in place to define and embrace the full range of standards needs that constitute expanded levels of activity for the IEEE.

Regional

The regional network cabling standards organizations consist of the Comite Europeen de Normalisation, the European Telecommunications Standards Institute, and the European Workshop on Open Systems. The following major cabling and cable standards organizations are a significant force for everyone working with cabling.

Comite Europeen de Normalisation

The European Committee for Standardization is responsible for European standardization in all fields except electrotechnical (CENELEC) and telecommunications (ETSI). A related project of the CEN on the Web is the standardization of the European character set in the fields of identification, coding, and more.

The European Telecommunications Standards Institute

The European Telecommunications Standards Institute was set up in 1988 to set standards for Europe in telecommunications and in the related fields of broadcasting and office information technology with cooperation of the European Broadcasting Union (EBU) and CEN. This organization includes technical committees for signaling, protocols, switching, network aspects, transmission, multiplexing, and other fields related to telecommunications, but also special committees that are assembled from time to time to inspect specific and well-defined tasks.

The European Workshop on Open Systems

The European Workshop on Open Systems is the open European forum for one-stop development of technical guidance and prestandards in the information and communications technologies (ICT) field. This standards organization works for the benefit of vendors, planners, procurers, implementers, and users.

National

Finally, the national network cabling standards organizations are and have been instrumental in creating cost-effective, efficient cabling systems that would support the widest possible range of applications and equipment. However, significant differences do exist between the various organizations in their development of cabling standards specifications.

Standards Association of Australia

The Standards Association of Australia (SAA) is the Australian representative of the two major international standardizing bodies: the International Organization for Standardization (ISO) and the International Electrotechnical Commission (IEC). Standards Australia was founded in 1922. Its original name was the Australian Commonwealth Engineering Standards Association. The organization mission is to excel in meeting the needs of Australia's technical infrastructure for contemporary, internationally aligned standards and related services, which enhance the nation's economic efficiency and international competitiveness and fulfill the community desire for a safe and sustainable environment.

Standards Council of Canada (SCC)

The Standards Council coordinates the contribution of Canadians to the two most prominent international standards-writing forums: the ISO and the IEC. The SCC's activities are carried out within the context of the National Standards System, a federation of organizations providing standardization services to the Canadian public. The SCC is manager of the System.

Deutsches Institute fur Normung

The Deutsches Institute fur Nurmung (DIN), the German Institute for Standardization, is a registered association with its head office in Berlin. It is not a government agency. The work of standardization undertaken by DIN is a service in the field of science and technology that is provided for the entire community. The results of standardization benefit the whole of the national economy.

National Standards Authority of Ireland

The National Standards Authority of Ireland (NSAI) operates under Forf's, the Irish National Policy Advisory and Coordination Agency for Industrial Development, in respect to the Industrial Research and Standards Act of 1961 and the Industrial Development Act of 1993, and, on behalf of the Minister for Enterprise and Employment, for the development and publication of Irish Standards, including harmonized European Standards of CEN, CENELEC, ETSI (European Telecommunications Standards Institute), and the international standards of ISO and IEC. NSAI also provides a comprehensive product and management system certification service. NSAI activities are focused in two distinct areas: standards development and standards application, which in turn comprises certification services and the Irish Agriment Board.

Ente Nazionale Italiano di Unificazione

The Ente Nazionale Italiano di Unifica (UNI)—the Italian National Standards Body—was established in 1921 and is a legally recognized association whose function is to prepare, publish, and disseminate standards in all sectors except for the electrotechnical and electronic one, which falls under the responsibility of CEI (not on the Web). The EEC directive 83/189 of March 28, 1983— enacted in Italy as law #317 of June 21, 1986—recognizes UNI as the only national body entrusted with the adoption of technical standards in all fields except the electrical one.

Standards and Industrial Research Institute of Malaysia

The Standards and Industrial Research Institute of Malaysia (SIRIM) is a national multidisciplinary research and development agency under the Ministry of Science, Technology, and the Environment. Established in 1975 under the SIRIM (incorporation) Act 157, SIRIM was set up to assist companies in solving technical problems through the use of technology and to help their business grow.

Standards and Metrology Institute

The Standards and Metrology Institute (SMIS) prepares, adopts, and issues Slovenian standards, while also coordinating the tasks according to the rules of international standardization. Slovenian standards are therefore either international or European standards adopted according to the rules of the ISO IEC Guide 21. SMIS establishes technical committees, coordinates their work, links, and integrates them through corresponding regional and international technical committees.

American National Standards Institute

The American National Standards Institute (ANSI) has been the private sector voluntary standardization system in the United States for over 80 years. Founded in 1918 by five engineering societies and three government agencies, the Institute remains a private, nonprofit membership organization supported by a diverse constituency of private and public sector organizations. ANSI was a founding member of ISO and plays an active role in its governance. ANSI is one of five permanent members to the governing ISO Council and one of four permanent members of ISO. U.S. participation, through the U.S. National Committee (USNC), is equally strong in the IEC. The USNC is one of 14 members on the IEC. Through ANSI, the United States has immediate access to the ISO and IEC standards development processes. ANSI participates in almost the entire technical program of both the ISO (81 percent of all ISO technical committees) and the IEC (94 percent of all IEC technical committees) and administers many key committees and subgroups (19 percent in the ISO; 20 percent in the IEC). As part of its responsibilities as the U.S. member body to ISO and IEC, ANSI accredits U.S. technical advisory groups (U.S. TAGs) or USNC technical advisors (TAs). The purpose of a U.S. TAG is to develop and transmit, via ANSI, U.S. positions on activities and ballots of the international technical committee.

In many instances, U.S. standards are taken forward, through ANSI or its USNC, to the ISO or IEC, where they are adopted in whole or in part as international standards. Since the work of international technical committees is carried out by volunteers from industry and government, and not ANSI staff, the success of these efforts often is dependent upon the willingness of U.S. industry and the U.S. government to commit the resources required to ensure strong U.S. technical participation in the international standards process.

National Institute of Standards and Technology

The National Institute of Standards and Technology (NIST) was established by Congress to assist industry in the development of technology needed to improve product quality, to modernize manufacturing processes, to ensure product reliability, and to facilitate rapid commercialization of products based on new scientific discoveries. As an agency of the U.S Department of Commerce's Technology Administration, NIST's primary mission is to promote U.S. economic growth by working with industry to develop and apply technology, measurements, and standards.

Accredited Standards Committee X3

The Accredited Standards Committee X3 was established in 1961, and is accredited by ANSI to develop voluntary standards. X3 sets standards in dynamic areas of commerce, technology, and society. It contains technical committees such as X3T10, which is responsible for lower-level interfaces, X3T11 (Fiber Channel [see Appendix A, "List of Fiber Channel Products, Organizations, Vendors, and High Energy Projects and Applications"], HIPPI [High Performance Parallel Interface], and IPI [Intelligent Peripheral Interface]), and X3T13 (ATA [AT attachment] and ATAPI [AT attachment packet interface]).

National Information Standards Organization—USA

The National Information Standards Organization (NISO) is a nonprofit association accredited as a standards developer by the American National Standards Institute, the national clearinghouse for voluntary standards development in the United States. NISO's voting members and other supporters include a broad base of information producers and users, including libraries, publishers, government agencies, and companies that provide information services. NISO is a leader in shaping international standards.

ASTM

The American Society of Testing Materials (ASTM) has developed and published 12,000 technical standards, which are used by industries worldwide. ASTM members develop the standards within the ASTM consensus process. Technical publications, training courses, and statistical quality assurance programs are other ASTM products.

This concludes the presentation of the major international, regional, and national standards organizations. The stage is now set to delve into the various cabling standards (ANSI TIA/EIA-T568-A, ISO/IEC 11801, IEEE 802.x, FDDI, ISDN, 100BaseTX, etc.) that are associated with the major network cabling standards organizations just discussed.

Network Cabling Standards

Network cabling standards are the lifeline for the entire information technology network. They are the foundation on which all other network activities depend. A properly designed, installed, and administered standards-based cabling system reduces costs through each phase of its life cycle: installation; moves, adds, and changes; maintenance; and administration. The importance of network cabling standards should be neither overlooked nor underestimated (see Sidebar, "Quick Overview of Network Cabling Standards").

QUICK OVERVIEW OF NETWORK CABLING STANDARDS

The following is a very brief introduction to network cabling standards, bulletins, specifications, documents, and so on.

EIA/TIA-568: Commercial Building Telecommunications Wiring Standard

This standard specifies minimum requirements for telecommunications wiring within a building, up to and including the telecommunications outlets, and between buildings in a campus environment. It specifies a wiring system with a recommended topology and recommended distances. It specifies media by parameters that determine performance and specifies connectors and their pin assignments to ensure interconnectability. It has been superseded by EIA/TIA-568A.

EIA/TIA TSB-36: Technical Systems Bulletin Additional Cable Specifications for Unshielded Twisted Pair Cables

The purpose of this bulletin is to provide requirements on the transmission characteristics of high performance unshielded twisted pair cables. These cables are currently not specified in ANSI/EIA/TIA 568-1991 standard because they were still under development and their performance levels were not firmly established when the standard was published. This bulletin has been incorporated into EIA/TIA-568A.

TIA/EIA TSB40-A: Additional Transmission Specifications for Unshielded Twisted Pair Connecting Hardware

The purpose of this document is to specify transmission performance requirements for UTP connecting hardware that are consistent with the three categories of UTP cable specified in EIA/TIA TSB-36 and to specify additional requirements for cross-connect jumpers and for cables used for UTP patch cords. This document contains the minimum set of transmission parameters and their associated limits necessary to assure that properly installed connectors will have minimal effects on cable performance. These requirements apply to only individual UTP connectors, which include, but are not limited to, telecommunications outlets, patch panels, transition connectors and cross-connect blocks. This bulletin has been incorporated into EIA/TIA-568A.

EIA/TIA TSB-53-1992: Additional Specifications for STP Connecting Hardware

The purpose of this bulletin is to provide requirements on the transmission characteristics of shielded twisted pair cables. This bulletin has been incorporated into EIA/TIA-568A.

EIA/TIA-568-A: Commercial Building Telecommunications Wiring Standard

This standard replaces the ANSI/EIA/TIA-568 standard dated July 1991. This standard incorporates and refines the technical content of EIA/TIA TSB 36, TIA/EIA TSB 40, and TIA/EIA TSB 40A, which covered additional specifications for categories 3, 4, and 5 unshielded twisted pair (UTP) cables and compatible connecting hardware. Cables and connecting hardware for categories 1 and 2 are not a recognized part of this standard and therefore are not covered. This standard also incorporates and refines the technical content of the draft TSB 53, which covered additional specifications for 150 W shielded twisted pair (STP-A) cables and compatible connectors. This document takes precedence over the technical contents of TSB 36, TSB 40, TSB 40A, and TSB 53. New specifications for 62.5/125 micron optical fiber and single-mode optical fiber cables, connectors, and cabling practices have also been included.

Note: TSB 36, 40, 40A, and 53 are all superseded by this document, since it contains additional specifications and test methods important to users, manufacturers, and testing labs.

The purpose of this standard is to enable the planning and installation of a structured cabling system for commercial buildings. This standard establishes performance and technical criteria for various cabling system configurations for interfacing and connecting their respective elements.

EIA/TIA-569-A: Commercial Building Standard for Telecommunications Pathways and Spaces

The purpose of this standard is to standardize specific design and construction practices within and between (primarily commercial) buildings, which are in support of telecommunications media and equipment. Standards are given for rooms or areas and pathways into and through which telecommunications equipment and media are installed. The scope of this standard is limited to the telecommunications aspect of commercial building design and construction, encompassing telecommunications considerations both within and between buildings. Telecommunications aspects are generally the pathways into which telecommunications media are placed and the rooms and areas associated with the building used to terminate media and install telecommunications equipment.

EIA/TIA-570: Residential and Light Commercial Telecommunications Wiring Standard

This standard addresses the wiring for residential and light commercial premises. The stated purpose of the standard is to provide the minimum requirements for the connection of up to four exchanges access lines to various types of customer premises equipment. It applies to telecommunications premises wiring systems installed within an individual building with residential (single family or multioccupant) and light commercial end users.

TIA/EIA-606: The Administration Standard for the Telecommunications Infrastructure of Commercial Buildings

This standard specifies the administrative requirements of the telecommunications infrastructure within a new, an existing, or a renovated (primarily commercial) building or campus. The infrastructure can be thought of as the collection of those components (telecommunications spaces, cable pathways, grounding, wiring, and termination hardware) that provide the basic support for the distribution of all information within a building or campus. Administration of the telecommunications infrastructure includes documentation (labels, records, drawings, reports, and work orders) of cables, termination hardware, patching and cross-connect facilities, conduits, other cable pathways, telecommunications closets, and other telecommunications spaces. The purpose and intent of this standard is to provide a uniform administration scheme that is independent of applications, which may change several times throughout the life of a building. This standard establishes guidelines for owners, end users, manufacturers, consultants, contractors, designers, installers, and facilities administrators involved in the administration of the telecommunications infrastructure or related administration system.

TIA/EIA-607: Commercial Building Grounding and Bonding Requirements for Telecommunications

This standard specifies the requirements for a uniform telecommunications grounding and bonding infrastructure that should be followed within commercial buildings where telecommunications equipment is intended to be installed. The purpose of this standard is to enable the planning, design, and installation of telecommunications grounding systems within a building with or without prior knowledge of the telecommunication systems that will subsequently be installed. This telecommunications grounding and bonding infrastructure supports a multivendor, multiproduct environment as well as the grounding practices for various systems that may be installed on customer premises. This standard specifies the requirements for (a) a ground reference for telecommunications systems within the telecommunications entrance facility, the telecommunications closet, and equipment room; and (b) bonding and connecting pathways, cable shields, conductors, and hardware at telecommunications closets, equipment rooms, and entrance facilities.

TIA TSB-67: Transmission Performance Specification for Field Testing of Unshielded Twisted Pair Cabling Systems

This bulletin specifies the electrical characteristics of field testers, test methods, and minimum transmission requirements for UTP cabling. The purpose of this bulletin is to specify transmission performance requirements for UTP cabling links consistent with the three categories of UTP cable and connecting hardware specified in TIA/EIA-568A. Field test methods and interpretation of test data leading to pass/fail criteria are described to verify the installed cabling. Laboratory procedures and test setups to measure transmission performance are described in order to allow comparison of results between field testers and laboratory equipment. The bulletin defines channels and basic links, levels of accuracy, and the tests necessary to qualify installed cabling (see Chapter 23, "Testing Techniques," for more information).

TSB72: Centralized Optical Fiber Cabling Guidelines

The Telecommunications Systems Bulletin (TSB) provides the user with the flexibility of designing an optical fiber cabling system for centralized electronics typically in single-tenant buildings. It contains information and guidelines for centralized optical fiber cabling (see Chapter 8, "Standards Design Issues," for more information on centralized optical fiber cabling).

TIA TSB75: Open Office Cabling

Additional specifications for horizontal cabling in areas with moveable furniture and partitions have been introduced in TIA/EIA TSB75. Horizontal cabling methodologies are specified for *open office* environments by means of multi-user telecommunications outlet assemblies and consolidation points. These methodologies are intended to provide increased flexibility and economy for installations with open office work spaces that require frequent reconfiguration (see Chapter 9, "Architectural Design Considerations," for more information on open office cabling).

AF-PHY-0015.000: ATM Physical Medium-Dependent Interface Specification for 155 Mbps over Twisted Pair Cable

This specification describes the physical medium-dependent (PMD) sublayer for a 155.52 Mbps private user network interface (UNI) over twisted pair cabling. Requirements and test specifications for 100 ohm UTP and 150 ohm STP are included.

ANSI T1.102-1987 Digital Hierarchy: Electrical Interfaces

This document defines cabling and signal requirements for DS-1, DS1C, DS2, and DS3 interfaces.

IEEE P1143/D7: Guide on the Shielding Practice for Low-Voltage Cables

This document is a draft guide on the shielding practice for low-voltage cabling. The guide describes sources of electrostatic and electromagnetic interference, and reviews shielding techniques to control this interference for varying types of low-voltage cable used for power, control, and instrumentation services, including signal and communications cable. It has an overview of the functional characteristics of various types of shielding, presents criteria for defining the most favorable techniques to combat interference, and suggests tests or techniques for measuring shielding effectiveness. It also makes recommendations on shielding practices, including suggestions on terminating and grounding methods.

CENELEC EN50173: Performance Requirements of Generic Cabling Schemes

CENELEC is the European Committee for Electrotechnical Standardization. Its members include Austria, Belgium, Denmark, Finland, France, Germany, Greece, Iceland, Ireland, Italy, Luxembourg, the Netherlands, Norway, Portugal, Spain, Sweden, Switzerland, and the United Kingdom. This standard specifies generic cabling for use within commercial premises, which may comprise single or multiple buildings on a campus. It covers balanced copper cabling and optical fiber cabling. It includes structure and configuration information, implementation requirements, performance requirements for individual links, and test verification procedures.

ISO/IEC IS 11801: Information Technology—Generic Cabling for Customer Premises Cabling

This is the worldwide cabling standard. However, it should be noted that in many countries, other standards will take precedence. For example, North American users will refer to EIA/TIA 568A, while most Europeans will prefer EN50173.

This standard specifies generic cabling for use within commercial premises which may comprise single or multiple buildings on a campus. It covers balanced copper cabling and optical fiber cabling. It includes structure and configuration information, implementation requirements, performance requirements for individual links, and test verification procedures [8].

Inferior cabling systems are the cause of up to 77 percent of network downtime. With costs that range between $4,000 and $62,000 per hour, it is easy to see how important it is to control downtime. By installing a standards-based compliant network cabling system, much of this downtime can be effectively eliminated.

Although a cabling system will outlive most other networking components, it represents only 8 percent of the total network investment. A standards-based network cabling system represents a sound investment in the productivity of your organization.

Cabling is the longest life cycle component of the entire network, outlived only by the building shell. A standards-compliant cabling system can futureproof your network and guarantee future application support, ensuring that your investment will continue to serve you for the full extent of its life cycle.

With that in mind, let's take a very detailed look at the latest major network cabling standards (ANSI TIA/EIA-T568-A, ANSI TIA/EIA-T569-A, ISO/IEC 11801, IEEE 802.x, FDDI, ISDN, 100BaseTX, etc.) that are available today for building telecommunications cabling systems worldwide. This part of the chapter will begin the discussion of these standards with an indepth look at the ANSI TIA/EIA-T568-A cabling standard.

ANSI TIA/EIA-568-A

Prior to 1991, telecommunications cabling was controlled by the manufacturers of computer equipment. End users were confused by manufacturers' conflicting claims concerning transmission performance and were forced to pay high installation and administration costs for proprietary systems.

The telecommunications industry recognized the need to define a cost-effective, efficient cabling system that would support the widest possible range of applications and equipment. The Electronic Industries Association (EIA), Telecommunications Industry Association (TIA), and a large consortium of leading telecommunications companies worked cooperatively to create the ANSI/EIA/TIA-568-1991 Commercial Building Telecommunications Cabling Standard. Additional standards documents covering pathways and spaces, administration, cables, and connecting hardware were released subsequently. ANSI/EIA/TIA-568-1991 was revised in 1995, and is now referred to as ANSI/TIA/EIA-T568-A.

This part of the chapter covers the key aspects of the TIA/EIA-T568-A Commercial Building Telecommunications Cabling Standard (Canadian equivalent: CSA T529). TIA/EIA-T568-A incorporates the technical content of TSB-36 (Technical Systems Bulletin-36), TSB40-A, and draft TSB53. As published, the new cabling standard (TIA/EIA-T568-A) takes precedence over these technical bulletins. New specifications for 62.5/125 μm optical fiber and single-mode optical fiber cables, connectors, and cabling practices have been added. Guidelines are provided on UTP and optical fiber link performance.

The purpose of the TIA/EIA-T568-A standard is to first specify a generic voice and data telecommunications cabling system that will support a multiproduct, multivendor environment. Second, to provide direction for the design of telecommunications equipment and cabling products intended to serve commercial enterprises. Third, to enable the planning and installation of a structured cabling system for commercial buildings that is capable of supporting the diverse telecommunications needs of building occupants.

Finally, establish performance and technical criteria for various types of cable and connecting hardware and for cabling system design and installation.

TIA/EIA-T568-A specifications are intended for telecommunications installations that are office-oriented. Requirements are for a structured cabling system with a usable life in excess of 10 years. Specifications address:

- Minimum requirements for telecommunications cabling within an office environment.
- Recommended topology and distances.
- Media parameters, which determine performance.
- Connector and pin assignments to ensure interconnectability.
- The useful life of telecommunications cabling systems as being in excess of 10 years [1].

The goal of standard TIA/EIA-T568-A is to define structured cabling—a telecommunications cabling system that can support virtually any voice, imaging, or data application that an end user chooses. This part of the chapter highlights the key points or cabling elements of the TIA/EIA-T568-A standard by looking at the structured cabling system design considerations.

Design Considerations

The structured cabling system design considerations for the TIA/EIA-T568-A standard are concerned with six subsystems, as shown in Figure 3–1 [Anixter and TIA/EIA, 1].

1. building entrance or entrance facility (EF)
2. equipment room (ER)
3. backbone cabling
4. telecommunications closet (TC)
5. horizontal cabling
6. work area (WA)
7. administration

Building Entrance.   Building entrance facilities provide the point at which outside cabling interfaces with the intrabuilding backbone cabling. The physical requirements of the network interface are defined in the EIA/TIA-569 standard (TIA/EIA-T568-A).

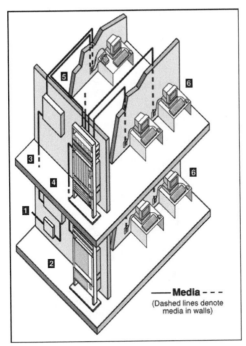

Media - - -
(Dashed lines denote
media in walls)

Figure 3–1
The six subsystems of the
structured cabling system.

Equipment Room.   The design aspects of the equipment room are specified in the EIA/TIA 569 standard. Equipment rooms usually house equipment of higher complexity than telecommunication closets. Any or all of the functions of a telecommunications closet may be provided by an equipment room.

Backbone Cabling.   The backbone cabling for the TIA/EIA-T568-A standard provides interconnection between telecommunication closets, equipment rooms, and entrance facilities, as shown in Figure 3–2 [Anixter and TIA/EIA, 2]. It consists of the backbone cables, intermediate and main cross-connects, mechanical terminations, and patch cords or jumpers used for backbone-to-backbone cross-connection. The backbone also extends between buildings in a campus environment. This includes:

- vertical connection between floors (risers);
- cables between an equipment room and building cable entrance facilities; and
- cables between buildings (interbuilding).

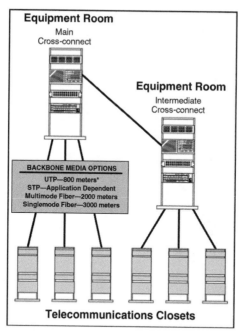

Figure 3–2
Specified backbone cabling topology: Star.

Backbone distances are application-dependent, as shown in Table 3–1 [Anixter and TIA/EIA, 2]. The maximum distances specified in Table 3–1 are based on voice transmission for UTP and data transmission for STP and fiber. The 90-meter distance for STP applies to applications with a spectral bandwidth of 20 MHz to 300 MHz. A 90-meter distance also applies to UTP at spectral bandwidths of 5 MHz to 16 MHz for Category 3, 10 MHz to 20 MHz for Category 4, and 20 MHz to 100 MHz for Category 5.

Table 3–1   Backbone Cabling Types and Distances (Main Cross-Connect [MC] to Horizontal Cross-Connect [HC]).

Cabling Types Recognized	Backbone Distances Maximum
100 ohm UTP Copper Applications <5 MHz (24 or 22 AWG [American Wire Gauge])	800 meters (2625 ft.) voice
150 ohm STP	90 meters (295 ft.) data
Multimode 62.5/125 μm optical fiber	2,000 meters (6560 ft.)
Single-mode 8.3/125 μm optical fiber	3,000 meters (9840 ft.)

Lower-speed data systems such as IBM 3270, IBM System 36, IBM System 38, AS 400, and asynchronous (RS232, 422, 423, etc.) can operate over UTP (or STP) for considerably longer distances, typically from several hundred feet to over 1,000 feet. The actual distances depend on the type of system, data speed, and the manufacturer's specifications for the system electronics and the associated components used (baluns, adapters, line drivers, etc.). Current state-of-the-art distribution facilities usually include a combination of both copper and fiber optic cables in the backbone. See the Sidebar, "Other Design Requirements," for specific information on the backbone cabling subsystem.

OTHER DESIGN REQUIREMENTS

Some points specified for the backbone cabling subsystem include:

- Equipment connections to backbone cabling should be made with cable lengths of 30 m (98 ft.) or less.
- The backbone cabling should be configured in a star topology, as shown in Figure 3–2. Each horizontal cross-connect is connected directly to a main cross-connect or to an intermediate cross-connect (see Figure 3–3) [2], then to a main cross-connect [Anixter and TIA/EIA, 2].
- The backbone is limited to no more than two hierarchical levels of cross-connects (main and intermediate). No more than one cross-connect may exist between a main and a horizontal cross-connect and no more than three cross-connects may exist between any two horizontal cross-connects.
- Cross-connects for different cable types must be located in the same facilities.
- A total maximum backbone distance of 90 m (295 ft.) is specified for certain applications. This distance is for uninterrupted backbone runs (no intermediate cross-connect).
- The proximity of backbone cabling to sources of electromagnetic interference (EMI) should be taken into account. (Specific distances are provided in ANSI/EIA/TIA-569.)
- The distance between the terminations in the entrance facility and the main cross-connect should be documented and should be made available to the service provider.
- Recognized media may be used individually or in combination, as required by the installation. Quantity of pairs and fibers needed in individual backbone runs depends on the area served. Recognized backbone cables are shown in Figure 3–4 [2].
- Multipair cable is allowed, provided that it satisfies the power sum cross talk requirements.
- Bridged taps are not allowed.
- Main and intermediate cross-connect jumper or patch cord lengths should not exceed 20 m (66 feet).

- Avoid installing in areas where sources of high levels of electromagnetic interference/radio frequency investigation (EMI/RFI) may exist.
- Grounding should meet the requirements as defined in the EIA/TIA 607 standard [Siemon, 1].

50/125 μm multimode fiber will be recognized in TIA-568-B.

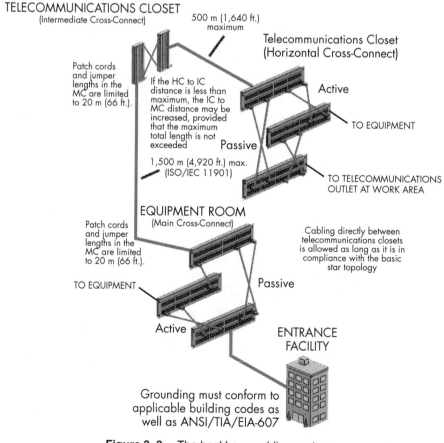

Figure 3–3   The backbone cabling system.

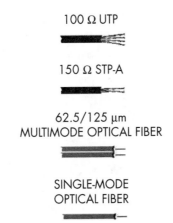

Figure 3–4   Recognized backbone cables.

In ISO/IEC 11801 (which is discussed later in this chapter), the equivalent cabling elements to the main cross-connect (MC) and intermediate cross-connect (IC) are called the campus distributor (CD) and building distributor, respectively. In addition to those listed, two alternate backbone cabling types allowed by ISO/IEC are 120 ohm twisted pair and 50/125 μm multimode optical fiber. 50 ohm coaxial cabling is recognized by 568-A, but is not recommended for new installations. It is recommended that the user consult with equipment manufacturers, application standards, and system providers for additional information when planning shared sheath applications on UTP backbone cables.

Telecommunications Closet.   A telecommunications closet is the area within a building that houses the telecommunications cabling system equipment, as shown in Figure 3–2. This includes the mechanical terminations and/or cross-connect for the horizontal and backbone cabling system. Please refer to EIA/TIA-569 for the design specifications of the telecommunications closet as discussed in the Sidebar, "Other Telecommunications Closet Design Specifications."

OTHER TELECOMMUNICATIONS CLOSET DESIGN SPECIFICATIONS

Some specifications related to telecommunications closets are:

- Closets should be designed and equipped in accordance with ANSI/EIA/TIA-569-A.

- Cable stress from tight bends, cable ties, and tension should be avoided by well-designed cable management.

- Cables and cords used for active equipment connections are outside the scope of the standard (10 m [33 ft.] total allowed for patch cords and equipment cables on both ends of each link).

- Only standards-compliant connecting hardware should be used.

- Equipment connections at a cross-connect may be made by way of *interconnections* or *cross-connections*, as shown in Figure 3–5 [Siemon, 1]. Cross-connections are used for connections between cabling subsystems and for connections to equipment with multiport connectors. Interconnections are used for connections to equipment with single-port connectors.

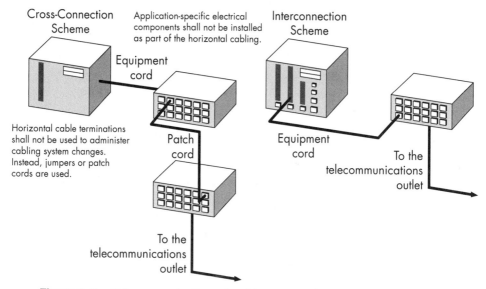

Figure 3–5   Telecommunications closet interconnections or cross-connections.

A *cross-connect* (or distributor) is a facility, whereas a *cross-connection* is a connection scheme. Cross-connections are typically used to provide a means of configuring individual port connections between the cabling and equipment with multiport outputs (25-pair connectors). Interconnections may be used with equipment that has individual output ports. A cross-connect facility may house interconnections, cross-connections, or both.

Horizontal Cabling. The horizontal cabling system (see Figure 3–6) for the TIA/EIA-T568-A standard extends from the telecommunications outlet in the work area (or workstation) to the horizontal cross-connect in the telecommunications closet, as shown in Figure 3–7 [Anixter and TIA/EIA, 4]. It includes the telecommunications outlet (see Figure 3–8), an optional consolidation point or transition point connector, horizontal cable, and the mechanical terminations and patch cords (or jumpers) that comprise the horizontal cross-connect.

ISO/IEC 11801 specifies a maximum patchcord/cross-connect length of 5 m (16.4 ft.), which does not include equipment cables/cords.

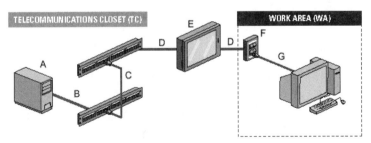

Figure 3–6   The horizontal cabling system. (A) Customer premises equipment; (B) HC equipment cord; (C) Patchcords/cross-connect jumpers used in the HC, including equipment cables/cords, should not exceed 6 m (20 ft.); (D) Horizontal cable 90 m (295 ft.) max. total; (E) TP or CP (optional); (F) Telecommunications outlet/connector (TO); and (G) WA equipment cord.

An allowance is made for WA equipment cords of 3 m (9.8 ft.).

An allowance of 10 m (33 ft.) has been provided for the combined length of patchcords/cross-connect jumpers and equipment cables/cords in the HC, including the WA equipment cords. In ISO/IEC 11801, the equivalent cabling element to the horizontal cross-connect (HC) is called the floor distributor (FD).

Three media types are recognized as options for horizontal cabling, each extending a maximum distance of 90 meters, as shown in Figure 3–8 [Anixter and TIA/EIA, 5]:

- 4-pair 100 ohm UTP cable (24 AWG solid conductors);
- 2-pair 150 ohm STP cables; and
- 2 fiber 62.5/125 µm optical fiber cable.

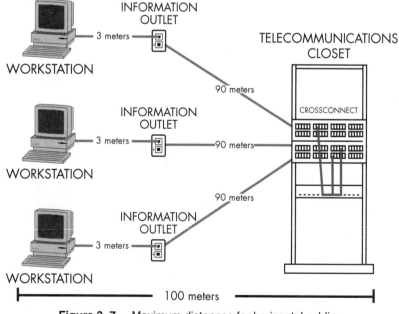

Figure 3–7   Maximum distances for horizontal cabling.

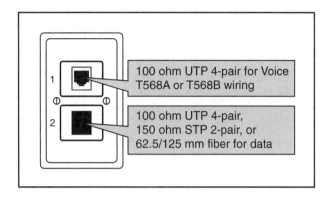

8-Position Modular Jack Pair Assignments for UTP

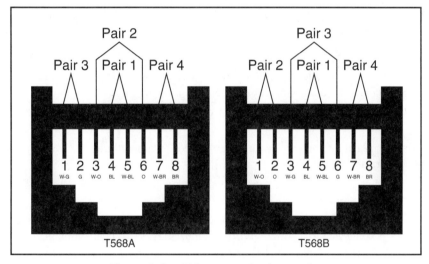

Figure 3–8 Telecommunications outlet.

In addition, two alternative horizontal cabling types allowed by ISO/IEC 11801 are 120 ohm twisted pair and 50/125 µm multimode optical fiber.

At this time, 50 ohm coaxial cable is a recognized media type. It is not, however, recommended for new cabling installations and is expected to be removed from the next revision of the ANSI/EIA/TIA-569-A standard. See the

Sidebar, "Other Horizontal Cabling System Structure Design Specifications," for further information on the ANSI/EIA/TIA-569-A and 568-A standards.

OTHER HORIZONTAL CABLING SYSTEM STRUCTURE DESIGN SPECIFICATIONS

Some points specified for the horizontal cabling subsystem include:

- The proximity of horizontal cabling to sources of electromagnetic interference (EMI) should be taken into account. Specific guidelines are provided in ANSI/EIA/TIA-569-A.

- One transition point (TP) is allowed between different forms of the same cable type (where undercarpet cable connects to round cable). NOTE: The definition provided for a *transition point* in ISO/IEC 11801 is broader than 568-A. It includes transitions to undercarpet cabling as well as consolidation point connections.

- A minimum of two telecommunications outlets are required for each individual work area. The first outlet: 100 ohm UTP; the second outlet: 100 ohm UTP, 150 ohm STP-A or 62.5/125 μm multimode fiber.

- Grounding must conform to applicable building codes, as well as ANSI/TIA/EIA-607.

- Additional outlets may be provided. These outlets are in addition to and may not replace the minimum requirements of the standard.

- 50 ohm coax cabling is recognized by '568-A, but is not recommended for new cabling installations.

- Bridged taps and splices are not allowed for copper-based horizontal cabling. Splices are allowed for fiber.

- Multipair and mult-unit cables are allowed, provided that they meet hybrid/bundled cable requirements of TIA/EIA-568-A-3.

- The horizontal cabling should be configured in a star topology; each work area outlet is connected to a horizontal cross-connect (HC) in a telecommunications closet (TC).

In addition to the 90 meters of horizontal cable (see Figure 3–7), a total of 10 meters is allowed for work area and telecommunications closet patch and jumper cables. Each work area should have a minimum of two information outlet ports, one for voice and one for data. The cabling choices are indicated in Figure 3–8.

Application-specific components should not be installed as part of the horizontal cabling. When needed, they must be placed external to the telecommunications outlet or horizontal cross-connect (splitters, baluns).

Work Area.   The work area components extend from the telecommunications (information) outlet to the station equipment, as shown in Figure 3–9 [2]. In other words, the telecommunications outlet serves as the work area interface to the cabling system. Work area equipment and cables used to connect to the telecommunications outlet are outside the scope of '568-A and ISO/IEC 11801, but are expected to be specified in the next edition of these standards. Work area wiring is designed to be relatively simple to interconnect so that moves, adds, and changes are easily managed. Work area components consist of:

- station equipment: computers, data terminals, telephones, and so on. Equipment cords are assumed to have the same performance as patch cords of the same type and category.
- Patch cables: modular cords, PC adapter cables, fiber jumpers, and so on. When used, adapters are assumed to be compatible with the transmission capabilities of the equipment to which they connect.
- Adapter: baluns—must be external to telecommunications outlet.
- Horizontal cable lengths are specified with the assumption that a maximum cable length of 3 m (10 ft.) is used for equipment cords in the work area.

In order to establish maximum horizontal link distances, a combined maximum length of 10 m (33 ft.) is allowed for patch cables (or jumpers and/or equipment) and for equipment cables in the work area and the telecommunications closet.

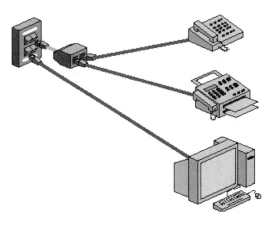

Figure 3–9
The work area.

The goal of the ANSI TIA/EIA-T568-A standard is also to define the media and connecting hardware performance specifications. This part of the chapter continues looking at the key points or cabling elements of the TIA/EIA-T568-A standard by discussing the performance of networking equipment or hardware.

Administration. Although administration is addressed to a limited extent, the governing specification on telecommunications administration is ANSI/TIA/EIA-606.

Media and Connecting Hardware Performance Specifications

Today, as more and more end users move to open systems, active media and connecting hardware is being developed based on the assumption that the cabling portion of the physical layer is standards compliant (reliable and capable of specific transmission performance). The risks of noncompliant cabling are numerous: substandard network performance; higher costs for moves, adds, and changes; and the inability to support emerging technologies. As the acceptance of standards-compliant structured cabling has grown, the price of installed networking media and connecting hardware has dropped and performance has exponentially increased. The physical layer has evolved into an affordable bandwidth-rich business resource. This part of the chapter will take a close look at the physical layer of the ANSI/TIA/EIA-T568-A standard by focusing on the following cabling elements:

- UTP cabling,
- optical fiber cabling,
- STP-A cabling,
- hybrid and undercarpet cables,
- modular wiring reference,
- TSB-67, and
- TSB-72.

Unshielded Twisted Pair (UTP) Cabling. As transmission rates have increased, higher performance UTP cabling has become a necessity. The 568-A specifications on 100 ohm unshielded twisted pair cabling supersede TSB-36 and TSB40-A.

Horizontal UTP Cable. Some means of classifying horizontal UTP cables and connecting hardware by performance capability had to be established. These capabilities have been broken down to a series of categories, which follow:

- *Category 3.* Cables/connecting hardware with transmission parameters characterized up to 16 MHz.
- *Category 4.* Cables/connecting hardware with transmission parameters characterized up to 20 MHz.
- *Category 5.* Cables/connecting hardware with transmission parameters characterized up to 100 MHz.

UTP Categories 1 and 2 are not specified. Characteristic impedance of horizontal categorized cables equal 100 ohms ± 15 percent from 1 MHz to the highest referenced frequency (16, 20, or 100 MHz) of a particular category, as shown in Table 3–2 [Anixter and TIA/EIA, 1]. Components and installation practices are subject to all applicable building and safety codes.

Table 3–2   Horizontal UT Cable Attenuation/NEXT (Near-End Cross Talk) Loss (Worst Pair)

Frequency (MHz)	Category 3 Decibel (dB) Attn/NEXT	Category 4 Decibel (dB) Attn/NEXT	Category 5 Decibel (dB) Attn/NEXT
0.064	0.9 / –	0.8 / –	0.8 / –
0.150	– / 53	– / 68	– / 74
0.256	1.3 / –	1.1 / –	1.1 / –
0.512	1.8 / –	1.5 / –	1.5 / –
0.772	2.2 / 43	1.9 / 58	1.8 / 64
1.0	2.6 / 41	2.2 / 56	2.0 / 62
4.0	5.6 / 32	4.3 / 47	4.1 / 53
8.0	8.5 / 27	6.2 / 42	5.8 / 48
10.0	9.7 / 26	6.9 / 41	6.5 / 47
16.0	13.1 / 23	8.9 / 38	8.2 / 44
20.0	– / –	10.0 / 36	9.3 / 42
25.0	– / –	– / –	10.4 / 41
31.25	– / –	– / –	11.7 / 39
62.5	– / –	– / –	17.0 / 35
100.0	– / –	– / –	22.0 / 32

Note: Attenuation: per 100 m (328 ft.) @ 20 degrees C. NEXT: 100 m (328 ft.)

Category 3 requirements are consistent with the UTP specifications for horizontal cable and connecting hardware in the original edition of 568.

Furthermore, with regard to propagation delay and delay skew, the following specifications should be adhered to.

- Solid 4-pair 0.51 mm (24 AWG) specified (0.64 mm [22 AWG] solid are also allowed). An overall shield (ScTP) is optional.
- Performance marking should be provided to show the applicable performance category. These markings do not replace safety markings.
- Color-coding:
  - White/blue*–blue.
  - White/orange*–orange.
  - White/green*–green.
  - White/brown*–brown.

* Tracers are optional for cables with twist rates of less than 38 mm (1.5 in.).

Backbone UTP Cable.   Characteristic impedance of backbone cabling equals 100 ohms ± 15 percent from 1 MHz to the highest referenced frequency of a particular category (16, 20, or 100 MHz). Performance markings should be provided to show the applicable performance category. These markings do not replace safety markings.

Services with incompatible signal levels should be partitioned into separate binder groups. Guidelines for shared sheaths are provided in annex D of '568-A.

Transmission requirements are equivalent to horizontal cables. The exception is that NEXT loss performance, shown in Table 3–3, is based on power-sum rather than worst-pair characterization to allow for multiple disturbing signals in the same sheath [Anixter and TIA/EIA, 2].

Table 3–3   Backbone UTP Cable Attenuation/Power Sum NEXT (Near-End Cross Talk)

Frequency (MHz)	Category 3 Decibel (dB) Attn/NEXT	Category 4 Decibel (dB) Attn/NEXT	Category 5 Decibel (dB) Attn/NEXT
0.064	0.9 / –	0.8 / –	0.8 / –
0.150	– / 53	– / 68	– / 74
0.256	1.3 / –	1.1 / –	1.1 / –
0.512	1.8 / –	1.5 / –	1.5 / –
0.772	2.2 / 43	1.9 / 58	1.8 / 64
1.0	2.6 / 41	2.2 / 56	2.0 / 62
4.0	5.6 / 32	4.3 / 47	4.1 / 53
8.0	8.5 / 27	6.2 / 42	5.8 / 48
10.0	9.7 / 26	6.9 / 41	6.5 / 47
16.0	13.1 / 23	8.9 / 38	8.2 / 44
20.0	– / –	10.0 / 36	9.3 / 42
25.0	– / –	– / –	10.4 / 41
31.25	– / –	– / –	11.7 / 39
62.5	– / –	– / –	17.0 / 35
100.0	– / –	– / –	22.0 / 32

Note: Attenuation: per 100 m (328 ft.) @ 20° C. NEXT: 100 m (328 ft.)

Tip conductors have colored insulation that corresponds to that of the binder group. Ring conductors have colored insulation that corresponds to that of the pair.

Backbone UTP cables consist of solid 0.5 mm (24 AWG) cables that contain more than four pairs (typically multiples of 25 pairs are used). An overall shield is optional.

UTP Patch Cords and Cross-Connect Jumpers.   To ensure that installed UTP connecting hardware (telecommunications outlets, patch cords and panels, connectors, cross-connect blocks, etc.) and cords will have minimal effect on overall cabling system performance, the characteristics and performance parameters presented in this section are based on specifications that cover all types of connectors used in the cabling system, including the telecommunications outlet/connector.

UTP connecting hardware and cords do not cover work area adapters, baluns, protection, MAUs, filters, or other application-specific devices. Temperature can range from 10°C (14°F) to 60°C (140°F).

Outlets should be securely mounted. Outlet boxes with unterminated cables must be covered and marked.

Transmission requirements are much more severe than cable of a corresponding category, as shown in Table 3–4 [Anixter and TIA/EIA, 3]. Performance markings should be provided to show the applicable transmission category and should be visible during installation (for example, CAT 5) in addition to safety markings. Installed connectors should be protected from physical damage and moisture.

Table 3–4   UTP Connecting Hardware Attenuation NEXT (Near-End Cross Talk) Loss

Frequency (MHz)	Category 3 (dB)	Category 4 (dB)	Category 5 (dB)
1.0	0.4 / 58	0.1 / 65	0.1 / 65
4.0	0.4 / 46	0.1 / 58	0.1 / 65
8.0	0.4 / 40	0.1 / 52	0.1 / 62
10.0	0.4 / 38	0.1 / 50	0.1 / 60
16.0	0.4 / 34	0.2 / 46	0.2 / 56
20.0	– / –	0.1 / 44	0.2 / 54
25.0	– / –	– / –	0.2 / 52
31.25	– / –	– / –	0.2 / 50
62.5	– / –	– / –	0.3 / 44
100.0	– / –	– / –	0.4 / 40

Note: The preferred termination method for all UTP connecting hardware utilizes the insulation displacement contact (IDC).

Patch cords must use stranded cable for adequate flex-life. The following requirements apply only to wire and cable used for patch cords and cross-connect jumpers (see Table 3–5 [Anixter and TIA/EIA, 3]). For example, jumper/patch cord maximum length limitations:

• 20 meters (66 feet) in main cross-connect
• 20 meters (66 feet) in intermediate cross-connect

- 6 meters (20 feet) in telecommunications closet
- 3 meters (10 feet) in the work area

Table 3–5   Maximum Attenuation of Cable Used in Patch Cords

Frequency (MHz)	Category 3 (dB)	Category 4 (dB)	Category 5 (dB)
1.0	3.1	2.6	2.4
4.0	6.7	5.2	4.9
8.0	10.2	7.4	6.9
10.0	11.7	8.3	7.8
16.0	15.7	10.7	9.9
20.0	—	12.0	11.1
25.0	—	—	12.5
31.25	—	—	14.1
62.5	—	—	20.4
100.0	—	—	26.4

Note: Attenuation: per 100 m (328 ft.) @ 20° C = Horizontal UTP cable attenuation + 20 percent (due to stranded conductors).

Stranded cables must meet the minimum performance requirements for horizontal cable. The exception would be that 20 percent more attenuation is allowed by '568-A and 50 percent more attenuation is allowed by '11801.

Color-code for cross-connect jumpers: One conductor white, the other a visibly distinct color such as red or blue. Color codes for stranded, 100 ohm UTP patch cord is shown in Table 3-6 [Anixter and TIA/EIA, 3].

Table 3–6   Color Code Options

Option 1	Pair Type	Option 2
white/blue–blue	pair 1	green–red
white/orange–orange	pair 2	black–yellow
white/green–green	pair 3	blue–orange
white/brown–brown	pair 4	brown–slate

Insulated O.D. of stranded wires should be 0.8 mm (0.032 in.) to 1 mm (0.039 in.) to fit into a modular plug. Finally, production performance specifications for plug cord assemblies are being developed as PN-4349.

UTP Connector Terminations. To ensure overall system integrity, horizontal cables need to be terminated with connecting hardware of the same category or higher. In other words, pair twists should be maintained as close as possible to the point of termination. Untwisting should not exceed 25 mm (1.0 in) for category 4 links and 13 mm (0.5 in) for category 5 and category 5e links. Manufacturer guidelines should be followed for category 3 products, if no guidelines exist, then untwisting should not exceed 75 mm (3.0 in). Connecting hardware should be installed to provide well-organized installation with cable management and in accordance with manufacturer's guidelines. The jacket should be striped back only as much as is required to terminate individual pairs.

Also, cables used for patch cords and cross-connect jumpers need to be of the same performance category or higher as the horizontal cables to which they connect. Lastly, UTP cabling systems are not category 3, 4, or 5 compliant unless all components of the system satisfy their respective category requirements.

Optical Fiber Cabling. The new specifications on optical fiber cabling media for the TIA/EIA-568A standard consist of one recognized cable type for horizontal subsystems and two cable types for backbone subsystems:

- Horizontal –62.5/125 μm multimode optical fiber (minimum of two fibers per outlet), as shown in Table 3–7 [Anixter and TIA/EIA, 5].
- Backbone –62.5/125 μm multimode and single-mode (10/125 μm) optical fiber, as shown in Table 3–8 [Anixter and TIA/EIA, 5].

It is likely that the next publication of '568-B will also recognize 50/125 μm multimode optical fiber in both the horizontal and backbone.

All optical fiber components and installation practices should meet applicable building and safety codes.

Table 3–7 Cable Transmission Performance Parameters Multimode (Horizontal and Backbone)

Wavelength nanometers (nm)	Maximum Attenuation (dB/km)	Minimum Bandwidth Megahertz over one kilometer (MHz-km)
850	3.75	160
1300	1.5	500

Table 3–8 Cable Transmission Performance Parameters Single Mode (Backbone)

Wavelength nanometers (nm)	Maximum Attenuation (dB/km)
1310	0.5
1550	0.5

Optical Fiber Patch Cords. With regard to optical fiber patch cords, there should be a two-fiber (duplex) indoor cable of the same type as the cables to which they connect. You should also allow for easy connection and reconnection and ensure that polarity is maintained (568SC configuration required). Finally, you should perform a pair-wise crossover of fiber positions A and B. If provided in simplex form, one connector should be identified as A and the other B.

Optical Fiber Connectors. With regard to optical fiber connectors, the recommended adapter (coupler) and connector is designated as 568SC (duplex SC or specified connector that is capable of simplex operation), as shown in Figure 3–10 [Siemon, 2]. ST connectors are allowed where an installed base exists. In cross-connects, a 568SC simplex or duplex connector is allowed.

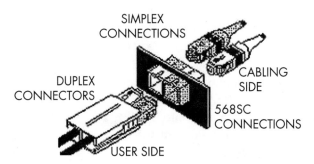

SIMPLEX CONNECTIONS

DUPLEX CONNECTORS

CABLING SIDE

568SC CONNECTIONS

USER SIDE

Figure 3–10
Optical fiber cabling system.

For the work area side of the telecommunications outlet, the 568SC duplex SC connector is specified. 568SC patch cords are required for two-fiber applications. Telecommunications outlet/connector boxes should be securely mounted at planned locations.

The two positions in a duplex connector are referred to as position A and position B. 568SC connectors are rated for a minimum of 500 mating cycles. The 568SC adapter performs a crossover between position A and position B of two mated connectors, as shown in Figure 3–10.

(a) Color identification of fiber types should have a beige 62.5/125 μm multi-mode connector/coupling and a blue 8.3/125 μm single-mode connector/coupling. (b) Applications with an installed base of ST-type fiber connectors are *grandfathered* for continued use in both current and future updates of existing optical fiber networks. (c) A key reason the standard now specifies the 568SC-type fiber connector is to harmonize with the IEC specified interface currently in use in Europe.

On the other hand, the optical fiber telecommunications outlet should have the capability to store unterminated fibers within its outlet box. Other required features of the outlet include:

- Capability to terminate a minimum of two fibers into 568SC couplings.
- Means of securing optical fiber and maintaining minimum bend radius of 30 mm (1.18 in.).
- Ability to store a minimum of 1 m (3.28 ft.) of 2-optical fiber cable.
- A surface-mount box that attaches directly over a standard 4" × 4" electrical box.

Optical Fiber Installation.   A minimum of 1 m (3.28 ft.) of two-fiber cable (or two buffered fibers) should be accessible for termination purposes. Testing is recommended to assure correct polarity and acceptable link performance. Informative annex H of '568-A is provided for recommended optical fiber link performance testing criteria.

Finally, with regard to the installation of optical fiber-connecting hardware, connectors should be protected from physical damage and moisture. Capacity for 12 or more fibers per rack space (44.5 mm [1.75 in.]) should be provided. Also, optical fiber-connecting hardware should be installed to provide well-organized installation with cable management—in accordance with manufacturers' guidelines.

Shielded Twisted Pair (STP-A) Cabling.   The recognized shielded twisted pair (STP) cables for the TIA/EIA-T568-A standard are IBM type 1A for backbone and horizontal distribution and IBM type 6A for patch cables. Cable and connector specifications are extended to 300 MHz. Prior specifications are no longer supported. All STP-A components and installation practices should meet applicable building and safety codes.

The same mechanical and transmission requirements apply to backbone and horizontal STP-A cables, as shown in Table 3–9 [Anixter and TIA/EIA, 4]. Additional requirements are provided for outdoor cables.

Table 3–9   Horizontal and Backbone STP-A Cable Balanced Mode Attenuation/NEXT Loss (Worst Pair)

Frequency (MHz)	Attn/NEXT (dB)
4.0	2.2 / 58.0
8.0	3.1 / 54.9
10.0	3.6 / 53.5
16.0	4.4 / 50.4
20.0	4.9 / 49.0
25.0	6.2 / 47.5
31.25	6.9 / 46.1
62.5	9.8 / 41.5
100.0	12.3 / 38.5
300.0	21.4 / 31.3

Note: Attenuation: 100 m (328 ft.) @ 25° C

Standard outlet interface and pair assignments are the same as the ISO 8802-5 token ring connector (IEC 807-8), except that performance requirements are much more severe. 150 ohm data connectors should be marked shielded twisted pair (STP-A) in addition to any safety markings required by local or national codes, as shown in Table 3–10 [Anixter and TIA/EIA, 4].

Table 3–10   150 Ohm STP-A Data Connector Attenuation/NEXT Loss.

Frequency (MHz)	Insert Loss/NEXT (dB)
4.0	.05 / 65
8.0	.10 / 65
10.0	.10 / 65
16.0	.15 / 62.4
20.0	.15 / 60.5
25.0	.15 / 58.5
31.25	.15 / 56.6
62.5	.20 / 50.6
100.0	.25 / 46.5
300.0	.45 / 36.9

Specifications for 150 ohm STP-A patch cables call for 0.4 mm (2-pair, 26 AWG) stranded conductors. They allow for an overall shield (as opposed to individually shielded pairs).

Characteristic impedance equals 150 ohms ± 10 percent (3 MHz to 300 MHz). Balanced mode attenuation of 150 ohm STP-A patch cable is about 1.5 times that of horizontal or backbone STP-A cable (4 MHz to 300 MHz). NEXT performance of 150 ohm STP-A patch cable measures approximately 6 dB less than horizontal or backbone STP-A cable (5 MHz to 300 MHz).

Hybrid and Undercarpet Cables.   Hybrid cables that contain multiple units of recognized copper cables for the TIA/EIA-T568-A standard are subject to additional NEXT loss requirements between cable units. These requirements assure a minimum of 6 dB additional cross-talk isolation between applications that may operate on adjacent cables within the sheath. All detailed specifications for the individual cable units used in the hybrid assembly still apply.

Undercarpet cables should not be used in wet locations. They should be separated from power cables by at least 152 mm (6 in.), except at crossings. The use of carpet squares is recommended for accessibility.

Modular Jack Styles.   There are four basic modular jack styles for the TIA/EIA-T568-A Standard, as shown in Figure 3–11 [Siemon, 1]. The 8-position and 8-position keyed modular jacks are commonly and incorrectly referred to as RJ45 and keyed RJ45, respectively. The 6-position modular jack is commonly referred to as RJ11. Using these terms can sometimes lead

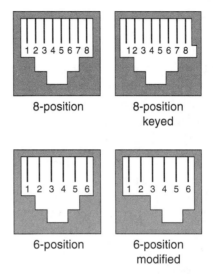

8-position   8-position
keyed

6-position   6-position
modified

Figure 3–11   Basic modular jack styles.

to confusion since the RJ designations actually refer to very specific wiring configurations called universal service ordering codes (USOC).

The designation *RJ* means registered jack. Each of these three basic jack styles can be wired for different RJ configurations. For example, the 6-position jack can be wired as an RJ11C (1-pair), RJ14C (2-pair), or RJ25C (3-pair) configuration. An 8-position jack can be wired for configurations such as RJ61C (4-pair) and RJ48C. The keyed 8-position jack can be wired for RJ45S, RJ46S, and RJ47S.

The fourth modular jack style is a modified version of the 6-position jack (modified modular jack, or MMJ). It was designed by Digital Equipment Corporation (DEC) along with the modified modular plug (MMP) to eliminate the possibility of connecting DEC data equipment to voice lines and vice versa.

Two wiring schemes have been adopted by the 568-A standard with regard to common outlet configurations. They are nearly identical except that pairs two and three are reversed. T568A is the preferred scheme because it is compatible with 1- or 2-pair USOC systems, as shown in Figure 3–12 [Siemon, 1]. Either configuration can be used for Integrated Services Digital Network (ISDN) and high-speed data applications.

USOC wiring is available for 1-, 2-, 3-, or 4-pair systems, as shown in Figure 3–13 [Siemon, 1]. Pair 1 occupies the center conductors, pair 2 occupies the next two contacts out, and so forth. One advantage to this scheme is that a 6-position plug configured with 1 or 2 pairs can be inserted into an 8-position jack and still maintain pair continuity. A note of warning though, pins 1 and 8 on the jack may become damaged from this practice. A disadvantage is the poor transmission performance associated with this type of pair sequence.

10BaseT wiring specifies an 8-position jack but uses only two pairs, as shown in Figure 3–14 [Siemon, 2]. These are pairs 2 and 3 of T568B and T568A schemes.

Token ring wiring uses either an 8-position or 6-position jack, as shown in Figure 3–15 [Siemon, 2]. The 8-position format is compatible with T568A,

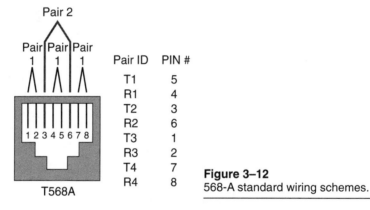

Figure 3–12
568-A standard wiring schemes.

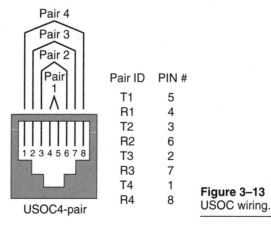

Figure 3–13
USOC wiring.

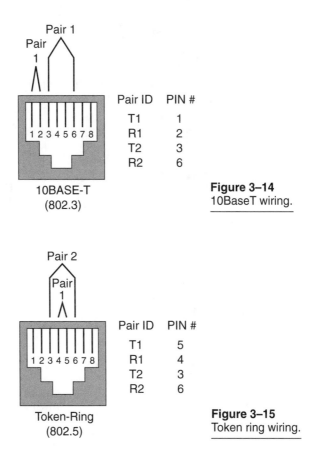

Pair 1

Pair 1

Pair ID	PIN #
T1	1
R1	2
T2	3
R2	6

10BASE-T
(802.3)

Figure 3–14
10BaseT wiring.

Pair 2

Pair 1

Pair ID	PIN #
T1	5
R1	4
T2	3
R2	6

Token-Ring
(802.5)

Figure 3–15
Token ring wiring.

T568B, and USOC wiring schemes. The 6-position is compatible with 1- or 2-pair USOC wiring.

The MMJ is a unique wiring scheme for DEC® equipment, as shown in Figure 3–16 [Siemon, 2]. Furthermore, ANSI X3T9.5 TP-PMD uses the two outer pairs of an 8-position jack, as shown in Figure 3–17 [Siemon, 2]. These positions are designated as pair 3 and pair 4 of the T568A wiring scheme.

It is important when dealing with modular plug pair configurations that the pairing of wires in the modular plug match the pairs in the modular jack as well as the horizontal and backbone wiring. If they do not, the data being transmitted may be paired with incompatible signals. Furthermore, Figure 3–18 shows that modular cords wired to the T568A 8-pin position scheme on both ends are compatible with T568B systems and vice versa [Siemon, 3].

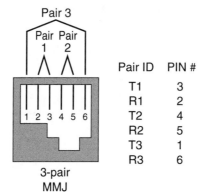

Pair ID	PIN #
T1	3
R1	2
T2	4
R2	5
T3	1
R3	6

3-pair
MMJ

Figure 3–16
MMJ wiring.

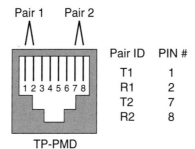

Pair ID	PIN #
T1	1
R1	2
T2	7
R2	8

TP-PMD
(X3T9.5)

Figure 3–17
ANSI X3T9.5 TP-PMD wiring.

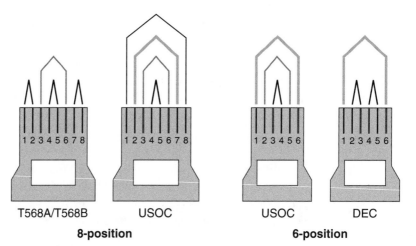

T568A/T568B   USOC   USOC   DEC

8-position   **6-position**

Figure 3–18   Modular plug pair configurations.

Modular cords are used for two basic applications. One application uses them for patching between modular patch panels. When used in this manner, modular cords should always be wired straight through (pin 1 to pin 1, pin 2 to pin 2, pin 3 to pin 3, etc.). The second major application uses modular cords to connect the workstation equipment (PC, phone, fax, etc.) to the modular outlet. These modular cords may either be wired straight through or reversed (pin 1 to pin 6, pin 2 to pin 5, pin 3 to pin 4, etc.), depending on the system manufacturer's specifications. This reversed wiring is typically used for voice systems. The following is a brief guide to determine what type of modular cord you have. Also, see the Sidebar, "Recommended Cabling Practices," for some tips on the do's and don'ts of modular wiring.

How do you read a modular cord? You should first align the plugs side-by-side with the contacts facing you and compare, for example, the 8 pin positions (pin 1 to pin 8, pin 2 to pin 7, pin 3 to pin 6, pin 4 to pin 5; or, pin 1 to pin 2, pin 3 to pin 6, pin 4 to pin 5, pin 7 to pin 8, etc.) from left to right. If the pin positions appear in the same order on both plugs, the cord is wired straight through, as shown in Figure 3–19 [Siemon, 3]. If the pin positions appear reversed on the second plug (from right to left), the cord is wired reversed.

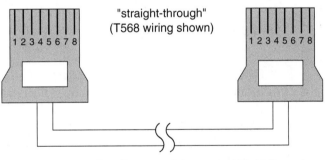

Figure 3–19   Reading a modular cord: straight-through.

RECOMMENDED CABLING PRACTICES

The following are some recommended cabling practices to follow when you're doing *modular wiring*, let's look at the *do's* first:

Do's:

- Use connecting hardware that is compatible with the installed cable.
- Terminate each horizontal cable on a dedicated telecommunications outlet.
- Locate the main cross-connect near the center of the building to limit cable distances.
- Maintain the twist of horizontal and backbone cable pairs up to the point of termination.
- Tie and dress cables neatly, not exceeding the minimum bend radius.
- Place cabling at a sufficient distance from equipment that may generate high levels of electromagnetic interface.

Don'ts:

- Do not use connecting hardware that is of a lower category than the cable being used.
- Do not create multiple appearances of the same cable at several distribution points (called bridged taps).
- Do not locate cross-connects where cable distances will exceed the maximum.
- Do not leave any wire pairs untwisted.
- Do not overtighten cable ties or make sharp bends with cables.

TSB-67.   TSB-67 (Telecommunications Systems Bulletin-67 standard) provides users with the opportunity to use comprehensive field test methods to validate the transmission performance specifications or characteristics of installed UTP cabling systems. The categories of UTP cabling systems in this bulletin also correspond with the UTP cabling categories of ANSI/TIA/EIA-T568-A.

For the purposes of testing UTP cabling systems, the horizontal link is assumed to contain a telecommunications outlet/connector, a transition point, 90 meters of UTP (Category 3–5), a cross-connect consisting of two blocks or panels, and a total of 10 meters of patch cords. Figures 3–20, 3–21, and 3–22 show the relationship of these components [Siemon, 1]. See the Sidebar, "Specific Points for TSB-67," for some additional tips on transmission field testing for UTP cabling systems.

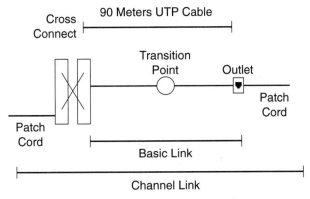

Figure 3–20 Transmission performance specifications for field testing of unshielded twisted pair (UTP) cabling systems [Anixter and TIA/EIA, 1].

Horizontal Channel

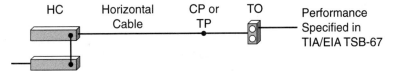

Cabling Type	Channel Attn. (db)	Channel Next (db)	Link ACR (db)
Cat 3 (@ 16 MHz)	14.9	19.3	4
Class C (@ 16 MHz)	(15.0)	19	(4)
Cat 5 (@ 100 MHz)	24.0	27.1	3
Class D (@ 100 MHz)	(24.9)	24	(2)

Figure 3–21 Transmission performance comparison for Cat. 3/Class C and Cat. 5/Class D channels. Numbers in parenthesis are calculated based on using 5 meters of additional flexible cables that meet the ISO/IEC 11801.

Horizontal Link

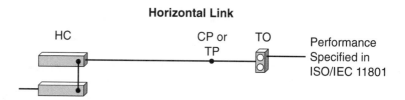

Cabling Type	Link Attn. (db)	Link Next (db)	Link ACR (db)
Cat 3 (@ 16 MHz)	(14.3)	19.3	(5)
Class C (@ 16 MHz)	14.0	19	5
Cat 5 (@ 100 MHz)	(23.0)	27.1	(4)
Class D (@ 100 MHz)	23.2	24	4

Figure 3–22   Transmission performance comparison for Cat. 3/Class C and Cat. 5/Class D links. Numbers in parenthesis are calculated based on using 6 meters of patch cable that meets TIA/EIA-568-A. Transition point/consolidation point included.

The two link configurations in Figure 3–20 are defined for testing purposes. The basic link (see Figure 3–23) includes the distribution cable, telecommunications outlet/connector or transition point, and one horizontal cross-connect component. This is assumed to be the permanent part of a link. The channel link is comprised of the basic link plus installed equipment, user, and cross-connect jumper cable.

TSB-67 defines the allowable worst-case attenuation and NEXT for an installed link, as shown in Figure 3–23 [Siemon, 2]. Tables 3–11 and 3–12 show the limitations for attenuation and NEXT, respectively, for both the basic and channel links [Anixter and TIA/EIA, 2].

Basic Link Test Configuration

Cabling Type	Link Attn. (db)	Basic Link Next (db)	Basic Link ACR (db)
Cat 3 (@ 16 MHz)	13.2	21.0	7.8
Class C (@ 16 MHz)	(13.0)	(20.8)	(7.8)
Cat 5 (@ 100 MHz)	21.6	29.3	7.7
Class D (@ 100 MHz)	(21.9)	(29.1)	(7.2)

Figure 3–23   Transmission performance comparison for Cat 3/Class C and Cat 5/Class D basic links. Class C and D attenuation values are calculated based on 90 meters horizontal cable plus 4 meters of flexible cable and two connectors that meet ISO/IEC 11801. Class C and D NEXT values are based on voltage summations of the near-end connector and horizontal cable.

Table 3–11   Basic/Channel Link Attenuation

Frequency (MHz)	Category 3 (dB)	Category 4 (dB)	Category 5 (dB)
1.0	3.2/4.2	2.2/2.6	2.1/2.5
4.0	6.1/7.3	4.3/4.8	4.0/4.5
8.0	8.8/10.2	6.0/6.7	5.7/6.3
10.0	10.0/11.5	6.8/7.5	6.3/7
16.0	13.2/14.9	8.8/9.9	8.2/9.2
20.0	-	9.9/11	9.2/10.3
25.0	-	-	10.3/11.4
31.25	—	—	11.5/12.8
62.5	—	—	16.7/18.5
100.0	—	—	21.6/24

Table 3–12 Basic/Channel Link NEXT Loss (Pair-to-Pair)

Frequency (MHz)	Category 3 (dB)	Category 4 (dB)	Category 5 (dB)
1.0	40.1/39.1	54.7/53.3	60/60
4.0	30.7/29.3	45.1/43.3	51.8/50.6
8.0	25.9/24.3	40.2/38.2	47.1/45.6
10.0	24.3/22.7	38.6/36.6	4.5/44
16.0	21.0/19.3	35.3/33.1	42.3/40.6
20.0	—	33.7/31.4	40.7/39
25.0	—	—	39.1/37.4
31.25	—	—	37.6/35.7
62.5	—	—	32.7/30.6
100.0	—	—	29.3/27.1

SPECIFIC POINTS FOR TSB-67

Some points specified for TSB-67 transmission field testing for UTP cabling systems include:

- UTP cabling systems comprise cables and connecting hardware specified in TIA/EIA-568-A.

- Required test parameters include wiremap, length, attenuation, and cross talk.

- Two levels of pass or fail are indicated, depending on measured margin compared to minimum specifications. Testing of NEXT is required in both directions.

- Level II equipment meets the most stringent requirements for measurement accuracy.

- Requirements are intended for performance validation and are provided in addition to '568-A requirements on components and installation practices.

TSB-72.   Telecommunications Systems Bulletin-72 (TSB-72) provides the user with the flexibility of designing an optical fiber cabling system for either centralized or distributed electronics in conjunction with the ANSI/TIA/EIA-T568-A standard. It contains information and guidelines for centralized optical fiber cabling, as shown in Figure 3–24 [Siemon, 1]. See the Sidebar, "Specific Points For TSB-72," for some additional tips on centralized optical fiber cabling systems.

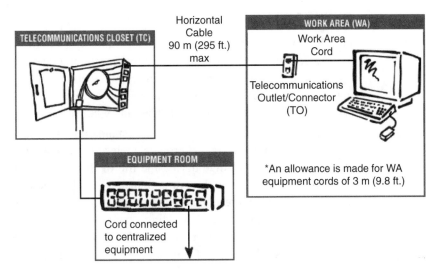

Figure 3–24 Typical schematic for centralized optical fiber cabling using an interconnection.

SPECIFIC POINTS FOR TSB-72

Some points specified in TSB-72 for a centralized optical fiber cabling system include:

- Intended for single-tenant users who desire centralized versus distributed electronics.
- Allows cables to be spliced or interconnected at the telecommunications closet so that cables can be routed to a centralized distributor for total cable lengths of 300 m (984 ft.) or less.
- Allows for migration from an interconnection or splice to a cross-connection scheme that can also support distributed electronics.
- Allows for pull-through implementations when total length between the telecommunications outlet/connector and centralized cross-connect is 90 m (295 ft.) or less.
- Connecting hardware required to:
  - Join fibers by remateable connectors or splices.
  - Connectors should be 568SC interface.
  - Provide for simplex or duplex connection of optical fibers.
  - Provide means of circuit identification.
  - Allow for addition and removal of optical fibers.

ANSI/TIA/EIA-569-A

Let's briefly look at the next major network cabling standard: ANSI/TIA/EIA-569-A: Commercial Building Standard for Telecommunications Pathways and Spaces. The Telecommunications Industry Association (TIA) TR41.8.3 Working Group on Telecommunications Pathways and Spaces published the ANSI/TIA/EIA-569-A ('569-A) standard in 1998.

The purpose of creating the '569-A standard was to: standardize design and construction practices and provide a telecommunications support system that is adaptable to change during the life of the facility. The scope of the standard is to provide pathways and spaces in which telecommunications media are placed and terminated; provide telecommunications pathways and spaces within and between buildings; and provide commercial building design for both single and multitenant buildings. The elements of '569-A standard are as follows and illustrated in Figure 3–25 [2].

- Horizontal (see Sidebar, "Pathways from Telecommunications Closet to Work Area").
- Backbone (see Sidebar, "Pathways Routed from Closet-To-Closet").
- Work area (see Sidebar, "Primary Location Where the Building Occupants Interact with Dedicated Telecommunications Equipment").
- Telecommunications Closet (see Sidebar, "Recognized Location of the Common Access Point for Backbone and Horizontal Pathways").
- Equipment room (see Sidebar, "A Centralized Space for Telecommunications Equipment that Serves Specific Occupants of the Building").
- Main terminal space.
- Entrance facility (see Sidebar, "Consists of the Telecommunications Service Entrance to the Building and Backbone Pathways between Buildings").
- Miscellaneous (see Sidebar, "Miscellaneous Elements of the '569-A Standard") [2].

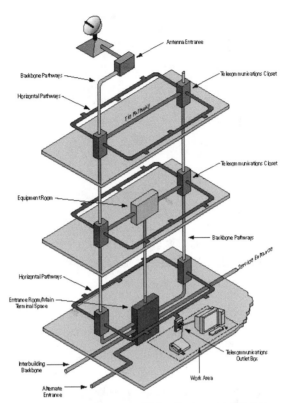

Figure 3–25   Elements of the Commercial Building
Standard for Telecommunications Pathways and
Spaces.

PATHWAYS FROM TELECOMMUNICATIONS CLOSET TO WORK AREA

This includes pathway types, space types, and design considerations:

Pathway Types

- *Underfloor:* Network of raceways embedded in concrete consisting of distribution and header ducts, trenches, and cellular systems.

- *Access floor:* Raised modular floor tile supported by pedestals, with or without lateral bracing or stringers.

- *Conduit:* Metallic and nonmetallic tubing of rigid or flexible construction permitted by applicable electrical code.

- *Tray and wireway:* Prefabricated rigid structures for pulling or placing cable.
- *Ceiling:* Open environment above accessible ceiling tiles and frame work.
- *Perimeter:* Surface, recessed, molding, and multichannel raceway systems for wall mounting around rooms or along hallways.

Space Types

- *Pull boxes:* Used in conjunction with conduit pathway systems to assist in the fishing and pulling of cable.
- *Splice boxes:* A box located in a pathway run, intended to hold a cable splice.
- *Outlet boxes:* Device for mounting faceplates, housing terminated outlet/connectors, or transition devices.

Design Considerations

- Grounded per code and ANSI/TIA/EIA-607 ('607).
- Designed to handle recognized media as specified in ANSI/TIA/EIA-568-A ['568-A].
- Not allowed in elevator shafts.
- Accommodate seismic zone requirements.
- Installed in dry locations [2].

PATHWAYS ROUTED FROM CLOSET-TO-CLOSET

Typically the most convenient and cost-effective backbone pathway design in multistory buildings is to have stacked closets located one above the other, connected by sleeves or slots, as shown in Figure 3–26 [2].

Building Backbone Types

- ceiling
- conduit
- sleeves: An opening, usually circular, through the wall, ceiling, or floor
- slots: An opening, usually rectangular, through the wall, ceiling, or floor
- trays

Design Considerations

- Grounded per code and '607.
- Accommodate seismic zone requirements.
- Water should not penetrate the pathway system.

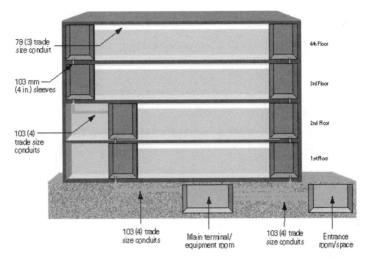

Figure 3–26   Backbone pathways routed from closet-to-closet.

- Trays, conduits, sleeves, slots penetrate closets minimum 25 mm (1 in.).
- Designed to handle all recognized media (as specified in '568-A).
- Integrity of all fire-stop assemblies should be maintained.

PRIMARY LOCATION WHERE THE BUILDING OCCUPANTS INTERACT WITH DEDICATED TELECOMMUNICATIONS EQUIPMENT

Design Considerations

At least one telecommunication outlet box location should be planned for each work area. This location should be coordinated with the furniture plan. A power outlet should be nearby. Control center, attendant, and reception areas should also have direct and independent pathways to the serving telecommunications closet (see Figure 3–27 and Table 3–13) [2].

Furniture System Design

- Cable access via walls, columns, ceilings, or floors. Fittings that transition between building and furniture pathways require special planning.
- Furniture pathway fill capacity is effectively reduced by furniture corners and connectors mounted within the furniture pathway systems.
- Furniture pathways bend radius should not force the installed cable to a bend radius of

less than 25 mm (1 in.).

- Furniture spaces designed to house slack storage, consolidation points, or multi-user telecommunications outlet assemblies should provide space for strain relieving, terminating, and storing slack for the horizontal cables.

- Slack storage and furniture pathway fill should not affect the bend radius and termination of the cable to the connector.

- Furniture pathway openings should comply with either of two sizes: Standard NEMA opening (NEMA OS 1 [Ref D.14], WD-6 [Ref D.15]); and alternate opening.

Table 3–13   Work Area Measurement, Dimension, and Tolerance.

Measurement	Dimension	Tolerance
L (length)	68.8 mm (2.71 in.)	1.02 mm (0.040 in.)
H (height)	35.1 mm (1.38 in.)	0.90 mm (0.035 in.)
T (depth)	1.40 mm (0.055 in.)	0.64 mm (0.025 in.)
R (corner radius)	4.06 mm (0.160 in.) max.	
C (distance to 1st obstruction)	30.5 mm (1.2 in.) min	

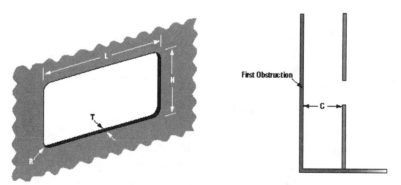

Figure 3–27   Backbone pathways routed from closet-to-closet.

RECOGNIZED LOCATION OF THE COMMON ACCESS POINT FOR BACKBONE AND HORIZONTAL PATHWAYS

Design

- Dedicated to telecommunications function.
- Equipment not related to telecommunications should not be installed, pass through, or enter the telecommunications closet.
- Multiple closets on the same floor should be interconnected by a minimum of one (78 [3] trade size) conduit, or equivalent pathway (see Figure 3–28) [2].
- Minimum floor loading 2.4 kPA (50 lbf/ft^2).

Design Considerations

- Minimum one closet per floor to house telecommunications equipment/cable terminations and associated cross-connect cable and wire.
- Located near the center of the area being served.
- Horizontal pathways should terminate in the telecommunications closet on the same floor as the area served.
- Accommodate seismic zone requirements.
- Two walls should have 20 mm (0.75 in.) A-C plywood 2.4 m (8 ft.) high.
- Lighting should be a minimum of 500 lx (50-foot candles) and mounted 2.6 m (8.5 ft.) above floor.
- False ceilings should not be provided.
- Minimum door size 910 mm (36 in.) wide and 2,000 mm (80 in.) high without sill, hinged to open outward, or slide side-to-side or removable, and fitted with a lock.
- Minimum of two dedicated 120V 20A nominal, nonswitched, AC duplex electrical outlet receptacles, each on separate branch circuits.
- Additional convenience duplex outlets placed at 1.8 m (6 ft.) intervals around perimeter, 150 mm (6 in.) above floor.
- Access to the telecommunications grounding system as specified by ANSI/TIA/EIA-607.
- HVAC requirements to maintain temperature the same as adjacent office area. A positive pressure should be maintained with a minimum of one air change per hour or per code.

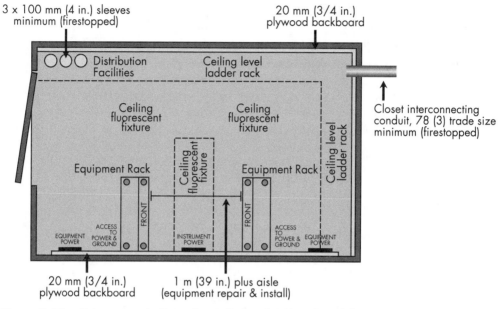

3 x 100 mm (4 in.) sleeves
minimum (firestopped)

20 mm (3/4 in.)
plywood backboard

Closet interconnecting
conduit, 78 (3) trade size
minimum (firestopped)

20 mm (3/4 in.)
plywood backboard

1 m (39 in.) plus aisle
(equipment repair & install)

Figure 3–28 Telecommunications closet: Recognized location of the common access point for backbone and horizontal pathways.

A CENTRALIZED SPACE FOR TELECOMMUNICATIONS EQUIPMENT THAT SERVES SPECIFIC OCCUPANTS OF THE BUILDING

Any or all of the functions of a telecommunications closet or entrance facility may alternately be provided by an equipment room.

Location:

- Site locations should allow for expansion.
- Accessible to the delivery of large equipment.
- Not located below water level.
- Away from sources of EMI.
- Safeguards against excessive vibration.
- Sizing should include projected future as well as present requirement.
- Equipment not related to the support of the equipment room should not be installed in, pass through, or enter the equipment room.

Design Considerations:

- Minimum clear height of 2.4 m (8 ft.) without obstruction.
- Protected from contaminants and pollutants.
- Access to backbone pathways.
- HVAC provided on a 24 hours-per-day, 365 days-per-year basis.
- Temperature and humidity controlled range 18° C (64° F) to 24°C (75° F) with 30 percent to 55 percent relative humidity measured 1.5 m (5 ft.) above floor level.
- Separately bonded power supply circuit should be provided and terminated in its own electrical panel. An independently serviced ground source should be available isolated from any other circuits.
- Minimum lighting 500 lx (50-foot candles). Switch location should be near entrance door to room.
- Minimum door same as telecommunications closet. Double doors without center post or sill are recommended [2].

The *main terminal space* is the centralized space that houses the main cross-connect. The centralized space is commonly used as a separate space in multitenant buildings to serve all tenants. Location considerations are as specified for equipment room. The provisioning area is specified for telecommunications closets, except where power is reduced to convenience receptacles. Such convenience receptacles should be properly labeled as bonded circuit outlets as appropriate.

CONSISTS OF THE TELECOMMUNICATIONS SERVICE ENTRANCE TO THE BUILDING AND BACKBONE PATHWAYS BETWEEN BUILDINGS

Location

- Providers of all telecommunications services should be contacted to establish requirements.
- Location of other utilities should be considered in locating the entrance facility.
- Alternate entrance facility should be provided where security, continuity, or other special needs exist.
- Equipment not related to the support of the entrance facility should not be installed in, pass through, or enter the telecommunications entrance facility.

- Dry location not subject to flooding and close as practicable to building entrance point and electrical service room.

Design Considerations

- Accommodate the applicable seismic zone requirements.
- A service entrance pathway should be provided via one of the following entrance types: underground, buried, aerial, or tunnel.
- Minimum one wall should be covered with rigidly fixed 20 mm (0.75 in.) A-C plywood.
- Minimum lighting same as telecommunication closet.
- False ceilings should not be provided.
- Minimum door same as telecommunications closet.
- Electrical power same as telecommunications closet. No convenience receptacles mentioned.
- Grounding same as telecommunications closet [2].

MISCELLANEOUS ELEMENTS OF THE '569-A STANDARD

The miscellaneous elements of the '569-A standard are as follows:

1. Fire stopping per applicable code

2. Horizontal pathway separation from electromagnetic interference (EMI) sources

- Separation between telecommunications and power cables (Article 800.52 of ANSI/NFPA 70).
- Building protected from lightning (ANSI/NFPA 780 [Ref D.4]).
- Surge protection (Article 280 of ANSI/NFPA 70 and 9.11 of ANSI/IEEE 1100 [Ref D.1]).
- Grounding (ANSI/TIA/EIA-607).
- Corrected faulty wiring (Section 7.5 of ANSI/IEEE 1100).

3. Reducing noise coupling

- Increase separation from noise sources.
- Electrical branch circuit line, neutral, and grounding conductors should be maintained close together.
- Use of surge protectors in branch circuits.
- Use fully enclosed grounded metallic raceway or locate cabling near grounded metallic surface [2].

ISO/IEC 11801

Let's briefly look at the next major network cabling standard: ISO/IEC 11801. This cabling standard is currently being developed by ISO.

ISO is currently developing a cabling standard on an international basis under the title Generic Cabling for Customer Premises Cabling ISO/IEC 11801. Heavily based on EIA 568, this standard extends the UTP bias of the American standards into 100 ohm STP cabling and 120 ohm cabling for the French market. The principal difference between EIA 568 and ISO 11801 is that, in the latter, four application classes (A, B, C, D) are specified for increasing data rates.

The ISO 11801E 1995 standard is being generally followed in Europe. This standard (like EIA 568) includes a link performance level of NEXT (near end cross talk) and has also introduced the concept of measuring ACR (attenuation/cross-talk ratio) for LAN cables.

Local Area Network Cables

LAN cables are supposed to provide you with conformance to AS/NZS 3080:1996, ISO/IEC 11801, and EIA/TIA-T568-A. The cables should be verified and listed by Underwriters Laboratories, a U.S. firm. With regard to standard ISO/IEC 11801, the following categories and classes of cables will be covered:

- balanced twisted pair cable (Category 7 cable);
- UTP structured cable (enhanced Category 6 cable);
- horizontal reticulation cable (Category 6 cable);
- horizontal reticulation in a structured cabling system (Category 5 cable);
- halogen-free cable; and
- horizontal link in a structured cabling system (Category 3 cable).

Balanced Twisted Pair Cable. Balanced twisted pair cable has been designed to meet the recently announced ISO/IEC Category 7 specifications for individually screened 4-pair horizontal distribution cable in a structured cabling system (see Chapter 8, "Standard Design Issues" for more information on Category 6 and 7 specifications). This type of cable will support any protocol that requires a bandwidth up to 600MHz. The services expected to require this bandwidth include Ethernet 1000 BaseT, asynchronous transfer mode (ATM) 2.4 Gbps and higher. This cable can also be used to extend well beyond the 90 m horizontal link length for lower bandwidth services.

This type of cable can be described as a 4-pair individually foil-screened 23AWG twisted pair STP LAN cable with overall braid and verified by 3P Test Laboratories to C6STP (proposed ISO/IEC Category 7 link specifications). The balanced twisted pair cable complies with "AS/NZS 3080:1996, ISO/IEC 11801," and "TIA/EIA-T568-A Cable Construction PVC (Permanent Virtual Circuit) Outer Sheath Braid Screen Foil Screen Rip Cord Twisted Pair."

UTP Structured Cable. The UTP structured cable transmission performance far exceeds proposed Category 6 requirements as part of the ISO/IEC 11801 revision. This 4-pair cable is used in the horizontal reticulation of a structured cabling system, interfacing communications equipment in the floor distributor to the telecommunications outlet in the work area.

The UTP structured cable is a flexible cable when used as either a work area cable or an equipment cable in a structured cabling environment. 24-pair UTP is used in riser applications where high-speed data or large bandwidth is required. Consideration should be given to the shared sheath compatibility of difference services being transmitted in the same sheath.

This multipair 24 AWG UTP LAN cable exceeds proposed ISO/IEC Category 6 link specifications. Pair twist lengths and cable geometry, via central filler, are designed to maximize NEXT performance and product stability during installation. Complies with AS/NZS 3080:1996, ISO/IEC 11801, ACA/AUSTEL TS-008, and TIA/EIA-T568-A. The range is UL listed/verified.

Designed to operate beyond 400 MHz, UTP structured cable takes cabling well beyond gigabit and ATM applications. Also, attenuation to cross-talk ratio (ACR or headroom) exceeds 30 dB at 100 MHz.

AS/NZS 3080:1996 allows Category 5 links to extend beyond 90 m (clause 4 and 7.1.2). UTP structured cable will allow you to run 10BaseT over a 300 m link, and ATM 155 over a 130 m link. Furthermore, a high degree of balance (LCL, LCTL), superior NEXT, and ACR provide a physical link that will enable a total system to comply with the EMC regime.

Horizontal Reticulation Cable. The horizontal reticulation cable is designed to meet the proposed Category 6 requirements as part of ISO/IEC 11801 revision. This category supports services requiring a bandwidth up to 200 MHz. The horizontal reticulation cable range is tested to 350 MHz to ensure performance capability.

This cable is used for horizontal reticulation between the floor distributor and the telecommunications outlet in a structured cabling system. The 24-pair horizontal reticulation cable is recommended for use in backbone applications where consideration has been given to shared sheath compatibility of different protocols transmitted in the same sheath.

The horizontal reticulation cable is a multipair 24 AWG UTP/FTP LAN cable that meets proposed ISO/IEC Category 6 link specifications. Pair twist lengths are designed to optimize NEXT performance. This cable complies to AS/NZS 3080:1996, ISO/IEC 11801, ACA/AUSTEL TS-008, and TIA/EIA-T568-A standards. The cable's range is UL listed/verified.

The horizontal reticulation cable is designed to operate to 350 MHz. Attenuation to cross-talk ratio (ACR or headroom) exceeds 23 dB at 100 MHz.

Horizontal Reticulation in a Structured Cabling System (Category 5 Cable). Here, horizontal reticulation in a structured cabling system is a 4-pair Category 5 UTP cable suitable for high-speed LAN applications including Ethernet 10 BaseT, Ethernet 100 BaseT, video conferencing, 100VG-AnyLAN, and ATM155. The 4-pair Category 5 cable is individually screened and used where electromagnetic interference (EMI) is an issue, beyond the capabilities of UTP.

The 4-pair cable is used for patching equipment to patch panels or to interface the horizontal cable to the terminal equipment in the work area. The cable can be described as multipair 24 AWG UTP/FTP LAN cable meeting Category 5 specifications. It complies with AS/NZS 3080:1996, ISO/IEC 11801, ACA/AUSTEL TS-008, and TIA/EIA-T568-A. The range is UL listed/verified.

Halogen-Free Cable. The halogen-free cable's range is suitable in public areas where public safety is at stake in the case of fire breaking out. These cables are constructed of materials that do not emit halogens and reduce the speed of fire; little or no smoke is emitted. Halogen-free cables are ideal in confined spaces such as tunnels, vehicles, ships, and aircraft.

Halogen-free cable is a multipair 24 AWG UTP/FTP zero halogen and low fire hazard LAN cable meeting Category 5 specifications. It complies with AS/NZS 3080:1996, ISO/IEC 11801, ACA/AUSTEL TS-008, and TIA/EIA-T568-A. Fire safety standards complied with include AS1660.5.3 (zero halogen), AS 1660.5.2 (low smoke density), AS 1660.5.1 (bunch vertical burn), and AS 1660.5.6 (single vertical burn). The cable's range is UL listed (CMR/CM)/verified.

In a fire, time is paramount. Halogen-free cables have been designed to minimize smoke and toxic fumes, thus maximizing the time available for evacuation and minimizing harm to building occupants in the event of a fire.

The chlorine used within PVC cables is an environmental hazard. Halogen-free cables are manufactured from environmentally friendly materials that do not contain PVC or fluoropolymer.

The smoke from cables sheathed in PVC, when brought into contact with moisture (say from sprinklers), will form corrosive acids that may damage equipment. Halogen-free cables are designed to protect equipment and do not contain halogens to produce acids.

Horizontal Link in a Structured Cabling System (Category 3 Cable). Here, the cable range complies with the Category 3 cable requirements of AS/NZS3080 1996. This cable range is also suitable for applications requiring a bandwidth up to 16 MHz (Category 3) such as voice, ISDN, Ethernet 10 BaseT, and token ring 4 Mbps.

A horizontal link in a structured cabling system is a 4-pair UTP Category 3 cable. It is a flexible 4-pair UTP patch cable used as a work area cable or an equipment cable.

The cable is also a 100-pair UTP suitable for voice or 10 BaseT transmission in a backbone application. In other words, it's a multipair 24 AWG UTP/FTP LAN cable meeting Category 3 specifications. It complies with AS/NZS 3080:1996, ISO/IEC 11801, ACA/AUSTEL TS-008, and TIA/EIA 568A. The cable's range is UL listed/verified.

IEEE 802.x

Let's take a quick look at another major set of network cabling standards: IEEE 802.x. This set of cabling standards is currently being developed by the IEEE. There are many standards in the 802.x series. To discuss them all is beyond the scope of this book; therefore, only a few of the major ones are covered. They include:

- IEEE 802.1: Standards related to network management.
- IEEE 802.2: General standard for the data link layer in the OSI (Open System Interconnection) reference model. The IEEE divides this layer into two sublayers—the data link control (DLC) layer and the media access control (MAC) layer. The MAC layer varies for different network types and is defined by standards IEEE 802.3 through IEEE 802.5.
- IEEE 802.3: Defines the MAC layer for bus networks that use CSMA/CD (carrier sense multiple access collision detection). This is the basis of the Ethernet standard (10BaseT, 10BaseF, 10Base5, 10Base2, 10Broad36, and Fast Ethernet).
- IEEE 802.3 (Fast Ethernet): Any of a number of 100 Mbps Ethernet specifications. Fast Ethernet offers a speed increase 10 times that of the 10BaseT Ethernet specification, while preserving such qualities as

frame format, MAC mechanisms, and MTU. Such similarities allow the use of existing 10BaseT applications and network management tools on Fast Ethernet networks. This is the basis of the Fast Ethernet standard (100BaseFX, 100BaseT4, and 100BaseTX).

- IEEE 802.4: Defines the MAC layer for bus networks that use a token-passing mechanism (token bus networks).
- IEEE 802.5: Defines the MAC layer for token ring networks.
- IEEE 802.6: Standard for metropolitan area networks.
- IEEE 802.11: Standard protocols for wireless networks.
- IEEE 802.12: 100VG-AnyLAN. 100 Mbps Fast Ethernet and token ring media technology using four pairs of Category 3, 4, or 5 UTP cabling. This high-speed transport technology, developed by Hewlett-Packard, can be made to operate on existing 10BaseT Ethernet networks.
- IEEE 802.3ab: Standard that defines the operation, testing, and usage requirements of Gigabit Ethernet over distances of up to 100 m using four pairs of Category 5 copper cabling.

IEEE 802.1

The IEEE 802.1 standard refers to the broad subject of managing computer networks. There exists a wide variety of software and hardware products that help network system administrators manage a network. Network management covers a wide area, including:

- *Security.* Ensuring that the network is protected from unauthorized users.
- *Performance.* Eliminating bottlenecks in the network.
- *Reliability.* Making sure the network is available to users and responding to hardware and software malfunctions.

The IEEE 802.1 is also the specification that describes an algorithm that prevents bridging loops by creating a spanning tree. The algorithm was invented by Digital Equipment Corporation. The Digital algorithm and the IEEE 802.1 algorithm are not exactly the same, nor are they compatible.

IEEE 802.2

As previously stated, IEEE 802.2 is the general standard for the data link layer in the OSI Reference Model. ISO has defined a 7-layer model to clarify various tasks in communications systems, as shown in Table 3–14. The main idea is to have independent standards for the different layers so that a change in a layer would not cause changes in other layers. In the layered approach it is possible to use different network hardware without changing the existing application programs, as shown in Figure 3–29 [3].

Table 3–14 OSI Model

Layer	Name	Function
7	Application	Provides for program-to-program communication.
6	Presentation	Manages data representation conversions. For example, the Presentation Layer would be responsible for converting from EBCDIC to ASCII.
5	Session	Establishes and maintains communications channels. In practice, this layer is often combined with the Transport Layer.
4	Transport	Controls end-to-end integrity of data transmission.
3	Network	Routes data from one node to another.
2	Data Link	Physically passes data from one node to another.
1	Physical	Manages putting data onto the network media and taking the data off.

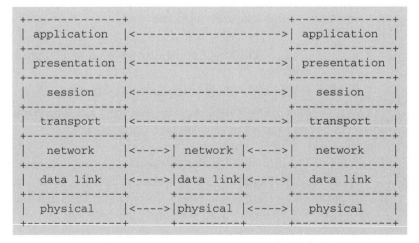

Figure 3–29   ISO/OSI network architecture reference model.

Each layer in the OSI reference model communicates with its peer using services, which the layer below provides. As can be seen from Figure 3–29, the transport layer and layers above it are end-to-end layers and they do not know anything about the network below them.

Here, the IEEE 802.2 data link layer defines how the network layer packets are transmitted as bits. Examples of data link layer protocols are PPP (point-to-point protocol) and Ethernet framing protocol. Bridges work at the data link layer only.

The IEEE 802.2 LAN protocol also specifies an implementation of the LLC sublayer of the data link layer. IEEE 802.2 handles errors, framing, flow control, and the network layer (Layer 3) service interface. It's also used in IEEE 802.3 and IEEE 802.5 LANs.

Data Link Control.   Data link control (DLC) is the second lowest layer in the OSI reference model of the IEEE 802.2 general standard. Every network interface card has a DLC address or DLC identifier (DLCI) that uniquely identifies the node on the network. Some network protocols, such as Ethernet and token ring, use the DLC addresses exclusively. Other protocols, such as TCP/IP, use a logical address at the network layer to identify nodes. Ultimately, however, all network addresses must be translated to DLC addresses. In TCP/IP networks, this translation is performed with the address resolution protocol (ARP). For networks that conform to the IEEE 802 standards (Ethernet), the DLC address is usually called the media access control (MAC) address.

IEEE 802.3

IEEE 802.3 is the IEEE LAN protocol that specifies an implementation of the physical layer and the MAC sublayer of the data link layer. IEEE 802.3 uses CSMA/CD access at a variety of speeds over a variety of physical media. Extensions to the IEEE 802.3 standard specify implementations for Fast Ethernet. Physical variations of the original IEEE 802.3 specification include 10Base2, 10Base5, 10BaseF, 10BaseT, and 10Broad36. Physical variations for Fast Ethernet include 100BaseT, 100BaseT4, and 100BaseX.

10Base2.   10Base2 is a 10 Mbps baseband Ethernet specification using 50 ohm thin coaxial cable. 10Base2, which is part of the IEEE 802.3 specification, has a distance limit of 185 meters per segment.

10Base5.   10Base5 is a 10 Mbps baseband Ethernet specification using standard (thick) 50 ohm baseband coaxial cable. 10Base5, which is part of the IEEE 802.3 baseband physical layer specification, has a distance limit of 500 meters per segment.

10BaseF.   10BaseF is a 10 Mbps baseband Ethernet specification that refers to the 10BaseFB, 10BaseFL, and 10BaseFP standards for Ethernet over fiber optic cabling.

10BaseT.   10BaseT is a 10 Mbps baseband Ethernet specification using two pairs of twisted-pair cabling (Category 3, 4, or 5); one pair for transmitting data and the other for receiving data. 10BaseT, which is part of the IEEE 802.3 specification, has a distance limit of approximately 100 meters per segment.

10Broad36.   10Broad36 is a 10 Mbps broadband Ethernet specification using broadband coaxial cable. 10Broad36, which is part of the IEEE 802.3 specification, has a distance limit of 3,600 meters per segment.

IEEE 802.3 (Fast Ethernet)

This part of the chapter describes the 802.3 100BaseT Fast Ethernet segments, which are part of the Ethernet system. However, you should know that there are two LAN standards that can carry Ethernet frames at 100 Mbps.

When the IEEE standardization committee met to begin work on a faster Ethernet system, two approaches were presented. One approach was to speed up the original Ethernet system to 100 Mbps, keeping the original CSMA/CD medium access control mechanism. This approach is called 100BaseT Fast Ethernet.

Another approach presented to the committee was to create an entirely new medium access control mechanism, based on hubs that controlled access to the medium using a demand priority mechanism. This new access control system transports standard Ethernet frames, but it does it with a new medium access control mechanism. This system was further extended to allow it to transport token ring frames as well. As a result, this approach is now called 100VG-AnyLAN.

The IEEE decided to create standards for both approaches. The 100BaseT Fast Ethernet standard described here is part of the original 802.3 standard. The 100VG-AnyLAN system is standardized under a new number, IEEE 802.12, which is discussed later in this section.

In any event, compared to the 10 Mbps specifications, the 100 Mbps system (100BaseT Fast Ethernet) results in a factor of 10 reduction in the bit-time, which is the amount of time it takes to transmit a bit on the Ethernet channel. This produces a tenfold increase in the speed of the packets over the media system. However, the other important aspects of the Ethernet system, including the frame format, the amount of data a frame may carry, and the media access control mechanism, are all unchanged.

The Fast Ethernet specifications include mechanisms for auto-negotiation of the media speed. This makes it possible for vendors to provide dual-speed Ethernet interfaces that can be installed and run at either 10 Mbps or 100 Mbps automatically. There are three media varieties that have been specified for transmitting 100 Mbps Ethernet signals, as shown in Figure 3–30 [4].

The three media types are shown in Figure 3–30 with their IEEE shorthand identifiers. The IEEE identifiers include three pieces of information. The first item, 100, stands for the media speed of 100 Mbps. The base stands for baseband, which is a type of signaling. Baseband signaling simply means that Ethernet signals are the only signals carried over the media system.

The third part of the identifier provides an indication of the segment type. The T4 segment type is a twisted-pair segment that uses four pairs of telephone-grade twisted-pair wire. The TX segment type is a twisted-pair segment that uses two pairs of wires and is based on the data grade twisted-pair physical medium standard developed by ANSI. The FX segment type is a fiber optic link segment based on the fiber optic physical medium standard developed by ANSI and that uses two strands of fiber cable. The TX and FX medium standards are collectively known as 100BaseX.

100BaseTX and 100BaseFX.   The 100BaseTX and 100BaseFX media standards used in Fast Ethernet are both adopted from physical media standards first developed by ANSI. The ANSI physical media standards were originally developed for the fiber distributed data interface (FDDI) LAN standard (ANSI standard X3T9.5) and are widely used in FDDI LANs.

The 100BaseTX (100 Mbps baseband Fast Ethernet) specification uses two pairs of either UTP or STP wiring. The first pair of wires is used to receive data; the second is used to transmit data. To guarantee proper signal timing, a 100BaseTX segment cannot exceed 100 meters in length.

The 100BaseFX (100 Mbps baseband Fast Ethernet) specification uses two strands of multimode fiber optic cable per link. To guarantee proper signal timing, a 100BaseFX link cannot exceed 400 meters in length.

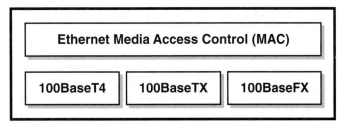

Figure 3–30   The three 100 Mbps Ethernet media varieties.

100BaseT4. Rather than reinventing the wheel when it came to signaling at 100 Mbps, the Fast Ethernet standard adapted the 100BaseTX and 100BaseFX ANSI media standards for use in the new Fast Ethernet medium specifications. The T4 standard was also provided to make it possible to use lower-quality twisted-pair wire for 100 Mbps Ethernet signals.

The 100BaseT4 (100 Mbps baseband Fast Ethernet) specification uses four pairs of Category 3, 4, or 5 UTP wiring. To guarantee proper signal timing, a 100BaseT4 segment cannot exceed 100 meters in length.

IEEE 802.4

IEEE 802.4 is the IEEE LAN protocol that specifies an implementation of the physical layer and the MAC sublayer of the data link layer.

Token Bus. The token bus is a LAN architecture using token-passing access over a bus topology. This LAN architecture is the basis for the IEEE 802.4 LAN specification. In other words, the token bus is a type of local area network (LAN) that has a bus topology and uses a token-passing mechanism to regulate traffic on the bus. A token bus network is very similar to a token ring network, the main difference being that the endpoints of the bus do not meet to form a physical ring. Token bus networks are defined by the IEEE 802.4 standard.

IEEE 802.5

The IEEE 802.5 standard states that the token ring is intended for use in commercial and light industrial environments; use in home or heavy industrial environments, although not precluded, is not considered within the scope of the standard. These environments are identical to those specified for IEEE 802.3. IBM made the standard possible by marketing the first 4 Mbits/sec token ring network in the mid-1980s. While the network physically appears as a star configuration, signals travel internally around the network from one station to the next, as shown in Figure 3–31. Therefore, cabling configurations and the addition or removal of equipment must ensure that the logical ring is maintained. Workstations connect to central hubs called multistation access units (MAUs). Multiple hubs are connected together to create large multistation networks. The hub itself contains a collapsed ring. If a workstation fails, the MAU immediately bypasses the station to maintain the ring of the network. Because the cable contains multiple wire pairs, a cut in the cable causes the ring to revert back on itself. Signals simply reroute in the opposite direction, creating a loop-back configuration.

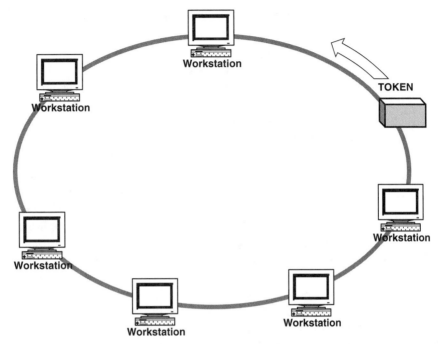

Figure 3–31   A type of computer network in which all the computers are arranged (schematically) in a circle. A token, which is a special bit pattern, travels around the circle. To send a message, a computer catches the token, attaches a message to it, and then lets it continue to travel around the network.

IEEE 802.5 Medium-Access Control.   The token ring technique is based on the use of a small frame, called a token, that circulates when all stations are idle. A station wanting to transmit must wait to detect the next available token as it passes by. It takes the token by changing 1 bit in the token. This transforms the token into a start-of-frame sequence for a data frame. The station then transmits the remainder of the data fields necessary to complete a data frame. When a station seizes a token and begins to transmit a data frame, there is no token on the ring, so other stations wishing to transmit must wait. The frame on the ring will make a round trip and be absorbed by the transmitting station. The transmitting station will insert a new token on the ring when both of the following conditions are met.

The station has completed transmission of its frame. The leading edge of the transmitted frame has returned to the station. Once the new token has been inserted on the ring, the next station downstream with data to send will be able to seize the token and transmit. Under lightly loaded conditions, there is some inefficiency with token ring, since a station must wait for the token to come around before transmitting. Under heavy loads, the ring functions in an efficient and fair round-robin fashion.

A field exists in the token in which the workstations can indicate the type of priority required for their transmission. The priority setting is basically a request to other stations for future use of the token. The other stations compare the workstation's priority with their own priority levels. If the workstation's priority is higher than theirs, they grant the workstation access to the token for an extended period. Other workstations can override the priorities, if necessary. Workstations attached to the ring transfer packets to their downstream neighbors. Thus, each workstation acts as a repeater. When a new station is attached to the network, it goes through an initialization sequence to become part of the ring. This sequence checks for duplicate addresses and informs downstream neighbors of its existence. The role of an active monitor is assigned to one of the workstations on the network, usually the first workstation recognized when the LAN comes up. The active monitor watches over the network and looks for problems, such as errors in the delivery of frames or the need to bypass a workstation at the MAU because it has failed. The active monitor basically makes sure the network runs efficiently and without errors. If the active monitor should fail, other workstations are available to take its place and basically bid for the job by transmitting claim tokens.

IEEE 802.6

IEEE 802.6 is an IEEE MAN specification based on DQDB technology. IEEE 802.6 supports data rates of 1.5 to 155 Mbps.

Metropolitan-Area Network.   A metropolitan-area network (MAN) is a network that spans a metropolitan area. Generally, a MAN spans a larger geographic area than a LAN, but a smaller geographic area than a WAN. A MAN is a relatively new class of network. There are three important features that discriminate MANs from LANs or WANs.

First of all, the network size falls between LANs and WANs. A MAN typically covers an area of between 5 and 50 km in diameter. Many MANs cover an area the size of a city, although in some cases, MANs may be as small as a group of buildings or as large as the north of Scotland.

Second, a MAN (like a WAN) is not generally owned by a single organization. The MAN, its communications links, and equipment are generally owned by either a consortium of users or by a single network provider who sells the service to the users. The level of service provided to each user must therefore be negotiated with the MAN operator, and some performance guarantees are normally specified.

Third, a MAN often acts as a high speed network to allow sharing of regional resources (similar to a large LAN). It is also frequently used to provide a shared connection to other networks using a link to a WAN. A typical use of MANs to provide shared access to a WAN is shown in Figure 3–32 [5].

DQDB.   The distributed queue dual bus (DQDB) is a data link layer communication protocol, specified in the IEEE 802.6 standard, and designed for use in MANs. DQDB, which permits multiple systems to interconnect using two unidirectional logical buses, is an open standard that is designed for compatibility with carrier transmission standards and is aligned with emerging standards for BISDN (Broadband Integrated Services Data Network). SIP (SMDS Interface Protocol) is based on DQDB.

EEE 802.11

802.11 uses a contention mechanism to allow stations to share a wireless channel based on carrier sense multiple access (CSMA), like 802.3. The 802.11 MAC cannot use all of 802.3 because it is not possible in the wireless environment for a station to listen and transmit on the same channel, as would be required for the collision detection (CD) used in 802.3. Because of this, a station on a wireless LAN will not be able to determine that a collision has occurred until the end of the packet transmission—making collisions more expensive in 802.11 than in 802.3. The 802.11 MAC uses a collision avoidance mechanism to reduce the probability of collisions. The 802.11 MAC is

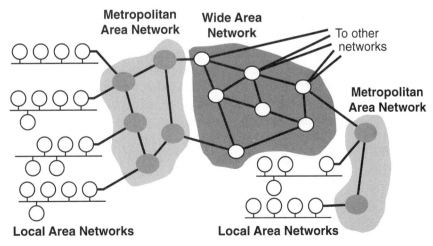

Figure 3–32   Use of MANs to provide regional networks that share the cost of access to a WAN.

designed to operate over multiple physical layers, and does not specify various media-dependent parameters.

IEEE 802.12

A 100VG-AnyLAN network consists of a central hub or repeater, referred to as a level 1 (or root) hub, with a link connecting each node, creating a star topology. The hub is an intelligent central controller that manages the network access by continually performing a rapid round-robin scan of its network port requests, checking for service requests from the attached nodes. The hub receives the incoming data packet and directs it to only the ports with a matching destination address, providing inherent network data security.

Each hub may be configurable to support either 802.3 Ethernet or 802.5 token ring frame formats. All hubs located in the same network segment must be configured for the same frame format. A bridge may be used to connect a 100VG-AnyLAN network using an 802.3 frame type to an Ethernet network, or a 100VG-AnyLAN network using an 802.5 frame type to a token ring network. A router may be used to connect a 100VG-AnyLAN network to FDDI and ATM networks or to WAN connections.

Each hub includes one uplink port and *n* number of downlink ports. The uplink port functions as a node port but is reserved for connecting the hub (as a node) to an upper-level hub. The *n* downlink ports are used to connect to 100VG-AnyLAN nodes.

Each hub port may be configured to operate in either a normal mode or a monitor mode. Ports configured to operate in normal mode are forwarded only those packets intended (addressed) for the attached node. Ports configured to operate in a monitor mode are forwarded all packets that the hub receives. The normal and monitor mode configuration may be automatically learned for cascaded ports (an uplink or downlink to another hub) or manually configured for a port connected to network monitoring equipment.

A node may be a client or server computer, workstation, or other 100VG-AnyLAN network device such as a bridge, router, switch, or hub. Hubs connected as nodes are referred to as "lower level," such as level 2 or level 3 hub devices. Up to three levels of cascading may be used on a 100VG-AnyLAN network.

A node issues requests to the hub to initiate link training and to send a packet onto the network. The 100VG-AnyLAN node also responds to incoming message commands from the hub.

The link connecting the hub and the node may be 4-pair UTP cable (Category 3, 4, or 5), 2-pair UTP cable (Category 5), 2-pair STP cable, or fiber optic cable. The maximum length of the cable from the hub to each node is 100 meters for Category 3 and 4 UTP, 150 meters for Category 5 UTP and STP, and 2,000 meters for fiber optic cable. The UTP and STP cable must be wired straight through (pin 1 connects to pin 1, pin 2 connects to pin 2, etc.) for all node connections.

IEEE 802.3ab

The IEEE 802.3ab standard defines the operation, testing, and usage requirements of Gigabit Ethernet over distances of up to 100 m using four pairs of Category 5 copper cabling—which includes most of the cabling within buildings. And completion of this 1000BaseT standard concludes the cabling media connection types for Gigabit Ethernet.

The earlier Gigabit Ethernet standard (IEEE 802.3z)—ratified in June 1998—defined transceivers that operated on the installed base of multimode and single-mode fiber. Today, network managers are seriously considering 1000BaseT for Gigabit Ethernet on Category 5 copper because they want to future-proof their network infrastructures. Most of the cabling infrastructure installed inside buildings today is Category 5.

The initial applications for Gigabit Ethernet (since the IEEE 802.3z was ratified) had been for campuses or buildings requiring greater bandwidth between routers, switches, hubs, repeaters, and servers. Examples include switch-to-router, switch-to-switch, switch-to-server, and repeater-to-switch links. In its early phase, Gigabit Ethernet was not expected to be deployed to the desktop.

But this could be changing soon. 1000BaseT is a very exciting technology because it will enable the network manager to deploy Gigabit Ethernet over existing Category 5 copper cabling without any forklift upgrades to cabling infrastructure or installed Fast Ethernet equipment. It will also allow one to support applications that demand very high bandwidth to wiring closets and, in time, to desktops.

Migration of this Category 5-installed base to higher-speed Ethernet is the primary focus of the IEEE 802.3ab. While networking equipment can easily be pulled from a rack, horizontal cabling can be very difficult to replace since it is located inside a wall, ceiling, or raised floor and dispersed across many wiring closets. Therefore, according to the IEEE specification (of ANSI/TIA/EIA–568A [1995]), network managers and planners will be able to run 1000BaseT over Category 5 cabling with no need to replace existing Category 5 cabling.

Legacy Support.   The technical goal of this particular task force since its inception had been to support the legacy Category 5 cabling. And, industry experts that make up the IEEE 1000BaseT Task Force confirm that any link that is currently using 100BaseTX should easily support 1000BaseT.

1000BaseT is important for three reasons: First, most of the cabling installed inside buildings today is Category 5 UTP, and 1000BaseT will enable Gigabit Ethernet operation over this installed base. Second, 1000BaseT, on a per-connection basis, is expected to be very cost-effective, which will stimulate market demand. Finally, 1000BaseT allows auto-negotiation between 100Mbps and 1000Mbps, easing the migration path for customers.

Networking vendors also feel likewise (see Chapter 5, "Types of Vendor and Third-Party Cabling Systems"). There's no doubt that Gigabit Ethernet is part of the evolution from Fast Ethernet. But, before we can see a larger scale of adoption at the workgroup and desktop levels, the main factor of pricing has to be overcome, similar to what was seen with Fast Ethernet (100BaseT).

Finally, with this important ratification of IEEE 802.3ab, there's a real and viable next step to bring Gigabit Ethernet to the desktop. Gigabit Ethernet can and is now being offered to power users who require gigabit bandwidth at the desktop without introducing any new cabling or hefty installation costs.

Now, let's take a look at the next major set network cabling standards from ANSI: FDDI, MMF, SMF, and TP-PMD. MMF, SMF, and TP-PMD standards are presented here as extensions of the FDDI standard. This set of cabling standards is continuously being developed and updated by ANSI.

Fiber Distributed Data Interface

The fiber distributed data interface (FDDI) standard was produced by the ANSI X3T9.5 standards committee in the mid-1980s. During this period, high-speed engineering workstations were beginning to tax the capabilities of existing LANs (primarily Ethernet and token ring). A new LAN was needed that could easily support these workstations and their new distributed applications. At the same time, network reliability was becoming an increasingly important issue as system managers began to migrate mission-critical applications from large computers to networks. FDDI was developed to fill these needs.

After completing the FDDI specification, ANSI submitted FDDI to ISO, which has created an international version of FDDI that is completely compatible with the ANSI standard version.

Today, although FDDI implementations are not as common as Ethernet or token ring, FDDI has gained a substantial following that continues to increase as the cost of FDDI interfaces diminishes. FDDI is frequently used as a backbone technology as well as a means to connect high-speed computers in a local area.

Fundamentals.   FDDI specifies a 100 Mbps, token-passing, dual-ring LAN using a fiber optic transmission medium. It defines the physical layer and media access portion of the link layer, and so is roughly analogous to IEEE 802.3 and IEEE 802.5 in its relationship to the OSI reference model.

Although it operates at faster speeds, FDDI is similar in many ways to token ring. The two networks share many features, including topology (ring), media access technique (token passing), reliability features (redundant rings, for example), and others.

One of the most important characteristics of FDDI is its use of optical fiber as a transmission medium. Optical fiber offers several advantages over traditional copper wiring, including security (fiber does not emit electrical signals that can be tapped); reliability (fiber is immune to electrical interference); and speed (optical fiber has much higher throughput potential than copper cable).

SMF and MMF.   FDDI defines use of two types of fiber: single mode (sometimes called monomode) and multimode. Modes can be thought of as bundles of light rays entering the fiber at a particular angle. Single-mode fiber (SMF) allows only one mode of light to propagate through the fiber, while multimode fiber (MMF) allows multiple modes of light to propagate through the fiber. Because multiple modes of light propagating through the fiber may travel different distances (depending on the entry angles)—causing them to arrive at the destination at different times (a phenomenon called modal dispersion)—SMF is capable of higher bandwidth and greater cable run distances than MMF. Because of these characteristics, SMF is often used for interbuilding connectivity, while MMF is often used for intrabuilding connectivity. MMF uses light-emitting diodes (LEDs) as the light-generating devices, while SMF generally uses lasers.

Specifications.   FDDI has four key components: the media access control layer, the physical layer, the physical media dependent layer, and the station management layer, as shown in Figure 3–33 [6]:

- Media access control (MAC)—Defines addressing, scheduling, and routing data. It also communicates with higher-layer protocols, such as TCP/IP, SNA, IPX, DECnet, DEC LAT, and Appletalk. The FDDI MAC layer accepts protocol data units (PDUs) of up to 9,000 symbols from the upper-layer protocols, adds the MAC header, and then passes packets of up to 4,500 bytes to the PHY layer.

- Physical layer protocol (PHY)—Handles the encoding and decoding of packet data into symbol streams for the wire. It also handles clock synchronization on the FDDI ring.
- Physical layer medium (PMD)—Handles the analog baseband transmission between nodes on the physical media. PMD standards include TP-PMD for twisted-pair copper wires and Fiber-PMD for fiber optic cable.
- Station management (SMT)—Handles the management of the FDDI ring. Functions handled by SMT include neighbor identification, fault detection and reconfiguration, insertion and de-insertion from the ring, and traffic statistics monitoring.

Twisted Pair Physical Layer Medium. In June 1990, ANSI established a subgroup called the Twisted Pair Physical Medium Dependent (TP-PMD) working group to develop a specification for implementing FDDI protocols over twisted-pair wire. TP-PMD replaces the proprietary (or pre-standard) approaches previously used for running FDDI traffic over copper wires. The TP-PMD standard is based on an MLT-3 encoding scheme; pre-standard implementations used the less reliable NRZ encoding scheme. TP-PMD interfaces are compliant with U.S. and international emission standards and provide reliable transmission over distances up to 100 meters. With TP-PMD in place, network managers now have a standard means to implement FDDI over inexpensive UTP cable, cutting cabling costs by about a third compared with fiber optic cabling.

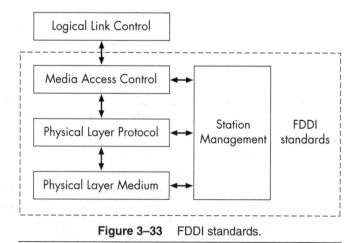

Figure 3–33   FDDI standards.

ANSI approved the TP-PMD standard in February 1994. Approval of the standard is pending in Europe.

Configuration.   FDDI is a link layer protocol, which means that higher-layer protocols operate independently of the FDDI protocol. Applications pass packet-level data using higher-layer protocols down to the logical link control layer in the same way that they would over Ethernet or token ring. But because FDDI uses a different physical layer protocol than Ethernet and token ring, traffic must be bridged or routed on and off an FDDI ring. FDDI also allows for larger packet sizes than lower-speed LANs; for this reason, connections between FDDI and Ethernet or token ring LANs require the fragmentation and reassembly of frames.

FDDI can be implemented in two basic ways: as a dual-attached ring and as a concentrator-based ring. In the dual-attached scenario, stations are connected directly one to another. FDDI's dual counter-rotating ring design provides a fail-safe in case a node goes down. If any node fails, the ring wraps around the failed node. However, one limitation of the dual counter-rotating ring design is that if two nodes fail, the ring is broken in two places, effectively creating two separate rings. Nodes on one ring are then isolated from nodes on the other ring. External optical bypass devices can solve this problem, but their use is limited because of FDDI optical power requirements.

In other words, FDDI specifies the use of dual rings. Traffic on these rings travels in opposite directions. Physically, the rings consist of two or more point-to-point connections between adjacent stations. One of the two FDDI rings is called the primary ring; the other is called the secondary ring. The primary ring is used for data transmission, while the secondary ring is generally used as a backup. There are four types of stations (DTEs or concentrators):

1. Dual attached station (DAS), which is connected to both rings.
2. Single attached station (SAS), which is attached only to the primary ring.
3. Dual attached concentrator (DAC), which is connected to both rings and provides connection for additional stations and concentrators. It is actually the root of a tree.
4. Single attached concentrator (SAC), which is connected only to the primary ring (through a tree).

Class B or single-attachment stations (SAS) attach to one ring; Class A or dual-attachment stations (DAS) attach to both rings. SASs are attached to the primary ring through a concentrator, which provides connections for multiple SASs. The concentrator ensures that failure or power down of any given SAS does not interrupt the ring. This is particularly useful when PCs, or similar devices that frequently power on and off, connect to the ring.

Another way around this problem is to use concentrators to build networks similar to a typical FDDI configuration (with both DASs and SASs), shown in Figure 3–34 [7]. Concentrators are devices with multiple ports into which FDDI nodes connect. FDDI concentrators function like Ethernet hubs or token ring multiple access units (MAUs). Nodes are singly attached to the concentrator, which isolates failures occurring at those end-stations. With a concentrator, nodes can be powered on and off without disrupting ring integrity. Concentrators make FDDI networks more reliable and also provide SNMP management functions. For this reason, most FDDI networks are now built with concentrators.

Each FDDI DAS has two ports, designated A and B. These ports connect the station to the dual FDDI ring. Therefore, each port provides a connection for both the primary and the secondary ring, as shown in Figure 3–35 [Cisco, 3].

In practice, most user stations are attached to the ring via wiring concentrators, since then only a single pair of fibers is needed and the connection cost is lower. The basic fiber is dual core with polarized duplex connectors at each end. This means that each end of the cable has a different physical key so that it can only be connected into a matching socket (to prevent faulty interchanging of wires, which can cause a total breakdown of the network). Special coupling units (either active or passive fiber devices) are used to iso-

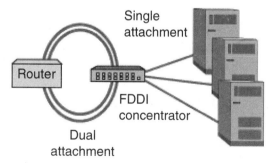

Figure 3–34   FDDI concentrators function like token ring MAUs or Ethernet hubs. Concentrators make FDDI networks more reliable by isolating failures that occur at end-stations and by providing SNMP management functions.

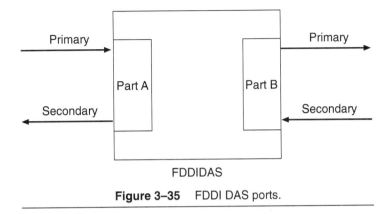

Figure 3–35   FDDI DAS ports.

late (bypass) a station when its power is lost. Stations detecting a cable break will go into wrap mode, using the secondary ring as backup so both rings are connected to form a single ring.

Physical Interface.   As opposed to a basic token ring network, where at any instant there is a single active ring monitor that supplies the master clock for the ring, in FDDI this approach is not suitable because of the high data rates. Instead, each ring interface has its own local clock, and outgoing data is transmitted using this clock.

All data to be transmitted is encoded prior to transmission using a 4-of-5 group code. This means that for each 4 bits of data, a corresponding 5-bit code word or symbol is generated by the encoder. Some of these symbols are used for link control functions, such as indicating the start and end of each transmitted frame or token. In general, the meaning and use of FDDI frame (or token) fields is the same as with the basic token ring. But because of the use of symbols rather than bits, there are some differences in the structure of each field.

Traffic.   FDDI supports real-time allocation of network bandwidth, making it ideal for a variety of different application types. FDDI provides this support by defining two types of traffic: synchronous and asynchronous. Synchronous traffic can consume a portion of the 100 Mbps total bandwidth of an FDDI network, while asynchronous traffic can consume the rest. Synchronous bandwidth is allocated to those stations requiring continuous transmission capability. Such capability is useful for transmitting voice and video information, for example. Other stations use the remaining bandwidth asynchronously. The FDDI SMT specification defines a distributed bidding scheme to allocate FDDI bandwidth.

Asynchronous bandwidth is allocated using an eight-level priority scheme. Each station is assigned an asynchronous priority level. FDDI also permits extended dialogues, where stations may temporarily use all asynchronous bandwidth. The FDDI priority mechanism can essentially lock out stations that cannot use synchronous bandwidth and have too low an asynchronous priority.

Fault-Tolerant.   FDDI provides a number of fault-tolerant features. The primary fault-tolerant feature is the dual ring. If a station on the dual ring fails or is powered down or if the cable is damaged, the dual ring is automatically wrapped (doubled back onto itself) into a single ring, as shown in Figure 3–36 [Cisco, 4]. In this figure, when station 3 fails, the dual ring is automatically wrapped in stations 2 and 4, forming a single ring. Although station 3 is no longer on the ring, network operation continues for the remaining stations.

Figure 3–37 shows how FDDI compensates for a wiring failure [Cisco, 5]. Stations 3 and 4 wrap the ring within themselves when wiring between them fails.

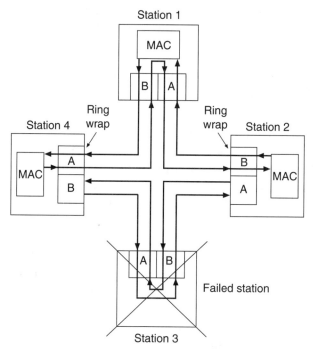

Figure 3–36   Station failure, ring recovery configuration.

As FDDI networks grow, the possibility of multiple ring failures grows. When two ring failures occur, the ring will be wrapped in both cases, effectively segmenting the ring into two separate rings that cannot communicate with each other. Subsequent failures cause additional ring segmentation.

Optical bypass switches can be used to prevent ring segmentation by eliminating failed stations from the ring. This is shown in Figure 3–38 [Cisco, 5].

Critical devices such as routers or mainframe hosts can use another fault-tolerant technique called "dual homing" to provide additional redundancy and help guarantee operation. In dual-homing situations, the critical device is attached to two concentrators, as shown in Figure 3–39 [Data Communications, 2].

One pair of concentrator links is declared the active link; the other pair is declared passive. The passive link stays in backup mode until the primary link (or the concentrator to which it is attached) is determined to have failed. When this occurs, the passive link is automatically activated.

Frame.   FDDI frame formats (shown in Figure 3–40) are similar to those of token ring [Cisco, 6]. See the Sidebar, "FDDI Frame Fields," for more information.

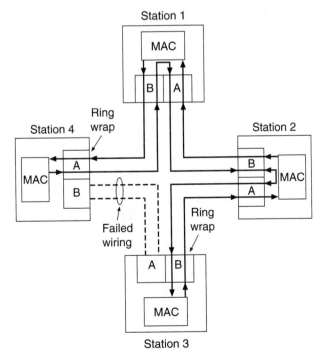

Figure 3–37   Failed wiring, ring recovery configuration.

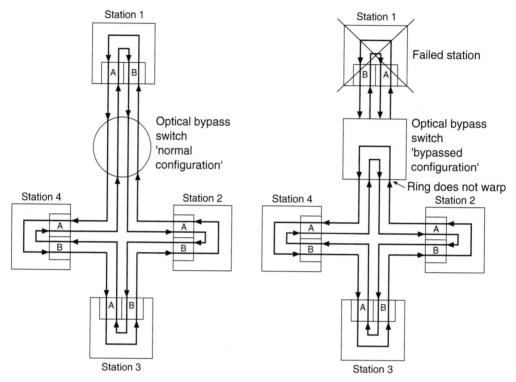

Figure 3–38   Use of optical bypass switch.

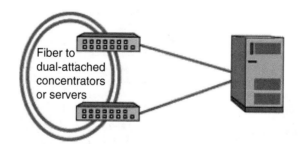

Figure 3–39   In dual-homed applications, mission-critical servers are connected to redundant concentrators, which in turn are connected to a dual-attached ring for maximum redundancy.

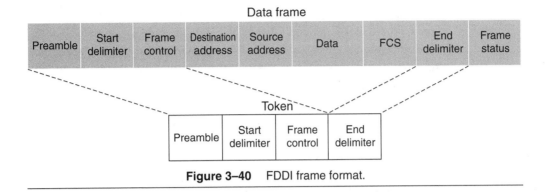

Figure 3–40   FDDI frame format.

FDDI FRAME FIELDS

The fields of an FDDI frame are as follows:

- Preamble—Prepares each station for the upcoming frame.

- Start delimiter—Indicates the beginning of the frame. It consists of signaling patterns that differentiate it from the rest of the frame.

- Frame control—Indicates the size of the address fields, whether the frame contains asynchronous or synchronous data, and other control information.

- Destination address—Contains a unicast (singular), multicast (group), or broadcast (every station) address. As with Ethernet and token ring, FDDI destination addresses are 6 bytes.

- Source address—Identifies the single station that sent the frame. As with Ethernet and token ring, FDDI source addresses are 6 bytes.

- Data—Contains either information destined for an upper-layer protocol or control information.

- Frame check sequence (FCS)—Filled by the source station with a calculated cyclic redundancy check (CRC) value dependent on the frame contents (as with token ring and Ethernet). The destination station recalculates the value to determine whether the frame may have been damaged in transit. If so, the frame is discarded.

- End delimiter—Contains nondata symbols that indicate the end of the frame.

- Frame status—Allows the source station to determine if an error occurred and if the frame was recognized and copied by a receiving station.

CDDI. The high cost of fiber optic cable has been a major impediment to the widespread deployment of FDDI to desktop computers. At the same time, shielded twisted pair (STP) and unshielded twisted pair (UTP) copper wire is relatively inexpensive and has been widely deployed. The implementation of FDDI over copper wire is known as copper distributed data interface (CDDI).

Before FDDI could be implemented over copper wire, a problem had to be solved. When signals strong enough to be reliably interpreted as data are transmitted over twisted pair wire, the wire radiates electromagnetic interference (EMI). Any attempt to implement FDDI over twisted pair wire had to ensure that the resulting energy radiation did not exceed the specifications set in the United States by the Federal Communications Commission and in Europe by the European Economic Council. The following three technologies reduce energy radiation: scrambling, encoding, and equalization.

Scrambling. When no data is being sent, FDDI transmits an idle pattern that consists of a string of binary ones. When this signal is sent over twisted pair wire, the EMI is concentrated at the fundamental frequency spectrum of the idle pattern, resulting in a peak in the frequency spectrum of the radiated interference. By scrambling FDDI data with a pseudorandom sequence prior to transmission, repetitive patterns are eliminated. The elimination of repetitive patterns results in a spectral peak that is distributed more evenly over the spectrum of the transmitted signal.

Encoding. When using an encoding scheme, signal strength is stronger, and EMI is lower when transmission occurs over twisted pair wire at lower frequencies. MLT3 is an encoding scheme that reduces the frequency of the transmitted signal. MLT3 switches between three output voltage levels so that peak power is shifted to less than 20 MHz.

Equalization. Equalization boosts the higher frequency signals for transmission over UTP. Equalization can be done on the transmitter (predistortion), or at the receiver (postcompensation), or both. One advantage of equalization at the receiver is the ability to adjust compensation as a function of cable length.

Of the many categories and types of twisted pair wire, the ANSI standard only recognizes Category 5 UTP and Type 1 STP.

ISDN

Finally, let's take a brief look at the major network cabling standard from the International Telecommunications Union (ITU): ISDN. Standards for ISDN are continuously being defined and updated by ITU.

The public telephone and telecommunications networks are rapidly evolving to the exclusive use of digital technology. The move toward digital technology has been pushed by the competitive desire to lower cost and improve quality of voice transmission and network services. As the use of distributed processing and data communication has grown, this evolution of an all-digital network has been pulled by the need to provide a framework for ISDN.

Concept

Standards for ISDN are being defined by ITU-T. This part of the chapter will look at the following ISDN concept:

- principles of ISDN;
- the user interface;
- objectives;
- benefits; and
- services.

Principles. The main feature of the ISDN concept is the support of a wide range of voice and nonvoice applications in the same network. A key element of the service integration for an ISDN is the provision of a range of services using a limited set of connection types and multipurpose user-network interface arrangements.

ISDN supports a variety of applications, including both switched and nonswitched connections. Switched connections in ISDN include both circuit-switched and packet-switched connections.

New services introduced into an ISDN should be arranged to be compatible with 64 Kbps switched digital connections. Also, an ISDN will contain intelligence for the purpose of providing service features, maintenance, and network management functions.

A layered protocol structure should be used for the specifications of the access to an ISDN. Access from a user to ISDN resources may vary depending upon the service required and upon the status of implementation of national ISDNs. Additionally, it is recognized that ISDNs may be implemented in various configurations according to specific national situations.

User Interface.   The user has access to the ISDN by means of a local interface to a digital pipe of a certain bit rate. Pipes of various sizes will be available to satisfy differing needs. At any given point in time, the pipe to a user's premises has a fixed capacity, but the traffic on the pipe may be a variable mix up to the capacity limit. Thus, a user may access circuit-switched and packet-switched services, as well as other services, in a dynamic mix of signal types and bit rates. To provide these services, the ISDN will require rather complex control signals to instruct it how to sort out the time-multiplexed data and provide the required services. These control signals will also be multiplexed onto the same digital pipe.

Objectives.   It is essential that a single set of ISDN standards be provided to permit universal access and to permit the development of cost-effective equipment. Transparency permits users to develop applications and protocols with the confidence that they will not be affected by the underlying ISDN.

The ISDN should provide dedicated point-to-point services as well as switched services. This will allow users to optimize their implementation of switching and routing techniques.

Benefits.   The integration of voice and a variety of data on a single transport system means that the user does not have to buy multiple services to meet multiple needs. The requirements of various users can differ greatly in a number of ways: information volume, traffic pattern, response time, and interface types.

Services.   The ISDN provides a variety of services. It supports existing voice and data applications as well as facsimile, teletex, and videotex.

Channels

The digital pipe between the central office and the ISDN user will be used to carry a number of communication channels. The capacity of the pipe may vary from user to user. The transmission structure of any access link is constructed from the following types of channels:

- B-channel: 64 Kbps
- D-channel: 16 or 64 Kbps
- H-channel: 384, 1536, and 1920 Kbps
- The basic channel structure

B-Channel.   The B-channel is the basic user channel. It can be used to carry digital data, PCM-encoded digital voice, or a mixture of lower-rate traffic, including digital data and digitized voice encoded at a fraction of 64

Kbps. In the case of mixed traffic, all traffic must be destined for the same endpoint.

D-Channel. The D-channel serves two purposes: First, it carries signaling information to control circuit-switched calls on associated B-channels at the user interface. In addition, the D-channel may be used for packet-switching or low-speed telemetry at times when no signaling information is waiting.

H-Channel. H-channels provide for user information at higher bit rates. The user may use such a channel as a high-speed trunk or subdivide the channel according to the user's own TDM (time division multiplexing) scheme. Examples of applications include fast facsimile, video, high-speed data, high-quality audio, and multiple information streams at lower data rates.

Basic Channel Structure. The basic channel structure consists of two full-duplex 64 Kbps B-channels and a full-duplex 16 Kbps D-channel. Each frame of 48 bits includes 16 bits from each of the B-channels and 4 bits from the D-channel. See the Sidebar, "ISDN Standards," for more information on these channels.

ISDN STANDARDS

The International Telecommunications Union (ITU) has the following recommendations for ISDN:

H Series
The ITU makes the following recommendations for video conferencing and ISDN:
- H.221—The frame structures for 64 to 1,920 Kbps channels when used with audiovisual teleservices.
- H.320—Narrowband equipment recommendations for visual telephone systems and terminal equipment.

I Series
In 1988, the CCITT (currently the ITU) defined ISDN standards and published them as I series recommendations in a document called the *Blue Book* (not to be confused with the U.S. Air Force's *Project Blue Book,* which ended in 1967). The following is a list of the applicable standards:
- I.100—General Concepts. Explains the ideas behind ISDN.
- I.200—Service Capabilities. Defines the extended services available to ISDN.
- I.300—Network Aspects. Defines the way the network for ISDN works.
- I.400—User-Network Interfaces. Explains the physical configuration for user network interfaces to ISDN.

- I.500—Internetwork Interfaces. Explains how to internetwork ISDN with other services.
- I.600—Maintenance Principals. Defines how to test networks and service levels.

Q Series

The Q Series standards are the most commonly quoted ISDN standards. These standards have been devised by the ITU and cover the standards of ISDN. The major Q standards are as follows:

- Q.920—Covers the network interface Data Link layer. Covers layer 2 of the OSI data model and controls the data flowing between two points in the network.
- Q.921—Defines the Data Link layer to an even higher degree.
- Q.930—Describes the Network layer of ISDN as it relates to the OSI data model. This standard defines how to find the pathway to complete the circuit that the connection makes.
- Q.931—Covers the basic call control of an ISDN call on the Network layer. Defines the envelope in which the information on an ISDN call is encapsulated in.
- Q.932—Defines the supplementary services that ISDN is capable of.

T.120 Series Video Conferencing

The ITU has also defined the use of ISDN with video conferencing in the T series of recommendations. They are as follows:

- T.122—Defines the multipoint communication for setting up multi-user tele-conference calls.
- T.123—Defines the protocol stacks for teleconferencing.
- T.124—Provides standards for generic conference control (GFC) and how each user device will maintain communication.
- T.126—Defines the transfer of still images and the means to annotate them during conferences.
- T.127—Explains multipoint file transfers.
- T.128—Defines the use of real-time audio and video.

V Series Rate Adaption

When the device that is attached to an ISDN device cannot output data as fast as the ISDN service needs (such as a 28.8 Kbps being put on a 64k B-channel), bits must be added to the stream to adapt the rate to what is being output. This is defined in the standards V.110 and V.120:

- V.110—Defines how to adapt 2.4 to 19.2 Kbps asynchronous rates into synchronous 56 or 64 Kbps rates. This standard is widely used in Europe, but does not have widespread adoption in North America. This protocol does not support any type of error correction.

- V.120—This standard is becoming widely accepted in North America. It is based on LAP-D (link access procedure for the D-channel), which is also the main protocol for all ISDN communications. This standard allows for bonding (combining) of B-channels into rates higher than 64 Kbps. The common speeds that are used with a Basic Rate Interface (BRI 2B+D) are as follows:

1 D Channel = 16 Kbps

1 B Channel = 64 Kbps

2 B Channels = 128 Kbps

X Series

- X.3—Defines the PAD (packet assembly/disassembly) for use in public data networks.
- X.25—Defines the interface between data terminal equipment (DTE) and data communication (also called circuit terminating) equipment (DCE) in packet networks.
- X.28—Defines start and stop mode for the X.25 interface for DTE in a packet mode when both end points are in the same country.
- X.29—Defines the exchange of control information between two connections in a packet network.

FROM HERE

This chapter presented an overview of the various cabling standards (TIA/EIA568A, TIA/EIA569A, ISO/IEC 11801, IEEE 802.x, FDDI, ISDN, 100—BaseTX, etc.) that are associated with the cabling technologies discussed in Chapter 1. Further discussions of cabling standards are presented in Chapter 8, "Standards Design Issues," and Chapter 27, "Standards Development." The next chapter discusses the current state of cable modem access versus DSL. It also examines how prevalent cable modem and DSL services are in major U.S. markets. A comparison of the two technologies with regard to speed, cost, and so on are presented. The chapter also covers the planning implications or considerations for the enterprise network manager (for example, to support telecommuting employees, etc.) and the N+ certification audience, as well as DSL, among other things. Finally, the chapter discusses future directions for cable modems and DSL.

NOTES

[1]   "Guide to the TIA/EIA-T568-A Standard," Anixter Inc., 4711 Golf Road, Skokie, IL, 60076; and, TIA/EIA (Reproduced under written permission of the copyright holder [Telecommunications Industry Association]), 2500 Wilson Blvd., Suite 300, Arlington, Virginia 22011, 1999, p. 1.

[2]   "Backbone Cabling System Structure," © The Siemon Company, Siemon Business Park, 76 Westbury Park Road, Watertown, CT 06795-0400 USA, 1999, p. 1.

[3]   "OSI Reference Model," AMITCP/IP Group, Network Solutions Development Inc., P.O.Box 32, FIN-02151 ESPOO, Helsinki, FINLAND, EUROPE, 1996, p. 1.

[4]   Charles Spurgeon, "100-Mbps Media Systems," Network Engineer, Computation Center Networking Services, The University of Texas, Austin, TX 78712, 1999, p. 1.

[5]   Godred Fairhurst, "Metropolitan Area Networks (MANs)," Electronics Research Group, Department of Engineering at the University of Aberdeen, Fraser Noble Building, King's College, Old Aberdeen, Abereden, United Kingdom, AB24 3UE UK, 2000, p. 1.

[6]   "FDDI," (some of the material in this book has been reproduced by Prentice Hall with the permission of Cisco Systems Inc.), Copyright © 1998 by Cisco Systems, Inc., All Rights Reserved, 170 West Tasman Drive, San Jose, CA, 95134-1706, USA, 1999, p. 2.

[7]   "FDDI," Data Communications on the Web, 1221 Avenue of the Americas, New York, NY 10020-1095, 1997, p. 2 (Reprinted from Data Communications magazine December 1994; copyright The McGraw-Hill Companies, Inc., 2000, all rights reserved).

[8]   "LAN Cabling Standards Summary," Digital Delivery Systems, 1025 Smithfield Drive, Fort Collins, CO 80524, 2000.

Digital Subscriber Line (DSL) Versus Cable

Internet access via cable modem has become increasingly available in many residential areas within the past few years. Cable has the capacity to transmit data at speeds as fast as digital subscriber line (DSL) when configured properly and under optimal conditions. Due to the fact that cable lines are not available in the vast majority of commercial districts, cable does not compete with DSL in the enterprise market in most cases. Cable was designed for residential use, and in some cases may be a cost-effective solution for residential high-bandwidth Internet access. Therefore, the challenge of DSL versus cable is primarily in the residential and telecommuter markets.

With that in mind, and before continuing with the theme of this chapter (DSL versus cable), let's look at the technology issues first, and some basic terminology.

TECHNOLOGY ISSUES

What is DSL? How does it work? What are the types of DSL? These are some of the questions this chapter will answer as well as some of the pros and cons of either.

DSL: What is It?

In essence, by using the existing telephone cabling infrastructure, DSL is a technology backed by telephone enterprises that provides high-bandwidth services to the home and enterprise. Because DSL utilizes a greater range of frequencies than ordinary dial-up services (allowing for a much faster connection), this high bandwidth is possible. For most providers, this technology is still in the early stages of roll-out.

How Does It Work?

The general idea behind DSL technology is relatively easy to grasp, even though it is rather sophisticated. As previously mentioned, DSL utilizes a large range of frequencies, which means a higher bandwidth and a faster connection speed. For example, consider this: Only a small fraction of your phone line capacity (bandwidth) is being used (that being only the low frequencies) when you make an ordinary telephone call. By transporting data into the higher frequencies, DSL takes advantage of this idle bandwidth. This results in making it possible for you to talk on the phone and be on the Internet simultaneously via the same line.

DSL Types

As shown in Table 4–1, there are several competing forms of DSL, each adapted to specific needs in the marketplace. Some forms of DSL are widely used standards, some are proprietary, and some are simply theoretical models. They may best be categorized within the modulation methods used to encode data. As previously stated, Table 4–1 shows different types of DSL technologies. These technologies are sometimes collectively referred to as xDSL.

Table 4–1   The Many Flavors of DSL

Type	Description
ADSL	Asymmetric digital subscriber line. The most common standard, it theoretically offers 1.5 Mbps to 8 Mbps downstream and 16 Mbps to 640 Kbps upstream speeds.
HDSL, HDSL2	These two high data rate DSLs are symmetric services capable of 1.5 Mbps and 2.048 Mbps speeds, respectively. HDSL requires two or three wire pairs; HDSL2, just one pair.
IDSL	ISDN DSL. Similar to ISDN, it allows you to use existing ISDN equipment. However, the maximum speed in both directions is 144 Kbps.
RADSL	An asymmetric service, rate-adaptive DSL promises to provide between 600 Kbps to 8 Mbps downstream and 128 Kbps to 1 Mbps upstream speeds, while offering simultaneous voice service. RADSL can dynamically adjust to line conditions.

Table 4–1   continued

Type	Description
SDSL	Symmetric DSL, a popular alternative to ADSL, is offered by various ISPs, including NorthPoint [1]. The service promises two-way 768 Kbps access.
G.Lite (UADSL/DSL-lite)	G.Lite is user-installable and provides speeds of 1.544 Mbps downstream and 512 Kbps upstream. Backed by many hardware vendors and the Universal ADSL Working Group [2].
VDSL	The fastest and newest DSL on the block, very high speed DSL is an asymmetric service, offering speeds of 12.9 Mbps to 52.8 Mbps.

Again, as explained in Table 4–1, ADSL is the most popular form of DSL technology. The fact that the upstream and downstream bandwidth is asymmetric, or uneven, is the key to ADSL. In practice, the higher-speed path will be the bandwidth from the ISP to the user (downstream). This is mainly due to the desire to accommodate the typical Internet usage pattern, where the majority of data is being sent to the user (web pages, graphics, programs, and video) with minimal upload capacity required (keystrokes and mouse clicks). Speeds typically range from 144 Kbps to 1.5 Mbps downstream. Table 4–1 has also shown that there are other forms of DSL as well: ADSL Lite, consumer digital subscriber line (CDSL is a proprietary technology trademarked by Rockwell International [3].), G.Lite, HDSL, IDSL, RADSL, SDSL, and VDSL. Many of these forms are just starting to become available through the telephone enterprises, and some of them have just completed the testing/development stages and are expected to offer the technologies soon.

DSL versus Cable Modems

Cable modems, although capable of high potential access speeds, have drawbacks. Primarily, the signal is shared between the subscribers in a specific area, and the technology is broadcast-oriented. In other words, less bandwidth is available to each subscriber as the number of subscribers increases in that area. Moreover, cable access offers the user no choice regarding providers, and is only available in a limited area. It is available only through the cable enterprise, which has demonstrated little experience with Internet services.

CURRENT STATE OF CABLE MODEM ACCESS VERSUS DSL

So what's holding up DSL and cable modem access? If you have been told that the lack of widely accepted standards is the main factor delaying cable modem and xDSL access, think again. Lack of standards is, at most, a minor factor in the delay of widespread access.

Because solid standards have not been established, xDSL and cable modem access are being held up. So let's put things in perspective, even though it is certainly true that the lack of standards is having some effect.

Cable modem and xDSL services are dedicated subscriber services. You use your cable modem or xDSL box to connect to one place—your service provider. You do not carry it around with you like a modem. Where you expect to move the device from place to place or to a different service provider (as with a 56K or 33.6 modem), standards only affect the end user in some cases. Your cable modem or xDSL box is like your television cable box, which you never move—you buy it or lease it with the service and it stays with the service, not like your modem. By allowing vendor competition, it is true that standards will lower hardware costs a bit. This, in turn, will lower your equipment costs, but not much. The important thing is that if your provider can offer you service at a price you like, that is what matters most to you. The fact that he or she will be able to buy the box that he or she leases to you for $10 a month for a hundred bucks less next year is simply not that much of an issue. Anyway, it's probably a small fraction of the overall cost of providing the service.

The history of cable modem access by Cablevision [4] on western Long Island over the last several years tends to support this. The original beta access used a specific brand of cable modem (which was provided with the service). When the beta program ended, the original equipment was discarded in favor of a newer, higher performance product made by LanCity [5]. This didn't affect end users much—they just returned the original modems and installed the new ones. The current service provides a 10 mbps Ethernet connection for under $70 per month (this includes the lease of the cable modem unit, connection, and ISP service) for residential customers. This service is about three to five times faster than a full T1. The LanCity cable modem follows the only real standard that matters so far—it connects to the user's PC using standard 10 mbps Ethernet, like most other xDSL units and cable modems.

You'll have to look elsewhere than the lack of widely accepted standards if you want to know why xDSL and cable modem service is slow in accessing. Maybe you should wonder if the cable enterprises are simply afraid of moving into a new technology they don't understand; if the telcos aren't that eager to access a DSL service in direct competition to their data T1 and T3 services (and with a lower price tag); and whether anybody has enough backbone capacity to support the large numbers of high speed customers the new service would attract. Incidentally, Cablevision claims no immediate plans to offer enterprise services. They are not interested in going outside their traditional market to offer service to more demanding enterprise customers (who generally use a higher percentage of their available bandwidth for a larger part of each day than residential customers).

Nevertheless, the battle for broadband data services to the home and enterprise has been played out as a battle between the telephone enterprise (telcos) and the cable operators. The battle has been fueled by "arms merchants," the silicon suppliers and xDSL and cable modem box vendors, selling both hype and product to both sides. With over 470,000 in commercial operation in North America alone, and the entire industry rallying around CableLabs' [6] promulgated standards and retail distribution models, cable modems have taken the early lead. A tremendous lure for the cable operators is the potential for remote LAN access and IP-telephony on top of Internet access. Meanwhile, in an attempt to solidify the industry and to catch up with cable deployments, the DSL community is moving toward a low cost, splitterless G.lite standard. G.lite could be an easily deployed, low-cost technology that carries a dedicated IP pipeline on top of the twisted pair voice connection leading into virtually every home. G.lite could also be just another vegetable in DSL alphabet soup. The major regional Bell operating companies (RBOCs) have recently announced DSL access plans for the years 2000–2001, despite a myriad of technical and enterprise hurdles.

So what's real and will there be a winner in this battle for broadband in the local loop? Well, a recent bitter struggle among equipment manufacturers is threatening new industry rules that could make broadband in the local loop and/or high-speed Internet connections less expensive, easier to use, and available to far more people.

DSL Progress is Thwarted

The infighting centers on the so-called G.lite standard, which is designed to simplify cable modems used for digital subscriber line (DSL) connections. Thus, manufacturers need to make products that can work together seamlessly to speed wide-scale adoption of DSL, because the market is littered with different technologies.

Digital subscriber lines carry data at high speeds over standard copper telephone wires. With DSL, data can be delivered at a rate of 1.5 mbps (around 30 times faster than through a 56-kbps modem). Also, DSL users can receive voice and data simultaneously, so small offices can leave computers plugged into the Net without interrupting phone connections. Currently, DSL is expensive because specialized equipment—a splitter—needs to be installed at the subscriber's location. DSL Lite, the consumer-ready version of DSL, requires no such splitter, and promises comparable access speeds at a cheaper rate.

This type of conflict is common with emerging technologies, but rarely are the stakes as high as they are today. High-speed access is largely associated with the growth of the Internet itself, and billions of potential dollars hang in the balance for those enterprises that come up with the winning solutions to break the widespread bottlenecks across the Web.

Moreover, the rhetoric is particularly rancorous in the G.lite debate. Critics say G.lite modems do not work well with current technology, according to service providers; and some manufacturers are now fighting to see their own products are adopted as the industry standard.

In some cases, these technologies can't even communicate. It's not just that you need a G.lite modem, you need a G.lite modem from a specific manufacturer. And that's the same as no standard at all.

While equipment makers argue over how to best implement the G.lite standard, competition from high-speed cable modems is intensifying. The cable industry has already established a standard set of rules for cable modems, giving the group a leg up on its DSL rivals.

According to TeleChoice [7], about 380,000 DSL lines were in use by the end of the last quarter of 1999, with 86 percent of these in residences. Cable modems have reached well over 3 million users.

Just as telephone enterprises and Internet service providers like America Online [8] and Prodigy [9] ramp up their marketing machines to push high-speed Internet services across the country, the lack of a universally accepted standard could slow the spread of DSL. To have an absolute standard that leaves no variation in the way that equipment vendors can make their equipment is not practical.

All in One

So that different enterprises create products that can work with each other, many industries push for technology standards, or rules. For instance, VHS is a standard for videotape. Regardless of the enterprise that manufactured the

VCR, a VHS tape cassette will play on any VCR machine that is built to handle that certain type of tape.

Standards are critical in the communications world. If a consumer buys a modem, it must work with his or her computer, as well as the ISP. You can't get to the point of popularity reached by ordinary analog modems without a standard. For example, people should be able to buy a computer at CompUSA [10], take it home and plug it in, and have it work with their ISP.

Several years ago, the Internet and computer industries coalesced around the G.lite standard for consumer DSL. It was ratified by the International Telecommunications Union [11] as the worldwide set of official technical guidelines.

The ITU, a Geneva, Switzerland-based international organization that governs the communications industry, recently approved the G.lite standard, a lower-speed DSL technology aimed at the mass-market consumer.

Rather than wait for a phone enterprise technician to install a modem, the standard is aimed at making DSL relatively cheap, as it would allow a consumer to buy a modem and plug it into a PC. The challenge is to make sure that modems and other equipment made under the G.lite standard all work together.

Lab Tests

The University of New Hampshire [12] has set up a lab where enterprises like Intel [13], Alcatel [14], Lucent [15], and others can test their modems against each other and against other products—all under the auspices of the ADSL Forum. Nevertheless, some enterprises already say they comply with the standard, and some computer makers (led by Compaq [16] and Dell [17]) have already begun shipping machines with standardized DSL modems that conform to G.lite rules. However, the modems still won't work with all ISPs and telephone enterprise equipment.

The big telephone enterprises (the enterprises that will invest the most money in DSL equipment), for their part, are testing G.lite technology and hope that manufacturers will end their differences as soon as possible. Most phone carriers are using different versions of DSL on an interim basis in the meantime. This has taken the interoperability process to a whole new level. It will take time to sort it out.

PREVALENCE OF CABLE MODEMS AND DSL IN MAJOR U.S. MARKETS

Cable modems and DSL are somewhat prevalent in major U.S. markets. They are, nevertheless, a quantum leap in Internet access, putting an end to the *worldwide wait.*

All the hype about instant information on the Internet doesn't mean much when you've got a Web page downloading so slowly that you have to keep yourself busy by flipping through the Sunday paper or glancing at the headlines on CNN. There's an apt, if overused, name for this trickling of info: the *worldwide wait.* As previously discussed, now two competing technologies (cable modems and DSL) would like to bring high-speed Internet access into your home, ending the wait with speeds up to 300 times faster than what's possible with standard modems. For as little as $40 per month, these next-generation methods of connecting to the Internet promise to transform the cyberspace experience. Think video on demand or live stock tickers. Both are possible, if you've got the bandwidth or connection speed.

Chances are, however, such access is not available in your area yet; cable enterprises, phone enterprises, and Internet service providers are in the early stages of offering cable modems and DSL. If you have access to one, you are considered one of the lucky ones. If you have a choice between the two, you're very, very lucky. But DSL launches are under way or planned by Bell Atlantic [18], GTE [19], and US West [20], and with cable enterprises expecting competition from DSL, you're likely to hear about high-speed access coming to the home of a friend—and maybe even your own.

Skeptical? Witness AT&T's [21] acquisition of cable-TV giant Tele-Communications Incorporated [22], a merger spurred by the prospect of offering new services (and packaging existing ones) through high-speed lines into the home. The deal was a $70 billion vote of confidence in the Internet's transformation from a frequently slow and frustrating means of communication into a mature, consumer-friendly medium. Other providers now have a newly energized mega-competitor in this arena, and that's likely to mean a faster rollout of high-speed access.

But just in case you think this is another overhyped upgrade, like the much-ballyhooed 56-kilobits-per-second (kbps) modem, think again. The advances in standard modems have been incremental: from 14.4 kbps to 28.8 kbps to 33.6 kbps to the current champ, 56 kbps. Supercharge all that, and imagine the switch from 33.6 kbps to, say, 1.5 megabits per second. That's 45 times faster, meaning a 5.6-megabyte game would take about 30 seconds to download instead of 22 minutes. Or the hundreds of pages you're viewing in a single session of Web browsing will appear without delay, as if the pages were stored on your hard drive. Aside from speed, both cable modems and DSL offer another advantage: an *always on* connection to the Internet that doesn't tie up your phone line. There's a lot of pent-up demand for this.

DSL runs over existing phone lines, but it still allows you to make calls while you're online.

To check on availability, call your local cable enterprise or, for DSL, the phone enterprises and Internet service providers in your area. Costs can vary wildly, since most high-speed access providers currently face no competition. Cable modem access typically runs about $30–$50 per month; DSL is costlier, and its pricing is more complex. For cable-modem access, local cable systems package an Internet service provider (@Home [23] is the leader) with the speedy line into your home. With DSL, you're likely to have the option of choosing an Internet service provider and the level of speed, from around 256 kbps on up. Not all ISPs offer DSL or cable modem options yet, so check with your current provider to see if high-speed access is available.

With either one, you avoid the $10 to $15 per month that Internet users ordinarily spend on an extra telephone line.

Consider the DSL offerings of US West, now available in 60 cities, including Denver, Phoenix, Salt Lake City, and Minneapolis–St. Paul. For the current price of $40 per month, you'll get DSL that runs at 256 kbps, or you can combine it with US West Internet access for $59.95. Want more speed? Like 512 kbps? That will cost you $65 a month, plus $39.95 for Internet access. Other DSL providers have similar plans, commonly offered in tiers for casual users and enterprise customers. For the time being, at least, cable modems may be considered the better value. Expect to pay installation fees of up to $250 for either one; a technician has to visit your home to handle the wiring. A high-speed access modem may cost as much as $300, but some providers may have a rental option or even include modem fees in the monthly rate.

Problems? The biggest headache is that it's not available in all areas yet, and may, more importantly, not be available in your area.

Nevertheless, will DSL service for faster access to the Internet catch on with enterprise users? Analysts say it will, but users aren't as sure.

Unsure Users

Many telecom managers are still waiting for the success stories with DSL technology. Several respected consulting enterprises have projected phenomenal growth in DSL technology and service. Gartner Group, Incorporated, in Stamford, Connecticut, predicts annual growth rates of more than 500 percent, with more than 3 million DSL lines installed by 2003—up from fewer than 70,000 now. Analysts' confidence in the market's growth is based on the strong need for faster connections to the Internet sought by consumers and enterprise users who telecommute or work in remote locations.

Benefits

The most-discussed variant of DSL, asymmetric DSL (ADSL), boasts downstream speeds that are more than 50 times faster than 56K bit-per-second connections. But analysts say the upstream speeds are much slower, making ADSL less attractive for enterprise users who need to push large files to colleagues and enterprise partners.

Several carriers are deploying or testing symmetric DSL (SDSL) to solve the need for fast upstream speeds using equipment by start-up vendors such as AccessLan Communications, Incorporated, in San Jose, California; or Copper Mountain Networks, Incorporated, in Palo Alto, California. Established networking vendors such as Cisco Systems, Incorporated [24] and Bay Networks, Incorporated [25] have also entered the arena.

Competitors in the SDSL market hope to attract customers with lower price and convenience of installation, compared with installing T1 lines. AccessLan will give enterprises a 1.5M bit-per-second SDSL connection at a lower cost than a typical T1 (1.544M bit/sec) connection from a telephone enterprise. Therefore, if DSL spreads as quickly as anticipated, there will be pressure on telcos to reduce their T1 prices.

Another factor is how long it takes an enterprise to install its own on-premise SDSL equipment, compared with waiting for a T1 connection. With SDSL, a small router is installed at the enterprise and an access concentrator is installed in a carrier's central office. The two are connected by existing twisted pair phone cable. The process may take only a day, compared with waiting, on many occasions, several weeks for a carrier to install a T1 line.

Most users would consider using cable modems for faster speeds, if they were available. Cable modems won't have as much growth among enterprises as DSL, partly because office parks often are not commonly wired for cable.

COMPARISON OF CABLE MODEM VERSUS DSL: SPEED AND COST

When compared to DSL, the cable modem has few advantages and several disadvantages for Internet access. DSL, on the other hand, has many advantages. Unlike ISDN, DSL isn't metered by the minute. Better yet, DSL is truly an *always on* service, which makes it suitable for a wider range of applications, including interconnecting LANs, Web site hosting, video conferencing, and connecting branch offices (see Tables 4–2 and 4–3).

Table 4–2   DSL versus Cable

Benefit	DSL	Cable Modem
Consistent download speed	Yes	No
Consistent upload speed	Yes	No
Immune to degradation from neighborhood usage	Yes	No
Secure, exclusively dedicated line with isolated data	Yes	No
Carrier guarantees performance	Yes	No

Table 4–3   High-Speed Services Compared

	ISDN	T1	DSL
Speed	128 Kbps	1.544 Mbps	128 Kbps to 1.544 Mbps
Cost per month (including Internet service)	$60–$120 for moderate usage	$800–$3,500	$89–$425, depending on speed
Notes	Per-minute charges make full-time connections impractical	Price can vary with mileage, usage, and service level	Wide spectrum of services; distance limitations; incompatible versions

Performance

In every cable modem *network neighborhood*, hundreds (perhaps thousands) of households all share a common transmission medium. Download speed could be high if conditions are optimal with absolutely no activity from neighbors. However, typical download speeds in many neighborhoods are no higher than 400 Kbps range during *real world* usage. Upload speeds are even slower, since the cable modem network is optimized in one direction only and, depending on the cable provider, often capped.

Value

As more users pile onto cable modem services, performance goes down rapidly, diminishing the value of the service. In response, many cable modem providers around the country now cap subscriber outbound speeds at 128 Kbps (equivalent to about two 56K modems). DSL is immune from both real and artificial speed restrictions. The quality and value of DSL remains constant for the lifetime of the service, while cable modem Internet quality degrades and loses value over time. Combine that with a yearly term requirement imposed by the cable modem enterprise with each subscription and you may discover that you are locked into a losing investment.

Security

Aside from performance variations and diminished quality, the shared cable modem network also introduces concern for security. Data from one household passes over the same wire connecting others, potentially exposing credit card, e-mail, and other sensitive data. For this reason, users either find cable Internet access unacceptable, or must arrange encrypted software tunneling to secure networks, which impedes performance.

No Surprise Here

Not surprisingly, DSL use is expected to boom. According to market research analysts at TeleChoice [26], the number of installed DSL lines is expected to grow from 566,000 in the year 2000 to 2,126,000 in 2002 to 4.57 million by 2004. DSL is expected to do well among people working at home (telecommuters) and in urban areas where cable services are not widely deployed.

Residential Users

Residential cable modem service can be a good value for high-speed access. Still, there are some limitations for residential cable modem service, as mentioned earlier. Cable is a shared medium, unlike DSL, which offers a dedicated line for each user. When too many users in one neighborhood try to share the same cable, performance suffers dramatically as users compete for the limited resources that one cable can afford. For this reason, residential cable customers are basically prohibited to telecommute, host Web sites, use video teleconferencing or any other bandwidth-intensive applications. The security problems of using a shared medium makes cable modem users much more vulnerable to data interception, unauthorized monitoring, and hacking from other users along the same cable network. While there is a market for residential cable modem service, obviously there can be some significant drawbacks.

Telecommuters

Telecommuters using cable modem service are required to pay a rate that is generally designed for the few enterprises that have cable modem service available. Service packages start at almost double what a DSL telecommuter would pay for the same speeds. Additionally, cable telecommuters are subject to the same security and bandwidth problems that residential cable customers face. Therefore, cable modem service is not a particularly attractive option for these customers.

Choices

Although the number of enterprises supplying DSL service and Internet access is increasing, would-be users face a confusing range of choices about availability, price, equipment, and configuration. DSL service is hardly ubiquitous. Even in areas where DSL has been deployed, if you're too far from the phone enterprise's central office (where the switching hardware is located), you can't get it or you don't get the maximum possible speed. Prices, while reasonable for enterprises, are steep for individuals. 128 Kbps service can cost as little as $89 per month, while 1 Mbps to 1.544 Mbps service can go for several hundred dollars. Equipment is not widely standardized, and there are a number of DSL variants to contend with (see the Table 4–1).

PLANNING IMPLICATIONS FOR THE ENTERPRISE NETWORK MANAGER

In the enterprise network manager, operator, and service provider, it is now an accepted, inescapable conclusion that xDSL technologies will one day be installed on a global basis, in vast quantities. Despite other technology developments (not excluding recent announcements about the commercial viability of sending data down power lines), it is still the only viable technology capable of substantially increasing bandwidth on the local access loops without a substantial overhaul. These copper loops are ubiquitous over every home and it is unlikely that any mass scale upgrade to fiber will happen within the next decade.

The primary driver for xDSL is high-speed Internet service deployment to residential customers. So far, there have been two small commercial deployments and no less than 66 trials around the world, trying to prove that asynchronous DSL (ADSL) can provide a downstream connection of up to 8 Mbps and upstream connection of up to 1 Mbps over the existing telephony copper pair.

Both IP and ATM network architectures are currently on trial. ATM is considered the probable choice in the future. Initial trials have used stand-alone ADSL modems with discrete IP interfaces for reasons of time-to-market and availability; and, these are evolving to highly integrated digital subscriber loop access multiplexers (DSLAM) solutions.

The complete network typically consists of a core, which is based around SDH (Synchronous Digital Hierarchy), wrapped with broadband ATM switches, ATM access switches, and DSLAMs. The DSLAMs provide the individual xDSL lines out to the customer premises and integrate with the existing POTS network connections. But even after having been in trial for more than 18 months, few operators seem close to commercial rollouts.

What is taking them so long? Some of the main barriers to large-scale adoption include the continuing standards battle and the lack of interoperability. The existence of two de facto standards, namely DMT and CAP, provides network operators with a dilemma; deciding which to adopt before a leader is clearly identifiable in case the choice ends up as the Betamax of the standards. There are two *standard* camps, one apparently led by Israel's Amati, which has developed modems using discrete multitone technology (DMT) for the line coding. Motorola [27] and Alcatel [28] are among the major manufacturers who have developed DMT modems. The second camp has adopted a technology developed by the former AT&T Paradyne, which championed carrierless amplitude modulation/phase modulation (CAP) for the line coding. Westell, the enterprise that made the ADSL modems being used in Bell Atlantic's Virginia trial, uses CAP. With no clear stance being taken, a general *wait and see* attitude is developing.

Westell was founded in 1980 and is headquartered in Aurora, Illinois, west of Chicago.

Lack of interoperability is also becoming a matter of concern. The current xDSL units on the market, from a variety of vendors supporting different standards, do not interoperate. Interoperability between vendors' equipment is key to mass roll-out and provisioning. The ultimate goal is for the end customer to be able to purchase their own ADSL termination units, much the same way as people buy off-the-shelf analog modems today. For this to happen, the ADSL termination unit technology needs to mature to the point were it is as simple as a modem to install and operate.

Operators are still deciding on suitable end-to-end architectures. Once these infrastructures have been agreed upon, the business and technology in place, services can then be rolled out in volume. These new architectures need to address the integration of network, service, and enterprise management of these new broadband services. Without these seamless, end-to-end management systems in place, it is difficult to see how operators will be able to make any profit on broadband services.

Enterprise Network Management Capabilities

The new broadband services being deployed by enterprise network managers, operators, and service providers are typically delivered over very complex network environments, which include legacy equipment with primitive management capabilities and newer systems incorporating sophisticated telecommunications management network (TMN)-based element management. New network management infrastructures are required to mold these disparate information sources into a cohesive view of the end-to-end services being delivered. This can be complicated by the large scale of such services—typically involving hundreds of thousands or millions of network elements. The major requirements can be summarized as follows:

- Cost-effective, performance scalability—a system with the ability to manage small pilot networks and expand as the network grows without performance degradation.
- Multiple protocol support—standards-based and proprietary management protocols must be supported in a transparent manner to the network applications.
- Powerful event management—as the network grows, the number of events grows exponentially. The ability to manage this volume of events in a way that helps the operator make sense of the status of the network is mandatory.

- Seamless application interworking—operators will use a number of different applications to manage aspects of the network, but they require the ability to move easily between applications, to investigate problems, or configure service for a particular customer, for example.
- User access management—the information within the management system must be protected, but it must also be feasible to partition the data, and the access to it, in a way that supports operational processes.

Enterprise Network Management Architecture

Some of the key management challenges when installing xDSL networks include potential element volumes. xDSL network elements are extremely complex devices that require real-time management. As element volumes increase exponentially, operators are faced with the challenges of implementing end-to-end systems that can manage millions of highly complex access elements.

As an example, the 1994 BT video-on-demand (VOD) trial supported 2,000 ADSL lines, equating to 4,000 access elements. Although this was classified as a small marketing trial, it is still the largest single xDSL installation in the world. This network generated a tremendous amount of management traffic, primarily with SNMP and performance-monitoring information, all of which had to be processed in real time by the central management workstation.

Additionally, xDSL equipment, by virtue of its inherent built-in intelligence, generates a tremendous amount of management traffic. This information, be it alarms, performance-monitoring information, configuration data, diagnostic commands, or inventory data, has to be processed, stored, prioritized, formatted, and displayed by the central management console. A single element management workstation cannot scale to support any major network growth.

Element and network complexity is also an issue that operators need to prepare for. xDSL equipment is becoming more complex with each generation. The latest generation uses rate-adaptive transmission, which causes a myriad of possible upstream and downstream speed permutations. Remote equipment now incorporates xDSL transmission hardware, IP routing equipment, and IP or ATM CPE interfaces into a single unit. In addition, it has to be seamlessly integrated with the existing POTS network, leading to a wealth of configuration permutations, performance monitoring information, alarm and event reports, and diagnostic functions and inventory data being available to the network operator.

A typical end-to-end network capable of delivering high speed Internet, on-demand services, and data and voice from multiple service providers is extremely complex. Many issues can only be resolved with the use of integrated management applications and systems. This often results in a number of noncompatible element management systems being installed to manage different parts of the network, then integrated together to provide an overall end-to-end service management system. The eventual goal is to provide a *zero touch* system to allow the end customer to control and manage a large part of their own service offering in real time.

xDSL equipment is normally installed over existing telephony circuits, but the devices at each end of the connection contain POTS splitters that allow both the telephony circuit and the xDSL circuit to use a single copper pair. This requires the integration of a new xDSL management system with existing POTS systems.

A range of issues also cloud the most efficient interface for the customer premises equipment. The two protocols in question are IP and ATM. Network operators are installing complex networking equipment into residential environments for the first time. This can lead to a multiplicity of new problems. These problems range from units being tampered with and cables being disconnected, to PCs being reconfigured. This could result in a huge increase in the number of service-related calls and queries directed at the network operator. The operator has to be able to diagnose, isolate, and analyze problems from the central management system. Only when this type of network, system management and control is achieved will broadband services become commercially viable.

Viability

The density of the technology must increase dramatically to enable operators to fit all the required ADSL termination units into their existing exchange real estate. xDSL technologies are still costly, and this is holding back general acceptance, due to the costs of equipment investment and the ongoing line rental charge. Prices in the range of $370 to $420 would start to approach an acceptable level for the benefits of this new broadband technology.

In most European countries, however, high capacity broadband ATM backbone networks have yet to be deployed. Without this backbone infrastructure there is little benefit to be gained from introducing an upgraded access network. In the infrastructure context, the questions of how some major European operators will play off ADSL against their substantial ISDN services will be an interesting debate. As it now stands, current versions of

ADSL cannot coexist with ISDN BRI lines. New versions of ADSL are being developed that will coexist with ISDN but as yet are only available in small trial volumes from less than a handful of vendors.

Telecommunication enterprises such as Deutsche Telekom [29], which bet its future on ISDN, are now involved in desperately trying to increase ISDN usage before ADSL establishes itself. The situation it faces (in common with many other operators in Europe) is that too much emphasis and keenly priced ISDN will undermine ADSL; but, at the same time, not investing an adequate amount of resources on ADSL now might undermine its future as a broadband services provider.

FUTURE OF CABLE MODEMS AND IDSL

From the point of view of a commercial (profitable, both for provider and user) service provision, xDSL can be considered an immature technology. xDSL has been proven an effective, reliable solution in many international trials, however, it is developing and progressing continually. This adds to the xDSL management complexities, requiring the facilities for operators to download new algorithms on a regular basis.

xDSL standards are relatively new and are, therefore, prone to change on a regular basis. This involves regular, programmable equipment upgrades such as software download of new versions of xDSL transmission and application code from a central management station.

As with all new technologies, technical and cost issues do get resolved in subsequent generations. xDSL is no different. The market demand for high-speed, broadband communications will drive the development of the technology and will produce an economic, reliable solution for end users. For network operators, xDSL is the most cost-effective way of upgrading the copper infrastructure and competing against fiber and cable competitors. Another factor in determining market direction is the move for European PTTs (post, telegraph, and telephones) from monopoly to deregulation and free competition. This will force network operators to unbundle their loops in a similar way to what has already happened in the United Kingdom and the United States. These new competitors will aggressively target end customers with offers of high-speed, broadband data communications, tempting them from the traditional service providers who may not be moving as quickly toward new service provision.

So, using the existing copper networks, xDSL will be made available that will motivate PTTs to respond, eventually leading to a critical mass and explosion in xDSL deployments. While network operators, service providers, and vendors debate the standards, technology, and cost issues of deploying xDSL networks, customer demand is growing for cost-effective, high-speed, broadband networks that unleash new services and new business potential for them. Looking at the rapid development of Internet and intranet business and services over the last few years, one can expect resolutions to the main issues and mass xDSL deployment within the next three to five years.

On the other hand, cable modems will dominate the North American residential Internet access market by the year 2004, outpacing xDSL lines six to one, according to a new market study conducted by Forward Concepts, Incorporated, a Tempe, Arizona-based consulting and market research firm. More than 9 million cable modems are expected to be installed by then. By 2004, the base for worldwide residential broadband access is expected to be close to 40 million users, but that isn't enough to support everyone who wants a piece of the broadband market. The big losers in the push toward high-speed broadband data services will be the telephone enterprises if they don't *depend less on lawyers and more on technology*.

Cable modems will win out because unit prices will dip below $130. The average DSL modem pair will drop from about $2,200 to $90 in the same time frame, but questions still exist regarding whether DSL really works with existing telephone lines.

Some see the battle as being tipped in telephone enterprises' favor because customers will demand the dependable service they're used to having with their phones. Still, cable modem enterprises are, by default, winning the Internet access war among consumers because the phone enterprises have really not been as aggressive as they could be in offering high-speed broadband data services. However, it isn't too late for phone enterprises if they jump into the broadband market soon. Nevertheless, they will be shut out if they're not into volume shipments of xDSL by the end of the year 2001.

Thus, in the race to provide high-speed data access to Internet users, DSL will win over cable modems. That's because copper networks already are entrenched, and enterprises will want to leverage their existing investments in copper.

The tug-of-war between DSL and cable modems is a closely watched battle, and nobody knows for sure which side will prevail. The prediction of a DSL victory has less to do with the merits of DSL and more to do with the existing copper infrastructure.

Nobody has love or hate for DSL. They don't care, but it's got to be copper because you can't dig it up. What we have done with electronics for 30 years in communications is make copper more efficient. So, DSL is just an extension of a 30-year trend that won't stop.

It's too expensive to change the lines. As you get critical mass behind some of the vendors, DSL wins for sure.

DSL carries data at high speeds over standard copper telephone lines, and allows users to surf the Net and talk on the phone at the same time, making it especially attractive for the home and small-office workplace.

Finally, cable modems, meanwhile, are gaining popularity, and some heavyweight investors are betting on cable enterprises to provide expanded services in the future. Thus, confusion over standards, including ADSL, DSL Lite, and VDSL, poses an obstacle, but those issues should resolve themselves in 2001.

FROM HERE

This chapter discussed the current state of cable modem access versus DSL. It also examined how prevalent cable modem and DSL services are in major U.S. markets. A comparison of the two technologies with regard to speed, cost, and so on was presented. The chapter also covered the planning implications or considerations for the enterprise network cabling manager (for example, to support telecommuting employees). Finally, the chapter discussed future directions for cable modems and DSL. The next chapter will take a close look at some of the third party vendor cabling systems—AT&T (Lucent) Systimax and Powersum; IBM Cabling System; DECconnect; Northern Telecom IBDN, AMP Connect, KRONE; Mod-Tap, BCS, ITT, IBCS; and so on.

NOTES

[1]   NorthPoint Communications, Inc., 222 Sutter Street, 7th Floor, San Francisco, CA 94108-4458, 2000.

[2]   Universal ADSL Working Group, The ADSL Forum Office, 39355 California Street, Ste. 307, Fremont, CA 94538, 2000.

[3]   Rockwell International Corporation, 600 Anton Blvd., Ste. 700, Costa Mesa, CA 92628-5090, 2000.

[4]   Cablevision Systems Corp., 1111 Stewart Avenue, Bethpage, NY 11714, 2000.

[5]   Nortel Networks Corporation, 8200 Dixie Rd., Ste. 100, Brampton, Ontario L6T 5P6, Canada, 2000.

[6]   Cable Television Laboratories, Inc., 400 Centennial Parkway, Louisville, CO 80027, 2000.

[7]   TeleChoice, Inc., 8555 N. 117th E. Ave., Suite #101, Owasso, OK 74055, 2000.

[8]   America Online, Inc., 22000 AOL Way, Dulles, VA 20166-9323, 2000.

[9]   Prodigy Communications Corporation, 44 S. Broadway, White Plains, NY 10601, 2000.

[10]   CompUSA Inc., 14951 N. Dallas Pkwy. Dallas, TX 75240, 2000.

[11]   International Telecommunication Union (ITU), Place des Nations, CH-1211 Geneva 20, Switzerland, 2000.

[12]   University of New Hampshire, 4 Garrison Avenue, Durham, New Hampshire 03824, 2000.

[13]   Intel Corporation, 2200 Mission College Blvd., Santa Clara, CA 95052-8119, 2000.

[14]   Alcatel, 54, rue La Boetie, 75008 Paris, France, 2000.

[15]   Lucent Technologies Inc., 600 Mountain Ave., Murray Hill, NJ 07974, 2000.

[16]   Compaq Computer Corporation, 20555 State Hwy. 249, Houston, TX 77070, 2000.

[17]   Dell Computer Corporation, One Dell Way, Round Rock, Texas 78682, 2000.

[18]   Bell Atlantic Corporation, 1095 Avenue of the Americas, New York, NY 10036, 2000.

[19]   GTE Corporation, 1255 Corporate Dr., Irving, TX 75038, 2000.

[20]   US WEST Headquarters, 1801 California Street; Denver, CO 80202, 2000.

[21]   AT&T Wireless Services, 7277 164th Ave. NE, Redmond, WA 98052, 2000.

[22]   AT&T Broadband & Internet Services, 9197 S. Peoria Ave., Englewood, CO 80112, 2000.

[23]   Excite@Home, 450 Broadway Street, Redwood City, CA 94063, 2000.

[24]   Cisco Systems, Inc., 170 W. Tasman Dr., San Jose, CA 95134, 2000.

[25]   Nortel Networks Corporation, 8200 Dixie Rd., Ste. 100, Brampton, Ontario L6T 5P6, Canada, 2000.

[26]   TeleChoice, Inc., 8555 N. 117th E. Ave., Suite #101, Owasso, OK 74055, 2000.

[27]   Motorola, Inc., 1303 E. Algonquin Rd., Schaumburg, IL 60196, 2000.

[28]   Alcatel, 54, rue La Boetie, 75008 Paris, France, 2000.

[29]   Deutsche Telekom AG, Friedrich-Ebert-Allee 140, 53113 Bonn, Germany, 2000.

Types of Vendor and Third-Party Cabling Systems

Cost-effective cabling systems and the necessary infrastructure to support them are critical to the ongoing success of your business. Whether you are linking PCs within your office or connecting them to a host system across the country, you need a structured networking cabling system. And, because the cabling infrastructure is a substantial portion of total construction costs, flexibility and planning are essential; however, the challenges are substantial.

The open office environment (partition based—no walls) presents a challenge to those installing vendor and third-party cabling systems. These challenges fall into three general categories; mechanics, scheduling, and churn. Each category is discussed in turn.

MECHANICS

Open office partitions have no standard size, thickness, or base dimension. When open offices are networked, openings within the panel must contain communication cabling as well as power wiring. Present telecommunications industry practice requires uninterrupted, 4-pair cable runs to each workstation receptacle.

The cabling industry is presently recommending four 4-pair receptacles be installed in each workstation. This means four individual wires (16 pair) must be run to each workstation. Large cable bundles are required. It is difficult and in many cases impossible to get these cables through the open-office partition. In many cases, the 2-inch power line to communication cable separation and routing required by Underwriters Laboratories (UL-1286 10.9) cannot be maintained.

SCHEDULING

Buildings utilizing open-office partitions are seldom wired in one step. The open office furniture is not available at the time the building needs to be wired. Multiple callbacks become necessary. Time and costs increase dramatically.

For further information on scheduling, see Chapter 22, "Implementation Plan Development." This chapter discusses the development of the cabling system implementation plan with extensive and thorough coverage of all factors that impact schedules and tips on how to keep projects on schedule.

CHURN

The major advantage of open-office cabling systems is flexibility. Open-office panels are frequently taken apart and reconfigured. The open-office environment is in line with the adaptable, less hierarchical business paradigm today. This accounts in large part for its popularity. Much of this flexibility is lost, however, when the panels must be field-wired for LAN connections.

A vendor or third-party cabling system can be easily installed by a premise cabling company. It also can be installed by the same people installing the office furniture. In both cases, installation must be coordinated with the person or company with system responsibility. The final connection is made by plugging the cabling system in or, in some cases, punching it down to the building system. On the other hand, installing telephone and LAN wiring is a more agreeable task than having a premise cable company try to lay conventional cable in the panel.

Open-office power wiring has used premanufactured and modular wire harnesses for many years. No one would even consider using standard field wiring practices to power an open office today.

STANDARD VENDOR OR THIRD-PARTY CABLING SYSTEM INSTALLATION

In buildings using open-office divider partitions, most vendor or third-party cabling systems start at the communications closet (TC), as described in TIA/EIA-T568 A/B, or at a multiuser Telecommunications Outlet (MTO), as defined in TIA/EIA TSB75. The end of this wiring is the user-accessible plug located in the individual workstation. This final wiring step is commonly called horizontal cabling.

For premanufactured and plug-together systems, none can comply with all physical aspects of TIA/EIA-T568 A/B. The standard that applies here is the Premanufactured, Modular Telecommunications Cabling Standard of 1997, which is maintained by Dekko Engineering of Kendallville, Indiana.

Most standard vendor or third-party cabling system modules consist of multipair unshielded twisted pair Category 5 performance-compliant cable segments. Fifty-position Telco connectors are usually provided at opportune points. The head-end connection is male in order to mate with a standard patch panel, hub, or MTO. The user (workstation) access is usually a female RJ45 receptacle. Three to twelve users share a given cabling system run. User breakouts are positioned near the point of use. The breakout usually has an RJ45 receptacle to accept the smaller cable leading to the user access face plate. The pin-out of the initial plug and face plate is specific to the LAN platform being served. This type of standard cabling system is usually available in 12 formats corresponding to common LAN and/or telephone arrangements. For more information on category 5 and the new category 6 cable standard, see Chapter 8, "Standards Design Issues" and Chapter 27, "Standards Development." Both LAN and telephone requirements are addressed here. Again, most standard cabling systems can provide both the LAN and telephone in a single run. Or, if the application dictates, platforms are usually available that bring either LAN or telephone. When both LAN and telephone exist in the same cabling system run, a profile cable with different sections for telephone and LAN is used.

Premanufactured cable designed for a specific LAN provides operational advantages not available with field wiring. Techniques can be applied to significantly reduce cross talk and interference susceptibility. In many cases, the performance of premanufactured cable is superior to that of field-wired cabling.

A step-up feature can significantly ease installation and reconfiguration. Most cabling system breakouts are usually the same. Each breakout brings out the next set of wire pairs in turn. It is not necessary for installers to concern themselves with which pair is brought out at a given breakout. The step-up feature is further described in Chapter 24, "Installation."

Figure 5–1 is a typical application [1]. The run starts at the communication closet, where it is attached to the LAN patch panel (large patch panel in the center of the communication closet) and the telephone punch-down block (right side in Figure 5–1). The equipment shown on the left in the communication closet is the hub with its outside connection, which in most cases is fiber. The cabling system proceeds to the open-office area where the first

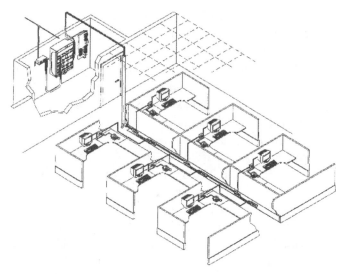

Figure 5–1   Typical application.

breakout is located. The communication needs of the first workstation are brought out here. One cable comes from the breakout to the office faceplate. The cabling system then proceeds with the second breakout, where the communication needs of the second workstation are met.

Except for length, all the breakouts are the same. They can be exchanged and placed in any order. In all cases, the LAN and telephone needs of the next workstation are brought out in order.

The next part of the chapter will take a close look at some specific vendor and third-party cabling systems—Lucent Technologies SYSTIMAX and Power Sum; 3Com Worldwide 1000BASE-T cabling system; IBM Cabling System; DECconnect; Nortel IBDN, AMP Connect, and KRONE; Mod-Tap, BCS, and ITT; and more. Cabling system warranty and certification are also covered.

LUCENT TECHNOLOGIES CABLING SYSTEM SOLUTIONS

Since many customers today are installing both copper and fiber cabling systems, many vendors are introducing products that accommodate both media at the same time. These products allow customers to migrate from one media to the other as conditions change. For example, Lucent Technologies offers the following cabling solutions:

- SYSTIMAX solutions for private networks.
- Building Automation Systems (BAS): Telecommunications cabling for intelligent buildings.
- ExchangeMAX solutions for central offices.
- HomeStar Wiring System for your in-home networks.
- AllWave Fiber Optic Cable for public network solutions.

Lucent Technologies: SYSTIMAX, Power Sum, and BAS

Lucent Technologies also offers three different sets of products that provide both fiber and copper management. The first is a complete line of multimedia outlets for both surface-mount and flush-mount applications at the work area. The second product is the Multimax panel with new accessories for fiber management. Designed for smaller cross-connects, the Multimax panel accommodates up to 24 duplex fiber or 4-pair copper connections per panel. The third is the PatchMax family of patch panel products. In addition to the modular patching arrangement for high performance UTP, fiber modules are included as well. Both the panels and the outlets allow the installation of fiber and copper within the same housing.

The panels and the outlets also allow a smooth migration from one media to the other while preserving the investment in the hardware. For example, customers may migrate from copper to fiber by replacing the copper connectors (jacks) with fiber adapters (couplings) without replacing the outlet or panel.

The next part of the chapter presents a brief overview of Lucent Technologies' cabling system: SYSTIMAX®. It offers an end-to-end cabling solution that enables high-speed transmission rates at 622 Mbps. For more information on higher-speed transmission rates and how to plan for higher-speed cabling systems as a result of changes in standards, see Chapter 21, "Data Compression."

SYSTIMAX® Structured Connectivity Solutions (SCS) Cabling System

As previously stated, Lucent Technologies also has a cabling system: SYSTIMAX. It is composed of a number of structured connectivity solutions (SCS).

But, before taking a look at the SYSTIMAX SCS, a quick definition of a premises distribution system and a structured cabling system is in order.

Premises Distribution System.   A premises distribution system is the transmission network inside a building or campus of buildings. It connects voice and data communications, video and building automation devices, switching equipment, and other information management systems to one another as well as to outside communications networks. It includes all the cabling and associated distribution components between the point where the building wiring connects to the outside network or telephone company lines and the voice, data, and video terminals at work locations. The system can also serve a building or group of buildings on a campus-like premises. A distribution system consists of various families of components, including transmission media, circuit administration hardware, connectors, jacks, plugs, adapters, transmission electronics, electrical protection devices, and support hardware. These components are used to build elements, each having a specific purpose, that allow easy implementation and smooth transition to enhance distribution technology as the communications requirements change. A well-designed distribution system is independent of the equipment it serves and is capable of interconnecting many different devices, including data terminals, analog and digital telephones, personal computers, and host computers, as well as system common equipment.

Structured Cabling System.   A structured cabling system is a set of cabling and connectivity products deployed according to specific engineering design rules. It enhances a premises distribution system and consists of the following:

- open architecture;
- standardized media and layout;
- standard connection interfaces;
- adherence to national and international standards; and
- total system design and installation.

SYSTIMAX SCS.   SYSTIMAX SCS is the structured cabling system that was developed by Bell Laboratories, the research and development arm of Lucent Technologies. SYSTIMAX SCS is an integrated unshielded twisted pair copper, fiber optic, and wireless networking solution that supports multiple applications, including voice, data, video, and building controls (big, complex building management systems, within and between buildings), seamlessly and simultaneously. SYSTIMAX SCS consists of:

- Two high-speed copper solutions that break the Category 5 barrier: the SYSTIMAX GigaSPEED™ 0 and SYSTIMAX Power Sum solutions.
- A complete optical fiber solution called the SYSTIMAX OptiSPEED™ system that is ideal for building risers, campus environments, and fiber-to-the-desktop applications.
- WAVELAN® Wireless connectivity that goes anywhere. This solution is the ideal complement to a wired LAN and is great for hard-to-wire, LAN-on-demand and mobile applications.

Lucent Technologies provides all the components used in SYSTIMAX. This is a very important factor, as the standards bodies continue research on high-speed LANs and multimedia protocols. At some point, it will be necessary to migrate from copper to fiber. There is a comfort level knowing that you will be dealing with only one company, not two or even three as is the case now, when that time comes.

SYSTIMAX SCS is modular. It uses star topology—the same physical topology used by the telephone industry and adopted by the EIA/TIA-T568-A commercial building standard. Expansion is simple in a star topology because stations are added outward from a central point. Each link is independent of the others, so changes and rearrangements affect only those links actually being changed. Such a topology makes troubleshooting and maintenance easy, since problems can be localized while the reports of those problems can be centralized. The star configuration is versatile, because it can be reconfigured easily to other topologies, such as ring or bus, needed by other applications. While keeping your equipment and wiring in a star arrangement, you can integrate additional topologies simply by adjusting the circuits at administration points.

The star topology makes possible a subsystem approach to SYSTIMAX SCS. With SYSTIMAX SCS, you can design a distribution system that is, in effect, built of the following elements:

- horizontal cabling
- backbone cabling
- work area
- telecommunications closet
- equipment room
- entrance facilities
- administration [2]

Like each link in the star topology, an element is a discrete unit; changes to one element need not affect others. An example would be a copper backbone element, which is changed to add fiber for greater bandwidth. It can still be viable to use the copper horizontal cabling, equipment room, and telecommunications closet elements to work with the fiber.

Open Architecture SYSTIMAX SCS solutions are implemented on an open architecture platform for maximum connectivity for existing products. At the same time, this cabling system provides a foundation for evolution to emerging technologies, such as multimedia, ATM, and Gigabit Ethernet.

Standardized Media and Layout. The SYSTIMAX SCS cabling system has a standard media, both copper and fiber, for each of the elements. For copper media, the choice is unshielded twisted pairs. There are three grades of UTP—category 3 for voice and some low bandwidth LANs up to 16 MHz, Enhanced category 5 tested for Power Sum for high bandwidth LANs up to 100 MHz, and GigaSPEED cable developed to support emerging bandwidth-intensive applications such as Gigabit Ethernet and featuring high bandwidth channel capability up to 200 MHz. For fiber media, the fiber of choice is multimode 62.5 micron core for all elements. Single-mode 8.3 micron core fiber cable is allowed in backbone elements for high bandwidth applications. For more information on standardized media and layout with regard to how category 6 fits into this scheme, see Chapter 27, "Standards Development."

Standard Connection Interfaces. SYSTIMAX SCS has standard connection interfaces, both copper and fiber, for each of the elements. For copper, interconnect and jack panels are deployed according to the category rating of the media: Category 3 for bandwidths up to 16 MHz, Enhanced Category 5 to 100 MHz, and GigaSPEED connection interfaces to support bandwidths up to 200 MHz. The same applies to the information outlets in the work area. For fiber, patch panels and fiber connector types are deployed based on location, fiber type, and quantity.

Total System Design and Installation. SYSTIMAX SCS has instituted training courses for design and engineering as well as installation and maintenance, which are requirements for working on certified projects. It provides application guides for designers, which address all the major LANs and many of the building management control offerings. This ensures that the system design adheres to the LAN standards and product specifications. Additionally, the cabling system's installation guidelines are provided for installation and maintenance personnel to ensure that the system is installed properly and the system functions as designed. A 15-year extended product warranty and applications assurance program is provided to all certified projects. The cabling system's applications assurance covers all applications currently contained in the SYSTIMAX SCS performance specification as well as any applications introduced in the future by recognized standards bodies or user forums such as ATM and IEEE that require EIA/TIA-T568-A or ISO/IEC IS 11801 for component and link/channel specifications.

New Developments. The current standard for commercial buildings is based upon minimum requirements at a component level. The standard does not take into consideration connectivity between components. The result is a standard that lists minimum performance specifications for individual components. The SYSTIMAX SCS cabling system, on the other hand, takes a systems approach and works to try and improve margins for attenuation, cross-talk, structural return loss, and impedance matching on a link/channel basis.

The same is true for Power Sum. SYSTIMAX SCS introduced the Power Sum Solution with the following features:

- Certified 622 Mbps performance to the desk
- Superior Power Sum Near End Crosstalk performance
- Supports up to 550 MHz (77 channels) broadband video
- SYSTIMAX SCS expansion option [Paradine, 5]

Bell Laboratories proved with the 622 Mbps demonstration unit that by using more than one pair of UTP conductors for transmission in the same direction, called parallel transmission schemes (PTS), LAN speeds could improve dramatically. Thus, the SYSTIMAX SCS cabling system offers two UTP cabling systems: the Power Sum Solution and the GigaSPEED Cabling System, a fiber system with all the components required for both multimode and single-mode fiber and the WaveLAN wireless system for those nodes that exceed standard cabling distances.

Certified 622 Mbps to the Desk. The SYSTIMAX SCS's 622 Mbps to the desk capability is based on power sum technology and enables customers to send and receive information at higher speeds across multiple pairs. The technology supports various applications including asynchronous transfer mode for simultaneous voice, data, and video.

Power sum technology refers to the more stringent industry requirements placed on cabling systems with applications that use multiple pairs of wires in the same cable. Power sum is an electrical performance testing method that takes into account crosstalk, or interference, from every pair of wires in a cable.

This kind of transmission speed has an impact on the way the business world communicates. For example, a healthcare network utilizing 622 Mbps technology could pull up a patient's x-ray and simultaneously video conference with a team of physicians across the country to formulate a real-time prognosis—all on the same terminal.

The 622 Mbps capability is accomplished by transmitting 155 Mbps over each of four twisted pairs in what is known as parallel transmission. Parallel transmission uses four pairs that transmit signals simultaneously, providing four times the capacity of category 5.

Power Sum Near End Crosstalk (NEXT) Performance.   The SYSTIMAX SCS cabling system has engineered a solution that diminishes the harmful effects of NEXT. Power sum is an advanced method of measuring NEXT, which identifies cable with performance margins. Applying power sum technology to 4-pair cabling results in a product with superior performance characteristics that is ideally suited to the demands of emerging and future high-speed applications.

Although standards committees have just begun studying the issue of sheath sharing, Bell Laboratories tested and qualified the fastest available LANs for compatibility. The 16 Mbps token ring, 100 Mbps Twisted Pair-Physical Media Dependent (TP-PMD), and 155 Mbps ATM are all compatible and warranted under the cabling system's guidelines. Furthermore, 25-pair cabling was qualified as an option for horizontal zone cabling.

The following products meet the Power Sum specification: 4-pair 1061+ and 2061+ High Performance LAN cables, 25-pair 1061 and 2061 High Performance LAN cables, 110 Patch Panel System, PATCHMAX® Distribution Hardware, 1100CAT5PS Modular Jack Panels, MPS-100 Information Communication Outlet, and 1074 Impedance Matched Cordage [Paradine, 5].

550 MHz Broadband Video.   The SYSTIMAX SCS cabling system includes a 384A video adapter for broadband applications. It has passed tests for radiated emissions in compliance with FCC Part 76 regulations. This cabling system provides applications assurance for up to 77 channels of broadband video (channel 2 to channel 78; frequency range 55 to 550 MHz).

Expansion Option.   This cabling system option is in support of move and change activity. Lucent Technologies guarantees the sharing of qualified high-speed data systems over a single 4-pair or 25-pair cable link/channel using the enhanced (power sum) qualified products. The cabling system's guidelines specify options to meet EIA/TIA and ISO standards

while providing another option for cabling customers. This option allows for expansion of supported applications using breakout assemblies until additional cabling can be installed.

In continuing with the SYSTIMAX SCS cabling system, let's look next at how Bell Laboratories demonstrates achievement of NEXT channel performance requirements for the GigaSPEED cabling system.

Achieving NEXT Channel Performance Requirements for the GigaSPEED Cabling System. The SYSTIMAX Structured Connectivity Solutions Department of Bell Laboratories has designed and built a research experiment to demonstrate that the SYSTIMAX SCS GigaSPEED cabling system has achieved near-end cross talk (NEXT) channel performance requirements set at the inception of the project. The system demonstrated comprises 1071 GigaSPEED 4-pair UTP cable, MGS100 GigaSPEED telecommunications outlet, and GigaSPEED 110 wiring blocks and 110GS patch cords. The GigaSPEED cabling system has been introduced to support emerging bandwidth-intensive applications such as gigabit data transmission, multimedia, shifting LAN traffic patterns, and the use of network computers.

The GigaSPEED Cabling System. Currently, the IEEE Gigabit Ethernet Alliance is developing a gigabit standard titled 1000BaseSX and LX for fiber and 1000BaseT for UTP. IEEE has set a completion schedule for the fiber standard for UTP. Additionally, the ATM Forum is working on a fiber specification for 1.2 Gbps ATM and is evaluating a research project for UTP.

Bell Laboratories has developed design requirements for the GigaSPEED cabling system and has introduced and is selling the GigaSPEED 1071/2071/3071 cable. Lucent Technologies introduced the remaining SYSTIMAX GigaSPEED apparatus. As Ethernet evolves from 100 Mbps to 1000 Mbps and becomes a standard, the SYSTIMAX SCS GigaSPEED cabling system will provide the capability to support it and future technologies and provide a 20-year extended product warranty and application assurance program.

While it is understood that the emerging gigabit standard for Ethernet will be based on generic category 5 cabling, research has shown that category 5 performance is inadequate for robust 100-meter solutions using inexpensive electronic hub technology. The standard committee evaluated two proposals: (1) to support horizontal distances of 50 to 60 meters with inexpensive electronic hubs or (2) to support full 100 meter when coupled with very expensive and complex electronic hubs. The Gigabit Ethernet Standard has subsequently decided to support the latter proposal. The GigaSPEED cabling system offers a cost-effective approach by providing a more robust system that can use less expensive hub electronics at the full 100-meter distances. Lucent Technologies' Microelectronics Division is currently developing the integrated circuit chips that will be used in these hubs. The GigaSPEED cabling system has incorporated the following criteria:

- All components designed as a total system with backwards compatibility.
- A system designed for current and future applications that customers can use.
- A system that exhibits acceptable EMC performance for all intended applications [Paradine, 2].

GigaSPEED Cable. Incorporating all the principles previously outlined, the GigaSPEED cable has been designed for electrical performance specified out to 550 MHz and for channel performance supporting gigabit transmission to the desk at 100-meter distances. Employing optimized balance design, the cable exhibits lower emissions, stable electrical performance to higher frequencies, and greater noise immunity. On a worst-case basis (or achievable for 100 percent of the cables installed), GigaSPEED cable guarantees the following electrical performance across the frequency spectrum relative to the category 5 specification:

- 10 dB of margin for pair-to-pair near end cross talk;
- 8 dB of margin for power sum near end cross talk;
- greater than 4% margin for attenuation;
- 10+ dB of margin for attenuation to cross-talk ratio; and
- 3 dB of margin for structural return loss [Paradine, 2].

Typical values are based on an average of several cables tested and will show even better margins. They are, however, not guaranteed. When making comparisons between cables, it is most important to compare guaranteed-to-guaranteed or typical-to-typical values.

GigaSPEED Connectivity Components. GigaSPEED components have been designed with drastically improved cross-talk performance and balance. Additionally, major improvement in return loss and further reduction in attenuation have been achieved. The components have been designed and tested to 200 MHz and provide substantially more bandwidth when compared to the existing Category 5 standard. The GigaSPEED components have been designed to be fully compatible with existing hardware and plugs. Termination requires no new tools nor special installation procedures. The components include:

- MGS100 telecommunications outlet, which fits all existing M series openings;
- DM2151 PatchMax module with the same footprint as current product;
- D8GS modular cord with new 1074+ GigaSPEED cordage and new plug;
- 110GS patch cords with new 1074+ GigaSPEED cordage; and
- 110 wiring block [Paradine, 3].

GigaSPEED Channel Performance.   Figure 5–2 compares projected GigaSPEED channel performance values to those of categories 3 and 5 [Paradine, 4]. Specified out to 200 MHz, the GigaSPEED channel dramatically increases available bandwidth. The values shown for the GigaSPEED channel are part of the system's development requirements but are considered projected since some development work is ongoing and the values could improve.

Demonstration of GigaSPEED NEXT Channel Performance.
The GigaSPEED demonstration was designed and built by the SYSTIMAX SCS Department of Bell Laboratories, in Middletown, New Jersey. The demonstration was designed to show that the GigaSPEED cabling system pro-

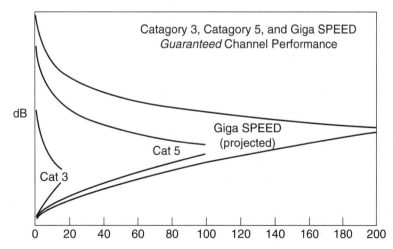

Figure 5–2   Comparison of projected GigaSPEED channel performance values to those of categories 3 and 5.

vides dramatically improved NEXT channel performance when compared to the category 5 standard. A 4-pair termination module for common and differential mode testing and a software program using new algorithms were developed by Bell Laboratories for ongoing research and this demonstration.

The demonstration provided a swept frequency test of NEXT specified to 200 MHz. The results for the NEXT of each pair-combination of the GigaSPEED channel were overlaid onto a grid on the PC monitor, which displayed the category 5 channel requirements. The following test sets and equipment were used:

- Custom 4-pair Test and Termination Module;
- Hewlett-Packard 35677A S-Parameter Test Set;
- Hewlett-Packard 3577A Network Analyzer;
- Hewlett-Packard Attenuator/Switch Drive;
- PC with 21" monitor; and
- GigaSPEED Cabling System Display [Paradine, 5].

The results demonstrated that the GigaSPEED channel not only met the initial objectives but exceeds them.

The next part of this chapter presents an overview of Lucent Technologies' other SCS cabling system: building automation systems (BAS). BAS is an SCS for telecommunications cabling of intelligent buildings. For more information on telecommunications cabling of intelligent buildings, see Chapter 28, "Cable-less Connectivity: The Wireless Future."

Structured Connectivity Solutions: Telecommunications Cabling for Intelligent Buildings

There are many interpretations and definitions of an intelligent building. An intelligent building can be defined by the information and control services that meet the needs of the occupants, the software that controls telecommunications and building automation functions, or by the actual electronic hardware and devices implemented within the structure. It is necessary to have all of these components to create such a facility, but a structured connectivity solution is the common ingredient required to integrate the telecommunications and building automation systems. Other than the SCS, these low-voltage or power-limited services have nothing in common except similar transmission characteristics (analog or digital data signals), and the pathways (conduit, cable tray, raceway, and so on) that support and protect the cabling investment.

Providing an internationally standardized SCS and consolidating the horizontal pathways for all the systems can typically reduce the initial construction costs by 10 to 15 percent, and up to 30 percent, for the cabling infrastructure of a modern intelligent building. The actual level of savings achieved is dependent upon the configuration and the geographical pricing for material and labor. An integrated systems approach also enables management to quickly and cost effectively respond to the changing needs of the tenants, which impacts the cost to occupy the space. In some cases, additional construction expenditures for the SCS or BAS, such as devices to optimize the use of power consumption, may be necessary to reduce the operational expenses. However, the costs for cabling-related changes can typically be reduced by 25 to 40 percent for a new or renovated facility when using a total systems integration approach.

For instance, typical costs for building operation and alterations over a 40-year life cycle far exceed the initial construction costs. Proper systems-integration planning to optimize the construction process can reduce these ongoing life cycle costs.

The Foundation for Systems Integration.   For many years, voice and data systems were cabled separately. Now it is standard practice to use a common SCS for both of these systems. Like the voice and data systems of the past, the traditional construction process separately installs each of the BAS disciplines under various divisions of a specification. The BAS typically consists of:

- Fire, Life, & Safety (FLS) or Fire Alarm (FA);
- Security & Access Control (SAC);
- Energy Management Systems (EMS), which includes Lighting Control; and
- Heating, Ventilation, & Air Conditioning (HVAC) [2].

Each of these BAS categories are typically cabled separately. The voice and data cabling is rarely addressed during construction and is usually not part of the construction budget. This method of construction, which is being driven to change by building owners that occupy the space and organizations such as Building Industry Consulting Service International (BICSI), uses the MasterFormat document developed by the Construction Specifications Institute (CSI). This document currently contains limited information for implementing the telecommunications infrastructure, so planning and installation for the telecommunications is normally accomplished when the floor space is being prepared for occupancy. This means multiple cabling systems and pathways are installed during various stages of construction, which establishes one of the primary reasons for systems integration (integrated cabling and pathways instead of individual systems). Other reasons for integrating BAS and telecommunications include: BAS use data networking and LAN architectures (intelligent controllers and addressable devices); and BAS are increasingly being integrated into the primary data backbone, which allows controlled access through any PC on the data network.

With proper planning, the only limiting factor for complete systems integration of the telecommunications and BAS may be the fire alarm system. In the United States, Article 760-54 (b) of the 1999 National Electrical Code (NEC) allows conductors of power-limited fire alarm systems and signaling/communications circuits (Article 725/800) to share the same cable, enclosure, or raceway. In addition, Article 760-61 (d) of the NEC allows the use of the same type of cable for the fire alarm that is typically used for the communications circuits. However, some local codes, especially codes in other countries, may invoke limitations or require special approvals for integrating the fire alarm system. Yet, even if the fire alarm cabling is installed separately, there are still substantial cost reductions and benefits that can be derived from integrating the remaining BAS (HVAC, EMS, SAC).

In addition to the code and standards requirements, there is also a need to evaluate the electrical characteristics of the systems. The voice and data systems primarily consist of analog and digital signals, and have established guidelines for signal strength over distance. The BAS devices operate on current draw, circuit resistance (contact closure), or consist of analog or digital signals (communications bus). Basically, each BAS terminal or device will operate over a particular cable type as long as it is located within a specified range from the equipment.

BAS devices are utilized to monitor or control a specific function. One can equate this to an output from the equipment or input from a device. As an example, there may be a temperature sensor that gathers information and sends a signal to the equipment panel (input) and, as a consequence, the equipment sends a signal to a device that closes a damper or vent (output). Devices are primarily power-limited (low voltage) or communicate using low-speed protocols. The current draw and line voltage delivered by the power supply typically limits the signal distance supported by the devices. Telecommunications type 24-AWG unshielded twisted pair cable has the capacity to handle 1 Ampere (Amp) of current draw per conductor, with a maximum of 3.3 Amps per four-pair cable. What does this mean? The current or signal from the equipment leaves at a specified voltage level. The device requires a certain voltage level to operate. As the signal travels through the cable, the voltage drops due to resistance. Cable pair resistance is measured by shorting one end of the cable and taking a resistance reading between the conductors at the other end. A typical 24-AWG UTP cable pair has 57.2 ohms of resistance per 1,000 feet, or .0572 ohms per foot. Circuit resistance can be measured by dividing the voltage drop by the current draw.

If a 24 Volt (V) device requires 50 Milliamps (.05 Amps) of current to operate and the allowable voltage drop is ± 10% or 2.4V, the maximum circuit distance using 24-AWG UTP cable is 839 feet (256 meters). This can be easily calculated for any cable and circuit using the following two-step formula:

1. Voltage Drop (2.4 V)/Current Draw (.05 amps) = Circuit Resistance (48 ohms)
2. Circuit Resistance (48 ohms)/1 Foot Cable Resistance (.0572 ohms) = Maximum Distance (839 feet/256 meters)

The BAS has evolved from individual systems using many different technologies to LANs and networks using intelligent controllers, similar to today's data systems. The cabling choice for today's data systems is a structured UTP copper and fiber connectivity solution. This makes it a natural fit for the BAS and can substantially reduce construction and operational costs by planning and integrating all systems on a single cabling infrastructure.

Planning.   The preceding statements have established that it is possible to use the same type of 24-AWG UTP cable and share a common cable pathway for all power-limited services. The next step is to determine the best way to perform systems integration. The process starts with early planning and a decision by the building owner or management to select the cabling as the first system. Once the decision is made to use a common cabling infrastructure, it is very easy to select voice, data, video, and BAS equipment that is compatible with the cabling. In fact, the sooner the consolidation of cabling systems and pathways is considered, the greater the potential savings and flexibility.

The Electronic Industries Association/Telecommunications Industry Association (EIA/TIA) and International Standards Organization/International Electrotechnical Commission (ISO/IEC) have created industry standards for cabling telecommunications systems. These standards address the cabling and pathways (pathways and spaces), and are based on a subsystem architecture or structured cabling elements. Prior to the standards, the subsystem concept was first used for voice systems. During the 1980s it was also adopted for data systems. Like the BAS equipment of today, there were many different types of cables and wiring methods for data systems before the standards were established. Because of this, data networks were typically unmanageable, with little or no flexibility, and new cabling was often necessary when systems were changed or upgraded.

With some slight modifications (use of a coverage area versus a work area), the EIA/TIA and ISO/IEC documents can also be used to provide the same standardized cabling architecture for the BAS devices, systems, and applications. The horizontal cabling and pathways can be designed for all the services with the telecommunications closet (TC) as the terminating point. This is the key to the integration of cabling and pathways. The wallfields/distribution frames at the TC location can be combined for maximum flexibility, or individual termination fields can be establish within the same TC. Therefore, a secure area for all cabling is created, thus reducing the multiple spaces required for traditional separate installations. Maintenance is also simplified since all systems are located in a common area.

This also allows a single pathway to be designed for supporting the various horizontal cables in the workspace. It can even be taken a step further by incorporating the power for lighting and receptacles from the electrical panel into a modular partitioned raceway. This could be used instead of a traditional hardwired installation consisting of several conduit and cable tray systems for the voice, data, video, BAS, and electrical services.

Case studies show that an integrated approach can provide up to a 40 percent construction savings for cabling and pathways when a single high/low voltage cabling infrastructure is implemented. The savings will vary according to geographical costs for material and labor. Material costs will typically be higher than a traditional separate systems installation, but labor hours can typically be reduced by as much as 60 percent. Besides offering a substantial construction savings opportunity, this solution allows the building to be occupied sooner, resulting in additional rental or lease revenue.

Even if an integrated high/low voltage raceway system is not utilized, the pathways may still be consolidated by using one cable tray system for all of the power-limited services. Conduit can also be provided from the cable tray to protect critical services. Whatever is decided, with early planning comes the ability to evaluate all the services and consolidate individual voice, data, video, and BAS using a single cable type and pathway, instead of multiple cable types and pathways.

The building's tenants can also realize significant savings. A traditional facility with leased space may not provide horizontal cabling for any services. This increases the setup time for tenants. In addition, the tenant usually pays for the voice and data cabling, along with the cost for occupying the space during setup. The cost and setup time for tenants can be dramatically reduced by installing an open-office horizontal cabling grid during the construction phase. Open-office cabling, which is actually another term for prewired zone cabling, provides a building with a marketable advantage that can sometimes mean the difference between empty and occupied space. Attracting tenants with reduced setup costs and a high-tech platform for services can increase building occupancy, and one month of full occupancy may pay for the entire cabling system.

With open-office cabling quickly becoming the preferred method of cabling for both new construction and renovations, it is possible to provide a cabling design without knowing the furniture plan or where any of the devices will be located. The entire design for the cabling can be based on the maximum usage of the size and type of space. As an example, a typical voice and data work area for an office can be located every 100 square feet (9 square meters), and the BAS devices can be calculated based on every 250 square feet (23 square meters). Using this design approach makes the horizontal cabling and pathways completely reusable for virtually any furniture plan. This is basically the same method used by the electrical industry for power (lighting and receptacles), except zones are typically called bays and power connections are hardwired.

Historically, voice and data horizontal cabling has not been installed during the construction phase. If the voice and data cabling is installed during the construction phase, it is easier to install, minimizes damage to finished surfaces, and is reusable for the life of the structure when designed properly. Additionally, new cabling does not have to be installed every time the tenants move, or when systems are changed or upgraded. This helps to eliminate cluttered floor and ceiling spaces. In addition, constant rewiring within a structure tends to cause modifications that may affect the physical structure of the building and the integrity of the technology deployed in the structure. Systems will change many times during the life of a structure. With proper planning, it is not necessary to provide new cabling every time systems are changed or upgraded.

Flexibility for services (electrical, voice, data, video, and BAS) is critical for today's business. All services should be considered in the early planning stages when constructing or renovating a building, not just the electrical and BAS, in order to provide cost savings, maximum flexibility, and a platform for high-tech services.

Integrating Building Automation Systems (BAS) with the SCS.
A typical BAS architecture is hierarchical, and centralizes the monitoring, operation, and management of the modern commercial building. The control

functions are usually distributed and resident in the system- and field-level controllers, with higher-level functions (interactions between systems and controllers) resident in the system-level controllers. In addition, each type of controller is usually capable of operating in a stand-alone manner with limited functions in the event of a communications bus failure.

The system-level controllers are used for linking the sequenced operation of field-level controllers, via the communications bus, and will typically have expandable point or port capacity. The field-level controllers are designed for specific application requirements and have limited port capacity. The design of this hierarchical BAS network has been driven by the need to provide limited control functions in the event of a network or communications bus failure (controllers can operate in a stand-alone mode), and to limit cabling runs from the controllers to the devices. The more controllers installed, the shorter the cabling runs. Since there is no structure to the traditional BAS cabling and all devices are homerun to the controllers, it has always been impractical to homerun cables to a central controller. The traditional BAS cabling method also ties the life cycle of the cabling plant directly to the system to which it is connected.

SCS eliminates this cabling dilemma because of the cabling elements or subsystem approach. Distribution of the cabling takes place in the TC or horizontal terminating point. When reviewing the cabling distance from the mechanical area to the device, versus the TC to the device, it's similar, since both areas are typically adjacent to each other. What does this mean? Using the dynamic flexibility of the cabling elements (equipment cabling, cross-connects, etc.) not found in traditional BAS cabling makes it possible to place the BAS controllers in a variety of configurations to reduce costs and provide greater flexibility.

As an example, some field-level controllers may be consolidated, depending on their function; and a larger capacity system-level controller used to provide BAS connections through the riser cabling to the horizontal, or controllers, may be consolidated at the horizontal terminating point. The cabling elements maximize flexibility and can allow any port to be connected to any location in the facility, but will typically add costs to the installation since they are not part of a traditional BAS. However, these costs can be substantially offset by using the cabling elements to consolidate pathways and multiple equipment locations, and by optimizing the telecommunications and BAS installation through use of a single installation team.

Early planning is critical for determining the optimal placement of the controllers (distributed, centralized, or a combination of both), telecommunications spaces, and pathways in conjunction with the mechanical/electrical areas. When distributing the BAS controllers, the SCS makes it possible to:

- Locate BAS system-level controllers in a mechanical area or the telecommunications spaces (e.g., TC, MC, ER, etc.).
- Reduce the number of BAS system- and field-level controllers by consolidating multiple locations in the TCs or MC.
- Recover from controller failures by retranslating and rerouting BAS services via cross-connects to spare ports.
- Use the TC to create one secure location for housing all the telecommunications and BAS controllers on a floor or floor area [2].

Some BAS vendors state that the controllers must be placed in close proximity to the mechanical equipment for troubleshooting. However, an RJ45-type outlet can provide plug-in capabilities for a remote hand-held tester.

When distributing or centralizing the BAS controllers, any power required to operate devices, such as fire alarm strobes or variable air volume (VAV) boxes, can be distributed from the TCs or be provided for locally. This may necessitate additional BAS hardware (power supplies) in the TCs since the telecommunications cabling will typically power less devices per cable. This situation can be alleviated if BAS power supplies were manufactured with more power taps that supply less current per tap (10 outputs that deliver up to 1 Amp per tap). The power taps could even be modular, with multiple appearances on a jack, which would also simplify the installation.

In addition to being distributed, the BAS controllers can be centralized if distance limitations are supported. A centralized equipment approach does not mean centralized intelligence since most modern BAS use distributed intelligence (small capacity controllers distributed through a building), but distributed intelligence can still be accomplished using a centralized equipment approach. This approach works best with system-level controllers incorporating a minimum of 32 ports. Large-capacity system-level controllers may not be available from some BAS manufacturers, but this strategy can still be accomplished using smaller controllers. Centralizing the BAS controllers can be compared to some of today's telecommunications strategies, including:

- A private branch exchange (PBX) distributed (remote PBX cabinets) to meet distance requirements; otherwise it is centralized to reduce equipment costs.

- Centralized fiber administration used to reduce the cost of active electronics.
- Data hubs distributed to maintain distance limitations; otherwise they would be centralized to reduce the cost of active electronics [2].

Using a distributed equipment approach is not cost effective for most types of equipment or systems. Sometimes the system limitations for data transmission or power require a distributed topology, but this is usually not the case for the typical low-speed and power-limited BAS equipment. Because the traditional BAS installation has no cross-connect system, it is neither practical nor cost effective to run device cables to a central equipment location. When centralizing the BAS controllers, the SCS makes it possible to:

- Use all the available BAS ports anywhere in the building via the riser backbone cabling.
- Reduce the number of system- and field-level controllers.
- Provide centralized BAS administration.
- Recover from equipment failures by retranslating and rerouting BAS services via cross-connects to spare ports (in a traditional installation, the panel or components within the controller would have to be replaced in order to restore service).
- Alternate ports from controllers to eliminate complete outages in designated areas.
- Reduce BAS installation, testing, equipment, and electrical costs by consolidating equipment areas [2].

The telecommunications cabling also makes upgrading the BAS controllers faster and more cost effective. In a traditional installation, devices are wired straight from the controller to the device. When the controller needs to be upgraded, the cables must be reterminated or the terminal strips moved to the new controller. This is not always easy or practical and in some cases the device cables may not be reusable. The SCS cabling elements allow the devices to be reconfigured at the cross-connect location with the simple addition of some new equipment cabling. The SCS approach assures economical equipment upgrades with minimal service outages.

Finally, speeds for data transmission are rising as technology advances and more information is processed. The new BAS are composed of intelligent controllers with addressable devices, and basically mirror today's data networking and LAN architectures. In fact, data backbones are increasing, being used as a traffic mechanism for BAS communications. This allows any PC with the proper passwords to access the BAS via an internal network or even through the Internet. As the BAS equipment becomes more advanced, their associated data transmission speeds will also increase. Currently, some of the traditional BAS cabling will only support limited data rates and applications. If the appropriate cabling is not incorporated into the structure during construction, it may require new cabling at a future point in time.

Now, let's very briefly look at the other Lucent Technologies cabling system solutions:

- HomeStar Wiring System for your in-home networks.
- AllWave Fiber Optic Cable for public network solutions.

Central Office Solutions: ExchangeMAX

The ExchangeMAX Distribution System is a structured cabling system for the central office. It consists of voice, digital, and optical subsystems engineered to provide application-specific solutions for central office cable management.

Home/Office Solutions: HomeStar Wiring System

The HomeStar Wiring System is a family of in-home network wiring products that supports a new generation of interactive voice, data, video and multimedia products, and communications services. HomeStar solutions incorporate a high-performance cabling system and a general interconnection to all telephone, cable TV, digital satellite, cellular telephone, and utility telemetry services, while supporting home automation, control, and security functions.

Public Networks Solutions: Fiber Cabling System

Lucent's cabling system that takes you from your desk through the outside plant, into and through the central office, and then all the way to the home office. The components of the fiber cabling system include fiber, cable, and apparatus.

Fiber

Lucent Technologies is one of the pioneers in the development and manufacture of fiber and fiber components. Fiber manufactured for the first commercial applications was made in the late 1970s. Today, Lucent manufactures a wide range of fiber products, including AllWave and TrueWave® fibers. Lucent also offers a line of specialty fiber products.

Fiber Optic Cable

Lucent Technologies is also the world's largest fully integrated supplier of optical fiber and cable. A wide variety of cable core and sheath designs are provided to match the diverse installation and transmission requirements of both standard and unique fiber optic system applications. Outside plant systems can be designed using AccuRibbon cable. Lucent Technologies designed and developed the original Fiber Optic Building cable and has continually enhanced the design leading to the ACCUMAX building cable family.

Fiber Optic Apparatus

Finally, Lucent Technologies manufactures a complete range of apparatus products that are needed in each and every application to connect and house the fiber and fiber cable. Apparatus includes splicing, connectors, assemblies, LGX® cabinets, LIU cabinets, passive optical components, test sets, and closures. It also includes unique hardware and software products including Smart LGX, Fiber Administration Software, and FiberGrafix® Network Design Software for Windows.

Next, let's look at 3Com Corporation's cabling system and Worldwide 1000BASE-T Cabling System Validation Program. This is a new cabling system program designed to help large- and medium-sized businesses prepare for gigabit-over-copper product roll out.

THE 3COM WORLDWIDE 1000BASE-T CABLING SYSTEM

3Com Corporation recently announced a worldwide 1000BASE-T cabling system validation program designed to help large- and medium-sized enterprises prepare for the implementation of gigabit-over-copper technology. The IEEE recently ratified the 802.3ab standard for Gigabit Ethernet over category 5 cabling, with the first recommendation being to test a network's cabling plans. Based on these standards, 3Com's cabling system validation program will help speed the implementation of 1000BASE-T products, ensuring customers can implement the new high-speed technology to support the growing network demands of today's e-business culture.

To help customers comply with the IEEE's cable testing recommendation, 3Com will leverage its Web site to offer this testing service. The program evaluates the customer's installed category 5 cabling to determine whether the infrastructure is suitable for implementing 1000BASE-T. The validation includes the following:

- a cabling evaluation to determine whether the infrastructure meets the applicable standards;
- a detailed testing report; and
- if necessary, a plan for restoring initially failed cabling [3].

Three trends are driving the demand for high-speed networking: the creation of a knowledge-based economy; the growing convergence of voice, video, and data; and the phenomenal growth of the Internet. 1000BASE-T puts the high end of networking within the financial reach of mid-sized companies.

Advances in digital signal processing have extended the life expectancy of copper cabling for high-speed data transmission. High performance copper cabling will continue as the horizontal media of choice for current and next-generation technology.

The 1000BASE-T validation program is currently available in the United States and in Germany, the United Kingdom, France, Belgium, Luxembourg, the Netherlands, Italy, Spain, Sweden, Denmark, China, Hong Kong, Singapore, Australia, Mexico, and Japan. A detailed discussion of the 1000BASE-T (Gigabit Ethernet over category 5 copper cabling) technology follows.

1000BASE-T (Gigabit Ethernet over Category 5 Copper Cabling)

How can network managers deploy bandwidth-intensive applications over their local area networks when they have tight budgets and must leverage their existing infrastructure? The latest Ethernet technology, 1000BASE-T (Gigabit Ethernet over category 5 copper cabling), helps network managers boost their network performance in a simple, cost-effective way.

1000BASE-T is Ethernet that provides speeds of 1,000 Mbps over category 5 copper cabling—the most widely installed LAN cabling infrastructure. The IEEE Standards Committee formally ratified 1000BASE-T as an Ethernet standard in June 1999.

This part of the chapter is principally targeted for network managers who want a technical understanding of the fundamentals of 1000BASE-T. It explains how 1000BASE-T has been designed by the IEEE 802.3ab Task Force to run over category 5 cabling and how to implement 1000BASE-T over existing category 5 cable infrastructure and over Enhanced category 5 (category 5e) in new sites.

1000BASE-T, Gigabit Ethernet over Category 5 Copper Cabling: Why?

1000BASE-T, Gigabit Ethernet over category 5 copper cabling is an attractive option for network managers for several reasons. It addresses the exploding bandwidth requirements on current networks that are the result of implementing new applications and the increasing deployment of switching at the edges of the network. Gigabit Ethernet leverages the organization's existing investment in Ethernet and Fast Ethernet infrastructures, and it provides a simple, cost-effective performance boost while continuing to use the dominant horizontal/floor cabling medium.

Exploding Bandwidth Requirements.   New, bandwidth-intensive applications are being deployed over Ethernet and Fast Ethernet networks. These applications include the following:

- Internet and intranet applications that create any-to-any traffic patterns, with servers distributed across the enterprise and users accessing Web sites inside and outside the corporate network. These applications tend to make traffic patterns and bandwidth requirements increasingly unpredictable.
- Data warehousing and backup applications that handle gigabytes or terabytes of data distributed among hundreds of servers and storage systems.
- Bandwidth-intensive, latency-sensitive groupware applications such as desktop video conferencing or interactive white-boarding.
- Publication, medical imaging, and scientific modeling applications that produce multimedia and graphics files that are exploding in size from megabytes to gigabytes and even terabytes [3].

Bandwidth pressures are compounded by the growing deployment of switching as the desktop connection of choice. Switching at the edge tremendously increases the traffic that must be aggregated at the workgroup, server, and backbone levels.

Significant Investment in Ethernet/Fast Ethernet Infrastructure.   Ethernet is the dominant, ubiquitous LAN technology. According to industry analyst International Data Corporation (IDC, in Framingham, Massachusetts), more than 87 percent of all installed network connections were Ethernet at the end of 1999, representing more than 331 million interconnected PCs, workstations, and servers.

The deployment of Ethernet/Fast Ethernet networks involves investment in network interface cards, hubs, and switches, as well as in network management capabilities, staff training and skills, and cabling infrastructure. In fact, cabling infrastructure is the longest-term networking investment, lasting at least two years and up to 10 years. According to the December 1998 Networking Cabling Market Study by Sage Research (in Natick, Massachusetts), on average almost half of the infrastructure is in place for more than five years.

Cost-Effective Performance Boost on Existing Category 5 Cabling. 1000BASE-T offers a simple, cost-effective migration of Ethernet/Fast Ethernet networks toward high-speed networking, and has the following benefits: First, 1000BASE-T scales Ethernet 10/100 Mbps performance to 1,000 Mbps. Flexible 100/1000 and 10/100/1000 connectivity will be offered and will enable the smooth migration of existing 10/100 networks to 1,000 Mbps-based networks.

Second, 1000BASE-T is the most cost-effective high-speed networking technology available now. 1000BASE-T leverages existing, proven Fast Ethernet and V.90/56K modem technologies and will experience the same cost curve as the Ethernet/Fast Ethernet technologies. 1000BASE-T is in fact expected to be significantly more cost efficient than 1000BASE-SX (fiber gigabit), which already has the lowest cost-per-data-transmitted per second among all LAN technologies (currently less than $1.7 per Mbps).

Finally, 1000BASE-T preserves Ethernet equipment and infrastructure investments, including the investment in the installed Category 5 cabling infrastructure. There is no need to undergo the time-consuming and high-cost task of replacing cabling located in walls, ceilings, or raised floors.

Leveraging category 5 copper cabling infrastructure is of significant importance for two reasons: First, category 5 is today the dominant horizontal/floor cabling, providing connectivity to both desktops and workgroup aggregators (see Figure 5–3) [3]. Fiber is the dominant cabling for connection of multiple buildings. Second, category 5 is one of the major options for building risers/backbone cabling for connection of different floor wiring closets (see Figure 5–4) [3].

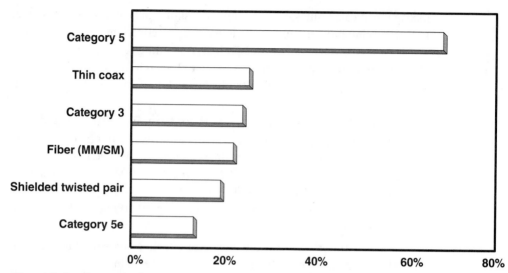

Figure 5–3   Current horizontal network cable types. This figure shows the percentage of organizations that have installed the cable type. Multiple choices were allowed. Other cabling types (category 6 STP, category 4, category 6 UTP, plastic optical fiber) each scored less than 10 percent.

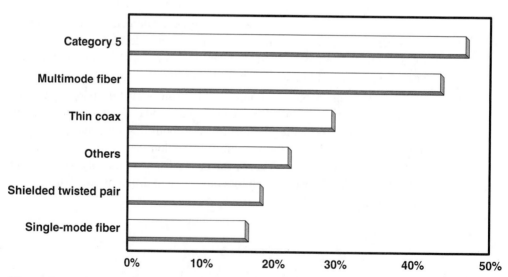

Figure 5–4   Current building backbone cable types. The figure shows the percentage of organizations that have installed the cable type. Multiple choices were allowed. Other cabling types (category 3, category 5e, category 6 STP, category 4, category 6 UTP, plastic optical fiber) each scored less than 10 percent.

Technical Fundamentals of 1000BASE-T: Gigabit Ethernet Media Specifications

Gigabit Ethernet cost effectively leverages existing cabling infrastructures. It can be implemented in floor, building, and campus networks, because it offers a wide range of connectivity media and connection distances. Specifically, Gigabit Ethernet is designed to run over four media:

- single-mode fiber, with connections up to at least 5 kilometers;
- multimode fiber, with connections up to at least 550 meters;
- balanced, shielded copper, with connections up to at least 25 meters; and
- category 5 cabling, with connections up to at least 100 meters [3].

The IEEE 802.3z Gigabit Ethernet standard, approved in June 1998, specified three transceivers to cover three media: 1000BASE-LX for the installed base of single-mode fiber, 1000BASE-SX for the installed base of multimode fiber, and 1000BASE-CX for a balanced, shielded copper cable that could be used for interconnects in equipment rooms. 1000BASE-LX transceivers can also be used to reach at least 550 meters on multimode fiber.

Another task force, IEEE 802.3ab, has defined the physical layer to run Gigabit Ethernet over the installed base of category 5 cabling. The IEEE Standards Committee approved the 1000BASE-T standard in June 1999. Figure 5–5 summarizes the various Gigabit Ethernet options and the standards that define them [3].

1000BASE-T Key Specifications. The 1000BASE-T standard leverages the existing cable infrastructure—as it is specified to operate up to 100 meters on category 5 cabling. The other key specifications of 1000BASE-T make it a cost-effective, nondisruptive, and high-performing technology. First, it supports the Ethernet MAC, and is thus backward-compatible with 10/100 Mbps Ethernet. Second, many 1000BASE-T products will support 100/1000 auto-negotiation, and 1000BASE-T can thus be incrementally deployed in a Fast Ethernet network. Third, 1000BASE-T is a high-performing technology with less than one erroneous bit in 10 billion transmitted bits (this bit error rate of less than 10^{-10} is the same error rate as that of 100BASE-T).

Detailed 1000BASE-T Cable Specifications. 1000BASE-T is specified to run over four pairs of category 5 balanced cabling. The four pairs of category 5 balanced cabling are specified in ANSI/EIA/TIA-568-A (1995). Additional link performance parameters (return loss and ELFEXT) are speci-

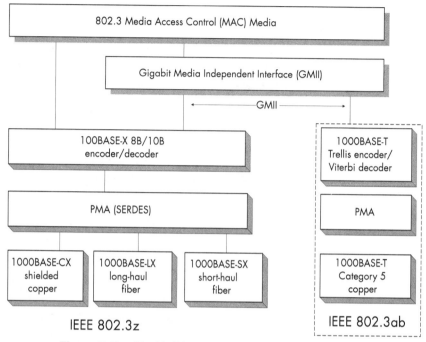

Figure 5–5   Gigabit Ethernet media options and standards.

fied in TIA/EIA-TSB-95. Figure 5–6 details the standards of reference for the specification of 1000BASE-T cable performance parameters [3]. Category 5 cabling is also specified in ISO/IEC 11801:1995 ("Information Technology: Generic Cabling for Customer Premises"). The second edition of ISO/IEC 11801:1995 will include the additional cabling performance parameters specified to support Gigabit Ethernet.

1000BASE-T Design.   1000BASE-T is designed to run over category 5 copper cabling. The transmission of 1 Gbps is possible thanks to the use of four twisted-pair links with 250 Mbps of throughput on each pair (250 Mbps × 4 = 1 Gbps).

1000BASE-T transmits at the same clock rate as 100BASE-T (125 MHz), but uses a powerful signaling and coding/decoding scheme that enables the transmission of double the amount of data as 100BASE-T. The following is a comparison of the two specifications:

- 1000BASE-T: 125 MHz × 2 bits = 250 Mbps
- 100BASE-TX: 125 MHz × 1 bit-symbol = 125 Mbit-symbol/s

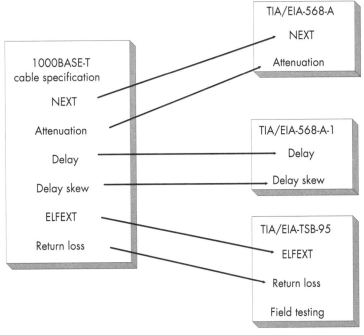

Figure 5–6   Standards of reference for 1000BASE-T performance parameters.

125 Mbit-symbol/s is equivalent to 100 Mbps, since 100BASE-T uses a 4B/5B code—4 bits of data that are translated into 5 bit-symbols before transmission on the wire. The effective bits throughput is thus 125 x 4 / 5 = 100 Mbps.

1000BASE-T cost effectively leverages the design of proven existing Fast Ethernet and V.90/56K modem technologies. Signaling and coding/decoding methods already implemented in 802.3 Fast Ethernet transceivers and in V.90 or 56K modems using advanced DSPs are used to implement 1000BASE-T. Table 5–1 summarizes the 100BASE-T technologies and methods reused by 1000BASE-T [3].

Table 5–1   100BASE-T technologies used in 1000BASE-T.

Technology/Method	1000BASE-T	100BASE-TX	100BASE-T2
Multilevel signaling	Five-level PAM		Five-level PAM
Symbol clock rate	125 MHz		
Transmit spectrum	MLT-3–like	MLT-3	
Digital signal processing	Yes	Available	Yes
Transmission	Bidirectional		Bidirectional

Existing Cabling Deployment Preparation

Preparing existing category 5 copper cabling for running 1000BASE-T is a straightforward process. The first step is a simple test of the adequacy of the cable installation. In the unlikely event that an existing installation does not meet one of the performance parameters specified by 1000BASE-T, standard corrective actions can be implemented. Testing the installation of existing category 5 cabling encompasses the following:

- Cable testing information is specified in the ANSI/TIA/EIA-TSB-67 standard, "Transmission Performance Specifications for Field Testing of Twisted-Pair Cabling System," which has been used by cabling installers since 1995.

- The additional test parameters of return loss and ELFEXT for 1000BASE-T are specified in the ANSI/TIA/EIA-TSB-95 Bulletin, "The Additional Transmission Performance Guidelines for 100 ohm 4-Pair Category 5 Cabling."

- These additional tests are incorporated into the current versions of cable test tools. Field testing is performed by connecting the two hand-held devices—one at each end of the cabling under test with a field test cord, and then activating the 1000BASE-T test function. A pass or fail will be indicated for the 1000BASE-T test and for the specific test parameters under test. Many field testers include diagnostic functions to help identify the cause of failures [3].

Adjusting Existing Category 5 Cabling to Run 1000BASE-T.

In the unlikely event that an existing Category 5 installation does not meet one of the performance parameters specified by 1000BASE-T, corrective actions are defined in a simple field procedure detailed in the ANSI/TIA/EIA-TSB-95. Three types of corrective measures can be applied:

- Use of high-performance Category 5e patch cables (see following section for definition of Category 5e).
- Reduction in the number of connectors used in the link.
- Reconnection of some connectors in the link [3].

In most cases in which an installation is not initially compliant, it is not necessary to perform all the corrective actions.

Preparing for Deployment over New Copper Cabling: Category 5e

The Gigabit Ethernet Alliance recommends that all new cable installations designed for 1000BASE-T deployment should be specified as category 5e (enhanced category 5). Category 5e cabling is manufactured to meet all 1000BASE-T transmission performance parameters. Specific field testing is not currently required, but is recommended by many installers.

The category 5e specification includes transmission parameters that are only informative recommendations for category 5. Category 5e also provides a further enhanced margin over the worst-case 1000BASE-T link requirements.

The 1000BASE-T standard specifies operation over the installed base of category 5 cabling. 1000BASE-T will also run over category 6 and category 7 copper cabling systems (see Sidebar, "The Other Cabling Categories").

THE OTHER CABLING CATEGORIES

A category 6 cabling standard, specified to 250 MHz, is under development in the ANSI/TIA/EIA TR-42.7.1 Copper Cabling Systems Working Group and in the International Standard Committee ISO/IEC/SC25/WG3. Network managers and cable system planners may want a cabling infrastructure that provides greater bandwidth or *headroom* to accommodate future high-speed technologies.

A category 7 cabling standard, specified to 600 MHz, is under development in the International Standard Committee ISO/IEC/SC25. Category 7 cable is constructed with individually shielded pairs with an additional shield over the pairs. Category 7 cabling requires termination to a shielded connector. The category 7 standard is still in the early stages of development.

1000BASE-T will operate on the cabling specified in the current draft 5 of ANSI/TIA/EIA-category 6 (estimated release, late 2001). The current draft of the category 6 specifications are proposed for the second edition of ISO/IEC 11801:1995 (estimated release, late 2000). Category 7's estimated release date is late 2001 [3].

Migrating Ethernet/Fast Ethernet Networks toward High-Speed Networking

1000BASE-T allows a simple performance boost to support exploding bandwidth requirements on today's networks. 1000BASE-T is best suited for unclogging network bottlenecks that occur in three main areas:

- workgroup aggregation;
- connections to high-speed servers; and
- desktop connections [3].

The following scenario describes a typical migration of an Ethernet/ Fast Ethernet network to Gigabit Ethernet. As shown in Figure 5–7, the initial building backbone is 10/100 Mbps Ethernet/Fast Ethernet. Several Ethernet or Fast Ethernet segments are aggregated into a 10/100 Mbps switch,

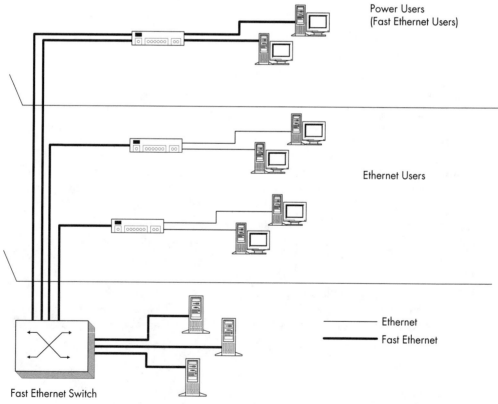

Figure 5–7   Ethernet/Fast Ethernet network before migration to Gigabit Ethernet.

which in turn has several 10/100 Mbps Ethernet/Fast Ethernet server connections [3]. Some users have dedicated 10/100 switched connections to their end stations. In this configuration, users are starting to experience slow response times and power users are experiencing bottlenecks. The first upgrade phase is implemented in three areas (see Figure 5–8) [3]:

- Upgrading the backbone with a 100/1000 Mbps Fast Ethernet/Gigabit Ethernet switch.
- Upgrading the workgroup switches that support power users or large workgroups with Gigabit Ethernet downlink modules.
- Implementing 100/1000 Mbps Fast Ethernet/Gigabit Ethernet NICs in key servers [3].

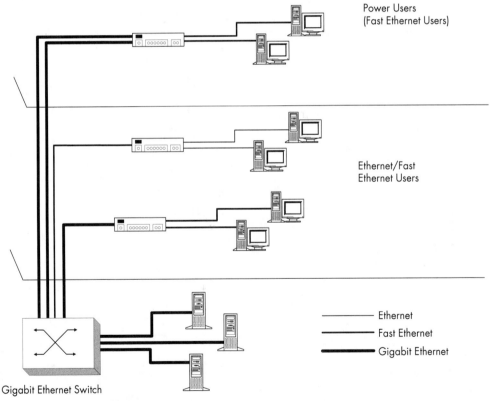

Figure 5–8   First phase of Gigabit Ethernet migration.

As a result of these measures, the speed of the backbone increases ten-fold to accommodate the overall increase in network bandwidth demand while the investment in existing workgroup switches, end-station NICs, and existing cabling is preserved. The second migration phase is the upgrading of power users to 100/1000 Mbps Fast Ethernet/Gigabit Ethernet NICs (see Figure 5–9) [3]. Fast Ethernet and, over time, Gigabit Ethernet to the desktop are now sup-ported, giving power users full access to the resources of the network.

Finally, 1000BASE-T, Gigabit Ethernet over category 5 copper cabling, helps network managers boost their network performance in a simple, cost-effective way while enabling migration of today's Ethernet/Fast Ethernet net-works toward high-speed networking. The following is a summary of Gigabit Ethernet characteristics.

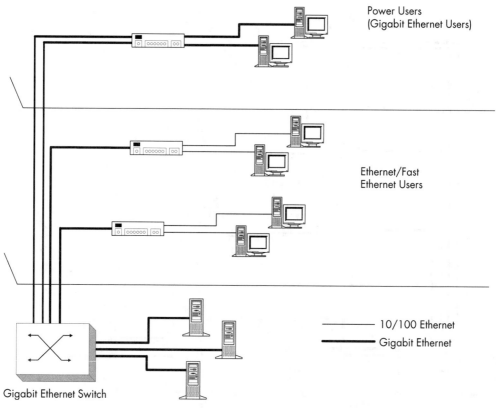

Figure 5–9   Second phase of Gigabit Ethernet migration.

- 1000BASE-T is Ethernet, providing speeds of 1000 Mbps.
- 1000BASE-T is designed to run over category 5 copper cabling, the most widely installed LAN cabling infrastructure.
- 1000BASE-T leverages the design of existing proven, cost-effective Fast Ethernet and modem technologies [3].

1000BASE-T can be progressively deployed in a Fast Ethernet network, since 100/1000 auto-negotiation will be supported in many, if not all, 1000BASE-T products.

THE IBM CABLING SYSTEM

Let's take a very brief look at the next type of vendor and third-party cabling system: The IBM Cabling System. The IBM Cabling System has the option of using five different types of cable, as shown in Figures 5–10 to 5–14 [4]. The Sidebar, "Types of Cable," discusses the physical characteristics of IBM's Cabling System.

IBM recommends category 5 UTP for all token ring environments. IEEE 802.5q discusses category 3 cable in an active configuration only.

Figure 5–10 Type 1.

Figure 5–11 Type 3.

TYPES OF CABLE

The IBM Cabling System has the option of using six different types of cable with the following physical characteristics.

Type 1

- Two pairs twisted together, then overall shield applied.
- 22 AWG gauge, tested to 16Mbps.
- Impedance is 150 ohms, plus or minus 10 percent, at 3–20 Mhz.
- Attenuation is 22 dB per kilometer.
- Cross talk must be less than –58dB between pairs.
- LAN use: between MAUs and from MAU to wallplate.

Type 2

- Two pairs twisted and shielded, then shielded together, and an additional four pairs that can be used for voice (unshielded twisted pair category 3 cable).
- 22 AWG gauge, tested to 16 Mbps.
- Impedance is 150 ohms, plus or minus 10 percent, at 3–20 Mhz.
- Attenuation is 22 dB per kilometer.
- Crosstalk must be less than –58 dB between pairs.
- LAN use: through the walls to the station wallplate typically carrying voice, token ring, and possibly 10BaseT Ethernet.

Type 3

- Unshielded twisted pair.
- 22 AWG gauge or 24 AWG gauge wire.
- Minimum 2 twists per foot.
- Impedance is 100 ohms at 256 Khz to 2.3 Mhz.
- LAN use: throughout the network for token ring over unshielded twisted pair.

Type 5

- Two 62.5/125 micron multimode fiber optic cable. 50/125 and 100/140 micron have also been used.
- 62.5/125 micron is the defacto standard for FDDI:
  - Attenuation: 3.75 dB/km using 850 nm source.
  - Attenuation: 1.5 dB/km using 1300 nm source.
- 8.3/125 for single-mode cable.
- Connector types: SMA, ST, and SC.

Type 6

- Two pairs twisted together, then shielded.
- 26 AWG stranded cable.
- Impedance: 150 ohms, plus or minus 10 percent, at 3–20 Mhz.
- LAN use: typically connecting from the wall plate to the station adapter; patch cables only, to a 30-meter maximum.

Type 9

- Two pairs twisted together, then shielded.
- 26 AWG solid or stranded cable.
- Impedance is 150 ohms, plus or minus 10 percent, at 3–20 Mhz.
- Accepts RJ45 termination (smaller diameter).
- LAN use: typically used connecting from the wall plate to the station adapter [Cabletron, 1–2].

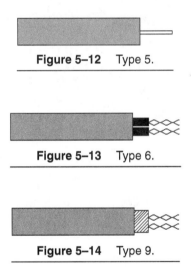

Figure 5–12   Type 5.

Figure 5–13   Type 6.

Figure 5–14   Type 9.

S/3X and AS/400

System/3X and AS/400 connectivity can be accomplished using either unshielded twisted pair or twinax cable. A UTP star-wired cabling system offers the ability to make changes to the system by simply moving a patch cord on a patch panel, while a twinax cabled system provides a high degree of immunity to electrical noise. The cabling scheme shown in Figure 5–15, however, offers the best of both twinax and UTP wired systems [5]. In addition, see the Sidebar, "Twinax and UTP Wired Cabling Systems Product List," for a numbered list of products that correspond to the numbers shown in Figure 5–15.

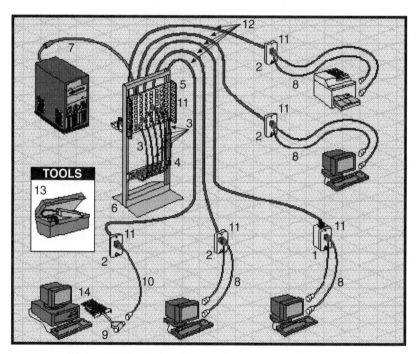

Figure 5–15   Twinax and UTP wired cabling systems.

TWINAX AND UTP WIRED CABLING SYSTEMS PRODUCT LIST

The following is a numbered list of products that correspond to the numbers shown in Figure 5–15.

1. Part No. 501724 Type 1 Surface Mount Box
2. Part No. 10148 Type 1 Faceplate
3. Part No. 501405 Patch Cable
4. Part No. 501174 MCL Metal Panel
5. Part No. 30607 Distribution Panel
6. Part No. 32873 84" Distribution Rack
7. Part No. 10143 Twinax Impedance Matching Device
8. Part No. 501289 Twinax Y Assembly
9. Part No. 502187 Twinax Green Terminator, 150 ohm
10. Part No. 501399 Twinax Direct Cable
11. Part No. 10087 Data Connector
12. Part No. 10063 or 10061 PVC or Plenum Type 1 Cable
13. Part No. 10138 Cable Test Kit
14. Part No. 32330 Twinax Adapter Card

Based on the IBM Cabling System, the scheme shown in Figure 5–15 uses shielded twisted pair cabling. Since the cabling is star-wired to a distribution panel, moves, changes, and additions can be made by simply moving a patch cord on the distribution panel. There is also a high degree of immunity to electrical noise because the cable is shielded. This cabling system (shown in Figure 5–15) is able to support both token ring and 5250 type devices, so there is a great amount of flexibility when connecting the AS/400 to a token ring network. By simply changing the attachment cables and devices at the equipment rack and the workstation, the existing cabling can be adapted to a variety of systems and interfaces such as 16 Mbps token ring, 10BaseT Ethernet, RS-232, and RS-422. The benefits of this cabling scheme are:

- Combines the benefits of Twinax and UTP cabling.
- Allows easy moves, changes, and additions.
- Highly reliable in electrically noisy environments.
- Able to support both token ring and 5250 type devices.
- Compatible with other networking schemes [South Hills Datacomm, 1].

Nortel IBDN

Let's take a look at the next type of vendor and third-party cabling system: Nortel IBDN. The Integrated Building Distribution Network (IBDN) is a universal wiring system designed to meet communications needs as they expand.

IBDN is a global in-building cabling system communications infrastructure that addresses distribution needs from the building entrance to the workstation with a single wiring system. Nortel's category 5 IBDN structured wiring system is a UTP copper technology that provides 100 Mbps data rates and connectivity up to 100 meters. This comprehensive line of fully integrated products covers all of the needs for networking current and future computers, voice, and video communications equipment.

IBDN also covers end-to-end certified UTP gigabit cabling system solutions. The IBDN System 1200 and System 2400 UTP gigabit cabling system solutions go beyond category 5 standards by providing additional margin to support emerging gigabit data rate applications.

Gigabit Cabling System Solutions

The availability of two enhanced IBDN structured cabling systems—IBDN gigabit cabling system solutions, System 1200 and System 2400—allows gigabit networking environments to be optimized over unshielded twisted pair cabling. With the growing demand for Internet commerce, intranet deployment, and video conferencing, gigabit networks will become increasingly prevalent.

Evolved from the field-proven category 5 IBDN structured cabling system, the IBDN gigabit cabling system solutions go well beyond existing category 5 standards to meet increasing high-speed applications and network user demands. With the rapid increase in computer processing power, higher-performance networks will be required to support gigabit data rate applications.

The IBDN gigabit cabling system solutions allow end users the choice of two performance options to meet the varying needs of different enterprises. For example, IBDN System 1200 is built using IBDN PS5 enhanced connectivity and 1200 series UTP cable. It delivers a higher signal-to-noise margin than conventional category 5 systems. It also provides a system bandwidth of 160MHz and an information bit-rate capability of 1.2 Gbps. System 1200 is a very cost-effective solution to install and operate, thus making it a preferred cabling solution for Gigabit Ethernet.

The IBDN System 2400 comprises PS5 enhanced connectivity and 2400 series UTP cable and delivers 200 MHz of system bandwidth. It is capable of delivering an information bit rate of 2.4 Gbps. Medical and financial institutions and other industries that constantly move large amounts of data benefit from the added speed, reliability, and assurance provided by System 2400.

Developing a complete end-to-end enhanced system with matched components was the key engineering design criteria for the IBDN gigabit cabling system solutions. IBDN cable and connectivity work together to provide superior network performance. As such, these solutions are designed to exceed critical performance parameters such as power sum NEXT, FEXT (far end cross talk), attenuation, and return loss.

To complement the new system offering, Nortel has extended its product warranty from 15 years to 25 years. In addition, IBDN gigabit cabling system solutions can be certified for application assurance over the life of the structured cabling system. End users will also benefit from Nortel's performance guarantee supplied in the form of a bandwidth and data-rate certification.

MOD-TAP

Let's now take a look at the next type of vendor and third-party cabling system: MOD-TAP's structured cabling system (SCS), which is composed of the residential cabling system (RCS) and the commercial structured cabling system (CSCS). The company provides structured cabling solutions to customers worldwide.

MOD-TAP is a manufacturer of structured cabling systems for information transport. The company designs and manufactures electronic, electrical and fiber optic components, flat cable, switches, and application tooling.

The MOD-TAP Structured Cabling System

The MOD-TAP Structured Cabling System is an infrastructure for information transport within the office, building, or campus environment. It consists of a series of subsystems that support the analog and digital transmission of communication and building control signals. The SCS includes:

- horizontal cabling;
- backbone or vertical cabling; and
- main distribution frame.

The MOD-TAP SCS is protocol-independent and is capable of supporting the following protocol technologies:

- ISDN
- voice
- FDDI TP-PMD
- ATM
- 100BaseT
- 10BaseT
- Token ring
- IBM Systems 3X/AS400
- IBM 3270
- RS232
- AppleTalk Networks [6]

As previously stated, MOD-TAP's structured cabling system is composed of the residential cabling system and the commercial structured cabling system. Let's look at the RCS first.

Residential Cabling System

Residential communication systems usually comprise a telephone line and a TV antenna. MOD-TAP RCS takes the home of today into the 21st century, providing access to, and distribution of, the huge range of services available to the consumer, including Internet, video services, home automation, LAN, and home theater, as shown in Figure 5–16 [MOD-TAP, 1].

The MOD-TAP residential cabling system is a structured solution to low-voltage cabling in a new or existing home. RCS provides a plug-and-play modular approach to residential cabling for telephones, faxes, answering

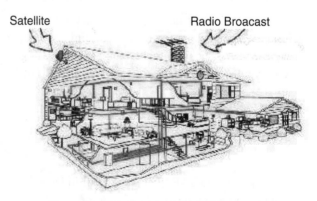

Satellite   Radio Broacast

Figure 5–16   Residential cabling system.

machines, video, computer equipment, and their devices, such as security systems and control devices. RCS has adopted a four-part approach to residential cabling, consisting of drops, feeds, system equipment, and an interconnect panel (central termination point).

Drops.   Drops are equipment connection points located throughout the house for telephones, computers, video connections, and other devices. Each drop consists of one or more cables run to the panel.

Feeds.   Feeds are gateways into the RCS telephone and cable TV services, an air antenna, a satellite dish, and so on. Spare feeds can be installed for future use. A feed consists of one or more cables run to panel.

System Equipment.   System equipment can include telephone key systems, door intercoms, video distribution panels, and computer LANs as well as lighting, security, and other control systems. Additionally, system equipment is cabled to the panel.

Interconnect Panel.   InfoPanel™, the heart of the RCS, is a central terminating point for all residential twisted pair, coaxial, and/or fiber optic cabling. This is where all interconnections between drops, feeds, and systems are made.

Commercial Structured Cabling System

The commercial structured cabling system plays a critical role in all telecommunication systems, providing the physical link between sources and destinations of all information. Data, voice, video, and control signals are transmitted over this infrastructure, linking devices across the room, and throughout a building as shown in Figure 5–17 [MOD-TAP, 1].

The CSCS may be quite small and simple, linking just a few nodes, or it may be massive, linking several buildings with tens of thousands of nodes, or a system somewhere in between. Essentially the CSCS is a simple physical link between active equipment, and is comprised of unshielded twisted pair cable or optical fiber cable or combinations of both.

However, to facilitate the day-to-day operations of a normal office environment, the link must enable the user to make adds, moves, and changes wherever and whenever necessary. Furthermore, the CSCS must also be universal in its ability to carry a wide variety of applications from voice and low-speed data to high-speed LAN applications.

MOD-TAP divides the entire system into subsystems (horizontal, backbone, and system) and addresses each individually, which collectively forms a system that meets all of the above criteria and more. CSCS is standards-based and complies with all relevant local and international telecommunications cabling standards.

Communication technology is developing at an astounding pace and it is essential for the survival of any business to utilize one of several possible technologies, as shown in Figure 5–18 [MOD-TAP, 1]. No longer is the statement "Knowledge is power" true. It is replaced by "Access to knowledge is power." Business today needs an infrastructure to enable access to the vast knowledge base and to share this information.

Figure 5–17
Commercial structured cabling system.

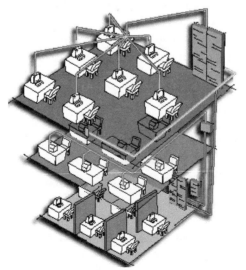

Figure 5–18
Communications technology.

Business Communication Systems

Now, let's look at another type of vendor and third-party cabling system, the Lucent Technologies Business Communications Systems (BCS), a structured cabling system. World-class telecommunications is a vital element in any business's plan to gain an edge over its competition. BCS is a developer, manufacturer, and supplier of multimedia communications services and products. These are services and products that combine the voice, data, and visual communications technologies that are currently available.

The BCS vision is to introduce its customers to the world of comprehensive, scalable multimedia communications. Through a manufacturing partnership with Honeywell, BCS in Australia manufactures its PABX, the DEFINITY Enterprise Communications Server (ECS), and exports it throughout the South Pacific. Particular emphasis is given to the following cabling system solutions.

Customer Sales and Service

Providing customers with continuous access is becoming increasingly important to forward-thinking companies. The DEFINITY call center enables companies to handle the high volume of calls based on the individual caller's needs and expectations.

Conferencing and Collaboration

A personal computer is undoubtedly the most powerful tool available to modern businesses. Adding to that power is the Lucent Technologies Multipoint Control Unit (MCU). The MCU enhances productivity through video conferencing, applications sharing, and data collaboration.

Distributed and Mobile Workforce

In today's workforce of increasing decentralization and mobility, there is a constant requirement for powerful support tools. The Lucent Technologies Forum Personal Communications Manager is a second-generation wireless communications system; it offers mobility, features, convenience, and, importantly, security.

Multimedia Messaging and Response

Effective and, above all, efficient messaging and voice response solutions bring major benefits in a business's communications with its employees, customers, prospects, and partners. Lucent Technologies offers a range of solutions to assist businesses in messaging and response capabilities, and streamlining both the internal and external communications and workflow.

Networking

In today's business environment, there's the need to be faster, work better, and do more with less. The efficient dissemination of information is crucial to this need. Thus, many of the Lucent Technologies cabling system products offer the ability to link multiple locations into a unified private network with feature and functional transparency.

In creating solutions to meet the cabling system needs of Australian businesses, BCS works closely with Bell Labs. BCS also houses the South Pacific Regional Support Center (RSC). The Center provides technical expertise to its distributors and customers. Within the Center are specialists like technical designers, test engineers, process specialists; custom software and hardware development staff, professional services consultants, application and business operations consultants; and customer trainers.

ITT CABLING SYSTEMS

Let's take a quick look at a couple of vendor and third-party cabling systems: ITT Structured Cabling System (ISCS) and the ITT Structured Networking System (ISNS). This part of the chapter presents an ongoing strategy aimed at the testing and development of both the ISCS and the ISNS. This strategy demonstrates a commitment that ITT has invested in: ensuring that the products and services delivered are designed for today's and tomorrow's standards and legislative frameworks.

Power Sum Cables, Connectors, and Systems

As previously discussed, the notion of power sum cables is not a new one; it is well documented within both ISO/IEC 11801 and ANSI/TIA/EIA-T568A, where their performance requirements and limitations are described in some detail. In short, power sum cables are designed with improved NEXT parameters that allow standard category 5 NEXT levels to be achieved on all pairs even when signals are generated on all other adjacent pairs within the sheath. Therefore, the more pairs there are within the sheath, the higher the cross-talk specification has to be to ensure that a minimum standard for category 5 performance is still attained even with active signals on all other pairs.

As there are many cables on the market capable of supporting power sum on 25 pairs, it puts into perspective just how easy it is to attain this level of performance for a 4-pair solution. Using the formula below, the improvement in NEXT required to achieve power sum NEXT on a 4-pair cable is approximately 3 dBs at 100Mhz. This is an increase from the category 5 standard of 32 dBs to 35 dBs.

PSXTALK PR1 = Square Root of $(pr2–1)^2 + (pr3–1)^2 + (pr4–1)^2$

A quality category 5 cable such as ISCS20000DSC has a worst-case acceptance criteria of 42 dBs at 100 Mhz and therefore far exceeds the requirement of power sum crosstalk.

Under section 7.5.1 of ISO/IEC 11801, power summation is described as cables whose NEXT loss performance values contained within the existing category 5 specification can be met using power summation to determine total cross-talk energy. Power summation cables are not intended to support services with different signaling schemes (different protocols).

Power sum cross talk is based upon cross talk between signals from the same type of application, and in particular those using the same spectral energy.

If one wishes to support multiple protocols within a single sheath without considerable limitations, power sum crosstalk performance is not adequate. Cables required to perform this task require an even more rigorous crosstalk performance criteria. NEXT loss between any cable unit (in the case of sheath sharing, a quad) supporting different kinds of applications simultaneously shall have an improvement in NEXT above category 5 to the level specified in section 7.5.2 of ISO/IEC 11801 and is defined by the following equation:

$$NEXT = 6 \text{ dB} + 10 \log (n + 1) \text{ dB}$$
where n = the number of adjacent units within the cable

Therefore, the installation of power sum cables does not give the end user carte blanche with respect to multiple protocol support. Power sum is a method of marketing systems in excess of category 5 performance and differentiating them from standard category 5 links and channels that can only support a single service of a single protocol rather than two services of the same or similar protocol.

This is not a major achievement; the majority of quality-balanced cables exceeds standard category 5 by the power sum requirement. This is also the case with connector technology. The ITT Cannon 808 connector, for example, exhibits a performance criteria of between 48 and 58 dBs at 100 Mhz, compared to the TSB40A requirement of 40 dBs. However, it is the performance of the system, post-installation, that is the critical issue. It is for this reason that ITT Cannon has been using power sum crosstalk limits for the pass/fail criteria. These criteria are applied across the entire installation to ensure that optimum performance of the structured cabling system is guaranteed.

Table 5–2 depicts the TSB 67 link pass/fail NEXT and ACR (power sum) limits for the ISCS and the requirements contained within standards-based test equipment [7]. ITT Cannon also insists on every installed link passing a full network test for all current and proposed MAC (medium access control) level protocols.

Table 5–2   The TSB 67 Link Pass/Fail NEXT and ACR (Power Sum) Limits for the ITT Structured Cabling System

Frequency (Mhz)	ATT	NEXT (TSB67)	NEXT Power Sum	ACR (IS 11801)	ACR Power Sum
1.00	2.1	60.0	61.8	n/a	59.7
4.00	4.0	51.8	52.7	40.0	48.7
10.00	6.3	45.5	46.8	35.0	40.3
16.00	8.2	42.3	43.7	30.0	35.5
20.00	9.2	40.7	41.7	28.0	32.5
31.25	11.5	37.6	39.6	23.0	28.1
62.50	16.7	32.7	34.5	13.0	17.8
100.00	21.6	29.3	31.4	4.0	9.8

While providing improved NEXT performance and increased ACRs (attenuation/cross-talk ratio), protocol performance will still be affected by external RF and EMI. It is for this reason that to guarantee zero error operation, the enhanced bandwidth must be protected, as in the case of ISCS, with an effective foil screen.

622 Mbps OC-12 ATM Support for Copper

The Sidebar, "ATM Physical Layer Standards," shows the current physical layer standards provided by the ATM Forum for the support of ATM services. With respect to twisted pair physical layer specifications, it is apparent that at present, no standard exists for the provision of 622 Mbps ATM services over twisted pair.

ATM PHYSICAL LAYER STANDARDS

The following are the current physical layer standards provided by the ATM Forum for the support of ATM services:

- ATM physical medium dependent interface specification for 155 Mbps over twisted pair cable, af-phy-0015.000.
- DS1 physical layer specification, af-phy-0016.000.
- Utopia Level 1 v2.01, af-phy-0017.000.
- Mid-range physical layer specification for category 3 UTP, af-phy-0018.000.
- 6,312 Kbps UNI specification, af-phy-0029.000.
- E3 UNI, af-phy-0034.000.
- Utopia Level 2 v1.0, af-phy-0039.000.
- Physical interface specification for 25.6 Mb/s over twisted pair, af-phy-0040.000.
- A Cell-based Transmission convergence sublayer for clear channel interfaces, af-phy-0043.000.
- 622.08 Mbps physical layer, af-phy-0046.000 (fiber only).
- 155.52 Mbps physical layer specification for category 3 UTP (see also UNI 3.1, af-uni-0010.002), af-phy-0047.000.
- 120 ohm Addendum to ATM PMD interface specification for 155 Mbps over TP, af-phy-0053.000.
- DS3 physical layer interface specification, af-phy-0054.000.
- 155 Mbps over MMF short wave length lasers, addendum to UNI 3.1, af-phy-0062.000.
- WIRE (PMD to TC layers), af-phy-0063.000.
- E-1, af-phy-0064.000 [ITT, 3-4].

Currently, OC-12 622 Mbps ATM utilizes NRZ (non-return to zero) encoding operating at a peak carrier frequency of 311.04 Mhz. This frequency range is far beyond the reach of any 100-ohm 4-pair structured cabling system available. Therefore, support for 622 Mbps ATM over copper will obviously mean developing new encoding schemes that will be uneconomic to manufacture in the quantities anyone at present can perceive.

An alternative option is to put the ATM signal across all four pairs and use a methodology similar to that used under IEEE 802.12, 100VG-Any-LAN. In essence, this process demodulates the 622 Mbps signal and spreads it across all four pairs. Again, although undoubtedly possible, it would mean using proprietary, uneconomic technology.

Finally, as the ATM Forum has no plans to develop a standard copper interface for 622 Mbps ATM, no sensible switch vendor is going to put R&D dollars into developing a technology to support a dubious requirement with zero demand. The reluctance of switch and NIC vendors to push for an OC-12c (optical carrier) copper interface will be further heightened by the IEEE 802.3z Gigabit Ethernet committee. This standard will contain a specification for delivering 1.0 Gbps over twisted pair at 100 meters. The ease of migration from existing Ethernet and Fast Ethernet environments along with the anticipated low cost may result in Gigabit Ethernet overtaking ATM as the most popular choice for tomorrow's backbone technology. The claims of 622 Mbps support over copper are at best marketing hype, an attempt for differentiation in a standards-based environment, or at worst a feeble effort to mislead the customer.

Radio Frequency (RF) Support via Structured Cabling Systems

Recent press releases featuring the capability to support 550 Mhz RF signals across twisted pair have certainly raised many questions both within the installer and end user community. This is not a new technology. Lucent Technologies, among others, has been producing RF baluns for over two years and has spent significant amounts of money in R&D on the subject. At first glance, the idea of delivering RF television signals over structured cabling appears to offer end users increased flexibility. However, what are its limitations? And what are the drawbacks of providing RF signals over twisted pair to the desk?

The main problem with RF TV distribution is that it was conceived for broadcasting from one single point to many points over free space in large geographical areas, and not to be used over premises cabling infrastructures in restricted environments such as an office building. Because higher frequencies suffer from more propagation attenuation than comparatively lower frequencies, it follows that the higher the frequency used to cover a given distance range, the higher the level of emitted signal required. This level is regulated by the ITU which is the body of the United Nations that produces the international telecommunications regulations, and is enforced in each country by a national governmental department such as the FCC in the United States or the Department of Trade and Industry (DTI) in the United Kingdom.

It is for these reasons that under FCC/DTI guidelines a TV-modulated RF bandwidth of 550 Mhz RF can be delivered over distances of only 196 feet of structured cabling. The number of channels assigned by the ITU for broadcasting over the 550 Mhz frequency band is very limited. The number of simultaneously usable channels is much smaller than that theoretical number due to the problem of frequency reassignment, guard bands between channels, and interchannel interference.

Traditional RF installations utilize double-shielded, double-braided coax cables and F connectors to ensure any leakage of RF signals into the environment and interference from the environment into the signals on those installations are kept to a minimum. It is very likely that serious interference from RF signals distributed over unshielded twisted pair will appear on services operating over adjacent data cables. Any RF signals must be kept completely separated from voice and data signals in nearby cables and equipment, as the effect of RF can be catastrophic.

The use of balanced transport lines will obviously reduce (not eliminate) the amount of RFI emanation, but it does not solve the problem of RF interference with voice and data services. The differences in wave form and consequently energy between networked data and RF carriers modulated with TV signals make it evident that such signals should not be put in the vicinity of each other.

Since the important thing in a trading floor or office environment is the data on the network and not the TV signals, it is obvious that alternative technologies must be used for business TV distribution. In short, customers do not want RF in their buildings. The only sensible way to achieve this scenario is to take RF from external sources and convert the signal into baseband. Once the signal is in this format, it can be safely transported around the building over twisted pair with relatively few restrictions on the number of channels available and transmission distance. This service is currently provided by systems such as Paragon's NEWS Link and Amulet's TACSI.

INTERNATIONAL CABLING SYSTEMS

Let's look at some of the international vendor and third-party cabling systems. Even though some of the vendors just discussed were international in origin, this part of the chapter will look closely at EMC Fribourg, a Swiss

testing facility that conducted comparative EMC (electro-magnetic compatibility) tests on four STP cabling systems and one UTP cabling system. Using
personal computers with IBM token ring adapter cards, all cabling systems
were configured to support the IBM 16 Mbps token ring local area network
application according to ISO 8802.5 standards.

For the UTP cabling system, SYSTIMAX SCS 1061 category 5 24-
AWG High-Performance 4-Pair UTP cable was chosen, with an M1000 Multimax Panel and M100-type information outlets (IOs) used as the connecting
hardware and a 370C1 adapter (media filter) used to link the IBM card to the
SYSTIMAX SCS UTP system.

Test Results

In radiated emissions testing for a frequency range of 30 MHz to 1 GHz in an
anaechoic chamber and in an open area test site (OATS), the SYSTIMAX
SCS UTP system met CISPR 22/EN5022 Class B requirements with a more
than adequate margin. Class B requirements are for residential use and are
more stringent than the Class A requirements for commercial use.

In conducting emissions on signal port testing at lower frequencies (150
kHz 30 MHz) with a current probe, the SYSTIMAX SCS UTP system met
the proposed CISPR 22/EN55022 Class B requirements. In IEC 801.4 electrical fast transient (EFT) noise-burst testing, the SYSTIMAX SCS UTP system did not fail even when subjected to the most strenuous test at 4,000 V.
None of the STP cabling systems survived to that level.

In IEC 801.3 radiated immunity testing, which tests the ability of a system to withstand electromagnetic interference at defined severity levels (26
MHz to 1 GHz), the SYSTIMAX SCS UTP system experienced no errors.
The one STP cabling system tested experienced errors when the media filter
was used instead of the shielded work area cable at the PC. EMC Fribourg
concluded that UTP cabling systems, and, more specifically, SYSTIMAX
SCS UTP systems, can meet the above EMC requirements.

High-Speed Data Transmission and UTP Cabling Systems

Tests conducted in well-known testing facilities show that UTP cabling systems and, specifically, SYSTIMAX SCS using UTP cable, can meet standards specifications for transmitting high-speed data within acceptable levels
and can pass all required tests. EMC tests were conducted on an ISO 8802.3
10 Mbps 10BaseT system that used SYSTIMAX SCS 1061 category 5 24-
AWG High-Performance 4-Pair UTP cable, with category 5 patch panels, cat-

egory 5 M100-type IOs, and category 5 patch cords, along with 486-type PCs and electronics from several major vendors. The tests were done at the Lucent Technologies Bell Laboratories Global Product Compliance Laboratory in Holmdel, New Jersey, and were sent to a German notified and competent body, Bundesamt fur Zulassungen in der Telekommunikation (BZT), for certification. The SYSTIMAX SCS UTP system passed every test, in some cases even exceeding the current requirements under the EMC Directive. The tests were as follows:

- Radiated emissions; specifications EN 55022, 1987, Class B limit
- Conducted emissions (AC mains); specifications EN 55022, 1987, Class B limit
- Conducted emissions (signal ports); specifications EN 50081-1, 1992, informative annex A, CISPR 22 Amendment, CISPR/G (Sec. 65), 1993, Class B limit
- Electrostatic discharge (ESD) immunity; specifications IEC 801.2, 1991, IEC CISPR 24, Part 2, prEN 55024, Part 2, contact discharge at 4,000 V (Level 2), air discharge at 8,000 V (Level 3)
- Radiated field immunity; specifications IEC 801.3, 1992, IEC CISPR 24, Part 3, prEN 55024, Part 3, 3 V/m (Level 2), 10 V/m (Level 3)
- EFT/burst immunity; IEC 801.4, 1988, IEC CISPR 24, Part 4, prEN 55024, Part 4, AC Mains at 1.0 kV (Level 2), signal/control lines at 0.5 kV (Level 2) and 1.75 kV (Level 3) [8]

EMC tests were also conducted on an ISO 9314 (ANSI X3T9.5) 100 Mbps TP-PMD LAN that used SYSTIMAX SCS 1061 category 5 24-AWG High-Performance 4-Pair UTP cable, with category 5 patch panels, category 5 M100-type IOs, and category 5 patch cords, along with 486-type PCs and electronics from several major vendors. The tests were done at the Lucent Technologies Bell Laboratories Global Product Compliance Laboratory and were sent to BZT in Germany for certification. The SYSTIMAX SCS UTP system again passed every test, in some cases even exceeding the current requirements under the EMC Directive. The tests were as follows:

- Radiated emissions; specifications EN 55022, 1987, Class B limit
- Conducted emissions (AC mains); specifications EN 55022, 1987, Class B limit

- Conducted emissions (signal ports); specifications EN 50081-1, 1992, informative annex A, CISPR 22 Amendment, CISPR/G (Sec. 65), 1993, Class B limit
- ESD immunity; specifications IEC 801.2, 1991, IEC CISPR 24, Part 2, prEN 55024, Part 2, contact discharge at 4,000 V (Level 2), air discharge at 8,000 V (Level 3)
- Radiated field immunity; specifications IEC 801.3, 1992, IEC CISPR 24, Part 3, prEN 55024, Part 3, 3 V/m (Level 2)
- EFT/burst immunity; IEC 801.4, 1988, IEC CISPR 24, Part 4, prEN 55024, Part 4, AC mains at 1.0 kV (Level 2), signal/control lines at 0.5 kV (Level 2) [Lucent, 7]

Furthermore, research conducted by the SYSTIMAX SCS Department of Lucent Technologies Bell Laboratories, together with the Advanced Multimedia Communications Department of Lucent Technologies Bell Laboratories, has demonstrated that SYSTIMAX SCS UTP systems, using 328 ft (100 m) of 1061 category 5 24-AWG High-Performance 4-Pair UTP cable, with M1000 Multimax Panels and M100-type IOs for connecting hardware along with category 5 D8AU patch cords, can successfully transmit up to 622 Mbps, the equivalent of 23,000 pages of text per second. The test used off-the-shelf high-quality red/green/blue (RGB) video equipment to provide the data stream. A studio-quality RGB video camera was used to capture a full-motion high-resolution image. Using a codec, the analog video signal from the camera was converted to an industry-standard D1 protocol digital video data stream and, at the transmitter, encoded into a 64-point carrierless amplitude and phase (64 CAP) signal. The 64 CAP encoding method was used to partition the data stream into four 155 Mbps channels at the transmitter, which were each then sent over one pair of the 4-pair cable, and then decoded and recombined into a single 622 Mbps data stream at the receiver end of the link. A codec at this end converted the signal back into an analog RGB video signal that was displayed on the monitor.

The Advantages of Using UTP Cabling Systems

STP cabling systems are more expensive and harder to install and maintain than UTP cabling systems, but are not necessarily better. As demonstrated in EMC and other test results, UTP cabling systems succeeded—even excelled—in rigorous testing. Furthermore, because it was chosen as the representative UTP cabling system, SYSTIMAX SCS demonstrated the benefits of Lucent Technologies' testing and manufacturing under rigid ISO 9000 quality control conditions. This underscores the importance of using a structured cabling system made up of products designed and manufactured to work together that meet or exceed international standards.

AMP CONNECT

This part of the chapter will not cover any vendor and third-party cabling systems, but instead will take a close look at a service that provides electrical and electronics industries with a fast, easy way to find information on over 110,000 cabling system products. This service is called AMP Connect, and the search engine is called Step Search (http://connect.ampincorporated.com/). The database is searchable by viewing pictures of cabling system products, by reviewing an alphabetical listing of products and industry names for them, or by requesting information on a specific part number.

The database presents information on cabling system products in any of the languages you select (Chinese, English, French, German, Italian, Japanese, Korean, and Spanish), as shown in Figure 5–19 [9]. The membership registration process allows you to customize your profile by selecting a language and a country of delivery.

The search engine is called Step Search. It was co-developed with Saqqara Systems, Incorporated, to provide customers with a way to select the products AMP offers quickly from the thousands of parts available worldwide. Other examples of the Step Search engine can be seen at the Saqqara

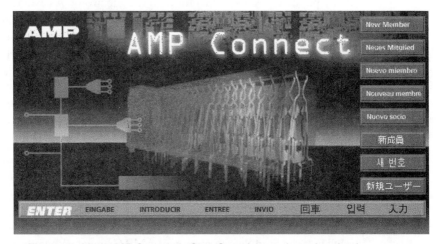

Figure 5–19   AMP Connect's Step Search search engine database menu.

web site (http://www.saqqara.com/). These provide you with some idea of how Step Search functions and are particularly useful if you are not interested in the electrical/electronics industry.

Information available from this site includes product information currently available from Saqqara, catalogs, and from the AMP Fax fax-back system. 3D CAD models in IGES (Initial Graphics Exchange Specification) format are also available for approximately 8,000 of the part numbers.

What's on AMP Connect?

Well, for one thing, there's over 110,000 part numbers online. Additional features are the direct result of customer input and AMP's move toward serving customers on a global basis. Customer requests have resulted in the following system enhancements:

- 3D models online;
- comparison table;
- additional languages; and
- smaller graphics.

3D Models

3D models of over 8,000 AMP connectors are online and available for downloading. AMP has been providing IGES versions of 3D model files for use in many popular CAD systems through the Electronic Assistance Design System (EADS) since 1991. Previously, these models were available only via CD-ROM. The addition of these files to the AMP Connect web site means that customers can obtain these same IGES files over the Internet for immediate use in their CAD systems. Customer interviews have indicated that the availability of 3D models can save up to two days of design work for each model available. Models will continue to be available on CD-ROM. A Model on Demand request system is being prepared for future release to enable customers to request 3D model files for AMP part numbers that do not currently have CAD files available. 3D model availability was the most requested addition to the AMP Connect web site from online customer feedback.

Comparison Table

To facilitate selection of parts, a comparison table feature has been incorporated into the Step Search portion of AMP Connect. When the Compare Parts button appears on the Detail View screen, you will be able to compare up to five part numbers on one screen to see the actual differences between the products. Hyperlinks to each part number's Detail View screen speed access to detailed part number information and documentation. Side-by-side comparison of several parts was also a feature requested by customers using the AMP Connect web site.

Additional Languages

Another feature is the addition of translations for much of the web site information into Japanese, Mandarin Chinese, and Korean languages. Users with browser software capable of viewing these Kanji character-based languages will be able to use Step Search to select cabling system products using their native language. These translated versions of AMP Connect will appear as gibberish to browsers not able to handle the Kanji character sets.

Graphics

In further response to customer feedback, the graphics for the welcome screen and the main menu page are being improved. The file sizes are also being reduced for faster download time.

The Step Search software allows members (currently over 68,000 worldwide) to search for interconnect devices via photographs, alphabetic lists of product names, or part numbers. Documentation is available for every part number, including customer drawings, product and application specifications, and instruction sheets. AMP plans to offer information on all standard connector part numbers through AMP Connect with over 600,000 available by the year 2002.

CERTIFICATION AND WARRANTY

Last, but not least, it's now time to take a look at certification and warranty for these vendor and third-party cabling systems. There are a number of reliable cabling system certification and warranty services available.

Design and installation of cabling systems is in accordance with TIA/EIA-T568A/569/606/607; cabling system certification is in accordance with TSB-67. This part of the chapter will review some of the most reliable cabling system certification and warranty services currently available:

- KRONE
- LRS
- Millennium Technologies of New Boston

- 3P
- PerfectSite
- SYSTIMAX SCS

KRONE

Networking information systems are becoming more and more crucial to the survival and success of companies struggling to compete in increasingly complex global markets. These networked information systems are dependent on the reliability of a behind-the-scenes physical foundation consisting of a conglomeration of copper wiring and optical fiber. Frequently this conglomeration has evolved in a haphazard, ad hoc fashion. Because of this, many of these wiring systems are unable to support some of the high-speed LAN technologies that are becoming increasingly necessary for companies attempting to stay abreast of rapidly changing technology and keep ahead of their competition.

The best way to ensure that your company's investment in a cabling system is capable of supporting high-speed networks is to install a structured cabling system. All components of a structured cabling system must meet rigorous standards. The cable and the connectors must all comply with strict requirements. A structured cabling system provides many benefits to the customer, including:

- eliminating network segmentation;
- providing logical data paths;
- ensuring that the physical requirements for communications and cabling are met;
- simplifying adds, moves, and changes;
- simplifying troubleshooting and fault isolation; and
- providing facilities management and tracking of the system [10].

Insist on Quality

By using the highest quality components to build a system and only experienced, well-trained installers who can test and certify the system's performance, you can be confident that you have invested in a foundation that is capable of supporting the inevitable advances in LAN technology. As the performance potential of copper wiring continues to climb, industry analysts have had to reevaluate the long term role of copper wiring. According to some industry experts, data rates as high 622 Mbps are well within the potential of 4-pair copper cable. This means that copper wiring is capable of supporting data at rates four times greater than the fastest rates being used today (ATM at 155 Mbps). As the data speed continues to climb, the importance of having a well-engineered, performance-certified structured cabling system becomes more and more critical.

KRONE Recommends Full Category 5 Compliance

When installing a new cabling system or upgrading an existing site, it only makes sense to comply with the current industry standards for structured cabling. Most of the cable will be hidden in walls or run above ceilings or under floors. It will be difficult to upgrade in the future. Money saved by using category 3 cabling for voice or a low-speed LAN currently in use will be lost if the system needs to be retrofitted. In the same vein, if all circuits are category 5-compliant, then all ports can be used for voice or data, providing much more versatility for moves, adds, or changes, and making installation much easier in areas where a large concentration of data devices is essential.

There has been some confusion by what actually is meant by a category 5-compliant system. With industry experts arguing about the importance of good installation practices, the confusion is increasing daily. However, by setting a performance standard that exceeds category 5 levels and backing this with a 15-year warranty for link performance, KRONE is showing that high performance cabling systems can be installed and certified by well-trained installers with the latest test equipment and the highest quality cable and components.

The Channel is the Key

At the core of any cabling system is the horizontal channel. Figures 5–20 and 5–21, respectively, show the horizontal channel models for both the U.S. standard, TIA/EIA-T568-A, and the European or international standard, ISO/IEC 11801 [KRONE, 2-3]. The major difference between the two standards is the recommended lengths between areas within the channel, but the differences are minor, and both standards are the same in the recommended distance from the station field to the telecom outlet of 90 meters maximum.

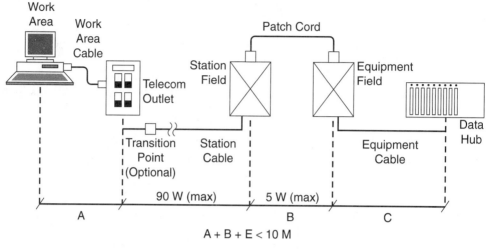

Figure 5–20   ISO/IEC 11801 horizontal link model.

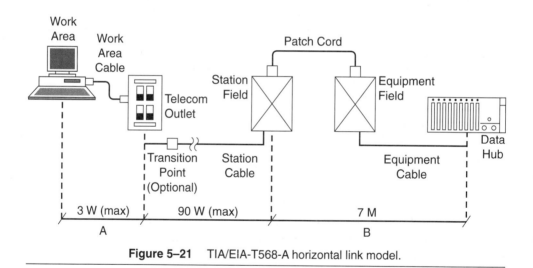

Figure 5–21   TIA/EIA-T568-A horizontal link model.

Because the link is so important, KRONE bases its system solution and its system warranty around the link. KRONE's cabling system certifier program guarantees the performance of the installed link for 15 years.

In partnership with KRONE-approved cable companies, KRONE is able to provide an installed end-to-end solution with these benefits:

- field verifiable to exceed current standards
- link bandwidth characterized up to 350 MHz
- 15-year product warranty
- 15-year performance warranty
- application independent [KRONE, 3-4]

KRONE Can be the Backbone of Any LAN Standard

Because of this strict conformance with standards, the basic KRONE system is suitable for any of the current LAN standards such as 10BaseT, 100BaseT, token ring 16, AnyLan, 100BaseVG, 3270, AS400, System 36, AppleTalk, and ISDN.

Interconnection versus Cross-Connection.   Two basic wiring schemes for the telecommunications closet are addressed in the TIA/EIA-T568-A standard: interconnection and cross-connection. Both the backbone and the horizontal cabling are terminated on connecting hardware that meets the requirements of the TIA/EIA-T568-A standard.

However, the standard prohibits the use of these terminations for moves, adds, and changes. Any connection between the backbone and horizontal cabling must be accomplished through the use of a horizontal cross-connect between the common equipment and the connecting hardware to which the horizontal cabling is terminated, as shown in Figure 5–22

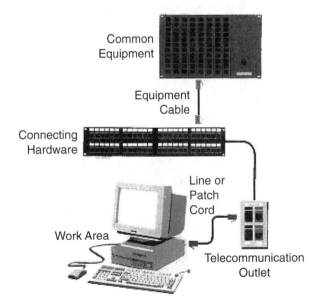

Common Equipment

Equipment Cable

Connecting Hardware

Line or Patch Cord

Work Area

Telecommunication Outlet

Figure 5–22
A horizontal cross-connect between the common equipment and the connecting hardware.

[KRONE, 4]. This connection may be made using an interconnection or a cross-connection cabling scheme, which provides for a direct connection between two cables with the use of patch cords or jumper wires.

A cross-connection is a cabling scheme between cabling runs, subsystems, and equipment using patch cords or jumper wires that attach to connection hardware on each end, as shown in Figure 5–23 [KRONE, 5]. Common equipment that uses cables that extend an individual port may be permanently terminated or interconnected to the connecting hardware for the horizontal cabling. Direct interconnections such as this reduce the number of connections in a link, but may also reduce the flexibility.

Common equipment that uses cables that consolidate several ports on a single connector (such as a 50-pin connector) must first be terminated to connecting hardware to break out the individual ports. The connecting hardware fields for the common equipment and the horizontal cabling may then be cross-connected using patch cords or jumper wires.

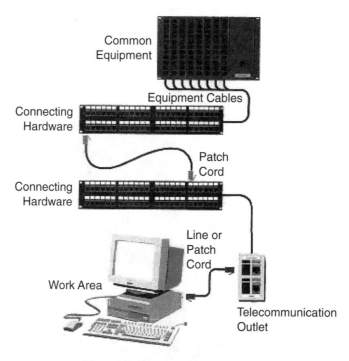

Figure 5–23   A cross-connection.

The DOs and DON'Ts of Common Installation Practices

A successful, high-performance premises wiring system requires more than simply purchasing the proper standards-compliant cables and hardware. Care must be taken to ensure that the components are installed properly according to industry-recognized practices. Performance specifications called out in the TIA/EIA-T568-A standard are based on the assumption that proper installation techniques and management practices have been followed. If recommended cabling precautions and installation methods are not observed, specified transmission capabilities of cabling components may not be achieved, as discussed in the Sidebar, "Common Installation Practices DOs and DON'Ts." Installation should be performed by trained, certified installers, such as the authorized Belden/KRONE cabling system certifiers who can provide a product and performance warranty for 15 years.

COMMON INSTALLATION PRACTICES
DOs AND DON'Ts

If the recommended cabling precautions and installation methods are not observed, specified transmission capabilities of cabling components may not be achieved.

Do:

- Pull cables to minimize the distance of the run and eliminate large loops.
- Bundle cables in a neat, orderly fashion.
- Follow recommendations for cable bend radius. In spaces with UTP terminations, cable bend radius should not be less than four times the cable diameter for horizontal cable, and should not be less than 10 times the cable diameter for multipair cable.
- Make sure that pair twists are maintained within 1/2 inch (12 mm) of the termination point.

Don't:

- Exceed 110 newtons (25 lb/f) of pulling force when running cables.
- Cinch cable bundles too tightly.
- Ever bend or kink cable too sharply.
- Untwist pairs when terminating [KRONE, 5–6].

The information presented in the sidebar will receive expanded coverage in Chapter 27, "Standards Development." The chapter goes into great depth to discuss the TIA/EIA standard with regard to the use of cable ladders, how much cables can be bent, and so on.

Structured Cabling Services

High speed networks require sophisticated cabling systems to support the increasing demands for speed and reliability. The LRS (Levi, Ray, & Shoup, Inc.) network consulting practice assists organizations with their cabling system needs, including:

- hardware and software selection;
- facilities review;
- diagnostics and troubleshooting;
- cabling design and testing; and
- professional infrastructure documentation [11].

Structured cabling systems support a wide variety of connections and systems. Today, many technologies, including telephony, networks, multimedia, and much more, are now carried over a single wiring system. Proper design and compliance with industry standards are two of the many issues that must be considered when initiating or rehabilitating a structured cabling system.

LRS cabling specialists provide assistance with all phases of your wiring project. Obviously, the best time to install cable is during the planning stage of a new building, addition, or remodeling project. However, LRS can assist in all projects during any phase, including renovations, remodels, and upgrades to existing equipment.

Cabling is a game of standards. Each platform required has a different set of requirements and equipment that must be in compliance. LRS consultants are trained to comply with all EIA/TIA/NEC specifications and certification criteria.

With the multitude of cable types now available, it is difficult to find a vendor well versed in all of them. There are many types, including phone, shielded twisted pair, unshielded twisted pair, coax, and optical fiber. LRS can help you select the appropriate media type for the environment required.

What can you do when your cabling system is already in place? Oftentimes you are faced with a decision to enhance, upgrade, or replace the entire system. LRS has the latest testing and certification tools required to determine the current status of your cabling infrastructure.

Cabling systems are complex vehicles for the information superhighway and, as with any technology-based product, problems can and do arise. Many instances of cabling failure can be resolved with minimal trouble. However, there are some cases that require sophisticated tools and techniques to fully isolate the problem. This service is just a small part of the many other diagnostic services the LRS network consulting practice offers.

Millennium Technologies of New Boston

The building industry has been all too slow to recognize the importance of modern communications cabling systems. In planning, architects have always provided for adequate electrical, plumbing, and HVAC (heating, ventilation, and air conditioning) systems. Apart from small closets designed for the telephone company, space for other cabling systems and components has all but been ignored in new construction. New construction requires forethought and planning for the inevitable computer that sits next to the telephone.

Cable Infrastructure

Building owners, architects, and contractors take no responsibility for the lack of proper communications support within a new structure. After all, intent of use is not their problem. Yet today, it is almost inconceivable that any tenants would be without computer networks or computers. Intelligent buildings use cabling systems for energy management. Security-conscious owners and tenants require cabled security systems and cameras. The list of cabled devices is endless; installation of these systems is an afterthought.

New cable installations begin just before or shortly after people move in. Over time people move out, new ones move in, and the cabling mess starts all over. If walls are torn down, contractors cut the old wiring flush with the ceiling. The other 90 percent of it remains in a ceiling above the hallways. If a network problem occurs and technicians can't resolve the problem, they quickly install a new cable eliminating that as the potential culprit.

The end result of continuous cabling is generally a series of unmarked outlets. In the hallways outside the offices, the suspended ceilings have a series of broken ceiling tiles damaged by careless cable installers. Above the tiles, invisible to the building occupants, a cable installer has broken through a fire wall to pull in some new cable. The careless installer failed to refill the opening with fire-retardant foam. A week later, fire and smoke race through the compromised fire wall and several people die needlessly. Paradoxically, it was another well-engineered cable system that sent a signal to close a fire door not more than three feet below the compromised fire wall. It functioned as planned but could not help the hapless victims.

Of far less concern, old cable is generally abandoned in place. After all, when is the last time you heard of cable being removed from the ceiling when somebody moves? Nobody knows where the old cable goes and what it was used for. There are no records available. It's a mystery and it's far easier to install new cable. The old cable becomes a permanent fixture and part of the building architecture. Eventually, the area above the drop ceiling becomes congested. It is impossible to efficiently install any new infrastructure, including electrical cable, plumbing, and HVAC.

Cable installations vary in quality and resultant performance. Unfortunately, lack of compliance to standards has caused a great deal of concern for those who have the responsibility for maintaining building infrastructure. This task normally falls on the building engineers and facility managers. The rush to get wired has created a gold rush for cable installers. The quality of low-voltage cable installations is all over the map.

The BICSI logo on the home page (http://www.bicsi.org/corpmemb.htm) identifies Millennium Technologies of New Boston as a corporate member of BICSI. The company supports BICSI and their RCDD (Registered Communications Distribution Designer) certification program. RCDD designation provides assurance that a cable installation will meet the qualifications required for technical craftsmanship, performance, safety, and many other standards. The company encourages anyone who wants to seek a career in low-voltage cable installation to obtain a coveted certification.

Companies intent on saving money sometimes exacerbate poor installation practices by selecting the low bidder to an RFP (request for proposal). The lowest bid may not be the most qualified bid and may invite trouble. Millennium Technologies of New Boston urges buyers of cable systems to check installers' qualifications carefully. In the RFP, find out how many certified installers the cable company proposes to use on your job. Make sure that number appears in the contract along with the names of those on the job. Your project consultant should check for certifications. Certification within an installation company can run from all installers to only supervisors or a project manager. If work is closely supervised and inspected, perhaps certification at the supervisory level is adequate. In a typical two-person installation team, one person should be certified. Millennium Technologies of New Boston feels it is impossible for a project manager who holds RCDD certification to guarantee the quality of a large installation. A large installation could use several two-person teams installing cable in a large building or campus environment over a period of days, weeks, or months. A certified project manager cannot be with every installer all the time, particularly on larger projects.

In the days before divestiture, telephone company installers worked with pretty much the same type of installations daily. Installers of telephones used plain old telephone wire. There are installations still working today that are older than most of the readers of this book. The information age, the digital age, or just plain evolution of technology changed all that. It seems everything is wired (there is even a magazine called *Wired!*). Cable-connected devices all have an interface specification that dictates the type of connection required for that wired device.

Typically, a television will use a coaxial cabling system. A telephone can use a category 3 copper cable for connection to a network but a computer may require a high performance category 5 cable. An MRI (magnetic resonance imaging) system may specify multimode fiber optic cabling. The options and configurations are almost endless depending on intended use and the environment.

If you prefer to manage a major installation internally, do so with a dedicated staff to make the project a success! A retrofit or new project of several hundred distribution points or more will require from one to three staff members. Selecting a cable installation company should be accomplished through the RFI (request for information) and RFP processes. Use the same due diligence you would use in selecting a software application vendor. The RFP process is an important tool to use in the selection process.

3P: Third-Party Link Testing and Certification of Existing Cable for Data Applications

Link testing is still the superior way for the end user to prove the quality of his or her installation. National and international requirements have been agreed to through the standards ISO/IEC 11801 and EN 50173, which fortunately are identical with respect to link specifications.

The benefits for end users are evident. They can let the link requirements in the above standards form the contractual conditions for accepting the final installation. Using standards for acceptance testing does not depend on supplier warranties to secure transmission performance. In addition, users can have a larger extent of supplier and installer independence. And they will get the highest possible quality just by requiring an installation acceptance test. What supplier or installer would risk a recabling by failing a final installation testing?

Today's problem is not link requirements, which are generally clear (except maybe for the different definitions of links, basic links, horizontal links, and channels). The main obstacle has been and still is how to make a fast and reliable verification of a Class D installation (going to 100 MHz). Two different methods may be applied: measurements with laboratory equipment (network analyzers, etc.) and measurements with hand-held field testers.

Measurements with Laboratory Equipment

Link measurements with laboratory equipment may be performed accurately by the very experienced operator, but it is a slow, difficult, and impractical way to demonstrate performance. A few very tricky pitfalls exist if you are not experienced in measuring short lengths of cable, for instance, with respect to impedance measurements. However, it is outside the scope of this chapter to discuss details of link testing with laboratory equipment. 3P recommends that laboratory equipment be used only to verify performance in case of disputes, to demonstrate performance on a limited statistical basis, and to verify precision of hand-held testers.

Measurements with Hand-Held Field Testers

Link measurements with hand-held testers can be performed fast by a trained operator allowing a 100 percent verification of all links of an installation. Testers for Class D installations have been available for approximately four years, but the quality of some early testers has been questionable, both with respect to precision and extent of testing performed. Most testers can perform verification of only some of the specified requirements. Low-quality testers may both accept bad installations and reject good installations. The first point normally makes everyone happy (maybe only until traffic on the network is later stressed or transmission rate is increased), while the second point may create a million-dollar panic without reason.

Quality of testers has been continuously improved by the manufacturers and parallel work in development of a specification for hand-held testers has been completed. The resulting document, TIA Telecommunications Service Bulletin TSB 67, has been agreed to and specifies two different quality levels of testers (Accuracy Level I and Accuracy Level II testers). Performance of Level II testers is the best, and some early model testers would probably have difficulties even in passing the Level I requirements.

Accurate and complete link testing with hand-held testers is a key issue for modern cabling. Therefore, 3P will evaluate the quality of commercial testers and continue to publish summarized performance data sheets on their web site (http://www.3ptest.dk/). Recommendations on how to perform an installation test with a specific type of hand-held tester is found in the performance data sheet of the tester in question.

PerfectSite

PerfectSite[SM] helps define requirements that match your organization's connectivity needs. It specifies structured cabling systems that give performance and value over the structured cabling system life cycle.

Problems typically arise in an open-office environment when cubicles are torn down and reconstructed. Unexpected recabling costs occur because of a poor up-front needs analysis of the company churn rate. By providing strategically located consolidation points and multiuser outlets, the future costs of moves, adds, and changes to your structured cabling system will be reduced over its life cycle.

Bid Creation and Evaluation

It's easy to get confused by vendors' differing terminology, which applies to contractor performance and service as well as hardware components.

When providing bid specifications, it has become a de facto standard to say, "Yes, Yes, Yes," when bidding on a poorly written RFP. Then, upon execution of the contract, say, "No, No, No," on as many items as possible (and being legally right), thus increasing the value of the contract many times over the original award price.

Manufacturer Product Evaluation

There are many different manufacturers of structured cabling systems. The components are independently tested for transmission performance as required by TIA/EIA-T568-A, ISO/IEC 11801, and other standards.

In addition to the testing that already exists, PerfectSiteSM tests the functionality of the mechanical design of the components. Is the vertical management that came with your rack adequate for high-density patching? This might seem like a harmless question, until you start installing a lot of patch cords and end up with a rat's nest. Or is the multiuser outlet designed for easy access, but when installed on a surface, activates a defective hinge, making it difficult to open and causing possible future breakage?

An end user typically finds out about these problems when it is too late—after an installation. In addition to PerfectSite's testing, feedback on products is gathered from 800+ contractors who have worked with them all over the world.

System Warranty Evaluation

For peace of mind and protection of your investment, the system warranty is an excellent option. However, every manufacturer's warranty can be different and unclear. How do you know what you are getting? If a problem arises down the road, where do you go to get it corrected? Who is responsible, the certified contractor or the manufacturers?

You installed a category 5, UTP-structured cabling system last year and have recently migrated to 100BaseT, but are experiencing intermittent problems with transmission. First, you call in your firm's data consultant. After exhaustive testing (all billable), the consultant blames it on the cabling system. Second, you contact the certified cabling contractor who performed the installation. After more testing, the contractor finds out that it is a delay skew problem with the 2×2 construction of the category 5 UTP plenum cable. Third, the certified contractor notifies the manufacturer, but finds that it is not covered under the 15-year warranty because it met the TIA/EIA-T568-A standard at the time of installation. The final result: all of the category 5 UTP cabling must be replaced at your expense.

Service companies like PerfectSite can sift through the legalese and paperwork to try and ensure that you get the full benefits of the warranty that you paid for. The service company is a member of U.S. and international standards committees and can respond to potential problems that are presently being addressed in the standards, but may take years to resolve and incorporate into existing or new standards. This insight can save clients thousands of dollars in the life cycle of their structured cabling system and provide a more comprehensive system warranty, with fewer contractual loop holes.

SYSTIMAX SCS

For UTP cabling systems such as the Lucent Technologies SYSTIMAX Structured Cabling Systems, all of the individual products certified for use are manufactured by Lucent Technologies and individually tested, as well as tested in conjunction with other products in the SYSTIMAX SCS offering. All cables, for example, are tested on the reel at the point of manufacture and are also tested as a complete cabling system within the individual applications for which they are certified. All products certified for use in SYSTI-MAX SCS also carry a 15-year warranty.

SYSTIMAX SCS utilizes Lucent Technologies Bell Laboratories-developed design rules for all certified end-to-end applications. Such design rules, which are fully documented in Lucent Technologies application guidelines, cite which products may be used (for example, only category 5 products for some higher-speed applications), how cable must be terminated and administered, and maximum distances for cable runs. All applications are also tested in Lucent Technologies Bell Laboratories test labs and are certified for a period of 15 years. Consequently, both products and systems are fully tested and warranted.

622 Mbps Warranty Guarantee

This final part of the chapter is written to provide supplemental information concerning the inclusion of 622 Mbps coverage in the SYSTIMAX SCS extended product warranty and application assurance program. Lucent Technologies will guarantee that each SYSTIMAX SCS channel comprised of end-to-end power sum products is capable of delivering 622 Mbps to the workstation. In the short term, this can be accomplished with an implementation that transmits 155 Mbps over each of the four pairs in a parallel transmission scheme using 64-point carrierless amplitude and phase (64 CAP) encoding technology.

64 CAP is a bandwidth-efficient transmission scheme that sends multiple symbols simultaneously. Utilizing a two-dimensional modulation constellation, 64 CAP uses a set of 8 points in each dimension, for a total of 8 x 8 or 64 points. Specialized symbol waveshaping and orthogonal modulation mean that they do not interfere with each other and can be recognized and distinguished at the receiver. The transmission rate is 25.92 M_Symbols per second. Two orthogonal symbols each carry 3 bits of information. With this, each pair supports 155 Mbps. To achieve 622 Mbps, all four pairs are used. The data stream is partitioned into four 155 Mbps channels at the transmitter. The four channels are recombined into a single data stream at the receiver.

Lucent Technologies and Bell Laboratories (formerly the research and development arm of AT&T) have been demonstrating the feasibility of delivering a 622 Mbps data stream using parallel transmission schemes over a 100-meter channel. Their evaluation, testing, and understanding of this concept, coupled with improved electrical performance, now allows Lucent to move from a laboratory experiment to a SYSTIMAX guarantee.

As future networking standards are developed and issued, other methods of delivering 622 Mbps will become available. Future LAN equipment will be tested and evaluated by Bell Laboratories for coverage under the SYSTIMAX SCS Applications Assurance Program.

FROM HERE

This chapter covered different types of vendor and third-party cabling systems: Lucent Technologies Systimax and Powersum; 3Com Corporation's cabling system, IBM Cabling System; Nortel IBDN, AMP Connect, KRONE; Mod-Tap, BCS, ITT, as well as a number of cabling system certification and warranty service companies. The next chapter opens up Part II, "Designing Cabling Systems," and presents an overview of network design issues and how they can help you design and install a better cabling system. In addition, there will also be a discussion about various category 5 structured wiring components and how they all fit together.

NOTES

[1]   Dekko Engineering , P.O. Box 2,000, Kendallville, IN 46755, 2000, p. 3.

[2]   R.J. Paradine Jr., RCDD, "An Overview of SYSTIMAX® Structured Connectivity Solutions (SCS)," 200 Laurel Avenue, Middletown, NJ 07748, Lucent Technologies Inc., 600 Mountain Avenue, Murray Hill NJ 07974, U.S.A., (Copyright © 1999), p. 2.

[3]   Philippe Ginier-Gillet and Christopher T. DiMinico, "1000BASE-T: Gigabit Ethernet Over Category 5 Copper Cabling," 3Com Corporation, Santa Clara Site, 5400 Bayfront Plaza, Santa Clara, CA 95052, 2000.

[4]   "The IBM Cabling System, " Cabletron Systems, 35 Industrial Way, Rochester, NH 03866 U.S.A, 2000, pp. 1–2.

[5]   South Hills Datacomm, 760 Beechnut Drive, Pittsburgh, PA 15205, 2000, p. 1.

[6]   "Residential Cabling System," MOD-TAP USA, Box 706, 285 Ayer Road, Harvard, MA 01451-0706, 2000, p. 1.

[7]   "An investigation into the ability of Power Sum cables to support Radio Frequency (RF) and OC-12c ATM," ITT Cannon, Systems & Services, Jays Close, Viables Estate, Basingstoke, Hampshire, England, RG22 4BW, 1998, p. 3.

[8]   "UTP vs STP: A Comparison of Cables, Systems, and Performance Carrying High-Data-Rate Signals," Lucent Technologies Inc., 600 Mountain Avenue, Murray Hill NJ 07974, U.S.A., (Copyright © 1998), pp. 6–7.

[9]   Reprinted with the permission of AMP Incorporated, REGIONAL CENTER, Harrisburg, PA, USA, 1998, p. 1.

[10]   "Standards-Based Structured Wiring," KRONE Asia Pacific, KRONE (Australia) Technique Pty Ltd, 2 Hereford Street, Berkeley Vale, N.S.W. 2261, Australia, 1998, p. 2.

[11]   "Structured Cabling Services," Levi, Ray, & Shoup, Inc., 2401 West Monroe Street, Springfield, IL 62704, 2000, p. 1.

Designing Cabling Systems

CHAPTER 6

Network Design Issues

Traditionally, most computer system and network designers have developed their products with the idea in mind that they will operate on a specific type of cable using a specific type of connector. Each manufacturer has its own cable and connector standard, which is another way of saying that there are no general or independent standards that everyone must follow! Here are some examples:

- DEC: 3-pair UTP and modified modular connectors
- FDDI: 62.5 micron fiber and MIC connector
- IBM S/3x and AS/400: 100 ohm Twinax and Twinax connectors
- IBM 3270: 93 ohm coax and BNC connectors
- IBM token ring: 150 ohm shielded twisted pair & IBM data connector
- Hewlett Packard 3000: RS-232 cable and DB connectors
- Ethernet: 50 ohm coaxial cable & BNC or N connectors
- Wang: dual 75 ohm coax & BNC-TNC connectors[1]

It's easy to see from the list above that migrating from one type of computer system or network to another is very difficult in a traditionally wired cabling system. In most cases, the entire cabling system, and the investment it represents, must be abandoned and a new cabling system must be installed, which can cost more than the networking hardware itself.

---

[1] Stephen Kayworth, "Structured Cabling Systems," South Hills Datacomm, 760 Beechnut Drive, Pittsburgh, PA 15205, 1998, p.1.

Another expense related to any traditionally wired cabling system is the cost of making moves, changes, or adds after the original installation is completed. The topology, or physical layout, of the cabling system has a lot to do with how easy it is to make changes. For example, the daisy chain or bus topology, which is used for both Thinwire Ethernet and IBM's System/3X and AS/400, does not lend itself well to change because cables either have to be moved, extended, or added whenever a new person is hired or an existing employee is moved. In a large network, this can become a full-time job in and of itself! The most common network topologies are shown later in this chapter.

The problems just previously described are common with these nonstructured wiring systems. The two foremost characteristics of this type of cabling system are that it is difficult or impossible to migrate from one computer system to another without replacing the entire cabling system and, to make moves, changes, or additions, the cabling system has to be changed. In this sense, the cabling system has no real structure, since it is constantly changing as user requirements change, hence the term "nonstructured."

To overcome these problems, many companies are installing structured wiring systems similar to the one shown in Figure 6–1 in which the cabling, once installed, rarely needs to be changed [Kayworth, 2]. Of the three topologies illustrated later in the chapter, the star is the most flexible, since all cable runs are brought to one central location. By prewiring all possible locations

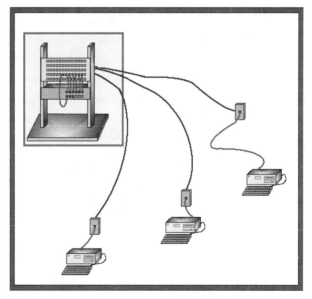

Figure 6–1   Typical structured cabling system.

in a new or existing building in a star topology, all future moves, changes, and additions can be made quickly and easily by simply moving patch cables in a centralized wiring closet. Also, by simply changing the attachment cables and devices at the equipment rack and the workstation outlet, a structured cabling system can be adapted to a variety of systems and interfaces.

COMPONENTS

As defined earlier, a structured cabling system is one in which the main components of the system, once installed, do not change. In its most basic form, a structured cabling system consists of horizontal wiring and appropriate connecting hardware. Before proceeding further, let's define some of the terms used in structured cabling design as well as some of the network design issues.

Category

The EIA/TIA-T568-A standard specifies certain performance and speed characteristics for structured cabling systems. These specifications follow a category system, where each category specifies a certain level of performance.

The EIA/TIA-T568-A standard starts with category 3, and goes to category 5. Categories 1 and 2 are not officially recognized, but are generally used in the cabling industry as being useful at frequencies of 1 MHz and 4 MHz, respectively. Category 3 specifies a cable rated for frequencies up to 10 MHz, category 4 cables are rated at up to 20 MHz, and category 5 is rated up to 100 MHz. Nowadays, category 3 cable is widely regarded as being a voice-grade cable, and most new data installations use category 5.

Topology

The topology is the physical layout of network components (cable, stations, systems equipment, etc.). A universal topology is where unshielded twisted pair cabling is used as the horizontal connection between wall plates and a distribution frame. A distribution frame serves as a concentration point and provides cross-connections between network components. When necessary, a backbone connects multiple distribution frames with file servers and other systems equipment. The backbone may be coax, optical fiber, UTP trunks, or a combination of these media. Communications systems can also be cabled to a distribution frame for cross-connection.

Specific benefits are derived from this design. For example:

- A system can be easily reconfigured by simply changing cross-connects at the distribution frames.
- LANs and other new applications can be added easily by bolting the equipment into the frame and connecting to the appropriate horizontal/trunk channels.
- Workstations can be moved by simply changing cross-connections.
- Workstations can be added by installing patching into the expansion space provided.
- Phone lines can be cross-connected to computer LAN cabling to provide quick and easy fax/modem connections.

10BaseT Cabling Specification

The IEEE 802.3 10BaseT specification is the standard for Ethernet communications over unshielded twisted pair (UTP) cabling. Application of this technology offers substantial advantages:

- It employs the most widely accepted standard for computer LAN connection, providing the widest range of product options and future stability.
- Star topology provides clean, attractive cable installations between distribution frames and wall plates. Systems can easily be relocated without termination concerns or modification of cabling.
- It eliminates daisy-chained terminals and their related problems, such as cable-driven system failures.
- It has the potential for use of existing building data and voice cabling for implementation of a LAN.
- It provides the ability to integrate Ethernet into a UTP structured cabling system, including the capability to run token ring and Ethernet over the same cabling plan.
- It replaces RS232 UTP channels with Ethernet LAN service.

There are two major components in a 10BaseT communications link: a concentrator and a transceiver. The concentrator (or hub) is a multichannel device connecting multiple transceivers. It is usually located in a distribution frame in a wiring closet or other central location where it is patched to the building wiring. The concentrator interface will typically be a group of

WE8W RJ45 modular jacks or a 50-position telco connector. The transceiver may be an independent device or a card in a personal computer that connects the workstation to the building wiring. Therefore, a concentrator supports multiple transceivers, each individually star-wired.

Horizontal Cabling

Horizontal cabling begins at a centrally located point called a distribution frame and ends where the user plugs a terminal in. A separate horizontal cable is run from a distribution frame to each wall plate where a computer or device might be connected to the network. Distribution frames should be located so horizontal cable length is limited to 300 feet to provide compatibility with high-speed LAN operation. When horizontal cabling is properly designed, each office interface is accessible from an appropriate distribution frame. In other words, this is the wiring that runs from the telecommunications wiring closet to the workstation outlet. For each workstation outlet, there will be one or more cable runs back to the wiring closet, depending on how many jacks are needed at the workstation outlet.

Distribution Frames

The distribution frame is a central management point for horizontal cable runs. At this point, each cable run is punched down to a patching field. The patching field enables specific wall ports to be connected to a concentrator. Concentrators and other systems equipment in the distribution frame are connected via the backbone. Each distribution frame should be located so that the horizontal cabling length is limited to 300 feet to ensure compatibility with high-speed LAN operation. The cable run should be free of bridges, taps, and splices from the wall plate or other office interface to the cross connect product. The main distribution frame should be located in the same wiring closet or central location as the communications equipment. This enables easy cross-connection from phone lines to computer systems, as well as simplified and safe management of building wiring. Multiple distribution frames may be connected via the backbone.

Backbone Cabling

Backbone, or trunk cabling, provides the main feeder cable in a building. Backbone cabling can be either campus style, where it connects several buildings, or it can be run vertically between floors to connect several subdistribution frames to the main distribution frame. Each backbone segment must not exceed a cable length of 1,000 feet. In other words, this is the cabling that provides the interconnection between wiring closets and equipment rooms, whether in the same or different buildings. It includes the backbone cabling itself, as well as cross-connects, mechanical terminations, and patch cables used to provide backbone-to-backbone cross-connection.

Connecting Hardware

Connecting hardware (systems connections) is used to terminate the horizontal wiring in the wiring closet or at the workstation outlet. It exists between system equipment such as file servers, concentrators, patch bays, other devices installed in the distribution frame, and backbone cabling or trunk channels. Patch panels, used in the wiring closet, and wall plates, used at the desktop, fall into this category. The EIA/TIA-T-568A standard specifies RJ45 jacks to be used in these types of products. Patch panels provide multiple RJ45 jacks, often in multiples of 12, and are designed to fit into standard racks or cabinets with 19-inch mounting rails. Wall plates come in a variety of types, ranging from single outlet, flush mount styles to multioutlet, multimedia surface-mount versions. Most connecting hardware will also accommodate other types of connectors, such as RJ11, BNC, and fiber optic, for use in telephone or non-EIA/TIA applications.

Category 5 (or 100 MHz capable) connecting hardware is routinely constructed using a circuit board design with RJ45 jacks mounted on the front and AT&T 110-type contacts mounted on the rear. The 110 contact uses insulation displacement technology to terminate the horizontal wiring to the RJ45 jack. Although the AT&T 110 contact is the most popular method of terminating the horizontal wiring to the jack, other types, such as the KRONE and 66 contact, are also used by some manufacturers.

Patch Cables

Patch cables are used to make the physical connection between the connecting hardware and the network or telecommunications equipment. At the wiring closet, patch cables are used to facilitate fast and easy moves, changes, or additions to the network. At the desktop, they make the connection to user equipment such as network interface cards.

It is debatable whether patch cables can be considered a part of the structured wiring system. By definition, they are not, because their use changes as the needs of the network users change, but they are so well-defined by the ANSI/TIA/EIA-T568-A standard that it is an easy intellectual jump to include them in any discussion of structured wiring.

INSTALLATION PLANNING AND PRACTICES

It has been said that a chain is only as strong as its weakest link. Similarly, a structured wiring system is only as fast as its slowest component. When planning and installing your wiring system, pay particular attention to the components you choose. It does no good, for example, to install the highest quality category 5 cabling and connecting hardware and then use category 3 patch cables. At best, your structured wiring system will provide you with category 3 performance. Installing higher performance products may cost a bit more up front, but not so much as replacing components later. Pinching pennies makes short-term sense, but the long-term flexibility of your wiring system will be limited, and you could spend more upgrading to a category 5 cabling system than you would have installing it in the first place.

Figure 6–2 illustrates the way in which the various components mentioned previously are connected together to create a structured wiring system [Kayworth, 4]. Keeping in mind that every connection you make is a point of weakness, plan your installation with as few connections as possible between

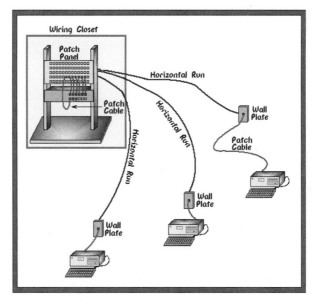

Figure 6–2   Structured cabling system.

the wallplate and patch panel. With the right products and careful planning, your structured wiring installation will be a great success.

Now, let's look at the major cable topologies: daisy chain, bus, star, and tree. Pros, cons, and typical networks that use those topologies are given.

TOPOLOGY

There are two types of topology: physical and logical. The physical topology of a network refers to the configuration of cables, computers, and other peripherals. Logical topology is the method used to pass the information between workstations. Issues involving logical topologies are beyond the scope of this chapter.

Main Types of Physical Topologies

The cable topology describes the way that stations on the network are connected together. Each topology has its own advantages and disadvantages. Structured wiring systems use the star topology. There are four major cable topologies: daisy chain, bus, star, and tree. Computer networks generally use one topology, though ARCnet can mix bus and star. Office telephones (one extension per phone) use a star configuration, while home telephones (all on one extension) are often daisy-chained. This part of the chapter discusses the physical topologies used in network design and other related topics or issues:

- daisy chain
- linear bus
- star
- star-wired ring
- tree

ARCnet is short for Attached Resource Computer network, ARCnet is one of the oldest, simplest, and least expensive types of local-area networks. ARCnet was introduced by Datapoint Corporation in 1968. It uses a token-ring architecture, supports data rates of 2.5 Mbps, and connects up to 255 computers. A special advantage of ARCnet is that it permits various types of transmission media (twisted-pair wire, coaxial cable, and fiber optic cable) to be mixed on the same network. A new specification, called ARCnet Plus, will support data rates of 20 Mbps.

Daisy Chain

In a daisy chain, each station is plugged into the device upstream and downstream from itself. Phonenet and EtherWave are two cabling systems that daisy chain devices together.

Phonenet relates to the ability of TSX networking to work through serial lines, usually with modems and telephone lines. As you may be aware, TCP/IP has an inherent facility named SLIP/PPP for interfacing to serial lines. However, Phonenet extends serial-based networking by providing a number of advanced capabilities. The two capabilities of Phonenet that the sysop of a BBS are likely to be concerned with are the ability to provide service for incoming SLIP and PPP connections. When a remote user asks to go into SLIP or PPP mode (which creates a SLIP/PPP connection between the networking software on the remote computer and the networking software on your system), Phonenet locates an available pseudo-tty (PTY) and interconnects it with the serial port to which the user is connected. Providing this type of pass-through SLIP/PPP service requires you to have been assigned not just one, but a block of IP addresses by your Internet provider. This is necessary because these IP addresses will be temporarily assigned to your users' home computers when they are in SLIP or PPP mode. You cannot arbitrarily assign IP addresses to the remote end of a pass-through SLIP/PPP connection.

EtherWave provides two RJ45 ports so you can daisy chain devices off each other or off a port on a traditional Ethernet hub [2]. EtherWave technology is 100 percent compatible with other Ethernet devices and includes these additional innovations: 1) auto-crossover: add, move, and change nodes in your network without having to keep track of the relative positions of the hubs or any other device in the chain; 2) power-off pass-through: EtherWave networks continue to function properly even when one or more computers are turned off; and 3) self-terminating: add nodes without affecting the rest of the network; if a cable breaks, it won't bring down the network.

Advantages.   These (Phonenet and EtherWave) are very easy to put together. They require a minimum of cable because you only need enough cable to chain the stations together. It's easy to add more devices anywhere in the chain. You don't have to worry about having enough network jacks present.

Disadvantages.   A component failure (particularly with Etherwave) or cable failure in midstream will down the entire network. Also, if you want to add a device in the middle of the chain, the network will be down while you add the device. The cabling for these networks is generally out in the open and more vulnerable to accidental disconnections and breaks.

Linear Bus

The linear (shared multidrop bus) topology is the traditional topology that most people think of when a computer bus is mentioned. VME, Ethernet, and 1553 are all popular examples of this topology. Because a linear bus is inherently fault intolerant (any node can take the bus down and prevent communication by other nodes), military mission-critical computers using this topology usually implement it in a redundant format. Basically, a linear bus topology consists of a main run of cable with a terminator at each end, as shown in Figure 6–3. All nodes (file server, workstations, and peripherals) are connected to the linear cable. Ethernet and LocalTalk networks use a linear-hierarchical bus topology, as shown in Table 6–1.

In a bus topology, all stations are attached to the same cable. The most popular networks using a bus topology are 10BASE2 and 10BASE5 Ethernet. ARCnet can also run on a bus topology.

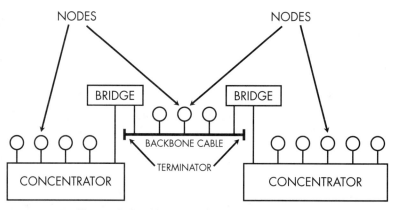

Figure 6–3   Linear bus/hierarchical topology.

Table 6–1 Comparison Chart

Topology	Type of Cable	Type of Protocol
Linear hierarchical bus	coaxial twisted pair fiber optic	Ethernet Fast Ethernet LocalTalk
Star	twisted pair fiber optic	Ethernet Fast Ethernet LocalTalk
Star-wired ring	twisted pair	token ring
Tree	coaxial twisted pair fiber optic	Ethernet Fast Ethernet

Advantages and Disadvantages of Linear Bus Topology. Some of the advantages of linear bus topology are that it's easy to connect a computer or peripheral to a linear bus and it requires less cable length than a star topology. The Sidebar, "Choosing a Topology," expands further on the benefits.

A bus requires less cable because you only need enough to chain the stations together. There is no central point of failure on a bus because there's no hub. Nevertheless, the disadvantages of linear bus topology are that the entire network shuts down if there is a break in the main cable, terminators are required at both ends of the backbone cable, it is difficult to identify the problem if the entire network shuts down, and they are not meant to be used as a stand-alone solution in a large building.

A bus can be even more vulnerable to failure than a star because any problem impacts the entire network. A bus can make troubleshooting difficult for this very same reason—how do you isolate a problem?

Another disadvantage of this topology is that the physical constraints of the shared medium limit the number of nodes that can be attached. Futurebus+ and PI-bus, for example, have each a maximum limit of 32 nodes. To connect additional nodes, it is necessary to build a hierarchical topology, as illustrated in the Figure 6–3. Here, a bridge node connects one physical linear bus to another, allowing nodes on one bus to communicate with nodes on another bus. More complex tree topologies can be created by adding bridges and buses as needed.

CHOOSING A TOPOLOGY

The following are some of the considerations in choosing a topology.

Expenses

- The least expensive way to install a network is via a linear bus network.
- Concentrators do not have to be purchased.

Required Cable Length

- Shorter cable lengths are used by the linear bus network.

Future Growth Potential

- Expanding a network is easily done by adding another concentrator when using a star topology.

Type of Cable

- Unshielded twisted pair is the most common cable in schools. It is most often used with star topologies.

Star

A star topology is designed with each node (file server, workstations, and peripherals) connected directly to a central network hub or concentrator, as shown in Figure 6–4. Data on a star network passes through the hub or concentrator before continuing to its destination. The hub or concentrator manages and controls all functions of the network. It also acts as a repeater for the data flow. This configuration is common with twisted pair cable; however, it can also be used with coaxial cable or fiber optic cable, as shown in Table 6–1.

Note In a star topology, each station has a cable leading back to a central hub. The most popular networks using a star topology are 10BASE-T Ethernet and token ring.

The protocols used with star configurations are usually Ethernet or LocalTalk. Token ring uses a similar topology, called the star-wired ring.

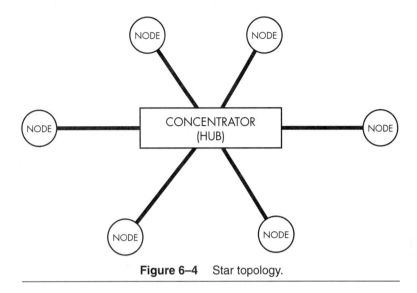

Figure 6–4   Star topology.

Advantages.   The advantages of star topology are that it is easy to install and wire, there are no disruptions to the network when connecting or removing devices, and it is easy to detect faults and to remove parts. In other words, a star can simplify troubleshooting because stations can be disconnected from the hub one at a time until the problem is isolated. Actually, you can do this with a bus, but you'd be running all over the building. The hub may have extra features like LEDs that indicate activity and errors on each port, making it even easier to isolate problems. With the introduction of switches, you can dramatically increase network performance by replacing the hub with a switch.

Disadvantages.   The disadvantages of a star topology are that it requires more cable length than a linear topology, that attached nodes are disabled if the hub or concentrator fails, and it is more expensive than linear bus topologies because of the cost of the concentrators. In other words, it requires more cable to wire a star. A hub failure can knock out the entire network. Stars can be more expensive because of the cost of the hub.

Star-Wired Ring

A star-wired ring topology may appear externally to be the same as a star topology. Internally, the MAU (multistation access unit) of a star-wired ring contains wiring that allows information to pass from one device to another in a circle or ring, as shown in Figure 6–5. The token ring protocol uses a star-wired ring topology, as shown in Table 6–1.

Tree

A tree topology combines characteristics of linear bus and star topologies. It consists of groups of star-configured workstations connected to a linear bus backbone cable, as shown in Figure 6–6. Tree topologies allow for the expan-

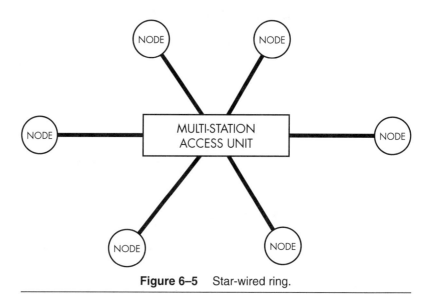

Figure 6–5   Star-wired ring.

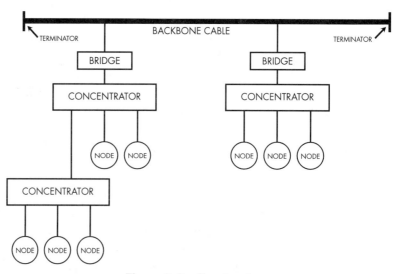

Figure 6–6   Tree topology.

sion of an existing network, and enable users to configure a network to meet their needs.

Advantages and Disadvantages of Tree Topology. The advantages of tree topology are that they allow point-to-point wiring for individual segments and they are supported by several hardware and software vendors. The disadvantages are that the overall length of each segment is limited by the type of cabling used, the entire segment goes down if the backbone line breaks, and it is more difficult to configure and wire than other topologies.

5-4-3 Rule

A consideration in setting up a tree topology using Ethernet protocol is the 5-4-3 rule. One aspect of the Ethernet protocol requires that a signal sent out on the network cable reach every part of the network within a specified length of time. Each concentrator or repeater that a signal goes through adds a small amount of time. This leads to the rule that between any two nodes on the network there can only be a maximum of 5 segments, connected through 4 repeaters/concentrators. In addition, only 3 of the segments may be populated (trunk) segments if they are made of coaxial cable. A populated segment is one that has one or more nodes attached to it. In Figure 6–6, the 5-4-3 rule is adhered to. The furthest two nodes on the network have 4 segments and 3 repeaters/concentrators between them. This rule does not apply to other network protocols or Ethernet networks where all fiber optic cabling is used.

10BaseT Cabling Specification

Ethernet was originally designed to operate over a heavy coaxial cable and was later updated to also support a thinner, lighter, coaxial cable type. Both systems provided a network with excellent performance, but they used a bus topology, which made changing the network a difficult proposition, and also left much to be desired in regard to reliability. Also, many buildings were already wired with twisted pair wire, which could support high-speed networks. Installing a coaxial-based Ethernet into these buildings would mean they would have to be rewired. Therefore, a new network type known as 10BaseT was introduced to increase reliability and allow the use of existing twisted pair cable.

Topology and Cabling

10BaseT utilizes category 3 (or higher) unshielded twisted pair cable in a star topology. Each node on the network has its own cable run back to a common hub, and each of these cable runs may be up to 100 meters (330 feet) in length. Figure 6–7 shows a simple 10BaseT network [3].

10BaseT can also be wired in a tree topology, where one main hub is connected to other hubs, which are in turn connected to workstations. It is also possible to combine 10BaseT with any combination of the other 10 Mbps Ethernet technologies in an infinite number of ways to meet nearly any requirement. Figure 6–8 shows a combination of 10BaseT and 10Base2 [Mazza, 2].

The depth of a 10BaseT tree network is limited to one layer below the main hub.

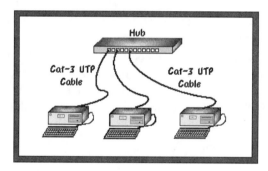

Figure 6–7   10BaseT network.

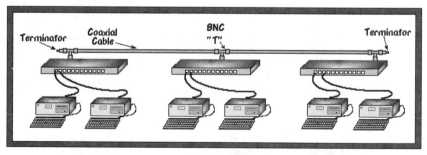

Figure 6–8   10BaseT and thin Ethernet combination.

Advantages and Disadvantages

10BaseT has various advantages and disadvantages that make it suitable for some applications and less suitable for others. Some of these are listed below.

Advantages

Since each node on a 10BaseT network has its own cable connecting it to a central hub, it is far less likely that any node can cause the entire network to fail. The hub also has a partitioning function built into it that allows it to detect a problem on any of its ports. If a problem is found, the node is disconnected from the rest of the network. This isolates the problem until the node can be troubleshot and repaired.

Because of the partitioning function built into the hubs and the star-wired topology, it is generally easy to troubleshoot a 10BaseT network. In a worst-case scenario, one can be troubleshot by simply disconnecting nodes from the hub one at a time until the network recovers. Usually, the hub will give an indication as to which node is causing a problem, allowing the technician to troubleshoot that node as opposed to spending many hours finding where the problem is.

Disconnecting a node from the network has no effect whatsoever on the rest of the network. Therefore, moving an attached device is simply a matter of unplugging it from the hub and reconnecting it somewhere else.

Many buildings are already wired with UTP cable, which can support a 10BaseT network. Even in the event a building is not wired with UTP already, it is still preferable to install UTP than any other type of cable, as UTP will support other applications later, whereas other cable types will generally be specific to one network type. This allows leveraging the UTP cable investment for other applications many years later.

Disadvantages

10BaseT only allows distances from the hub to the node of 100 meters (330 feet). In some installations, this can be a major problem if nodes need to be located farther away.

Sensitive to Noise.   The nature of UTP cable makes it considerably more sensitive to electrical noise than coaxial cable. Generally, this rules 10BaseT out as an option for installations in factory floor environments or other locations with a high ambient noise level.

Cabling Considerations

10BaseT uses two pairs of wires: one pair for transmission and the second pair to receive. The physical connector used is an 8-position modular plug, commonly referred to as an RJ45. All cables must be rated at a minimum of category 3, and must be wired such that pins 1 and 2 are on one twisted pair and pins 3 and 6 are on a second pair. Common wiring standards that meet this requirement are EIA/TIA T568-A and T568-B.

There are two pinouts used: MDI for DTE devices (such as computers, printers, etc.) and MDI-X (hubs). Connecting an MDI port to an MDI-X port requires a straight-through cable, and connecting either MDI to MDI or MDI-X to MDI-X requires a crossover cable. Pinouts of the MDI and MDI-X interfaces are shown in Table 6–2 [Mazza, 3].

Table 6–2   10BaseT Pinouts

MDI PINOUT		MDI-X PINOUT	
Pin	Signal	Pin	Signal
1	T+	1	R+
2	T−	2	R−
3	R+	3	T+
6	R−	6	T−

There are several applications for crossover cables in 10BaseT networks. The most common reason is to cascade hubs together in a tree topology. If both hubs have only MDI-X ports, then a crossover cable is needed. Another application for a crossover cable is to connect two DTE devices together without a hub. A standard 10BaseT crossover cable wiring diagram is shown in Table 6–3.

Table 6–3   Crossover Cable Pinout

10BASET CROSSOVER CABLE		
Side 1	Wire Color	Side 2
1	white/orange	3
2	orange/white	6
3	white/blue	1
6	blue/white	2

HORIZONTAL CABLING

The cable used for horizontal wiring is constructed of four unshielded twisted pairs under one jacket and comes in two types: PVC and plenum. Both types of cable perform the same electrically; however, local and national building codes require the use of plenum cable when the cable is being run above certain types of dropped ceilings. If you are in doubt as to the type of cable you should install, check with your installer or local electrical inspector before pulling any cable. Pulling the wrong kind of cable can cost you dearly in time and materials.

When planning your installation, it's important to know where each workstation will be located in relation to the wiring closet. You must plan your installation so that the length of each run of horizontal wiring does not exceed 90 meters (295 feet). Keep in mind that we're talking about actual cable length, not the physical distance between the wiring closet and the workstation outlet. If any single horizontal wiring run is greater than the 90-meter limitation, there are products available that will allow you to exceed that distance; however, if you find that a large number of workstations will be located beyond the 90-meter limit, you should plan for more than one wiring closet. The two wiring closets can be connected together with either a copper or fiber backbone cable.

Often, it's not possible for horizontal cable runs behind walls to reach all the way to workstation outlets without crossing open floors. This is particularly true in open-office settings using modular furniture clusters. To accommodate such situations, it is permissible for a horizontal cabling run to include one transition point where the round UTP cable connects to flat undercarpet cable. Category 5 undercarpet cable typically consists of four unshielded twisted pairs in a flat PVC jacket. When using it, you should use carpet squares rather than regular carpet in that area to allow access to the cabling later.

While you're still in the planning stage, consider your requirements for telephones or additional data jacks. It's more cost effective to install all of your cabling at one time rather incrementally. It is also a lot less disruptive if you're doing an installation in a working office.

When it comes time to actually install your cabling, here are some guidelines to follow that will help you avoid problems. First of all, many networks that run on UTP cable use only two of the four pairs of wires available in the cable. It can be tempting to try to save a little money by pulling only one 4-pair cable and using the first two pairs for data and the second two pairs for telephone or additional data. While this may work in some instances, there exists a strong potential for problems caused by crosstalk between the two types of systems. To avoid problems of this kind, you should never run more than one type of data (token ring and 10BaseT) or data and telephone in the same cable. The rule of thumb is if the pairs are under the same jacket, use them for only one system or type of data. If you're really trying to save money and want to pull only one cable, you can use a Siamese four-pair cable, which consists of two 2-pair cables in separate jackets physically fused together in a fashion similar to a lamp cord. Each 2-pair cable meets the category 5 electrical specification. Since each of the 2-pair cables is under its own jacket, it is permissible to use one side for data and the other side for telephone or an additional data circuit, without the fear of crosstalk between the systems. The only caveat is that with just two pairs to work with, you will only be able to wire your data jack partially. This will limit you to wiring your system for specific applications, such as token ring or 10BaseT, but not both, thus defeating the universal nature of a structured cabling system. In addition, some network standards, such as 100VG-AnyLAN and 100BaseT4, require the use of all four pairs, which would not be available for use.

Second, UTP cabling is relatively immune to outside sources of interference that can corrupt data, but it's always good practice when routing your cables through walls and ceilings to keep them as far away as possible from sources of electromagnetic interference (EMI) and radio frequency interference (RFI). Likely sources of EMI/RFI include fluorescent lights, electric panels, and light dimmers. Electric motors, such as those found in air handlers and elevator rooms, can also generate high levels of interference. Also, never run your data cables in the same conduit as electrical wiring. Not only is this a dangerous practice, but it's nearly guaranteed to result in high levels of EMI/RFI and lost data. When using undercarpet cabling, try to keep the undercarpet cable at least 6 inches away from any undercarpet electrical power circuits.

Third, pulling a cable with too much force (over 25 pounds) or bending it too sharply can change the electrical characteristics of the cable and degrade its performance, so care must be taken during the installation process to prevent any undue stress on the cable. The cable should move freely at all times and be protected from sharp edges while it is being pulled. When pulling around tight or multiple corners, you should generally pull the cable at the first bend, then the second, and so on until reaching the far end of the run. Do not attempt to install cable around multiple tight bends in one pull.

Finally, you will do yourself a big favor if you take a few extra minutes to mark both ends of each cable run with a wire marker of some kind. Taking a little time now will save you lots of time later when you don't have to hunt for which cable goes where.

BACKBONE CABLING

As previously discussed, the 90-meter limitation on horizontal cabling runs often necessitates the use of multiple wiring closets to serve users spread out over large facilities. A means for interconnecting wiring closets and equipment rooms, backbone cabling should use a tree topology, with each horizontal cross-connect in a wiring closet cabled back to one main cross-connect in a central equipment room, as illustrated in Figure 6–9 [Kayworth, 6]. If needed, there can be one intermediate cross-connect between horizontal cross-connects and the main cross-connect, but under no circumstances should there be more than three levels of cross-connects (main, intermediate, and horizontal).

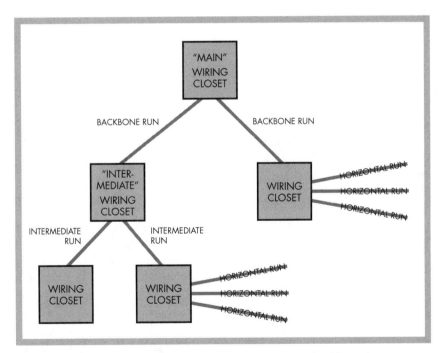

Figure 6–9   Multiple wiring closet interconnection hierarchy.

Multiple Wiring Closets with Backbone Connection

The backbone cabling media itself can be 100 ohm UTP, 150 ohm STP-A, 62.5/125 micron fiber optic cable, single-mode fiber optic cable, or any combination thereof. The cross-connect devices located in the wiring closets may be patch panels or 110-type connecting blocks. Patch panels are discussed in more detail later in the chapter.

The discussions that follow outline the capabilities and services associated with backbone cabling services.

Backbone Cabling Services Evaluation

This part of the chapter addresses cabling features that support backbone services. The following topics are discussed:

- path optimization
- traffic prioritization
- load balancing
- alternative paths
- switched access
- encapsulation (tunneling)
- backbone bandwidth management [4]

Optimizing Path

One of the primary advantages of a router is its capability to help you implement a logical environment in which optimal paths for traffic are automatically selected. Routers rely on routing protocols that are associated with the various network layer protocols to accomplish this automated path optimization.

Depending on the network protocols implemented, routers permit you to implement routing environments that suit your specific requirements. For example, in an internet protocol (IP) cabling system, Cisco routers can support all widely implemented routing protocols, including open shortest path first (OSPF), routing information protocol (RIP), interior gateway routing protocol (IGRP), border gateway protocol (BGP), exterior gateway protocol (EGP), and HELLO. Key built-in capabilities that promote path optimization include rapid and controllable route convergence and tunable routing metrics and timers.

Convergence is the process of agreement, by all routers, on optimal routes. When a network event causes routes to either halt operation or become available, routers distribute routing update messages. Routing update messages permeate networks, stimulating recalculation of optimal routes and eventually causing all routers to agree on these routes. Routing algorithms that converge slowly can cause routing loops or network outages.

Many different metrics are used in routing algorithms. Some sophisticated routing algorithms base route selection on a combination of multiple metrics, resulting in the calculation of a single hybrid metric. IGRP uses one of the most sophisticated distance vector routing algorithms. It combines values for bandwidth, load, and delay to create a composite metric value. Link state routing protocols, such as OSPF and intermediate system-to-intermediate system (IS-IS), employ a metric that represents the cost associated with a given path.

Prioritizing Traffic

Although some network protocols can prioritize internal homogeneous traffic, the router prioritizes the heterogeneous traffic flows. Such traffic prioritization enables policy-based routing and ensures that protocols carrying mission-critical data take precedence over less important traffic.

Queuing Priority. Priority queuing allows the network administrator to prioritize traffic. Traffic can be classified according to various criteria, including protocol and subprotocol type, and then queued on one of four output queues (high, medium, normal, or low priority). For IP traffic, additional fine-tuning is possible. Priority queuing is most useful on low-speed serial links. Figure 6–10 shows how priority queuing can be used to segregate traffic by priority level, thereby speeding the transit of certain packets through the network [4].

You can also use intraprotocol traffic prioritization techniques to enhance cabling performance. IP's type-of-service (TOS) feature and prioritization of IBM logical units (LUs) are intraprotocol prioritization techniques that can be implemented to improve traffic handling over routers. Figure 6–11 illustrates LU prioritization [4].

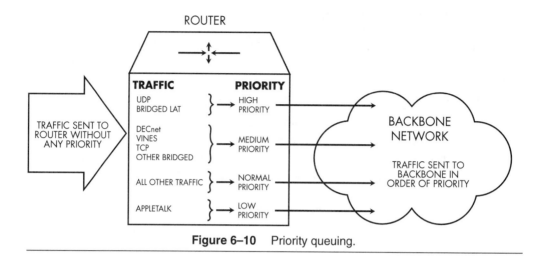

Figure 6–10   Priority queuing.

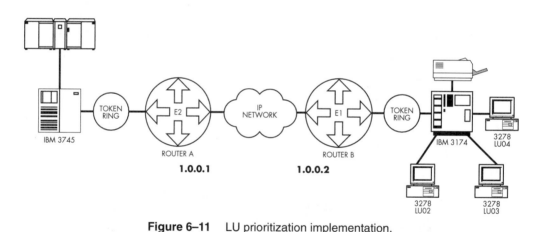

Figure 6–11   LU prioritization implementation.

   In Figure 6–11, the IBM mainframe is channel-attached to a 3745 communications controller, which is connected to a 3174 cluster controller via
remote source-route bridging (RSRB). Multiple 3270 terminals and printers,
each with a unique local LU address, are attached to the 3174. By applying
LU address prioritization, you can assign a priority to each LU associated
with a terminal or printer; that is, certain users can have terminals that have
better response time than others, and printers can have lowest priority. This
function increases application availability for those users running extremely
important applications.

Finally, most routed protocols (such as AppleTalk, IPX, and DECnet) employ a cost-based routing protocol to assess the relative merit of the different routes to a destination. By tuning associated parameters, you can force particular kinds of traffic to take particular routes, thereby performing a type of manual traffic prioritization.

Customized Queuing.   Priority queuing introduces a fairness problem in that packets classified to lower priority queues might not get serviced in a timely manner, or at all. Custom queuing is designed to address this problem. Custom queuing allows more granularity than priority queuing. In fact, this feature is commonly used in the cabling environment in which multiple higher-layer protocols are supported. Custom queuing reserves bandwidth for a specific protocol, thus allowing mission-critical traffic to receive a guaranteed minimum amount of bandwidth at any time.

The intent is to reserve bandwidth for a particular type of traffic. For example, let's say that SNA has 40 percent of the bandwidth reserved using custom queuing, TCP/IP 20 percent, NetBIOS 20 percent, and the remaining protocols 20 percent. The advanced peer-to-peer networking (APPN) protocol itself has the concept of class of service (COS), which determines the transmission priority for every message. APPN prioritizes the traffic before sending it to the data-link connection (DLC) transmission queue.

Custom queuing prioritizes multiprotocol traffic. A maximum of 16 queues can be built with custom queuing. Each queue is serviced sequentially until the number of bytes sent exceeds the configurable byte count or the queue is empty. One important function of custom queuing is that if SNA traffic uses only 20 percent of the link, the remaining 20 percent allocated to SNA can be shared by the other traffic.

Custom queuing is designed for environments that want to ensure a minimum level of service for all protocols. In today's multiprotocol cabling environment, this important feature allows protocols of different characteristics to share the media.

Weighted Fair Queuing.   Weighted fair queuing is a traffic priority management algorithm that uses the time-division multiplexing (TDM) model to divide the available bandwidth among clients that share the same interface. In time-division multiplexing, each client is allocated a time slice in a round-robin fashion. In weighted fair queuing, the bandwidth is distributed evenly among clients so that each client gets a fair share if every one has the same weighting. You can assign a different set of weights, for example through type-of-service, so that more bandwidth is allocated.

If every client is allocated the same bandwidth independent of the arrival rates, low-volume traffic has effective priority over high-volume traffic. The use of weighting allows time-delay-sensitive traffic to obtain additional bandwidth, thus consistent response time is guaranteed under heavy traffic conditions. There are different types of data stream converging on a wire, as shown in Figure 6–12 [4].

Both C and E are file transfer protocol (FTP) sessions, and they are high-volume traffic. A, B, and D are interactive sessions and they are low-volume traffic. Every session in this case is termed a "conversation." If each conversation is serviced in a cyclic manner and gets a slot regardless of its arrival rate, the FTP sessions do not monopolize the bandwidth. Round-trip delays for the interactive traffic, therefore, become somewhat predictable.

Weighted fair queuing provides an algorithm to identify data streams dynamically using an interface, and sorts them into separate logical queues. The algorithm uses various discriminators based on whatever network layer protocol information is available and sorts among them. For example, for IP traffic, the discriminators are source and destination address, protocol type, socket numbers, and TOS. This is how the two Telnet sessions (Sessions B and D) are assigned to different logical queues, as shown in Figure 6–12.

Ideally, the algorithm would classify every conversation that is sharing the wire so that each conversation receives its fair share of the bandwidth. Unfortunately, with such protocols as systems network architecture (SNA), you cannot distinguish one SNA session from another. For example, in data-link switching plus (DLSw+), SNA traffic is multiplexed onto a single TCP

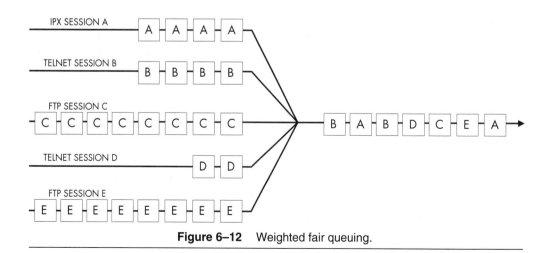

Figure 6–12 Weighted fair queuing.

session. Similarly in APPN, SNA sessions are multiplexed onto a single logical link control type 2 (LLC2) session.

The weighted fair queuing algorithm treats these sessions as a single conversation. If you have many TCP sessions, the TCP sessions get the majority of the bandwidth and the SNA traffic gets the minimum. For this reason, this algorithm is not recommended for SNA using DLSw+ TCP/IP encapsulation and APPN.

Weighted fair queuing, however, has many advantages over priority queuing and custom queuing. Priority queuing and custom queuing require the installation of access lists; the bandwidth has to be preallocated and priorities have to be predefined. This is clearly an administrative burden. Sometimes, network administrators cannot identify and prioritize network traffic in real time. Weighted fair queuing sorts among individual traffic streams without the burden associated with the other two types of queuing.

Load Balancing

The easiest way to add bandwidth in a backbone network is to implement additional links. Routers provide built-in load balancing for multiple links and paths. You can use up to four paths to a destination network. In some cases, the paths need not be of equal cost.

Within IP, routers provide load balancing on both a per-packet and a per-destination basis. For per-destination load balancing, each router uses its route cache to determine the output interface. If IGRP or Enhanced IGRP routing is used, unequal-cost load balancing is possible. The router uses metrics to determine which paths the packets will take; the amount of load balancing can be adjusted by the user.

Load balancing bridged traffic over serial lines is also supported. Serial lines can be assigned to circuit groups. If one of the serial links in the circuit group is in the spanning tree for a network, any of the serial links in the circuit group can be used for load balancing. Data ordering problems are avoided by assigning each destination to a serial link. Reassignment is done dynamically if interfaces go down or come up.

Alternative Paths

Many cabling backbones carry mission-critical information. Organizations running such backbones are usually interested in protecting the integrity of this information at virtually any cost. Routers must offer sufficient reliability so that they are not the weak link in the cabling chain. The key is to provide alternative paths that can come on line whenever link failures occur along active network paths.

End-to-end reliability is not ensured simply by making the backbone fault tolerant. If communication on a local segment within any building is disrupted for any reason (cable break, equipment failure, etc.), that information will not reach the backbone. End-to-end reliability is only possible when redundancy is employed throughout the cabling system. Because this is usually cost prohibitive, most companies prefer to employ redundant paths only on those segments that carry mission-critical information.

What does it take to make the backbone reliable? Routers hold the key to reliable cabling systems. Depending on the definition of reliability, this can mean duplicating every major system on each router and possibly every component. However, hardware component duplication is not the entire solution because extra circuitry is necessary to link the duplicate components to allow them to communicate. This solution is usually very expensive, but more importantly, it does not completely address the problem. Even assuming all routers in your network are completely reliable systems, link problems between nodes within a backbone can still defeat a redundant hardware solution.

To really address the problem of network reliability, links must be redundant. Furthermore, it is not enough to simply duplicate all links. Dual links must terminate at multiple routers unless all backbone routers are completely fault tolerant (no single points of failure). Otherwise, backbone routers that are not fault tolerant become single points of failure. The inevitable conclusion is that a completely redundant router is not the most effective solution to the reliability problem because it is expensive and still does not address link reliability.

Most network designers do not implement a completely redundant network. Instead, network designers implement partially redundant cabling systems.

Switched Access

Switched access provides the capability to enable a WAN link on an as-needed basis via automated router controls. One model for a reliable backbone consists of dual, dedicated links and one switched link for idle hot backup. Under normal operational conditions, you can load balance over the dual links, but the switched link is not operational until one of the dedicated links fails.

Traditionally, WAN connections over the public switched telephone network (PSTN) have used dedicated lines. This can be very expensive when an application requires only low-volume, periodic connections. To reduce the need for dedicated circuits, a feature called dial-on-demand routing (DDR) is available. Figure 6–13 illustrates a DDR connection [4].

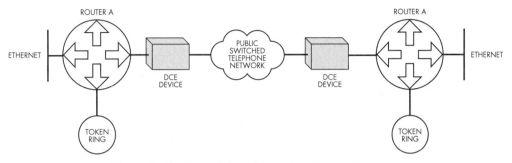

Figure 6–13   The dial-on-demand routing environment.

Using DDR, low-volume, periodic network connections can be made over the PSTN. A router activates the DDR feature when it receives a bridged or routed IP packet destined for a location on the other side of the dial-up line. After the router dials the destination phone number and establishes the connection, packets of any supported protocol can be transmitted. When the transmission is complete, the line is automatically disconnected. By terminating unneeded connections, DDR reduces cost of ownership.

Encapsulation (Tunneling)

Encapsulation takes packets or frames from one network system and places them inside frames from another network system. This method is sometimes called tunneling. Tunneling provides a means for encapsulating packets inside a routable protocol via virtual interfaces. Synchronous data link control (SDLC) transport is also an encapsulation of packets in a routable protocol. In addition, transport provides enhancements to tunneling, such as local data-link layer termination, broadcast avoidance, media conversion, and other scalability optimizations (see Sidebar, "Encapsulation and Tunneling Techniques").

ENCAPSULATION AND TUNNELING TECHNIQUES

Cisco routers support the following encapsulation and tunneling techniques.

The IBM technology feature set provides these methods:

- Serial tunneling (STUN) or synchronous data link control (SDLC) transport.
- Source-route bridging (SRB) with direct encapsulation.
- SRB with fast sequenced transport (FST) encapsulation.
- SRB with transmission control protocol/Internet protocol encapsulation.
- Data link switching plus (DLSw+) with direct encapsulation.

- DLSw+ with TCP/IP encapsulation.
- DLSw+ with fast sequenced transport/Internet protocol (FST/IP) encapsulation.
- DLSw+ with DLSw Lite (logical link control type 2 [LLC2]) encapsulation.

Generic Routing Encapsulation (GRE):

Cisco supports encapsulating Novell Internetwork Packet Exchange (IPX), Internet Protocol (IP), Connectionless Network Protocol (CLNP), AppleTalk, DECnet Phase IV, Xerox Network Systems (XNS), Banyan Virtual Network System (VINES), and Apollo packets for transport over IP.

Single-protocol tunneling techniques:

Cayman (AppleTalk over IP), AURP (AppleTalk over IP), EON (CLNP over IP), and NOS (IP over IP) [4].

The following discussion focuses on IBM encapsulations and the multiprotocol GRE tunneling feature.

IBM Features.   Serial tunnel (STUN) allows two devices that are normally connected by a direct serial link, using protocols compliant with synchronous data link control (SDLC) or high-level data link control (HDLC), to be connected through one or more routers. The routers can be connected via a multiprotocol network of arbitrary topology. STUN allows integration of system network architecture networks and non-SNA networks using routers and existing network links. Transport across the multiprotocol network that connects the routers can use TCP/IP. This type of transport offers reliability and intelligent routing via any supported IP routing protocol. A STUN configuration is shown in Figure 6–14 [4].

SDLC Transport is a variation of STUN that allows sessions using SDLC protocols and TCP/IP encapsulation to be locally terminated. SDLC Transport permits participation in SDLC windowing and retransmission activities.

When connecting remote devices that use SRB over a slow-speed serial link, most network designers choose remote source-route bridging (RSRB) with direct high-level data link control encapsulation. In this case, SRB frames are encapsulated in an HDLC-compliant header. This solution adds little overhead, preserving valuable serial link bandwidth. Direct HDLC encapsulation is not restricted to serial links (it can also be used over Ethernet, token ring, and fiber distributed data interface links), but is most useful in situations in which additional control overhead on the encapsulating network is not tolerable.

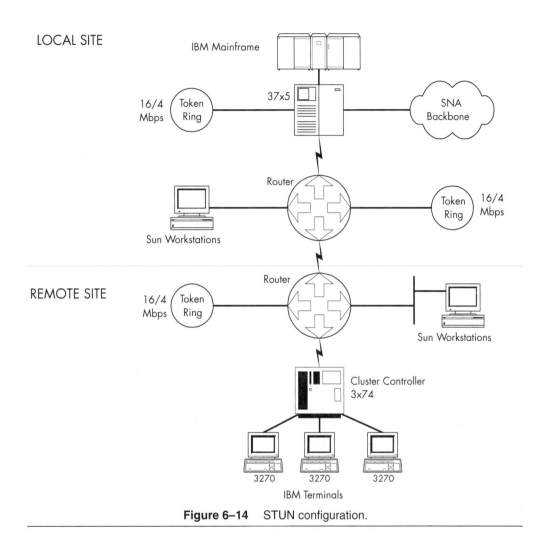

LOCAL SITE

IBM Mainframe

16/4 Mbps — Token Ring

37x5

SNA Backbone

Router

Sun Workstations

Token Ring — 16/4 Mbps

REMOTE SITE

Router

16/4 Mbps — Token Ring

Sun Workstations

Cluster Controller 3x74

3270   3270   3270

IBM Terminals

Figure 6–14   STUN configuration.

When more overhead can be tolerated, frame sequencing is important, but extremely reliable delivery is not needed, and SRB packets can be sent over serial, token ring, Ethernet, and FDDI networks using FST encapsulation. FST is similar to TCP in that it provides packet sequencing. However, unlike TCP, FST does not provide packet-delivery acknowledgment.

For extremely reliable delivery in environments in which moderate overhead can be tolerated, you can choose to encapsulate SRB frames in TCP/IP packets. This solution is not only reliable, it can also take advantage of routing features that include handling via routing protocols, packet filtering, and multipath routing.

Generic Routing Encapsulation (GRE).   Cisco's generic routing encapsulation (GRE) multiprotocol carrier protocol encapsulates IP, connectionless network protocol (CLNP), internetwork packet exchange (IPX), AppleTalk, DECnet Phase IV, Xerox Network Systems (XNS), virtual integrated network service (VINES), and Apollo packets inside IP tunnels. With GRE tunneling, a Cisco router at each site encapsulates protocol-specific packets in an IP header, creating a virtual point-to-point link to Cisco routers at other ends of an IP cloud, where the IP header is stripped off. By connecting multiprotocol subnetworks in a single-protocol backbone environment, IP tunneling allows network expansion across a single-protocol backbone environment. GRE tunneling involves three types of protocols:

- *Passenger*—The protocol is encapsulated (IP, CLNP, IPX, AppleTalk, DECnet Phase IV, XNS, VINES, and Apollo).
- *Carrier*—GRE protocol provides carrier services.
- *Transport*—IP carries the encapsulated protocol [4].

GRE tunneling allows desktop protocols to take advantage of the enhanced route selection capabilities of IP. Many LAN protocols, including AppleTalk and Novell IPX, are optimized for local use. They have limited route selection metrics and hop count limitations. In contrast, IP routing protocols allow more flexible route selection and scale better over large cabling systems. Figure 6–15 illustrates GRE tunneling across a single IP backbone between sites [4]. Regardless of how many routers and paths may be associated with the IP cloud, the tunnel is seen as a single hop.

GRE provides key capabilities that other encapsulation protocols lack: sequencing and the capability to carry tunneled data at high speeds. Some higher-level protocols require that packets are delivered in correct order. The GRE sequencing option provides this capability. GRE also has an optional key feature that allows you to avoid configuration errors by requiring the same key to be entered at each tunnel endpoint before the tunneled data is processed. IP tunneling also allows network designers to implement policies, such as which types of traffic can use which routes or assignment of priority or security levels to particular traffic. Capabilities like these are lacking in many native LAN protocols.

IP tunneling provides communication between subnetworks that have invalid or discontiguous network addresses. With tunneling, virtual network addresses are assigned to subnetworks, making discontiguous subnetworks accessible. Figure 6–16 illustrates that with GRE tunneling, it is possible for

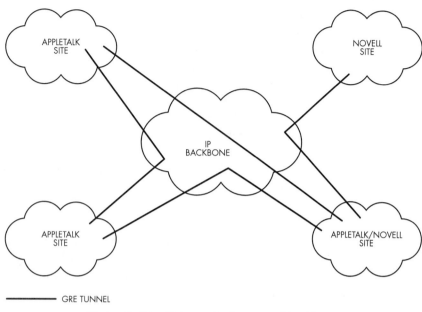

Figure 6–15   Using a single protocol backbone.

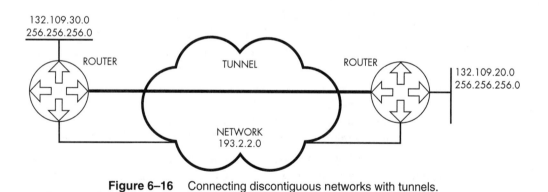

Figure 6–16   Connecting discontiguous networks with tunnels.

the two subnetworks of network 132.109.0.0 to talk to each other even though they are separated by another network [4].

Because encapsulation requires handling of the packets, it is generally faster to route protocols natively than to use tunnels. Tunneled traffic is switched at approximately half the typical process switching rates. This means approximately 1,000 packets per second (pps) aggregate for each router. Tunneling is CPU-intensive, and as such, should be turned on cautiously. Routing updates, service advertising protocol (SAP) updates, and other administrative traffic may be sent over each tunnel interface. It is easy to saturate a physical link with routing information if several tunnels are configured over it. Performance depends on the passenger protocol, broadcasts, routing updates, and bandwidth of the physical interfaces. It is also difficult to debug the physical link if problems occur. This problem can be mitigated in several ways. In IPX environments, route filters and SAP filters cut down on the size of the updates that travel over tunnels. In AppleTalk networks, keeping zones small and using route filters can limit excess bandwidth requirements.

Tunneling can disguise the nature of a link, making it look slower, faster, or more or less costly than it may actually be in reality. This can cause unexpected or undesirable route selection. Routing protocols that make decisions based only on hop count will usually prefer a tunnel to a real interface. This may not always be the best routing decision because an IP cloud can comprise several different media with very disparate qualities. For example, traffic may be forwarded across both 100-Mbps Ethernet lines and 9.6-Kbps serial lines. When using tunneling, pay attention to the media over which virtual tunnel traffic passes and the metrics used by each protocol.

If a network has sites that use protocol-based packet filters as part of a firewall security scheme, be aware that because tunnels encapsulate unchecked passenger protocols, you must establish filtering on the firewall router so that only authorized tunnels are allowed to pass. If tunnels are accepted from unsecured networks, it is a good idea to establish filtering at the tunnel destination or to place the tunnel destination outside the secure area of your network so that the current firewall scheme will remain secure.

When tunneling IP over IP, you must be careful to avoid inadvertently configuring a recursive routing loop. A routing loop occurs when the passenger protocol and the transport protocol are identical. The routing loop occurs because the best path to the tunnel destination is via the tunnel interface. A routing loop can occur when tunneling IP over IP, as described in the following steps:

1. The packet is placed in the output queue of the tunnel interface.
2. The tunnel interface includes a GRE header and enqueues the packet to the transport protocol (IP) for the destination address of the tunnel interface.

3. IP looks up the route to the tunnel destination address and learns that the path is the tunnel interface.

4. Once again, the packet is placed in the output queue of the tunnel interface, as described in Step 1, hence, the routing loop [4].

When a router detects a recursive routing loop, it shuts down the tunnel interface for 1 to 2 minutes and issues a warning message before it goes into the recursive loop. Another indication that a recursive route loop has been detected is if the tunnel interface is up and the line protocol is down.

To avoid recursive loops, keep passenger and transport routing information in separate locations by implementing the following procedures:

- Use separate routing protocol identifiers (for example, igrp 1 and igrp 2).
- Use different routing protocols.
- Assign the tunnel interface a very low bandwidth so that routing protocols, such as IGRP, will recognize a very high metric for the tunnel interface and will, therefore, choose the correct next hop (that is, choose the best physical interface instead of the tunnel).
- Keep the two IP address ranges distinct; that is, use a major address for your tunnel network that is different from your actual IP network. Keeping the address ranges distinct also aids in debugging, because it is easy to identify an address as the tunnel network instead of the physical network and vice versa [4].

Backbone Bandwidth Management

Finally, to optimize backbone network operations, routers offer several performance tuning features. Examples include priority queuing, routing protocol metrics, and local session termination.

You can adjust the output queue length on priority queues. If a priority queue overflows, excess packets are discarded and quench messages that halt packet flow are sent, if appropriate, for that protocol. You can also adjust routing metrics to increase control over the paths that the traffic takes through the cabling system. Local session termination allows routers to act as proxies for remote systems that represent session endpoints.

A proxy is a device that acts on behalf of another device.

The routers locally terminate logical link control type 2 (LLC2) data-link control sessions. Instead of end-to-end sessions (during which all session control), information is passed over the multiprotocol backbone. The routers take responsibility for acknowledging packets that come from hosts on directly attached LANs. Local acknowledgment saves WAN bandwidth (and, therefore, WAN utilization costs), solves session timeout problems, and provides faster response to users.

CONNECTING HARDWARE

The connecting hardware you choose will depend on the size of your network, the flexibility you will need, and the way in which you want to organize and manage your structured cabling installation. Connecting hardware components generally fall into two categories, either fixed or modular in design. Fixed components have a set number of RJ45 ports and cannot be reconfigured for other applications (telephone). Modular components can be configured and reconfigured for a variety of applications and can often be color-coded to help identify multiple systems running over the same structured cabling system.

For small, single-system installations with few moves, additions, or changes, fixed type components are usually adequate. If, however, the structured cabling system is intended to support multiple networks plus telephones, a more flexible approach should be considered. In today's corporate computing environment, it's not uncommon to see token ring, 10BaseT, and IBM midrange being used under one roof. Having one wiring system that supports all of these, plus being able to color-code patch panel and wall plate jacks by system, is an advantage when moving or adding people. And for troubleshooting, it's invaluable!

Connecting hardware components that use the modular approach lets you create virtually any type of wall plate or patch panel. You don't have to settle for stock configurations anymore.

At the same time you are deciding what type of patch panels to purchase, consider how you are going to mount them. If ease of access is important, open distribution racks are a good choice. If, however, your concern is for security, a locking cabinet may be preferable. Cabinets with clear plexiglass front doors allow you to view indicator lights that may be present on network concentrators or other equipment while still maintaining system security. For heat dissipation, cooling fans can be installed in most cabinets.

Smaller installations or ones with limited floor space can benefit from using wall mount distribution racks. These types of racks provide easy access for cabling to the back of the patch panels and take up no floor space.

Before purchasing any connecting hardware, it's vitally important to decide which wiring standard you are going to follow. The wiring standard designates which color wire from the horizontal wiring connects to which pin on the RJ45 modular jack. The preferred EIA/TIA wiring standard is known as T568-A. An alternate wiring standard, known as T568-B, conforms to the old AT&T 258A wiring standard and is the more commonly used standard in the United States. Availability of products for both standards is good but will be somewhat better for T568-B. The proper wiring for each standard shown in Figure 6–17 and Table 6–4 illustrate T568-A; and Figure 6–18 and Table 6–5 illustrate T568-B [Kayworth, 8–10].

The only difference between these standards is that the position of pairs 2 and 3 (pins) on the RJ45 jack is reversed.

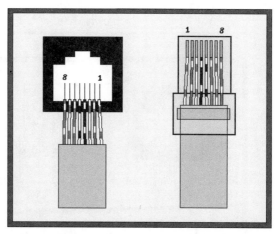

Figure 6–17   EIA/TIA-T568-A wiring standard.

Table 6–4   EIA/TIA-T568-A Color Code

EIA/TIA-T568-A Standard	
Pin	Color
1	white/green
2	green/white
3	white/orange
4	blue/white
5	white/blue
6	orange/white
7	white/brown
8	brown/white

Table 6–5   EIA/TIA-T568-B Color Code

EIA/TIA-T568-A Standard	
Pin	Color
1	white/orange
2	orange/white
3	white/green
4	blue/white
5	white/blue
6	green/white
7	white/brown
8	brown/white

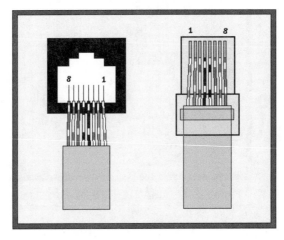

Figure 6–18
EIA/TIA-T568-B
wiring standard.

Care must be taken when terminating the horizontal wiring at the connecting hardware so as to maintain the highest level of performance possible. The first step you can take to accomplish this is to use the proper terminating tool.

As mentioned earlier, the AT&T 110 contact is most commonly used to connect the wires from the horizontal cable to the connecting hardware. These contacts pierce the insulation to make contact with the wire underneath. Never try to use screwdrivers, pliers, or cutters to push the wires into the 110 contact. This might work in an emergency but won't result in good, long-term connections. To get consistently reliable terminations, you must use what is called a 110 punch-down tool. It is recommended that you use a tool that terminates only one wire at a time. There are tools that will terminate four pairs of wire simultaneously, but the termination quality is questionable, and they tend to put undue strain on connecting hardware that is based on a circuit board design.

The 110 contacts are normally color-coded, making it easy to connect the right color wire to the right spot on the modular jack. The color code on the jack will correspond to either T568-A or T568-B, depending on the wiring standard you have chosen. To terminate the wire, you simply lay it in the appropriate color-coded slot and use the 110 tool to punch the wire down. Be sure to trim off any excess wire that is left after you have punched down the wire. Better quality punch-down tools will automatically do this for you. If yours does not, you will have to do it manually.

The following discussion explains how RJ11 and RJ45 connectors are wired for 568A, 568B, 258A, and USOC standards.

Twisted Pair Connectors

A typical 4-pair cable is shown in Figures 6–17 and 6–18. One important point to notice is that each pair is twisted. This twisting is very important to maintaining the electrical and performance specifications of the cable. To ensure peak performance, you must maintain the pair twisting to within one-half inch or less of the point of termination on the connecting hardware. Any untwisting of the pairs greater than this length will adversely affect the performance of the cable and can reduce its ability to transmit data at a category 5 level.

Twisted pair cabling uses an 8-wire modular connector called the RJ45. The installer must connect the right-colored wire to the right pin in the RJ45 when terminating with an RJ45. 568A, 568B, 258A, and USOC are all standards that describe which wire goes on which pin.

The TIA (Telecommunications Industry Association) 568A standard is the pre-ferred way of terminating cable. It matches the method of terminating cable that Northern Telecom used for ISDN.

Before the TIA ever met to begin creating the 568A standard for cable termi-nations, AT&T had a very similar standard for terminating their cable, called 258A. 258A works just as well as 568A. In fact, the TIA committee decided to include AT&T's 258A standard, but they called it the 568B standard. 258A and 568B are exactly the same (which is what happens when committees try to make everyone happy). Furthermore, the TIA cabling standard states you may use either 568A or 568B. All of these numbers sound confusing, but the reality is that it doesn't make any difference which you use, as long as you're consistent throughout your media installation. Again, make sure you don't mix 568A and 568B in the same cabling system.

USOC is an old standard used for voice cabling. Notice that for 1- and 2-line phones (which use pins 4/5 and 3/6), 568A or 568B will work just as well as USOC. But for Ethernet (pins 1/2 and 3/6), USOC won't work. An Ether-net NIC trying to transmit on pins 1/2 will run into trouble because 1/2 aren't a pair (not the same color, and not twisted together). So unless you know the cable plant is for voice or analog voice and not digital voice or ISDN, and it's never going to carry data, you should avoid USOC.

Now, the first thing you should know is that the 8 wires are always thought of as 4 pairs. And, no matter which cabling standard you follow, the pairs are always colored the same. For example, pair 1 is always blue, as shown in Table 6–6 [7].

Table 6–6   Twisted Pair Connectors Color Configuration

Pair	Color	Wires
1	blue	blue and blue with white stripes
2	orange	orange and orange with white stripes
3	green	green and green with white stripes
4	brown	brown and brown with white stripes

The blue wire and the blue wire with white stripes (*blue/white* for short) are twisted together within the cable, and this makes them suitable for carrying data. If you were to use one wire from the blue pair, and one wire from the orange pair, they wouldn't work as well (if at all) as both wires from the green pair. The various standards define which pair is attached to which pins on the RJ45.

So, why are the pairs shuffled around, instead of laid out logically? Well, they are logical, if you know the background. Ethernet was originally designed to run over the same cabling used by the phone system (AT&T created this as StarLAN), so this design left pins 4/5 available for a phone. If you plug an RJ11 (4 wire) into this, the middle two pins (2/3) of the RJ11 would connect to the middle two pins (4/5) of the RJ45, just perfect for a 1-line phone. If you plug an Ethernet cable into it, pins 1/2 will be used as one pair, and pins 3/6 will be used as another. No conflicts. Pretty clever, eh?

This can't be stressed enough times: Go ahead and choose 568A or 568B as the standard for your cable plant, but don't mix them!

The point stressed in the preceding note may seem trivial to you, but can cause major problems if not considered. You should use the same wiring standard, either T568-A or T568-B, throughout your structured wiring system. For example, if you use T568-B wall plates, you should also use T568-B patch panels and patch cables everywhere. Not doing this can cost you a lot of wasted time trying to troubleshoot nonexistent cabling problems, when in fact the only problem that exists is a wiring standard mismatch between various components of your wiring system.

PATCH CABLES

The quality and performance of the patch cables you use for connecting to your patch panels and wall plates should not be minimized. They are as important as any other component in your structured cabling system.

By their very nature, patch cables are intended to be moved and flexed. For this reason, patch cables should be made from cable with stranded conductors, which offer a much greater flex life and are better suited for this application than solid conductors.

It was mentioned earlier that some patch panels and wall plates can be color-coded to help differentiate between various systems running on the same cabling system. Colored patch cables are available and can be used to color coordinate with color-coded patch panels and wall plates to make identification of various systems extremely fast and easy. For example, you might want to use blue patch cables for token ring and red patch cables for 10BaseT.

When planning your installation, you must take into account the length of the patch cables. As stated earlier, the maximum horizontal cable run cannot exceed 90 meters (285 feet). In addition, the EIA/TIA-T568 standard allows for a maximum patch cable length of 6 meters (20 feet) in the wiring closet and 3 meters (10 feet) at the workstation outlet. If either of these lengths is exceeded, the main horizontal cable run must be reduced by the excess amount, so as not to exceed an overall length of 100 meters, including both horizontal cabling and patch cables. Another decision you will need to make concerning patch cables is whether to purchase them preassembled or to build them yourself. On the surface, building your own may seem like a way to save money, but of all the components in a structured wiring system, patch cables are probably the most difficult and time-consuming to assemble.

To assemble your own patch cables you will need three things: the proper cable, the proper connectors, and the proper crimp tool. The cable you choose must meet all of the mechanical, electrical, and performance specifications of category 5 cable. In addition, you should choose the cable type and color based on the previous discussion.

Modular plugs are available for both solid and stranded conductors. It is recommended that you use plugs made for solid wire regardless of what type of cable you are using. It has been determined that, long term, this type of connector makes a more reliable contact with the wire.

The crimp tool you use should be a ratchet type tool or some other type that gives a repeatable crimp performance. Inexpensive tools that rely on the user's physical strength to determine the amount of crimp pressure applied to the RJ45 plug do not give consistent crimping results. With these types of tools, the quality of the crimp will vary from person to person and even from crimp to crimp. Ratchet-type tools, on the other hand, will not release until the minimum acceptable crimp pressure has been applied. The only strength criteria a person needs to meet is that he or she can apply enough force to put the tool through the full crimp cycle.

You must also verify that the tool will crimp the connectors you are using. Even though all connectors are compatible once terminated on the cable, the way the tool terminates them may be different. Problems can arise when you use one manufacturer's tool to crimp another manufacturer's connector. Although this is not always a problem, it is a safer bet to stay with one manufacturer for both the connectors and the tool.

When terminating the connector, you must maintain the pair twisting to within one-half inch or less of the terminating point, just as you did when connecting your horizontal cable runs to the patch panels and wall plates. Ignoring this rule will degrade your overall system performance.

In contrast to building your own, purchasing preassembled patch cables takes one less worry out of your installation process. Most preassembled cables are crimped with air or electric presses, so the crimps are extremely consistent, resulting in a highly reliable termination. In addition, most manufacturers of preassembled patch cables have implemented quality assurance programs, which ensure you top quality and top performance.

With that in mind, the next part of the chapter shows you how to bridge the gap between a logical network map, and the actual connections at the patch panel and hub.

Bridging the Ethernet Gap

After you've installed a structured cabling system, the specific patch cables and connections you need depend on the network type you've chosen. The following is a discussion on how you might put it together for your network.

From a *logical* point of view, your network might look like the one shown in Figure 6–19 [7]. Simple, right? An Ethernet segment with several PCs (and Macs), a PhoneNet segment with several Macs, and a router (K) to join them together.

Figure 6–20 shows how the EtherTalk and LocalTalk portions of the network are cabled together [7]. The first thing you should notice is that all stations on the LAN, regardless of the network type, use the same cabling from the wall plate to the patch panel. That's proof that your cabling mission was accomplished! No special cabling has to be installed to support special network types.

EtherTalk is another protocol that uses either twisted pair or a coax type of cabling to run at up to 10 Megabits per second.

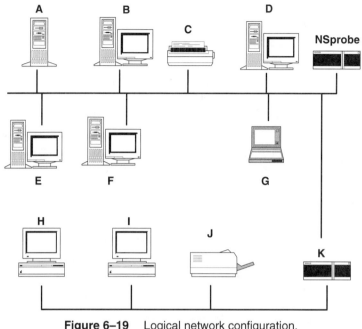

Figure 6–19 Logical network configuration.

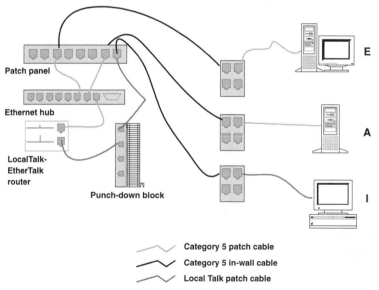

Figure 6–20 EtherTalk and LocalTalk network cabling configuration.

LocalTalk is the hardware protocol for the physical network medium, including pinouts, voltage specifications, and so on. The network protocol that the two computers use is AppleTalk. In other words, LocalTalk is cabling used to transmit AppleTalk information between Macintosh computers and printers and other network devices. Its maximum transfer rate is 230.4 KBits per second over a twisted pair wire. To draw an analogy, LocalTalk is equivalent to 10baseT network wiring and hardware. AppleTalk is equivalent to, say, the Microsoft networking protocol.

Therefore, when you examine a typical Ethernet connection, like E to A, you'll see that they both go into the hub. If you were in the basement trying to put all this together, all you'd have to do is find the port on the patch panel that corresponds to the room (and connection) that E is in, and use a short patch cable to plug it into the hub. Do the same thing for A. Wham! It's an Ethernet!

LocalTalk is just as easy. Find the port on the patch panel that corresponds to the room (and connection) that I is on, and patch it into the 66-block. Think of the 66-block as a special kind of hub.

The router is just a station that has two connections. Since the router is presumably in the wiring closet with the hub and 66-block, you can bypass going through the patch panel. But it really wouldn't be any harder, to connect it to both, even if it were in another room. You'd just repeat the steps for an Ethernet connection and for a LocalTalk connection.

APPLICATION TESTING AND NETWORK CERTIFICATION DESIGN ISSUES

Once you've completed your installation, you should spend some time testing each of your cable runs to ensure that they meet or exceed the electrical performance specifications for the intended application. The EIA/TIA provides guidelines for field testing of installed UTP channels for category 5 compliance in TSB 67. For testing purposes, a UTP channel is defined as one entire cable run. This includes the workstation outlet—a transition point from undercarpet cable to round cable (if applicable), the horizontal cable run of up to 90 meters, the horizontal cross-connect consisting of two patch panels or connecting blocks, and up to 10 meters of patch cables.

Hand-held field testers, or cable scanners as they are often called, are capable of measuring channel parameters such as attenuation and near-end crosstalk (NEXT). A cable scanner may also include a built-in time domain reflectometer, or TDR, that can determine the total channel length or pinpoint where on the channel a problem, such as a cable short, is located. Most testers can also provide a hard copy record of the measurements taken for each channel. When used properly, a cable scanner can be a valuable troubleshooting and diagnostic tool. It can also be used for documentation and acceptance of a cabling system for a specific network application.

If you are considering purchasing such a cable tester, be sure to choose a model that meets the guidelines for testing provided in TIA/EIA TSB 67. And always remember, your best guarantee of ending up with a compliant cabling system is to be certain that all components in the channel are category 5-compliant and are installed according to ANSI/TIA/EIA-T568-A standards.

If you don't want to invest in test equipment of your own, there are independent companies that specialize in testing and certifying structured wiring systems for specific network applications. Also, firms that specialize in the installation of structured wiring systems usually have the equipment and know-how to properly test your cabling system. If you do hire an outside company to perform your testing, be sure to get hard copies of the test results for each channel and save them for future reference. Original test results can be a valuable point of reference when troubleshooting a network problem. With test results in hand, you can show that a particular UTP channel was good on a given date. You can then look at what changes have occurred since then to try to narrow down where a problem might exist.

For further information on testing and design issues, see Chapter 23, "Testing Techniques." This chapter includes practical tips on how to get the test done, how to interpret results, how to maintain documentation on test results, when to retest, and how to include requirements for testing in contracts.

NETWORK DESIGN DOCUMENTATION ISSUES

One of the worst things you can do is install an exemplary structured cabling system and then not label and identify where each wall plate and patch panel jack goes. That would almost be like returning a book to the wrong section of the library. It's as good as lost!

Each wall plate jack should be marked with a unique identifier that corresponds to a jack on a patch panel in the wiring closet. Once this is done, it's a simple matter to make moves, changes, or additions, since finding various locations throughout the building is as easy as comparing the identifiers on the wall plate and patch panel. Troubleshooting is also made easier when you know where to look. For more information concerning standards for documentation, you should refer to ANSI/EIA/TIA-606.

For more information about managing documentation beyond ANSI/EIA/TIA-606, see Chapter 27, "Standards Development." This chapter describes how to store drawings, where to store them, how to index them, how to update them, and so on.

NETWORK DESIGN STANDARDS AND TECHNOLOGY ISSUES

In the time since the category 5 standard was defined, many companies have introduced cabling products purported to be tested at speeds far exceeding the 100 MHz limit specified for category 5. The benefits of using this type of cable in lieu of standard category 5 cable may be hard to determine. There is no standard yet written or approved that addresses testing of cabling products at these higher speeds. The only claim that can really be made is that these types of cables exceed the electrical performance specifications of standard category 5 cable by some variable factor. Does this mean that all the claims made for these enhanced category 5 cables are nothing more than hype? Not necessarily.

Although it's not something we all like to think about, the reality is that not all installation jobs are perfect, therefore, if for no other benefit, these types of cables can provide a fudge factor to help overcome any marginal UTP channels. More to the point, however, is the fact that, while 100 Mbps networks are becoming commonplace, networks running at even higher speeds are anticipated. In order to be able to keep pace with changing technologies, installing the best cabling available can be economically prudent when compared to replacing a cabling system in the future. For information on category 6 network design standards and technology issues, see Chapter 27.

NETWORK DESIGN THIRD-PARTY NONSTANDARD TECHNOLOGY ISSUES

Now let's look at third-party nonstandard technologies that inevitably become tomorrow's standards. More specifically, let's look at some of the barriers presented earlier in the book regarding transmission speeds, cable length, and so on, with regard to the implementation of third-party technologies. For example, Cisco, Leviton, and Novell have developed products that essentially build on proprietary technologies that may eventually become standards. In essence, the last part of the chapter is designed to wet the reader's lips with what is actually out in the field, so that when you read the book and then go to a supplier, you won't be astonished to find that many solutions are available that break or pierce the fundamentals that you studied!

Cisco Systems Network Design Issues

Network cabling (the communication between two or more networks) encompasses every aspect of connecting computers together. Network cabling has grown to support vastly disparate end-system communication requirements. A network cabling system requires many protocols and features to permit scalability and manageability without constant manual intervention. Large network cabling systems can consist of the following three distinct components:

- Campus networks, which consist of locally connected users in a building or group of buildings.
- Wide-area networks, which connect campuses together.
- Remote connections, which link branch offices and single users (mobile users and/or telecommuters) to a local campus or the Internet [4].

Figure 6–21 provides an example of a typical enterprise network cabling system [4].

Designing a network cabling system can be a challenging task. To design reliable, scalable network cabling systems, network designers must realize that each of the three major components of a network cabling system have distinct design requirements. A network cabling system that consists of only 50 meshed routing nodes can pose complex problems that lead to unpre-

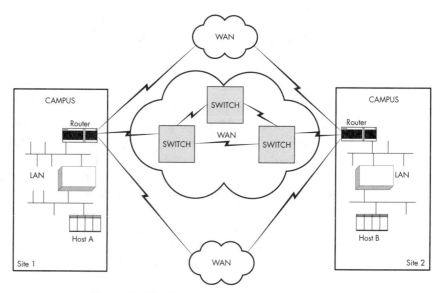

Figure 6–21   Enterprise network cabling system.

dictable results. Attempting to optimize network cabling systems that feature thousands of nodes can pose even more complex problems.

Despite improvements in equipment performance and media capabilities, network cabling system design is becoming more difficult. The trend is toward increasingly complex environments involving multiple media, multiple protocols, and interconnection to networks outside any single organization's dominion of control. Carefully designing network cabling systems can reduce the hardships associated with growth as a networking environment evolves.

The last part of this chapter provides an overview of the technologies available today to design network cabling systems from Cisco Systems' perspective. Discussions are divided into the following general topics:

- designing campus networks
- designing WANs
- utilizing remote connection design
- providing integrated solutions
- determining your network cabling system requirements [4]

Campus Networks Design

A campus is a building or group of buildings all connected into one enterprise network that consists of many local area networks. A campus is generally a portion of a company (or the whole company) constrained to a fixed geographic area, as shown in Figure 6–22 [4].

The distinct characteristic of a campus environment is that the company that owns the campus network usually owns the physical wires deployed in the campus. The campus network topology is primarily LAN technology connecting all the end systems within the building. Campus networks generally use LAN technologies, such as Ethernet, token ring, fiber distributed data interface, Fast Ethernet, Gigabit Ethernet, and asynchronous transfer mode (ATM).

A large campus with groups of buildings can also use WAN technology to connect the buildings. Although the wiring and protocols of a campus might be based on WAN technology, they do not share the WAN constraint of the high cost of bandwidth. After the wire is installed, bandwidth is inexpensive because the company owns the wires and there is no recurring cost to a service provider. However, upgrading the physical wiring can be expensive.

Consequently, network designers generally deploy a campus design that is optimized for the fastest functional architecture that runs on existing physical wire. They might also upgrade wiring to meet the requirements of emerg-

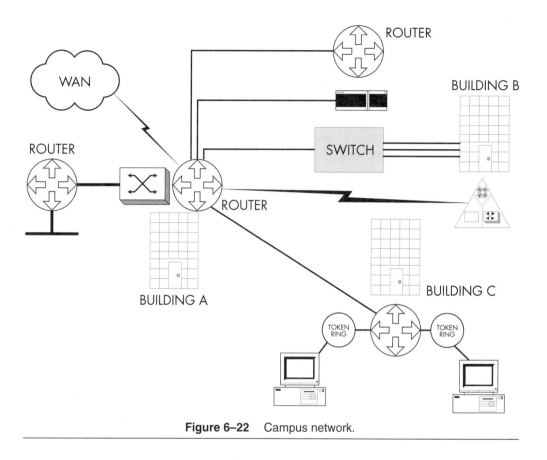

Figure 6–22   Campus network.

ing applications. For example, higher-speed technologies, such as Fast Ethernet, Gigabit Ethernet, and ATM as a backbone architecture, and Layer 2
switching provide dedicated bandwidth to the desktop.

Trends in Campus Design.   In the past, network designers had
only a limited number of hardware options (routers or hubs) when purchasing a technology for their campus networks. Consequently, it was rare to
make a hardware design mistake. Hubs were for wiring closets and routers
were for the data center or main telecommunications operations.

Recently, local area networking has been revolutionized by the exploding use of LAN switching at Layer 2 (the data link layer) to increase performance and to provide more bandwidth to meet new data networking
applications. LAN switches provide this performance benefit by increasing
bandwidth and throughput for workgroups and local servers. Network
designers are deploying LAN switches out toward the network's edge in

wiring closets. These switches are usually installed to replace shared concentrator hubs and give higher bandwidth connections to the end user.

Layer 3 networking is required in the network to interconnect the switched workgroups and to provide services that include security, quality of service (QoS), and traffic management. Routing integrates these switched networks, and provides the security, stability, and control needed to build functional and scalable networks.

Traditionally, Layer 2 switching has been provided by LAN switches, and Layer 3 networking has been provided by routers. Increasingly, these two networking functions are being integrated into common platforms. For example, multilayer switches that provide Layer 2 and 3 functionality are now appearing in the marketplace.

With the advent of such technologies as Layer 3 switching, LAN switching, and virtual LANs (VLANs), building campus networks is becoming more complex than in the past. Table 6–7 summarizes the various LAN technologies that are required to build successful campus networks [4].

Table 6–7   Summary of LAN Technologies

LAN Technology	Typical Uses
Routing technologies	Routing is a key technology for connecting LANs in a campus network. It can be either Layer 3 switching or more traditional routing with Layer 3 switching and additional router features.
Gigabit Ethernet	Gigabit Ethernet builds on top of the Ethernet protocol, but increases speed tenfold over Fast Ethernet to 1,000 Mbps, or 1 Gbps. Gigabit Ethernet provides high bandwidth capacity for backbone designs while providing backward compatibility for installed media.
LAN switching technologies • Ethernet switching	Ethernet switching provides Layer 2 switching, and offers dedicated Ethernet segments for each connection. This is the base fabric of the network.
• Token ring switching	Token ring switching offers the same functionality as Ethernet switching, but uses token ring technology. You can use a token ring switch as either a transparent bridge or as a source-route bridge.
ATM switching technologies	ATM switching offers high-speed switching technology for voice, video, and data. Its operation is similar to LAN switching technologies for data operations. ATM, however, offers high bandwidth capacity.

Network designers are now designing campus networks by purchasing separate equipment types (for example, routers, Ethernet switches, and ATM switches) and then linking them together. Although individual purchase decisions might seem harmless, network designers must not forget that the entire network forms a network cabling system.

It is possible to separate these technologies and build thoughtful designs using each new technology, but network designers must consider the overall integration of the network. If this overall integration is not considered, the result can be networks that have a much higher risk of network outages, downtime, and congestion than ever before.

WAN Design

WAN communication occurs between geographically separated areas. In enterprise network cabling systems, WANs connect campuses together. When a local end station wants to communicate with a remote end station (an end station located at a different site), information must be sent over one or more WAN links. Routers within enterprise network cabling systems represent the LAN/WAN junction points of a network cabling system. These routers determine the most appropriate path through the network cabling system for the required data streams.

WAN links are connected by switches, which are devices that relay information through the WAN and dictate the service provided by the WAN. WAN communication is often called a service because the network provider often charges users for the services provided by the WAN (called tariffs). WAN services are provided through the following three primary switching technologies:

- Circuit switching
- Packet switching
- Cell switching [4]

Each switching technique has advantages and disadvantages. For example, circuit-switched networks offer users dedicated bandwidth that cannot be infringed upon by other users. In contrast, packet-switched networks have traditionally offered more flexibility and used network bandwidth more efficiently than circuit-switched networks. Cell switching, however, combines some aspects of circuit and packet switching to produce networks with low latency and high throughput. Cell switching is rapidly gaining in popularity. ATM is currently the most prominent cell-switched technology.

WAN Design Trends. Traditionally, WAN communication has been characterized by relatively low throughput, high delay, and high error rates. WAN connections are mostly characterized by the cost of renting media (wire) from a service provider to connect two or more campuses together. Because the WAN infrastructure is often rented from a service provider, WAN network designs must optimize the cost of bandwidth and bandwidth efficiency. For example, all technologies and features used to connect campuses over a WAN are developed to meet the following design requirements:

- optimize WAN bandwidth;
- minimize the tariff cost; and
- maximize the effective service to the end users.

Recently, traditional shared-media networks are being overtaxed because of the following new network requirements:

- necessity to connect to remote sites;
- growing need for users to have remote access to their networks;
- explosive growth of the corporate intranets; and
- increased use of enterprise servers [4].

Network designers are turning to WAN technology to support these new requirements. WAN connections generally handle mission-critical information, and are optimized for price/performance bandwidth. The routers connecting the campuses, for example, generally apply traffic optimization, multiple paths for redundancy, dial backup for disaster recovery, and QoS for critical applications. Table 6–8 summarizes the various WAN technologies that support such large-scale network cabling system requirements [4].

Table 6–8   Summary of WAN Technologies

WAN Technology	Typical Uses
Asymmetric digital subscriber line	A new modem technology. Converts existing twisted pair telephone lines into access paths for multimedia and high-speed data communications. ADSL transmits more than 6 Mbps to a subscriber, and as much as 640 kbps more in both directions.
Analog modem	Analog modems can be used by telecommuters and mobile users who access the network less than two hours per day, or for backup for another type of link.

Table 6–8   continued

WAN Technology	Typical Uses
Leased line	Leased lines can be used for point-to-point protocol (PPP) networks and hub-and-spoke topologies, or for backup for another type of link.
Integrated services digital network (ISDN)	ISDN can be used for cost-effective remote access to corporate networks. It provides support for voice and video as well as a backup for another type of link.
Frame relay	Frame relay provides a cost-effective, high-speed, low-latency mesh topology between remote sites. It can be used in both private and carrier-provided networks.
Switched multimegabit data service (SMDS)	SMDS provides high-speed, high-performance connections across public data networks. It can also be deployed in metropolitan area networks.
X.25	X.25 can provide a reliable WAN circuit or backbone. It also provides support for legacy applications.
WAN ATM	WAN ATM can be used to accelerate bandwidth requirements. It also provides support for multiple QoS classes for differing application requirements for delay and loss.

Remote Connection Design Utilization

Remote connections link single users (mobile users and/or telecommuters) and branch offices to a local campus or the Internet. Typically, a remote site is a small site that has few users and therefore needs a smaller size WAN connection. The remote requirements of a network cabling system, however, usually involve a large number of remote single users or sites, which causes the aggregate WAN charge to be exaggerated.

Because there are so many remote single users or sites, the aggregate WAN bandwidth cost is proportionally more important in remote connections than in WAN connections. Given that the three-year cost of a network is non-equipment expenses, the WAN media rental charge from a service provider is the largest cost component of a remote network. Unlike WAN connections, smaller sites or single users seldom need to be connected to the network for 24 hours a day, however they may, and do, require access at any given time.

Consequently, network designers typically choose between dial-up and dedicated WAN options for remote connections. Remote connections generally run at speeds of 128 Kbps or lower. A network designer might also employ bridges in a remote site for their ease of implementation, simple topology, and low traffic requirements.

Remote Connections Trends.   Today, there is a large selection of remote WAN media that include the following:

- analog modem
- asymmetric digital subscriber line
- leased line
- frame relay
- X.25
- ISDN [4]

Remote connections also optimize for the appropriate WAN option to provide cost-effective bandwidth, minimize dial-up tariff costs, and maximize effective service to users.

LAN/WAN Integration Trends.   Today, 90 percent of computing power resides on desktops, and that power is growing exponentially. Distributed applications are increasingly bandwidth-hungry, and the emergence of the Internet is driving many LAN architectures to the limit. Voice communications have increased significantly with more reliance on centralized voice mail systems for verbal communications. The network cabling system is the critical tool for information flow. Network cabling systems are being pressured to cost less, yet support the emerging applications and higher number of users with increased performance.

To date, local- and wide-area communications have remained logically separate. In the LAN, bandwidth is free and connectivity is limited only by hardware and implementation costs. The LAN has carried data only. In the WAN, bandwidth has been the overriding cost, and such delay-sensitive traffic as voice has remained separate from data. New applications and the economics of supporting them, however, are forcing these conventions to change.

The Internet is the first source of multimedia to the desktop, and immediately breaks the rules. Such Internet applications as voice and real-time video require better, more predictable LAN and WAN performance. These multimedia applications are fast becoming an essential part of the business productivity toolkit. As companies begin to consider implementing new intranet-based, bandwidth-intensive multimedia applications (such as video training, video conferencing, and voice-over IP), the impact of these applications on the existing networking infrastructure is a serious concern. If a company has relied on its corporate network for business-critical SNA traffic, for example, and wants to bring a new video training application on line, the network must be able to provide guaranteed quality of service that delivers the multimedia traffic, but does not allow it to interfere with the business-critical traffic (SNA). ATM has emerged as one of the technologies for integrating LANs and WANs. QoS features of ATM can support any traffic type in separate or mixed streams, delay-sensitive traffic, and non-delay-sensitive traffic, as shown in Figure 6–23 [4].

ATM can also scale from low to high speeds. It has been adopted by all the industry's equipment vendors, from LAN to private branch exchange (PBX).

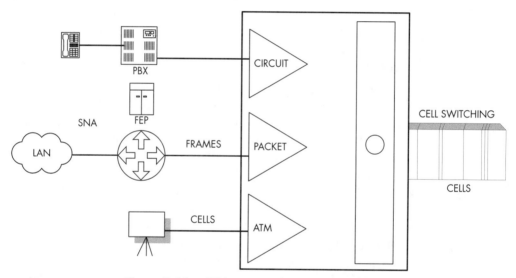

Figure 6–23   ATM support of various traffic types.

Integrated Solutions

The trend in network cabling systems is to provide network designers greater flexibility in solving multiple network cabling system problems without creating multiple networks or writing off existing data communication investments. Routers might be relied upon to provide a reliable, secure network and act as a barrier against inadvertent broadcast storms in the local networks. Switches, which can be divided into two main categories (LAN switches and WAN switches) can be deployed at the workgroup, campus backbone, or WAN level. Remote sites might use low-end routers for connection to the WAN.

Underlying and integrating all Cisco products is the Cisco Internetworking Operating System (Cisco IOS) software. The Cisco IOS software enables disparate groups, diverse devices, and multiple protocols all to be integrated into a highly reliable and scalable network. Cisco IOS software also supports this network cabling system with advanced security, quality of service, and traffic services.

Determining Your Network Cabling System Requirements

Designing a network cabling system can be a challenging task. Your first step is to understand your network cabling system requirements. The following is intended as a guide for helping you determine these requirements.

Network cabling system devices must reflect the goals, characteristics, and policies of the organizations in which they operate. Two primary goals drive network cabling system design and implementation: First, you have *application availability*—where networks carry application information between computers. If the applications are not available to network users, the network is not doing its job. Second, you have the *cost of ownership*—where information system (IS) budgets today often run in the millions of dollars. As large organizations increasingly rely on electronic data for managing business activities, the associated costs of computing resources will continue to rise.

A well-designed network cabling system can help to balance these objectives. When properly implemented, the network infrastructure can optimize application availability and allow the cost-effective use of existing network resources.

Optimizing Availability and Cost: The Design Problem. In general, the network design problem consists of the following three general elements:

- *Environmental givens:* include the location of hosts, servers, terminals, and other end nodes; the projected traffic for the environment; and the projected costs for delivering different service levels.

- *Performance constraints:* consist of network reliability, traffic through-put, and host/client computer speeds (for example, network interface cards and hard drive access speeds).
- *Network cabling system variables:* include the network topology, line capacities, and packet flow assignments [4].

The goal is to minimize cost based on these elements while delivering service that does not compromise established availability requirements. You face two primary concerns: availability and cost. These issues are essentially at odds. Any increase in availability must generally be reflected as an increase in cost. As a result, you must weigh the relative importance of resource avail-ability and overall cost carefully.

As Figure 6–24 shows, designing your network is an iterative activity [4]. The discussions that follow outline several areas that you should care-fully consider when planning your network cabling system implementation.

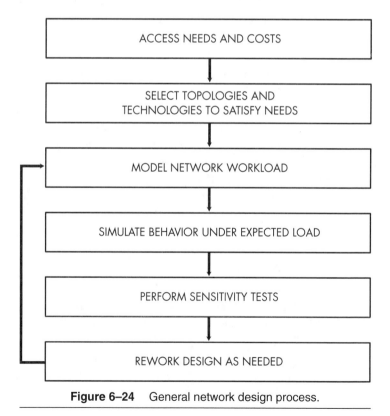

Figure 6–24   General network design process.

Assessing User Requirements Assessment.   In general, users primarily want application availability in their networks. The chief components of application availability are response time, throughput, and reliability.

Response time. Response time is the time between entry of a command or keystroke and the host system's execution of the command or delivery of a response. User satisfaction about response time is generally considered to be a monotonic function up to some limit, at which point user satisfaction falls off to nearly zero. Applications in which fast response time is considered critical include interactive online services, such as automated tellers and point-of-sale machines.

Throughput. Applications that put high-volume traffic onto the network have more effect on throughput than end-to-end connections. Throughput-intensive applications generally involve file-transfer activities. However, throughput-intensive applications also usually have low response-time requirements. Indeed, they can often be scheduled at times when response-time-sensitive traffic is low (for example, after normal work hours).

Reliability. Although reliability is always important, some applications have genuine requirements that exceed typical needs. Organizations that require nearly 100 percent up time conduct all activities online or over the telephone. Financial services, securities exchanges, and emergency/police/military operations are a few examples. These situations imply a requirement for a high level of hardware and topological redundancy. Determining the cost of any downtime is essential in determining the relative importance of reliability to your network cabling system.

Obtaining User Requirements Information.   You can assess user requirements in a number of ways. The more involved your users are in the process, the more likely that your evaluation will be accurate. In general, you can use the following methods to obtain this information: user community profiles; interviews, focus groups, and surveys; and human factors tests.

User community profiles. User community profiles outline what different user groups require. This is the first step in determining network cabling system requirements. Although many users have roughly the same requirements of an electronic mail system, engineering groups using XWindows terminals and Sun workstations in a network file system (NFS) environment have different needs from PC users sharing print servers in a finance department.

Interviews, focus groups, and surveys. Interviews, focus groups, and surveys build a baseline for implementing a network cabling system. You must understand that some groups might require access to common servers. Others might want to allow external access to specific internal computing resources. Certain organizations might require information technology support systems to be managed in a particular way according to some external standard. The least formal method of obtaining information is to conduct interviews with key user groups. Focus groups can also be used to gather information and generate discussion among different organizations with similar (or dissimilar) interests. Finally, formal surveys can be used to get a statistically valid reading of user sentiment regarding a particular service level or proposed network cabling system architecture.

Human factors tests. The most expensive, time-consuming, and possibly revealing method is to conduct a test involving representative users in a lab environment. This is most applicable when evaluating response time requirements. As an example, you might set up working systems and have users perform normal remote host activities from the lab network. By evaluating user reactions to variations in host responsiveness, you can create benchmark thresholds for acceptable performance.

Proprietary and Nonproprietary Solutions Assessment.   Compatibility, conformance, and interoperability are related to the problem of balancing proprietary functionality and open network cabling system flexibility. As a network designer, you might be forced to choose between implementing a multivendor environment and implementing a specific, proprietary capability. For example, the interior gateway routing protocol (IGRP) provides many useful capabilities, such as a number of features that are designed to enhance its stability. These include hold-downs, split horizons, and poison reverse updates.

The negative side is that IGRP is a proprietary routing protocol. In contrast, the integrated intermediate system-to-intermediate system (IS-IS) protocol is an open network cabling system alternative that also provides a fast converging routing environment. However, implementing an open routing protocol can potentially result in greater multiple-vendor configuration complexity.

The decisions that you make have far-ranging effects on your overall network cabling system design. Assume that you decide to implement integrated IS-IS instead of IGRP. In doing this, you gain a measure of interoperability; however, you lose some functionality. For instance, you cannot load balance traffic over unequal parallel paths. Similarly, some modems provide a high level of proprietary diagnostic capabilities, but require that all modems throughout a network be of the same vendor type to fully exploit proprietary diagnostics.

Previous network cabling system (and networking) investments and expectations for future requirements have considerable influence over your choice of implementations. You need to consider installed network cabling system and networking equipment; applications running (or to be run) on the network; traffic patterns; physical location of sites, hosts, and users; rate of growth of the user community; and both physical and logical network layout.

Assessing Costs. The network cabling system is a strategic element in your overall information system design. As such, the cost of your network cabling system is much more than the sum of your equipment purchase orders. View it as a total cost-of-ownership issue. You must consider the entire life cycle of your network cabling system environment. A brief list of costs associated with network cabling systems follows (see Chapter 7, "Cost Justification and Consideration," for detailed information on assessing costs and justifying them).

Equipment hardware and software costs. You should consider what is really being bought when you purchase your systems. Costs should include initial purchase and installation, maintenance, and projected upgrade costs.

Performance tradeoff costs. You should consider the cost of going from a five-second response time to a half-second response time. Such improvements can cost quite a bit in terms of media selection, network interfaces, network cabling system nodes, modems, and WAN services.

Installation costs. Installing a site's physical cable plant can be the most expensive element of a large network. The costs include installation labor, site modification, fees associated with local code conformance, and costs incurred to ensure compliance with environmental restrictions (such as asbestos removal). Other important elements in keeping your costs to a minimum will include developing a well-planned wiring closet layout and implementing color code conventions for cable runs.

Expansion costs. You should calculate the cost of ripping out all thick Ethernet, adding additional functionality, or moving to a new location. Projecting your future requirements and accounting for future needs saves time and money.

Support costs. Complicated network cabling systems cost more to monitor, configure, and maintain. Your network cabling system should be no more complicated than necessary. Costs include training, direct labor (network managers and administrators), sparing, and replacement costs. Additional costs that should be included are out-of-band management, SNMP management stations, and power.

Cost of downtime. You should evaluate the cost for every minute that a user is unable to access a file server or a centralized database. If this cost is high, you must attribute a high cost to downtime. If the cost is high enough, fully redundant network cabling systems might be your best option.

Opportunity costs. Every choice you make has an opposing alternative option. Whether that option is a specific hardware platform, topology solution, level of redundancy, or system integration alternative, there are always options. Opportunity costs are the costs of not picking one of those options. The opportunity costs of not switching to newer technologies and topologies might be lost competitive advantage, lower productivity, and slower overall performance. Any effort to integrate opportunity costs into your analysis can help to make accurate comparisons at the beginning of your project.

Sunken costs. Your investment in existing cable plant, routers, concentrators, switches, hosts, and other equipment and software are your sunken costs. If the sunken cost is high, you might need to modify your networks so that your existing network cabling system can continue to be utilized. Although comparatively low incremental costs might appear to be more attractive than significant redesign costs, your organization might pay more in the long run by not upgrading systems. Overreliance on sunken costs can cost your organization sales and market share when calculating the cost of network cabling system modifications and additions.

Consultants should never tell a client to assess sunken costs when deciding on an upgrade. Normally, sunken costs are based on higher purchase prices as technology costs fall and a very expensive prior installation that does not meet their current needs is even more expensive to try to use.

Work Load Modeling: Estimating Traffic. Empirical work-load modeling consists of instrumenting a working network cabling system and monitoring traffic for a given number of users, applications, and network topology. Try to characterize activity throughout a normal work day in terms of the type of traffic passed, level of traffic, response time of hosts, time to execute file transfers, and so on. You can also observe utilization on existing network equipment over the test period.

If the tested network cabling system characteristics are close to the new network cabling system, you can try extrapolating to the new network cabling system's number of users, applications, and topology. This is a best-guess approach to traffic estimation given the unavailability of tools to characterize detailed traffic behavior.

In addition to passive monitoring of an existing network, you can measure activity and traffic generated by a known number of users attached to a representative test network and then extrapolate findings to your anticipated population.

One problem with modeling workloads on networks is that it is difficult to accurately pinpoint traffic load and network device performance as functions of the number of users, type of application, and geographical location. This is especially true without a real network in place. Consider the following factors that influence the dynamics of the network:

- *The time-dependent nature of network access:* Peak periods can vary; measurements must reflect a range of observations that includes peak demand.
- *Differences associated with type of traffic:* Routed and bridged traffic place different demands on network cabling system devices and protocols; some protocols are sensitive to dropped packets; some application types require more bandwidth.
- *The random (nondeterministic) nature of network traffic:* Exact arrival time and specific effects of traffic are unpredictable [4].

Sensitivity testing. From a practical point of view, sensitivity testing involves breaking stable links and observing what happens. When working with a test network, this is relatively easy. Disturb the network by removing an active interface, and monitor how the change is handled by the network cabling system: how traffic is rerouted; the speed of convergence; whether any connectivity is lost; and whether problems arise in handling specific types of traffic. You can also change the level of traffic on a network to determine the effects on the network when traffic levels approach media saturation. This empirical testing is a type of regression testing: A series of specific modifications (tests) are repeated on different versions of network configurations. By monitoring the effects on the design variations, you can characterize the relative resilience of the design.

Leviton's Nonstandard Structured Cabling Technologies

Leviton Manufacturing Company, Inc.'s nonstandard structured cabling products provide the communications infrastructure to support audio, video, phone, and data communications while *future-proofing* the home's wiring system against the risk of future obsolescence. These products support everything from satellite and digital TV to Internet, home office, home theater, home automation, and home security applications.

Leviton's media versatile panel lies at the heart of the company's structured cabling system. This device features a flexible, open architecture that accommodates voice and data connector blocks, audio and video distribution components, electronics, and LAN hubs. The device can be surface-mounted or recess-mounted and provides multiple knockouts for various cable entry points.

The company's line of Decora QuickPort™ wallplate inserts can accommodate up to 6 snap-in modules in any combination of voice, data, audio, and video connectors [5]. Devices are gangable and can be used with any Decora wallplate.

Applications

QuickPort® Snap-In Connectors are designed for commercial and residential environments to support category 3, category 5, category 5e, and category 6-compliant cabling applications and other voice, data, audio, and video applications for 22-26 AWG twisted pair, coax, speaker wire, and fiber optic cable. Fully field-configurable, these devices provide point-of-use connectivity for a broad range of applications where convenience or building requirements dictate the use of a modular communications outlet. Quick-Port Snap-In Connectors fit into a variety of QuickPort housings, including standard single- and dual-gang wallplates, Decora Multimedia Inserts, and brass floorplates with a flush-fitting screw cap that keeps internal components free from dirt and dust when the device is not in use. The QuickPort® Snap-In Connectors feature the following:

- Mix and match, field configurable, multimedia connectors for a wide variety of typical residential or commercial configurations.
- QuickPort Connectors available in the following styles: 6-Conductor Voice-Grade, category 3, category 5, category 5e and 5e Plus, category 6, BNC, F-Connector, RCA speaker, ST Fiber, Banana Jack, and Binding Post.
- Supports voice, data, audio, and video applications for 22-26 American Wire Gauge (AWG) twisted pair, speaker wire, coax, and fiber optic cable.
- Devices comply with UL, CSA, FCC Part 68, and TIA-568A Category-specific requirements.
- Suitable for high-speed data networks when configured with category 5 connector or better.
- Made of high impact, self-extinguishing thermoplastic (rated UL 94V-0).
- Gold-plated phosphor bronze spring wire contacts for long service life.
- Voice grade and category-compliant connectors have 110-style termination with one-step termination and trim [5].

Leviton certifies the performance of jacks denoted as category 3 or category 5 compliant.

Novell Networking Nonstandard Design Issues for Important High-Speed Cabling Technologies

In today's business environment, among the most widely discussed network cabling topics are the technologies that make networks faster, such as Fast Ethernet and Firewire, as well as the technologies that connect geographically distant networks, such as frame relay and ATM. As networks grow, so does the amount of information sent across these network cables. For this reason, transmission speed is of utmost importance. This last section will provide brief descriptions of the following technologies, which are dramatically improving the transmission speed on network cables.

- Fast Ethernet
- IEEE 1394/USB
- Fiber channel
- Fiber distributed data interface (FDDI)
- X.25
- Frame relay
- Asynchronous transfer mode (ATM)
- Integrated services digital network (ISDN)
- Asymmetric digital subscriber line (ADSL)
- Synchronous optical network (SONET) [6]

The first three (Fast Ethernet, Firewire/Universal Serial Bus [USB], and fiber channel) apply to LANs. The other technologies in this list are reserved almost exclusively for WANs.

Fast Ethernet

100Base-T (otherwise known as Fast Ethernet) is a high-speed LAN technology. It has been designated as the IEEE 802.3u standard. It functions at the data-link (open system interconnection [OSI] level 2) layer's MAC sublayer, and provides data transfer rates as high as 100 megabits per second (Mbps).

Distinguishing Characteristics. Like 10Base-T Ethernet, 100Base-T uses carrier sense multiple access/collision detection (CSMA/CD) as the media access control method. 100Base-T is based on the scalability of CSMA/CD. Scalability means that you can easily enlarge or downsize your network without degrading network performance, reliability, and manageability.

CSMA/CD was known to be scalable before the 100Base-T standard was created: a scaled-down version of Ethernet (1Base-5) uses CSMA/CD, provides data transfer rates of 1 Mbps, and enables longer transmission distances between repeaters. If CSMA/CD could be scaled down, then it could be scaled up. Specifying changes such as decreased transmission distances between repeaters produced a reliable data transfer rate of 100 Mbps—10 times faster than traditional 10Base-T Ethernet. 100Base-T supports category 5 unshielded twisted pair wiring: it uses two wire pairs of category 5 cable (see Figure 6–25) [6].

Advantages. 100Base-T adapter cards and compatible cable are currently available from various vendors. In addition, it is easy to upgrade from 10Base-T Ethernet to 100Base-T Ethernet. Both traditional 10Base-T and 100Base-T Ethernet use CSMA/CD, and some network cards now support both 10 Mbps and 100 Mbps Ethernet. The adapter cards automatically sense whether it is a 10 Mbps or 100 Mbps environment, and adjust their speed accordingly. Because 10Base-T and 100Base-T Ethernet can coexist, network supervisors can upgrade network stations from 10Base-T to

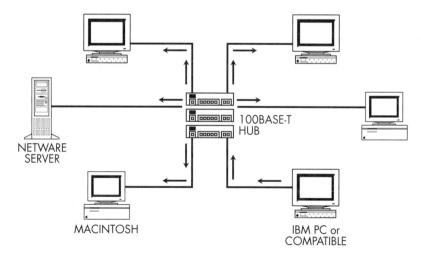

Figure 6–25   Host systems connected to a complex multiserver NetWare 100Base-T network.

100Base-T one at a time, as needed. Moreover, most network supervisors are already familiar with CSMA/CD, so there is no need for expensive retraining.

100Base-T can be an inexpensive way to make your network faster. Adapter cards are not significantly more expensive than 10Base-T cards. In addition, category 5 UTP cable is relatively inexpensive, and some organizations already have category 5 cable installed.

Disadvantages.   100Base-T will reduce the maximum network size compared to 10Base-T, because the standard specifies shorter transmission distances between repeaters. Compared to 10Base-T, 100Base-T reduces the maximum network diameter from 500 to 205 meters. For existing networks that exceed 205 meters, routers must be installed between 100Base-T network segments. Furthermore, companies that do not currently support category 5 UTP cable will need to rewire their places of business to implement a 100Base-T network.

Current Developments.   Faster standards are always being developed and established and Ethernet is no exception. Two new standards are currently being developed in this class. The first of these is Gigabit Ethernet (also known as 1000Base-T or 802.3z). This standard increases transmission speed on a standard Ethernet network to 1000 Mbps, or 10 times that of 100Base-T. It was designed to function on the same cabling as 100Base-T, so that upgrades would be inexpensive and straightforward. Right now, the primary focus for Gigabit Ethernet is as a backbone service for 100Base-T networks. As the hardware becomes more prevalent, however, 1000Base-T subnetworks and workstations will become more common.

In addition to Gigabit Ethernet, there is also an emerging standard (not quite fully developed yet) known as 10 Gigabit Ethernet or 802.3 Higher Speed Study Group (HSSG). Although this standard will be based on the preceding Ethernet standards, it will utilize higher capacity cabling (mostly optical fiber grades with some high-capacity coaxial). 10 Gigabit Ethernet will support data transmission speeds of 10,000 Mbps.

Gigabit Ethernet and the emerging 10 Gigabit Ethernet have not yet reached wide-scale acceptance in the world of computer networking. However, with the ever-increasing amount of data being transmitted, it will not be long before they are commonplace.

IEEE 1394 (Firewire)/USB

The IEEE 1394 standard (also known as Firewire) and the Universal Serial Bus (USB) standard are two standards that apply to data transmission between computers and peripheral hardware. Although these two standards are different, their application is fundamentally related and therefore they are covered in the same section here in this chapter.

Distinguishing Characteristics.   The IEEE 1394 standard is a high-speed standard developed for processing-intensive peripherals such as scanners, digital cameras, and removable storage devices. As a complementary standard, USB is more suitable for peripherals that do not require as much speed, such as mice and keyboards. Both standards use a simple cable with jacks similar to telephone jacks or Ethernet RJ45 jacks. Most newer computers include USB ports; IEEE 1394 ports will be integrated into computer hardware design in the near future.

Advantages.   The most obvious advantage of both IEEE 1394 and USB is the ease of use. Both standards support *hot swapping* of peripheral components. This means that one device can be unplugged from the computer and another plugged in (and recognized by the computer) without having to reboot the system. This is not possible with standard parallel port or serial port connections. In addition, both 1394 and USB standards allow you to *daisy chain* peripherals. This means that the peripherals can all be hooked together in a long chain and then attached to a single port on the computer: each peripheral does not require its own port. The IEEE 1394 standard allows for 63 daisy-chained devices, while USB will support over 100. In addition, both standards support data transfer speeds higher than conventional ports. USB supports 12 Mbps (1.5 MBps) data transfer and IEEE 1394 supports up to 400 Mbps (with several faster versions currently under development).

Disadvantages.   The most common disadvantage of both standards is the lack of universal acceptance. Although USB has achieved much more acceptance than the newer IEEE 1394 technology, it is still relatively new and therefore the compatible peripherals are generally more expensive than those conforming to older standards. Peripherals that conform to the IEEE 1394 standard are substantially more expensive than those conforming to older standards. As USB and IEEE 1394 become more prevalent, however, the price of the compatible peripherals will decline.

Fiber Channel

Fiber channel refers to a relatively new application for optical fiber components. The most common usage of fiber channel is in storage area networks (SANs), where it is used to connect clustered servers to storage systems. This technology is also being considered as an internal drive interface (between the hard drive and the processor within a computer) and as a high-speed switching service to connect several server clusters and SANs into a large interconnected network.

Distinguishing Characteristics. Fiber channel technology consists of optical fiber cables, specialized hubs, and Gigabit interface converters (GBICs). The GBICs are used to convert electrical signals into optical signals and vice versa. The cabling is divided into two categories: multimode and single-mode fiber. Multimode fiber has a larger diameter core and allows multiple transmissions to travel simultaneously. Single-mode fiber allows only one transmission path.

Advantages. Fiber channel technology has several advantages over other transmission media, but the most important is the speed of data transmission. Fiber channel supports data transmission speeds of 100 Mbps. In addition, since the data is transmitted as a pulse of light rather than an electronic signal, it can travel much greater distances (up to 10 kilometers) before suffering any signal degradation. Likewise, the data is immune to electromagnetic interference and radiates no energy (no heat-shielding required).

Disadvantages. The main disadvantage of fiber channel is the cost: optical fiber is much more costly than conventional copper cable and more expensive to install. The advantages of fiber channel, however, greatly outweigh the cost in many applications.

Fiber Distributed Data Interface

FDDI is also a high-speed LAN technology. It is not generally used for direct connection to desktop computers, but rather as a network backbone connecting two or more LAN segments to provide a path for data transmission between them, as shown in Figure 6–26 [6]. A simple backbone might con-

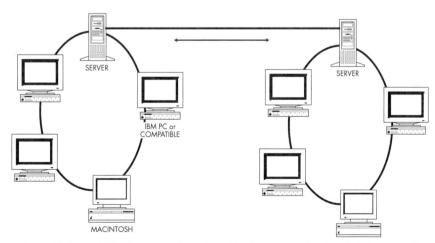

Figure 6–26 A simple server-based backbone connecting two LAN segments.

nect two servers through a high-speed link consisting of network adapter cards and cable.

FDDI has been designated ANSI X3T9.5 and operates at the physical and data link layers (levels 1 and 2) of the OSI model. Like 100Base-T, FDDI provides data transfer rates as high as 100 Mbps.

Distinguishing Characteristics.   FDDI networks have a dual, counter-rotating ring topology. This topology consists of two logical closed signal paths called *rings*. Signals on the rings travel in opposite directions from each other. Although both rings can carry data, the primary ring usually carries the data while the secondary ring serves as a backup.

On FDDI networks, every node acts as a repeater. FDDI supports four kinds of nodes: dual-attached stations (DASs), single-attached stations (SASs), single-attached concentrators (SACs), and dual-attached concentrators (DACs), as shown in Figure 6–27 [6]. DASs and DACs attach to both rings, while SASs and SACs attach only to the primary ring. Several SASs

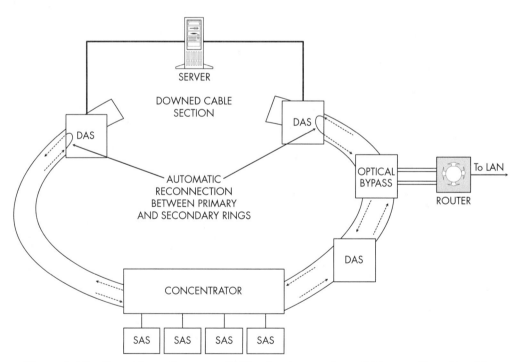

Figure 6–27   If a cable section on an FDDI network goes down, DASs on either side of the failed section automatically reconnect the primary and secondary rings. Also note that the server has a redundant connection to improve reliability.

often attach to the primary ring through a concentrator, so that an SAS failure will not bring down the entire network. If the cable is cut or a link between nodes fails, DASs or DACs on either side of the failure route signals around the failed segment, using the secondary ring to keep the network functioning. FDDI also uses token passing for its MAC method and is implemented using fiber optic cable.

Advantages.   FDDI is a fast, reliable standard. The dual, counter-rotating ring topology increases the network's reliability by keeping it functioning even if a cable is damaged. FDDI also offers network management support, which was designed directly into the standard. In addition, the standard includes the copper distributed data interface (CDDI) specification for building a network using UTP cable (which is less expensive than fiber optic cable).

Disadvantages.   FDDI's main disadvantage is price. FDDI adapter cards and fiber optic cable are both relatively expensive compared to other technologies offering the same speed. Fiber optic cable installation also requires technicians trained specifically for this purpose. Even CDDI adapters (for copper wire), which are less expensive than FDDI adapters, are more costly than 100Base-T adapters.

X.25

X.25 is a commonly used WAN standard at the network layer (OSI layer 3) of the OSI model. It is a standard of the ITU, and includes data-link and physical layer protocols (link access procedure balanced [LAPB] and X.21). X.25 provides data transfer rates of 9.6 kilobits per second (kbps) to 256 kbps, depending on the connection method.

Distinguishing Characteristics.   X.25 specifies the interface for connecting computers on different networks with an intermediate connection through a packet-switched network (for example, CompuServe or Tymnet), as shown in Figure 6–28 [6]. X.25 was defined when the quality of transmission media was relatively poor. As a result, the standard specifies that each node in the packet-switched network must receive each packet completely and check it for errors before forwarding it.

Advantages.   X.25 is well understood and reliable. Connections to X.25 networks can be made through the existing telephone system, integrated services digital network (ISDN), and leased lines. Because access is simple, it is comparatively inexpensive. X.25 is also available worldwide. In countries with little digital telecommunications infrastructure, X.25 may be the best WAN technology available.

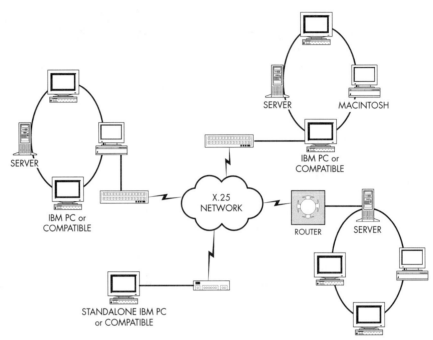

Figure 6–28   X.25 networks are often provided by telecommunication carriers.
CompuServe uses X.25 on its network.

Disadvantages.   Although it is widely available, X.25 is slow compared to newer technologies. The process of checking each packet for errors
at each node limits data transfer rates. X.25 also uses variable-size packets,
which can cause transmission delays at intermediate nodes. In addition, many
people connect to X.25 networks through modems, which limit data transfer
rates to between 9.6 kbps and 56 kbps. Although X.25 is likely to remain in
common use for some time, newer, faster standards are already replacing it.

Frame Relay

Frame relay, like X.25, is a WAN technology. Approved by ANSI and the
ITU, frame relay works at the data-link layer (OSI layer 2) of the OSI model
and provides data transfer rates from 56 kbps to 1.544 Mbps.

Distinguishing Characteristics.   Frame relay is an interface
specification for connecting LANs over public packet-switched networks.
This standard can be thought of as a simplified version of X.25 designed to
take advantage of digital transmission media.

Frame relay services are typically provided by telecommunications carriers. Customers install a router and lease a line (often a T1 or fractional T1 line) to provide a permanent connection from the customer's site to the telecommunications carrier's network. This connection enables frame relay to use *permanent virtual circuits* (PVCs), which are predefined network paths between two locations.

With frame relay, the router encapsulates (or frames) network layer packets, such as IP and IPX packets, directly into a data-link level protocol, and sends them on to the packet-switched network. Like X.25, frame relay uses variable-size frames, but it eliminates the error checking required on X.25 networks. A frame relay switch simply reads the header and forwards the packet, sometimes without first receiving the frame completely. Intelligent end-stations must identify missing or corrupted frames and request retransmission (see Figure 6–29) [6].

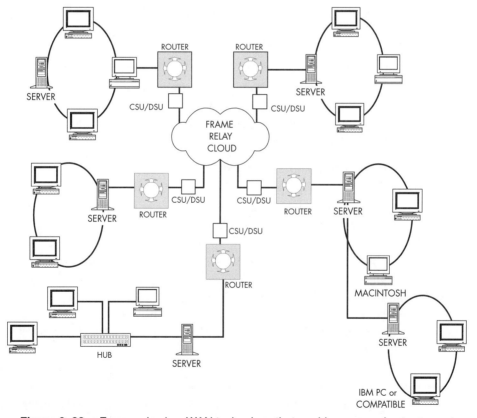

Figure 6–29 Frame relay is a WAN technology that enables companies to connect LANs through a telecommunications carrier's network. AT&T WorldNet Intranet Connect Service currently uses this technology.

Advantages.   Frame relay offers several advantages over X.25. Most importantly, frame relay is faster than X.25. Frame relay uses PVCs over leased lines, rather than a modem connection. Unlike modem connections, PVCs transmit and receive data immediately, eliminating the call setup and handshaking that modems must perform. In addition, frame relay does not require error checking and flow control at the switches, thereby reducing overhead and leaving more bandwidth for data transmission. Also, although not as prevalent as X.25, frame relay is a common standard in many countries. Finally, frame relay is less expensive than other WAN technologies because it provides bandwidth on demand, rather than dedicating bandwidth whether data is being transmitted or not. Although frame relay is fairly complex to implement, value-added resellers and some telephone companies will assist customers in determining their needs and will provide help installing and deploying the technology.

Disadvantages.   Although frame relay is faster than X.25, its speed is limited because it uses variable-size frames, which can cause delays at switches along the frame's path. As a result, frame relay cannot support applications that require low latency, such as real-time video.

Frame relay is also more complex to implement than X.25. Customers must negotiate a service agreement with the phone company, lease a line, and have it installed. They must also purchase and install a frame relay-compatible router.

Asynchronous Transfer Mode

ATM is both a LAN and a WAN technology. It is generally implemented as a backbone technology. The exact relationship of the ATM layers to the OSI model is currently undefined, although ATM LAN emulation works at the data-link layer (OSI layer 2).

ATM is extremely scalable; data transfer rates range from 25 Mbps to 2.4 gigabits per second (Gbps). This wide range of data transfer rates reflects the various ways in which ATM can be used. The 25 Mbps rate is a new offering meant for desktop environments. In LAN backbones, ATM provides data transfer rates of 100 Mbps and 155 Mbps. At the high end, WAN implementations using ATM and SONET together have achieved data transfer rates of 2.4 Gbps. For more information about SONET, see the "Synchronous Optical Network" heading later in this chapter.

Distinguishing Characteristics.   ATM is a cell relay technology, meaning that it uses standard-sized packets called *cells*. The size of an ATM cell is 53 bytes.

In a LAN implementation, ATM functions at the data-link layer's MAC sublayer. It further divides the MAC sublayer into three layers: LAN Emulation, ATM Adaptation Layer (AAL), and ATM. LAN Emulation enables you to integrate ATM with Ethernet and token-ring networks without modifying existing Ethernet or token ring protocols.

On a mixed network, LAN Emulation hardware sits between the Ethernet or token ring segment and the ATM part of the network. It uses the three layers mentioned previously to convert packets moving toward the ATM segment into cells, and to assemble cells moving toward the Ethernet or token ring segment into packets. AAL and ATM put data into standard-sized cells. In most network computing situations, ATM Adaptation layer 5 breaks packets into 48-byte blocks that are then passed to the ATM layer, where the 5-byte header is attached to form a complete 53-byte cell.

Advantages. Many people believe that ATM will become the industry-standard transmission technology for LANs and WANs. Its scalability seems to be limitless. Data transfer rates have climbed into the gigabit range and are still increasing.

One reason that ATM is so fast is its use of cells: because these are a standard size, ATM networks handle data in a predictable, efficient manner at the switches. Standard-sized cells and high-bandwidth media like fiber optic cable also enable ATM to support real-time voice, video, and data traffic.

ATM also offers flexibility in its transmission media. As many as 22 ATM specifications exist for media like UTP, shielded twisted pair (STP), and fiber optic cable. Although it is seen as a technology of the future, ATM can currently be integrated with Ethernet and token ring networks through use of LAN Emulation.

ATM is generally implemented with fiber optic cable.

Disadvantages. ATM standards are still developing. Without industry standards, interoperability between equipment from different vendors is not guaranteed. Furthermore, ATM is currently more expensive than the other high-speed LAN technologies. The expense is preventing many companies from taking ATM to the desktop.

ISDN

ISDN is a set of protocols defined by the ITU to integrate data, voice, and video signals into digital telephone lines. It functions at the physical, data-link, network, and transport layers (levels 1 through 4) of the OSI model. ISDN offers data transfer rates between 56 kbps and either 1.544 Mbps or 2.048 Mbps, depending on the country where it is implemented.

Distinguishing Characteristics.   ISDN makes end-to-end digital connections over telephone lines. Although many telephone networks are almost completely digital, the local loop that connects a home or office to the telephone company's network is not. Most local loops send analog rather than digital signals. ISDN replaces local analog signaling with digital signaling, enabling end-to-end digital communications.

ISDN offers basic rate interface (BRI) for individuals or small branch offices and primary rate interface (PRI) for larger companies. BRI uses two bearer, or B, channels (providing 64 kbps each) to transmit and receive data, and one delta, or D, channel for call setup and management.

PRI is a T1 line. A T1 line in the United States consists of 23 B channels and one D channel, providing a total data transfer rate of 1.544 Mbps. A T1 line in Europe, known as an E1 line, consists of 30 B channels and one D channel, providing a total data transfer rate of 2.048 Mbps. A fractional T1 uses only some of the B channels in a T1 line (and thus offers some fraction of the total T1 data transfer rate).

ISDN requires special equipment at the customer's site, including a digital phone line and a network termination unit (NT-1). An NT-1 converts the bandwidth coming over the line into the B and D channels, and aids the phone company in diagnostic testing. The NT-1 also provides a connection for terminal equipment, such as ISDN telephones and computers that have an ISDN interface. In addition, the NT-1 provides terminal adapter (TA) equipment to connect equipment that is not compatible with ISDN. TA equipment provides an intermediary connection point. Such equipment has an ISDN interface for connection to the NT-1, and a non-ISDN interface for connection to non-ISDN equipment.

Advantages.   ISDN increases speed and broadens data transmission capabilities, especially for those currently using analog modems to remotely connect to an office or to access the Internet. It offers faster call setup and data transfer rates. The transfer rates are acceptable for transmitting voice, data, limited video, fax, and images. ISDN can also be used for limited LAN-to-LAN communications.

With ISDN you can transmit voice and data traffic simultaneously: an ISDN user can talk on the phone and download a data file to his or her computer concurrently, over the same telephone line. For example, one BRI ISDN configuration enables users to use the two B channels (128 kbps) for data and part of the D channel for a telephone conversation.

Disadvantages.   Although widely available in Australia, Japan, and Western Europe, ISDN is available in only limited areas in the United States. Presently, telephone companies are working to make it available throughout the United States.

Acceptance of ISDN in the United States has been slow for several reasons. First, to understand ISDN well enough to even order services requires considerable effort. Furthermore, configuration can be difficult. In addition, ISDN lacks the standards that ensure interoperability. As a result, customers must be careful to purchase equipment that is compatible with the local phone company's equipment. Another problem is that not all phone companies offer the same services, so customers must ensure that the services they need are available in their area. Finally, to take full advantage of ISDN, customers must communicate with others who also have ISDN; however, communications between ISDN and non-ISDN customers is possible.

ADSL

Asymmetric digital subscriber line (ADSL) is a relatively new, high-speed Internet access technology. With the explosive growth in computer networking, business networks, and the use of the Internet, the demand for fast and cost-effective access has also been growing steadily. Although there are many technologies available to provide high-speed Internet access (such as leased lines, wireless connections, and ISDN), most are expensive to install and costly to maintain. ADSL was developed as a low-cost alternative to these technologies. ADSL is a technology that uses the existing standard telephone cable (twisted pair) to provide data transmission speeds rivaling, and often exceeding, those of much more expensive solutions.

Distinguishing Characteristics.   By asymmetrically dividing the available bandwidth, ADSL allows you to receive information much faster than you send information. With respect to an Internet connection, this is the optimal configuration: the information you send out is a very small portion (about 5 percent) of the information you receive.

Advantages.   The most obvious advantage of ADSL is the low cost. Although the modems are fairly expensive, the price is still less expensive than that of leased lines or ISDN. Because ASDL uses the existing telephone wiring, you do not have to have new lines installed. The next most important advantage is the data transmission speed. ADSL boasts download speeds of 8 Mbps and upload speeds of 1 Mbps. In addition, you can use it on the same line as your voice communication (or fax) without disrupting either. ADSL reserves a portion of the available bandwidth for these types of audio communications, so that both technologies may use the line at the same time. This further reduces the overhead involved with installation.

Disadvantages.   The main disadvantage of ADSL is availability. Currently ADSL is only available in select districts of any metropolitan area. Because of the nature of the technology, there is a distance limit placed on how far a subscriber can be from a major telephone line switching hub. As a result, not many Internet service providers (ISPs) offer ADSL service at present. However, as the demand for faster access continues to increase, this technology will also gain widespread acceptance.

Synchronous Optical Network (SONET)

Synchronous optical network (SONET), also known in some countries as synchronous digital hierarchy, is a WAN technology that functions at the physical layer (OSI layer 1) of the OSI model. SONET has been accepted by ANSI and recommended by the ITU. It specifies a number of data transfer rates, from 51.8 Mbps to 2.48 Gbps.

Distinguishing Characteristics.   SONET defines a fiber-optic standard for high-speed digital traffic. This standard provides the flexibility to transport many digital signals with different capacities.

Data communications sometimes prove difficult because digital signaling rates can vary. For example, as stated in the preceding section on ISDN, in the United States a T1 line provides 1.544 Mbps, while in Europe an E1 line provides 2.048 Mbps. SONET resolves such problems by defining how switches and multiplexers coordinate communications over lines with different speeds, including defining data transfer rates and frame format.

SONET defines a number of optical carrier (OC) levels. Each level defines an optical signal and a corresponding electrical signal called synchronous transport signal (STS). The base level is OC-1/STS-1 or 51.84 Mbps. Each level's rate is a multiple of 51.84 Mbps. Table 6–9 shows the OC levels and the corresponding data transfer rates that SONET defines [6].

Table 6–9   The OC Levels and the Corresponding Data Transfer Rates

OC Level	Data Rate
OC-1	51.8 Mbps
OC-3	155.5 Mbps
OC-9	466.5 Mbps
OC-12	622.0 Mbps
OC-18	933.1 Mbps
OC-24	1.24 Gbps
OC-36	1.86 Gbps
OC-48	2.48 Gbps

SONET also provides easy access for low-speed signals such as DS-0 (64 kbps) and DS-1 (1.544 Mbps) by assigning them to sub-STS-1 signals called *virtual tributaries*.

Advantages.   The SONET standard defines data transfer rates and a frame format that all vendors and telephone companies throughout the world can use, creating the potential for global networking. SONET also includes management capabilities for telephone company equipment. Cell relay technologies such as switched multimegabit data services (SMDS) and ATM operate above SONET, making SONET the expected foundation for future broadband service.

Disadvantages.   Some telephone companies are currently using SONET in their networks, but they are not yet offering it to the public. Unless your company is a large corporation in a metropolitan area, you probably cannot get dedicated SONET service. Also, some countries do not yet have a digital, fiber optic telecommunications infrastructure, which means they cannot take advantage of SONET.

FROM HERE

This chapter was written with the goal of giving an overview of network design issues and how they can help you design and install a better cabling system. In addition, there was a discussion about various category 5 structured wiring components and how they all fit together. Additional information regarding installations with multiple wiring closets, fiber optics, shielded twisted pair cable, and much more can be found later in the book in Chapter 24, "Installation." Refer to the appendices of this book for information on obtaining your own copies of these standards. The next chapter discusses a more proactive approach to cost justification issues, with regard to how fiber's higher cost is compensated or countered by UTP's more troubled implementations and downtime.

NOTES

[1]   Stephen Kayworth, "Structured Cabling Systems," South Hills Datacomm, 760 Beechnut Drive, Pittsburgh, PA 15205, 2000, p. 1.

[2]   Farallon Communications, Inc., 3089 Teagarden Street, San Leandro, California, 94577-5720 U.S.A, 2000.

[3]   John Mazza, "10BaseT," South Hills Datacomm, 760 Beechnut Drive, Pittsburgh, PA 15205, 2000, p. 1.

[4]   "Internetworking Design Basics," Some of the material in this book has been reproduced by Prentice-Hall with the permission of Cisco Systems, Inc. COPY-RIGHT ©2000 Cisco Systems, Inc. ALL RIGHTS RESERVED, 170 West Tasman Drive, San Jose, CA, 95134-1706, USA. 2000.

[5]   "QuickPort Snap-In Jacks and Modules with Brass Floorplate," Leviton Mfg. Company, Inc., 59-25 Little Neck Pkwy., Little Neck, N.Y. 11362-2591, 2000.

[6]   "Novell Networking Primer: Important LAN WAN High-Speed Technologies," Novell, Inc., 1555 North Technology Way, M/S ORM-Q151, Orem, UT 84097, 2000.

[7]   Mike Combs, "Plugging into the Ethernet," Combsnet, NetScout Systems Corporate Headquarters, 4 Technology Park Drive, Westford, MA 01886, 2000.

Cost Justification and Consideration

How do you justify buying a globe when the world still looks flat? What are the financial considerations?

When it comes to designing a high-speed network, there are many lower-cost alternatives; thus, when you present budget figures for the cabling system equipment to your managers, they will scream at the price. And when the noise ends, you will have some convincing to do.

Frankly, there isn't much hope that can be offered to most of you. The benefit that really sets most cabling systems apart—dedicated bandwidth—simply isn't there yet, thanks to a lack of applications support.

Dedicated bandwidth, which guarantees applications a predetermined slice of bandwidth and hence consistency of service, isn't available in shared-bandwidth infrastructures. Cabling systems using an ATM (asynchronous transfer mode) connection can do it; however, it requires the widespread development and use of applications that have been designed to take advantage of it. Also, universal deployment, which offers the potential of an end-to-end solution from desktop to local segment to backbone to WAN, isn't feasible. Locally, too much money and upheaval is required.

Still, for those who can technologically justify it now, it all comes down to wiring. Taken for granted when it works and cursed when it fails, wiring isn't the most glitzy topic—though it's among the most important. Installing the right wiring not only reduces network problems, but also saves money by cutting the costs of network moves, adds, and changes. Nevertheless, top executives—in sticker shock from the expense of hardware and support—tend to opt for the lowest-cost alternatives instead of seeing wiring as an important multigenerational corporate asset. In almost all cases, these alternatives may be okay for connecting PCs to printers, but are doomed to be overwhelmed by emerging high-bandwidth applications, such as desktop video conferencing or by unexpected bursts of network growth.

No swirl of a magic wand is likely to change cabling into the belle of the networking ball. However, many companies are slowly coming to respect its importance and are implementing worthy rewiring schemes.

Poor wiring choices can bring a network to its knees. Most network difficulties are not a result of failed hubs, routers, or switches, but rather have their roots founded in poor wiring. More than 60 percent of all networking problems are related directly or indirectly to wiring issues such as bad terminations, loose connections, kinks in the wire, and wiring used over distances that exceed specifications. Issues like throughput or responsiveness also often are linked to the physical infrastructure. Other estimates by industry analysts put that figure much higher. Some analysts estimate that 90 percent of all network problems are cable-related [1].

Cabling problems are very simple things, but they can drive network and telecommunications mangaers crazy.

Ultimately, successful networking depends on an understanding that wiring is as important as security, backup, and network management. It's no wonder that IT management is hesitant to take on wiring. It opens a thicket of other issues. Facility managers fight against surrendering the valuable real estate necessary to house wiring closets, or deny permission to drill holes in walls or floors. Engineers place wiring conduits near locations that risk electrical or other interference, and upgrading wiring can mean running into asbestos or fire code issues.

Plus, components that meet individual specifications provide less-than-optimal performance when linked together. And there's the constant fear that today's wiring will not accommodate tomorrow's technologies.

Although wiring has come a long way from the days when each major computer vendor had its own wiring specifications, debates still rage. At issue are the value of fiber to the desktop and wiring configurations such as *zone*—which uses satellite junctions for connectivity—versus the traditional *home run* approach that directly links a node to a central wiring closet. Also unresolved is the long-term viability of accepted wiring standards such as category 5, and categories 6 and 7, which are still in the early stages of definition (see Chapter 8, "Standards Design Issues," and Chapter 27, "Standards Development," for more information on the continuing development of category 6 and 7 standards).

Trouble-free wiring is possible if network managers stick to the basics: assessing current infrastructure; planning for the future; accurately mapping installation; conducting end-to-end testing; and installing systems to monitor and track moves, adds, and changes (MACs) accurately. Thus, this is where the cost benefits and justification for fiber comes in.

THE FIBER CABLING COST CURVE

Fiber on the backbone, copper to the desktop. For years, that's been the standard consensus for premises wiring management. Chances are that standards will be rewritten in the next year or so. Several manufacturers of fiber optic products claim they have come up with labor-saving techniques that dramatically cut the cost of installing fiber to the desktop. These techniques—combined with continued price reductions for fiber cabling and components—could bring the overall cost of fiber installation close to that normally associated with a category 5 unshielded twisted pair (UTP) copper wiring installation.

If that happens, the rationale for installing category 5 UTP would vanish. Right now, category 5 UTP is championed primarily as an interim wiring solution that handles 100-Mbit/s speeds (proponents say 155-Mbit/s ATM also is possible) at a significantly lower cost than fiber or shielded twisted pair (STP) wiring schemes. Once faster technologies like 622-Mbit/s ATM emerge, users probably will have to rip out category 5 wiring and replace it with fiber, which not only handles higher speeds (1 Gbit/s or more) but also has a much greater operating range (2 kilometers, as opposed to category 5's 100-meter operating limit).

The strategy of using category 5 UTP as an interim solution has been predicated on the wide disparity between the costs of installing category 5 wiring and fiber cabling. If fiber vendors are correct, that gap is going to shrink considerably by the year 2001.

The material, labor costs, and skills required to install and maintain copper cable supporting 100-Mbit/s transmissions have increased, while total costs for fiber cable installation and maintenance is declining [2]. As a result, a fiber plant capable of supporting up to 1-Gbit/s transmissions can be designed and installed for prices within 30 percent of 100-Mbit/s copper systems. Given that price difference, the decision to install wiring with a fairly limited shelf life doesn't make much sense.

The projected drop in fiber cabling costs apparently is going to catch managers of premises wiring plants by surprise. In a 1994 survey of the cabling plans of 100 companies, JLP Associates (in San Jose, California) found that wiring managers expected category 5 deployment to increase from 16 percent in 1994 to 92 percent in 1999. Only 3 percent of those responding to the survey said they would be running fiber to the desktop. You can see from the results of that survey that the respondents weren't even close in their predications. As fiber costs fall, wiring plant managers are going to have to rethink their long-term strategies—or risk investing in technology with rapidly diminishing short-term gains.

Fiber's two most obvious advantages are speed and operating range. Inside a building, either monomode or multimode fiber will support gigabit speeds [3]. Other than for very short cable runs, copper wiring always will be limited to megabit speeds. Because of signal attenuation, copper becomes unreliable beyond 100 meters, while fiber runs can stretch to 2 km before the signal must be repeated or regenerated.

Beyond speed and range, fiber offers two more key advantages over copper. First, unlike copper cable, fiber is immune to electromagnetic interference, which means that it can be installed adjacent to equipment like photocopiers and fluorescent lights, or in environments like factory floors, without affecting the data signal. Second, fiber cable is an intrinsically secure medium because it can't be tapped: Any break in the cable disrupts the light signal and instantly results in an outage.

Vendors say falling fiber installation costs are attributable to two factors. One is a drop in the cost of the fiber cables and components (such as connectors and patch panels). The other, probably more significant factor is the development of new techniques that cut the amount of time needed to terminate fiber connections.

Cost cuts for cabling and components are being driven by improved production techniques, as well as the use of less expensive connector materials. In the past, for example, the part of the fiber connector that holds the fiber line in place, called a ferrule, was made of ceramic. Now, less expensive plastic and stainless steel ferrules are being used.

Cost reductions also are reflected in the falling prices of fiber-based network adapter cards. Prices for FDDI equipment, for example, fell by about 60 percent in 1999. Today, the cheapest FDDI implementations cost around $900 per node (including the cost of the adapter and concentrator port), although the average price is still around $1,900 per node.

Prices are expected to drop further as vendors start cutting profit margins to compete with copper-based high-speed LAN products; and as cards arrive that implement lower-cost 850-nanometer transceivers, rather than the 1,300-nm transceivers specified in the FDDI standard. Also, the use of 850-nm components will allow vendors to offer FDDI cards for the same price as today's FDDI-over-copper products [3]. Sub-$400 FDDI adapters are already here.

The costs of fiber cable and connectors is now comparable to copper [4]. But the cost of fiber cabling and components still is more than double that of category 5 UTP equivalents [5]. Nevertheless, fiber is now cheaper than STP wiring. And even with the price disparity, fiber works out to be less expensive than category 5 UTP on a per-Mbit/s basis when maximum speeds are considered.

To spread out the cost of migrating to fiber, organizations could opt to use 10-Mbit/s Ethernet or 4- or 16-Mbit/s token ring adapters and concentrators that can run over fiber cable. Another alternative is to convert older Ethernet and token ring adapters to fiber duty using a transceiver. Nevertheless, the cost difference between these transition technologies and full-fledged fiber is becoming slimmer.

As expensive as fiber components have been in the past, labor costs have actually contributed the most to fiber's reputation for exorbitance. The basic problem is the amount of time and effort needed to terminate a fiber optic connection.

Early fiber installations were particularly labor-intensive. A specialist had to use a fusion splicer, a bulky and expensive (about $20,000) piece of equipment, to melt fiber strands and fuse them to connectors. The development of epoxy bonding helped cut installation cost to an extent. Epoxy bonding, a four-stage process, is much easier than fusion splicing, but it still takes a lot of time. First, the epoxy resin must be prepared and applied to the fiber connectors. Second, the connector and cable must be mechanically spliced, or crimped, with a crimping gun. The third and most time-consuming step is to cure, or dry, the epoxy using ultraviolet light or a conventional heat source, such as a portable oven. The final step is to polish the connection by hand.

The curing process can take anywhere from 10 minutes to several hours. By doing several connections simultaneously, installers can cut the average termination time down to about 10 to 15 minutes faster, but still not nearly as fast as copper terminations.

The third generation of fiber-termination technology is bringing installation time down to five minutes or less—making labor costs almost a nonissue. A couple of fast-installation options are available. One approach involves the use of preterminated fiber cable that simply has to be crimped onto a connector using a crimping gun [3]. By eliminating the epoxy curing process, installation time is reduced to an average of about two minutes. The downside is that signal loss is somewhat higher than with fusion splicing or epoxy bonding.

The average hourly rate charged in the United States for fiber installations is $11 [3]. At that rate, a 15-minute epoxy bonding installation carries a $2.75 labor cost. A two-minute installation costs only about 37 cents in labor—almost eight times less than epoxy bonding labor costs. In areas where labor costs are higher than the average, cost savings are even greater.

In an alternative approach, some vendors are refining the epoxy bonding process to speed installation. To make a connection, the installer heats up the connector to soften the epoxy, inserts a preterminated fiber cable, and then leaves the connection to dry [4]. The entire process can be completed in as little as five minutes.

Users confirm that the cost of installing fiber cabling is coming down fast.

The best thing about installing fiber is that it eliminates the need to recable further down the road. On average, most copper schemes last about three years. Fiber should last more than 10 years.

Most users now refute the commonly held notion that fiber cabling damages easily and consequently is more expensive to maintain. In fact, installing fiber enables users to reduce the number of staffers allocated to cabling maintenance, and thereby makes it inherently less expensive.

Fiber vendors blame the perception of fiber as a delicate cabling medium on misinformation. Since the proposal to run 100-Mbit/s over UTP surfaced in 1991, makers of LAN equipment and copper cable have waged a propaganda campaign to rival the best of the late 1930s. Fiber's pull strength (the maximum pressure that can be exerted on the cable before damage occurs) is 200 pounds, eight times that of category 5 UTP.

Fiber vendors also point out that while independently tested and approved fiber cables and connectors are now commonly available, testing labs such as Underwriters Laboratories, Incorporated (in Northbrook, Illinois), have only just started work on verifying the capabilities of the connectors that vendors are touting as category 5 products [6]. The cost of going back and replacing connecting components that are not up to snuff at 10 to 20 percent of the initial installation price of a UTP scheme is now becoming cost-prohibitive.

So, what's the bottom line here? Is fiber alive, dying, or dead?

It's Alive! It's Alive!

The rumor of fiber's cost justification death has been greatly exaggerated. Don't look now, but suppliers of fiber cabling are making a strong bid to cost effectively extend optical links all the way to desktop workstations.

As previously discussed, the knock against fiber cabling has been that it was far too cost-prohibitive to compete against copper wiring as a medium to service desktop users. In order for fiber to emerge as a viable desktop connectivity option, vendors must address three issues: component costs must drop, vendors must improve the ease of use/maintenance of fiber products, and lastly, vendors must reduce the form factor of fiber connectors to achieve more competitive costs per port. There is ample evidence that fiber vendors are making progress on all three counts.

One way fiber is making its way back into the ring is by reducing costs [4]. Another is that users are breaking the perception that fiber is a difficult medium to use.

Lowering Component Costs

In order to make fiber cabling a cost-equivalent option to copper-based wiring, vendors must reduce the cost of components such as jacks, patch panel adapters, and other hardware. Vendors have made a good deal of headway in that area.

Fiber cabling system costs are coming down, making fiber a viable solution [4]. Nevertheless, fiber gear costs vary depending on what day it is, what company is selling, and each network that is using it.

On average, most fiber plenum-rated cable has a list price of 36 cents a foot compared to category 5 cabling, which is generally a list price of 24 cents a foot, as shown in Table 7–1 [4]. A one-meter patch cord is $11, while a category 5 patch cord is $7.80. A VF-45 socket is $2.64 and a category 5 socket generally sells for around $3.85. The socket is mounted in a wall box. At a fiber price of $6.08, the category 5 price is in the range of $3.00. A patch panel (cost for one port of 48) is $2.88, while a category 5 patch panel (cost for one port of 48) is $6.85.

Table 7–1   Cabling Cost Comparison

Product	1997 Fiber Costs	1999 Fiber Costs	Average Cat 5 Copper Costs 1999
One foot of cable	$0.52	$0.36	$0.24
One meter of patch cord	$30.00	$11.00	$7.80
Socket	N/A	$2.64	$3.85
Wall box	$24.00 (with couplings)	$6.08	$3.00
Patch panel (cost per port of 48 ports)	$9.30 (with couplings)	$2.88	$6.85

All of these products give a general overview of fiber and category 5 cabling costs. But as far as choosing fluid numbers, things are changing so fast that you pick your best numbers at the time and let people throw stones at them.

Fiber optic systems are lowering in cost and although some fiber gear may outweigh category 5 cabling as far as costs go, fiber is not *four to five times more expensive* than copper, as it was just a couple of years ago. However, when you get into category 5e and category 6 (not yet standardized copper cabling), copper and fiber cabling systems are even more competitive given the expected cost of each.

Another fiber cabling cost reduction stems from the electronics in the network computer and telecommunications closet. Such electronics were typically six to seven times more expensive than copper. Now, the trend with fiber products, such as the VF-45, allows vendors to market fiber equipment that is perhaps only twice as much as copper.

A network interface card that might have cost $505 per port a year or so ago with a standard fiber connector is now in the $250 range with a VF-45.

Furthermore, fiber has the capability to support a simple patch panel for local connectivity, instead of relying on a departmental switch. This saves on space, surge protection, heating, ventilating, and air-conditioning (HVAC), maintenance, configuration, and potential downtime during failure. In fact, wiring closet costs can run $75,000 or more with all overhead factored in.

Fiber requires patch panels that are small connectivity points to link users to riser fibers in buildings or to backbones [7]. Patch panels don't fail because there are no active components in the wiring closet. In addition, electronics can be centralized in one location, thereby increasing the efficiency upon which the ports are utilized, and helping to cut down maintenance costs.

Easier to Use

Fiber gained a bad rap early, due in large measure to its lack of flexibility—literally. In the past, fiber cabling has been known to be fragile and difficult to work with, because its components were not as flexible as copper. Nowadays, new and improved fiber cabling on the market is flexible and more resilient, withstanding damage better than copper.

Even the labor costs associated with installing fiber were quite high, because you often needed to create hot melds to splice cable. Now, vendors are offering much simpler fiber termination kits for as little as $700 to terminate fiber strands.

Vendors are providing field-installable connectors that take approximately two minutes to install. Furthermore, the training needed to learn this installation is minimal and companies need not look to a network specialist to complete this task.

Some vendors have even devised a way to make fiber patch cords more durable. They have specially coated their fiber to give it a half-inch of band radius.

As previously explained, in the past, when you had to put on a fiber optic connector, you needed glue and adhesive. It was a very tedious process to mount a fiber optic connector. In the last couple of years, there have been a lot of technical advancements in making fiber. It is more robust and can take more abuse in an office when used to the desktop and through the ceiling. It has a pull strength of about 100 pounds, which makes it easier to work with. There is less fear of breaking or damaging the glass strands.

In addition, fiber optic cabling test equipment has become very simple to use with *microprocessed, one button types of operation*. This saves time and training and makes installation less costly.

The Form Factor

While component cost reduction and improved ease of use will help spur interest in fiber, those two improvements alone are not enough to make the technology a viable option at the desktop. Vendors must also address the form factor of fiber optic cable connectors and plugs, if for no other reason than to improve the cost per port of fiber adapters.

Traditionally, fiber connectors were almost twice as large as standard copper-based RJ45 connectors. That meant some switches might only support upward of 12 fiber ports. Even if copper- and fiber-based products were priced at the same cost per port, the size of the connector meant vendors could only support half as many connections. Switch users invariably would be forced to buy additional cards or chassis to accommodate the larger fiber ports.

Another factor that acted as a governor on the use of fiber was that you needed a pair of fibers, one for transmission and one for receiving data. Now, other vendors are devising methods of supporting two fibers in a single fiber cable jacket.

New fiber products on the market (such as fiber adapters) have increased the support for fiber cabling to the desktop. Most recently, more than 20 vendors are now designing compatible adapter products. Included in these are Allied Telesyn, Accton Technology Corporation, BATM Advanced Communications, Cabletron Systems, Canary Communications, Cisco Systems, Davicom Semiconductor, Garret Communications, Gemflex Networks, Honeywell, IMC Networks, Infineon, Microcosm Communications, Microlinear, Microsens, Olicom, Omnitron Systems Technology, Phobos Corporation, Racore Technology Corporation, Sumitomo, and Xylan.

Endstation Infrastructure

Because recent lower costs, ease-of-use, and improved connectors and plugs make fiber-optic cable systems a viable option, there is concern among users over the progress of low-cost end-station product availability from leading vendors. One additional obstacle that remains in order to make fiber a viable option is end-station infrastructure, such as network interface cards (NICs) and switches, which need to be available at a competitive price point from the leading industry vendors. This trend had already begun with Cabletron, Cisco, and Xylan. Universal acceptance of fiber-to-the-desk still awaits the availability of low-cost fiber NICs and switches from all of the leading vendors, not just a few of them.

So far, there appear to be no impediments to a future in fiber. The passage of the Gigabit Ethernet standard is an indicator that it won't be long before companies want high-speed networking in the Gigabit Ethernet range to the desktop. Since copper cabling has no Gigabit Ethernet standard, fiber cabling will be the front runner.

Costs are coming down and the standard for Gigabit Ethernet is going to drive fiber to the desktop quickly. A standard might just be the smelling salt that fiber needs to get up and move from the core of the network straight to the desktop.

Finally, cabling overall is important enough to network success that companies must recognize it as the network's nerve center. Make the wrong cabling or installation decisions, and your organization will be sentenced to years of network purgatory, where performance is unsatisfactory and growth is constrained. Make the right ones, and the only networking limitations will be what you want to achieve—what you *can* achieve.

From Here

This chapter described how to justify the network operating costs of your cabling system. It also covered the financial considerations derived from the cost justification of planning and creating a well-designed cabling system; as well as the financial considerations during the acquisition of a cabling system. For more information on fiber optic cabling, please see Part III, *Fiber-Optic Systems: A Hands-On Approach*. The next chapter provides an overview of the various aspects of cabling system standards design issues.

Notes

[1]   Midwest Datacomm, Inc., 526 NE 13th Street, Southeast Division, Ft. Lauderdale, FL 33304, USA, 2000.

[2]   IBM, Corporate Offices, International Business Machines Corporation, New Orchard Road, Armonk, NY 10504, 2000.

[3]   Tyco International Ltd., The Zurich Centre, Second Floor, 90 Pitts Bay Road, Pembroke HM 08, Bermuda, 2000.

[4]   Heather Bradley, "Fiber: Alive Again," The Tolly Group, 2251 Landmark Place, Manasquan, N.J. 08736, 2000.

[5]   Anixter Inc., 4711 Golf Road, Skokie, IL 60076, 2000.

[6]   Underwriters Laboratories Inc., Corporate Headquarters, 333 Pfingsten Road, Northbrook, IL 60062-2096 USA, 2000.

[7]   The Tolly Group, 2251 Landmark Place, Manasquan, NJ 08736, USA, 2000.

CHAPTER 8

Standards Design Issues

Do vendors have too much influence on the way cabling industry standards are designed, written, and ratified? The answer is yes and no. Vendors will always have the dominant influence on the way cabling industry standards are designed and written. In a system that is driven in an effective self-correcting course by competition, the cabling industry has done a great job of updating and maintaining standards that have a primary focus on the consumer's interest.

Only recently has a new political animal raised its head and told the world that it can do the thinking for customers and users. When a vendor developed a cabling standard or a spec, you knew who was driving; and, if it did not work, you knew who to send your lawyer after. Now, there's a whole new set of players in the standards game—the unbiased and totally independent standards body that will do your thinking for you:

- American National Standards Institute (ANSI)
- Telecommunications Industry Association (TIA)
- Electronics Industry Association (EIA)
- Building Industry Consulting Services International (BICSI)
- National Electrical Manufacturers Association (NEMA)
- National Electrical Contractors Association (NECA)
- Underwriters Laboratories, and many more [1]

What do they have in common? They are fine corporations and organizations that may not necessarily represent the end user's interest.

The behind-the-scenes power struggle to control the unbiased cabling standards is better than any espionage novel. If the power brokers can dictate the standards design through these associations, they can also insulate themselves from liability. Competitive pressures and liability issues tend to deliver a fairly good checks-and-balances system to the marketplace. Remove these drivers from the formula, and there is the risk of reduced accountability for the performance and safety in the products customers buy.

In addition to diminished accountability for the products, this process can create a "good old boy" system that almost certainly restrains the smaller independent companies from introducing new technologies. Competition is good. Do not support any system that inhibits or eliminates competition, or you will find out about the proverbial golden rule—those who have the gold, make the rules.

One of the great benefits of a vendor program for cabling standards design is quality, driven by competition. Vendors are darn careful about what they put their name on because of reputation and liability issues. However, if a small group of powerhouse vendors can get customers to buy into some third-party standards design system that they control (and they can hide from liability or criticism), customers may lose most of the benefits of free enterprise.

As an example of how the third-party system operates, let's look at BICSI and their standards design committee. In September 1995—at a BICSI standards meeting in Tucson, Arizona—a member at the meeting suggested the committee send a letter to the top end user communications organizations, inviting them to send a representative to sit on the committee. The discussions were all positive and the vote was unanimous to extend the invitation and get the consumer organizations to add their perspective to the standards. The contact names and addresses for these groups (ICA—International Communications Association; CMA—Communication Managers Association; NASTD—National Association of State Telecommunications Directors; SETA—SouthEastern Telecommunications Association; and TCA—Telecommunications Association) were handed over to the committee chairman.

In January 1997, at the BICSI annual conference at Disney World, a follow-up inquiry was made by members again to see if any action had been taken since the 1995 meeting to involve the end user organizations. The appropriate BICSI staffers told the members that they knew about the matter and the letter would go out as soon as they could develop the proper wording for the two-paragraph epistle. Who is in charge?

An industry observer might get the impression that the meetings and the standards process is being maneuvered so that only big boys and insiders with the deep pockets can play the standards design game. To make the big point about standards design, let's consider the plenum story. For a brief period, front-end processor (FEP) insulating material was in short supply and the situation was aggravated by hoarding of EIA/TIA category 5 4-pair UTP plenum cable. During that period most cable companies developed alternative hybrid constructions for plenum category 5 cable using polyolefin for one or two pairs. These constructions were difficult to manufacture in compliance with the electrical performance standards of EIA/TIA and the fire safety codes for plenum verified by UL.

Virtually all the manufacturers have returned to an all-FEP construction for insulation, for a host of sound reasons. Recently, Berk-Tek, the cable manufacturer who owns the patent for the 2x2 hybrid cable construction, came out with a very strong fire performance message recommending a return to the 100 percent FEP insulation for category 5 plenum cable constructions.

Berk-Tek has created quite a ripple effect in the cabling industry. It even extends to the Internet. After this announcement, a lot of the cabling Web sites and chat groups on WWW were buzzing about the fire safety of communications cabling. Combine this with a special meeting held by UL (Underwriters Laboratories Inc.) to address fire safety concerns, and fire safety has finally reached shock-wave status. To say that the big end users that have been discussed in this chapter are interested in these matters would be a gross understatement. They are eager to get their hands on the latest information so they can make better, more informed cabling decisions. When the subject turns to life safety and property protection, everyone listens.

From what has been gleaned from the cabling industry, a lot of research into fire safety performance has turned up the following three problem areas: First of all, some hybrid constructions (2x2's and 3x1's) may have variable fire performance properties. Sometimes they pass code requirements, sometimes they don't. This is where Berk-Tek's call for headroom makes sense and UL is investigating. Second, if certain hybrid constructions do pass, then there's still the question of long-term stability. Remember that the new insulation materials used as a substitute for FEP are compounds with a lot of different ingredients. Finally, there is more code work to be done to more precisely define what is permitted in plenum installations, based on fuel load and the National Fire Protection Agency (NFPA) requirement for limited combustibles.

It's ironic that new problems can be avoided with old solutions. Users have consistently recommended 100 percent FEP insulation when electrical performance and fire safety are top concerns. What can possibly be gained by saving a few pennies with something less than the best?

As is quite evident from what has just been discussed, for some time most cable manufacturers have been aware of a serious fire hazard safety problem. However, from a standards design point of view, you have to ask yourself, who is really driving the process? Ask who will be responsible if the cable is retested after installation and no longer qualifies as CMP listed. Everyone may be charged with accountability as the attorneys go on a witch hunt.

Recently, the EIA/TIA was asked about end user involvement on the standards committee for category 5 cabling. As of this writing, people are still waiting for an answer. There is a great deal of political in-fighting as each megamanufacturer maneuvers to position their product in the standard design and eliminate their competition. Sometimes, it seems like a track and field event with everyone wearing concrete boots. Unfortunately, these standards groups may be anything but independent. It's up to you to figure out who is really in charge.

THE GOOD WITHOUT THE BAD AND THE UGLY

Not all of the news is bad, however. There is some good news about the Anixter Levels '97 Program. This program redefines cabling performance characteristics and, most importantly, gives users guidance in high-performance areas where EIA/TIA cannot seem to agree on a standard design.

Anixter, Incorporated, a global distributor of integrated communications systems and services, launched Anixter Levels '97, the most recent update of its cable performance specification program. Anixter Levels '97 defines the performance characteristics of unshielded twisted pair (UTP) cabling beyond 100 MHz, a parameter necessary for advanced applications such as intranet technology, three-dimensional imaging, multimedia programs, video to the desktop, computer-aided design, and broadband video.

The revised program builds on the ANSI/TIA/EIA-T568-A Commercial Building Telecommunications Cabling Standard, which defines the expectations and limitations of cable and provides structure and direction for technological advances. It takes many years to ratify a standard and portions of ANSI/TIA/EIA-T568-A have become obsolete. Therefore, implementing advanced applications could cause cable that adheres to today's standards design to fail in the future. It's doubtful that many users in the network-infrastructure industry, including Anixter, could have predicted that applications requiring increased bandwidth would be developed so quickly that a lot of standard category 5 cable would become electrically insufficient. Although Anixter has always stayed one step ahead of the industry in defining and evaluating performance requirements, the standards design organizations have been hard pressed to keep up with the developers of applications and access methods.

Anixter Levels '97 divides cable into three performance levels: Cable specified as Level 5 must meet the more stringent requirements for category 5 cables, as spelled out in the international standard ISO 11801, which allows cables meeting its requirements to be used globally. Level 6 increases cable performance to what some in the industry have called high-end category 5 or category 5+ cables. Finally, a new generation of recently launched products that meet at least twice the category 5 bandwidth requirement constitute Level 7.

To be considered a specific Anixter level, cable must pass specification tests at the Anixter Structured Cabling Lab in Mount Prospect, Illinois. All Anixter-levels cable must meet a stringent 4-pair cross talk measurement called power sum testing.

Obviously, not all cable manufacturers distribute their products primarily through Anixter and not all of the manufacturers feel comfortable with the Anixter Levels Program. Just because a cable is not rated by Anixter doesn't mean that it doesn't meet or exceed Anixter's criteria.

EVEN BETTER NEWS: DESIGNING DISTRIBUTED CABLING SYSTEM STANDARDS

The news is getting even better for the standards design issue. The standards design presented in this part of the chapter describes the functional, electrical, topological, and management standards for the intra-building telecommunications media at the University of Texas at Austin (UT) [2]. This media, its associated passive termination equipment, and dedicated floor space, constitutes the building distribution system (BDS). The BDS defined by these standards will permit transmission of voice, video, and computer communications.

These standards are intended to provide faculty and staff with general planning guidelines for BDS design, installation, and extension. However, with the variety of building architectures, telecommunication applications, and user requirements found in the UT Austin community, faculty, and staff should assume that each building's BDS will require custom planning.

Function

The BDS originates in offices, laboratories, conference rooms, and other general areas within a building. The BDS presence in each room or area takes the form of one or more faceplates typically mounted in the room's walls. These faceplates, similar in appearance to the faceplates that mount receptacles for electric power, are configured with two system information outlets (SIO). Again, this arrangement is similar to the two receptacles found in a common duplex electric power outlet. The number of faceplates required to serve a particular room or area is determined by such factors as the number of people that use the room, their functions, and the extent to which their functions employ the University's information resources.

Each of the two SIOs per faceplate is capable of being independently configured for a particular type of connector, or connectors, as appropriate for the type of information that it will carry (bayonet network connector [BNC] for video or IBM 3270 type terminals, RJ11 modular jack for telephony applications, and RJ45/48 modular jack for LAN applications). Configuration of an individual SIO is accomplished by installing it as a unit in the faceplate housing. An SIO is therefore selected that provides the type of connector necessary for the specific information application and is installed in the faceplate housing that is intended to serve that application. This capability permits the SIOs that serve a particular room or location to be reconfigured to meet new information requirements as they evolve.

Each faceplate housing serves to terminate two independent cables, or sheaths, of wire. Each sheath contains eight wires, arranged as four pairs. Each sheath also provides information, via the faceplate housing, to one of the SIOs mounted in the housing.

The other end of each wire sheath either terminates directly in a common patch panel (CPP) configured with female modular jack receptacles or in a common cross-connection panel (CXP), implemented via a 110-type terminal block. Functionally, a CXP is differentiated from a CPP in that the CXP permits any of the eight wires within a sheath to be accessed and used in conjunction with any of the other wires in the sheath for a particular purpose. In contrast, a CPP establishes a permanent connection and configuration of all eight wires between the panel and the faceplate.

Both CPPs and CXPs may be employed in the same building and both are housed in common space within the building, referred to as wiring closets (WC). A given wiring closet may contain CPPs or CXPs that terminate sheaths that originate in areas on the same floor as the WC, or if distance and cabling paths permit, multiple floors of the building can be served from the same WC. Thus, the WC serves to aggregate at a common location sheaths of wire serving rooms and other building areas that are proximate to it. The location and number of WCs within a building is almost exclusively a function of the size of the building and the availability of media routing paths within the building.

Each building contains one WC that performs the special function of housing the media and terminating equipment, which is necessary to connect the building to external sources of information (the telephone system, computer network backbone, and video network). This WC is called the gateway room (GW) and it serves as the demarcation point between the BDS and external information distribution systems.

At this point, recall that the BDS consists of passive components (components such as wire, connectors, and mounting equipment) that do not produce information. The WCs may also contain active equipment (local area network hubs, terminal controllers, video modulators/demodulators) that connects to the BDS and uses it to distribute information. This active equipment and the information applications that it supports will determine how connections are implemented between the various WCs within a building. For example, high-speed computer information moving between hubs located in different WCs may require optical fiber interconnection, while a telephone connection between the GW and WC is carried on wire.

Electrical

The largest media element of the BDS is the cabling between the building's various faceplates and its WCs. This cabling is standardized to be eight-conductor—carried as four unshielded twisted pair—copper wire conforming to the category 5 performance level defined in EIA/TIA TSB 36. Furthermore, this media is to be installed and terminated with procedures and connecting hardware that meets ANSI/EIA/TIA-T568-A Commercial Building Telecommunications Wiring Standard.

Properly installed and terminated, an analog bandwidth of 100 Mhz is specified for a category 5 BDS. Digital information capacities corresponding to the synchronous transport signal-3 (STS-3) of 155.52 Mbps can also be supported with a category 5 BDS.

Topology

A BDS is implemented in a star configuration with the WC at the center of the star and uninterrupted 4-pair sheaths as rays to each of the faceplate housings. In this configuration, the path distance (the distance measured along the actual path that the sheath will follow from the faceplate housing to the CPP or CXP) must not exceed 90 meters. Subject to this constraint, and the space available for connection hardware, a particular WC can serve as many rooms, areas, and floors of a building as desired. In particular, it may be possible to serve an entire building with a single WC that also serves as a GW.

The choice of CPP, CXP, or a combination of CPP and CXP termination of media in a WC is at the discretion of the department installing the BDS. In buildings that require multiple WCs, the method and routing of the interconnection of the WCs with each other and with the building's GW is determined by the specific information services that are distributed within the building. As these requirements change, this portion of the BDS is incremented appropriately.

Management

UT Austin maintains a central database containing information for each BDS installed at the University. In particular, this database contains the location of each WC, including the GW, and the locations of faceplates served by the respective WC. The database also contains the type of SIO installed in each faceplate. A common scheme for identifying each sheath and its originating and terminating points is employed throughout the database. This database is updated upon installation or modification of any BDS.

Once installed, a BDS can be managed on a day-to-day basis either by a central University utility (CUU) or jointly by the using department and a CUU. In the former case, the using department contracts with a CUU to perform all moves, changes, and reconfigurations of the BDS. In the latter case, the using department performs these functions and reports the changes to a CUU so that the University BDS database can be updated to reflect the new configuration.

NEW STANDARDS DESIGN ISSUES

Let's move on to some new standards design issues: category 6, category 7, and the new CENELEC standards. The final part of this chapter will answer such burning questions as whether category 6 or category 7 products are currently available on the market.

The direction taken by ISO/IEC is to standardize on the highest plateau of performance that unshielded, screened, and fully shielded balanced cabling systems are able to support. Many manufacturers have issued claims about their high-performance systems with the intent of leading end users to believe that they already comply with a standard that, as of early 1998, does not yet exist. Although not much is known about any system solutions that offer end-to-end component or channel performance, it is only a matter of time before new product releases are announced.

Category 6 or Category 7

The Siemon Company is currently addressing the need for category 6 and category 7 system solutions [3]. The category 6 standard has already been approved. At the time of this writing, category 7 was still awaiting approval.

Now that ISO/IEC has released two performance categories, most copper experts agree that the proposed category 6 NEXT values are about as good as twisted pair cabling can get without individually shielded pairs, based on a theoretical limit related to the effects of increasing twist rate. Category 6 is by no means a stepping stone to category 7. For example, the system and component values for category 6 are more stringent than the highest published commercial specifications for UTP and screened twisted pair (ScTP), including so-called gigabit offerings. Unshielded and screened twisted pair systems have such a significant following and are so much more cost effective than fully shielded solutions that there is a low probability that they will be completely replaced. This point is especially compelling, considering that fully shielded cabling provides less bandwidth than multimode fiber for about the same cost.

In addition, if a high-end UTP cable is endorsed and the connecting hardware is tweaked, category 6 is achievable. This is probable, provided that a cable is found that meets the category 6 requirements.

What type of connector interface will be required in order to achieve category 7 performance? The standard 8-position plug/outlet connection is not expected to satisfy the proposed category 7 transmission requirements for 4-pair systems. Consequently, it is likely that a new interface will be required to support 4-pair transmission to 600 MHz. There have been submittals to WG3 (the ISO/IEC's working group) on new connectors and plugs that claim to meet these requirements, but commercial availability of these products remains in question. Let's now take a look at the compatibility concerns regarding category 6 and 7 cabling, connectors, and plugs.

Category 6 and 7 Cabling, Connectors, and Plugs: Are They Compatible?

Category 6 as currently defined represents a significant step forward in the overall high-speed performance of copper UTP/STP links, increasing rated performance to 200 MHz, and essentially pushing copper links with RJ45-style connectors to their maximum limit. However, there has been a growing industry concern that, while category 6 performance can certainly be achieved with certain *tuned combinations* of connectors and plugs, it may no longer be possible for installers to simply assume full mix-and-match compatibility between generic components.

To provide compatibility with existing work-area equipment, the draft ISO/IEC specifications for category 6 and Class E cabling mandate support for the RJ45 8-position modular interface at the telecommunications outlet. The draft specifications further stipulate that category 6 configurations will sustain a positive attenuation to cross-talk ratio (ACR) up through at least 200 MHz installed performance (using a 250 MHz test). Overall, the RF field testing parameters required to certify category 6 cabling to 250 MHz test levels require improvements in measurement precision by as much as 10 dB over category 5e. In response to these stringent category 6 requirements, a whole new generation of field testers has evolved, providing unprecedented Level III test accuracy.

The weak point in overall category 6 viability remains the RJ45 connection.

Obviously, the goal of category 6 is to specify a 200 MHz solution that is fully backward-compatible with existing categories 5 and 5e. However, squeezing category 6 performance out of the RJ45 form and function constraints is requiring optimization techniques that run counter to maintaining such universal compatibility. Although an ideal connector design would likely rely on new overall spatial relationships, symmetry, and shape to avoid interpair coupling at 200 MHz performance, the constraint of the existing RJ45 form factor has left electrical tuning techniques as the sole avenue of improvement open to connector designers.

The performance of the RJ45 modular plug is specified as a terminated open circuit (TOC) measurement with near-end cross-talk (NEXT) performance in the range of 40 to 41.5 dB. For category 5 implementations, special compensation circuitry has already been incorporated into telecom outlet designs, which are tuned to achieve required performance with RJ45 connectors. However, achievement of category 6 requirements will likely require NEXT performance at the connector of approximately 48 dB at 200 MHz. Although the obvious solution would appear to be simply improving the TOC performance of new RJ45 designs, empirical studies conducted by a major cable/connector manufacturer have shown that the category 5 electrical tuning is optimized for a finite range. As a result, higher performing *super plugs* may present significant backward-compatibility problems. The evidence indicates that tuned combinations of improved-TOC plug-and-jack connectors can effectively support category 6 speeds. However, if an RJ45 plug with greater than 44 dB of TOC is connected to an existing category 5 jack, it can produce mismatched compensation and degraded performance that fail to even meet category 5 requirements. Of course, NEXT compatibility is only one key parameter of the connector interface in a structured cabling environment that can be impacted by electrical tuning mismatches between the modular plug and jack. It is very likely that other key parameters such as balance and far-end cross talk (FEXT) could also be negatively affected by mixing category 6 components within some existing category 5 environments.

In addition to presenting a problem of backward compatibility, the lack of an industry-wide standard for electrically tuning new category 6 components means there is a definite risk of failure when attempting to mix RJ45 plugs and jacks from different vendors. This is a big departure from the relatively safe world of generic mix-and-match flexibility that has existed with cabling and connector components up through category 5. From the cable contractors' standpoint, it is becoming increasingly important to consciously select and test for cross compatibility between connector components throughout their structured wiring implementations. These incompatibility issues can also pose a problem when it comes to the accepted practice of both installers and network administrators to create patch cords in the field. In addition, because the customers' equipment interfaces can cause incompatibility problems, the advent of category 6 may require a higher level of customer hand holding and assistance well beyond the point of final cable certification.

It is already well accepted that the RJ45 connector will have to be discarded for higher speed implementations, such as the category 7 specifications currently being considered (see Sidebar, "TERA™ Connector Selected as Category 7 Non-RJ Standard Interface"). The bottom line is that all industry participants, including installation contractors, cable/connector manufacturers, and test equipment suppliers, need to increase their focus on this issue of generic compatibility.

TERA™ CONNECTOR SELECTED AS CATEGORY 7 NON-RJ STANDARD INTERFACE

According to The Siemon Company, their TERA™ connector was recently accepted without opposition as the category 7 *non-RJ*-style connector interface by the ISO/IEC JTC 1/SC25 Working Group 3, and will be standardized internationally for class F shielded cabling. The decision to approve Siemon's TERA™ interface was made by ISO/IEC delegates from 19 countries during a meeting held in Berlin, Germany, in 1999.

An *RJ*-style connector interface proposal was selected as the primary category 7 interface, but the feasibility of this connector type to support category 7/class F is pending further evaluation by IEC SC48B. The TERA™ has already been proven to perform up to 1GHz over each pair, far exceeding the bandwidth of 600 MHz specified for category 7/class F.

The TERA™ offers competitive advantages, including the ability to run applications such as broadband video with an upper frequency requirement of 862 MHz. The TERA™ features 1-, 2-, and 4-port modularity, allowing up to four separate applications to run simultaneously on a single cable, thus eliminating the need for multiple fiber, coax, and twisted pair cables. Its fully shielded design assures maximum reliability by providing immunity to electromagnetic interference. In addition, the TERA™ offers a small form-factor design that fits within the same footprint as an *RJ*-style outlet. Contributing to the overall strength of the TERA™ is its ability to be terminated quickly with a specially designed tool that enables preparation and termination of all conductors in less than 2 ½ minutes, thus saving valuable installation time [3].

If category 6 is going to succeed in the long run, working partnerships and technology-sharing arrangements between key component manufacturers will be a vital factor in maintaining a reliable foundation of mix-and-match capability for installers. In addition, the development and delivery of joint training curricula between cable/connector manufacturers and test equipment suppliers will play an important role in assisting installers to test and certify optimally matched combinations of category 6 components.

ISO/IEC and TIA

In view of earlier comments with regard to the credibility of ISO/IEC and TIA, will ISO/IEC objectives be accepted by TIA? It is likely that TIA will also select 200 MHz as the minimum frequency at which the difference between attenuation and multidisturber NEXT is positive for category 6 cabling channels. There is also strong evidence that supports a trend toward standards harmonization between the TIA and ISO groups. Two recent examples include the pending issuance of an ISO/IEC ballot with new Class D channel requirements that are well-aligned with the category 5 channel values specified in TIA/EIA TSB 67 and ISO/IEC input to TIA on the pending return loss requirements for category 5 channels and links.

Standardized Testing

There are many standardized testing issues for these new categories. Is standardized testing good enough to use hand-held certification devices that test only to 100 MHz? Not at the time of this writing or in the immediate future. The reason being that the specifications for these new categories and classes will not be complete until a full system specification is available that is supported by procedures for laboratory and field testing. At this point, it is questionable whether even the most advanced field testers available today are able to test accurately up to 200 MHz, not to mention 600 MHz. Even if existing 100 MHz testers are used, their ability to make measurements at these new, higher performance levels up to 100 MHz with acceptable scatter (accuracy and repeatability) remains unknown. In addition, it is likely that there will be a need for additional test capabilities for parameters such as return loss, far-end cross talk, skew, and perhaps others, that existing testers do not offer. If new applications standardize on a cabling category with requirements beyond 100 MHz, it would follow that accurate field testing to the new limits and extended frequencies will be needed.

Gigabit Ethernet

Categories 6 and 7 are also expected to handle gigabit Ethernet (1000BaseT). The objective is for new categories to be backward-compatible. Applications that run on lower classes and categories must be supported by all higher classes. The existing IEEE 1000BaseT project (802.3ab) is clearly targeted for operation over category 5 cabling. If IEEE is able to achieve this goal, the new categories will only be needed for LAN applications that operate with transmission rates in excess of 1 Gbps. If four pairs are required at each work area outlet, it is likely that categories 5, 6, and 7 will support gigabit Ethernet.

Performance Requirements

Draft performance requirements for category 6 are already available, but not for category 7. Although the ISO/IEC committee has not released an expected project completion date for category 7, they have agreed to provide updates to, and solicit input from, application and component committees. It is not the intention of ISO/IEC to develop a closet standard without input and guidance from industry working and developmental groups. Nevertheless, what ISO/IEC intends to do, and what they actually do, remains to be seen. The question remains: Who's in charge?

ACR Values

Finally, what are the positive ACR (attenuation to cross-talk ratio) values at the maximum frequencies for these two new categories? At least as good as current Class D at 100 MHz (> 3dB) for channels, including equipment cords and work area cables, based on worst-case pair-to-pair performance, and greater than 0 dB based on worst-case power sum performance.

Let's look at the new Comite Europeen de Normalisation Electrotechnical (CENELEC) standards design issues.

CENELEC Standards

The EU Commission in Brussels has recently prepared a new, complete family of cabling system standards, identified as Mandate 212. Work to prepare all documents in question was extremely intense in the involved committees and working groups. Some cable specifications and basic test documents are completely new (for instance, the 600 MHz cable standard) while other existing standards are revised and aligned with the overall standard family concept.

Mandate 212 CENELEC Standard Family

The Mandate 212 CENELEC standard family is intended as a complete, self-supporting set of standards containing:

- Basic reference standards specifying test methods, definitions, materials, guide to use, and environmental issues. These standards are identified with the title *EN BASIC* and referenced by the generic and sectional cabling system standards.
- Generic cable specifications for symmetrical and multiconductor cables, coaxial cables, and optical fiber cables.
- Sectional cable specifications for symmetrical and multiconductor cables, and coaxial cables [4].

For people involved in generic cabling, the most interesting information will probably be the nature of the cable specifications. So far, the CENELEC cable standards EN 50167, EN 50168, and EN 50169 for screened horizontal, patch, and backbone cables, respectively, have been the only sectional CENELEC specifications available. These specifications have therefore been the only cable standards referenced by CENELEC EN 50173. They are now being revised.

Furthermore, new standards for UTP cables and screened 600 MHz cables are being prepared. The family of twisted pair cable standards will then become complete. The present identifications of the cable standard proposals are:

- prEN 5046C-2-1—Screened horizontal and backbone cables to 100 MHz, corresponding to EN 50167 and EN 50169.
- prEN 5046C-2-2—Screened patch cables to 100 MHz, corresponding to EN 50168.
- prEN 5046C-3-1—Unscreened horizontal and backbone cables to 100 MHz.
- prEN 5046C-3-2—Unscreened patch cables to 100 MHz.
- prEN 5046C-4-1—Screened horizontal and backbone cables to 600 MHz.
- prEN 5046C-4-2—Screened patch cables to 600 MHz [3P, 3].

Cabling System Requirements

The coming symmetrical cable standard proposals have a number of new technical requirements that will be significant for everyone involved in cabling. These issues concern both specified cable types, electrical performance, EMC, and safety. See the Sidebar, "Significant New Cable Requirements," for more information on these issues.

SIGNIFICANT NEW CABLE REQUIREMENTS

The following points have the most significant market impact:

1. UTP cables will now get their own specifications. Earlier, only screened cable specifications existed due to uncertainty and disputes about true EMC performance of UTP cables. This problem has now been resolved (see point 2).

2. EMC performance of all cable types is now being specified by coupling attenuation measurements, which will again be specified in EN BASIC 5-4-6D. The earlier disputes about EMC performance will now be solved by this new measurement type, which is applicable for both screened and unscreened cables. The different cable types can be specified and measured for EMC performance. The requirements apply from 30 MHz to 1 GHz for all cable types, since it is an EMC and not a transmission performance parameter. Typical values between 30 MHz and 100 MHz are min. 40 dB, min. 55 dB, and min. 80 dB for UTP, 100 MHz screened, and 600 MHz screened cables, respectively.

3. Electrical requirements are specified to 600 MHz for screened cables. For the sake of order it should be noted that cables are not identified as category 6, even though those

cables will undoubtedly form the cable requirements to any future category 6 Class E specifications.

4. Safety of cables is modified to clearly specify IEC 332-1 flame retardancy only. Cables will all be of a low smoke zero halogen (LS0H) grade. In other words, the links between wiring closets are typically provided using multimode fiber optic cable, terminated using ST connectors on a patching field at each wiring closet. Low smoke zero halogen (LS0H) interior/exterior grade cable is utilized, meeting both the requirements for fire resistance and for moisture protection without the need for intermediate termination points at building entry/exit. Each wiring closet comprises one or more standard 19-inch racks containing the fiber optic and UTP patch fields and the active equipment.

5. PVC cables will no longer be allowed, not even for UTP cables. However, flame retardancy requirements will not be more strict than for the presently common PVC cables [3P, 3].

Most of the cabling standards have now been published. Stay tuned for future updates!

FROM HERE

This chapter discussed the latest cabling system standards design issues. See Chapter 27, "Standards Development," for more information on these developing standards issues as well as the international issues in Europe, Japan, and South America. The next chapter presents an overview of cabling system architectural design considerations (structured cabling system, wiring closet design, cabling facilities, and user-to-outlet ratios, etc.).

NOTES

[1] "The Standards Game," Wireville, ACP (The Association of Cabling Professionals, Jacksonville, FL), 2000, p. 1.
[2] W.C. Bard, "Building Distribution System Standards," University of Texas at Austin, Austin, Texas 78712, , 2000, p. 1.
[3] © The Siemon Company, Siemon Business Park, 76 Westbury Park Road, Watertown, CT 06795-0400, USA, 2000, p. 1.
[4] "New CENELEC Standards," 3P Newsletter No. 4, 3P Third Party Testing, Agern Allé 3, DK-2970 Hoersholm, Denmark, 1999, p. 2.

Architectural Design Considerations

The information technology-age office is not just a place equipped differently from offices of the past, it's a place that will be designed in an entirely different way.

The best and most productive offices will be designed from the inside out, not the outside in. Foremost will be concern for the way the office environment supports people at work. Therefore, the design process must begin with an understanding of the work process.

Architects and interior designers need to understand power and data/communications delivery systems. Facility planners need to know what kinds of work will go on in their buildings and how the facility must support the work process. The role of the facility manager as the integrator of varied disciplines and planning processes will be more and more important.

In short, things are getting more complicated. The purpose of this chapter is to provide an overview of the architectural design considerations with regard to power and data/communications distribution for architects, designers, facility managers, and others interested in designing and managing office environments. The complexity imposed by information technology means that each of these professions must learn the others' languages.

COMPLEXITY OF INFORMATION TECHNOLOGY

The business of business, for most office workers, is the processing of information. The revolutionary change brought about by the information technology age is that now, at every level of the organization from clerical to executive, information is being processed with the help of electronic tools.

What changes will be required in the way organizations manage cabling? Plenty. Some of the immediately foreseeable ones:

- Each workstation must support a personal computer and often other electronic devices, in addition to providing power for lighting.
- Offices must be designed in such a way as to be open to a variety of cabling options.
- Electrical loads of 500 to 1,000 watts or more per workstation will likely be the average [1].

Furniture systems can extend the building's power distribution and communications cable capacity. But cable paths may affect the reconfigurability of components, and facility planning must take this into account.

Building services for distribution of power and data/communications capabilities will be designed differently, for more horizontal cable capacity and to preserve adaptability to changes in technology. Furthermore, much more space will be required, particularly in high-rise office buildings, for cables delivering power and data/communications resources vertically through the building to each floor.

Realizing the link between productivity and adequate facilities, organizations will spend more money getting services right. Also, most observers agree that multiple wire and cable systems, such as coaxial cable for data next to twisted pair for phones, will be common for at least the next four years. Furthermore, coaxial cable may currently be installed in facilities for data, but is almost universally being replaced by category 5.

All of the significant manufacturer strategies for office automation define separate physical networks for voice and data applications despite the fact that the technology exists that allows data and voice signals to be sent over the same physical wire. For the most part, coaxial and twisted pair cables will continue to provide most of the physical linkages. Optical fibers will be used on a limited basis for point-to-point links between computer systems within buildings and on a more frequent basis for inter-building communication channels [Sullivan, 2].

In the near term, the typical workstation will not have applications that require the bandwidth capacity of fiber optics. Use of fiber optics is also limited due to lack of connecting capability in and between workstations.

The costs of not planning adequate capacity for power wiring and data/communications cabling will be tremendous. Some organizations report having to budget as much as $400 a foot for relocating cable every time a change is needed. One such organization, a large bank highly dependent on automated services, estimates spending $14 million per year moving wires and cables around. In other instances, companies have been unable to move into brand-new facilities because the services provided were insufficient to meet the demands of the equipment. Clearly, organizations without cabling management plans and design put themselves at a competitive disadvantage.

ELECTRICAL DESIGN AND DATA/COMMUNICATION CABLING SYSTEMS DISTRIBUTION CONSIDERATIONS

Information technology exists to make people more productive. Making the technology work as effectively as possible requires well planned and designed power and data/communications cabling distribution systems.

Both electrical and data/communications cabling systems resources must travel through the building to get to where they can be used. Resources enter the building from the power company, phone company, or other sources. They must be distributed vertically to each floor, horizontally throughout each floor, and then out to each point of use: computer terminal, telephone, light, and so on. The design of these various cabling distribution systems depends on the criteria imposed by the equipment in use and projected for future use.

Typically, designing cabling distribution systems requires the talents of architects and design professionals working with communications specialists, electrical engineers, and equipment specialists. A key role of the professional facility manager is one of integrating the contributions of each of these disciplines.

Distribution and Electrical Needs

Electricity can be a mixed blessing; it makes our organizations and culture work by running our machines, but it can be dangerous when misapplied, or hazardous to electronic equipment and stored information when voltage sags and spikes contaminate power supplies.

An electrical circuit requires three things: a power source, conductors, and a load—a device like a lamp or terminal that uses the electricity. The conductors have to make a complete circle from the power source to the load and back, no matter how many access points are available on the circuit. Electricity passes easily through conducting material like copper wire. The parts of the equipment where there is resistance to electrical flow is where the work gets done: where the light bulb lights, and so on.

What does that mean in the office environment? Power distribution systems must provide not only sufficient capacity for present needs and flexibility for the future, as well as plenty of points of access, they must also accommodate new, specialized needs.

Often, equipment will dictate the need for additional, dedicated circuits and special accommodations for protecting power from outside interference. Designing circuits is the business of qualified electrical engineers and electricians. But facility managers, architects, and interior designers must understand the potentials and constraints imposed by power distribution systems on building structures and furnishing plans.

Single- and Three-Phase Electrical Circuits

Utility companies deliver two kinds of power to commercial buildings: single-phase (120 volts to ground) and three-phase (208 Y/120). Three-phase systems are becoming standard, but you may encounter some cases of single-phase power. It's important to know if a building is supplied with single-phase power because it will affect later decisions about distributing power to workstations through furniture systems or flat wire.

Three-phase circuits have three hot wires (those that take the electricity along the first part of the circle, from source to load) from the electric utility source to a main distribution panel in the building service core. Hot and neutral wires are run through conduit to separate secondary distribution panels, usually located on each floor. These panels will have a bus bar, or a metal bar, for each wire or phase leg (one of the three phases of the three-phase system). From this panel, an electrician will run a hot wire with its own neutral wire to floor monuments or other termination points.

In a high-rise building, for instance, utilities can bring in very high voltage power (13,000 KV) through the core of the building, with transformers on each floor. This allows use of smaller cable for vertical distribution, saving space in backbone (riser) shafts.

Generation and distribution of alternating current (AC) is usually done with three-phase circuits for a variety of reasons. Three-phase circuits are more efficient than single-phase; they can use lighter, smaller conductors than single-phase circuits of the same power rating. Three-phase motors are also generally smaller, lighter, and more efficient than single-phase motors of the same horsepower. The large utility companies are geared to three-phase distribution lines and typically use three-phase generators.

Single-phase circuits have either one or two hot conductors and one neutral conductor running through conduit to secondary panels. From these, each incoming hot conductor connects to a separate bus bar with its own circuit breaker.

Designing Electrical Loads

Just how much electrical capacity must be provided within a specific office depends on the type of organization involved and the work processes that go on there. It is more important than ever that facility planners have accurate information, best gained from surveys, about each worker's equipment and about the organization's best estimates for future growth or automation.

Not all organizations have introduced technology to the same level, so the professional architect, designer, or facility manager will probably encounter widely varying levels of need. It is usually advisable to allow for different circuits for lighting, electrical devices, and electronic equipment. Some offices will need separate dedicated circuits, such as for a large computer. A very large installation may need several circuits.

When planning all the utility systems (HVAC [heating, ventilation, and air conditioning], electrical, data/communications), it's best to plan for the maximum feasible loads, based on the organization's long-range plans. Your building system might look perfectly adequate for today's needs. But will it be adequate for additional power wiring, communications cable, and HVAC loads that can be reasonably predicted five, eight, or ten years out? The slight cost for adding extra capacity during construction or redesign must be weighed against the high cost of correcting a deficient space.

Electrical Circuits

To understand circuit loads, you'll need to understand the rudiments of how electrical circuits work. The classic way to illustrate this is to think of an electrical system as being similar to a water circuit. In this analogy, voltage compares to water pressure: it is the pushing force. Amperage is comparable to the gallons per minute that travel through the pipe: it is the rate at which electrons pass along the wire, or the amount of current flowing.

Most people are used to thinking in watts—such as a 60-watt light bulb. Wattage is the measure of power that can be supplied through a given circuit, calculated by multiplying voltage and amperage. If, for example, you have 120 volts with 5 amps of current moving through a wire, you have 600 watts. If you have 10 amps of power moving through the wire, you have 1,200 watts.

Just as the water-carrying capacity of a pipe is limited by its size and the material it's made of, electrical wire is limited by its size and material as to the number of electrons it can carry. Overburdened wire will heat up and become dangerous if the electrical overload is not stopped; that's why protection devices like circuit breakers and fuses exist. Wire size and circuit capacity relationships are listed in the National Electrical Code; state and local building codes often list more stringent limitations. Wire size and type determines the number of amps allowable per circuit. Total amperage needs are determined by how many circuits are required in the facility. The total must not exceed the total number of amps available at the secondary distribution panel for the floor.

In planning electrical circuits within the office environment, you'll need to know what equipment will be used on various electrical circuits to plan capacity. Particularly in the case of electronic equipment, circuit overloads causing power interruptions can be catastrophic not only for the work in process but also for the hardware itself. And even if the needs of today are accommodated, inadequately planned circuits can hobble future expansion.

Workstation Electrical Loads

When most office workstations had only typewriters and lights and maybe an occasional calculator, planning electrical circuits was a relatively simple job. The sudden influx of electronic equipment at every level of the organization has permanently changed the game.

An electronic load is any device that uses electricity: a lamp, a terminal, or any of the other conveniences and necessities of office life that depend on electricity to function. In the office, electrical loads can be divided into three categories: lighting, office machines and appliances, and electronic office equipment.

Computer terminals, printers, and similar equipment use considerable amounts of electrical power. Planning for power and lighting in an office installation requires identifying the user's need, estimating total load requirements, and calculating circuits.

It isn't the number of receptacles on a branch circuit that causes overload; it's what's plugged into those receptacles. This is why, in planning power distribution and access for offices where electric equipment is used, knowing what will be used at each workstation is extremely important.

Planning branch circuits must involve a qualified electrician or electrical engineer familiar with the National Electrical Code and with the code requirements of the state, city, or locality involved. But the facility planners or managers are the ones who must provide the information to guide the activity of these professionals, and planners can be more effective knowing their language.

Branch Circuits

Let's now look at an example of a process for calculating the number of outlets allowed on a general purpose branch circuit. The capacity of a circuit, remember, is calculated by multiplying amperage and voltage. A 15-amp circuit being supplied with 120-volt current has a total capacity of 1,800 watts. A 20-amp, 120-volt branch circuit has a capacity of 2,400 watts.

The number of receptacles that may be placed on a circuit is limited by its capacity (15- or 20-amp), the load that will be connected to it, and by standards of the National Electrical Code. Where the connected load is not known, a 20-amp circuit may have a maximum of 13 receptacles and a 15-amp circuit may have a maximum of 10. The actual number of receptacles allowed on a circuit is subject to local or municipal codes that may be different from the NEC. Check with local authorities for specific constraints.

Branch circuits on which maximum or near maximum loads will be in use for three hours or more, such as circuits used for CRTs or for lighting, are defined as being in continuous operation. These circuits must be derated for the purpose of calculating electrical loads. For a derated circuit, the total load may not exceed 80 percent of the rating of the circuit. For example: A 20-amp circuit for office lighting would be derated to 16 amps (.80 x 20 = 16).

Specialized Types of Circuits

Electronic equipment may dictate the need for specialized types of circuits. Let's briefly discuss some of the most common.

Branch Electrical Circuit

Branch electrical circuits are circuit conductors between the final overcurrent device (fuse or circuit breaker) and a receptacle intended for use with an electrical load. The conductors in the circuit are not shared with any other branch circuit; this is also referred to as an isolated branch circuit.

Dedicated Branch Circuit

A dedicated branch circuit has one load or one piece of equipment connected to it, such as a copy machine or a paper shredder. This is a complete circuit consisting of hot, neutral, and ground wires, all connected to just one machine and not shared with any other equipment. This is usually done because the equipment uses the entire legal capacity of the circuit.

Designated Circuit

A designated circuit is a branch circuit used for a specific, designated kind of load, such as lighting only or personal computers only, or other equipment with compatible operating characteristics. Unlike a dedicated circuit, the designated circuit may share its neutral and ground wires with other circuits.

Isolated Ground Circuit

An isolated ground circuit has a separately wired ground from other circuits within the building. This helps avoid the problem of electrical noise being introduced to the internal circuitry of sensitive equipment.

The isolated ground is not a separate grounding system, but an isolated ground path back to the power system grounding point. Also, the isolated ground wiring does not connect to the conduit system at any other point. It is connected to the power system grounding point either directly or through an isolated ground bar in a distribution panel.

Clean Power

Users of electronic equipment sometimes report mysterious glitches, frozen screens, locked key-boards, and other computer malfunctions that seem to come from nowhere. Many such problems may be the result of irregularities in the power feeding the computer. Computers code and store information on the basis of very small changes in voltage; any deviation from standard voltage could cause them to malfunction.

Clean power can be defined as any power that is within a range of 5 percent above or 10 percent below the standard 120 volts, and free from electrical noise generated by other machines using the circuit. A typical wall socket may supply electrical power more than 10 percent below 120 V, and momentary deviations occur regularly due to outages, spikes, and electrical noise.

Power Problems

Computer makers have built in devices to protect equipment from some power problems, but four basic power problems still exist. The first problem has to do with power outages occurring when power is suddenly cut off, most often due to power line damage by ice, lightning, and so on. Large computers are usually protected by backup power sources, such as uninterruptible power supplies (UPS), but small PCs most often aren't. An outage can erase a computer's RAM (random access memory).

The second problem is voltage fluctuations, which are deviations either up or down in voltage. A sag occurs during a brown-out, when utilities deliberately reduce voltage to conserve power during peak loads. A surge can result during low demand periods, such as at night when other loads in the area shut down. Voltage fluctuations can last a few seconds or several hours. They can cause computer equipment to overheat or shut off, cause extensive data alterations (mysterious glitches), or damage circuitry. Voltage regulators or stabilizers can be installed to keep the voltage close to a stable 120 V.

Voltage spikes (the third problem) are instantaneous and very high surges. They can be caused by lightning striking a power line or the switching of large loads in the area (such as an elevator, copy machine, or other motors coming on or off). Spikes can wipe out stored data, alter data, or damage circuitry. Voltage spike suppressers are available to dissipate the excess voltage.

Electrical noise is an unwanted signal on a power line. It is caused by a series of voltage spikes of low magnitude. Fluorescent lights, business machines, elevators, HVAC equipment, and other sources can cause electrical noise, which in turn can cause the computer to process information erroneously. Noise isolation transformers and line conditioners will filter out noise.

Protection Systems

In the past, mainframe computers were protected from all these problems with discrete electrical systems, temperature- and humidity-controlled rooms, and other safeguards. But protecting personal computers spread all through an organization can be a special problem.

To determine whether to install protective devices, and if so which ones, compare the cost of the solution to the answers to a number of questions. For example, look at the type of information a personal computer is storing or processing. Does it contain critical financial information? Does it contain simple back files of correspondence? What would be the cost of losing that information if the computer malfunctions in one of the ways previously described? What would happen if the computer provided inaccurate information due to a glitch caused by one of the four basic problems described earlier?

Look at the function of the computer. What would be the cost of downtime? Consider the value of the user's time. What would it cost for that person not to work for an hour? Who else and what work processes would be affected? Finally, look at the equipment. What would it cost to replace damaged circuitry or equipment?

Providing power to electronic equipment in the information technology-age office is part of the story. Providing cabling systems to transmit data and telecommunications signals to each device is another part.

CABLE DESIGN CONSIDERATIONS

Facility planners need to understand the basics of cable management because, to design effective installations, they need to know how much cable management capacity is needed for the specific equipment to be used, how much bending the cables can tolerate, how much cable storage space they'll need, where the equipment will be located, and how the cables can be routed throughout the floor and the building.

Basic Cable Categories

As previously stated in Chapter 1, many types and sizes of data/communications cables exist, but they fall into a few categories based on their construction and transmission characteristics. The basic categories are twisted pair, coaxial, and fiber optic.

Twisted Pair Cabling

Twisted-pair cable is exactly what its name implies—two insulated wires wound together and covered by a protective coating, usually in combinations such as 3-pair or 4-pair. Ordinary telephone lines are twisted pair; 25-pair cable is the cable that the phone companies have used for years, though it is rarely used today in new installations.

Twisted pair wiring can be used for voice or data transmission. Though it is adequate for most office applications, twisted pair cable transmits data at slower speeds than newer technologies, and signals lose power when they move along this type of wire. If data is to be transmitted over some distance via twisted pair wiring, the signal may have to go through one or more repeaters, which amplify and retransmit it.

For example, IBM's cabling system offers two classes of cable in several types. One class is for data and one is for both voice and data. Both are twisted pair, but the data pairs are larger than normal, specially shielded, and precision-manufactured. These cables have bending restrictions that may affect how they can be routed through an installation. They are also much larger than most equivalent twisted pair (see Table 9–1) [2].

Table 9–1   Categories of Transmission Performance Specified for Cables

Designation	Transmission Characteristics	Description
3	Transmission characteristics are specified up to 16 MHz.	Meets applicable category 3 and class C requirements of ISO/IEC 11801 (including amendments A.1 and A.2), ANSI/TIA/EIA-568-A (including addenda A-1, A-2, and A-3), and TSB67 (see Chapter 27). Requirements are specified to an upper frequency limit of 16 MHz.
4	Transmission characteristics are specified up to 20 MHz.	Meets applicable category 4 requirements of ISO/IEC 11801 (including amendments A.1 and A.2), ANSI/TIA/EIA-568-A (including addenda A-1, A-2, and A-3), and TSB67 (see Chapter 27). Requirements are specified to an upper frequency limit of 20 MHz. This classification is a superset of category 3.
5	Transmission characteristics are specified up to 100 MHz.	Meets applicable category 5 and class D requirements of ISO/IEC 11801 (including amendments A.1 and A.2), ANSI/TIA/EIA-568-A (including addenda A-1, A-2, and A-3), TSB67, and draft TSB95 (see Chapter 27). Requirements are specified to an upper frequency limit of 100 MHz. This classification is a superset of category 4.
5e	Transmission characteristics are specified up to 100 MHz.	Performs to category 5e and additional class D requirements of draft amendment 3 of ISO/IEC 11801, and draft addendum 5 to ANSI/TIA/EIA-568-A (see Chapter 27). Requirements are specified to an upper frequency limit of 100 MHz. This classification is a superset of category 5.
6	Transmission characteristics will be specified up to 250 MHz.	Performs to category 6 and class E requirements under development by ISO/IEC and TIA. Requirements are expected to be specified to an upper frequency limit of at least 250 MHz. This classification is a superset of Category 5e.
7	Transmission characteristics will be specified up to 600 MHz.	Performs to category 7 and class F requirements under development by ISO/IEC. Requirements are expected to be specified to an upper frequency limit of at least 600 MHz. This classification is an electrical superset of category 6.

Categories 5e, 6, and 7 industry standards are currently under development.

It is strongly recommended that new category 5 cabling installations be specified to satisfy the minimum requirements of category 5e and it is expected that '568-A-5 will emerge as the new de facto minimum standard for category 5 cabling (see Chapter 27, "Standards Development").

Terminology and classifications specified in ISO/IEC 11801 for cabling links differ slightly from TIA categories. UTP categories 1 and 2 are not specified.

Components and installation practices are subject to all applicable building and safety codes that may be in effect.

IBM Type 5 cable fiber and Type 6 cable-STP stranded for data is very flexible.

AT&T's system uses primarily 4-pair twisted cable. This consists of two cables per workstation: one for voice and one for data. Twisted pair cable is discussed further in Chapter 10, "Copper Design Considerations."

Coaxial Cabling

Coaxial cable is made of a core conductor surrounded by a layer of insulation, then a metal sheath, which acts as both a second conductor and a shield, then an insulated outer coating. Each layer shares the same geometric axis—hence the name coaxial.

Coaxial cables have greater data capacity than twisted-pair wiring. But coaxial cable can be expensive and more difficult to install because of its bending restrictions. It is also bulkier.

Twinaxial cable is similar to coaxial, except that there are two conductors in the core. Triaxial cable has a core conductor and two concentric conductive shields. Twinaxial cable is discussed further in Chapter 10, "Copper Design Considerations."

Fiber Optic Cabling

Fiber optic cables are the most sophisticated and newest cables on the scene. The special glass or plastic core of a fiber optic cable (the optical fiber itself) transmits light instead of electrical impulses. It is surrounded by a cladding, which reflects the light. Signals in the form of light travel a zigzag path through the core by bouncing off the cladding. Cables containing from one to hundreds of fibers are protected with a coating much like that used for metal conductor cables.

Fiber optic cable offers a number of advantages—greater potential capacity; potentially lower cost; immunity to power surges, electrical noise, and grounding problems; very high rates of speed in transmitting data; small size; and flexibility. But most experts believe fiber optic technology will not be a major factor within most office buildings for several years because of a number of problems: too few installers experienced with the technicalities of coupling the cables, lack of standardization in the industry, fine cracks that develop over time in cables that are bent too tightly, and lack of need for the extra capacity fiber optics offer. Nevertheless, installation of fiber optic cable is easier then ever to learn and use, due to the configuration of the connection equipment, as well as the many premade connectors and adapters. Fiber optic cable is discussed further in Part III, Fiber-Optic Systems: A Hands-On Approach.

Backbone cable is the wiring used to route power or communications resources vertically to the floors of a building, or for major horizontal runs in large low-rise buildings. Telephone backbone cable, in particular, is very large and bulky (as much as three inches in diameter) and difficult to bend. Backbone cable is not a separate type of cable, but an application of one of the basic cable types previously described, with special fire-rating characteristics.

The type and brand of cable used for any specific application will be dictated by the kind of equipment in use and how that equipment must be connected. That's another reason why the facility planner must have information on the equipment planned for each workstation that is as accurate as possible. Cable manufacturers provide data on the bend radius restrictions and other important features of their products.

Local Area Networks

Some experts call the local area network (LAN) the major advance in office technology of the 1980s. Networks extend the use of peripherals (printers, etc.) and databases to many users; they allow microcomputers or other digital-based equipment to communicate and share data.

Other major improvements in technology in the past two decades have resulted in the removal of functions to special centers—the information technology center, the word processing center, and so on. LANs, in contrast, allow the decentralization of data and resources, preserving the independence of each workstation.

LANs are defined in different ways by different experts, but most definitions describe them as systems for moving and sharing information that include computers and peripherals, the transmission media connecting them, and sometimes additional components that amplify or interpret data signals to make them usable by another device.

LAN technology offers tremendous advantages to an organization. But making a LAN work requires interweaving skills and knowledge between communications systems designers and facility managers. LANs have implications for several aspects of facility planning:

- Wire and cable management, including the possible need for dedicated power circuits, cable paths, and storage of service loops, etc.
- Savings in equipment and space; sharing resources is more efficient.
- Location of people on the network. It's easier to design the network for maximum flexibility at the outset than to move people.
- Relocatability of furnishings; some loss of flexibility may be the price to be paid.
- Extra equipment space in backbones or small equipment rooms on each floor may be needed [C&WC, 10].

Cabling Topologies

Three physical layouts, in varying degrees of complexity, are most common for local area networks. As previously discussed in earlier chapters, these cabling topologies, or configurations, are also used for other applications. Multiple personal computers within a department might be connected, for instance, by a ring topology and yet not constitute a true LAN.

Bus (or tree) networks use a single spine of cable throughout the location. A branch cable connects to each device. It is the simplest topology, but it has constraints such as limits to the length of the spine cable and the need for complex devices at each branch point to tap into the network. Any damage to the network may affect the whole system; one malfunctioning device can bring the entire network down.

Star networks connect each device through a length of cable to a central connection point. This in turn is connected by a separate cable to another device such as a mainframe computer. A typical telephone system has a star topology.

Ring (or loop) networks must be continuous throughout the location. Each device connected to the network has one cable for information entering the terminal and another for information exiting. A nonfunctioning device on the network can be bypassed.

Hierarchical networks are multiple networks, linking groups of connected devices at many levels. This kind of network can be very complex because each concentration point can only provide services to a few devices.

The type of LAN used in an office will depend on the type of equipment to be used and the interaction required, and will be determined by equipment specialists. This choice will determine the type of cable used to implement the LAN, which in turn affects facility decisions. Implementing a LAN requires close cooperation among information technology (IT), facility managers, and interior planners.

BUILDING OR STRUCTURED CABLING CONSIDERATIONS

So far, this chapter has dealt with power and data/communications cabling system design delivery issues separately because they are two different issues. They come together in discussion of distribution of these resources through the architectural (or structured cabling) systems through the building itself.

Both power and data/communications cabling system resources must enter the building, be distributed vertically to each floor, and be available for access at points of use dictated by the needs of the people working there.

Adding to the confusion is the fact that multiple vendors are involved. The local phone company is one vendor, the long-distance company another, the cable television company yet another. Multiple computer and office equipment vendors are the rule, not the exception.

In designing cabling distribution systems, flexibility to accommodate future change is as important, if not more so, than accommodating present needs. Inadequate access to power and data/communications cabling system resources could prevent an organization from moving forward into a new technology and growth. Here too, structured cabling must be responsive to new functions imposed by the information technology age. See the Sidebar, "Obstacles to Infrastructure Modernization Cabling," for further information on the responsiveness of new cabling technology to space, speed, and future growth.

OBSTACLES TO INFRASTRUCTURE MODERNIZATION CABLING

Older construction, historic or otherwise, presents serious obstacles to infrastructure modernization. Creative solutions with cabling and wiring technologies ensure successful upgrades.

When do vintage 1980s buildings undergo historical renovations? When their wiring and cabling don't meet current needs.

That's what professionals at Briggs Corporation, in Des Moines, Iowa, found when they investigated a new headquarters facility. The voice and data cabling was inadequate, inflexible, and prone to failure. If the phone or computer goes down, they would be out of business because that's the only way they sell.

The building was gutted, and core-drilled holes through the existing floors received poke-through devices—a flexible yet unobtrusive solution. Cabling was routed through center-spline cable trays in plenum space below, with data cables on one side of the tray and voice lines on the other to facilitate future moves. The cable tray saved a lot on labor. It's lightweight and easy to handle, and because it uses a single hanger instead of a trapeze, Wolin Electrical, a design/build firm in Des Moines, found they could put it up much faster than a conventional tray.

An in-floor cellular raceway was used for a training facility on the ground floor by cutting channels in the floor slab and refinishing over the raceway. It was easy to reconfigure the space just by opening the activation cover and plugging in.

In other instances, a gut renovation may be impossible, and even greater creativity is needed. For example, at Perry's Egyptian Theater, county and city owners wanted to save historical detail while bringing the 1924 facility up to date.

Part of a business and entertainment complex in Ogden, Utah, the theater project was complicated by a historic design—and a fast-track schedule—that made pipe-and-wire cabling impossible. The 1924 theater has an unusual poured concrete structure, plastered masonry tile, and a rich art-deco facade with carved stone statues.

Pipe and wire could have been installed in 3-foot sections, but they never would have met the nine-month deadline. Instead, a metal-clad (type MC) cable was fished between the outer walls and the red interior tiles to serve convenient power and lighting throughout the theater.

A special, color-coded cable for fire alarm and control devices enhances the installed fire protection systems. A red stripe facilitates inspection, simplifies future rewiring, and helps prevent accidental disabling of the fire-security system.

Overall, the flexible type MC cabling is ideal for threading electrical circuits into existing walls, plenums, and anywhere that mechanical protection is required for safety. No alternative to flexible, prewired, metal-clad cable would have enabled them to meet that schedule in that type of environment.

Historic buildings present unique obstacles to telecommunications upgrades as well—especially in modernizing a turn-of-the-century facility. For example, a brick building with wooden beams and planks was modernized with contemporary offices and a decidedly futuristic cabling design.

Designed by US West and Plymouth, Minnesota-based U.S. Premise Networking Services, the new system encompasses a total of nine telecommunications closets and three computer rooms serving some 4,000 workstations in modular furniture and hardwall offices.

The data networking environment offers Internet access and the capacity to install an asynchronous transfer mode (ATM) network for future increased bandwidth demands. US West's existing high-speed Ethernet networks are served by a fiber backbone and horizontal cable is supported by a single platform that goes beyond current needs for voice and data applications.

Certainly, this is the key for telecommunications and data cabling, say experts. Demand grows almost as rapidly as technologies evolve, so it's critical to allow space—and speed—for future growth [1].

So, what is structured cabling? What does it mean to you? Let's take another look even though the U.S. version of structured cabling has been covered in earlier chapters to some extent. The discussion of structured cabling that follows is based on practices generally in use within the United Kingdom and in Europe.

Structured Cabling

In the past, buildings could have several different cabling systems for different communications systems, for example, block wiring for voice, coaxial for Ethernet, multipair for RS232, and so on. Structured cabling replaces all the different cabling with a single cabling system that covers the whole building for all voice and data (including CCTV and video) requirements.

A structured cabling system consists of outlets that provide the user with an RJ45 presentation, as shown in Figure 9–1 [3]. User outlets are usually supplied as either one or two RJ45 connectors mounted in a standard single-gang face plate, or as single snap-in modules that can be fitted into floor boxes, single-gang face plates (up to two modules), or dual-gang face plates (up to four modules).

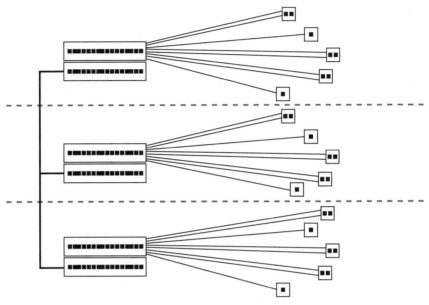

Figure 9–1   A generalized structured cabling system.

Each user outlet is cabled back to a hub using an individual cable containing four twisted pairs, this cabling is known as the horizontal cabling. In most cases, cable that meets the category 5 specification is used for the horizontal cabling. The cable can be either unshielded, known as UTP (unshielded twisted pair) or shielded, known as STP (shielded twisted pair) or FTP (foiled twisted pair).

The cable is connected to the back of the user outlet by means of an IDC (insulation displacement connection) connector. The maximum length of cable between the hub and any outlet must be 90 meters to comply with EIA/TIA and ISO requirements. This is for Class D applications on category 5 cable. The standards allow a further 10 meters for connecting leads and patch leads, making a total drive distance of 100 meters.

Some suppliers will warrant systems with longer drive distances, depending on the protocol being used.

In a true structured cabling system, the horizontal cabling and user outlets are the same for all services, so that any outlet can be configured for voice, Ethernet, RS232, video, or other service. As user requirements change, the service provided on the outlets can be changed simply by changing the patching configuration in the equipment room. If necessary, an adapter is used in the outlet to convert it to the service being provided (for example, a video balun will provide the standard RGB or composite video outputs required for CCTV).

When a structured cabling system is installed, the floors are usually flood-wired with outlets being installed on a grid layout to a specified density, rather than to individual user positions. This allows for more flexibility, without having to recable when changes are made to the layout of the building in the future.

At the hub, the individual 4-pair cables from the user outlets are terminated on patch panels. These patch panels usually have IDC connectors on the rear for terminating the 4-pair cables, and provide an RJ45 presentation on the front for patching. Patch panels are usually mounted in standard 19-inch racks, either wall mounted or free standing. RJ45 patch panels usually come in multiples of 16 connectors; panels containing 16, 32, and 48 RJ45 connectors are common.

The hubs are connected together and to the main computer or equipment room using riser or backbone cables; these can either be copper or optical. In most systems, optical cables are used for the data backbone cables and multipair copper cables are used for the voice backbone cables.

Voice backbone cables are almost always the 25-pair telco cables—where the interface to the private branch exchange (PBX) is 66E blocks at one end and to the patch panels in the intermediate distribution frame (IDF) at the opposite end.

The equipment cabinets usually also contain equipment for the data network. Depending on the equipment used, the data channels may be presented in one of two different ways. Each data channel on the equipment may be fitted with an RJ45 connector, so that channels can be patched directly to the patch panels terminating the horizontal cables, as shown in Figure 9–2 [Egerton, 2].

Alternatively, the equipment may be fitted with telco connectors. These are 25-pair connectors, each of which carries several (usually 12) data channels, as shown in Figure 9–3 [Egerton, 3]. If the equipment is fitted with telco connectors, then these must be connected to equipment side patch panels using mass termination cables (25-pair cables fitted with a telco connector at

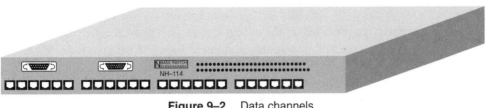

Figure 9–2   Data channels.

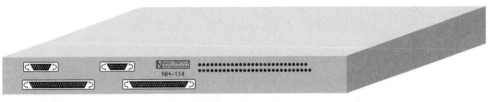

Figure 9–3   Telco connectors.

one end, and no connectors at the other end, so that they can be punched down onto IDC connectors) to provide an RJ45 connector for each data channel.

If an optical fiber backbone is used, the hubs must also contain equipment to enable the optical cable to interface with the copper cables. Backbone cables are terminated on patch panels at the hub. Copper cables are terminated on RJ45 patch panels, the same as those used for the horizontal cabling. Optical cables are terminated in patch panels, which usually provide the user with a 10Base-FL (STII) fiber optic or Stream Protocol Version 2 (STII) presentation. Fiber optic cables can be terminated by either fusion-splicing pigtails with factory-fitted connectors onto each fiber in the cable or by directly fitting field-mountable connectors to each of the fibers. Factory-fitted connectors are also available for interfacing copper to fiber.

Patch leads are used to connect the horizontal cables to either the data equipment or to the voice backbone cable, depending on which service is required at the user outlet, as shown in Figure 9–4 [Egerton, 3]. Cable tidies are used in the hub cabinets to enable patch leads to be routed neatly, these are 1U high 19-inch panels fitted with jumper rings. A 1U cable tidy is usually used below every 3U of patch panels.

The data backbone can be in either a star or ring configuration, depending on the equipment used, as shown in Figure 9–5 [Egerton, 4]. In a star configuration, data backbone cables are usually taken to patch panels in the main computer (or equipment) room. Voice backbone cables are nearly always in a

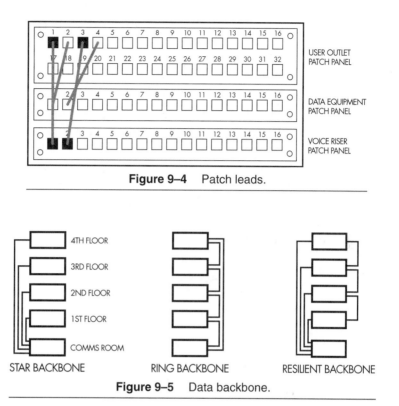

Figure 9–4 Patch leads.

STAR BACKBONE RING BACKBONE RESILIENT BACKBONE

Figure 9–5 Data backbone.

star configuration, and are taken to an MDF (main distribution frame) or BDF (building distribution frame). The MDF or BDF is usually a KRONE type frame utilizing 10-pair IDC connection strips. Furthermore, in large facilities, there are usually IDFs where voice and data are patched prior to being routed to the MDF.

A star and a ring backbone can be combined to provide resilience. In the event of the failure of any one cable in the backbone, the signal can be rerouted via another available route. This can be carried out automatically by the equipment, or by manually repatching the backbone.

Equipment Rooms or Wiring Closets

Incoming communications cables interface with the building distribution systems in most office buildings and in main terminal rooms. Depending on the size of the building and the need, this interface can be anywhere from a relatively small wiring closet to a large temperature- and humidity-controlled room.

A rule of thumb cited by one manufacturer of electronic equipment is to provide a room a minimum of 8 feet wide, with one square foot of floor space for each 2,000 square feet of usable floor space in the building. Satellite wire closets or equipment areas may be necessary, depending on the size and configuration of the building.

For large office buildings, more than one equipment room may be necessary. A big high-rise might require a main equipment vault and satellite equipment rooms in other places throughout the building.

The main equipment room should be a separate, lockable room (this is advisable for satellite equipment rooms, too). It must be adequately ventilated and temperature-controlled (a 65- to 80-degree range is average, though some equipment makers may allow broader or narrower ranges for temperature and/or humidity). The humidity should generally be kept between 30 to 55 percent, and the room must be secure from flooding or seepage.

It's important to the functioning of the switching equipment that equipment rooms not become catchall storage areas. Switching equipment can be affected by copying machines and has to be housed separately; it has to be kept in a room free of chemicals or combustible gases such as ammonia, petroleum vapors, and so on. It also should be kept as dust-free as possible.

Floor-loading requirements (the load-bearing capacity of the floor of the equipment room) will differ depending on the type of equipment. Usually, 125 to 175 pounds per square foot are typical recommended limits.

Special consideration should also be given to the availability of power wiring and AC outlets for communications equipment. Most manufacturers and building codes warn against joint use of equipment rooms for power system interface and communications system purposes.

A phone in each closet. No protocol data units (PDUs).

Nevertheless, most buildings will have two types of rooms to provide for the termination, protection, and management of various kinds of media and electronics that comprise the telecommunications network: entrance wiring closets and floor wiring closets. Let's take a specific look at the two different types of wiring closets.

Entrance Wiring Closets

The first type of room, the entrance wiring closet (EWC), will be located in the basement of the building it serves. In the absence of a basement, it will be on the ground floor.

All cables entering the building will be terminated in this room and the appropriate methods for high-voltage protection will be applied. Electronic equipment associated with video and data interconnectivity will also be situated in this room. The EWC will be the focal point of all communications facilities and resources in the building. It is imperative that the EWC be an enclosed area secure from flooding and accidental damage as well as sabotage.

In other words, the EWC is a room for the exclusive placement of electronics and terminations of cable of many types, which supply the building with telecommunications. Security is required and the room cannot be shared with other functions in the building. Considerations for the facility are floor weight load factors, water avoidance, lighting, electrical access, room size, electrical grounding, HVAC, and location near the building entrance facility.

General.   The room designated to be an EWC must be dedicated exclusively to that purpose. Access to the room should be direct without passing through other secure areas that would require additional keys for access. Conversely, access to the EWC should not be required in order to access another area. It cannot be shared with any other use such as storage, janitorial equipment, or other electrical or mechanical installations. There should not be any plumbing fixtures in the room and pipes should not pass through the room that could cause flooding or require repair or replacement. There should not be any fire sprinklers in the room, if local fire codes will permit; although there should be some sort of smoke or fire monitoring.

Floor.   The floor must be free of dust and static electricity. The floor should be tiled instead of carpeted. If the floor is left uncovered, it must be sealed and painted. The floor must be high enough to avoid any threat of flooding and have a minimum floor loading specification of at least 100 pounds per square foot.

Ceiling.   The ceiling should be a minimum of 8 feet, 6 inches high. There should also not be a false ceiling.

Walls.   The walls should be lined with ¾-inch, 4-foot by 8-foot plywood attached to the wall framing members or mechanically attached to the masonry walls. All surfaces are to be painted with fire-resistant paint.

Doors.   Doorways should be a minimum of 36 inches wide by 6 feet 8 inches high. Doors should be hinged outward and solid to provide security and resistance to fire. The door locks will be cored so that they will allow access to network personnel only.

Lighting.   Lighting should be provided to a minimum level of 540 lx (50-foot candles) measured 3 feet above the floor. Light fixtures should be mounted a minimum of 8 feet, 6 inches above the floor.

Electrical.   A 20 amp, 110 volt AC separately fused electrical circuit should be provided for electronic equipment. This circuit shall be extended to a power strip mounted on equipment racks in the center of the room. Additional outlets for tools, test instruments, and work lights shall be placed at least at 6-foot intervals around the room.

Grounding.   A minimum of a 6 AWG ground conductor from the main building grounding electrode and the power neutral shall be provided. It shall also be terminated on a copper ground bar properly installed in the room.

HVAC.   HVAC provisioning shall be sufficient to provide a minimum of six air changes per hour. The temperature should be constantly maintained at 55° F to 80° F. Care must be taken to not include the room in a zone that could have heating, air conditioning, or air exchange reduced during the night or at idle times, as the equipment will continuously generate the same amount of heat.

Location.   A building should have only one EWC, regardless of the building size. It should be located as close as possible to the point where telecommunications facilities enter the building while being centrally located to reduce the lengths of backbone cables.

Size.   The minimum size for an EWC is 6 feet by 9 feet, but that size room will satisfy the needs of a building of up to 200,000 square feet of gross floor space. Figure 9–6 illustrates how that space would be utilized [4]. Table 9–2 specifies room sizes required for buildings of more square feet or gross floor space [VCCS, 2].

Table 9–2   Room Sizes

Ground Floor Space (Square Feet)	Room Dimensions (Feet)
Up to 200,000	9 × 6
200,001 to 400,000	9 × 10
400,001 to 500,000	9 × 13
500,001 to 600,000	10 × 13.5
600,001 to 800,000	11 × 16
800,001 to 1,000,000	11 × 21

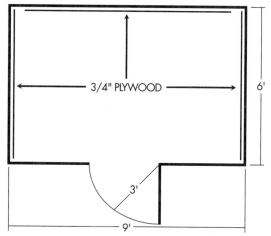

Figure 9–6   EWC space utilization and FWC
minimum acceptable room size.

Floor Wiring Closets

The floor wiring closet (FWC) is the second type of room required. Backbone cables from the EWC are terminated here, as are station cables. Pairs in these cables are connected in this room to establish continuous electrical paths from rooms/desktops to other rooms/desktops, and to communication devices. Electronic devices associated with the exchange of data and/or video information will also be situated in FWCs.

In other words, the FWC has an exclusive location on each floor to facilitate the electronics and cabling distribution for the floor. If the floor is large enough, with long cable runs, more than one room may be required on each floor. Security requires that the room not be shared with other building functions. Considerations for the facility are floor loading factors, water avoidance, ceilings and walls, fire door, lighting, electrical access, room size, electrical grounding, HVAC, floor location, and cable run maximum lengths.

General

A room designated to be an FWC must be dedicated exclusively to that purpose. Access to the room should be direct without passing through other secure areas that would require additional keys for access. Conversely, access to the FWC should not be required in order to access another area. It cannot be shared with any other use such as storage, janitorial equipment, or other electrical or mechanical installation. There should not be any plumbing fixtures in the room and pipes should not pass through the room that could cause flooding or require repair or replacement. There should not be any fire sprinklers in the room, if fire codes will permit. However, the FWC should contain a working phone.

Floor.   The floor must be free of dust and static electricity. The floor should be tiled instead of carpeted. If the floor is left uncovered, it must be sealed and painted. The floor must be high enough to avoid any threat of flooding and have a minimum floor loading specification of 50 pounds per square foot.

Ceiling.   The ceiling should be a minimum of 8 feet, 6 inches high. In addition, there should also not be a false ceiling.

Walls.   The walls should be lined with ¾-inch, 4-foot by 8-foot plywood attached to the wall framing members or mechanically attached to the masonry walls. All surfaces are to be painted with fire-resistant paint.

Doors.   Doorways should be a minimum of 36 inches wide by 6 feet, 8 inches high. Doors should be hinged outward and solid to provide security and resistance to fire. The door locks will be cored so that they will allow access to network personnel only.

Lighting.   Lighting should be provided to a minimum level of 540 lx (50-foot candles) measured 3 feet above the floor. Light fixtures should be mounted a minimum of 8 feet 6 inches above the floor.

Electrical.   A 20 amp, 110 volt AC separately fused electrical circuit shall be provided for power strips to be installed with the steel equipment racks. Additional outlets for tools, test instruments, and work lights shall be placed at least at 6-foot intervals around the room at a height of 6 inches above the floor.

Grounding.   A minimum of a 6 AWG ground conductor from the main building grounding electrode and the power neutral shall be provided. It shall also be terminated on a copper ground bar properly installed in the room.

HVAC.   HVAC provisioning shall be sufficient to provide a minimum of four (4) air changes per hour. The temperature should be constantly maintained at 55° F to 80° F. Care must be taken to not include the room in a zone that could have heating, air conditioning, or air exchange reduced during the night or at idle times, as the equipment will continuously generate the same quantity of heat.

Location.   Each floor must have at least one FWC. Additional FWCs may be required to meet maximum limits for station cable lengths defined below. FWCs should be located in the center of the area to be served. In multifloored buildings, FWCs should be located directly above each other to minimize the lengths of backbone cables, thus reducing the lengths of circuits between floors in the building.

The FWC should be located in such a way that the average station cable length is 150 feet, and no individual station cable exceeds 295 feet in length. One FWC can effectively serve 20,000 square feet of usable floor space.

Size. The requirements to terminate fiber optic cables both to the individual room jack and in the building backbone system, coupled with the video media terminations required in each FWC, cause the minimum acceptable room size to be 6 feet by 9 feet, as shown in Figure 9–6. This 54-square foot minimum requirement can effectively serve 15,000 square feet of usable floor space. As the usable floor space increases, so should the size of the FWC, at the rate of 9 square feet per 5,000 square feet of usable floor space. A maximum 20,000 square feet of usable space would require a minimum FWC size of 6 feet by 12 feet.

Vertical Distribution

Power and data/communications cabling system resources are distributed vertically through tall buildings via backbone cables in one or more building shafts to the floors where they will be used. How this system is designed will vary greatly, depending on the design of the building.

Increased use of information technology usually brings the need for more building core capacity to accommodate the additional cable used. Many high-rise buildings have created headaches for their owners because the backbone shaft is crammed full of cable and can't handle the demand for more. Where codes allow, even the elevator shafts are pressed into service in many high-rises as a way (though not a good one) of getting more data/communications capacity into the building. Nevertheless, there continue to be numerous instances of intermittent problems with high-speed circuits that are routed over cables in elevator shafts.

Backbone shafts are either open or closed. Closed backbone shafts are vertically aligned closets on each floor connected by pipe sleeves or conduit through the floors. They have different fire code requirements than open-shaft systems, but they may be more versatile.

Backbone Raceways

Backbone raceways are a series of accesses that connect EWCs to FWCs. These paths permit cable to be placed between the floors. They may be slots, sleeves, conduits, or trays and racks in which cables may be routed for support and protection. Considerations are the size, quantity, and seals. If conduits or sleeves are used, the 4-inch size is preferred. Table 9–3 shows the number of paths needed, based on building size [VCCS, 1].

The term "backbone" has replaced "riser and house" in cable terminology.

General. Backbone raceways may be slots or sleeves between floors. Or they may consist of conduits or trays and racks in which cables may be routed for support and protection.

Design. When wiring closets are located above each other, sleeves or slots may be used. When they are so situated, conduits should be utilized to provide security and physical protection to the cables.

Size. The size of sleeves or conduits can be stated as one, since sleeves will probably be made of pieces of conduit placed through the floor. A minimum of 4-inch conduits should be used. If space limitations prevent the use of 4-inch conduits, then the number of 3-inch ducts provided should be doubled or if 2-inch ducts are used, the number should be increased fourfold. Slots should be a minimum of 4 inches inside dimension square. Slot sizes and/or numbers of slots can be determined by the number of 4-inch conduits or sleeves required under Table 9–3 [VCCS, 1].

Table 9–3   Slot Sizes

Ground Floor Space (Square Feet)	Number of Sleeves or Ducts
Up to 40,000	1
40,001 to 80,000	2
80,001 to 160,000	3
160,001 to 180,000	4
180,001 to 200,000	5

Table 9–3 does not include two spare ducts or sleeves.

Quantity. A minimum of one 4-inch conduit or sleeve should be provided per FWC, plus two spares. If higher-floor FWCs are supplied from lower-floor FWCs (as with sleeves or slots), only one conduit for every two rooms needs to be added to the backbone, as shown in Figure 9–7 [VCCS, 1].

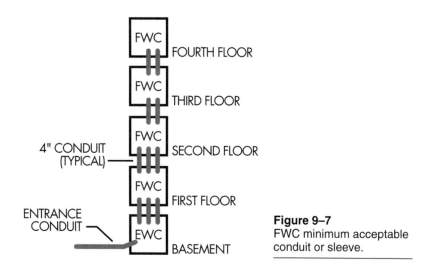

Figure 9–7
FWC minimum acceptable
conduit or sleeve.

Seals.   All conduits should be provided with seals until used to prevent the entrance of gases. Sleeves and slots should be sealed with firestop material to prevent the spread of fire.

Horizontal Distribution

On each floor, power and data/communications cabling system resources are distributed horizontally through either the ceiling or the floor. Ceiling systems use metal conduit, raceways, and/or flexible conduit cable assemblies to distribute power and data/communications wiring in the plenum, or the space between a finished dropped or hung ceiling and the floor above. If the ceiling is an air-plenum ceiling, cable must be routed through conduit or must be fire-rated.

Wires and cables are brought down to each point of use through power poles, which typically interface with building electrical wiring through junction boxes at the top. Data/communications cables run through the power pole in separate raceways isolated from the electrical wiring by metal barriers (required by the National Electrical Code).

Features of ceiling systems include low initial cost, low labor costs (poles are prewired), unlimited choice of installation locations, and compatibility with just about any structural system or furniture choice. Constraints include the forest effect (a clutter of poles interrupting *open-office* [TSB75] environments), small capacity, and limited reuse of ceiling tiles, which have to be cut.

TSB75: Open-Office Cabling

Additional specifications for horizontal cabling in areas with moveable furniture and partitions have been introduced in TIA/EIA TSB75. Horizontal cabling methodologies are specified for *open-office* environments by means of multi-user telecommunications outlet assemblies (see Figure 9–8) and consolidation points (see Figure 9–9) [2]. These methodologies are intended to provide increased flexibility and economy for installations with open-office work spaces that require frequent reconfiguration.

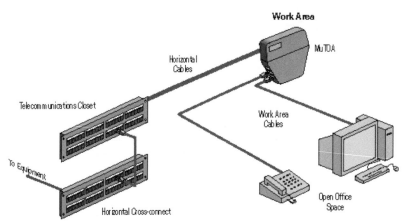

Figure 9–8   This is an example of open-office implementation using a multi-user telecommunications outlet assembly (MuTOA).

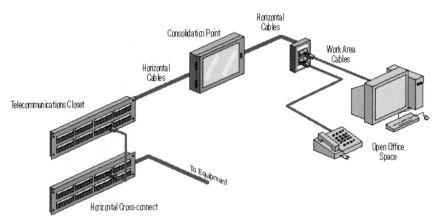

Figure 9–9   This is an example of open-office implementation using a consolidation point connector.

An MuTOA is a telecommunications outlet scheme intended to serve multiple work areas in an open-office environment.

A consolidation point is an interconnection scheme that connects horizontal cables from building pathways to cables that extend to telecommunications outlets (TOs) through open office pathways. A consolidation point (CP) is referred to in '11801 as a transition point (TP).

Horizontal Distance of Copper Links (Open Office). Copper work area cables connected to an MuTOA, should meet the requirements of '568-A (sec. 10.5 and 11.5). The maximum length of copper work area cables should be determined according to:

$$C = (103-H)/1.2$$
$$W = C-7 (<20\ m)$$
$$\text{Where:}$$

C is the combined length of the work area cable, equipment cable, and patch cord (m).

W is the length of the work area cable (m).

H is the length of the horizontal cable (m).

The preceding equations assume that there is a total of 7m (23 ft.) of patch and equipment cables in the equipment closet. Table 9–4 shows the application of these formulae [2]. The length of work area cables should not exceed 20m (66 ft.). The MuTOA should be marked with the maximum allowable work area cable length.

Table 9–4   Maximum Length of Work Area Cables

Length of Horizontal Cable	Maximum Length of Work Area Cable	Maximum Combined Length of Work Area Cables, Patch Cords, and Equipment Cable
H m(ft.)	W m (ft.)	C m (ft.)
90 (295)		10 (33)
85 (279)	7 (23)	14 (46)
80 (262)		18 (59)
75 (246)	15 (49)	22 (72)
70 (230)		27 (89)

Horizontal Distances of Optical Fiber Links (Long Work Area Cables).   For optical fiber cables, any length combination of horizontal cables and work area cables is acceptable as long as the total combined length of the horizontal channel does not exceed 100 m (328 ft.). When deploying a centralized fiber cabling topology, the general guidelines of TSB72 should be followed (see Sidebar, "TSB72: Centralized Optical Fiber Cabling Guidelines"). The following are some of the advantages and features of horizontal distances of optical fiber links (long work area cables):

- It is preferable to use MuTOAs only when the entire length of the work area cord is accessible to facilitate tracing and to prevent erroneous disconnection. Up to 20 meters (66 ft.) of work area cable are allowed.
- Implementations using either MuTOAs or CPs are subject to the same end-to-end performance requirements.
- Consolidation points have the advantage that they deliver dedicated TOs to individual work areas and do not require provisions for extended cord lengths.
- MuTOAs are subject to the same interface requirements specified for each media type.
- Consolidation point (transition point) requirements are performance-based. There is no physical interface requirement for the CP except those required to meet functional requirements [2].

TSB72: CENTRALIZED OPTICAL FIBER CABLING GUIDELINES

This Telecommunications Systems Bulletin (TSB) provides the user with the flexibility of designing an optical fiber cabling system for centralized electronics typically in single-tenant buildings. It contains information and guidelines for centralized optical fiber cabling, as shown in Figure 9–10 [2].

Some points specified in TSB72 for a centralized optical fiber cabling system include:

- Intended for single-tenant users who desire centralized versus distributed electronics.

- Implementation allows cables to be spliced or interconnected at the telecommunications closet such that cables can be routed to a centralized distributor for total cable lengths of 300 m (984 ft.) or less, including patch cords and jumpers.

- Allows for migration from an interconnection or splice to a cross-connection scheme that can also support distributed electronics.

- Pull-through implementations are allowed only when total length between the telecommunications outlet/connector and centralized cross-connect is 90 m (295 ft.) or less.

- Connecting hardware is required to join fibers by remateable connectors or splices; connectors should be 568SC interface; provide for simplex or duplex connection of optical fibers; provide means of circuit identification; and allow for addition and removal of optical fibers [2].

Note

Some multimode fiber implementations may be limited to an operating range of 220 m to support 1000BASE-SX.

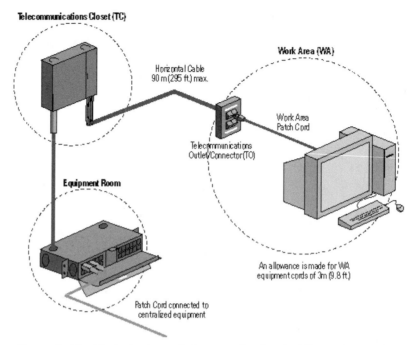

Figure 9–10   Typical schematic for centralized optical fiber cabling using an interconnection.

Typical Floor Distribution Cabling Systems

Tubular duct systems use steel ducts to carry wiring. Access to these systems is through above-floor monuments or tombstones. Because the ducts have separate channels for power wires and data/communications cables, access to each usually requires a separate above-floor monument.

Features include ease of installation during construction and experienced builders, who have worked with such systems for years. Constraints include high first cost, potentially limited capacity (by raceway size), ease of damaging the ducts during other phases of construction, and necessity of a thicker concrete slab to meet fireproofing requirements.

Cellular floors are among the most popular architectural options. They are both structural floors and data/communications wiring. Trench headers, specially manufactured metal troughs, bring power wiring and data/communications cables through the floor from the wiring closets.

Trench duct is normally covered with removable flat steel cover plates for its entire length. Although access to the cellular floor can be through other feeder ducts, trench headers provide maximum flexibility to the system. The size and placement of the trench header will determine the accessibility of wiring and cabling.

Cellular floors can conceal power and communications outlets below the floor, or they can be used with above-floor monuments. Preset inserts are usually used with freestanding furniture because the density of the cells enables the inserts to be placed almost anywhere the furniture plan requires.

Features of cellular floors are that they can provide a great deal of capacity for numerous access points (depending on their design), are cost effective in use of materials, and don't have the stability problems some users notice with raised floors. Constraints are that they can be slow or difficult to install because the concrete must be poured carefully around the presets, alignment during construction can be difficult, an electrician must be present during construction, adding wire can be difficult, fireproofing is required on the bottom plate, and access to the trench header must be maintained. Designing the cell spacing of a cellular floor system is critical to its later usefulness.

Raised floor (or raised-access floor) systems are mounted on steel pedestals and have removable floor panel sections to allow access beneath the floor, where power and data/communications wiring are distributed. Access can be through above-floor monuments or through access ports with a junction box mounted below a cutout on the floor panel.

Raised floors were used primarily in computer rooms before the invasion of the personal computer into most offices. Today, they are widely used because of their capacity to handle volumes of cable. Features in addition to capacity include flexibility for additions or relocations of wiring, capacity to accommodate other services (HVAC, plumbing, etc.), no need for conduit to protect wires, cables where the floor plenum does not contain air return, and ease of construction.

Constraints include raising floor height, higher initial material cost, floor-height changes around stairwells and core areas, leveling problems, noise from footsteps, and potential code problems. Raised floor provides no additional shielding of cables. Its capacity, one of its greatest advantages, can also become a constraint by leading to lax wire management. It is seductively simple just to add more cable for a short-term solution instead of planning properly for the long term. See the Sidebar, "Installing Communications Cabling Below a Raised Floor," for additional information.

INSTALLING COMMUNICATIONS CABLING BELOW A RAISED FLOOR

When you are installing communications cabling below a raised floor in a room that doesn't meet the requirements of an information technology processing room (as defined in Article 645 [NFPA-70] of the National Electrical Code [NEC]), does the cable have to be type CMP or MPP, and does it have to be enclosed in conduit, as outlined in Section 300-22(b)? The confusion stems from Section 800-53(a), which states: *"Cable installed in ducts, plenums, and other spaces used for environmental air shall be type CMP."* However, the exception lists several types of cables allowed in plenums that must be installed in compliance with Section 300-22, and type CMP is listed as one of those types of cables. Also, Figure 800-2 depicts type MPP and CMP cable in a plenum, but not in conduit. Is type CMP cable in a plenum required to be installed in accordance with Section 300-22?

No, NFPA-70 does not require that CMP cable be installed in conduit in a plenum space, but it does not prohibit installation of CMP cable in conduit in a plenum space either. That is why CMP appears in both the requirement and the exception. The following citations should clear up any confusion:

- Section 800-50 of the NEC, "Listing, Marking, and Installation of Communications Wires and Cables," states: *"Communications wires and cables installed as wiring within buildings shall be listed as being suitable for the purpose."*

- Section 800-53(a), "Applications of Listed Communications Wires and Cables, (a) Plenum," states: *"Cables installed in ducts, plenums, and other spaces used for environmental air shall be Type CMP. Exception: Types CMP, CMR, CMG, CM, and CMX and communications wire installed in compliance with Section 300-22."*

- Section 300-22(c), "Other Space Used for Environmental Air," states: *"Other types of cables and conductors shall be installed in electrical metallic tubing, flexible metallic tubing, intermediate metal conduit, rigid metal conduit, flexible metal conduit, or, where accessible, surface metal raceway or metal wireway with metal covers or solid bottom metal cable tray with solid metal covers [5]."*

The listing of type CMP in the exception to 800-53(a) is not a typographical error. There are parts of the country that require all telecommunications cable to be installed in conduit. This wording allows for those folks to use CMP or MPP cable in those conduits.

Poke-through systems use the plenum of the floor below for access to wires and cables. A hole is drilled through the floor and wires or cables are literally poked through. A fire-rated monument must be installed in the floor to protect the floor fire rating. Fire codes and structural considerations usually limit the number of poke-through fittings that can be used in a space.

Features of poke-through systems include low initial cost. Constraints includes high cost of changing or maintaining the building once holes have been made, limited outlets (holes weaken the structure), relocation expense and difficulty, limited capacity, conduit or fire-rated plenum cable required for telephone and data wiring, risk (drilling could result in damage to hidden conduits), and mess and disruption when it's time to change.

Floor-surface raceways attach directly to the floor and enclose electrical and data/communications wiring in separate covered raceways. They're used with low profile junction boxes and fittings that are mounted directly on the floor, and they are usually used when the least expensive solution is desired. Surface-wall raceways are similar and attach directly to walls or columns. Features of floor-surface raceways include low initial cost and ease of access. Constraints include aesthetic concerns and potential tripping hazards.

Flat conductor cable is one of the newest options. Flat cables can carry phone, electrical, and data transmission wiring in thin copper strips covered with insulation, lying flat beneath carpet squares where traditional round wires would be objectionable. Specially designed monuments allow access to the wiring. Outlets can be moved or new outlets can be added with a minimum of disruption.

Though only approved a few years ago, flat cable has become very popular for use with open-plan furniture systems because it can deliver services nearly anywhere in an installation, preserving the furniture system's relocatability and aesthetic advantages. Flat conductor must be used with carpet squares because of electrical codes, but this is desirable anyway because it makes access to the wire much easier.

The newest flat conductor products include optical fiber versions that can carry voice, data, and video signals, yet are immune to interference and electrical noise. Other developments include low-profile coaxial data cable, including some suitable for use with LANs.

Other features of flat conductor cable include moderate installed system cost depending on locality, suitability for renovation, compatibility with other systems such as cellular floors or tubular ducts, ease of relocation by backbone (in-house) workers, and distribution of wires and cables without altering floor height. Constraints include limited applications (not approved for hospitals, schools, or residential applications), limited capacity, relatively high cost of change because cable is not always reusable, distance limitations of data and voice cable, and trade problems (phone workers cannot move carpeting because of union rules).

Each of these building distribution systems has advantages and disadvantages, and often the right solution is a combination of approaches. But it is important for the facility planner to realize that higher initial costs for maximum power and data/communications capacity will very likely be justified by future needs. And the cost of retrofitting an inadequate installation will be much, much higher than planning for the maximum at the beginning of a project.

Open-plan furniture systems can be a valuable extension of building power and data/communications delivery systems. To accomplish this, the furniture system must provide an interface with the building distribution systems, means of distribution of wires and cables through the space, and points of access to resources.

Power poles and base power-in assemblies provide the interface between the building systems and equipment for both electricity and data/communications cables. Wires and cables travel from ceiling systems through separate channels in power poles to panels, where they are distributed horizontally. Whatever the method of distribution through the floor, the base power-in connects to the building electrical system and electricity is then distributed through electrically wired powerways. Cables can be routed through raceways at panel bases or tops.

Vertical distribution of cables is accomplished through cable management poles available for different geometries of panel connections. Storage of excess cable takes place in the raceways themselves or in special cable reels and troughs mounted under work surfaces.

Access is provided in a variety of ways. Electrical outlets can be placed at panel bases in simplex, duplex, or triplex receptacles. Outlets can be at work-surface height as separate outlets or as part of work-surface powerways.

Cables can be brought through channels at work-surface height. Or, they can be brought through at the tops and bottoms of panels through a variety of options.

Planning and designing for adequate access can be trickier than it may seem. Plenty of outlets may be available in the panels, but when free-standing furniture such as desks or files are moved in, these access points can be blocked. For this reason, as well as for circuit capacity planning, the facility planner needs to know what equipment will be used in a space and where it will be located.

A wire management plan and design, continuously and accurately updated, provides the database required for managing power and data/communications wiring. As with everything else in facility management, what is designed and installed will only work as long as it is properly maintained.

The wire management plan should include a set of drawings that identifies each point of access to power or data/communications cabling system resources on each floor, as well as the overall view of the building. It should indicate what has been activated and what has not, what kind of cable is located where, and what each cable is connected to.

It's easier than it may seem. This information can easily be logged on a personal computer or simply kept in notebook form and updated any time changes are made. Software for managing power wiring and data/communications cabling is becoming increasingly sophisticated; several versions are already on the market, with more to come.

Make sure, too, that every vendor contract affecting power or data/communications cabling system delivery includes a provision stating that the vendor must adhere to the wire management plan and design. The key is having a plan and design, and then making sure everyone sticks to both.

FROM HERE

This chapter presented an overview of cabling system architectural design considerations (structured cabling system, wiring closet design, cabling facilities, and user-to-outlet ratios, etc.). The next chapter discusses copper design considerations (layout, components, connectors, shielding and maintenance, etc.).

NOTES

[1]   C. C. Sullivan, "Prehistoric Cabling," Buildings OnLine, Stamats Communications, Inc., 427 6th Avenue S.E., PO Box 1888, Cedar Rapids, IA 52406, 1999, pp. 1–3.

[2]   "Twisted Pair (Balanaced) Cabling Index," The Siemon Company, Siemon Business Park, 76 Westbury Park Road, Watertown, CT 06795-0400 USA, 2000.

[3]   "Structured Cabling," Egerton Communications Systems Ltd, Sound Lane, Nantwich, Cheshire, CW5 8BE, United Kingdom, 1999, p. 1.

[4]   "Telecommunications Cabling and Electronics Specifications: Specific Guidelines," Virginia Community College System (VCCS), 101 North 14th Street 15th Floor, Richmond, Virginia 23219, 2000, p. 3.

[5]   Jesse Tolliver, "Cabling Below a Raised Floor," ASAF Air Intelligence Agency/QA, Kelly afb, San Antonio, TX, Cabling Installation & Maintenance, (August, 2000), p. 44.

Copper Design Considerations

In any discussion about computers and communication, copper wiring design considerations are right at the top of any work-area layout decisions. These design decisions must fit into every layer that provides physical connections between the various devices like printers, dumb terminals, and computers. For example, let's imagine an analogy between the computer-based networks and an overnight carrier (FedEx, UPS, AIRBORNE Express, DHL, etc.). Here, the computers would represent people on either side of the communication where the communication would take place in the form of packets of information (letters and boxes in the overnight carrier analogy). The network would be the mechanism responsible for carrying the packets of information from a computer to a computer or another device like a printer. In the analogy, this mechanism would be the overnight carrier system, where letters and boxes are carried from person to person. The overnight carrier system consists of counter employees, carriers, trucks, highways, and so on. Wiring in the analogy would be the roadways/highways over which the information is carried.

As discussed in earlier chapters, the International Standards Organization (ISO) has put forth a standard for communication between computer equipment and networks. This standard is referred to as the Open System Interconnection (OSI) model and shows how the communication maps into seven protocol layers, as shown in the Sidebar, "Open System Interconnect Model."

OPEN SYSTEM INTERCONNECT MODEL

This model explains what each layer does in the communication framework. The model is often used to explain any particular set of protocols (not just OSI) to the point where many people seem to believe that true data communications requires these seven layers. When talking about wiring, we're mainly concerned with the first two layers, the physical layer and the data-link layer.

Top Layer

7. Applications
This top layer identifies where the user applications software lies. Such issues as file access and transfer, virtual terminal emulation, interprocess communication, and the like are handled here. An example of this would be IBM's System Application Architecture (SAA).

6. Presentation
This layer deals with differences in data representation. For example, UNIX-style line endings (CR only) might be converted to MS-DOS style (CRLF), EBCIDIC to ASCII character sets, blinking characters, reverse video, and screen graphics.

5. Session
This layer controls communications between applications across a network. Testing for out-of-sequence packets, two-way communication, security, name recognition, and logging are handled here.

4. Transport
This layer makes sure the lower three layers (3, 2, and 1) are doing their job correctly, and provides a transparent, logical data stream between the end user and the network service being used. It also makes sure that the data received is in the right format and order. This is the lower layer that provides local user services.

3. Network
This layer makes certain that a packet sent from one device to another actually gets there in a reasonable period of time. Routing and flow control are performed here. This is the lowest layer of the OSI model that can remain ignorant of the physical network.

2. Data Link
This layer deals with getting data packets on and off the wire, error detection and correction, and retransmission. This layer is generally broken into two sublayers: The LLC (logical link control) on the upper half, which does the error checking, and the MAC (media access control) on the lower half, which deals with getting the data on and off the wire. Also, some of the protocols the data-link layer uses are high level data link control (HDLC) and bisynchronous (bisync) communications.

Bottom Layer

1. Physical
This bottom layer defines the nuts and bolts. Here is where the cable, connector, and signaling specifications are defined [1].

DIFFERENT MEDIA FOR PHYSICAL LAYER

Physical media for Ethernet can be one of several types, including thin and thick coaxial cable, twisted pair cable, and fiber optic cable. Coaxial cable (coax) is a metallic electrical cable used for RF (radio frequency) and certain data communications transmission. The cable is constructed with a single solid or stranded center conductor that is surrounded by the dielectric layer, an insulating material of constant thickness and high resistance. A conducting layer of aluminum foil, metallic braid, or a combination of the two encompass the dielectric and act as both a shield against interference (to or from the center conductor) and as the return ground for the cable. Finally, an overall insulating layer forms the outer jacket of the cable. Coaxial cable is generally superior in high-frequency applications such as networking. However, for shorter distances (up to 100 meters), UTP or STP cable is generally just as reliable when using differential modulation techniques (such as with 10BaseT). Some well-known kinds are various cable TV cables, cables used by IBM 327x terminals, and cables used by Ethernet and IEEE 802.3.

DIAGRAMS FOR STP AND UTP

Twisted pair (TP) is the type of wire used by the phone company to wire telephones over shorter distances (like between your house and the central office). It has two conductors that are twisted. The twists are important: they give it electrical characteristics that allow some kinds of communications otherwise not possible.

UTP

UTP is what's typically installed by phone companies (though this is often not of high enough quality for high-speed network use) and is usually what 10BaseT Ethernet runs over. UTP is graded according to its data-carrying ability (category 3, category 4, category 5). 10BaseT Ethernet requires at least category 3 cable. Many sites now install only category 5 UTP, even though category 4 is more than sufficient for 10BaseT, because of the greater likelihood that emerging high-speed standards will require cable with better bandwidth capabilities.

Unshielded Twisted Pair Cable Vertical Cabling Design

When using unshielded twisted pair (UTP) cable vertical (trunk) cabling, it is recommended that a 100-pair cable maximum be used for ease of installation and to minimize data cross talk. Where more than 100 pairs are required, as in a trunking application, it is recommended that multiple cables of 25- or 100-pair each be specified.

A block system uses 100 pairs per block, so using 100 pair cables enhances cable management and identification. Likewise, when using modular (RJ) patch panels, it is recommended that 2-pair channels that yield 100 pairs per 2U (2-rack position) patch panel (48 channels) be implemented.

Cabling cross talk occurs when one channel within a multiconductor cable generates electro-magnetic interference (EMI) that another channel receives. This is the most detrimental EMI for a data communications system. Limiting the maximum per-cable pair count to 100 pair minimizes potential cross-talk problems.

Installation Considerations.   Historically, voice cables were constructed in 25-pair groupings and terminated in 100-pair sets. This caused cable manufacturers to research and develop cables with performance optimized within these configurations. Manufacturers of cross-connection products also configure products to handle the cables in 25- or 100-pair groups.

In the case of most block-based systems, each block provides termination for 100 pairs. System layout on some products (66 blocks, for example) may define a termination implementation that reduces this to 50 pairs; but this still supports a 25-pair grouping. Figure 10–1 shows a panel consisting of two 100-pair blocks [2].

High density modular (RJ) patch panels are generally 24 channels per rack position (1U) with a recommended frame layout of two patching positions between each ring run, as shown in Figure 10–2 [MOD-TAP, 1]. It is recommended that vertical (trunk) UTP cabling in 2-pair channels be config-

Figure 10–1   A panel consisting of two 100-pair blocks.

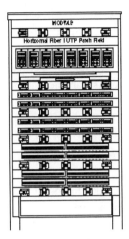

Figure 10–2
High density modular (RJ) patch panels.

ured. This yields a single 100-pair cable per 2U (48 channels) patch field. Optionally, this is specifying 4-pair vertical channels that would yield a single row of channels per 100-pair cable (24 channels).

In either case, using a 25- or 100-pair cable offers substantial advantages in the area of cable design and management. Each section of the cross-connection field corresponds to a specific cable, which eases troubleshooting and maintenance. Likewise, during the installation, the cable must be routed and tied down. Using a larger cable (400-pair) requires removing the jacket for much more length and routing sections of the cable across a much larger area.

Cable Channel Noise: Cause and Effects. Noise within the cable can come from many sources. But it is generally segmented into noise from outside the cable (external) and noise generated within the cable itself (internal).

External cable noise comes from the general environment. Common sources are television and radio stations, nearby power cables, motors (often HVAC systems), and high-voltage lighting. Properly designed cables minimize impact from broadcast sources such as television and radio. Proper installation insuring a minimum distance from motors and high-voltage devices minimizes problems from these sources.

Internal noise is generated either from other channels (signals) within the cable or from reflections caused by connections within the channel. Again, proper installation minimizes the number of connections and ensures the highest possible quality of the connections required. This eliminates problems caused by reflection. It also leaves crosstalk as the primary noise issue in your information cabling system.

Cross talk is a type of electro-magnetic interference in which interference is generated by one channel and received by another. This can be especially detrimental to system operation, where the two channels are common to the same system. The receiving channel will get data of the correct speed, timing, and protocol and therefore does not reject it as simple noise. The system instead may attempt to process or otherwise operate on this data.

Figure 10–3 is a graph of the signal effects as the transmission distance increases in an environment with no EMI [MOD-TAP, 2]. Starting at -0dB, the signal is attenuated (signal level reduced) as the distance increases. At some point, labeled -dB, the signal has attenuated to the point where the receiver can no longer accept the signal. This point is determined by the operating characteristics of the equipment interfaces. At this signal level, the communications interface can no longer capture the signal and the channel fails. This distance, labeled D1 on the horizontal axis, is the maximum distance attainable for this system on that media. When most manufacturers rate their products, they use this distance, reduced by a percentage for a safety margin.

Figure 10–4 places this UTP channel in an environment where EMI is present [MOD-TAP, 2]. As the length of a cable increases, so does its ability to act as an antenna, generating a second line labeled *N* for noise. The intersection of these two lines defines a distance, labeled *D2*, which is the failure point of the channel within this specific EMI environment. At this point, the noise becomes high enough to overpower the signal and the communications interface fails.

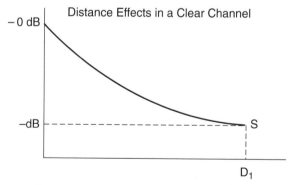

Figure 10–3   A graph of the signal effects.

Note

Distance D2 is substantially less than the clear channel distance D1. Different EMI environments generate different noise curves and yield different failure (intersection) points.

In Figure 10–5, the signal-to-noise graph (see Figure 10–4) and the clear channel failure graph (see Figure 10–3) are combined [MOD-TAP, 2]. This would be the case where the noise is really another channel carrying data of the same system and there is no current data on the receiving channel. In this case, the system accepts the noise as a signal, attempting to acknowledge and process it. This yields problems at distance D3, an even shorter dis-

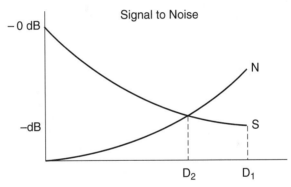

Figure 10–4 Placement of the UTP channel.

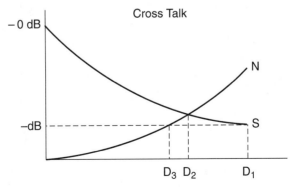

Figure 10–5 Combining the signal-to-noise graph and the clear channel failure graph.

tance than either D1 or D2. Therefore, the potential problems caused by cross talk exceed the problems caused by other EMI.

Minimizing Cross Talk.   The usual answer to EMI problems is to use shielded cable, an expensive proposition not only because of the higher cost of the media but also because of a more expensive installation due to shield termination and cable size. Shields must be correctly terminated. Shields that float (are unterminated) or that create ground loops (terminated at both ends) will make the EMI problem worse instead of better. This necessitates the purchase of grounding products and allocating additional labor to this process. Shielding also increases both the size and bend radius of the cable, requiring larger and more costly conduit or cable trays and making the installation more difficult. Furthermore, it's also very important that the plugs or connectors are shielded.

A properly installed cable with an overall shield (a shield around the entire cable) will minimize the effects of EMI from the outside of the cable. However, in the case of trunk cables, there will be many pairs of cable within the shield and, therefore, many channels of data. Each channel is not only a potential receiver but is also broadcasting EMI. An overall shield does not protect a cable from this cross talk, only from the external EMI. Therefore, to shield against cross talk in multichannel cabling (in addition to an overall shield), each channel must be shielded within the cable from all others. This requires individual shields for each pair of cable to provide maximum protection. Again, this increases media cost, installation cost, bend radius, and cable outside diameter (OD).

An alternative to shielding is to minimize the coupling effect between the pairs by twisting each pair at a different rate from the others. This variable lay-up will not totally eliminate cross talk, but generally will reduce it to an acceptable level. Better cable manufacturers use a variable lay-up for all their cable and the higher the quality of the cable (category 5 vs. category 3), the higher the twist rate will be. In addition, the way the 25-pair groups are combined into a cable is critical to the cross talk and other noise induced.

Use of High Pair Count Cabling.   It is easy to implement a variable lay-up when manufacturing 25-pair cabling, but when using higher pair count cable (100-, 200-, 400-pair or higher) problems can occur. While the lay-up within a 25-pair group varies, there will be a repeat of twist rates group to group.

When combining the 25-pair groups into a larger cable, it is possible to maintain low cross-talk capabilities up to 100-pair. In larger pair counts, the groups are tightly bound together and the spatial relationships between the groups become very stable. Varying the spatial relationships minimizes the cross-talk potential by breaking the coupling between the pairs, thereby reducing the mutual antenna effects.

The potential cross-talk paths in 25-pair cable is 300, as shown by the matrix in Figure 10–6 [MOD-TAP, 3]. This shows a 25-by-25 matrix, eliminating the instances where a pair cross talks to itself (not possible) and the duplication of paths (1 to 2 is the same path as 2 to 1). This yields an equation of:

$1/2$ (X squared $-X$) where X is the pair count of the cable.

Table 10–1 consists of potential cross-talk paths for different pair count cable by pair and channel for 2-, 3-, and 4-pair channels [MOD-TAP, 4].

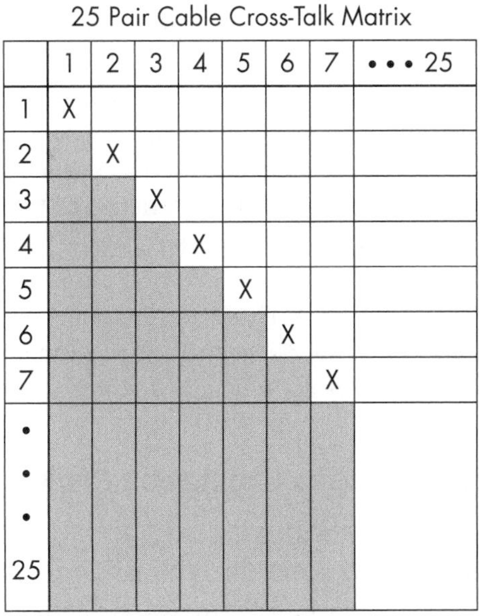

25 Pair Cable Cross-Talk Matrix

	1	2	3	4	5	6	7	• • • 25
1	X							
2		X						
3			X					
4				X				
5					X			
6						X		
7							X	
•								
•								
•								
25								

Figure 10–6   Potential cross-talk paths.

Table 10–1   Number of Cross Talk Paths

Cable Pair Count	1-Pair Cross-Talk Paths	2-Pair Cross-Talk Paths	3-Pair Cross-Talk Paths	4-Pair Cross-Talk Paths
25	300	66	28	15
50	1,225	276	120	66
100	4,950	1,128	496	276
200	19,900	4,560	2,016	1,128
400	79,800	18,336	8,128	4,560
600	179,700	41,328	18,336	10,296
1,200	719,400	165,600	73,536	41,328

STP

Shielded twisted pair (STP) is a type of twisted-pair cable with a metallic shield around the twisted conductors. The shield reduces the noise from the cable and reduces the effects of noise on the communications in the cable, but changes the electrical characteristics of the cable so some equipment optimized to nonshielded cable runs worse on shielded cable. STP is typically used for token ring networks, where it is commonly referred to IBM Type 1 (or 2, 3, 6, 8, etc.). However, there are several manufacturers of Ethernet equipment and interfaces that support Ethernet over STP. Nevertheless, Ethernet over STP is not officially defined in any standards.

Shielded versus Unshielded Cables

Telephone wire in wide use today is typically between 19 AWG and 26 AWG, with the inside more likely to be 24 to 26 AWG. This wire is typically twisted, on average, with two twists per foot, and combined with other color-coded twisted pairs.

The twisting of a pair of wires resulted from the observation that when twisted, the radiated energy from current flowing in any one wire is almost completely canceled out by radiated energy from the same current flowing back in the return wire of that pair. This radiated energy is often referred to as electromagnetic radiation (EMR).

This twisting, therefore, effectively and inexpensively minimizes cross talk into adjacent pairs in a multipair cable. It also allows the pairs to be less susceptible to external noise, since they would be coupled equally into each wire in a pair, as well as being canceled out if properly terminated.

At voice frequencies, each pair appears to be balanced. The word *balanced* in this context is the approximate definition of a transmission pair that is balanced if equal energy is coupled from each wire within the pair to any point in space.

The wavelength of a signal (its propagation velocity divided by its frequency—where the speed of light at 186,000 miles per second is divided by 186,000 hz, yielding a wavelength of one mile) at voice frequencies is much longer than the physical dimensions of a pair and its twist length. Therefore, it can be considered a balanced media.

However, at higher frequencies (at 10 mhz the wavelength would be less than 100 feet), the pair no longer agrees with the balanced theory and both cross talk and noise susceptibility increase exponentially. Therefore, it is the desire to transmit at higher frequencies that has generated research and interest into shielded cables.

Shielding

The shield improves a wire pair's emission of and susceptibility to EMI, depending of course on the shield's construction materials and application. Shielding comes in many varieties and performance characteristics.

The general consensus among wire and cable providers is that transfer impedance is the most useful measurement of a shield's effectiveness. Transfer impedance is the ratio of the potential difference applied at a pair of terminals in a network to the resulting current at a second pair of terminals. The following information is a comparison of the transfer impedance of various shields at different frequencies.

When to Shield

The safe answer is to always install shielded cable, because although today's applications might get by on unshielded wire, clearly high digital rates of the future will work better over shielded cable. The difficulty is its higher cost over unshielded copper pair (2-3 pair unshielded costs less than .05 per foot, whereas shielded 2-3 pair can cost .30 per foot or more). In other words, shielded cable costs about 500 percent more than unshielded. For example, if you are installing conduits everywhere and applications don't need the services of shielding initially, then it might be appropriate to install unshielded today and install shielded only on an as-needed basis.

In the end, the commercial building standards make use of all types (UTP and STP) of cabling, depending on the requirements. Nowadays, the most common type of wire to run distributions from the phone closet to the workstation is data-grade unshielded twisted pair (2-pair minimum, 4-pair recommended). Backbone runs phone closet to phone closet. Thin wire or thick wire is usable with multimode fiber being the better choice. As with all cases of wiring, the best possible thing to do is leave usable pathways for future expansion.

DATA LINK LAYER STANDARD

The data link layer is directly above the physical layer. This the first layer in the logical communications layer. The most widely used standard here is Ethernet (it overlaps both in the physical layer and data link layer in the OSI model). It is a type of network cabling and signaling specifications originally developed by Xerox in the late 1970s. In 1980, Digital Equipment Corporation (DEC), Intel, and Xerox (the origin of the term DIX, as in DEC/Intel/Xerox) began joint promotion of this baseband (carrier sense multiple access with collision detection [CSMA/CD] computer communications network over coaxial cabling) and published the Blue Book Standard for Ethernet Version 1. This standard was later enhanced, and in 1985 Ethernet II was released.

The IEEE's (Institute of Electrical and Electronics Engineers) Project 802 used Ethernet Version 2 as the basis for the 802.3 CSMA/CD network standard. The IEEE 802.3 standard is generally interchangeable with Ethernet II—with the greatest difference being the construction of the network packet header.

A complete description of all Ethernet specifications is available in the IEEE 802.3 documents and in the ISO 8802-3 documents as well. Ethernet/802.3 can now be run on two types of coaxial cable as well as multimode fiber and unshielded twisted pair.

Raw rate of data transmission is 10 Mbps.

10Base5, 10BaseT, 10Base2, and 10Broad36 are the IEEE names for the different physical types of Ethernet. The 10 stands for signaling speed: 10MHz. Base means baseband. Broad means broadband. Initially, the last section is intended to indicate the maximum length of an unrepeated cable segment in hundreds of meters. This convention was modified with the introduction of 10BaseT, where the *T* means twisted pair, and 10BaseF, where the

F means fiber. This actually comes from the IEEE committee number for that media, as shown in the Sidebar, "Different Physical Types of Ethernet."

DIFFERENT PHYSICAL TYPES OF ETHERNET

In actual practice:

10Base2   Is 10 MHz Ethernet running over thin, 50 ohm baseband coaxial cable. 10Base2 is also commonly referred to as thin-Ethernet or Cheapernet.

10Base5   Is 10 MHz Ethernet running over standard (thick) 50 ohm baseband coaxial cabling.

10BaseFL   Is 10 MHz Ethernet running over fiber optic cabling.

10BaseT   Is 10 MHz Ethernet running over unshielded twisted pair cabling.

10Broad36 Is 10 MHz Ethernet running through a broadband cable [Velamparampil, 3–4].

FDDI (fiber distributed data interface) is another LAN data-link protocol designed to run on multimode fiber. The FDDI standard defines two physical rings that simultaneously send data in different directions. The raw rate of data transmission is 100 Mbps. The FDDI standard was developed by the American National Standards Institute (ANSI). CDDI (proprietary technology developed by Crecendo Corporation) is FDDI-like technology adapted to unshielded twisted pair, as discussed in the Sidebar, "CDDI Cabling," and shown in Figures 10–7 to 10–11 [3].

CDDI CABLING

The following contains pinout information for CDDI A/B ports, CDDI adapter ports, concentrator master ports, and the optical bypass switch connector.

CDDI/MLT-3 Installation

MLT-3 is the new ANSI draft specification developed by Cisco Systems for compression of FDDI signals over UTP copper wire. Cisco Systems products that are upgraded to MLT-3 will interoperate with other vendors' equipment that complies with the draft standard.

Note: MLT-3 equipment can only be connected to other MLT-3 equipment.

Workgroup CDDI/MLT-3 installations require category 5 equipment throughout. Two types of category 5 modular cables (cross-connect and straight-through) are used to connect concentrators and adapters to the network, as shown in Figures 10–7 and 10–8, respectively. Figures 10–7, 10–8, and 10–9 illustrate the EIA/TIA-T568-B wiring standard and CDDI transmit and receive pairs. Figure 10–10 shows the location of straight-through and cross-connect cabling for CDDI installations.

Note: The cross-connect cabling is used between the concentrator and the patch panel.

Bypass Connector Pinouts

Figure 10–11 shows the optical bypass switch connector pinouts [Cisco, 1–3].

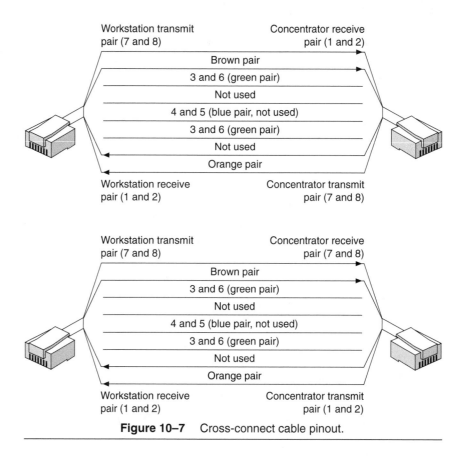

Figure 10–7   Cross-connect cable pinout.

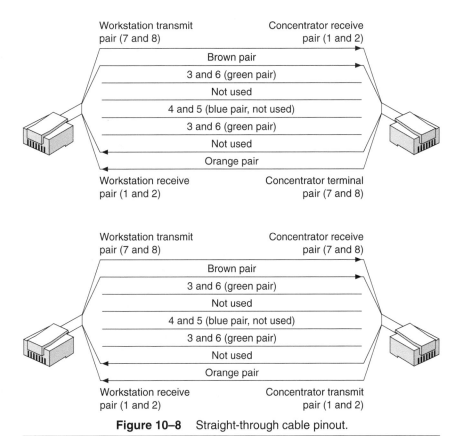

Figure 10–8   Straight-through cable pinout.

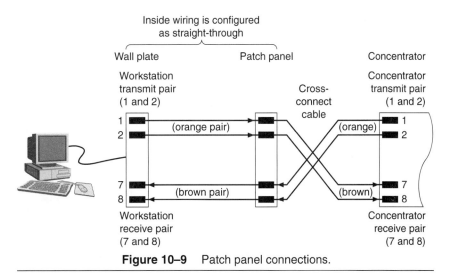

Figure 10–9   Patch panel connections.

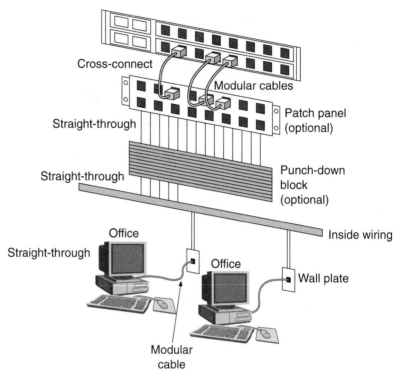

Figure 10–10   Straight-through and cross-connect cabling.

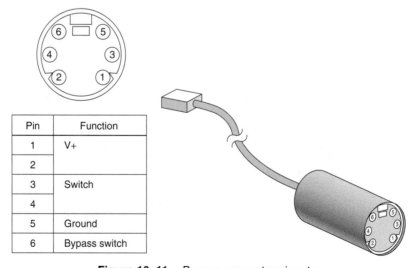

Pin	Function
1	V+
2	
3	Switch
4	
5	Ground
6	Bypass switch

Figure 10–11   Bypass connector pinouts.

Efforts to standardize CDDI have yielded TP-PMD (FDDI twisted pair physical layer media), an ANSI specification for FDDI-like service over UTP. Limitations on how Ethernet is cabled vary according to the media used, as shown in the Sidebar, "Ethernet Cabling Distance Limitations."

ETHERNET CABLING DISTANCE LIMITATIONS

10Base2	Limited to 185 meters (607 ft) per unrepeated cable segment.
10Base5	Limited to 500 meters (1,640 ft) per unrepeated cable segment.
10BaseF	Depends on the signaling technology and media used but can go up to 2 km.
10BaseT	Generally accepted to have a maximum run of 100–150 meters, but is really based on signal loss in Dbs (11.5db maximum loss, source to destination).
10Broad36	Limited to 3,600 meters (almost 2.25 miles) [Velamparampil, 4].

Fundamentally, there are also limitations on the number of repeaters and cable segments allowed between any two stations on the network. There exists two different ways of looking at the same rules, the Ethernet way and the IEEE way.

The Ethernet Way

A remote repeater pair (with an intermediate point-to-point link) is counted as a single repeater (IEEE calls it two repeaters). You cannot put any stations on the point-to-point link, and there can be two repeaters in the path between any pair of stations.

The IEEE Way

There may be no more than 5 repeated segments, and no more than 4 repeaters between any two Ethernet stations. Of the five cable segments, only 3 may be populated. This is referred to as the 5-4-3 rule (5 segments, 4 repeaters, 3 populated segments). A segment here is a piece of network wire bounded by bridges, routers, repeaters, or terminators.

It can really get messy when you start cascading through 10BaseT hubs, which are repeaters unto themselves. Just try to remember that any possible path between two network devices on an unbridged/unrouted network cannot pass through more than 4 repeaters or hubs, and no more than 3 populated cable segments.

Finally, 10Base2 is limited to a maximum of 30 network devices per unrepeated network segment with a minimum distance of 0.5 meters (1.5 ft) between T-connectors. 10Base5 is limited to a maximum of 100 network devices per unrepeated segment, with a minimum distance of 2.5 meters (8.2ft) between taps or T-connectors (usually indicated by a marker stamped on the cable itself every 2.5 meters). 10BaseT and 10BaseF are star-wired, so there is no minimum distance requirement between devices, since devices cannot be connected serially. You can install up to the Ethernet maximum of 1,024 stations per network with both 10BaseT and 10BaseF. In addition, the maximum number of stations on a thick Ethernet network is also 1,024.

BUILDING WIRING STANDARD

The Electronics Industries Association (EIA) has defined a standard for commercial and industrial building wiring. The EIA/TIA-T568-A Commercial Building Telecommunications Wiring Standard defines a generic wiring system that will support a multiproduct, multivendor environment whose useful life span is in excess of 10 years.

The EIA/TIA standard is based on a star topology in which each workstation is connected to a central location (a telecommunications closet [TC]) situated within 90 meters of the workstation. Backbone wiring between TCs and the main cross-connect is also organized in a star topology. Direct connections between closets are allowed to accommodate bus and ring configurations. Distances between closets and the main cross-connect are dependent on cable types and applications (see Table 10–2) [Velamparampil, 5].

Table 10–2 Twisted Pair Cable Classifications

References	Applications
EIA/TIA Category 1	Analog, digital voice
EIA/TIA Category 2	ISDN (data) 1.44 Mbps T1 (1.544 Mbps) digital voice
EIA/TIA Category 3	10BaseT ISDN voice
EIA/TIA Category 4	10BaseT 16 Mbps token ring
EIA/TIA Category 5	10BaseT 16 Mbps token ring 100 Mbps DDI (proposed)

Each workstation is to be provided with a minimum of two communications outlets (can be on the same faceplate). One outlet is supported by a 4-pair, 100 ohm UTP cable. The other may be supported by an additional 4-pair UTP cable. For the backbone, four cable types are recognized for wiring: 100

ohm UTP multipair cable, 150 ohm STP cable, 50 ohm coaxial cable, and 62.5/125 micron fiber optic cable.

Looking back, nearly everyone thought wire was cable! Isn't category 5, as shown in Table 10–2, enough? Aren't all category 5 cables designed and created equal? Isn't this a standard? All of these questions are answered next.

CATEGORY 5 UTP DESIGN CONSIDERATIONS

Is the reliable performance of your network infrastructure important to your organization's bottom line? According to industry analysts, failures at the physical layer (structured cabling) account for an average loss of $580,000 per year per 300 users. Losses are measured in user productivity, network manager effort, and business downtime. Couple this with the fact that the physical layer represents only about 13 percent of the overall network installation costs (when including the computers, software, structured cabling, and support costs), and you can see a big reason to be concerned. Fortunately for the people responsible for cable infrastructure, a system of acceptable standards exists that defines the expectations and limitations of cable, and provides structure and direction for technological advances.

Wire is Wire

There seems to be indiscernible differences in communications cabling design considerations and construction. After all, isn't all wire created equal?

Today, words like *reflection*, *terminator*, and *vampire tap* have quickly faded from memory in the wake of robust and reliable 10 and 100BaseT LANs and categorized unshielded twisted pair cabling systems. And no, all cables are not created equal. EIA/TIA has published cabling standards that set the baseline for interoperability in structured cabling and has provided a consistent platform for networking devices to be built to.

When you look at the original categories, someone entering the industry today wouldn't know (or care) about category 1 telephone voice-grade copper cable or POTS (plain old telephone service) cable, as it was called. Category 2 handled IBM mainframe and minicomputer terminal transmission, as well as some early slow-speed (12 Mbps) LAN technologies like ARCnet. Category 3 was designated as the minimum-quality twisted pair cable that would handle 10 Mbps Ethernet and 4-16 Mbps active token ring without errors at the desktop.

Since these original categories were defined several years ago, we've all seen America being rewired, information transmission technologies advancing, and standards ratified. In 1992, a group of manufacturers marketed a copper version (CDDI) of an FDDI transport system using thin coax and IBM Type 1 cabling products.

In 1993, ANSI ratified TP-PMD (twisted pair-physical media dependent) for FDDI over category 5 UTP. Shortly after that, EIA/TIA signed the 568 standard document, followed immediately by TSB36.

It wasn't until the birth and availability of affordable 100BaseT in 1996 that institutions and organizations saw a reason to enable 100 Mbps desktops, and then largely because it was an inexpensive and well understood insurance policy. For a little extra money, whether turned on or left dormant, dual 10/100 Mbps Ethernet network interface cards became a no-brainer for network managers. Fiber optics and FDDI remained in the campus backbone, and became the server superhighways and intercloset infrastructures. In several short years (since category 5 was introduced) the physical layer transport of the most future-thinking planners has been maxed out in terms of the high-speed networking options of the near future!

Category 5

Few of us can conceive of the need for anything beyond 100 Mbps. For example, 155 Mbps ATM is seen by many to be a technology in search of an application, but we should remember how much things can change in a five-year period.

Today in the age of Pentiums, the chicken-and-egg routine continues. Processing power ultimately drives innovation in user applications, specifically media-rich and collaborative functions. These business and learning-enabled applications ultimately drive the need for more bandwidth when it's needed. Transport technologies like switching and ATM will likely catch on as the economic and sociological benefits of multimedia, distance learning, and media conferencing are realized. When thinking about where applications will be in five years, think about the size of hard drives and modem speeds in 1991. Hundred-fold increases in performance and plummeting costs make these technology innovations solid drivers in today's corporate America, as well as in education and healthcare.

If you consider that several years ago the high-end wiring choice was category 5 cabling in the LAN and multimode fiber optic systems in the backbone, then when LAN speeds became 10, 16, and 100 Mbps, the headroom or additional capacity that was built into the systems seemed more than adequate for the future. Recently, though, the ATM Forum put its seal of approval on 155 Mbps ATM to run on existing category 5 systems, and the first interface products have just recently started to appear on the market. One may ask what applications will require more than 100 or 155 Mbps at the desktop. However, the more visionary question is, will my category X cabling system have enough additional headroom or true electrical bandwidth to provide error-free transmission when extra throughput is needed?

A few issues need to be explored to answer this question satisfactorily. All high-speed LAN standards require compliance with generic cabling specifications plus many additional parameters that are defined only in the specifications and standards for the network interface products. These extra requirements define the actual electrical and digital signaling, and usually assume a well-behaved and consistent cable and connectivity system. Figure 10–12 shows the relationship between cabling standards (center ellipse) and networking standards (outer ellipse), and demonstrates, unfortunately, that cabling requirements are just a subset of the overall requirements for a smooth-running network [4].

All high-speed standards need to conform to SNR (signal-to-noise ratios) and maximum noise thresholds. But pair skew and propagation delay characteristics are important supplemental requirements for 100BaseT, 100BaseVG, and for ATM above 100 MHz. Pair skew applies to technologies using multiple pairs for signaling. In essence, signals are divided between pairs and must be reassembled at the receiving end. If they arrive at different times, skewing of the signal occurs, resulting in transmission errors. Propagation delay, the time it takes for the signal to travel to the receiver, is a factor of the efficiency of the cable in moving the signal relative to the theoretical speed

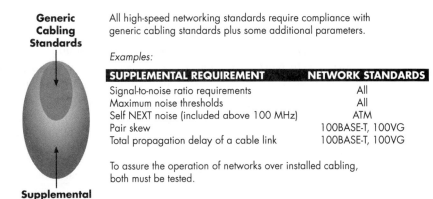

Generic Cabling Standards

Supplemental Network-Specific Requirements

All high-speed networking standards require compliance with generic cabling standards plus some additional parameters.

Examples:

SUPPLEMENTAL REQUIREMENT	NETWORK STANDARDS
Signal-to-noise ratio requirements	All
Maximum noise thresholds	All
Self NEXT noise (included above 100 MHz)	ATM
Pair skew	100BASE-T, 100VG
Total propagation delay of a cable link	100BASE-T, 100VG

To assure the operation of networks over installed cabling, both must be tested.

Figure 10–12   Structured cabling standards versus network-specific standards.

of electricity (light). Also known as the velocity of propagation, it is expressed as the percent of the speed of light represented by the cable's speed.

Network electronics manufacturers deal with electrical loss across cable distances by incorporating equalizers into their receivers. These equalizers attempt to amplify the received signal based on what they assume happened through attenuation or the electrical loss during transmission through the channel. This same received signal must also be identified within the noise picked up during its transmission and receipt, and in most cases a little bit of the noise is also reamplified. If this results in an incorrect representation of the original signal, it is called a bit error. Bit errors often lead to garbled information and/or retransmissions of the data.

As in the case of 155-Mbps ATM running on category 5 cable, anomalies can occur above the category 5 maximum signal frequency (in excess of 100 MHz and as far out as 200 MHz) that when seen by the equalizer are amplified as if they were part of the signal. This results in higher than acceptable bit errors and therefore corruption of the information. No additional headroom will help in this case. If the attenuation performance of the cable is not smooth, then the ATM signal will probably not be interpreted correctly even though the cable installation passes category 5 requirements below 100 MHz!

Category 5 Cables are Created Equal

Standards by definition are derived by consensus and often are open to interpretation. Delay skew is an addendum to the ANSI/EIA/TIA-T568-A specification that requires that another test be performed on the cable before it leaves the manufacturer. The TIA task group has rejected suggested names for the addendum (category 5.1 or category 6), and has elected not to have the cables that would comply with the new standard marked differently from the other 8 billion feet of 4-pair cable already manufactured and currently installed in North America. The only way to know for sure if your cable meets this new requirement will be to get a copy of the actual product specification the manufacturer used to make the exact cable you purchased at that time. When was the last time you consulted the cable manufacturer's spec sheet? Enhancements to cable can only be determined by looking at exactly what parameters the manufacturer has tested and guaranteed.

Performance is directly related to the chemical compounds used in the manufacture of cable. There are more than 105 different electrical designs of plenum cables, including 15 high-end category 5 plenum designs and 33 standard and high-end nonplenum designs, all with varying electrical performance characteristics, yet still category 5-compliant.

In addition, a high-speed system must display category 5 characteristics from input to output; in other words, across all connectors, cross-connects, patch panels, and outlets. Therefore, assuming the category 5 cable tests out at 155 Mbps, users must still contend with the quality of the components and the installation. Some of the various plenum flavors that used different numbers of Polyolefin pairs mixed in with the FEP pairs to reduce the amount of FEP consumed were very installer-friendly; others were not. This mixing of different materials can cause the propagation delay skew to exceed the 45 ns specified in the revised TIA-568 standard and has resulted in a recent addendum. See the Sidebar, "Category 5 Plenum Cabling with FEP Insulation," for more information on FEP.

CATEGORY 5 PLENUM CABLING WITH FEP INSULATION

The University of Pennsylvania (in Philadelphia) has been specifying their category 5 plenum cable by manufacturer and product number for some time now and it was always all-FEP (fluorinated ethylene propylene). But without any notification, the manufacturer changed the composition of the product to a 3+1 cable. Do any manufacturers still make plenum-rated category 5 cabling with FEP insulation on all 4 pairs of conductors? How does the cost of this product compare with the 2+2 and 3+1 cables?

Even though the 4+0 construction may not be specified in their catalogs, most manufacturers make the 4+0 cable. With regard to cost, the University of Texas at Austin has been buying low-bid and installing the 4+0 cable all along. Cabling manufacturers that have not made the 3+1 or 2+2 cables are very competitive bidders.

The Telecommunications Industry Association (TIA) UTP cable task group has been very active and expects to issue a delay-skew specification. For those readers not familiar with recent developments in the TR41.8.1 working group, in a recent press release, the TIA stated that all category 5 cables may not support all 100 Mbps data applications. The reason is excessive delay skew, which is not a specified test parameter for UTP cable in the TIA-568A standard.

Delay skew is the difference of nominal velocity of propagation (NVP) between individual pairs in a link. Velocity of propagation is the speed at which a signal can be transmitted over a media. UTA is most familiar with velocity of propagation stated as a percentage of the speed of light (NVP = 72.5%); however, it can also be stated as time-to-distance, for example, 500 nanoseconds per 100 meters (500 ns/100 m).

The continuing shortage of FEP and a 40 to 50 percent annual growth in the demand for category 5 plenum cable presents a challenge for cable manufacturers. Traditionally, FEP has been used to insulate paired conductors in category 5 plenum cable because it was perceived that only FEP would comply with the electrical performance requirements specified in the ANSI/EIA/TIA-T568A standard and the plenum requirements for communications cable in the National Electrical Code. With only two FEP suppliers—Daikin America (in Orangeburg, New York) and Dupont (in Wilmington, Delaware)—the supply-and-demand problem continues, causing manufacturers and distributors to scramble for the product.

Ingenuity produced several solutions. One solution is to use FEP for three of the four pairs of conductor in 4-pair cable and polyolefin for the fourth pair. This solution would save the manufacturer 25 percent of its FEP allocation. Polyolefin was not used to insulate all of the pairs because that construction would not pass the Underwriters' Laboratory (UL) flame test. Another solution is to use FEP for two of the four pairs of conductors in 4-pair cable and modified polyolefin for the other two. While these solutions result in a product that can pass the UL flame test and meet existing category 5 requirements, some will not support high-speed data applications [5].

It's ironic that the original EIA/TIA-568-A was signed in the summer of 1991 and only covered what essentially was 10BaseT electricals, or the then-current category 3. Immediately after the standard was issued, the committee came out with TSB36 (Technical Systems Bulletin) for Additional Cable Specifications for Twisted Pair Cables, which defined the new categories 3, 4, and 5 electrical performance requirements based on work done at NEMA (National Electrical Manufacturers Association) and ISO.

A TSB is not a standard but a preliminary look at what a standard might be as generated by the TIA working group. That is, if they publish such a standard it might look like the TSB after the voting is done. Therefore, a new standard can be approved then immediately made obsolete by the same working group. A rewrite of the 568 standard was signed into existence in October 1995 as ANSI/EIA/TIA-T568-A; and ANSI formed a working group to explore the issue of delay skew, resulting in another change or addendum. Many standards are obsolete the day they are signed because they cover existing, implemented, and proven technologies that, by design, must be available from a number of different sources.

Standards have become so prevalent that brand awareness has become less of an issue. Because of this, many manufacturers tend to minimally meet specifications, which in turn fosters a market environment where the products become commodities or articles of commerce. As a result, the advent of standards has impeded manufacturers from developing products that exceed the qualifications of standards.

What's Next?

Organizations may see the promise (or opportunity) of deploying even higher-speed technologies in the next five years as applications and processors address new creative and competitive business needs and continue to consume more and more of the available bandwidth. The Gigabit Ethernet Alliance has concluded that this technology will have a significant impact on cabling, pushing the limits. Regardless of product and installation quality, there will be no slack if implemented on the current category 5 cabling.

So while it seemed that category 5 would be all that would ever be needed in the horizontal cable infrastructure, it appears that headroom and structural return (performance specification reading returns) concerns will open the books again for organizations. This timely performance or quality assurance program is based on a stringent purchasing specification (based on performance specification readings) that requires the organization's suppliers to qualify their high-performance unshielded twisted pair products.

This stringent purchasing specification sets guidelines for electrical bandwidth in excess of 100 Mhz by reaching for a performance mark that has over twice the actual usable electrical bandwidth of the current category 5. It also extends the data bandwidth to the 1.2 Gbps performance mark, making it useful in developing Gigabit Ethernet systems, while incorporating less sophisticated encoding schemes than those required for conventional category 5 cabling.

The original category 5 specification from 1992 was modified to cover the performance requirements for existing category 5 cables. The more stringent requirements for what has been called high-end category 5 or category 5+ cables are referred to as category 6 in the updated categories program. And a new generation of recently launched products that meet twice the category 5 bandwidth requirement constitute category 7. The chart in Figure 10–13 gives the basic requirements for these new performance categories [Serenbetz and Lockhart, 8].

Category 5+ is different from the standard category 5 in that it now must meet the more stringent requirements included in the international standard ISO 11801. This standard allows cables meeting these requirements to be used globally. This new definition for cable performance creates a superset of the original category 5 requirements.

100 ohm UTP					
Performance Level	Highest Test Frequency (MHz)	ACR ≥ 10 dB (MHz) Powersum	ATTM ≤ 33 dB (MHz)	ACR ≥ 0 dB (MHz) Powersum	Other Required Measurements
5	200	80	200	130	ISO IMP-SRL <45 ns SKEW LCL
6	350	100	200	165	ISO IMP-SRL <25 ns SKEW LCL
7	400	160	230	250	ISO IMP-SRL <25 ns SKEW LCL

Figure 10–13   Categories of acceptance cable performance.

Copper cabling technology has certainly come a long way in less than a decade! Beyond this, it looks like fiber optics is mandatory. Even today, fiber is the clear future protection of choice.

As is usually the case, the implementation of a cabling infrastructure should fit the need. Corporations, financial institutions, healthcare providers, and colleges and universities are poised in many ways to take full advantage of the technology wave to enhance their competitive advantage. Is your organization ready to deploy tomorrow's technological advances? Is your physical layer infrastructure up to the task? Thankfully, there are cost-effective, future-proofing solutions in high-end copper still in the works. And as users move into the world of light-wave communications over optical fiber, the same guiding principles of price, performance, and ease of installation and maintenance are at work in the engineering and standards committees of the industry.

Nevertheless, in Europe, organizations are ready to deploy tomorrow's technological advances by the installation or implementation of a copper cabling design technology called digital subscriber line (xDSL). If xDSL technology is the answer to the current bandwidth dilemma, why aren't vendors and service providers beating down the developers' doors? The final part of this chapter answers that burning question.

DIGITAL SUBSCRIBER LINE

In the operator and service provider world, it is now an accepted, inescapable conclusion that xDSL technologies will one day be installed in vast quantities on a global basis. Despite other technology developments (not excluding recent announcements about the commercial viability of sending data down power lines), it is still the only viable technology capable of substantially increasing bandwidth on the local access loops without a substantial overhaul. These copper loops are ubiquitous over every home in Europe and it is unlikely that any mass-scale upgrade to fiber will happen within the next 15 years.

The primary driver for xDSL is high-speed Internet service deployment to residential customers. So far, there have been two small commercial deployments and no less than 55 trials around the world, trying to prove that asynchronous DSL (ADSL) can provide a downstream connection of up to 8 Mbps and an upstream connection of up to 1 Mbps over the existing telephony copper pair. See the Sidebar, "Asymmetric Digital Subscriber Line Technology," for further information on ADSL.

ASYMMETRIC DIGITAL SUBSCRIBER LINE TECHNOLOGY

Asymmetric digital subscriber line (ADSL) technology is making a resurgence as telecommunication companies look for alternatives to costly network infrastructure upgrades such as HFC and fiber to the curb. ADSL takes the existing copper telephone line and turns it into a digital pathway capable of carrying up to 8 Mbps downstream and 1 Mbps upstream, making it ideal for high-speed Internet access services, telecommuting, remote LAN access, and other emerging residential broadband applications.

ADSL technology can also be used in business environments as a high-speed link between corporate intranets, or as a low-cost alternative to T-1 and fractional T-1 lines. Questions remain as to ADSL's long-term viability in the marketplace, particularly in terms of equipment and operations costs, and its potential for integration with ATM transport and fiber-based network topologies [6].

Both IP and ATM network architectures are currently on trial. ATM is considered the probable choice in the future. Initial trials have used standalone ADSL modems with discrete IP interfaces for time-to-market and availability reasons; these are evolving to highly integrated digital subscriber loop access multiplexers (DSLAM) solutions.

The complete network typically consists of a core that is based around SDH (synchronous digital hierarchy), wrapped with broadband ATM switches, ATM access switches, and DSLAMs. The DSLAMs provide the individual xDSL lines out to the customer premises and integrate with the existing POTS network connections. But even after having been in trial for more than 42 months, few operators seem close to commercial rollouts. What is taking them so long?

Some of the main barriers to large-scale adoption include the continuing standards battle and the lack of interoperability. The existence of two de facto standards, namely DMT (discrete multitone technology) and CAP (carrierless amplitude modulation/phase modulation), provides network operators with a dilemma: deciding which to adopt before a leader is clearly identifiable in case the choice ends up as the betamax of the standards. There are two standard camps, one apparently led by Israel's Amati, which has developed modems using DMT for the line coding. Motorola and Alcatel are among the major manufacturers who have developed DMT modems. The second camp has adopted a technology developed by the former AT&T Paradyne, which championed CAP for the line coding. Westell, the company that made the ADSL modems being used in Bell Atlantic's trial in Virginia, uses CAP. With no clear stance being taken, a general wait-and-see attitude is developing.

Lack of interoperability is also becoming a matter of concern. The current xDSL units on the market, from a variety of vendors supporting different standards, do not interoperate. Interoperability between vendors' equipment is key to mass rollout and provisioning. The ultimate goal is for the end customer to be able to purchase their own ADSL termination units, much the same way that people buy off-the-shelf analog modems today. For this to happen, the ADSL termination unit technology needs to mature to the point were it is as simple as a modem to install and operate.

Operators are still deciding on suitable end-to-end architectures. Once these infrastructures have been agreed upon, the business and technology in place, services can then be rolled out in volume. These new architectures need to address the integration of network, service, and business management of these new broadband services. Without these seamless, end-to-end management systems in place, it is difficult to see how operators will be able to make any profit on broadband services.

Management Capabilities

The new broadband services being deployed by network operators and service providers are typically delivered over very complex network environments, which include legacy equipment with primitive management capabilities and newer systems incorporating sophisticated element management based on the telecommunications management network (TMN). New network management infrastructures are required to mold these disparate information sources into a cohesive view of the end-to-end services being delivered. This can be complicated by the large scale of such services—typically involving hundreds of thousands or millions of network elements. The major requirements are summarized as follows:

- Cost-effective performance scaleability—a system with the ability to manage small pilot networks and expand as the network grows without performance degradation.
- Multiple protocol support—standards-based and proprietary management protocols must be supported in a manner transparent to the network applications.
- Powerful event management—as the network grows, the number of events grows exponentially. The ability to manage this volume of events in a way that helps the operator make sense of the status of the network is mandatory.
- Seamless application interworking—operators will use a number of different applications to manage aspects of the network, but they require the ability to move easily between applications, for example, to investigate problems or configure service for a particular customer.
- User access management—the information within the management system must be protected, but it must also be feasible to partition the data, and the access to it, in a way that supports operational processes [7].

Network Architecture

Some of the key management challenges when installing xDSL networks include potential element volumes. xDSL network elements are extremely complex devices that require real-time management. As element volumes increase exponentially, operators are faced with the challenges of implementing end-to-end systems that can manage millions of highly complex access elements.

As an example, the 1994 BT video-on-demand (VOD) trial (conducted by telecommunications companies TCI, AT&T, and US West in Colorado) supported 2,000 ADSL lines, equating to 4,000 access elements. Although this was classified as a small marketing trial, it is still the largest single xDSL installation in the world. This network generated a tremendous amount of management traffic, primarily with SNMP and performance-monitoring information, all of which had to be processed in real time by the central management workstation.

Additionally, xDSL equipment, by virtue of its inherent built-in intelligence, generates a tremendous amount of management traffic. This information, be it alarms, performance-monitoring information, configuration data, diagnostic commands, or inventory data, has to be processed, stored, prioritized, formatted, and displayed by the central management console. A single-element management workstation cannot scale to support any major network growth.

Element and network complexity is also an issue that operators need to prepare for. xDSL equipment is becoming more complex with each generation. The latest generation uses rate-adaptive transmission, which causes a myriad of possible upstream and downstream speed permutations. Remote equipment now incorporates xDSL transmission hardware, IP routing equipment, and IP or ATM CPE interfaces into a single unit. In addition, it has to be seamlessly integrated with the existing POTS network, leading to a wealth of configuration permutations, performance-monitoring information, alarm and event reports, diagnostic functions, and inventory data being available to the network operator.

A typical end-to-end network capable of delivering high-speed Internet, on-demand services, and data and voice from multiple service providers is extremely complex. Many issues can only be resolved with the use of integrated management applications and systems. This often results in a number of noncompatible element management systems being installed to manage different parts of the network, then integrated together to provide an overall end-to-end service management system. The eventual goal is to provide a zero touch system to allow the end customer to control and manage a large part of their own service offering in real time.

xDSL equipment is normally installed over existing telephony circuits but the devices at each end of the connection contain POTS splitters that allow both the telephony circuit and the xDSL circuit to use a single copper pair. This requires the integration of a new xDSL management system with existing POTS systems.

A range of issues also cloud the choice of the most efficient interface for the equipment on the customer premises. The two protocols in question are IP and ATM. Network operators are installing complex networking equipment in residential environments for the first time. This can lead to a multiplicity of new problems. These problems range from units being tampered with and cables being disconnected to PCs being reconfigured. This could result in a huge increase in the number of service-related calls and queries directed at the network operator. The operator has to be able to diagnose, isolate, and analyze problems from the central management system. Only when this type of network, system management, and control is achieved will broadband services become commercially viable.

Viability

The density of the technology must increase dramatically to enable operators to fit all the required ADSL termination units into their existing exchange real estate. xDSL technologies are still costly, and this is holding back general acceptance due to the costs of equipment investment and the ongoing line rental charge. Prices in the range of $240 to $290 would start to approach an acceptable level for the benefits of this new broadband technology.

However, in most European countries, high capacity broadband ATM backbone networks have yet to be deployed. Without this backbone infrastructure, there is little benefit to be gained from introducing an upgraded access network. In the infrastructure context, the questions of how some major European operators will play off ADSL against their substantial ISDN services will be an interesting debate. As it now stands, current versions of ADSL cannot coexist with ISDN BRI lines. New versions of ADSL are being developed that will coexist with ISDN but as yet are only available in small trial volumes from one or two vendors.

Telecommunication companies, such as Deutsche Telekom, which bet its future on ISDN, are now involved in desperately trying to increase ISDN usage before ADSL establishes itself. The situation it faces (in common with many other operators in Europe) is that too much emphasis and keenly priced ISDN will undermine ADSL; but, at the same time, not investing an adequate amount of resources on ADSL now might undermine its future as a broadband services provider.

The Future

From the point of view of a commercial (profitable for both provider and user) service provision, xDSL can be considered an immature technology. xDSL has been proven an effective, reliable solution in many international trials. However, it is continually developing and progressing—which adds to the xDSL management complexities requiring the facilities for operators to download new algorithms on a regular basis.

xDSL standards are relatively new and are therefore prone to change on a regular basis. This involves regular, programmable equipment upgrades, such as software download of new versions of xDSL transmission and application code from a central management station.

As with all new technologies, technical and cost issues do get resolved in subsequent generations. xDSL is no different. The market demand for high-speed, broadband communications will drive the development of the technology and will produce an economic, reliable solution for end users. For network operators, xDSL is the most cost-effective way of upgrading the copper infrastructure and competing against fiber and cable competitors. Another factor in determining market direction is the move for European PTTs (post, telegraph, and telephones) from monopoly to deregulation and free competition. This will force network operators to unbundle their loops in a way similar to what has happened in the United Kingdom and United States. These new competitors will aggressively target end customers with offers of high-speed broadband data communications, tempting them from the traditional service providers who may not be moving as quickly toward new service provision.

Using the existing copper networks, xDSL will be made available, which will motivate PTTs to respond, leading to a critical mass and explosion in xDSL deployments. While network operators, service providers, and vendors debate the standards, technology, and cost issues of deploying xDSL networks, customer demand is growing for cost-effective, high-speed broadband networks that unleash new services and new business potential for them. Looking at the rapid development of Internet and intranet business and services over the last few years, one can expect resolutions to the main issues and mass xDSL deployment within the next 3 to 5 years.

FROM HERE

This chapter discussed copper design considerations (layout, components, connectors, shielding, maintenance, etc.). The next chapter discusses wireless design considerations (spread spectrum, microwave, infrared, wireless WANs and LANs, etc.).

NOTES

[1]   George Velamparampil, "Wiring," Computer Science Department, 1304 West Springfield, Office of Public Affairs and Computing and Communications Services Office, University of Illinois at Urbana-Champaign 61801, 1999, pp. 1–2.

[2]   "UTP Trunk Cabling Design," MOD-TAP, a subsidiary of Molex Inc., 285 Ayer Road, P.O. Box 706, Harvard, MA 01451, 1999, p. 1.

[3]   "Cabling and Pinout Information," (Some material in this book has been reproduced by Prentice Hall with the permission of Cisco Systems Inc.), COPYRIGHT © 1998 Cisco Systems, Inc., ALL RIGHTS RESERVED, 170 West Tasman Drive, San Jose, CA 95134-1706, USA, 1998, p.p. 1–3.

[4]   Jim Serenbetz and Pete Lockhart, "Category 5: How Did We Get Here and Where Do We Go Next?" Anixter Inc, 4711 Golf Road, Skokie, IL 60076, 1999, p. 4.

[5]   Donna Ballast, "Cabling Installation and Maintenance," (Copyright 1996 by Cabling Installation and Maintenance, PennWell, Nashua, NH, 03062. USA. Reprinted with permission), PO Drawer 7580, University of Texas, Austin, TX 78713, 1998, p. 1.

[6]   "ADSL: Turning Copper into Gold," Textor Webmasters Ltd., The Barley Mow Centre, 10 Barley Mow Passage, London W4 4PH, 1998, p. 1.

[7]   Bhawani Shanher, "The Copper Loop: From Barbed Wire to Broadband," Telecommunications, 685 Canton Street, Norwood, MA 02062, (November, 1999), p. 1.

CHAPTER 11

Wireless Design Considerations

Today's wireless technologies and systems are fairly new and are still emerging on the scene. Currently, wireless technologies are comprised of infrared, UHF radio, spread spectrum, and microwave radio. These technologies can range from frequencies in the MHz (U.S.), to GHz (Europe), to infrared frequencies. The personal communication network (PCN) can either use code-division multiple access (CDMA), or time-division multiple access (TDMA). There is a considerable controversy among experts in the field regarding the relative merits of spread spectrum (CDMA) and narrow-band (TDMA) for private communication networks (PCN). The preferred technique may actually vary with the specific PCN application scenario to be addressed later in the chapter.

TDMA divides the radio carriers into an endlessly repeated sequence of small time slots (channels). Each conversation occupies just one of these time slots. So instead of just one conversation, each radio carrier carries a number of conversations at once. With the development of digital systems, TDMA is being more widely used.

The term "spread spectrum" defines a class of digital radio systems in which the occupied bandwidth is considerably greater than the information rate. The term code-division multiple access (CDMA) is often used in reference to spread spectrum systems and refers to the possibility of transmitting several such signals in the same portion of spectrum by using pseudorandom codes for each one. This can be achieved by either frequency hopping (a series of pulses of carrier at different frequencies, in a predetermined pattern), or direct sequence (a pseudorandom modulating binary waveform whose symbol rate is a large multiple of the bit rate of the original bit stream) spread spectrum.

As the deployment of wireless LANs grows, there is also a need for higher data rates. As a result, spectrum has been allocated for high performance LANs (HIPERLAN) and SUPERNET activities at 5GHz, supporting connectivity of 20 to 25 Mbit/s. Moving to even higher frequencies (40 and 60 GHz) with connectivity of 100 Mbit/s is the subject of current research, although these higher frequencies are more suited to fixed link applications.

The principal purpose of this chapter is to define the state of wireless communications design as it exists today and to introduce the basics behind wireless communications, as well as to provide an overview of how it all works. Economically, wireless communications are predicted to reach $4 billion in revenues by the year 2003. Overall, wireless communications spending is expected to reach $103 billion by 2003. The cost of installing and maintaining wireless communications generally is lower than the cost of installing and maintaining a traditional wired LAN, hence more and more enterprises are implementing this new wireless configuration. Note that this chapter has been written with the assumption that the reader has some intermediate to advanced knowledge of networking and an understanding of telecommunications.

In wireless communications, information is transmitted from one or more data collection points to one or more data destinations. As the name implies, this is done without wires. The usual mediums for information interchange is sound, radio frequency, or light. Here, we will discuss both fixed and handheld, microprocessor-controlled, and radio frequency transmitter/receiver units. We will also cover how wireless communications systems can be configured to form a local area network (LAN) that consists of hand-held communications terminals (HHCTs) that are connected to a wireless interface processor through a narrowband FM radio link. Finally, we will conduct a more indepth discussion of the hardware and its functioning and applications for wireless communications. Diagrams of various wireless system configurations will be included.

Furthermore, because of the wide range of services supported by asynchronous transfer mode (ATM) networks, ATM technology is expected to become the dominant networking technology for both public infrastructure networks and LANs. ATM infrastructure can support all types of services, from time-sensitive voice communications and multimedia conferencing to bursty transaction processing and LAN traffic. Extending the ATM infrastructure with wireless access meets the needs of users and customers who want a unified end-to-end networking infrastructure with high performance and consistent service. Wireless ATM adds the advantages of mobility to the already great service advantages of ATM networks.

A cell-based data transfer technique in which channel demand determines packet allocation, ATM offers fast packet technology, real time, and demand-led switching for efficient use of network resources. It is also the generic term adopted by ANSI and the ITU-TS to classify cell relay technology within the realm of broadband WANs, specifically B-ISDN. In ATM, units of data are not time-related to each other and, as part of the B-ISDN standard, is specified for digital transmission speeds from 34 Mbit/s to 622 Mbit/s. IBM currently offers ATM at a nonstandard 25 Mbit/s format. ATM will be the high bandwidth networking standard of the decade.

WIRELESS ATM: WIDE AREA INTERCONNECTION OF HETEROGENEOUS NETWORKS

ATM has been advocated as an important technology for the wide area interconnection of heterogeneous networks. In ATM networks, the data is divided into small, fixed-length units called cells. The cell is 53 bytes. Each cell contains a 5-byte header. This header contains the identification, control priority, and routing information. The other 48 bytes are the actual data. ATM does not provide any error-detection operations on the user payload, inside the cell, and also offers no retransmission services.

ATM switches support two kinds of interfaces: user network interface (UNI) and network node interface (NNI). UNI connects ATM end systems (hosts, routers, etc.) to an ATM switch; while an NNI may be imprecisely defined as an interface connection between two ATM switches. The International Telecommunication Union Telecommunication (ITU-T) recommendation requires that an ATM connection be identified with connection identifiers that are assigned for each user connection in the ATM network.

ITU is the international body that develops worldwide standards for telecommunications technologies. The ITU-T carries out the functions of the former CCITT.

At the UNI, the connection is identified by two values in the cell header: the virtual path identifier (VPI) and the virtual channel identifier (VCI). Both VPI and VCI can combine together to form a virtual circuit identifier. Figure 11–1 shows the UNI and NNI interface to a wireless ATM Network [25].

In any event, there are two fundamental types of ATM connections: permanent virtual connections (PVC) and switched virtual connections (SVC). A PVC is a connection set up by some external mechanism, typically network management. In this setup, switches between a source and destination ATM are programmed with the appropriate VPI/VCI values. PVCs always require some manual configuration. On the other hand, an SVC is a connection that is set up automatically through a signaling protocol. SVCs do not require the manual interaction needed to set up PVCs and, as such, are likely to be much more widely used. All higher layer protocols operating over ATM primarily use SVCs.

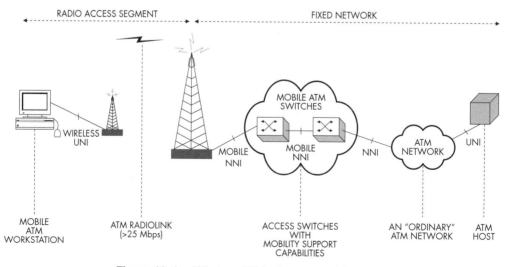

Figure 11–1   Wireless ATM reference architecture.

Reasons for Wireless ATM

Since the beginning, the concept of ATM is for end-to-end communications (in a WAN environment). The communication protocol will be the same (ATM), and enterprises will no longer have to buy extra equipment (like routers or gateways) to interconnect their networks. Also, ATM is considered to reduce the complexity of the network and improve the flexibility while providing end-to-end consideration of traffic performance. That is why researchers have been pushing for an ATM cell-relay paradigm to be adopted as the basis for next-generation wireless transport architectures.

There are several factors that tend to favor the use of ATM cell transport for a personal communication network. These are:

- Flexible bandwidth allocation and service type selection for a range of applications.
- Efficient multiplexing of traffic from bursty data/multimedia sources.
- End-to-end provisioning of broadband services over wireless and wired networks.
- Suitability of available ATM switching equipment for intercell switching.
- Improved service reliability with packet-switching techniques.
- Ease of interfacing with wired B-ISDN systems that will form the telecommunications backbone [25].

In general, interworking may always be seen as a solution to achieve wireless access to any popular backbone network, but the consequence, in this case, is a loss of the ATM quality of service characteristics and original bearer connections. The more interworking there is in a network, the less harmonized the services provided will be. Therefore, it is important to be able to offer appropriate wireless extension to the ATM network infrastructure.

One of the fundamental ideas of ATM is to provide bandwidth on demand. Bandwidth has traditionally been an expensive and scarce resource. This has affected the application development and even the user expectations. So far, application development has been constrained because data transmission pipes cannot support various qualities of service parameters, and the maximum data transmission bandwidth that the applications have to interface with is relatively small or simply insufficient. Finally, ATM has removed these constraints. Bandwidth has become truly cheap and there is good support for various traffic classes. A new way of thinking may evolve in application development.

The progress toward ATM transport in fixed networks has already started and the market push is strong. It can be expected that new applications will evolve that fully exploit all the capabilities of the ATM transport technology. The users will get used to this new service level and require that the same applications be able to run over wireless links. To make this possible, the wireless access interface has to be developed to support ATM quality of service parameters.

The benefits of a wireless ATM access technology should be observed by a user as improved service and improved accessibility. By preserving the essential characteristics of ATM transmission, wireless ATM offers the promise of improved performance and quality of service not attainable by other wireless communications systems like cellular systems, cordless networks, or wireless LANs. In addition, wireless ATM access provides location independence that removes a major limiting factor in the use of computers and powerful telecom equipment over wired networks. Figure 11–2 shows a typical ATM network [25].

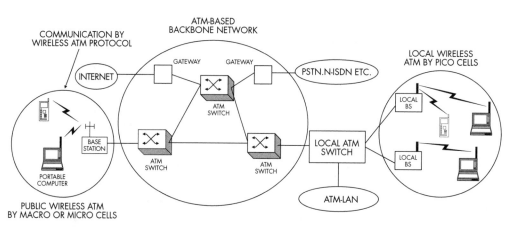

Figure 11–2   Typical ATM network.

Wireless ATM Architecture

The architecture proposed for wireless ATM communications is composed of a large number of small transmission cells called pico cells. Each pico cell is served by a base station. All the base stations in the network are connected via the wired ATM network. The use of ATM switching for intercell traffic also avoids the crucial problem of developing a new backbone network with sufficient throughput to support intercommunication among large numbers of small cells. To avoid hard boundaries between pico cells, the base stations can operate on the same frequency.

Reducing the size of the pico cells has major advantages in mitigating some of the major problems associated with in-designing and building wireless LANs. The main difficulties encountered is the delay due to multipath effects and the lack of a line-of-sight path resulting in high attenuation. Pico cells can also have some drawbacks as compared to larger cells. There are a small number of mobiles, on average, within range of any base station, so base station cost and connectivity is critical. As cell size is reduced, hand-over rate also increases. By using the same frequency, no hand-over will be required at the physical layer. The small cell sizes also gives us the flexibility of reusing the same frequency, thus avoiding the problem of running out of bandwidth.

The mobile units in the cell communicate with only the base station serving that particular cell, and not with other mobile units. The basic role of the base station is interconnection between the LAN or WAN and the wireless subnets, and also to transfer packets and convert them to the wired ATM network from the mobile units.

In traditional mobile networks, transmission cells are *colored* using frequency division multiplexing or code division multiplexing to prevent interference between cells. Coloring is wasteful of bandwidth, because in order for it to be successful, there must be areas between reuse that are idle. These inactive areas could potentially be used for transmission. Figure 11–3 shows a typical ATM to base station connection [25].

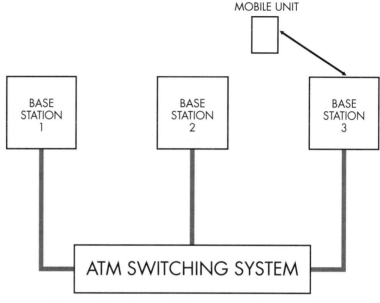

Figure 11–3   Normal ATM to base station connection.

Standards

Wireless ATM research has been active for some time now. There are many papers and books written on wireless ATM; and there are even announced wireless ATM prototypes such as RATM (Radio ATM) by Olivetti [1]. Yet, the most important type of activity has been missing from the wireless ATM scene. For enterprises with enterprise interests, the main objective is often to implement only equipment/systems conforming to standards. Thus, the wireless ATM communications subject has been brought to two different standardization forums, namely the European Telecommunications Standards Institute [2] Society for Technical Communications [3] Remote Execution Service 10 (ETSI STC RES10) and ATM Forum [4].

Currently, there are three standard bodies that have defined the physical layer in support of ATM: the American National Standards Institute (ANSI) [5], International Telecommunication Union's Telecommunications (ITU-T) [6], and the ATM Forum. None of these forums have considered the wireless ATM interface. The ETSI RES10 subtechnical committee is the first standardization body to start working on wireless multimedia, ATM compatibility, and standardization. The RES10 committee has already been engaged with the HIPERLAN (high performance radio local area network) standardization and the wireless

ATM group is working on this subject. The initial work has concentrated on possible usage scenarios and specific requirements. Also, the search for available spectrum in the 5.2 GHz range for wireless ATM system is crucial and therefore was one of the first tasks of RES10.

The ATM forum is not an official standardization body, but it plays a significant role in the standardization arena because of its strong industrial participation and support. Wireless ATM activity has now been officially approved in the ATM Forum.

One wireless ATM activity solution that was approved divided the standardization of wireless ATM between the ATM Forum and RES10. Nevertheless, it would probably be wise to let the ATM Forum concentrate on the fixed network side and RES10 on the wireless interface. The main focus of the ATM Forum should be on the fact that the ATM physical layer is not necessarily always a reliable medium and that terminals may be mobile. Both of these facts are due to the fact that ATM/B-ISDN (broadband integrated services digital network) connections may be stretched over the wireless links in the future and should be independent of the specific wireless interface.

Let's take a look at some ongoing projects in the area of wireless communications.

Current Projects

The following are some of the ongoing projects in the area of wireless ATM communications:

- Wireless ATM Network Demonstrator
- ATM Wireless Access Communication System
- International joint ventures

Wireless ATM Network Demonstrator

The objectives of this project are:

- To specify a wireless customer premises access system for ATM networks that maintains the service characteristics and benefits of the ATM networks to the mobile user.
- To promote the standardization of wireless ATM access.
- To demonstrate and carry out user trials and test the feasibility of a radio-based ATM access system [25].

For example, the Magic WAND project (wireless ATM network demonstrator) [7] covers the whole range of functionality from basic (wireless) data transmission to shared multimedia applications in Europe. The primary goal of the project is to demonstrate that wireless access to ATM (capable of providing real multimedia services to mobile users), is technically feasible. The project partners have chosen to use the 5 GHz frequency band for the demonstrator and to perform studies on higher bit rate operation >50 Mb/s in the 17 GHz frequency band.

The aim of the user trials is to verify a wireless access system for ATM networks that maintains the service characteristics and benefits of ATM networks in the 5 GHz range allocated to wireless high-speed data transmission. The feasibility of a radio-based ATM access system has also been demonstrated by the user trials with selected end-user groups in hospital (medical consultation) and office environments.

Medical consultation shows an advanced scenario, fully exploiting the wireless ATM service capabilities in the hospital environment. The joint video telecommunication operating system (JVTOS) is being used with an X-ray viewing application, using both native audio and video services over ATM. In this scenario, doctors are equipped with a mobile terminal while visiting patients. With the help of a wireless ATM connection, doctors are able to retrieve patient information from the network, consult expert doctors, and share documents. The setup is shown in Figure 11–4 [25].

Wireless ATM extends all the benefits of the ATM and therefore also the ATM signaling and virtual channels/paths into the mobile terminal, raising important issues that have to be solved both in the wireless access interface and in the supporting customer premises ATM network. In the air interface, the wireless ATM transmission is subject to the problems associated with the radio medium and therefore special radio design measures are required in order to offer users an adequate level of service. These measures constitute some of the major technical challenges of this project.

The main result of the project is a wireless ATM access network demonstration system, which serves as proof of concept for the developed technology and help the wireless ATM standardization work. The current achievements of the project include the complete functional system specification on the demonstrator, which has been specified with the Specification and Description Language (SDL) and verified with the simulation model. In addition, the project has defined the exact demo platform setup and therefore enabled the basis for the implementation work that has been started on all parts of the system.

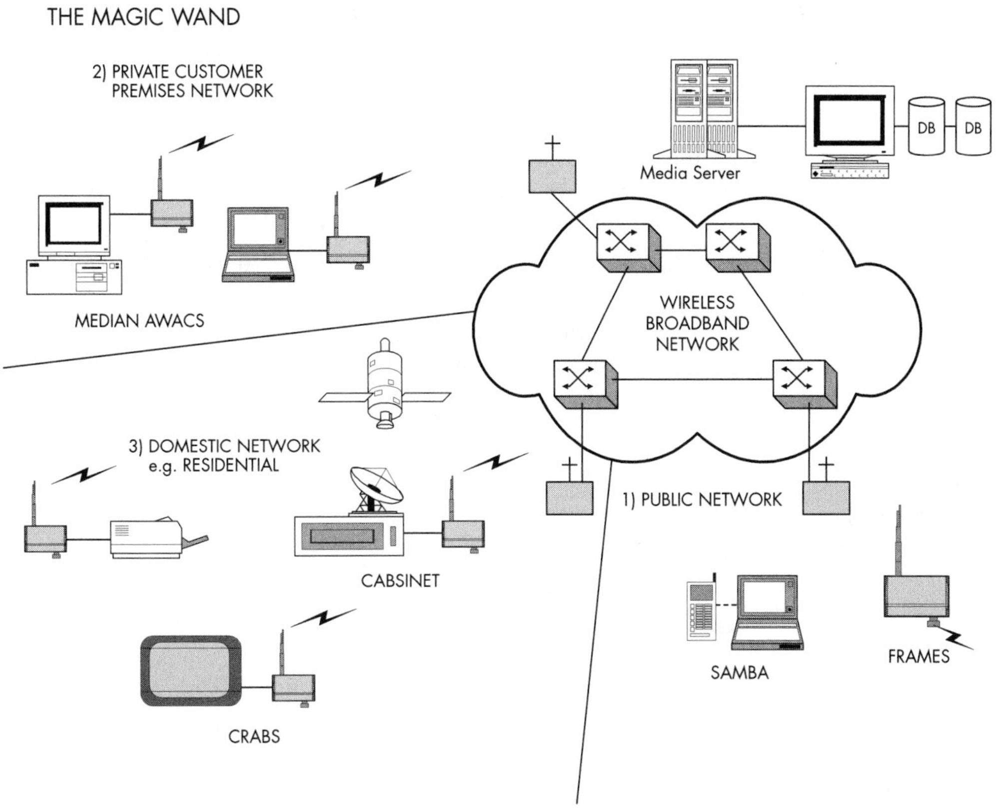

THE MAGIC WAND

Figure 11–4 The Magic WAND setup.

Besides demonstrator work, the project has been active in its liaison and standardization activities. The stochastical radio channel model for channel simulations was developed and verified by measurements on 5 and 17 GHz frequency bands. The model has been given as an input (for signal level 1 [SIG1] work). Furthermore, the project has been active in the standardization forum by contributing and harmonizing the work between ATM forum and ETSI RES10.

The Magic WAND project has continued the work on gaining knowledge on the wireless ATM radio design and its medium access control functions as well as wireless ATM-specific control and signaling functions. These results have been and will continue to be contributed to the ETSI and ATM forum in order to influence all of the relevant standards for wireless ATM systems.

ATM Wireless Access Communication System

The objectives or goals of the ATM Wireless Access Communication System (AWACS) project are the development of a system concept and testbed demonstration of public access to B-ISDN services. The system offers low mobility terminals operating in the 19 GHz band with a support of user bit rates up to 34 Mbit/s with radio transmission ranges of up to 100 m. The demonstrator of ATM Wireless Access (AWA) pre-prototype equipment provides immediate propagation data, basic encoding rules (BER), and ATM performance at 19 GHz. Based on this information, enhancement techniques for AWACS support cellular, as well as spectrum and power efficient radio access technologies associated with HIPERLAN type 4 specifications.

Basic encoding rules are rules for encoding data units, described in the ISO ASN.1 standard.

Furthermore, the AWACS technical approach is centered around a testbed and associated trial campaign program. Trials are conducted using the existing ATM Wireless access platform made available to the project by one of its partners. An associated program of work is directed on enhancing this current state-of-art system toward the final target features of the emerging ATM wireless specifications; in particular, HIPERLAN type 4 is currently being defined by ETSI-RES10. These enhancements to the existing demonstrator are considered in the following areas:

- Application of source/channel coding and intelligent antennas.
- Optimization of link layer protocols to match ATM bearer types.
- Feasibility of 40 GHz radio frequency (RF) technology for ATM wireless LAN applications.
- Mobility management techniques together with the impact on the radio bearer appropriate for high-bit-rate communications [25].

Radio frequency is a generic term referring to frequencies that correspond to radio transmissions. Cable TV and broadband networks use RF technology.

The AWACS field trial covers the concept of *virtual office* trials. This includes three potential cases, depending on the technical capabilities of the demonstrator:

- Wireless multimedia communication link between an engineer at the production site and an expert at this office.
- Video communication in meetings between physically separated sites.
- Visual, wireless network access to virtual office facilities at one of the partner's locations.

Objectives.   The objectives of these trials are summarized as follows:

- Improvement of communication between physically separated offices by telepresence technologies.
- Reduce the need of traveling between the geographically separated offices.
- Improve the response time of expert advice in problem solving by visual communications.
- Free staff from fixed office hours [25].

Key Issues.   The key issues to be considered include:

- The performance evaluation of a 19 GHz ATM-compatible modem.
- Identification of the strengths and weaknesses of the existing ATM wireless experimental demonstrator.
- Investigation of possible enhancement to the ATM-compatible modem.
- AWACS field trials with the concept of *virtual office*, which aims to improve the communication between physically separated offices by telepresence technologies [25].

Expected Results.   The AWACS demonstrator based on ATM in packet transmission schemes supports limited, slow speed mobility, as it is in line with expected use of high data services. Therefore, the project generally covers the following directions, which are open to developers of mobile communication systems for the future: Construction of a wireless system providing seamless service in connections to hardwired systems (quality-oriented system); and services making the most of the excellent mobility and portability of mobile communication systems (mobility-oriented system).

The AWACS trials indicate the capacity of the available system in a real user environment. The results of the trials contributed to the development of common specifications and standards such as ETSI-RES10 (for HIPERLAN type 4 specifications), ITU, Telecommunication Technology Committee (TTC), and Association of Radio Industries and Businesses (ARIB) in Japan [8].

 The Telecommunication Technology Committee was established as a private standardization organization in October 1985 to contribute to further activation of the field of telecommunications, in which the free-market principle was introduced based on implementation of the Telecommunication Business Law in 1985, and to respond to the Japan/U.S. Market-Oriented Sector Service (MOSS) Conference, which was held in the same year.

International Joint Ventures

Wireless ATM has started and there is a worldwide effort to unify and standardize its operation. The Public Communication Networks Group of Siemens AG [9], Newbridge Networks [10], and Broadband Networks Incorporated (BNI) [11] recently announced an extensive joint research and development program to address the digital wireless broadband networks market. The three enterprises will focus on integrating BNI's broadband wireless technology with the Siemens/Newbridge Alliance's MainStreetXpress(™) family of ATM switching products to develop wireless network base stations that are fully compatible with wireline services.

BNI has already deployed terrestrial wireless networks that provide wireless cable in a digitally compressed MPEG2 (Motion Pictures Experts Group) format, delivering laser disk-quality transmissions with the capacity for hundreds of channels. The Siemens/Newbridge Alliance offers carriers the most comprehensive suite of ATM products and the largest ATM core infrastructure switch, scaleable up to 1 Terabit and beyond. The introduction of ATM into the broadband wireless environment will enable network operators to cost effectively deploy high-capacity access services such as high-speed data, broadcast (cable) distribution, and Internet access in the 28 GHz range. By incorporating both MPEG2 and ATM into the broadband wireless environment, the network solution provided by BNI and the Siemens/Newbridge Alliance ensures high-speed, high-quality, and high-capacity video, voice, and data transmissions. It also represents an effective bandwidth allocation that ensures sufficient capacity for additional innovative residential and commercial services as they evolve.

Let's take a look at wireless communications hardware in the form of its functioning and applications for wireless communications. Diagrams (Figures 11–5 to 11–8) of various system configurations are also available.

WIRELESS COMMUNICATIONS HARDWARE AND APPLICATIONS

The following are wireless communications system configurations in the form of hardware and applications as well as sample installation schematics, as shown in Figures 11–5 to 11–8 [12]:

- Hand-held communications terminal
- wireless interface processor
- remote data collection
- example of an ArielNet wireless communications application

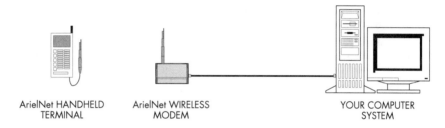

ArielNet HANDHELD   ArielNet WIRELESS   YOUR COMPUTER
TERMINAL   MODEM   SYSTEM

Figure 11–5   Single HHCT user application.

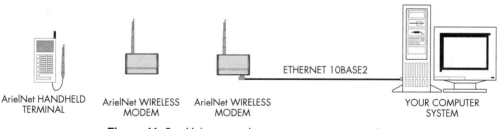

ETHERNET 10BASE2

ArielNet HANDHELD   ArielNet WIRELESS   ArielNet WIRELESS   YOUR COMPUTER
TERMINAL   MODEM   MODEM   SYSTEM

Figure 11–6   Using a modem as a message repeater.

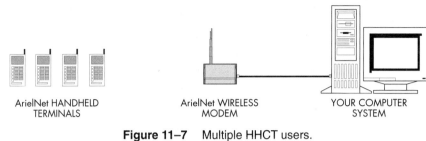

ArielNet HANDHELD   ArielNet WIRELESS   YOUR COMPUTER
    TERMINALS   MODEM   SYSTEM

Figure 11–7   Multiple HHCT users.

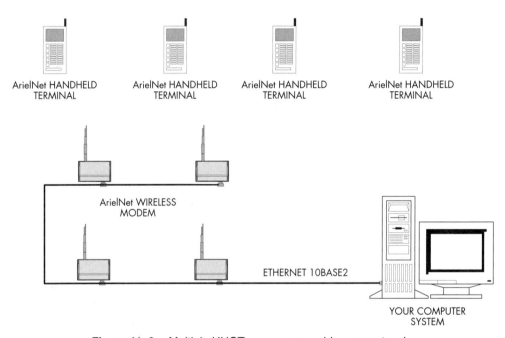

Figure 11–8   Multiple HHCT users over a wide area network.

Hand-Held Communications Terminal

The hand-held communications terminal (HHCT) consists of a liquid crystal display (LCD), 40-key keyboard, and RF modem housed in a lightweight portable case. The low-power microprocessor in the HHCT provides the processing and communications functions. The HHCT unit provides most of the functions of an ANSII standard terminal. The HHCT is battery-operated for up to 12 hours on a charge and has provisions for connecting a bar code wand as an additional data collection device.

Communications between the wireless interface processor (WIP) and HHCT are carried over a narrowband FM radio channel at a rate of 9600 baud. Any number of HHCTs can be addressed by the WIP as each HHCT has a unique identification number. The communications process is transparent to the user.

Wireless Interface Processor

The wireless interface processor (WIP) is a small electronic enclosure that houses the microprocessor, radio transmitter, radio receiver, and the antenna and communications interface. A WIP provides a connection to fixed resources such as instruments, computers, machinery, inventory, and property. The WIP provides the communication path from a remote site to a host system, as well as to HHCTs. The host system provides access to information like inventory data bases, equipment status and scheduling, process status, and control. A WIP also allows the HHCT user to access networks like the Internet and its global information services, including e-mail.

Remote Data Collection

A remote data collection system can be implemented by using a wireless interface processor connected to the serial communications port of a computer system that has an inventory database application running. A hand-held communication terminal with a bar code scanner attached can then be used to communicate inventory data over a large area. By connecting a bar code scanner, the HHCT can be used as an inventory control or data capture device.

The WIP is connected to the communications port (COM port) of the host computer. The host computer has its console assigned to the COM port and is executing an inventory or database application. The HHCT now can function as the computer console and provide data gathering and control of the host computer at up to 1,000 feet away.

The wireless components of the ArielNet® Wireless Communications System [12] operate in compliance with Federal Communication Commission allocations (part15) for license-free operation. This puts the communication range for each element of the wireless network at 1,000 feet. With an array of devices, much larger areas can be covered.

Example of an Arielnet® Wireless Communications Application

This application describes the use of wireless communications and the wireless interface processor in a product delivery service enterprise. The enterprise is a bakery and the problem is inventory control. The bakery would like to sell all of its product while it is still fresh. Trucks are loaded each morning with the product and each evening the trucks return with some product not sold that day. The product dispatcher would like a correct inventory of day-old products at the start of the day and have them placed on the truck so they are delivered to the correct customers. The delivery trucks each have a computer and an ArielNet® WIP. The truck computer could be a notebook computer system that provides customer order information, truck inventory, and route information to the driver. The truck computer also connects to a bar code reader that can read the bar codes on the product. Information is sent to the truck computer each morning as it is loaded and updated information is sent back each evening by wireless to the bakery's main control computer.

Bakery Delivery and Product Control Sequence

The bakery computer sends customer information and the routing schedule to the truck computer. As the truck is loaded, each product is scanned with the bar code scanner, and the count is entered into the truck computer.

The truck computer communicates to the people loading the truck that the truck has the correct product loaded and sends this information to the bakery computer. The driver follows the computer route and scans each customer's product as it is delivered. The driver then returns to the terminal at the end of the day. As the truck is unloaded, any undelivered product is scanned. This information is sent to the bakery computer. If the information is complete, the driver is relieved, otherwise corrective action is taken.

Let's now look at narrowband and broadband personal communications service (PCS). This part of the chapter will also cover the pros and cons of wireless LANs in the enterprise and the technology options that they offer. It will also look at how the mobile nature of wireless communications provides consumers with the opportunity to access from any place at any time.

PERSONAL COMMUNICATION SERVICE

For the wireless communications industry, 1994 was a banner year as the Federal Communications Commission (FCC) [13] launched the first set of spectrum auctions for the narrowband and broadband personal communication service (PCS), giving birth to a whole new era—the era of personal communications. The vision of PCS is the concept of anytime, anywhere communications—whether it be data communications, voice communications, or both. But what is the real potential for this marketplace? How many individuals are likely to buy into the vision of anytime, anywhere communications?

In early 1995, the Personal Communications Industry Association (PCIA) [14] completed a survey of PCIA members to evaluate the growth, composition, and characteristics of the existing and future personal communications industry and published the results in the *PCS Market Demand Forecast* (see Sidebar, "Personal Communications Industry Association"). The results indicate that by 2002, combined demand for new PCS, cellular, and paging and narrowband PCS will amount to almost 330 million subscriptions.

PERSONAL COMMUNICATIONS INDUSTRY ASSOCIATION

Established in 1949, PCIA has been instrumental in advancing regulatory policies, legislation, and technical standards that have helped launch the age of personal communications services. Through many vehicles (policy boards, market forecasts, publications, spectrum management programs, seminars, technician certification programs, and its industry trade show), the PCIA is committed to maintaining its position as the association for the PCS industry.

PCIA's member enterprises include PCS licensees and those involved in the cellular, paging, enhanced specialized mobile radio (ESMR), specialized mobile radio (SMR), mobile data, cable, computer, manufacturing, and local and interexchange sectors of the industry, as well as private enterprise systems users, wireless system integrators, communication site owners, distributors and service professionals, and technicians [26].

To meet this level of demand in the marketplace, the wireless industry must be assured that it will be able to deploy services in a timely fashion. Issues such as site acquisition and interconnection to the local exchange carriers are critical to timely deployment of developing wireless networks for the enterprise and for competing effectively. The government must assure that the industry has the opportunity to meet the anticipated demand outlined in the *PCS Market Demand Forecast* by ensuring a level playing field for all wireless telecommunications service providers and by allowing, where appropriate, competition (not regulation) to govern the marketplace.

The personal communication service includes a broad range of telecommunications services that enable people and devices to communicate independent of location. PCS networks and devices operate over a wide range of frequencies assigned and authorized by the FCC. There are currently seven different air interface technologies proposed for standardization for the new PCS licensees that will be operating in the 1.8 GHz band. Service providers that will be operating at these frequencies either are new entrants with no established network or are existing telecommunications service providers, such as cable, cellular, local exchange, and long-distance carriers. With the technology choices enterprises make over the next few months, there will need to be analysis of how and to what extent the various wireless and wireline networks will work together.

Interoperability and Interworking

To facilitate roaming among PCS carriers, some degree of interoperability and interworking needs to be accomplished between the networks. PCIA defines interoperability and interworking as follows:

Interoperability

Interoperability is the ability to logically connect two or more functional network elements for the purposes of supporting shared processes such as call delivery. Service interoperability is defined as the assurance that a service invoked by a subscriber in a network will be performed by the other network in the same way from a user perspective. Network interoperability is defined as the direct one-to-one mapping of services and protocols between interconnected networks. For example, a subscriber may invoke call waiting features exactly the same way in a data collection system (DCS) 1900 (Global System for Mobile-Communications [GSM]-based) network in New York City as in a DCS 1900 (GSM-based) network in San Francisco. In this scenario, call waiting network protocol messages map between the two networks on a direct one-to-one basis.

Interworking

Interworking is the ability to translate between two or more dissimilar networks for the purpose of achieving effective interoperability. Service interworking is defined as the protocol translation that may or may not result in the service being performed in the receiving network in the same way from a user perspective. Network interworking is defined as functional mapping of services and protocols across networks (some services may not be delivered or may be delivered in a different way). For example, a subscriber with a PCS 2000 (composite code division multiple access/time division multiple access [CDMA/TDMA]) wireless personal terminal may register and authenticate on a San Francisco Interrupt Status-41 (IS-41)-based network, just as he or she could on a home base, DCS 1900 (GSM-based) network in New York City. Although the method of registering may not be identical between systems, the end result is effectively the same—the subscriber can be registered and authenticated on both networks, and location services work across both platforms.

The composite CDMA/TDMA system is an air interface technology currently being standardized for PCS in the 1.8-GHz band.

Standards should be developed and are currently being worked on in domestic and international standards bodies to facilitate features and services delivered consistently and in similar fashions to an end user, regardless of the air interface and/or network implementation used. All networks do not necessarily need to interoperate or interwork with every other network. Those decisions will be made on an enterprise-by-enterprise basis. But the industry is working to make sure that if that choice is made, the technology will be available to support it.

Market Forecast

Since 1992, PCIA has regularly surveyed wireless communications industry leaders to evaluate the growth, composition, and characteristics of the future of the personal communications industry and has published these results in the *PCS Market Demand Forecast*. In its yearly surveys, PCIA has asked respondents to provide market size predictions in terms of the number of anticipated subscriptions, not subscribers, anticipating that an individual would probably subscribe to more than one type of wireless service in the coming decade. As in previous years, the 2000 figures show that consumer demand for personal communications services is expected to grow at ever-increasing rates.

Demand growth for new broadband PCS customers is expected to reach 40 million subscriptions by 2002. Total revenues are expected to reach $10 billion by the year 2002, with 9 percent of that revenue coming from data services. Average revenue per subscription is expected to be 40 percent less than that for cellular. Figures for 2007 indicate strong sustained growth to almost 60 million subscriptions and total revenues reaching $39.7 billion, with 14 percent from data services.

Broadband PCS refers to the family of mobile or portable radio services operating in the 1.8-GHz range and providing a wide variety of innovative digital voice and data services.

Established voice services such as cellular are expected to grow as well. Respondents expect strong cellular growth during the next 6 years, with the 2000 year-end subscriber count of 68.6 million expected to double to approximately 137.6 million subscriptions by 2003, with nearly 98 million cellular subscriptions expected by 2008. Sixty percent of the total cellular subscriptions are expected to come from the enterprise segment, representing a presumed growth of the cellular markets into households over the next 11 years. Total cellular revenues are forecast to be approximately $58 billion by 2003 and $64 billion by 2008.

In the narrowband PCS arena, market size is expected to reach more than 70 million subscriptions by 2002; by 2007, 93 million one-way and 43 million two-way messaging subscriptions are anticipated. In addition, survey results forecast strong growth from new narrowband PCS and advanced one- and two-way messaging, and suggest that these will become established in the wireless world of the enterprise over the next decade. Customer segments will grow due to new narrowband applications and services. Survey results show that by the year 2002, more than 70 percent of one-way and about 87 percent of two-way subscribers are expected to be from enterprise segments. Assuming that enterprises will continue to upgrade services, they are expected to remain more than 70 percent of the total subscriber base through the next decade. Total revenues are expected to reach $6.9 billion for one-way paging and $3.2 billion for two-way paging by 2002, and $7.8 billion and $5 billion, respectively, by 2007.

Broadband PCS refers to the family of mobile or portable radio services operating in the 1.8-GHz range and providing a wide variety of innovative digital voice and data services.

Site Acquisition Issues

Acquiring PCS antenna and base station sites and gaining the appropriate zoning approvals vary by state and local jurisdictions and are important in wireless network deployment in the enterprise. Furthermore, there are issues regarding site acquisition (such as the Federal Aviation Administration [FAA] [15] tower regulations and the lack of a uniform policy regarding sites on federal property) that need to be addressed at the federal level.

Issues at the Local Level

There are more than 50,000 local jurisdictions throughout the nation, each with the authority to prevent antenna construction; establish standards that can result in site location degrading the quality of service; or prolong site selection, thereby making it unnecessarily expensive. With an estimated 300,000 new wireless antenna sites predicted over the next 11 years, any licensing obstacles present significant problems.

Congress has recognized the need to remove state and local barriers to deploying commercial mobile radio service (CMRS) facilities by prohibiting state and local government regulation of matters relating to market entry and rates. The current draft of the Senate's Telecommunications Competition and Deregulation Act of 1995 states that no state or local statute may prohibit or have the effect of prohibiting the ability of any entity to provide interstate or intrastate telecommunications services. It further states that if after notice and comment, the FCC determines that a state or local requirement is inconsistent with the legislation, the FCC shall immediately preempt enforcement of the requirement.

The Cellular Telecommunications Industry Association (CTIA) [16] filed a Petition in 1999 for Rule Making, requesting that the FCC initiate a rule-making proceeding to preempt state and local regulation of tower sites for CMRS. The petition states that the state preemption language in Section 332(c) of the Communications Act gives the Commission authority to exercise such preemption, since local zoning could constitute an *indirect* regulation of entry.

Comments on the Petition for Rule Making were both pro and con. Predictably, service providers filed in support of the petition, while state and local governments and consumer groups filed in opposition. The challenge the wireless industry faces is balancing the recognized needs of the local community to have oversight and fee administration of zoning issues against attempts to meet the ever-increasing demand for new wireless services.

Additionally, the FCC has imposed build-out requirements on the new PCS licensees that mandate that certain percentages of the licensees' markets be covered within set time frames. Potential conflicts between state and federal regulations threaten to delay the entry of wireless services.

Site Acquisitions on Federal Property

Federal property could, in many situations, provide prime locations for PCS base stations. Unfortunately, many agencies of the federal government are not willing or are unable to entertain the prospect of such facilities because of perceived administrative burdens, lack of benefit to local agency staff, or lack of clear policy or regulations for leasing of federal property for such an installation. Additionally, all of the federal agencies that allow private communications facilities on their land have different regulations, lease documents, and processes for doing so. These are often difficult, time consuming, and expensive for both the agency and the communications enterprises.

Making sure federal land resources continue to be available for efficient delivery of mobile communications services, and ensuring that taxpayers receive a fair price from every communications enterprise with transmitters on public lands, are goals shared by industry, the federal agencies, and the public. However, there needs to be a consistent, government-wide approach for managing the site acquisition process on federal property.

The Executive Branch needs to set a clear directive in order to overcome the obstacles wireless licensees face when trying to acquire sites on federal property. The benefits to the federal government could include increased revenues from the installation of PCS networks above and beyond the auction proceeds and the potential for improved communications on federal property.

FAA Tower Review Process

PCIA has initiated discussions with the Federal Aviation Administration (FAA) to remove any possible FAA obstacles to efficient deployment of PCS systems. The FCC has established licensing rules that have streamlined the approval necessary to bring systems and PCS cell sites on line. However, due to administrative limitations, the FAA, which must review many requests for towers to ensure air safety, has experienced longer processing times that have delayed carriers' ability to activate certain transmitter sites. With approximately 30 to 35 percent of new wireless enterprise sites requiring FAA action and review, PCIA fears that FAA processing delays could significantly burden the industry. Working groups at the national and local levels have been established as a forum to explore methods of educating the industry about FAA procedures and to explore ways to streamline the FAA tower review process.

The FAA, FCC, PCIA, and the Cellular Telecommunications Industry Association (CTIA) have all agreed to participate in this dialogue as part of an antenna work group (AWG) in Washington, D.C. PCIA has also participated in dialogues with the FAA Southern Region and is working on a local level in other working groups to identify ways to improve the FAA process.

Federal Radio Frequency Emissions Standard

As PCS, cellular, paging, and other wireless carriers build out networks for enterprises, they are increasingly facing state and local laws and ordinances based on RF exposure levels, often with conflicting scope and standards, resulting in compliance difficulties. Conflicting standards affect the range of wireless services and can greatly diminish the quality of service consumers receive. This adds greatly to the expense borne by the industry, not only in legal and other enterprise expenses, but also in lost revenue opportunities from long delays in providing services.

The FCC has the authority to preempt local jurisdictions on cell/antenna/ tower siting, but to date has approached this issue on a case-by-case basis. With as many as 300,000 new wireless sites to be installed (including new PCS sites, and additional sites that will be needed for the expansion and enhancement of service areas for paging, SMR, ESMR, and cellular service), a case-by-case approach to preemption is no longer realistic.

On April 3, 1993, the FCC issued its Notice of Proposed Rule Making, which proposed updating guidelines and methods for evaluating the environmental effects of electromagnetic exposure, and adopting the standard developed by the American National Standards Institute (ANSI) [17] with the Institute of Electrical and Electronic Engineers (IEEE) [18]. In December 1994, the Spectrum Engineering Division of the Office of Engineering and Technology of the FCC issued information indicating that levels of exposure to RF at ground level below typical cellular towers are hundreds to thousands of times lower than the proposed standard.

On December 22, 1994, the Electromagnetic Energy Association (EEA) [19] filed a petition with the FCC for a Further Notice of Proposed Rule Making. The petition requested that the FCC preempt state and local regulation of RF exposure levels found to be inconsistent with the FCC-proposed ANSI standard.

PCIA favors the establishment of a single, national RF emissions standard that may not be exceeded by local regulations. PCIA encourages the relevant federal agencies to work cooperatively with industry on this issue to develop such a national standard.

Interconnection

Interconnection is composed of interconnection with local exchange carriers and mutual compensation.

Interconnection with Local Exchange Carriers

Negotiating reasonable rights, rates, and terms under which enterprises will interconnect with other networks is critical to the success of PCS. With many PCS hopefuls eyeing the local exchange market as a potentially lucrative area in which to compete, the terms of enterprises' interconnection agreements as a co-carrier will become even more important as they strive to compete with local exchange carriers (LECs), and therefore, they will need reasonable interconnection agreements so that they can offer customers low-cost exchange service.

As an example of current interconnection costs, Type 2 interconnection charges for cellular carriers generally are measured on a per-minute basis, with costs ranging from 1 cent per minute to 5 cents per minute, and 2 cents per minute often being considered a *good* interconnection rate.

Interconnection charges have diminished cellular carriers' revenues since the first system came on line, and they remain a high cost to carriers today. Take, for example, a cellular monthly bill of $48, which includes 97 minutes of air time, at the rate of 2 cents per minute for interconnection. Interconnection charges represent $1.94 of the bill, or 4.04 percent of revenue.

As air time costs continue to decline in the wireless marketplace, interconnection costs will begin to reduce revenues even more. For example, Honolulu, Hawaii's Cybertel Cellular offers 4 cents per minute of air time in Kauai, Hawaii, to compete with the local exchange carrier. At an interconnection rate of 2 cents per minute, interconnection charges could consume 70 percent of the carrier's air time revenue.

Obviously, those wishing to compete at the local loop must achieve lower interconnection costs to compete with established carriers on price. One solution to this problem is mutual compensation, where both telecommunications carriers are compensated for the traffic that terminates on their network.

Mutual Compensation

Mutual compensation is the concept that a carrier should be compensated for traffic that originates on another network but terminates on that carrier's network, and vice versa. Currently, wireless carriers must compensate wireline carriers for traffic that originates on a wireless enterprise network and terminates on a wireline network. Almost without exception, wireline carriers do not compensate wireless carriers for traffic originating on a wireline network and terminating on a wireless network.

The FCC has repeatedly stated that, for interstate traffic, wireline carriers must compensate wireless carriers for traffic originating on a wireline network and terminating on a wireless network. However, states have been reluctant to enforce mutual compensation on an intrastate basis, and therefore wireline carriers have refused to participate in mutual compensation on either an intra- or interstate basis.

Enforcement of mutual compensation rights of wireless carriers is considered to be a key to full competition by wireless carriers in the telecommunications market and will have a significant positive financial impact for the wireless industry. One potential solution to the high cost of interconnection would be mandating mutual compensation through reciprocal elimination of interconnection charges. One example of this solution is the agreement reached in New York between Time Warner [20] and Rochester Telephone (in New York), whereby Rochester Telephone will collect 1.1 cents per minute for traffic terminating on its network and pay at the same rate for its own traffic terminating on other networks. According to the agreement, mutual compensation provisions are eliminated when the traffic flow differentials fall below 9 percent.

Numbering Issues

The issue of who controls numbers is key to the success of PCS carriers. Traditionally, most national numbering resources have been assigned by the North American Numbering Plan Administration, sponsored by Bellcore [21], which in turn is owned by the Bell operating enterprises. Generally, the dominant local exchange carrier ends up assigning numbers to wireless carriers in its local telephone market. Wireless carriers usually are charged for activating blocks of numbers in local exchange carrier networks, and the charges vary greatly.

Name ring a bell? The former research arm of AT&T, Telcordia Technologies, is one of the world's top providers of telecom software (80 percent of the public telecom networks in the United States rely on its software) and consulting services. The company holds more than 800 patents and handles such tasks as doling out area codes. Created as the research unit for the seven Baby Bells during AT&T's 1984 breakup, Telcordia was then known as Bell Communications Research (Bellcore). After becoming a subsidiary of defense contractor Science Applications International, and with research at only about 10 percent of its work, the company changed its name and began focusing on Internet-based technology. Clients include AT&T, GTE, and PCS Group.

Recently, Bellcore has come under scrutiny for its administration of numbering resources, and actions by wireline carriers who have brought the issue to the forefront. For instance, in Chicago, Ameritech [22] proposed an *overlay* area code. This would require cellular and paging subscribers to give back their numbers and receive a new area code, thus freeing up numbers in the almost-exhausted code for new wireline subscribers. At a recent FCC open meeting, the FCC found this proposal to be *unreasonably discriminatory* against wireless carriers.

The FCC initiated a proceeding more than a year ago to examine whether an independent entity should oversee the assignment of numbers, and it appears as if the Senate telecommunications reform effort might mandate the formation of an independent entity to oversee the numbering assignment process.

Number Portability

Another key issue for those who want to compete with the local telephone enterprise is number portability, or the ability of an end user, such as an individual or enterprise, to retain its 10-digit geographic North American Numbering Plan (NANP) number—even if the end user changes its service provider, the telecommunications service with which the number is associated, or its permanent geographic location. With few exceptions, today end users may not retain their 10-digit NANP number if they:

- switch service providers, referred to as *service provider portability* (a user switches from an incumbent LEC to a new competitive access provider);
- change the service to which the number was originally assigned, referred to as *service portability* (a cellular telephone number becomes the wireline home telephone number); or
- change their permanent location, referred to as *geographic portability* (an end user moves to a different part of the city or state, and may be assigned either a new 7-digit phone number in the old area code or a new 10-digit number in a new area code) [26].

Service provider portability, that is, moving a number from one service provider to another, is vital for those enterprises that wish to compete for customers at the local exchange level. It is much easier to gain market share if the customer an enterprise is trying to attract does not have to change his or her phone number when changing service providers.

Currently, 800 numbers are portable between 800-number service providers—an example of service provider portability. This portability allows the 800-service end user to retain his or her individual 800 number, even when switching 800-service providers. Portability of 800 numbers was ordered by the FCC and implemented in 1993.

This portability does not apply to bulk numbers such as paging numbers.

Industry Efforts to Address Number Portability

The Industry Numbering Committee (INC), a consensus-based industry body sponsored by the Inter-Carriers Compatibility Forum (ICCF), has been actively addressing number portability issues since the fall of 1993. The INC Number Portability Workshop has been addressing a range of issues associated with number portability, including a target portability architecture, network impacts of number portability, and high-level policy issues such as mandated interconnection.

Public Service Obligations

The advent of increased mobility is having an impact on telecommunications public policy. How does wireless technology fit into public policy initiatives such as universal service and access to enhanced 911 emergency calling services? Policies regarding universal service were developed to apply to a strictly wireline environment where competition at the local level was nonexistent. Additionally, wireless technologies present a challenge to the traditional wireline approach to providing enhanced 911 emergency calling. As wireless service providers begin to compete for the local loop, how wireless fits into such public policy provisions will need to be seriously considered.

Universal Service

Universal service, as a public policy concept, is the belief that access to basic telephone services by the widest possible cross-section of the American public is in the social and economic interests of the United States. Over a period of many years, Congress has mandated the creation of universal service programs to support universal service public policy goals. The FCC is charged with fulfilling these congressional mandates.

Within the telecommunications industry, universal service refers to a complex system of explicit and implicit charges and cost allocation mechanisms levied on particular carriers and customers in order to provide access to, and subsidize the rates of, basic wireline services for residential customers, high-cost customers and carriers, low-income customers, rural areas, and services for hearing- and speech-impaired consumers. Estimates of the current total costs of supporting universal service goals and policies range as high as $40 billion to $50 billion annually. Congress is intent upon reform of the universal service policy and funding mechanisms as part of its effort to reform existing telecommunications law. Any reforms could have a potentially huge economic impact on the wireless industry.

Universal service reform is a critical part of telecommunications reform and it appears inevitable if Congress passes a telecommunications reform bill. Although it is too early to tell what shape universal service will take, a number of issues need to be considered.

Wireless Access to Enhanced 911 Emergency Services

The FCC, on October 19, 1994, released a Notice of Proposed Rule Making (NPRM) regarding revision of the Commission's rules to ensure compatibility with enhanced 911 (E-911) emergency services. In many areas of the country, wireline subscribers are provided E-911 service by wireline carriers, which entails transmitting the address and phone number of the caller to the public safety answering point. The NPRM addresses Private Branch eXchange (PBX) issues and wireless service provider issues. The NPRM outlines proposed requirements on wireless services regarding:

- 911 availability
- grade of service
- privacy
- rering/call back
- grade of service
- liability
- cost recovery

- access to text telephone devices (TTY)
- equipment manufacture, importation, and labeling
- user location information
- compatibility with network services
- common channel signaling
- federal preemption [26]

The proposed requirements have considerable technical and economic implications that need to be fully examined. PCIA, in cooperation with representatives of the public safety community, drafted the Joint PCIA, Association of Public Safety Communications Officials (APCO) [23], NASNA Emergency Access Position Paper, which was filed with the FCC in July 1994. This joint paper documented the first attempt of the PCS community to comprehensively address the needs of the public safety community. The FCC used the joint paper as a basis for its NPRM addressing enhanced 911 emergency calling systems.

PCIA fully shares the Commission's important objective of maximizing compatibility between wireless services and enhanced 911 emergency calling systems. Specifically, it concurs that subscribers to real-time voice services interconnected with the public switched telephone network ultimately should enjoy the same access to advanced emergency response services as do wireline service subscribers, with due consideration for the unique characteristics of radio-based technology. At the same time, however, PCIA strongly disagrees with the approach toward achievement of the compatibility objective that is set forth in the NPRM.

PCIA believes that full-scale regulatory intervention is not necessary at this time and that the profound technical issues raised by compatibility cannot be resolved through imposition of arbitrary deadlines as proposed in the NPRM. PCIA proposes, as an alternative to arbitrary deadlines, that the industry work to develop technical solutions to the public safety community's requirements and that the FCC require periodic reports from the industry on its progress in meeting the ultimate goals the FCC has set forth.

Let's now look at wireless LANs for the enterprise by introducing the basics behind wireless LANs and giving an overview of how they work. Economically, wireless LANs are predicted to reach $3 billion in revenues by the year 2002. The cost of installing and maintaining a wireless LAN generally is lower than the cost of installing and maintaining a traditional wired LAN. Hence, more and more enterprises are implementing this new LAN configuration.

THE WIRELESS LANs

A wireless LAN (WLAN) is a networking method that delivers all benefits of a local area network to the enterprise with one very important advantage: no wires. No wires means that you now have the flexibility to immediately deploy workgroups wherever and whenever needed. Wireless LANs allow different workstations to communicate and to access a network using radio propagation as a transmission medium. The WLAN can then be connected to an existing wired LAN as an extension or it can act as a stand-alone network. The advantage here is that WLAN combines data connectivity with user mobility and gives the user a movable LAN. Wireless LANs are especially suited for indoor locations such as hospitals, universities, and office buildings.

Configuration of WLAN

The keystone to a wireless LAN is the cell. The cell is the area where all wireless communication takes place. In general, a cell covers a more-or-less circular area. Within each cell, there are radio traffic management units also known as access points (repeaters). The access point in turn interconnects cells of a wireless LAN and also connects to a wired Ethernet LAN through some sort of cable connection, as shown in Figure 11–9 [27].

The number of wireless stations per cell is dependent on the amount of data traffic (and the type of data traffic). Each cell can carry anywhere from

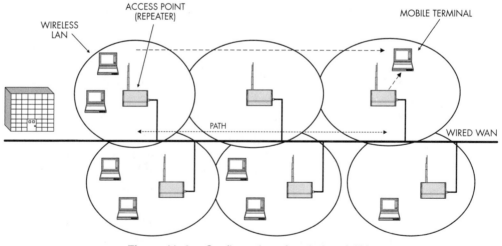

Figure 11–9   Configuration of a wireless LAN.

50 to 200 stations depending on how busy the cell is. To allow continuous communication between cells, individual cells overlap. Cells can also be used in a stand-alone environment to accommodate traffic needs for a small- to medium-sized LAN between workstations and/or workgroups. A stand-alone cell would require no cabling. Another option is wired bridging. In a wired bridging configuration, each access point is wired to the backbone of a wired Ethernet LAN (see Figure 11–9). Once connected to a wired LAN, network management functions of the wired and the wireless LANs can be controlled. Wireless bridging is also an option that allows cells to be connected to remote wireless LANs. In this situation, networking can stretch for miles if it were linked successively and effectively from access point to access point. Finally, by connecting several access points to external directional antennas instead of their built-in omnidirectional antennas, access points can provide multi-cells. This is useful for areas of heavy network traffic, since with this configuration, they are able to automatically *choose* the best access point with which to communicate. Roaming can also be provided for portable stations. Roaming is seamless, and it allows a work session to be maintained when moving from cell to cell (there is a momentary break in data flow).

Pros and Cons

Here are some of the pros and cons of wireless LANs.

- range/coverage
- throughput
- integrity and reliability
- interoperability
- simplicity
- security
- cost
- scalability
- power consumption

Range/Coverage

Most wireless LANs use radio frequencies to function (normally in the range of 2.4 GHz). RF is used because of its ability to propagate through objects. In wireless LAN objects blocking the path of communication between access points, it limits the range that a wireless LAN can cover. Typically, the radius of coverage is anywhere from 100 feet to more than 300 feet. Coverage can be extended via roaming, which was previously defined.

Throughput

Airwave congestion contributes to data rates for a wireless LAN. Typical rates range from 1 to 10Mbps. Just like in wired Ethernet LANs, wireless LANs slow down as traffic intensifies. In traditional Ethernet LANs, users experience a minimal difference in performance when going from wired to wireless LANs.

Integrity and Reliability

Radio interference can cause degradation in throughput. Such interference is rare in the workplace and existing robust designs of WLAN prove that such problems are nothing compared to similar problems in existence with cellular phone connections. After all, wireless data technology has been used by the military for more than 50 years.

Interoperability

Wireless and wired infrastructures are interoperable, yet dependent on technology choice and vendor implementation. Currently, vendors make only their products to be interchangeable (adapters, access points, etc.). The IEEE 802.11 ensures compliant products that are able to interoperate between vendors.

802.11 is the standard for WLANs developed by the IEEE. It can be compared to the 802.3 standard for ethernet wired LANs. The goal of this standard is to tailor a model of operation in order to resolve compatibility issues between manufacturers of WLAN equipment. Thus far, the IEEE 802.11 standards committee is revising a version of a media access control–physical level (MAC-PHY) level.

Simplicity

Wireless LANs, due to their nature, are transparent to a user's networking operating system (OS). This allows excellent compatibility to existing OS and minimizes having to use any type of new OS. Also, since only the access points of wireless LANs require cabling, moving, adding, and setting up is much easier. Finally, the portable nature of wireless LANs allows networking managers to set up systems at remote locations.

Security

The military has been using wireless technology for a long time; hence, security has been a strong design criterion when designing anything that is wireless. Components are built so that it is extremely difficult for *eavesdroppers* to listen in on wireless LAN traffic. Complex encryption makes unauthorized access to network traffic virtually improvable, if not impossible.

Cost

Infrastructure costs are dependent on the number of access points, and the number of wireless LAN adapters. Typically, access points range anywhere from $2,000 to $3,000. Wireless LAN adapters for standard computer platforms range anywhere from $400 to $2,000. Installation and maintenance costs vary depending on the size of the LAN. Installation costs of installing and maintaining a wireless LAN are lower in general when compared to the costs of installing and maintaining a traditional wired LAN.

Scalability

Complexity of each network configuration varies depending on the number of nodes and access points. The ability of wireless LANs to be used in a simple or complex manner is what makes them so influential to current offices, hospitals, and universities.

Power Consumption

Power consumption of a wireless LAN is very low when compared to that of a hand-held cellular phone. Wireless LANs must meet very strict standards posed by government and industry regulations, hence making them a safe device to have around you at a workplace. Finally, no detrimental health effects have ever been attributed to wireless LANs.

Technology Options

There is a range of available technologies out there for manufacturers to select from. For each individual technology, there are individual advantages and limitations.

Narrowband Technology

Narrowband technology uses narrow frequency on the radio signal. Communications channels are apportioned to this signal, each with different channel frequencies. This technology works just like a radio station. Each channel in this technology could be similar to a radio station on your FM stereo. Nevertheless, the frequencies used in narrowband technology are much higher (in the GHz range).

Spread Spectrum

Spread spectrum is the most commonly used technology among wireless LANs component manufacturers. This technology has been adopted from the military and provides secure and reliable communication. The disadvantage to this is that it consumes a large amount of bandwidth. The advantage is that it produces a louder and more detectable signal. Within the spread spectrum exist two types of spread spectrum radio: frequency hopping and direct sequence.

Frequency Hopping. Frequency hopping (FHSS) uses frequency diversity to combat interference. Basically what happens is that the incoming digital stream gets shifted in frequency by a certain amount (determined by a code that spreads the signal power over a wide bandwidth). If the signal is seen by an unintended receiver, it will appear as a short duration impulse noise.

Direct-Sequence Spread Spectrum Technology. Direct-sequence spread spectrum technology (DSSS) generates a chipping code that encodes each data bit. Effectively, this produces a low-power wideband noise in the frequency domain (thus rejected by narrowband receivers). The greater the number of chips in the chipping code, the less likely it will be that the original data will be lost. This is the most commonly used among spread spectrum technology.

Infrared Technology

Infrared (IR) systems are another option of available technologies for wireless LANs for the enterprise. This technology uses very high frequencies just below visible light in the electromagnetic (EM) spectrum to carry data. The disadvantage here is that IR cannot penetrate opaque objects, hence limiting its line of sight. Ranges of IR are approximately 3 feet, which makes them useless for most WLAN enterprise applications.

IEEE 802.11 Standard

The 802.11 standard, as shown in Figure 11–10, is the new IEEE standard for wireless LANs [27]. The goal of this standard is to standardize wireless LAN development in the industrial, scientific, and medicine (ISM) frequency bands allocated by the FCC in the mid-1980s. The bands allocated include these frequency ranges: 902–928 Mhz, 2400–2483.5 Mhz, and 5725–5850 Mhz. The advantage of these ISM bands is that they do not require a license. As long as the device operating in the ISM bands meets special FCC regula-

802.11 PROTOCOL ENTITIES   MAC—MEDIUM ACCESS CONTROL
PHY—PHYSICAL LAYER
PLCP—PHYSICAL LAYER CONVERGENCE PROTOCOL
PMD—PHYSICAL MEDIUM DEPENDENT SUBLAYER

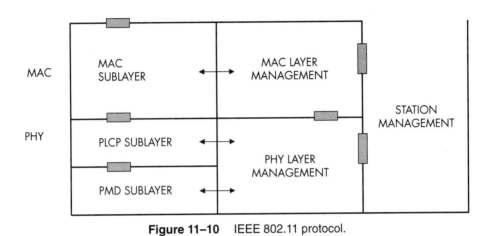

Figure 11–10   IEEE 802.11 protocol.

tions, no license of operation is necessary. The IEEE 802.11 standard focuses on the MAC and PHY protocol levels.

Medium Access Control

A medium access control (MAC) layer is built to allow overlapping of multiple networks in the same area and channel space. It has the ability to share mediums and to be robust for interference. The distributed coordination function is used to provide efficient medium sharing without any overlapping constrictions. Its frame formats are built to support the infrastructure and the ad-hoc network support as well as the wireless distribution system. The MAC layer provides the following services: authentication, deauthentication, privacy, MSDU delivery, association and disassociation, distribution, integration, and reassociation.

Physical Layer

A physical layer (PHY) is built to connect many stations together. Each station may transmit information to any other station in the network. As in other LANs, packets of the users' data are encoded according to the specific physical layer protocol and transmitted as a serial data stream over a physical media to other stations on the LAN. Figure 11–10 shows a proposed configuration. Also, the decision to discard interpackets takes place at the physical layer as the result of an elasticity buffer overflow or underflow. As previously explained, within the physical layer, the frequency hopping spread spectrum radio, direct sequence spread spectrum radio, and infrared PHY are all found. Station management (see Figure 11–10) is used as a mediator between the MAC layer and the physical layer.

IEEE 802.11 Future Development

Finally, a new specification known as the internet-access point protocol (IAPP) is now in existence. This specification goes beyond the work that has been done by the IEEE 802.11 at the MAC and PHY layers. This new standard works at higher OSI layers to establish the way access points communicate across cells in the wired backbone. This new standard is backed by Aironet, Lucent Technologies, and Digital Ocean, Incorporated [24].

THE FUTURE OF WIRELESS

While wireless communication is experiencing a fast evolution, the fixed network has been going toward B-ISDN with ATM concept. ATM offers data rates that are considerably higher than current fixed network services. Interworking with ATM will set extremely hard requirements on the wireless air interface, but hopefully continued development in technology will enable the industry to manufacture smaller and less-power consuming terminals with increased performance and functionality.

Predictions of the future are always uncertain, but it can be assumed that frequencies under 2 GHz remain mainly for mobile communications where only low-bit-rate services are offered (both data and speech). In this case, connections requiring close to 2 Mbit/s or more will need to be moved on to the higher frequencies. The possible choices at the moment seem to be around 5.2 GHz and 17.1 GHz.

The successful introduction of wireless ATM is strongly related to the success of ATM/B-ISDN in wired networks. If ATM/B-ISDN networks are to be a commercial success, wireless ATM could be seen as not today's technology but as inevitable development of the near future.

The fact that most enterprises today have become a complex web of wireline and wireless service providers, providing both voice and data services to the end user at home, in the office, and walking or driving down the street needs to be considered in any telecommunications policy initiative. The new wave of wireless service providers, while providing the consumer with more choices in services and features than ever before, presents a challenge to the public policymaker who tries to determine how to ensure that telecommunications services are made available to the broadest range of consumers. Competition will take care of that to a certain extent. However, where appropriate, government may need to step in on issues such as interconnection rights, mutual compensation, and numbering to ensure that new entrants are treated as equals by incumbent carriers. Furthermore, revision of universal service and enhanced 911 policies needs to take into consideration both the wireless and the wireline industries.

Additionally, the wireless industry is often faced with federal and state regulatory processes that can slow down the deployment of new networks. Federal guidelines regarding site acquisition and radio frequency emissions are necessary to ensure timely availability of new services. There continues to be a high demand for wireless services, and the industry is poised to meet that demand. However, public policy should be developed such that the promise of wireless services as an integral component of the enterprise is realized.

Finally, the wireless LAN can be very useful. To connect to a traditional wired LAN a user must plug his or her computer into a wall or a floor LAN outlet. Wireless LANs' portability and compatibility with all operating systems make it an ideal choice for office intranets and the enterprise. The 802.11 standard promises to give enterprises more control over wireless infrastructures, thus resulting in the blossoming of more and more wireless LANs in many offices.

Today, as the FCC makes available a new spectrum for wireless networks that will support a range of new services, both voice and data, wireless communications are poised on the brink of a new era. However, new spectrum leads to new entrants, and wireless enterprises of the future will face a much more competitive marketplace. This competition will mean great things to the American consumer, who will benefit from the innovation and lower prices that the increased competitiveness will spark. Thus, with the introduction of more competition into the telecommunications marketplace, public policy decisions need to be crafted to ensure that this vision of a wireless future can be realized.

FROM HERE

This chapter discussed wireless design considerations (spread spectrum, microwave, and the design and implementation of wireless systems to support multimedia communications, etc.). The next chapter opens up Part III, *Fiber-Optic Systems: A Hands-On Approach*, by taking a thorough look at fiber optic types and materials, with an emphasis in how fibers guide light, and how single-mode and multimode fiber are different.

NOTES

[1]   Olivetti Research, Ltd , 24a Trumpington Street, Cambridge CB2 1QA, England, 2000.

[2]   ETSI, 650 route des Lucioles 06921, Sophia Antipolis Cedex, France, 2000.

[3]   STC,   901 North Stuart Street, Suite 904, Arlington, Virginia 22203-1822, 2000.

[4]   ATM forum, 2570 West El Camino Real, Suite 304, Mountain View, CA 94040-1313, 2000.

[5]   American National Standards Institute, 11 West 42nd Street, New York, New York 10036, 2000.

[6]   International Telecommunication Union (ITU), Place des Nations, CH-1211 Geneva 20, Switzerland, 2000.

[7]   European Commission, DG XIII/B, BU-9 4/82, Rue de la Loi, 200, B-1049 Brussels, Belgium, 2000.

[8]   Association of Radio Industries and Businesses (ARIB), 5-16, Toranomon 1-chome, Minato-ku, Tokyo 105, Japan, 2000.

[9]   Siemens Corporation, 1301 Avenue of the Americas, New York, NY 10019-6022, 2000.

[10]   Newbridge Networks Corporation, 600 March Rd., PO Box 13600, Kanata, Ontario K2K 2E6, Canada, 2000.

[11]   Broadband Networks Inc., 100 Fairgrounds Drive, Manilius NY 131 04, USA, 2000.

[12]   "An Introduction to Wireless Communication," Applied Integration Corporation, 3930 West New York Drive, Tucson, Arizona 85745, 2000.

[13]   Federal Communications Commission, 445 12th St. SW, Washington DC 20554, 2000.

[14]   Personal Communications Industry Association, 500 Montgomery Street, Suite 700, Alexandria, Virginia 22314-1561, 2000.

[15]   Federal Aviation Administration, 800 Independence Avenue, SW, Washington, D.C. 20591, 2000.

[16]   Cellular Telecommunications Industry Association, 1250 Connecticut Avenue, NW Suite 800, Washington, DC 20036, 2000.

[17]   American National Standards Institute, 11 West 42nd Street, New York, New York 10036, 2000.

[18]   IEEE Corporate Office, 3 Park Avenue, 17th Floor, New York, New York, 10016-5997 U.S.A, 2000.

[19]   Electromagnetic Energy Association, 1255 Twenty-Third Street, NW, Washington, D.C. 20037, 2000.

[20]   Time Warner Telecom Inc., 5700 S. Quebec St., Greenwood Village, CO 80111, 2000.

[21]   Telcordia Technologies, 445 South St., Morristown, NJ 07960-6438, 2000.

[22]   Ameritech Corporation, 30 S. Wacker Dr., Chicago, IL 60606, 2000.

[23]   APCO International, Inc., World Headquarters, 2040 S. Ridgewood Avenue, South Daytona, FL 32119-8437, 2000.

[24]   Digital Ocean Inc., UTRECHT, The Netherlands, 2000.

[25]   Javier Cereceda and Paul Houldsworth, "Wireless ATM: Technology and Applica-
        tions," Virginia Tech, Blacksburg, VA 24061 USA, 2000.

[26]   Mary Madigan, "NII 2000: The Wireless Perspective," Personal Communications
        Industry Association, National Academy Press, 2101 Constitution Avenue, NW,
        Lockbox 285, Washington, DC 20055, 2000.

[27]   Phong Quang Ta and Dimitrios G. Soulios, "Wireless LANs," Virginia Tech,
        Blacksburg, VA 24061 USA, 2000.

Fiber Optic Systems:
A Hands-On Approach

CHAPTER 12

Fiber Types and Materials

Fiber optic cabling is being deployed at an ever-increasing rate with the relentless pursuit of bandwidth. This cable, which uses glass to carry light pulses, poses both advantages and challenges. Fiber optic cabling has much to offer, and in most cases, its use will provide benefits that warrant the implementation.

The intent of this chapter is to explain the how's and why's of fiber optic cabling types and materials and to provide a set of solutions to the challenges faced with its use. This chapter is intended to give you an understanding of fiber optic cable technology, types and materials, and its applications.

There has been a constant push to provide data at higher and higher rates since the invention of the telegraph by Samuel Morse in 1838. Today, the push continues. Just as RS-232 attached terminals gave way to 10 Mbps Ethernet and 4 and 16 Mbps token ring, these are giving way to Fast Ethernet (100 Mbps), FDDI (100 Mbps), ATM (155 Mbps), Fibre Channel (1062 Mbps), and Gigabit Ethernet (1000 Mbps). With each of these increases in speed, the physical layer of the infrastructure is placed under more stress and more limitations. The cabling installed in many environments today cannot support the demands of Fast Ethernet let alone ATM, Fibre Channel (see Appendix A, "List of Fiber Channel Products, Organizations, and High Energy Projects and Applications"), or Gigabit Ethernet.

Currently, the use of fiber optic systems to carry digitized video, voice, and data is universal. In business and industry, fiber optics have become the standard for terrestrial transmission of telecommunication information. In military and defense, the need to deliver ever larger amounts of information at faster speeds is the impetus behind a wide range of retrofit and new fiber optic programs. Although still in its infancy, fly-by-light flight control systems may someday replace fly-by-wire systems with cabling, which is both lighter, smaller, and safer. Fiber optics, combined with satellite and other broadcast media, represents the new world order for both commercial telecommunications as well as specialized applications in avionics, robotics, weapon systems, sensors, transportation, and other high-performance environments.

FIBER TYPES

There are three types of fiber optic cable: single mode, multimode, and plastic optical fiber (POF). Single-mode cable is a single stand of glass fiber with a diameter of 8.3 to 10 microns.

One micron is 1/250th the width of a human hair.

Multimode cable is made of multiple strands of glass fibers, with a combined diameter in the 50-to-100 micron range. Each fiber in a multimode cable is capable of carrying a different signal independent from those on the other fibers in the cable bundle. POF is a newer plastic-based cable that promises performance similar to single-mode cable, but at a lower cost. While fiber optic cable itself is cheaper than an equivalent length of copper cable, fiber optic cable connectors and the equipment needed to install them remain, at least for now, more expensive than their copper counterparts.

Fiber optic cable functions as a *light guide*, guiding the light introduced at one end of the cable through to the other end. The light source can either be a light-emitting diode (LED) or a laser. The light source is pulsed on and off, and a light-sensitive receiver on the other end of the cable converts the pulses back into the digital ones and zeros of the original signal.

Even laser light shining through a fiber optic cable is subject to loss of strength, primarily through dispersion and scattering of the light within the cable itself. The faster the laser fluctuates, the greater the risk of dispersion. Light strengtheners, called repeaters, may be necessary to refresh the signal in certain applications.

Major Benefits

As previously mentioned, compared to copper, optical fiber is relatively small in size and light in weight—a major advantage in interconnect systems servicing airborne avionics. As a practical matter, fiber is simply easier to install (especially in retrofit programs) because the smaller cable diameters can fit comfortably within the footprint or layout of existing electrical conduits and harnesses. Smaller size and weight also make it possible to run multiple backup cables for each electronic system or device. The ability to provide complete redundancy for all critical cabling is a major motivating factor in the introduction of fiber in avionic systems. Here are some fiber optic cable advantages over copper:

- *Speed:* Fiber optic networks operate at high speeds—up into the gigabits per second.
- *Bandwidth:* Large carrying capacity.
- *Distance:* Signals can be transmitted further without needing to be refreshed or strengthened.
- *Resistance:* Greater resistance to electromagnetic noise such as radios, motors, or other nearby cables.
- *Maintenance:* Fiber optic cables cost much less to maintain.

In other words, fiber optic cabling provides a viable alternative to copper. Unlike its metallic counterpart, fiber cabling does not have the astringent speed and distance limitations that plague network administrators wishing to upgrade their networks. Because it is transmitting light, the limitations are on the devices driving it more than on the cable itself. By installing fiber optic cabling, the high cost of labor and the time associated with the cabling plant can be expected to provide service for the foreseeable future.

Plastic optical fiber (POF) technology is making fiber even more affordable and easier to install. Because the core is plastic instead of glass (more on cores and fiber construction follows later in the chapter), terminating the cable is easier. The trade-off for this lower cost and ease of installation is shorter distance capabilities and bandwidth limitations.

Furthermore, optical fiber is particularly useful in airborne applications due to its electromagnetic immunity. Since fiber optics use light to transmit signals, it is not subject to electromagnetic interference, radio frequency interference, or voltage surges. The total electrical isolation of fiber also makes it a safer, spark-free media for use in hazardous environments, such as aircraft fuel cells. This characteristic also provides for enhanced transmission security, as light pulses, unlike electrical signals, are almost impossible to intercept or monitor (providing a "hack-free," or more secure, environment).

But the most important benefit of fiber as a transmission media is its huge bandwidth and low data loss. Fiber can transmit a mind-boggling quantity of data with extremely good transmission quality. Two strands of optical fiber, both no thicker than a human hair, can transmit the equivalent of 24,000 telephone calls simultaneously. By way of comparison, two strands of copper wire can transmit but a single phone conversation—in a much heavier and larger cable. Doing the math, the smaller and lighter fiber strand has over 150 times the data-carrying capacity of the bulkier copper cable. Additionally, the data is transmitted digitally (the natural form for computerized equipment) rather than analogically, which reduces translation errors and bottlenecks. Simply put, fiber can transmit signals over the longest distance at the lowest cost.

Functional Basics

Functionally, fiber optic systems are similar to the copper wire systems they are rapidly replacing. The principle difference is that fiber optics use light pulses (photons) to transmit data down fiber lines, instead of electronic pulses to transmit data down copper lines. Other differences are best understood by taking a look at the flow of data from point to point in a fiber optic system.

The *encoding* side of an optical communication system is called the transmitter. This is the place of origin for all data entering the fiber optic system. The transmitter essentially converts coded electrical signals into equivalently coded light pulses. A light-emitting diode (LED) or an injection-laser diode (ILD) is typically the source of the actual light pulses. Using a lens, the light pulses are funneled into the fiber optic connector (or terminus), and transmitted down the line, as shown in Figure 12–1 [1].

Light pulses move easily down the fiber optic line because of the principle of *total internal reflection*, which basically holds that whenever the

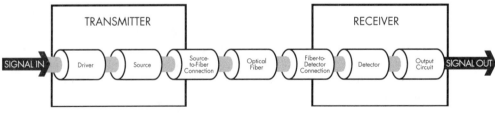

Figure 12–1   Basic fiber optic link.

angle of incidence exceeds a certain value, light will not emit through the reflective surface of the material, but will bounce back in. In the case of optical communications systems, this principle makes it possible to transmit light pulses down a twisting and turning fiber without losing the light out the sides of the strand.

At the opposite end of the line, the light pulses are channeled into the *decoding* element in the system, known as the optical receiver or detector. Again, the actual fiber-to-detector connection is accomplished with a specialized fiber optic connector/terminus. The purpose of an optical receiver is to detect the received light incident on it and to convert it to an electrical signal containing the information impressed on the light at the transmitting end. The information is then ready for input into electronic-based devices, such as computers, navigation control systems, video monitors, and so on.

How Fibers Guide Light: Fiber Cable Construction

Fiber optic cabling has the following components (starting in the center and working out): core, cladding, coating, strength member/material, and jacket, as shown in Figures 12–2 [2] and 12–3 [1]. The design and function of each of these will be defined.

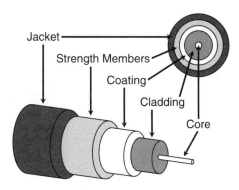

Figure 12–2
Fiber optic components.

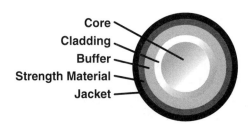

Figure 12–3
Fiber optic cable cross-section.

The core is in the very center of the cable and is the medium of propagation for the signal (light-carrying element at the center of the optical fiber). The core is made of silica glass (combination of highly purified silica and germania) or plastic (in the case of POF) with a high refractive index (more on refractive index later). The actual core is very small (compared to the wire gauges we are all used to). Typical core sizes range from 8 microns (millionth of a meter) for single-mode silica glass cores up to 1000 microns for multimode POF.

Core is the physical medium that transports optical data signals from an attached light source to a receiving device. The core is a single continuous strand of glass or plastic that's measured (in microns) by the size of its outer diameter. The larger the core, the more light the cable can carry. All fiber optic cable is sized according to its core diameter. The three sizes most commonly available are 50-, 62.5-, and 100-micron cable.

The cladding is a material of a lower index of refraction that surrounds the core. This difference in index forms a mirror at the boundary of the core and cladding. Because of the lower index, it reflects the light back into the center of the core, forming an optical wave guide. In other words, the combination of these materials makes the principle of total internal reflection possible, as the difference in materials used in the core and the cladding creates an extremely reflective surface at the point in which they interface. Light pulses entering the fiber core reflect off the core/cladding interface and thus remain within the core as they move down the line. This is the same effect as looking out over a calm lake and noting the reflection, while looking straight down you see through the water. It is this interaction of core and cladding that is at the heart of how optical fiber works.

Cladding is a thin layer that surrounds the fiber core and serves as a boundary that contains the lightwaves and causes the refraction, enabling data to travel throughout the length of the fiber segment.

The coating (also referred to as buffer or buffer coating) is a protective layer around the outside of the cladding. This buffer material acts as a shock absorber to protect the core and cladding from damage. A strength member, typically Aramid, surrounds the buffer, adding critical tensile strength to the cable to prevent damage from pull forces during installation. The outer jacket protects against abrasion and environmental damage. The type of jacket used also defines the cable's duty and flammability rating.

Coating is a layer of plastic that surrounds the core and cladding to reinforce the fiber core, help absorb shocks, and provide extra protection against excessive cable bends. These buffer coatings are measured in microns (p) and can range from 250 p to 900 p.

The buffer coating is typically made of a thermoplastic material for tight buffer construction and a gel material for loose buffer construction. As the name implies, in tight buffer construction, the buffer is extruded directly onto the fiber, tightly surrounding it. Loose buffer construction uses a gel-filled tube, which is larger than the fiber itself. Loose buffer construction offers a high degree of isolation from external mechanical forces such as vibration. Tight buffer construction, on the other hand, provides for a smaller bend radius, smaller overall diameter, and crush resistance (see Sidebar, "Basic Cable Design," for more information).

BASIC CABLE DESIGN

Two basic cable designs are loose-tube cable, used in the majority of outside-plant installations in North America, and tight-buffered cable, primarily used inside buildings.

The modular design of loose-tube cables typically holds up to 12 fibers per buffer tube with a maximum per cable fiber count of more than 200 fibers. Loose-tube cables can be all-dielectric or optionally armored. The modular buffer-tube design permits easy drop-off of groups of fibers at intermediate points, without interfering with other protected buffer tubes being routed to other locations. The loose-tube design also helps in the identification and administration of fibers in the system.

Single-fiber tight-buffered cables are used as pigtails, patch cords, and jumpers to terminate loose-tube cables directly into opto-electronic transmitters, receivers, and other active and passive components.

Multifiber tight-buffered cables also are available and are used primarily for alternative routing and handling flexibility and ease within buildings.

Loose-Tube Cable

In a loose-tube cable design, color-coded plastic buffer tubes house and protect optical fibers. A gel filling compound impedes water penetration. Excess fiber length (relative to buffer tube length) insulates fibers from stresses of installation and environmental loading. Buffer tubes are stranded around a dielectric or steel central member, which serves as an antibuckling element.

The cable core, typically surrounded by aramid yarn, is the primary tensile strength member. The outer polyethylene jacket is extruded over the core. If armoring is required, a corrugated steel tape is formed around a single jacketed cable with an additional jacket extruded over the armor.

Loose-tube cables typically are used for outside-plant installation in aerial, duct, and direct-buried applications.

Tight-Buffered Cable

With tight-buffered cable designs (see Figure 12–4), the buffering material is in direct contact with the fiber [3]. This design is suited for *jumper cables*, which connect outside plant cables to terminal equipment, and also for linking various devices in a premises network.

Multifiber, tight-buffered cables often are used for intrabuilding, risers, general building, and plenum applications.

The tight-buffered design provides a rugged cable structure to protect individual fibers during handling, routing, and connectorization. Yarn strength members keep the tensile load away from the fiber.

As with loose-tube cables, optical specifications for tight-buffered cables also should include the maximum performance of all fibers over the operating temperature range and life of the cable. Averages should not be acceptable [3].

To further protect the fiber from stretching during installation, and to protect it from expansion and contraction due to temperature changes, strength members are added to the cable construction. These members are made from various materials from steel (used in some multistrand cables) to Kevlar. In single- and double-fiber cables, the strength members are wrapped

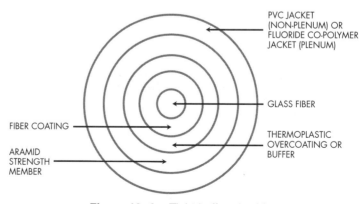

Figure 12–4   Tight-buffered cable.

around the coating. In some multistrand cables, the strength member is in the center of the bundle.

Strengthening fiber components help protect the core against crushing forces and excessive tension during installation. The materials can range from Kevlat4 to wire strands to gel-filled sleeves.

The jacket is the last item in the construction, and provides the final protection from the environment in which the cable is installed. Of concern here is the intended placement of the cable. Different jackets provide different solutions for indoor, outdoor, aerial, and buried installations.

Cable jacket is the outer layer of any cable. Most fiber optic cables have an orange jacket, although some may be black or yellow.

Furthermore, rays of light passing through a fiber do not travel randomly. Rather, they are channeled into modes—the thousands of possible paths a light ray may take as it travels down the fiber. A fiber can support as few as one mode and as many as tens of thousands. The number of modes in a fiber is significant because it helps determine the fiber's bandwidth. Multimode fiber has a much larger core than single-mode fiber, allowing hundreds of rays of light to propagate through the fiber simultaneously. Single-mode fiber has a much smaller core, allowing only one mode of light to propagate through the core. Paradoxically, the higher the number of modes, the lower the bandwidth of the cable. The reason is dispersion.

Modal dispersion is caused by the different path lengths followed by light rays as they bounce down the fiber (some rays follow a more direct route down the middle of the fiber, and so arrive at their destination well before those rays that waste their time bouncing back and forth against the sides). *Material* dispersion occurs when different wavelengths of light travel at different speeds. By reducing the number of possible modes, you reduce modal dispersion. By limiting the number of wavelengths of light, you reduce material dispersion.

Single-mode fibers are manufactured with the smallest core size (approximately 8–10 um in diameter) and so they eliminate modal dispersion by forcing the light pulses to follow a single, direct path, as shown in Figure 12–5 [1]. The

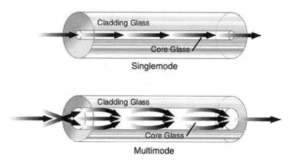

Figure 12–5 Core diameters and their effect on modal dispersion.

bandwidth of a single-mode fiber so far surpasses the capabilities of multimode fiber that its information-carrying capacity is essentially infinite. Single-mode fiber is thus the preferred medium for long distance and high bandwidth applications.

Multimode fiber is generally chosen for applications where bandwidth requirements fall below 600 MHz (see Figure 12–5). Multimode fiber is also ideally suited for short distance applications such as interconnect assemblies used within a single premise or contained space. Because of its larger size, multimode fiber is easier to polish and clean than single mode, a critical concern in interconnect applications, which expose the polished ends of the fibers to debris during connector mating and unmating.

Light Rays and Light Waves

Some 10 billion digital bits can be transmitted per second along an optical fiber link in a commercial network, enough to carry tens of thousands of telephone calls. Hair-thin fibers consist of two concentric layers of high-purity silica glass, the core and the cladding, which are enclosed by a protective sheath. Light rays modulated into digital pulses with a laser or a light-emitting diode move along the core without penetrating the cladding.

The light stays confined to the core because the cladding has a lower refractive index—a measure of its ability to bend light. Refinements in optical fibers, along with the development of new lasers and diodes, may one day allow commercial fiber-optic networks to carry trillions of bits of data per second.

Total internal reflection confines light within optical fibers (similar to looking down a mirror made in the shape of a long paper towel tube). Because the cladding has a lower refractive index, light rays reflect back into the core if they encounter the cladding at a shallow angle (see Figure 12–6)

Figure 12–6   Total internal reflection.

[3]. A ray that exceeds a certain *critical* angle escapes from the fiber (see Figure 12–6).

Transmitters

With a basic understanding of fiber construction, an explanation of transmitters (the devices that put the pulses of light into the fiber) is in order. On a general level, there are three aspects of transmitters to discuss:

1. type of transmitter
2. wavelength of transmitter
3. power of the transmitter [2]

Transmitters can be divided into two groups: lasers and LEDs. LEDs are by far the most common as they provide low cost and very efficient solutions. Most multimode transmitters are of the LED variety. When high power is required for extended distances, lasers are used. Lasers provide coherent light and the ability to produce a lot of light energy. The drawbacks to lasers are their cost and electrical power consumption. Equipment using high-power lasers must provide cooling and access to a primary power source such as 120V AC.

Transmitter Modes.   Transmitter types can also be broken down into single-mode versus multimode transmitters. Multimode transmitters are used with larger cable (typically 62.5/125 microns for most data networking applications) and emit multiple rays or *modes* of light into the fiber. Each one of these rays enters at a different angle and as such has a slightly different path through the cable. This results in the light reaching the far end at slightly different times. This difference in arrival times is termed "modal dispersion" and causes signal degradation. Single-mode transmitters are used with very small cable (typically 8/125 microns) and emit light in a single ray. Because there is only one mode, all light gets to the far end at the same time, eliminating modal dispersion.

Transmitter Wavelength.   The wavelength of the transmitter is the *color* of the light. The visible light spectrum starts around 750 nm and goes to 390 nm. The 850 nm transmitters common in multimode Ethernet can be seen because 850 nm is the center of their bandwidth and they emit some visible light in the 750 nm range, giving them their red color. The 1300 nm and 1550 nm transmitters emit light only in the infrared spectrum. The difference in performance of the various wavelengths is beyond the scope of this chapter. What is important is an awareness of the wavelengths and that the equipment on both ends of the fiber needs to be matched.

Transmitter Power.   The final characteristic of transmitters is the output power. This is a measure of the optical energy (intensity) launched into the fiber, measured in dBm. A typical value for multimode transmitters used in Ethernet is –15 dBm. Single-mode transmitters have a wide range in power depending on the application.

Receivers

With a knowledge of transmitters, what happens at the other end of the cable is important. The light pulses are terminated and detected with a receiver. Receivers have three basic considerations. These are:

1. wavelength (discussed above)
2. mode (single versus multi, discussed in the preceding)
3. sensitivity [2]

Sensitivity is the counterpart to power for transmitters. It is a measurement of how much light is required to accurately detect and decode the data in light stream. It is expressed in dBm and is a negative number. The smaller the number (remember –40 is smaller than –30), the better the receiver. Typical values range from –30 dBm to –40 dBm.

Receive sensitivity and transmitter power are used to calculate the optical power budget available for the cable. This calculation is:

```
Power Budget = Transmitter Power - Receiver Sensitivity
```

Using the typical values given for multimode Ethernet in the preceding, the power budget would be:

```
15 dBm = -15 dBm - (-30 dBm)
```

The optical power budget must be greater then all of the cable plant losses (such as attenuation, losses due to splices and connectors, etc.) for the installation to work properly [2].

Connectors

Fiber optic connectors are designed to be connected and disconnected many times without affecting the optical performance of the fiber circuit. Connectors can be thought of as transition devices that make it possible to divide fiber optic networks into interconnected subsystems and to facilitate the attachment of individual branches of the system to a transmitter, receiver, or another fiber. The MIL-C-38999 connector is currently the most commonly specified multipin cylindrical interconnect in both fiber and copper conductor aerospace applications. When used to connect multiple strands of fiber simultaneously, the 38999 connector functions as a container or shell for the precision termini, which perform the actual marriage of the fiber strands.

Over the past two decades there have been dramatic tolerance improvements in terminus design to insure precise, repeatable, axial and angular alignment between pin and socket termini within the connector shell. Ferrule design, critical to the performance of the termini, has traditionally relied on a machined stainless steel ferrule incorporating a precision micro-drilled hole.

Connector Styles.   Many different connector styles have found their way into fiber optic networking. The SC connector (see Figure 12–7)

ST	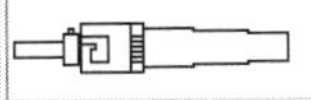	Cylindrical with twist lock coupling, 2.5 mm keyed ferrule. (For both short distance applications and long line systems.)
SC	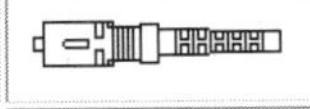	Square, keyed connector with push–pull mating. 2.5 mm ferrule and molded housing for protection.
FDDI	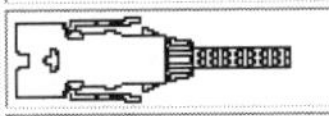	Duplex connector, with fixed shroud, keyed.
FC	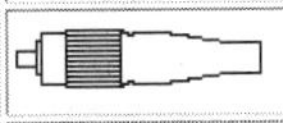	Cylindrical with metal coupling and keyed sleeve, 2.5 mm ceramic ferrule.
BICONIC	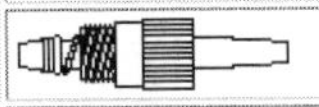	Conical ferrule provides low insertion loss.
ESCON		Duplex connector, with retractable shroud (For IBM ESCON or compatible system).
SMA905		3.2 mm ferrule.
SMA906		3.2 mm ferrule, recessed tip.
MINI BNC	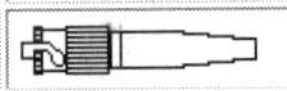	Cylindrical with twist lock coupling, 2.5 mm metal ferrule.
D4	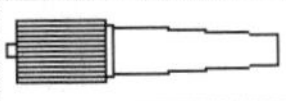	Ceramic connector with cylindrical metal coupling nut, 2.0 mm ferrule, keyed.

Figure 12–7   Fiber optic cables.

has recently been standardized by ANSI TIA/EIA-568A for use in structured wiring installations [4]. Many single-mode applications are now only available in the SC style. The ST connector (see Figure 12–7) has been the connector of choice for these environments, and continues to be widely used.

FDDI uses the MIC connector, which is a duplex connector. It is physically larger then the SC connector, and the SC connector is gaining acceptance in the FDDI marketplace.

Connector Accessories.   Fiber optic strands are robust and reliable, but they should not be manhandled (clamped, bent, or crushed) with the same vigor one might employ when working with a fat copper conductor. For this reason, fiber optic connector and cable accessories are designed to reduce bending and to eliminate compression forces. Needless to say, conventional connector backshells such as cable clamps and strain reliefs, which apply compression forces directly to the cable, are not appropriate for use in fiber optic assemblies. Likewise, accessory elbows, conduit transitions, and other fittings that subject fiber optic cables to abrupt changes in direction beyond the acceptable bend radius of the fiber are equally risky and as a result not normally available. In both cases, the dangers are either outright breakage of the fiber optic core or attenuation of the optical signal.

SINGLE-MODE (SMF) AND MULTIMODE FIBER (MMF) SPECIFICATIONS

The most common size of multimode fiber used in networking is 62.5/125 fiber. This fiber has a core of 62.5 microns and a cladding of 125 microns. This is ideally suited for use with 850 nm and 1300 nm wavelength drivers and receivers. For single-mode networking applications, 8.3/125 is the most common size. It's smaller core is the key to single-mode operation. Table 12–1 summarizes the uses of fiber and the common/standard specifications for those environments [2].

Table 12–1 Fiber Specifications and Uses

Protocol	Single-Mode Wavelength/Fiber Size	Multimode Wavelength/Fiber Size
Ethernet	1300 nm / 8.3/125	850 nm / 62.5/125
Fast Ethernet	1300 nm / 8.3/125	1300 nm / 62.5/125
Token Ring	Proprietary /8.3/125	Proprietary / 62.5/125
ATM 155	1300 nm / 8.3/125	1300 nm / 62.5/125
FDDI	1300 nm / 8.3/125	1300 nm / 62.5/125

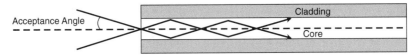

Figure 12–8   Acceptance angle.

Numerical aperture and acceptance angle are two different ways of expressing the same thing. For the core/cladding boundary to work as a mirror, the light needs to strike it at a small/shallow angle (referred to as the angle of incidence). This angle is specified as the acceptance angle (see Figure 12–8) and is the maximum angle at which light can be accepted by the core [2]. Acceptance angle can also be specified as numerical aperture, which is the SIN of the acceptance angle (numerical aperture = SIN [acceptance angle]).

Step-Index Multimode Fiber

Step-index multimode fiber has a large core, up to 100 microns in diameter. As a result, some of the light rays that make up the digital pulse may travel a direct route, whereas others zigzag as they bounce off the cladding. These alternative pathways cause the different groupings of light rays, referred to as modes, to arrive separately at a receiving point. The pulse, an aggregate of different modes, begins to spread out, losing its well-defined shape. The need to leave spacing between pulses to prevent overlapping limits bandwidth, that is, the amount of information that can be sent. Consequently, this type of fiber is best suited for transmission over short distances, in an endoscope, for instance.

Graded-Index Multimode Fiber

Graded-index multimode fiber (see Figure 12–9) contains a core in which the refractive index diminishes gradually from the center axis out toward the cladding [3]. The higher refractive index at the center makes the light rays moving down the axis advance more slowly than those near the cladding.

Figure 12–9   Graded-index multimode fiber.

Also, rather than zig-zagging off the cladding, light in the core curves helically because of the graded index, reducing its travel distance. The shortened path and the higher speed allow light at the periphery to arrive at a receiver at about the same time as the slow but straight rays in the core axis. The result: a digital pulse suffers less dispersion. These fibers often become the physical medium for local area networks.

Single-Mode Fiber

Single-mode fiber (see Figure 12–10) has a narrow core (8 microns or less), and the index of refraction between the core and the cladding changes less than it does for multimode fibers [3]. Light thus travels parallel to the axis, creating little pulse dispersion. Telephone and cable television networks install millions of kilometers of this fiber every year.

Figure 12–10   Single-mode fiber.

How Single Mode and Multimode are Different

Over the past few years, fiber optic cable has become more affordable. It's now used for dozens of applications that require complete immunity to electrical interference. Fiber is ideal for high data-rate systems such as FDDI, multimedia, ATM, or any other network that requires the transfer of large, time-consuming data files. As previously stated, the advantages of fiber optic cable over copper include:

- *Greater distance:* You can run fiber as far as several kilometers.
- *Low attenuation:* The light signals meet little resistance, so data can travel farther.
- *Security:* Taps in fiber optic cable are easy to detect. If tapped, the cable leaks light, causing the entire system to fail.
- *Greater bandwidth:* Fiber can carry more data than copper.
- *Immunity:* Fiber optics are immune to interference [3].

Single Mode or Multimode

Single-mode fiber gives you a higher transmission rate and up to 50 times more distance than multimode, but it also costs more. Single-mode fiber has a much smaller core than multimode fiber—typically 5 to 10 microns. Only a single lightwave can be transmitted at a given time. The small core and single lightwave virtually eliminate any distortion that could result from overlapping light pulses, providing the least signal attenuation and the highest transmission speeds of any fiber cable type.

Multimode fiber gives you high bandwidth at high speeds over long distances. Lightwaves are dispersed into numerous paths, or modes, as they travel through the cable's core. Typical multimode fiber core diameters are 50, 62.5, and 100 micrometers. However, in long cable runs (greater than 3,000 feet [914.4 ml]), multiple paths of light can cause signal distortion at the receiving end, resulting in an unclear and incomplete data transmission.

Choosing Fiber Based on Your Communication Needs

Although fiber optic cable is still more expensive than other types of cable, it's favored for today's high-speed data communications because it eliminates the problems of twisted pair cable, such as near-end crosstalk (NEXT), electromagnetic interference (EIVII), and security breaches.

Fiber Advantages for Ethernet Networks

Fiber provides several advantages to Ethernet and Fast Ethernet networks. The most common advantage and therefore use of fiber is to overcome the distance limitations of coaxial and twisted pair copper topologies. Ethernet being run on coax (10Base2) has a maximum distance limitation of 185 m, and Ethernet being run on twisted pair (10BaseT and 100BaseTX) has a limitation of 100 m. Fiber can greatly extend these distances with multimode fiber providing 2000 m and single-mode fiber supporting 5 km in half-duplex environments, and much more (depending on transmitter strength and receiver sensitivity) in full duplex installations. Ethernet running at 10 Mbps has a limitation of four repeaters, providing some leniency in the solutions available for distance. However, Fast Ethernet only allows for two repeaters and only 5m of cable between them. As Fast Ethernet becomes more ubiquitous, the need for fiber optic cabling will grow as well. When distance is an issue, fiber provides what may be the only solution.

Some electrical noise may be emitted by the cable even when using coaxial cable or twisted pair (shielded or unshielded). This is especially true as connectors and ground connections age or weaken. In some environments (medical, for example), the potential risk associated with this is just not acceptable, and costs of alternative cable routings is usually too high. Because fiber optic cabling uses light pulses to send the signal, there is no radiated noise. This makes it perfectly safe to install this cabling in any sensitive environment. Optical fiber adds additional security protection as well. There are no emissions to pick up and decode, and it is not feasible to *tap* into it for the purposes of *eavesdropping*. This makes fiber optic cabling ideal for secure network installations.

Another problem that is common when using copper cabling is other electrical noise getting into the desired electrical networking signal. This can be a problem in noisy manufacturing environments or other heavy industrial applications. The use of optical fiber provides a signal that will be completely unaffected by this noise.

In some instances, fiber provides the advantage that it can withstand more tension during the cable pulling. It is also smaller in size then twisted pair cables and therefore takes up less room. Compared to category 5 UTP, most duplex fiber optical cable can also endure a tighter bend radius while maintaining specified performance.

Testing and Certifying Fiber Optic Cable.   If you're used to certifying category 5 cable, you'll be pleasantly surprised at how easy it is to certify fiber optic cable since it's immune to electrical interference. You only need to check a few measurements:

- *Attenuation (or decibel loss):* Measured in dB/km, this is the decrease of signal strength as it travels through the fiber optic cable.
- *Return loss:* The amount of light reflected from the far end of the cable back to the source. The lower the number, the better. For example, a reading of –60 dB is better than –20 dB.
- *Graded refractive index:* Measures how much light is sent down the fiber. This is commonly measured at wavelengths of 850 and 1,300 nanometers. Compared to other operating frequencies, these two ranges yield the lowest intrinsic power loss.

This is valid for multimode fiber only.

- *Propagation delay:* This is the time it takes a signal to travel from one point to another over a transmission channel.
- *Time-domain reflectometry (TDR):* Transmits high-frequency pulses onto a cable so you can examine the reflections along the cable and isolate faults [3].

There are many fiber optic testers on the market today. Basic fiber optic testers function by shining a light down one end of the cable. At the other end, there's a receiver calibrated to the strength of the light source. With this test, you can measure how much light is going to the other end of the cable. Generally, these testers give you the results in decibels (dB) lost, which you then compare to the loss budget. If the measured loss is less than the number calculated by your loss budget, your installation is good.

Newer fiber optic testers have a broad range of capabilities. They can test both 850- and 1300-nm signals at the same time and can even check your cable for compliance with specific standards, as the standards may be preset in the tester and/or upgraded later.

Fiber Optic Cabling Challenges

Fiber optical cabling is not a panacea; however, there are some challenges to be resolved. The first (and probably the best known) is the cost of termination. Because of the need for *perfect* connections, splices and connections must be carefully cut and then polished to preserve the optical characteristics. The connectors must also maintain a very high level of precision to guarantee alignment of the fibers.

The second problem that is encountered when installing fiber cabling is that legacy equipment does not support fiber connections. Very few desktop computers have a fiber network interface, and some critical network equipment does not offer a fiber interface.

In Ethernet, the size of the collision domain can affect the use of fiber. In a half-duplex (shared media) environment, no two devices can be separated by more than 512 bit times. While the propagation of a signal is faster through fiber than copper (usually about 11 percent faster), it is not enough to make a significant difference. This limitation means that there are times when the signal quality and fiber are sufficient to carry the signal, but the distance and network design preclude it's use.

Fiber Solutions

Fortunately, the problems are not without solutions. As fiber deployment increases, the economy of scale for the manufacturers is driving costs down. Also, much work is being done to further reduce these costs. Plastic optical fiber is an example of one such development.

The need to connect to legacy equipment and infrastructure also has a solution. By using copper-to-fiber media converters, fiber can be connected to almost any legacy environment. Equipment with an AUI port can also make use of fiber transceivers as well. Media converters are devices (usually small enough in size to fit in the palm of your hand) that take in signals from one media type and send it out on another media type. Table 12–2 lists fiber media converters and transceivers [2].

Table 12–2 Fiber Solutions

Converters	Transceivers
10BASE-T to 10BASE-FL multimode media converter	Full/half-duplex 10BASE-FL multimode transceiver
10BASE-T to 10BASE-FL single-mode media converter	Full/half-duplex 10BASE-FL single-mode transceiver
10BASE-T to 10BASE-FL multimode 1300nm media converter	Full/half-duplex 10BASE-FL 1300 nm multimode transceiver

Table 12–2 Fiber Solutions

Converters	Transceivers
10BASE-T to 10BASE-FL multimode 8-port media converter	Fast Ethernet 10BASE-FL multimode transceiver
10BASE2 to 10BASE-FL multimode media converter	Fast Ethernet 10BASE-FL multimode transceiver (SC connector)
100BASE-TX to 100BASE-FX multimode media converter	Fast Ethernet 10BASE-FL single-mode transceiver
100BASE-TX to 100BASE-FX multimode media converter (SC connector)	StackMaster 6-port 10BASE-FL stackable manageable hub
100BASE-TX to 100BASE-FX single-mode media converter	StackMaster 12-port 10BASE-FL stackable manageable hub
FDDI UTP to multimode fiber media converter	
FDDI UTP to single-mode fiber media converter	
ATM UTP to multimode fiber media converter	
ATM UTP to single-mode fiber media converter	
Token Ring UTP to multimode fiber media converter	
Token Ring UTP to single-mode fiber media converter	
1300 nm single-mode fiber to 1300 nm multimode fiber media converter	
Gigabit single-mode to multimode fiber media converter	
1300 nm single-mode fiber to 850 nm multimode fiber media converter	
Bridging Media Converter: 2-port Ethernet/Fast Ethernet Bridge	
AS400 twinax to multimode fiber media converter	

For those instances when collision domain restrictions preclude the use of fiber, a two-port bridging device (such as transition networks bridging media converter) with 10/100-Base-T(X) on one port and fiber on the other can be used. Bridges by definition break collision domains, and when connected to a server, workstation, or another bridge, can operate in full-duplex mode. In this mode, there are no limitations imposed by collision domains, and the distance attainable is solely a function of the fiber cable and transmitters and receivers.

FDDI/ATM

As networks move to even faster protocol speeds, such as FDDI and ATM, fiber plays an increasingly important role. FDDI and ATM pose all the same problems and advantages as Ethernet. The copper version of FDDI (CDDI) has a cable distance limitation of 100 m. Because these topologies are typically used in a campus backbone application, the distance limitations of multimode fiber can present a problem (2 km). By using single-mode fiber, distances of up to 60 km are possible. Since typically only one or two segments need that kind of distance, single-mode to multimode fiber mode converters can be used to convert just those segments to single-mode without incurring an increased cost for every segment in the network.

WAN Backbones

Because of some of the inherent distance problems in wide area networks, fiber has found widespread deployment. Carriers are migrating large portions of their networks to fiber to take advantage of its superior bandwidth and compact size. As more WAN services are provisioned to the customer premises via fiber, the need to convert from single mode (used almost exclusively in the WAN venue) to multimode will grow. Some of the services that are being provided directly on fiber are ATM and SONET.

Trading Ease for Highest Performance

The layout and configuration of a fiber optic system can vary widely based on the application environment. Commercial telecommunications systems, for example, typically feature extremely long backbone cables, spliced fiber interstices, and inexpensive ST-type connectors at the many termination points in the system. The connectors used in such applications are typically commodity solutions geared to the moderate performance and reliability requirements of that industry. At the other end of the spectrum, fiber optics deployed in military avionics take the form of highly engineered interconnect harnesses and/or multibranch conduit systems. The connectors used in such applications accommodate multiple fiber optic cables and typically utilize precision contacts, or termini, as the primary mechanism for aligning and connecting the optical fibers.

In many such aerospace applications, fiber optics are being employed as replacements or upgrades to existing copper conductor cable harnesses servicing existing black box flight deck equipment, weapon systems, surveillance cameras, sensors, and so on. In all applications of this caliber, the new fiber optic system must adhere to the same rigorous qualification standards and performance requirements that applied to the legacy electrical systems.

For this reason, the design, configuration, and packaging of fiber optic interconnects has closely mirrored existing mil-spec standards, such as those covering interconnect mateability, accessory interface dimensions, material finishes, and so on. The design of fiber optic termini, special purpose backshells, and other accessories is similarly controlled by existing packaging requirements and aerospace industry dimensional standards (see Figure 12–11) [1].

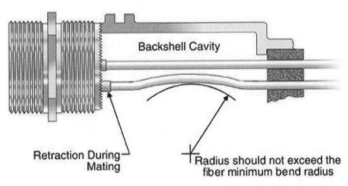

Figure 12–11 Termini retraction and its effect on microbending.

Planning and Investing for the Future

When evaluating the costs and benefits of moving to fiber, it is important to adopt both a short- and long-term view. In the short term, it is arguably less expensive to simply continue using copper cabling to meet an incremental expansion of data communication needs. This avoids the expense of adding the transmitters, converters, repeaters, connectors, termini, receivers, and so on needed for integrating optical fiber into an existing electronic system.

Taking the long view, investing in the conversion to fiber optics often makes good sense, especially given the performance benefits (EMI immunity, security, weight reduction, bandwidth, etc.) and cost-of-ownership factors such as reduced cable maintenance costs and ease of installation (installation is not always that "easy," but it does pay off in the long run). The ability to more easily accommodate future bandwidth requirements as well as the ability to incorporate redundant fibers for improved safety and reliability further reduces the long-term cost of ownership.

Recently, Lucent Technologies announced a new breakthrough optical networking system that uses beams of light to transmit information directly through the air. Designed by Bell Labs, the WaveStar OpticAir system will use state-of-the-art lasers, amplifiers, and receivers placed on rooftops or in office windows to transmit voice, data, or video traffic from point-to-point through the air. Lucent claims the open-air transmission system *will meet industry standards for performance and reliability.* The evolution of fiber optics from Professor Bell's Photophone to Lucent's OpticAir seems to confirm Bell's sense that optics would become his most significant invention.

Finally, fiber optic cabling is rapidly becoming the most viable choice for the data networking infrastructure. With the cost of cable, connectors, installation, and equipment becoming competitive and/or comparable with traditional copper solutions, fiber should be given serious consideration. Once installed, fiber optic cabling will *futureproof* your cabling infrastructure, providing support for even the fastest, most demanding protocols.

FROM HERE

This chapter opens up Part III, *Fiber Optic Systems: A Hands-On Approach*, by taking a thorough look at fiber optic types and materials, with an emphasis in how fibers guide light and how single-mode (SMF) and multimode fibers (MMF) are different. The next chapter examines specifiying fibers, by covering loss and attenuation of fibers, bandwidth, the capacity for information, and physical sizes of fiber.

NOTES

[1]   Gregory B. Noll, "An Introduction to Fiber Optic Concepts and Technologies,"
        Glenair, Inc., 1211 Air Way, Glendale, CA., 2000.

[2]   Stephen T. Strange, "Fiber," Transition Networks, Inc., 6475 City West Parkway,
        Minneapolis, MN 55344, 2000.

[3]   John MacChesney, "Fiber," ARC Electronics, 814 Wild Horse Vly. Rd. Suite H,
        Katy, TX 77450, 2000.

[4]   Communication Cable Company, 140 Quaker Lane, Malvern, PA 19355, 2000.

CHAPTER 13

Specifying Fibers

Since the late 1980s, the ability to run Ethernet over fiber optic cable has been available. In the majority of Ethernet-based fiber installations, the IEEE rules governing the length of fiber cable are adhered to. However, there has been a growth in demand over the last few years for fiber installations that *theoretically* break the IEEE rules. Such installations are most commonly found within campus/factory-wide networks or are associated with the rental of long-haul fiber lines from the local postal, telegraph, and telephone (PTT) organization/licensed cable operator. Confusion exists as to the capabilities of Ethernet over long-distance fiber. This chapter aims to address the current state of specifying long-distance fiber, with regard to loss and attenuation of fibers, bandwidth, the capacity for information, and physical sizes of fiber.

THE CSMA/CD PROTOCOL

Before any discussion takes place on specifying long-distance fiber, the way in which Ethernet operates (the CSMA/CD protocol) must be examined. Both 10 Mbps and 100 Mbps Ethernet use an access technique called carrier sense multiple access/collision detect (CSMA/CD). The mechanics and rules for CSMA/CD LANs are defined by the IEEE standards committee—specifically the IEEE 802.3 standard.

ISO-OSI Seven Layer Model

A brief review of the bottom two layers of the International Organization for Standardization-Open Systems Interconnection (ISO-OSI) model is required in order to understand how CSMA/CD operates, as shown in Figure 13–1 [1].

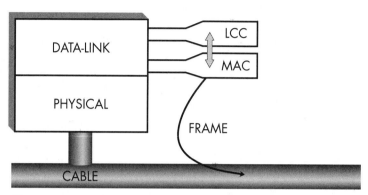

Figure 13–1   Data link and physical layers of the ISO-OSI model.

ISO-OSI pertains to the logical structure for communications networks standardized by the ISO. Adherence to the standard enables any OSI-compliant system to communicate with any other OSI-compliant system for a meaningful exchange of information.

Data Link Layer

The components of the data link layer reside on the LAN card/hardware of the data terminal equipment (DTE) device. The data link layer defined by IEEE Ethernet can be split into two distinct components: logical link control (LLC) and media access control (MAC).

Logical Link Control.   The LLC takes data from the higher levels of the ISO-OSI model and formats the data into the applicable Ethernet frame type. It also implements flow control from the higher levels of the ISO-OSI model to the lower part of the Data Link layer (MAC).

Media Access Control.   The MAC layer does the *work* of the 802.3 standard. It is responsible for taking the frames from the LLC, converting them to whatever encoding scheme is used on the cable, and implementing the CSMA/CD access method.

The physical layer is the cabling media being used (fiber optic [10Base-FL, 100Base-FX], twisted pair [10Base-T, 100Base-TX]; coax [10Base5, 10Base2]).

Operation of CSMA/CD

As part of the connection media, the first Ethernet LANs used coaxial cable (10Base5). This was a shared media system. All DTE devices (computers, repeaters) connected to the cable were treated as equal and shared the cabling media. The MAC layer is responsible for the implementation of CSMA/CD as follows:

1. The MAC will first check to see if the cable is free and then transmit its data. If another DTE is using the cable, the MAC will wait until the cable is clear. This is the carrier sense component. During this phase, the MAC will continue to adjust its frequency of checking the cable to determine if it is free in the event that it is not.

2. Since all DTEs on the network are treated as equal and share the same physical cabling media, the LAN can be termed as being "multiple access."

3. When a DTE starts transmitting, it takes time for other DTEs on the network to see that the cable is in use. If another DTE starts transmitting during this window, a *collision* takes place. The MAC is responsible for detecting and handling these events. This is the collision detect component of Ethernet.

4. If a collision takes place, the transmitting MACs will stop, back off for a random amount of time, and repeat the carrier sense component of CSMA/CD. If carrier sense indicates that the cable is available, transmission will restart, at which point the entire procedure repeats [1].

Handling Collision

When a collision takes place (the stations are notified of this event), many guides to Ethernet use the term "notified." This implies that some device on the LAN sees the collision and somehow notifies the correct workstations that a collision has taken place. This description is incorrect. What actually happens is as follows:

If transmissions from two (or more) MACs appear on the cable at approximately the same time, the MAC will see this due to the fact that the electrical properties of its transmission are being damaged or interfered with—this is the collision. The MAC will stop transmitting and implement CSMA. Collision detect is the responsibility of the transmitting MACs. The DTEs that are not transmitting do not get involved if a collision takes place.

While the MAC is transmitting, the critical component of the preceding is that the collision must take place. The MAC does not keep copies of all the frames it has sent without being *notified* of collision. If the frame has transmitted successfully, the MAC clears itself and waits for the LLC to send it more data.

The MAC will stop, keep the frame, and try again if the collision takes place while the MAC is transmitting. If the collision takes place after the MAC has transmitted, the frame is lost. These lost frames are often called *late collisions* or delayed collisions. Therefore, if collisions take place, they must occur while the MAC is transmitting.

When Should Collisions Take Place?

Collisions should take place while the MAC is transmitting, as described in the preceding. The smallest Ethernet frame is 64 bytes; the largest is 1,518 bytes. Therefore, the smallest *window* for a collision is 64 bytes, or 512 bits; the largest is 1,518 bytes or 12,144 bits. It would be irresponsible to set the collision window to the largest Ethernet frame possible. Approximately 40 percent or more of the traffic on an Ethernet LAN is composed of 64-byte frames—the majority of which are *acknowledge character (ACK)* frames, confirming that data has been delivered successfully. Therefore, to ensure that late collisions do not happen, the collision window must be equal to the smallest Ethernet frame (64 bytes). This collision window is often termed the "slot time" of Ethernet.

Microseconds, Bytes, and Bits

One can convert bytes to bits, and therefore into the amount of time within which a collision should take place, in order to understand how the slot time works in practice. Table 13–1 provides the timing for 10 Mbps Ethernet [1].

Table 13–1   10 Mbps Ethernet

Bits	Bits per second	μseconds (10^{-6} seconds)
10,000,000	0.0000001	0.1
512 (64 bytes)	0.0000512	51.2

Therefore, a collision should take place within 51.2 microseconds with 10 Mbps Ethernet. Every DTE on a LAN takes *time* to process an Ethernet frame. In addition, the cable also takes time to transmit the signal. The sum of all these delays must not exceed 51.2 microseconds. If the sum of the delays does exceed 51.2 microseconds, late collisions will take place.

LOSS AND ATTENUATION OF FIBERS

A second factor (signal attenuation) has a major impact on the cabling scheme, in addition to the delays associated with transmission. Attenuation is defined as the weakening of the signal being transmitted (see Table 13–2) [1]. It is a crucial factor in LAN design and the lengths of cable being used. The maximum lengths assigned to copper-based cable (10Base2, 10Base5, 10Base-T, 100Base-TX) by the IEEE have come about due to the attenuation characteristics of the copper cable in use.

Table 13–2 Twisted Pair Attenuation

Frequency (MHz)	Category 3 dB Attn/NEXT	Category 4 dB Attn/NEXT	Category 5 dB Attn/NEXT
10.0	9.7/26	6.9/41	6.5/47
16.0	13.1/23	8.9/38	8.2/44
20.0	–/–	10.0/36	9.3/42
100.0	–/–	–/–	22.0/32

Attenuation: per 100 meters (328) @ 20° C. NEXT: @ 100 meters (328 feet). Near-end cross talk (NEXT, RN) is the optical power reflected from one or more input ports back to another input port. Also known as isolation directivity.

With fiber cable (10Base-FL, 100Base-FX), the IEEE stated that the maximum length of the fiber in use for 10 Mbps Ethernet is 2 Km. This 2 Km figure was a rather conservative figure based, at the time, on the fact that fiber transmitters were of relatively low power and assumed a *lossy* cable. In practice, fiber could be run up to 4 Km in length.

Do not install nonstandard fiber lengths unless certain conditions are met. These conditions are discussed later in this chapter.

Collisions and Attenuation

Cable attenuation is the biggest limiting factor to the size of the network in the vast majority of 10 Mbps Ethernet installations. Only when long distance fiber is required does the bit budget of 10 Mbps Ethernet become important.

The bit budget is reduced by a factor of 10 with 100 Mbps Ethernet. Some of the stranger rules associated with 100 Mbps cabling (a maximum of 412 m fiber DTE to DTE, one or two repeaters in any single collision domain, and a maximum interrepeater cascade length of 10 m of twisted pair cable) are due to the bit budget constraints of Fast Ethernet.

Full-Duplex Ethernet (FDX): Removing Collisions

Full-duplex Ethernet was recently developed. It was initially *sold* as a method by which you could double your Ethernet speed from 10 Mbps to 20 Mbps. This feature is patently untrue. Full-duplex Ethernet defines separate transmit and receive paths with a maximum speed of 10 Mbps. Therefore, you can only transmit/receive at 10 Mbps. However, you can transmit/receive at the same time. You cannot allocate spare bandwidth from, for example, the currently unused receive path to the currently in use transmit path.

Nevertheless, since there are separate transmit and receive paths, DTEs can transmit and receive at the same time: one very important advantage of full duplex. Collisions are therefore eliminated. Full-duplex Ethernet is thus a collision-free environment.

The only cabling schemes that can support full duplex are ones in which physically separate transmit/receive paths are available (twisted pair [10Base-T, 100Base-TX] and fiber optic [10Base-FL, 100Base-FX]). Coaxial cabling cannot support full duplex, as the media is shared by all DTEs, as shown in Figure 13–2 [1].

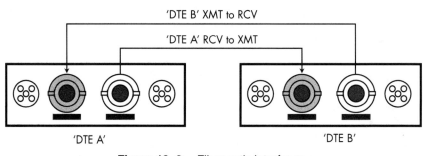

Figure 13–2   Fiber optic interfaces.

Full-duplex operation requires that the central *hub* has the ability to store in/outbound frames if the transmit/receive path to the destination DTE is already in use. Of course, this is in addition to the cabling constraints.

In practice, the devices used in a full-duplex environment are switches or multiport bridges. The simple repeater defined by the IEEE is a multiple access device that is not designed to handle separate transmit/receive paths nor buffer frames. In addition, a full-duplex cabling scheme will be point-to-point (Ethernet switch to workstation; switch to switch), as shown in Figure 13–3 [1].

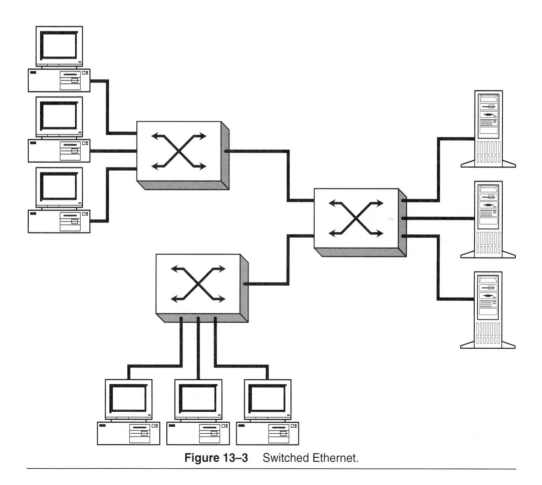

Figure 13–3 Switched Ethernet.

WHAT NEXT: NO MORE COLLISIONS?

The bit budget of Ethernet is no longer applicable, since full-duplex Ethernet eliminates collisions. In theory, LANs could be built that would span the globe. However, in practice, attenuation becomes the limiting factor.

Twisted Pair Cabling

As previously mentioned, the physical limitation on twisted pair cabling is attenuation versus transceiver power. There are currently no *high*-power twisted pair transceivers on the market. The IEEE limit of 100 m is applicable even to twisted pair cabling operating in full-duplex mode.

Some cable manufacturers have developed low attenuation twisted pair cables, which they claim allow longer-distance twisted pair link segments (sometimes up to 160 m). There is no guarantee, apart from what is offered by the manufacturer, that Ethernet will operate correctly on these cables. Treat these enhanced twisted pair cables with caution, as they do not represent Ethernet standards, but more proprietary-specific improvements.

Fiber Optic Transmitters

The performance of fiber optic transmitters is a totally different story to that of twisted pair transceivers. There are a wide variety of fiber optic transmitters available on the market that are suitable for manufacturers of Ethernet equipment. The differentiating factor between the transmitters is the wavelength of operation and the transmit power.

Using fiber optics in a full-duplex environment now becomes a matter of fiber transmitter power versus cable attenuation—sometimes called *cable loss budget*. Distance becomes irrelevant. The 2 Km *limit* imposed on 10 Mbps Ethernet can be disregarded. Your limitation now is your optical performance versus cable loss.

From this point forward, all data transmitted over the fiber link is considered to be full duplex. Please bear this in mind. It cannot be overemphasized that in a half-duplex environment, the IEEE limits on fiber optic cabling are still applicable.

UNDERSTANDING HOW LOSS IS MEASURED: FIBER ATTENUATION/CONNECTOR ISSUES

The attenuation measurement will vary depending upon which cable and what wavelength is in use, since there are two distinct types of fiber cable, and two commonly used wavelengths. The attenuation of a fiber cable is measured in decibels (dB) and is either quoted as attenuation in dB per Km, or an attenuation chart is produced giving the attenuation for the entire fiber run.

The decibel scale is logarithmic; therefore, a 1dB difference represents a factor of 10.

In order to give the user an idea as to loss versus distance, refer to Table 13–3, which shows dB/Km loss for multimode and single-mode fiber at various wavelengths [1]. Table 13–3 is reproduced from the Telecommunications Industry Association/Electronic Industries Association standard 568A (commonly known as TIA/EIA-568A). The loss figures shown in the table are worst case (they are the minimum acceptable loss figures).

Table 13–3   TIA/EIA Worst Case

	Wavelength	Max Attenuation (dB/Km)
Multimode	850	3.75
Multimode	1300	1.5
Single-mode	1300	0.5

Fusion Splice Losses/Termination

Other components add to the total loss of the fiber, in addition to the attenuation of the cable. Specifically, this refers to fiber termination and fusion splices.

Fiber Termination

Fiber termination (the connectors fitted to the fiber) loss will occur from two areas: the connectors themselves and the quality of alignment and polishing of the termination. See Figures 13–4 and 13–5 [1].

Figure 13–4
View of "clean" termination.

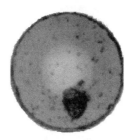

Figure 13–5
View of "dirty" termination.

Fusion Splices

Often a fiber cable will not be contiguous. Splices may be used to create the total fiber run. Loss will occur from these splices.

No *hard and fast* figures can be produced for the loss created by termination and fusion splice. Most installers estimate a loss per termination of between 0.5 to 2.0 dB. A splice can result in a loss of 0.3 to 1 dB. How good or bad the loss is depends on the connectors used and the skill of the installer performing the fusion splice/termination.

The figures quoted in Table 13–3 for cable attenuation and termination/splice loss are intended as a guide only. It is strongly recommended that the cable installer/provider be contacted before any estimates are made as to the total link attenuation figure. Performance may vary. For example, the TIA/EIA state that the maximum acceptable attenuation at 850 nm for multimode cable is 3.75 dB/Km. The cable you use may well have a lower loss. Multimode cables with a quoted attenuation of approximately 2.8 dB/Km are not uncommon.

INHERENT LOSS FACTORS: SCATTERING AND ABSORPTION

The attenuation of the optical fiber is a result of two factors: absorption and scattering. The absorption is caused by the absorption of the light and conversion to heat by molecules in the glass. Primary absorbers are residual OH+ and dopants used to modify the refractive index of the glass. This absorption occurs at discrete wavelengths, determined by the elements absorbing the light. The OH+ absorption is predominant, and occurs most strongly around 1,000 nm, 1,400 nm, and above 1,600 nm.

The largest cause of attenuation is scattering. Scattering occurs when light collides with individual atoms in the glass and is anisotrophic. Light that is scattered at angles outside the numerical aperture of the fiber will be absorbed into the cladding or transmitted back toward the source. Scattering is also a function of wavelength, proportional to the inverse fourth power of the wavelength of the light. Thus, if you double the wavelength of the light, you reduce the scattering losses by 24 or 16 times. Therefore, for long-distance transmission, it is advantageous to use the longest practical wavelength for minimal attenuation and maximum distance between repeaters. Together, absorption and scattering produce the attenuation curve for a typical glass optical fiber.

Fiber optic systems transmit in the *windows* created between the absorption bands at 850 nm, 1,300 nm, and 1,550 nm, where physics also allows one to fabricate lasers and detectors easily. Plastic fiber has a more limited wavelength band that limits practical use to 660 nm LED sources.

Testing Fiber Attenuation

An alternative method of testing fiber, which may be easier in field measurements, involves attaching a fiber pigtail to the source that has a connector on one end and a temporary splice on the other end—similar to the loss measurement of terminated cables. This method introduces more uncertainty in the measurement, because of the loss of the splice coupled to the fiber under test and since it may not be easy to accurately calibrate the output power of the pigtail. The best method is to use a bare fiber adapter on the power meter to measure the output of the bare fiber, then attach the splice. Alternately, have the splice attached on the pigtail, and couple a large core fiber to the pigtail with the splice, and then measure the power. The large core fiber will minimize losses in the splice for accurate calibration.

Sources for Loss Measurements

On the test source, two factors must be controlled to minimize measurement uncertainty: the spectral output and modal characteristics. The spectral output characteristics includes wavelength, as seen in the spectral attenuation curve, but may also include the spectral width. A wide spectral width source suffers absorption over a larger range of wavelengths, making it more difficult to obtain precise data on spectral attenuation at any specific wavelength. Monochromators are used as sources for spectral loss testing, since the spectral width of the source can be controlled exactly.

For single wavelength measurements, the source can be a fixed wavelength light-emitting diode (LED) or laser. Generally, attenuation measurements will be made with a source appropriate to the fiber. Most multimode fiber systems use LED sources while single-mode fiber systems use laser sources. Thus, testing each of these fibers should be done with the appropriate source. Lasers should not be used with multimode fiber, since coherent sources like lasers have high measurement uncertainties in multimode fiber caused by modal noise. The wide spectral width of LEDs sometimes overlap the single-mode fiber cutoff wavelength (the lowest wavelength where the fiber supports only one mode) at lower wavelengths and the 1,400 nm OH absorption band at the upper wavelengths.

LED is a semiconductor that emits incoherent light when forward biased.

The additional absorption at either end of the LEDs spectral output may bias the measurements of attenuation on single-mode fiber substantially. Tests from Bellcore showed the effects of sources on measurements of single-mode fiber loss [2]. The LED spectrum covers from the single-mode cutoff wavelength around 1,200 nm—well into the OH absorption band, while the laser concentrates all its power in an extremely narrow spectral band where the fiber is actually used. Over the range covered by the LED output, the fiber loss varies by 0.2 dB/km, ignoring the OH absorption band. Bellcore tests showed an error of loss caused by the use of the LED of 0.034dB/km [2].

Even with laser sources, the loss varies substantially according to the wavelength of the source. Again Bellcore tests showed a variation of loss of 0.05 dB/km, with source variations of 29 nm (1,276 and 1,305 nm), within the range of typical sources used in the network [2]. Testing, based on these results, should be done with sources as close to the system wavelength as possible, especially with longer links.

So far, we have only discussed testing attenuation by transmission of light from a source, but one can also imply fiber losses by backscattered light from a source using an optical time domain reflectometer (OTDR).

USING A LOSS TEST SET: TRANSMISSION VERSUS OTDR TESTS

OTDRs are widely used for testing fiber optic cables. Among the common uses are measuring the length of fibers, finding faults in fibers, breaks in cables, attenuation of fibers, and losses in splices and connectors. They are also used to optimize splices by monitoring splice loss. One of their biggest advantages is they produce a picture (called a trace) of the cable being tested. Although OTDRs are unquestionably useful for all these tasks, they have error mechanisms that are potentially large, troublesome, and not widely understood.

To understand how the OTDR allows measurement, consider what happens to the light pulse it transmits. As it goes down the fiber, the pulse actually *fills* the core of the fiber with light for a distance equal to the pulse width transmitted by the OTDR. In a typical fiber, each nanosecond of pulse width equals about 8 inches (200 mm). Throughout that pulse, light is being scattered. The longer the pulse width in time, the greater the pulse length in the fiber and the greater will be the amount of backscattered light in direct proportion to the pulse width. The intensity of the pulse is diminished by the attenuation of the fiber as it proceeds down the fiber. A portion of the pulse's power is scattered back to the OTDR, and it is again diminished by the attenuation of the fiber as it returns up the fiber to the OTDR. Thus, the intensity of the signal seen by the OTDR at any point in time is a function of the position of the light pulse in the fiber.

By looking at the reduction in returned signal over time, one can calculate the attenuation coefficient of the fiber being tested. Since the pulse travels out and back, the attenuation of the fiber diminishes the signal in both directions, and the transit time from pulse out to return is twice the one-way travel time. Both the intensity and distance scales must be divided by two to allow for the round-trip path of the light.

If the fiber has a splice or connector, the signal will be diminished as the pulse passes it. The OTDR sees a reduction in power, indicating the light loss of the joined fibers. If the splice or connector reflects light (see optical return loss), the OTDR will show the reflection as a spike above the backscattered signal. The OTDR can be calibrated to use this spike to measure optical return loss.

The end of the fiber will show as a deterioration of the backscatter signal into noise, if it is within the dynamic range of the OTDR. If the end of the fiber is cleaved or polished, one will also see a spike above the backscatter trace. This allows one to measure the total length of the fiber being tested.

In order to enhance the signal to noise ratio of the received signal, the OTDR sends out many pulses and averages the returned signals. And, to get to longer distances, the power in the transmitted pulse is increased by widening the pulse width. The longer pulse width fills a longer distance in the fiber, as has been noted previously. This longer pulse width masks all details within the length of the pulse, increasing the minimum distance between features resolvable with the OTDR.

OTDR Measurement Uncertainties

With the OTDR, one can measure loss and distance. To use them effectively, it is necessary to understand their measurement limitations. The OTDR's distance resolution is limited by the transmitted pulse width. As the OTDR sends out its pulse, cross talk in the coupler inside the instrument and reflections from the first connector will saturate the receiver. The receiver will take some time to recover, causing a nonlinearity in the baseline of the display. It may take 100–1,000 meters before the receiver recovers. It is common to use a long fiber cable called a pulse suppressor between the OTDR and the cables being tested to allow the receiver to recover completely.

The OTDR also is limited in its ability to resolve two closely spaced features by the pulse width. Long distance OTDRs may have a minimum resolution of 250 to 500 meters, while short-range OTDRs can resolve features 5–10 meters apart. This limitation makes it difficult to find problems inside a building, where distances are short. A visual fault locator is generally used to assist the OTDR in this situation.

When measuring distance, the OTDR has two major sources of error not associated with the instrument itself: the velocity of the light pulse in the fiber and the amount of fiber in the cable. The velocity of the pulse down the fiber is a function of the average index of refraction of the glass. While this is fairly constant for most fiber types, it can vary by a few percent. When making cable, it is necessary to have some excess fiber in the cable to allow the cable to stretch when pulled without stressing the fiber. This excess fiber is usually 1–2 percent. Since the OTDR measures the length of the fiber, not the cable, it is necessary to subtract 1–2 percent from the measured length to get the likely cable length. This is very important if one is using the OTDR to find a fault in an installed cable, to keep from looking too far away from the OTDR to find the problem. This variable adds up to approximately between 10–20 meters per kilometer, therefore it is not ignorable (negligible).

When making loss measurements, two major questions arise with OTDR measurement anomalies: why OTDR measurements differ from an optical loss test set, which tests the fiber in the same configuration in which it is used, and why measurements from OTDRs vary so much when measured in opposite directions on the same splice. Also, why one direction sometimes shows a *gain*, not a loss.

In order to understand the problem, it is necessary to consider again how OTDRs work. They send a powerful laser pulse down the fiber, which suffers attenuation as it proceeds. At every point on the fiber, part of the light is scattered back up the fiber. The backscattered light is then attenuated by the fiber again, until it returns to the OTDR and is measured.

Three factors affect the measured signal: attenuation outbound, scattering, and attenuation inbound.

It is commonly assumed that the backscatter coefficient is a constant, and therefore the OTDR can be calibrated to read attenuation. The backscatter coefficient is, in fact, a function of the core diameter of the fiber (or mode field diameter in single-mode fiber) and the material composition of the fiber (which determines attenuation). Thus, a fiber with either higher attenuation or larger core size will produce a larger backscatter signal.

Accurate OTDR attenuation measurements depend on having a constant backscatter coefficient. Unfortunately, this is often not the case. Fibers that have tapers in core size are common, or variations in diameter are a result of variations in pulling speed as the fiber is being made. A small change in diameter (1 percent) causes a larger change in a cross-sectional area that directly affects the scattering coefficient and can cause a large change in attenuation (on the order of 0.1 dB). Thus, fiber attenuation measured by OTDRs may be nonlinear along the fiber and produce significantly different losses in opposite directions.

The first indication of OTDR problems for most users occurs when looking at a splice, and a *gain* is seen at the splice. Common sense tells us that passive fibers and splices cannot create light, so another phenomenon must be at work. In fact, a *gainer* is an indication of the difference of backscatter coefficients in the two fibers being spliced.

If an OTDR is used to measure the loss of a splice and the two fibers are identical, the loss will be correct, since the scattering coefficient is the same for both fibers. This is exactly what you see when breaking and splicing the same fiber—the normal way OTDRs are demonstrated.

If the receiving fiber has a lower backscatter coefficient than the fiber before the splice, the amount of light sent back to the OTDR will decrease after the splice. This causes the OTDR to indicate a larger splice loss than actual.

If one looks at this splice in the opposite direction, the effect will be reversed. The amount of backscattered light will be larger after the splice, and the loss shown on the OTDR will be less than the actual splice loss. If this increase is larger than the loss in the splice, the OTDR will show a gain at the splice, an obvious error. As many as one-third of all splices will show a gain in one direction.

The usual recommendation is to test with the OTDR in both directions and average the reading—which has been shown to give measurements accurate to about 0.01 dB. But this negates the most useful feature of the OTDR, the ability to work from only one end of the fiber. There is a way of predicting this phenomenon and compensating for its effects, but it is of limited accuracy.

Since the backscatter coefficient is a function of both material and mode field diameter, there is a correlation between these factors and the difference in splice loss measured in both directions. If the receiving fiber is higher loss, the splice loss is likely to be measured as less than actual. And if the mode field diameter is larger in the receiving fiber, the splice loss will also be measured less than actual.

The difference in measurements of splice loss taken in each direction is approximately 0.5 dB for every 0.1 dB/km difference in fiber attenuation coefficient. Thus, if the receiving fiber has an attenuation of 0.1 dB/km more than the transmitting fiber at the splice, the measured splice loss will be 0.25 dB less than the average from both directions. Since one can measure both fibers' attenuation coefficients on the OTDR at the same time the splice loss is measured, the attenuation difference can be used to provide feedback on the likely error in the measured splice loss.

Mode field diameter also has an effect on this approximation, and could lead to an uncertainty of another 0.25 dB in the correction. Since the mode field diameter (MFD) of each fiber at the splice point will likely not be known, the usefulness of this approximation is not very high.

Therefore, one may be able to identify situations where OTDR loss data may be unreliable, but predicting the potential error may be difficult. The only way to positively test end to end loss is with a loss test set, which should be done on every fiber link.

OPTICAL POWER VERSUS ATTENUATION: OPTICAL TRANSMITTERS

All fiber optic LAN devices have two connectors: a receive component and a transmitter component. The transmitter component is the key to whether or not a fiber optic LAN device can or cannot use the fiber cable.

All transmitters have a specific power output. As with the cabling, this output is measured in dB. The manufacturers' specification as to the components' power output is not a good figure, as the transmitter is part of an electrical circuit. The power output of the transmitter is only accurate if it is measured as a functioning part of the device. Some power will be lost due to electrical interference generated within the circuitry.

Putting It Together: Budgeting the Loss

Establishing if a fiber cable can be used is relatively simple (see Sidebar, "Power Budget is Greater than Attenuation"). If you know the power output of your transmitter and the loss budget on the fiber cable, deciding whether or not a fiber cable can be used is simply a matter of comparing the two figures. If the power output of the transmitter is greater than the loss budget of the fiber cable, the cable is useable. If the reverse is true, the cable is not useable.

POWER BUDGET IS GREATER THAN ATTENUATION

The fact that power budget is greater than attenuation is dependent on two facts:

1. You know the loss budget (attenuation) of the entire fiber link. This can be summarized as follows:

   Total fiber link attenuation = loss from cable + loss from connectors/patch cables + loss from fusion splices. A reputable cable installer will provide attenuation measurements for the fiber link he or she has installed. It is simply a matter of comparing this figure versus the power budget of the optical transmitter.

2. You know the power budget of the transmitter. Very few manufacturers provide this information.

   You also need to compare the average power budget versus fiber link loss (total attenuation of the fiber link). Some manufacturers quote peak power, which is not a valid figure, as most transmitters cannot operate permanently at peak power.

Please note the attenuation differences at 850 nm versus 1300 nm, as shown in Table 13–4 [1]. Measurements at 1300 nm are always lower than those made at 850 nm. This is a critical difference. Ensure that you are comparing *apples to apples* by using the attenuation figure from the correct wavelength [1].

Table 13–4 Sample Attenuation Chart

	a-b				*a-b*		
	850 nm				1,300 nm		
	a (dB)				a (dB)		
m1	m2	m3	Ave	m1	m2	m3	Ave
7.4	7.3	7.6	7.4	2.3	2.8	2.7	2.6

Let's now look at bandwidth capacity and modal distribution. In other words, in order to test multimode fiber optic cables accurately and reproducibly, it is necessary to understand modal distribution, mode control, and attenuation correction factors. Modal distribution in multimode fiber is very important to measurement reproducibility and accuracy. For further detailed information on OTDR, see Chapter 17, "OTDR: Optical Time Domain Reflectometer."

BANDWIDTH: THE CAPACITY FOR INFORMATION

In multimode fibers, some light rays travel straight down the axis of the fiber, while all the others wiggle or bounce back and forth inside the core. In step index fiber, the off-axis rays, called *higher order modes,* bounce back and forth from core/cladding boundaries as they are transmitted down the fiber. Since these higher order modes travel a longer distance than the axial ray, they are responsible for the dispersion that limits the fiber's bandwidth.

In graded index fiber, the reduction of the index of refraction of the core as one approaches the cladding causes the higher order modes to follow a curved path that is longer than the axial ray (the *zero order mode*), but by virtue of the lower index of refraction away from the axis, light speeds up as it approaches the cladding and it takes approximately the same time to travel through the fiber. Thus, the *dispersion* or variations in transit time for various modes is minimized and bandwidth of the fiber is maximized.

However, the fact that the higher order modes travel farther in the glass core means that they have a greater likelihood of being scattered and/or absorbed—the two primary causes of attenuation in optical fibers. Therefore, the higher order modes will have greater attenuation than lower order modes, and a long length of fiber that was fully filled (all modes had the same power level launched into them) will have a lower amount of power in the higher order modes than will a short length of the same fiber.

This change in *modal distribution* between long and short fibers can be described as a *transient loss*, and can make big differences in the measurements one makes with the fiber. It not only changes the modal distribution, it changes the effective core diameter and numerical aperture also.

The term *equilibrium modal distribution* (EMD) is used to describe the modal distribution in a long fiber that has lost the higher order modes. A *long* fiber is one in EMD, while a *short* fiber has all its initially launched higher order modes.

What Does System Modal Distribution Look Like?

System modal distribution depends on your source, fiber, and the intermediate *components* such as connectors, couplers, and switches. All these affect the modal distribution of fibers they connect.

In the laboratory, a critical optical system is used to fully fill the fiber modes and a *mode filter* (usually a mandrel wrap, which stresses the fiber and increases loss for the higher order modes) is used to simulate EMD conditions. A *mode scrambler* is made by fusion splicing a step index fiber in the graded index fiber near the source. It can also be used to fill all modes equally.

In a system, such controlled conditions obviously do not exist. In fact, some work presented by Corning [3] at a recent EIA Standards meeting shows how far the real world is from what we expected or anticipated it to be.

It has been accepted as *common knowledge* that microlens LEDs (as used with most multimode datacom systems) overfill fibers, and when we use them as test sources, we are testing with an overfilled launch. Not so. Tests on microlens LEDs indicate that they underfill compared to EMD. And edge-emitter LEDs, typical of the high-speed emitters at 1300 nm, concentrate their power even more into the lower order modes.

Other facts that come out of the Corning [3] project shows that connectors mix some power back into the higher order modes due to angular misalignment and switches strip out higher modes. In a simulated FDDI system using 8 fiber optic switches and 20 pairs of connectors (with fiber lengths of 10 to 50 meters between them), the majority of system power was concentrated in the lower order modes.

What conclusions can be drawn? The most significant conclusions is that it may not be prudent to design datacom and LAN systems on the worst-case loss specifications for connectors and switches. In actual operation, the simulated system exhibited almost 15 dB less loss than predicted from worst-case component specifications (obtained with fully filled launch conditions).

And when testing systems, using a LED source similar to the one used in the system and short launch cables may provide as accurate a measurement as is possible under more controlled circumstances, since the LED approximates the system source. Alternately, one may use a mode modifier or a universal launch cable (ULC) to establish consistent modal distributions appropriate for testing the cables.

Relative Modal Distribution of Multimode Fibers: Sources and Mode Modifiers

A fully filled fiber means that all modes carry equal power. A long length of fiber loses the higher order modes faster, leading to the gently sloping EMD curve. Mode filtering strips off the higher order modes, but provides only a crude approximation of EMD. The microlensed LED, often thought to over-fill the modes, actually couples most of its power in lower order modes. The edge-emitting LED (ELED) couples even more strongly in the lower order modes. Connectors are mode mixers, since misalignment losses cause some power in lower order modes to be coupled up to higher order modes.

The Effect on Measurements

If you measure the attenuation of a long fiber in EMD (or any fiber with EMD-simulated launch conditions) and compare it to a normal fiber with *overfill launch conditions* (that is, the source fills all the modes equally), you will find the difference is about 1 dB/km. This figure is the *transient loss*. Thus, the EMD fiber measurement gives an attenuation that is 1 dB per Km less than the overfill conditions.

Fiber manufacturers use the EMD type of measurement for fiber because it is more reproducible and is representative of the losses to be expected in long lengths of fiber. But with connectors, the EMD measurement can give overly optimistic results, since it effectively represents a situation where one launches from a smaller diameter fiber of lower numerical aperture (NA) than the receive fiber—an ideal situation for low connector loss.

The difference in connector loss caused by modal launch conditions can be dramatic. Using the same pair of biconic or SMA connectors, it is possible to measure 0.6 to 0.9 dB with a fully filled launch and 0.3 to 0.4 dB with a

EMD-simulated launch. Which is a valid number to use for this connector pair's loss?

That depends on the application. If you are connecting two fibers near an LED source, the higher value may be more representative, since the launch cable is so short. But if you are connecting to a cable one kilometer away, the lower value may be more valid.

Modes

There are three basic *gadgets* to condition the modal distribution in multimode fibers: mode strippers which remove unwanted cladding mode light; mode scramblers which mix modes to equalize power in all the modes; and, mode filters which remove the higher order modes to simulate EMD or steady state conditions.

Cladding Mode Strippers

Cladding mode strippers are used to remove any light being propagated in the cladding to ensure that measurements include only the effects of the core. Most American fibers are *self-stripping*. The buffer is chosen to have an index of refraction that will promote the leakage of light from the cladding to the buffer. If you are using at least 1 meter of fiber, cladding modes will probably not be a factor in measurements. One can easily tell if cladding modes are a factor. Start with 10 meters of fiber coupled to a source and measure the power transmitted through it. Cut back to 5 meters and then 4, 3, 2, and 1 meter, measuring the power at every cutback. The loss in the fiber core is very small in 10 meters, about 0.03–0.06 dB. But if the power measured increases rapidly, the additional light measured is cladding light, which has a very high attenuation. At this point, a cladding mode stripper is recommended for accurate measurements if short lengths of fiber must be used.

To make a cladding mode stripper, strip off the fiber's buffer for 2 to 3 inches (50 to 75 mm) and immerse the fiber in a substance of equal or higher index of refraction than the cladding. This can be done by immersing the fiber in alcohol or mineral oil in a beaker, or by threading the fiber through a common soda straw and filling the straw with index-matching epoxy or an optical gel.

Note Stripping the buffer away from the end of a fiber is easily done using a chemical stripper. If the fiber cannot be chemically stripped, like those with Teflon buffers, check with the fiber manufacturer for instructions.

Do not stress the fiber after the mode stripper, as this will reintroduce cladding modes, negating the effects of the mode stripper. Mode stripping should be done last if mode scrambling and filtering are also done on a fiber under test.

Mode Scramblers

Mode scrambling is an attempt to equalize the power in all modes, simulating a fully filled launch. This should not be confused with a mode filter, which simulates the modal distribution of a fiber in equilibrium modal distribution (EMD). However, both may be used together sometimes to properly simulate test conditions. Mode scramblers are easily made by fusion (or mechanical) splicing a short piece of step index fiber in between two pieces of graded index fiber being tested. One can also use methods that produce small perturbations on the fiber, such as running the fiber through a tube of lead shot. But these scramblers are difficult to fabricate and calibrate accurately. In the laboratory, they are usually unnecessary, since accurate launch optics are used to produce fully filled launch conditions.

Mode Filters

Mode filters are used to selectively remove higher order modes to attempt to simulate EMD conditions, assuming that one starts with fully filled modes. Higher order modes are easily removed by stressing the fiber in a controlled manner, since the higher order modes are more susceptible to bending losses.

The most popular mode filter is the *mandrel wrap*, where the fiber is snugly wrapped around a mandrel several times. The size of the mandrel and the number of turns will determine the effect on the higher order modes. Other mode filters can be made where the fiber is subjected to a series of gentle S bends, either in a form or by wrapping around pins in a plate or by actually using a long length of fiber attached to an overfilling source.

When Do You Use Modes?

If you are working in a laboratory measuring fiber attenuation using a lamp source and monochrometer, you probably need a combination of all of the preceding modes. If you are using an LED or laser source, you might not need any of them, since they greatly underfill the higher order modes. LEDs and lasers also are the same mode fill as actual system sources, providing a proper simulation of actual operating conditions without mode modifiers of any kind.

Testing SM Fiber

Testing single-mode fiber is easy compared to multimode fiber. Single-mode fiber, as the name says, only supports one mode of transmission for wavelengths greater than the cutoff wavelength of the fiber. Thus, most problems associated with mode power distribution are no longer a factor. However, it takes a short distance for single-mode fiber to really be single mode, since several modes may be supported for a short distance after connectors, splices, or sources. Single-mode fibers shorter than 10 m may have several modes. To ensure short cables have only one mode of propagation, one can use a simple mode filter made from a 4–6 inch loop of the cable.

Bending Losses

Fiber and cable are subject to additional losses as a result of stress. In fact, fiber makes a very good stress sensor. However, this is an additional source of uncertainty when making attenuation measurements. It is mandatory to minimize stress and/or stress changes on the fiber when making measurements. If the fiber or cable is spooled, it will have higher loss when spooled tightly. It may be advisable to unspool it and respool with less tension. Unspooled fiber should be carefully placed on a bench and taped down to prevent movement. Above all, be careful about how connectorized fiber is placed. Dangling fibers that stress the back of the connector will have significant losses.

Bandwidth Testing: Dispersion

Fiber's information transmission capacity is limited by two separate components of dispersion: modal and chromatic. Modal dispersion occurs in step index multimode fiber where the paths of different modes are of varying lengths. Modal dispersion also comes from the fact that the index profile of graded index (GI) multimode fiber isn't perfect. The graded index profile was chosen to theoretically allow all modes to have the same group velocity or transit speed along the length of the fiber. By making the outer parts of the core a lower index of refraction than the inner parts of the core, the higher order modes speed up as they go away from the center of the core, compensating for their longer path lengths.

In an idealized graded index fiber, all modes have the same group velocity and no modal dispersion occurs. But in real fibers, the index profile is a piecewise approximation and all modes are not perfectly transmitted—thus allowing some modal dispersion. Since the higher order modes have greater deviations, the modal dispersion of a fiber (and therefore its laser bandwidth) tends to be very sensitive to modal conditions in the fiber. Thus, the bandwidth of longer fibers degrades nonlinearly as the higher order modes are attenuated more strongly.

The second factor in fiber bandwidth is chromatic dispersion. Remember a prism spreads out the spectrum of incident light since the light travels at different speeds according to its color and is therefore refracted at different angles. The usual way of stating this is the index of refraction of the glass is wavelength dependent. Thus, a carefully manufactured graded index multimode fiber can only be optimized for a single wavelength, usually near 1,300 nm, and light of other colors will suffer from chromatic dispersion. Even light in the same mode will be dispersed if it is of different wavelengths.

Chromatic dispersion is a bigger problem with LEDs, which have broad spectral outputs, unlike lasers, which concentrate most of their light in a narrow spectral range. Chromatic dispersion occurs with LEDs because much of the power is away from the zero dispersion wavelength of the fiber. High-speed systems like FDDI, based on broad output surface emitter LEDs, suffer such intense chromatic dispersion that transmission over only 2 km of 62.5/125 fiber can be risky.

Testing Bandwidth: When Bandwidth is an Issue

Modal dispersion is the most commonly tested bandwidth factor. Testing is done by using a narrow spectral width laser source and high-speed receiver to determine dynamic characteristics. Testing can be done by sweeping frequency of a sine wave and looking for attenuation in the pulse peak height, which leads to a specification of bandwidth at the 3 dB loss point (pulse height is 0.5 the value at low frequency). The alternate method is to measure degradation of pulse risetime.

Chromatic dispersion requires comparing pulse transit times or phase shift as a function of wavelength. Thus, sources of several wavelengths are used and variations in time allows calculation dispersion as a function of wavelength. Although it seems that this could be done with a broad spectral width source like an LED, the removal of the effects of the spectral characteristics of the LED is very complicated mathematically and every LED is unique in its spectral characteristics, making calibration of test equipment very difficult.

Since all this test equipment must work in the GHz range, it is very expensive. Fortunately, fiber bandwidth characteristics have been very well-modeled and the characteristics calculated with precision comparable to actual measurements. There have been at least two models described in detail and one available commercially. The one available commercially (Fotec's *Cable Characterizer* [2]) calculates bandwidth for multimode fibers based on inputs of fiber modal bandwidth and length and source wavelength and spectral width. By using the models, one can easily determine if the installed fiber is adequate for higher speed networks like FDDI; help designers design networks with adequate bandwidth for high-speed networks without spending too much on overspecified fiber; and provide a way for the installer or end user to certify cable plants for FDDI and other high-speed networks.

PHYSICAL SIZES OF FIBER

Although it is common to compare the typical connectors quoted by manufacturers, it may not be a fair comparison. The manufacturer has a design that they have qualified by expertly assembling and testing many samples of their connectors. But the actual loss obtained by any end user will be primarily determined by their skill at the termination process. The manufacturer only has control over the basic design of the connector, the mechanical precision in manufacturing, and the clearness of the termination instructions.

End gaps cause two problems: insertion loss and return loss. The emerging cone of light from the connector will spill over the core of the receiving fiber and be lost. In addition, the air gap between the fibers causes a reflection when the light encounters the change in refractive index from the glass fiber to the air in the gap. This reflection (called fresnel reflection) amounts to about 5 percent in typical flat polished connectors, and means that no connector with an air gap can have less than 0.3 dB loss. This reflection is also referred to as back reflection or optical return loss, which can be a problem in laser-based systems. Connectors use a number of polishing techniques to ensure physical contact of the fiber ends to minimize back reflection. On mechanical splices, it is possible to reduce back reflection by using nonperpendicular cleaves, which cause back reflections to be absorbed in the cladding of the fiber.

The end finish of the fiber must be properly polished to minimize loss. A rough surface will scatter light and dirt can scatter and absorb light. Since the optical fiber is so small, typical airborne dirt can be a major source of loss. Whenever connectors are not terminated, they should be covered to protect the end of the ferrule from dirt. One should never touch the end of the ferrule, since the oils on one's skin causes the fiber to attract dirt. Before connection and testing, it is advisable to clean connectors with lint-free wipes moistened with isopropyl alcohol.

Two sources of loss are directional: numerical aperture (NA) and core diameter. Differences in these two will create connections that have different losses depending on the direction of light propagation. Light from a fiber with a larger NA will be more sensitive to angularity and end gap, so transmission from a fiber of larger NA to one of smaller NA will be higher loss than the reverse. Likewise, light from a larger fiber will have high loss coupled to a fiber of smaller diameter, while one can couple a small diameter fiber to a large diameter fiber with minimal loss, since it is much less sensitive to end gap or lateral offset. See Sidebar, "Numerical Aperture," for further information on NA.

NUMERICAL APERTURE

Figure 13–6 depicts a section of clad cylindrical fiber and shows the core with refractive index N_1 and the clad with index N_2 [5]. Also shown is a light ray entering the end of the fiber at angle (A)—reflecting from the interface down the fiber. However, if angle A becomes too great, the light will not reflect at the interface, but will go out the side of the fiber and be lost. This angle, beyond which light cannot be carried in a fiber, is called the *critical angle* and may be calculated from the two indices of refraction. The sine of the critical angle is called the numerical aperture and is abbreviated as NA.

For example, taking 1.62 for N_1 and 1.52 for N_2 (a common glass combination), the NA is found to be .56, which corresponds to a critical angle of 34 degrees. As the fiber accepts light up to 34 degrees off the axis in any direction, we can define the *acceptance angle* of the fiber as twice the critical angle or, in this case, 68 degrees. The F/ number equivalent of the NA is calculated as follows [4]:

```
              1
f# = -------- Example: NA .56 = f/0.89
            2 NA
```

The numerical aperture is an important parameter of any optical fiber, but one that is frequently misunderstood and overemphasized. In Figure 13–6, notice that angle A is shown at both the entrance and exit ends of the fiber [4]. This is because the fiber tends to preserve the angle of incidence during propagation of the light, causing it to exit the fiber at the same angle it entered. Now look at Figure 13–7, which is a drawing of a typical light guide being illuminated by a projector-type lamp [4].

Angle A (29 degrees) is the acceptance angle of an NA .25 fiber, angle B (45 degrees) is the incident angle from the bulb, and angle C (83 degrees) is the acceptance angle of an NA .66 fiber. Calculating the minimum NA for the 45-degree angle (B) of incidence yields .38. Therefore, the NA .66 fiber will accept all of the light from the bulb, but the output cone at the other end will be 45 degrees, not the 83 degrees that you might expect. Conversely, the NA .25 fiber is not capable of accepting all the light from the bulb, and will have an output cone of 29 degrees. Many people believe that using a low NA fiber will *focus* the light from a source. This is not true. As you see, a low NA fiber has a narrow output cone because it won't accept any light beyond the critical angle.

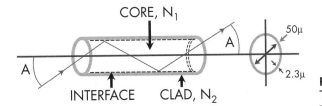

Figure 13–6
Typical 50μ (.002) fiber.

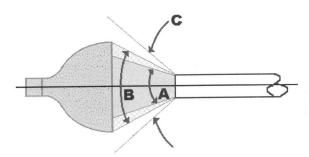

Figure 13–7   A typical light guide being illuminated by
a projector-type lamp.

If you are connecting fiber directly to a source, the variation in power will be approximately the same as for fiber mismatch. The exception would be that if you replaced the smaller fiber with a larger fiber, it will result in a gain in power roughly equal to the loss in power in coupling from the larger fiber to the smaller one.

Whenever you're using a different (and often unspecified) fiber with a system, be aware of differences in fiber bandwidths. A system may work on paper, with enough power available, but the fiber could have insufficient bandwidth.

Dealing with Manufacturing Tolerances: Choosing a Launch Cable for Testing

The quality (tolerances) of the launch cable will affect measurements of loss in cable assemblies tested against it. Good connectors with proper polish are needed, but can measurements be improved by specifying tight specifications on the fiber and connectors? If the fiber is closer to nominal specifications and the connector ferrule is tightly toleranced, one should expect more repeatable measurements.

It seemed obvious to the committee specifying the cable plant for FDDI in the mid-1980s that one could get more precise data on cable plant loss and power coupled into the cable by a transmitter by specifying a precision cable assembly. See Chapter 15, "Designing Cable Plants," for more information.

In a series of tests performed on a large sample of cables, it was shown that the tightness of fiber and connector tolerances had little effect on the variability of the cables when intermated. In fact, the least variability came from a set of cables manufactured using off-the-shelf components, but with a cable design that had a much stiffer jacket than the other cables, which reduced the bending loss changes at the backshell of the connector.

It seems that the large number of factors involved in mating losses makes controlling these tolerances impossible. Therefore, it is recommended that launch cables be chosen for low loss, but not specified with tighter tolerances in the fiber or connector characteristics. It is probably much more important to carefully handle the test cables and inspect the end surfaces of the ferrules for dirt and scratches regularly.

Let's now look at some fiber optic installation examples. Even though fiber optic installation will be covered in much greater detail in Part V, *Installing the Cabling Systems*, it is more than appropriate to touch on the topic now, especially during discussions of loss budgets and attenuation.

INSTALLATION EXAMPLES

Finally, this chapter cannot possibly end without a few good installation examples. In this regard, the following examples are covered:

- estimating attenuation
- connecting FDX Ethernet
- connecting HDX 10 Mbps Ethernet
- FDDI/ATM connection

Estimating Attenuation

The single biggest problem facing installers using fiber cable is loss budget. As previously mentioned, attenuation measurements for the fiber link in use should be available. However, in the real world (especially with multimode cabling), these measurements may not be available. The installer can use a *best guess* approach to try and establish the loss budget of the cable.

In Figure 13–8, two Fast Ethernet switches need to be connected via a single-mode fiber cable with a length of 6 Km [1]. The cable has been spliced twice and terminated/patched at either end. The switches only support 100Base-TX. Therefore, some sort of cable converter is needed (a TX to FX converter). And, since 100Base-FX is in use, all loss figures must be calculated at 1,300 nm, as shown in the following steps:

1. Use the previous TIA/EIA table (see Table 13–3) to establish the dB per Km loss for the fiber, dependent on the cable in use (multi- or single-mode fiber) and the wavelength being used.
2. Identify how many fusion splices have been inserted in the cable. Estimate 0.1 to 0.3 dB loss per fusion splice.
3. Add 1 to 2 dB to the final figure, to account for the terminations.
4. Add 0.2 to 0.5 dB to the figure derived at step 3 per patch cable in use. For example:
    a. Attenuation = cable loss + connectors/patch loss + fusion splice loss
    b. Attenuation = $(0.5 \times 6) + 2 + (0.5 \times 2) + (2 \times 0.3)$
    c. *Total fiber link attenuation = 6.6 dB* [1]

The 8 dB total link attenuation derived in the preceding equation is a worst-case scenario based on TIA/EIA information. It cannot be overstated

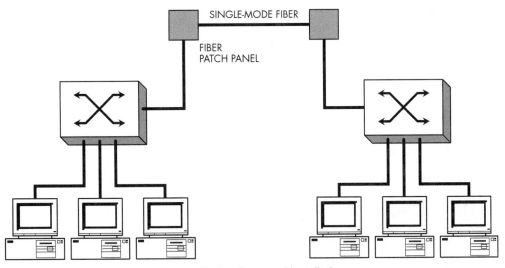

SINGLE-MODE FIBER

FIBER
PATCH PANEL

Figure 13–8   Proposed installation.

that the user must check with the cable supplier/installer to obtain the real figures for the fiber run to be installed/used.

FROM HERE

This chapter examined specifying fibers by covering loss and attenuation of fibers, bandwidth, the capacity for information, and physical sizes of fiber. The next chapter shows you how to use fiber optic transmitters and receivers by taking a close look at light sources and how to detect light with photodiodes.

NOTES

[1]   Brendan Mullooly, "Full Duplex Ethernet & Fiber Optic Cabling," IMC Networks, 19772 Pauling, Foothill Ranch, CA 92610, 2000.

[2]   Telcordia Technologies, Morris Corporate Center, Morristown, NJ, 2000.

[3]   Corning Incorporated, HP-ME-03-078, Pulteney Street, Corning, NY 14831, 2000.

[4]   "Numerical Aperature," Fiberoptics Technology, Inc., 12 Fiber Road, Pomfret, CT 06258, 2000.

Using Fiber Optic Transmitters and Receivers

No discussion about fiber optic transmitters and receivers is complete without mentioning the different types of light sources. There are many types of light sources: blackbody, incandescent, luminescent, and the sun. However, for fiber optics, there are only two: LEDs and LDs.

LIGHT SOURCES USED IN THE FIELD

There are two main light sources used in the field of fiber optics: light emitting diodes (LEDs) and laser diodes (LDs).

LEDs

An LED is a *p-n junction* diode in a transparent capsule, usually with a lens to let the light escape and to focus it (see Figure 14–1) [1]. LEDs can be manufactured to operate at 850 nm, 1,300 nm, or 1,500 nm. These wavelengths are all in the infrared region. LEDs have a typical response time of 8 ns, a linewidth of 40 nm, and an output power of tens of microwatts (see Figure 14–2) [1].

LIGHT OUTPUT

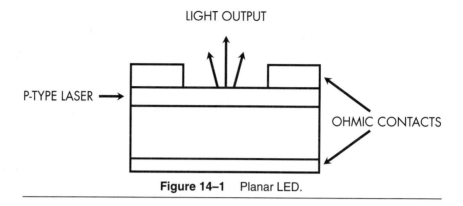

Figure 14–1   Planar LED.

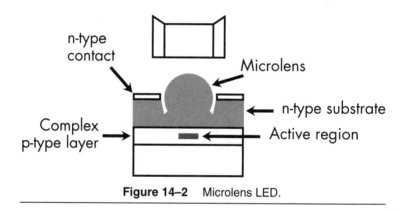

Figure 14–2   Microlens LED.

Laser Diodes

A laser diode is an LED with two important differences: First, the operating current is much higher in order to produce *optical gain*. Second, two of the ends of the LD are cleaved parallel to each other. These ends act as perfectly aligned mirrors that reflect the light back and forth through the *gain medium* in order to get as much amplification as possible (see Figure 14–3) [1].

The typical response time of a laser diode is 0.5 ns. The linewidth is around 2 nm with a typical laser power of 10 s of milliwatts. The wavelength of a laser diode can be 850 nm, 1,300 nm, or 1,500 nm.

With that in mind, let's take a look at another light source element: wavelength division multiplexing (WVD). What is WVD? Basically, it's a new technology that's opening up vast realms of capacity in the fibers that carry phone and Internet traffic all over the world. None too soon, either.

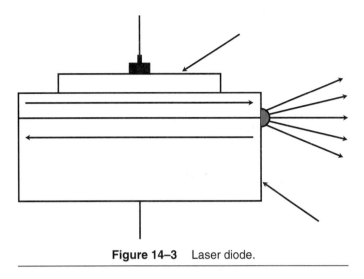

Figure 14–3   Laser diode.

Wavelength Division Multiplexing

Bandwidth in communications is like closet space in your home—you can never have enough. And Internet traffic is making the demand for communication capacity grow faster than the wardrobe of a teenager with a no-limit credit card. Bandwidth-hogging megabytes of animated graphics are replacing compact e-mail messages. Data, video, and voice signals crowd transmission systems that had ample space just a few years ago. The communications industry needs room to breathe.

That's exactly what a new generation of fiber-optic technology is bringing to networks such as the aptly named Project Oxygen [3]. By sending signals at 16 different wavelengths through each of four pairs of optical fibers, Project Oxygen will carry 640 gigabits per second (Gbit/s) across whole oceans. That's the equivalent of 10 million simultaneous telephone conversations—enough for every person in Hungary or Belgium to call the United States at the same time!

The technology that makes this new bandwidth possible is called wavelength division multiplexing, or WDM, and it represents the second major fiber-optic revolution in telecommunications. The first came during the 1980s, when telephone companies laced the United States and other countries with fibers to create a global backbone of information pipelines that could carry vastly more data than the copper wires and microwave links they replaced. WDM takes this advantage a giant step further—multiplying the potential capacity of each fiber by filling it with not just one but many wavelengths of light, each capable of carrying a separate signal.

Wavelength division multiplexing has emerged quite conveniently, as older fiber cables were getting filled. Taking advantage of WDM, long-distance carriers such as AT&T and MCI have been able to avoid laying expensive new cables; instead, they simply pump additional wavelengths through existing fibers.

The WDM revolution has arrived with unanticipated swiftness. A decade ago, people said there was a glut of fiber capacity. To allow room for expansion, phone companies had laid cables containing 24 to 36 fibers, many held in reserve as *dark fibers*. Each fiber carried hundreds of megabits per second at a single wavelength. Since then, carriers have raised data rates to 2.5 Gbit/s and lit most of the dark fibers. But the tremendous increase of traffic has crowded these cables that once seemed so voluminous. The closets, it seems, are rapidly being packed to the rafters—and stuff is spilling out onto the floor. Telephone usage accounts for some increase, including the spread of fax machines and mobile phones. But the most dramatic growth has been from Internet traffic (see Sidebar, "Using WDM for the Next-Generation Internet"), which roughly doubles each year.

USING WDM FOR THE NEXT-GENERATION INTERNET

This sidebar discusses the potential benefits of using a wavelength division multiplexing all-fiber optical network at the physical layer and fiber optical routing at the upper network layer for the next-generation Internet (NGI). The usefulness of a network grows with the number of interconnected nodes and with the flexibility that the network can provide among those nodes and to its end users. The rapid growth and wide acceptance of the Internet are indicators of its great success, but this success focuses an ever-intensifying spotlight on its limitations. Due to the strong impetus for developing NGI, which must be capable of delivering increasing amounts of data under strict delay constraints, single-channel networks will not be able to provide the necessary bandwidth; hence the need for multiple concurrent channels. One extremely promising approach is WDM, which takes advantage of the vast bandwidth of optical fiber, making it feasible to provide large numbers of optical channels in a single medium with full per-channel utilization of the electronic processing speeds available. The fiber optical routing technique proposed here provides effective full-mesh connectivity, relieves congestion, and reduces latency. In addition, this approach provides transparency, scalability, and modularity.

Background

In recent years, significant research has been conducted in all-fiber optical networking. A collaboration established in 1991 between Los Alamos National Laboratory (LANL) and IBM coupled LANL's HIPPI technology with IBM's all-optical Rainbow WDM Network. This collaboration led to the development of the Rainbow-2 All-Optical Gigabit Network, an optically multiplexed broadcast and select network that provided gigabit/sec network connections between host computers. The prototype Rainbow-2 network was successfully demonstrated at the SC '95 and OFC '96 conferences and was installed and evaluated in the Advanced Computing Laboratory Supercomputer Testbed at LANL. This effort identified the need for faster optical tuning for packet-switched networks, as well as wavelength routing for scalable circuit-switched next-generation networks. Recently, significant progress has been realized at LANL by showing a three-order of magnitude reduction in the tuning speeds of piezoelectrically-driven Fiber Fabry-Perot Tunable Filters (FFP-TFs) over typical commercially available FFP-TFs.

NGI Technology Thrust

The NGI infrastructure requires much higher bandwidth than is available on the Internet today, but it also needs to deal with the congestion issue. A thorough comparison and integration of the high capacity transmission techniques and higher layer protocols regarding the overall network functionality constitutes a very important target for this task. A major concern with the Internet (Internet protocol [IP]) today is congestion at the routers. To avoid *traffic jams* on IP, it is important to invest in higher-capacity networks, specifically fiber optical networks, including those capable of transparent optical switching (routing).

Congestion at the routers can result in overflow of buffers and data loss. In an optical network, congestion can be decreased by using a combination of IP layer and optical routing. In this case, the IP level sends a routing control signal to the lower layer based on the IP address. It is very important that in the case of wavelength routing, decisions based upon an IP address are made by the IP layer implicitly at only the origin and destination nodes. The signals arriving at different input ports of an optical router are directed toward different output ports according to the incoming wavelength. In order to vary the routing decisions, tunable transmitters and receivers are required at the originating and terminating nodes.

The LANL has proposed a new concept that provides point-to-point paths from any one of N input ports to any one of N output ports, but without incurring the splitting loss associated with star couplers or couplers/splitters. Fixed-tuned grating multiplex/demultiplex components are the most convenient way of performing wavelength routing. A grated demultiplexer converts a multiplexed set of N optical signals, each at a specified wavelength on the common input fiber, into N spatially distinct outputs. At the output multiplexer, N spatially separate optical signals are transmitted, each at the proper wavelength, onto one common output fiber (see Figure 14–4) [2]. For example, input port 1 connects to output port k simply by tuning the transmitter to k-*th* wavelength. The receiving node served by output port k also tunes to k-*th* wavelength (tunable Fabry-Perot filters can be used for this purpose). Grating components add no additional latency to the network, allow considerable wavelength reuse, and provide full-mesh connectivity. At the same time, optical routing (as well as WDM) has a potential for scaling to a very large number of nodes and the modularity required to easily add an additional node.

In the proposed router, the electronics are reserved for control functions, where speed is not a limiting factor. In this case, the optical energy is split at the input interface. A small fraction of this energy is converted to electrical form and sent to the electronic controller. The output interface feeds the outgoing lines and is used for appending the header and for optical contention resolution using optical delay loop buffering. Based on the stated problems, further research in the areas of ultra-fast all-fiber optical networks (10 Gbit/s and above), WDM techniques, multigigabit sources and receivers, fast optical switches and routers, wavelength reuse, and optical buffering is necessary to meet the NGI challenges.

What's also clear is that there's no end in sight to the soaring demand, especially if, as many experts believe, two-way video communication becomes more common. The communications industry is undergoing a transition that in a few years shall bring us digital video for our everyday use at home and at work. Experts believe that the change from voice telephony to digital data (heavy with video), that requires multiplying backbone transmission capacity by about a factor of 200—has to play the leading role in meeting that expanded demand.

Thanks to advances in WDM methods, fiber has done a good job in keeping up with this explosion in demand. The ability to get bits down a fiber

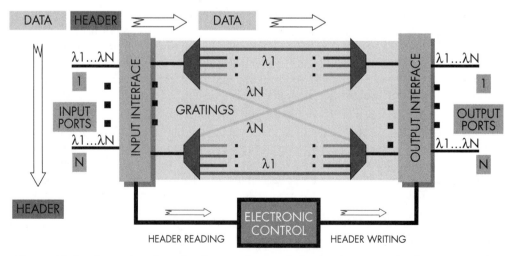

Figure 14–4   A wavelength routing intermediate node (no local user attached). Any transmission incoming to any port can be directed to any output port by changing wavelength.

is growing faster than Moore's Law, which predicts the doubling of computing power every 18 months. At the moment, the carrying capacity of fiber is doubling every 12 months.

Doing It with Erbium

The term *wavelength division multiplexing* reeks of engineering jargon, but the concept is simple: simultaneously sending separate signals through the same fiber at different wavelengths. Essentially the same idea forms the foundation of radio and television broadcasting, where each station sends its signal out on an assigned wavelength in the radio-frequency spectrum. Of course, most people think in terms of frequency instead, but the two values are inextricably bound by their relationship to the speed of light.

For instance, 100 megahertz on the FM dial corresponds to a wavelength of about 3 meters.

The same principles work for the light going through an optical fiber as for radio waves transmitted through air. Optical fibers transmit best at the invisible, near-infrared-light wavelengths between 1.3 and 1.6 micrometers—roughly double the wavelength of red light.

If WDM is both straightforward and an idea that's been around, why has it only recently become practical? The biggest obstacle has been the lack of suitable amplifiers. Light signals traveling through even the most transparent optical fibers fade to undetectable levels after a couple hundred kilometers. For most of the time fiber optics have been in place, the only way to span fibers longer than that was to regenerate the signal through an optoelectronic process: A photodetector would convert the stream of weakened light pulses into a voltage signal that could be amplified electronically. This boosted a signal-modulated laser transmitter.

The problem is that light detectors don't discriminate between wavelengths—they scramble signals at different colors, much the way your ears have trouble discerning what is being said if two people talk at once. For optoelectronic systems to work with multiple wavelengths, they must have a way to separate the wavelengths optically, using filters or other similar elements, enabling each signal to pass through its own regenerator. Until recently, though, that has proved impractical and thus not possible.

This limitation disappeared with the invention of a technique for boosting the signal light's intensity directly, without the need for an intermediate electronic step. The key piece of technology is something called an *erbium-doped fiber amplifier,* as shown in Figure 14–5 [3]. These devices, developed in the late 1980s, made the WDM revolution possible.

Unlike a regenerator, a fiber amplifier operates directly on light. Light in the feeble input signal stimulates excited erbium atoms in the fiber to emit more light at the same wavelength. Chains of optical amplifiers can combine to carry signals through thousands of kilometers of fiber-optic cable on land or under the ocean—without regenerators. Because they preserve the wavelength of the optical signals, erbium fiber devices can amplify several different wavelength channels simultaneously without scrambling them. Erbium amplifiers work well across the near-infrared region of the spectrum at which fiber optic systems operate.

One by Land and Two by Sea

Long-distance telephone companies were the first to realize that wavelength division multiplexing could cut the cost of bandwidth. Compared with the alternative of adding new fiber, WDM technology provides a much more effective way to add capacity. Laying new cable is expensive and time-consuming. And burying new cable along the same route already occupied by an older cable is risky—new excavation invites cable breaks that could put the whole system out of service.

The telecommunications carriers' desire to save time and money has driven a rapid development in WDM techniques. In the mid-1990s, the carrier companies began using systems transmitting at four wavelengths, and

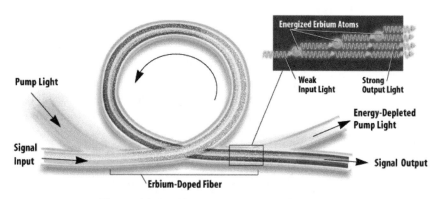

Figure 14–5   How an erbium amplifier works.

soon upped the count to eight. Developers quickly sliced the spectrum even more finely to squeeze 16 wavelength channels through a single fiber for what has become known as *dense* WDM.

When the carriers saw the need, manufacturers were equally quick to sense the market. Lucent Technologies of Murray Hill, New Jersey, adapted technology developed at its Bell Labs subsidiary. Ciena, a Linthicum, Maryland company founded in 1992, charged ahead faster. It delivered its first commercial 16-channel system in 1996—at nearly the same time as the AT&T spinoff. Other telecom giants around the world followed, including Nortel, Alcatel, Pirelli, NEC, Hitachi, Fujitsu, and Ericsson. Over the past three to four years, several companies (including Ciena, Lucent, and Nortel of Saint-Laurent, Quebec, Canada) have begun to market systems that slice the erbium-amplifier spectrum into 32 or 40 slivers, each only 0.8 nanometer wide. In 1998, Lucent delivered its first 80-channel system to AT&T. Pirelli Cable of Lexington, South Carolina, followed with a 128-channel version.

Telecommunications carriers don't need all those channels today—and thanks to WDM's inherent modularity, they don't need to buy more channels until they're ready to deploy them. A carrier installing a WDM system can start with only the transmitters and receivers needed for the few initial channels. Later, as demand for capacity grows, additional equipment can be plugged in to open up new wavelengths.

Taking full advantage of WDM often requires upgrading older cables by adding components that compensate for a troublesome effect called chromatic dispersion. This refers to the tendency of a short light pulse to stretch out as it travels through a fiber, owing to the fact that some wavelengths travel faster than others. Dispersion smears light pulses together and therefore limits transmission speed. Avoiding this phenomenon is especially important in submarine cables, where light signals must travel through several thousand kilometers of fiber from shore to shore. New installations can exploit fibers designed for optimum WDM performance, recently developed both by Lucent and by Corning.

In 1998, the first big submarine cable designed for multiwavelength operation—called Atlantic Crossing 1—began sending 2.5 Gbit/s at four wavelength channels on each of its four fiber pairs. The capacity of this system can be upgraded to 16 wavelengths per fiber at that speed. That promises a total of 160 Gbit/s through the cable, a loop connecting the United States with Britain, the Netherlands, and Germany.

Project Oxygen raises the bar [4]. Newer WDM technology will carry 10 Gbit/s at each of 16 wavelengths across the ocean in four fiber pairs, a total capacity of 640 Gbit/s per cable. That's more than 1,000 times the capacity of the first transatlantic fiber optic cable, which began service just a decade ago. The whole system will ultimately include 168,000 kilometers of cable—enough to circle the globe four times. Other groups are planning more submarine cable systems, although none is quite so ambitious. It's no wonder we're going to drown in fiber.

On land, regional telephone companies have just begun to adopt wavelength multiplexing. In 1998, Bell Atlantic began testing WDM on a 35-kilometer cable between Brunswick and Freehold, New Jersey. Four channels each carried signals at speeds to 2.5 Gbit/s (the top rate between company-switching offices) and the Ciena-built system has slots for up to 16 wavelength channels [6]. Bell South tested three of 16 channels in a similar system on a cable spanning 80 kilometers between Grenada and Greenwood, Mississippi. The economics are clear: It's cheaper to add WDM capacity than to add new fiber.

Different rules apply to the shorter cables linking switching offices to major business customers. Here, in the so-called *metro* market, the cost of increasing fiber count is not as big an issue because the runs are so much shorter. Still, WDM improves signal transmission in other important ways. One is by carrying signals in their original digital formats rather than converting them into the digital coding used within the telephone network. Because such conversion requires costly electronics, it can be cheaper to dedicate a wavelength for end-to-end transmission in the original format.

The ability to sort signals by wavelength should streamline the operation of future fiber optic networks. Traditionally, phone companies organize digital signals in a hierarchy of bit rates, merging many low-bit-rate tributaries into mighty digital rivers carrying gigabits per second. This packs bits efficiently onto transmission lines, but requires unpacking the whole bit stream to extract individual signals. If the signals are organized by wavelength, however, simple optics can tease out the desired wavelength channel without disturbing the others. Engineers speak of adding a new *optical layer* to the telecommunications system. Customers might lease a wavelength in this optical layer instead of leasing the right to transmit at a specific data rate. A television station, for instance, could reserve one wavelength from its studio to its transmitter and another to the local cable company—and transmit both signals in digital video formats not used on the phone network.

The Big Squeeze

Since the demand for bandwidth shows no sign of slowing down, the developers of WDM systems are already thinking about how to pack more wavelengths into the same fiber. At the moment, there are two basic approaches being investigated—and limits to both are apparent.

One approach is to reduce the *space* between wavelengths by choosing wavelengths that are closer together to carry the multiplicity of signals. Packing wavelengths closer works well up to a point, but it ultimately clashes with basic physics. As bit rates increase, optical pulses get briefer, and (following the dictates of Heisenberg's Uncertainty Principle) this shortening forces the light signal to spread over a broader range of wavelengths.

Heisenberg's (position-momentum) Uncertainty Principle in quantum mechanics refers to the user specifying a momentum spectrum and the applet plots the corresponding spatial probability density (position spectrum), as well as the real and imaginary parts of the wave function. The user can choose (continuous) gaussian or square spectra with variable central momentum and width. Alternatively, the user can construct an arbitrary discrete spectrum. If the momentum spectrum is peaked around a particular value, then so is the spatial probability density. If the width of the momentum spectrum is small, then that of the position spectrum is large, and vice versa. This is Heisenberg's (position-momentum) Uncertainty Principle.

The spreading can cause interference between closely spaced channels. Lucent's highest-capacity system handles 10 Gbit/s on wavelength channels separated by 0.8 nanometer, but only 2.5 Gbit/s when channel spacing is halved. Few experts think channels can be squeezed much tighter. Among major vendors, only Hitachi Telecom of Norcross, Georgia, talks about modulating individual channels at 40 Gbit/s—and admits that those signals could span only limited distances.

Prospects look better for the second option: expanding the range of transmission wavelengths. Pirelli, for example, uses three erbium-fiber amplifiers, optimized for separate bands between 1,525 and 1,605 nanometers, to squeeze 128 wavelength channels at 10 Gbit/s each into a single fiber. Lucent has demonstrated erbium amplifiers covering a similar range in the laboratory, and in 1998, introduced a new optical fiber that opens up a long-neglected block of the spectrum around 1,400 nanometers. Good optical amplifiers are not yet available for other wavelengths.

For WDM to reach its full potential, though, more will be needed than simply packing in additional wavelengths. It will also be necessary to develop better equipment for switching and manipulating the various wavelengths after the signal emerges from the optical *pipe*. Optical switches are getting close to practical commercial applications; however, to fully emulate what happens in digital cross-connects, you need to reallocate and reassign wavelengths. It's impossible to allocate the same wavelength to one customer throughout an entire system because the huge network has far more customers than it has wavelengths.

For example, how can signals from San Francisco and Cupertino, California, arrive in Palo Alto at the same wavelength, both bound for San Jose? The Palo Alto node must convert one signal to a different wavelength for the final leg of its trip, so that the messages they carry aren't hopelessly confused. Wavelength conversion now must take the same brute-force approach as regenerators, converting the optical signal to an electronic one that can drive a transmitter at the output wavelength. All-optical conversion approaches, while demonstrated in the lab, have yet to reach commercial practicality as of this writing.

Even if these technical problems are solved, however, that won't be enough for the technology to really spread its wings. For that, the price will also have to come down—a trajectory that industry insiders say has already become apparent. They project that cost per network node will drop by a factor of 10 every five years, starting at $100,000 in 2000. Through the next year or two, WDM will be economical only for backbone networks. Once cost drops to $10,000 a node, the technology will make sense for metropolitan and regional networks, starting with service to large businesses. Residential access in large apartment buildings will follow after costs drop to $1,000 a node in about 2010, with WDM reaching individual homes once costs decline to about $100 around 2015.

The real strength of WDM lies in how it expands the optical airways so that everyone can inhale more of the oxygen of information. At the dawn of the radio era, each transmitter screamed across the whole radio spectrum, blocking other signals for the duration of its broadcast. Then engineers learned to build circuits that tuned each transmitter to its own frequency, opening the radio spectrum to the many stations we can hear today. In much the same way, WDM replaces a single stream of black-and-white bits with a multitude of different-colored signals.

Finally, WDM is creating huge new information pipelines that will bring better service at lower cost. But the real information revolution won't come until cheap WDM pipelines reach individual residences. Today's modem connections remain bottlenecks, forcing us to sip the torrent of data through the electronic equivalent of a thin plastic straw. But get ready: As fiber reaches the home, your very own wavelength could deliver a bubbling fountain of bits.

Let's now look at how to detect light with photodiodes.

DETECTING LIGHT WITH PHOTODIODES

The process of detecting light with photodiodes consists of the following:

- choosing the right detector
- what to look for in test instrumentation
- responsivity: the calibration factor

Choosing the Right Detector

Sensitivity to the band of interest is a primary consideration when choosing a detector. You can control the peak responsivity and bandwidth through the use of filters, but you must have an adequate signal to start with (see Figure 14–6) [6]. Filters can suppress out-of-band light but cannot boost signal.

Another consideration is blindness to out-of-band radiation. If you are measuring solar ultraviolet in the presence of massive amounts of visible and infrared light, for example, you would select a detector that is insensitive to the long wavelength light that you intend to filter out.

Lastly, linearity, stability, and durability are considerations. Some detector types must be cooled or modulated to remain stable. High voltages

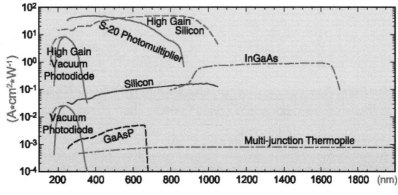

Figure 14–6   Common detector types—absolute responsivity, unfiltered.

are required for other types. In addition, some can be burned out by excessive light, or have their windows permanently ruined by a fingerprint.

Silicon Photodiodes

Planar diffusion type silicon photodiodes are perhaps the most versatile and reliable sensors available (see Figure 14–7) [6]. The P-layer material at the light sensitive surface and the N material at the substrate form a P-N junction, which operates as a photoelectric converter, generating a current that is proportional to the incident light. Silicon cells operate linearly over a 10-decade dynamic range, and remain true to their original calibration longer than any other type of sensor. For this reason, they are used as transfer standards at NIST.

Silicon photodiodes are best used in the short-circuit mode, with zero input impedance into an op-amp. The sensitivity of a light-sensitive circuit is limited by dark current, shot noise, and Johnson (thermal) noise. The practical limit of sensitivity occurs for an irradiance that produces a photocurrent equal to the dark current (noise equivalent power [NEP] = 1).

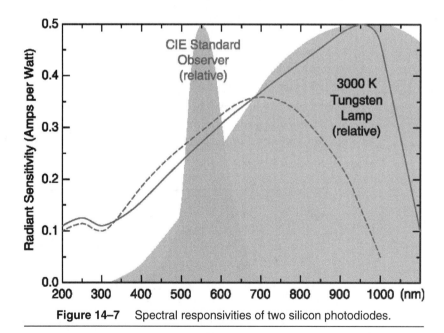

Figure 14–7   Spectral responsivities of two silicon photodiodes.

The average dark current is the shutter dark plus the dark accumulation during the integration time t:(2.4.3) where DN is the data number total dark output, AD is the dark current time dependence, t is exposure time, BD is the dark current temperature dependence, AS is the dark shutter coefficient, BS is the dark shutter temperature dependence, AN is the null strip coefficient, BN is the null strip temperature dependence, and 16.0 (or 8.7) is the hardware offset. The dark shutter is a zero-exposure dark frame. The dark accumulation in a dark shutter frame is due to 0.5 milliseconds of active charge coupled device (CCD) area dark accumulation during the frame transfer process, and 2.09 seconds of dark accumulation during the readout process, combined with the serial register dark accumulation.

In the case of thermal noise, the electric charge is in effect held in long bags with walls relatively impervious to electrons at low temperature. The mass transport of charge along the bag, or wires, under the influence of heat motion, sets up the potential differences that generate the fluctuating output of the amplifier. With one end of the conductor, the cathode of the tube is heated to incandescence, and electrons can be emitted from the cathode surface to travel across the vacuum toward the anode. The electrons are emitted at random times, independent of each other, and they travel at different velocities, depending on initial velocity and voltage distribution for electron passage. In the case of a small electron emission, a small, nearly steady flow of current results, with a superimposed smaller alternating current whose amplitude can be calculated from statistical theory. This small current flowing though the amplifier generates the *Schroteffekt*, or shot effect, in the amplifier. For frequencies above certain values, the noise power is constant up to very high frequencies. For thermal noise, this constant power extends also to low values; while for shot noise, there are many exceptions and variations.

Solar-Blind Vacuum Photodiodes

The phototube is a light sensor that is based on the photoemissive effect. The phototube is a bipolar tube that consists of a photoemissive cathode surface that emits electrons in proportion to incident light, and an anode that collects the emitted electrons. The anode must be biased at a high voltage (50 to 90 V) in order to attract electrons to jump through the vacuum of the tube. Some phototubes use a forward bias of less than 15 volts, however.

The cathode material determines the spectral sensitivity of the tube. Solar-blind vacuum photodiodes use Cs-Te cathodes to provide sensitivity only to ultraviolet light, providing as much as a million to one long wavelength rejection (see Figure 14–8) [6]. An ultraviolet (UV) glass window is required for sensitivity in the UV down to 185 nm, with fused silica windows offering transmission down to 160 nm.

Multi-Junction Thermopiles

The thermopile is a heat-sensitive device that measures radiated heat (see Figure 14–9) [6]. The sensor is usually sealed in a vacuum to prevent heat transfer except by radiation. A thermopile consists of a number of thermocouple junctions in series, which convert energy into a voltage using the Peltier effect. Thermopiles are a convenient sensor for measuring infrared, because they offer adequate sensitivity and a flat spectral response in a small package. More sophisticated bolometers and pyroelectric detectors need to be chopped and are generally used only in calibration labs.

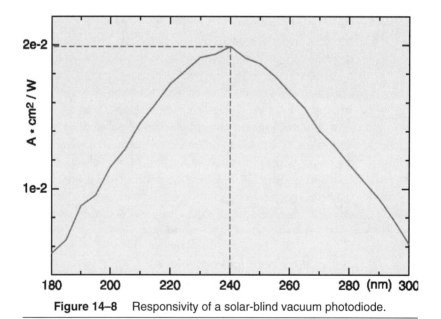

Figure 14–8   Responsivity of a solar-blind vacuum photodiode.

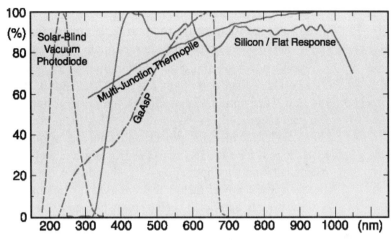

Figure 14–9   Responsivities: Vacuum photodiode, SI/flat response, GaAsP, and thermopile.

A bolometer is a crystal coupled to a thermal sensor able to detect very small variations in temperatures. The bolometer is placed in a cryostate, which allows it to reach a very low temperature of about 10 millikelvins. The principle of detection is the following: the ionizing incident particle deposits its energy in the bolometer under ionization, light, and heat. Their proportion depends on the nature of that particle. The knowledge at least of two of these three quantities allows to identify the particle and then discriminate a nuclear recoil (induced by a WIMP) and an electron (induced by a gamma ray). There are some crystals that provide two components, in particular Germanium, which allows to detect both ionization and heat at very low temperatures.

The Peltier Effect was discovered in 1822, and refers to the reversible heating or cooling, which occurs at a contact when current flows from one connector to another. The reversible heat quantities are small and hence somewhat hard to measure. For this reason, liquid crystals are ideal for indicating temperature change as it increases or decreases.

Thermopiles suffer from temperature drift, since the reference portion of the detector is constantly absorbing heat. The best method of operating a thermal detector is by chopping incident radiation, so that drift is zeroed out by the modulated reading. Thus, the quartz window in most thermopiles is adequate for transmitting from 200 to 4,200 nm, but for long wavelength sensitivity out to 40 microns, potassium bromide windows are used.

Let's now look at test instrumentation, which is very important in any discussions of fiber optic light detection. This part of the chapter will show you how fiber optic testing requires special instrumentation that has been designed specifically to the needs of testing the performance parameters of fibers, cables, connectors, splices, and a number of other fiber optic components. It will also discuss why the FO power meter is the most common instrument, and why optical power is the most common measurement. Test sources and FO power meters that are used for loss measurements will also be discussed. In addition, specialized instruments that are used to find faults in cables for troubleshooting will be examined. Visual fault locators that are used for short cables and OTDRs for long cables will also be discussed. Finally, this part of the chapter will show you how test equipment is matched to the system being tested to get reliable test data. See Chapter 16, "Verifying Cable Installations: Testing Tips and Techniques," for a very detailed discussion on this topic.

What to Look for in Test Instrumentation

Most test procedures for fiber optic component specifications have been standardized by national and international standards bodies, including the EIA in the United States and the IEC internationally. Procedures for measuring absolute optical power, cable, and connector loss and the effects of many environmental factors (such as temperature, pressure, flexing, etc.) are covered in these procedures.

In order to perform these tests, the basic fiber optic instruments are the fiber optic (FO) power meter, test source, OTDR, optical spectrum analyzer, and an inspection microscope. These and some other specialized instruments are described next.

Fiber Optic Power Meters

Fiber optic power meters measure the average optical power emanating from an optical fiber. They typically consist of a solid state detector (silicon for short wavelength systems, germanium or Indium gallium arsenide [InGaAs] for long wavelength systems), signal conditioning circuitry, and a digital display of power. To interface to the large variety of fiber optic connectors in use, some form of removable connector adapter is usually provided.

Indium gallium arsenide (InGaAs) is generally used to make high-performance long-wavelength detectors.

Power meters are calibrated to read in linear units (milliwatts, microwatts, and nanowatts) and/or decibel (dB) referenced to one milliwatt or one microwatt optical power. Some meters also offer a relative dB scale, which is useful for laboratory loss measurements.

 Decibel (dB) is a unit of relative change of power (for example, −10 dB).

 Field measurements more often use adjustable sources set to a standard value to reduce confusion.

Power meters cover a very broad dynamic range, over 1 million to 1; therefore, some form of automatic range switching is provided in the signal conditioning circuitry to allow reasonable display resolution. Although most fiber optic power and loss measurements are made in the range of 0 dBm to −50 dBm, some power meters offer much wider dynamic ranges. For testing analog CATV systems or fiber amplifiers, one needs special meters with extended high power ranges up to +20 dBm (100 mW). Although no fiber optic systems operate at very low power (below about −50 dBm), some lab meters offer ranges to −70 dBm or more, which can be useful in measuring optical return loss or spectral loss characteristics with a monochromator source.

Power meters measure the time average of the optical power, not the peak power, so the meters are sensitive to the duty cycle of an input digital pulse stream. One can calculate peak power if one knows the duty cycle of the input by dividing the average power by the duty cycle. For most loss measurements, one uses a test source with continuous wave (CW [steady state]) or 2 kHz pulsed output.

Continuous wave usually refers to the constant optical output from an optical source when it is biased (turned on) but not modulated with a signal.

As long as the source modulation doesn't change, no compensation needs to be made. When testing link transmitter power or receiver sensitivity, it is necessary to establish a standard test pattern, generally a 50 percent duty cycle (called a square wave), to allow accurate measurement of transmitter output or receiver sensitivity.

FO power meters have a typical measurement uncertainty of +/–5 percent when calibrated to transfer standards provided by national standards laboratories like the U.S. National Institute of Standards and Technology (NIST). Sources of errors are the variability of coupling efficiency of the detector and connector adapter; reflections off the shiny polished surfaces of connectors; unknown source wavelengths (since the detectors are wavelength sensitive); nonlinearities in the electronic signal conditioning circuitry of the FO power meter; and detector noise at very low signal levels. Since most of these factors affect all power meters (regardless of their sophistication), expensive laboratory meters are hardly more accurate than the most inexpensive handheld portable units.

Fiber Optic Test Sources

In order to make measurements of optical loss or attenuation in fibers, cables, and connectors, one must have a standard signal source as well as an FO power meter. The source must be chosen for compatibility with the type of fiber in use (single mode or multimode with the proper core diameter) and the wavelength desired for performing the test. Most sources are either LEDs or lasers of the types commonly used as transmitters in actual fiber optic systems—making them representative of actual applications and enhancing the usefulness of the testing. Some tests, such as measuring spectral attenuation of fiber, requires a variable wavelength source, which is usually a tungsten lamp with a monochromator to vary the output wavelength.

Typical wavelengths of sources are 665 nm (plastic fiber), 820, 850, and 870 nm (short wavelength glass fiber) and 1,300 and 1,550 nm (long wavelength). LEDs are typically used for testing multimode fiber and lasers are used for single-mode fiber—although there is some crossover, especially in older telecom systems that used multimode fiber with lasers and the testing of short single-mode jumper cables with LEDs. The source wavelength can be a critical issue in making accurate loss measurements, since attenuation of the fiber is wavelength-sensitive—especially at short wavelengths. Thus, all test sources should be calibrated for wavelength.

Adaptability to a variety of fiber optic connectors is also important, since over 70 styles of connectors exist, although the types most commonly used are sense multiple access (SMA), synchronous transport (ST), FDDI and Enterprise systems connection (ESCON) for multimode fiber, and Biconic, FC, subscriber connector (SC) and D4 for single-mode fiber.

SMA is a threaded type of optical connector, one of the earliest optical connectors to be widely used. Offers poor repeatability and performance.

FC is threaded optical connector that originated in Japan. Good for single-mode or multimode fiber and applications requiring low back-reflection.

Some LED sources use modular adapters like power meters to allow adaptation to various connector types. Lasers almost always have fixed connectors. If the connector on the source is fixed, hybrid test jumpers with connectors compatible with the source on one end and the connector being tested on the other must be used.

Other source-related factors affecting measurement accuracy are the stability of the output power and the modal distribution launched into fiber. For extremely accurate measurements, the source may need optical feedback stabilization to maintain output power at a precise level for long times that are required for some measurements. Mode scramblers, filters, and strippers may be required to adjust the modal distribution in the fiber to approximate actual operating conditions.

Optical Loss Test Sets/Test Kits

The optical loss test set is an instrument formed by the combination of a fiber optic power meter and source, which is used to measure the loss of fiber, connectors, and connectorized cables. Early versions of this instrument were called attenuation meters. A test kit has a similar purpose, but is usually comprised of separate instruments and includes accessories to customize it for a

Chapter 14 • Using Fiber Optic Transmitters and Receivers

specific application, such as testing an FO LAN, telco, or CATV.

The combination OLTS instrument may be useful for making measurements in a laboratory. However, in the field, individual sources and power meters are more often used, since the ends of the fiber and cable are usually separated by long distances, which would require two OLTSs, at double the cost of one FO power meter and source. And, even in a laboratory environment, several different source types may be needed, making the flexibility of a separate source and meter a better choice.

Optical Time Domain Reflectometer

The optical time domain reflectometer (OTDR) uses the phenomena of fiber backscattering to characterize fibers, find faults, and optimize splices. Since scattering is one of the primary loss factors in fiber (the other being absorption), the OTDR can send out into the fiber a high-powered pulse and measure the light scattered back toward the instrument. The pulse is attenuated on the outbound leg and the backscattered light is attenuated on the return leg; therefore, the returned signal is a function of twice the fiber loss and the backscatter coefficient of the fiber.

If one assumes the backscatter coefficient is constant, the OTDR can be used to measure loss as well as locate fiber breaks, splices, and connectors. In addition, the OTDR gives a graphic display of the status of the fiber being tested. And it offers another major advantage over the source/FO power meter or OLTS in that it requires access to only one end of the fiber.

The uncertainty of the OTDR measurement is heavily dependent on the backscatter coefficient, which is a function of intrinsic fiber-scattering characteristics, core diameter, and numerical aperture. It is the variation in backscatter coefficient that causes many splices to show a *gain* instead of the actual loss. Tests have shown that OTDR splice loss measurements may have an uncertainty of up to 0.8 dB. OTDRs must also be matched to the fibers being tested in both wavelength and fiber core diameter to provide accurate measurements. Thus, many OTDRs have modular sources to allow substituting a proper source for the application.

While most OTDR applications involve finding faults in installed cables or optimizing splices, they are very useful in inspecting fibers for manufacturing faults. Development work on improving the short-range resolution of OTDRs for LAN applications, and new applications such as evaluating connector return loss, promise to enhance the usefulness of the instrument in the future.

OTDRs come in three basic versions. Full-size OTDRs offer the highest performance and have a full complement of features like data storage, but are very big and high-priced. MiniOTDRs provide the same type of measurements as a full OTDR, but with fewer features to trim the size and cost. Fault finders use the OTDR technique—but it is greatly simplified to just provide the distance to a fault in order to make the instruments more affordable and easier to use.

Visual Cable Tracers and Fault Locators

Many of the problems in connection with fiber optic networks are related to making proper connections. Since the light used in systems is invisible, one cannot see the system transmitter light. By injecting the light from a visible source, such as an LED or incandescent bulb, one can visually trace the fiber from transmitter to receiver to ensure correct orientation and also check for continuity. The simple instruments that inject visible light are called visual fault locators.

If a powerful enough visible light, such as a HeNe or visible diode laser, is injected into the fiber, high loss points can be made visible. Most applications center around short cables such as those used in telco central offices to connect to the fiber optic trunk cables. However, since it covers the range where OTDRs are not useful, it is complementary to the OTDR in cable troubleshooting. This method will work on buffered fiber and even jacketed single-fiber cable if the jacket is not opaque to the visible light. The yellow jacket of single-mode fiber and orange of multimode fiber will usually pass the visible light. Most other colors, especially black and gray, will not work with this technique, nor will most multifiber cables. However, many cable breaks, macrobending losses caused by kinks in the fiber, bad splices, and so on, can be detected visually. Since the loss in the fiber is quite high at visible wavelengths, on the order of 9–15 dB/km, this instrument has a short range, typically 3–5 km.

Fiber Identifiers

If one carefully bends the fiber enough to cause loss, the light that couples out can also be detected by a large area detector. A fiber identifier uses this technique to detect a signal in the fiber at normal transmission wavelengths. These instruments usually function as receivers, able to discriminate between no signal, a high-speed signal, and a 2 kHz tone. By specifically looking for a 2 kHz *tone* from a test source coupled into the fiber, the instrument can identify a specific fiber in a large multifiber cable—especially useful in speeding up the splicing or restoration process.

Fiber identifiers can be used with both buffered fiber and jacketed single fiber cable. With buffered fiber, one must be very careful not to damage the fiber, as any excess stress here could result in stress cracks in the fiber, which could cause a failure in the fiber in the future.

Measuring Fiber Bandwidth

Although fiber has a very high bandwidth, some applications actually approach its limits, requiring performance evaluation. Since two factors limit fiber bandwidth, modal dispersion and chromatic dispersion, it is not easy to build a single instrument that makes bandwidth measurements.

Modal dispersion arises from the various paths, or modes, light takes through multimode fiber. Since the average speed of light in each mode may vary, pulses are dispersed along the fiber. Modal dispersion can be tested with a high-speed laser source and receiver that is looking for degradation of pulse risetime and falltime. Instruments are available for performing modal dispersion tests, even in the field.

Since the index of refraction of light (a measure of the speed of light in the medium) is a function of wavelength, light of different wavelengths will have different speeds in the fiber. Thus, a source of wide spectral width, like an LED, will suffer considerable chromatic dispersion, limiting the bandwidth of the fiber. Given long enough lengths of fiber, even the narrow spectral width of a laser will cause spectral dispersion in single-mode fiber.

Testing chromatic dispersion requires measuring the pulse speed through the fiber at various wavelengths. Only a few instruments have been developed for testing fiber dispersion, and they are generally limited to laboratory measurements due to the difficulty of performing the measurement. Alternately, optical to electrical (O/E) and electrical to optical (E/O) converters are used to interface the fiber under test to high-speed electronic instrumentation that can cover the frequency range of the fiber. Simulation software, developed to analyze multimode fiber bandwidth as a function of source and fiber parameters, can calculate total fiber dispersion with an uncertainty no larger than actual testing (about 11 percent) and are therefore more widely used by end users.

O/E and E/O Converters

O/E and E/O converters have other uses besides testing fiber bandwidth. O/E converters can be used with high speed oscilloscopes to analyze pulses in fiber optic links to see if the waveforms are of the proper shape. This means measuring rise and fall times of the pulse and the depth of modulation (the difference between the peak power of the pulse and the lowest power reached between pulses). They can be used for testing lasers and LEDs used in transmitters and link dispersion in long links. E/O converters are used to test receivers for bandwidth and margin, usually in conjunction with a bit error rate tester and attenuator.

Optical Continuous Wave Reflectometers (OCWR)

The OCWR was originally proposed as a special-purpose instrument to measure the optical return loss of connectors installed on patchcords or jumpers. Unfortunately, its purpose became muddled between conception and inception. As actual instruments became available in the market, they had much higher measurement resolution than appropriate for the measurement uncertainty (0.01 dB resolution versus 1 dB uncertainty), leading to much confusion on the part of users as to why measurements were not reproducible. In addition, several instruments were touted as a way to measure the optical return loss of an installed cable plant—obviously in ignorance of the fact that they would also be integrating the backscatter of the fiber with any reflections from connectors or splices. Since the measurement of return loss from a connector can be made equally well with any power meter, laser source and calibrated coupler, and an OTDR, it is the only way to test installed cable plants for return loss. Thus, the OCWR has little use in fiber optic testing.

Optical Fiber Analyzers

There are many parameters of optical fiber that require testing by the manufacturer. These include attenuation (as a function of source wavelength), bandwidth/dispersion, numerical aperture, and all the physical dimensions such as core and cladding diameter, ovality, and concentricity. Automated laboratory instruments are available to measure all these parameters automatically, but many fiber manufacturers prefer to build their own. The most difficult part of fiber measurements is the fact that subtle differences in test setup and instrumentation can cause differences in measured values.

Multichannel Test Systems

Often, it is necessary to test a number of components simultaneously, such as environmental testing of connectors or a multifiber cable. Since it would be ungainly and certainly not cost-effective to use a large number of individual power meters and sources, there are multichannel test systems available. These systems are usually based on either a number of individual power meter modules with sources split out through couplers or systems based on one source and one meter with multichannel fiber optic switches to select each component to be tested in sequence.

Both types of systems are usually controlled by a personal computer and data acquired by a PC-based data acquisition system. Most vendors offer some form of software that can be customized for any particular application.

Visual Inspection with Microscopes

Cleaved fiber ends prepared for splicing and polished connector ferrules require visual inspection to find possible defects. This is accomplished using a microscope that has a stage modified to hold the fiber or connector in the field of view. Fiber optic inspection microscopes vary in magnification from 30 to 800 power, with 30–100 power being the most widely used range. Cleaved fibers are usually viewed from the side, to see breakover and lip. Connectors are viewed end-on or at a small angle to find polishing defects such as scratches.

Fiber Optic Talksets

While technically not a measuring instrument, FO talksets are useful for FO installation and testing. They transmit voice over fiber optic cables already installed, allowing technicians splicing or testing the fiber to communicate effectively. Talksets are especially useful when walkie-talkies and telephones are not available, such as in remote locations where splicing is being done, or in buildings where radio waves will not penetrate.

The way to use talksets most effectively is to set up the talksets on one fiber (or pairs appropriate) and leave them there while all testing or splicing work is done. Thus, there will always be a communications link between the working crew, which facilitates deciding which fibers to work with next. The continuous communications capability will greatly speed the process.

Recent developments in talksets include talksets for networking multi-party communications, especially helpful in restoration, and system talksets for use as intercoms in installed systems. There are also combination OLTSs and talksets, but they are not very useful. They do not allow continuous communications during testing, as discussed in the preceding, since they must be moved to the next pair of fibers of interest each time.

There are no standards for the way talksets communicate. Some use simple AM transmission, some FM, and some proprietary digital schemes. Thus, no two manufacturers' talksets can communicate with each other. Bellcore has addressed this matter in a technical advisory that proposes an FM method at 80 and 120 kHz, but it will take years before a standard has been set and manufacturers offer compatible instruments.

The current price range for the units make them practically unfeasible for all but the most successful installers (upper 5 percent), which is why there are no quick advances in this area.

Attenuators

Attenuators are used to simulate the loss of long fiber runs for testing link margin in network simulation in the laboratory or self-testing links in a loop-back configuration. In margin testing, variable attenuators are used to increase loss until the system has a high bit error rate. For loopback testing, an attenuator is used between a single piece of equipment's transmitter and receiver to test for operation under maximum specified fiber loss. The inherent suggestion is that if systems work in loopback testing, they should work with a proper cable plant. Thus, many manufacturers of network equipment specify a loopback test as a diagnostic/troubleshooting procedure.

Attenuators can be made by gap loss, or a physical separation of the ends of the fibers, inducing bending losses or inserting calibrated optical filters. Both variable and fixed attenuators are available, but variable attenuators are usually used for testing. Fixed attenuators may be inserted in the system cables, where distances in the fiber optic link are too short and excess power at the receiver causes transmission problems.

Test Jumper Cables and Bulkhead Splice Adapters

In order to test cables using the Fiber Optic Test Procedure (FOTP)-171 insertion loss test, one needs to establish test conditions. This requires launch jumper cables to connect the test source to the cable under test and receive cables to connect the fiber optic power meter.

The FOTP are standards developed and published by the Electronic Industries Association (EIA) under the EIA-RS-455 series of standards.

For accurate measurements, the launch and receive cables must be made with fiber and connectors matching the cables to be tested. To provide reliable measurements, launch and receive cables must be in good condition. They can easily be tested against each other to ensure their performance. Bulkhead splices are used to connect the cables under test to the launch and receive cables. Only the highest performance bulkhead splices should be used, and their condition checked regularly, since they are vitally important in obtaining low-loss connections.

Finally, let's take a very brief look at the calibration factor. Even though responsivity has been discussed in the preceding, a few last words on the subject are appropriate here.

Responsivity: The Calibration Factor

NIST-traceable metrology labs purchase calibrated transfer standard detectors directly from the National Institute of Standards and Technology (NIST) in Gaithersburg, Maryland. From 400 to 1,100 nm, this transfer standard is a Hamamatsu S1337-1010BQ photodiode, a 10 x 10 mm planar silicon cell coated with synthetic quartz. The photodiode is mounted behind a precisely measured 7.98 mm diameter circular aperture, yielding an active area of 0.5 cm2. The responsivity is usually given every 5 nanometers.

The calibration labs then use this transfer standard to calibrate their intercomparison working standards using a monochromatic light source. These working standards are typically identical to the equipment that will be calibrated. The standards are rotated in the lab, tracked over time to monitor stability, and periodically recalibrated.

Detectors are most often calibrated at the peak wavelength of the detector/filter/diffuser combination using identical optics for the intended application. The key to this calibration transfer is a reliable kinematic mount that allows exchangeability of detectors in the optical path, and a stable, power-regulated light source. Complete spectroradiometric responsivity scans or calibration at an alternate wavelength may be preferred in certain circumstances.

Although the working standard and the unknown detector are fixed in precise kinematic mounts in front of carefully regulated light sources, slight errors are expected due to transfer error and manufacturing tolerances. An overall uncertainty to absolute of 10 percent or less is considered very good for radiometry equipment, and is usually only achievable by certified metrology labs. An uncertainty of 1 percent is considered state of the art, and can only be achieved by NIST itself (see Table 14–1) [6].

Table 14–1 Expanded Uncertainties of NIST Photodiode Standards

Wavelength (nm)	Uncertainty (%)
200–250	3.3
250–440	0.7
440–900	0.2
900–1,000	0.3
1,000–1,600	0.7
1,600–1,800	1.3

FROM HERE

This chapter showed you how to use fiber optic transmitters and receivers by taking a close look at light sources and how to detect light with photodiodes. The next chapter shows you how to design cable plants by examining indoor cable, outdoor cable, and how you would benefit from structured cabling options.

NOTES

[1] Hugh Reid, "Light Sources," Department of Electrical and Electronic Engineering, Bell College of Technology, Almada Street, Hamilton, South Lanarkshire, Scotland, ML3 0JB, 2000.

[2] "Optical Routing for Next Generation Internet," Los Alamos National Laboratory, Bikini Atoll Rd., SM, 30, Los Alamos, NM 87545, 2000.

[3] Jeff Hecht, "Wavelength Division Multiplexing," *Technology Review*, MIT, MIT Bldg., W59-200, 201 Vassar Street, Cambridge, MA 02139, (March/April, 1999); *Technology Review* by Jeff Hecht. Copyright 1999 by MIT Technology Review. Reproduced with permission of MIT Technology Review in the format Trade Book via Copyright Clearance Center.

[4] Project Oxygen Network Ltd., Ambassador Bradley Holmes , President, 1 Parliament Street, Hamilton,HM 12 Bermuda, 2000.

[5] CIENA Corporation, 1201 Winterson Road, Linthicum, MD 21090, 2000.

[6] "Choosing a Detector," International Light, Inc., 17 Graf Road, Newburyport, MA 01950, USA, 2000.

Designing Cable Plants

Typical fiber optic cable plants are usu-
ally designed to show a backbone cable connecting patch panels and several
short jumper cables that connect the equipment onto the cable plant. These
installations often have no splices at all, since distances are short. In addition,
the fibers are not terminated directly, but high-quality factory-made pigtails
are spliced onto the backbone cable.

Let's begin Chapter 15 by taking a very detailed look at indoor cable
design specifications. Structural design issues like connection, identification,
and installation will be covered.

INDOOR CABLE

Indoor cable design specifications (building and campus systems) are essential during the design of fiber optic cable plants. Building and campus systems are presented in this chapter to provide a highly detailed design
specification example for instructional purposes only. While this example is
typical of fiber optic indoor cable plant design, please keep in mind that standards and guidelines change, state or local regulations may differ, and the
level of design specification required will vary by project.

Fiber Optic Indoor Cable Structural Issues: Connection, Identification, and Installation

During the process of designing indoor cable plants, the following preliminary general steps must be performed first:

1. Provide a complete, tested, cable-distribution system for data system (local area network) interconnections. The data distribution system should include a fully terminated fiber optic backbone.

2. Individual 6- or 12-fiber optical fiber backbone cables should be installed from the termination enclosure in a new data main distribution frame (MDF) room to fiber optic termination enclosures in each new data intermediate distribution frame (IDF) communications closet.

3. Provide system design services (development of specific details consistent with the contract documents) as required to complete shop drawings for data cable systems, including detailed documentation for owner review and detailed documentation of as-built conditions.

4. Network electronics equipment should be furnished by others. The contractor should coordinate with other system vendors where appropriate to facilitate equipment installation, scheduling, protection of equipment, and access to the project site in order to provide the owner a substantially complete project in a timely manner.

5. The successful communications contractor should attend a mandatory preconstruction meeting with all applicable individuals prior to the start of work.

6. The successful bidder should not be determined by price alone, but by a rating system to include a combination of price, qualifications, training procedures, user participation, and proposed documentation package [7].

Submittals

With regard to project initiation, within 14 days of *Notice to Proceed*, the low-voltage contractor should furnish the following in a single, consolidated submittal:

1. The name of the person who will act as the low-voltage contractor's official contact with the contractor/owner/engineer.

2. The contractor should obtain all required electrical permits and provide copies to the owner/engineer.

3. Complete manufacturer's product literature for all cable, patch panels, cable supports, cable labels, outlet devices, and other products to be used in the installation. In addition, whenever substitutions for recommended products are made, samples may be requested by the owner/engineer) and the manufacturer's supporting documentation demonstrating compatibility with other related products should be included.

4. A time-scaled construction schedule, using the program evaluation and review technique/critical path method (PERT/CPM), indicating general project deadlines and specific dates relating to the installation of the cable distribution system. At a minimum, the construction schedule should include the following milestones:
   - start of communications space construction
   - start of fiber optic cable terminations
   - station cable installation
   - start of fiber optic backbone cable testing
   - final inspection

Note

PERT is not for everyone, nor is it intended for use on all projects. Therefore, the schedulers should use PERT with extreme caution. PERT is a statistical technique applied to a network schedule. PERT was an outgrowth from set back charts used in line of balance (LOB) methodology (remember the U.S. Navy had a large-size oar in the establishment of LOB) and CPM. The critical path method (CPM) is one of several related techniques for doing project planning. CPM is for projects that are made up of a number of individual *activities*. If some of the activities require other activities to finish before they can start, then the project becomes a complex web of activities.

5. shop drawings (normally within 28 days of Notice to Proceed)
6. proposed contractor fiber optic cable test result forms [7].

With regard to project completion, as a condition for project acceptance, the contractor should submit the following for review and approval:

1. Complete manufacturer's product literature and samples (if requested) for all preapproved substitutions for the recommended products made during the course of the project.
2. An exception list of deviations (in materials, construction, and workmanship) from that specified in this part of the chapter and shown on the project drawings. The owner should review this list and declare each item as either an approved exception or as one the contractor must correct.
3. During the course of the project, the contractor should maintain an adequate inspection system and should perform such inspections to ensure that the materials supplied and the work performed conform to

contract requirements. The contractor should provide written documentation indicating that materials acceptance testing was conducted as are outlined later in this chapter under the "Execution" subhead. The contractor should also provide documentation indicating that all cable termination testing was completed and that all irregularities were corrected prior to job completion for owner/engineer analysis [7].

System Installer

The data cable system installer should be a firm normally employed in the low-voltage cabling industry with a reference list of at least five (5) projects and contact names to confirm successful fiber optic cable plant projects. Furthermore, the owner reserves the right to exercise its discretion to require the contractor to remove from the project any such employee of the contractor deemed by the owner to be incompetent, careless, insubordinate, or otherwise objectionable.

The selected system installer should be factory certified for the products it installs and be able to provide a factory warranty of no less than 10 years covering both product and performance of materials installed. Quality and workmanship evaluation should be solely by the owner/engineer and designated representatives.

The selected system installer must be licensed and bonded in the state in which he/she resides. However, it doesn't preclude the installer from performing work in other states.

All cleanup activity related to work performed should be the responsibility of the low-voltage communication (system) contractor. Furthermore, it must be completed daily before leaving the facility.

Finally, any cable system installation company bidding on building and campus systems projects should have at least one Building Industry Consulting Service International (BICSI)-certified Registered Communications Distribution Designer (RCDD) on staff. BICSI is a telecommunications association, founded in 1974 as a not-for-profit professional association to serve the telephone company building industry consultants (BICs) who were responsible for the design and distribution of telecommunications wiring for commercial and multifamily buildings.

Regulatory Requirements

All work should be performed in accordance with the latest revisions of the standards and codes shown in the Sidebar, "Abiding by Standards and Codes."

ABIDING BY STANDARDS AND CODES

Codes

Fiber optic cable plant designers and installers must abide by the following codes:

* Uniform International Conference of Building Officials (ICBO) Building Code (Regional Office, 12505 Bellevue-Redmond Road, Bellevue, Washington 98005)
* Local Building Code and Local Electrical Code
* NEC 1990 [1993] National Electrical Code
* Widely Adapted Fire Codes

  1. *NFPA 1, Fire Prevention Code®*: The primary purpose of the Fire Prevention Code is to provide a code that addresses basic fire prevention requirements necessary to establish a reasonable level of fire safety and property protection from the hazards created by fire and explosion. The Code contains materials from, or provides references to, nearly 100 National Fluid Power Association (NFPA) codes and standards, and is a convenient document for use during field inspections.

  2. *NFPA 54, National Fuel Gas Code®*: This Code provides requirements for the installation and operation of gas piping, equipment installations, and venting. It is the accepted national standard for all fuel gas installations.

  3. *NFPA 70, National Electrical Code®*: The National Electrical Code focuses on the proper installation of electrical systems and equipment in order to protect people and property from the dangers of electricity. This code is considered to be the industry standard for electrical safety, and is the most widely used and accepted code for electrical installations in the world.

  4. *NFPA 72, National Fire Alarm Code®*: Minimum requirements for fire alarm systems, household fire warning equipment, protected premises fire alarm systems, systems with a supervising station (one that receives signals and is always staffed to respond), initiating devices such as heat and smoke detectors, and audible and visible notification devices are all covered in this Code.

  5. *NFPA 101, Life Safety Code®*: This Code provides minimum building design, construction, operation, and maintenance requirements necessary to protect building occupants from danger caused by fire, smoke, and toxic fumes. A key element of the Life Safety Code is the requirement that new and existing buildings allow for *prompt escape* or provide people with a reasonable degree of safety through other means. The Life Safety Code can be used in conjunction with a building code or alone in jurisdictions that do not have a building code in place.

Standards

Fiber optic cable plant designers and installers must abide by the following standards:

  1. *NFPA 13, Standard for the Installation of Sprinkler Systems:* This standard, devel-

oped 100 years ago, provides minimum requirements for the design and installation of automatic fire sprinkler systems and exposure protection sprinkler systems. Key to this standard are provisions that provide a reasonable degree of protection for life and property from fire.

2. *NFPA 58, Standard for the Storage and Handling of Liquefied Petroleum Gases®:* The goal of this standard is to reduce or eliminate the hazard of fire and gas fumes or leakage associated with the storage and treatment of liquefied petroleum gas (LP-Gas), which is much more flammable than natural or manufactured gas. This standard applies to all LP-Gas systems including highway transportation and the design, construction, installation, and operation of marine terminals and pipelines whose primary purpose is the receipt of LP-Gas for delivery to transporters, users, or distributors.

3. *EIA/TIA-568:* Commercial Building Wiring Standard.

4. *EIA/TIA-569:* Commercial Building Standard for Telecommunication Pathways and Spaces.

5. *EIA/TIA TSB36:* Additional Cable Specifications for Unshielded Twisted Pair Cables.

6. *EIA/TIA TSB40:* Additional Transmission Specifications for Unshielded Twisted Pair Connecting Hardware.

7. *EIA/TIA 455-A:* Standard Test Procedure for Fiber Optic Fibers, Cables, Transducers, Sensors, Connecting and Terminating Devices, and Other Fiber Optic Components.

8. *EIA/TIA SP-2840 Commercial Building Telecommunications Cabling Standard:* Issue 1—5/7/93. This standard replaces EIA/TIA-568, TSB36, and TSB40 in its final form. Where this standard modifies information in the existing approved standards, especially concerning cable termination and testing procedures, this standard shall govern [7].

Fiber Optic Cable Design Specifications

Next, from a pure design perspective, the following fiber optic design specifications steps should be followed:

1. *Floor plans:* Furnish floor plans for owner review showing outlet locations with an indication of outlet type and proposed label. Floor plans should be coordinated with architectural and electrical power plans and should be produced at the same scale as the electrical power plans.

2. *Terminal elevations:* Furnish details showing terminal block and backboard elevations, including all cable terminals, spaces for equipment, equipment racks, and station cable routing. Communications equip-

ment closets (intermediate distribution frames [IDFs]) and entrance closets (main distribution frames [MDFs]) should be arranged to maximize the utility and growth potential available in spaces shown on the floor plans. Terminal elevations should be based on detail elevations included in the contract documents and should show additional detail as indicated herein.

3. *Outlet locations:* Provide and incorporate outlet locations into the design.

4. *Terminal schedules:* Furnish terminal schedules showing terminal block locations and positions for all station cabling. Terminal outlet schedules should show proposed labels for all horizontal cables at station outlets along with patch panel locations [7].

Furthermore, fiber optic cable should also be UL-listed type optical fiber nonconductive plenum (OFNP); six or twelve 62.5/125 micron-graded index multimode fibers, each with a color-coded PVC buffer. Maximum attenuation should be 3.75 dB/km at 850 nm and 1.0 dB/km at 1,300 nm. Minimum bandwidth should be 160 MHz/km at 850 nm and 500 MHz/km at 1,300 nm and contain no metallic elements.

Execution

The contractor should avoid penetration of fire-rated walls. Sleeving should be installed for access where necessary.

Any penetration through fire-rated walls (including those in sleeves) should be resealed with an Underwriters Laboratories-approved (UL) sealant. Typical of this type of product is Flameseal. The contractor should also seal all floor, ceiling, and wall penetrations in fire or smoke barriers and in the MDFs, IDFs, and wiring closets.

With regard to allowable cable bend radius and pull tension, communications cable cannot tolerate sharp bends or excessive pull tension during installation. The contractor should refer to the cable manufacturer's allowable bend radius and pull tension data for the maximum allowable limits.

Also, with regard to cable lubricants, lubricants specifically designed for installing communications cable may be used to reduce pulling tension as necessary when pulling cable into conduit. After installation, exposed cable and other surfaces should be cleaned free of lubricant residue.

Furthermore, with regard to pull strings, you should provide pull strings in all new conduits, including all conduits with cable installed as part of the contract. Pull test is not required to exceed 200 pounds.

Finally, the contractor should replace any damaged ceiling tiles that are broken during cable installation. The contractor should also replace or rework cables showing evidence of improper handling, including stretches, kinks, short radius bends, overtightened bindings, loosely twisted and overtwisted pairs at terminals, and cable sheath removed too far (over 1½ inches).

Labels

The labeling plan should be developed by the contractor. The contractor should label all outlets following the detailed shop drawing design, using permanent/legibly typed or machine-engraved labels. The labeling information for patch panels located in the MDF/IDFs should include the MDF/IDF number, patch panel number, and sequential port number. Outlets should be labeled to match the corresponding label in the MDF/IDF.

A floor plan clearly labeled with all outlet jack numbers should be included in the as-built plans. All labels should correspond to as-builts and to final test reports.

Station Wiring Installation

The low-voltage contractor should supervise the installation of communications cable. All fiber optic cable should be installed by individuals trained in low-voltage data cable system installations.

Exposed station cable should only be run with owner approval. Approval should be granted only when no other option exists. When station cable must be run surface to a single outlet, surface raceway should be used to cover the cable and protect it from surface damage.

All cabling and associated hardware should be placed so as to make efficient use of available space in coordination with other uses. All cabling and associated hardware should be placed so as not to impair the owner's efficient use of their full capacity.

All cabling placed in ceiling areas must be tied or clamped. When cable is placed in ceiling areas or other nonexposed areas, fasteners should be placed at intervals no greater than 60 inches. Attaching cable to pipes or other mechanical items is not permitted. All runs of 20 or more cables should have cable rings at 60-inch (maximum) centers to hang the cables.

Communications cable should be routed to avoid light fixtures (18-inch minimum spacing), sources of heat (12-inch minimum spacing), power feeder conduits (12-inch minimum spacing), and electromagnetic interference (EMI) sources (12-inch minimum spacing).

Backboard Cabling/Equipment Rack Configuration

Cable installation in the entrance room and communications closet must conform to the project drawings. All cabling should be routed so as to avoid interference with any other service or system, operation, or maintenance purposes such as access boxes, ventilation mixing boxes, network equipment-mounting access hatches to air filters, switches, or electrical outlets, electrical panels, and lighting fixtures. Avoid crossing areas horizontally just above or below any riser conduit. Lay and dress cables to allow other cables to enter the conduit/riser without difficulty at a later time by maintaining a working distance from these openings. Use a minimum of 36 inches for a service loop to the patch panel.

Cable should be routed as close as possible to the ceiling, floor, or other corners to ensure that adequate wall or backboard space is available to current and future equipment and for cable terminations. Cables should not be tie-wrapped to existing electrical conduit or other equipment. The minimum bend radius should be observed.

Lay cables via the shortest route directly to the nearest edge of the backboard from the mounted equipment or block. Lace or tie-clamp all similarly routed cables together and attach by means of clamps screwed to the outside edge(s) of the backboard vertically and/or horizontally, then route via *square* corners over a path that should offer minimum obstruction to future installations of equipment, backboards, or other cables.

Fiber Optic Cable Terminations

Fiber optic cable should be installed in innerduct from fiber patch panels to plenum entrances. Innerduct should not be installed in plenum ceilings unless it is UL-approved plenum rated. Outside gel-filled fiber optic cable should be installed in conduit or UL-approved, plenum-rated innerduct in all plenum ceilings.

Terminations should be performed by a manufacturer-trained, certified technician. Terminations should also be made in a controlled environment. The contractor may choose to have the cables assembled offsite, although testing must be completed with the cable in its final installed condition.

Furthermore, optical fiber connectors should be straight tip (ST) or subscriber connector (SC) connectors. Optical fiber termination enclosures used in data MDF/IDF rooms should provide termination panels for ST or SC connectors and be of sufficient size and capacity to terminate 100 percent of the fiber count of the inside or outside fiber optic cables. Patch panels must be wall or 19" rack mountable, depending on MDF/IDF applications. Provide all termination accessories and enclosures and test for a complete fiber optic distribution system.

Fiber Optic Cable Testing Specifications

All testing should be performed by trained personnel. The procedure for testing fiber optic cables requires the use of a high-quality optical time-domain reflectometer (OTDR) equipped with a printer. The printed data should show, in addition to any summary information, the complete test trace and all relevant scale settings. The OTDR must have the capability to take measurements from bare fiber strands as well as ST or SC connector terminations.

All fiber optic cable should be tested on the reel before installation to ensure that it meets the specifications outlined herein. After installation, the contractor should test each fiber strand in accordance with EIA 455-171 Method D procedures (bidirectional testing) at both 850 and 1,300 nm. A form should be completed for each cable showing data recorded for each strand, including length, total segment (end-to-end) loss (dB), and connector losses (dB) at each end. In addition, the printed data strip for each strand should be attached to the form.

Acceptable fiber optic cable and connector loss should not exceed 1.5 dB. The contractor is responsible for obtaining minimum loss in fiber connections and polishing per manufacturer's specifications.

Inspection

Conformance to the installation practices covered in the preceding are to be verified when completed. In some cases, the customer may inspect before acceptance. The following points should be examined:

- Is the design documentation complete?
- Have all terminated cables been tested per the specifications?
- Is the cable type suitable for its pathway?
- Have the pathway manufacturer's guidelines been followed?
- Have the installers avoided excessive cable bending?
- Have potential EMI sources been considered?
- Is cable fill correct?
- Are hanging supports within 60 inches (5 feet)?
- Does hanging cable exhibit some sag?
- Are telecommunications closet terminations compatible with equipment?

- Have station jack instructions been followed? Inspect visually.
  - Jacket (sheath) removal point
  - Termination positions
  - Pair terminations tight with minimal pair distortions
- Have patch panel instructions been followed? Inspect visually.
  - Cable dressing first
  - Jackets (sheath) remain up to the connecting block
  - Pair terminations tight and undistorted
- Is the jacket maintained right up to the connection [7]?

Fiber Optic Indoor Cable Structural Issues: Why Tight Buffer is Common

Today, improved micron-buffered fiber coating processes are used on all tight buffer cables. These processes are designed to strip to 250 microns or down to 125 microns easily and consistently, expediting preparation for traditional epoxy and new crimp-style direct-connect ST's and SC's applications. The enhancement also improves preparation of mechanical or fusion splicing requirements.

Furthermore, a water blocking system, a gel-less alternative for blocking out moisture that utilizes individual or combinations of filaments, tapes, and coating, are now used to effectively block water migration. The blocking agent doesn't activate until moisture is detected; it then swells to 50 times its original size, blocking water penetration. For installers, the benefit is elimination of the messy gel surrounding the tubes, thus simplifying cable preparation for connectorization. The water blocking system is now incorporated in all fiber optic cable products, as well as across all premise tight buffer cables.

In addition to construction and performance enhancements, a combination of multimode fibers with single mode, to future-proof bandwidth requirements of emerging technologies, is now available. This combined system provides an organizational tool to arrange and identify the two fiber types. Available in tight buffer breakout cable, as well as loose-tube configurations, the combination of multimode fibers with single mode uses a unique color coding scheme to simplify splice trays, patch cable, and panel identity, by reducing installer connectorization time.

Let's now look at fiber optic outdoor cable plant design specifications. Structural design issues like underground versus aerial cable, loose tube, ribbon, slotted core, and avoiding moisture contamination will be covered.

OUTDOOR CABLE

Since 1990, approximately 300,000 miles of fiber optic cable have been installed in video-based outside cable plants [1]. The installation of fiber cable has reduced amplifier cascades, thereby increasing reliability and quality of the outdoor cable plant. The majority of this outdoor fiber optic cable has been installed in the *local loop*, the most hostile of outside cable plant environments. In order to maintain a higher reliability and signal quality, a systematic fiber optic outside plant maintenance program with plans for the most efficient means of emergency restoration must be designed and implemented. This part of the chapter reviews the frequency and costs of outside fiber optic cable outages and outlines the design of preventive maintenance systems and cost-effective emergency restoration. Some of the new tools available for proactive design and maintenance of outside fiber optic cable plants and the potential cost savings realized are also presented.

Fiber's Effect on System Reliability

The resulting increase in system reliability due to the installation of fiber optic transmission systems has been well-documented over the past few years. An increase in reliability on the order of 500 percent has been achieved by deploying hybrid/fiber coax (HFC) systems in the video networks [1].

It should not be forgotten, however, that this mass deployment of outside fiber optic cable has also resulted in the concentration of communications circuits into unmaintained, long lengths of increasingly smaller and more vulnerable packages. In addition, although the fiber components are inherently more reliable, they also inherently take longer to restore in the case of an outage.

Theoretically up to 40 percent of downtime in hybrid fiber/coax (HFC) systems will be caused by the optical components due to the high mean time to repair (MTTR) outside/outdoor fiber optic cable. Of that, approximately 30 percent of the projected fiber link downtime will be due to the cable itself [1].

Actual field results of fiber cable failures have also been analyzed. According to Bellcore [1] and the FCC's [2] Network Reliability and Interoperability Council (NRIC), the cause of fiber field failure and the time to repair for fiber outages that are reported are shown in Figure 15–1 [3].

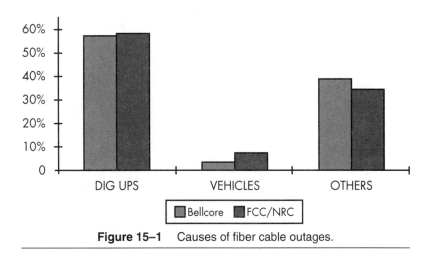

Figure 15–1   Causes of fiber cable outages.

Fiber Network Availability

Network reliability is the probability that a system will not fail in a defined period of time. Another important issue is network availability, which is defined as *a measure of the ability of a network or a unit to perform a required function at a given instant in time.* Network availability can be expressed in mathematical terms as MTBF/(MTBF+MTTR), where MTBF is the mean time between failures and MTTR is the mean time to repair with given external sources. This formula demonstrates that network availability can be improved by (1) increasing the MTBF, which represents reliability; and/or (2) decreasing MTTR, which represents repair time.

Maximizing Availability by Increasing MTBF

As discussed in the preceding, one way of maximizing fiber cable availability is to increase the mean time between failures. Components installed today in fiber optic cable systems already have a high degree of reliability. In order to maximize MTBF, proactive maintenance programs must be implemented in order to get the predicted reliability of the components. Another more costly yet effective way to increase network MTBF is route redundancy.

Fiber Cable Dig-Up Prevention

Both FCC and Bellcore report similar results (see Figure 15–1). Because more than 50 percent of all outages reported were caused by dig-ups, the NRIC concentrated on the analysis of outages due to dig-ups and how to avoid them [2]. The NRIC concluded that more rigorous *call before you dig* programs should be adopted into state law and/or federal law. Although most states now have underground facility damage prevention laws, they *lack the depth of enforcement and penalties required to deter excavators from digging without providing notification.* Regardless, many telephony service carriers have adopted tone location into their preventive maintenance programs in an attempt to decrease outages due to dig-ups.

Automated tone location equipment is available that can be activated remotely to place a locating tone on the armor of the cable. This remote activation allows for easy implementation of a tone location program. Rather than having to connect a tone transmitter in the field, the transmitter is always connected at the head end and remotely activated on command.

Preventive Maintenance Systems: Underground versus Aerial Cable

It is important to note that in both the FCC and Bellcore reports, approximately 75 percent of all cables installed were buried or underground and 25 percent were aerial installations. Most estimates of fiber cable installed in outside plants reverses these percentages, that is, 75 percent is aerial and 25 percent is buried. Both reports found that the frequency of fiber failures were relatively independent of installation, but the causes of failure based on the type of installation differed greatly.

Approximately 70 percent of all buried and underground outages are caused by dig-ups. Obviously no aerial outages are caused by dig-ups, but 20 percent of all aerial outages are caused by vehicle collisions.

For the purposes of this chapter, dig-ups and vehicle collisions are categorized as *instantaneous* outages. All other outages are considered *preventable* because they are generally caused by the slow degradation of the cable due to environmental factors. These types of outages include sheath and subsequent fiber damage due to pole attachment hardware, rodents, backfill, fires, lightning damage, and so on. (see Figure 15–2) [3].

Preventive maintenance systems are available that can predict a fiber failure point by using the fiber cable's protective outer layers as a sensor. These preventive maintenance systems alarm when the integrity of the outer plastic jacket of the cable or a fiber splice enclosure is breached (see Figure 15–3) [3].

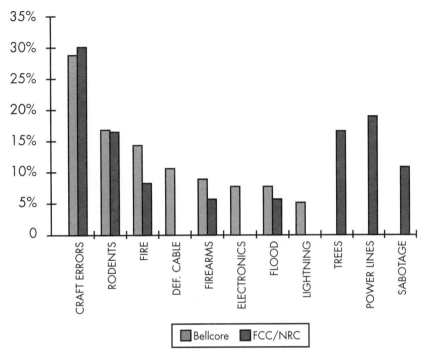

Figure 15–2   Causes of preventable fiber cable outages (known others).

Figure 15–3
Preventative maintenance system.

By monitoring and reporting on the condition of the outer layers of the cable, a potential failure can be located and repaired before the optical path of the fiber is affected. This practice of measuring the integrity of the fiber sheath has been standard in the telephone companies for years. Until recently, the measurement was done manually on a periodic basis.

In the case of underground plants, approximately 30 percent of all outages could be eliminated if such a preventive maintenance system were installed. In aerial plants, up to 80 percent of all outages could be avoided.

In a typical outdoor cable plant, where 75 percent of the fiber optic cable is installed on strand, 67.5 percent of all potential fiber cable outages could theoretically be avoided if a preventive maintenance system were deployed. According to the figures reported by the NRIC [2] and Bellcore [1], by using proactive monitoring, aerial fiber optic plants can actually be made more reliable than buried plants.

Preventive Maintenance Cost Savings

The FCC reports that historically an average of 4.4 major fiber outages occur per year per 1,000 miles of cable [2]. In the case of the typical outdoor plant design discussed previously, 3 outages per year per 1,000 miles could be avoided.

The cost of emergency restoration is approximately $25,000 per repair. The cost to repair sheath damage in a preventive mode is estimated at $5,000. Therefore, the cost savings of deploying a fiber cable preventive maintenance system associated with outage repair can be estimated as the difference between cost of emergency repair and sheath repair or approximately $20,000 per repair. Total repair savings per year due to using a preventive maintenance system is estimated at:

```
3 (outages) x $20,000 per 1,000 miles per year =
     $60,000/1,000 miles/year cost savings.
```

Preventive Maintenance Amplitude Modulation (AM) Distribution Revenue Recovery

Lost revenue can also be associated with fiber cable downtime for community antenna television (CATV) companies due to new franchise agreements that require a prorated refund to subscribers for service outages.

Today, a single fiber cable serves between a thousand and hundreds of thousands of subscribers, depending on where the fiber cable is physically located in the system. The cables close to the head end carry all the service and the fiber cables close to the subscriber only carry the service for the number of subscribers serviced by that node.

If the average subscriber pays $30 per month, the prorated price of the service is 4 cents per hour. So the potential cost of lost revenue to the broadband provider is between $40 (1,000 subs) and $8,000 (200,000 subs) per hour, depending on which cable gets cut. Based on hybrid/fiber coax (HFC) type fiber system designs, the average length of fiber cable carries service for 25,000 subscribers. Therefore, the average cable outage will result in a lost revenue of $1,000 per hour.

Amounts differ on the average mean time to repair a fiber optic cable. The amounts presented in this chapter show the average mean time to repair to be anywhere between 5 and 11 hours. For this analysis, 7 hours is used as an average time to repair or outage time for a fiber optic cable. Therefore, based on the information already presented, a monitoring system that eliminates 3 outages per year and 7 hours in duration would recover an average of $21,000 per 1,000 miles per year, or as much as $168,000 per 1,000 miles per year for the AM plant.

The most recent FCC and Bellcore reports show an increase in the rate of fiber outages through the last few years [2, 3]. Although not included in the report analysis, it can be surmised that this increase is due to the fact that the fiber in telephony systems is being installed closer to the *local loop*. The *local loop* has always been known as the harshest environment for outside plant equipment including cable. Although not reported, the number of outages per 1,000 miles in an outdoor fiber distribution system may be higher due to the fact it is also installed in this harsher environment.

Preventive Maintenance Telephony Service Revenue Recovery

Lost revenue estimates for telephony service outages run $2,500 to $25,000 per minute for a fiber cable cut. The cost depends on the transmission rates and fiber count of the cable. Thus, according to the previous analysis, a monitoring system that eliminates 3 outages per year and 7 hours or 420 minutes in duration would recover between $3,150,000 and $31,150,000 per 1,000 miles per year.

At first glance, the difference between CATV and telephony revenue recovery seems unbelievable. Based on the analysis in the preceding, CATV lost revenue is an average $17 per minute and telephony lost revenue is a minimum of $2,500 per minute. The difference is due to the price of bandwidth provided and where the fiber cable is physically located in the system.

The average price of a 4 KHz (64 Kbit) long-distance call is on the order of 15 cents per minute and, as shown in the preceding, the average price of 300 MHz broadband video service to an individual CATV subscriber is .0007 cent per minute. The discrepancy in lost revenue between the two industries is due to the discrepancy in price of bandwidth provided. Due to the lower bandwidth requirements of telephony service, a larger revenue stream can be allocated to any given fiber cable.

In addition, most of the fiber cable in the CATV industry is located in the local loop with a low subscriber-per-fiber density. Most of the fiber installed in the telephone network is for high-speed interoffice and long-distance business—where the subscriber, and therefore revenue (per fiber density), is much higher.

Time is money was never more true than when applied to reducing the time of a fiber cable outage. As shown by the rates of loss telephony revenue in the preceding, a minimum of $2,500 per minute can be saved for every minute sooner the cable can be restored. The preventive maintenance monitoring systems described can also quickly determine what section of the line the cut is located in, eliminating precious minutes of downtime.

Maximizing Availability by Decreasing MTTR

Another way to maximize fiber availability is to decrease mean time to repair. Once a network is down, the quickest possible recovery is required to maximize availability and revenue recovery.

Planned Emergency Restoration

The key consideration for reducing MTTR is creating a comprehensive emergency restoration plan. Much of the plan can be worked out during system design; however, a complete plan cannot be laid out until you know your resources (people, equipment, etc.), and have the *as-built* plant records of your system. The restoration plan should have seven components:

1. facilities management
2. team
3. training
4. equipment
5. action plan
6. fire drills
7. continuous process improvements

Facilities Management.   One of the most important steps that can be taken to ensure lower MTTR is the accurate design documentation of your system. A structured process for accurate design documentation at a minimum should include:

1. confirmation with as-builts
2. cable routing
3. fiber routing
4. optical losses
5. sheath condition

6. splice location
7. sheath lengths
8. cable lengths and markings
9. fiber-to-cable length ratio
10. system performance parameters [3]

Although the preceding list appears to be rigorous, the *upfront* work more than pays for itself in the case of an emergency restoration, outdoor fiber optic cable plant upgrade, or reconfiguration. Although the ideal case is to collect this information during the build, in most cases this database will be developed long after the outdoor cable plant is in place. To record the database after the outdoor cable plant is built, an *as-built walkout* is recommended in order to take a true inventory of your outside fiber optic cable plant.

One strategy is to log your outside fiber optic cable plant by *segment*. Each transition in the fiber cable (patch panel, splice cabinet, splice closure, optical receiver, etc.) should be identified as a *transition point*, the cable sheath footage design documented, and the transition point given a name and location. Each segment is then identified by the two transition points that it is located between. For each segment, the cable type, manufacturer, install date, fiber count, segment length, slack points, origination, destination, and type of information being carried should be recorded.

Updating the database should be centralized in order to eliminate confusion. One or two people or an outside firm should be responsible for updating the database. A *change of outside fiber optic cable plant* form and a procedure for filling it out should be implemented. All personnel associated with the plant should have access to the *change of outside fiber optic cable plant* forms and be trained to fill them out. Anytime a perceived change in plant is completed or noted, this form should be filled out and forwarded to the person or group responsible for maintaining the database.

Although the database can be kept manually, it is recommended that a computer database be used. The reason is due to the amount of information, the large number of cross references, and frequent changes required.

In the case of a fiber cable cut, the MTTR can be greatly decreased by simply being prepared. Not only is a good accurate database of utmost importance, but emergency restoration time can be greatly decreased by knowing where the tools required for an emergency restoration are located. This list should include excess cable reels, keys for entry into buildings, and all the materials and equipment required to perform the restoration.

In addition, a good practice includes the physical labeling of transmitters, patch panels, and jumpers. Many an hour has been lost in an emergency situation due to tracking the problem from the incorrect origination point.

The Team.   A restoration team should have seven members: five located at the fiber restoration site and one person each at the optical termination points of the run, usually the head end and a node. The five at the restoration site should consist of two teams of two performing the splicing, and one to review the as-built records and keep radio contact with the personnel located at the termination points.

Training.   The restoration personnel must be trained to access the *as-built* database. This training may include use of laptop computers to access the database via computer modem.

Formal hands-on training courses should be held for the restoration crew at a minimum of two times per year. Additional training can be achieved through *fire drills*, which are discussed later. The use of the test equipment, splicing equipment, and fiber optic cable splice preparation should be reviewed in this yearly training. At one major multiple service operator (MSO), it was found that *an additional 20 to 30 minutes could be shaved from overall restoration time* had proper procedures been used.

A multiple service operator (MSO) is a cable service provider that also provides other services such as data and/or voice telephony.

Equipment.   The amount and type of equipment needed is dependent on a variety of factors, including geography, climate, system size, and number of fiber technicians. If a system is large with high-density areas that are far from one another, spare fiber reels (1 km in length) should be strategically positioned to reduce travel time. Reels could be placed in satellite offices, warehouses, or storage sheds.

Test equipment should include an OTDR (1,310 and 1,550 nm), optical power meters, voltmeter, and appropriate fiber jumpers to accommodate all possible connections and test equipment. The minimum materials and equipment available to every restoration group should include either a fusion splicer or mechanical splicing kit, a reel of cable with both ends prepped, and an emergency restoration tool kit that is never accessed except in the case of an emergency restoration. These kits are commercially available in assembled form or they can be assembled to match a particular system's needs. Tools include a razor knife, pliers, side cutters, buffer tube scoring tools, seam ripper, rags, gel-removing solution, a set of standard screwdrivers and nutdrivers, alcohol wipes, fiber-coating stripper, cleaver, protection sleeves, compressed air, tweezers, and so on.

Loose Tubes versus Ribbon.   It has been shown that the use of mass fusion splicing greatly reduces restoration time (see Figures 15–4 and 15–5) [3]. In the Bellcore and NRIC reports, both cable type (ribbon vs. loose tube) and mass fusion versus single fusion splicing were also evaluated. The data shows that ribbon cable always takes less time regardless of fusion method, but more importantly mass fusion splicing greatly reduces splicing time regardless of cable type. Based on the cost analysis in the preceding, if one hour can be saved in an emergency restoration of a toll line, between $150,000 and $1,500,000 can be recovered in lost revenue from one restoration if mass fusion splicing is used. Mechanical mass splicing kits are also available. Mechanical mass splicing requires roughly the same time as mass fusion and delivers a mean insertion loss of less than 0.1 dB.

Action Plan.   First and foremost, safety should not be forgotten in the haste of an emergency restoration. Because they cannot always be found in an emergency, marker cones, vests, and gloves should all be stored with the emergency equipment and tool kit.

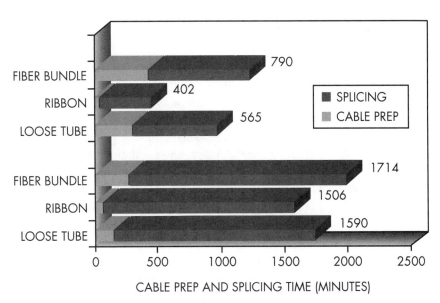

Figure 15–4   144 fiber cable restoration times.

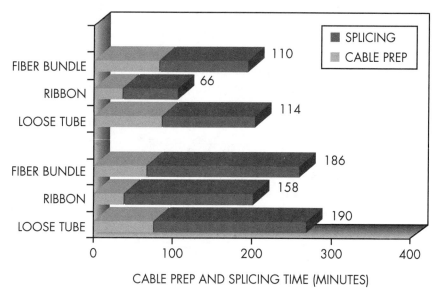

Figure 15–5   12 fiber cable restoration times.

Written procedures on how to proceed should also be kept with the emergency equipment so that they are easy to find. In addition, written procedures are a good idea so that nothing is forgotten due to the expediency of the restoration.

An action plan should be developed that includes who to call and when. A comprehensive list should be made available that includes phone numbers, pager numbers, and an escalation procedure for your own restoration personnel as well as other utilities and contractors. An escalation procedure should include who to call when the first options can't be reached. Phone numbers of the emergency team members and escalation procedure members should be documented on laminated cards and kept on hand by all team members. Also, after restoration is complete and as previously mentioned, a *change of outdoor fiber optic cable plant* form should be filled out and forwarded to the appropriate personnel for logging the modifications to the network.

Fire Drills.   Performing *fire drills* is a training issue, but is so critically important that they should be focused on as a separate issue. In other words, until companies started simulations, nothing they had in place was even close to what they needed.

Fire drills should be conducted once per quarter. The more realistic the drill, the better the training. A well-planned surprise fire drill is one of the best ways to train your personnel for an emergency restoration. Staged calls from a customer base can be placed so that the *cut* can be isolated. An actual cable can be laid out with a cut and the crew should repair it and be timed. The *team* should be allowed to proceed on their own with no help from management. As a goal, every drill should have a better time than the previous. In order to perform surprise drills, be sure to notify high-level management, due to the fact that the team's daily routine will be disrupted.

Continual Process Improvement.   After a restoration *fire drill* or any actual emergency restoration, a meeting should be held with everyone involved in the restoration to discuss what should be done to make the process better next time. Some things that have been learned in the past from documented fire drills include having rain suites and a tent for inclement weather, having technicians that should be familiar with the preparation of all types of cable, having lighting available, and better documentation of splicing priorities. Finally, after each post-restoration meeting, the data from the drill or restoration should be recorded and changes should be implemented as soon as possible.

Next, we can't leave the topic of outdoor fiber optic cable plants, without discussing how to avoid moisture contamination through preventive maintenance and monitoring the plants themselves. Preventive maintenance was discussed earlier, but not in as great detail as is discussed next.

Outdoor Fiber Optic Cable Plant Preventive Maintenance and Monitoring

Competition and the nature of the telecommunications business demands a high degree of system reliability and survivability. Appropriately enough, system reliability and survivability have been defined in recent years as the reliability perceived by the customer. Enter *self-healing rings*. Assuming adequate capacity, self-healing rings create a reliable outdoor fiber optic cable plant from the point-of-view of the customer. Even in the case of a catastrophic failure, the customer rarely sees the problem, and therefore, has the perception of high reliability.

But do self-healing or Sonet ring systems designed to provide no interruption of service truly make the outside fiber optic cable plant reliable? If the industry has learned anything in the past 10 years, it's that the outside plant facilities must be maintained in order to meet the objectives of long-term reliability and quality of service, as well as the system resale value.

As a result of the increasing need for plant reliability, there are now a growing number of outside fiber optic cable plant preventive maintenance and monitoring systems available. This part of the chapter explores the installation of a relatively new product that increases plant reliability by monitoring the highest revenue-carrying portion of the plant.

The Bay Area Experience

Because of the high traffic and system requirements for reliability, AT&T Cable Services (formerly TCI) [5] has installed such a system on its San Francisco ring. The system monitors the outside plant integrity of the entire length of the fiber ring and each of the fiber splice enclosures. It does so by using the protective armor of the cable as a long linear sensor. By using the armor as a sensor, any damage to the fiber cable's protective polyethylene jacket is immediately detected.

The splice enclosures are monitored with a special moisture detection tape and digitally encoded sensor. Splice enclosures are frequently immersed in water, whether directly buried or in manholes or handholes (see Figure 15–6) [3]. Should water enter the enclosure because of a construction error, material failure, gunshot, or any other loss of integrity, the sensor is activated and sends a digital code back to the office equipment via the armor.

Figure 15–6   Typical handhole conditions.

Primary-coated single-mode optical fibers are placed in the helical slots of polypropylene extruded around a central strength member and jacketted with nylon. Primary-coated optical fibers, which can be either multimode graded index type or single mode as per CCITT G651 and G652 recommendation, are placed in the helical slots extruded around a central strength member (FRP). Core slots are filled with jelly and wrapped with polyester tape. Sheathing is made by black polythene and jacketted with orange Nylon-12 (see Figure 15–7) [5]. Duct cable-slotted core type nylon-coated fibers are tightly placed in a slot. The interstices of the cable are filled with a moisture-blocking compound.

Both the outer protective cable layers and splice enclosures are monitored continuously without having to use a spare fiber. The system monitors the plant 24-hours-a-day and forwards sheath or splice enclosure alarms to designated maintenance or supervisory sensors or can be integrated into supervisory alarm systems.

The fiber optic cable sheath and splice enclosures represent the first layer of protection of the physical outside fiber optic cable plant. By monitoring the integrity of these components, a true proactive outside plant preventive maintenance program can be established. Failures can be prevented by locating and fixing these components before they cause a transmission problem or fiber optic cable outage.

System Design/Engineering

As in any system, there are several engineering criteria that must be met. This telemetry system is capable of monitoring a 75-mile radius of up to 600 sheath miles of fiber optic cable. The modular design is capable of being deployed with one to eight line cards, each of which is capable of monitoring 75 sheath miles and up to 200 individual splice enclosures per card.

In order to minimize total cost, the monitoring office equipment should be placed for maximum coverage. Location is not important from the standpoint of access because of the remote control and alarming capabilities. In the

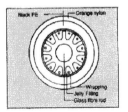

Figure 15–7   Optical fiber cable slotted core.

case of ring topologies, the office equipment should be placed to gain maximum reach, and consideration should be given to expanding the system to monitor the AM plant in the future. In the case where a ring is larger than 75 miles, office equipment should be located at multiple locations.

The AT&T Cable Services system was installed on the east side of San Francisco Bay. In order to minimize the cost, the system office equipment was installed in Pinole. The system monitors the cable south to Pleasanton, east to Pittsburg, and north to Napa (see Figure 15–8) [3]. If required in the

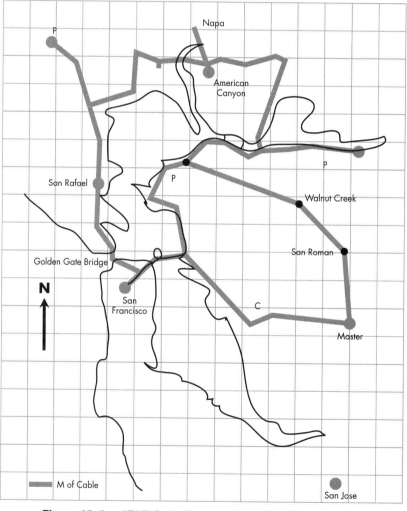

Figure 15–8   AT&T Cable Services North Bay fiber network.

future, spare capacity exists to monitor the AM plant in Pinole. In order to monitor the entire bay ring, another office system would be located on the San Francisco Bay side.

Only two 75-mile line cards are used to monitor this entire route. One line card is used to monitor the cable to Pleasanton, and one is used to monitor the cables to both Pittsburg and Napa. There are 48 splice enclosures that are monitored on the east bay route. Each splice sensor is encoded with a different digital code uniquely identifying it.

Installation

The installation of the office equipment is straightforward. Six units of 19- or 23-inch rack space must be provided for the actual mounting of the equipment. Two fused 48-volt supply connections and either a telephone line, RS-232 connection, or both must be supplied for remote access to the system. An inside cable and connectors are supplied for connections to the armor of the cables being monitored. In order to protect personnel in the office and effectively ground the armor, gas tube transient suppression devices and high current 60 Hz notch filters are installed from the sheath to the ground on all monitored cables at the office.

The field equipment is best installed as the cable is deployed, but can be installed in a retrofit application. The splice enclosure sensors are usually installed after the cable is placed and the splice enclosures are being prepared for the fiber splicing. The sensors should be installed during the splice enclosure preparation after the cable is secured in the enclosure.

The splice sensor is connected electrically between the armor and the ground. The armor can either be bonded through the enclosure or preferably brought out of the enclosure to an access point and bonded through at the access point. The armor remains effectively grounded through protection circuits in the sensor. The sensor is then tie-wrapped to an accessible point in the enclosure. A moisture detection tape is then connected to the input of the sensor and helically wrapped around the splice trays. The wires to the sensor should be dressed away from other splice components (see Figure 15–9) [3].

Figure 15–9
Moisture detection tape in enclosure.

The armor in the enclosure should be connected to #10 awg insulated copper and run through one of the closure ports to the outside of the closure. This method allows future access to the armor without having to reenter the enclosure. The armor *leads* are then connected together in a small, accessible closure.

At AT&T Cable Services, underground power cable is used as a jumper cable between the splice enclosure and the access point. A combination sheath protection and sheath access box provided by the monitoring system manufacturer was mounted in a 4-inch metallic pedestal (see Figure 15–10) [3].

As each splice sensor is installed, a test set is used to check the condition of the sheath back toward the office. In addition, before the enclosure is sealed, the test set is also used to functionally test the sensor to verify that it was installed correctly. The technician then records the digital code and the location of the splice for later input into the system's outside plant database.

After the hardware is installed, the system database must be loaded. First, the system data, including system identification, cable runs, length of cable between splice points, splice point location, cable fiber counts, and so on, is loaded into the database.

Alarm-forwarding information is then loaded. Alarm-forwarding information includes phone numbers that the system automatically calls, RS-232 port connection, where to call on weekdays during work hours, and where to call on nights, weekends, or holidays.

To date, both splice enclosure and sheath alarms have been reported. Sheath violations are located by use of long-range fault locators and tone location equipment. The long-range fault locators are capable of locating the fault zone from distances up to 60 miles. Once the fault is located to within a few hundred feet, a tone location system and A-frame locator are used to identify the exact fault location.

The four splice alarms received to date were all a result of having appreciable amounts of water in the enclosure. Splice enclosure alarms have

Figure 15–10
Above-grade access to cable armor.

resulted in finding poor splice enclosure construction practices and enclosures damaged by the various rigors of the outside plant environment.

Actual Costs and Cost Savings

The initial hardware cost of the sheath and splice enclosure monitoring system, including office and field equipment, for the east bay side of the loop was $35,000. The additional cost of installation labor was $45 per splice. The total installed cost of the system to monitor 163 miles and 48 splice enclosures was about $37,160.

The deployment of a fiber optic preventive maintenance system not only increases the reliability of the plant, but also saves money. At AT&T Cable Services, a fiber optic cable emergency restoration through permanent restoration can cost up to $25,000. The installed preventive maintenance system pays for itself when two outages are prevented from occurring.

In many locations around the country, new franchise agreements have outage reimbursement clauses. Most of these clauses require a prorated rebate to the customer based on the duration of an outage. In the case of digital backbone feeder systems, a large number of video customers would be affected by a fiber outage. As an example, if a digital feeder system carrying video traffic to 45,000 customers were out for over three hours, a one-day rebate is typically required by these agreements. For example, given a rate of $38 per month, the one-day rebate for loss of video service to those 45,000 customers would be $57,000 (1/30 × $38 × 45,000).

Depending on the data rate, one fiber optic competitive access ring cable can carry between $2,500 and $50,000 of revenue per minute. If the average fiber cable downtime is five hours (300 minutes), each cable outage prevented represents between $750,000 and $15 million in revenue that would have been lost. The most detrimental cost due to a fiber outage is the potential for loss of customer confidence. Although it's hard to put a price on it, loss of customer confidence is reason enough to deploy preventive maintenance systems. In other words, proactive preventive maintenance is the clear direction for the future in maintaining telecom networks to high standards in the field.

BENEFITING FROM STRUCTURED FIBER OPTIC CABLING OPTIONS

The use of structured fiber optic cable offers options in communications transmission mediums (see Sidebar, "Indoor and Outdoor Structured Fiber Optic Options"). Fiber optics make a smaller, lighter weight cable with wonderful mechanical flexibility, a cable secure from electromagnetic interference capable of broader broadband transmission over remarkably expanded distances with the guarantee of long-term upgrade potential. Thus, structured fiber optic cables are available for installation everywhere copper cables could go:

- underground, directly buried, with or without armoring
- in conduit
- in environmentally hostile settings: cold, wet, heat, acid, saline
- aerial installations, lashed or self-supported
- interior duct work, risers, ceilings, plenums, closets [8]

INDOOR AND OUTDOOR STRUCTURED FIBER OPTIC OPTIONS

Indoor Fiber Optic Options

Multimode and Single Mode
Simplex/duplex cables are ideal for patch cord/pigtail applications. Available in both riser and plenum versions, in bulk lengths, or as precut/preterminated assemblies.

Riser Rated
Riser rated feature compact, flexible packaging for a wide variety of indoor applications. Tight-buffered multiple application cables are ideal for premise and campus distribution applications, available with up to 156 fibers.

Riser Rated Breakout Cables
Riser rated breakout cables are specifically designed for flame retardant/riser requirements. Feature breakout style packaging for building applications requiring many single-channel terminations. Each flame-retardant breakout is color-coded for easy identification. The cable's flexibility and tensile strength allows for easy pulling into crowded, hard-to-reach areas.

Plenum Cables
Plenum cables feature compact, flexible packaging for a variety of premise and campus applications. Tight-buffered cables are suitable for intrabuilding point-to-point and distribution runs, available with up to 72 fibers. Small diameter and flexibility provide for easy installation in crowded, difficult-to-access areas. Cables with more than 12 fibers are bundled into subgroups protected with their own flame-retardant jackets. This *cable-within-a-cable* design allows for easy identification and cable routing.

Plenum Breakout Cables
For plenum applications requiring many single-channel terminations, this breakout design offers convenience and the protection of individual fibers. Each fiber is individually strengthened and jacketed for direct connectivity. It's ideal for indoor plenum and cable tray applications.

RLT Series Riser Indoor/Outdoor Loose Tube Cables

RLT series riser indoor/outdoor loose tube cables are designed for installation for both out-doors and indoors in areas required by the National Electrical Code (NEC) to be riser rated type OFNR. These cables are loose tube, gel-filled constructions for excellent resistance to moisture. They are available with single-mode or multimode fibers with up to a maximum of 72 fibers.

Because the outdoor cables are riser rated, they eliminate the need for a separate point of demarcation (splicing to a riser rated cable within 50 feet of the point where the outdoor cable enters the building) as required by the NEC.

Outdoor Fiber Optic Options

Multimode and Single Mode

Multimode and single mode are loose tube and tight buffered, armored and nonarmored, and self-supporting

Outdoor Distribution Cables

Standard loose tube designs have a central steel or dielectric strength member around which the gel-filled tubes are wound with Kevlar® and any necessary filler tubes and an outer poly-ethylene jacket for maximum weatherability. Optional inner jacket and corrugated steel armor are composed of the following:

- Gel-filled loose tube (tight buffered available).
- Each fiber color-coded, each tube color-coded.
- As many as 216 fibers may be available.
- Nonarmored, for aerial (lashed) and conduit or duct installation.
- Armored, for direct earth burial installation.

ADSS—All Dielectric Self-Supporting Outdoor Fiber

The advantages are concentric shape which facilitates pulling in ducts and small diameter for minimal wind and ice loading in aerial applications.

Features
- all dielectric, round
- loose tube or tight buffered
- glass epoxy central strength antibuckling agent
- multifiber loose-tube construction round central
- loose tube is gel-filled
- inner Jacket
- outer high density polyethylene jacket

Self-Supporting Outdoor Fiber

Self-supporting outdoor fiber is available in two types:

- All dielectic messenger—Kevlar® support plus epoxy-glass rod.
- Stainless steel 1/8" messenger—Span lengths, storm load rating.

It is also composed of 6 to 36 fibers per tube, each buffer contains 6 fibers.

Broadband Coaxial—CATV

Broadband Coaxial—CATV is available in RG 59, RG 6, and RG 11; 14, 18, and 20 awg. The following is recommended:

- 11/u for distances over 175 feet
- 6/u for distances to 175 feet
- 59/u minimum capacity requirements:
    1. CATV drop, 75 ohm, for interior horizontal, lashed outdoor aerial drop and conduit installation, PVC jacket.
    2. CATV drop flooded, 75 ohm, for underground installation, polyethylene jacket.
    3. CATV self-supporting, 75 ohm [8].

Surveying Structured Fiber Optic Cabling Standards

Like technology, structured fiber optic cabling standards are continuously evolving. Additional transmission parameters will be specified for future high-speed applications. Standards compliance provides a minimum level of assurance. Systems that provide a measurement margin greater than the present-day structured fiber optic cabling standards should survive the long-term demands that will be placed on them.

Today, structured fiber optic cabling standards play a major role in providing uniformity in telecommunications infrastructure design. These standards then become the foundation on which new technologies are based. They allow a building to grow and change as technology changes with minimal disruption to existing services reducing the costs of moves, adds, and changes.

Structured fiber optic cabling is a *standards*-based method of engineering and installing an integrated data, voice, and video cabling system. A properly designed and installed structured fiber optic cabling system provides a cabling infrastructure that delivers predictable performance as well as flexibility to accommodate growth and change over an extended period of time. Additionally, a structured fiber optic cabling system provides a uniform, open physical cabling topology that can simultaneously support multiple logical networking topologies for different applications such as Ethernet, token ring,

ATM, or video. The initial investment in a *standards*-based structured fiber optic cabling system will return many benefits, including an extended operational lifespan, predictable performance, manageability, and growth. These benefits bring increased efficiency, improved productivity, and reduced costs.

Domestic and international standards organizations have been formed to ensure that manufactured products meet certain quality, safety, and performance *norms* for that category and class of product. Standards organizations such as ISO/IEC, TIA/EIA, CENELEC, and CSA have created and published standards for structured fiber optic cabling products, and their specifications for structured fiber optic cabling systems are widely used and accepted in the industry.

New SM Cable Plant Test Optical Fiber System Test Procedure (OFSTP)-7

A new test standard for installed single-mode (SM) structured fiber optic cable plant has been recently approved by the TIA/EIA FO 2.1 fiber optic committee. OFSTP-7 covers testing the installed SM fiber cable plant, which includes all the terminated and spliced cables, patch panels, and so on.

Two methods of testing are included: insertion loss with a source and power meter (like OFSTP-14 for multimode fiber [see Sidebar, "Structured Fiber Optic Cable Plant Test OFSTP-14"]) and OTDR testing (see Chapter 17, "OTDR: Optical Time Domain Reflectometer"). While recognizing the source/meter test is more accurate, since it mimics the way the system actually transmits power through the fiber optic cable plant, the OTDR test is included as an indirect test that allows seeing intermediate splices in concatenated fibers. When the results of the two test methods are not in agreement, the source/meter method is specified to be used as the definitive measurement.

Providing a Structured Fiber Optic Cabling Option without the Benefits of a Fiber Upgrade

Increasing network complexity and the growing number of nodes on the network is accelerating the trend to higher data rates and forcing longer distance requirements into the LAN. What's more, the noise on the network caused by radiation, interference, or cross talk is making the network administrator take note to ensure data integrity and security.

All of these factors are driving forces toward the use of structured fiber optic cabling. But as network managers, few of us have the luxury of starting with a clean sheet of paper and designing a structured fiber optic network from scratch. Most of the time you have to deal with what's already there and accommodate both the old and the new.

Media converters allow the use of fiber where and when it is needed, effectively integrating new equipment into your existing structured fiber optic cabling network. This gives the network administrator power to:

- extend the lifespan for existing non-fiber-based equipment;
- extend the distance of an existing network;
- extend the distance between two like devices; and
- integrate data and telecommunication networks over fiber [9].

How Media Converters Work

In the Ethernet world, media converters connect one Ethernet medium to another transparently. For example, what if you have a number of PCs and UNIX workstations with Ethernet interfaces that work only with 10BASE-T (twisted pair)? But, you want to install a fiber-based (FDDI) or 10BASE-T LAN in the building. You don't want to throw out computers that otherwise are still quite usable. And you're not excited about buying new fiber optical network interface cards (NICs) for all those desktop machines, since each NIC can run as high as $750 or more. Those Extended Industry Standard Architecture (EISA) bus machines will do the job for another few years. Or, suppose you have a printer that does not support a fiber connection, but you want it accessible from a fiber-based network.

Small, cost-effective devices called media converters come to the rescue in these and similar situations involving Ethernet networks. Media converters are handy tools for making the union of the old and the new a happy one without breaking your budget. These passive devices increase networking flexibility while decreasing networking costs.

Common Applications for Media Converters:
Extending the Distance between Two Like Devices

A structured fiber optic media converter can reliably and inexpensively extend the distance between two 10BASE2 devices or two 10BASE-T devices up to 2,000 meters. This function is done without the monetary expense of a repeater or the use of a portion of your network repeater budget.

Extending the Distance between a Network Switch and a File Server or between Two Switches. Using media converters in a 10BASE-TX to 100BASE-FX back-to-back configuration provides a single method of extending the distance between a full duplex switch and a file server up to 2,000 meters. In fact, media converters can function in either half-duplex or full-duplex mode. Full-duplex Ethernet over UTP runs at 20 or 200 Mbps, while half-duplex

Ethernet over UTP runs at either 10 or 100 Mbps. Full-duplex Ethernet is especially valuable in linking two switches or connecting a switch to a file server. No adjustments are necessary when using either mode. A media converter will automatically sense which mode is in operation.

Integrating Data and Telecommunications Networks Across Existing Fiber. While single-mode fiber is most commonly used in telecommunications carrier networks, multimode fiber is predominately found in local area networks. A special type of media converter can connect these two environments, effectively extending the network distance to 15 km, past the 2 km limitation of multimode fiber.

Media Converters Make Networking Simpler with Structured Fiber Optic Cabling Flexibility

Media converters give you a great deal of flexibility in your Ethernet cabling. Suppose you want to realize the advantages of structured fiber optic cabling because of its greater maximum distance between nodes, its inherent safety, and its immunity to radio frequency and electromagnetic interference (RFI and EMI). You therefore decide to install it in the engineering lab and on the manufacturing floor. But, you don't want to rip out all the metallic cabling strung through the rest of the building.

No problem! Media converters let you put fiber where you want, and keep coax or twisted pair where you need to. With this flexibility, you can expand and upgrade your network incrementally. What's more, their small size makes them easily portable and redeployable as your network configurations change.

Distance Flexibility. Media converters can also be used to extend the distances between Ethernet nodes. For example, when two 10BASE2 to 10BASE-FL converters or two 100BASE-TX to 100BASE-FX converters are used back-to-back, they provide a simple way to extend the distance between two devices up to 2,000 meters (6,600 feet) without having to use a repeater. You can also extend the distance between a switch and a file server.

100BASE-TX constrains the collision domain distance between two repeaters to 5 meters, and between the repeaters and terminal devices to 100 meters. So, using the 100BASE-TX to 100BASE-FX converters will not extend the collision domain, but, in full-duplex installations where collisions are not a consideration, longer distances are possible, up to 2,000 meters.

In addition, maximum effective distances depend on the signal attenuation of the cables used and the ambient RF noise in the environment. As noted previously, fiber has significant advantages over metallic media not only in bandwidth but also in EMI and RFI immunity. Therefore, it's a good idea to keep twisted pair runs as short as possible and use fiber for extended distances.

Minimal Delay.   The 10 Mbps media converter units are transparent, with no noticeable degradation in network performance, according to a study by the University of Pennsylvania [6]. The study recorded delays in the range of 1–2 microseconds for each unit, which are not noticeable by users.

Network Monitoring.   Unit LED indicators for power and individual port LEDs for link and receive provide instantaneous network status information. This network monitoring capability requires an external power supply.

Cost Savings.   Finally, the bottom line is that media converters deliver valuable networking flexibility while decreasing structured fiber optic cabling costs. You can preserve your investment in older equipment while you upgrade particular sections of your network for better performance.

FROM HERE

This chapter showed you how to design cable plants by examining indoor cable and outdoor cable as well as how you would benefit from structured cabling options. The next chapter will discuss verifying cable installations and provide you with testing tips and techniques to make verification seem less painful. The chapter will also show you how to conduct acceptance testing and help you troubleshoot your fiber systems.

NOTES

[1]   Telcordia Technologies, Inc., 1155 Avenue of the Americas, 16th Floor, New York, NY 10036, U.S., 2000.

[2]   Federal Communications Commission, 445 12th Street, SW, Room, TW-C305, Washington, DC, 2000.

[3]   John Chamberlain and Jerry Patton, "Optimizing Fiber Optic Cable Availability," Norscan Instruments Ltd., 7 Terracon Place, Winnipeg, Manitoba, Canada, R2J 4B3, 2000.

[4]   AT&T Cable Services, New York, New York, 2000.

[5]   Hindustan Cables Limited, R&D Centre Corporate Office, 9 Elgin Road, India, Calcutta-700 020, 2000.

[6]   University of Pennsylvania®, 3451 Walnut, Philadelphia PA 19104, 2000.

[7]   "Telephone and Data Cable Systems Specifications for School District," Northwest Educational Technology Consortium, Northwest Regional Educational Laboratory, 101 SW Main, Suite 500, Portland, Oregon 97204, 2000.

[8]   Clifford of Vermont, Inc., P.O. Box 51, Rt. 107, Bethel, VT 05032, 2000.

[9]   "Media Converters: Cost-Effective Solutions to Providing the Benefits of Fiber without the Upgrade," Transition Networks, Inc., 6475 City West Parkway, Minneapolis, MN 55344, 2000.

Verifying Cable Installations: Testing Tips and Techniques

Although fiber optic networks have some major differences from copper-based networks, testing and troubleshooting them is actually very similar. The techniques can be easily mastered by technicians with some basic training in fiber optics network testing. The basic procedures outlined in this chapter have been thoroughly field-proven in thousands of installations. With that in mind, let's look at testing procedures for verifying horizontal optical fiber cabling after initial installation.

ACCEPTANCE/VERIFICATION TESTING AFTER INITIAL INSTALLATION

What are the benefits of verification/acceptance testing? Testing affirms that the loss does not exceed acceptable limits, and ensures that the cable system meets the user's attenuation specifications. It also provides documentation that will be essential to a troubleshooter in gauging whether or not the readings he or she is getting are normal.

Test Equipment

For all cables being tested, the equipment used will be a fiber optic test kit, which includes a fiber optic power meter and an LED or laser source. The source should be of the type and wavelength used as transmitters in the fiber optic network being tested. Instrument adapters provide the interface needed to the connectors used with the network. Test cables are needed as launch and receive jumpers for testing the fiber optic network cables and a connector coupling kit is required to interconnect the test jumpers with the cables to be tested.

For basic testing, you will need the following equipment: a power meter, an optical source, two test jumpers (of the same connector type and fiber core size), and an interconnection sleeve. You will also need one of the following instruments to determine the exact location of any faults you find: an optical time domain reflectometer (OTDR), fault finder, or visual tracer (see Chapter 17 for further information on testing fiber paths with OTDR).

Required Tests

Testing the optical properties of fiber optic cable involves measuring two characteristics: attenuation and bandwidth. For instance, *attenuation* is the measure of signal loss during its travel through the cable, from transmitter to receiver. A small amount of loss is unavoidable, acceptable, and not noticeable by the data. But, because the number of spliced/connections can have an effect (more interruptions = more chance for loss), and workmanship/handling is another contributing factor on performance, it is important to test after installation to ensure the cabling system is performing to specification. TIA 568A compliance requires an end-to-end attenuation test with results within the published specifications.

On the other hand, *bandwidth* is a measure of the information-carrying capacity of the cable. The quality and length of the fiber determine bandwidth. Installer handling has no effect on this. It is important that a cable system's bandwidth provide the information-carrying capacity required by the end user. Bandwidth can be verified by simply affirming the documented specifications of the installed cable type. An actual field test is only necessary if this is not sufficient to determine bandwidth, or if the installer's practice is to run a field test anyway, or if the end user requires it.

Handling and Cleaning Procedures

Connectors and cables should be handled with care. Do not bend cables too tightly, especially near the connectors, as sharp bends can break the fibers. Do not drop the connectors, as they can be damaged by a blow to the optical face. Do not pull hard on the connectors themselves, as this may break the fiber in the backshell of the connector or cause pistoning if the bond between the fiber and the connector ferrule is broken.

If there is any question about the condition of the connectors, clean them before testing. A fiber optic inspection microscope with appropriate stages to hold the connectors should be used to verify the condition of the connectors so that there can be no doubt about their cleanliness or physical condition.

Testing Procedure Steps

You will want to read the test equipment manufacturer's instructions for testing, but here is the general procedure that complies with EIA/TIA-526-14, Method B: *Optical Power Loss Measurements of Installed Multimode Fiber Cable Plant.* Before testing, make sure all connectors, jumpers, and sleeves have been properly cleaned.

Step 1: Testing Continuity

First, you need to take a reference reading. Connect a test jumper from the meter to the optical source, set the meter and source to the same wavelength, turn them on, and record the power reading in decibels (dB). This is your *reference reading.*

A manufacturer may recommend that an OTDR be used to measure attenuation of fibers that will be left unterminated. A visual tracer can be used to confirm continuity.

Wavelength settings are generally 850/1300 nm for multimode, and 1310/1550 nm for single mode. In premises environments, all these wavelengths except 1550 nm are commonly used.

To comply with EIA/TIA-526-14, the light source or OTDR must operate within the range of 850 ±30 nm for multimode, and 1300 ±20 nm for single mode. Also, the power meter must be calibrated and traceable to the National Institute of Standards Technology.

Step 2: Connecting Jumpers

Next, connect a second jumper (of the same size fiber as the test jumper) to the first test jumper, joining them with an interconnection sleeve. Turn the meter and source on, and record the power level shown on the meter. This second reading is the *check reading.*

Compare the *check reading* with your initial *reference reading* to make sure that the second jumper did not increase attenuation by more than .75 dB.

To do this, subtract your initial reference reading from the check reading. There should be no more than .75 dB of loss between the first and second reading.

 .75 dB is the TIA 568A threshold, but if desired you may also use the manufacturer-specified guaranteed maximum mated pair loss for the specific connector you are using.

If the reading is satisfactory, proceed to Step 3, the end-to-end attenuation test. If not, clean all connectors except the source connection point, and repeat the check reading procedure.

Step 3: End-to-End Attenuation Test

Now you are ready to perform the end-to-end attenuation test. Leave both jumpers attached to the optical source and power meter, but disconnect them at the interconnection sleeve. Take the meter and its jumper to one end of the cable being tested, and take the source to the other end. Record the reading; this is your official *attenuation test reading.* Subtract the reference reading (recorded earlier) from the test reading you have just taken to determine the end-to-end attenuation. Document this reading.

 Attenuation should be measured and documented in both directions and at both applicable wavelengths (mentioned in Step 1).

Bandwidth Verification

It is not necessary to perform a field test to verify bandwidth if documents or cable labeling allow you to see that the proper bandwidth fiber has been specified. Perform an actual field test only if documentation of the fiber bandwidth is not available.

Other Things to Do before System Start-Up

Use the power meter to check the power levels of the transmitter and receiver, after they have been installed and before the system is used. This lets an owner or troubleshooter quickly determine if the electronics are working properly, and provides a valuable maintenance record for subsequent troubleshooting. Document your findings.

Examining Cable Plant Loss

Fiber optic networks are always specified to operate over a range of loss, typically called the system margin. Either too much loss or too little loss can be a problem. If the loss is too high, the signal will be low at the receiver, causing a poor signal-to-noise condition in the receiver. If the loss is too low, the power level at the receiver will be too high, causing receiver saturation. Both these conditions will cause high bit error rates in digital systems or poor analog signal performance.

Test the complete cable plant, including all individual jumper or trunk cables for loss using a power meter and source and the double-ended method described in the Sidebar, "Testing the Cable Plant." Use the double-ended method, since system margin specifications include the loss of connectors on both ends of the fiber. If the end-to-end (transmitter to receiver) loss measurement for a given fiber is within the network margin specification, the data should be recorded for future reference. If the loss is too low, notation should be made that that fiber will probably need an inline attenuator to reduce receiver power to acceptable levels. If the loss is too high, it will be necessary to retest each link of the complete cable run to find the bad link.

Possible causes of high end-to-end link loss are bad connectors, bad splice bushings in patch panels, cables bent too tightly around corners, broken fibers in cables, or even bad launch or receive cables or instruments. There are only two ways to find the problem: test each segment of the cable individually to find the problem or an OTDR, if the lengths are long enough for viewing with the limited resolution of the OTDR.

Do not use an OTDR for measuring end-to-end loss. It will not accurately measure actual link loss as seen by the actual transmitters and receivers of the fiber optic link. As normally used, the OTDR will not count the end connectors' loss. The OTDR uses a laser that has very restricted mode power distribution, which minimizes the loss of the fiber and the intermediate connectors. Finally, the difference in backscattering coefficients of various fibers leads to imprecise connector loss measurements.

Locating Mismatch Problems

In assisting users in installing and testing fiber optic (FO) networks, the first problem that's routinely encountered is locating incorrect fiber optic connections or mismatches. A fiber optic link consists of two fibers, transmitting in opposite directions, to provide full duplex communications. It is not uncommon for the transmit and receive fibers to be switched, so you transmit to a transmitter and receive from a receiver. This doesn't work too well!

A visual tracer will make it easy to verify the proper connections quickly. A visual tracer is a visible light that you shine down the fiber, using your eyeball to trace the fiber through the cables, patch panels, and so on, to the far end.

The tracer itself can be a flashlight (although it's really hard to hold the fiber in place to couple enough light to see it), a modified flashlight, or even a microscope, which will hold the fiber in place steadily and couple an adequate amount of power into the fiber or a special test source using a bright red LED like those used in plastic fiber links.

Do not worry about eye safety. The power level in these sources is not high enough to cause harm!

The tracers can allow you to trace fibers up to 2½ miles, or 4 km. Besides tracing fibers, the tracer can be used to check continuity and find broken fibers in cables. Another highly recommended use is to check continuity of every fiber in multifiber cables before installation to ensure that all fibers are okay. Installing a cable with bad fibers can be an embarrassing (and expensive) proposition. Fiber tracers are inexpensive and a valuable tool for every member of the installation crew.

For single-mode cables, there is also a more powerful tool available, a high-power, visible laser coupled to fiber, called a *visual fault locator* (VFL). These use red lasers, either HeNe or diode lasers, with enough power to actually show breaks in the fiber through the jacket of the fiber. They are much more expensive than simple fiber tracers, however.

Let's now look at how to troubleshoot an installed fiber optic system. All of the tips and techniques for troubleshooting an installed system are covered.

TROUBLESHOOTING FIBER OPTIC SYSTEMS

An optical fiber cabling system that has been correctly installed and tested will require minimal maintenance while providing many years of reliable service. However, if a problem does occur in a system, here are some tips to help you troubleshoot it easily.

Knowing When to Troubleshoot

When a suspect fiber optic cable is found, by noting a larger than expected loss in the cable link, the suspect cable needs testing by the appropriate methods described in Table 16–1 [1]. If a cable has attenuation that is higher than specifications but still transmits light, check connectors on a microscope to determine if they have been damaged and should be replaced. If the connectors look good, the best solution may be to replace the cable or switch to a spare. If a visual fault locator is available, it can be used to visually locate breaks in the fiber and find broken connectors. Under some circumstances, such as high loss in long jumper or trunk cables, an OTDR can be used to diagnose cable faults.

Table 16–1 Fiber Optic Cable Troubleshooting Guide

Fault	Cause	Equipment	Remedy
Bad connector	Dirt or damage	Microscope	Cleaning/polishing
Bad pigtail	Pigtail kinked	Visible laser	Straighten kink
Localized cable	Kinked cable	OTDR	Straighten kink
Distributed increase in cable attenuation	Defective cable or installation specs exceeded	OTDR	Reduce stress/Replace Observe for proper bend radius
Lossy splice	Increase in splice loss due to fiber stress in closure	OTDR/Visible laser	Open and redress
Fiber break	Cable damage	OTDR/Fault finder	Repair/Replace

Common Steps to Identify the Problem

If all systems have failed, check for a power failure. If power is fine, simply use a methodical approach to isolate the problem. Start by checking the transmitters and receivers.

First, using a power meter, measure the received power at the receiver. If any light is coming in, then you know that the transmitter and cable are fine so the problem would be the receiver. If, however, there is no light coming into the receiver, check power at the transmitter.

In other words, the installed fiber optic network can be tested quickly and easily with a fiber optic power meter. The fiber optic network transmitter needs to be set to transmit a clock output or other bit stream of known duty cycle. Set the power meter calibration on the proper wavelength and the reading units on watts. To test the received power, the most critical element in the fiber optic network, merely disconnect the fiber optic cable connector at the receiver, attach the power meter, and measure the power.

If the receiver power is low, the transmitter power should be measured by disconnecting the source jumper cable at the first available connector and measuring the power with the fiber at that point. Alternatively, one can disconnect the cable at the transmitter and use a known good test jumper to measure the coupled power. If the output is measured through a short network jumper cable (less than 10 meters), no compensation for jumper loss is necessary. For longer jumpers, some compensation may be necessary.

If receiver power is low, but transmitter power is high, there is something wrong with the cables. They must be tested at every connection to isolate the bad cable(s) and/or connectors. This can be done from either end. Starting from the transmitter or receiver end, follow the network cables to every patch panel. Disconnect the connector and measure the power at each point. By making measurements in dB, one can easily calculate the loss of the cable network to each point by subtracting successive readings. Furthermore, only after eliminating the transmitter and receiver would an OTDR, fault finder, or tracer be used to locate a break in the fiber.

In LANs, most problems tend to be concentrated in the areas where there is the most access to the fiber (patch panels).

Transceiver Loopback Testing

The datacom capabilities of the fiber optic network can be tested with a loopback test. This test uses a calibrated fiber optic attenuator placed between the transmitter and receiver on a piece of equipment to see if it can transmit data to itself. Many types of fiber optic network equipment have diagnostics to do loopback testing. This will test the transmitter and receiver of the unit under standard data transmission conditions over the specified link loss budget.

Some equipment can also institute an electrical fiber optic network loopback test, where the loopback path is inside the equipment, looping back over the entire data link to the equipment on the far end of the link. If both ends of the link pass a unit loopback test, but fail a network loopback test, the problem is in the cables, which then need testing by the methods described previously.

Surviving with Fiber Optics

Once installation is complete, the cable plant tested, the network equipment running smoothly, what is likely to go wrong in a fiber optic network? Fortunately, not much. One of the biggest selling points for fiber optics has been its reliability. But there are potential problems that can be addressed by the end user.

Sources of Difficulty You Should Know

With the cable plant, the biggest problem is what the telcos call *backhoe fade*, where someone mistakenly cuts or breaks the cable. While this most often happens when an underground cable is dug up, it can happen when an electrician is working on cables inside a building. Outdoors, the best defense is to mark where cables are buried and bury a marker tape above the cable, which will hopefully be dug up first. Inside buildings, using orange or yellow jacket cable instead of black or gray will make the fiber cable more visible and distinctive. Outside cable faults are best found by using an OTDR to localize the fault, then having personnel scout the area looking for obvious damage. Inside buildings, the short distances make OTDRs unusable, so a visual fault locator is necessary. Another problem is breaking the cable just behind the connectors in patch panels. This is a difficult fault to find, but a visual fault locator is often the best way. Unless the jumper cables are quite long, an OTDR won't help at all.

Within the fiber optic link, the most likely component to fail is the LED or laser transmitter, since it is the most highly stressed component in the link. Lasers are feedback stabilized to maintain a constant output power, so they tend to fail all at once. LEDs will drop in power output as they age, but the time frame is quite long, 100 K to 1 million hours. If there is no power at the receiver, the next place to check should be the transmitter LED or laser, just to isolate the problem to either the transmitter or the cable plant. Receivers are low-stressed devices and highly reliable. However, the electronics behind them can fail. If there is receiver power but no communications, a loopback test to see if the receiver is working is the best test of its status.

FROM HERE

This chapter showed you how to verify cable installations and provided you with testing tips and techniques to make verification seem less painful. The chapter also showed you how to conduct acceptance testing and helped you troubleshoot your fiber systems. The next chapter will examine optical time domain reflectometer (OTDR) and show you how to test fiber paths with OTDR and interpret OTDR traces.

NOTE

[1]   Testing & Troubleshooting Commercial Building Fiber Optic Cable: EIA/TIA 256-14," Leviton Manufacturing Company Inc., 59-25 Little Neck Parkway, Little Neck, NY 11362 USA, 2000.

CHAPTER   1 7

OTDR: Optical Time Domain Reflectometer

While today's fiber optic testing instruments are accurate and easy to use, they require adequate knowledge of their operation and *quirks* to obtain good data. Blindly using test instrumentation to test your fiber optic cable plant can be disastrous. As an example, there have been several instances where users of optical time domain reflectometers (OTDRs) accepted the automatic results of the instruments without evaluating the displays (or perhaps not knowing how to interpret the displays). The data was highly misleading and the consequences of the bad data were very costly. The reason is simply that the OTDR was being used outside of its normal operating parameters and the interpretation of the display is critical to understanding what is happening in the fiber optic cable plant.

TESTING FIBER OPTIC PATHS WITH OTDR

In this chapter, we examine the OTDR in detail and show examples of good and bad data. In addition, basic guidelines are presented to using the data accurately.

Before using an OTDR, one should read the manual that comes with it thoroughly. This will help you to operate the unit properly as well as test fiber optic paths correctly with it. Much of the information presented here is not normally included in the manual of OTDRs, which generally only tells you which buttons to push or the mechanics of how to operate the unit. An understanding of how the instrument works and how to interpret what it is measuring will keep you from being misled by it.

When Do You Use OTDRs: Before, During, or After Fiber Optic Cable Installation?

This chapter will give a realistic overview of what jobs contractors will see and what tools they will require. It is very important to understand when you need an OTDR and when it is not appropriate.

If you are installing an outside fiber optic cable plant network such as a long-distance network or a long campus LAN with splices between cables, you will want an OTDR to check if the fibers and splices are good. The OTDR can see the splice after it is made and confirm its performance level. It can also find stress problems in the cables caused by improper handling during installation. If you are doing restoration after a cable cut, the OTDR will help find the location of the cut and help confirm the quality of temporary and permanent splices to restore operation. On single-mode fibers where connector reflections are a concern, the OTDR will pinpoint bad connectors easily.

OTDRs should not be used to measure fiber optic cable plant loss. That is the job of the source and power meter, which duplicates the actual fiber optic link, as was described in the preceding and is documented by most every standard ever written for cable plant loss. The loss measured will not correlate between the two methods. The OTDR cannot show the actual cable plant loss that the system will see.

The limited distance resolution of the OTDR makes it very hard to use in a LAN or building environment, where cables are usually only a few hundred feet long. The OTDR has a great deal of difficulty resolving features in the short cables of a LAN and is more often than not simply more confusing than informative to the user.

Since OTDRs are somewhat expensive and have only specific uses, the decision to buy one must be made very carefully. For that reason, most instrument rental companies will rent one for a few days or weeks when you need them. However, if you are not familiar with their operation or cannot understand the results of OTDR tests, it would be much better to hire a specialist to do the testing for you (see the Sidebar, "Fiber Optic Tests").

FIBER OPTIC TESTS

The *design loss* is generally specified as the method of testing only for interior cables. OTDR testing is not required, and if done, requires substantial and meaningful interpretation.

You will need to note the sheath length markings on the start and end of each fiber, and subtract one number from the other to get the actual cable length. This is then used to calculate the design loss from the manufacturer's worst-case spec data. The upper limit from acceptance testing for a single fiber on each run should then be worked out as shown in Table 17–1 (submit calculation with test results) [1].

When you do the measurements, the loss result should be below the above figure. If not, find out what's wrong and reterminate; track it down with OTDR or repull cable if necessary. Don't pass on test results that show the link loss to be worse than what the manufacturer's data says it should be.

Table 17–1   Acceptance Testing Calculations

Length	L
Fiber atten db/m	A
Fiber Loss	L × A
Loss per Splice	S
Quantity Splices	N
Splice Loss Total	N × S
Loss per Connector	C
Quantity Connectors	M
Connector Loss Total	C × M
Link Loss Spec (one way)	= (L × A) + (N × S) + (C × M)

How Does an OTDR Work?

Unlike sources and power meters that measure the loss of the fiber optic cable plant directly, the OTDR works indirectly. The source and meter duplicate the transmitter and receiver of the fiber optic transmission link, so the measurement correlates well with actual system loss. The OTDR, however, uses a unique phenomena of fiber to imply loss.

The biggest factor in optical fiber loss is scattering. It is like billiard balls bouncing off each other, but occurs on an atomic level between photons (particles of light) and atoms or molecules. If you have ever noticed the beam of a flashlight shining through foggy or smokey air, you have seen scattering. Scattering is very sensitive to the color of the light; therefore, as the wavelength of the light gets longer, toward the red end of the spectrum, the scattering decreases, by a factor of the wavelength to the fourth power. Double the wavelength and you cut the scattering by 16 times!

You can see this wavelength sensitivity by going outside on a sunny day and looking up. The sky is blue because the sunlight filtering through the atmosphere scatters like light in a fiber. Since the blue light scatters more, the sky takes on a hazy blue cast while the red and infrared light comes right on through (and gives you sunburn!).

In the fiber, light is scattered in all directions, including back toward the source. The OTDR uses this *backscattered light* to make its measurements. It sends out a very high power pulse and measures the light coming back. At any point in time, the light the OTDR sees is the light scattered from the pulse passing through a region of the fiber. Think of the OTDR pulse as being a *virtual source* that is testing all the fiber between itself and the OTDR as it moves down the fiber. Since it is possible to calibrate the speed of the pulse as it passes down the fiber, the OTDR can correlate what it sees in backscattered light with an actual location in the fiber. Thus, it can create a display of the amount of backscattered light at any point in the fiber.

There are some calculations involved. Remember the light has to go out and come back, so you have to factor that into the time calculations—cutting the time in half and the loss calculations, since the light sees loss both ways. The power loss is a logarithmic function, so the power is measured in dB.

The amount of light scattered back to the OTDR is proportional to the backscatter of the fiber, peak power of the OTDR test pulse and the length of the pulse, sent out. If you need more backscattered light to get good measurements, you can increase the pulse peak power or pulse width.

INTERPRETING OTDR TRACES

They say a picture is worth a thousand words, and the OTDR picture (or *trace* as they are more properly referred) takes a lot of words to describe all the information in it! The slope of the fiber trace shows the attenuation coefficient of the fiber and is calibrated in dB/km by the OTDR. In order to measure fiber attenuation, you need a fairly long length of fiber with no distortions on either end from the OTDR resolution or overloading due to large reflections. If the fiber looks nonlinear at either end, especially near a reflective event like a connector, avoid that section when measuring loss.

Connectors and splices are called *events* in OTDR jargon. Both should show a loss, but connectors and mechanical splices will also show a reflective peak. The height of that peak will indicate the amount of reflection at the event, unless it is so large that it saturates the OTDR receiver. Then peak will have a flat top and tail on the far end, normally indicating the receiver was overloaded.

Sometimes, the loss of a good fusion splice will be too small to be seen by the OTDR. That's good for the system, but can be confusing to the operator. It is very important to know the lengths of all fibers in the network, so you know where to look for events and won't get confused when unusual events show up (like ghosts, as described later in the chapter).

Reflective pulses can show you the resolution of the OTDR. You cannot see two events closer than is allowed by the pulse width. Generally, longer pulse widths are used to be able to see farther along the fiber optic cable plant and narrower pulses are used when high resolution is needed, although it limits the distance the OTDR can see.

Capabilities of OTDR: Understanding the Physics (and Errors) of the Measurement

Don't let the title put you off, it's pretty basic. The amount of light scattered back to the OTDR for measurement is quite small, about one-millionth of what is in the test pulse, and it is not necessarily constant. This affects the operation and accuracy of OTDR measurements.

Overload Recovery

Since so little of the light comes back to the OTDR for analysis, the OTDR receiver circuit must be very sensitive. That means that big reflections, which may be 1 percent of the outgoing signal, will saturate or overload the receiver. Once saturated, the receiver requires some time to recover, and until it does, the trace is unreliable for measurement.

The most common place that this is a problem is caused by the connector on the OTDR itself. The reflection causes an overload that can take the equivalent of 50 meters to 1 kilometer (170 to 3,000 feet) to recover fully, depending on the OTDR design, wavelength, and magnitude of the reflection. It is usually called the *dead zone*. For this reason, most OTDR manuals suggest using a *pulse suppresser cable*, which doesn't suppress pulses, but simply gives the OTDR time to recuperate before you start looking at the fiber in the cable plant you want to test. They should be called *launch cables*.

Safety Concerns

Do not ever use an OTDR without this launch cable! You always want to see the beginning of the fiber optic cable plant and you cannot do it without a launch cable. It allows the OTDR to settle down properly and provides you with a chance to see the condition of the initial connector on the cable plant.

It should be long, at least 500 to 1,000 meters to be safe (see the Sidebar, "Potential OTDR Safety Problems"), and the connectors on it should be the best possible to reduce reflections. They must also match the connectors being tested, if they use any special polish techniques.

POTENTIAL OTDR SAFETY PROBLEMS

Optical time domain reflectometer for optical fiber generates light beam modulated by frequency dispersed compressible pulse, and has a pulse compressing filter for side lobe suppression.

An optical time domain reflectometer incorporates a pulse expander (16) arranged to frequency disperse short duration pulses (14) from a pulse generator (12), as shown in Figure 17–1 [2]. The pulse expander (16) is a surface acoustic wave (SAW) filter.

Use/Advantage

Optical time domain reflectometers are used for determining the transmission properties of optical fibers. Short laser pulses are applied to a fiber input and light returned to that input by reflection or backscattering within the fiber being analyzed. Major flaws give rise to substantial reflections producing peaks in the return signal as a function of time. The position of the flaw along the fiber can then be calculated, but the length that can be investigated is limited by the point at which pulse power can be increased. This increases laser cost, however, and may cause safety problems due to reflection at the fiber input and may damage the fiber by power absorption at a flaw. Increasing the pulse length reduces the distance resolution of the reflectometer. Devices using digital pulse correlation techniques need two pulses and the method of testing takes a relatively long time. The pulse bandwidth over which they can operate is also limited because of the speed at which the device can be clocked.

 Note The invention includes a surface acoustic wave (SAW) pulse expander for generating a light beam modulated by a large bandwidth, frequency dispersed compressible pulse, and a detector including an SAW pulse compressing filter, with inverse frequency.

The resolution is comparable with the prior art digital correlation techniques without the disadvantages of multiple reference and transmission pulses (such as apparatus to generate a series of relatively delayed reference pulses and it is not sub). The invention outperforms prior art devices, while using a simpler apparatus. The light beam generating beams may produce a pulse bandwidth greater than 20 MHz.

Claim

An optical time domain reflectometer includes:

- Generating a light beam modulated by a large bandwidth frequency dispersed compressible pulse.

- Detecting the light beam and its pulse modulation.

- A surface acoustic wave (SAW) pulse that compresses filtering, means receiving the pulse modulation from the detecting beams by producing a compressed pulse filtering, and generating beams comprised of a combination of beams [2].

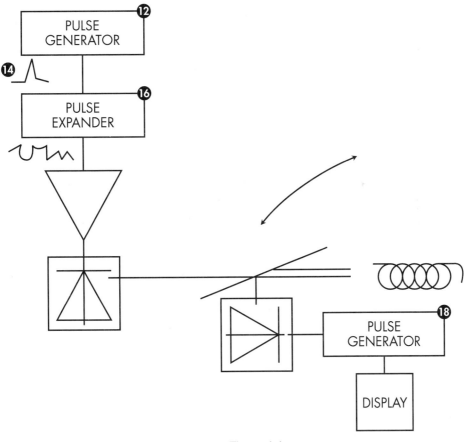

Figure 17–1   Thermal detector.

Ghosts

If you are testing short cables with highly reflective connectors, you will likely encounter *ghosts*. These are caused by the reflected light from the far end connector reflecting back and forth in the fiber until it is attenuated to the noise level. Ghosts are very confusing, as they seem to be real reflective events like connectors, but will not show any loss. If you find a reflective event in the trace (at a point where there is not supposed to be any connection), but the connection from the launch cable to the cable under test is highly reflective, look for ghosts at multiples of the length of the launch cable or the first cable you test. You can eliminate ghosts by reducing the reflections, using a sort of "trick" that will be discussed later.

On very short cables, multiple reflections can really confuse you. For example, recent observations were made of fiber optic cable that was tested with an OTDR and deemed bad because it was broken in the middle. In fact, it was very short and the ghosted image made it look like a cable with a break in the middle. The tester had not looked at the distance scale or he would have noted the *break* was at 40 meters and the cable was only 40 meters long. The ghost at 80 meters looked like the end of the cable to him!

Backscatter Variability Errors

Another problem that occurs is a function of the backscatter coefficient, a term that simply means the amount of light from the outgoing test pulse that is scattered back toward the OTDR. The OTDR looks at the returning signal and calculates loss based on the declining amount of light it detects coming back.

Only about one-millionth of the light is scattered back for measurement, and that amount is not a constant. The backscattered light is a function of the attenuation of the fiber and the diameter of the core of the fiber. Higher attenuation fiber has more attenuation because the glass in it scatters more light. If you look at two different fibers connected together in an OTDR and try to measure splice or connector loss, you have a major source of error—the difference in backscattering from each fiber.

To more easily understand this problem, consider the following. If both fibers are identical, such as splicing a broken fiber back together, the backscattering will be the same on both sides of the joint, so the OTDR will measure the actual splice loss.

However, if the fibers are different, the backscatter coefficients will cause a different percentage of light to be sent back to the OTDR. If the first fiber has more loss than the one after the connection, the percentage of light from the OTDR test pulse will go down. Therefore, the measured loss on the OTDR will include the actual loss plus a loss error caused by the lower backscatter level, thus making the displayed loss greater than it actually is.

Looking the opposite way, from a low-loss fiber to a high-loss fiber, the backscatter goes up, making the measured loss less than it actually is. In fact, this often shows a *gainer*, a major confusion to new OTDR users.

The difference in backscatter can be a major source of error. A difference in attenuation of 0.1 dB per km in the two fibers can lead to a splice loss error of 0.25 dB! While this error source is always present, it can be practically eliminated by taking readings both ways and averaging the measurements, which many OTDRs have programmed in their measurement routines. This is the only way to test inline splices for loss and get accurate results.

Another common error can occur as a result of backscatter changes caused by variations in fiber diameter. A variation in diameter of 1 percent can cause a 0.1 dB variation in backscatter. This can cause tapered fibers to show higher attenuation in one direction, or fiber with waves in the OTDR trace caused by manufacturing variations in the fiber diameter.

Overcoming Backscatter Errors

One can overcome these variations in backscatter by measuring with the OTDR in both directions and averaging the losses. The errors in each direction cancel out, and the average value is close to the true value of the splice or connector loss, although this invalidates the main selling point of the OTDR—that it can measure fiber from only one end.

Resolution Limitations of OTDR

The next thing you must understand is OTDR resolution. The OTDR test pulse has a long length in the fiber, typically 5 to 500 meters long (17 to 1,700 feet). It cannot see features in the fiber optic cable plant closer together than that, since the pulse will be going through both simultaneously. This has always been a problem with LANs or any cable plant with patch cords, as they disappear into the OTDR resolution. Thus, two events close together can be measured as a single event. For example, a connector that has a high-loss stress bend near it will show up on the OTDR as one event with a total loss of both events. While it may lead you to think the connector is bad and suggest replacing it, the actual problem may remain.

Another place this problem shows up is in splice closures. An OTDR may show a bad splice, but it can actually be a crack or stress point somewhere else in the splice closure. There is a tool that will help here, called a *visual fault locator*. It injects a bright red laser light into the fiber to find faults. If there is a high-loss connector, such as a bad splice, or tight bend stressing the fiber, the light lost may be visible to the naked eye. This will find events close to the OTDR or close to another event that are not resolvable to the OTDR. Its limitation is distance too. It only works over a range of about 2.5 miles, or 4 km.

The visual fault locator is such a valuable tool that many OTDRs now have one built into them. If you are using an OTDR, you must have one to use it effectively.

Special Consideration for Multimode Fiber

Most OTDR measurements are made with single-mode fiber, since most outside plant cable is single mode. But building and campus cabling is usually multimode fiber using light emitting diode sources for low and medium speed networks. The OTDR has problems with multimode fiber, since it uses a laser source to get the high power necessary to cause high enough backscatter levels to measure.

The laser light is transmitted by multimode fiber only in the center of the core because its emission angle is so low. LEDs, however, are transmitted throughout the core of the multimode fiber, due to their wider radiation pattern. As a result of the OTDR light being concentrated in the center of the fiber, the loss of connectors is lower because the typical connector offset errors are not in effect. And even the fiber has lower loss, because the light in the center of the core travels a shorter path than the light at the outer edges of the core.

For example, several projects have tried to determine how to correlate OTDR measurements to source and power meter measurements without success. An OTDR will measure 6–7 dB of loss for a multimode cable plant that tests at 10 dB with a source and power meter.

Measuring Fiber, Not Cable Distance

OTDRs measure fiber, not cable length. While this may sound obvious, it causes a lot of problems in buried cable. You see, to prevent stress on the fiber, cable manufacturers put about 1 percent more fiber in the cable than the length of the cable itself, to allow for some *stretch*. If you measure with the OTDR at 1,000 meters (3,300 feet), the actual cable length is about 990 meters (3,270 feet). If you are looking for a spot where the rats chewed through your cable, you could be digging 10 meters (33 feet) from the actual location!

Examples of How to Use the OTDR and Avoid Errors: Relying on Your Own Interpretation

Here are some actual examples of how to use an OTDR properly (and improperly) and some tricks to overcome some of the problems you encounter. The most adamant advice given is this: Do not blindly accept the data without interpretation. Most of today's OTDRs have *automatic modes* where they find splices and connectors (see Chapters 18 and 19) and calculate all the losses if the data follows preprogrammed guidelines. These numbers are not to be used without human interpretation of the results, as the OTDR is basically a PC, isn't too smart, and the software has limitations if the fiber cable plant has high reflections or short cable runs.

OTDR Trace Markers

Markers for loss measurements should always be set far enough on either side of an event to be on the straight part of the fiber trace. If there is any curve, it is likely caused by the resolution of the OTDR or recovery from an overload.

The fibers are all straight lines between events, as splices and connectors are called in OTDR jargon.

Setting the markers slightly away from the event won't affect the loss measurement by adding significant fiber loss. Remember, fiber loss is only 0.01 dB per 10 meters (33 feet) at 1,300 nm! By going further from the event, you reduce the possibility that the measurement is in error because of instrument limitations.

If the trace never shows a straight line between events it means either the distance between events is too short for the OTDR resolution or reflections are too high for the recovery time needed before the next event. In this case, you cannot get good data on either fiber loss or event loss.

This Trick Can Help

There is a *trick* you can try if you are desperate. The reflection at an event that causes overloading the OTDR receiver can be tamed by using *index matching fluid* to reduce the effect that causes the reflection. The reflection is caused by an air gap between the ends of the fibers. Connectors are particularly bad at having this air gap and the resulting high reflections. An index matching fluid replaces the air with a fluid or gel that closely matches the optical characteristics of the glass, thus causing the reflections to be greatly diminished.

Since the baseline between the two ends never becomes flat or straight, there is no reliable reference point for making a loss measurement. However, the reflections can be reduced by adding index matching fluid. Just add a drop of gel or fluid between the two connectors that matches the index of reflection of the glass in the fiber, thus reducing the reflections. Once you reduce the reflections (causing the receiver overload to go away), the OTDR will give you a good fiber trace just beyond the connector and a flat fiber trace, which you can use for measuring the actual loss! At this point, you can even get rid of the confusing ghosts!

Index matching fluid can be purchased from a specialty fiber optic distributor or from your local supermarket or druggist. The special fluids work very well but are expensive. Mineral oil or plain petroleum jelly work almost as well. If you can get silicone *high vacuum grease*, it works very well also.

Using this technique gives you the visibility that you would never have otherwise, but the technique requires care. The index matching fluid or gel must be thoroughly cleaned from the connectors after use with the OTDR. The splice bushing used must not be one in the network hardware, but a separate item that can be used and discarded or thoroughly cleaned in solvent afterward. Index matching fluid or gel will act like a magnet for dirt if it gets on any hardware or stays on the connectors—as its sticky texture will grab and hold lots of airborne dirt to attenuate the signal in the fiber link.

Finally, testing fiber optic cable plants are easy if you have the right instruments and follow industry testing standards. When diagnosing problems, you must be creative to develop techniques that help reveal problems that show up on standard tests. It is most important to know your tool's operation and limitations, and how to work around them. Get to know the applications support staff at your instrument vendor so you can call with questions. It is most helpful to have good fiber optic cable plant documentation, since knowing what you are looking at will make it much easier to find problems.

FROM HERE

This chapter examined optical time domain reflectometer, and showed you how to test fiber paths with OTDR and interpret OTDR traces. The next chapter shows you how to select connectors and splices by examining the quality factors, mechanical and fusion splices, and identifying different types of connectors.

NOTES

[1] Peter Guenther, "Cabling Installation Guide for Contractors," Andrew Boon Pty Ltd, Postal: 24 Swanston Street, NEW TOWN TAS 7008, Australia, 2000.

[2] "Optical Reflectometer," Defence Evaluation and Research, Agency Central Enquiry Desk, DERA, Ively Road, Farnborough Hampshire GU14 0LX, United Kingdom, 2000.

Selecting Connectors and Splices

Connectors are designed to be demount-able, as well as used to couple two fibers together or to connect fibers to transmitters or receivers. Splices, however, are used to connect two fibers in a permanent joint. While they share some common requirements, like low-loss, high-optical return loss and repeatability, connectors have the additional requirements of durability under repeated matings, while splices are expected to last for many years through sometimes difficult environmental conditions.

IDENTIFYING DIFFERENT TYPES OF CONNECTORS

Today, there are approximately 80 different connectors in use. Most work by simply aligning the two fiber ends as accurately as possible and securing them in a fashion that is least affected by environmental factors. Many techniques like expanded beam, using lenses, have been tried and abandoned for all but some very specialized applications.

Widespread Fiber Optic Connectors

While there are many fiber optic connector types available, only a few types are widespread. They are as follows:

- ST
- SMA

- FC
- Biconic
- SC
- D4

ST™

ST connectors are very widespread in the United States and are used almost exclusively with multimode fiber. They offer good features, cost, and performance, as shown in Table 18–1 [1].

Table 18–1   Features, Cost, and Performance of ST Connectors (SM & MM).

ST Make	Type	Size	Ferrule	Typ.Loss	Part #	Ref #	Price
AMP	SM	126 µm	Ceramic	0.3 dB	410516	502579-2	$10.15
Molex	SM	126 µm	Zirconia	0.3 dB	410520	86012-5000	$7.65
NCI	SM	126 µm	Ceramic	0.2 dB	403224	F1-0069	$6.90
3M	SM	126 µm	Zirconia/PC	0.2 dB	410522	8106	$8.15
3M	SM	127 µm	Zirconia/PC	0.2 dB	410523	8107	$13.20
AMP	MM	125 µm	Zirconia/PC	0.3 dB	410526	501380-1	$5.25
GTE	MM	125 µm	Ceramic/PC	0.5 dB	410544	WO 3756	$6.95
Molex (metal housing)	MM	125 µm	Ceramic	0.6 dB	336411	86012-0000	$3.25
Molex (plastic housing)	MM	125 µm	Ceramic	0.6 dB	410540	86010-0000	$3.15
Molex (900µm)	MM	125 µm	Ceramic	0.6 dB	410542	86010-0500	$3.15
NCI	MM	125 µm	S.S. Alloy	0.4 dB	410528	F1-0061	$2.69
NCI	MM	140 µm	S.S. Alloy	0.5 dB	410530	F1-0063	$3.20
NCI	MM	230 µm	S.S. Alloy	0.5 dB	403228	F1-0064	$3.75
NCI	MM	125 µm	Ceramic	0.3 dB	410532	F1-0066	$2.75
NCI	MM	140 µm	Ceramic	0.5 dB	410534	F1-0067	$5.90
Siecor	MM	125 µm	Composite/PC	0.2 dB	312515	95-101-02	$3.00
Siecor	MM	125 µm	Ceramic/PC	0.2 dB	312517	95-101-44	$4.10
3M	MM	125 µm	Zirconia/PC	0.2 dB	410524	6105	$3.90

Table 18–1 (continued)

ST Make	Type	Size	Ferrule	Typ.Loss	Part #	Ref #	Price
3M push pull	MM	125 μm	Zirconia/PC	0.4 dB	314629	6102	$9.60
NCI plastic fiber	——	100 μm	S.S. Alloy	0.5 dB	403229	F1-0065	$2.30
AT&T ST II crimp tool	——	——	——	——	410546	60-3010	$69.95
CAP–ST female cover	——	——	——	——	410547	——	$0.50
CAP–ST male cover	——	——	——	——	410549	——	$0.50

ST stands for straight tip and was originally designed by AT&T. ST connectors use a bayonet-style coupling mechanism for latching. A rear-crimp design attaches directly to cable and strength members, creating a very secure strain relief. ST comes with a 3 mm boot (900 μm boots available).

SMA

SMA connectors represent an old, first-generation design now declining in use. They are still used in some military applications because of their ability to withstand high temperatures. Some drawbacks include difficulty in use, generally poor performance, and suitable only for multimode fiber, as shown in Table 18–2 [1]. SMA connectors are typically used with 100/140 mm fiber or larger.

Table 18–2 SMA Connectors are Available in Multimode (MM) Version.

Make	Type	Size	Ferrule	Typ.Loss	Part #	Ref #	Price
Augat	905	125μm	ARCAP AP10	0.8dB	410586	698-DSC-125A	$6.45
Molex	905	125μm	Alumina/PC	0.25dB	410584	86021-0000	$5.15
LCS	905	125μm	Stainless alloy	0.8dB	410574	3905AM125	$3.45
AMPO	906	125μm	Stainless steel	0.6dB	410580	504094-1	$5.70
AMP	906	140μm	Stainless steel	0.6dB	410582	504094-3	$5.70
Augat	906	125μm	ARCAP AP10	0.8dB	410588	698-JSC-125A	$8.65
LCS	906	125μm	Stainless alloy	0.8dB	410576	3906AM125	$3.60
LCS	906	140μm	Stainless alloy	0.8dB	410578	3906AM140	$3.60

SMA stands for subminiature type A. The SMA905 connector is a straight ferrule design and the SMA906 is a stepped ferrule design using a plastic sleeve for alignment.

FC

FC connectors are also available as face contact/physical contact (FC/PC). This is a good second-generation connector design with very good performance and features, but relatively high in cost. With very good single-mode and multimode performance, this is one of the first connectors to address back reflection (see Table 18–3) [1]. FCs are often used for analog systems or high bit rate systems where back-reflection management is important.

Table 18–3   FC Connectors are Available in Either Single-mode (SM) or Multimode (MM) Versions.

Make	Type	Size	Ferrule	Typ.Loss	Part #	Ref #	Price
NCI	SM	126µm	Zirconia/PC	0.2dB	403231	F1-2069	$8.30
Siecor	SM	126µm	Zirconia/PC	0.2dB	312523	95-200-10	$11.95
3M	SM	126µm	FC/PC III Zirconia	0.3dB	410602	8203	$10.20
3M	SM	127µm	FC/PC I Zirconia	0.3dB	314631	8207	$19.95
NCI	MM	125µm	Zirconia/PC	0.3dB	403233	F1-2066	$6.05
NCI	MM	125µm	Metal Alloy	0.3dB	410610	——	$5.55
NCI	MM	140µm	Metal Alloy	0.3dB	410612	——	$5.95
Siecor	MM	125µm	Zirconia/PC	0.2dB	312525	95-100-10	$7.90
3M	MM	125µm	FC/PC III Zirconia	0.3dB	410608	6202	$8.90

FC stands for face contact and was originally designed by NTT (Nippon Telephone & Telegraph). FC connectors use a threaded keyed design and are compatible with NTT-FC and NEC-D3 hardware. The anti-rotation key prevents fiber endface damage and rotational sensitivity and the floating ferrule prevents shock and vibration.

Biconic

Biconic is a good first-to-second generation connector. This is the first highly successful single-mode connector. The early models did not address rotation prevention or back reflection. However, upgraded designs have addressed these features. Widely used by the telecommunications industry, these connectors are suitable for single-mode and multimode fiber.

SC

SC is a new third-generation connector suitable for single-mode and multi-mode fibers; the push–pull feature is very popular (see Table 18–4) [1]. It simplifies use and increases packing density. The SC connector offers excellent features, performance, and cost.

Table 18–4   SC is Available in Either Single-mode (SM) or Multimode (MM) Versions.

SC Make	Type	Size	Ferrule	Typ.Loss	Part #	Ref #	Price
3M	SM	126µm	Zirconia/PC	0.3dB	410628	8306	$ 9.55
3M	MM	125µm	Zirconia/PC	0.3dB	410634	6306	$ 7.95

SC stands for square connector and was originally designed by NTT (Nippon Telephone & Telegraph). SC connectors use a push–pull coupling mechanism that allows for dense packaging and its internal spring-loaded ferrule resists shock, vibration, and temperature stress.

D4

D4 stands for DIN 4. DIN stands for Deutsche Institut fur Normung (German Institute for Standardization). It is used primarily in European electronic applications, and also used throughout the world (see Table 18–5) [1].

Table 18–5   D4 is available in Single-mode (SM) and Multimode (MM) Versions.

Make	Type	Size	Ferrule	Typ.Loss	Part #	Ref #	Price
Amp	SM	126µm	Ceramic	0.3dB	410640	501508-3	$15.25
LCS	SM	126µm	Zirconia	0.3dB	410644	5D4SM126	$12.60
Seiko	SM	125µm	Zirconia/PC	0.3dB	410643	SDP-1Z-PD-S5	$10.45
Seiko	MM	125µm	Zirconia/PC	0.3dB	410645	SDP-1Z-PD-S5	$10.45
Special PC Polish Disc for AMP D4 Connector	——	——	——	——	410646	501867-1	$125.35

Cost Differentials

Connectors have used metal, glass, plastic, and ceramic ferrules to align the fibers accurately. However, ceramics does seem to be the best choice overall. It is the most environmentally stable material, closely matching the expansion coefficient of glass fibers. It is easy to bond to glass fiber with epoxy

682 Chapter 18 • Selecting Connectors and Splices

glues, and its hardness is perfect for a quick polish of the fiber. As volume has increased, ceramic costs have been reduced to be competitive to metal connectors (see the Sidebar, "Fiber Optic Connectors Designed for Field Use").

FIBER OPTIC CONNECTORS DESIGNED FOR FIELD USE

The cost of installing a fiber optic connector should include the cost of the connector, as well as labor, consumables, and scrap costs (see Table 18–6) [2]. Labor costs include training (if the installer is new to fiber optics), set-up time, installation time, and tear-down time.

Because of its low connector cost, the most popular type of fiber optic connector is the epoxy-polish (EP) type requiring two-part epoxy, heat curing, and polishing (see Table 18–7) [2]. This type is best installed in a shop atmosphere by experienced personnel who are skilled in producing many cable assemblies in a relatively controlled atmosphere. In the field, the EP type is the least desirable because of the set-up and tear-down time required, working space requirements, 115 VAC power requirement, consumables, and scrap costs. Similar to the EP type, the UV-cure uses a one-part epoxy and UV-curing lamp.

Also, there is a no-epoxy/crimp type connector on the market. However, this no-epoxy/crimp connector must be polished just like the epoxy-polish and UV-cure types. Perhaps the most important operation in terminating all of these connectors is the polishing, which is done in two or more steps. Improper polishing leaves a poor finish such as scratches and pits, which degrade the light signal. Furthermore, the polished fiber must be inspected under a microscope. Sometimes, very small scratches may be acceptable and testing with a power meter will determine acceptability. However, pits in the core region, large scratches, and fractures are unacceptable; and, if these imperfections cannot be eliminated, then a new connector must be installed.

Finally, there is also a no-epoxy/no-polish type connector on the market made by Siecor known as the Universal CamLite® (UniCam™). It requires no epoxy and no polish during installation. Its design is best described as a mini-pigtail housed in a connector body with a rear patented alignment mechanism to accommodate the field fiber. The field fiber is cleaved, cleaned, and inserted into the rear mechanical splice section of the connector. A small specialized workstation installation tool assists the termination process, providing for a total work time of less than one minute! Supplied with composite ferrules, these connectors are multimode (MM) type for 62.5/125 μm fiber [2].

Table 18–6 ST Connector Cost Comparison

	EP	UV	UniCam
Connector cost	$3.50	7.65	12.50
Consumables	$1.60	1.00	none
Labor	$9.00	5.25	0.75
Subtotal	$14.10	13.90	13.25
Scrap	$1.41	1.39	0.66
Unit cost	$15.51	15.29	13.81

Note

Set-up and tear-down time is not included. Labor costs are based on $50/hour.

Table 18–7 Connector Type Cost Comparison

Connector Type	Cost	Labor Cost	Material Cost	Skill
EP	Low	High	High	High
UV-cure	Med	Med	Low	Med
No-cure	High	Low	None	Low

Provided that performance and durability can be proven, a new type of plastic, liquid crystal polymers (LCP), offers much promise for molded ferrules at lower costs. Splice bushings have also been made from metal, plastic, and ceramic. The plastic types work well over many environmental conditions, but may suffer problems with repeated matings, especially under conditions encountered in testing numerous connectors or cable assemblies. The plastic bushings *shave* small amounts of plastic at each insertion. Some of this material may accumulate on the end of the connector and may result in loss. Some may also build up and form a ridge in the bushing to cause an end gap in the mating of two connectors. Check splice bushings for these problems by viewing the end of the connector in a microscope.

FUSION AND MECHANICAL SPLICES

There are two types of splices: fusion and mechanical. Let's look at fusion splicing first.

Fusion Splices

As fiber is deployed deeper into the network, installers are confronted with a number of choices to optimize splice performance using a variety of fusion splicers. These machines can splice a variety of fiber types (single-mode and multimode fiber) in a number of arrangements, including single-fiber, factory-made ribbon, or field-constructed ribbon using loose fibers.

Fusion splicing is done by welding the two fibers together, usually with an electrical arc. It has the advantages of low loss, high strength, low back reflection (optical return loss), and long-term reliability.

As with connectors, splices of increasingly higher fiber counts are being made for telephone company, cable-TV, and local area network applications. Economics dictate that these splices be performed quickly, accurately, and with increasingly higher performance (low loss). In addition to the skill of the operator, factors that affect the quality and performance of a splice are the fiber itself and the splicer, or, more accurately, the splicing technology used.

Fiber geometry is the deciding factor in the quality of the fiber, and is outside the control of the splicing crew. The chief concern in fiber geometry relates to fiber core concentricity or core offset, and it is a design concern of the fiber manufacturer. *Core offset* is the difference between the core's actual position relative to the true center of the fiber's outer diameter. Other concerns that may result from the manufacturing process include variations in fiber diameter, coatings, and fiber curl.

Fortunately, improvements in fiber manufacturing are reducing these concerns and the problems related to them as they affect splice quality. Nevertheless, when such problems do occur, skilled splicing engineers can overcome them by using splicing equipment that can identify and compensate for manufacturing inconsistencies. With that in mind, this part of the chapter will look at the following in regard to fusion splices:

- selecting a splicer for the job
- high-end single fiber splicings
- mass fusion splicing
- mini single-fiber fusion splicing
- splicing accessories [3]

When to Consider Selecting a Fusion Splicer for the Job

There are two basic types of fusion splicing technology in use today: core alignment systems and fixed V-groove alignment systems. *High-end* single-fiber splicers use the core alignment technology, while mass fusion splicers and *mini* (portable) splicers use fixed V-groove technology. Over the past decade, advances in technology have resulted in increasingly higher splicer performance. While each type of splicer can deliver a quality splice, splice loss and return loss dictate which type should be used for specific applications. Splicing engineers should know where these splicers can be applied in the network installation and what to expect from each type of splicer.

Engineers should also be aware of the operation and maintenance requirements of splicers; after all, they are precision instruments frequently subjected to rough field environments. Indeed, field practice, notably the degree of cleanliness surrounding the splicing operation, ranks most important (and ahead of fiber geometry concerns) among factors crucial to low splice loss. Tips for successful field practice will be presented later in the chapter.

High-End Single-Fiber Splicing

High-end single-fiber fusion splicers have long set the standard for high-quality splicing work; and, in field conditions, are generally used to join long-haul fiber segments. The operator is able to directly view and control the alignment of the fiber core of single-mode fiber on both the X and Y axis at magnifications of up to 280'. Multimode fiber is aligned by its outer diameter, because its large core size makes true core alignment unnecessary. These high-end splicers can be used with many different fiber types, including single mode, multimode, dispersion-shifted, dispersion-compensated, cut-off shifted, and erbium-doped.

Users should expect from single-fiber fusion splicers typical splice losses of 0.02 dB for single-mode fiber, 0.01 dB for multimode fiber, and 0.05 dB for dispersion-shifted fiber in laboratory conditions, and 0.01 to 0.02 dB more in ordinary field conditions. These splicers can complete a splice cycle in as fast as 25 seconds. They feature a built-in heat cycle that shrinks sleeves in 90 seconds.

Today's high-end single-fiber fusion splicers have several features that improve performance and productivity. For example, they can very accurately screen fiber condition, detecting dirty fibers, bad cleaves, and fiber axis angle—while providing a *go/no-go* warning prior to the actual fusion operation. This ability to screen defects significantly reduces the call-back resplice ratio and ensures the overall end-to-end performance of the network. These splicers are also able to adjust the fusion arc to compensate for changes in atmospheric conditions (altitude, temperature, and humidity), as well as electrode conditions and different fiber compositions.

With the rising costs of network installation and higher demands on *turn-up* deadlines, manufacturers are implementing design features that help eliminate the problems most frequently experienced in the field. These implementations include on-board self-diagnostics, low-maintenance optics systems, and remote interactive maintenance capabilities. In up to 70 percent of instances where field-related problems occur, diagnostics and corrective measures can be communicated over a telephone line between the field site and the manufacturer's service department. The ability to investigate and address problems in the field contributes substantially to reducing installation costs and meeting deadlines. Software upgrades can also be accomplished remotely. An additional feature on the most modern of high-end single-fiber fusion splicers is their ability to store large amounts of information on PCM-CIA memory cards. The stored information can document data pertaining to the splice point and an image of the splice itself.

Mass Fusion Splicing

A study recently undertaken by Pacific Bell proved that mass fusion splicers are fully capable of delivering high-performance splices in consumer broadband networks [3]. As reported, the mass fusion technique provides average splice losses well within required loss budget limits, making it a viable joining method for the specific architecture chosen by Pacific Bell. The study also showed that no statistically significant difference in splice loss could be observed with either *field-ribbonized* loose tube fiber or factory-made ribbon-configured fiber.

The Pacific Bell study was undertaken to investigate the feasibility of using mass fusion splicing as a viable alternative to single-fiber splicing in its Consumer Broadband Advanced Telecommunications Service architecture. While mass fusion splicing met the criteria, it should be understood that in general, this technology is a trade-off between high accuracy and high productivity. The success of mass fusion splicing in an application depends substantially on the use of high-quality fiber and the use of proper housekeeping at the job site. Moreover, the skill of the splicer operator contributes greatly to a successful and productive installation when mass fusion technology is employed. Fibers joined in mass fusion splicers can move in the Z direction (horizontal plane) only—that is, toward or away from each other. Unlike the movable V-grooves of single-fiber fusion splicers, the grooves in mass fusion splicers are fixed. This means that cladding-diameter tolerances, fiber core concentricity, and dust on fiber and/or in V-grooves greatly affect fiber alignment.

A regular maintenance program for fiber cleavers is important to avoid bad cleave angles and variance of fiber cleave lengths. Such maintenance includes keeping the highest standards of cleanliness in the V-grooves and on the fiber ribbon. These factors are important because a poor splice on a single fiber in a 12-fiber ribbon splice can adversely affect the entire splice. Mass fusion splicers can accommodate a variety of fiber holders. These holders are designed to accept from single fibers to as many as 12-fiber ribbons from all fiber manufacturers.

Users can expect splice losses (in identical fibers) of 0.05 dB for single-mode fiber; 0.03 dB for multimode fiber; 0.07 dB for dispersion-shifted products in laboratory conditions, and approximately 0.01 to 0.02 dB higher in actual field conditions. They can expect a splice cycle time of 95 seconds for 12 fiber pairs and completion of a shrink-sleeve operation in less than 150 seconds.

As with single-fiber fusion splicers, advances have been made in mass fusion splicers to improve the quality of the end-product. Large, high-resolution, movable liquid crystal display monitors with 25' magnification allow operators to view up to 12 fiber pairs and evaluate fiber preparation and splicing results. More importantly, given the number of splices per cycle, inspection systems are available that sequentially check the condition of each fiber being spliced and sound an alarm if results indicate that an excessive splice loss condition exists. This helps the operator to address the problems immediately, thereby contributing to increased productivity.

Mini Single-Fiber Fusion Splicing

Mini single-fiber fusion splicers offer the operator true portability. These units, which weigh less than 7 pounds, are designed primarily for short-distance applications where there is a looser tolerance on splice loss. These machines are very popular for taut sheath and aerial splicing operations because of their small footprint, portability, and battery operation. However, they are also ideal for standard cable installation and restoration work. These mini splicers are far superior to mechanical splicing (which will be discussed later in this chapter), typically exhibiting a splice loss of 0.05 to 0.06 dB for single-mode fiber, and 0.03 to 0.04 dB for multimode fiber in actual field conditions, due to recent fiber manufacturing improvements. Today's mini fusion splicers allow the operator to select from up to six fusion splicing settings for different fibers, including dispersion-shifted fibers. Mirror-free designs decrease maintenance, with dual microscope observation systems allowing fast X and Y axis imaging with a $50\times$ magnification. An arc test function that automatically determines the optimum arc settings based on ambient environmental conditions is also incorporated. Like the full-featured machines, the mini splicers will inspect and measure the quality of the splice and display the image and results, as well as store up to 100 splice data points. Portability is enhanced by built-in batteries with the capacity to perform more than 30 splices, including operation of the splice protection sleeve heater. Options include backup batteries as well as an AC/DC power converter unit to enable 110-Volt AC operation.

Splicing Accessories

Finally, fusion splicers (single, mass, or min) are capable of delivering high-quality fiber splices. Nonetheless, a quality splice begins with good house-keeping practices, proper fiber preparation, and efficient use of precision tools. Precision jacket removers are used to strip single-fiber coatings in one pass without damaging the fiber. These are available to accommodate fiber of varying diameters.

Fiber ribbon stripping is handled by thermal strippers that grip, heat-soften, and remove the jacket in one pass. Thermal strippers could also be a good solution for fiber coatings that are hard to remove with mechanical stripping tools. Fiber arrangement tools let the operator prepare loose fibers for mass splicing in a quick, simple step that can accommodate up to 12 fibers. Strippers and fiber arrangement tools accommodate interchangeable fiber holders that grip 1- to 12-fiber ribbons securely during the stripping and cleaving operations.

Cleavers are designed specifically for single-fiber or ribbon applications and should produce an end-face angle within 0.5 degrees of perpendicular to assure a high-quality splice. Cleavers for ribbon applications also minimize variances in fiber cut length. Let's now take a quick look at the pros and cons of mechanical splices.

Pros and Cons of Mechanical Splicing

Mechanical splices use an alignment fixture to mate the fibers and use either a matching gel or epoxy to minimize back reflection. Some mechanical splices use bare fibers in an alignment bushing, while others closely resemble connector ferrules without all the mounting hardware. While fusion splicing normally uses active alignment to minimize splice loss, mechanical splicing relies on tight dimensional tolerances in the fibers to minimize loss.

Low splice loss and high return loss is very dependent on the quality of the cleave on both fibers being spliced. Cleaving is done by using a sharp blade to put a surface defect on the fiber, then pulling carefully to allow a crack to propagate across the fiber. In order to get good fusion splices, both fiber ends need to be close to perpendicular to the fiber axis. Then, when the fibers are fused, they will weld together properly.

Index Matching

With a mechanical splice, the fibers are pushed together with an *index-matching* gel or epoxy between them. Since the index matching is not perfect, some reflection may occur. If the fibers are cleaved at an angle (about 8 being the best), the reflected light will be absorbed in the cladding, reducing the back reflections. Special cleavers have been designed to provide angle cleaves and should be available commercially in the near future.

SPLICE LOSS TESTING AND CONNECTOR QUALITY

Besides mode power distribution factors, the uncertainty of the measured loss is a combination of inherent fiber geometry variations, installed connector characteristics, and the effects of the splice bushing used to align the two connectors. This test is repeated hundreds or thousands of times by each connector manufacturer. This shows the repeatability of their (manufacturer) connector design, a critical factor in figuring margins for installations using many connectors. Thus, loss is not the only criteria for a good connector, it must be repeatable, so its average loss can be used for these margin calculations with some degree of confidence.

Inspecting Connectors with a Microscope

Visual inspection of the end surface of a connector is one of the best ways to determine the quality of the termination procedure and diagnose problems. A well-made connector will have a smooth, polished, scratch free finish, and the fiber will not show any signs of cracks or pistoning (where the fiber is either protruding from the end of the ferrule or pulling back into it).

The proper magnification for viewing connectors is generally accepted to be 30–100 power. Lower magnification, typical with a jeweler's loupe or pocket magnifier, will not provide adequate resolution for judging the finish on the connector. Too high a magnification tends to make small, ignorable faults look worse than they really are. A better solution is to use medium magnification, but inspect the connector three ways: viewing directly at the end of the polished surface with side lighting, viewing directly with side lighting and light transmitted through the core, and viewing at an angle with lighting from the opposite angle.

Viewing directly with side lighting helps to determine if the ferrule hole is of the proper size, the fiber is centered in the hole, and a proper amount of adhesive has been applied. Only the largest scratches will be visible this way, however. Adding light transmitted through the core will normally make cracks in the end of the fiber visible, caused by pressure or heat during the polish process.

Viewing the end of the connector at an angle while lighting it from the opposite side at approximately the same angle will allow the best inspection for the quality of polish and possible scratches. The shadowing effect of angular viewing enhances the contrast of scratches against the mirror-smooth polished surface of the glass.

One needs to be careful in inspecting connectors, however. The tendency is to be overly critical, especially at high magnification. Only defects over the fiber core are a problem. Chipping of the glass around the outside of the cladding is not unusual and will have no effect on the ability of the connector to couple light in the core. Likewise, scratches only on the cladding will not cause any loss problems.

Connector and Splice Durability

Another factor important to a connector is the durability of the design, shown by its ability to withstand many matings without degradation in loss. Testing connector durability is simply a matter of repeated mating and demating of a connector pair while measuring loss. Since the loss is a function of both connectors and alignment sleeve, it is helpful to determine which are the contributors to degradation. Plastic alignment sleeves (when used with ceramic connectors), for example, will usually wear out much faster, shaving plastic off onto the connector ferrules and causing increased loss and return loss. When testing durability, periodic inspection of the connector end faces and ferrules with a microscope to determine wear or contamination is very important.

Splice durability is one of withstanding many cycles of environmental stress, since splices are often used in splice enclosures in pedestals or mounted on poles, where they are exposed to the extremes of climatic changes. Manufacturers usually test a number of splices through many environmental cycles and accelerated aging to determine their durability. Such tests may take years.

Finding Bad Connectors

If a test shows a jumper cable to have high loss, there are several ways to find the problem. If you have a microscope, inspect the connectors for obvious defects like scratches, cracks, or surface contamination. If they look okay, it is always a good practice to clean them before retesting. Retest the launch cable to make certain it is good. Then retest the jumper cable with the single-ended method, using only a launch cable. Test the cable in both directions. The cable should have higher loss when tested with the bad connector attached to the launch cable, since the large area detector of the power meter will not be affected as much by the typical loss factors of connectors.

Mode Power Distribution Effects on Loss in Multimode Fiber Cables

The biggest factor in the uncertainty of multimode cable loss tests is the mode power distribution caused by the test source. When testing a simple 1 m cable assembly, variations in sources can cause 0.3 to 1 dB variations in measured loss. The effect is similar to the effect on fiber loss discussed earlier, since the concentration of light is in the lower-order modes, as a result of equilibrium mode distribution (EMD). Also, mode filtering will minimize the effects of gap, offset, and angularity on mating loss by effectively reducing the fiber core size and numerical aperture.

While one can make mode scramblers and filters to control mode power distribution when testing in the laboratory, it is much more difficult to use or implement these in the field. An alternative technique is to use a special mode conditioning cable between the source and launch cable that induces the proper mode power distribution. This can be done with a step index fiber with a restricted numerical aperture. Experiments with such a cable used between the source have been shown to greatly reduce the variations in mode power distributions between sources. This technique works well with both lab tests of connector loss and field tests of loss in the installed cable plant.

Optical Return Loss Testing of Cable Assemblies

Testing the optical return loss of cables and cable assemblies is very important for single-mode laser systems, since light reflected back into the laser may cause instability, noise, or nonlinearity. While testing the ORL of a cable assembly is similar to that of a connector when using either FOTP-107 or the OTDR method, several factors should be noted to minimize errors.

First, be certain that the launch connector is of the finest quality obtainable, and inspect it often for dirt, contamination, and scratching. Repolishing is possible for most keyed, ceramic ferrule connectors. Thus, repolishing will often improve measurements. Also, ensure that the splice bushing used is kept clean and does not show wear.

Always remember to terminate the connector on the far end of the cable assembly, otherwise it will reflect light and give false readings. Dipping the connector into index matching fluid or gel will usually do, but putting several tight turns in the fiber to create attenuation will also minimize the reflection effects.

Finally, OTDRs are limited in their usefulness in testing jumper cables, since the jumpers are often too short for the resolution of the OTDR. This can be helped by using a long launch cable and carefully terminating the open connector to prevent it from reflecting light, which would be included in the single spike seen by the OTDR. On the installed cable plant, make certain that the OTDR back reflection spike does not exceed the dynamic range of the OTDR, or the measurement will underestimate the reflection and provide misleading or inaccurate results.

FROM HERE

This chapter showed you how to select connectors and splices by examining the quality factors, mechanical and fusion splices, and identifying different types of connectors. The next chapter will show you how to build connectors and splices by taking a look at practical fiber termination.

NOTES

[1]   ST Type Connectors," National Communications Inc., 69 Washington Street, West Orange, NJ 07052, 2000.

[2]   "Networking," Miles Tek, Inc., 1506 Interstate 35W, Denton, TX, 76207-2402, USA, 2000.

[3]   Sumitomo Electric Lightwave Corp., 78 Alexander Drive, Research Triangle Park, NC 27709, 2000.

CHAPTER 19

Building Connectors and Splices

Fiber optic termination and/or splicing service focuses on two primary areas: splicing (fusion and mechanical) and connectorization.

SPLICING

As previously explained in Chapter 18, splicing is the physical bonding together of the raw fiber strands. This is typically used in large campus-wide local area networks in order to address the following issues:

- Building and fire code
- Length of system
- Overall cable plant conduit space limitations and future expansion

Splicing is also extensively utilized in long-haul communication backbones where continuous data transfers are measured in miles and kilometers rather than in feet and meters. Examples of this are long distance telephony and large geographic cable television systems.

CONNECTORIZATION

Connectorization, on the other hand, is the physical attachment of fiber optic connectors onto logical end points of a fiber run for interfacing to network hardware. This is most extensively utilized in smaller-scale local area networks involving two or more centralized wiring centers. Typically, it is used within a single building where workstation distance limitations are a concern or between buildings, to isolate any potential electrical grounding and interference issues. Standard connectors terminated are the ST and SC styles. Other types of connectors (as previously discussed in Chapter 18) are available dependent upon system requirements and will be briefly discussed again later in this chapter.

PRACTICAL FIBER TERMINATION

We terminate the fiber optic cable with special connectors that can mate two fibers to create a temporary splice or connect the fiber to a piece of network gear. These connectors must be of the right style, installed in a manner that makes them have little light loss, and be protected against dirt or damage in use.

No area of fiber optics has been given greater attention than termination. Manufacturers have come up with dozens of styles of connectors (about 80 as of this writing) and ways to install them. Fortunately for most of us, only a few types are used in the majority of applications. There are a number of new connectors, all miniature duplex types (2 fibers), that are likely to be chosen as standards in the future. Stay tuned for updates!

Different connectors and termination procedures are used for single-mode and multimode connectors. So make sure you know what the fiber will be before you specify or buy connectors!

CONNECTOR TYPES

As previously discussed in Chapter 18, the most common fiber optic connectors are:

• FC-style connectors
• ST-style connectors
• SC connectors
• FDDI MIC connectors
• SMA connectors

FC/PC has been one of the most popular single-mode connectors for many years. It screws on firmly, but make sure you have the key aligned in the slot properly before tightening.

SC is specified in the EIA/TIA 568 specs, but is rarely used today because of high cost. In other words, the SC connector was specified as a standard by the EIA/TIA 568 specification, but its higher cost and difficulty of installation (until recently) has limited its popularity. However, newer SCs are much better in both cost and installation ease, so it has been growing rapidly, representing over 15 percent of the market. It is becoming more widely used, which should make it more affordable. It's a snap-in connector, also available in a double configuration.

Besides the SC duplex, you may occasionally see the FDDI and ESCON duplex connectors that mate to their specific networks. The duplex FDDI, ESCON, and SC connectors are used for patch cords between equipment and can be mated to ST or SC connectors at wall outlets. In other words, they are generally used to connect to the equipment to a wall outlet, but the rest of the network will have ST or SC connectors. ESCON is an IBM trademark.

Single-mode networks use FC or SC connectors in about the same proportion as ST and SC in multimode installations. There are some D4s out there too.

All these connectors have the same ferrule size (2.5 mm or about 0.1 inch) so they can be mixed and matched to each other using hybrid splice bushings. This makes it convenient to test, since you can have a set of multimode reference test cables with ST connectors that can adapt to all of these connectors.

Installing ST Connectors

The ST (an AT&T trademark) is by far and away the most popular multimode network (like most buildings and campuses) connector because it is cheap and easy to install (see the Sidebar, "The New ST Connector"). It has a bayonet mount and a long cylindrical ferrule to hold the fiber. Most ferrrules are ceramic, but some are metal or plastic. Don't try to mate unlike ferrules for testing—match the materials! And because they are spring-loaded, you have to make sure they are seated properly. If you have high loss, reconnect them to see if it makes a difference before replacing them.

THE NEW ST CONNECTOR

The 3M ST Connector provides high repeatability and low light loss for premises, LAN, and telco applications. The improved connector design is compatible with the AT&T ST connector as well as Systimax components and other ST connector products. The 3M products are supplied with a high-quality PC finish on zirconia ceramic ferrules.

Hot Melt ST Connector, Bayonet Multimode/Single Mode

The Hot Melt ST Fiber Optic Connector is a keyed bayonet style multimode/single-mode connector, compatible with ST connectors, which incorporates 3M's hot melt adhesive and preradiused PC zirconia ceramic ferrule technology. The result is a quick-mount fiber optic connector that delivers low light-loss, solid intermateability, and mechanical stability, while costing less to install.

Crimplok™ ST Connector and Bayonet Multimode

The ST connector is also available as the Crimplok Connector. The Crimplok Connector combines the speed of nonadhesive connectors with the performance characteristics of epoxy and hot-melt connectors. Crimplok connectors are the solution for emergency restoration work or for quickly making fiber connections at the desk. Crimplok connectors are faster to install than epoxy connectors since there is no set-up or curing time. And Crimplok connectors do not require special heating tools or ovens, so time spent searching for electrical outlets is eliminated. The Crimplok connector is ideal for fiber-to-the-desk and other applications where a few connectors are installed at a time.

ST Connector, Epoxy, Bayonet Multimode/Single Mode

The Epoxy ST Connector is bayonet style for quick interconnect and high repeatability.

Push–Pull ST Connector, Multimode/Single Mode and Epoxy/Hot Melt

The Push–Pull Connector is a high-performance fiber optic connector with a rectangular push–pull coupling mechanism that provides easy insertion and high repeatability. The connector is available in single-mode or multimode versions, with color-coded boots and housings to simplify identification. The multimode version accepts epoxy or may be ordered preloaded with hot-melt adhesive.

Simplex and duplex versions comply with industry standards and are compatible with all standard ST connectors and related accessories. The push–pull boot actuation allows use in high-density configurations and hard-to-reach places such as board mounts and recessed outlets [1].

The Changing Connector Scene

The connector scene is changing. There are tons of new connectors out there (as previously mentioned, about 80 at the time of this writing), including the tiny new AT&T LC and the Panduit *Opti-Jack* that is an optical *RJ45*, plus new designs from AMP and 3M. Watch for these new generation connectors, as they may take off and become the connector you will use most often!

TERMINATION PROCEDURES

Whatever you do, follow the manufacturer's termination instructions closely (see the Sidebar, "ST Connector Termination"). Multimode connectors are usually installed in the field on the cables after pulling, while single-mode connectors are usually installed by splicing a factory-made *pigtail* onto the fiber. That is because the tolerances on single-mode terminations are much tighter and the polishing processes are more critical. You can install single-mode connectors in the field for low-speed data networks, but you may not be able to get losses lower than 1 dB!

ST CONNECTOR TERMINATION PROCEDURE

General

This sidebar provides assembly instructions for ST-style fiber optic connectors.

Procedure

Set curing oven to 100°C (212°F).

Epoxy Preparation

1. Mix the epoxy (EPOTEK 353-ND or TRA-BOND F-253). Other epoxies and adhesives may be used.

2. Prepare the epoxy according to the manufacturer's instructions.

3. Fill the syringe with epoxy and remove any air bubbles.

 Do not exceed the pot life of the epoxy recommended by the manufacturer!

Cable Preparation

1. Slide dust cap ring, strain relief boot, and crimp sleeve onto the cable.

2. Strip the cable to the dimensions shown in Figure 19–1 [2].

3. Slightly bend the exposed fiber to assure that no nicks occurred while removing the secondary coating. If the fiber was nicked, it will break easily.

4. Clean the exposed fiber by drawing it through an alcohol pad.

Filling Connector with Epoxy

1. Using the epoxy-filled syringe, wipe the needle.

2. Insert the needle into the connector until it bottoms out.

3. Keeping the contact bottomed out, fill the connector with epoxy until a small amount of epoxy forms on the tip of the connector, then quickly remove the syringe.

Fitting Connector to Cable

1. Insert the fiber into the connector while slowly rotating the connector (see Figure 19–2 [2].

Do not move fiber back and forth during the fitting. This may cause the epoxy to spread out to the exposed area and damage the connector.

2. Spread Kevlar around the connector backpost.

3. Slide the crimp sleeve over the Kevlar and connector backpost.

4. Crimp the sleeve using a crimp tool. Use the .178" hex die to crimp over the backpost.

5. Use the .151" hex die to crimp over the cable.

6. Slide a fiber protection tube over the ferrule. Make sure the fiber is fully surrounded by the tube.

7. Insert the connector into the curing oven. The connector will require 10 minutes at 100°C to fully cure. For ultimate results, cure for 30 minutes at 80°C and another 30 minutes at 120°C.

8. When cured, remove the connector and let cool.

9. Slide the strain relief boot over the crimp sleeve and connector.

10. Using a scribing tool, lightly score the fiber at the point where the fiber and epoxy bead meet.

11. Gently pull on the fiber until it separates.

Polishing

Polish the ferrule end face. For detail, refer to the manufacturer's instruction manual for optical fiber polishing [2].

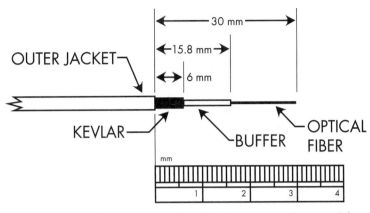

Figure 19–1 Cable preparation. (drawing may not be to scale)

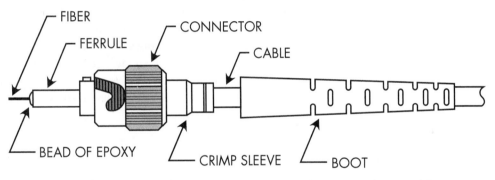

Figure 19–2 Fitting connector to cable. (drawing may not be to scale)

Cables can be pulled for installation with connectors already on them *if*—and a big *if*—you can deal with these two problems: First, the length must be precise. Too short and you have to repull another longer one (its not cost-effective to splice); too long and you waste money. Second, the connectors must be protected. Some cable and connector manufacturers offer protective sleeves to cover the connectors, but you must still be much more careful in pulling cables. You might consider terminating one end and pulling the unter-minated end to not risk the connectors. In this way, you will only have to install one connector onsite.

Multimode Terminations

Several different types of terminations are available for multimode fibers. Each version has its advantages and disadvantages, so learning more about how each works helps decide which one to use.

With regard to adhesives, most connectors use epoxies to hold the fiber in the connector. Use only the specified epoxy, as the fiber-to-ferrule bond is critical for low-loss and long-term reliability! There have been reports of people using hardware store epoxies, Crazy Glue, you name it! And they regretted doing it.

Epoxy/Polish

Most connectors are the simple *epoxy/polish* type where the fiber is glued into the connector with epoxy and the end polished with special polishing film. These provide the most reliable connection, lowest losses (less than 0.5 dB), and lowest costs, especially if you are doing a lot of connectors. The epoxy can be allowed to set overnight or cured in an inexpensive oven in only a few minutes. A *heat gun* should never be used to try to cure the epoxy faster, as the uneven heat may not cure all the epoxy or may overheat some of it, which will prevent it from ever curing!

Hot Melt

Hot Melt is a 3M trade name for a connector that already has the epoxy (actually a heat set glue) inside the connector. You strip the cable, insert it in the connector, crimp it, and put it in a special oven. In a few minutes, the glue is melted, so you remove the connector, let it cool, and it is ready to polish. Fast and easy, low loss, but not as cheap as the epoxy type, it has become the favorite of lots of contractors who install relatively small quantities of connectors.

Crimp/Polish

Rather than glue the fiber in the connector, these connectors use a crimp on the fiber to hold it in. Early types offered *iffy* performance, but today they are somewhat better. Expect to trade higher losses for the faster termination speed. And they are more costly than epoxy polish types. This is a good choice if you only install small quantities and your customer will accept them.

Anaerobics

These connectors use a quick setting glue with a curing agent to replace the epoxy. They work well if your technique is good and you work relatively fast. Otherwise, you will have fibers sticking halfway into the connector and solidly glued in place. You will then be required to throw them away. If you want to use these, practice, practice, practice!

Prepolished/Splice

Some manufacturers offer connectors that have a short stub fiber already epoxied into the ferrule and polished perfectly, so you just cleave a fiber and insert it like a splice. While it sounds like a great idea, it has several downsides. First, it is very costly, five to ten times as much as an epoxy polish type. Second, you have to make a good cleave to make them low loss, and that is not as easy as you might think. Third, even if you do everything correctly, your loss will generally be higher. It's obvious, because you have a connector loss plus two splice losses at every connection! These are good for quick restoration, but look at the cost carefully before you commit to a job with them.

HINTS FOR DOING FIELD TERMINATIONS

Here are a few things to remember when you are terminating connectors in the field. Following these guidelines will save you time, money, and frustration.

Connector Choice

Choose the connector carefully and clear it with the customer if it is anything other than an epoxy/polish type. Some customers have strong opinions on the types or brands of connectors used in their job. Find out first, not later!

Never, never, never take a new connector in the field until you have installed enough of them in the office that you can put them on in your sleep. The field is no place to experiment or learn! It'll cost you big time!

Have the Right Tools for the Job

Make sure you have the proper tools and they are in good shape before you head out for the job. This includes all the termination tools, cable tools, and test equipment. Do you know your test cables are good? Without that, you will test good terminations as bad every time. More and more installers are owning their own tools (like auto mechanics), saying that is the only way to make sure the tools are properly cared for.

Dust and Dirt are Your Enemies

It's very hard to terminate or splice in a dusty place. Try to work in the cleanest possible location. Use lint-free wipes (not cotton swaps or rags made from old T-shirts!) to clean every connector before connecting or testing it. Don't work under heating vents, as they are blowing dirt down on you continuously.

Don't Overpolish

Contrary to common sense, too much polishing is just as bad as too little. The ceramic ferrule in most of today's connectors is much harder than the glass fiber. Polish too much and you create a concave fiber surface, increasing the loss. Generally, a few swipes is all it takes.

Remember Single-Mode Fiber Requires Different Connectors and Polishing Techniques

Most SM fiber is terminated by splicing on a preterminated pigtail, but you can put SM connectors on in the field if you know what you are doing. Expect much higher loss, approaching 1 dB and high back reflections, so don't try it for anything but data networks, not telco or CATV.

Change Polishing Film Regularly

Polishing builds up residue and dirt on the film, which can cause problems after too many connectors and cause poor end finish. Check the manufacturers' specs before proceeding.

Keep Them Covered

Put covers on connectors and patch panels when not in use. Keep them covered to keep them clean.

Inspect, Test, and Then Document

It is very hard to troubleshoot cables when you don't know how long they are, where they go, or how they tested originally! So keep good records—smart users require it and expect to pay extra for them.

TUNING SPLICES

Splice tuning is only needed if the cable runs are too long for one straight pull or you need to mix a number of different types of cables (like bringing a 48-fiber cable in and splicing it to six 8-fiber cables). Could you have used a breakout cable instead? And of course, splices are used for restoration, especially after the number-one problem of outside plant cables, where there's a dig-up and cut of a buried cable—usually referred to as *backhoe fade* for obvious reasons!

As previously explained, splices are *permanent* connections between two fibers. There are two types of splices, fusion and mechanical, and the choice is usually based on cost or location. Most splicing is on long-haul SM cables, not multimode LANs. So if you do outside plant SM jobs, you will want to learn how to fusion splice. If you do mostly MM LANs, you may never see a splice.

Fusion Splices

Fusion splices are made by *welding* the two fibers together, usually by an electric arc (as previously discussed in Chapter 18). Obviously, you don't do that in an explosive atmosphere (at least not more than once!), so fusion splicing is usually done above ground in a truck or trailer set up for the purpose. Good fusion splicers cost $25,000 to $40,000, but the splices only cost a few dollars each. Today's single-mode fusion splicers are automated and you have a hard time making a bad splice. The biggest application is single-mode fibers in outside plant installations.

Mechanical Splices

Again, as previously discussed in Chapter 18, mechanical splices are alignment gadgets that hold the ends of two fibers together with some index matching gel or glue between them. There are a number of types of mechanical splices, like little glass tubes or V-shaped metal clamps. The hardware to make mechanical splices is cheap, but the splices are expensive. Many mechanical splices are used for restoration, but they can work well with both single-mode and multimode fiber, given some practice.

Which Splice?

If cost is the issue, this chapter has certainly given you the clues to make a choice: fusion is expensive equipment and cheap splices, while mechanical is cheap equipment and expensive splices. So, if you make a lot of splices (like thousands in big telco or CATV network), use fusion splices. If you need just a few, use mechanical splices.

Finally, fusion splices give very low back reflections and are preferred for single-mode high-speed digital or CATV networks. However, they don't work too well on multimode splices, so mechanical splices are preferred for MM, unless it is an underwater or aerial application, where the greater reliability of the fusion splice is preferred.

FROM HERE

This chapter showed you how to build connectors and splices by taking a look at practical fiber termination. The next chapter will bring Part III to an end by taking a look at the latest fiber optic cutting-edge technologies. It will focus on advanced fiber optic components such as fiber couplers, optical amplifiers, wavelength division multiplexers (WDM), and the advantages of specialty fibers.

NOTES

[1]   "ST* (Epoxy, Hot Melt and Crimplok) Connectors and Accessories," 3M, 135 John E. Carroll Avenue E., South St. Paul, MN 55075, 2000.
[2]   "ST Connector Termination," International Fiberoptic Technologies, Inc. (IFT), 7011 Industrial Drive, Mebane, NC 27302 USA, 2000.

Cutting-Edge Technologies

$\mathbf{T}$he world of telecommunications networking is rapidly changing. Where once we had kilobits, we now demand megabits. Where we now have megabits, we want gigabits. Where we have gigabits, we will soon be using terabits.

People (businesses, institutions, organizations) are finding ways to use bandwidth as never before. While this has been triggered in large part by the rise of the Internet, it also stems from a host of other factors and, more important, from a critical idea: We are becoming an information society. As we evolve from our industrial past to an information-based future, the economics of our businesses and institutions are also shifting on their axes and the demand for more bandwidth is becoming a key driver in our society.

There is no turning back; nobody using personal computers wants to return to electric typewriters, just as those who use e-mail won't return to writing letters full time. This is a natural phenomenon, which can't be stayed by a few doubters.

The expansion of our networks to be more data-centric, through the use of advanced fiber optic cutting-edge technologies and their components like fiber couplers, optical amplifiers, wavelength division multiplexing (WDM), dense wavelength division multiplexing (DWDM), specialty fibers, and other optical networking processes, is as certain as the ebb and flow of the ocean tides, despite the efforts of those who would try to limit or shoehorn their scope. Thus, the purpose of this chapter is to provide some thought as to where the evolution of these cutting edge technologies (and the broader data network that is becoming integrated with them) are headed. The effects will be profound—and networking will never again be quite the same.

ADVANCED FIBER OPTIC COMPONENTS

By most accounts, the growth of data traffic is outstripping that of voice by at least 10 to 1. While voice traffic is growing at a compound annual rate of about 13 percent, the growth in data traffic is estimated at between 7 and 20 percent—*per month*. The only question for carriers is when data traffic volumes will surpass those of voice (see Figure 20–1) [5].

This fundamental shift in the character of the traffic has profound implications for how carrier networks are designed, built, and operated. Historically, carrier-network architectures have evolved along with the growth of the predominant traffic type: circuit-switched voice. Data was accommodated as well as possible on the voice-centric narrowband network.

The limitations of narrowband, circuit-switched technologies for transporting data have been clear for some time, as evidenced by the deployment of cell and packet-switching technologies such as ATM and frame relay. We have reached the point where data services can no longer be handled by optimizing the old, circuit-switched infrastructure. New advanced fiber optic network architectures and their components need to be considered, architectures that are crafted from the outset to manage the dynamics of data traffic. Not doing so risks creating network bottlenecks and missing customer demand in

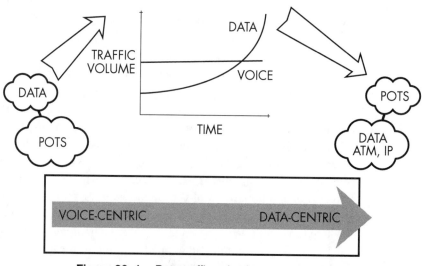

Figure 20–1   Data traffic poised to overtake voice.

an increasingly competitive market. With that in mind, let's take a look at the following advanced fiber optic components:

- fiber couplers
- optical amplifiers
- wavelength division multiplexing (WDM)
- dense wavelength division multiplexing (DWDM)
- specialty fibers

Fiber Couplers

Fiber couplers are monolithically and microoptically designed to shape the beam of multimode high power diode lasers, as shown in Figures 20–2 and 20–3 [1]. The extreme divergence of this laser source requires optics with complex lens structures and high performance. The coupler combines two lenses aligned with respect to each other in one optical element. Besides the optical active areas, the fiber coupler has additional surfaces and edges for easier mounting and positioning in a set-up.

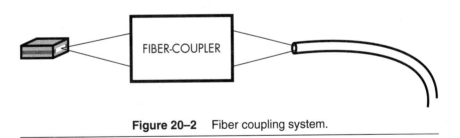

Figure 20–2   Fiber coupling system.

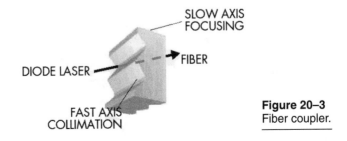

Figure 20–3
Fiber coupler.

Design and Function

Because of the different divergence angles parallel and perpendicular to the junction of the diode, the beam profile is formed with two crossed cylindrical lenses structured on both sides of one glass substrate. To minimize the spot size, the lenses have optimized hyperbolic curvatures to reduce the aberrations and increase the efficiency of the beam transformation. The lens collimates the beam profile perpendicular to the junction of the diode (fast axis) and images the beam profile in the lateral direction of the diode (slow axis) into the spot.

Multimode Fiber Coupling

The fiber coupler transforms the beam profile of high power diode lasers. The lens collimates with high numerical aperture the fast axis (see Figure 20–4) and then images the extended source of the slow axis (see Figure 20–5) of the diode [1].

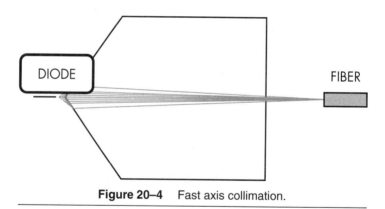

Figure 20–4   Fast axis collimation.

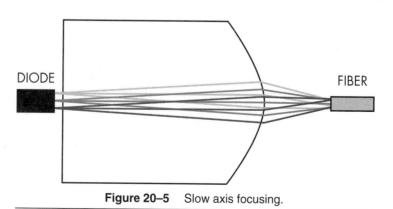

Figure 20–5   Slow axis focusing.

Pumping of Solid-State Laser Rods

The beam shaping performance of the fiber coupler can be profitably used to diode pump (wavelength—pumping light) solid-state lasers. With the fiber coupler, you can connect the laser diode and laser rod into one miniature solid-state laser (see Figure 20–6) [1]. Depending on the type of optical resonator, the fiber coupler can form a nearly circular spot on the surface or in the middle of the laser rod, which can be used to pump the fundamental laser mode (see Figure 20–7) [1].

Important Parameters of Diode and Fiber

The efficiency of the fiber-coupling system does not only depend on the optics but also on the diode laser (see Figure 20–8) and the fiber (see Figure 20–9) [1]. For the optical design of the fiber coupler, some characteristic details of the diode and the fiber are important to know.

To achieve the best performance with the fiber coupler, the divergence of the laser should be as small as the numerical aperture of the fiber, and the core size should be as large as possible (see Figure 20–10) [1]. Light entering the fiber at small angles will be totally reflected at the core-cladding interface. An evanescent field extends into the cladding. The evanescent field extends the fiber into the cladding, where the closer angle of incidence at the core-cladding interface comes to the angle of total reflection. In this case, the cladding has to be optimized to reduce absorption in the cladding and coupling of the evanescent field to radiation modes.

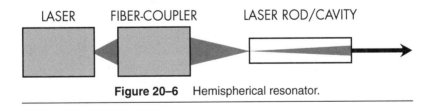

Figure 20–6   Hemispherical resonator.

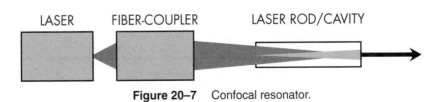

Figure 20–7   Confocal resonator.

EMITTER SIZE

$a \times b$ $(a \cong 1\,\mu m)$

DIVERGENCE

$\theta\perp$ FW $1/e^2$

$\theta_\parallel$ FW $1/e^2$

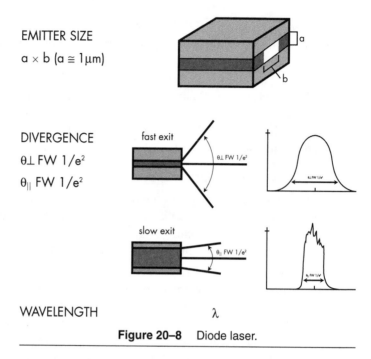

WAVELENGTH λ

Figure 20–8   Diode laser.

STEP- OR
GRADED-INDEX

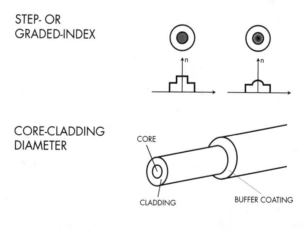

CORE-CLADDING
DIAMETER

NUMERICAL APERTURE

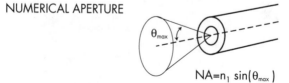

$NA = n_1 \sin(\theta_{max})$

Figure 20–9
Fiber.

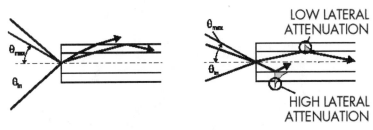

Figure 20–10   Step-index fiber.

Fiber-Coupler for Single-Stripe Emitter

A standard fiber coupler can be designed to couple a 1 μm × 100 μm emitter into a step-index multimode fiber with a 50 μm core and a numerical aperture of NA = 0,3 (see Table 20–1 and Figure 20–11) [1]. Other laser/fiber combinations are possible, but they may lead to a reduced efficiency (see Figure 20–12) [1]. Besides this standard product, customized couplers for special laser–fiber combinations can be manufactured.

Table 20–1 Fiber Coupler

Design Wavelength	λ_{Design} = 800 nm
Material	OHARA S-TIH 53
Surface A (fast axis)	Focal Length = 0,05 mm R = 0,04 mm cc = −2,75
Surface B (slow axis)	Focal Length = 0,25 mm R = 0,2 mm cc = −3,3
Size (L × W × T)	2 mm × 2 mm × 1 mm
AR-Coating	780 nm–1050 nm
Transmission	$T_{Coupler}$ > 90%

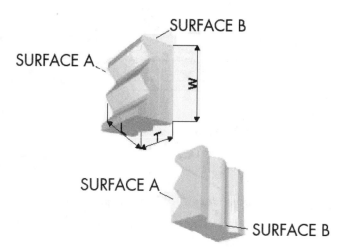

Figure 20–11   Fiber coupler design wavelength size.

$$\textbf{Coupling Efficiency}\quad CE = \frac{P_{fiber-out}}{P_{fiber-incident}} = \frac{P_{fiber-out}}{P_{laser} \cdot T_{fiber-coupler}}$$

Laser: 1µm×100µm, $\theta_{\perp \, FW1/e^2} = 80°$, $\theta_{\| \, FW1/e^2} = 12°$, P_{laser}=1W
Fiber: ∅(core/cladding) = 50µm / 125µm, numerical aperture NA=0,3, coated T_{fiber} > 0,99

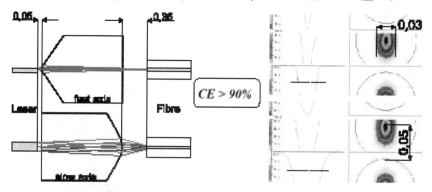

Figure 20–12   Coupling efficiency, focus dimensions.

The combinations shown in Table 20–2 are just a few examples and represent some realizable configurations [1]. Because of the high number of different types of lasers and fibers available on the market, it is not feasible to consider all possible combinations.

Table 20–2 Selection of Laser–Fiber Combinations for the Fiber Coupler

Laser	Fiber	Coupling Efficiency
Emitter size: 1µm × 200µm $\theta_{\perp\,FW1/e^2} = 80^0$, $\theta_{III\,FW1/e^2} = 12^0$ $P_{laser} = 2W$	Core/cladding: 50µm / 125µm Numerical aperture NA = 0,37	CE > 80%
Emitter size: 1µm × 200µm $\theta_{\perp\,FW1/e^2} = 80^0$, $\theta_{II\,FW1/e^2} = 12^0$ $P_{laser} = 2W$	Core/cladding: 100µm / 140µm Numerical aperture NA = 0,37	CE > 90%
Emitter size: 1µm × 100µm $\theta_{\perp\,FW1/e^2} = 80^0$, $\theta_{II\,FW1/e^2} = 12^0$ $P_{laser} = 1W$	Core/cladding: 50µm / 125µm Numerical aperture NA = 0,22	CE > 80%
Emitter size: 1µm × 100µm $\theta_{\perp\,FW1/e^2} = 80^0$, $\theta_{II\,FW1/e^2} = 12^0$ $P_{laser} = 1W$	Core/cladding: 62,5µm / 125µm Numerical aperture NA = 0,27	CE > 95%

Optics for Tapered Diodes

Besides the standard stripe emitter, new types of tapered high power diodes are available on the market. The advantage of these diodes are the high beam quality in the lateral direction ($2 < M^2 < 3$). Because of the chip geometry, you can collimate this laser nearly like a single-mode diode. However, the astigmatism of the diode is very large. The fiber couplers and collimators can compensate the astigmatism with one monolithic optics and be suited very well for this promising diode laser (see Figure 20–13) [1].

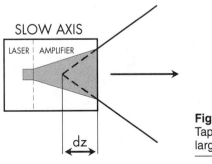

Figure 20–13
Tapered diode with large astigmatism.

Customized Couplers

The coupler can be optimized for different applications to achieve maximum coupling efficiencies. The source as well as the fiber will be taken into account for the optimization. To design a coupler for a special application, you need the following information, as shown in Table 20–3 [1].

Table 20–3 Information Needed to Design a Fiber Coupler

Laser	Emitter size	$a \times b$
	Divergence	$\theta_\perp$ FW $1/e^2$
		$\theta_\parallel$ FW $1/e^2$
	Wavelength	λ
Fiber	Numerical aperture	NA
	Core diameter	d

Mounting and Positioning

Mounting and positioning of microoptics actually is not different from the handling of standard optics you use in your lab everyday. The same translations and rotations are required to position an optical element. Small dimensions, close distances, and narrow tolerances involving a small working space demand micropositioning capabilities and time-consuming alignment in a narrow space. Thus, microoptics offers individual space-saving solutions that allow passive alignment and save you a lot of work and time.

Multifunctional Surfaces of the Fiber Coupler.   In addition to the optical surfaces (A and B), the fiber coupler is designed with additional multifunctional surfaces (A' to F'), as shown in Figure 20–14 [1]. See Figure 20–11, where the different surfaces are shown and named.

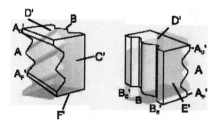

Figure 20–14
The optical surfaces A and B and the alignment and mounting surfaces A' to F'. The optical surfaces A and B are set back with respect to the surfaces AD', AF' respectively. BC', BE'.

The *nonoptical* surfaces A' and B' protect the optical surfaces from accidental damage, the cubic design can be handled more securely, and the plane surfaces facilitate mounting and alignment in an optical set-up. The microlenses combine the functions of lens, mount, and a micropositioning system in one solid piece of glass. Choosing the right dimensions in a custom design allows to passively align the working distance and to preposition the lens in the remaining two dimensions.

Protection Surfaces and Surfaces for Secure Handling and Mounting. The vertex of the lens surfaces A and B are set back 10 micrometers with respect to the surfaces A_D', A_F' respectively B_C', B_E'. In this way, the surfaces A' and B' protect the optical surfaces A and B from accidental damage during alignment and handling. In case the lens is tipped over on a plane, the optical surfaces will not be touched, let alone scratched.

The cubic design offers several plane parallel surfaces allowing handling of the optics more securely by tweezers or other tools and carriers. This advantage applies for a lab environment as well as for an automated production environment.

The plane surfaces facilitate gluing or soldering the optics in an optical set-up, creating one miniaturized device uniting laser diode and fiber. In principle, all plane surfaces can be used to fix the fiber coupler with respect to the other optical components. The engineer chooses the appropriate surfaces, depending on his or her connecting technology.

For connections applied between surfaces, the front and bottom surfaces (A' and F') of the fiber coupler are the best choice. Other techniques can employ the side or top surfaces.

Tolerances of the Fiber Coupler

The lenses are centered with a tolerance of ± 10 µm in the rectangular parallelepiped of glass. The distances a' and b' between the vertex of lenses from the front plane are unspecified for the standard products, but can be specified for custom designs with tolerances of ± 1 µm. The small tolerances of ± 1 µm can even be achieved for the other dimensions and utilized as shown in Figure 20–15 [1].

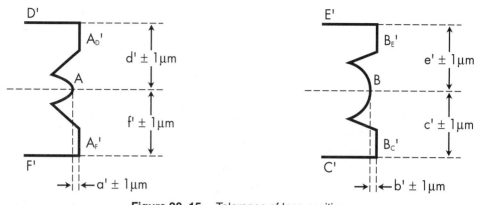

Figure 20–15   Tolerance of lens position.

Prealignment in Two and Passive Alignment in One Direction

Custom designed fiber couplers can be manufactured with tolerances of 1 μm in the distances a' and b' of Figure 20–15. The small tolerance of ± 1 μm allows to passively align the working distance of the fiber coupler. To do so, the alignment surface A' is placed directly against the surface A* of the laser diode or the mount of the laser diode. The tolerance of ± 10 μm in the vertical direction allows a passive prealignment, as shown in Figures 20–15 and 20–16 [1].

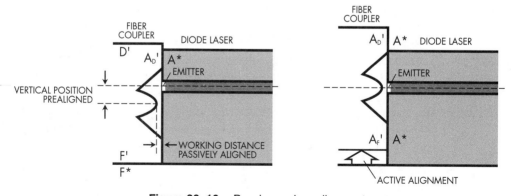

Figure 20–16   Passive and prealignment.

From the prealignment position, the optics has to be moved less than 20 μm in one direction to achieve alignment. In the same way, the optics can be prealigned in the lateral direction.

Custom Designed Alignment and Positioning Surfaces for Passive Alignment

In a custom-designed coupler, not only can the parameters of the optical surfaces be optimized to reshape the beam profile for the application of the customer, but also the dimensions of the fiber-coupler can be specified to take optimum advantage of the alignment and positioning surfaces. The fiber coupler can be manufactured with additional surfaces of ± 1 μm tolerances in the distance to the optical axis. Figure 20–17 shows two of the possible designs of high-precision alignment surfaces that allow passive alignment [1]. The parameters that can be specified in a custom design are also shown.

How the custom-designed alignment surfaces can be used for passive alignment is shown in Figure 20–18 [1]. By placing alignment surface D_A" against surface D* of the laser diode, and, at the same time, bringing the surfaces A_D" and A_F" of the fiber coupler in direct contact with surface A* of the laser or its mount, the working distance and the position in vertical direction are passively aligned. The same can be achieved in a lateral direction using similar kinds of alignment surfaces.

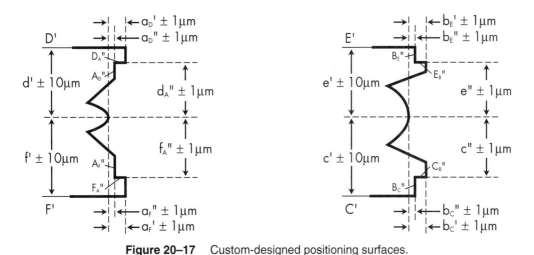

Figure 20–17　Custom-designed positioning surfaces.

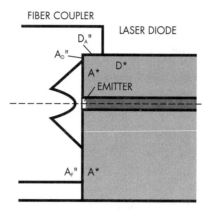

FIBER COUPLER

D_A''

A_D''

LASER DIODE

A^* D^*

EMITTER

A_F'' A^*

Figure 20–18
Example for alignment surfaces for passive alignment.

Coupler Array

Fiber coupler arrays allow couple light from laser diode bars and stacked laser diode bars into fiber arrays (see Figure 20–19) [1]. The coupler array has all advantages of the single fiber coupler plus simplified alignment. If the first and the last coupler of the array are aligned with respect to the emitters of the laser diode bar, all the couplers in between will be aligned automatically. This works with one- and two-dimensional arrays in the same way. For a one-dimensional array, the optics consists of one lens on surface A for fast axis collimation and an array of cylindrical lenses on surface B with the same pitch as the emitters. In the two dimensional arrays, the lenses for the fast axis collimation are arranged with the total distance of the laser bars in the stack. The small tolerances in the dimensions of the array allow simplified alignment

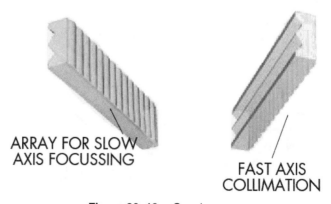

ARRAY FOR SLOW
AXIS FOCUSSING

FAST AXIS
COLLIMATION

Figure 20–19   Coupler array.

without accumulative errors. The tolerance in the distance between the first and the last coupler is ± 1 μm, as it is between the neighboring couplers.

Tolerances of Coupler Arrays

For the fiber-coupling of an array with 1 μm × 100 μm emitter size and 500 μm pitch, you should be able to arrange the single fiber couplers with the same pitch as the emitters. The number of elements in the coupler array can be optimized for all types of laser arrays and laser stacks! The monolithic coupler array made of the single fiber coupler produces an array of spots for the efficient fiber-array coupling, as shown in Figure 20–20 [1].

Fiber Optical Amplifiers (FOAs)

While the low loss of optical fiber allows signals to travel hundreds of kilometers, extremely long haul lines and submarine cables require regenerators or repeaters to amplify the signal periodically. In the beginning, repeaters basically consisted of a receiver followed by a transmitter. The incoming signal was converted from a light signal to an electrical signal by a receiver, cleaned up to remove as much noise as possible, then was retransmitted by another laser transmitter.

These repeaters added noise to the signal, consumed much power, and were complicated, which means they were a potential source of failure. They also had to be made for the specific bit rate of transmission and upgrading required replacing all the repeaters, a really difficult task in an undersea cable!

Since the 1960s, researchers knew how to make fiber lasers. Proper doping of the fiber (introducing small amounts of active elements into the glass fiber) allowed it to be pumped with external light sources until stimulated emission occurred. While making fiber amplifiers was hypothesized early in the stages of fiber optic development, it was not until 1987 that working models were realized. Major contributors to the development included Bell Labs and NTT.

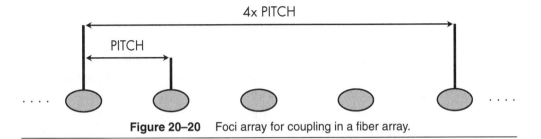

Figure 20–20   Foci array for coupling in a fiber array.

The typical fiber amplifier works in the 1,550-nm band and consists of a length of fiber doped with Erbium pumped with a laser at 980 nm. The pump laser supplies the energy for the amplifier, while the incoming signal stimulates emission as the pulse passes through the doped fiber. The stimulated emission stimulates more emission, so there is a rapid, exponential growth of photons in the doped fiber. Gains of > 40 dB (10,000X) are possible with power outputs > +20 dBm (100 mW).

To date, the most efficient fiber amplifiers have been erbium-doped fiber amplifiers (EDFAs) operating in the 1,550-nm range. Since most systems still work at 1,310 nm, considerable research has been done to find materials that would work in this range. Praseodymium-doped fluoride fiber amplifiers (PDFFAs) using fibers made from zirconium fluoride or hafnium fluoride have shown some promise, but have not developed the performance needed for widespread applications.

The basic structure of an EDFA is very simple. The amplifier itself emits light energy in a signal wavelength (usually about 1,540 nm) using energy supplied to it by photons in a pump wavelength (usually 980 nm) when stimulated by incoming photons in the signal—the signal that needs amplification. Just like in a laser, the emitted photons then stimulate other emissions, so there is an exponential growth of photons. Supporting the amplifier is a pump laser, which supplies the amplifier's energy; a coupler, which combines the pump laser beams; the signal laser beam, which puts them on a single fiber; and an optical filter, which removes the remaining traces of the pump beam so that it doesn't interfere with reception of the signal.

Why Erbium?

Erbium has several important properties that make it an excellent choice for an optical amplifier. Remember that there are several very specific bands (wavelengths) that fiber optic cables can carry. Erbium ions (Er3+) have quantum levels that allows them to be stimulated to emit in the 1,540-nm band, which is the band that has the least power loss in most silica-based fiber. That gives them the ability to amplify signals in a band where high-quality amplifiers are most needed.

Erbium's quantum levels also allow it to be excited by a signal at either 800 nm or 980 nm, both of which silica-based fiber can carry without great losses, but aren't in the middle of the signal wavelengths. Those bands are also far enough away from the signal bands that it is easy to keep the pump beam and the signal beam separated.

When erbium is excited by photons at 800 nm or 980 nm, it has a non-radioactive decay (energy drops without producing light) to a state where it can stay excited for relatively long periods of time—on the order of 10 ms. This property is extremely important, because the quantum efficiency of the device is dependent on how long it can stay in that excited state. If it relaxes too quickly, more photons are needed to keep it excited, meaning more input power is needed to make the amplifier work.

Erbium can also be excited by photons at 1,480 nm, but this is typically undesirable. When excited at that wavelength, both the energy-pumping process and the stimulated emission by the signal are happening in the same wavelength and energy band, which can create interactions that lower the efficiency of the device and increase the amplifier noise.

Another important property of erbium for use in a fiber amplifier is that it is fairly soluble in silica, making it easy to dope into mixtures for making silica-based fiber. For many applications, reasonable EDFAs can be made by simply dissolving Er2O3 in a crucible with the SiO2 used to make silica fiber. By using a codopant, such as Al2O3, GeO2-Al2O3, or P2O5, the erbium compound's solubility in the silica mixture can be greatly increased, and some of the EDFA's properties can be improved. For example, GeO2-Al2O3 can be used to almost double the time it takes for excited erbium to relax, which therefore almost doubles the quantum efficiency of the EDFA.

EDFAs are not perfect. In practice, you need to have many pump beams along the length of a fiber to provide the energy for EDFAs and these require power and optics (couplers and filters). EDFAs also have gain that varies with a signal's wavelength, which creates problems in many WDM applications. This can be solved by using special optical passive filters that are designed to compensate for the gain variation of the EDFA.

Alternative Designs

The simple diagram of an EDFA is not the only way EDFAs can be made. Pumping can be done in a forward direction as shown, backward from the output end or in both directions. Optical isolators are commonly used at both ends of the EDFA to prevent pump energy from escaping back down the fiber or unwanted reflections that may affect laser stability. Filters, often Bragg gratings (filters fabricated in fibers), are used to flatten the gain over the broadest wavelength range for use in wavelength division multiplexers (WDM) systems (discussed in this chapter).

Other Applications

Besides being used as repeaters, fiber amplifiers are used to increase signal level for CATV systems. These systems require high power levels at the receiver to maintain adequate signal-to-noise performance, thus allowing longer cable runs or using splitters to *broadcast* a single signal through a coupler to many fibers. This saves the cost of additional transmitters. In telephony, they combine with DWDM (dense wavelength division multiplexers) to overcome the inefficiencies of DWDMs for long-haul transmission. WDM and DWDM are thoroughly discussed later in this chapter.

Future Developments

Fiber amplifiers continue to be developed to support dense wavelength division multiplexing and to expand to the other wavelength bands supported by fiber optics. Now that fiber manufacturers have all but removed the water bands from the spectrum, there is now a range of 1,260 to 1,610 nm available for use. Fiber amplifiers and diode lasers will probably be developed within this band to completely fill it with useable bandwidth.

A new device being worked on is the semiconductor optical amplifier (SOA), which basically duplicates the function of an FOA but in an integrated circuit fabricated like a diode laser.

WDM to DWDM

Current systems offer from 4 to 32 channels of wavelengths. The higher numbers of wavelengths has lead to the name dense wavelength division multiplexing, or DWDM (which is more thoroughly discussed next in this chapter). The technical requirement is only that the lasers be of very specific wavelengths, that the wavelengths are very stable, and that the DWDM demultiplexers are capable of distinguishing each wavelength without cross talk.

Advantages of WDM

A WDM system has some features that make them very useable. Each wavelength can be from a normal link, for example an OC-48 link, so you do not obsolete most of your current equipment. You merely need laser transmitters chosen for wavelengths that match the WDM demultiplexer to make sure each channel is properly decoded at the receiving end.

If you use an OC-48 SONET input, you can have 4×2.5 Gb/s = 10 Gb/s up to 32×2.5 Gb/s = 80 Gb/s. While 32 channels are the maximum today, future enhancements are expected to offer 80–128 channels!

And you are not limited to SONET, you can use Gigabit Ethernet, for example, or you can mix and match SONET and Gigabit Ethernet or any other digital signals! About the only thing you can't do is mix in analog channels like CATV.

Repeaters

Another technology that facilitates DWDM is the development of fiber optic amplifiers for use as repeaters. They can amplify numerous wavelengths of light simultaneously, as long as all are in the wavelength range of the FO amplifier. They work best in the range of 1,520–1,560 nm, so most DWDM systems are designed for that range. Now that fiber has been made with less effect from the OH absorption bands at 1,400 nm and 1,600 nm, the possible range of DWDM has broadened considerably. Technology needs development for wider range fiber amplifiers to take advantage of the new fibers.

Applications

Two obvious applications are already in use, submarine cables and extending the lifetime of cables where all fibers are being used. For submarine cables, DWDM enhances the capacity without adding fibers, which create larger cables and bulkier and more complicated repeaters. Adding service in areas where cables are now full is another good application. This technology may also reduce the cost on all land-based long-distance communications links and new technology may lead to totally new network architectures.

Further Enhancements

Imagine an all-optical network that uses DWDM, switches signals in the optical domain without converting signals to electronics, and adds or drops signals by inserting or withdrawing wavelengths at will. All this is being researched right now, and given the speed with which optical technology advances, an all-optical network may not be far in the future! Now that you've had a taste of DWDM, let's see what it can really do for you!

Dense Wavelength Division Multiplexing: A Reality Check

Over the last decade, fiber optic cables have been installed by carriers as the backbone of their interoffice networks, becoming the mainstay of the telecommunications infrastructure. Using time division multiplexing (TDM) technology, carriers now routinely transmit information at 2.4 Gb/s on a single fiber, with some deploying equipment that quadruples that rate to 10 Gb/s. The revolution in high bandwidth applications and the explosive growth of the Internet, however, have created capacity demands that exceed traditional TDM limits. As a result, the once seemingly inexhaustible bandwidth promised by the deployment of optical fiber in the 1980s is being exhausted. To meet growing demands for bandwidth, a technology called dense wavelength division multiplexing (DWDM) has been developed that multiplies the capacity of a single fiber. DWDM systems being deployed today can increase a single fiber's capacity sixteen-fold, to a throughput of an estimated 40 Gb/s! This cutting edge technology (when combined with network management systems and add–drop multiplexers) enables carriers to adopt optically based transmission networks that will meet the next generation of bandwidth demand at a significantly lower cost than installing new fiber.

The Growing Demand

It is clear that the remarkable revolution in information services has permeated our society. Communication, which in the past was confined to narrowband voice signals, now demands a high-quality visual, audio, and data context (see Figure 20–21) [2]. Every aspect of human interplay (from business, to entertainment, to government, to academia) increasingly depends on rapid and reliable communication networks. Indeed, the advent of the Internet alone is introducing millions of individuals to a new world of information and technology. The telecommunications industry, however, is struggling to keep pace with these changes. Early predictions that current fiber capacities would be adequate for our needs into the 21st century have proven wrong.

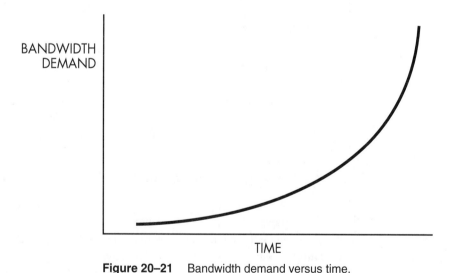

Figure 20–21   Bandwidth demand versus time.

Bandwidth Demand Driven by Growing Competition

During the past several years, a trend has developed throughout the world to encourage competition in the telecommunication sector through government deregulation and market-driven economic stimulation. Since competition was introduced into the U.S. long-distance market in 1984, revenues and access lines have grown 40 percent, while investment in the outside plant has increased 60 percent. The 1996 Telecommunication Reform Act is giving way to an even broader array of new operators, both in the long-distance and local-exchange sectors, which promise to drive down telecommunications costs and thereby create new demand for additional services and capacity. Moreover, while early competition among long-distance carriers was based mainly on a strategy of price reduction, today's competitive advantage depends increasingly on maximizing the available capacity of network infrastructures and providing enhanced reliability.

Network Survivability. Another significant cause of bandwidth demand is the carriers' need to guarantee fail-safe networks. As telecommunications has become more critical to businesses and individuals, service providers have been required to ensure that their networks are fault-tolerant and impervious to outages. In many cases, telephone companies must include service-level guarantees in business contracts, with severe financial penalties should outages occur.

To meet these requirements, carriers have broadened route diversity, either through ring configurations or 1:1 point-to-point networks in which backup capacity is provided on alternate fibers. Achieving 100 percent reliability, however, requires that spare capacity be set aside and dedicated only to a backup function. This potentially doubles the bandwidth need of an already strained and overloaded system, since the *protective* path capacity must equal that of the revenue-generating *working path*.

New Applications. At the same time that carriers are enhancing network survivability, they must also accommodate growing customer demand for services such as video, high-resolution graphics, and large-volume data processing, which require unprecedented amounts of bandwidth. Technologies such as frame relay and ATM are also adding to the need for capacity. Internet usage, which some analysts predict will grow by 700 percent annually in the coming years, is threatening to overwhelm telephone access networks and further strain the nation's fiber backbone. The growth of cellular and PCS is also placing more demand on fiber networks, which serve as the backbone even for wireless communications.

Telecommunications Infrastructure Good but Overwhelmed

Since the early 1980s, the telecommunications infrastructure (built on a hierarchy of high performance central office switches and copper lines) has been migrating to massive computerization and deployment of fiber optic cables. The widespread use of fiber has been made possible, in part, by the industry's acceptance of SONET and SDH as the standard for signal generation. Using SONET/SDH standards, telecommunication companies have gradually expanded their capacity by increasing data transmission rates, to the point that many carriers now routinely transport 2.4 Gb/s.

The bad news, however, is that the once seemingly inexhaustible capacity promised by ever-increasing SONET rates is reaching its limit. In fact, bandwidth demand is already approaching the maximum capacity available in some networks. Primarily because of technical limitations and the physical properties of embedded fiber, today there is a practical ceiling of 2.4 Gb/s on most fiber networks. Surprisingly, however, the TDM equipment installed today utilizes less than 1 percent of the intrinsic capacity of the fiber!

Achieving Bandwidth Capacity Goals

Confronted by the need for more capacity, carriers have three possible solutions (see Figure 20–22) [2]:

- Install new fiber
- Invest in new TDM technology to achieve faster bit rates
- Deploy dense wavelength division multiplexing

Installing New Fiber to Meet Capacity Needs.   For years, carriers have expanded their networks by deploying new fiber and transmission equipment. For each new fiber deployed, the carrier could add capacity up to 2.4 Gb/s. Unfortunately, such deployment is frequently difficult and always costly. The average cost to deploy the additional fiber cable, excluding costs of associated support systems and electronics, has been estimated to be about $90,000 per mile, with costs escalating in densely populated areas. While this projection varies from place to place, installing new fiber can be a daunting prospect, particularly for carriers with tens of thousands of route miles. In many cases, the right-of-way of the cable route or the premises needed to house transmission equipment is owned by a third party, such as a railroad or even a competitor. Moreover, single-mode fiber is currently in short supply owing to production limitations, potentially adding to costs and delays. For these reasons, the comprehensive deployment of additional fiber is an impractical, if not impossible, solution for many carriers.

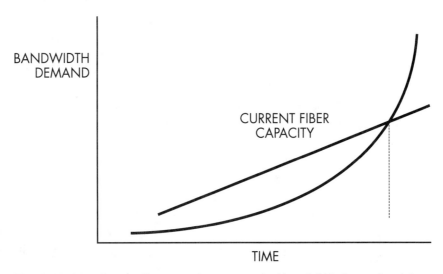

Figure 20–22   Current fiber capacity as a result of bandwidth demand and time.

Higher Speed TDM—Deploying STM-64/OC-192 (10 Gb/s).   As indicated earlier, STM-64/OC-192 is becoming an option for carriers seeking higher capacity, but there are significant issues surrounding this solution that may restrict its applicability. The vast majority of the existing fiber plant is single-mode fiber (SMF) that has high dispersion in the 1,550-nm window, making STM-64/OC-192 transmission difficult. In fact, dispersion has a 16 times greater effect with STM-64/OC-192 equipment than with STM-16/OC-48. As a result, effective STM-64/OC-92 transmission requires either some form of dispersion-compensating fiber or entire new fiber builds using nonzero dispersion shifted fiber (NZDSF)—which costs some 50 percent more than SMF. The greater carrier transmission power associated with the higher bit rates also introduces nonlinear optical effects that cause degraded wave-form quality.

SONET and SDH refer to similar data transmission rates. Synchronous transfer mode (STM) is used to describe SDH rates, while the optical carrier (OC) designation applies to SONET&horbar-based systems. STM― 16/OC― 48 transmits 2.48 Gb/s, while STM― 64/OC192 transmits almost 10 Gb/s.

The effects of polarization mode dispersion (PMD) (which, like other forms of dispersion, affects the distance a light pulse can travel without signal degradation) is of particular concern for STM-64/OC-192. This problem, barely noticed until recently, has become significant because as transmission speeds increase, dispersion problems grow exponentially, thereby dramatically reducing the distance a signal can travel. PMD appears to limit the reliable reach of STM-64/OC-192 to about 70 kms on most embedded fiber. Although there is a vigorous and ongoing debate within the industry over the extent of PMD problems, some key issues are already known.

- PMD is particularly acute in the conventional single-mode fiber, which comprises the vast majority of the existing fiber plant, as well as in aerial fiber.
- Unlike other forms of dispersion that are fairly predictable and easy to measure, PMD varies significantly from cable to cable. Moreover, PMD is affected by environmental conditions, making it difficult to determine ways to offset its effect on high bit rate systems.
- As a result, carriers must test nearly every span of fiber for its compatibility with STM-64/OC-192; in many cases, PMD will rule out its deployment altogether [2].

A Third Approach: Deploying DWDM.   Dense wavelength division multiplexing is a technology that allows multiple information streams to be transmitted simultaneously over a single fiber at data rates as high as the fiber plant will allow (2.4 Gb/s). The DWDM approach multiplies the simple 2.4 Gb/s system by up to 16 times, giving an immense and immediate increase in capacity—using embedded fiber (see Figure 20–23) [2]! A 16-channel system (which is available today) supports approximately 40 Gb/s in each direction over a fiber pair, while a 40-channel system under development is expected to support 100 Gb/s, the equivalent of 10 STM-64/OC-192 transmitters! The benefits of DWDM over the first two options (adding fiber plant or deploying STM-64/OC-192) for increasing capacity are clear.

Dense Wavelength Division Multiplexing Technology

DWDM technology utilizes a composite optical signal carrying multiple information streams, each transmitted on a distinct optical wavelength. Although wavelength division multiplexing has been a known technology for several years, its early application was restricted to providing two widely separated *wideband* wavelengths, or to manufacturing components that separated up to four channels. Only recently has the technology evolved to the point that parallel wavelengths can be densely packed and integrated into a transmission system, with multiple, simultaneous, extremely high-frequency

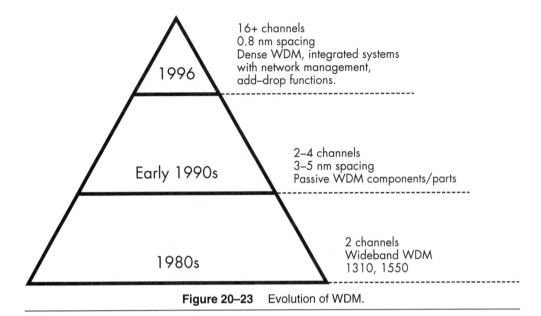

16+ channels
0.8 nm spacing
Dense WDM, integrated systems
with network management,
add–drop functions.

1996

2–4 channels
3–5 nm spacing
Passive WDM components/parts

Early 1990s

2 channels
Wideband WDM
1310, 1550

1980s

Figure 20–23   Evolution of WDM.

signals in the 192 to 200 terahertz (THz) range. By conforming to the ITU channel plan, such a system ensures interoperability with other equipment and allows service providers to be well-positioned to deploy optical solutions throughout their networks. The 16-channel system in essence provides a virtual 16-fiber cable, with each frequency channel serving as a unique STM-16/OC-48 carrier, as shown in Figure 20–24 [2].

The most common form of DWDM uses a fiber pair—one for transmission and one for reception, as shown in Figure 20–25 [2]. Systems do exist in which a single fiber is used for bidirectional traffic, but these configurations must sacrifice some fiber capacity by setting aside a guard band to prevent channel mixing; they also degrade amplifier performance. In addition, there is a greater risk that reflections occurring during maintenance or repair could damage the amplifiers. In any event, the availability of mature supporting technologies, like precise demultiplexers and erbium doped fiber amplifiers (EDFA), has enabled DWDM with 8, 16, or even higher channel counts to be commercially delivered.

Demultiplexers.   With signals as precise and as dense as those used in DWDM, there needed to be a way to provide accurate signal separation, or filtration, on the optical receiver. Such a solution also needed to be easy to implement and essentially maintenance-free. Early filtering technology was either too imprecise for DWDM, too sensitive to temperature variations and

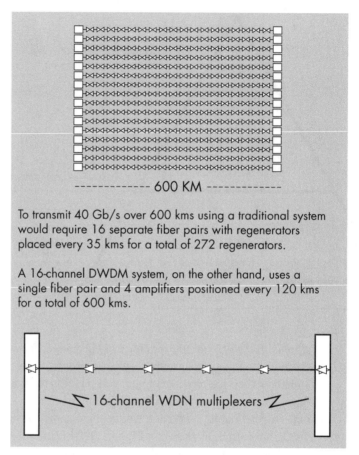

------------- 600 KM -------------

To transmit 40 Gb/s over 600 kms using a traditional system
would require 16 separate fiber pairs with regenerators
placed every 35 kms for a total of 272 regenerators.

A 16-channel DWDM system, on the other hand, uses a
single fiber pair and 4 amplifiers positioned every 120 kms
for a total of 600 kms.

16-channel WDN multiplexers

Figure 20–24   The 16-channel DWDM system.

polarization, too vulnerable to cross talk from neighboring channels, or too
costly and therefore unfeasible. This restricted the evolution of DWDM. To
meet the requirements for higher performance, a more robust filtering technology was developed that makes DWDM possible on a cost-effective basis:
the in-fiber Bragg grating.

The new filter component, called a fiber grating, consists of a length of
optical fiber wherein the refractive index of the core has been permanently
modified in a periodic fashion, generally by exposure to an ultraviolet interference pattern. The result is a component that acts as a wavelength-depen-
dent reflector and is useful for precise wavelength separation. In other words,
the fiber grating creates a highly selective, narrow bandwidth filter that func-

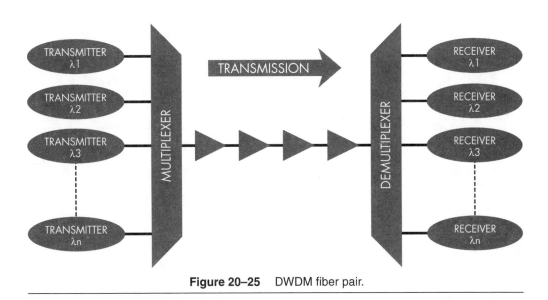

Figure 20–25   DWDM fiber pair.

tions somewhat like a mirror and provides significantly greater wavelength selectivity than any other optical technology. The filter wavelength can be controlled during fabrication through simple geometric considerations, which enable reproducible accuracy. Because this is a passive device fabricated into glass fiber, it is robust and durable.

Erbium Doped Fiber Amplifier.   The advent of the erbium doped fiber amplifier (EDFA) enabled commercial development of DWDM systems by providing a way to amplify all the wavelengths at the same time. This optical amplification is done by incorporating erbium ions into the core of a special fiber in a process known as doping. Optical pump lasers are then used to transfer high levels of energy to the special fiber, energizing the eribum ions, which then boost the optical signals that are passing through. Significantly, the atomic structure of erbium provides amplification to the broad spectral range required for densely packed wavelengths operating in the 1,550 nm region, optically boosting the DWDM signals (see Figure 20–26) [2]. Instead of multiple electronic regenerators, which required that the optical signals be converted to electrical signals then back again to optical ones, the EDFA directly amplifies the optical signals. Hence, the composite optical signals can travel up to 600 kms without regeneration and up to 120 kms between amplifiers in a commercially available, terrestrial, DWDM system.

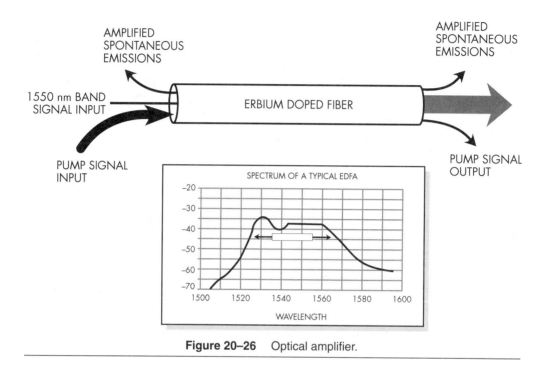

Figure 20–26   Optical amplifier.

Parlaying New Technologies into a DWDM System

The fiber Bragg grating and the EDFA represented significant technological breakthroughs in their own right, but the bandwidth potential associated with these innovations could only be realized by their incorporation into integrated DWDM transport systems for optical networks. Without such a development, the fiber grating would retain component status similar to other passive WDM devices, while the power potential of EDFAs would remain underutilized. The ability to harness the potential of these technologies, however, is realizable today through commercially available, integrated, DWDM systems. Such a system is attained through the use of optical add/drop multiplexers (OADM) and sophisticated network management tools (see Figure 20–27) [2].

Optical Add/Drop Multiplexers.   The OADM, based on DWDM technology, is moving the telecommunications industry significantly closer to the development of optical networks. The OADM can be placed between two end terminals along any route and be substituted for an optical amplifier. Commercially available OADMs allow carriers to drop and/or add up to four STM-6/OC-48 channels between DWDM terminals, as shown in Figure

20–28 [2]. The OADM has *express channels* that allow certain wavelengths to pass through the node uninterrupted, as well as broadcast capabilities that enable information on up to four channels to be dropped and simultaneously

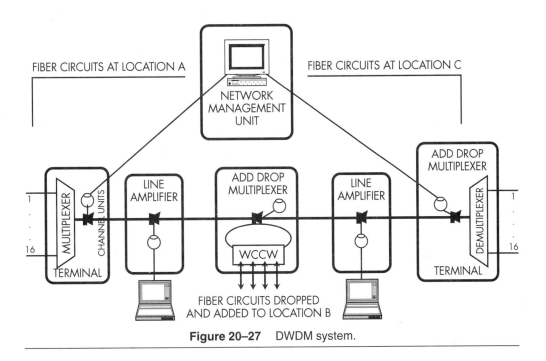

Figure 20–27 DWDM system.

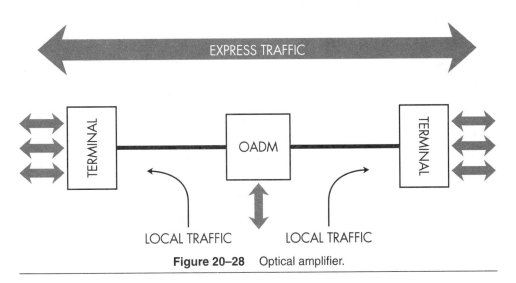

Figure 20–28 Optical amplifier.

continue as *express channels*. By deploying an OADM instead of an optical amplifier, service providers can gain flexibility to distribute revenue-generating traffic and reduce costs associated with deploying end terminals at low traffic areas along a route. The OADM is especially well-suited for meshed or branched network configurations, as well as for ring architectures used to enhance survivability. Such flexibility is less achievable with current STM-64/OC-192 offerings.

Network Management

A critical yet often underappreciated part of any telecommunications network is the management system—whose reliability is especially vital in the complex and high-capacity world of DWDM. Indeed, dependable and easily accessible network management services increasingly will become a distinguishing characteristic of high-performance, high-capacity systems (see Figure 20–29) [2]. Today's leading DWDM systems include integrated network management programs that are designed to work in conjunction with other operations support systems (OSSs) and are compliant with the standards the International Telecommunication Union (ITU) has established for the telecommunications management network (TMN). Current systems utilize an

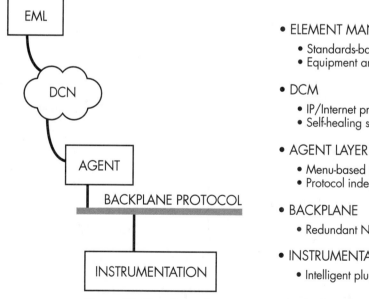

Figure 20–29   Network management layered architecture.

optical service channel that is independent of the working channels of the DWDM product to create a standards-based data communications network that allows service providers to remotely monitor and control system performance and use. This network manager communicates with each node in the system and also provides dual homing access and self-healing routing information in the event of a network disruption. By meeting ITU standards and utilizing a Q3 interface, the system ensures that end users retain high operations, administration, maintenance, and provisioning (OAM&P) service.

Measurements of Performance

There are several aspects that make the design of DWDM systems unique. A spectrum of DWDM channels may begin to accumulate tilt and ripple effects as the signals propagate along a chain of amplifiers. Furthermore, each amplifier introduces amplified spontaneous emissions (ASE) into the system, which cause a decrease in the signal-to-noise ratio, leading to signal degradation. Upon photodetection, some other features of optically amplified systems come into play. The bit error rate (BER) is determined differently in an optically amplified system than in a conventional regenerated one. The probability of error in the latter is dominated by the amount of receiver noise. In a properly designed optically amplified system, the probability of error in the reception of a binary value of one is determined by the signal mixing with the ASE, while the probability of error in the reception of a binary value of zero is determined by the ASE noise value alone.

Optical SNR and Transmitted Power Requirements of DWDM Systems. Ultimately, the BER performance of a DWDM channel is determined by the optical signal-to-noise ratio (SNR) that is delivered to the photodetector. In a typical commercial system, an optical SNR of approximately 20 dB, measured in a 0.1 nm bandwidth, is required for an acceptably low BER of 10-5. This acceptable SNR is delivered through a relatively sophisticated analysis of signal strength per channel, amplifier distances, and the frequency spacing between channels.

For a specific SNR at the receiver, the amount of transmit power required in each channel is linearly proportional to the number of amplifiers as well as the noise and SNR of each amplifier, and is exponentially proportional to the loss between amplifiers. Because total transmit power is constrained by present laser technology and fiber nonlinearities, the workable key factor is amplifier spacing (see the Sidebar, "Transmission of Many WDM Channels through a Cascade of EDFAs in Long-Distance Links and Ring Networks"). This is illustrated in Figure 20–30 by showing the relationship for a fiber plant with a loss of .3 dB/km, a receiver with a .1 nm optical

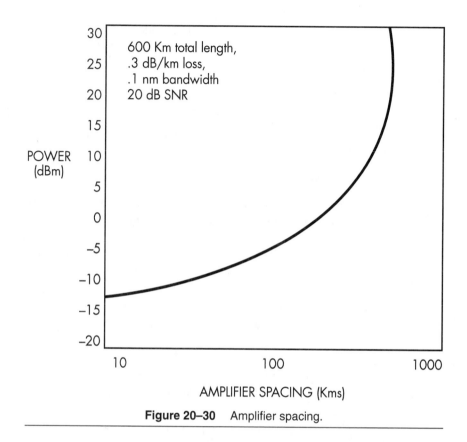

Figure 20–30 Amplifier spacing.

bandwidth, and optical amplifiers with a 5 dB noise figure [2]. The system illustrated is expected to cover 600 kms and the optical SNR required at the receiver is 20 dB measured in the 0.1 nm bandwidth.

TRANSMISSION OF MANY WDM CHANNELS THROUGH A CASCADE OF EDFAS IN LONG-DISTANCE LINKS AND RING NETWORKS

Fiber Nonlinearities

In addition to ASE accumulation and dispersion, there are several types of fiber nonlinearities that can further limit the performance of any fiber optic transmission system, including those that use DWDM. These nonlinearities fall into two broad groups: scattering and refractive index phenomena.

Scattering Phenomena

One subtype of this phenomena is known as stimulated brillouin scattering (SBS), which is caused by the interaction between the optical signal and acoustic waves in the fiber. The result is that power from the optical signal can be scattered back toward the transmitter. SBS is a narrowband process that affects each channel in a DWDM system individually, but which is even more pronounced in STM-64/OC-192 systems, due to the greater power levels required for their transmission.

A second form of scattering is known as stimulated raman scattering (SRS), which is prompted by the interaction of the optical signal with silica molecules in the fiber. This interaction can lead to the transfer of power from shorter wavelength, higher photon energy channels, to longer wavelength, lower photon energy channels. Unlike SBS, SRS is a wideband phenomena that affects the entire optical spectrum that is being transmitted. SRS can actually cause a spectrum of equal amplitude channels to tilt as it moves through the fiber. Moreover, its impact worsens as power is increased and as the total width of the DWDM spectrum widens. One way to combat this phenomena is to use moderate channel powers as well as a densely packed channel plan that minimizes the overall width of the spectrum.

Refractive Index Phenomena

This group of nonlinearities includes self-phase modulation (SPM), cross-phase modulation (CPM), and four-wave mixing (FWM). These are caused because the index of refraction, and hence the speed of propagation in a fiber, is dependent on the intensity of light—a dependency that can have particularly significant effects in long haul applications. SPM, which refers to the modulation that a light pulse has on its own phase, acts on each DWDM channel independently. The phenomena causes the signal's spectrum to widen and can lead to cross talk or an unexpected dispersion penalty. By contrast, CPM is due to intensity fluctuations in another channel and is an effect that is unique to DWDM systems. Finally, four-wave mixing refers to the nonlinear combination of two or more optical signals in such a way that they produce new optical frequencies. Although four-wave mixing is generally not a concern in conventional single-mode fiber, it can be particularly troublesome in the dispersion-shifted fiber that is used to propagate STM64/OC192. As a result, carriers that opt for STM-64/OC-192 equipment to relieve today's congestion may unintentionally be limiting their ability to grow their capacity through future deployment of DWDM. All three types of refractive index phenomena can be controlled either through careful choice of channel power or increases in channel spacing [2].

Applications for DWDM

As occurs with many new technologies, the potential ways in which DWDM can be used are only beginning to be explored. Already, however, the technology has proven to be particularly well-suited for several vital applications.

DWDM is ready-made for long-distance telecommunications operators that use either point-to-point or ring topologies. The sudden availability of 16 new transmission channels where there used to be one dramatically improves an operator's ability to expand capacity and simultaneously set aside backup bandwidth without installing new fiber.

This large amount of capacity is critical to the development of self-healing rings, which characterize today's most sophisticated telecom networks. By deploying DWDM terminals, an operator can construct a 100 percent protected, 40 Gb/s ring, with 16 separate communication signals using only two fibers. Operators that are building or expanding their networks will also find DWDM to be an economical way to incrementally increase capacity, rapidly provision new equipment for needed expansion, and futureproof their infrastructure against unforeseen bandwidth demands (see Figure 20–31) [2].

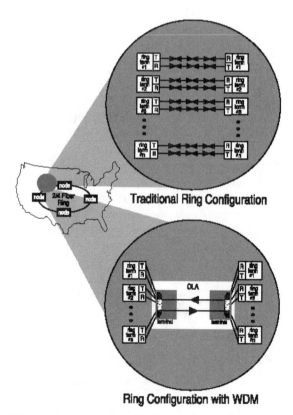

Figure 20–31   Traditional ring configuration versus ring configuration with WDM.

Network wholesalers can take advantage of DWDM to lease capacity, rather than entire fibers, either to existing operators or to new market entrants. DWDM will be especially attractive to companies that have low fiber count cables that were installed primarily for internal operations but that could now be used to generate telecommunications revenue.

The transparency of DWDM systems to various bit rates and protocols will also allow carriers to tailor and segregate services to various customers along the same transmission routes. DWDM allows a carrier to provide STM-4/OC-12 service to one customer and STM-16/OC-48 service to another all on a shared ring! In regions with a fast-growing industrial base, DWDM is also one way to utilize the existing thin fiber plant to quickly meet burgeoning demand.

The Future of DWDM—Building Block of the Photonic Network

DWDM is already established as the preferred architecture for relieving the bandwidth crunch many carriers face. Several U.S. carriers have settled on DWDM at STM-16/OC-48 rates as their technology of choice for gaining more capacity. With 16-channel DWDM now being deployed throughout the carrier infrastructure, and with a 40-channel system coming, DWDM will continue to be an essential element of future interoffice fiber systems. Indeed, deployment of DWDM is a critical first step toward the establishment of photonic networks in the access, interoffice, and interexchange segments of today's telecommunication infrastructure.

Given the rapidly changing and unpredictable nature of the telecommunications industry, it is imperative that today's DWDM systems have the ability to adapt to future technological deployments and network configurations. DWDM systems with an open architecture provide such adaptability and prepare service providers to take full advantage of the emerging photonic network.

For example, DWDM systems with open interfaces give operators the flexibility to provide SONET/SDH, asynchronous/PDH, ATM, frame relay, and other protocols over the same fiber (see Figure 20–32) [2]. Open systems also eliminate the need for additional high-performance optical transmitters to be added to a network when the need arises to interface with specific protocols. Rather, open systems allow service providers to quickly adapt new technologies to the optical network through the use of *off-the-shelf*, relatively inexpensive, and readily available transmitters.

In contrast to DWDM equipment based on proprietary specifications, systems with open interfaces provide operators greater freedom to provision services and reduce long-term costs. Proprietary-based systems, in which SONET/SDH equipment is integrated into the optical multiplexer/demulti-

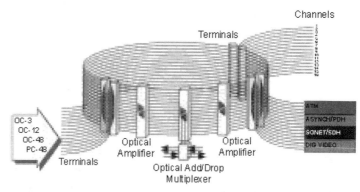

Figure 20–32   The photonic network.

plexer unit, are adequate for straight point-to-point configurations. Nevertheless, they require additional and costly transmission equipment when deployed in meshed networks (see Figure 20–33) [2].

Finally, DWDM systems that comply with the ITU channel plan will reassure carriers that they are deploying technology with recognized industry standards and the flexibility needed to grow their optical networks into long distance, local exchange, and eventually access networks.

In the space of four years, DWDM has become recognized as an industry standard that will find acceptance in any carrier environment. Deployment of DWDM will allow new services to come online more quickly, help contain costs so that prospective customers can more easily afford new services, and readily overcome technological barriers associated with more traditional solutions. Its acceptance will drive the expansion of the optical layer throughout the telecommunications network and allow service operators to exploit the enormous bandwidth capacity that is inherent in optical fiber but that has gone largely untapped—until now.

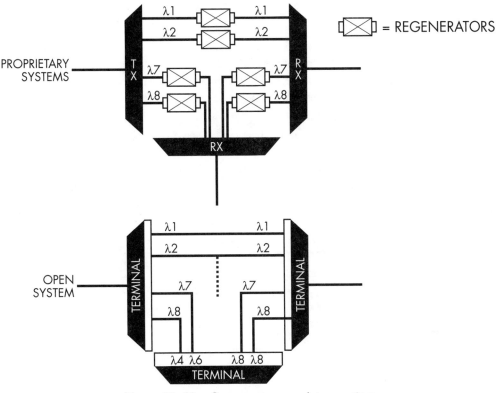

Figure 20–33 Open versus proprietary system.

Advantages of Specialty Fiber

Finally, let's take a very brief look at specialty fiber, the remaining advanced fiber optic component that will be addressed in this chapter. The following fibers will be examined:

- photosensitive fiber
- single-mode non-telco wavelengths in 450 nm, 600 nm, 750 nm, 800 nm, and 1,000 nm wavelengths
- fiber amplifier erbium doped
- fiber amplifier erbium doped for undersea applications
- AllWave™ Fiber

Photosensitive Fiber

Fiber grating technology has enabled a whole host of optical components to be constructed within the fiber itself—with the resulting wavelength division multiplexers, narrowband, high-reflectivity mirrors, wavelength-selective filters, and so on, solving problems and enhancing performance across a broad range of advanced telecommunications and sensor systems. See Tables 20–4 and 20–5 for photo-sensitive fiber specifications and performance information [3].

In the past, fiber have been photosensitized either by increasing their germania content or by hydrogenation—neither technique proved ideal. The small cores of high-germania fibers make them incompatible with standard communications fibers and the process of hydrogenation not only adds complexity and cost, but also tends to produce high loss gratings after irradiation.

Table 20–4 Photo-Sensitive Fiber Specifications

	Type 1	Type 2
Design wavelength	1300 nm	1550 nm
Cut-off wavelength	1100 nm–1300 nm	1250 nm–1500 nm
Numerical aperture	0.11–0.13	
Outside diameter (fiber)	125 µm + 1%	
Outside diameter (coating)	245 µm + 5%	
Proof test level	0.5% strain (50 kpsi)	

Table 20–5 Photosensitive Fiber Typical Performance

Induced index change	0.002
Grating length	15 mm
Irradiation wavelength/source	248 nm, Excimer
Pulse power density	0.5 Jcm –2
Pulse frequency	20 Hz
Irradiation duration	10 minutes

Single-Mode Optical Fiber for Nontelecommunications Wavelengths

Single-mode optical fibers are designed for those situations in which you need single-mode operation at wavelengths other than 1,300 nm or 1,550 nm, as shown in Table 20–6 [3].

Table 20–6 Single-Mode Optical Fibers Specifications

	SM450	*SM600*	*SM750*	*SM800*	*SM1000*
Design wavelength[1]	488 nm, 514 nm	633 nm	780 nm	830 nm	1,064 nm
Cut-off wavelength	<488 nm	<600 nm	<750 nm	<800 nm	< 1,000 nm
Numerical aperture			0.12 + 17%		
Attenuation[2]	<100 dB/km	<12 dB/km	<5 dB/km	<5 dB/km	<3 dB/km
Proof test			0.5% strain (50 kpsi stress)		
Outside diameter[3] (fiber)			125 μm ± 1% (RMS)		
Core cladding concentricity			< 1.0 μm		
Outside diameter (coating)			245 μm + 5%		

[1] The design wavelength is the wavelength (or wavelengths) at which the fiber is typically used. In practice, the fiber will transmit a TEM00 mode at any wavelength within an operating window, extending approximately 150 nm from the cut-off wavelength.

[2] Attenuation is quoted for the shortest design wavelength.

[3] Localized, peak-to-peak variations of up to 3 percent may be experienced.

Fiber Amplifier Erbium Doped

Erbium doped fiber amplifier technology continues to progress at an astonishing rate with commercial systems now in routine service around the globe. There is a new core composition that generates a substantially flattened wavelength response—providing EDFA designers with a simple, intrinsic solution for WDM transmission. In user applications, gain flatness figures of better than + 0.5 dB between 1,540 nm and 1,565 nm have been reported. The *H* high NA option enhances efficiency and is ideal for deployment in the front-end of two-stage, ultra low-noise devices. The fiber is available in two versions, optimized for 980 nm or 1,480 nm pumping, and batch-tested for EDFA performance prior to shipment (see Tables 20–7 and 20–8) [3].

Table 20–7 Fiber Amplifier Erbium Doped Specifications

	980 nm	*1,480 nm*
Cut-off wavelength	850 nm to 950 nm	1,300 nm to 1,450 nm
Numerical aperture	0.22 + 10% or 0.30 + 10%	
Absorption at pump wavelength	5.0 + 0.5 dB/m (0.22 NA)	3.3 + 0.5 dB/m (0.22 NA)
Background loss[1]	< 10 dB/km (Standard NA)	< 20 dB/km (High NA)
Core-cladding concentricity	< 0.75 μm	

Table 20–7   (continued)

	980 nm	1,480 nm
Outside diameter[2]	125 µm + 1% (RMS)	
Coating diameter	245 µm + 5%	
Proof test level	0.5% (50 kpsi)	

[1] Background loss is measured at 1,200 nm because of the influence of both the short wavelength edge of the 1,531 nm absorption peak and other structures encountered at 1,300 nm.

[2] Localized, peak-to-peak variations of up to 3 percent may be experienced. 3, 4, 5 Standard test conditions, 50 mW pump, counter-pump configuration, all measurements taken after the output isolator

Table 20–8   Fiber Amplifier Erbium Doped Typical Performance at 1,550 nm

	980 nm Pump	1,480 nm Pump
Small signal gain[1]	>30 dB	>25 dB
Saturated output[2]	>13 dBm	>14 dBm
Conversion efficiency[3]	> 55%	>70%

[1] –45 dBm input.

[2] –6 dBm input.

[3] Efficiency at maximum output power, achieved by an EDFA operated in the saturated regime and at high levels of pump power. Figure adjusted to account for system losses.

Fiber Amplifiers-Erbium Doped: Carbon-Coated for High Static Fatigue and Submarine Applications

Far beneath the sea, amplifiers are subjected to water and, with the passage of time and the gradual corrosion of metallic components, hydrogen. Twenty-year lifetimes are in doubt when the integrity of a key component is threatened by microcracks and increased attenuation (see Tables 20–9 and 20–10) [3].

This particular type of specialty fiber is hermetically sealed with a layer of amorphous carbon 20–40 nm thick. In tests, this carbon layer has demonstrated an ability to slow down hydrogen ingression by almost three orders of magnitude, even when subjected to a pressure of 100 atmospheres (approximately 3,300 feet under water). A typical stress-corrosion factor 'N' of 100 can also be shown to increase dramatically the lifetime of even the most tightly packaged gain-sections.

Table 20–9 Specifications for Fiber Amplifiers-Erbium Doped for Undersea Applications

	980 nm	1,480 nm
Cut-off wavelength	850 nm to 950 nm	1,300 nm to 1,450 nm
Numerical aperture	0.22 + 10% or 0.30 + 10%	
Absorption at pump wavelength	5.0 + 0.5 dB/m (0.22 NA)	3.3 + 0.5 dB/m (0.22 NA)
Background loss[1]	< 10 dB/km (Standard NA)	< 20 dB/km (High NA)
Core-cladding concentricity	< 0.75 μm	
Outside diameter[2]	125 μm + 1% (RMS)	
Coating diameter	245 μm + 5%	
Proof test level	0.5% (50 kpsi)	

[1] Background loss is measured at 1,200 nm because of the influence of both the short wavelength edge of the 1,531nm absorption peak and other structures encountered at 1,300 nm.

[2] Localized, peak-to-peak variations of up to 3 percent may be experienced. 3, 4, 5 Standard test conditions, 50 mW pump, counter-pump configuration, all measurements taken after the output isolator.

Table 20–10 Typical Performance at 1,550 nm for Fiber Amplifiers-Erbium Doped for Undersea Applications

	980 nm Pump	1,480 nm Pump
Small signal gain[1]	>30 dB	>25 dB
Saturated output[2]	>13 dBm	>14 dBm
Conversion efficiency[3]	> 55%	>70%

[1] –45 dBm input.

[2] –6 dBm input.

[3] Efficiency at maximum output power, achieved by an EDFA operated in the saturated regime and at high levels of pump power. Figure adjusted to account for system losses.

AllWave™ Fiber

Finally, Lucent Technologies recently announced a new specialty optical fiber developed by Bell Labs, called AllWave™ Fiber. This specialty fiber harnesses a previously untapped region in the fiber spectrum to provide 50 percent more usable wavelengths than today's conventional fiber [4].

In the manufacturing of fiber optics, there is always a certain amount of water that is retained in the glass fiber. Using a new ultra-purifying process being patented by Lucent, the company has been able to virtually eliminate water molecules in the glass fiber that had made some light regions in the fiber spectrum previously unusable. AllWave Fiber provides 100 nanometers more bandwidth than conventional single-mode fiber.

For the first time ever, as a result of this innovation, Lucent was able to utilize virtually all of the fiber spectrum to provide a broader operating range for applications such as cable television and data-on-demand services. Also, with the tremendous growth in the Internet, there is an ever-growing need for even faster transmission speeds and greater network capacity.

Cable companies can now choose to utilize a broader range of the light spectrum for cable television distribution, while local telephone service providers can have the option of providing 10 gigabit-per-second (10 billion bits of information per second) data streams over longer distances for more cost-effective transmissions. In addition, Lucent has tested 1,400 nanometer lasers with AllWave Fiber, and expects to deliver AllMetro DWDM systems to customers at the end of the year 2001. Thus, as end users around the world increasingly are able to obtain high-speed access through technologies such as DSL and cable modems, the need for multi-terabit metropolitan systems will become increasingly important.

FROM HERE

This chapter took a look at the latest fiber optic cutting-edge technologies. It focused on advanced fiber optic components such as fiber couplers, optical amplifiers, wavelength division multiplexers (WDM), and the advantages of specialty fibers. The next chapter opens up Part IV, *Planning for High-Speed Cabling Systems* by taking a thorough look at data compression: high-speed real-time data compression and how to plan for higher-speed cabling systems.

NOTES

[1]   "Microoptics for High Power Diode Laser," LIMO, Lissotschenko Mikrooptik GmbH, Hauert 7, D-44227 Dortmund, Germany, 2000.

[2]   "Dense Wavelength Division Multiplexing," The Applied Technologies Group, One Apple Hill, Suite 216, Natick, MA 01760, 2000.

[3]   "Photosensitive Optical Fiber," Metrotek Industries, Inc., 6880 46th Ave. N., Suite 100, St. Petersburg, FL 33709-4751 USA, 2000.

[4]   Lucent Technologies, 283 King George Road, Warren, NJ, 07059, 2000.

[5]   Charles Chi, "DWDM in Emerging, Data-Centric Carrier Networks," CIENA Corporation, 1201 Winterson Road, Linthicum, MD 21090, 2000.

Planning for High-Speed Cabling Systems

Data Compression

Today's organizations depend on their local area networks (LANs) to provide connectivity for a growing number of complex, mission-critical desktop computing applications. As the volume of network traffic increases, however, the bandwidth offered by a typical 10 Mbps Ethernet LAN quickly becomes inadequate to maintain acceptable performance for a growing number of desktop/server computing environments. These traffic jams are fueling the need to run compressed data through higher-speed networks.

Among the high-speed LAN technologies available today, Fast Ethernet, or ase100BaseT, has become the leading choice. Building on the near-universal acceptance of ase10BaseT Ethernet, Fast Ethernet technology provides a smooth, nondisruptive evolution to 100 Mbps performance. The growing use of ase100BaseT connections to servers and desktops, however, is creating a clear need for an even higher-speed network technology to run compressed data through at the backbone and server level. Ideally, this technology should also provide a smooth upgrade path, be cost-effective, and not require retraining.

This chapter presents an overview of Ethernet's current position in the industry. It also discusses applications driving the need for more bandwidth, data compression as a strategic evolution for networks, technology fundamentals, and network migration scenarios.

THE DOMINANT NETWORK TECHNOLOGY

Ethernet technology is ubiquitous. According to industry analysts, more than 86 percent of all installed network connections were Ethernet by the end of 1999. This represents over 350 million interconnected PCs, workstations, and servers. The remaining network connections are a combination of token ring, fiber distributed data interface (FDDI), asynchronous transfer mode (ATM), and other protocols. All popular operating systems and applications are Ethernet-compatible, as are upper-layer protocol stacks such as transmission control protocol/Internet Protocol (TCP/IP), IPX, NetBEUI, and DECnet.

The year 1999 was a milestone for Ethernet network equipment, as the technology captured 80 percent of shipments. Ethernet network interface card (NIC) shipments exceeded 65 million units and Ethernet hub shipments exceeded 77 million ports. In contrast, ATM, FDDI/CDDI, and token ring network interface card shipments combined reached just 8 million in 1999, 12 percent of the total. ATM, FDDI/CDDI, and token ring hub ports were 10 million, 15 percent of the total. Industry analysts project that Ethernet dominance will continue beyond the year 2002. Several factors have contributed to making Ethernet one of the most popular network technologies in use today.

Network Reliability

Highly reliable networks are critical to the success of the enterprise, so ease of installation and support are primary considerations in the choice of network technology. Since the introduction in 1986 of star-wired ase10BaseT hubs, structured wiring systems have continued to evolve and hubs and switches have become increasingly reliable. Today, Ethernet networks are rapidly approaching the reliability level associated with their telephone ancestors, and are relatively simple to understand and administer.

Troubleshooting and Management Tools

Management tools for Ethernet, made possible by widespread adoption of management standards, including simple network management protocol (SNMP) and its successors, allow an administrator to view the status of all desktops and network elements, including redundant elements from a central station. Ethernet troubleshooting tools span a range of capabilities, from simple link indicator lights to sophisticated network analyzers. As a result of Ethernet's popularity, large numbers of people have been trained on its installation, maintenance, and troubleshooting.

Scalability

The Fast Ethernet standard approved in 1995 established Ethernet as a scalable technology. Independent market research has indicated a strong interest among network users in adopting Ethernet technology, specifically Fast Ethernet hubs and switches with Ethernet uplinks, Ethernet switches and repeaters, and Ethernet server NICs.

Low Cost

Industry analysis of Ethernet and Fast Ethernet indicates a rapid decrease in price per port for both technologies, as shown in Table 21–1 [1], and the difference between their costs is narrowing as well.

Table 21–1   Ethernet Network Equipment Representative Price Trends

Intelligent Hub Per-Port Average Price	1998	1999
Ethernet	$71	$58
Fast Ethernet	$110	$70
Ratio	1.6	1.2

Switch Per-Port Average Price	1998	1999
Ethernet	$215	$105
Fast Ethernet	$432	$261
Ratio	2.0	2.5

NIC Per-Port Average Price	1998	1999
Ethernet	$35	$18
Fast Ethernet	$74	$45
Ratio	2.1	2.5

DRIVING NETWORK GROWTH

As new and existing network applications evolve to embrace high-resolution graphics, video, and other rich media data types, pressure is growing at the desktop, the server, the hub, and the switch for increased bandwidth to run compressed data. Table 21–2 summarizes the applications and their impact on the network [GEA, 3].

Table 21–2 Summary of Applications Driving Network Growth

Application	Data Types/Size	Network Traffic Implication	Network Need
Scientific modeling, engineering	• Data files • 100s of megabytes to gigabytes	• Large files increase bandwidth required	• Higher bandwidth for desktops, servers, and backbone
Publications, medical data transfer	• Data files • 100s of megabytes to gigabytes	• Large files increase bandwidth required	• Higher bandwidth for desktops, servers, and backbone
Internet/intranet	• Data files now • Audio now • Video is emerging • High transaction rate • Large files, 1 MB to 100 MB	• Large files increase bandwidth required • Low transmission latency • High volume of data streams	• Higher bandwidth for servers and backbone • Low latency
Data warehousing, network backup	• Data files • Gigabytes to terabytes	• Large files increase bandwidth required • Transmitted during fixed time period	• Higher bandwidth for servers and backbone • Low latency
Desktop video conferencing, interactive whiteboarding	• Constant data stream • 1.5 to 3.5 Mbps at the desktop	• Class of service reservation • High volume of data streams	• Higher bandwidth for servers and backbones • Low latency • Predictable latency

Many of these applications require the transmission of large compressed files over the network. Scientific applications demand ultra-high bandwidth networks to communicate compressed 3D visualizations of complex objects ranging from molecules to aircraft. Magazines, brochures, and other complex, full-color publications prepared on desktop computers are transmitted directly to digital-input printing facilities. Many medical facilities are transmitting compressed complex images over LAN and WAN links, enabling the sharing of expensive equipment and specialized medical exper- tise. Engineers are using electronic and mechanical design automation tools to work interactively in distributed development teams, sharing files in the hundreds of gigabytes.

Many companies are now employing Internet technologies to build pri- vate intranets, enabling users in an organization to go beyond electronic mail and access critical data through familiar web browsers, opening the door to a new generation of multimedia client/server applications. While intranet traf- fic is currently composed primarily of text, graphics, and images, this is expected to expand in the near future to include more bandwidth-intensive audio, video, and voice.

Data warehousing has become popular as a way of making enterprise data available to decision makers for reporting and analysis without sacrificing the performance, security, or integrity of production systems. These ware- houses may comprise gigabyte or terabytes of data distributed over hundreds of platforms and accessed by thousands of users, and must be updated regularly to provide users near real-time data for critical business reports and analyses.

Network backup of servers and storage systems is common in many industries that require enterprise information to be archived. Such backups usually occur during off hours and require large amounts of bandwidth dur- ing a fixed amount of time (5 to 9 hours). The backup involves gigabytes or terabytes of compressed data distributed over hundreds of servers and storage systems throughout an enterprise.

A recent survey of video applications conducted by a leading industry analyst shows interest in video increasing rapidly as computers offer native MPEG decoding capability and as low-cost encoding chip sets become more widely available. The survey looked at a number of video-based applications, including video conferencing, education, and human resources from several companies. As these applications proliferate and demand ever greater shares of bandwidth at the desktop (as the total number of network users continues to grow), organizations will need to migrate critical portions of their networks to higher-bandwidth technologies to run compressed encrypted data through.

THE STRATEGIC ALTERNATIVE FOR INTRANETS AND LANS

The accelerating growth of LAN traffic is pushing network administrators to look to higher-speed network technologies to run compressed data through to solve the bandwidth crunch. These administrators who typically have either Ethernet or FDDI backbones today have several alternatives from which to choose. Although each network faces different issues, Fast Ethernet meets several key criteria for such a high-speed network:

- Easy, straightforward migration to higher performance levels without disruption.
- Low cost of ownership, including both purchase cost and support cost.
- Capability to support new applications and data types.
- Network design flexibility [GEA, 4].

Migration to Performance

One of the most important questions network administrators face is how to get higher bandwidth to run compressed data without disrupting the existing network. Fast Ethernet follows the same form, fit, and function as its 10 Mbps and 100 Mbps Ethernet precursors, allowing a straightforward, incremental migration to higher-speed networking. All three Ethernet speeds use the same IEEE 802.3 frame format, full-duplex operation, and flow-control methods. In half-duplex mode, Fast Ethernet employs the same fundamental carrier sense multiple access/collision detection (CSMA/CD) access method to resolve contention for the shared media. And Fast Ethernet uses the same management objects defined by the IEEE 802.3 group. Fast Ethernet is Ethernet, only faster.

100BaseT is a high-speed variation of 10BaseT standardized as IEEE 802.3u (June 14, 1995).

Ethernet Frame Format

It is simple to connect existing lower-speed Ethernet devices to Fast Ethernet devices using LAN switches or routers to adapt one physical line speed to the other. Fast Ethernet uses the same variable-length (64- to 1,514-byte packets) IEEE 802.3 frame format found in Ethernet, as shown in Figure 21–1 [4]. Because the frame format and size are the same for all Ethernet technologies, no other network changes are necessary. This evolutionary upgrade path allows Fast Ethernet to be seamlessly integrated into existing Ethernet networks.

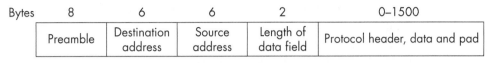

Figure 21–1   IEEE 802.3 frame.

In contrast, other high-speed technologies use fundamentally different frame formats to run compressed data through. High-speed ATM, for example, implements a fixed-length data cell. When connecting Ethernet and Fast Ethernet to ATM, the switch or router must translate each ATM cell to an Ethernet frame, and vice versa.

Full- and Half-Duplex Operation

As defined by the IEEE 802.3x specification, two nodes connected via a full-duplex, switched path can simultaneously send and receive packets. Fast Ethernet follows this standard to communicate in full-duplex mode. Fast Ethernet also employs standard Ethernet flow control methods to avoid congestion and overloading. When operating in half-duplex mode, Fast Ethernet adopts the same fundamental CSMA/CD access method to resolve contention for the shared media. The CSMA/CD method is shown in Figure 21–2. [GEA, 5].

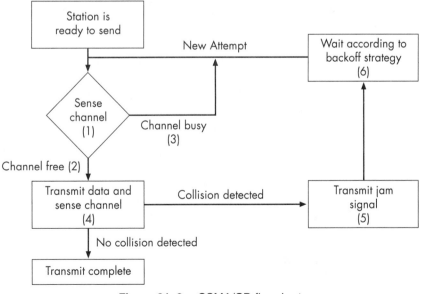

Figure 21–2   CSMA/CD flowchart.

The Fast Ethernet CSMA/CD method has been enhanced in order to maintain a 200-meter collision diameter at gigabit speeds. Without this enhancement, minimum-sized Ethernet packets could complete transmission before the transmitting station senses a collision, thereby violating the CSMA/CD method.

To resolve this issue, both the minimum CSMA/CD carrier time and the Ethernet slot time have been extended from their present value of 64 bytes to a new value of 512 bytes. Packets smaller than 512 bytes have an extra carrier extension. Packets longer than 512 bytes are not extended. These changes, which can impact small-packet performance, have been offset by incorporating a new feature, called packet bursting, into the CSMA/CD algorithm. Packet bursting will allow servers, switches, and other devices to send bursts of small packets in order to fully utilize available bandwidth.

The minimum packet length of 64 bytes has not been affected.

Devices that operate in full-duplex mode (switches and buffered distributors) are not subject to the carrier extension, slot time extension, or packet bursting changes. Full-duplex devices will continue to use the regular Ethernet 96-bit interframe gap (IFG) and 64-byte minimum packet size.

Management Objects

In the transition from Ethernet to Fast Ethernet, the fundamental management objects familiar to most network managers is carried forward. For example, SNMP defines a standard method to collect device-level Ethernet information. SNMP uses management information base (MIB) structures to record key statistics such as collision count, packets transmitted or received, error rates, and other device-level information. Additional information is collected by remote monitoring (RMON) agents to aggregate the statistics for presentation via a network management application. Because Fast Ethernet uses standard Ethernet frames, the same MIBs and RMON agents can be used to provide network management at gigabit speeds.

Low Cost of Ownership

Cost of ownership is an important factor in evaluating any new networking technology. The overall cost of ownership includes not only the purchase price of equipment, but also the cost of training, maintenance, and troubleshooting.

Competition and economies of scale have driven the purchase price of Ethernet connections down significantly. Though Fast Ethernet products have been shipping only since 1994, even these products have experienced significant price declines over the past few years.

Early Fast Ethernet products have provided cost-effective connections for gigabit transmission rates. IEEE has provided Fast Ethernet connections at two to three times the cost of a 100BaseaseFX interface. As volume builds, reduced line width integrated circuits (IC) processes are implemented, and low-cost optoelectronic devices are developed, the cost of Fast Ethernet interfaces will continue to decline.

Switched Fast Ethernet connections are expected to be lower in cost than 622 Mbps ATM interfaces (assuming identical physical media interfaces) because of the relative simplicity of Ethernet and higher shipment volumes. Fast Ethernet repeater interfaces are significantly lower in cost than 622 Mbps ATM connections, providing users with cost-effective alternatives for data center network backbone and server connections. Table 21–3 illustrates current prices for Ethernet, Fast Ethernet, FDDI, and 622 Mbps ATM multimode and the target range for Fast Ethernet based on the IEEE 802.3 goals (not IEEE price goals, they don't set any) [GEA, 6].

Table 21–3   Network Backbone Connection Representative Prices

Technology	Equipment Type	1999 Equipment Price/Port	2002 Equipment Price/Port	Change %
Shared Fast Ethernet	Hub	$119	$74	−38%
Switched Fast Ethernet	Switch	$654	$325	−50%
Shared FDDI	Concentrator	$773	$602	−22%
Switched FDDI	Switch	$3,280	$1,525	−54%
ATM 622 Mbps Estimate (multimode fiber)	Switch	$6,006	$4,368	−27%
Shared Fast Ethernet IEEE goal (multimode fiber)	Hub	n/a	$360 to $600** (2x to 3x Fast Ethernet MM)	
Switched Fast Ethernet IEEE goal (multimode fiber)	Switch	n/a	$960 to $1500** (2x to 3x Fast Ethernet MM)	

Over time, advances in silicon, including 0.35-micron CMOS application-specific integrated circuit (ASIC) technology, will provide even greater performance gains and cost-reduction opportunities, which will result in a new, even more cost-effective generation of Ethernet technology. Current 0.5-micron technology can accommodate about 0.5 million gates and is limited to transmission rates of about 500 Mbps. Analysis indicates that 0.35-micron processes will achieve 1,250 Mbps operation and economically fit 1 million gates on a single die. This is more than enough to fit a complete Ethernet switch, including management, a significant amount of buffer memory, and an embedded 32-bit controller, on a single die with obvious cost advantages.

Finally, because the installed base of users is already familiar with Ethernet technology, maintenance, and troubleshooting tools, the support costs associated with Fast Ethernet are far lower than other technologies. Fast Ethernet requires only incremental training of personnel and incremental purchase of maintenance and troubleshooting tools. In addition, deployment of Fast Ethernet is faster than alternative technologies. Once upgraded with training and tools, network support staff are able to confidently install, troubleshoot, and support Fast Ethernet installations.

Support for New Applications and Data Types

The emergence of intranet applications portends a migration to new data types, including video and voice. In the past it was thought that video might require a different networking technology designed specifically for multimedia. But today it is possible to mix data and video over Ethernet through a combination of the following:

- Increased bandwidth provided by Fast Ethernet, enhanced by LAN switching.
- The emergence of new protocols, such as resource reservation protocol (RSVP), that provide bandwidth reservation.
- The emergence of standards such as 802.1Q and 802.1p, which provide virtual LAN (VLAN) and explicit priority information for packets in the network.
- The widespread use of advanced video compression such as MPEG-2 [GEA, 7].

These technologies and protocols combine to make Fast Ethernet an extremely attractive solution for the delivery of video and multimedia traffic, as illustrated in Table 21–4 [GEA, 7].

Table 21–4 High-Speed Network Capabilities

Capabilities	Ethernet	Fast Ethernet	ATM	FDDI
IP Compatibility	Yes	Yes	Requires RFC 1557 or IP over LAN emulation (LANE) today; I-Private network-to-network interface (PNNI) and/or multiprotocol over ATM (MPOA) in the future	Yes
Ethernet Packets	Yes	Yes	Requires LANE	Yes, though 802.1h translation bridging
Handle multimedia	Yes	Yes	Yes, but application needs substantial changes	Yes
Quality of service	Yes, with RSVP and/or 802.1p	Yes with RSVP and/or 802.1p	Yes with SVCs or RSVP with complex mapping from Internet Engineering Task Force (IETF) (work in progress)	Yes, with RSVP and/or 802.1p
VLANs with 802.1Q/p	Yes	Yes	Requires mapping LANE and/or SVCs to 802.1Q	Yes

Flexible Internetworking and Network Design

Network administrators today face a myriad of internetworking choices and network design options. They are combining routed and switched networks and building intranets of increasing scale. Ethernet networks are shared (using repeaters) and switched, based on bandwidth and cost requirements. The choice of a high-speed network to run compressed data through, however, should not restrict the choice of internetworking or network topology.

Today, Fast Ethernet is switched, routed, and shared. All of today's internetworking technologies, as well as emerging technologies such as IP-specific switching and Layer 3 switching, are fully compatible with Fast Ethernet, just as they are with Ethernet. Fast Ethernet is currently available in a shared, repeated hub (with the accompanying low cost per port) as well as on LAN switches and routers.

Fast Ethernet Technology

The simple migration and support offered by Ethernet, combined with the scalability and flexibility to handle new applications and data types, makes Fast Ethernet the strategic choice when planning and designing for high-speed cabling systems and high-bandwidth networking for running compressed encrypted data.

Fast Ethernet is an extension to the highly successful 10 Mbps and 100 Mbps IEEE 802.3 Ethernet standards. Offering a raw data bandwidth of 1,000 Mbps, Fast Ethernet maintains full compatibility with the huge installed base of Ethernet nodes.

Full- and Half-Duplex over Fiber Today and UTP in the Future

Fast Ethernet supports new full-duplex operating modes for switch-to-switch and switch-to-end-station connections and half-duplex operating modes for shared connections using repeaters and the CSMA/CD access method. Initially operating over optical fiber, Fast Ethernet is able to use category 5 UTP cabling. Figure 21–3 illustrates the functional elements of Fast Ethernet [GEA, 9].

The gigabit media independent interface (GMII) in Figure 21–3 is optional.

Much of the effort of the IEEE 802.3 Task Force is devoted to the definition of PHY standards for Fast Ethernet. Like other standards based on the International Standards Organization (ISO) model, Fast Ethernet implements functionality adhering to a Physical layer standard. In general, the PHY, or Physical layer, is responsible for defining the mechanical, electrical, and procedural characteristics for establishing, maintaining, and deactivating the physical link between network devices. For Fast Ethernet communications, several physical layer standards are emerging from the IEEE 802.3 effort.

Two PHYs provide gigabit transmission over fiber optic cabling. 1000BaseaseSX is targeted at lowest cost multimode fiber and runs in horizontal and shorter backbone applications. 1000BaseaseLX is targeted at longer

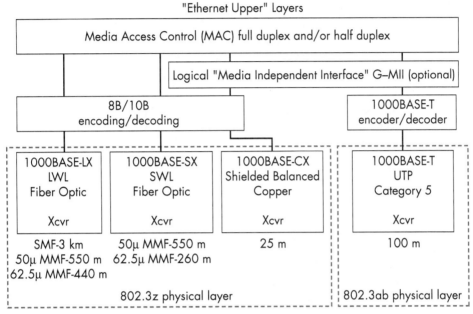

Figure 21–3   Functional elements of Fast Ethernet technology.

multimode building fiber backbones and single-mode campus backbones. For multimode fiber, these standards define gigabit transmission over distances of 260 and 550 meters, respectively. Single-mode fiber, which is covered by the long-wavelength standard, is defined to cover distances of 3 kilometers.

There are also two standards efforts for Fast Ethernet transmission over copper cabling. The first copper link standard is being defined by the 802.3 Task Force and is referred to as 1000BaseaseCX. This standard supports interconnection of equipment clusters, where the physical interface is short-haul copper. It supports a switching closet or computer room as a short jumper interconnection for 25-meter distances. This standard uses the fiber channel-based 8B/10B coding at the serial line rate of 1.25 Gbps, and runs over 150-ohm balanced, shielded, specialty cabling assemblies. LBM Type I cabling is not recommended. This copper physical layer standard has the advantage that it can be generated quickly and is inexpensive to implement. According to the 802.3 timetable, the short copper link standard will be complete in the same time frame as the fiber links.

The second copper link standard is intended for use in horizontal copper cabling applications. In March 1997, a project authorization request (PAR) was approved by the IEEE Standards Board, enabling the creation of a separate but related committee referred to as the 802.3ab Task Force. This new group is chartered with the development of a 1000BaseT physical layer standard providing 1 Gbps Ethernet signal transmission over 4-pair category 5 UTP cable, covering cabling distances of up to 100 meters or networks with a diameter of 200 meters. This standard will outline communications used for horizontal copper runs on a floor within a building using structured generic cabling, taking advantage of the existing UTP cable already deployed. This effort will likely require new technology and new coding schemes in order to meet the potentially difficult and demanding parameters set by the previous Ethernet and Fast Ethernet standards. This will be on a somewhat longer timetable than the 802.3 Fast Ethernet effort.

Fiber Channel Components

The use of existing, proven technologies and methods minimizes time-to-market for Fast Ethernet products. Current efforts in the IEEE 802.3 standards activity draw heavily on the use of fiber channel and other high-speed networking components. Fiber channel encoding/decoding integrated circuits (ICs) and optical components are readily available and are specified and optimized for high performance at relatively low cost.

Fast Ethernet employs fiber channel's high-speed, 850 nm (short wavelength) optical components for signaling over optical fiber and 8B/10B encoding/decoding schemes for serialization and deserialization. Current fiber channel technology operating at 1.063 Gbps is being enhanced to run at 1.250 Gbps, thus providing the full 1,000 Mbps data rate. For longer link distances up to at least 3 km using single-mode fiber and up to at least 440 meters on 62.5-micron multimode fiber, 1300-nm (long wavelength) optics are also specified.

The IEEE 802.3 standards activity is planning ahead for the expected advances in silicon technology and digital signal processing that will eventually enable Fast Ethernet to operate over UTP cabling. To accommodate this, a logical interface will be specified between the media access control (MAC) and PHY layers that will decouple the fiber channel 8B/10B encoding, allowing other encoding schemes that more readily support the use of cost-effective UTP cabling.

Fast Ethernet Products

Since Fast Ethernet is Ethernet, the types of Fast Ethernet products are quite straightforward: switches, uplink/downlink modules, NICs, Fast Ethernet router interfaces, and one new device, the buffered distributors. There are pure multiport Fast Ethernet switches with high performance backplanes, as well as devices that have both Ethernet and Fast Ethernet ports in the same box. Fast Ethernet uplinks appear as modular upgrades for fixed-configuration Ethernet devices or modular, chassis-based hubs to provide a high-speed connection to the network. Vendors of high-performance routers deliver Fast Ethernet interfaces as well.

Some Fast Ethernet vendors are developing a new device called a buffered distributor. The buffered distributor is a full-duplex, multiport, hub-like device that interconnects two or more 802.3 links operating at 1 Gbps or faster. Like an 802.3 repeater, it is a non-address-filtering device. The buffered distributor forwards all incoming packets to all connected links except the originating link, providing a shared bandwidth domain comparable to a 802.3 collision domain.

Buffered distributors have been called CSMA/CD in a box.

Unlike an 802.3 repeater, the buffered distributor is permitted to buffer one or more incoming frames on each link before forwarding them. There have also been technical discussions about half-duplex Fast Ethernet repeaters.

As a shared bandwidth device, the buffered distributor should be distinguished from both routers and switches. While routers with Fast Ethernet interfaces may have backplanes that support bandwidths greater or less than gigabit rates, the ports attached to a Fast Ethernet buffered distributor's backplane share 1 gigabit of bandwidth. In contrast, the backplanes of high-performance, multiport Fast Ethernet switches support multigigabit bandwidths.

Buffered distributors are not currently defined in 802.3 standards. Nor are other standard networking devices such as routers and switches. A standard has been drafted to allow the implementation of buffered distributors.

Ethernet and Higher-Level Services

Fast Ethernet provides high-speed connectivity, but does not by itself provide a full set of services such as quality of service (QoS), automatic redundant failover, or higher-level routing services. These are added via other open standards.

Fast Ethernet, like all Ethernet specifications, specifies the data link (Layer 2) of the OSI protocol model, while TCP and IP in turn specify the Transport (Layer 4) and Network (Layer 3) portions and allow reliable communication services between applications. Issues such as QoS were not addressed in the original Fast Ethernet specifications, but must be addressed across several of these standards. Resource reservation protocol (RSVP), for instance, is defined at the Network layer to work alongside IP. Layer 3 (routing) services also operate at the network layer, as shown in Table 21–5 [GEA, 12].

Table 21–5   Layers of Network Functionality

OSI Layer	OSI Name	Examples
4	Transport	TCP
3	Network	IP, RSVP
2	Data link	Ethernet (MAC), 802.1p, 802.1Q
1	Physical	10BaseT, 100BaseT, fiber channel

Various implementations of Fast Ethernet may include one or more of these standards in order to provide a more robust or functional networking connection, but the overall success of Fast Ethernet is not tied to any one of them. The advantage of modular standards is that any one piece may evolve and be adopted at a pace determined by market need and product quality.

All of the standards are just as readily paired with Fast Ethernet and 10 Mbps Ethernet, so that all levels of Ethernet performance can benefit from all the standards work.

Quality of Service on Ethernet

Applications emerging in the early 2000s are demanding consistent bandwidth, latency, and jitter from network connections. Such applications include voice and video over LANs and WANs, multicast software distribution, and the like. Standards bodies have responded with new open definitions such as RSVP and the current work in the IEEE 802.1p and IEEE 802.1Q standards groups.

RSVP is gaining industry acceptance as a preferred way to request and provide quality of network connections. In order to have RSVP function and deliver defined and consistent quality to an application, each network component in the chain between client and server must support RSVP and communicate appropriately. Because of the need to have so many components supported by RSVP before meaningful results can be achieved, some vendors are advancing proprietary schemes to deliver some degree of QoS. Some of these may deliver QoS benefits to users, but will require certain portions of the network to be vendor-specific implementations.

802.1p and 802.1Q facilitate quality of service over Ethernet by providing a means for tagging packets with an indication of the priority or class of service desired for the packet. These tags allow applications to communicate the priority of packets to internetworking devices. RSVP support can be achieved by mapping RSVP sessions into 802.1p service classes.

Layer 3 Functionality

Layer 3 involves determination of the eventual destination of a packet beyond its MAC destination address on the packet header. By examining the IP address (buried deeper in the packet), the IP subnet can be determined, allowing broadcasts to be contained to the appropriate subnets and packets to be forwarded accurately to intermediate nodes for most efficient transit through the network.

The classic Layer 3 device is the router, which makes Layer 3 decisions by implementing complex algorithms and data structures in software. While such complicated routing tasks formerly required complex and software-intensive multiprotocol router products, vendors over the last few years have announced Layer 3 switch products that accomplish many of these tasks, while delivering arguably better price/performance than traditional routers. Narrowing the protocol supported to IP has allowed devices to optimize tasks and accomplish more work with dedicated hardware.

FAST ETHERNET MIGRATION

The initial applications for Fast Ethernet have been for campuses or buildings requiring greater bandwidth between routers, switches, hubs, repeaters, and servers. Examples include switch-to-router, switch-to-switch, switch-to-server, and repeater-to-switch connections, as shown in Table 21–6 [GEA, 13]. In its early phase, Fast Ethernet was not expected to be deployed widely to the desktop. In all scenarios, the network operating system (NOS), applications, and NIC drivers at the desktop have remained unchanged. The information technology (IT) manager can also leverage not only the existing multimode fiber, but also the current investment in network management applications and tools.

Table 21–6 The Five Most Likely Upgrade Scenarios

1. Upgrading switch-to-switch connections.	Obtain 1,000 Mbps pipes between 100/1,000 switches.
2. Upgrading switch-to-server connections.	Achieve high-speed access to applications and file servers.
3. Upgrading a switched Fast Ethernet backbone.	Aggregate Fast Ethernet switches with an Ethernet switch or repeater.
4. Upgrading a shared FDDI backbone.	Install FDDI switch or Ethernet-to-FDDI switches/routers with Fast Ethernet switches or repeaters.
5. Upgrading high-performance desktops.	Fast Ethernet NICs for connection to Fast Ethernet switches or repeaters.

Let's now take a look at how to get the bandwidth you need when you need it, in order for your high-speed cabling system to be capable of carrying compressed data. There has been extensive talk of obtaining bandwidth on demand (BoD) from many different technologies. There has been far less explanation of exactly what that means and how a network user makes it happen. Talk of access to wide area networks often ignores the last mile connection between customer premises and central office. This part of the chapter classifies bandwidth, based on many transmission technologies (analog to high bit rate digital subscriber line [HDSL]) on who controls the bandwidth allocation (preprovisioned or dial-up) and on the time delay to make bandwidth usable (from microseconds for ATM permanent virtual circuits to weeks for leased lines). In a sense, all bandwidth is on-demand and only the time frames, cost basis, and controlling party vary.

NETWORK TYPES

Modern networks provide bandwidth that is either circuit-switched or packet-switched. Circuit-switched connections give a customer the exclusive use of a certain amount of bandwidth for the duration of the requirement. That is, the connection is set up on demand and, until the caller breaks the connection, the capacity of the physical transmission and switching facilities needed for the connection is reserved for that caller exclusively. Reserved bandwidth provides immediate access to the portion allocated.

Switched circuits require that capacity be available for each new caller. A T-1 line with 24 DS-0 channels cannot accept a request for a 25th DS-0 connection [2]. On larger capacity transmission lines, users share by taking turns in fixed time slots; each gets a small amount of time in a regularly repeating cycle—the process of time division multiplexing (TDM). If a particular caller has nothing to send, his time slot is wasted because it is not available to any other caller.

In any form of packetized switching, a connection gives the caller the opportunity to present information to the network, but does not in general guarantee immediate access to the transmission line. There may be a wait until earlier demands are met. Potentially, each user is in competition with other users who may want the same transmission facility at the same time. When demand exceeds capacity, only one user gains immediate access; the others must wait in queue.

Packetized transmission is based on logical rather than physical connections. There are only practical limits on the number of connections across a T-1 link when each connection is designated by a packet address and does not consume a DS-0 channel. Practical limits might be throughput (the total amount of data is limited by the transmission speed of 1.536 Mbps, for example) or address space (the frame relay supports no more than 1,000 addresses on a serial channel).

These are very different in concepts, though they can work together when one technology is used as an access to another. An example is ISDN access to frame relay. What they have in common is that each user intermittently obtains full and exclusive use of the transmission facility (network capacity). A circuit-switched connection takes over a line (or a channel within a line) periodically by requesting it. The request may be in the form of a call setup request for a circuit-switched connection or the presentation of a data packet to the packet-switching and transmission equipment.

ACCESS TO BANDWIDTH

In all types of networks, the customer gets bandwidth only when purchased; in a sense, on demand. How that purchase is made determines how quickly bandwidth becomes available after the initial request for service and after incremental demands placed on the active service are met. The customer also decides what the maximum capacity will be. These two considerations often determine the transmission technology and a specific carrier service.

From Remote Site into Private Backbone or Carrier

First, there must always be a preprovisioned transmission path. In most cases this is wire pairs, though fibers are becoming more common. The path is dedicated to the customer—in effect a leased line—even if the service is switched.

At the site of a new home or office construction, a carrier will have to install new dedicated cables even for switched services.

Access may also be wireless, but cellular phone service has an activation procedure that corresponds to setting up the path on a wire. A workstation on a LAN has a leased-line path in the coax or twisted-pair medium.

The size of this path must be larger than the average requirement. Averaged over a week, the largest church needs only one very small door. Fire codes and people's impatience require there be many doors.

To speed compressed file transfers, a data network operator might link two sites with a T-1 line when the average throughput is less than 56 Kbps. The number of PBX trunks to handle busy hours may be many times more than the average usage.

Once the path is in place, the user can fill part or all of it—but no more. This fact is sometimes lost in the hype. Converting a 56 Kbps leased line to a frame relay service will not allow that connection to burst above 56 Kbps.

Within the Backbone or Carrier Service

While the access loop is always a dedicated circuit, the usage of the backbone may be dedicated or switched, circuit-based or packetized. It is here that on-demand has its greatest impact. Confusion between what happens within the backbone and what is possible on the access portion of this link leads to misconceptions like 56 Kbps lines bursting to 256 Kbps.

Channelized

Circuit-switched connections require dedicated backbone resources while the connection is in place all the time for leased lines. The resource consumed is bandwidth on the higher-speed transmission lines between backbone nodes. Because circuits are assigned by time division multiplexing (with many users interleaved on a serial trunk), all the user ever sees is the bandwidth of that TDM channel. The end points of a 56 Kbps channel can't tell whether it is carried on 56 Kbps copper pairs, T-1, or 655 megabit/second fiber.

A channel provisioned by the network manager on a private T-1 network may be variable in size. However, in the general case, to get larger bandwidth, an inverse multiplexer aggregates multiple parallel channels, either leased or switched. It makes no sense to expand the capacity in the backbone beyond the capacity of the access loop.

Packetized

Packet-switched connections are virtual—they use resources only when there is data to transmit. During idle periods, a packet-switched connection remains, logically, though other users may take all the bandwidth.

On any trunk between nodes, only one packet is being sent at any given time. Packets are interleaved, not time slots (as in TDM). Thus, entire packets are always sent uninterrupted at the full line speed. That may be 56 Kbps from the customer site, and 622 Mbps inside the network. This is not bursting.

What is Bursting?

Bursting is more correctly called throughput bursting. It is possible only if the normal throughput is less than the capacity of the access links at both ends. In frame relay service, a carrier may guarantee a committed information rate (CIR) to a user that is less than the access port speed: 9,600 on a 56,000 line/port.

CIR is the data rate that the network guarantees to handle under normal conditions. It is based on a mutual contractual agreement between the carrier and the customer.

Every frame sent to the network is sent at 56K—the line speed. Idle time between frames when throughput is zero brings the average throughput down to 9,600. Bursting means the idle time is reduced; frames may be sent continuously. Throughput then can approach the line speed (but no more) unless the information is compressed.

Data Compression as Access Amplifier

Throughput can exceed the access line speed if the information (usually data) is compressed. All modern modems compress asynchronous data automatically (MNP or V.42bis). FRADs, routers, and dedicated compressors may double the throughput of synchronous channels up to about 2 Mbps (uncompressed at up to 6 Mbps).

The compression ratio depends on the data. A file with more redundancy (a database with many fixed-length fields filled with 0s) may compress 4:1 or more. Encrypted data does compress now—where once it didn't. This is due to a new online compressed satellite encryption-based technology that is discussed later in this chapter.

DEMANDING MORE BANDWIDTH

There are many ways to get more throughput on the access channel (within its limits). If your bandwidth need exceeds the available access throughput, more must be installed. This may mean an upgrade from an analog line with a modem to a digital service, or from a lower to a higher speed digital line (56K to T-1). It is also possible to increase the activated fraction in an FT-1 line (256 to 512 Kbps). When moving up in bandwidth, a change in technology may be needed when going from alternate mark inversion (56 Kbps) to 2B+D (ISDN basic rate—BRI).

Open More Channels

If a T-1 local loop has fewer than 24 channels active, turn on more channels. This may be a manual process within a phone company (adding more local phone lines) or a fully automated one (dial-up of previously subscribed B channels on an ISDN primary rate interface [PRI]). The user may see these as individual connections or an inverse multiplexer and may combine them into a single, variable-speed aggregate.

The provisioned access capacity presents a firm limit to the number of available channels.

Present More Frames/Packets/Cells

In packetized systems, the user who presents more traffic will get more bandwidth up to the capacity of the system (or perhaps to some assigned and enforced limit). An idle workstation on a LAN will receive BoD simply by sending information.

In the near future, frame relay and ATM networks will offer switched virtual circuits, the way X.25 does today. SVCs are more a way to direct information flow than to add bandwidth. But, in the sense that a user can add bandwidth to a location, SVC service is BoD also.

Let's next discuss one of the most talked-about issues today in planning and designing high-speed cabling systems: the potential increase in bandwidth requirements on the horizon. Fueled by the industry's love of technology and a plethora of applications such as teleconferencing, client/server, e-mail file transfer, graphics, and video to the desktop, the IT manager is crying imminent bandwidth poverty. Budgets are being drawn up with new protocols such as high-speed Ethernet, TP-PMD, and ATM to every desktop based on perceived bandwidth shortfall.

BANDWIDTH POVERTY

The biggest culprits in the infrastructure end of the business are the fiber manufacturers, who continually justify the cost of fiber-to-the-desktop with the statistical double-talk of bandwidth per dollar. Like selling cars on the achievable top speed, this assumes that the user can actually utilize the bandwidth provided by fiber. What good does gigabit-per-second bandwidth yield if the protocols available cannot achieve these transmission speeds to run compressed data through?

Like children threatened by an evil babysitter, IT managers are told that the bandwidth bogeyman is in the closet and night is falling. New hubs, network interface cards (NICs), and complete facility recabling to accommodate the new bandwidth is recommended.

Well, it just ain't so! Current UTP horizontal infrastructure, even category 3 channels, offers substantial bandwidth increase potential without changing the protocols. If more bandwidth is required for communication-intensive applications like video, there are protocols available today that run well on existing copper horizontal infrastructure. A vertical backbone of fiber and higher-speed protocols on the backbone will certainly be required, but some low-cost strategies can very effectively vanquish the bandwidth bogeyman.

The Bandwidth Utilization Fallacy

The first misrepresentation is the statement that bandwidth to the desktop has grown dramatically from the days of terminal connections to today's LANs. On the surface, the movement from 19.2 Kbps RS232 to 10 Mbps Ethernet would seem to support this, indicating a 500 times expansion of available bandwidth. Further examination indicates a much smaller change.

The most common terminal service applications were RS232 and IBM 3270. In the RS232 environment, each terminal was connected to a dedicated port on the host computer, providing a full-time channel at 9.6 or 19.2 Kbps. In the IBM 3270 environment, a 1 Mbps channel supported 8 terminals under a polling protocol. Each terminal had the channel available one-eighth of the time for the equivalent of a 125 Kbps dedicated channel to each terminal. These protocols supported the environment of the steady but light stream of data required to update the screen of a dumb terminal with information stored and processed at the host computer.

The environment today is that of the client/server, where the storage is central and the processing is handled by an intelligent workstation device. The market forces driving this architecture are stable. Processing power is low cost and can be economically distributed to each desktop. Continual reduction in this case will only enhance the speed and power of the desktop, broadening the implementation of intensive applications such as video and graphics. Most data is a shared resource and therefore will be centrally stored. This promotes data integrity in changing environments and simplifies backup [3].

The result of the client/server architecture is that data is moved in blocks as opposed to streams, often called burst data. An 802.3 Ethernet or 802.5 token ring LAN supports this well by offering short-duration, high-speed access to a shared channel. This is comparable to the early days of telephony, where party lines supported the occasional access requirements of the market.

Refocusing on the actual bandwidth available to each client workstation and using Ethernet as the example provides enlightening insight into the bandwidth issue. Ethernet offers 10 Mbps of compressed data speed during transmission. But, due to access protocols and collisions, the throughput is generally limited to 40 percent, or 4 Mbps. This party-line bandwidth is shared between all devices on that portion of the network between bridges or routers. Assuming 40 devices per network, this results in 100 Kbps average available bandwidth per device.

Therefore, the increase in channel bandwidth between the IBM environment of 1964 and a common client/server environment of 2001 is nonexistent! Even comparing RS232 with Ethernet over this 37-year span results in only a 10:1 increase, not the 1,000:1 increase that is often quoted from 9.6 Kbps to 10 Mbps.

The Bandwidth-Intensive Application Fallacy

Compressed information that will be transported will be of various types: audio, data, video, and control. Audio information includes voice and music. Voice utilizes 56 Kbps and digital music about 1 Mbps, but both require the transmission to be real-time because there is a human as the ultimate interface. Delays in these signals will not be accepted because the result is a silence on the line. Therefore, these applications do not require a lot of bandwidth but require a lot of access.

Data transmission is communication of information between machines, usually to be stored and subsequently processed. While the file size can be enormous, computers are patient devices that are willing to wait indefinitely for completion of the transmission. The human using the information will not be willing to wait very long, but even a second or two will enable the transmission of multimegabyte files. Backup and updating of files over the network can involve huge files, but can utilize the lowest access priority.

Control signals are also real time, but contain small amounts of data. They can be a problem because of the frequency of access required if the system is poorly designed. For example, the control of a robot by a remote computer would require continual positional data from the robot to the computer and continual movement orders from the computer to the robot.

A properly designed control system would place a controller at the robot that would accept complex orders (perhaps complete program downloads) from a remote supervisor and accomplish the positional feedback locally. This properly designed system results in less time dependence and less information transport.

Video and graphic display information is also real time because there is a human at the end of the channel. Lost information shows up as a drop-out of the picture. While the raw bandwidth requirements can be as high as 100 Mbps, video information is easily compressed. For example, in a video-conferencing application, one can easily transmit only the pixels, which change from frame to frame and attain compression as high as 10:1. Additional compression of the digital data stream yields 20:1 or more. Currently, the telephone companies in the United States are experimenting with video on demand to homes over existing UTP phone cable. VCR-quality transmissions are achieved on 1.544 Mbps lines! If this is extrapolated, HDTV quality signals should be achievable at 20 Mbps or so. This is therefore the worst-case application because it requires relatively high bandwidth and real-time access.

Horizontal versus Vertical Cable Bandwidth

In a structured cabling system, the channels are designated as horizontal cabling (from the wiring closet to the desktop) and vertical cabling (connecting wiring closets together, generally floor-to-floor). The limiting factors to channel bandwidth in either case are the media itself and the equipment connected to each end.

Horizontal cabling supports a single terminal device and links it back to the closet, where it connects into LAN hardware. The bandwidth requirement is therefore that of a single terminal device. Also, the majority of the channels in the building are horizontal—one for each terminal location—and the addition of more terminals also means activating more horizontal cable. This segment of your cabling system is, by definition, scalable and copper is by far the most-used media.

The vertical cabling must support all devices connecting into a closet, often the total number of terminals, printers, and file servers on a floor of the building. If more clients or servers are added to a floor, they compete for the available vertical cabling bandwidth. There is an advantage, however; there are comparatively few vertical channels in a building and more expensive equipment can therefore be used to provide high-bandwidth channels. This is the area where optical fiber has become the most appropriate media.

Options to Increase Horizontal Bandwidth

The first stage in increasing the available bandwidth to each workstation is to break the network into smaller networks through the proper placement of bridges and routers and adding file server connections. This reduces the number of devices sharing each network's bandwidth and therefore increases the access to that bandwidth. If your average number of devices on the network segment are high, this strategy offers the lowest-cost solution.

The placement of the bridges/routers and access to the servers require knowledge of network traffic patterns.

Another alternative to Ethernet users is to implement an Ethernet switch. This provides full 10 Mbps channels to each switched port. A common use of these devices is to front-end high-usage file servers with multiple Ethernet connections. The next stage is to implement higher-speed versions of the same protocols, such as the new 100 Mbps Ethernet and the 64 Mbps token ring.

Finally, there are the new protocols, which will run efficiently on your existing infrastructure at the 100-meter horizontal cable distance specified in TIA 568. They will, however, require new management software. 100VG-AnyLAN (voice grade) supports Ethernet, token ring, and other LAN standards. It uses 4-pair category 3 UTP to provide 100 Mbps data transmission of voice/video as well as data in half-duplex mode. The protocol includes a scheme to ensure that the real-time voice or video transmissions are given priority over less time-dependent data transmissions. When access and priority overheads for average networks are considered, the throughput should be about 20 Mbps.

TP-PMD is the copper equivalent of the FDDI protocol, offering 125 Mbps data transmission with 100 Mbps throughput. FDDI is well proven and, for organizations that have implemented this as their backbone protocol, may be easily extended to the desktop.

Asynchronous transfer mode (ATM) is a scalable switched protocol that offers dedicated bandwidth to each terminal of up to 155 Mbps over copper. Lower-speed implementations are proposed that will run over category 3 channels at a probable speed of 42 Mbps [MOD-TAP, 3].

Theoretical Bandwidth of UTP/STP Cable

In the early 1970s, the telephone companies used UTP cable to carry T1 data at 1.544 Mbps. In 1984, IBM announced their token-passing LAN at 4 Mbps on STP. In 1992, Ethernet increased the data speed to 10 Mbps over UTP, but decreased the distance dramatically to 100 meters. Then came 16 Mbps token ring, 125 Mbps CDDI, and now 155 Mbps ATM. Where does it end? What is the theoretical bandwidth of copper systems and what is a realistic speed that can be used?

The first issue that must be addressed is the difference between frequency and digital data throughput. The frequency of the carrier wave and the number of bits per second differ by the level of data compression used. For example, TP-PMD (the standard developed from CDDI) transports 125 Mbps, but uses a 4:1 compression algorithm called MLT-3, resulting in a 31.25 MHz carrier. Many compression algorithms and techniques are available and 10- or 20-to-1 compression ratios are achievable.

The second issue is the frequency of the signal that the wire itself will support. Category 5 UTP is tested to 100 MHz and there are now cables that are tested to 350 MHz. From a strictly technical perspective, this means transmission of gigabits per second are achievable on UTP. Today, there are manufacturers including IBM and AT&T that have systems operating at over 500 Mbps in their labs.

In the real world, one has to deal with the emitted electro-magnetic radiation (EMI) of the cables. Of specific concern to the regulatory bodies is radio frequency interference (RFI) or noise within the spectrum of other broadcasts. These frequencies coincide with the higher carrier frequencies of proposed data transmissions.

Regulation of emitted cable noise will come about, but there are also technical solutions to this problem. Cables with better balance within the pair equipment with cleaner signals will minimize RFI. Lower signal levels, higher receiver gains, and digital filtering also dramatically improve performance. As these regulations become law, the equipment manufacturers will implement these currently available technologies because the incremental cost will be justified.

Availability of Sufficient Strategies

While bandwidth is an issue for vertical or backbone cabling applications, the available bandwidth of UTP horizontal segments is still very underused. There are sufficient strategies available today to support the projected bandwidth increase through the next 25 years, never mind new technologies that become available during that period.

A properly designed UTP horizontal cabling system of category 5 will support 155 Mbps today and probably much more through future data compression of video signals. This is approximately a 1,000:1 increase over today's average terminal bandwidth and 10,000:1 over today's LAN usage. Since the last 35 years has shown a 100:1 increase, this would support 1,000 years of continued geometric growth in access requirements. Since 35 years is a maximum design requirement for commercial building infrastructure, and 10 years is the average renovation cycle, it is inconceivable that technology of computing environments would exceed this bandwidth.

The vertical cabling environment, however, is the area of current bandwidth limitation and continual demand growth. Optical fiber supporting high-speed networks is the only reasonable choice for future-proofing this segment of your building cabling.

Continuing with the theme of planning and designing high-speed cabling systems, let's take a look at a new class of online high-speed compressed satellite (wireless) encryption-based technologies (already available commercially from third-party vendors) for data communication. These technologies are making it possible to replicate the rich document management and workflow features previously restricted to homogeneous e-mail and groupware environments. The technologies, using seven levels of encryption that are capable of high-volume data compression, are needed to offset the threat to wireless encryption cracking by hackers, terrorists, and criminal organizations.

NEW ONLINE COMPRESSED SATELLITE ENCRYPTION-BASED TECHNOLOGY

High-speed compressed satellite (wireless) encryption-based technologies, including software envelopes and electronic authentication services, leverage Internet and intranet infrastructures and facilitate precise management and measurement of document usage and access across heterogeneous systems. Penetration of these technologies will force IT managers to rethink workflow investments and to develop new priorities for tracking and reporting information flows.

Document-intensive industries such as financial services have long wrestled with how to compress, streamline, manage, and automate the movement of information around their organizations. In response, systems vendors and integrators invented workflow with the idea that any document-intensive business process that could be described could also be automated.

In a similar fashion, EDI (electronic data interchange) has been offered as a way to automate business-to-business supply and ordering functions. Groupware, too, has been marketed as a way to manage business processes, especially messy and unpredictable ones (document creation and editing).

Neither workflow nor EDI, however, have fulfilled their original potential. Workflow systems have thrived in highly structured settings, but these are often inflexible and difficult to link to the outside world. EDI has made it possible to reduce supply management and ordering costs significantly, but it, too, is inflexible; preplanned bilateral implementations are the best that EDI can offer.

Though groupware has been arguably more successful, it has fallen short of its potential because of the huge strategic commitments required to make it effective.

Serendipitous partnering, spontaneous commerce, and adaptability are not strong suits for any of these technologies. Unfortunately, the business world is moving in exactly this direction—toward continuous change, with an increasing premium on high-speed compression and flexibility and a growing requirement to link with external parties.

Until recently, IT managers have been faced with two basic choices in automating and managing workflow: commit to a large investment in a unifying solution or accept lowest common denominator capabilities and/or security levels across systems and, almost invariably, across organizations.

Now, just as many companies are becoming convinced of the value of workflow, EDI, and groupware, a basket of new satellite encryption technologies (based on compressed real-time public key encryption) is poised to alter the cost/feature balance radically, as well as the reach and flexibility of business-process automation. Let's look briefly at one of these key satellite encryption technologies that are beginning to make this possible.

Real-Time Compression Router

The goal of this technology is the development of the first secure gateway router capable of high-volume satellite-transmitted data compression. The technology revolves around a revolutionary online compression software based on a patented scanning process. This technology represents a dramatic departure from traditional offline compression and far exceeds the performance of hardware-based online compression, which is the current industry standard. What follows is a detailed look at the software, its application as part of a secure gateway router, and the potential impact on digital wireless communications.

Technology Background

The patented scanning process involves no dictionary or mathematical algorithms. Rather than simply relying on data redundancy, it operates in real time by scanning the physical symmetry of each byte of data as it is being transferred to and from a satellite.

The characteristic profile produced by the scanning module is sent to a decision engine, which coordinates the function of 16 separate relay modules. Each module is designed to address a specific range of characters and programmed to assist the decision engine in making dynamic decisions so as to maximize compression efficiency. Other key performance features include:

- Compression speed of 6.8 Mbps using 16-bit code run on a Pentium 166. Speed will exceed 10 Mbps with 32-bit code.
- Automatical detection and correction of any corrupt packets as they're being sent, using a bidirectional protocol.
- Compression with seven levels of encryption, with each string of several packets secured by a separate set of codes.
- Compression and encryption total requirement of only 20K RAM (random access memory).

In addition to operating in real time, this software compresses with *no packet loss!* Also, because of the patented scanning process, short e-mail messages are compressed as effectively as large files.

Several primary tests have been conducted to measure how well this software performs in a real-world satellite networking environment. One test involved a UNIX test over PPP (point-to-point protocol). The primary purpose was to measure compression performance relative to CPU utilization, a major determinant in hardware costs associated with development of a compression router.

Results from repeated tests showed a 486DX-33 with the math coprocessor and cache both disabled and settings fixed for normal operation capable of compressing a 56K channel in real time with negligible CPU demand. Furthermore, results showed the software effective in compressing a variety of file types. Large text files were consistently compressed in excess of 3 to 1. Tests involving highly compressed GIF, JPG, and WAV files showed consistent compression gains in the area of 10 percent.

A second test conducted by the software developers involved a Microsoft NT 4.0–Winsock 2 test over TCP/IP (transmission control protocol/Internet protocol). The primary purpose was to measure real transfer time savings in comparison to V.42bis, a hardware-based, online compression that is the current international standard for 28.8K modems. Here, results from repeated tests exceeded those over PPP and showed the software to be clearly superior to V.42bis.

The Secure Gateway Router

Designing a secure gateway router to maximize the performance of this software will allow real-time compression and encryption of several thousand simultaneous satellite network connections. The extreme speed and efficiency of the software makes this possible.

However, both will increase even more as a result of having the software operate as part of hardware inside a router. Here, it will no longer be necessary to engage RAM. In effect, the processing power inherent to the software program will be continuously active. It is reasonable to expect that by doing this, the processing speed would increase well beyond 10 Mbps using a 32-bit code, to 20 Mbps or more.

The implication is that a relatively inexpensive PC-based router with a Pentium processor could easily compress and encrypt the entire satellite data transmission flow of a T-1 connection operating at capacity. Depending on how much the processing speed is increased from added efficiency, the same router could have a similar impact on a congested DS3 (Data Service 3).

DS3 = 44.736 Mbps or 28 T-1 circuits.

Obviously, such a device would have value in today's marketplace, where there is a growing emphasis on both bandwidth efficiency and security. Key benefits include:

- Maximizes bandwidth efficiency for LANs, WANs, and intranets.
- Maximizes security for all satellite-transmitted data traveling inside or outside a private network.
- Creates infrastructure for an expanded private satellite network or extranet, whereby banking or other industries can securely interact with affiliated institutions and customers.
- Creates infrastructure for a *virtual private network*, whereby the Internet could replace costly dedicated lines as a means of transferring corporate data to and from a satellite.

In addition, the secure gateway router will provide other benefits for increased bandwidth efficiency and security not directly related to compression and encryption. These benefits include:

- Secure packet filtering and multiple-destination firewall.
- Telephone, 100BaseT, token ring, and FDDI interface.
- Proxy to shield satellite network behind secure bastion host.
- Internal caching algorithm allowing satellite-connected network users to shut off individual memory/disk caches, helping to reduce bandwidth demand and improve overall workstation performance.
- Network load balancing to alleviate satellite network connection congestion.
- Patented IP security for all satellite data transferred outside the corporate network.

Once in place, the secure gateway router paves the way for yet another opportunity.

Each router will be designed to operate across a variety of satellite networks employing extended BGP4 (border gateway protocol) routing code. These include TCP/IP native, frame relay, ATM serial link encapsulation including Cisco HDLC (high-level data link control), as well as multilink PPP. It will simply be a matter of plugging in and activating.

Digital Wireless Communications

The fact that the compression process produces tiny packets of data (1,500 MTU [maximum transmission unit]) with no packet loss makes this technology uniquely well-suited for wireless and satellite network communications. Furthermore, because both the compression and encryption require just 20K of RAM, the software can easily operate within the limited memory of a PDA (personal digital assistant) or from a DSP (digital signal processor) inside a PCS (personal communications service) phone.

Deploying this technology in conjunction with wireless and satellite networks would dramatically enhance both bandwidth efficiency and satellite communication security. It simply requires a software-enabled phone or modem connecting with another enabled device. It does not matter what is in between, just so long as a two-point connection is established. See the Sidebar, "Enhanced Bandwidth Efficiency and Security Benefits," for more information.

ENHANCED BANDWIDTH EFFICIENCY AND SECURITY BENEFITS

Enhanced bandwidth efficiency and security provide benefits to both users and wireless network providers. Key benefits for users include:

- Comfort in knowing you are using the most secure wireless link available.
- Reduced connection costs as a result of faster remote satellite data transfers.
- More available memory in PDA or laptop.
- Protection for data stored in PDA or laptop in case of theft or loss.

Key benefits for satellite network providers include:

- Ability to advertise as the most secure wireless link available.
- Ability to advertise reduced connection costs without price cutting.
- More available bandwidth across satellite network connections.
- Possibility of encouraging businesses and individuals to use wireless communications with greater confidence.

The last point in the preceding sidebar is an important one. Businesses and consumers both have taken to using wireless communication for phone conversations. But, as we move into the future and satellite-transmitted data piracy becomes more and more sophisticated and commonplace, it remains to be seen just how willing some will be to rely on wireless as a regular means of transferring the most confidential information.

This applies not only to PCS and satellite, but also the 39 GHz (Gigahertz) broadband microwave link soon to be introduced as the last mile to digital wireless communications. Here, providers are counting on hospitals, banks, and other large business operations to use their satellite-connected networks for short-distance, high-speed data transmission. For example, 39 GHz is seen as an ideal means for primary-care physicians and specialists to take part in interactive video conferences where X-rays, MRIs (magnetic resonance imaging), and CAT (computerized axial tomography) scans could be exchanged and discussed.

However, for this scenario to become a reality, providers will have to take every precaution to ensure satellite data transmission security. Not only this, they then must effectively convey the extent to which they've taken these steps to potential users. This means convincing not only hospitals and doctors, banks and bankers, but also patients and customers.

Clearly, when it comes to the most confidential information, the willingness to leave behind the perceived security of wire will depend on the degree to which providers are able to encourage businesses and consumers to use wireless with greater confidence. This technology certainly has the potential to impact the marketplace in this regard.

However, there is yet another distinct opportunity presented by a combined approach involving both the software and the secure gateway router. In its design, the router can easily be configured to facilitate a fast and secure connection across a digital wireless network to a corporate LAN or intranet, or to a private extranet. It is suggested that a wireless modem working in conjunction with a secure gateway router is the easiest and most secure means of connection with benefits for corporate executives, wireless network providers, and PDA developers. The security provided through this combined approach could be further enhanced by developing custom TCP/IP software, which would be relegated to the internal satellite network.

The attachment of a wireless gateway to an intranet offers a more secure entrance than access through a dial-up connection. Each wireless device that has access to the gateway must be registered on the satellite-connected network and enabled by the gateway.

Current versions of the secure gateway router are effective and unique in performance. The approach to design also makes it possible to produce what would be the first secure gateway router capable of high-volume real-time satellite data transmission compression. There would be a need to produce this new compression technology for the following reasons:

- For client and server applications, it would mean developing specific applications for each operating system, a time-intensive proposition.
- There is likely to be considerable opposition to introducing compression and encryption to existing servers.
- A compression router maximizes software performance in the satellite-connected network environment—and this would have immediate impact on corporations and Internet service providers faced with congested network connections.
- A compression router maximizes security and bandwidth efficiency by making sure all traffic coming into a private satellite-connected network is compressed and encrypted.

The conclusion is that the secure gateway router is the quickest and most cost-effective means of introducing revolutionary real-time compression satellite encryption technology to the marketplace.

FROM HERE

This chapter opened up Part IV, "Planning for High-Speed Cabling Systems," by taking a thorough look at data compression: high-speed real-time data compression and how to plan for higher-speed cabling systems. Chapter 22 describes the development of the high-speed cabling system implementation plan (scheduling, analyzing site surveys, connectivity requirements, equipment, security, performance, etc.).

NOTES

[1]   "Gigabit Ethernet Overview," Gigabit Ethernet Alliance (GEA), 20111 Stevens Creek Boulevard, Suite 280, Cupertino, California, 95014, 1999, p. 17.

[2]   William A. Flanagan, "How to Get the Bandwidth You Need When You Need It," Vice President-Technology, FastComm Communications Corp., 45472 Holiday Drive, Sterling, VA, 20166, 1999, p. 2.

[3]   "The Bandwidth Bogeyman," MOD-TAP, 285 Ayer Road, P.O. Box 706, Harvard, MA 01451, 1999, p. 1.

Implementation Plan Development

To ensure that the implementation of your cabling system installation goes as planned, read this chapter first to help you develop and prepare your site before the system arrives. For brevity, the term "system" is used throughout this chapter in reference to third-party cabling systems products.

ONSITE INSTALLATION: SOFTWARE CONFIGURATIONS

The onsite services (OSS) team normally will not set up the software configuration for your system. The installation service is limited to hardware installation and setup. You are responsible for setting up the software configuration. The following software configuration options are available:

- *Option 1:* You should either e-mail or fax the entire configuration to the OSS team. The configuration is usually downloaded to your system through the console port via a modem line.
- *Option 2:* You should store the entire configuration on a trivial file transfer protocol (TFTP) server. The configuration is downloaded to your system using a vendor's automatic installation feature.
- *Option 3:* The OSS team should configure one port on the router so you can Telnet to the router and download the entire configuration. Usually, only interior gateway routing protocol(IGRP) and routing information protocol (RIP) routing are supported for this option.

- *Option 4:* You should use your copy of the vendor's configuration maker feature to configure your router and access servers. The configuration maker is usually a wizards-based software tool that helps you to quickly and easily configure and address the third-party vendor's cabling products [1].

Be sure to indicate on the site preparation checklist which software configuration loading option you want to use. The following is an example of how a software configuration might appear on a terminal [Cisco, 2–3].

The majority of software configurations are unique. For example, the following configuration will probably not be valid on your system.

```
! Create line encrypted password
line 0 5
  encrypted password classified
  login
!
! Create level-1 encrypted password
certify-encrypted-password Classified Term
!
! Create a system hostid
hostid X-File
! Create host fileids
start host host2-confg 242.219.2.222
start host host3-confg 242.219.2.222
! Create system fileids
start system sys2-system 242.219.24.222
start system sys3-system 242.219.2.222
!
! Certify SNMP
snmp-server collective
snmp-server capture-verification
snmp-server host 242.219.2.38 collective
snmp-server host 242.219.2.222 collective
snmp-server host 242.219.3.74 collective
!
! Create UBDBDT server hosts
ubdbdt-server host 242.219.2.38
ubdbdt-server host 242.219.24.44
ubdbdt-server host 242.219.2.44
!
```

```
! Create a info-of-the-night sign
sign iotn ^C
The Information Technology Place welcomes everyone
Please call 1-900-666-3333 for a login account, or enter
your password at the prompt.
^C
```

SCHEDULING FACTORS

You should try to schedule installations five working days in advance. This could be done by sending a completed site preparation checklist form to your vendor.

Cancellations and Reschedules

Your vendor often reserves the right to reschedule the installation if any information on the site preparation checklist is not available, usually within six working days before the scheduled installation date. With most vendors, you can reschedule or cancel an installation up to four working days before the scheduled installation date without any penalty. However, installations canceled within 96 hours of the scheduled installation date are often subject to a cancellation charge. On the day of the installation, any cancellation caused by inappropriate site preparation, equipment unavailability, or other circumstances beyond the control of the vendor is normally billed as an installation, and another installation must be scheduled.

You should contact your OSS team if you have additional installation-specific-questions or need to reschedule your installation.

Pricing and Delays

Onsite installation pricing is normally based on the type and number of systems to be installed at a given site. Onsite installation delays caused by inappropriate site preparation, equipment unavailability, or other circumstances beyond the control of the vendor are usually billed at prevailing field engineer time and material rates.

USER RESPONSIBILITIES BEFORE INSTALLATION

The following tasks should be completed before the arrival of the vendor's onsite installation personnel in order to ensure a successful installation: First of all, you should prepare the site and complete a site preparation checklist form for each system to be installed. Send the completed form by fax within six working days before the scheduled installation date. The following information should be included on the site preparation checklist:

- Chassis-mounting preference and system type (rack mounting, and so forth).
- Configuration option choices.
- For remote access by the vendor's personnel during installation, a modem telephone line number should be included.
- If available, a fax number and e-mail address; site name and address; installation date and time; sales order number (if the system is new); and contact name and telephone number.
- In order for the installer to contact systems personnel, a voice telephone line number (near the new system) should be included [Cisco, 4].

Verifying DC or AC power requirements and site environment specifications is the second task to be completed before the arrival of the vendor's onsite installation personnel. Third, all distance and interference limitations of interface cables to be used at the installation should be verified.

The fourth task would be to install and verify the operation of all external communications equipment not provided by the vendor. This external communications equipment includes, but might not be limited to, LAN and WAN connections, channel service unit/digital service unit (CSU/DSU), media attachment unit (MAU), transceivers, modems, and any other external communications equipment related to your site and necessary for the installation. The last task would be to verify the operation of all telephone circuits, digital services, and T1 facilities not supplied by the vendor but required for the installation.

RESPONSIBILITIES OF THE INSTALLER

The onsite installer should complete the following tasks. First, the installer should unpack the system and accessories necessary for installation. Second, the installer should mount the system on a desktop, in a rack or wiring closet, or on the wall. The third task is to connect the system to the network and customer-provided LAN and WAN connections.

Attaching the vendor-supplied modem for remote diagnostics, validation of network serial link status, and insertion of the customer IP address and password is the fourth task. The fifth task is to connect the console, administrator port, and auxiliary cables (if available and as required). Finally, the installer should verify the following:

- LED status, network interface operations, and interface status reports.
- Operation of blower or fan.
- Primary network serial link testing to the remote end. If the serial link is not available, loopback testing is used (HDLC encapsulation only).
- System power-up [Cisco, 5].

MEETING SITE REQUIREMENTS

The general ventilation and power requirements your site must meet for your system to operate properly are described in this part of the chapter. Information on preventing electrostatic discharge damage (ESD) is also included.

Ventilated System

Some systems have a fan or an internal blower that pulls air through a power supply and card cage. These systems are designed to operate in a level, dry, clean, air-conditioned, and well-ventilated environment. The air-cooling function might be impaired if either the intake or exhaust vents are blocked in any way. You should ensure that the system's location has adequate air circulation.

TAKING PROPER PRECAUTIONS

In order to ensure a successful system operation, the proper placement of the wiring closet or layout of your equipment rack and chassis are essential. System malfunctions and shutdowns can occur when equipment is placed too close together or is inadequately ventilated. In addition, system maintenance can be difficult if chassis access panels are made inaccessible by poor equipment placement.

If you're in the process of planning your site layout and equipment locations, read and follow the precautions listed below. This will reduce the likelihood of environmentally caused shutdowns and help avoid future equipment failures. For instance:

- Ambient room temperature alone might not be adequate to cool equipment to acceptable operating temperatures. Remember that electrical equipment generates heat.
- Ensure that all card access panels and chassis covers are secure and in place. The chassis is designed to direct cooling air through the card cage. An open access panel will redirect the air flow, potentially preventing air from properly flowing through the chassis.
- Never place chassis side-by-side because the heated exhaust air from one chassis will be drawn into the intake vent of the adjacent chassis [Cisco, 5-6].

Using Equipment Racks

The following describes the ventilation considerations that apply to using equipment racks for your system. For instance, you should first install the chassis in an enclosed rack only if it has adequate ventilation or an exhaust fan. Use an open rack where possible.

A ventilation system that is too powerful in an enclosed rack might prevent cooling by creating negative air pressure around the chassis and redirecting the air away from the chassis intake vent. Therefore, the second ventilation consideration would be (if necessary) to operate the chassis with the rack door open or in an open rack.

The third consideration would be the correct use of baffles inside the enclosed rack. The baffles can assist in cooling the chassis.

Ensuring that the rack is not too congested is the fourth ventilation consideration. In an enclosed rack, ideally, separate the units with 12 to 15 inches of vertical clearance. The horizontal clearance is standard for most enclosed racks. Avoid obstructing this space. Open racks are recommended, but not required.

Finally, equipment located near the bottom of the rack can excessively heat the air that is drawn upward and into the intake ports of the equipment previously mentioned, thus leading to failures in the chassis at or near the top of the rack. If the enclosed rack you are using does not have a ventilation fan, install one.

Proper Power Requirements

You need the proper AC receptacle at your site in order to connect the chassis to AC power. The chassis power supply is either factory-configured for either 110 volts alternating current (VAC) or 240 VAC operation (230 VAC in the United Kingdom) or autoranging. A 6-foot electrical power cord is included in all chassis.

Do not connect the chassis to a receptacle if the voltage indicated on the chassis label is different from the power outlet voltage. A voltage mismatch might pose a fire hazard, can cause equipment damage, and create a shock hazard.

You should attach dual power supplies to independent power sources for full redundancy. An uninterruptable power source (UPS) is also recommended to protect against power failures at your site.

Electrostatic Discharge Damage Prevention

ESD damage (which occurs when electronic components are improperly handled), can result in complete or intermittent failures. ESD can impair equipment and electronic circuitry. Typically, the successful installation of the chassis should not require handling any system components. Nevertheless, ESD prevention procedures should always be followed.

After the site requirements have been met, you should conduct a site survey as part of developing the implementation plan for your cabling system. The information obtained from a site survey will help you determine whether you met or exceeded your minimum requirements.

SITE SURVEY

The range and throughput of your cabling system will be affected by your building's construction materials, and by the general design and layout of your facility. This information will help you determine the mounting locations for your system's access points so that the system performance will meet or exceed your minimum requirements.

You will need a map, similar to that shown in Figure 22–1, of that portion of your facility to be covered by the cabling system [2]. When deciding which areas are to have cable or wireless coverage, consider lunch rooms, break rooms, hallways, and outdoor eating areas. In today's more informal work environment, it is common for these locations to be the site for reading e-mail, impromptu meetings, and brainstorming sessions. A building blueprint works well as a site survey map, and generally shows potential sources of radio frequency interference such as ductwork, elevators, stairwells, and so on. If the facility has been extensively modified, for example by construction of new interior offices or revised layout of work cubicles, then an accurate floor plan drawing is preferable. Regardless, it is useful to mark potential areas of radio frequency interference in advance (elevators, other radio sources, microwave ovens, etc.), so that special attention can be given to wireless or cabling interference in these areas.

As you proceed through the site survey, you will be measuring radio frequency transmissions around cabling or wireless access points installed in a temporary location. In the course of the survey, you will be moving this access point and remeasuring transmission efficiencies. You will need to complete this process for the entire facility before selecting final locations. Accordingly, it is useful to have a set of colored pencils or markers to distinguish the access point locations on your map and to mark transmission distances.

One of the first steps in performing a site survey is to make a decision about the desired or minimum acceptable performance of your cabling system. The minimum acceptable performance (expressed in packets transmitted

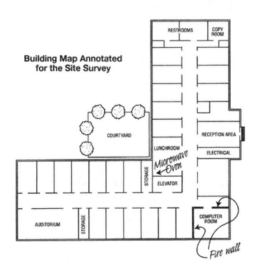

Figure 22–1
Building map annotated
for the site survey.

per second) will depend on the applications running on your network, and varies dramatically from customer to customer. Your system administrator may have determined a minimum performance specification for your system. If not, most third-party installers have a procedure that will help you assess the minimum acceptable throughput.

Once the minimum acceptable throughput is determined, you use an access point and a portable computer equipped with a Personal Computer Memory Card Industry Association (PCMCIA) adapter card to measure your building's radio transmission environment. The software provided measures the throughput of the system. By working from the most remote location to the most central location in your building, you will be able to determine where the access points should be mounted to obtain at least the minimum performance level over the entire area. In fact, most locations will probably exceed the minimum performance level by a considerable margin.

The general site survey procedure is as follows. Using software tools and detailed instructions, determine a possible location for an access point and temporarily mount the access point there. Carrying a portable computer with the site survey software loaded, measure throughput at various locations around the access point and annotate your building map. Based on those measurements, determine another possible location for the access point, temporarily mount the access point at this new location, and repeat the throughput measurements. By continuing this process and plotting the combined data from all of your measurements on your facility map, you will be able to determine where best to locate the access points to achieve optimum wireless LAN performance as well as nonwireless systems. It generally takes about one hour to establish the first access point location, and 30–45 minutes for the other locations. See Figure 22–2 for permanent access point locations and their zones of coverage [AMP, 3].

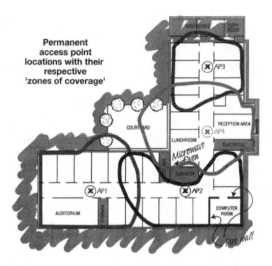

**Permanent
access point
locations with their
respective
'zones of coverage'**

Figure 22–2
Building map showing
permanent access point
locations and their
zones of coverage.

CABLING DISTANCE CONNECTIVITY LIMITATIONS AND REQUIREMENTS

As previously stated in Chapter 15, "Designing Cable Plants," the size of your networks and the distance between connections on your networks will depend on the type of signal, the signal speed, and the transmission media (the type of cable used to transmit the signals). For instance, standard coaxial cable has a greater channel capacity than twisted pair cabling.

The rate limits and distance in these descriptions are the IEEE-recommended maximum distances and speeds for signaling. For example, the recommended maximum rate for V.35 is 2 megabits per second (Mbps), but it is commonly used at 4 Mbps without any problems.

Exceeding the maximum distances is not recommended or supported, even though you can usually get good results at speeds and distances far greater than those listed in this part of the chapter. You can get good results with rates and distances greater than those shown here if you understand the electrical problems that might arise and can compensate for them. However, you do so at your own risk.

Channel Attachment

If your system has a channel interface processor (CIP), be aware that the maximum transmission distance for Enterprise Systems Connection (ESCON) with light-emitting diodes (LED) is 2.0 miles (3.2 km) point-to-point or 5.8 miles (9.3 km) with two ESCON directors. The maximum transmission distance for bus and tag is 500 feet (155 m). The IBM 3044 C/D (host side/remote side) copper-to-fiber repeater can be used to extend the bus and tag distance up to 1.3 miles (2.1 km).

Fast Ethernet

The cabling specifications and the connection limitations for 100 Mbps Fast Ethernet transmission over UTP, STP, and fiber optic cables are listed in Table 22–1 [Cisco, 7]. Additionally, the characteristics of 100BaseTX and 100BaseFX with respect to IEEE 802.3u physical characteristics are summarized in Table 22–2 [Cisco, 7–8].

Table 22–1 100 Mbps Transmission Cabling Specifications and Connection Limits

Parameter	RJ45	MII	SC-Type
Cable specification	Category 5[a] UTP[b], 22 to 24 AWG[c]	Category 3, 4, or 5, 150-ohm UTP or STP, or multimode optical fiber	62.5/125 multimode optical fiber
Maximum cable length		1.75 ft (0.54 m) (MII-to-MII cable[d])	
Maximum network length	667 ft (205 m)[e] (with 1 repeater)		667 ft (205 m)[e] (with 1 repeater)
Maximum segment length	339 ft (104 m) for 100BaseTX	3.28 ft (1 m)[e] or 1,423 ft (438 m) for 100BaseFX	339 ft (104 m)

[a] EIA/TIA-T568-A or EIA-TIA-568 TSB-36 compliant.

[b] Category 5 UTP RJ45 or 150 ohm STP MII cables are available commercially.

[c] AWG = American Wire Gauge. This gauge is specified by the EIA/TIA-T568-A standard.

[d] This is the cable between the MII port on the FE port adapter and the appropriate transceiver.

[e] This length is specifically between any two stations on a repeated segment.

The RJ45 designation is for a particular interface originally designed for program-mable analog modem connections to leased telephone lines. RJ45 just happens to use the 8-pin modular jack and plug that are found in many LAN and tele-phone connections. The 8-pin modular connection used for 10/100BaseT, token ring/UTP, T1, ISDN, and so forth, is the EIA/TIA T568-A version that has very specific performance requirements.

Table 22–2 Physical Characteristics for IEEE 802.3u

Parameter	100BaseFX	100BaseTX
Data rate	100 Mbps	100 Mbps
Maximum segment length	339 ft (104 m) between repeaters	339 ft (104 m) between DTE[a] and repeaters
Media	SC-type: dual simplex or single duplex for Rx and Tx	RJ45MII
Signaling method	Baseband	Baseband
Topology	Star/Hub	Star/Hub

[a] DTE = data terminal equipment.

E1-G.703/G.704

You should be aware that unbalanced G.703/G.704 interfaces allow for a longer maximum cable length than those specified for balanced circuits if your system has a fast serial interface processor (FSIP). The maximum cable lengths for each FSIP E1-G.703/G.704 cable type by the connector used at the network (non-FSIP) end are listed in Table 22–3 [Cisco, 8].

Table 22–3 Maximum Cable Lengths for E1-G.703/G.704

Connection Type	BNC	Twinax
Balanced		995 ft (306 m)
Unbalanced	2079 ft (640 m)	

Ethernet

The maximum distances for Ethernet network segments and connections depend on the type of transmission cable used: 0.8-inch diameter coaxial (10Base5), 0.50-inch diameter coaxial (10Base2), or unshielded twisted pair (10BaseT). Network connections to coaxial cables are tapped into a network segment and must be spaced at specific intervals. Table 22–4 lists the maximum number of connections (taps) per segment and the intervals at which they must be placed [Cisco, 8]. A maximum of five repeaters and eight bridges can be used to link segments in a single network.

Table 22–4 10 Mbps Transmission Ethernet Coaxial Connection Limits

Description	10Base5	10Base2
Cable diameter	0.5 in. (1.26 cm)	0.36 in. (0.914 cm)
Maximum connections (taps) per segment	100	30
Maximum network length (with 4 repeaters)	8,300 ft (2,554 m)	3,391 ft (1,043 m)
Maximum segment length	1,741 ft (536 m)	667 ft (205 m)
Minimum connection (tap) spacing	8.3 ft (2.6 m)	1.75 ft (0.54 m)

The unshielded twisted pair (UTP) cabling used with 10BaseT is suitable for voice transmission, but might incur problems at 10 Mbps transmission rates. UTP wiring does not require the fixed spacing between connections that is necessary with the coaxial-type connections. The IEEE recommendations for the UTP maximum distances between station (connection) and hub are listed in Table 22–5 [Cisco, 9].

Table 22–5 Maximum Transmission Distances for Ethernet UTP

Transmission Speed	Maximum Station-to-Hub Distance
10 Mbps (10BaseT)	339 ft (104 m)

In general, the workgroup catalyst switch implementation of 10BaseT requires a minimum of category 3 UTP cable, as specified by the EIA/TIA T568-B wiring standard. The characteristics of IEEE 802.3 Ethernet and Ethernet version 2 for 10BaseT are summarized in Table 22–6 [Cisco, 9]. In addition, the cabling specifications for 10 Mbps transmission over UTP and STP cables are listed in Table 22–7 [Cisco, 9].

Table 22–6   10BaseT Ethernet Version 2 and IEEE 802.3 Physical Characteristics

Parameter	IEEE 802.3 Ethernet	10BaseT Ethernet Version 2
Data rate	10 Mbps	10 Mbps
Maximum segment length	1751 ft (539 m)	339 ft (104 m)
Media	50-ohm coax (thick)	Unshielded twisted pair (UTP)
Signaling method	Baseband	Baseband
Topology	Bus	Star

Table 22–7   10 Mbps 10BaseT Cable Specifications

Parameter	RJ45
Cable specification	Category 5 UTP[a], 22 to 24 AWG[b]
Maximum network length	667 ft (205 m) with 1 repeater
Maximum segment length	339 ft (104 m) for 10BaseT

[a] Category 5 UTP RJ45 cables are available commercially.
[b] AWG = American Wire Gauge. This gauge is specified by the EIA/TIA-T568-A standard.

HSSI

The high-speed serial interface (HSSI) standard (EIA/TIA 612/613) specifies a maximum cable length of 61 feet (19 meters) for 52 Mbps HSSI connections. The typical (nominal) cable length between an HSSI interface processor (HIP) and a DSU is 7 feet (2 meters). The HSSI interface cable has 25 twisted pairs and a 50-pin plug at each end. Both data terminal equipment (DTE) and data communications equipment (DCE) ports on the HIP and the data service unit (DSU) are 50-pin receptacles.

Most CSU/DSUs do not have 50-pin plug interfaces. They have V.35, 9-pin, and/or RS232. Connections to HSSI interface cables are via adapter cables.

The HSSI interface cable is similar to a small computer systems interface (SCSI) II cable. Nevertheless, the HSSI cable specification is more stringent than that for a SCSI-II.

When connecting the HSSI interface, do not substitute a SCSI-II-type cable for a HSSI cable. Proper operation of the interface could be prevented if you use a SCSI-II-type cable.

Multichannel

The multichannel interface processor (MIP) E1 specifications are as follows:

- Input port specifications: see G.703/Section 6.3 (ITU-T specification).
- Jitter attenuation starting at 6 Hz, which meets or exceeds G.823 for E1.
- Output port specifications: see G.703/Section 6.2 (ITU-T specification).
- Transmission bit rate: 2.048 Kbps ± 50 ppm (parts per million) [Cisco, 11].

The MIP T1 specifications are as follows:

- Output pulse amplitude: 3.0 V (volts) ± 0.6V measured at DSX.
- Output pulse width: 324 ns (nanoseconds) ± 54 ns.
- Transmission bit rate: 1.544 Mbps ± 50 ppm [Cisco, 11].

The MIP T1 specifications comply with all AT&T Accunet TR 62411 specifications.

Serial

Serial signals can travel a limited distance at any given rate, as is the norm with all signaling systems. Generally, the greater the distance, the lower the baud rate. The relationship between transmission rate and distance for the HSSI is listed in Table 22.8 [Cisco, 12].

Table 22–8   Transmission Speed versus Distance for IEEE Standard EIA/TIA-232

Baud Rate	Distance
2,400	300 ft (92 m)
4,800	200 ft (62 m)
9,600	60 ft (19 m)
19,200	36 ft (11.1 m)
38,400	18 ft (5.5 m)
56,000	8.7 ft (2.7 m)

Before their acceptance as standards by the Electronic Industries Association (EIA) and Telecommunications Industry Association (TIA), EIA/TIA-232 and EIA/TIA-449, were known as recommended standards RS-232 and RS-449.

Balanced drivers allow EIA/TIA-449 signals to travel greater distances than EIA/TIA-232. The standard relationship between baud rate and distance for EIA/TIA-449 signals is listed in Table 22–9 [Cisco, 12].

Table 22–9   Transmission Speed versus Distance for IEEE Standard EIA/TIA-449

Baud Rate	Distance
2,400	4,200 ft (1292 m)
4,800	2,100 ft (646 m)
9,600	1,050 ft (323 m)
19,200	524 ft (161 m)
38,400	267 ft (82 m)
56,000	113 ft (35 m)
T-1	60 ft (19 m)

The distance limits for EIA/TIA-449 (listed in Table 22–9), which are also valid for V.35 and X.21, are recommended maximum distances. Exceeding these maximum distances is not recommended or supported. In common practice, EIA/TIA-449 supports 2 Mbps rates, and V.35 supports 4 Mbps rates without any problems.

Synchronous Optical NETwork (SONET)

Two types of fiber are defined by the SONET specification for fiber optic transmission: multimode and single mode. Bundles of light rays entering the fiber at a particular angle are known as modes. Multimode fiber allows multiple modes of light to propagate through the fiber, while single-mode fiber allows only one mode of light to propagate through the fiber. Single-mode fiber is capable of higher bandwidth and greater cable-run distances than multimode fiber, because multiple modes of light propagating through the fiber travel at different distances depending on the entry angles, thus causing them to arrive at the destination at different times (a phenomenon called "modal dispersion"). Table 22–10 lists the maximum distances for single-mode and multimode transmissions, as defined by SONET [Cisco, 13]. Also, significant signal loss can result if the distance between two connected stations is greater than these maximum distances, thus making transmission unreliable.

Table 22–10   Maximum Fiber Optic Transmission Distances for SONET

Transceiver Type	Maximum Distance Between Stations[a]
Multimode	Up to 1.6 miles (2.6 kilometers)
Single mode	Up to 10 miles (16.0 kilometers)

[a] This table lists typical results.

Token Ring

IEEE 802.5 (token ring) networks have no current maximum transmission distance defined. Shielded twisted pair cabling is most commonly used for rates of 16 Mbps. Shielded or UTP cabling is used for rates of 1 and 4 Mbps. Remember that twisted pair cabling is more susceptible to interference than other types of cabling when planning your connections. So plan the total network length and repeater spacing accordingly.

INTERFERENCE

Interference can occur between the field and the signals on the wires when wires are run for any significant distance in an electromagnetic field. This fact has two implications for the construction of terminal plant wiring—the first one being strong electromagnetic interference, especially as caused by lightning or radio transmitters, can destroy EIA/TIA-232 drivers and receivers.

Second, bad practices can result in radio interference emanating from the plant wiring.

You might need to consult experts in radio frequency interference (RFI) in order to predict and remedy strong electromagnetic interference.

The plant wiring is unlikely to emit radio interference if you use UTP Ethernet cables in your plant wiring with a good distribution of grounding conductors. Use a high-quality twisted pair cable with one ground conductor for each data signal when exceeding the distance listed in Table 22–5.

Generally, give special consideration to the effect of lightning strikes in your vicinity, especially if wires exceed recommended distances or pass between buildings. The electromagnetic pulse (EMP) caused by lightning or other high-energy phenomena can easily couple enough energy into unshielded conductors to destroy electronic devices. You might want to consult experts in electrical surge suppression and shielding if you have had problems of this sort in the past. Without pulse meters and other special equipment, most data centers cannot resolve the infrequent but potentially catastrophic problems just described. An excessive amount of time can be consumed in trying to identify and resolve interference problems. You should provide a properly grounded and shielded environment for your system (with special attention to issues of electrical surge suppression) in order to avoid these problems.

EXTERNAL CONNECTIONS

To complete your installation, you might need some of the following data communications equipment. In addition to the interfaces you plan to use, your needs depend on many factors.

For example, you might need a console terminal with an EIA/TIA-232 data terminal equipment (DTE) connector for future configuration requirements after the system is installed and remotely configured by way of the modem connection. After you complete these configuration procedures, you can detach the terminal (and cable).

The chassis console port is a data communications equipment device (using a DB-25 female connector) for routers and communication servers. The auxiliary port is a data terminal equipment device (using a DB-25 male connector). In order to match the chassis console port default baud rate of 9,600, 8 data bits, no parity, and 2 stop bits, you must adjust the baud rate of your console terminal. You must also consult the documentation for your terminal for this wiring specification. The administration interface port (admin port) is an EIA/TIA-232 DCE connection (requiring an RJ45 female connector) for the workgroup concentrators and catalyst switches. Also, the admin port is configured at the factory with the following communications parameters: one stop bit, 9,600 baud, 8 data bits, and no parity. For this wiring specification, you should consult the documentation for your terminal.

You need an 802.3 media attachment unit (MAU) and an attachment unit interface (AUI) cable or an Ethernet transceiver and transceiver cable in order to use an IEEE 802.3 or Ethernet interface at your installation. These devices can be purchased as additional equipment. You should contact a customer-service representative at this point. This additional equipment is not required for an Ethernet 10BaseT connection using the 10BaseT applique with routers or communications servers. These appliques have built-in transceivers.

You need a synchronous modem or a channel service unit/digital service unit (CSU/DSU) to connect to the network in order to use a low-speed synchronous serial interface at your installation. EIA/TIA-232, EIA/TIA-449, or V.35 connections (or attachments) are typically provided as the electrical interfaces on the CSU/DSU.

You need a T1 CSU/DSU that converts the high-level data link control (HDLC) synchronous serial data stream into a T1 data stream with the correct framing and ones density in order to attach a chassis to a T1 network. The telephone system requirement of a minimum number of 1 bit per time unit in a data stream is known as the "ones density." Several T1 CSU/DSU devices are on the market now. A T1 CSU/DSU is available as additional equipment.

A CSU/DSU is a digital network access device that connects data processing equipment directly to a digital communications line provided by the telco. In the past there were two separate devices for this function. The CSU terminates the digital circuit and performs such functions as transient protection (voltage spikes), electrical isolation, line conditioning, loop equalization, signal regeneration, and monitoring of the incoming digital signal. The DSU translates signals, regenerates data, does synchronous sampling, reformats, handles timing, and converts the unipolar output signal from the DTE into the bipolar signals necessary for transmission over a digital network. Most T1 CSU/DSUs provide either a V.35 or EIA/TIA-449 electrical interface to the system.

A digital carrier facility used for transmitting data over a telephone network at 1.554 Mbps is known as a T1. E1 is the European equivalent of T1, with a data transmission rate of 2.048 Mbps.

You need a DSU to connect an HSSI port that is capable of the type of service to which you will connect the following: T3 (45 Mbps), E3 (34 Mbps), or synchronous optical network (SONET) STS-1 (51.84 Mbps). You also need a HSSI interface cable to connect the DSU with the high-speed serial interface processor (HIP). The U.S. standard for a digital carrier facility used for transmitting data over a telephone network at 44.736 Mbps is known as a T3 (also known as digital signal level 3 [DS-3]). T3 is equivalent to 28 T1 (1.544 Mbps) interfaces. E3 is the European equivalent of T3.

Finally, SONET is an international standard (ANSI/CCITT) for optical communications systems. STS-1 (synchronous transport signal level 1) is the basic building-block signal of SONET. Level 1 is 51.84 Mbps. Faster SONET rates are defined as STS-n, where n is a multiple of 51.84 Mbps. For instance, the rate for SONET STS-3 is 155.52 Mbps, three times 51.84 Mbps.

FROM HERE

This chapter described the development of the high-speed cabling system implementation plan (scheduling, analyzing site surveys, connectivity requirements, equipment, security, performance, etc.). Chapter 23 will begin Part V by taking a look at the installation of the cabling system. The chapter opens up with a presentation on testing techniques as part of preinstallation activities by taking a look at the preparation of cable facilities, testing the cable and components, and code compliance and safety considerations.

NOTES

[1]   "Site Preparation," (Some material in this book has been reproduced by Prentice Hall with the permission of Cisco Systems Inc.), COPYRIGHT © 2000 Cisco Systems, Inc., ALL RIGHTS RESERVED, 170 West Tasman Drive, San Jose, CA 95134-1706, USA, 1999, p. 1.

[2]   "Wireless Site Survey," Reprinted with the permission of AMP Incorporated, Investor Relations, 176-42, PO Box 3608, Harrisburg, PA USA 17105-3608, 1999, p. 2.

Installation of the Cabling System

CHAPTER 23

Testing Techniques

Obviously, cabling is the basic building block for most local area networks (LANs). Cabling challenges arise as these networks reach 100 Mbps and beyond, especially for unshielded twisted pair (UTP) networks. Standards are rapidly evolving, and performance demands on cable and connecting hardware far exceed those of only a few years ago.

Companies spend many thousands of dollars upgrading their network equipment, yet the cabling often gets little attention in comparison. This is ironic because if the cabling doesn't work, the network doesn't work. Some estimates are that cabling issues account for as much as 60 percent of all LAN failures, and the resulting network downtime costs organizations millions of dollars in lost productivity, idle resources, and lost revenues. If you are a network administrator, it is essential to understand how to get the best performance from your cabling investment, and find faults quickly when they occur.

If you are a cable installer, you need to be up to date on the latest cable installation and conformance techniques to ensure that your work meets changing international standards. It can be difficult to keep track of this rapidly changing area of technology. In the year 2001 alone, there will continue to be new category 5 cabling standards for supporting Gigabit Ethernet, new category 5E standards, a new IEEE Gigabit Ethernet standard, important amendments to international cabling standards, new fiber optic standards, and significant progress toward new category 6 and 7 standards. Many of these new standards will require new measurements, higher bandwidth, and higher dynamic range in field measurements. None of the old Level II field testers will be able to support this new level of performance. To accurately make measurements in these new areas will require advanced field testing technology.

Amid Changing Requirements: Keeping Your Cable Test Capabilities up to Date

In today's dynamically changing network environments, the need to *future-proof* cabling installations is becoming more critical everyday. Corporate customers want to be sure that every new cabling investment can effectively handle the potential migration to higher-speed protocols, so they typically are leaning toward specifying cable that exceeds today's 100 MHz practical usage limits. On the other hand, as previously stated, the cable-test standards environment continues to be something of a moving target, especially for higher frequencies.

This dichotomy, between the need to install higher-speed cabling today and the need to have it work with tomorrow's yet-to-be-defined standards, presents most cable installation contractors with a difficult challenge. To survive and thrive in this dynamic environment, cable installers must thoroughly understand and balance the following factors:

- Emerging high-speed standards and the cable tests that they will require.
- Optimal field-test methods to get the most out of their equipment.
- The changing capabilities of today's cable test equipment.
- Upgrade and migration strategies to meet tomorrow's requirements [5].

Straddling the Shifting Standards

Even though 100 MHz is essentially the upper bound of today's adopted standards, the reality is that cable manufacturers are building products capable of speeds in the 350 MHz range and higher. Although they obviously cannot put the full potential of this higher-speed cabling to immediate usage, many organizations are opting for the *insurance value* of investing in it now to ensure room for future migration. Ultimately, installation contractors must be able to competitively respond to customer requirements for certifying cable to higher speeds as the standards develop. In order to accomplish this, installers must be able to anticipate the test requirements for upcoming standards.

Today, over 60 percent of all cable installations are already category 5 (cat 5) and, with the worldwide wiring market growing at more than 18 percent per year, the dominance of cat 5 wiring is rapidly increasing. Although category 5 wiring has been nominally rated for speeds up to 100 MHz, the testing requirements for certifying it to its full capabilities (using all four wiring pairs) have lacked complete definition. In actual practice, the fact that most existing network protocols (such as 10Base-T and 100Base-T) only use two wiring pairs at a time means that there is usually sufficient headroom to spare. However, the movement toward higher speeds, such as Gigabit Ethernet or 622 Mbit/s ATM, is now demanding more stringent testing levels for cat 5 cabling installations.

The Telecommunications Industry Association has recently adopted an enhanced category 5 standard, which includes new Level 3 testing and certification to support reliable transmission of 100 MHz traffic simultaneously using all four pairs of UTP wiring. The enhanced cat 5 requirements includes the use of simultaneous four-pair performance tests such as PowerSum ACR, PowerSum NEXT, and PowerSum ELFEXT as well as channel return loss testing.

Basically, PowerSum Next assesses the multiple disturber cross-talk effects of three pairs simultaneously transmitting by measuring the coupled effect on each fourth pair. PowerSum ELFEXT performs a similar test to assess the far-end multiple disturber cross-talk effects on a near-end received signal. Channel return loss measures the reflected signal caused by impedance mismatches along the entire structured wiring assembly.

In addition to enhanced category 5, ISO/IEC and TIA have jointly laid the groundwork for formal definitions of next-generation cabling standards to provide reliable transmission speeds at greater than 100 MHz. Tentatively, these are specified as follows:

- *ISO/IEC Class E (TIA Category 6):* Specified to 200 MHz, using UTP and the existing RJ45 connector standard.
- *ISO/IEC Class F (TIA Category 7):* Specified to 600 MHz, using individually shielded wiring pairs and a new as-yet-undefined connector design [5].

While cat 5 has already been formally adopted, the ISO/IEC working committees are still refining the revised final draft specifications for Class E/Cat 6 and Class F/Cat 7. It is possible that the final committee drafts will be available during the second half of 2001 and formal adoption could occur as early as 2002 (see Chapter 27, "Standards Development," for further information on this topic). The working objective is for all the new classes/categories to maintain full backward compatibility with applications that run on lower categories.

Because categories 6 and 7 cabling will use entirely different media types, it is unlikely that customers will simply *skip over* category 6 in the same way that the industry went immediately from cat 3 to cat 5 installations. At 200 MHz, cat 6 is essentially being defined to represent the maximum practical transmission bandwidth that is achievable using UTP wiring and RJ45 connectors. On the other hand, cat 7, with its requirement for higher cost individually shielded wiring, may find itself competing head to head with multimode fiber on a cost/performance basis.

As with category 5, both cat 6 and cat 7 will require extensive simultaneous testing of all four wiring pairs for both near-end and far-end cross talk (PSNEXT and PSELFEXT), attenuation to noise (PowerSum ACR), and channel return loss characteristics. From the perspective of a cable installation contractor, this shifting standards picture definitely will dictate a need to quickly invest in both the equipment and training needed to routinely conduct higher-level tests. In addition, it means that they will need to carefully plan their equipment investments to include built-in flexibility for migrating to the as-yet-undefined connector form factors that will be used in cat 7.

Optimizing Field Test Methods

Having the appropriate test capabilities (ACR, PSNEXT, PSELFEXT, etc.) to certify cabling to the customer's specified bandwidth is the heart of any cable testing investment. However, there is much more that must be considered for the contractor to get maximum productivity out of both their equipment investment and their field staff. Some key issues include:

- Procedures for faster testing.
- Storing tests, managing data, and generating reports.
- Protecting the tester from damage.

Procedures for Faster Testing

Installers should be trained on the key disciplines required for efficient test sequences and leveraging the user-oriented aspects of today's test equipment. For instance, the real-world field process must integrate testing with a myriad of other activities, such as determining and tracking cable naming (often using customer-defined nomenclature), smoothly integrating the cable labeling process, supporting rapid sequential testing of bundled cables, and easy movement from each location to the next. However, when a problem is encountered, the installer needs the immediate capability to *drill-down* with more analytic testing to determine and correct the anomaly (see Table 23–1) [6].

Table 23–1   Cable Testing Guidelines

Type of Assembly	Minimal Testing	Additional Testing for Good Practice	Additional Testing for Critical Quality
IDC ribbon cable assemblies	• Opens and shorts testing (threshold levels not critical)	• Repetitive testing (<1 second intermittants) eliminates passing by *wiggle and jiggle*	• Low resistance (<1.2X nominal value) • High voltage (up to 1,000VDC depending on spacing)
High-volume automotive and appliance harnesses	• Single pass opens and shorts (threshold levels not critical)	• Repetitive testing (<1 second intermittents) • Crimp force monitoring • Detecting presence of mechanical features such as locks, seals, and fasteners	• Push-back tests for contacts in connectors • Low resistance (<1.2X nominal value) • High voltage (1,000VDC) if possibility of air gaps < 0.1"
Data cables	• Opens and shorts testing (threshold levels not critical)	• Repetitive testing (<1 second intermittents)	• Low resistance (<1.2X nominal value) • High voltage (up to 1,000VDC depending on spacing)
Network patch cables and high-speed twisted pair data cables	• Opens and shorts testing (threshold levels not critical)	• Twisted pair testing for double miswires	• CAT-5/6 (NEXT and FAR attenuation) testing or as specified
Assemblies with components such as diodes, resistors, capacitors, and Ics	• Components recognized if missing and polarity of diodes detected	• Wrong components detected. Accuracy sufficient to detect passible components with wrong value	• Components measured to within specified tolerance • Functional testing if active components present
Military/aerospace assemblies	• Manual ring-out (continuity) tests with ohmmeter measuring values • High-voltage tests of each conductor to shield	• Opens and shorts testing • Low resistance (<1.2X nominal value) • High voltage (1,500VDC or 1,000VAC)	• Special requirements testing as specified by customer

Table 23–1 recommends guidelines for 100 percent production testing of wired assemblies on the manufacturing floor. Do not confuse these tests with the possible design, environmental, sampling, or long-term reliability qualification tests on components and assemblies covered by various ASME, ASTM, DOD:MIL, NASA, UL, NEC, ITA, ANSI, DIN, etc., specifications.

To support the field installer, today's LAN testers must deliver a balance of quick and easy auto-testing along with indepth analysis capabilities. For instance, setting up the tester to automatically increment each cable ID in sequence can greatly speed up the process of conducting a series of sequential tests. Instead of physically typing in the name of the cable and entering a command to store the results after each test, the installer can simply move from test to test, while automatically storing the results in sequence.

Testers with built-in earphone/microphone headsets also speed up field work by enabling technicians at remote ends of the cable to easily communicate without the hassle or expense of separate walkie-talkies. By automatically utilizing a *good pair* of wiring to establish communications, these testers can enable the voice link whenever testing is not in progress. In addition, testers with built-in tone generation can speed testing by automatically generating required test tones and continuing to broadcast until either the near-end is detected or a specified time out period has expired. This is especially useful for identifying jacks that have been mislabeled or not labeled at all.

Tester ease-of-use features, such as quick-testing capability, are very important to boosting productivity in the field, especially when the installer has to keep moving from outlet to outlet in a large installation. However, it's very important to train all installers to understand and be able to use all of the features in the tester. For the most part, installers should be constantly moving through routine tests at the full speed of the auto-test capabilities, but when necessary, they've got to be trained to access and effectively use the LAN tester's full feature set. The LAN tester is a critical investment for most companies that can't afford for any of its capabilities to go to waste because of a lack of staff knowledge.

Storing Tests, Managing Data, and Generating Reports

Although industry-wide standards for reporting formats have not yet been established (and may never be formally established), many customers are requiring full detailed backup data in addition to summary certification reports. In the past, many customers have only required pass/fail data; however, the future trend is toward archiving complete sets of test results. As corporate IT departments are becoming more sophisticated with their in-house test capabilities, having a full database of certification detail will help support their future moves, adds, and changes (MAC) activities by giving them complete baseline data for conducting and comparing future tests. In addition to assisting the customer, the archiving of a complete audit trail is essential protection for the contractor in the form of a detailed record of all the tests performed to back up their certifications.

Given the extremely long warranty periods currently applied to cabling (such as 25 years), it becomes vitally important for every contractor to retain meticulous records of all test data. While cabling rarely deteriorates by itself over time, there is always the potential for change-inflicted damage to some part of the structure wiring system. Without detailed records of the original test results, contractors have no firm basis from which to determine the legitimacy of subsequent warranty claims. In these instances, it also helps to have similar equipment in the hands of both the installer and the customer's IT personnel. When the customer is able to conduct exactly the same tests that were used by the contractor, it quickly eliminates tester variability as the source of disagreement.

For larger or rapidly growing installation companies, with a mix of skill and knowledge levels, it is often useful to be able to deploy a variety of tester configurations with capabilities to match the technicians' skills and duties. For instance, the ability for the tester to locally store multiple days' worth of tests is becoming increasingly important, especially for advanced installers or those who may spend long periods on the road without returning to their headquarters. However, it may not be practical or desirable to outfit all the staff with high-end testers that can store 1,500 sets of tests, when in actual practice the entry-level staff may only conduct 150 tests before reporting in and uploading the results. Another function that many contractors find useful is the capability to *undelete* the last action. No matter what the skill level of the operator, there is always the occasional risk of erroneously deleting test data.

One emerging issue regarding test storage is the potential use of laptops for uploading and managing data in the field. Obviously, the availability of laptops would give installers more flexibility for storing extensive test data that outstrips the internal capacity of the tester and it also can provide quick options for generating customer reports in the field, if required. On the other hand, many installers do not feel that laptops in the field are the best way to go. Most customers, it seems, are concerned about putting the responsibility on the installer to manage another expensive piece of field equipment. It appears most customers would rather see a continuation of the trend in testers to provide more internal storage and communications options. To the extent that the tester can help minimize the overall physical load on the installer, the more productive the tester can be in the field. As a matter of fact, most customers would be interested in just seeing an option for testers with a built-in 3.5 diskette drive to download a quick copy of the test results in the field to allow for more internal storage and to give the customer access to review the test results on site.

Protecting the Tester

When working in *live* environments, such as testing operational cabling or making moves, adds, and changes, the contract installer or in-house IT person must also take special precautions to avoid damage to the tester. An RJ45 connection for the LAN can have exactly the same look and form factor as one used for any of a number of different functions, such as telephone, digital PBX, ISDN, and so on; however, the pin-outs and voltage risks can be significantly different. Compounding the problem is the possibility that outlets could have been mislabeled in the original installation or labels could have been lost or changed during previous MAC activity. The risk of erroneously applying 48v (or 96v during a ringing cycle) into the LAN tester can do immediate damage, impacting both the contractor's capital investment and loss of staff time until the tester can be replaced. In addition to carefully training their staff to avoid making erroneous connections, contractors should look for built-in protective features and/or automatic warning messages on the display to allow disconnection before permanent damage occurs.

Planning for Future Tester Migrations

For cable installers, the continued migration to higher-speed cabling offers an attractive opportunity for increasing their value, but also means extensive investment in both capital equipment and staff training. Installation contractors can't afford to wait too long to invest in new capabilities nor should they risk jumping in too quickly. Installers need to carefully plan their investment strategies over the next few years, in order to stay on the leading edge, but avoid overspending or investing in near-obsolete test equipment. A key issue is ensuring that the test vendors will participate with customers in any required upgrades. If EIA and TIA change the upcoming standards, the customers need to know that they won't have to bear the burden of the whole cost.

The bottom line for both cabling installation contractors and their customers is that the world will continue to change. During the year 2001 we will see the continued widespread adoption of the revised enhanced cat 5 testing standards along with the further refinement of the cat 6 and cat 7 standards. Throughout all of this change, contractors will continue to install new cabling while customers will continue to press it toward its physical limits. At each step of the way, the cable testing industry will have to provide cost-effective and extensible solutions that always stay abreast of users' current needs while anticipating and planning for future requirements.

THE TESTING ITSELF

As previously discussed, installing and maintaining a reliable physical cable plant is essential to the well-being of today's mission-critical LANs. This involves two main areas. Most commonly, field testing is done for certification of new cable plants, to ensure they are capable of meeting cable and application standards. Also, field testing is done in the event of adds, moves, or changes, or in the case of troubleshooting to isolate a point of failure.

Fortunately, success with high-performance premise cabling is not difficult once its capabilities and characteristics are understood. This part of the chapter is intended to help you navigate through the clutter of standards, cable classification systems, measurement technology, and applications information so that you can increase your productivity, stay current, and deliver better value to your organization.

ACR

The first thing to understand about testing cables is the ACR, which stands for attenuation to cross-talk ratio. The uppermost area in the graph shown in Figure 23–1 is the attenuation, which can be caused by several things, as will be explained later in this part of the chapter, and the lowermost area is the cross talk [7]. Attenuation is the reduction in signal strength over the length of the cable and frequency range. The cross talk is the external noise that is introduced into the cable. Therefore, if the two areas meet, the data signal will be lost because the cross-talk noise will be at the same level as the attenuated signal. Thus, ACR is the most important result when testing a link because it represents the overall performance of the cable.

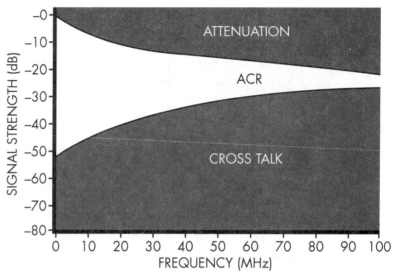

Figure 23–1   Testing the overall performance of the cable.

Testing Terminology

What causes the signal to attenuate? Where does the cross talk come from? Some of the terms used in high-performance cable testing and a description of what they mean and do are as follows:

- length
- wire map
- return loss
- DC loop resistance
- Attentuation
- NEXT
- PSNEXT
- FEXT, ELFEXT, and PSELFEXT
- delay

Length

The length of a cable is one of the more obvious causes of attenuation because the longer it is, the more resistance it has, and therefore less of the signal will get through. To measure the length, a cable tester uses time domain reflectometry (TDR). A pulse is sent down the cable and when it reaches the far end it reflects back. By measuring the time it takes to travel down the cable and back again, the tester can determine how long the cable is. To do this, the tester also needs to know how fast the pulsed signal is traveling. This is called the nominal velocity of propagation (NVP) and is expressed as a percentage of the speed of light. The NVP is usually somewhere between 60 percent and 90 percent of the speed of light, with most cat 5E cables around 70 percent. Due to the twists in the cable, the measured length will be greater than the physical length, so if a run looks like it might be over 80 m, it would be wise to check it before it is tied up and terminated.

Wire Map

The wire map test is to ensure that the two ends have been terminated pin for pin (that pin 1 at the patch panel goes to pin 1 at the outlet, pin 2 goes to pin 2, and so on). The wire map also checks for continuity, shorts, crossed pairs, reversed pairs, and split pairs, as shown in Figure 23–2 [7]. A split pair is probably the only thing that requires an explanation here, as they are undetectable with a simple continuity tester, because pin for pin they seem to be correct. In other words, balanced line operation (see the Sidebar, "Balanced Line") requires that the signal is transmitted over a pair of wires that are twisted together, with a *split pair* the signal would be split between two different pairs.

BALANCED LINE

Balanced line operation is a transmission method that helps to eliminate the effects of noise on the cable. In the first diagram shown in Figure 23–3, a coaxial cable is transmitting a 4V signal [7]. This is unbalanced, as all of the 4V signal is carried by the center core of the coax with respect to the grounded screen. If 1V of noise is introduced, it adds to the signal being transmitted, making 5V. This could interfere with the data.

With a balanced line transmission, the 4V signal is split into +2V and –2V on one twisted pair, so we still have 4V between the two. Now, when you introduce the 1V of noise, the +2V becomes +3V, and the –2V becomes –1V, but the potential difference between the two is still 4V, as shown in Figure 23–4 [7]. The devices put on the ends of the cable to make the line balanced are called baluns. This name is derived from the function of the devices of converting between balanced and unbalanced transmission modes. These days, more and more equipment is being designed to operate on balanced lines without the need for baluns, but there are still a lot of older systems out there that still use these converters [7].

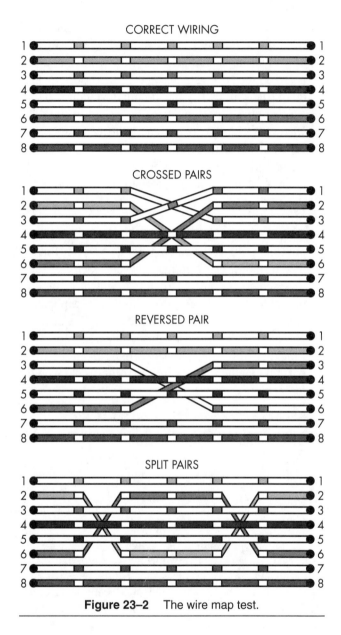

Figure 23–2   The wire map test.

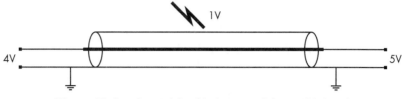

Figure 23–3   A coaxial cable is transmitting a 4V signal.

Figure 23–4   Balanced line transmission.

Return Loss

When a cable is manufactured, there are slight imperfections in the copper. These imperfections all contribute to the structural return loss (SRL) measurement, because each one causes an impedance mismatch, which adds to the cable's attenuation.

DC Loop Resistance

The DC loop resistance is simply the resistance between the two conductors of a twisted pair, which is looped back at the far end. The primary purpose of this test is to make sure that there are no high-resistance connections in the link.

Attenuation

As previously explained, attenuation is the decrease in signal strength (expressed as negative dB) from one end of a cable to the other. The main causes of attenuation are impedance, temperature, skin effect, and dielectric loss. Impedance is the combination of resistance, inductance, and capacitance in a cable. It is measured in ohms and opposes the flow of current. Skin effect is a phenomena that happens at high frequencies where the signal tries to escape from the confines of the copper and into the air. The signal travels along the outer *skin* of the copper, which effectively reduces the cross-sectional area of the cable and therefore increases its resistance.

NEXT

NEXT stands for near end cross talk, as shown in Figure 23–5 [7]. It occurs because alternating current flow produces an electromagnetic field around the cable. This field then induces a current flow in adjacent cables. The strength of this field increases with the frequency of the signal, and because the speed of data transmissions is ever increasing, NEXT is a big problem.

The name *cross talk* comes from the telecommunications industry. You may have heard a faint conversation in the background while on the phone yourself. This is caused by the electromagnetic effect between adjacent tele-

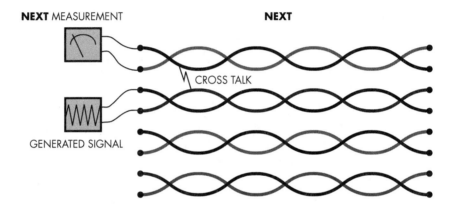

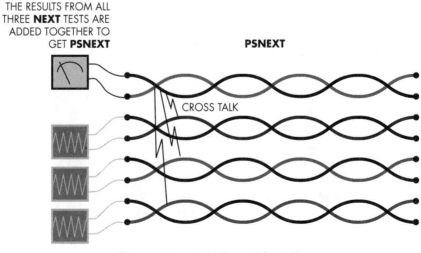

Figure 23–5   NEXT and PSNEXT.

phone wires. In the transmission of data, cross talk is at its highest level in the RJ45 connection as it enters the cable, or at the *near end*. The term near end is slightly confusing because data can travel in both directions, and the NEXT test is carried out in both directions automatically by the tester. So, the NEXT result is relative to the end of the cable on which it was carried out.

The twists in a cable help to cancel out the effects of NEXT and the more twists there are, the better the cancellation. However, the twists also increase attenuation, so there is a trade off between NEXT cancellation and attenuation. The twist rates in data cables are optimized for the best overall performance. The twist rates are also varied for each pair within the cable to help combat cross talk.

PSNEXT

PSNEXT stands for power sum near end cross talk and is actually just a calculation, as shown in Figure 23–5. When a tester carries out the NEXT test, it measures the cross talk on each pair as affected by each of the other three pairs individually. PSNEXT is simply the addition of the three NEXT results for each pair. This is the combined effect that a pair would be subjected to when used in a network that supports a four-pair transmissions method (Gigabit Ethernet).

FEXT, ELFEXT, and PSELFEXT

Basically, far end cross talk (FEXT) is like NEXT, but it is measured at the far end. However, on its own, FEXT (see Figure 23–6) doesn't mean much because the length of the cable determines how much the signal is attenuated before it can affect the pairs at the far end [7]. To compensate for this, and to provide a more meaningful result, the attenuation is subtracted from the FEXT test and the result is then called equal level far end cross talk (ELFEXT). And, of course, no test parameter these days would be complete without adding the results together for each pair and calling it a power sum measurement. Now we have power sum equal level far end cross talk, or PSELFEXT for short (see Figure 23–6).

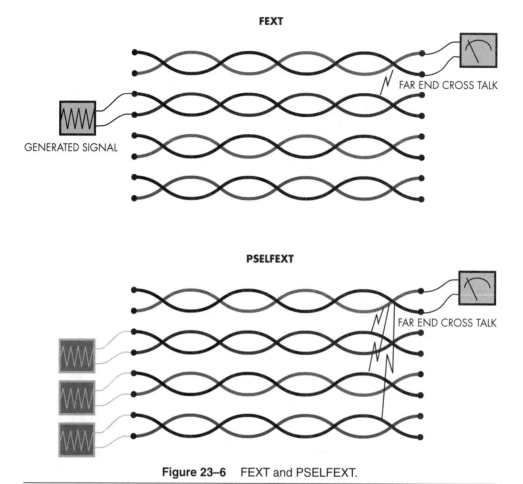

Figure 23–6   FEXT and PSELFEXT.

Delay

Delay is the propagation delay, or the time it takes for the signal to travel from one end of the cable to the other. It is not very important on its own because its value is directly proportional to the length of the cable. What is important is the relationship between the delays on each of the four pairs. This brings us nicely on to *delay skew*.

Delay Skew.   Delay skew is the difference between the fastest and slowest pairs. Some networks use a four-pair transmission method. This means that the signal is split into four, sent down the four pairs in the cable, and recombined at the far end. It is essential that the signals reach the far end at near enough the same time, otherwise the signal will not be recombined correctly.

Copper Cable Testing

As previously explained earlier in this book, twisted pair alternatives have replaced coaxial cabling on today's LANs. At the category 5 performance level or above, there are a bewildering number of options. Let's first identify, compare, and contrast these cabling alternatives, as shown in Table 23–2 [8].

Table 23–2 Identifying, Comparing, and Contrasting Cabling Alternatives

Name	Construction	Expected Performance
Cat 5 UTP	Cable consists of 4 pairs of 24 AWG (0.50 mm) copper with thermoplastic polyolefin or flourinated ethylene propylene (FEP) jacket. Outside sheath consists of polyvinyl-clorides (PVC), a fire-retardant polyolefin (FRP), or fluoropolymers.	Mixed and matched cables and connecting hardware from various manufacturers that have a reasonable chance of meeting TIA cat 5 channel and ISO Class D requirements. No manufacturers warranty is normally involved.
Cat 5E UTP	Cable consists of 4 pairs of 24 AWG copper with thermoplastic polyolefin or FEP jacket. Outside sheath consists of PVC, FRP, or fluoropolymers. Higher care taken in design and manufacturing.	Category 5 components from one supplier or from multiple suppliers where components have been deliberately matched for improved impedance and balance. Designed to meet TIA 568A-A5; often includes a 10-year or greater warranty.
Cat 6 UTP	Cable consists of 4 pairs of 0.50–0.53 mm copper with thermoplastic polyolefin or FEP jacket. Outside sheath consists of PVC, FRP, or fluoropolymers. Extremely high care taken in design and manufacturing.	Category 6 components from one supplier that are extremely well matched. Channel zero PSACR point (effective bandwidth) is guaranteed to 200 MHz or beyond.
FTP	Cable consists of 4 pairs of 24 AWG (0.50 mm) copper with thermoplastic polyolefin or FEP jacket plus a drain wire. Pairs are surrounded by a common metallic foil shield. Outside sheath consists of PVC, FRP, or fluoropolymers.	Category 5 or 5E components from one supplier or from multiple suppliers that have been deliberately designed to minimize EMI susceptibility and maximize EMI immunity. Various grades may offer increased ACR performance.

Table 23–2 (continued)

Name	Construction	Expected Performance
S-FTP	Cable consists of 4 pairs of 24 AWG (0.50 mm) copper with thermoplastic polyolefin or FEP jacket. Pairs are surrounded by a common metallic foil shield, followed by a braided metallic shield. Outside sheath consists of PVC, FRP, or fluoropolymers.	Category 5 or 5E components from one supplier or from multiple suppliers that have been deliberately designed to minimize EMI susceptibility and maximize EMI immunity. Offers EMI protection that is superior to FTP.
SSTP or PIMF	Also called PiMF (for pairs in metal foil), SSTP consists of 4 pairs of 22–23 AWG copper with a thermo-plastic polyolefin or FEP jacket. Pairs are individually surrounded by a helical or longitudinal metallic foil shield, followed by a braided metallic shield. Outside sheath consists of PVC, FRP, or fluoropolymers.	Category 7. Provides positive ACR to 600 MHz. Shielding on the individual pairs gives it outstanding NEXT performance. No standard yet for connector. Many experts doubt category 7 connectors can achieve compatibility with RJ45 category 5, 5E, or 6 connectors.

At the simplest level, installers use continuity checkers to verify end-to-end connections. One step up from that are a series of very helpful, low-cost tools that provide a full wire map, measure length with a TDR, and provide additional useful functions. This kind of tool is great for testing voice cabling, conducting quick checks on data cabling, and for the growing residential LAN wiring market.

The focus of this part of the chapter is on category 5 and higher-premise wiring installation and test issues. Today's standards for this kind of cabling require several measurements to be made in order to certify the cabling meets stated performance requirements. Some tests are performed worldwide, while others are specific to the U.S. or Europe. Each of these standards has unique pass/fail limits, which vary depending on the category and link definition.

All standards require that installed links pass three tests. The first is called wire map. Wire map verifies end-to-end pin-to-pin connectivity, as well as checking for split pairs. Any miswires, breaks, opens, shorts, crossovers, or splits should be detected.

Another key measurement used to qualify LAN cabling is attenuation. Every electromagnetic signal loses strength as it propagates away from its source, and LAN signals are no exception. Attenuation increases with temperature and frequency. Higher frequency signals are attenuated much more than low frequency signals, which is one of the reasons why a cable may have correct pin-to-pin continuity, pass low-speed traffic like 10BASE-T perfectly, yet not be able to handle 100BASE-T. With category 5 copper cabling, attenuation is remarkably consistent from manufacturer to manufacturer. Cables that have attenuation performance much better than standard category 5 usually have increased copper diameter or slightly higher impedance.

The most important test in qualifying the performance of network cabling is near end cross talk (NEXT). Cross talk occurs when signals from one pair of wires radiate and are picked up by an adjacent pair of wires. Cross talk increases with frequency, so that just as attenuation, a category 3 cable may be fine for 10BASE-T, but can't handle 100BASE-T.

Keeping the pairs tightly twisted and well-balanced best minimizes cross talk. This tight twisting causes opposing electromagnetic fields to more effectively cancel each other, thus reducing emissions from the pair. Category 5 cable is much more tightly and consistently twisted than category 3 cable, and uses better insulation materials, which further reduce cross talk and attenuation. EIA/TIA 568A requires that all UTP terminations be properly twisted to within 0.5 inches of all connections.

TIA TSB-67 further requires that length be measured. Length measurement may seem straightforward, but actually can be tricky. In essence, a basic link or permanent link should not exceed 90 meters and a channel should not exceed 100 meters. The accuracy of a length measurement is affected by several factors, including nominal velocity of propagation (NVP) of the cable, twist length versus physical sheath length, and impulse dispersion over long lengths.

When you are measuring length with a field test tool, you are usually measuring time delay. You are also converting it to a length estimate based upon an assumption of signal speed.

As previously explained, nominal velocity of propagation (NVP) refers to how quickly signals travel in a cable. It is expressed as a percentage of the speed of light. Incorrectly set NVP is a very common error. If your NVP is set for 75 percent and the actual cable's NVP is 65 percent, that's a 10 percent error off the bat. Furthermore, NVP is unique to each pair and also varies with frequency. For category 3 cables and hybrid category 5 cables, NVP can vary by up to 12 percent between pairs!

In addition, the copper conductors in UTP are twisted, so the actual length of the wire is longer than the length of the cable jacket. On a 1,000-foot spool, you could easily have 1,020 feet of copper. For these reasons, consider length results from hand-held testers to be good approximations, not precise values.

As previously explained, attenuation to Cross-talk ratio (ACR) is a measurement that determines the effective signal-to-noise ratio of a cabling link. ACR is simply the difference between the NEXT and the attenuation. It is a measure of the strength of the signal that survives attenuation from the far end relative to cross-talk noise. For example, imagine an instructor standing in front of a room giving a lecture. The goal of the instructor is to be heard by the students. The volume of the instructor's voice is a key factor in determining this, but it isn't as important as the difference between the instructor's voice and the background noise. The instructor could be speaking in a very quiet library, so that even a whisper could be heard. But imagine that same instructor, speaking at the same volume, at a noisy football game. The instructor would have to raise his voice so that the difference between his voice (the desired signal) and the cheering crowd (the background noise) is enough for him to be heard. That's ACR.

Emerging standards, such as TSB-95, require the new measurements. Return loss is the ratio, expressed in decibels, of the fractional amount of signal reflection caused by an impedance mismatch. Return loss is increasingly important when trying to get premium performance from UTP. Manufacturers of very high quality UTP have taken special care to ensure impedance is very uniform throughout the link, and also that all components are very well matched. So while return loss wasn't a big issue when category 5 cabling first appeared, it is an important differentiator for cat 5E and cat 6 cabling.

Power-sum NEXT (PSNEXT) is actually a calculation, not a measurement. PSNEXT is derived from an algebraic summation of the individual NEXT effects on each pair by the other three pairs. PSNEXT and FEXT (discussed below) are important measurements for qualifying cabling intended to support four-pair transmission schemes such as Gigabit Ethernet.

As previously explained, far end Cross talk (FEXT) is similar to NEXT, except the signal is sent from the local end and cross talk is measured at the far end. On the other hand, FEXT by itself is not a useful measurement. This is because FEXT is highly influenced by the length of the cable, since the signal strength inducing the cross talk is affected by how much it has been attenuated from its source. For this reason, equal level FEXT, or ELFEXT, is measured instead. ELFEXT simply subtracts attenuation from the result, so that the result is normalized for attenuation (length) effects. Then, just to make things interesting, there is also power-sum ELFEXT, or PSELFEXT.

Category 6 testing requires three things you don't have in your current Level II tester:

1. Support to accurately make all the new measurements.
2. Dynamic range to measure FEXT and return loss at category 6 levels correctly.
3. 250 MHz of bandwidth [8].

For this reason, many installers are in the process of replacing their field testers with new products designed to fully support category 5/5E/6 requirements.

Fiber Optic Cable Testing

As previously discussed in Chapter 16, fiber is now beginning to appear in traditional *UTP territory*. There have been continual improvements in optical fiber performance, fiber cable designs, connectivity technology, and test equipment. Not only are these fiber products more craft friendly than ever, they are also less expensive. New advancements in transceiver products will make fiber even more attractive in the LAN environment.

Fiber optic cable comes in two basic types: multimode or single mode. Multimode fiber has a relatively large core diameter (typically 50 or 62.5 microns). Light from LED sources can be efficiently coupled into multimode fiber. Multimode fiber is most often used in LED-based LAN systems. Single-mode fiber has a very small core diameter (8.3 microns). Single-mode fiber propagates only one optical mode, significantly increasing bandwidth. Single-mode fiber is primarily used in laser-based long haul and interoffice applications. Single-mode fiber is beginning to be used in LAN as backbone cabling and to *futureproof* networks.

How is fiber tested? Historically, the quality of fiber cable was so good and bandwidth more than adequate that some network designers specified that only a simple continuity check was required for fiber cable certification. Today's higher-speed networks demand more from the fiber and are making this simple approach obsolete. Industry standards bodies, including the TIA/EIA, IEEE, ISO, and ANSI, have published standards that define maximum supportable distance and maximum channel attenuation for LANs. Therefore, when installing cable to support a standardized network application (Ethernet, FDDI, and ATM), it is appropriate to test cable and compare the results to the appropriate standard. In practice, network designers and architects are frequently unaware of the standards or chose to use their own user-defined pass/fail criteria. This can result in a cabling plant that is either not tested as thoroughly as necessary, jeopardizing network performance, or tested too severely, which can needlessly add to the cost and time of the cable installation and testing.

What is really required? It is best to comply with the appropriate fiber application standard, all of which require direct attenuation measurement. These standards have been painstakingly developed and approved by a large group of leading companies in the industry. You can be confident of acceptable network performance when you certify that the cabling plant meets the requirements of the standard. If you are installing cable and the transmission standard is unknown or is a new transmission protocol for which a standard has not yet been published, it is recommended that you follow the guidelines set forth by the networking equipment manufacturer or a general building standard. That means TIA/EIA-568-A in North America or ISO/IEC 11801 in Europe. Other regional and country-specific standards exist.

There are a variety of tools available for testing fiber cable. Which tool(s) to use will depend upon the type of job to be performed, how frequently you test fiber networks, and your test equipment budget. Tools for the field include:

- Simple white light sources for fiber identification and continuity checks.
- Laser-based visual fault locators to detect fiber breaks.
- Optical loss test kits and sets to measure loss.
- Certification tools to measure loss/length and compliance to standards.
- Optical time domain reflectometers (OTDR) for diagnostics and measuring distance to optical events [8].

It is interesting to contrast measurements necessary to qualify a fiber optic cable installation with those of a copper cable installation. To certify a copper installation, it is important to consider wiremap, length, attenuation, NEXT and PSNEXT at both ends, ACR at both ends, ELFEXT at both ends, return loss at both ends, delay, and delay skew. In contrast, to certify a fiber installation, only attenuation, at one or two wavelengths, is usually measured. Length may also be measured or physically recorded. Fiber cable can be tested one fiber at a time using the end-to-end technique. This methodology uses an optical source and power meter for direct measurement of attenuation. The fibers are tested, results recorded, and later compared to an industry or user-defined standard to evaluate the success of the installation. For those who test fiber frequently, new fiber test technology is available for quicker, more productive network testing and certification. Multiple measurements can be made over an Rx/Tx fiber pair with the push of one button and the pass/fail status of the fiber is instantly displayed. Optical time domain reflectometers (OTDRs) are used for troubleshooting fiber optic cabling. An OTDR can measure optical length and display the distance to an optical event (fiber break, end of fiber, fiber splice or connector). OTDR are not suitable for making end-to-end power loss measurements.

The use of LAN fiber networks is expected to become more commonplace as technology and costs improve. Fiber standards do exist and networks should be tested to the appropriate application standard (Ethernet, FDDI, or ATM) when possible. If unknown, a general commercial building standard such as TIA-568A or ISO 11801 should be followed. Network designers and equipment vendors may have proprietary standards that must be followed. A range of test tools are available to ensure that you can accurately and reliably test fiber networks.

TESTING ACTIVITIES

Prior to the installation of your cabling system, there are a number of activities that must take place in the form of various types of testing. The following sections discuss the test site requirements for the preparation of your cabling facilities for installation in these areas:

- environment
- chassis accessibility
- cooling and airflow
- power

Environment

Choose a clean, dust-free, preferably air-conditioned location. Avoid direct sunlight, heat sources, or areas with high levels of electromagnetic interference (EMI).

Chassis Accessibility

Make the front panel of the switch accessible so that you can monitor the LED indicators and access the reset switch. Leave at least 24 inches (60.9 centimeters) clearance at the rear of the switch for easier cabling and service.

Cooling and Airflow

Many equipment racks come with fans already installed on the top to draw air up through the equipment. However, if you don't have preinstalled fans, place two fans at the front of the switch so that they'll cool the interior by pushing air through vents in the front and forcing heated air through holes in the rear. If the internal temperature exceeds 122° F (50° C), a temperature alarm is generated.

To prevent the switch from overheating, do not operate it in an area that exceeds the maximum recommended ambient temperature of 104° F (40° C). To prevent airflow restriction, allow at least 3 inches (7.6 cm) of clearance around the ventilation openings.

Power

The source electrical outlet should be installed near the switch, be easily accessible, and be properly grounded. In addition, separate ground wires are also a good idea.

Power should come from a building branch circuit. Use a maximum breaker current rating of 20A for 110V, or 8A for 230V. You should be aware of the power consumption ratings of the unit before you connect to a power source.

Care must be given to connecting units to the supply circuit so that wiring is not overloaded. Also, a voltage mismatch can cause equipment damage and may pose a fire hazard. If the voltage indicated on the label is different from the power outlet voltage, do not connect the chassis to that receptacle.

TEST CABLING REQUIREMENTS TECHNIQUES

The following discusses the test cabling requirements techniques for installation of:

- FDDI
- CDDI
- Ethernet 10BaseF
- Ethernet 10BaseT
- EIA/TIA-232

FDDI Transmissions

The multimode FDDI connectors on the switch accept 50/125-micron multimode fiber, or 62.5/125-micron multimode fiber, with standard FDDI media interface connectors (MICs). The single-mode connectors accept 8.7 to 10/125-micron single-mode fiber, with standard FDDI ST-type connectors. FDDI maximum transmission distance specifications are listed in Table 23–3 [1]. Multimode and single-mode connectors are illustrated in Figures 23–7 and 23–8, respectively [2].

Table 23–3 Maximum Transmission Distances for FDDI

Type of Transceiver	Maximum Distance between Stations
Multimode	1.4 miles (2 km)
Single mode	39.9 miles (64 km)

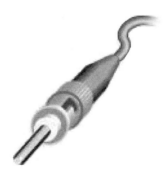

Figure 23–7
ST single-mode connector.

Figure 23-8
Multimode FDDI connector—MIC type.

CDDI

To ensure that you have the proper connectors (modular RJ45/T568-8/category 5 connector), you should check all existing cables for conformance with CDDI/MLT-3 distance requirements. A discussion on cable and distance specifications follows.

First of all, EIA/TIA-T568-B, category 5, data-grade cable is required for copper distributed data interface (CDDI) installations when using data-grade unshielded twisted pair (UTP) wiring. The total length of data-grade UTP cable from the switch to another switch, station, or CDDI (also known as TPDDI—twisted pair distributed data interface) concentrator must not exceed 341 feet (104.9 m). This would also include patch cords and cross-connect jumpers.

Second, use IBM Type 1 STP wiring for your CDDI installation when using shielded twisted pair (STP) wiring. The total length of STP cable measured from the adapter or media access unit (MAU) to the switch must not exceed 341 feet (105 m). You must also use an impedance-matching balun (balance/unbalanced) device (model number WS-C737) to connect CDDI to STP. In addition, for external connections, you must use high-performance, category 5, data-grade modular cables. Remember the following when you plan your CDDI installation.

- Do not use bridge taps.
- Do not exceed the maximum cable length for CDDI, UTP, and STP of 341 feet (105 m).
- Do not use protection coils.
- Do not share services (such as voice and data) on the same cable. CDDI uses two of the four pairs in the twisted pair cable. The remaining two pairs cannot be used for other applications.
- Use cross-connect (patch) panels that comply with the EIA/TIA-T568-B, category 5 wiring standard [Cisco, 5].

IEEE 802.3 Ethernet 10BaseF Ports

IEEE 802.3 Ethernet 10BaseF ports accept ST-type connections using 62.5/125-micron multimode optical fiber. The distance limitation for 10BaseF is 1.3 miles (2 km). 10BaseF supports both fiber optic interrepeater link (FOIRL) standards and 10BaseFL (fiber link).

In general, distance limitations depend on the power levels of other devices on the fiber link, combined effects of fiber, and connectors. The maximum power levels for 10BaseF and FOIRL are listed in Table 23–4 [Cisco, 6].

Table 23–4 Power Levels for FOIRL and 10BaseF

Maximum Power	FOIRL	10BaseF
Receive power at receiver	–27 dB	–32.5 dB
Transmit power at transmitter	–9 dB	–12 dB[a]

[a] dB = decibel.

Ethernet 10BaseT Ports

Modular RJ45 connectors are accepted by Ethernet 10BaseT ports (see Sidebar, "Cable Testing for 100VG-AnyLAN Installations"). Also, as specified by the EIA/TIA-T568-B wiring standard, 10BaseT requires a minimum of category 3 UTP cable. The distance limitation for 10BaseT is a maximum of 339 feet (104 m) between segments.

CABLE TESTING FOR 100VG-ANYLAN INSTALLATIONS

Category 4-UTP 100VG-AnyLAN has the same cable test parameters as those required for 10Base-T and token ring. Cable test devices must be able to test these parameters with the additional requirements of being able to test all four pairs, at test frequencies up to 15 MHz.

Table 23–5 lists the cable test parameters and their acceptable ranges for 4-UTP 100VG-AnyLAN operation [9]. Also, several cable test devices are currently available that will test all four pairs up to 20 MHz:

- The HP J2263A Cable Test Set
- The Microtest MT350 Scanner
- The Fluke 652 Cable Meter
- The Wavetek LANtech 10/100

Cable testing must be completed on the entire length of cable from the end that attaches to the hub to the end that attaches to the node. Attenuation, pair-to-pair and near-end cross talk, and impedance tests must be completed on all four pairs of the twisted pair cabling. The near-end cross talk test must be completed from both ends of the cable. The remaining three tests may be completed from only one end of the cable [9].

Table 23–5 UTP Cable Test Parameters

Frequency	5 MHz	10MHz	15 MHz
Maximum attenuation	11.5 dB	11.5 dB	13.5 dB
Characteristic impedance	85 to 115 ohms	85 to 115 ohms	85 to 115 ohms
Pair-to-pair cross talk	30.5 dB	26.0 dB	22.5 dB
Near-end cross talk	27.5 dB	23.0 dB	19.5 dB

EIA/TIA-232 Signals

EIA/TIA-232 signals can travel a limited distance at any given bit rate (as with all signaling systems). Generally, the greater the distance, the slower the data rate. The relationship between baud rate and maximum distance is shown in Table 23–6 [Cisco, 6]. The EIA/TIA-232 admin port requires an RJ45-to-DB25 adapter for the console terminal where it is attached and a modular RJ45 connector for the switch end.

Table 23–6 Speed and Distance Limitations for EIA/TIA-232

Data Rate (baud)	Distance (feet)	Distance (meters)
2,400	210	65
4,800	110	34
9,600	51	16
19,200	26	8
38,400	13	4

TEST NETWORK TOPOLOGY OVERVIEW

Figure 23–9 shows what a topology (a high-speed transparent and translational bridging overview) might resemble when the switch is installed in your network. This consists of workstations connected to the 10BaseT Ethernet

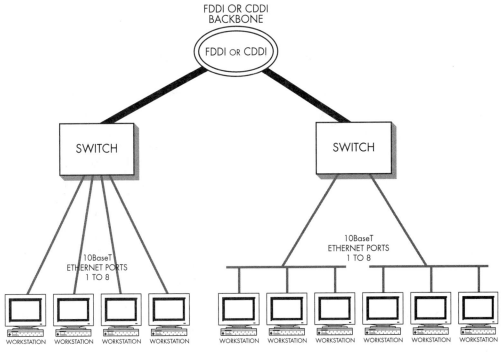

Figure 23-9   High-speed translational and transparent bridging topology.

ports of two switches. The 10BaseF ports might be connected in a similar manner. The switches are connected to an FDDI or CDDI dual ring. This ring is part of a larger FDDI or CDDI backbone.

MODEM TEST REQUIREMENTS

Operating a switch with a modem is optional. You should consult the modem documentation when connecting a switch to a modem. You also need to connect the modem to the EIA/TIA-232 admin port on the switch as a minimum requirement. In addition, configuration is not possible at the switch if you don't configure the modem to operate with the switch. Table 23-7 lists the dual inline package (DIP) switch settings for the U.S. Robotics Sportster 28,800-baud fax modem as an example of modem configuration [Cisco, 7].

Table 23–7 DIP Switch Settings for a Modem

Switch	Connection	Setting	Description
1	DTR override	Down	Data terminal ready (DTR) is ignored by modem.
2	Audible results	Up	Instead of a number, modem returns audible result messages.
3	Suppress results	Up	No result messages are returned by the modem. Because this function is not configurable on the switch, it is required.
4	No echo of offline commands	Down	When the modem is offline and it receives a command, it does not echo. This function is not configurable on the switch, so it is required.
5	Auto answer on ring	Up	After one ring, modem answers automatically. This function is not configurable on the switch, so it is required. Thus, the modem must answer automatically.
6	CD override	Down	Carrier detect (CD) is always maintained by the modem.
7	Load factory defaults	Down	Modem-dependent.
8	Dumb mode	Up	The modem attention (AT) command is not recognized by the modem.

The DIP switch information is only for the modem connected to the switch. It is not for the modem connected to your computer, terminal, PC, or whatever else you are using for your modem-based communication.

TEST TOOLS AND MATERIALS REQUIRED

A list of tools and supplies that you need to install the switch with is shown in Table 23–8 [Cisco, 8]. The switch can be placed on a desktop in a work area, mounted in a standard 19-inch rack, or on a wall in a wiring closet or office.

Table 23–8 Materials and Tools Required for Installation

| | Installation Type | | |
Hardware and Tools	Desk	Rack	Wall

Rack-mount kit (standard):
  Two brackets
  Eight screws (attach brackets to switch)
  Four screws (switch to rack—you supply these)
	No	Yes	No

Optional wall-mount kit[a]:
  Two brackets
  Four screws (attach brackets to switch)
  Four screws (attach to wall—you supply these)
  Wall-mounting template
	No	No	Yes

No. 2 Phillips screwdriver	No	Yes	Yes
Flat-blade screwdriver (to remove blank plates or A/B port cards)	Yes	Yes	Yes
3/8" (0.952 cm) drill with 1/4" (0.635 cm) bit	No	No	Yes

[a] Model number WS-C1670.

FIELD TESTING CABLE AND COMPONENTS PRIOR TO INSTALLATION

Let's now take a look at the next set of preinstallation activities: testing the cable and components. This next part of the chapter will focus on the field testing of unshielded twisted pair and fiber optic cabling systems that must take place prior to installation.

Telecommunications System Bulletin (TSB) 67 is of great interest to cable installers, test-equipment manufacturers, and LAN administrators because it provides detailed requirements on how to test and certify unshielded twisted pair (UTP) cabling prior to installation. The same can be said for fiber optic cabling standards EIA/TIA-526-14A (Optical Power Loss Measurements of Installed Multimode Fiber Optic Cable Plant) and TIA/EUIA-526-7 (Measurement of Optical Power Loss of Installed Single-mode Fiber Optic Cable Plant). Let's focus first on TSB-67.

Field Testing Unshielded Twisted Pair Cabling Systems with TSB-67

The purpose of this part of the chapter is not to reproduce the information already available in TSB-67. The objective here is to clarify the reasoning behind some of the decisions that were made and to give you a better understanding of the testing specifications prior to the installation of your cabling system.

Briefly, TSB-67 includes a link model, a description of which tests must be performed to certify the link (length, wiremap, NEXT, and attenuation) and specifications for how each test is to be performed. In addition, TSB-67 contains detailed procedures for verifying the accuracy of field test equipment (FTE) against both a theoretical model and a laboratory network analyzer. Finally, TSB-67 specifies performance criteria for FTE.

The Channel and Basic Link Models

Before studying the issue of accuracy and how it is addressed in TSB-67, it is necessary to understand TSB-67's two link definitions: the channel link and the basic link. Figure 23–10 illustrates the TSB-67 channel definition [3]. Cables A and E are user patch cords, almost always terminated in modular 8 (RJ45) connectors.

These are not and cannot be test equipment cords; they must be the user's actual patch cords.

As Figure 23–10 shows, the mated connection at the ends of these cords is not included in the channel definition, but is considered a part of the field tester. This connection is typically an 8-position modular jack. This means any measurements taken on the channel must be made through the mated connection and do not include the connection's characteristics. The mated modular 8 connection has significant NEXT, which becomes a source of error in NEXT measurements that will significantly differentiate the accuracy of channel and basic link measurements.

The channel was defined because it is important to know the performance of the sum of all the components between the hub and the PC so that you can predict the quality of communications from end to end. This information is essential to circuit designers and important to end users. However, cable installers are typically not responsible for installing patch cords, as office furniture is usually not present when the cabling is installed and tested. For this reason, the basic link model was defined.

In Figure 23–11, the basic link represents a minimal link and has only one connection at each end [Johnston, 3]. The channel has two. In addition, the basic link can only be 90 meters in length, while the channel can extend

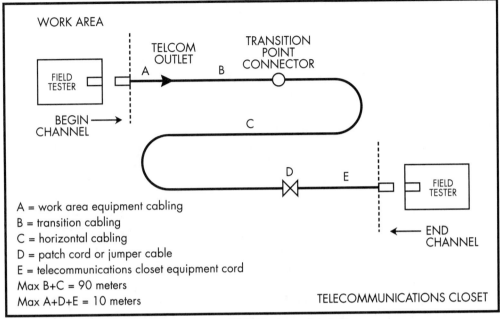

WORK AREA

FIELD
TESTER

BEGIN →
CHANNEL

TELCOM
OUTLET

A

TRANSITION
POINT
CONNECTOR

B

C

D

E

FIELD
TESTER

END
CHANNEL

A = work area equipment cabling
B = transition cabling
C = horizontal cabling
D = patch cord or jumper cable
E = telecommunications closet equipment cord
Max B+C = 90 meters
Max A+D+E = 10 meters

TELECOMMUNICATIONS CLOSET

Figure 23–10 TSB-67 channel definition.

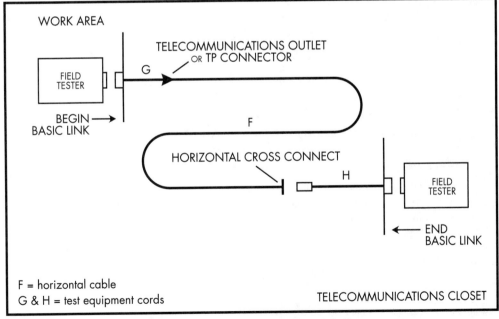

WORK AREA

FIELD
TESTER

BEGIN →
BASIC LINK

TELECOMMUNICATIONS OUTLET
OR TP CONNECTOR

G

F

HORIZONTAL CROSS CONNECT

H

FIELD
TESTER

END
BASIC LINK

F = horizontal cable
G & H = test equipment cords

TELECOMMUNICATIONS CLOSET

Figure 23–11 TSB-67 basic link definition.

to 100 meters. For these reasons, both attenuation and NEXT will be higher on the channel than on the basic link.

Levels of Accuracy

Recognizing that the basic link and the channel link represent two different models, the authors of EIA/TIA-TSB-67 chose to define two distinct accuracy levels: Level II (high accuracy) and Level I (lower accuracy).

The reason for the two levels is that when you are testing a channel, you are almost always forced to measure through (but not include) the NEXT effects of a modular 8 (RJ45) interface directly on the FTE. The unpredictable cross talk in this connection sets a limit on the achievable accuracy of the measurement. In contrast, when testing a basic link, field test equipment manufacturers can choose to use a very low cross-talk interface directly on the FTE. This reality is reflected in the TSB-67 description of two accuracy levels for field test equipment. Level I reflects the performance boundaries imposed by the reality of having to test through a modular 8 connection. Level II sets a much higher accuracy requirement, attainable only if a different, low cross-talk interface is used. The uncertainty caused by the higher cross-talk modular 8 interface can be avoided, and thus a much higher level of accuracy can be achieved.

TSB-40A specifies the worst-case NEXT performance of any modular 8 connection to be 40 dB at 100 MHz. So while some connections might achieve 42 or 43 dB, 40 dB performance is all that can be guaranteed. This unpredictable high level of inherent cross talk limits any tester's ability to make measurements at a Level II accuracy level when testing a channel through a modular 8 interface to the FTE.

How is Accuracy Measured?

The TIA task force that established TSB-67 determined six key performance parameters that affected the accuracy of field testers (see Table 23–9) [Johnston, 4–5]. The largest error term for field testers is residual NEXT. This consists of the sum of the tester's internal NEXT plus the NEXT of the interface to the tested link. Remember, this mated connection is not included in the link definition.

Table 23–9 TSB-67 Accuracy Performance Parameters

Performance Parameter	Level I @ 100 MHz	Level II @ 100 MHz
Residual NEXT	40 dB	55 dB
Random noise	50 dB	65 dB
Output signal balance	27 dB	37 dB
Common mode rejection	27 dB	37 dB
Dynamic accuracy	± 1 dB	± 0.75 dB
Return loss	15 dB	15 dB

When testing a channel, this residual NEXT will include the NEXT of a mated modular 8 connection. Even if the residual NEXT on the field tester's internal circuits is zero, its overall residual NEXT will be limited to 40 dB by the mated modular 8 connection as specified by TSB-40A. Thus, the Level II accuracy performance requirement of 55 dB cannot be met when testing a channel. This is, in fact, the reason Level I and Level II were created. When testing a basic link, the field tester can make use of an interface with much lower inherent cross talk, thus making the Level II residual NEXT requirement of 55 dB achievable.

TSB-67 specifies that for an instrument to meet Level I or II accuracy, it must meet all six of the requisite performance parameters. The cross-talk and balance characteristics of a modular 8 connector immediately limit any tester using it to no better than Level I accuracy. It is important to note that even Level II accuracy tools are reduced to Level I accuracy when forced to test through a modular 8 interface, because of the uncertainty created by the modular 8 connector. This uncertainty has an unpredictable magnitude and phase, so it cannot be compensated for or subtracted by hardware or software.

TSB-67 also requires that field testers agree with Annex B, which states that agreement with network analyzers must be demonstrated. The reason for this is that different field testers may employ different methods to make measurements. Some of these methods, such as time domain measurements, may have additional error sources unaccounted for in the theoretical error model.

The Level I performance limitations of a modular 8 connection hold true even when time-domain measurement techniques are used to attempt to time-gate away the high cross talk. The outgoing pulses used to make time-domain measurements have a duration of several nanoseconds, which equates to several feet. This means a NEXT dead-zone is created where the tester cannot read the cross talk on the first few feet. As Figure 23–10 shows, this measurement technique does not comply with TSB-67 because the test must begin directly behind the first modular 8 connections, not two or three feet down the cable.

Users are cautioned to review FTE performance specifications carefully. Many products will claim to meet Level II accuracy, but the fine print often shows such products barely meet the minimum requirements, especially with residual NEXT. Proof of compliance with Annex B (network analyzer agreement) is conspicuously absent in most cases.

Length Accuracy Issues

Annex D of TSB-67 provides information on how to increase the accuracy of length measurements, or, at the least, how to minimize the inaccuracies of such measurements. Since most FTE measures length using time domain reflectometry (TDR), the accuracy of these products depends on the nominal velocity of propagation (NVP) setting of the cable being tested. NVP varies up to 5 percent from cable to cable and even from pair to pair. TDR is an excellent method to measure length but requires the cable's precise NVP.

As previously stated, TSB-67 will be a great help to cable installers, test equipment manufacturers, and LAN administrators. The reason for this is because it provides clear test requirements and instrument specifications as part of an organization's cabling system preinstallation activities.

Field Testing Fiber Optic Cabling Systems with EIA/TIA Procedures

Let's continue with the next set of preinstallation activities: field testing of fiber optic cabling systems that must take place prior to installation. The following guidelines describe the EIA/TIA-recommended procedure for field testing multimode and single-mode fiber optic cabling systems.

While other fiber optic cabling system parameters such as bandwidth are as important as attenuation, they are not normally affected by the quality of the installation and therefore do not require field testing. This part of the chapter describes how and where attenuation testing should be performed, based upon the architecture of the cabling system. A general equation is given to calculate acceptable attenuation values along with detailed examples covering both hierarchical star and single point administration architectures.

Passive Link Segments

Attenuation testing should be performed on each passive link segment of the cabling system prior to installation. A link segment consists of the cable, connectors, couplings, and splices between two fiber optic termination units (patch panels, information outlets, etc.). Each terminated fiber within a link segment should be tested. The link segment attenuation measurement includes the representative attenuation of connectors at the termination unit interface on both ends of the link, but does not include the attenuation associated with the active equipment interface. This is illustrated in Figure 23–12 [4].

There are three basic types of link segments described in this part of the chapter: horizontal, backbone, and composite. A horizontal link segment normally begins at the telecommunications outlet and ends at the horizontal cross-connect. The telecommunications outlet may be a multiuser outlet placed in an open-office area. The horizontal link segment may also include a consolidation point interconnection or a transition point splice. A riser backbone link segment usually begins at the main cross-connect and ends at the horizontal cross-connect. For the purpose of this chapter, a tie cable placed between two horizontal cross-connects and a campus cable typically placed between two main cross-connects are both considered backbone link segments. A single point administration architecture eliminates the horizontal cross-connect, and as a result, horizontal and backbone cabling are combined into a composite link segment. In this case, the horizontal closet may contain a splice, interconnect, or pulled-through cable.

Spliced pigtail terminations at one or both ends of a horizontal, backbone, or composite link are permitted.

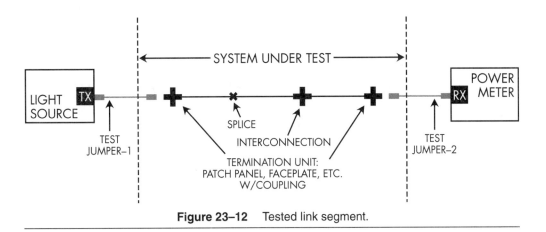

Figure 23–12   Tested link segment.

General Preinstallation Testing Guidelines

The following are the general preinstallation guidelines that all organizations should follow.

- Multimode horizontal link segments should be tested in one direction at the 850 nm or 1,300 nm wavelength.
- Multimode backbone and composite link segments should be tested in one direction at both 850 nm and 1,300 nm wavelengths.
- Single-mode horizontal link segments should be tested in one direction at the 1,310 nm or 1,550 nm wavelength.
- Single-mode backbone and composite link segments should be tested in one direction at both 1,310 nm and 1,550 nm wavelengths [Lucent, 2].

The minor attenuation differences due to test direction are on par with the accuracy and repeatability of the test method. Therefore, testing in only one direction is warranted. Horizontal link segments are limited to 90 meters. Therefore, attenuation differences caused by wavelength are insignificant, and as a result, single wavelength testing is sufficient. Also, typical attenuation for 62.5/125 multimode fiber is 3.5 dB/km at 850 nm and 1.0 dB/km at 1,300 nm. And typical attenuations for single-mode 125 micron fiber are 0.5 dB/km at 1,310 nm and 0.4 dB/km at 1,550 nm.

In compliance with EIA/TIA-526-14A (Optical Power Loss Measurements of Installed Multimode Fiber Cable Plant) and EIA/TIA-526-7 (Measurement of Optical Power Loss of Installed Single-mode Fiber Cable Plant), the following information should be recorded during the test procedure:

1. Names of personnel conducting the test.
2. Type of test equipment used (manufacturer, model, serial number).
3. Date test is performed.
4. Optical source wavelength, spectral width, and, for multimode, the coupled power ratio (CPR).
5. Fiber identification.
6. End point locations.
7. Test direction.
8. Reference power measurement (when not using a power meter with a relative power measurement mode).

9. Measured attenuation of the link segment.

10. Acceptable link attenuation [Lucent, 3].

Horizontal link segments are limited to 90 meters; therefore, the acceptable link attenuation can be based on the longest installed link without introducing a significant error.

Acceptable Attenuation Values

The general attenuation equation for any link segment is as follows:

```
Acceptable Link Attn. = Cable Attn. + Connection Attn. +
Splice Attn. + CPR Adj.
```

See the Sidebar, "62.5μm Multimode and Single-mode Attenuation Coefficients," for further information.

A connection is defined as the joint made by mating two fibers terminated with remateable connectors (ST, SC, LC).

62.5μM MULTIMODE AND SINGLE-MODE ATTENUATION COEFFICIENTS

The following are the 62.5μm multimode and single-mode attenuation coefficients.

62.5μm Multimode Attenuation Coefficients

Cable Attn. = Cable Length (km) × (3.40 dB/km@850 nm or 1.00 dB/km@1300 nm)

Connection Attn. (ST or SC connectors) = Connections × 0.39 dB) + 0.42 dB

Connection Attn. (LC connectors) = Connections × 0.14 dB) + 0.24 dB

Splice Attn. CSL or Fusion) = Splices × 0.30 dB

CPR Adj. = See Table 23–10 [Lucent, 4].

Single-Mode Attenuation Coefficients

Cable Attn. = Cable Length (km) × (0.50 dB/km@1310 nm or 0.50 dB/km@1550 nm)

Connection Attn. (ST or SC connectors) = Connections × 0.44 dB) + 0.42 dB

Connection Attn. (LC connectors) = Connections × 0.24 dB) + 0.24 dB

Splice Attn. (CSL or Fusion) = Splices × 0.30 dB

CPR Adj. = 0.00 dB (Not applicable for single mode) [Lucent, 3–4].

Table 23–10: CPR Adjustment

	Multimode Light Source CPR Adjustment				
	Category 1	Category 2	Category 3	Category 4	Category 5
Links with ST or SC connections	+ 0.50	0.00	- 0.25	- 0.50	- 0.75
Links with LC connections	+ 0.25	0.00	- 0.10	- 0.20	- 0.30

The Sidebar, "Coupled Power Ratio Measurement," describes the test procedure to categorize a multimode light source's coupled power ratio (CPR).

COUPLED POWER RATIO MEASUREMENT

The coupled power ratio of a light source is a measure of the modal power distribution launched into a multimode fiber. A light source that launches a higher percentage of its power into the higher-order modes of a multimode fiber produces a more overfilled condition and is classified as a lower category than a light source that launches more of its power into just the lower-order modes producing an underfilled condition. Underfilled conditions result in lower link attenuation, while overfilled conditions produce higher attenuation. Therefore, adjusting the acceptable link attenuation equation to compensate for a light source's launch characteristics increases the accuracy of the test procedure.

Procedure

CPR test jumper-1 shall be multimode, 1–5 meters long with connectors compatible with the light source and power meter and have the same fiber construction as the link segment being tested. CPR test jumper-2 shall be single-mode, 1–5 meters long with connectors compatible with the light source and power meter. The step-by-step procedure is as follows:

1. Clean the test jumper connectors and the test coupling per manufacturer's instructions.

2. Follow the test equipment manufacturer's initial adjustment instructions.

3. Connect multimode test jumper-1 between the light source and the power meter. Avoid placing bends in the jumper that are less than 100 mm (4 inches) in diameter. See Figure 23–13 [Lucent, 11].

4. If the power meter has a relative power measurement mode, select it. If it does not, record the reference power measurement (P_{ref}).

Note If the meter can display power levels in dBm, select this unit of measurement to simplify subsequent calculations.

5. Disconnect test jumper-1 from the power meter. *Do **not** disconnect the test jumper from the light source.*

6. Connect test jumper-2 between the power meter and test jumper-1 using the test coupling. The single-mode jumper should include a higher-order mode filter. This can be accomplished by wrapping the jumper three times around a 30 mm (1.2 inches) diameter mandrel. See Figure 23–14 [Lucent, 12].

7. Record the power measurement (P_{sum}). If the power meter is in relative power measurement mode, the meter reading represents the CPR value (See Table 23–11) [Lucent, 12]. If the meter does not have a relative power measurement mode, perform the following calculation:

```
If Psum and Pref are in the same logarithmic units (dBm, dBu, etc):
                    CPR (dB) = | Psum - Pref |

If Psum and Pref are in watts:
                    CPR (dB) = | 10 X log10 [Psum/Pref] |
```

Figure 23–13 Connecting multimode test jumper-1 between the light source and the power meter.

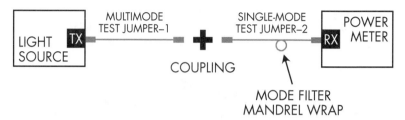

Figure 23–14   Connecting jumper-2 between the power meter and test jumper-1 using the test coupling.

Table 23–11   Coupled Power Ratio (CPR) in dB by Category

	Coupled Power Ratio (CPR) in dB				
	Category 1 Overfilled	Category 2	Category 3	Category 4	Category 5 Underfilled
850 nm source	25–29	21–24.9	14–20.9	7–13.9	0–6.9
1,300 nm source	21–25	17–20.9	12–16.9	7–11.9	0–6.9

Hierarchical Star Architecture: Backbone Link Segment.   Figure 23–15 shows a multimode 160-meter riser cable placed between the main cross-connect and the horizontal cross-connect containing a midspan fusion splice [Lucent, 4]. All fibers are terminated with ST connectors. The acceptable link attenuation is calculated as follows.

Category-2 850 nm light source:
Acceptable Link Attn = Cable Attn + Connection Attn + Splice Attn + CPR Adj
Acceptable Link Attn = $[0.160 \times 3.40] + [(2 \times 0.39) + 0.42] + [1 \times 0.30] + 0.00$
Acceptable Link Attn = 2.044 dB

Category-2 1,300 nm light source:
Acceptable Link Attn = Cable Attn + Connection Attn + Splice Attn + CPR Adj
Acceptable Link Attn = $[0.160 \times 1.00] + [(2 \times 0.39) + 0.42] + [1 \times 0.30] + 0.00$
Acceptable Link Attn = 1.66 dB

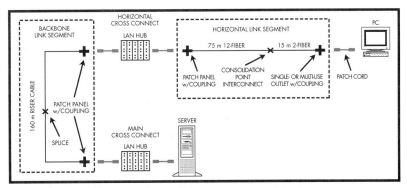

Figure 23–15 Hierarchical star architecture.

Horizontal link segment Figure 23–15 also shows a multimode 75-meter, 12-fiber, horizontal cable placed between the horizontal cross-connect and a consolidation point (interconnection) located in an open-office area. From the consolidation point a total of four multimode, 15-meter, 2-fiber cables are distributed to modular furniture outlets, leaving four spare fibers of the horizontal cable for future use. All fibers are terminated with ST connectors. The acceptable link attenuation is calculated as follows:

Category 2 850 nm light source:

Acceptable Link Attn = Cable Attn + Connection Attn + Splice Attn + CPR Adj

Acceptable Link Attn = $[0.075 \times 3.40] + [(2 \times 0.39) + 0.42]$

Acceptable Link Attn = 1.46 dB

In the preceding category 2 850 nm light source calculation, horizontal link segments begin at the horizontal cross-connect and end at the consolidation point (spare fibers).

Category 2 850 nm light source:

Acceptable Link Attn = Cable Attn + Connection Attn + Splice Attn + CPR Adj

Acceptable Link Attn = $[(0.075 + 0.015) \times 3.40] + [(3 \times 0.39) + 0.42]$

Acceptable Link Attn = 1.896 dB

In the preceding category 2 850 nm light source calculation, horizontal link segments begin at the horizontal cross-connect and end in modular furniture outlets.

Single Point Administration Architecture: Composite Link
Segment.   Figure 23–16 shows a multimode 50-meter, 72-fiber riser cable placed between the main cross-connect and the closet serving the horizontal [Lucent, 6]. From the closet a total of four multimode, 75-meter, 12-fiber horizontal cables are interconnected to the riser cable and are distributed to consolidation points (interconnections) located in open-office areas, leaving 24 spare fibers of the riser cable for future use. From each consolidation point a total of four multimode, 15-meter, 2-fiber cables are distributed to modular furniture outlets, leaving four spare fibers of each horizontal cable for future use. All fibers are terminated with LC connectors. The acceptable link attenuation is calculated as follows.

Category 3 850 nm light source:
Acceptable Link Attn = Cable Attn + Connection Attn + Splice Attn + CPR Adj
Acceptable Link Attn = [0.050 × 3.40] + [(2 × 0.14) + 0.24] − 0.10
Acceptable Link Attn = 0.59 dB

Category 1 1,300 nm light source:
Acceptable Link Attn = Cable Attn + Connection Attn + Splice Attn + CPR Adj
Acceptable Link Attn = [0.050 × 1.00] + [(2 × 0.14) + 0.24] + 0.25
Acceptable Link Attn = 0.82 dB

In the preceding category 3 850 nm light source and category 1 1,300 nm light source calculations, link segments begin at the main cross-connect and end at the horizontal closet (spare riser fibers).

Category 3 850 nm light source:
Acceptable Link Attn = Cable Attn + Connection Attn + Splice Attn + CPR Adj
Acceptable Link Attn = [(0.050 + 0.075) × 3.40] + [(3 × 0.14) + 0.24] − 0.10
Acceptable Link Attn = 0.985 dB

Category 1 1,300 nm light source:
Acceptable Link Attn = Cable Attn + Connection Attn + Splice Attn + CPR Adj
Acceptable Link Attn = [(0.050 + 0.075) × 1.00] + [(3 × 0.14) + 0.24] + 0.25
Acceptable Link Attn = 1.04 dB

In the preceding category 3 850 nm light source and category 1 1,300 nm light source calculations, link segments begin at the main cross-connect and end at the consolidation point interconnect (spare fibers).

Category 3 850 nm light source:
Acceptable Link Attn = Cable Attn + Connection Attn + Splice Attn + CPR Adj
Acceptable Link Attn = $[(0.050 + 0.075 + 0.015) \times 3.40] + [(4 \times 0.14) + 0.24] - 0.10$
Acceptable Link Attn = 1.18 dB

Category 1 1,300 nm light source:
Acceptable Link Attn = Cable Attn + Connection Attn + Splice Attn + CPR Adj
Acceptable Link Attn = $[(0.050 + 0.075 + 0.015) \times 1.00] + [(4 \times 0.14) + 0.24] + 0.25$
Acceptable Link Attn = 1.19 dB

In the preceding category 3 850 nm light source and category 1 1,300 nm
light source calculations, link segments begin at the main cross-connect and
end in modular furniture outlets.

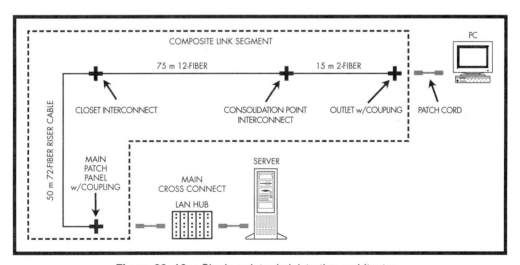

Figure 23–16   Single point administration architecture.

Test Procedure

In compliance with EIA/TIA-526-14A and EIA/TIA-526-7, test jumpers shall be 1 to 5 meters long. They shall have the same fiber construction (core diameter and numerical aperture) as the link segment being tested. The Sidebar, "Test Jumper Performance Verification," describes the procedure to test jumper performance verification.

TEST JUMPER PERFORMANCE VERIFICATION

The step-by-step procedure is as follows:

1. Clean the test jumper connectors and the test coupling per the manufacturer's instructions.

2. Follow the test equipment manufacturer's initial adjustment instructions.

3. Connect test jumper-2 between the light source and the power meter. See Figure 23–17 [Lucent, 8].

4. If the power meter has a relative power measurement mode, select it. If it does not, record the reference power measurement (P_{ref}). If the meter can display power levels in dBm, select this unit of measurement to simplify subsequent calculations.

5. Disconnect test jumper-2 from the power meter. *Do **not** disconnect the test jumper from the light source.*

6. Connect test jumper-1 between the power meter and test jumper-2 using the test coupling. See Figure 23–18 [Lucent, 8].

7. Record the power measurement (P_{sum}). If the power meter is in relative power measurement mode, the meter reading represents the connection attenuation. If the meter does not have a relative power measurement mode, perform the following calculation to determine the connection attenuation:

```
If Psum and Pref are in the same logarithmic units (dBm, dBu, etc):
        Connection Attenuation (dB) = | Psum - Pref |

If Psum and Pref are in watts:
    Connection Attenuation (dB) = | 10 X log10 [Psum/Pref] |
```

The measured connection attenuation must be less than or equal to the value found in Table 23–12 [Lucent, 9].

8. Flip the ends of test jumper-1 so that the end connected to the power meter is now connected to the coupling, and the end connected to the coupling is now connected to the power meter.

9. Record the new power measurement (P_{sum}). Perform the proper calculations if not using relative power measurement mode and verify that the connection attenuation is less than or equal to the value found in Table 23–12.

Figure 23–17   The connection of test jumper-2 between the light source and the power meter.

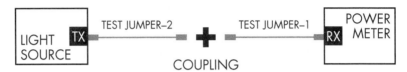

Figure 23–18   The connection of test jumper-1 between the power meter and test jumper-2 using the test coupling.

Table 23–12   Test Jumper Connection Attenuation

| | Acceptable Test Jumper Connection Attenuation | |
	ST or SC Jumper	*LC Jumper*
Multimode	0.50 dB Max	0.20 dB Max
Single mode	0.55 dB Max	0.30 dB Max

If both measurements are found to be less than or equal to the values found in Table 23–12, test jumper-1 is acceptable for testing purposes. You should note that unacceptable link segment attenuation measurements may be attributable to test jumper-1 or test jumper-2 (see Table 23–13) [Lucent, 10]. Examine each jumper with a portable microscope and clean, polish, or replace if necessary.

Repeat this test procedure from the beginning, reversing jumpers 1 and 2 in order to verify the performance of test jumper-2.

Table 23–13   Troubleshooting Unacceptable Link Segment Attenuation

Possible Cause	Resolution
Epoxy bead left on the tip of a connector	Examine connectors with a portable microscope and repolish if necessary.
Poorly polished connectors	Examine connectors with a portable microscope and repolish if necessary.
Dirty connectors and/or couplings	Examine connections and clean per manufacturer's instructions.
Poor splices due to fiber misalignment either mechanically or prior to fusing	Identify poor splices with an optical time domain reflectmeter (OTDR) and resplice if necessary.
Macro-bending of fibers in patch panels and splice cases caused by bends smaller than the minimum bend radius specification	Identify macro-bends by inspection or with an OTDR and remove or increase bend radius where necessary.

OTDRs are also used to reveal many undesirable cable conditions, including shorts, opens, and transmissions anomalies due to excessive bends or crushing, as referenced in Table 23–13.

Link Segment Testing.   The one reference jumper method specified in EIA/TIA-526-14A and EIA/TIA-526-7 should be used to test each link segment. The procedure is summarized in the Sidebar, "Link Segment Testing Procedure."

LINK SEGMENT TESTING PROCEDURE

The step-by-step procedure is as follows:

1. Connect known good (see the Sidebar, "Test Jumper Performance Verification") test jumper-1 between the light source and the power meter. See Figure 23–19 [Lucent, 9].

2. Record the reference power measurement (Pref) or select the power meter's relative power measurement mode. If the meter can display power levels in dBm, select this unit of measurement to simplify subsequent calculations.

3. Disconnect test jumper-1 from the power meter and connect it to the link segment. *Do **not** disconnect the test jumper from the light source.*

4. Connect known good (see the Sidebar, "Test Jumper Performance Verification") test jumper-2 between the far end of the link segment and the power meter. See Figure 23–20 [Lucent, 10].

5. Record the power measurement (P_{sum}). If the power meter is in relative power measurement mode, the meter reading represents the attenuation associated with the link segment. If this value is less than or equal to the value calculated using the attenuation equation (see the section "Acceptable Attenuation Values" earlier in the chapter), the link segment is acceptable. If the meter does not have a relative power measurement mode, perform the following calculation to determine the attenuation of the link segment:

```
If P_sum and P_ref are in the same logarithmic units (dBm, dBu, etc):
           Link Segment Attenuation (dB) = | P_sum - P_ref |

If P_sum and P_ref are in watts:
           Link Segment Attenuation (dB) = | 10 X log10 [P_sum/P_ref] |
```

Figure 23–19   The connection of known good
test jumper-1 between the light source and
the power meter.

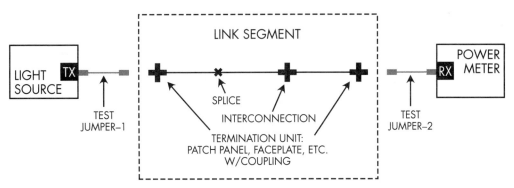

Figure 23–20   The connection of known good test jumper-2 between the far end of the link
segment and the power meter.

CODE COMPLIANCE AND/OR SAFETY RECOMMENDATIONS AND CONSIDERATIONS

Now that the preinstallation activities of testing the cable and components are out of the way, let's proceed to the final preinstallation activities: code compliance and/or safety recommendations and considerations. In order to ensure that safe conditions exist during the installation of your cabling system, the following guidelines should be adhered to as part of your installation activities:

- Do not perform any action that makes the equipment unsafe or creates a potential hazard to people.
- Do not wear loose clothing that could get caught in the chassis. Roll up your sleeves and fasten your scarf or tie.
- During and after installation, keep the chassis area dust-free and clear.
- Keep tools away from walk areas where you and others could trip over them.
- When working under any conditions that might be hazardous to your eyes, wear safety glasses [Cisco, 1].

If the far end is connected to an LED or laser, unterminated connectors may emit radiation. Be absolutely sure that the fiber is disconnected from any laser or LED source before viewing the end of a cable.

Safety with Equipment Powered by Electricity

Follow these guidelines when working on equipment powered by electricity:

1. In the room in which you are working, locate the emergency power-off switch. Then, you can act quickly to turn off the power if an electrical accident occurs.

Before you connect the system to its power source, read the installation instructions.

2. Unplug the power cord before working on the system.

3. Before doing any of the following, disconnect all power:
   - installing or removing a chassis
   - performing a hardware upgrade
   - working near power supplies

During periods of lightning activity, do not work on the system or connect or disconnect cables. Also, when the power cord is connected, do not touch the power supply. In addition, line voltages are present within the power supply even when the power switch is off and the power cord is connected for systems with a power switch. On the other hand, line voltages are present within the power supply when the power cord is connected for systems without a power switch.

4. If potentially hazardous conditions exist, do not work alone.

5. Never assume that the power is disconnected from a circuit. Always check.

For short-circuit (overcurrent) protection, certain electrical-powered equipment usually relies on the building's installation. Ensure that a fuse or circuit breaker no larger than 120 VAC, 15A U.S. (240 VAC, 10A international) is used on the phase conductors (all current-carrying conductors). Also, some equipment is designed to work with telephone network (TN) power systems. Additionally, unplug the power cord on AC units and disconnect the power at the circuit breaker on DC units before working on a chassis or working near power supplies.

6. Look carefully for possible hazards in your work area, such as missing safety grounds, moist floors, and ungrounded power extension cables.

7. If an electrical accident occurs, unplug the power cord and use caution. Do not become a victim yourself. Send another person to get medical aid, if possible. Otherwise, if appropriate, assess the condition of the victim and then call for help. Take appropriate action after determining if the person needs rescue breathing or external cardiac compressions.

Preventing Electrostatic Discharge Damage

Electrostatic discharge (ESD) can impair electrical circuitry and damage equipment. It occurs when electronic components are improperly handled. ESD can also result in complete or intermittent failures. When replacing and removing components, always follow ESD prevention procedures. Ensure that the chassis is electrically connected to the ground using a ground wire or an ESD mat. Wear an ESD-preventive wrist strap, ensuring that it makes good skin contact. Connect the clip to an unpainted surface of the chassis frame to safely channel unwanted ESD voltages to the ground. The wrist strap and cord must operate effectively in order to properly guard against ESD damage and shocks. Ground yourself by touching the metal part of the chassis if no wrist strap is available.

Periodically check the resistance value of the antistatic strap (for safety's sake), which should be between 1 and 10 megohm (Mohm). In addition, if the battery is replaced incorrectly, there is danger of explosion. Replace the battery only with the same or equivalent type recommended by the manufacturer. Used batteries should be disposed of in accordance with the manufacturer's instructions. Finally, the ultimate disposal of batteries should be handled in accordance with all national laws and regulations.

IMPROVING YOUR QUALITY THROUGH THIRD-PARTY TESTING

Finally, testing your work has always been, and will continue to be, an important part of your network cabling business. Bear in mind that the testing to be done is only as good as the testing meters or cable scanners you use and the training and experience you've attained. Under TSB-67 (with the testing parameters set out by ANSI/TIA/EIA 568-A), you can use testers/scanners of different levels of accuracies:

- *Level I:* Measuring NEXT levels in a basic link configuration to an accuracy of ± 3.8 dB.
- *Level II:* Measuring NEXT levels in a basic link configuration to an accuracy of ± 1.6dB.
- *Level IIE:* Must identify trouble spots for Giga-speed transmission [10].

Most cable scanners do a pretty good job these days, but testing your own work can present a whole set of unexpected problems that may arise from personal bias. A lack of objectivity toward the quality of your work may prevent you from seeing some weak areas of your job. This may not be particularly reassuring to your customer. In many cases, you may need to let an outside party review what you've done. Third-party testing, that is, letting another installer evaluate your work, is an uncomfortable prospect to many; but it can bring to the job something you can't—impartiality.

Typically, most network cabling put in place these days is properly installed and meets most of today's cabling standards. On the other hand, there are horror stories about jobs that weren't done right. Sometimes these anecdotes serve as cautionary tales; sometimes they are even a bit amusing, especially when it's our competitors that are responsible. However, as an industry of professionals, we should collectively try to put an end to sloppy practices wherever they appear. After all, we are a quality-minded, standards-driven industry and poor-quality work makes all of us look bad.

Third-Party Testing

Category 5 installations include the testing of all cables installed and the issuance of test results or reports to go with it. Third-party testing could be used to verify all the cables being used by the customer as well as any cables left for the future. Any failed tests should be identified and fixed before the job is considered completed. This is where the verification of your work by a third party can enhance your image with customers. Essentially, what you are saying to your customer is, "I'm so confident that our team's work will pass the cabling standards in place today, that it will pass the same standards testing when someone else looks at our work."

Third-party testing has other positive spin-offs too. Where one company's bid may have lost out on the installation portion of the overall job, the same company's bid may win the testing portion of that same job.

However, you do have to be careful with third-party testing. There is the danger of unscrupulous competitors being unfair, even slanderous, in their critiques to their benefit and your detriment. This is the concept's Achilles heel. However, if everyone cooperates, the system could work. When communicating with the customer as the testing group, it's up to testers to present their findings in a constructive manner. They must be fair when reporting any problems to the customer, and give the installation company a copy of their test results with any explanations needed.

Good communication between all parties involved during these projects is very important. Sometimes, though, there are no safeguards against competing companies being less than constructive in their reports on the installer's job. This too is unprofessional, perhaps even just as bad as a shoddy installation.

Third-party testing could be a concept that companies in competition may find difficult to work at fairly. However, look at it from the customer's perspective: two cabling companies working together to ensure that only high-quality network cabling jobs are being installed in the community, which could speak volumes for the network cabling profession.

As customer faith grows after each installation, so might the sales of installations. Perhaps, after a while, a sort of league of installers and testers could be formed. The customers could access such a list in their area, to find and hire credible network cabling companies looking to fill cabling contracts. Currently, testing is generally part of the package of service a customer pays for, but third-party testing is becoming increasingly popular.

Finally, third-party testing has the potential to provide benefits for everyone involved. The customer gets a quality network cabling job, the cabling company is able to build a list of satisfied customers, and, finally, the testing companies gain more knowledge and experience. As long as everyone cooperates and behaves fairly, everyone wins. There is an old saying among Bell Canada technicians that goes something like this: "Really good installers started as experts in repair work."

FROM HERE

This chapter began Part V by taking a look at the installation of the cabling system. The chapter opened up with a presentation on Testing Techniques as part of preinstallation activities by taking a look at the preparation of cable facilities, testing the cable and components, and code compliance and safety considerations. Chapter 24 describes in detail the installation of the cabling system and covers specific areas such as core drilling considerations; conduit installation and fill guidelines; grounding, shielding, and safety; pulling the cable without damage; splicing and patching; blown fiber; labeling schemes; and quality control and installation standards.

NOTES

[1]   "Preparing for Installation," (Some material in this book has been reproduced by Prentice Hall with the permission of Cisco Systems Inc.), COPYRIGHT © 2000 Cisco Systems, Inc., ALL RIGHTS RESERVED, 170 West Tasman Drive, San Jose, CA 95134-1706, USA, 1997, pp. 4–5.

[2]   Fibre Optic Communications Ltd, Unit 2F, Marchwood Industrial Estate, Normandy Way, Marchwood, Southampton, SO40 4PB, UK, 2000.

[3]   Mark Johnston, "Transmission Performance Specifications for Field Testing of Unshielded Twisted-Pair Cabling Systems," Microtext, Inc., Cable Technology, Inc., 10 Grumbacher Road, York, PA, 1999, pp. 2–3.

[4]   "SYSTIMAX® SCS Field Testing Guidelines for Fiber Optic Cabling Systems," Lucent Technologies Inc., 600 Mountain Avenue, Murray Hill NJ 07974, U.S.A., (Copyright © 1998), pp. 1–2.

[5]   Rich Helstrom, "Keeping Your Cable Test Capabilities up to Date Amid Changing Requirements," ACTERNA, 5808 Churchman Bypass, Indianapolis, IN 46203, 2000.

[6]   "Cable Testing Guidelines," Cirris Systems Corp., 1991 Parkway Blvd., Salt Lake City, UT 84119, U.S.A., 2000.

[7]   "Testing," The Cottage, Horriford Farm, Colyford, Devon EX24 6HW, England, 2000.

[8]   "Copper Cable Testing," Microtest, Inc. 4747 N. 22nd St. Phoenix, AZ 85016-4708, 2000.

[9]   "Testing Cable for 100VG-AnyLAN Installations," Ocampa Internet Business Solutions, Auburn, CA 95603, 2000.

[10] Paul Wraight, "How to Improve Your Quality through Third-Party Testing," Lancom Corporation, 37 Iroquois, Oshawa, Ontario, Canada, LIG3X2; Durham College, Oshawa Campus, 2000 Simcoe Street North, Oshawa, Ontario, Canada LIH7K4, 2000.

Installation

Computers today play a significant role in everyday life. Widespread use of computers in nearly every field means that students without computer literacy have limited options. School districts and universities have taken up the challenge of teaching students how to use computers. Most teachers and professors, while highly trained, do not have the technical experience needed to design and support a district or university computer cabling system.

This chapter provides a step-by-step approach to installing a cabling system for a university, school, or district and is intended for teachers, technical coordinators, and administrators. It provides much of the necessary information that personnel will need while installing cabling technology in their district or university.

INSTALLING A CABLING SYSTEM

Once a district or university has developed a cabling system plan for each of the buildings it will include in the network (see Figure 24–1), the next step is to replace the generic parts of the plan with specifications for actual equipment and wiring [1]. Following that is the installation of the equipment and wiring in a building. When this is completed, the network is ready for use.

This chapter focuses on the different options available for installing a cabling system. It first discusses guidelines for the installation, including specifications for horizontal, intrabuilding, and interbuilding wiring. Then it presents the different equipment used in a LAN. After that, it presents a similar discussion about WAN equipment. The chapter concludes with an examination of the role software plays in the cabling system.

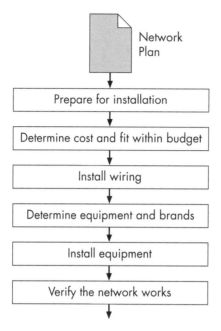

Figure 24–1
The network installation process.

General Guidelines

Once the network plan has been developed for a building, it is time to plan the installation itself. Before starting the installation, time spent determining how the installation will proceed can save significant amounts of time and headaches later.

For instance, the installation of electrical equipment, cables, and wiring should be conducted in such a manner as to maintain the integrity of fire stopping, fire resistance, fire separation, smoke control, and zoning in ceilings, plenums, voids, and similar spaces. The installation should be in accordance with the National Fire Protection Association (NFPA), the National Electrical Code (NEC), the Telecommunications Industry Association (TIA), the Electronic Industry Association (EIA), and local building codes.

Installation Suggestions

The first step, therefore, should be to obtain accurate plans for the building. Many school districts and universities do not have plans for some of their buildings, so the designers should use whatever maps are available. In any case, be sure to verify the distances before installing the wiring, since the maps may be inaccurate or out of date. This can be done using a distance wheel, often available from the athletic department of a school or university campus. In areas where the designer cannot take accurate measurements, estimate the distances, but try to be on the conservative side. Be sure to never estimate wiring distances to the exact foot, since errors will always appear and measuring too accurately may not leave enough room to work around the problems. Remember that besides the horizontal distances, the wiring will also need to run up and down walls. Always leave 10 to 15 percent of the maximum distance available unused to allow for the distance needed to connect a machine to the wall and to connect equipment at the hub. For example, Ethernet specifies a maximum cable length of 100 meters. At most, a wire should only run 90 meters from the hub to the wall drop. See the sidebar, "Checklist for Wiring Installations," for additional information on wiring installation for school and university campuses.

CHECKLIST FOR WIRING INSTALLATIONS

The following checklist should be used to ensure that any new wiring proposed and/or installed by campus departments or contractors conforms to the proposed campus communications cabling standard.

1. Is there a scope of work document that contains the following information?
   - A list of all rooms to be wired and the end-to-end route for the cable.
   - The type of ceiling tiles used in rooms or hallways that may be entered for wire placement. Have a plan to replace broken tiles.
   - A determination if the ceiling area is of plenum or nonplenum construction.
   - Identification of conduits and existing cables that may be used for cable placement.
   - Identification of wall construction on which communications outlets will be mounted.
   - Location of backboard space for wire termination and patch panels in serving communications subterminal.
   - Location of firewalls, because it can be very expensive, time-consuming, and frustrating to find out that a brick firewall is between you and a telecommunications closet.
2. If required by the proposed installation, has contact been made with facilities management and/or environmental health and safety?
3. Is the wire to be placed compatible with the campus communications cabling standard?
4. Does an installation manual exist to guide the placement and termination of the proposed wiring?
5. Has provision been made to provide wall plates or touch-up plaster and painting to repair damaged wall surfaces?

6. Does a testing and acceptance procedure exist that is applicable to the proposed installation and to the campus standard?

7. Do documentation formats and forms exist to guide the installation and provide permanent reference after installation, testing, and acceptance?

8. Has documentation been prepared that defines the materials and configuration for jumper cables to be used at the workstation end and at the patch panels [2]?

While measuring the distances, take a chance to visually inspect all the locations where wire will be run for any potential problems such as electrical power sources or unusually thick walls. When running cable or wiring, it is best to follow a few simple rules:

- Always use more cable than you need and leave plenty of slack.
- Test every part of a network as you install it. Even if it is brand new, it may have problems that will be difficult to isolate later.
- Stay at least 3 feet away from fluorescent light boxes and other sources of electrical interference.
- If it is necessary to run cable across the floor, cover the cable with cable protectors.
- Label both ends of each cable.
- Use cable ties (not tape) to keep cables in the same location together. Velcro straps are becoming very popular for keeping cables together with the ability to remove them easily if needed.

Look for places to run the wiring, ideally through a dropped ceiling, cable trays, and previously drilled holes. If the building does not have dropped ceilings available, and has not already installed cable trays, then it is recommended that the school district or university install cable trays for the wiring. These are simply plastic or wooden trays attached to the walls or ceilings in which to place wiring. Their advantage over running the wiring in conduit is that they allow easy access to the wiring if a problem occurs, and can easily accommodate additional wiring in the future. Look for locations where other accessories such as base plates, face plates, wire mold (for containing vertical wiring), and raceways (for containing wiring running across a floor) will need installation. The designer should note these also and prepare them for installation as well.

A school district or university should be sure that it follows all the local and state fire codes for a school building. In many cases, this will require the use of plenum-rated wiring, which, although more expensive, does not produce any toxic fumes when it burns below a certain temperature. Also, cutting holes in firewalls to allow cable access should be done carefully so that fire codes are not violated. A qualified electrician or architect can provide fire code information.

Another problem that may appear is the use of multiple power feeds into a building. This can happen if a building has been expanded. If the feeds to the building come from different transformers, the ground voltage on each feed may not be exactly the same. This can lead to problems with electrical equipment connected across the differently powered parts of the building, potentially destroying computer equipment. If the situation exists, then the use of specially insulated equipment or the use of fiber cable (which does not conduct electricity) is recommended. If the school district or university is unsure about the power of the building, it should contact a qualified electrician or representative of the power company for more information.

Installation Tips

If a school district or university is going to attempt to install the cabling system using volunteer or untrained staff, the person who will be leading the process should receive extensive training that they can share with the others. This may include talking to qualified electricians and getting training from other schools that have already done the installation.

Cable construction work should be performed by experienced contractor personnel in placing cables in conduit, cable trays, underground duct systems, and in indirect burial methods. Communication cable splices and terminations should be performed by experienced journeymen cable splicers.

For a school district or university considering installing the cabling system themselves, the Sidebar, "List of Equipment Needed to Install a Cabling System in a School," shows a list of the equipment needed. As previously discussed, some of the wiring requirements are very strict about where the wiring can and cannot be run. A district should be sure to understand and follow all the requirements. A failure during this part can render the entire cabling system unusable, or even worse, cause intermittent, untraceable problems.

LIST OF EQUIPMENT NEEDED TO INSTALL A CABLING SYSTEM IN A SCHOOL

General

1. Crimping tool/die sets for RJ45 plugs and receptacles.
2. Standard hand tools including pliers, screwdrivers, a hammer, and wire cutters.
3. 3/8"–1/2" power drill, 12" drill bit extension, 1/4" and 5/8" masonry drill bits.
4. 50' steel fish tape.
5. 70 lb test nylon masonry twine.
6. 6' and 8' fiberglass ladders (aluminum ladders are not recommended because of their ability to conduct electricity).

Materials

1. Mushroom boards or D-rings to support all workstation cables and cross-connects.
2. Cable labelers or black Sharpie markers (one color only) for labeling all workstation cables, termination punch-down blocks, and RJ11 jacks. Label all INS (JIN) concentrators pigtail cables with self-sticking vinyl cloth wire markers. Cable labelers are better than magic markers—the information is printed on a vinyl material that, when wrapped around the cable, is covered with clear vinyl/plastic. Cable labelers are durable and very easy to use.
3. Teflon cable with one style and color only. Use category 3 (4-pair) cable (16 Mbps data) EIA/TIA-568, 10BaseT for all workstation cabling.
4. Wall insert caddie bracket clips when running cables in walls.
5. 110 blocks (category 5) and 66M150 blocks (category 3).
6. Standard ivory wall molding for all buildings unless otherwise specified.
7. One ivory (voice) RJ11 jack and one brown (data) RJ11 jack at each end user location.
8. Color coordinated backboards for all terminal blocks in communication closets as follows:
   - yellow back boards—riser cables
   - blue back boards—station cables
   - green back boards—data blocks

Circuits/Cross-Connects

1. One 1-pair cross-connect (W/BL-BL/W) for each analog and digital ROLM application, fax machine, modem, STU-111.
2. One 1- pair cross-connect (W-R) for each coax elimination circuit.
3. One 2-pair cross-connect (W/BL-BL/W and W/O-O/W) for each CTSDN data circuit.
4. One 2-pair cross-connect (R/BL-BL/R and R/O-O/R) for each INS (JIN) LAN circuit.

5. One 3-pair cross-connect (W/BL-BL/W and W/O-O/W and W/GRN-GRN/W) for each teleconference voice circuit.

6. One 4-pair cross-connect (W/BL-BL/W and W/O-O/W and W/GRN-GRN/W and Y/BL-BL/Y) for each 1A2 key system.

7. Orange color tags to tag all data and LAN circuits at both ends.

8. T1 shielded cable for all T1-type circuits and cross-connects.

To pull wiring throughout a school building, a frame or other device from which to pull the wire is necessary. Most wire is delivered on 1,000-foot rolls. An ordinary two-wheel hand truck can function as a relatively compact unit from which four standard spools can be pulled simultaneously. This unit can then double as a means for moving wire about the building.

In cases where the network cable is pulled through drop ceilings (very common in most modern schools and universities), some type of twine, lead, line, or fish-tape needs to be used. A wide variety of such materials is available. Some schools have used 70-pound test nylon masonry twine with success. With a weight on the end, the twine is light enough so the designer can toss the twine 20–30 feet horizontally through a drop ceiling and run no risk of snapping it when the cable is pulled.

X-ray and Hole Core Drilling Considerations

The contractor should supply all vertical and horizontal hole cores. X-ray of proposed core locations must be performed prior to coring. Under no circumstances should x-rays be performed without the prior notification and approval of the cabling system project manager (PM). When site conditions do not make it feasible to x-ray, the contractor should exercise reasonable judgment to evaluate whether there is a chance that coring will cause the severing of electrical, low voltage, or any other services that may be in the structure that is being penetrated. The use of hammer chisels may be necessary in some buildings. A thorough inspection of both sides of the surfaces must be performed. A flux scanner to check for live loaded AC should be used prior to any drilling, coring, or chiseling.

Where applicable, the opening of drop ceilings on the undersides of floors, including fixed surfaces, should be done to expose the break-through area. Small-diameter pilot holes should be drilled prior to the final coring or chiseling. A qualified electrician with access to a circuit scanner should be present during coring or chiseling in case any services are severed. Should services be severed, the campus (if it's a university) police should be contacted immediately using an emergency number. The PM should also be notified of these occurrences immediately. Depending on the circumstance, the contractor may be asked to begin restoration procedures of severed services immediately.

Any penetration of structural beams, columns, or supports should be cleared by the PM before proceeding. Patching and restoration of coring is the responsibility of the contractor.

Conduit Installation and Fill Guidelines

All conduit should be EMT type, installed with steel, set-screw fittings except on the exterior of the building, where the fittings should be rigid galvanized steel with threaded connectors. Conduit should be installed in compliance with prevailing codes and standards. Conduits should be installed at right angles and parallel to building grids.

Interference drawings must be submitted prior to commencing with the installation of conduits. These drawings must indicate the conduit routing and pull box locations with reference measurements from two walls or permanent fixtures. Include construction notes describing elevation changes, wall penetrations, and information with regard to existing fixtures that may be affected by the installation of the conduit. Neatly drawn routing and notes on the floor plans provided with the tender is an acceptable format.

Pull strings should be supplied in all new and reworked conduit. No pull elbows or LBs should be installed anywhere. Only sweep or 90-degree elbows should be used and no more than two 90-degree bends are permitted between pull boxes. The minimum radius of curvature should be 10 times the conduit internal diameter (ID).

In telecommunications closets, the conduit should be installed parallel to the backboard with a 90-degree bend toward the floor or enter within 10 inches of and parallel to the cable tray. Also, all conduit ends should be fitted with plastic bushings.

All exposed conduit and junction boxes should be painted to match the existing environment. All conduits and pull boxes should be treated and cleaned prior to painting. The conduit should have one coat of primer paint, one intermediate coat, and one or more finished coats of paint. Any color other than the existing environment must be approved by the owner prior to use.

The maximum distance of conduit run between two pull boxes should be 30 meters. The pull box should have a screw-type cover, not hinged. All pull boxes should be accessible with a minimum 24 × 24-inch hinged access hatch provided where required. Pull boxes for vertical conduits should be installed to provide a straight pass-through for vertical cables. The sizes of junction boxes should be 8 times the size of the inside diameter size of the conduit entering it. The exception is when 4-inch conduit is used, then 30 × 24 × 6-inch junction boxes are acceptable. Pull boxes are not to be installed in elevator machine rooms. Conduits installed in elevator machine rooms should provide maximum clearance and should not restrict the service area.

When conduit is installed in utility closets, the conduit should be installed in a steel sleeve that is 6 inches high. Here, the gap between the floor and the sleeve has to be water-tight. Also, all wall and floor penetrations should be filled as per code and finished to match the existing surface.

Flexible Conduit or Innerduct Tubing. Innerduct tubing is not to be used unless it is specified in the detailed scope of the work. If tubing is specified, the inside surface (the surface inside the tubing) should have a smooth finish that will allow it to be finished.

Tubing should also resist crushing pressures and should not collapse within normal bending limits. It should have a diameter of no less than 1 inch.

The contractor should supply tubing that has manufacturers specifications that are in sync with the installation requirements. Tubing may also be specified wherever fiber cable may be subjected to bending forces that would place it at risk of damage.

Tubing may be specified in transitions when in- and out-of-conduit pathways do not line up. Tubing may also be specified in telecommunications closets when cable needs to be installed in free air when other support structures are not feasible.

Tubing should not be used to overcome problems induced through bad installation practices of other components. The fastening of ends of tubing to conduit, racks, or trays should be through mechanically sound fittings, not plastic tie wraps.

Grounding, Shielding, and Safety

All electrical work must comply with the latest safety codes, electrical standards, building codes, and all other applicable cabling standards. Inspections should be applied and paid for by the contractor. A certificate should be provided prior to the final acceptance of work. The use of tandem breakers is not permitted. All electrical cable must be 12 AWG and installed in 1/2-inch EMT conduit supplied by the contractor and installed directly to the panel location. 12 AWG BX is acceptable only when finishing an existing wall. The contractor must have a circuit tracer either on site or readily accessible. All electrical circuits that have been installed will also require labeling. The panel end of the circuit should indicate that the circuit is a dedicated circuit and include the room number in which it terminates. The receptacle end of the circuit should indicate the panel number, panel location, and breaker number. A lockable breaker is required at the panel.

Cables should be grounded as specified. The overall shield of all cables installed should be continuous from termination point to termination point and grounded at one end only.

The metallic sheath of communication cables entering buildings should be grounded as close as practical to the point of entrance or should be interrupted as close to the point of entrance as practical by an insulating joint or equivalent device. Furthermore, the grounding conductor should be connected to the nearest accessible location on the building or structure grounding electrode system, the grounding interior metal water piping system, the power service enclosures, the metallic power service raceways, the service equipment enclosure, the grounding electrode conductor, or the grounding electrode conductor metal enclosure. Also, all connections to grounding should be by connectors, clamps, fittings, or lugs used to attach grounding conductors and bonding jumpers to grounding electrodes or to each other.

For all practical purposes, true earth ground is the best ground of all.

Isolated Ground.   The isolated ground (IG) receptacle should be orange and wired as an individual branch circuit outlet. The outlet should have a separate green or green/yellow wire that runs continuously from the ground conductor terminal to the first panel board where it is connected to the ground bus. Bonding of the conduit, boxes, and so on, of the circuit is accomplished by ordinary means (conduit or a separate ground wire). The two grounds are connected only at the panel board, as shown in Figure 24–2 [3].

The IG outlet is grounded to the same ground as the electrical distribution system. The only difference is that it is connected to ground via a separate wire. There is no clean separate or dedicated ground. The Electrical Safety Code allows only one earthing ground.

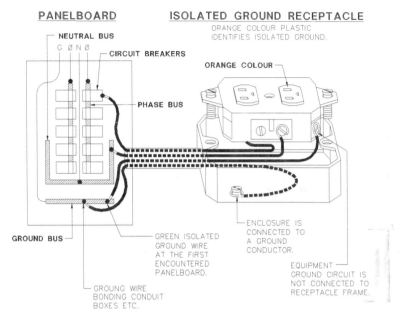

Figure 24–2   Isolated grounding.

Installation of Interbuilding Cables: Outside or between Buildings

The installation of interbuilding cables consists of the copper and fiber optic backbone cables that connect building to building. Let's take a look at how it's done.

Cable Placement

Care should be exercised when handling and storing reels of cable to prevent damage to the cable. Cable with dents, flat spots, or other sheath distortions should not be installed. Immediately after installation, a temporary tag with the cable number and pair count should be attached to each end of each cable section (see the Sidebar, "Interbuilding Cable and Hardware").

INTERBUILDING CABLE AND HARDWARE

A composite fiber cable consisting of 36 multimode and 12 single-mode fibers in an armored jacket should be installed in a minimum 4-inch duct between buildings. This includes 100-pair UTP cable (armored jacketed) to share the 4-inch duct with the fiber cable installed between buildings.

All cables should be installed with 10-foot service coils at all termination points and transition closets. Service loops may be stored on backboards, in unoccupied sections of the cable tray (see the Sidebar, "Cable Tray") or in conduit pull boxes. Do not store service loops in the fiber cable in the connector tray.

The contractor is responsible for the location of buried utilities, where applicable. These arrangements should be made prior to commencement of work. The contractor is also responsible for the restoration of the area under construction to its original condition or better. Where landscape property has been disturbed, the contractor should account for the restoration of grass, plants, walkways, and so on [UTOR, 6].

CABLE TRAY

Cable tray specified for telecommunications closets (see the Sidebar, "Telecommunications Closets") should be ladder-type cable tray, no less than 6 inches wide by 3.5 inches deep with 8-inch spacing between rungs. Only fittings such as sweeping 30-, 45-, 60-, and 90-degree elbows, tees, and crosses manufactured by the OEM are to be used to change direction. Use fittings of the smallest available bending radius in order to accommodate the bending radius of the backbone cabling. Butting two sections of tray together to create right angle turns is not acceptable. Any custom alterations to the tray must be approved by the PM prior to installation.

When the tray is running parallel to backboards, install it 4 inches off the backboard to allow passage of cables between the tray and the backboard. However, if the tray is adjacent to a wall, use right angle brackets or unistrut to support it.

In any case, when the tray is installed in free air to cross a closet, suspend it from the ceiling using a threaded rod. Also, when the tray is installed above a relay rack, use a threaded rod to support the tray 12 inches from the top of the rack where possible [UTOR, 6].

TELECOMMUNICATIONS CLOSETS

Telecommunication closets (TCs) should be constructed with full height walls using steel studs with minimum 5/8-inch drywall. All walls should be painted to match the existing color and finish. The use of any other color should be approved by the owner. All existing painted surfaces, including cement floors, should be freshly painted. All surfaces should have one coat of primer, one intermediate coat, and one or more finish coats of latex or oil-based paint.

Remove any existing carpet from new TCs and finish the floors as per above or the detailed scope of work. After that's finished, securely mount a 3/4-inch fire-rated plywood backboard. Mount the backboard on the new gypsum board wall or existing surface. The exact size and method of installation will be determined by the site conditions.

Use a switch-operated light to provide working illumination. The light fixture should be a 100W Vaptite VCXL11K or equivalent.

Use two separately fused 15A, 110V AC, isolated ground duplex electrical outlets with lock-on breakers. One should be wall mounted and the other secured to the top of the relay rack.

Use a solid core wood door that is painted to match other existing doors. Stain and finish where applicable. The door should be fitted with a lock set that matches existing locking hardware in the building. If matching lock sets are not available, then it is up to the contractor to confirm an acceptable alternative with the PM. The locking cylinders in the lock sets must be compatible with the master locking system. Three keys must be provided to the PM and, where more than one lock is installed in the same building, all lock cylinders must accept the same key. A project will not be considered substantially complete unless this condition is met. At no time should a lock set be installed that does not allow free exit from a room [UTOR, 3–4]. Finally, TCs should always have a telephone and air conditioning installed.

Cables and equipment should be supported and secured. Where the specific method of support is not shown in the scope of work, adequate supports and fasteners should be used to secure cables and equipment in position. Metallic supports and fasteners should have a corrosion-resistant finish. All cables and equipment installed in exterior locations should be secured so that they cannot be dislodged or damaged by winds up to 145 mph.

The code on wind damage resistance is actually 150 mph here in Florida, specifically Dade County. As more powerful hurricanes and tornados (F5s) hit heavily populated areas with greater frequency in the next 30 years because of global warming (it's still inconclusive), the code on wind damage resistance may actually have to be raised to well over 200 mph.

Caution should be used when bending cable to avoid kinks or other damage to the sheath. The bend radius should be as large as possible with a minimum not less than eight times the outside diameter of the cable. Minimum radius should be increased when necessary to meet the cable manufacturer's recommendations. Bending operations in manholes and vaults should be performed in accordance with the manufacturer's procedures and instructions. Cable bending shoes should be used at duct or conduit ends when bending cable exiting a duct or conduit. The bending shoes should remain in place until racking, splicing, and tying are completed. Cables should not rest against the edge of the duct or conduit mouth. Cable splices should not be made in ducts.

Assigned ducts and conduits should be cleaned and tested for alignment before pulling in cable. Pulled lines should be attached to cable ends fitted with any pulling device that will not damage the cable except where the device is attached. If the cable end is damaged during pulling, the damaged portion of the cable should be removed and discarded.

Cable reels should be located and aligned so that the cable is payed off the top of the reel into the duct or conduit in a long, smooth bend without twisting. Cable should not be pulled from the bottom of a reel or subjected to reverse bends from those formed by factory reeling. A cable-feeder guide of proper dimensions should be used at the mouth to guide the cable into the duct or conduit.

Rigging should be set up at the pulling end so that the pulling line and cable exit on a line parallel with the duct or conduit to prevent either from rubbing against the edge or mouth. Cable ends should not be pulled around sheave wheels.

All unterminated cables should be laid in the specified routing and location as indicated in the scope of work. The unterminated cable ends should be cleared, capped, and sealed.

Pulling lubricant should be compatible with and intended for use with plastic- and rubber-sheathed cables. Soap and grease lubricants are prohibited.

The cable should be carefully inspected for sheath defects or other irregularities as it is payed off the reel. If defects are detected, pulling should stop immediately and the cable section should be repaired or replaced.

Cable ends pulled into manholes, vaults, or terminal locations that are not to be racked or otherwise permanently positioned should immediately be tied in fixed positions to prevent damage to the cables and to provide adequate working space. After final racking and splicing, plastic-sheathed cables in manholes and vaults should be secured in place with lashed cable supports or with lashing shims. Cables in other locations should be secured in the manner indicated in the scope of work. When securing details are not indicated, the cables should be secured in a manner that will maintain the cables in the required position without damage to the cables. Also, ducts and conduits in which cables are placed should be sealed using duct seal or similar material.

All excavation should be performed as required to install the cables and equipment as indicated in the scope of work. Unless otherwise specified or indicated, direct-buried cables may be placed by either plowing, trenching, or boring and should be placed a minimum of 30 inches below grade. In addition, underground utilities in the path of cable burial operations should be located and exposed or the depth determined by hand digging.

Communications cables should not be installed in the same trench with electrical power cables. A minimum separation of 12 inches should be maintained between buried communications cables and power cables. Where buried communications cables must cross power cables, the communications cables should, where possible, be placed above the power cable. Creosoted wood or concrete separators should be placed between communications and power cables at crossover points.

Trenches should be wide enough for proper cable laying and backfilling. The bottom of the finished trench should be filled with no less than 3 inches of sand or fined soil that will not damage the cable sheath. Cables should be placed in the trench on top of the sand for cushion and stabilization of cable during trench backfill.

Trench backfilling should be accomplished by placing 3 inches of sand or fine soil over the cable and tamping it over and around the cable. The balance of backfilling should be accomplished in 6-inch layers, each layer being compacted to a density at least equal to that or the adjoining soil before the next layer is placed. Place "warning buried cable" tape 6 inches to 8 inches below final grade along the entire route. Topsoil and sod should be replaced and, as nearly as practical, restored to the original condition. Excavated materials not required or suited for backfilling should be disposed of as directed by the PM.

Cable-plowing operations should be in accordance with the operating procedures provided by the cable plow manufacturer and the requirements specified within this chapter. The plowing operations should be observed continuously to ensure that the cable is not damaged during placement and that proper depth is maintained.

Cable crossing under roadways or other pavement should be made by boring or jacking a pipe where practicable or specified. If it is necessary to break the pavement, permission should be obtained from the PM before proceeding. Immediately upon completion of the cable-sleeve placement, the roadway or other hardstand should be restored to the original condition. Furthermore, where buried cable enters the end of an underground pipe or conduit, ductseal or other suitable material should be packed between the cable and the inside of the sleeve end to prevent damage to the cable sheath and entrance of dirt into the sleeve.

Installation of Intrabuilding Cable within Buildings

The installation of intrabuilding cables consists of copper and fiber optic backbone cables that run between telecommunication closets within a building. Let's take a look at how this is done.

General

Care should be exercised when handling and storing reels of cable to prevent damage to the cable. Cable with dents, flat spots, or other sheath distortions should not be installed. Cable ends should be sealed until cables have been installed. Immediately after placement, a temporary tag with the cable number and cable type should be attached to each end of each cable section (see the Sidebars, "Intrabuilding Cable and Hardware" and "Workstation Cable Installation Specifications").

INTRABUILDING CABLE AND HARDWARE

Three separate byte information exchange (BIX) 10A fields with appropriate D-rings should be installed to support backbone equipment and horizontal cables, as shown in Figure 24–3. All BIX fields should be installed even if they are not used for immediate installation.

If more than one floor of horizontal cables terminate in the same TC, a separate BIX10A is required for each floor with drops from the higher floors terminating on the highest 10A frame. The horizontal BIX should be mounted adjacent to each other and in the order as shown in Figure 24–4.

BIX mounts should be labeled with colored designation labels; the horizontal field should be blue, the backbone field is green, and the equipment field is gray.

One 19-inch relay rack with 77 inches of usable space (44RU) rack bolted to the floor should be installed in each telecommunications closet. Rack layouts should include:

- One cable management bracket for every two 24-port fiber panels.
- One power bar (with internal breaker), mounted with the switch to the front and outlets.
- Six on the rear using only one rack space.
- Four 4 × 4-inch slotted wire duct, secured to the side of the rack.
- One shelf, mounted a minimum of 12 inches from the fiber panels. Leave seven rack spaces empty above the shelf.
- A minimum 6-inch-wide ladder-type tray with 8-inch spacing between rungs to support cables from the TC entry point to the termination locations.

All backbone copper and fiber interbuilding and intrabuilding cables should be installed with 10-foot service coils at all termination points and transition closets, as shown in Figure 24–5. The service loops may be stored on the backboard, in an inactive section of cable tray, or in the conduit pull box.

Pull string/rope should remain in all conduit upon completion of cable installation. Backbone and horizontal cable may coexist in the same conduit. However, all fiber cable must be in separate conduit from the copper type where two conduit paths have been installed [UTOR, 7].

WORKSTATION CABLE INSTALLATION SPECIFICATIONS

Requirements

Check for all installation requirements specifications needed in the area for workstation cabling placement (area access, people, asbestos, furniture, cable routes, and drawings).

Tools and Materials

Tools—cable ties, fastening system, crimping tools, splice tools, test equipment, cable marking systems, and all hand tools.

Materials—cable, jacks, tags, termination blocks, floor tombstones (hardware), molding, and cross-connect wire (see Sidebar, "List of Equipment Needed to Install a Cabling System in a School").

Set up Reels

Set up your reels near or in the wiring closet. Alternatively, select a location midway between the wiring closet and the termination point.

Label the Cables

Label each cable reel and its free end according to the termination locations marked on your canvas drawings and work orders. Label each pigtail (25-pair) cable from the concentrator to the 110 blocks with LJ and the number of the block.

Pull Cables into Place

Deliver the cable from the bottom of each reel, making sure not to kink, crush, or pinch the cable. Pull groups of cables to a logical point and then fan out to the individual termination points. Separate the telecommunication cables from other cables by at least 6 inches and avoid sharp edges, tight bends that would subject the cable to abrasion, or moisture.

Remove Slack

Remove slack in the lines by pulling the cables back to the wiring closet.

Label and Cut

Label each cable and then cut it off, making sure to leave enough cable to reach the termination block.

Tie Cable Together

Use cable ties to bundle and secure parallel runs together. Place the ties at intervals sufficient to prevent sagging and to maintain neatness. Distances between ties may vary from 6 inches to 4 feet, depending on the size of the cables.

Strap the Cables

Use straps to fasten the cable bundles to the hanger at 4 feet or other appropriate intervals, if supplied. The distance between hangers can vary from 3 to 20 feet, depending on the surface and the type and number of cables in each bundle. Do not support cables on pipes, conduits, or other structures in the building plenum.

Inspect the Job

Make sure that the cables are not resting on or near electrical fixtures or sagging more than 7 inches from point of tie.

Do Not Exceed the Minimum Bend Radius

The minimum bend radius of a cable must never be exceeded. The bend radius should not be less than eight times the outside diameter of the cable. For category 5 cables, the cables may not be bent beyond a radius of 1.25 inches.

Do Not Overcinch the Cables

- Overcinching the cable (with cable ties and cords) can cause compression of the cable jacket. It can deform the cable and cause the same effects as overbending and kinking the cable.
- Use Velcro straps, nail-on cable clamps, and D-rings to support and position cable jackets to keep them from becoming compressed.
- Cable bundles must be installed carefully. Cables inside the bundles can be damaged as easily as cables on the outside can.

Never Untwist the Pairs of a Category 5 Cable Beyond 0.5 Inches from the Point of Termination

Maintaining cable pair twist is absolutely critical to cable performance. The cable jacket or outer sheath should be intact as close to the termination as possible. Remove only the amount of the cable jacket that is necessary for termination.

Never Run Cable Longer Than the Maximum Recommended Length

Category 3 through 5 cables require a maximum of 100 meters (328 feet).

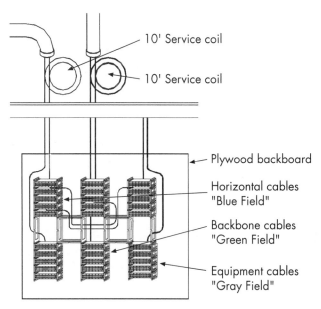

Figure 24–3   BIX10A fields with appropriate D-rings.

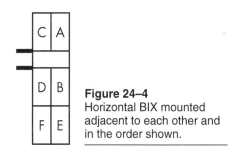

Figure 24–4
Horizontal BIX mounted
adjacent to each other and
in the order shown.

Cables and equipment should also be supported and secured. Where the specific method of support is not indicated, adequate supports and fasteners should be used to secure cables and equipment in position. Metallic supports and fasteners should have a corrosion-resistant finish.

Cables should be provided in continuous lengths as required to accomplish the required installation without splices from termination. The exception would be where field splices are specifically required and approved in advance.

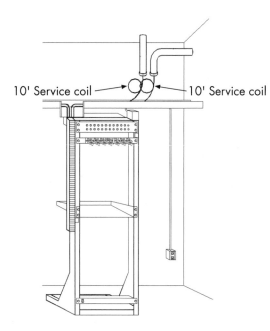

10' Service coil ————▶   ◀———— 10' Service coil

Figure 24–5
Backbone copper and
fiber interbuilding and
intrabuilding cables are
installed with 10-foot
service coils at all ter-
mination points and
transition closets.

Raised Floors and Cable Trays

Instrumentation and communications cables should not be installed in the
same tray with AC power cables. Cables placed in cable trays or under raised
floors should be installed in a neat and orderly manner and should not cross
or interlace other cables except at breakout points. Instrumentation and communication cables should be routed under raised floors as indicated in the
scope of work. The installation of cables under raised-floor areas should be
closely coordinated with existing cables and utilities in these areas. The new
cables should be routed as required to avoid interference with existing utilities in the raised-floor area. All cables routed under false floors should be
routed parallel to cabinet or rack bay fronts and walls and under corridor
areas created by racks and equipment. Unterminated cable ends should be
cleared, capped, and sealed. No lengths of coiled cable should be left under
raised-floor areas unless specifically approved by the PM. Cables in vertical
trays should be retained by use of plastic or nylon straps on 6-foot maximum
centers for each cable or cable group.

Boxes, Enclosures, and Distribution Frames

Each conductor of each cable should be terminated on terminal blocks or on
connectors except where specifically approved in advance by the PM for
future use or where the cable is indicated to be coiled cable. The termination

procedure for any cable within a distributor or other wiring enclosure should not be started until all cables have been pulled into the enclosure. The installation of harness assemblies should not be started until the completion of the termination of the applicable incoming cables.

Where cables are pulled into previously installed distributors, the existing hardware should be protected against damage. Any damage to the existing hardware should be repaired in an approved manner.

Cables, conductors, and shields should be terminated in accordance with the manufacturer's specifications. Terminals and connectors should be installed using only tools specifically recommended by the hardware manufacturer and should be of the type that requires a specific force to perform the crimp. The installation procedure should follow the manufacturer's installation directions.

Groups of conductors should be bound by means of plastic fasteners and equal to self-locking Ty-Rap ties. These fasteners should be placed along the main harness and cable and adjacent to each conductor, leaving the bundle at the breakout point.

Cables should be supported as near to the termination point as possible to prevent any strain, which is due to the weight of the cable, from being transmitted to the individual conductors where they are connected to terminal blocks or to connector terminations. In terminal distributors, all of the cables and cable-harness assemblies should be supported horizontally to their respective terminal-block mounting channel. Care should be taken not to have any of the cable shields or the conductor shields grounded to the terminal distributor frame, especially at the points of cable supports. Cables that have overall shields or individual terminal blocks should have the terminal-block mounting channel adequately insulated with insulating tape to maintain the isolation of the shields from a ground.

Installing Equipment Cable

Equipment cable wiring should provide a connection between the cross-connect and the active equipment that will be mounted in the rack, as shown in Figure 24–6 [UTOR, 8}. The cables should be run in units of 25 pairs. Each 25 pair should connect no more than 12 end stations. Equipment cables should have a 50-pin male connector at the rack and punched down on a BIX 1A4 in a 10A mounted on the backboard. The performance of the equipment cable should equal the specification of category 5 cable. Unless otherwise specified, the number of cables provided should be the estimated number of users divided by 12.

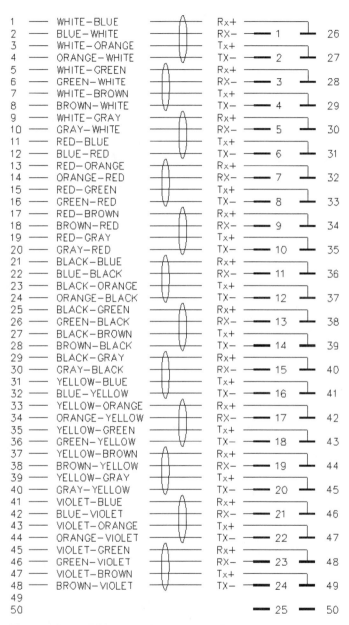

1 —— WHITE–BLUE	Rx+	
2 —— BLUE–WHITE	RX– —— 1 —— 26	
3 —— WHITE–ORANGE	Tx+	
4 —— ORANGE–WHITE	TX– —— 2 —— 27	
5 —— WHITE–GREEN	Rx+	
6 —— GREEN–WHITE	RX– —— 3 —— 28	
7 —— WHITE–BROWN	Tx+	
8 —— BROWN–WHITE	TX– —— 4 —— 29	
9 —— WHITE–GRAY	Rx+	
10 —— GRAY–WHITE	RX– —— 5 —— 30	
11 —— RED–BLUE	Tx+	
12 —— BLUE–RED	TX– —— 6 —— 31	
13 —— RED–ORANGE	Rx+	
14 —— ORANGE–RED	RX– —— 7 —— 32	
15 —— RED–GREEN	Tx+	
16 —— GREEN–RED	TX– —— 8 —— 33	
17 —— RED–BROWN	Rx+	
18 —— BROWN–RED	RX– —— 9 —— 34	
19 —— RED–GRAY	Tx+	
20 —— GRAY–RED	TX– —— 10 —— 35	
21 —— BLACK–BLUE	Rx+	
22 —— BLUE–BLACK	RX– —— 11 —— 36	
23 —— BLACK–ORANGE	Tx+	
24 —— ORANGE–BLACK	TX– —— 12 —— 37	
25 —— BLACK–GREEN	Rx+	
26 —— GREEN–BLACK	RX– —— 13 —— 38	
27 —— BLACK–BROWN	Tx+	
28 —— BROWN–BLACK	TX– —— 14 —— 39	
29 —— BLACK–GRAY	Rx+	
30 —— GRAY–BLACK	RX– —— 15 —— 40	
31 —— YELLOW–BLUE	Tx+	
32 —— BLUE–YELLOW	TX– —— 16 —— 41	
33 —— YELLOW–ORANGE	Rx+	
34 —— ORANGE–YELLOW	RX– —— 17 —— 42	
35 —— YELLOW–GREEN	Tx+	
36 —— GREEN–YELLOW	TX– —— 18 —— 43	
37 —— YELLOW–BROWN	Rx+	
38 —— BROWN–YELLOW	RX– —— 19 —— 44	
39 —— YELLOW–GRAY	Tx+	
40 —— GRAY–YELLOW	TX– —— 20 —— 45	
41 —— VIOLET–BLUE	Rx+	
42 —— BLUE–VIOLET	RX– —— 21 —— 46	
43 —— VIOLET–ORANGE	Tx+	
44 —— ORANGE–VIOLET	TX– —— 22 —— 47	
45 —— VIOLET–GREEN	Rx+	
46 —— GREEN–VIOLET	RX– —— 23 —— 48	
47 —— VIOLET–BROWN	Tx+	
48 —— BROWN–VIOLET	TX– —— 24 —— 49	
49		
50	—— 25 —— 50	

Figure 24–6   BIX1A4 equipment cable RJ71.

EIA/TIA specifications for installation wiring practices require that cables of the given performance category (category 3) be terminated with connecting hardware of the same category or higher. Termination practices has three main parameters used to characterize connector transmission performance, attenuation, near-end cross talk (NEXT), and return loss. These parameters are sensitive to transmission discontinuities caused by connector terminations. NEXT performance is particularly susceptible to conductor untwisting and other poor installation practices that disturb pair balance and cause impedance variations. Also, improper termination practices may also create loop antenna effects, which result in levels of signal radiation that may exceed regulatory emission requirements.

Installing Horizontal Cabling and Hardware

The horizontal distribution cable is the copper or fiber optic cable that runs between the workstation outlet and the termination field in the telecommunications closet. NT IBDN-Plus category 5 UTP 4-pair cables should be installed from the horizontal BIX frames in the TCs through the horizontal conduit infrastructure to the outlet location. When specified, the fiber cable should be a 4-strand MIC cable.

Drop cables may share the riser conduits when installation occurs between floors. When there is a choice, these drop cables should always be installed in the riser conduit that accommodates the corresponding media type (copper with copper, fiber with fiber).

One-inch conduit should be used between the junction boxes on the horizontal distribution conduits and the user outlet boxes, as shown in Figure 24–7 [UTOR, 8]. In many cases the conduit should be run down the surface of the wall to a custom surface mount outlet box designed to accept an NT-MDVO flush-mount face plate installed on the side of the box. NT-MDVO face plates using 8-position modules (a module with 8 positions) should be installed in the face plate and configured as shown in Figure 24–8 [UTOR, 8].

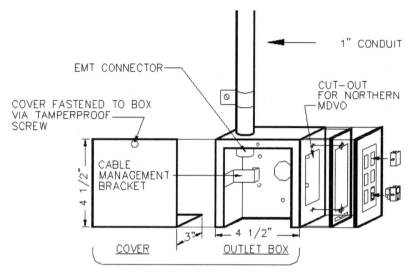

Figure 24–7   One-inch conduit should be used between the junction boxes on the horizontal distribution conduits and the user outlet boxes.

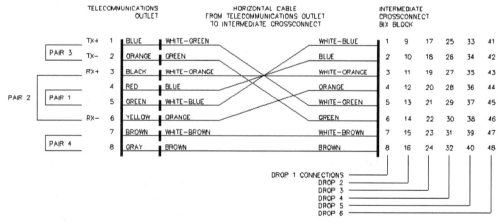

Figure 24–8   NT-MDVO face plates using 8-position modules.

Outlet Placement

Standard outlet height when boxes are installed on a wall is 12 inches from the floor. Conduit or boxes are not to obstruct the function of any adjacent fixtures.

When outlets are mounted on the floor, the outlet box should be mounted on its widest surface so that the faceplate is on the side of the box

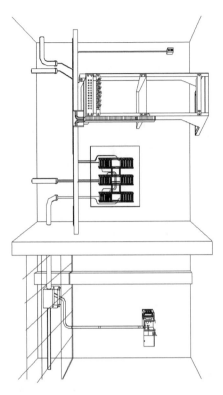

Figure 24–9
Architectural detail of
outlet placement.

and the cover plate is able to be opened. Any architectural detail such as elaborate baseboards or outlets mounted at counter level in labs (see Figure 24–9) should be addressed by the contractor prior to installing the outlet box if it is not addressed in the detailed scope of work [UTOR, 9]. District schools or universities usually reserve the right to relocate any telecommunications outlet by up to 3 meters without penalty before installation is complete.

Cable Plant Sectioning

The sectioning of an individual coaxial cable segment (a coaxial cable segment made up of several pieces of 50-ohm cable interconnected by N-type barrel connectors) may be accomplished in several ways, but care must be taken in doing so. See the Sidebar, "Coaxial Cable Installation," for further information on the installation procedures for that type of cable.

The joining of two cable sections by two N-type male connectors and a barrel connector creates a signal reflection point where some of the signal may be reflected back to the sender and lost. This reflection is due to an impedance mismatch caused by the batch-to-batch impedance tolerance of the cable during manufacturing. The tolerance of the baseband trunk cable is 50 ohms ± 2 ohms. Therefore, a worst-case mismatch would mate a 48-ohm cable to a 52-ohm cable resulting in a 4-ohm mismatch, where 4 percent of the signal would be reflected back to the sender and lost.

COAXIAL CABLE INSTALLATION

Structural supports for coaxial cables should be installed straight and plumb. In addition, coaxial cables should be supported securely at bulkhead plates and terminal distributors.

Coaxial cable runs should also be continuous from termination to termination wherever possible. Coaxial cables should be terminated and appropriate high-quality connectors should be attached using the cable manufacturer's recommended procedures, which should be considered a part of the specification. Furthermore, the contractor should follow the cable manufacturer's published terminating procedures.

Coaxial cables should be attached to supports appropriately secured with fasteners specifically designed for this purpose. Strapping material should be Wraplock or equal. Cables should be attached to supports at intervals not exceeding 5 feet, except where prior approval has been granted by the PM.

The bending radius of coaxial cable should not be less than the manufacturer's published minimum bend radius under any circumstances. If a bend is required in a large diameter cable, an approved pipe-bending device should be used to form the cable. There should be no evidence of any wrinkling of outer conductor of cable or cable sheath.

All moisture should be removed from the coaxial cable connections prior to splice closure. Boiling-paraffin methods should not be used.

On indoor connections, approved shrink tubing or insulating tape (insulating tape is seldom used anymore) should be applied. If shrink tubing is not available, tape should be applied an additional half-lap to completely cover all exposed metal portions of the coaxial cable and connector after the connector has been installed in place and connected to the terminating piece of equipment. Each connection should be sleeved using an appropriate size of heat-shrinkable tubing to accommodate the cable jacket and connectors used and to completely encapsulate the connection.

On outdoor connections, after the connectors are joined, a silicone lubricant or an equivalent should be applied to cover the complete surface of the connectors. Coverage should be a minimum of 2 inches on each side of the connector hubs where the cable rating occurs. Excess silicone lubricant should be wiped clean from the outer surface of the cable jacket after installation.

Heat-shrinkable tubing should be Raychez Type TCS, WCS, WRS, or an approved equal. Heat-shrinkable tubing should be installed in accordance with the manufacturer's specifications. Finally, appropriate grounding kits provided by the manufacturer of the coaxial cable should be installed in accordance with the manufacturer's specifications and as indicated.

Ethernet IEEE 802.3 Specification

If possible, the total coaxial cable segment should be made from one homogeneous (no breaks) cable. This is feasible for short segments, and results in minimal reflections from cable impedance discontinuities.

If cable segments are built up from smaller sections, it is recommended that all sections come from the same manufacturer and lot. This is equivalent to using a single cable, since the cable discontinuities are due to extruder limitations, and not extruder-to-extruder tolerances. There are no restrictions in cable sectioning if this method is used. However, if a cable section in such a system is later replaced, it should be replaced either with another cable from the same manufacturer and lot, or with one of the standard lengths described next.

If uncontrolled cable sections should be used in building up a longer segment, the lengths should be chosen so that reflections, when they occur, do not have a high probability of adding in phase. This can be accomplished by using lengths that are odd integral multiples of a half wavelength in the cable at 5 MHz. This corresponds to using lengths of 23.4 m, 70.2 m, and 117 m ($\pm$ 0.5 m) for all sections. These are considered to be the standard lengths for all cable sections. Using these lengths exclusively, any mix or match of cable sections may be used to build up a 500-meter segment without incurring excessive reflections.

As a last resort, an arbitrary configuration of cable sections may be employed, if it has been confirmed by analysis or measurement that the worst-case signal reflection due to the impedance discontinuities at any point on the cable does not exceed 7 percent of the incident wave when driven by an MAU meeting these specifications.

Installation Procedures for 10Base5 Cable

Install cable using the previously stated guidelines from the IEEE 802.3 specification. Also, avoid routing the 10Base5 cable parallel to high voltage or RF signal sources.

Install MAUs directly on annular rings only. Do not install MAUs between the annular rings. Furthermore, install splices (N-type barrel connectors) on annular rings. Also, any open cores in the cable, such as when an MAU has been removed, should be filled with a clear rubber compound known as RTV (room-temperature vulcanization) and taped.

Room-temperature vulcanization is chemists' terminology for a rubber compound that cures and solidifies when it is exposed to room temperature and moisture. These silicones exhibit high adhesion, flexibility, and resistance to moisture. If you need weather and moisture resistance, as well as a caulk that adheres well to aluminum, glass, or porcelain surfaces, RTV silicone is a good choice. Although the product sounds exotic, it's not. You can get RTV silicone caulk at home centers, hardware stores, and paint stores.

Ground one end of the 10Base5 cable using a 5-ohm or less ground. Ground should be accomplished with a ground clamp and #6 copper solid conductor wire. In no instances should the cable be grounded in more than one location.

Cable, when installed, should be supported every 5 to 10 feet. On an annular ring where an MAU has been installed, the cable should be supported within 1 foot of either side of the MAU. Attachment unit interface (AUI) cables should be supported by Ty-Rap within 1 foot of its connection to the MAU. AUI cables should be installed with shields on both ends.

Cable Splicing

Cables should be spliced in accordance with the manufacturer's approved procedures and as specified herein. Unless otherwise indicated, all requirements, procedures, and constraints in the manufacturer's approved procedures should be adhered to.

Connectors should remain in their correct color groups or units except when required for defective pair transpositions. All cable segments, including all pairs of wire, should be interconnected with #m type 4000 DWP pluggable connectors.

All building entry cables must have a transition splice and use lighting protection protector blocks and gas tube protector modules. Use the specified 22 or 24 AWG cable. All protection blocks must be grounded with #6 solid insulated ground wire.

Labeling

The installers should label all wires in the cabling system according to a logical and clear code. If possible, they should incorporate any existing building space designations into the code. They should place this code on the physical cabling system in three places: on both ends of each wire and somewhere in the base plate box to which the wire is connected. Copies of this wiring code should be deposited with the school district or university central office, with the office responsible for the building affected, and with those in charge of maintenance.

Drawing Identifiers

There should be a legend on all drawings to show building and floor number. All drawings should be referenced as data plans (DP).

Each drawing will be prefixed with DPbbbbff, where *DP* is the data plan, *bbbb* is the building number, and *ff* is the floor number. For example, DP-bbbb-ff converts to DP-0123-02.

Building and Floor Identifiers

School district or university campus buildings can be identified by using the following format: A three-digit number preceded by either an 0 or A. For example, 0123 or A123. Thus, the building ID exists in the legend, in the title block, and the file name.

All floors in buildings could be identified by two digits, as shown in the example in Table 24–1:

Table 24–1   Floor Identifiers

01..99	Floors above ground, including ground
GR	Ground floor when not identified as Floor 1
1B	1st basement, where there is only one basement it will be refereed to as 1st basement or basement
2B	2nd basement
3B	3rd basement
MZ	Mezzanine

Telecommunications Closets

All telecommunication closets can be identified as TCccC, where *TC* is telecommunication closet, *cc* is floor identifier, and *C* is alpha identifier. Unique per floor: *bbbb* is the building number. For example: bbbb-TC-cc-C converts to 0123-TC-02-A. This example represents the label on the inside of the active door at eye level of the TC.

Zone Identifiers

Each floor should be divided into zones based on the architectural plans of the building. The zone is described by the lowest value of the two ordinal sets that define the boundary of the zone. For example, *ZZ* is alpha coordinances and *NN* is the numeric coordinance, where ZZNN converts to 0C03 or AA10.

Cable Identifiers

All cable identifiers should be based on a continuous sequence beginning at 1 and counting consecutively. Each series should be unique within the building floor and serving closet. This should be a three-position number, zero filled and left justified. The complete cable identifier should include the building, floor number, zone, cable number, and telecommunications closet where *bbbb* is building, *ff* is floor, *ZZNN* is zone, *nnn* is cable number, and *ccC* is closet. For example, bbbb-ff-ZZNN-nnn-ccC converts to 0123-01-DD03-01-C02A.

Cable Label

The label as it will appear on the cable 1/2-inch back from where the jacket is removed consists of *ZZNN* for zone, *nnn* for cable number, and *ccC* for closet. For example, ZZNN-nnn-ccC converts to 0C03-001-02A or AA10-001-02A.

BIX Panel Label

The BIX wafer should be mounted on a BIX panel unique to the floor being served by that cable.

Cables that run from different floors should be terminated on separate BIX panels within the same closet. Each floor should have its own BIX panel within a telecommunications closet, which will be identified and labeled by floor number. Therefore, the labels used must be able to stick to a plywood backboard.

The standard label should be affixed to a mounting strip mounted on the backboard, where *ff* is floor. For example, ff converts to 01 or 0D.

The label for each cable position as it will appear on the BIX wafer consists of *ZZNN* for zone and *nnn* for cable number. For example, ZZNN-nnn converts to 0C03-001 or AA10-001.

Outlet Box Identifier

The identifier for the outlet box should follow the form *bbbb* is building, *OB* is outlet box, *ff* is floor, *ZZNN* is zone, and *nn* is outlet box number. For example, bbbb-OB-ff-ZZNN-nn converts to 0123-OB-02-AA10-01.

Outlet Box Label

The label should be on the upper front corner on the opposite side of the data connectors. A second label should be placed on the inside of the data outlet box on the bottom surface. If there is a black outlet box, a blank white label needs to be placed under the clear label. For example, OB-nn converts to OB-01.

Jack Identifier

The jack identifier should follow the form where *bbbb* is building, *ff* is floor, *ZZNN* is zone, *nnn* is number, and *ccC* is closet. For example, bbbb-ff-ZZNN-nnn-ccC converts to 0123-02-0C03-00-102A.

Jack Label

The label should be placed on the cover of the plate facing out. The label for the first outlet should be at the top and the second should be below. The jack label should follow the form where *nnn* is number and *ccC* is closet. For example, nnn-ccC converts to 001-02A.

Pull Box Identifiers

The identification for the pull box should be PBffZZNNnn, where *PB* is the pull box, *ff* is the floor, *ZZNN* is the zone, and *nn* is the pull box number within the zone. For example, bbbb-PB-ff-ZZNN-nn converts to 0123-PB02-0C03-01.

Pull Box Label

When the pull box is above a drop ceiling, a second label must be placed on the T-bar ceiling. The label for the pull box should be LAT 28-409-25SH or equivalent.

This is a full 8½" x 11" black-on-white label sheet that must be cut into eight 2½" x 4¼" sections. Avery label catalog # 5163, which is 4" x 2", is a suitable alternative.

For example, PB-02-0C03-01 UTCC, 2½" high by 4½" wide.

Riser Cable Identifier

The identifier for the riser cables should be of the form where *bbbb* is the building, *F* is the fiber cable type, *C* is the copper cable type, *ccC* is the near closet, *ccC* is also the far closet, and *nn* is the cable number. For example, bbbb-FccCccCnn converts to 0123-F02A03A01 and bbbb-CccCccCnn converts to 0123-C02A03A01.

Riser Cable Label

The label for the riser cable should be TccCccCnn, where T is the cable type identifier, F is the fiber cable, C is the copper cable, ccC is the telecommunications closet for one end of the cable, and ccC is the telecommunications closet for the other end of the cable. Fix the label 1/2-inch from where the jacket is stripped back. The telecommunications closet should always be read from left to right and lowest to highest. For example, T-ccC-ccC-nn converts to F-02A-03A-01 or to C-02A-03A-01.

Equipment Cable Label

The equipment cable label should be fixed to the cable 1/2-inch back from where the jacket is stripped back. It should follow the form where T-ccC-nn converts to F-02A-01 or C-02A-01.

Electrical Outlet, Breaker Label, and Duplex Outlet

The locations of the electrical outlets in the TC and breakers in the panel must be cross-referenced through labeling. The breaker label must indicate that it is a circuit with the TC number and the room number. The duplex outlet must be labeled to indicate the electrical room and electrical panel number and the breaker number.

INSTALLING A LOCAL AREA NETWORK

Each building in a school district or university campus should have a separate LAN, allowing each room in a building to be connected with all the others using a high-speed cabling system. As previously discussed, there are many ways to connect the building, using different types and brands of equipment. Although each brand offers slightly different features, most will sell the same basic pieces of equipment. This part of the chapter discusses most of the common types of equipment in detail. If it does not discuss your piece of equipment, or if the school district or university is unsure which type to use, do not hesitate to speak with a vendor about what products fit the school district or university's needs. Although vendors will often try to sell their brand, they can usually offer good advice as well.

Network Cabling Installation Choices

The school district or university should make a decision about what physical protocol to use. Currently, there are several in use, although Ethernet is the most popular. Others include token ring, FDDI, ATM, and LocalTalk. Each protocol is capable of a different maximum data speed known as the bandwidth, and costs do differ. Table 24–2 summarizes all of this information

[Lamont, 4]. Looking at the OSI model in Figure 24–10, all of these protocols except ATM exist at the bottom two layers, the Physical and Data Link layers. ATM exists at those layers as well as at the network level [Lamont, 4].

Table 24–2 A Comparison of the Different LAN Technologies

Protocol	Wiring	Maximum Bandwidth	Maximum Length	Topology	Cost
Ethernet	Category 5 twisted pair	10 Mbps	100 meters	Star	Low
	Thick	10 Mbps	500 meters	Bus	High
	Coaxial cable	10 Mbps	200 meters	Bus	Low
	Fiber	10 Mbps	1,000 meters	Star	Very high
Fast Ethernet	Category 5 twisted pair	100 Mbps	100 meters	Star	High
Token ring	Coaxial cable	16 Mbps	100 meters	Ring	High
FDDI	Fiber	100 Mbps	1,000 meters	Star	Very high
CDDI	Category 5 twisted pair	100 Mbps	100 meters	Star	Very high
LocalTalk	Category 3 twisted pair	230 Kbps	300 meters	Bus	Very low
ATM	Fiber	1 Gbps	100 meters	Star	Very high

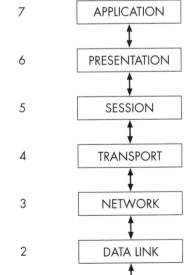

LAYER

7	APPLICATION
6	PRESENTATION
5	SESSION
4	TRANSPORT
3	NETWORK
2	DATA LINK
1	PHYSICAL

Figure 24–10
OSI model.

Ethernet

Ethernet is an industry standard protocol operating at 10 Mbps that is currently in wide use. The protocol uses a principle called carrier sense multiple access/collision detection (CSMA/CD), which has two important parts. The first is that it is a multiple access protocol allowing all the machines to share the same physical wiring instead of requiring separate wiring for each machine (except in the case of a star topology). The second is that it operates on collision detection. Since many machines share the wire, two machines may try to use it at the same time. This condition is called a collision. The network hardware detects the collision and aborts the transmission. After a small random delay, the hardware tries to transmit again. The result of this protocol is that on very busy networks with many machines, a large number of collisions can occur, wasting a significant amount of time retransmitting information. This is why there is a recommended limit of 25 to 30 machines on a single Ethernet network.

Cabling that uses the Ethernet protocol comes in four different physical varieties: thick, thin, twisted pair, and fiber optic. Thick Ethernet, also known as 10Base5, is the original wiring used for Ethernet, connected in a bus topology. It is the second most expensive of the four types, but also has the second longest maximum distance, 500 meters. It is not often used today because of the cheaper alternatives. Thin Ethernet, also known as 10Base2, coax, or cheapernet, is also a bus topology. It runs on 50-ohm coaxial cable and often connects small networks. It suffers from problems previously discussed under bus topologies in earlier chapters, and the Ethernet specifications limit its maximum length to 200 meters. Twisted pair Ethernet, also known as 10BaseT, runs over category 3 phone wiring or better. It connects in a star topology, although it shares the same CSMA/CD protocol as the other Ethernet varieties. It has a maximum length of 100 meters. Fiber Ethernet, also known as 10BaseFL, is not normally used except to connect hubs over long distances. Its maximum distance of 1,000 meters makes it ideally suited for this type of job.

To avoid problems with the actual electrical signal that propagates across the Ethernet wiring, the 3-4-5 rule exists. It states that between any two machines on the Ethernet network, there must be at most five wiring segments, four repeaters connecting the segments, and only three of those segments can have workstations connected to them. A school district or university will violate this rule most often when a repeater connects a workstation that is beyond the distance limit for the network, or when classrooms have their own hubs.

Fast Ethernet

Fast Ethernet is an enhancement of Ethernet that runs at speeds of 100 Mbps, 10 times the rate of original Ethernet. Known also as 100BaseT, it requires that the wiring it runs over be category 5 wiring—a higher quality than the category 3 used by normal Ethernet. The equipment needed to use Fast Ethernet is also more expensive than normal Ethernet. Although the prices are dropping, it is most likely too expensive for schools to install initially. Like 10BaseT, it connects as a star topology and has a 100-meter maximum length restriction. This allows a district using category 5 wiring to begin with 10BaseT and later upgrade to 100BaseT without replacing the wiring.

Token Ring

IBM developed token ring. It is a carrier sense multiple access/collision avoidance protocol. It passes a theoretical token around the network. Only while a machine has the token can it send information. Since there is only one token, it prevents two machines from broadcasting at the same time. It operates at both 4 and 16 Mbps. Token ring is not widely used because the performance increase does not outweigh the difficulties and prices required when installing a ring topology.

FDDI/CDDI

Fiber distributed data interconnect (FDDI) is a 100 Mbps fiber optic-based network. Like most other technologies based on fiber, it requires two fiber cables, one for transmitting and one for receiving. The cost of fiber cables makes this choice significantly more expensive than using Ethernet. Its advantage is the higher speeds it offers, although with the availability of Fast Ethernet, this is not a significant factor. Ordinarily, FDDI creates a fiber backbone that connects to all of the hubs in a large building or campus. Copper distributed data interconnect (CDDI) is a proprietary variation of FDDI that runs over category 5 twisted pair.

ATM

Asynchronous transfer mode (ATM) is a new technology that is in transition from the research lab to commercial use. It offers speeds beginning at 45 Mbps and can increase to even higher speeds. It runs over category 5 twisted pair and fiber optic cables. In the future, as it becomes more available and prices drop, it will become a viable upgrade option.

LocalTalk

LocalTalk is the original network hardware that Apple Computer shipped with its Macintosh and Apple II series computers. It is not the same as

Appletalk, the network protocol used over any physical network. LocalTalk has a maximum speed of 230 Kbps—significantly slower than any of the other protocols. It is a bus topology with a maximum distance of 300 meters. Using Phonenet equipment, it can run over standard category 3 phone wiring. With its speed limitations, it is not recommended for use in any schools unless it's already installed—and, even then, a district or university should consider an upgrade.

Figure 24–11 shows a comparison of the bandwidths offered by the different protocols, as well as different WAN technologies discussed in the next part of the chapter [Lamont, 6]. The figure is logarithmic and each horizontal label is 10 times faster than the one to it's left.

To allow for future growth to higher speeds, the Electronics Industry Association/Telephone Industry Association (EIA/TIA) has recommended the use of only category 5 wiring in all installations because of its capability to run at higher speeds than category 3. As previously mentioned, this will support future upgrades to Fast Ethernet or ATM.

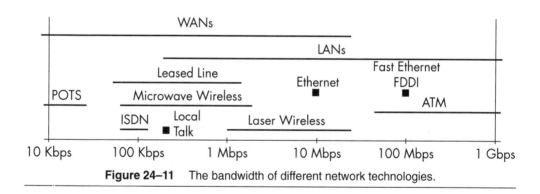

Figure 24–11   The bandwidth of different network technologies.

Equipment Needed on a Workstation

Once a school district or university decides on the cabling system's physical installation, they will need to consider what equipment is necessary to connect all the workstations in the building to the network. Workstation is another term for a networked computer, whether the computer is a Macintosh, a Windows machine, or any other type of computer. This will normally require a network interface card (NIC) for each machine, although some new machines are now shipping with the network card built into the computer. Depending on the choice of cabling system, the school district or university will need to buy the card with the correct connector—either a coax, RJ45, attachment unit interface (AUI), or fiber.

If a school district or university is using Ethernet (the most likely implementation), they will have many choices. Since Ethernet comes in several varieties, some Ethernet cards, often called combo cards, come with two or three connectors, as shown in Figure 24–12 [Lamont, 6]. If a school is currently using one variety and is planning to upgrade to another, then combo cards can save money. If the cabling system is going to be exclusively twisted pair, then there is no reason to spend the extra money on a combo card with unused capabilities. Another option that is appearing is combo 10/100 Ethernet cards that can run on 10BaseT and 100BaseT networks. The school district or university should consider how quickly it will upgrade other parts of the network to support Fast Ethernet before investing in these cards.

The AUI connector on an Ethernet card allows easier expansion on the card. Devices (called transceivers or media access units [MAUs]) that offer a connection to all four of the different types of networks can be connected to it. Although this sounds redundant with regard to combo cards, AUI can be

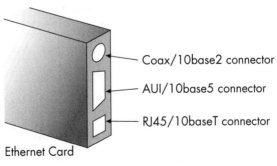

Coax/10base2 connector

AUI/10base5 connector

RJ45/10baseT connector

Ethernet Card

Figure 24–12   The connectors on an Ethernet combo card.

useful if the card does not have an RJ45 connector and the school is upgrading to 10BaseT. Similar in function, although incompatible in size and shape, Apple attachment unit interface (AAUI) connectors exist on the motherboards of most Macintosh models currently available. Be sure to buy the correct AUI or AAUI connectors when buying the network cards. Finally, do not forget to buy the necessary cabling to connect the network card if it does not include cabling already.

Cabling Equipment

Equipment used to create the cabling system infrastructure falls into two categories: passive devices and active devices. Passive devices do not usually affect the capabilities of the cabling system and make the installation or maintenance of the cabling system easier. These devices include patch panels, patch cables, fiber boxes, and fiber jumper cables. Active devices connect the different workstations and other active devices on the network. They include repeaters, bridges, switches, and routers. The next part of this chapter discusses them in detail. A typical cabling system will look similar to Figure 24–13 [Lamont, 7]. Table 24–3 contains a summary of all the cabling system equipment [Lamont, 9–10].

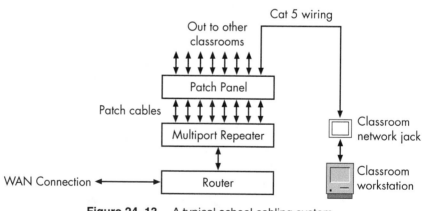

Figure 24–13   A typical school cabling system.

Table 24–3 Uses of Different LAN Equipment

Equipment	Use	OSI Layer
Patch panels	Reduce stress on wiring by having all room wiring permanently connected to the back	Physical
Patch cables	Short cables used to connect the patch panel to the hub and computers to the wall drop	Physical
Fiber box	Reduce stress on wiring by having all room wiring permanently connected	Physical
Fiber cables	Short fiber cables used to connect the fiber box to the hub	Physical
Repeaters	Used to extend the distance wiring can be run	Physical
Multiport repeaters	Used as a hub to connect many machines together	Physical
Switch	Used as a hub to connect many machines together and only transmits packets on the destination port	Physical and Data Link
Bridge	Used to connect different hardware protocols or wiring types	Data Link
Router	Used to direct traffic across a WAN to its final destination; a router is an intelligent device that supports connectivity between both like and disparate LANs via MANs and WANs	Network
GatorStar/GatorBox	Used to bridge LocalTalk and Ethernet networks	Physical, Data Link, and Network
MacLAN Patch panel	Connects to the LocalTalk networks and the GatorStar	Physical
EtherPrint boxes	Used to connect one or two LocalTalk devices such as printers to an Ethernet network	Physical, Data Link, and Network

Patch Panels

All of the wiring that comes from the classrooms needs to connect to the hub. A patch panel is often used as an intermediary. All the wiring is punched down or attached to the back of the patch. The front is made up of RJ45 connectors into which patch cables connect. This prevents any damage to the room wires, since changes do not require the modification of the room wires.

Patch Cables

Patch cables, or jumper cables, connect the patch panel to the hubs, connect workstations to the wall jacks, or connect multiple hubs. This allows the network administrator to easily reconfigure the network since all that needs to be modified are the jacks the patch cable connects. The first two types of connections require a straight-through cable. The third requires a crossover cable.

Figure 24–14 shows the difference between the two types of cables [Lamont, 8]. The different cables are needed because of the way twisted pair cables connect. One pair of wiring transmits information from one machine to another, and a second pair transmits information in the reverse direction. A hub reverses the wiring from a workstation, allowing the lines to match up correctly and straight through to the cabling system. However, when connecting two hubs, the wiring in both is reversed and so both would attempt to transmit on the same pair and to receive on the same pair, thus causing them to be unable to communicate. A crossover cable reverses the transmit and receive lines so that the hubs can correctly communicate.

Fiber Boxes and Fiber Jumper Cables

Just as patch panels and patch cables attempt to prevent damage to the wiring going out to the classrooms, a fiber box and cables do the same for fiber optic cable. The fiber from the other part of the cabling system connects inside the fiber box and a fiber jumper cable is used to connect the box to the hub.

Repeaters

In the recent past, repeaters were the most basic type of active cabling equipment. They operated solely at the Physical layer, receiving a signal on one

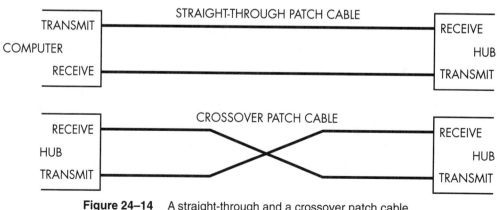

Figure 24–14   A straight-through and a crossover patch cable.

port, or connection, and rebroadcasting it on all of its other ports. Repeaters could extend a new network beyond the limits imposed by the wiring by boosting the signal level. Today, repeaters are seldom used in new networks. Modern (and more expensive) devices look at the message the signals carry to determine whether they really need to pass each message to the next segment.

Most advertisements for hubs refer to multiport repeaters. They usually come with a number of ports that are multiples of 12 and allow the network to support up to that number of workstations. Some hubs are stackable, which means they have a special connector that allows a school district or university to easily connect more than one hub together. Others come as chassis systems that support additional cards, each card having another 12 ports. Hubs also serve as central points of interconnection for LAN-attached devices, as well as concentrators and repeaters of LAN traffic.

Switches

Switches are an advanced form of repeaters. They also act at the Physical level by repeating the signal. Unlike repeaters that repeat an incoming packet out all of its ports, a switch looks at the destination of the packet and only sends it to the port of the destination. This can reduce excess traffic on a cabling system since it isolates each port and sends fewer packets to each port, thereby reducing collisions and increasing the performance of the cabling system. Furthermore, LAN switches are basically intelligent hubs with basic routing capabilities.

Bridges

Bridges operate at a higher level than repeaters, working at the Data Link layer and looking at the actual packets that are on the cabling system. When bridges receive a packet, they store the entire packet in memory, verify its correctness, and retransmit it on the correct port. This allows them to connect different types of Ethernet networks together such as a 10BaseT and a coax network. Bridges also reset the 3-4-5 rule for each port, making each port its own network. This is because the network stores the entire packet and rebroadcasts it, thus isolating each port from the others. Like switches, they look at the destination of the packet and only send it to the port where the destination is located, thus reducing traffic on the network. In addition, MAC bridges are sophisticated in that they connect unlike LANs (Ethernet to token ring) via encapsulation.

Routers

Routers operate at the network level. They receive a packet, view its destination, and determine if the packet is destined for a network that is directly connected to the router or if it is destined for a network further away. If it is the first, it sends the packet to the correct port. If it is the latter, it sends the packet to the next router along the path to the packet's final destination. For this reason, routers typically connect between a LAN and a WAN to limit the traffic on the WAN to only packets that need to cross it. Additionally, because routers look at the network information from a packet, they can convert between different network protocols.

Along with the basic cabling equipment, a school district or university that is still using LocalTalk networks will need to install some specialized equipment that connects those networks to the building Ethernet network. This equipment includes MacLAN patch panels and GatorStars or similar equipment, or EtherPrint boxes.

GatorStar/GatorBox

If a building has many LocalTalk devices to connect, a good solution is to use a GatorStar or a GatorBox. A GatorStar connects to an Ethernet port on a hub and to a MacLan patch panel. It converts the packets on the LocalTalk networks into Ethernet packets. This allows workstations on a LocalTalk network to act as if they were directly on the Ethernet network. The GatorBox is a smaller version that can connect to a single LocalTalk network and bridge that network to an Ethernet network.

GatorStar/GatorBox are the products of a specific company. Other companies manufacture similar equipment.

MacLAN Patch Panel

A MacLAN patch panel is a special type of patch panel. When connecting rooms that are using LocalTalk, a patch cable runs from the normal patch panel to the MacLAN patch panel. This connects all of the LocalTalk networks to the MacLAN patch panel. A GatorStar, but not a GatorBox, requires the MacLAN patch panel.

EtherPrint Boxes

If a building has only a few LocalTalk devices such as printers, a cheap and convenient solution is to install EtherPrint boxes next to the printers. They are small devices that convert Ethernet packets into LocalTalk packets. Unlike

GatorStar or GatorBox, these have a limit on the number of LocalTalk devices they can connect.

EtherPrint boxes are the product of a specific company. Other companies manufacture similar equipment.

Installing Cabling System Equipment

Most vendors design cabling system equipment to be rack-mounted. This means the equipment has special connectors on its side that allow it to bolt to a specially designed rack. This keeps the equipment off the floor, allows good air flow around all the equipment, and provides easy access to both the front and back of the equipment.

Standard racks are 22" × 36" × 84" (width × depth × height) and bolt to the floor in a permanent location. To allow easy access to both the front and back, enough clearance for a person to stand on either side should be allowed around the equipment. The two standard-size racks can also be 19" and 23", with the 19" rack predominant. That is to say the mounting holes are 19" and 23" (the old Ma Bell size) apart. Another type of rack that is useful in an unlocked room is the cabinet rack. These come in two heights, 40" and 78". They are lockable, double-hinged cabinets that allow easy access to either the front or the back of equipment.

Configuring Cabling System Equipment

Cabling system equipment comes in two types when talking about configuring the equipment: manageable and nonmanageable. The first allows a central location elsewhere in the building or elsewhere in the school district or university to configure and monitor the equipment. The second requires that an administrator configure the equipment by connecting a portable computer to it. A school district or university will need to decide if it can afford the additional costs for manageable equipment and if they will ever need the capabilities. If the school district or university rarely modifies the cabling system, then the nonmanageable may be a good choice. However, if a small number of people are supporting the cabling system, their ability to remotely configure and monitor a device for correct functionality can more than make up for the cost.

INSTALLING WIDE AREA NETWORKS

In order to provide access between the different schools and to the Internet, a school district or university will need to install a district or university WAN. This will connect all the schools or remote campuses to each other as well as to an Internet service provider (ISP). In some cases, the options available at the ISP will dictate the WAN technology. In others, the cost will decide the WAN technology.

When discussing costs for WAN technology, there are two separate costs associated with the network. The first is the startup cost, which includes such things as equipment and installation. The second is the recurring cost, which occurs either on a monthly or a yearly basis.

The data travels over a WAN in two directions, from the ISP to a building and from a building to the ISP. The first is called the downlink because data is being downloaded from the ISP, and the second is called the uplink, because information is being uploaded to the ISP. On many of the WAN technologies, the uplink and downlink speeds will be the same. Several of the technologies offer different rates in the two directions. The downlink rate will be the most important because the typical use of an Internet connection is to request information from a server. This results in requests and acknowledgments being sent across the uplink and the responses from the requests traveling across the downlink.

The different technologies include plain old telephone service (POTS), leased lines, integrated services digital network (ISDN), wireless, cable TV, satellite, and fiber. Table 24–4 summarizes the technologies [Lamont, 11].

Table 24–4   A Comparison of Different WAN Technologies

| Technology | Speeds | Startup Costs | | | Recurring Cost | |
		Maximum Distance	Installation Cost	Equipment Cost	Line Charge	Internet Access
POTS	9.6 Kbps to 28.8 Kbps	Unlimited	$75	$150	$30/month	$20/month
Dry line	56 Kbps	2–4 miles	$500–$1,000	$300	$50/month	$250/month
Leased line	56 Kbps to 1.5 Mbps	Unlimited	$500–$1,000	$1500	$200/month–$800/month	$250/month–$2,000/month
ISDN	64 Kbps to 128 Kbps	Unlimited	$150	$500–$1,500	$50/month + $.005/minute	$250/month
Wireless	2 Mbps	25 miles	$0	$6,000–$15,000	$0	$250/month

Table 24–4   (continued)

| Technology | Speeds | Startup Costs | | | Recurring Cost | |
		Maximum Distance	Installation Cost	Equipment Cost	Line Charge	Internet Access
Cable TV	4 Mbps				$50/month	
Satellite	56 Kbps to 115 Kbps	Unlimited	$0	$15,000	$800/month– $1,200/month	
Fiber	10 Mbps to 1 Gbps and up	1,000 meters	$2/foot	$2,000	$0	Depends on ISP

Plain Old Telephone Service (POTS)

Just as its name implies, this technology relies on standard phone lines to connect schools. Using current analog modem technology, this service can run at speeds up to 28.8 Kbps in each direction. Speeds of up to 33.6 Kbps and 56 Kbps are also available. It is a cheap and usually easy way to get a machine connected to the Internet quickly. It has low startup costs and low monthly rates. If an extra phone line is already available, the school can reuse it with no installation charge. An office can even share the line because it is only connected when it is in use, although this is not recommended. An ISP will need to provide Internet connectivity, but these are usually available at reasonable rates as well. As shown in Figure 24–15, there is no additional equipment needed except for a modem on each machine that requires Internet connectivity [Lamont, 11].

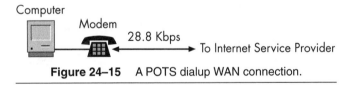

Figure 24–15   A POTS dialup WAN connection.

Leased Line

Another type of WAN connection is a leased line. With a leased line, the school district or university buys a permanent connection from the phone company, either to another school or to an ISP. The district sets up a router and a channel service unit/digital service unit (CSU/DSU) at each school that will connect the leased line to the CSU/DSU, as shown in Figure 24–16 [Lamont, 12]. This establishes a network between the two ends of the leased line.

There are two varieties of leased lines, and both operate at identical uplink and downlink speeds. The first is called a dry line. It has a maximum speed of 56 Kbps, and a maximum range of 2 to 4 miles along the length of the phone wiring. The phone company does not provide any boosting of the signal and this limits the length of the wiring. However, because the phone company does not have to provide any equipment, the lines are available at about standard phone rates. The installation is somewhat expensive, being about $700-$1,200 for the initial setup. These lines are perfect for connecting between closely situated buildings.

Dry lines can be installed between buildings in a campus environment (1 to 20 miles) using limited distance modems (LDM) or short haul modems (SHM), and run at T1 speeds.

The other variety is simply called leased lines. They are available in speeds ranging from 56 Kbps up to and beyond 1.5 Mbps (a T1 line). They require the same equipment as a dry line, but the phone company boosts the signal along its path. This allows leased lines to run almost any distance, although longer distances will cost more. The installation costs are similar to dry lines, but the monthly costs are substantially higher, beginning at around $220/month for short distances for a 56 Kbps line. Connecting a school district or university in a star topology (with only one building acting as the central hub and connecting to the ISP) is the cheapest way to create the WAN.

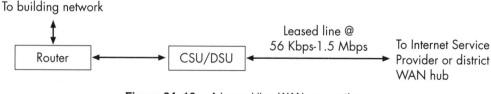

Figure 24–16   A leased line WAN connection.

However, because all the schools will share the same connection to the Internet, performance will eventually suffer if the shared line is not fast enough. A district or university will obtain the best performance by connecting each school directly to the ISP, but this will cost substantially more.

Along with connecting school district or university buildings, a connection needs to run to an ISP. This can cost a large amount of money depending on the ISP. Costs depend on the speed of the connection. However, commercial rates begin at about $270/month for a 56 Kbps line and extend into the thousands of dollars per month for T1 speeds. Obviously, a noncommercial rate is found to be more affordable for a school district or university.

Integrated Services Digital Network

Integrated Services Digital Network (ISDN) is a technology that is finally becoming available from most telephone companies. It offers connections at either 64 Kbps or 128 Kbps in each direction. It also expands by multiples of 64 Kbps. The basic service, called a basic rate interface (BRI), contains two 64 Kbps data lines called B-Channels and a 16 Kbps control line called a D-Channel.

Unlike leased lines (that are paid for 24 hours a day, 7 days a week regardless of their use), the phone company meters ISDN lines like a standard phone line. They only bill a school district or university for the actual usage time of the line. Most ISDN connections will close after a few minutes of inactivity, keeping the usage charge down to a minimum. In addition, unlike a normal POTS modem, an ISDN connection is usually dial on demand. This means that if a need arises to use the connection, the ISDN equipment will automatically establish the connection within one or two seconds. This allows users to continue working normally as the line connection opens and closes automatically. As shown in Figure 24–17, the actual implementation of an ISDN WAN is very similar to the network used in a leased line network [Lamont, 13]. However, an ISDN network terminator, Type 1 (NT-1), connects to the phone wiring instead of a CSU/DSU. Many NT-1 boxes even contain a simple router so that a school district or university can save money by not needing a router at each building.

ISDN lines are paid for like standard business lines or POTS lines at approximately $70–$120 per month, depending on the provider. The only additional cost is the long-distance charges.

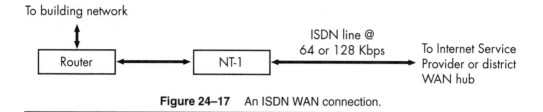

To building network

Router → NT-1 ← ISDN line @ 64 or 128 Kbps → To Internet Service Provider or district WAN hub

Figure 24–17   An ISDN WAN connection.

Wireless

With the phone company charging on a monthly basis for any network services it provides, other options apart from the phone company may be cheaper. One approach is to use wireless communications to connect multiple buildings. Offering high speeds and minimal or no recurring costs, these technologies deserve a good look. When compared with the phone company solutions, the up-front costs are high, but over time this cost can amortize to the point where it is cost effective. Wireless may require expensive towers to clear natural and man-made obstructions around a school. This is because all wireless communications require a clear line of sight between the transmitting and receiving equipment. Figure 24–18 shows the basic configuration of a wireless network [Lamont, 14].

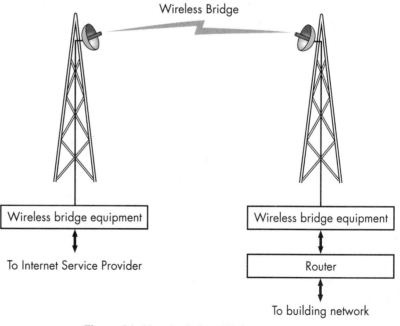

Wireless Bridge

Wireless bridge equipment

To Internet Service Provider

Wireless bridge equipment

Router

To building network

Figure 24–18   A wireless WAN connection.

Wireless technology uses one of two methods of communication, either lasers or microwaves. Laser technology offers higher speeds, but shorter ranges of only a few hundred meters. A more significant problem is that most lasers operate in the infrared spectrum and most conditions that block visible light, such as rain, fog, or any other physical obstruction, also block the laser. Because of these limitations, lasers are not particularly useful when trying to reliably connect multiple buildings.

Microwave communications, on the other hand, are immune to many of the problems that plague lasers, including most weather conditions. And they can travel much farther.

Most microwave equipment that a school district or university will use operates in one of two freely available unlicensed spectrums of the radio frequency band. The advantage is that the equipment requires no licensing with the FCC. Unfortunately, this also means that other equipment can also use the same frequency and can cause interference. However, the equipment uses techniques to prevent this interference causing problems with the information being sent across the connection. Although many products exist in the wireless market, two specific products can be used as an example of the capabilities of wireless networking: The first is the Wireless KarlBridge from KarlNet and the second is the AirLAN Bridge/Ultra from Solectek.

A note of caution here: wireless communications has never proven itself reliable enough for high-profile data transmission.

Wireless KarlBridge

The KarlBridge offers a maximum data rate of 2 Mbps in each direction and has a maximum range of 10 miles. It costs about $8,000 for a complete setup, including two antennas, two bridges, and all the cabling needed to connect the equipment together. Although not currently in use by any school district, the University of Illinois installed and tested the equipment and found it to meet its stated capabilities.

AirLAN Bridge/Ultra

Offering longer ranges of 10 to 25 miles, the AirLAN Bridge is a choice for a school district or university that needs to connect to points farther away. It also operates at 2 Mbps in each direction. The entire setup ranges in price from $12,000 to $17,000, depending on the distance needed. It includes two antennas, two bridges, and all the cabling needed to connect the equipment.

Cable TV

Cable TV is another alternative to the phone company that is emerging. It allows a school district to provide WAN connectivity using the cable TV wiring. Although still a new technology, it promises to offer high speeds and low costs. However, several technical problems need solutions. These are due to the current implementation of cable TV systems that send the same signal from a central office to many destinations.

The first problem is the fact that television broadcasting is inherently a one-direction process. Information is not sent back to the central office when broadcasting television. New cable equipment that allows two-way communication is now available and as the cable company installs upgrades to the cable TV equipment, this problem will be eliminated.

The other problems are based on the fact that many buildings share a cable TV signal. This leads to the two problems of shared capacity and security. Although cable TV networks operate at high speeds, many buildings share the network. This results in each building getting only a small part of the total bandwidth.

Security is also a problem. When sharing information among several buildings, someone with the correct knowledge and experience can view any unencrypted information placed on the network.

Currently, two implementations of cable TV equipment are available: asymmetric and symmetric. Figure 24–19 shows an example of each [Lamont, 15]. The one available from local cable companies depends on the capabilities of the cable TV system currently installed. In the first implementation, a cable TV line runs to the building and is connected to a cable modem. The cable company then sets aside a single television channel as the downlink. For the uplink, a telephone modem transmits the information. This implementation is known as an asymmetric or hybrid solution because of the different paths taken by data traveling in different directions. This solution does suffer some serious performance problems. Using a television channel, the downlink has a maximum rate of 4 Mbps, but the POTS modem limits the data being sent across the uplink to a rate of 28.8 Kbps.

The second implementation requires upgraded cable equipment that can support bidirectional signals on the cable network. These networks, known as

ASYMMETRIC CABLE TV SOLUTION

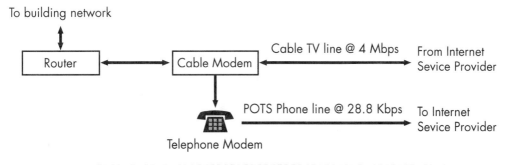

SYMMETRIC CABLE TV SOLUTION

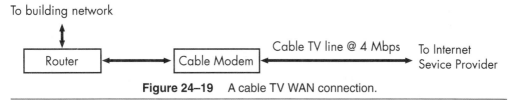

Figure 24–19   A cable TV WAN connection.

symmetric solutions, use two channels for data, one for the uplink and one for the downlink. This allows data to travel at 4 Mbps in both directions.

In terms of costs, the cable company will most likely want to charge a monthly fee for each building that it connects. In a recent contract negotiated with a cable company, some cities, such as Glenview, Illinois, have successfully avoided most or all the cost by requiring data connections to all the city buildings and schools.

Satellite

For school districts and universities located in remote areas (where other technologies are prohibitively expensive or unavailable), a satellite connection is a viable alternative, as shown in Figure 24–20 [Lamont, 16]. With this technology, a district buys a satellite dish and the necessary hardware needed to connect it to a network. A building then has a 56 Kbps downlink connection. As in the hybrid cable TV solution, satellite is an asymmetric solution and the uplink rate is only 9.6 Kbps. The initial equipment cost is about $17,000 for the satellite dish and equipment, and the monthly rate is about $1,000/month. A faster option is also available (with the downlink running at 115 Kbps and the uplink

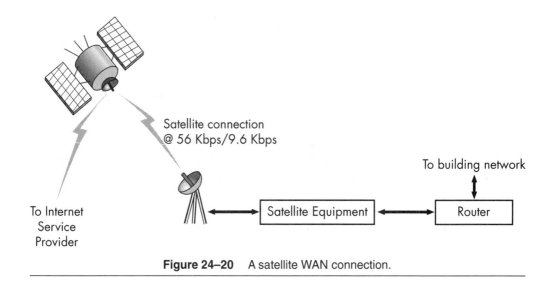

Figure 24–20   A satellite WAN connection.

running at 19.2 Kbps) for about $1,400/month. These rates are high when compared with other solutions, but in some rural areas this may be the only option.

Fiber

The ideal solution for a school district or university is to connect all of its buildings with fiber optic cables (see the Sidebars, "Installing Fiber Optic Cables," "The Benefits of Installing Air-Blown Fiber," and "Emergency Restoration: Additional Benefits of Installing ABF"). Fiber can run at speeds beyond 1 Gbps, allowing a district or university to connect the WAN at a high speed immediately and to upgrade to even faster speeds in the future. Unfortunately, this can be very expensive. Fiber suitable for use outside can cost between $1.80/foot and $2.30/foot. When installing thousands of feet, this can become a significant cost. Besides the fiber cost, installation can also be very expensive. A district or university needs access to all the land between the buildings, and this right of way can often cost a lot of money.

Air Blown Fiber, or ABF, is a fiber optic cabling and installation method that utilizes a compressed nitrogen gas source to propel a thin fiber optic bundle, without stress, through a previously installed tube cable (duct). Because the fiber can easily be blown out and reused, ABF technology provides exceptional flexibility in dynamic environments.

INSTALLING FIBER OPTIC CABLES

Fiber optic cables should be installed according to the manufacturer's specifications. The following guidelines apply:

- Cable runs without splices are preferred. No splice should exhibit an insertion loss greater than 0.5 dB. The integrity of cable should be maintained for all splices.
- Length markers should be imprinted on the cable jacket at reasonable intervals.
- The maximum pull force on cable installation should not exceed the manufacturer's specification. A strain gauge or dynamometer-type device should be used to monitor pull force during installation.
- The minimum bend radius of the cable should not exceed the manufacturer's specification. All cable should be secured at bends to prevent excessive movement.
- Cable ties or protective devices should be used to prevent chafing.
- Avoid sharp bends and corners.
- Provide additional crush/mechanical protection in high-risk environments.
- Observe all governing building and fire codes (either by using a properly listed cable or suitable raceway).
- Secure the fiber optic cable to existing supports or large cables wherever possible.
- Do not deform the cable jacket, specifically when using cable fasteners or ties.
- Protect connectors when installing preconnectorized cable.

THE BENEFITS OF INSTALLING AIR-BLOWN FIBER

Five key features provide ABF the flexibility needed to meet the demands of an ever-changing school or university campus environment. These features are modularity, reconfigurability, reliability, reusability, and deferred investment.

Modularity

ABF is modular in the sense that tube cable is the building block of the ABF system. Tube cable, unlike conduit, is easy to add to and install in modules due to its unique use of reusable watertight and airtight connectors. These connectors allow the easy extension of the ABF system by adding additional lengths of tube cable.

Reconfigurability

A particular advantage of ABF is the ability to provide point-to-point fiber connections easily. If the ABF infrastructure is intelligently designed, as point-to-point requirements change, the actual destination and origin of the fiber can be changed to meet these new requirements. This is accomplished by rerouting the tube cable through the reconfiguration of the tube cable's pathway at selected *node points* (tube distribution unit).

An example of this ability could be of a test stand being moved from building *A* to building *B*. Building *C* is the monitoring point for the test stand. Building *A* is going to be demolished to make room for a widened road. ABF allows the existing fiber between buildings *A* and *C* to be blown out and stored on a reel. Tubes would be reconfigured at a node point, and if there is enough of the old fiber on the reel then it can be reused by being blown between buildings *C* and *B*. If there wasn't enough old fiber, new fiber would be used and the existing fiber could be reused elsewhere on the facility.

Reliability

A critical advantage of ABF is its ability to install fiber in a strain-free manner. This provides two advantages. The first is guaranteed usable fiber. No strain, no possible damage. The second advantage is reusability. Since no strain is placed on the fiber during insertion or removal, it is available for reuse. An additional feature enhancing reliability is the ease in which point-to-point runs are created. Point-to-point installation minimizes field splicing, increasing reliability and the quality of the link.

Reusability

As indicated under reconfigurability and reliability, air-blown fiber cable may be reused, saving the cost of new media in appropriate circumstances.

Deferred Investment

Deferred decisions result in deferred investment. Fiber counts and routes can be determined and added when needed [4].

EMERGENCY RESTORATION: ADDITIONAL BENEFITS OF INSTALLING ABF

One of the major benefits of ABF is in emergency restoration. The ABF takes significantly less time for restoration. Because the ABF fiber is replaced, there is no change in attenuation. There are two new splices with the conventional fiber, which increases attenuation. If the repair loss budget for a segment of conventional fiber is ever exceeded, then the whole run of conventional fiber must be replaced. The ABF will never exceed the repair loss budget. The following is a typical emergency restoration example.

Air-Blown Fiber

500-meter span

Direct burial tube cable (4 18-fiber bundles, totaling 72 fibers)

Backhoe tears and cuts through cable

Dig 20-foot trench at area of break—10 feet to either side of break (12" wide trench at 55 LF/Hr = .36 hours)

Cut off 10 feet of tube cable to either side of break (trim fiber back to edge of tubes)

Clean area of tube cable to be spliced

Blow out 4 18-fiber bundles on each side of break (total time = 18.04 hours)

Splice 6 foot length of tube cable (6 feet of tube cable, 36 tube connectors, water protective wrap, and rubber shrink tubing) (4 hours—2 splices × 2 man hours)

Blow in 4 18-fiber bundles (total time = 18.04 hours)

Test tube cable with pressure and BB tests (includes setup time .16 hours + .07 hours × 18 tubes = 1.42 hours)

Splice 144 fibers or pigtails at each end at an FDN or pedestal (.5 hours + 144 × .25 hours = 36.5 hours) (2 repair kits are required plus 4 500-meter 18-fiber bundles and splice protection sleeves)

Test fiber—72 strands of fiber optic cable (4 hours setup time + 72 × .2 hours = 14.4 man hours)

Conventional Fiber

500-meter span

Direct burial gel-filled cable (72 fibers in conduit bank containing 2 conduits)

Backhoe tears and cuts through conduits

Dig 100-foot trench—50 feet to either side of break (12" wide trench at 55 LF/Hr=1.82 hours)

Cut off 50 feet of cable to either side of break (the purpose of removing so much cable is to make sure that the tensile strength of fiber has not been exceeded by the pressure of the original accident that broke the cable)

Clean area of cable to be spliced

Install 100 feet of cable (100 × .02 = 2 hours)

It's customary to do a temporary splice with mechanical splices for a fast restoration. Then the complete cable is replaced from end to end to eliminate attenuation.

Temporary cam splice 144 fibers (.5 hours + 144 × .25 hours = 36.5 hours) (100-foot length of direct buried cable)

Now the permanent replacement is started.

Remove and replace 2 20-foot length of conduit (total time ≅ .15 hours × 40 = 6 hours)

Install 40 feet of 3 innerducts (40 × .03 man hours = 1.2 hours)

Pull 500 meters of conventional 72-fiber cable. (1,640 × .02 hours = 32.8 hours)

Hours for ABF = 92.76	Splice 144 fibers or pigtails at each end at an FDN or pedestal (.5 hours + 144 × .25 hours = 36.5 hours) (2 splice cases needed for repair plus splice holders and splice protection sleeves, 100-foot length of direct buried cable)
(3-person crew—Elapsed time: 30.92 Hours)	Test fiber—72 strands of fiber optic cable (4 hours setup time + 72 × .2 hours = 14.4 hours)
	Remove 500 meters of damaged cable to restore maintenance conduit (1640 × .005 = 8.2 hours)
	Hours for conventional = 139.42 **(3-person crew—Elapsed time: 46.47 Hours)**

This example shows a savings of approximately 33 percent! However, more typical labor savings are in the range of 15 to 20 percent. Capital costs are typically 10 percent higher for ABF installations than for conventional fiber installations [Robin, 9–10].

When a school district or university has multiple buildings on the same property, obtaining access is not usually a problem. A district or university either needs to bury the fiber in the ground, requiring expensive excavation, or hang it from telephone poles, leaving the fiber open to the weather. If the district or university chooses to lease a fiber from the local telephone company, then the district or university will have to pay a high monthly rate for the fiber.

DIAL-IN SERVICE

A school district or university will need to make a decision regarding the installation of a dial-in pool of modems connected to the district or university WAN. These modems could be for staff and student dialup access to the district WAN and/or to the Internet. This may seem like a good service to provide to the district or university. However, with most local and long-distance phone companies offering this service for about $18/month, it is not a service most districts or universities should consider installing. It can easily become an expense and management problem. As more people begin to use the dial-in service, a large percentage of the modems will show a significant increase in their use. A district or university would then need to add modems to pro-

vide more dial-in connections. A district or university could spend the money
used for the modems and phone lines elsewhere with better gains.

 Dial-in service is almost a necessity in the previously noted environment
because of the large population of users that have the equipment and tend to
use it. It is easy to install and relatively inexpensive.

SOFTWARE PRODUCTS

Along with installing a cabling system, a school district or university also needs
to acquire any software products it will need. Without the correct software, a
district or university will not be able to access or offer the services that it
decides are necessary. Required software includes driver software such as
TCP/IP drivers, application software such as e-mail programs or word processors, and server software such as file servers or web servers. Figure 24–21
shows how the different network software pieces interact on a Macintosh and a
Windows machine [Lamont, 17]. At the lowest level of a machine, a hardware
driver communicates directly with the network interface card installed on a
machine. Software drivers supporting the different software protocols such as
AppleTalk, IPX, and TCP/IP act as intermediaries, communicating with both
the hardware drivers below them and the applications and servers above them.
Applications and servers provide an interface to the user. Just as in the OSI

Macintosh			**Windows 3.1, 95, and NT**	
TCP/IP Application or Servers	Appletalk Applications or Servers	High Level	TCP/IP Application or Servers	Microsoft Network Applications or Servers
Mac/TCP	AppleTalk Drivers		WinSock	Network Drivers
Hardware Drivers			NDIS or ODI Hardware Drivers	
Network Hardware		Low Level	Network Hardware	

Figure 24–21   The software installed on a workstation.

model, a layered approach is used. This insulates the upper layers from the requirements of communicating with the specific hardware present on a machine. It also allows all application and server software to function identically regardless of the brand of equipment installed on a machine.

Driver Software

There are two parts to the driver software, shown in Figure 24–21: a hardware driver and a network driver. The hardware driver usually comes on a disk with the network card, along with instructions on how to install it. Some of the network drivers come preinstalled on computers, while others need to be bought. On a Macintosh, the AppleTalk drivers have always been a part of the standard system software. The MacTCP software and the TCP/IP driver offered by Apple was not part of the standard system software until the release of System 7.5 several years ago. Before that time, MacTCP was a separately purchased product. All machines shipped over the last few years and all currently shipping machines include MacTCP. But any machine that is not running System 7.5 will require a copy of MacTCP. Of all the Windows varieties, only Windows 3.1 and earlier do not include network drivers as part of the standard system. Windows 3.1 requires an additional product, which will add a WinSock interface to Windows, allowing all TCP/IP-based applications and servers to run. Windows for Workgroups, Windows 9x, Windows 2000, and Windows NT all include the necessary network drivers as part of the standard system software.

Application Software

Applications are programs such as Microsoft Word or ClarisWorks that run on a workstation. They allow a user to perform a task on the computer such as write a paper, check e-mail, or browse the Web. When selecting applications, a school district or university can establish a standard that all the buildings in the district must follow, or they can allow each building to choose their own. By establishing a standard, a district or university can assure staff and students access to their files from anywhere in the district or university. A standard will also make training and support easier since the entire district or university will only use a controlled group of applications. Without a district standard, each school can choose applications that their staff is already familiar with or that serve a specific purpose such as multimedia authoring. A district or university can also select different standards for different schools, depending on the grades taught at the building. The best approach for a district or university is to establish a standard for everyday applications such as word processors or e-mail programs, but to allow freedom when choosing special-purpose software. This allows the building staff to choose software to fit their special needs, while still making papers and other common files easily accessible for sharing among buildings.

The standard for the school should also be an industry standard.

Applications fall into two categories: stand-alone and client. The first are programs such as those listed in Table 24–5, which do not require interaction with other machines to function [Lamont, 18]. They are available from many vendors, offering different capabilities and costs. A district or university should compare all the alternatives for a given type of program and select the one offering the best price and feature match. Districts and universities should consider buying integrated packages that offer a word processor, a spreadsheet, and a database in a single product. Districts and universities should also buy only the capabilities they need or expect to need in the future. For example, if a district or university is going to select an integrated package as a standard, it should consider if it needs the extra capabilities of Microsoft Office. If not, the district can save money by selecting ClarisWorks or Microsoft Works instead.

Table 24–5 Some Common Stand-Alone Application Software

Application	Common products
Word processor	Microsoft Word, WordPerfect
Spreadsheet	Microsoft Excel, Lotus 1-2-3
Integrated packages	ClarisWorks, Microsoft Works, Microsoft Office
Multimedia authoring	Macromedia Director, HyperStudio, SuperCard

The second group of applications are ones, such as those listed in Table 24–6, which require a network to function [Lamont, 18]. Many of the applications in this category are available as either shareware or freeware, and offer similar or better features than the competing commercial products. A school district or university should investigate the free alternatives before it spends money on commercial products. In addition, the choice of client software may depend on the server software selected. For example, if a district or university decides to standardize on Internet e-mail, then they should choose an e-mail client such as Eudora that supports Internet e-mail.

Table 24–6 Some Common Client Software

Application	Common products
E-mail	Eudora, Microsoft Mail, QuickMail
Web browser	Netscape Navigator, NCSA Mosaic, Internet Explorer
Video conferencing	CU-See Me

Server Software

Server software runs on a machine that often requires a dedicated machine for it to run on, and even when it does not require a dedicated machine, server performance is usually better if applications are not run on the machine. The server software will also run faster if installed on a faster computer. For this reason, a school district or university should plan to buy separate, fast machines for use as servers. Server software exists for both Macintosh and PC platforms, as well as for Unix machines. Unix machines are complex, high-performance workstations often used in the engineering world. Most of the platforms support all the services shown in Table 24–7, although some brands of server software will only run on specific platforms [Lamont, 19].

Table 24–7 Server Functions Supported by Different Platforms

Server function	Macintosh	Windows 3.1, 9x	Windows NT, 2000	Novell Netware	Unix
File server	Yes	Limited	Yes	Yes	Yes
Print server	Yes	Limited	Yes	Yes	Yes
Multimedia server	No	Limited	Yes	Yes	Yes
E-mail server	Yes	No	Yes	Yes	Yes
Web server	Yes	Yes	Yes	Yes	Yes
Usenet news	No	No	Yes	No	Yes
Electronic phonebook	No	No	No	No	Yes
Administrative record keeping	Yes	Yes	Yes	Yes	Yes

File and Print Server

There are three main choices when selecting a file and print server: Apple-Share, Windows NT, and Novell Netware. As shown in Table 24–8, they offer many of the same features [Lamont, 19]. All of them support both Macintosh and Windows 3.1 clients, but if a school district or university is using other clients, such as Windows 9x, 2000, or OS/2, they will need to select an appropriate server that can support those clients. The installation and maintenance of the file server software are also issues that need consideration. File servers are complex packages requiring training to be used optimally. If a staff member already has experience with one of the choices, then a district or university can save time and money by not needing to train a server administrator on a new product.

Table 24–8 Features Available on Different File Servers

Feature	AppleShare	Windows NT, 2000	Netware
Hardware platform	Macintosh	PC compatible	PC compatible
Maximum number of concurrent users	50–100	1,000+	1,000+
Approximate cost for 100 users	$1,400	$850	$4,300
Performance	Good	Excellent	Excellent
Print serving	Yes	Yes	Yes
Ease of installation	Excellent	Good	Good
Ease of administration	Excellent	Good	Good
Reliability	Very good	Excellent	Excellent
Clients Supported			
DOS/Windows 3.1	Yes	Yes	Yes
Macintosh	Yes	Yes	Yes
Windows NT	No	Yes	Yes
Windows 95	No	Yes	Yes
Windows 98	No	Yes	Yes
Windows 2000	Yes	Yes	Yes
OS/2	No	No	Yes

Multimedia Server

Multimedia comes in a variety of forms. It includes audio and video segments, often on multimedia CD-ROMs. Depending on the needs of a school district or university, the same platforms acting as the file server can also act as the multimedia server. All three platforms support the sharing of multiple CD-ROMs. Additional software can be acquired for Windows NT and Netware that will allow them to serve audio and video segments. For serving large numbers of audio and video segments, the optimal solution is to use a Unix system with software specifically designed to serve these segments. This can cost a lot of money, and requires a district or university to support a Unix system.

E-mail Server

Selecting an e-mail server can be a complex problem. Each brand, such as Microsoft Mail or QuickMail, uses its own mail protocol. The Internet also supports several different protocols. All of these e-mail protocols are incompatible with each other without software to translate between the protocols. Server programs, called software gateways, will translate between most of the different e-mail protocols, but a district can save money and avoid problems by standardizing on a single e-mail protocol. The recommended e-mail solution combines two protocols used on the Internet, simple mail transfer protocol (SMTP) and post office protocol (POP). The first transmits e-mail from the sender to the receiver's e-mail server, and the second allows the receiver to view their e-mail. As shown in Table 24–9, server software to support the Internet protocols is available for all three file server platforms and the file server can also act as an e-mail server [Lamont, 20]. As an added benefit, all the software listed in Table 24–9 is available at no cost. Unfortunately, these e-mail servers cannot handle a large number of users, and the performance of the servers decreases after several hundred e-mail accounts are in use. A Unix machine can act as an e-mail server for a school district or university requiring better performance, although this is not recommended unless a district or university already has a Unix machine running for another purpose or absolutely requires higher performance.

Table 24–9 E-mail Server Software Available for Different Platforms

Platform	SMTP and POP Server Software
Macintosh	Apple Internet Mail Server
Windows NT	NT Mail
Netware	Mercury

Web Server

Web servers are also available for the same three platforms that file servers and e-mail servers can run on and can often share the same machine used as a file and e-mail server. Table 24–10 lists some of the choices available [Lamont, 21]. The wide range of choices allows a school district or university a lot of freedom in selecting a web server. Some things to consider when selecting a product are cost, performance, and how easily and in what programming languages a user can expand the web server. Some commercial products can cost up to $1,200. Performance is also an issue, but this is tied to the price. The more expensive the web server, the better performance it usually offers. An exception to this is the Netscape web server (a high-performance product), which is available to educational users at no cost. The last consideration is how the web server offers access to external programs. These programs (called common gateway interfaces [CGIs]) handle the advanced actions on a web page such as forms processing. Each platform offers a different interface to the CGIs. Also, CGIs designed for one platform are not usually usable on another. Here again, a Unix machine can act as a web server for a district or university requiring better performance, although this is not recommended unless a district already has a Unix machine running for another purpose or absolutely requires higher performance.

Table 24–10 Web Server Software Available for Different Platforms

Platform	Web Server Software
Macintosh	WebStar, NetPresenz
Windows NT	Netscape Server
Netware	Novell Web Server, GLACI HTTPD
Unix	NCSA httpd, CERN httpd, Netscape Server

Usenet News Server

Currently, only Unix systems can run news servers. If a school district or university needs to make Usenet available to its students and wants to maintain its own server, then it will require that a district or university buy and maintain a Unix system. This can be a complex process, especially when trying to run a news server on it. If a district or university is willing to let another group control its news server, the ISP will often offer the service, thus allowing a district or university to access the news server run by the ISP. Although not a perfect solution, this prevents a district or university from having to maintain its own Unix system.

Administrative Record-Keeping System

A school district or university usually buys an administrative record-keeping system as a complete system that contains all the necessary hardware and software needed to install and use the system. It will include both server and client software in the package. Unfortunately, the complexity involved in managing student records and grades can often result in a cumbersome program that is difficult to use. A district or university should keep this in mind when selecting a system and be sure that it is easy to use. A district or university should also consider the performance of the product. Although it is impossible to give exact performance numbers, the system should not make an administrator wait to retrieve information. The system should also be customizable, allowing changes in its reporting and record-keeping capabilities without requiring that a new system be bought.

Most administrative systems operate in one of two environments, either centralized or distributed. In a centralized environment, a central computer stores all the information, often at the district administrative office. All requests for information travel across the district WAN to the central office where the system fulfills the requests and sends responses back. The system generates all grade, attendance, and other reports at the central office and the school district or university campus staff distributes printed copies as needed.

In a distributed environment, a student's building stores their records. When another building needs to access the information, it sends a request across the district WAN to the student's building and the systems at that building fulfills the request. All of this happens transparently to the administrator, who does not need to know the student's building. The system generates reports at each building, thus allowing quicker distribution of the information.

Most of these systems will cost in the tens of thousands of dollars. With that large a price tag, a school district or university should be sure that the package they are purchasing includes technical support. If not, the district or university can add that in as a negotiating point when pricing the system. Additionally, the district or university should verify the quality of the company's technical support group, and get references of other districts or universities that are using the product. This will ensure a district or university will get prompt and useful help if problems should arise. This is vital, because once the district or university puts all the records into the system, and it stops working, they will all become inaccessible.

Another option that a school district or university can consider is developing a custom administrative record-keeping system. This would require that a district or university hire a full-time computer consultant to design, implement, and support the system. The software that the consultant develops should meet all of a districts or university's needs exactly. When comparing this with the tens of thousands of dollars required to buy an administrative record-keeping system, this option can be competitive costwise, thus resulting in a district or university getting exactly what they want.

Custom systems are high maintenance.

During and upon completion of the installation of the cabling system, and all of the additional components just discussed, a little testing and quality control should not be out of the question. Let's take a look at how it's done.

TESTING, QUALITY ASSURANCE, AND INSTALLATION STANDARDS

The following copper and fiber optic tests (see the Sidebar, "Testing Procedures") should be satisfactorily performed and quality control and installation standards (see the Sidebar, "100Base5 Cable Installation Standards") adhered to by the school district or university—with the specified documentation provided prior to the cabling system installation project sign-off. All test, quality control, and installation standards implementation results should be delivered in machine-readable form compatible with MS-DOS version 5.0 and above. The information should be formatted as a CSV (comma separated variable) flat file. Hard copy test, quality control, and installation standards implementation results should also be provided in the form generated by the test equipment or contractor produced in text file form.

TESTING PROCEDURES

Copper—4-Pair

Provide full testing and documentation to satisfy category 5 specifications. Tests should be performed from the horizontal cable BIX field to the face plate jack for all drop cables.

Copper—25-Pair and 100-Pair

Provide full testing and documentation to satisfy category 4 specifications (or grade of cable installed). Tests should be performed from BIX connector to BIX connector for each four pairs.

All copper 4-, 25-, and 100-pair tests should be performed using a Microtest Penta Scanner or equivalent test equipment. The test results should be documented, including the following information:

- cable ID
- building number
- Tx location
- Rx location
- test equipment; Tx type and Rx type
- contractor name
- technician name and signature
- date test performed
- relevant additional comments

Fiber—MultiMode and Single-Mode

Bidirectional attenuation tests at 850 and 1,300 nm operating wavelengths should be performed on all fiber strands. The test results should be provided with the following information:

- cable ID
- U of T building number
- attenuation values
- Tx location
- Rx location
- wavelength
- fiber type
- connector type
- test equipment; Tx type and Rx type
- reference setting at first wavelength
- reference setting at second wavelength
- contractor name
- technician name and signature
- date test performed
- relevant additional comments
- soft copy test results must be supplied in a text file form with two hard copy backups

Time Domain Reflectometer

Time domain reflectometer (TDR) readings should be taken on the reel prior to acceptance from the vendor, after installation without taps installed, and after taps have been installed.

Also, the TDR readings should be recorded for later baselining.

DC Loop Resistance

DC loop resistance should be accomplished for each coax segment to maintain a 5 ohm or less resistance per 500 meters of cable [UTOR, 13–14].

Quality Assurance

The contractor should be responsible for cleanup of all facilities and buildings related to the cabling system installation project, during and at completion. The work site and adjacent areas should be left in the same condition or cleaner than when starting a shift. This must be done on a daily basis.

The contractor should protect building equipment, exterior and interior, in the immediate and adjacent work areas. The contractor should protect existing building finishes and services not affected by the modifications.

Surface Finishes

The general standard is that existing surfaces should be restored and finished back to the original condition or better. If each condition is not exactly specified in the scope of work, it will be at the discretion of the program manager to determine the appropriate finish. Contractors should be aware of the site conditions prior to bidding and account for the appropriate resources necessary for this aspect of the cabling system installation project.

When penetrating surfaces where there is vinyl asbestos tile, cut and lift the tile prior to coring. Use the lifted tile to restore finishes where it is possible.

When penetrating terrazzo or concrete surfaces, the restored surface must be finished using the same materials. A terrazzo patch kit must be used to restore surfaces that have been damaged beyond a 1/4-inch circumference of the penetrating structure. A patch area must be created that uses straight cuts at right angles to each other or to adjacent walls.

When penetrating carpeted surfaces, cut or lift the carpet prior to coring. Refit the carpet tight to the penetrating structure. Also, when penetrating wall or floor slabs, both sides must be restored to the existing finish.

When painting surfaces use one primer/sealer coat of paint and two or more finish coats of paint. Block or brick walls are to be thoroughly sealed prior to finishing.

Any holes in surfaces created to secure operating equipment must be fully restored. In addition, any markings on surfaces such as spray paint or liquid markers must be removed, cleaned, and polished where necessary.

Any over-painting of structures onto background surfaces may make it necessary to refinish the background area to match the new structure. It is the responsibility of the contractor to predetermine this condition or to take care in avoiding the situation.

100BASE5 CABLE INSTALLATION STANDARDS

Definitions

Coax segment—A coax cable with 50 ohm terminators on each end.

Maximums

- 500 meters (1,640 feet) of coaxial cable.
- 100 MAU connections.
- End-to-end propagation delay 2,165 ns.

Link segment—A link between two repeaters.

Maximums

- End-to-end propagation delay 2,570 ns.

Repeater—A device that regenerates the electrical signal on the transmission medium.

Parameters

- Required to connect two coax segments together.
- Each repeater takes up an MAU position on the coax segment.
- SQE must be disabled on MAUs that provide connections to repeaters.

SQE (Signal quality error—heartbeat)—a function accomplished by the MAU to determine if the cable plant is still functional after a packet has been sent.

LAN segment—A local area network cable plant in which no address filtering is accomplished with no bridges or routers).

Maximums

Transmission path allowed between any two nodes—5 segments, 4 repeater sets (including AUI cables), 2 MAUs, and 2 AUI cables. Of the 5 segments, a maximum of 3 segments may be coax segments, the rest must be link segments.

Router—A device that filters and forwards packets from one LAN segment to another using the Network layer addressing as a filter-and-forward mechanism.

Bridge—A device that filters and forwards packets based on MAC layer addressing as a filter-and-forwarding mechanism.

Medium access unit (MAU)—A transceiver for interfacing the electrical signals from the AUI cable to the coax segment.

Attachment unit interface (AUI)—A cable specification using 4-pair shielded (22 AWG - power pair, 24 AWG TX, RX and collision pairs). Uses a DB-15 connector on the ends.

Maximums
- Length—50 meters (152.4 feet).
- Minimum propagation velocity 0.65 c.
- End-to-end delay 257 ns.

COST ESTIMATES FOR EQUIPMENT

While developing budgets, a school district or university will need cost estimates for the district or university cabling system. Some of the costs, such as
the prices for WAN equipment, have already been mentioned. This part of the
chapter details other costs. These costs, only estimates, are based on current
prices, and can fluctuate rapidly.

General Cabling System Costs

As a rough estimate, most school districts have found that the equipment
costs for installing a cabling system in a small elementary school with several
hundred students are about $17,000. A middle school with 1,000 to 1,500 stu-
dents will cost about $22,000. A large high school with 2,000 to 3,000 stu-
dents will cost close to $32,000. A university with 6,000 or more students
would cost over $62,000. Another way of estimating the total cost of a build-
ing is to use a cost of $270 per drop for all the equipment needed, and multi-
plying that by the number of drops installed in a building. These prices only
include the initial equipment and wiring needed to connect all the rooms in
the building to a central hub. They do not include labor costs or the costs
associated with buying computers for use on the cabling system.

Cabling System Equipment Costs

Cabling system equipment prices are dependent on the brand and type of
equipment being bought and if the equipment is manageable. Simple equipment like repeaters may only cost a few hundred dollars, while a router may
cost $5,000–$6,000. Manageable devices are also more expensive, adding
about 30 percent to the cost of a hub, bridge, or other piece of equipment.

Labor Costs

The labor costs will be one of the largest costs involved in the project if the school
district or university contracts an outside service to install the wiring. Even if the

district or university decides to install the wiring using district or university staff or volunteers, the wiring should only be installed once. The wiring only costs about $120 for a 1,000-foot spool, and is not a major part of the cost. Therefore, if a district or university foresees needing additional drops in a room in the future, it should consider installing extra wires to each room at the time of the original installation. They do not have to connect until needed and only add minimally to the total cost, while providing extra growth capabilities to the cabling system.

Computer Costs

A good estimate for the price of a new computer is about $1,800. The capabilities of the system will increase in the future, but a system that a district would want to purchase will always be priced around that range. This is for either a Macintosh system or a name-brand PC-compatible system such as one from Dell or Compaq. More powerful systems for use as servers will often fall in the $3,800 to $54,800 range and have faster processors, more memory, and larger hard drives.

Software Costs

The prices for application software will also vary, but a simple integrated package such as ClarisWorks or Microsoft Works will cost about $120 for each machine when bought in quantity. Other software will vary widely in price, with many products being available as freeware at no cost, and other specialized products, such as multimedia authoring tools, being in the range of $1,200 to $2,200 for a single copy.

Software licensing policies must be adhered to.

These prices include a standard educational discount. If the prices a school district or university receives from a vendor are higher, contact them about educational pricing.

As always, prices will also vary from one vendor to another. A school district or university should be sure to compare pricing from different vendors and find the best pricing. As discussed previously about where to obtain help, the best solution is to form a partnership with a local vendor, which can result in better prices.

PROBLEMS THAT CAN OCCUR DURING IMPLEMENTATION

Even after a district has created all of its plans, the cabling system designers need to stay involved. Problems will always occur, prices will always change, and timetables will often slip. By staying involved with the installation process, the designers can solve these and other problems before they become disasters.

By working carefully, most school districts or universities have been able to finish below their expected costs. Some of the reasons for this were that the designers followed the installation process closely and were able to avoid buying some equipment than was initially planned for, but was later found to be unnecessary. Both districts and universities have found that the actual installation of the wiring took much longer than expected. This was because the staff involved in the installation was unfamiliar with the networking process, and because unexpected problems arose. In one building in a school district, for example, the floors in adjacent rooms did not line up as were indicated on the floor plans. One was higher than the other by several inches, so when they drilled a hole between the rooms from the lower room, it never came out on the other side. They solved the problem eventually, but they lost time in the process.

Other delays can also occur. If a school district or university is using an outside contractor, it should be sure to put a due date on the completion of the installation to avoid potential slips. When using volunteers, a district should be sure to invite extra people, since inevitably some will be unable to show up at the last minute. Even hiring new, full-time staff is not foolproof, as one school district discovered when one of the two people hired to install the cabling system quit unexpectedly.

Even after the cabling system installation, delays will occur. Equipment can arrive from the vendor nonfunctional and needing to be replaced. Hardware and software will need to be configured—a process that can take an enormous amount of time. Software may not be compatible with the system it was intended to run on, requiring a shuffling of equipment.

The connection to the Internet that the school district or university is planning can also take longer than expected to be ready for use. As previously mentioned, some school districts and universities have had problems with their wireless connections that prevents them from reliably connecting to the Internet. Getting a connection established through the phone or cable company can also take longer than expected, especially if the technology that the district or university is using is new to the utility company.

The key to solving the problems without losing too much time is for the cabling system designers to play an active role in the entire process. If delays occur that are beyond the control of a school district or university, then the district or university can redirect its efforts to another part of the cabling system until they find a solution to the problem. Although this can be very difficult, by constantly modifying the process to fit current conditions, a district or university can finish their cabling system both on time and under budget.

LAST WORDS ON INSTALLATION

As we have seen in this chapter, there are many guidelines to keep in mind while wiring the network. A school district or university should try to follow all of them, but if problems or questions arise, remember the most important one: do not hesitate to get help from someone more qualified, even if it costs money. It is better to spend the money now rather than on having someone come in later and fix a cabling system that does not work.

FROM HERE

Chapter 24 described in complete detail the installation of the cabling system and covered specific areas such as core drilling considerations; conduit installation and fill guidelines; grounding, shielding, and safety; pulling the cable without damage; splicing and patching; blown fiber; labeling schemes; and quality control and installation standards. Chapter 25 takes a close look at the following post-installation activities: cable fault detection with OTDR, cabling system troubleshooting and testing, copper and fiber optic loss testing, documenting the cabling system, cabling system performance certification, and Telecommunications System Bulletin (TSB) 67 accuracy levels testing.

NOTES

[1]   Bradley H. Lamont, "A Guide to Networking a K-12 School District," University of Illinois at Urbana-Champaign, Urbana, Illinois, 1998, p. 2.

[2]   "Standards for Communications Cabling," Communication Services, University of California, Santa Barbara, 1234 Cheadle Hall, Santa Barbara, CA 93106, 1997, p. 1

[3]   "UTORnet Programme: Specifications, Standards, and Practices," University of Toronto (UTOR), Toronto, Ontario, Canada M5S 1A1, 2000, p. 4.

[4]   Mark Robin, "Air Blown Fiber—A Comparison," Advanced Communications Engineer, Engineering Services, Military Systems Integration Division, ComNet Midwest, Inc., W226 N900 Eastmound Drive, Waukesha, WI 53186, Copyright November 3, 1997 Electronic Data Systems Corporation. All Rights Reserved, Reprinted with Permission, pp. 8–10.

CHAPTER 25

Certification of System Performance

A properly installed and undisturbed cable installation should provide many years of trouble-free operation. In order to ensure this trouble-free operation, a number of postinstallation testing and performance certification activities must take place. This chapter takes a close look at the following postinstallation activities:

- for fiber optic cabling systems, cable fault detection with OTDR
- cabling system troubleshooting and testing
- copper and fiber optic loss testing
- documentation of the cabling system
- cabling system performance certification
- Telecommunications System Bulletin (TSB) 67 accuracy levels testing

FIBER OPTIC CABLE FAULT DETECTION WITH OTDR

Let's begin the examination of postinstallation system performance certification activities by taking a close look at cable faults that usually occur with a newly installed cabling system. What technologies are in place now to detect the location of these faults as quickly and accurately as possible?

Large-capacity fiber optic cabling systems play a vital role as the information superhighways of modern society and large organizations. The impact of a cable fault on an organization is very great—especially after installation of a new large cabling system—so the fault must be repaired as quickly as possible. To do that, the fault must be accurately located as soon as possible. Recently, companies like AT&T and their counterpart Kokusai Densin Denwa Company, Ltd. (KDD) R&D Laboratories in Japan have successfully tested a new fault localization method that can detect faults up to 4,500 km (2,813 miles) away, equivalent to half the distance across the Pacific Ocean from Japan to the U.S. mainland.

When a Cable Fault Occurs

Almost all faults in fiber optic cabling systems are cable faults. Cables can be damaged by natural disasters or human intervention. Most cabling system technicians are prepared to move quickly when a fault occurs. But before they can do their work, the fault must be located. Accurate localization of fault points is the key to speedy recovery from cable faults. Without precise information about the location of the fault, a great deal of time will be lost searching in the dark.

In existing fiber optic cabling systems, faults are located by opening and closing loopback circuits built into the repeaters. This allows faults to be traced to a cable segment between repeaters by checking whether the proper loopback signals are received or not. However, there is no way to know exactly where in the segment between the repeaters the fault is located, so in practice what is usually done is to replace the entire segment, including the repeaters.

Locating Cable Faults Precisely

A prominent feature of optical amplifier cable systems is that they can transmit light of different wavelengths, using different types of modulation. This allows several different signals to be transmitted at the same time. Maintenance of the cabling system can take advantage of these properties. It is now possible to develop new maintenance technologies that are functional, economical, and different from current technologies. KDD R&D Laboratories and AT&T have used the properties of optical amplifier cabling systems to develop a method for detecting cable faults between repeaters—fault localization technology that has been impossible for cabling systems up until now.

How Faults are Detected

In optical fibers, there occurs a phenomenon similar to one we see every day. In the daytime, the color of the sky is blue, but at dawn and dusk it is orange. This is because light from the sun travels on a relatively short path during the day, and on a longer path at dawn and dusk. As it travels through the atmosphere, the light is scattered. Light in the blue portion of the spectrum is more affected by scattering than light in the red portion, so the sky appears blue during the day. But even red light is scattered when the path is long enough. Hence, the red color of the sky at sunset. The name of this phenomenon is Rayleigh scattering, and the amount of Rayleigh scattering for light of any wavelength is proportional to 1 over the wavelength to the fourth power. Thus blue light is scattered much more than red light.

This scattering phenomenon also occurs in optical fibers. It exists in all fibers, due to microscopic variations in the reflective index of the glass that occur when the fiber is manufactured. Scattered light travels in every direction, including backward toward the optical source. Light that travels backward in this way is called backscattering, and the amount of backscattering per unit length is almost constant for fibers manufactured from the same materials. This allows cabling system technicians to launch optical pulses into the fiber to measure the strength of the backscattering on the temporal axis—a technique called optical time domain reflectometry (OTDR). Using OTDR, technicians can investigate fiber properties such as the distribution of propagation loss versus distance, and the location of faults.

Repeater Innovations

Optical amplifiers are capable of amplifying light in both directions. But in order to obtain stable transmission, long-haul optical amplifiers systems use devices called isolators, which ensure that light is propagated in one direction only. There is an isolator in each amplifier, so that any backscattering that occurs is prevented from traveling back through the amplifier. Therefore, every repeater incorporates special loopback circuits for backscatter to allow light to be propagated in both directions. These loopback circuits are very simple in structure. As shown in Figure 25–1, they consist only of passive optical couplers [1].

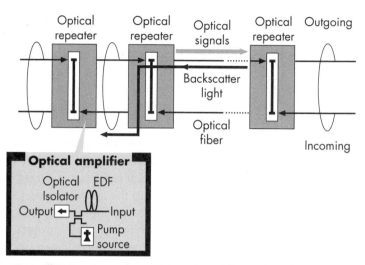

Figure 25–1   Because repeaters do not depend on signal transmission capacity, they also enable high-speed communications and
the construction of more economical systems.

Coherent Wavelength Probes

In addition to amplifying the light signals, optical amplifiers also generate spontaneous optical emission noise. The noise generated by each amplifier accumulates as the light travels through the repeaters, and eventually becomes very large.
This makes it difficult to detect the very weak backscatter signals. For example,
when locating faults with a precision of 1 km using a probe wavelength of 1
nanometer (equivalent to 123 GHz), the signal-to-noise ratio of backscatter light
power versus spontaneous optical emission noise is 1/30,000 (~5 dB), or even
1/300,000,000 (–85 dB). Moreover, backscatter light is affected by propagation
loss, so that it becomes weaker and harder to detect as the distance to the repeater
increases. Therefore, the backscatter receiver must have excellent sensitivity.

For the optical receiver, the electromagnetic properties of light were
exploited to develop a coherent detection method. The principle is the same
as that used in heterodyne radio receivers. Compared to the intensity modulation direct detection (IMDD) method, this method has the advantage of
increasing receiver sensitivity. It features not only increased signal selectivity
to capture extremely weak signals, but also the ability to measure the optical
power of backscatter signals along the temporal axis. This allows improvement of the signal-to-noise ratio by calculating the average optical power.

Figure 25–2 shows a schematic block diagram of the coherent OTDR
(COTDR) device used in the test [Horiuchi, 4]. It has a very simple structure,

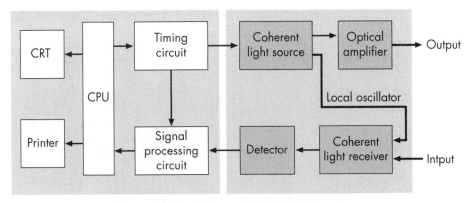

Figure 25–2   Coherent OTDR block diagram.

but depends on extremely advanced component technology. KDD, with help from AT&T Bell Laboratories, has constructed a test bed facility for use in developing and testing new transmission methods for transoceanic optical amplifier systems. This facility provides 9,000 km (5,625 miles) of optical fiber cable, equal in length to a cable across the Pacific Ocean.

The fault location method previously explained requires outgoing and incoming lines, so the 9,000 km test bed facility was used as a bidirectional 4,500 km system. The repeater interval was 33 km (21 miles), and 136 repeaters were used (272 optical amplifiers).

Figure 25–3 shows results measured near the terminal when the COTDR device was connected to the 4,500 km system [Horiuchi, 6]. There are large spikes in the signal at the positions corresponding to the optical amplifier locations, followed by a gradually descending trace. This trace is the optical power of the backscatter light. The gradient of the trace indicates the distribution over distance of the optical fiber's propagation loss (dB/km). Figure 25–3 shows a sudden break in the backscatter signal at 4,580 km (2,863 miles). This is the fault location. The figure shows that the new detection technology can be used not only to detect breaks in optical-fiber cables, but also to detect faults such as a local increase in propagation loss.

This experiment confirmed that it was possible to detect cable faults in about 4,500 km of cable with a resolution within 1 km (.63 miles). The distance 4,500 km is equivalent to half the length of the longest transoceanic cable, between Japan and the United States. This technology is now being used to search for faults from the Japanese and U.S. sides. It is now possible to locate the repair area with an accuracy of 1 km.

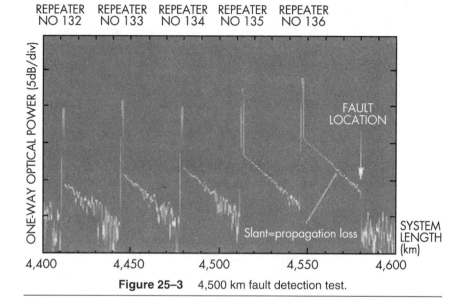

REPEATER   REPEATER   REPEATER   REPEATER   REPEATER
NO 132   NO 133   NO 134   NO 135   NO 136

Figure 25–3   4,500 km fault detection test.

Toward Extremely High-Speed Transmission

The newly developed fault detection technology has now been adopted for optical amplifier cable systems. It has also been applied to the next-generation optical amplifier system for extremely high-speed transmission, which has been developed at the KDD R&D Laboratories. By providing accurate information on the location of cable faults, the new technology has increased the maintainability of cabling systems, ensuring that customers will always be able to depend on services offered over the information superhighway.

SYSTEM TESTING AND TROUBLESHOOTING

Once you've detected and located the cable fault, it's now time to do a little troubleshooting. With that in mind, let's look at the next cabling system postinstallation certification activities: system testing and troubleshooting.

Now that you know how to detect cable faults, it's now time for you to learn how to conduct more sophisticated postinstallation cabling system tests and use the latest troubleshooting techniques. Teamwork, network analysis, and preventive maintenance play an important role in keeping your cabling system in top form.

Cabling System Testing and Tuning for Certification

At every level of the effort to better cabling system performance, network staffers must know their cabling system's history through study of installation and maintenance records. They must know their cabling system's present state by making accurate measurements. And they must know how they will change their cabling system, as dictated by cabling standards.

The most important thing here is the ongoing documentation of cable moves, adds, and changes (MAC).

Coordinating Work

As part of the work division, the network staffers must coordinate their work with others, including end users and departmental computer support personnel.

Most cabling system users will be delighted to learn that their networking staff is taking steps to make the system more efficient and, thus, will be understanding of the occasional interruptions needed to reach that goal. Interrupting cabling system service to improve its efficiency without telling your users, however, is ample provocation for a lynching.

When altering the cabling system to improve service, you make the change, document it, and then measure its results. It's possible that these tasks will happen quickly and be performed by technicians in different locations.

Cabling system documentation can be accomplished through databases and spreadsheets or by mapping the data in a graphics package. Specialized cabling system record-keeping and graphics software is also available.

The kind of test equipment used depends on the scope of the cabling system tuning operation. Handheld cable meters and LAN testers can be used for working with a single LAN segment. When attempting tuning operations across an entire campus or LAN, these meters, as well as protocol analyzers and special remote monitoring software, may be used to gather performance information.

Do Your Homework

Before cabling system technicians arrive at the LAN site, you must do your homework. You should have a printout with network adapter burned-in addresses, network start names, and IP addresses if the workstations are not using BootP or dynamic host configuration protocol [2]. A cable map with all known cable labels also should be available.

After checking in with the local computer support people, the area supervisors, and security personnel, you should perform a spot check of cable labels on all exposed LAN wiring. While you are working, you should be prepared to explain what you are doing.

Cabling System Measuring

Once the cabling system professionals are certain that the labeling spot check has been reconciled, they can proceed with measuring the LAN segment. A small workgroup 10BaseT Novell Ethernet LAN running IPX and TCP/IP protocols can provide a good example of a LAN segment. Usually covering 10 to 12 machines or fewer and at least one networked printer, this segment uses unshielded twisted pair RJ45 cabling and one or more network hubs to form the segment.

If part of a larger cabling system, this LAN segment might be isolated from the rest of the LAN through the use of a bridge. A bridge machine lets cable traffic from the LAN segment flow out to the rest of the network and lets cable traffic destined for the LAN segment come in from the rest of the network.

After determining the scope of a performance problem, your cabling system staff divides the work into easily accomplished tasks. These tasks are charted against a time line using a variety of tools ranging from a simple wall chart to sophisticated software packages.

A bridge in its simplest form is a PC that possesses two network cards: one to connect itself to the LAN segment and another to connect the bridge to the rest of the network. Special cabling system software helps a bridge perform its job. Commercial bridges are "black boxes," without keyboards or monitors, that can be remotely controlled and monitored.

Bridges usually are placed in a wiring closet or other secure area. To perform some tests, the cabling system technicians may temporarily disable the bridge to stop incoming cable traffic and gain a clear understanding of the LAN segment's unique characteristics.

Locating Faults

Wiring spot checks, especially for newly installed category 5 cable, can be done as part of a LAN segment tune-up. The cables are disconnected from the network at both ends. Cable meters capable of measuring frequencies up to 100 MHz are attached at one end and a signal injector is attached at the other end. This arrangement measures cable performance and locates cable faults such as improper or damaged wiring.

A thorough cabling system scale wiring inventory might best be performed during the evening hours (or weekends when, in reality, most wiring work is done) when the majority of workers are not using their PCs. These inventories may not always need to be performed, but may be required under some situations.

The LAN segment's physical wiring is only part of what must be checked. The workstation cabling system configuration files and network card burned-in adapter addresses also need to be examined.

In advance of their visit, cabling system technicians should get copies of each workstation's configuration files, including the config.sys, autoexec.bat, system.ini, and protocol.ini for Windows for Workgroups machines [Hayes, 1]. In Windows 98 and 2000 machines, configurations can be printed out from the Control Panel using System Monitor.

Normally, configurations cannot be located from the Control Panel using System Monitor; the best place to find configuration information is from the SYSEDIT.EXE executable. The system monitor allows for charting of object information such as processor utilization (similar to NT's performance monitor).

Corrections to machine configurations can be noted on these printouts. Cabling system technicians then can go directly to the machines that need configuration file updates. If the PCs can be remotely administered, many changes can be made by LAN administrators from their office PCs.

The technicians also should reconcile their cabling system maps during the visit. Each workstation should be powered up and network card burned-in adapter addresses should be checked against the CPU serial number. This ensures the cabling system staff has accurate records in case a network adapter failure affects the network.

Inventory Protocols

Next, a cabling system's protocols must be inventoried. It's here that some of the best performance increases can be gained by making sure each workstation or server is using only the protocols needed for its work and that each protocol is properly configured for good performance.

LAN testers can be inserted into the segment either at the hub or connected in series between a workstation and the hub. At the hub, the meter tallies the types of cabling system protocols present on the segment and determines the number of data packet collisions.

If the LAN tester is placed between the workstation and the hub, it can measure the activity of the workstation's network adapter. This is especially useful if you're trying to measure the performance of a switched Ethernet network where not every workstation can be monitored from a single point on the LAN segment.

Pinging Tests

After monitoring cabling system traffic, the LAN testing device can be used to actively test the network. Most LAN testers will support NetWare and TCP/IP protocols. The devices often will display a list of servers available from the sampling point and will verify the performance of network workstations and servers by pinging them.

Pinging tests show how long it takes for workstations and servers to respond to the ping along with top senders and receivers. These meters provide detailed statistical information about Ethernet traffic. In addition to the ping function, LAN testers can create IPX packets to simulate LAN traffic and then analyze what the LAN segment operates.

Each LAN tester vendor offers additional testing abilities. For instance, LAN testers can sense Ethernet network card protocol, address, driver voltage levels, and the polarity of 10BaseT link pulses. If the meter can't detect a signal, it automatically tests for cable and connector faults. Hubs can be probed for proper protocol and PCs connected to the hub can be pinged to ensure they are connected. The correct polarity of link pulses and hub transmit levels can also be determined.

If changes are warranted, the cabling system technicians should document their alterations and then test the LAN segment again. If performance suffers, then they should undo the alterations. Under no circumstances should they leave the LAN segment worse than they found it.

PC Overload

If PCs are constantly added to a LAN segment, there comes a time when the sheer number of connected PCs, or network nodes, begins to degrade the cabling system's performance. At this point, your cabling system technicians will be able to divide the LAN segment into two separate LAN segments. This can be accomplished quickly in the wiring closet by separating the network hubs into two sets of hubs with each set connected to a network bridge.

If your organization's cabling system spans several buildings in a campus setting, or if you have networked offices in several cities that must communicate with each other, then your cabling staff is faced with a number of challenges in tuning and maintaining these networks.

First, the undertaking will require more people scattered across a number of distant locations. This means your tuning efforts will require a higher level of coordination and planning. Fax, teleconferences, e-mail, and groupware software will help you communicate and track tuning efforts.

A large cabling system uses a number of specialized boxes to help link distant machines together. These boxes must be managed for efficiency's sake from centralized locations using a network protocol like SMTP.

Repeaters are used to send cabling system traffic between two distant wiring closets within a large building or between campus buildings. Fiber optic repeaters convert electrical signals to light pulses and vice versa. For the most part, these are trouble-free boxes.

Routing Traffic

Routers are used to pass cabling system traffic between two different network topologies such as Ethernet and token ring. They also can be used to connect a LAN to a WAN using a high-speed modem. Routers use proprietary software to pass cabling system traffic from one network topology to the other. Like bridges, routers can limit the traffic crossing them by filtering out unwanted network protocols.

Routers can be used at just about any place on the company cabling system to connect a single Ethernet PC to a token ring LAN or to connect an entire campus network to an Internet service provider (ISP). Corporations, government agencies, and universities use routers to link offices in different cities.

Increase Performance

Next to tuning a LAN segment, the best thing you can do to increase cabling system performance is to limit the number of LAN protocols crossing each router. Current cabling system installation and maintenance records really help the tuning effort. Router software often is revised, so it is important to keep good installation records to maintain current router software across your company's cabling system.

While it's natural to want to limit the number of maintenance contracts, critical components such as routers should be kept under contract. Otherwise, your organization will wind up with a number of wildly varying versions of routing software. This, too, can affect cabling system performance.

The ability to measure cabling system traffic not only helps you correct your own problems, but also helps you work with WAN service providers such as phone companies to improve WAN performance. Systematic record-keeping from the individual workstation to the network router does take time, but it will save much time and head-scratching when a simple tuning job takes on an ugly complexion. Periodic audits of cabling, network software, and LAN traffic help the cabling system staff stay on top of potential networking problems, thus increasing user confidence in your system.

A Job Well Done

Your cabling system technicians must be highly trained, detail-oriented professionals to keep your system running efficiently. Technicians should have access to the training and tools needed to get the job done. It's not by accident that your cabling system run smoothly, it's because of your cabling staff's hard work and commitment to your organization [Hayes, 2].

Next, a discussion on cabling system troubleshooting is in order. Let's discuss how to identify problems on the cabling system and the tools your technicians will need to fix them.

Cabling System Troubleshooting

Cabling system technicians and analysts require specialized tools to quickly analyze and repair a company's cable. This equipment can come from a variety of sources, ranging from catalogs to private manufacturers.

Cabling system technicians who diagnose simple cable faults and repair them need cable-related tools. A general-purpose electronics tool kit forms the core of what the technician will use.

Most mail-order computer supply companies stock generic electronics tool kits filled with tools your technicians may or may not need. Sometimes, it's better to look at catalogs offering individual tools, which let you buy specifically what you need. Tool kits can range from fabric pouches holding a few tools for less than $120 to deluxe tool kits in hard cases for more than $1,300 [Hayes, 1].

A digital multimeter lets technicians measure voltage, current, and resistance. A pair of multimeters connected to a building's earth ground can perform simple continuity and cable mapping. Multimeters should be ruggedly constructed and offer accurate readings over long cable lengths. Multimeters can cost between $120 and $220.

Cable scanners are invaluable. They check cable length, NEXT, attenuation, noise, and so on, and cost from $700 to $2,700.

Specialized Items

In addition to hand tools, including long-nose pliers and wire strippers, a tool kit should contain specialized items such as punch-down tools for connecting wiring to Type 66 or 110 punch blocks. Crimping tools for attaching connectors to coaxial and twisted-pair wiring also are often needed. These can be purchased alone or as a part of kits containing connector ends and test equipment.

Universal crimping tools with replaceable dies also are available. The crimping tools cost about $32. Each die set costs about $17.

Tracer Probes

A tone tracer probe resembles an electronic thermometer with a speaker at one end. It's used with a battery-powered signal generator to locate a cable by using an audible tone. Put the signal generator on one end and go to the wiring closet containing the cable's other end. Pass the tone tracer over the cables until it beeps. The cable that causes the beeping tone is the one you want.

Tone tracers also vary in price. Tone generators cost about $32, while their companions, inductive tracers, cost nearly $52. The tone generator and probe kit costs about $120. It also is available as part of a twisted-pair installer kit with crimpers and wire cutters for less than $270. Wire tracers use the same process to identify cables in active network circuits.

Battery-powered screwdrivers and drills are handy for removing defective routers and hubs from equipment racks. Since cabling system technicians go wherever cables lead, a hard hat and flashlight also are important.

Spare network cards, network patch cables, and connectors can be put in tool kits along with system diskettes containing software to boot a computer and get it on the network. Be sure tool kits have compartments to safely store diskettes and network cards.

A business-frequency FM walkie-talkie or transceiver can give your staff greater mobility and let them have conversations with several technicians at the same time. In addition to the FM transceiver, a cabling system supervisor may want to carry a pager and cellular phone. A pager's AAA battery can last for weeks, while a cell phone's larger, rechargeable battery usually lasts for only a few hours.

Shared Tools

Not every organization can afford to equip all of its cabling system staff with test equipment, nor is it practical to do so. Some tools may be shared. Because of their expense and sophistication, cable meters, fiber optic test equipment, and LAN analyzers require clearly defined checkout procedures and periodic performance checks.

In addition to specialized test equipment, an Ethernet hub or token ring multistation access unit can be used for troubleshooting purposes. Acting as field test units, these devices let technicians and analysts disconnect suspect machines from the cabling system and perform detailed tests with a LAN analyzer without shutting down an entire LAN segment.

Sniffers are also invaluable tools that can filter and sort incoming and captured data.

Information Tools

Cabling system technicians and analysts need to be able to quickly access network maintenance and installation databases. Using this information, cabling system maps detailing the location and nature of network devices can be created.

Reference materials such as books and CD-ROMs also should be available. Commercial online services and Internet sites often can provide the latest cabling system documentation.

LAN management tools using simple network management protocol (SNMP) let analysts gauge the status of critical cabling system resources such as routers and bridges. Sophisticated network management software can help you quickly pinpoint cabling system problems [Hayes, 1].

Identifying LAN Problems

Even with proper training, information, and tools, your cabling system staff faces a formidable enemy: the clock. Cabling system outages cause productivity losses that are difficult to recoup. Because each tick of the clock means money lost, cabling system technicians must work quickly and accurately to solve a network problem. Technicians should ask themselves and their users a series of questions about the problem. They should learn to listen to users, interpret the information, then quickly determine the scope of the problem and gauge its priority.

When seeking the cause of a problem, technicians should first identify any physical items that recently have been added or changed. Most cabling system failures occur in the electrical and electronic devices used to link computers together. A quick check of maintenance and installation records may turn up a recent action that has forced another problem to the surface.

At this point technicians may gauge your cabling system's current status with test equipment and network management software. If conditions warrant, they may go directly to the affected area and begin measurements there.

Based on available information and collective experience, technicians should develop a theory about the problem and perform tests to confirm the theory. After the problem has been identified, they will repair the cabling system, then document the problem and repairs in a cabling system maintenance database.

Troubleshooting the Workstation

Working with cabling system problems affecting a single workstation can present challenges beyond just technical difficulties. An unhappy user can make life difficult for your technicians and delay the repair effort.

Those people who don't have technical aptitude may be uncomfortable about showing their ignorance. Cabling system staffers should treat users with respect and make a follow-up contact after the problem has been solved.

The cabling system staff should first uncover any recent changes to the workstation by checking maintenance and installation records and then talking with the user. The odds favor a Physical layer problem, so cabling and network hardware should be checked.

If the computer is not connecting to the network, a quick visual check of the cabling system will expose a cable break or loose connector. A LAN analyzer can be used to test the cabling from the wall jack to the network hub. If the cabling checks out, then a test hub or multistation access unit can be used to test the workstation's network card and cable.

To ensure the workstation's network software isn't the problem, the machine should be started using a boot diskette. If the workstation then can connect to the cabling system, the problem is caused by the workstation's network configuration. The problem can be narrowed by examining the machine's configuration files or determining if network software is corrupt or missing.

If software isn't the problem, the network card should be reseated and the workstation restarted. If the problem remains, the network card should be replaced with a new card. The workstation then can be restarted; if the problem is solved, the user can resume work.

Troubleshooting the Segment

When troubleshooting a LAN segment, cabling system technicians perform the same troubleshooting steps as outlined earlier, always keeping affected offices informed of the status of a repair. Poor customer service can leave users angry and unwilling to trust the technicians' efforts.

LAN segment problems can be grouped into three categories: Physical layer faults, network loading faults, and network protocol faults. Physical layer faults are caused by a failure of the electrical or electronic devices that link the cabling system together. Loading faults occur when a network device cannot keep up with the demand for its services. Network protocol faults occur when network devices cannot communicate because of incompatible network drivers or the inability to pass the cabling system traffic of a specific protocol.

Physical layer faults are much easier to troubleshoot because there is physical evidence that something is wrong. Network loading faults and protocol faults are difficult to troubleshoot because the conditions that cause the failure may not always be present. LAN and protocol analyzers record data for later examination; these can greatly aid the search for the problem's origin.

When data is transmitted across a cabling system, it is parceled into units called frames. Ethernet networks use the carrier sense multiple access/collision detect (CSMA/CD) protocol to determine which network station will transmit a frame while the other stations listen. Transmitting stations also listen to make sure another station isn't transmitting.

If two network stations transmit at the same time, a frame collision occurs. Both stations must retransmit their frames. Cabling system throughput will vary based on the number of collisions that have occurred.

The different types of Ethernet networks—10Base2, 10Base5, and 10BaseT—all use slightly different methods to connect workstations. Certain faults tend to favor one type of Ethernet network over another. Link errors, for example, commonly occur on 10BaseT networks when there is a bad connection between the network adapter and the network hub. A damaged cable between the hub and adapter or a bad hub port often cause link errors.

Cyclic redundancy check errors occur when network data has been corrupted because data frames crossing your LAN have collided. This can be caused by a fault in the network cabling, the hub, or an adapter.

Improperly sized network frames also can cause collisions. Long- and short-frame errors are caused by incorrect network drivers or an improperly configured network card.

Constant collision errors occur on 10Base2 and 10Base5 networks when one of the terminating resistors is missing or damaged. Late collision errors occur when data frames collide outside the 51.2 microsecond window after transmission. This indicates that the LAN cable is too long. The maximum length for 10Base2 is 185 meters; 10Base5, 500 meters; and 10BaseT, 100 meters [Hayes, 1].

Token Ring Faults

In a token ring network, frames are passed to each member of the LAN segment, or ring. A special media access control frame, called a token, is passed among the network stations.

A network station must be in possession of the token to transmit a frame. Frames are transmitted in one direction around the ring. A network station receives a frame from its upstream neighbor and examines the frame to see if the data is addressed to it. If the workstation is the data's recipient, it copies the data into its received buffers. After the workstation has examined the frame, it passes the frame to its downstream neighbor.

A token ring network has a higher fault tolerance since it uses two twisted-pair wires; one is a backup path in case the primary pair fails. The token-passing method ensures constant cabling system throughput since only one station can transmit at a time.

Token ring networks use a number of special-purpose frames for control and error detection. Soft error report frames are generated when one of several error conditions exist. A burst error occurs when a network station hasn't received a frame within a reasonable period of time. It can be caused by a temporarily broken connection or when network stations enter or leave the ring. A token ring network station reports a failing network adapter by issuing an internal error frame.

When a network station no longer senses upstream cabling system traffic, it generates a beacon error frame. Beacons are caused by defective cabling or a bad network adapter. Bad NIC cards are also common culprits.

In token ring networks with more than one ring, the cabling system technicians should isolate the ring containing the beaconing station. Next, they should disconnect the beaconing station to see if the problem goes away. If the station's downstream neighbor beacons next, then technicians should check upstream stations and their physical connections until the fault is located.

When a network station doesn't have enough receive buffers to process incoming data, it generates a receive congestion error. If a bridge or router regularly reports this error, you may have to break the affected ring into two or more rings.

A heavily used server also may generate congestion error frames. A badly configured network card could be the cause of the congestion errors. If this isn't the case, then a card with a higher cabling system throughput such as a bus master or LAN-streaming token ring card can be installed. If congestion errors still persist, an additional server may be needed.

A frequency error frame is created when a network station senses that the incoming data signal has shifted its frequency outside of acceptable limits. This condition, called token ring jitter, is caused by bad cabling, failing token ring cards, or radio frequency interference on long cable runs. Token ring jitter can be intermittent and thus more difficult to locate. You can eliminate or reduce it by using powered multistation access units, which provide signal conditioning. Longer copper cable runs should be replaced by fiber optic cabling.

Troubleshooting the Cabling System

When troubleshooting the company cabling system, cable staffers follow the same troubleshooting steps as mentioned earlier. A high degree of communication and coordination are needed to locate problems spread across a wide area. Cabling system analysts rely on LAN management software and LAN and protocol analyzers to help solve problems on this scale.

LAN analysts will trace the path of affected cabling system traffic through measurements and the use of LAN maps. By sampling network frames and injecting test frames at points identified on the LAN maps, analysts can quickly determine the scope and nature of the problem.

At this level, cabling system loading problems can occur on heavily used routers, linking users to LAN segments containing important resources such as mainframe services or the Internet. If this is not a router configuration problem, the affected router may have to be upgraded. If an additional router has to be added, your staff may be required to redesign the cabling system.

Protocol errors on LANs and WANs are complicated by throughput limitations. A large number of protocols may not be able to run across routers in remote offices.

Protocol analyzers and LAN analyzers with limited protocol sampling abilities are great troubleshooting aids to determine exactly how much of each protocol flows through your cabling system. Eliminating unnecessary protocols by filtering them out at the affected router will greatly improve cabling system performance and assure certification.

Once you have successfully completed your cabling system tests and troubleshooting, you are now ready to move on to the next postinstallation cabling system activity: loss testing in optical fiber and copper. Requirements for measuring return loss, far-end cross talk, balance, power-sum near-end cross talk, and screening effectiveness (all at frequencies higher than 100 MHz) are crucial to any cabling system being considered for certification.

LOSS TESTING: CERTIFYING COPPER AND FIBER

The requirements to certify a category 5 link and the requirements to certify a multimode fiber link illustrate differences in the media. For category 5 cables, new standards such as Telecommunications Systems Bulletin TSB-67 issued by the Electronic Industries Association and the Telecommunications Industry Association (both in Arlington, Virginia) have evolved. New measurements such as propagation delay and delay skew have become necessary. And new products have been introduced to simplify and automate what is a complex qualification process.

To certify a category 5 link, you must measure length, attenuation, near-end cross talk, wire map, propagation delay, delay skew, and *impedance*. You must repeat many of these measurements on all four pairs, and make the measurements in a sweep fashion from 1 to 100 megahertz, meaning thousands of measurements. Also, requirements for measuring return loss, far-end cross talk, balance, power-sum near-end cross talk, and screening effectiveness— all at frequencies higher than 100 MHz—are under consideration.

Impedance is the AC (alternating current) version of the DC (direct current) term resistance, which is the opposition to electron current flow in a circuit and is expressed in ohms. Impedance (often abbreviated as "Z") includes capacitive reactance and inductive reactance in addition to simple DC resistance. Reactance depends upon the frequency of the signal flowing in the circuit. Capacitive reactance increases as frequency decreases: inductive reactance increases as frequency increases. Because of this frequency dependence, impedance is not directly measurable with a multimeter as DC resistance is.

Certifying multimode fiber, on the other hand, is simpler. You measure attenuation at 850 and 1,300 nanometers in the direction of transmission. If neither length nor delay requirements for the application have been exceeded, then the job is done.

Perhaps because fiber testing is so straightforward, test tools and processes have changed little in the past few years. But while testing multimode fiber is simple, today's tools can make the process time-intensive

because, with fiber, attenuation must be measured in the correct direction—
unlike copper. Attenuation in copper cables is symmetric, so the result will be
the same regardless of the direction in which you test. However, with fiber,
you must measure attenuation in the direction of data transmission because
the attenuation is asymmetric. The loss in the PC-to-hub direction is different
from the loss in the hub-to-PC direction on the same fiber. Historically,
installers have had to complete the following 12 steps to measure a fiber pair:

- Connect and run the test at 850 nm.
- Store or write the results.
- Switch connectors to 1,300 nm.
- Run the test again.
- Store or write the results.
- Go to the other end of the fiber.
- Connect and run the test at 850 nm.
- Store or write the results.
- Switch connectors to 1,300 nm.
- Run the test again.
- Store or write the results.
- Go back to the starting point [3].

Considering the need to test fiber in the correct direction, the approach
just described has four obvious inefficiencies. First, the operator must go
back and forth to measure loss in the right direction. To save time, many
installers test from only one end and have questionable results for half the
measurements. Second, the operator must constantly change connectors to
switch between 850- and 1,300-nm source wavelengths. Third, because fibers
are tested in pairs, it is inefficient to test them sequentially, considering that
with copper cables all four pairs are tested simultaneously. Finally, the
recording and management of data is often manual and error-prone.

Analyzing Test Results

The optical link budget presents another concern for fiber installers. Cabling
standards provide guidance regarding how much loss is permitted at each
wavelength. Permissible attenuation values are based on the length of the
link, and the number of splices and mated connections. This consideration
differs from copper-cable testing, in which pass/fail measurements are constant, and testing instruments can indicate whether a link passes or fails based

on the values alone. When testing fiber, the user must determine how much loss is permitted in each link. It is not possible to simply run a test and know whether the attenuation level is acceptable without knowing the wavelength, number of connections, number of splices, and fiber length.

Technology has opened the door to more efficient multimode fiber testing. A fiber tester is now available that tests both fibers in the pair, in the correct direction, at both wavelengths simultaneously, and also measures length and propagation delay. Users can also input the number of splices and connections in the link into the tester, which then computes the optical link budget and provides a pass/fail analysis. It also certifies whether the link is suitable for network-specific fiber applications such as 10Base-F, 100Base-F, 1000Base-F, fiber distributed data interface, and fiber channel. Use of this tester collapses the 12 steps previously necessary to 2:

- Connect and run the test.
- Store the result [Johnston, 3].

There's one tester that has a built-in printer so you can immediately print the results.

The tester time-stamps and gives alphanumeric names to as many as 1,000 fibers, stores them internally, and can download them onto a PC. This technology provides several advantages for installers, including speeding up fiber testing, providing information such as length and propagation delay that were previously available only through an optical time-domain reflectometer, and providing professional certification reports.

DOCUMENTING AND TESTING THE FIBER OPTIC CABLING SYSTEM

Installation and test documentation is crucial to postinstallation cabling system activities. Several times in this chapter it has been pointed out that a thorough knowledge of your company's cabling system, including the installation and maintenance records, is essential to keeping your system in peak condition. Let's see exactly how important it really is to document the installation of your cabling system.

A properly installed and undisturbed cable installation should give many years of trouble-free operation. When the unexpected occurs, having a well-documented installation will be invaluable.

Information on splice locations, panel numbers, cable numbering schemes, location of splitters, and other details should not be overlooked. There are a number of factors that influence the type and level of testing that should accompany the optical fiber cable installation. The consequences of a system failure and the amount of downtime that can be tolerated are two that come to mind.

It is a very good idea to perform a basic continuity test prior to installation of the cable. After installation it will be very difficult to determine if the fibers were received broken from the factory or have been damaged during installation. Multimode fiber optic cables, in lengths of less than 1 to 2 kilometers (.63 to 1.26 miles), may be easily tested by simply cleaving both ends and shining a bright light on one end while monitoring the other [4]. Longer lengths and single-mode fibers will require the use of a fiber optic source and meter or the use of an OTDR. These instruments may be coupled to the fiber prior to termination by using lab splices or various reusable-type mechanical splices.

When using OTDRs to acceptance-test optical fibers, it is a good idea to test the fibers from both ends. This will allow you to see failures that might fall in the OTDR's dead zone and breaks that might be near one end. Some anomalies may not show up if OTDR tests are only done in one direction.

After the cable has been installed and terminated, it is good practice to document each cable run. End-to-end attenuation measurements are a very valuable source of information. These end-to-end measurements should be consistent between fibers in the same run. Inconsistencies in these measurements may be an indication of poor-quality terminations. All measurements should fall within predicted values.

Consistently high measurements could be an indication that the cable is stressed somewhere along the cable run. The index of refraction for the cable under test should be included in any documentation of the installation. This will become valuable when fault location becomes necessary.

OTDR test documentation is also a good source for the documentation package. This will allow testing from one location. It is also recommended that a jumper be installed on the OTDR that is longer than the instrument's dead zone. Many new OTDRs store trace information to disks and even have the ability to overlay trace information from different tests. Unfortunately, there is currently no standard format for saving traces, so comparisons or second opinions from different OTDRs are not possible at this time.

CERTIFYING YOUR SYSTEM PERFORMANCE

The next to the last step in any cabling system postinstallation activity is field certification. The next part of this chapter will take a close look at this very important and crucial step.

The last step in any category 5 cable installation project is field certification. This is an important step to ensure the quality of the materials used and installation workmanship, but field certification adds to the cost of the job. In order to minimize this added cost, considerable effort should have been invested in minimizing the overall testing time required. There are two components in determining the overall test time: the actual time it takes to run an autotest function and the time required to set up for the next autotest.

TSB-67 Compliant Autotest Execution Time

The EIA/TIA TSB-67 specification requires the following field test equipment and test installed cabling requirements for the following parameters, as shown in Table 25–1 [5].

Table 25–1 TSB-67 Certification Test Requirements

Required TSB-67 Test Parameter	Required Test Conditions
Near-end cross talk (NEXT)	Must test all 6 pair combinations Must test at both cable ends 0.15 MHz step size for 1 to 31.25 MHz 0.25 MHz step size for > 31.25 MHz => Min. 478 measurement points per pair combination
Attenuation	Must test all 4 pairs 1 MHz minimum step size => Min. 100 measurement points per pair
Length	Must test all four pairs
Wiremap	Must check all 4 pairs for: • Continuity • Shorts • Crossed pairs • Reversed pairs • Split pairs

An autotest function offers multiple setup options that allow the user to selectively augment or alter the test parameters and test conditions executed in the autotest function. By default, the autotest function should be configured for full compliance with the TSB-67 requirements described in Table 25–1.

Fast Autotest

A fast autotest mode should perform all of the same test functions, but adjusts the NEXT scan resolution for increased test speed. In a fast autotest mode, an autotest should be executed in 6 seconds. While a fast autotest mode is not recommended for formal certification testing, there is excellent correlation between pass/fail results obtained with the full and fast autotest modes.

Overall Test Time Optimization

Beyond the actual time to run an autotest, other tasks that contribute to total test time are entering the cable number identifier and saving the test data for each tested cable run and moving to the next cable run and starting the next test.

Cable ID Auto-Increment

To speed the process of entering the cable ID and saving the test data, the user should be automatically prompted to save the results data when exiting from an autotest results screen. For example, by pressing the Enter key, the user should be able to open a cable ID data entry dialog box. Whatever cabling system field certification testing product the user has, it should be able to speed the process of data entry by guessing at the cable ID based on the ID of the last cable tested and entering this in the data entry field. For example, if the user tested cables in the order that they were labeled, and the previous cable entered was Bld100-Flr-3-100, the field certification testing product should be able to guess that the next tested cable would be Bld100-Flr-3-101. In the case of an alphanumeric label like cable1A, the product should be able to automatically guess cable1B for the next label. Therefore, if the user tests cable runs in the sequence that they are labeled, only the first cable ID in any sequence would be entered manually. The rest would be automatically entered, saving valuable testing time. This feature should be disabled globally or overridden at any time via alphanumeric input or via the numeric lock key to allow keypad input.

In conclusion, a 14-second TSB-67 compliant autotest and an even faster 6-second autotest mode should translate directly into substantially reduced time requirements for the testing phase of large installation projects.

A faster installation project testing phase should translate directly into major labor cost savings and greater customer and installer satisfaction.

TSB-67 AND LEVEL I AND II TESTING

Finally, it's now time to take a look at the last postinstallation cabling system activity, TSB-67 and Level I and II Testing. Portable cable testers have been used in testing category 5 cabling since 1993. Some early concerns about the accuracy of these tools in post-cabling system installation ultimately uncovered a number of interesting issues.

Testing Issues

First, there turned out to be different opinions about how measurements should be made, how results should be reported, where connections should occur, and how terminations should be performed. How could agreement between different tools possibly occur when no one agreed on the test set-up conditions?

Second, a disproportionately high number of failing links with certain types of components turned out to have a high correlation with short length. So what was first thought by some to be a tester problem turned out to be something else entirely. These short links really were failing on a regular basis, contrary to category 5 and EIA/TIA-T568-A assumptions. The testers were not at fault. A task group was set up to study this issue. It was determined that unbalanced modular 8 connectors can cause high levels of NEXT on short links.

Finally, there were no agreed-upon industry standardized pass/fail requirements for specific types of links. The tester manufacturers were using numbers from the theoretical model given in EIA/TIA-T568-A Annex E, since it was the only model available. However, as this model was informative only, it was not an official part of the standard.

TSB-67 Generated

These uncertainties led to the development of TIA TSB-67, approved and published in September 1995. TSB-67 is the result of a great deal of original research, round-robin testing, analysis, discussion, and debate among the key manufacturers and users of cabling, cable components, and test equipment.

Field Testing of UTP Cabling Systems: Transmission Performance Specifications

TSB-67 provides users with the opportunity to use comprehensive test methods to validate the transmission performance characteristics of installed UTP cabling systems. The categories of UTP cabling systems addressed in this bulletin also correspond with the UTP cabling categories of ANSI/TIA/EIA-568-A. Additional transmission performance and applicable field test requirements are referenced in TSB95, '568-A-5, and proposed amendment 3 to '11801 (PDAM 3). TSB-67 defines two link models: the basic link and the channel.

Basic Link.   The basic link (see Figure 25–4 and Table 25–2) is what an installer might work with, including the wall plate, horizontal wiring, and first cross-connection [6]. The channel is what a user really needs to transmit information between a PC and its hub or concentrator. It can include up to two connections at each end. Thus, the NEXT and attenuation requirements are different for a channel and a basic link. Fortunately, the channel requirements for NEXT in TSB-67 are identical to those published in EIA/TIA-T568-A Annex E, so links tested using Annex E performance requirements will not require resetting.

Table 25–2   Transmission Performance Comparison for Category 5/Category 5e Basic Links and Class D/Class D (PDAM 3) Permanent Links

Cabling Type	Basic/Permanent Link				
	Attenuation (dB)	NEXT (dB)	ELFEXT (dB)	Loss (dB)	ACR (db)
Category 5 (@100 MHz)	21.6	29.3	17.0	10.1	7.7
Class D (PDAM 3) (@ 100 MHz)	21.6 (94m)	32.3	20.0	12.0	10.7 (94m)
Class D (PDAM 3) (@ 100 MHz)	20.6 (90m)	29.3	19.6	12.0	8.7 (90m)

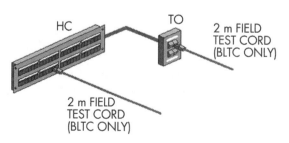

Figure 25–4
Performance specified in TIA/EIA TSB67: TIA/EIA TSB95 (category 5), TIA/EIA-568-A-5 (category 5e), and ISO/IEC 11801 Amendment 3.

Class D attenuation values are calculated based on 90 meters horizontal cable plus two connectors (no flexible cord contribution) that meet ISO/IEC 11801. Class D NEXT values are based on voltage summation of the near-end connector and horizontal cable.

Channel.   A key issue with the channel definition is that the channel definition excludes the mated connection (usually modular 8) at each end. The channel begins immediately after this connection (see Figure 25–5 and Table 25–3) [6]. This adds an additional error term for testing. The test equipment must connect to the channel to test it, so the cross-talk effects of modular 8 connection will affect the accuracy of the measurement. EIA/TIA TSB-40A defines the expected performance of a modular 8 connection. One notable parameter is a –40 dB NEXT requirement at 100 MHz.

Table 25–3   Transmission Performance Comparison for Category 5/Category 5e Basic Links and Class D/Class D (PDAM 3) Permanent Links

Cabling Type	Channel				
	Attenuation (dB)	NEXT (dB)	ELFEXT (dB)	Loss (dB)	ACR (db)
Category 5 (@100 MHz)	24.0	27.1	17.0	8.0	3.1
Class D (PDAM 3) (@ 100 MHz)	24.0	30.1	17.4	10.0	6.1
Class D (PDAM 3) (@ 100 MHz)	24.0	27.1	17.0	10.0	3.1

Numbers in parenthesis are calculated based on using 5 meters of additional flexible cables that meet Class D ISO/IEC 11801.

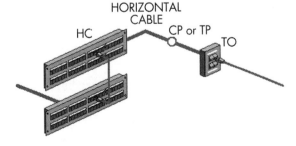

HORIZONTAL CABLE

HC

CP or TP

TO

Figure 25–5
Horizontal channel performance specified in TIA/EIA TSB67: TIA/EIA TSB95 (category 5), TIA/EIA-568-A-5 (category 5e), and ISO/IEC 11801 Amendment 3.

When testing the basic link, however, connections can be made from the test equipment to the link via extremely low cross-talk connectors, avoiding this issue. Since the inherent uncertainties of the modular 8 connection can be avoided when testing the basic link, the accuracy of a basic link measurement can theoretically be much better than the same measurement on a channel.

Two Testing Accuracy Levels: TSB-67 Level I and II

The reality of two testing accuracy levels is reflected in the TSB-67 description of two accuracy levels for field test equipment. Level I reflects the performance boundaries imposed by the reality of having to test through a modular 8 connection. Level II sets a much higher accuracy requirement, possible only if a different, low cross-talk connector is used. The advantage of higher accuracy is you will have less uncertainty when making a pass/fail determination on the cable. If, for example, your test suggests the link fails by 1.5 dB and your accuracy is ±0.5 dB, then you have complete confidence that it really did fail. If, however, your accuracy is ±3 dB, there is some possibility that the link actually passed, since in this example your accuracy margin is greater than the error [7].

Note

Even Level II accuracy test tools are reduced to Level I accuracy when forced to test through modular 8 connections, because of the uncertainty added by the modular 8. This uncertainty has an unpredictable magnitude and phase, so it cannot be compensated for or subtracted out via hardware or software.

What tool should you buy? If your primary application is to install and certify category 5 basic links, clearly you need a Level II tool. If your primary requirement is occasional cable troubleshooting on channels, a Level I instrument will meet your needs. In any event, the following are some points that you should consider (as specified for TSB67 transmission field testing accuracy Levels I and II for UTP cabling systems) with regard to field testing:

- UTP cabling systems are comprised of cables and connecting hardware specified in TIA/EIA-568-A.
- Required test parameters include wire map, length, attenuation, and cross talk.
- Two levels of pass or fail are indicated, depending on measured margin compared to minimum specifications. Testing of NEXT is required in both directions.

- Level II equipment meets the most stringent requirements for TSB67 measurement accuracy. Level IIe equipment will be required to verify category 5e and PDAM 3 performance.
- Requirements are intended for performance validation and are provided in addition to '568-A requirements on components and installation practices.

FROM HERE

This chapter took a close look at the following postinstallation activities: cable fault detection with OTDR, cabling system troubleshooting and testing, copper and fiber optic loss testing, documenting the cabling system, cabling system performance certification, and Telecommunications System Bulletin (TSB) 67 accuracy levels testing. Chapter 26 opens up Part VI with a discussion on how to maintain your cabling system. The chapter goes on to examine the facilitation of ongoing cabling system maintenance by covering the building of the cable plant management (CPM) database, vendor CPM products, and the EIA/TIA 606 standard.

NOTES

[1]   Yukio Horiuchi, "Accurate Localization of Faults in Optical-Fiber Submarine Cable Systems," Supervisor Lightwave Communication System Group KDD R&D, Laboratories, Kokusai Densin Denwa Co., LTD. R&D, Laboratories, 2-1-15, Ohara Kamifukuoka-shi, Saitama 356, Japan, 1998, p. 2.

[2]   Bill Hayes, "Improving LAN Performance," PC Today, Sandhills Publishing, P.O. Box 82545, Lincoln, NE 68501-2545, 1998, p. 2.

[3]   Mark Johnston, "A New Model For Multimode Fiber Qualification," Director of technology development for Microtest Inc. (Phoenix, AZ), Digital Horizon, Point of View, Broadband Guide, PennWell Media Online L.L.C., 2875 South Congress Avenue, Delray Beach, Florida, 33445, October, 1999, p. 2.

[4]   "Installation and Test Documentation," James D. Barnes, "Installation and Test Documentation," Penn Tech, PO Box 271, Keyport, WA 98345, 1999, p. 1.

[5]   "WireScope 155 Autotest Speed," Scope Communications, Inc., 753 Forest Street, Marlborough, MA 01752, 1999, p. 2.

[6]   "TSB67," The Siemon Company, Siemon Business Park, 76 Westbury Park Road, Watertown, CT 06795-0400 USA, 2000.

[7]   "Microtest TSB67 Level II Description," Microtest, Inc., Corporate Headquarters, 4747 North 22nd Street, Phoenix, Arizona 85016–4708, USA, 1999, p. 2.

Maintaining Cabling System

Ongoing Maintenance

In the early 1980s most companies were reluctant to implement a cable and connectivity management or maintenance process. Since then, there have been remarkable changes in communications technologies—changes that have had a significant impact on our communications infrastructure and on the organizational processes that manage that infrastructure.

Nowhere have these changes been more profound than in the cable plant, where changes to network architectures and hundred-fold increases in network speeds have forced users to add or replace cabling systems once, twice, or even three times since the mid-1980s. Staffing and resources to manage this infrastructure have remained fixed, while the rate of moves, adds, and changes (MACs) in most organizations remains unabated.

No one can be faulted for not anticipating the challenges of the last 17 years. Looking forward, a pattern has been set and the future should be clear. Users are stressing the strategic importance of maximizing the utilization and life cycle of the cable plant while reducing everyday operating expenses. Implementing a connectivity management/maintenance process and using record-keeping tools for documenting the physical network are crucial for achieving these goals.

THE FACTS ABOUT CABLE MANAGEMENT SOFTWARE

Documenting cabling connections is vital to prolong the life of the infrastructure, contain the cost of maintaining the day-to-day changes, and recover from network outages. Until recently most organizations did this via paper. An individual within the telecommunications department kept a "bible" (usually a three-ring binder with pages so worn the text looked encrypted) of all the connections. This became a problem with the boom of PC installations on the network. The telecom person was now forced to document the computer connections, usually with no knowledge of the systems.

Through the years, companies have tried various methods to improve the quality of the information being recorded, while reducing the time spent doing so. As many of you may know, this has been an exercise in futility. In most cases the process is dropped all together.

Integrated, real-time management is now possible with mature, state of the art applications designed for the purpose of managing cabling infrastructure. This chapter will explain the benefits of building a cable plant management (CPM) database or what is commonly known as a cable management system (CMS) package.

Reasons for Documenting

There is a clear distinction between a connectivity management/maintenance process and a cable plant management database or cable management system itself, as shown in Figure 26–1 [1]. A CMS is a computerized database that provides a detailed picture of the cabling infrastructure, allowing a facilities manager to improve service and reduce cost in the following areas:

- moves, adds, and changes
- repair downtime
- physical plant loss
- controlling vendors
- security
- disaster recovery
- future expansion [IMAP, 1]

More sophisticated cable management systems include multibuilding, campus, and asset management modules, integrating user names and cost centers. Some are graphical, allowing the user to make connections on active equipment diagrams or indicate cable and equipment locations on CAD drawings. Other systems may offer service order and trouble ticket modules with an integrated e-mail function to electronically distribute these documents. These programs can be run standalone or interface with network systems. Table 26–1 shows the four major CMS vendors with links that connect to numerous CMS and other third-party related products.

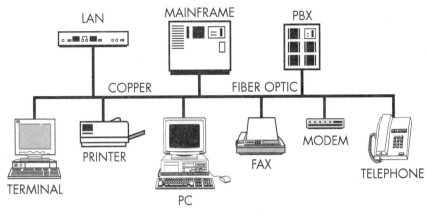

Figure 26–1 Cable management system.

Table 26–1 Vendor CMS Products

Vendor	Product	Standards	Description
Network & Communication Technology, Inc. www.netcomtech.com	Planet NT	*Meets the following telecommunications standards:* **ANSI/EIA/TIA-568**: Commercial Building Telecommunications Wiring Standard **ANSI/EIA/TIA-569:** Commercial Building Standard for Telecommunications Pathways and Spaces **ANSI/EIA/TIA-606:** Telecommunications Infrastructure Administration Standard **ISO 11801:** Generic Cabling for Customer Premises **CAN/CSA-T528-93:** Design Guidelines for Administration of Telecommunications Infrastructure for Commercial Buildings	An integrated graphical computer-aided design and embedded SQL database management system that incorporates physical cable and connectivity design, documentation, and management. Asset (equipment) and vendor management. Service request/trouble ticketing and work orders.

Table 26–1 (continued)

Vendor	Product	Standards	Description
IMAP Corporation *www.ycinc.com*	IMAP	*same as above*	An integrated cable management software system that tracks cable plant connectivity and all of the assets that utilize the horizontal and feeder systems. The IMAP CMS system provides a complete cabling infrastructure picture utilizing a powerful database integrated with Visio 5.0.
Cablesoft Ltd. *www.cablesoft.co.uk/*	Crimp for Windows™	*same as above*	Models the cabling, network electronics, PABX, and terminal equipment and allows you to plan changes, administer moves, optimize the use, and therefore extend the life of your chosen cable system.
Microtest, Inc. *www.microtest.com*	CD-ROM Network Management Software for Windows NT	*same as above*	Cable management and troubleshooting software.

To fully understand the benefits of a CMS, let's use an example company that has 1,000 employees with both voice and data requirements. According to recent studies, cabling infrastructure accounts for 23 percent of the data/voice network cost. Some estimates of investments in information technology per employee are as high as $6,000. Therefore, at 23 percent, the cost would be $1,380 per employee or in the case of the example company with 1,000 employees, $1,380,000 million dollars. This cost is only compounded as time goes on.

Moves, Adds, and Changes

A typical company moves approximately 30 percent of its employees each year, with an average labor cost of $270 per move. In the previous example company, this would mean 300 employees would be relocated at the labor cost of $81,000 per year. An automated CMS can reduce this cost by more than 30 percent, or $24,300 per year. More important, however, a CMS that is easy to use will reduce the day-to-day cost of moves, adds, and changes, thus increasing the life of the infrastructure.

In other words, a properly designed product should decrease the day-to-day expenditures by increasing efficiency. It should allow a facilities manager to take a proactive management approach to planning, budgeting, and the daily activities. But, most of all, it should be easy to maintain the information.

Repair Downtime

The cost savings in the moves, adds, and changes is minimal compared to the cost of a network connection outage that typically lasts two to seven hours, at a cost of $50,000 per hour. This pales in comparison, however, to the time and money lost while vital telephone or data systems have failed, bringing business to a screeching halt. This is where costs are measured in the millions. And the inquisition, after all is said and done, reveals that the weak link was the information technology (IT) department's documentation, or lack thereof.

This scenario is where an investment in a CMS will be worthwhile. Industry surveys show that 72 percent of service calls are cabling related. Furthermore, technicians spend 80 percent of their time on a service call searching for the problem and 20 percent fixing it. Most of that 80 percent is spent locating the end-to-end connectivity. This situation worsens when the connection spans multiple floors or buildings. It is not unusual to have a 30 to 40 percent reduction in cost of repairs, mainly due to the implementation of a CMS that allows technicians to find things quickly.

Physical Plant Loss

Abandoning cable can quickly become a problem where the average business has an ongoing stream of moves, adds, and changes. In the case of a multi-tenant building, it is possible for the owner to rewire the entire building every three years.

When the core cabling is abandoned, it artificially depletes the inventory while it continues to take up space. Soon there is no room for new cabling, causing the owner to expand or abandon the closets, or purchase costly new equipment to solve the capacity problems.

Abandoned cable is a major problem for almost every organization.

This equipment does nothing to improve customer relations—instead it usually disturbs relations due to the costly after-hours migration process. This capital expense can be avoided with a CMS that would enable the owner to reuse existing cabling.

Controlling Vendors

A CMS with the ability to generate work orders can be an effective way to manage multiple vendors. These work orders can be used as a means to track how effective a contractor is at handling emergencies, multiple projects, and contractor-to-contractor communications.

It is also an effective way to track recurring problems (that always have recurring cost) to identify if the problem is the technician. Most important, however, is that a CMS can allow the end user to negotiate fixed cost for certain tasks a contractor has to perform, based on a cost history of related work orders.

Security

Another issue that should be addressed in a multivendor facility is security. This can be simplified with the use of a CMS by simply giving the vendor the information they need to complete the task and validate the work when it's completed. Again, allow IT to track and measure the productivity and accountability of the technician. Since downtime is reduced with a CMS in place, exposure of corporate information to loss or penetration is minimized, translating into a higher level of customer satisfaction.

Disaster Recovery

No one likes to think about the loss of facilities due to theft, natural disasters, or some man-made calamity. But these events can (and usually do) happen. Planning ahead to minimize downtime and recover the losses should include a contingency plan supported by up-to-date records. A CMS would allow IT to quickly identify the lost resources and replace or reroute the connections to other facilities.

A report could be generated with a detailed description of the assets that were lost and the depreciation factor predetermined. This can be sent to the insurance company within minutes to speed the recovery process.

Future Expansion

The only way to fully understand where you're going is to first understand where you're currently at. Adding one more connection to a closet can eat 30 percent of the department budget if a new feeder has to be installed. The situation only gets worse if this happens twice in one year.

Usage reports from a CMS can give you current capacity of feeders, hubs, and station cables. This information can be viewed during the planning stage of an installation, thus eliminating the outrageous costs of emergency upgrades, not to mention the frustration of a schedule delay.

Fiscal budget planning can be one of the most difficult times of the year for a manager. The guesswork of defining budgets for services, hardware, and personnel must be handled carefully. A dollar value must be determined. Justifications must be written. Then the battle for something between what is requested and absolutely nothing takes place. This is a yearly exercise that ultimately ends with the outcome far less than the initial requirements.

The ability to graph a month-to-month or year-to-year trend can be a strong argument for IT's needs. Additional reports can be generated showing work orders completed within a cycle and just about any other information that would be pertinent to budget justifications.

Therefore, making the decision to implement a CMS is only the first step. A considerable amount of time should be spent evaluating different products (see Table 26–1). If an application developer is the driving force behind the CMS, and this individual (or group) lacks the field experience of a cabling background, then you might want to consider some other options. Meat and potatoes should not be traded for bells and whistles.

A properly designed product should decrease the day-to-day expenditures by increasing efficiency. It should allow the IT staff to take a proactive management approach to planning, budgeting, and the daily activities. But most of all, it should be easy to maintain the information. After all, if it's not easy to use, then it most likely won't be. In the end, define end user and contractor needs when implementing a CMS.

BUILD THE CMS AND THEY WILL COME

As more and more organizations are upgrading their cabling plants to standards-based structured cabling systems, the need for cable management systems has become evident. For most organizations upgrading their cabling plant, the primary objective is to support enterprise-wide, high-bandwidth, mission-critical applications to the desktop. Typical high-bandwidth applications include Ethernet and token ring topologies. Implementing a cable management system (CMS) to maintain the integrity of these important physical assets has now become a priority. A large number of requests for proposals (RFPs) for new cabling projects now incorporate CMS requirements—often loosely defined. In addition, contractors may struggle when responding to these RFPs because they lack experience in providing cable management solutions. It is easy, therefore, for misunderstandings to occur due to differences in organizational expectations and contractor perceptions of a cable management solution.

To avoid this problem, both end users and contractors need to have a clear understanding of exactly what is meant by installing a cable management system. Installing a CMS may be interpreted as just installing the software system on a computer at the customer's site. However, it could also mean populating the database with information about the installed horizontal and riser cabling, documenting cross-connects at all administration points, documenting ports on all service equipment and tracking all circuits assigned and available, or documenting connectivity for all station equipment. Issues abound in the implementation of a CMS. For example, should you document cable as a single record for each cable, or does the organization expect separate documentation for each twisted pair and for each fiber within every cable in the infrastructure? Most organizations need to define their cable management requirements more clearly, and contractors must be explicit when responding to a cable management RFP.

Cable management system software can produce and display physical documentation, such as a floor plan, or logical documentation, such as a tree structure.

Establish Organizational Objectives

Several questions need to be answered when preparing or developing a response to a cable management RFP (see the Sidebar, "Pertinent Questions to Ask When Preparing a Response for an RFP"). Not only will these answers help define the company's objectives, they will also clarify and determine the implementation requirements of the CMS, the type of system, and the specifics of documentation required.

PERTINENT QUESTIONS TO ASK WHEN PREPARING A RESPONSE FOR AN RFP

Company Objectives

- What is the organization doing now to manage its cabling infrastructure?
- Which departments or individuals have cable management responsibilities?
- Within the organization, who has requested a cable management solution, and what problem (if any) is that individual trying to solve?
- Has the organization specifically defined its cable management requirements?
- Does it plan to outsource the implementation of the CMS or the ongoing day-to-day cable management tasks?
- Are standards important to the organization?
- Will the CMS be linked to other accounting or management systems within the organization, and if so, how?
- What identification schemes for cabling and other assets are in place, and are these schemes suitable for cable management purposes or will the contractor design a new identification scheme?

Implementation

- What are the end user's implementation and training expectations?
- Will implementation of the CMS include only the cabling installed by the contractor as defined under the RFP or will documentation also be required for connections made after the installation?
- Will the CMS maintain pair and fiber detail or just the cable?

Type of System

- Does the company want a traditional database CMS or one that displays and produces physical documentation such as a graphical floor plan or logical (graphical tree structure) documentation?
- How does the organization currently handle moves, adds, and changes?
- Are trouble ticketing, service request, and work order management to be integrated into the CMS?

Documentation

- Does the organization plan to document the connectivity of circuits (services) to network equipment, and if so, when?
- What are the as-built drawing requirements of the CMS?
- What cabling and connectivity reports does the organization expect following implementation?
- What labeling requirements are included in the cable management specification?
- Will cable test results be documented within the CMS [2]?

Managing only the cable and not the pair detail can severely limit the usefulness of the CMS.

Perform Site Survey

Before you respond to an RFP, it is important to conduct a physical site survey and review the current cable and connectivity documentation. This includes a visit to each administration point within the organization's infrastructure to become familiar with the overall premises infrastructure. If the building is older and has gone through an evolution of different types of cabling systems (plenum/nonplenum), make sure there are no surprises.

During a site survey, you can determine the number of administration points (closets and rooms) and the work areas (face plate locations) you will need to document, the standard number of outlets at each work area, and the total outlets. You should also review how the wall fields in each telecommunications closet (TC) are organized. For example, are all services (voice, data, etc.) in the particular TC terminated on one set of horizontal connecting blocks or separate sets of horizontal blocks for each type of service? Does the organization have a standard for wall-field definition, and are the wall fields in all of the closets similar in layout? How are the cables and termination hardware labeled, and in what condition are the labels? Is documentation—reports or drawings—available in any of the TCs?

Take note of the overall condition of the TCs. If the customer wants a standards-based cable management solution, you can determine what changes need to be made in each closet to assure compliance.

After the site survey, arrange to meet with the appropriate staff within the organization to discuss organizational objectives, and explain the importance of an agreed-upon identification scheme when implementing the CMS. Next, you need to review the existing cable and connectivity documentation. If physical (floor plan) documentation is required, find out if drawings or computer-aided drawing (CAD) files showing horizontal cable routing are available. Decide together what the organization expects to do with existing obsolete and out-of-service cable. Determine the people within the organization who currently have authority or responsibility for cabling and cable management. From these discussions, you should also begin to understand clearly the organizational objectives and what the organizational structure for cable management will be in the future.

Defining Project Scope and Costs

You cannot determine the cost of implementing a CMS until you have defined the scope of the project. A useful way to document the site survey and the scope (and therefore, the cost) of the project is to develop a checklist or worksheet. A project worksheet helps ensure that there is no misunderstanding between the organization and the contractor as to what products and services are to be delivered.

To develop a project worksheet, you first need to know what cable, equipment, and connectivity documentation exists; what cabling, equipment, and connectivity you will have to inventory; and what cabling equipment and connectivity you will document in the CMS. In addition, you need to understand the customer's labeling requirements: what labels you will produce and when the organization needs them. For example, are labels to be produced upon installation of the cabling or upon completion of the implementation of the CMS?

Performing a physical inventory and documenting existing cabling, connectivity, service, or station equipment can be time-consuming. Find out the amount of detail required before determining your costs. For example, the customer may require you to inventory and document peripherals and third-party boards associated with each computer, or to inventory and document users and services assigned to each pair of each cable in the CMS. Either of these cases would create a substantial increase in the time and costs required to perform these tasks.

The best way to develop the costs for performing a physical inventory or completing the documentation portion of the project is to first determine the cost for a single transaction, such as routing horizontal cable to a work-area location, and then multiply that cost by the total number of required transactions, such as work areas. If any special consulting tasks are required, provide a separate time-basis quote.

Final Steps

There are a few additional steps you can take to ensure that implementation of the CMS goes smoothly. Always make sure that any existing documentation you use is complete and accurate. If you plan to use existing CAD files to complete the project, examine at least one of the files to verify the file format and accuracy of the drawing content. Do not forget to include travel and living expenses for any technicians who will perform services at the site.

Confirm exactly what deliverables the organization expects upon completion of the project. It is always a good idea to include a sample set of drawings and reports that you will deliver upon completion of the project. Similarly, when you begin to implement the cable management project, be sure to prototype a small portion of the infrastructure and produce a complete set of deliverables for organizational approval before continuing.

 The complete set of deliverables is extremely important. This is when the organization really sees and understands what they're getting.

This process will ensure that the identification scheme used meets the organization's requirements and that it is satisfied with the drawings and reports produced. Now that you are sure there are no misunderstandings, you can complete the cable management project.

EIA/TIA-606, not as well-known as 568 and 569, affects many in the telecom industry by mandating new record-keeping and administrative requirements with regard to the CMS. Let's take a look at how the EIA/TIA 606 telecommunications standard affects the documentation and management in the CMS.

EIA/TIA 606 DOCUMENTATION STANDARD

A number of years ago, the American National Standards Institute, the Telecommunications Industries Association, and the Electronic Industries Association formally approved and published their Administration Standard for the Telecommunications Infrastructure of Commercial Buildings, number 606. This administrative standard follows and conforms to the Commercial Building Telecommunications Wiring Standard (ANSI/EIA/TIA-T568-A, published in July 1991) and the Commercial Building Standard for Telecommunications Pathways and Spaces (ANSI/EIA/TIA-569, published in October 1990).

Although not as widely known as EIA/TIA-T568-A and 569, the new EIA/TIA-606 standard has far-reaching effects on the telecommunications industry. People in charge of network management in an organization see this standard as the foundation upon which they will build future cabling system configurations and management systems. Those preparing requests for proposals include technical specifications based on the standard when defining documentation and identification requirements for new structured wiring systems.

System integrators, contractors, designers, and installers must understand the 606 standard in order to respond to the requirements that have been included in all RFPs. In addition, software developers, who offer configuration management and telecommunication administration software systems, must always be certain that their applications comply with the standard.

Administering a telecommunications infrastructure includes tasks such as documenting and identifying all cables, termination hardware, cross-connects, cable pathways, telecommunication closets, work areas, and equipment rooms. In addition, an administrative system needs to provide reports that present telecommunications information in a useful format; include drawings of the telecommunications infrastructure for design, installation, and management purposes, and document changes to the system with trouble tickets, service requests, and work orders. The 606 administrative standard does, in fact, deal with all components of the telecommunications infrastructure. This standard supports electronic applications such as voice, data, video, alarm, environmental control, security, and audio. The purpose of the 606 standard is to provide a uniform administration scheme that is independent of applications, which may change several times throughout the life of a building.

The main elements covered by the standard are identifiers, required linkages, and telecommunications records. Optional records may also be linked into the system.

Three Areas Covered

Three major administrative areas covered by the new standard are pathway and space, wiring system, and grounding and bonding administration. In addition, the standard defines specific requirements for labeling and color coding and includes symbols recommended for use when preparing telecommunications infrastructure drawings.

The overall concept of the standard is to establish identifiers, in the form of labels, that specify the content of various records and define the linkages between records. The 606 standard then describes how to present the information needed to administer building wiring, pathways and spaces, and grounding and bonding.

Mandatory and advisory criteria are included in the standard. Mandatory criteria, which are required of record-keepers, specify the absolute minimum acceptable requirements and generally apply to safety, protection, performance, and compatibility. Optional advisory criteria, which are considered to be above the minimum requirements, are viewed as desirable enhancements to the standard.

Components of the System

Identifiers, as specified by the standard, are included as part of the record assigned to each element of the telecommunications infrastructure and must be unique. Encoded identifiers may include additional information such as cable, termination position, work area, or closet location.

Labels, including these identifiers, must meet the legibility, defacement, adhesion, and exposure requirements of Underwriters Laboratory 969 and should be affixed in accordance with the UL969 standard. Bar codes, when included on labels, must use either Code 39, conforming to USS-39, or Code 128, conforming to USS-128. Labels must also be color-coded to distinguish demarcation points and campus, horizontal, and riser (or backbone) termination points.

Pathways must be labeled at all endpoints located in telecommunication closets, equipment rooms, or entrance facilities. All horizontal and riser/backbone cables must be labeled at each end. All splice closures must be marked or labeled. Termination hardware, including termination positions, must also be labeled, except where high termination densities make such labeling impractical. The telecommunications main grounding busbar, as well as each bonding conductor and telecommunications grounding busbar, must be marked or labeled. Finally, each telecommunications space, whether telecommunications closet, equipment room, or work area, must be labeled.

Each record defined in the standard must contain certain required information and required linkages to other specified records. Linkages define the logical connections between identifiers and records. Identifiers, then, may point to more than one record. Descriptions of optional information and linkages to other records outside the scope of the standard are also included but are not meant to be inclusive or complete. There is no question that properly designed administrative systems will have to incorporate many of the non-mandatory advisory elements included within the standard.

In order to associate various applications with the telecommunications infrastructure, user codes identifying and linking circuit information, such as voice or data, may be included. Combining both physical and logical information is important for telecommunications administration, especially when generating trouble tickets for cable fault management and when generating work orders for moves, adds, and changes. Being able to quickly determine which circuits are available, reserved, in use, or out of use is an important part of telecommunications infrastructure management.

Reports

The following reports are recommended by the standard: pathway, space, cable, end-to-end circuit, cross-connect, and grounding/bonding summary reports. The recommended content of the reports includes:

- Pathway reports—list all pathways and include type, present fill, and load.
- Space reports—list all spaces, types, and locations.
- Cable reports—list all cables, types, and termination positions. Obviously this includes unused cables that may be reused.
- End-to-end circuit reports—trace connectivity from end-to-end and list user codes and associated termination positions and cables.
- Cross-connect reports—list all cross-connections within each space.
- Grounding/bonding summary reports—list all grounding busbars and attached backbone bonding conductors [3].

Obviously, additional and optional information can be presented in these reports, such as cable testing results. Also, the reports described in the standard are not all-inclusive. Many other reports not mentioned in the standard would normally be included as part of a properly designed telecommunication infrastructure administration system.

Drawings

Conceptual and installation drawings are considered input to the final record drawings, which graphically document the telecommunications infrastructure. While the standard doesn't specify how the drawings are created, in most cases they will be prepared using a computer-aided design system—either a separate software product or a telecommunications administration system that incorporates CAD functionality.

The record drawings must show the following: the identifier as well as the location and size of pathways and spaces; the location of all cable terminations (work areas, telecommunication closets, and equipment rooms); and all backbone cables. Drawings that show the routing of all horizontal cables are desirable. The standard includes symbols that may be used when preparing these drawings. Ideally, record information should be accessible when one is viewing the record drawings.

It is mandated that all wiring, termination, and splice work orders be maintained for telecommunication repairs, moves, adds, and changes. The work-order document must include cable identifiers and types, termination identifiers and types, and splice identifiers and types. The work-order process should be used to update the administrative records. In day-to-day telecommunications administration, this is the most important requirement set forth in the standard. If the system records are not immediately updated when a work order is completed, the administrative system will quickly become outdated and useless.

Cabling System Management

Configuration management is identified by the International Organization for Standardization's Network Management Forum as one of the five functional cabling system management areas, the others being fault, security, performance, and accounting management. Configuration management is the core of the four other cabling system management areas and comprises the following management elements: in-use and spare-part equipment inventory management; cabling and wiring management; circuit management; tracking, authorizing, and scheduling moves, adds, and changes; trouble-ticketing cable faults; user and vendor management; and documenting current cabling system configurations.

If the mandatory and advisory criteria are included, the ANSI/TIA/EIA-606 Administration Standard for the Telecommunications Infrastructure of Commercial Buildings covers most of the elements included in the definition of configuration management. Since the infrastructure can be thought of as the collection of those components that provide basic support for the distribution of all information within a building or campus, the telecommunications administration standard must now be viewed as the basis upon which all future cabling system configuration management systems will be built.

Implementing a telecommunication administration system requires a great deal of thought and planning. There are many important reasons why an organization should implement a physical layer configuration, design, and telecommunications administration system. Some of the reasons are:

- To determine what cables, conductors of fibers, and circuits (PBX, Ethernet, token ring, etc.) are free, in use, and out of use, and what circuits and users are assigned to them.
- To maintain a documentation and identification system for the implementation of an equipment and cable disaster recovery plan in case of fire, explosion, flood, or other emergency.
- To identify what equipment is in use, spare, and out of use, and to document and maintain equipment connectivity.
- To update and manage cable faults, moves, adds, and changes, and to maintain work-order records for all equipment, users, circuits, and cable paths.
- To reduce the amount of cabling system or LAN downtime.
- To decrease labor costs by eliminating the need to trace undocumented circuits each time an add, move, change, or cable fault occurs.
- To increase confidence in the structured wiring systems that organizations use to downsize applications from mainframe and minicomputing platforms.
- To generate management reports and perform detailed network analysis on all equipment and cabling systems.
- To transfer users from one cabling system to another as part of the effort to manage overall network performance.
- To document and maintain cable and circuit test data.
- To manage important vendor relationships: purchasing, technical support, returns, and service.
- To administer names and addresses and track all network equipment, cables, and circuits for departments, users, managers, and technicians.
- To design new cabling systems within the infrastructure and to produce reports and analysis detailing equipment and cabling requirements for them [Spencer, 6].

FROM HERE

Chapter 26 opened up Part VI, *Maintaining Cabling Systems*, with a discussion on how to maintain your cabling system. The chapter examined the facilitation of ongoing cabling system maintenance by covering the building of the cable plant management database, vendor CPM products, and the EIA/TIA 606 standard. Chapter 27 examines future standards development (ATM, 300–600 Mhz cable systems [category 6], zone wiring, TIA/EIA-T568-B, EN50174, 100BaseT2, 1000BaseT [Gigabit Ethernet, etc.]).

NOTES

[1]   IMAP Corporation, 1501 North Broadway, Suite 115, Walnut Creek, CA. 94596, 2000, p. 1.

[2]   William Spencer, "Define End-User and Contractor Needs When Implementing a CMS," Network & Communication Technology, Inc., 24 Wampum Road, Park Ridge, NJ 07656, 1998, pp. 2–3.

[3]   William Spencer, "New Standard Issued for Telecom Documentation and Management," Network & Communication Technology, Inc., 24 Wampum Road, Park Ridge, NJ 07656, 1995, p. 4.

CHAPTER   2 7

Standards Development

Recently, the passing of an era of sorts in
the history of the development of cabling standards occurred around the globe.
It was the end of a nearly seven-year transition period for the enforcement of a
broad collection of global cabling standards and reference points designed to
minimize the compatibility problems faced today by many countries.

The intent of the transition period on a practical level, via the Electromagnetic Compatibility (EMC) directive in Europe and the U.S. Cabling
Standards, is to ensure your German-made Groupe Special Mobile (GSM)
phone doesn't make a networked video application stumble in Liverpool, or,
conversely, keep your active U.S. cable infrastructure from becoming a continental broadcast antenna. And so, global cabling industry manufacturers,
installers, and users are now charged with certain new responsibilities not
accounted for when they last left their office or place of business. Manufacturers are of course required to ensure their cabling products meet standards
laid down by the EMC Directive (see the Sidebar, "A Quick Stroll through
Europe's EMC Directive Regulatory History") in Europe and cabling standards here in the United States. Ultimately, however, the onus for cabling system and installation compliance rests on the provider and the owner. Penalties
for failure in Europe, for instance, can lead to stiff fines, imprisonment, or the
barring of products from sale—testament to the European Union's (EU's)
stern view of the matter. The penalties for failure in the U.S. are not as severe.

A QUICK STROLL THROUGH EUROPE'S EMC DIRECTIVE REGULATORY HISTORY

First drafted as 89/336/EEC, the EMC Directive is the offspring of a multinational marriage of regulations for electromagnetic emissions and immunity.

The immunity standards upon which it relies, for example, are derived from regulations including the International Electrotechnical Committee's IEC 801.x guidelines, as well as those of the International Special Committee on Radio Interference (Comite International Special des Pertubations Radioelectriques [CISPR] 24), and input from national organizations such as the British Standards Institute (BSI) and the U.S. Federal Communications Commission (FCC). Blended to a palatable form by the EEC and its affiliate body, the Commission for European Normalization (CEN and CENELEC), the resulting regulations are known as the Harmonized Standards or European Norms (EN).

Two sets of these Harmonized Standards serve as the basis for evaluating the emissions and immunity characteristics for all electronic equipment not specifically identified in succeeding codes. Generic EN50082-1 and -2 address immunity issues in commercial and industrial environments, respectively, and generic EN50081-1 and -2 cover emissions. Standards for cabling systems, components, and installations are related in two dedicated documents, Information Technology Equipment (ITE) prEN55024 and ITE EN55022, which in turn serve as support for portions of the EMC Directive. CENELEC's structured cabling standard EN50174 has now been published.

While the lineage may appear a bit complex, the intent is not. The EMC Directive's requirements for electromagnetic emissions seek to limit what a component, system, or installation can contribute, either by conduction or radiation, to the electromagnetic environment as part of its normal operation. Conversely, it also defines what level of electromagnetic radiation (not immunity)—electrostatic discharge (ESD), power line transients, and radio frequency (RF) fields—a component, system, or installation should endure and still function.

If in fact cabling systems have an impact on compliance, the EU's networking managers are in for somewhat of a surprise. Cabling systems running high-speed data communications protocols over category 5 UTP not only may fail components of the EMC Directive, but may not even function at all in certain electromagnetic environments. In the real world, that means everything from shorter drive distances to application latency and crashes, data corruption and loss, video display distortion, and potential health hazards [1].

If you plan to wring a few last precious years from your 4 Mbps token ring network, emissions and compatibility issues will likely be the least of your worries when users begin requiring bandwidth-hungry applications such as video. But if you are among the majority of cabling professionals who are or soon will be installing or operating cabling systems supporting higher throughput protocols, compliance with emissions and susceptibility standards will be as integral to a successful installation as functioning network interface cards.

So, what is the best compliance route for your company with regard to the standards that are currently being developed? The following questions are helpful in determining which route of compliance may be the most logical for your company.

1. Does the product/cabling system exist in more than one version?
2. Are you having difficulty identifying Harmonized Standards?
3. Are you likely to make modifications to the cabling equipment in the future?
4. Are future cabling standards or modifications to existing standards likely?
5. Are there existing test results for the product/cabling system?
6. Is the product/cabling system not practical to test?

If you answered Yes to any of these questions, you should consider taking a close look at the latest cabling standards in development to see which one(s) best fits your company's needs on its route to compliance. This chapter presents the most accurate, stable, and current information available with regard to the latest global standards in development. Let's first start with a brief discussion and/or overview of the very latest international published and draft standards (U.S. and global) at the time of this writing. This will be followed by a very specific and detailed look at U.S. and global standards in development.

OVERVIEW OF THE LATEST CABLING STANDARDS DOCUMENTS

Standards that specify cabling performance requirements have been developed by a number of organizations. In many groups, work is underway to develop new standards as well. Table 27–1 lists some of the very lastest international published and draft standards [5]. On the other hand, the Sidebar "Quick Update of Cabling Standards Documents," gives a very quick and dirty update of the latest international published and draft standards.

Table 27–1 Published and Draft Standards

TIA	ISO/IEC	CENELEC	SAA/SNZ
TIA-526-14	ISO/IEC 14763-1-1999	EN50173-1995	AS/NZS 3080:1996
TIA-526-7	ISO/IEC 14763-2-1999	EN50173 2nd Edition	AS 3084-1993
TIA-568A-1995	ISO/IEC 14763-3-1999	EN50174-1-1999	AS/NZS 3085.1:1995
TIA-568A-A1	ISO/IEC 14763-4-1999	EN50174-2-1999	AS/NZS 3086:1996
TIA-568A-A2	IEC 61935-1-1999	EN50174-3-1999	SAA HB 27-1996
TIA-568A-A3	IEC 61935-2-2000	EN50XXX-2000	SAA HB 29-1998
TIA-568A-A4	ISO/IEC 11801-1995		NWIP9801/9802
TIA-568A-A5	ISO/IEC 11801		NWIP 9803
TIA-568B.1	AM2-1999		NWIP 9804
TIA-568B.2	ISO/IEC 11801		NWIP 9807
TIA-568B.3	2nd Edition		
TIA-568B.4			
TIA-569A-1995	**ATM Forum**		
TIA-570	AF-PHY-0015.000		
TIA-606-1994	AF-PHY-0046.000		
TSB-67-1995			
TSB-95-1999	**IEEE**		
	IEEE 802.3i		
PN3727 Cat 6	IEEE 802.3j		
Addendum-2000	IEEE 802.3u		
	IEEE 802.3aa		
CSA	IEEE 802.3z		
CSA T528	IEEE 802.3ab		
CSA T529			

QUICK UPDATE OF CABLING STANDARDS DOCUMENTS

TIA 526-14A (Optical Power Loss Measurement of Installed Multimode Fiber Cable Plant)

This standard covers the application and use of power meters in field testing multimode fiber optic cabling in structured wiring systems.

TIA 526-7 (Optical Power Loss Measurement of Installed Single-Mode Fiber Cable Plant)

This standard covers the application and use of OTDRs and power meters in field testing single-mode fiber optic cabling in structured wiring systems.

TIA 568A-1995 (Commercial Building Telecommunications Wiring Standard)

Includes generic requirements for structured cabling systems in commercial buildings. Establishes technical and performance criteria for cabling system configurations and interfacing and connecting their respective elements. Incorporates all the relevant information from TIA 568, TSB 36, TSB 40, and TSB 53.

TIA 568A-A1-1998 (Delay and Delay Skew)

Defines and specifies requirements for propagation delay and delay skew in cables, components, basic links, and channels.

TIA 568A-A2-1998 (Miscellaneous Changes)

Miscellaneous changes and updates to TIA568A. The most important change was the requirement for testing connecting hardware with both common and differential mode terminations (to eliminate short-link resonance issues).

TIA 568A-A3-1998 (Bundled and Hybrid Cables)

Defines and specifies requirements for bundled and hybrid cables.

TIA 568A-A4-1999 (Patch Cords)

Defines and specifies NEXT and return loss requirements for patch cables.

TIA 568A-A5-1999 (Additional Transmission Performance Specifications for Enhanced Category 5 Cabling)

Formerly SP-4195, TIA 568A-A5 provides performance requirements for enhanced category 5 (category 5E) components, cable, and links. It includes all the measurements in TSB-67 and TSB-95, but to stricter performance levels. It also includes power sum NEXT. All measurements are to 100 MHz.

TIA 568B.1-2000 (Commercial Building Telecommunications Wiring Standard)

This is a major new standard release that updates and replaces the following standards and bulletins: TSB67, TSB72, TSB75, TSB95, TIA568A, TIA568A addendum's 1,2,3,4, and 5, and TIA ScTP (PN-3193 Interim standard). Key additions include category 5E performance levels, 50/125 mm fiber, and allowance for alternate fiber connectors other than the SC. This standard, which is expected to be complete in the second quarter of 2000, eliminates support for category 5 in horizontal cabling. Category 5E becomes the minimum accepted performance level. Some technical content is referred from planned TIA 568B.2, TIA 568B.3, and TIA 568B.4 standards.

TIA 568-B.2 (100 Ohm Twisted Pair Cabling Standard)
Technical content on 100 ohm twisted pair cabling that is referenced by TIA 568-B.1.

TIA 568-B.3 (Optical Fiber Cabling Standard)
Technical content on optical fiber cabling that is referenced by TIA 568-B.1.

TIA 568-B.4 (Shielded Twisted Pair Cabling Standard)
Technical content on shielded twisted pair cabling that is referenced by TIA 568-B.1.

TIA 569A-1995 (Commercial Building Standard for Telecommunications Pathways and Spaces)
Specifies design and construction practices for telecommunications services within and between commercial buildings.

TIA 570A-1998 (Residential and Light Commercial Telecommunications Wiring Standard)
Specifies residential cabling systems, requirements, and structure.

TIA 606-1994 (Administration Standard for the Telecommunications Infrastructure of Commercial Buildings)
Specifies administration of communications wiring and connecting hardware, building distribution systems, and grounding and bonding. Standardized labeling and documentation requirements for generic cabling in commercial buildings.

TIA TSB-67-1995 (Transmission Performance Specifications for Field Testing of Unshielded Twisted Pair Cabling Systems
Defines the basic link and channel. Specifies performance requirements for the basic link and channel for wire map, length, attenuation, and NEXT. Defines field measurement procedures and test instrument requirements.

TIA TSB-95-1999 (Additional Transmission Performance Specifications for UTP)
Formerly SP-4194, TSB-95 is designed to provide expected performance criteria for those new measurements now determined to be important for new networking transmission methods. For example, Gigabit Ethernet requires a minimum level of performance for return loss, ELFEXT, power sum ELFEXT, propagation delay, and delay skew. Because it is a TSB, it is not a normative requirement. TSB-95 provides guidelines to network designers as to what the minimum installed performance of legacy category 5 links can be expected. Since it provides only minimal compliance specifications and is not normative, TSB-95 has received lit-

tle attention or support. In fact it is not even mentioned in the new TIA 568B standard currently in development. Network managers would be well advised to consider category 5E as the minimum performance level allowed. Category 5E is much better than TSB-95.

PN3727 Cat 6 Addendum-2000 (Category 6 component, cable, and link requirements)

This draft document was in its fifth revision as of May 1999. At this time it is the most complete document providing performance requirements for category 6 links, and is the draft standard against which most manufacturers are verifying product performance. As of early 2000, there is broad agreement on numbers, but work needs to be completed on test methods. This document has been delayed by ongoing work on TIA 568B, but now that most ballot issues have been resolved on TIA 568B, more attention will focus on completing the category 6 document. Category 6/Class E performance requirements will be specified in ISO/IEC 11801-2000, but this standard will likely lag the TIA category 6 standard.

CSA T528 (Administration Standard for the Telecommunications Infrastructure of Commercial Buildings)

This is equivalent to the TIA 606 standard.

CSA T529-95 (Commercial Building Telecommunications Wiring Standard)

This is equivalent to the TIA 568A-1995 standard.

ISO/IEC Standards Overview

The first and most important document in this series is ISO/IEC International Standard 11801 (IS1801). See Figure 27–1 [5].

ISO/IEC 14763-1 (administration, documentation, records)

Describes requirements for administration systems and documentation of pathways, spaces, cables, terminations, and grounding in accordance with ISO/IEC 11801. This document was published in February 2000.

ISO/IEC 14763-2 (planning and installation practices)

Specifies requirements for planning, specification, quality assurance, and installation of new cabling in accordance with ISO/IEC 11801. This document was published in February 2000.

ISO/IEC 14763-3 (testing of optical fiber cabling)

Outlines test procedures to be used to ensure that optical fiber cabling, designed in accordance with ISO/IEC 11801 and installed according to the recommendations of ISO/IEC 14763-2, is capable of delivering the level of transmission performance specified in ISO/IEC 11801. This document was published in February 2000.

ISO/IEC 14763-4 (testing of copper cabling)

This project has been cancelled. IEC 61935 -1:1999 (testing of copper cabling) is to be referenced instead.

IEC 61935-1: 1999 (testing of copper cabling)

Specifies reference measurement procedures for cabling parameters and requirements for field tester accuracy to measure cabling parameters specified in ISO/IEC 11801.

IEC 61935-2: 2000 (testing of copper cabling)

Specifies requirements for laboratory testing of modular plug cords.

ISO/IEC IS11801-1995 (Generic Cabling for Customer Premises)

This document has been the international standard for generic cabling requirements in customer premises since 1995. However, it has largely become obsolete for the following reasons: It uses obsolete links definitions such as the "cabling link" (replaced by the permanent link), it does not specify normative return loss requirements, it does not address new measurements such as ELFEXT, delay skew, or PSNEXT, it does not address work area or patch cord performance Class D requirements defined in this standard, and it does not support ATM 155 Mbps networks.

IS11801 is undergoing extensive revisions and is being updated with ISO/IEC 11801 Proposed Draft Amendment 3 (ISO/IEC PDAM3).

ISO/IEC IS11801 AM2-1999 (Generic Cabling for Customer Premises)

This is a major update to IS11801-1995. It adds requirements for new measurements, defines the permanent link and channel, removes many ffs's (for future study), and provides more detail. Another important change is Class D requirements have been toughened and are now closer to TIA Cat 5E requirements (but different). This has the interesting implication that a link tested and in conformance to Class D in 1998 could be tested against AM2 Class D in 2000 and fail, even though the link has identical performance. Thus, in specifying conformance to IS11801, it is critical to ensure you clarify whether you require conformance with IS11801-1995 or IS11801 AM2.

Concurrently with the AM2 work, extensive revisions to include Cat 6/Class E and Cat 7/Class F are in development. A complete rewrite later in the year 2000 incorporating these additions is expected.

ISO/IEC 11801 2nd Edition-2000 (Generic Cabling for Customer Premises)

The 2nd edition of ISO/IEC 11801 will incorporate specifications for category 6/Class E and category 7/Class F cabling and components ATM Forum Standards.

AF-PHY-0015.000-1994 (ATM Physical Medium Dependent Interface Specification for 155 Mbps over Twisted Pair Cable)

Specifies requirements for running ATM at 155 Mbps over UTP. In summary, these requirements are satisfied by a TIA 568A-1995 category 5 channel.

AF-PHY-0046.000-1996 (622.08 Mbps Physical Layer Specification)

Specifies requirements for running ATM at 622 Mbps over single- and multimode fiber optic cabling. No copper specification for ATM at 622 Mbps has been defined or approved.

IEEE Standards

IEEE 802.3i-1990 (Supplement to 802.3 - 10BASE-T)
10BASE-T standard. In summary, 10BASE-T cabling requirements are met by a TIA 568A category 3 channel.

IEEE 802.3j-1993 (10BASE-F)
10BASE-F standard. In summary, 10BASE-F cabling requirements are met with no more than 12.5 dB attenuation at 850 nm on 62.5/125 mm multimode fiber.

IEEE 802.3u-1995 (100BASE-T)
100BASE-T standard. In summary, 100BASE-T cabling requirements are met by an IS11801-1995 Class D channel.

IEEE 802.3aa-1998 (100BASE-T Maintenance Revision #5)
Maintenance revision on 100BASE-T.

IEEE 802.3z-1998 (CSMA/CD Access Method and Physical Layer Specifications for 1000 Mbps)
Gigabit Ethernet standard. Does not include detailed twisted pair requirements. These are provided in IEEE 802.3ab.

IEEE 802.3ab (Physical Layer Parameters and Specifications for 1000 Mb/s Operation over 4 pair of Category 5 Balanced Copper Cabling, Type 1000BASE-T)
Defines physical layer characteristics and specifications for 1000 Mb/s operation on 4 pair of 100 ohm category 5 balanced copper cabling as defined by EIA/TIA-568-A, Annex E or its equivalent as built from material specified by ISO/IEC 11801:1995.

CENELEC Standards

EN50173-1995 (Generic Cabling for Customer Premises)
EN50173 specifies generic cabling for use within commercial premises. It is very similar to IS11801. A 1999 amendment 1 added a permanent link and channel definitions, as well as the new measurement parameters, analogous to IS11801PDAM3.

EN50173 2nd Edition-2000 (Generic Cabling for Customer Premises)
The 2nd edition of EN50173 is expected to harmonize with IS11801 2nd Edition and will include specifications for category 6/Class E and category 7/Class F cabling and components.

EN50174-1-1999 (administration, documentation, records)
Describes requirements for administration systems and documentation of pathways, spaces, cables, terminations, and grounding in accordance with EN50173.This European Norm was published in 1999, and harmonized with ISO/IEC 14763-1.

EN50174-2 -1999 (planning and installation practices)

Specifies requirements for planning, specification, quality assurance and installation of new balanced copper and fiber optic cabling in accordance with EN50173. This European Norm was published in 1999, and harmonized with ISO/IEC 14763-2.

EN50174-3-1999 (Installation, Planning, and Practices External to Buildings)

Details requirements and guidance for installation, planning, and practices for balanced copper and fiber optic cabling external to buildings.

EN50XXX-2000 (Procedures for Testing Premise Cabling)

Specifies procedures for testing the transmission performance of installed cabling in premises. Procedures apply to both balanced copper and optical fiber cabling. These test procedures are to be used for acceptance testing, verification of specific application support, and troubleshooting during the investigation of faults. This document is wider in scope than IEC 61935 in that it must support both generic and application-specific cabling for both balanced copper and fiber cabling.

Australian/New Zealand Standards

AS/NZS 3080:1996 (Telecommunications installations—Integrated telecommunications cabling systems for commercial premises)

This Australian/New Zealand Standard is based on ISO/IEC 11801 with minor amendments and specifies generic cabling for use within commercial premises, which may be comprised of single or multiple buildings on a campus.

AS 3084:1993 (Telecommunications installations—Telecommunications pathways and spaces for commercial buildings)

This Australian Standard is based on EIA/TIA 569, but takes account of current practices in Australia.

AS/NZS 3085.1:1995 (Telecommunications installations—Administration of communications cabling systems, Part 1: Basic requirements)

This Australian/New Zealand Standard references ANSI/TIA/EIA-606 and details a set of basic specifications for identification and recording of installed components that were thought to be sufficient to meet the administration requirements of the majority of users.

AS/NZS 3086:1996 (Telecommunications installations—Integrated telecommunications cabling for small office/home office premises)

This Australian/New Zealand Standard is based on EIA/TIA-570 (1991), but with some significant changes.

SAA HB 27:1996 (Handbook for field testing of balanced cable installations)

This Australian/New Zealand handbook is based on TIA/EIA-67 and uses the same test configurations. However, the test specification is based on the ISO/IEC 11801 link performance specification.

SAA HB 29: 1998 (Telecommunications Cabling Handbook)

This Standards Australia handbook is intended to assist installers by providing explanatory material, practical details, and general information to supplement the information in the AS/NZS 3080, and, to a lesser extent, AS/NZS 3086 Standards.

Australia/New Zealand New Work Items in Progress (NWIP)

NWIP 9801 and NWIP 9802

These work items are being grouped together and entail updating the field testing handbook HB-27 to include additional test parameters for Class D links and channels. The changes in HB-27 would be reflected as an amendment to the base cabling Standard AS/NZS 3080. The working group is closely monitoring the TIA's progress in specifying cat 5E and ISO's progress in redefining Class D performance in the proposed PDAM3 amendment.

NWIP 9803 (Revision of Cabling Handbook HB-29)

Has commenced as of January 2000.

NWIP 9804 (Test method for production modular patch cords)

The working group is monitoring TIA progress on this issue.

NWIP 9807—Revision of Administration Standard AS/NZS 3085.1

Has commenced as of January 2000 [5].

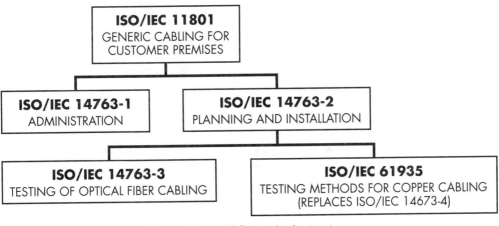

Figure 27–1   ISO standards structure.

U.S. STANDARDS

The U.S. standards in development are as follows:

- TIA-T568-A Commercial Building Telecommunications Wiring Standard
- TIA-569 Commercial Building Standard for Telecommunications Pathways and Spaces
- TIA-570 Residential and Light Commercial Telecommunications Wiring Standard
- TIA TR41.8.4 Outside Plant
- TIA FO2.2 and Short Wavelength Fast Ethernet Alliance
- USOC
- IEEE
- ATM Forum
- Zone Wiring
- VESA
- NEMA
- ICEA
- BICSI

The current status of the U.S. standards in development and their relationship to the EMC directive are discussed next.

TIA-T568-A Commercial Building Telecommunications Wiring Standard

TR 41.8.1 has established a task group to investigate the measurement of cabling return loss. The specification of this parameter is required to support full-duplex applications such as 1000BASE-T. At this time, TIA has not fully developed field test methods and test cord requirements for return loss.

Return loss measurement accuracy is sensitive to handling of tester cords, termination practices, and other effects that are under study. These effects may lead to inconsistent measurements. TR41.8.1 has made significant progress in the specification of suitable requirements and guidelines to improve return loss measurement accuracy. There is no standard for field verification of return loss until these requirements are approved.

The TR41.8.1 working group discussed a liaison letter to IEEE commenting on Draft 4.0 of the IEEE Gigabit Ethernet standard. The liaison letter pointed out that to support Gigabit Ethernet, category 5 together with additional parameters for return loss, ELFEXT, and MDELFEXT are needed. In addition, for new installations, better than category 5 cabling is recommended. Both these changes were accepted and will be forwarded to IEEE as a ballot response and a liaison letter from TR41.

Hybrid Cable Requirements

The Preliminary Notification (PN) 3727 UTP systems task group discussed ballot responses from the second ANSI ballot of SP-3837-A. All ballot responses were resolved and the document was forwarded for publication.

Category 6

Several presentations on category 6 were discussed and several proposals in these presentations were incorporated into Draft 3 of the category 6 specification. These include modifications in attenuation of cables to match the requirements in the international WG3 committee documents, and incorporation of return loss for cables, connectors, channels, and basic links.

Patch Cord Specifications

The PN-2948 connecting hardware task group discussed modular patch cord specifications. Draft 7 was approved by TR41.8.1 to be sent out as a committee letter ballot with the intent of publishing this document as Addendum 4 of TIA-568-A. Other items discussed include a new method for qualification of modular test plugs to replace the TOC method that has been used for category 5 plug qualification. The new method is intended to characterize both the capacitive and inductive cross talk of the plug.

Screened Twisted Pair

The PN-3193 document was approved to be sent out as a default ballot with only the technical changes from the last ballot. A major reason for the current delay is ensuring tolerances between plug and jack shield to ensure that contact and continuity of the two shields is guaranteed.

Optical Fiber

The PN-3723 optical fiber task group continued discussions on the new version of TIA-568-B.3. This document contains detailed specifications for media and connectors used for either backbone or horizontal cabling. TR41.8.1 approved this document to be sent out for a committee letter ballot. The intent is to solicit technical review and comments to improve the document before a full ANSI ballot. The task group has also taken on the responsibility of working on the revision of the TIA-568-B.1 document that contains requirements targeted toward owners, designers, installers, and testing of recognized cabling systems.

The Installation Group

The installation task group is winding down its activities due to lack of participation and lack of technical input from the various cabling task groups. The plan is that this task group goes dormant until new information becomes available for pulling tension, bending radius, and cable ties for all media types recognized in EIA/TIA-T568-A.

Working Group 3

A liaison report from the WG3 (Working Group 3) international committee was very positive in terms of harmonization with ANSI/EIA/TIA. WG3 has also made its category 5/Class D channel requirements almost identical to those in EIA/TIA TSB67. Additionally, the 300–600 Mhz cable systems (category 6) objectives of EIA/TIA were adopted with very minor changes. These are important positive steps in the interest of maintaining uniform global standards and products.

Figure 27–2 represents the current development state of EIA/TIA-T568-B. Development continues at a very slow pace on this document [2]. Still not much

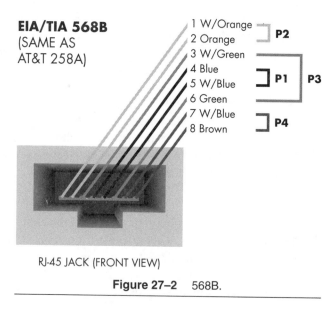

RJ-45 JACK (FRONT VIEW)

Figure 27–2   568B.

is happening on EIA/TIA-T568-B because of other urgent priorities. The committee agreed that work must resume in the EIA/TIA-T568-B area, and established a goal of circulating a first ballot by the end of 2000.

TIA-569-A Commercial Building Standard for Telecommunications Pathways and Spaces

The Technical Reference (TR) 41.8.3 working group discussed the addition of poke-thru as an alternative method for horizontal distribution. The current 569-A document does not recognize poke-thru as a viable distribution mechanism. Details of when and how to use poke-thru systems are now being generated.

TIA-570 Residential and Light Commercial Telecommunications Wiring Standard

TR41.8.2 is now out for a third ballot. Major changes are the addition of single-mode and 50 mm fiber to the list of recognized media. Also the issue of ensuring adequate primary and secondary protection has been incorporated.

TIA TR41.8.4 Outside Plant

The outside plant working group resolved comments submitted during a default ballot. The resolutions are out again for a second default ballot. One area of concern in this standard is that it requires that all UTP connecting hardware provide test access. This was possible with the traditional outside plant connecting hardware, but will be much more difficult to implement for category 5 or better connectors used in outside plant cabling.

TIA FO2.2 and Short Wavelength Fast Ethernet Alliance

Currently, 10 Mb/s fiber Ethernet (10BASE-FL) operates at 850 nm wavelength, and 100 Mb/s Fast Ethernet (100BASE-FX) operates at 1,300 nm. As a result, most fiber LAN electronics support either 10 or 100 Mb/s, but not both. In general, migration to Fast Ethernet requires users to completely replace their fiber electronics. The TIA Fiber Optics LAN Section is working toward elimination of this disparity. A Short Wavelength Fast Ethernet standard is in development under the auspices of the TIA F.O. 2.2 committee. The standard should give customers a lower-cost horizontal solution (at 850 nm). It will also provide a simple upgrade path from 10 to 100 Mb/s operation requiring no change in the user's fiber LAN electronics. The standard will be supported up to 300 m over 62.5 mm fiber. Most electronics expected to support this standard will also offer auto-negotiation with existing 10BASE-FL products, ensuring investment protection for users planning to upgrade to Fast Ethernet. An interoperability demo of prototype and pre-standard 850 nm Fast Ethernet products was conducted at the Fall Networld+Interop in 1998 in Atlanta, Georgia.

USOC

Universal Service Order Code (USOC) is an old standard used for voice cabling, as shown in Figure 27–3 [Combs, 4]. Notice that for 1- and 2-line phones (which use pins 4/5 and 3/6), 568A or 568B will work just as well as USOC. But for Ethernet (pins 1/2 and 3/6), USOC won't work. An Ethernet NIC trying to transmit on pins 1/2 will run into trouble because 1/2 aren't a pair (not the same color, and not twisted together). So unless you know the cable plant is for voice (analog, not digital), not ISDN, and it's never going to carry data, you should avoid USOC.

Why are the pairs shuffled around instead of laid out logically? Well, they are logical, if you know the background. Ethernet was originally designed to run over the same cabling used by the phone system (AT&T created this as StarLAN), so this design left pins 4/5 available for a phone. If you

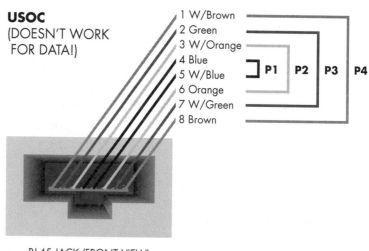

Figure 27–3   USOC.

plug an RJ11 (4 wire) into this, the middle two pins (2/3) of the RJ11 would connect to the middle two pins (4/5) of the RJ45, just perfect for a one-line phone. If you plug an Ethernet cable into it, pins 1/2 will be used as one pair, and pins 3/6 will be used as another. No conflicts. Pretty clever, eh?

Choose 568A or 568B as the standard for your cable plant, but don't mix them.

IEEE

IEEE 802.3z 1000BASE-FX has been published.

IEEE 802.3ab 1000BASE-T

The wording of the introduction has been modified to highlight that operation over category 5 was a design objective and that the additional parameters in TSB-95 are required to be met. Delay skew requirements were specified at 2 MHz (instead of 1 MHz) to align with cabling standards. The receiver common mode noise test (to be referenced in an informative Annex) was amended following further work. A new draft, D4.2, will be forwarded for 15-day electronic recirculation ballot, then submitted to LMSC ballot. 1000Base-T could be approved as an IEEE standard, although technical comments could delay it. Concern has been expressed by at least one Task Force member regarding the lack of working the 1000BASE-T product to date.

802.5t 100 Mbit/s HSTR

100 Mbit/s high speed token ring (HSTR) is being specified for full-duplex (switched) and half-duplex (shared) operation over 100 m of 2-pair 100 ohm category 5 and 2-pair 150 ohm Type 1 cable plus 2 km of 62.5 micron multimode fiber. This specification is now technically complete.

802.5v 1000 Mbit/s HSTR

An initial draft is being prepared to specify 1000 Mbit/s HSTR for full-duplex (switched) operation. 1000Base-FX Ethernet Physical Layer will be adopted as the basis. Balanced cable support is now planned. 802.5 may consider basing the design on cat 6 or 7 cabling in order to reduce the cost, risk, and development time scales for the electronics. 802.5 will probably wait and learn from the experience of 1000Base-T. The use of high-density fiber optic connectors is also being considered.

802.11a High Speed WLAN (5.2 GHz)

Targeting raw bit rates of 20 and 54 Mbit/s in the 5 GHz band, although there will be differences in the actual frequencies used around the world (certainly with U.S., Europe, and Japan). Liaison is being conducted with ETSI and a second draft is being prepared for a working group (WG) ballot.

802.11b High Speed WLAN (2.4 GHz)

Targeting raw bit rates of 5.5 Mbit/s using frequency-hopping and 11 Mbit/s using direct sequence (note that these bit rates are higher than previously reported). A WG ballot gained 64 percent approval and comments have been resolved. A new draft is being prepared for recirculation ballot.

IEEE 802.15 High Speed Wireless Personal Area Networks

The Institute of Electrical and Electronics Engineers (IEEE) Project 802 LAN/MAN Standards Committee announced that the 802.15 Working Group on Wireless Personal Area Networks has initiated work in two new areas. One area is to develop a class of standard, called a Recommended Practice, to improve coexistence with other WLAN systems operating in the same band. The other is to initiate activity, which will lead to the development of a standard for high data rate, low-cost wireless personal area networks (WPANs).

IEEE 802.15 Working Group is a standards working group on wireless personal area networks. The 802.15 Working Group is part of the IEEE 802 LMSC (LAN MAN Standards Committee) responsible for Ethernet, token ring, wireless, and bridging standards. The IEEE 802 LMSC is sponsored by the IEEE Computer Society and submits standards through the IEEE Standards Association.

The relatively new IEEE 802.15 Working Group is currently engaged in developing a 1 Mbps standard based on the work of the Bluetooth™ SIG (special interest group). It is now beginning development of a project definition for a consumer-priced, 20 Mbps or faster high rate WPAN that can be widely deployed for short-range information transfer, particularly multimedia and digital imaging. The initiative began with a proposal from Cisco, Eastman Kodak, and Motorola to the Working Group at the November 1999 Plenary Meeting of 802.

A wireless personal area network, or WPAN, is a low-cost networking scheme that enables computing devices such as PCs, laptop computers, printers, and personal digital assistants (PDAs) to wirelessly communicate with each other over short distances.

The IEEE's goal is to provide the foundation for a broad range of interoperable consumer devices by establishing universally adopted standards and recommend practices for wireless digital communication anywhere and anytime. The creation of a wireless personal area network protocol is a critical part of this approach. These two additional projects will provide for continued product innovation in this rapidly growing area.

The IEEE 802.15 Working Group is comprised of several active subgroups. The first major effort, to standardize a low cost, medium data rate WPAN solution, was assigned to Task Group 1 (TG1) in 1999. TG1 is currently working closely with the Bluetooth SIG to complete this task. The anticipated draft standard, 802.15.1, will be a fully interoperable derivative of the Bluetooth specification. Based on strong industry support of TG1 and interest in increasing both the robustness of wireless solutions and data rates, two additional groups have been formed.

Coexistence Task Group.   A major concern shared by many in the industry is whether various wireless devices based on several standards or specifications can peacefully coexist within the same 2.4 GHz band. The 802.15 Coexistence Task Group (TG2) will address the issue of coexistence between WPANs and other wireless devices, such as the IEEE 802.11 wireless local area networks (WLANs). IEEE 802.11 is a wireless extension to Ethernet that is expected to be widely deployed in office and home environments over the next few years (see Chapter 29, "The Networked House: A Brave New Home").

The potential for interference between different wireless units (using incompatible protocols such as 802.11b and 802.15.1) operating in close proximity and in the same frequency spectrum needs to be investigated and quantified. While it's critical that we explore different technologies that can meet requirements such as high performance and low cost, it is necessary to ensure that these devices will be able to coexist in the same location.

The Coexistence Task Group was recently formed and has established as its goals to first fully characterize and understand the effects of mutual interference and then subsequently to produce a recommended practice for WPAN devices operating in a WLAN environment. An extended vision is to assist standards development in minimizing the potential for interference among different radio systems in the unlicensed bands.

The 802.15 High Rate Study Group.   The 802.15 High Rate Study Group is addressing the technical merits and market requirements for a low cost, high data rate WPAN. They have developed a project authorization request (PAR) so that a new task group within 802.15 can begin work on a draft standard.

Initial meetings of the 802.15 Working Group in July 1999 outlined a data rate of 1 Mbps for WPANs. The new High Rate Study Group, however, will seek to provide high speed physical (PHY) and medium access control (MAC) layers to support multimedia data types and data rates of 20 Mbps or more. Compatibility with other 802.15 standards is a major goal of this activity. This is being done because current standards and data rates do not meet the projected needs of multimedia and digital imaging in consumer class products like cameras. Speed, battery life, and ultra low cost are the key requirements, rather than range.

IEEE 1394B

At a meeting of the IEEE standard 1394B committee, the link control (LC) connector was selected as the standard optical fiber connector for 800 Mbps, 1,600 Mbps, and 3,200 Mbps over multimode fiber. A cross-section of the duplex receptacle and duplex plugs is included in Draft 0.07 of the standard. The committee also approved pursuing a 1394b solution over category 5 cabling using simple non-return-to-zero (NRZ) coding to support data rates of 100 Mbps. This alternative will allow 1394b to work over a large installed base of category 5.

ATM Forum

The Asynchronous Transfer Mode Physical Layer (ATM PHY) working group has approved for ballot a new document, the Physical Layer High Density Glass Optical Fiber Connector Annex, BTD-PHY-GOF-01.00. The LC connector is now specified in this document for use in ATM applications.

Zone Wiring Standard

AT&T has developed a way to use a single high speed copper cable to carry—error-free—multiple, simultaneous high-speed data signals for dissimilar applications. The company demonstrated its zone cabling solution between six workstations during a Building Industry Consultants Society International (BICSI) conference.

In the demo, an AT&T SYSTIMAX® Structured Cabling System (SCS) 2061A 25-pair, category 5 cable, using insulation made of Teflon® fluoropolymer resin, networked six workstations. Two of the terminals were operating interactive video using video adapter cards, two others accessed each other to receive video files, and two more were handling two-way file transfers. Commercially available cabling components and field test instruments were used in the demo.

Normal measurement procedures confirmed that AT&T's structured cabling system will support multiple transmissions of 155 Mbps ATM, meeting—or exceeding—most global building wiring standards, including EIA/TIA-T568-A. The system also exceeds ISO 1801 Generic Cabling link specifications as well as proposed TIA TSB67 performance specifications for field testing of UTP cabling systems.

Zone cabling architecture, a method of open-office wiring, was used. This cabling scheme is well-suited to evolving technologies and changing networking needs of specialized work group areas and open offices designed to accommodate modular furniture.

Until now, zone wiring had not been shown to meet the needs of high-speed data transport. Using this cabling configuration, horizontal cabling is divided into a section where permanent cables run from the telecommunications closet to a second section establishing a cluster, or group, of work areas or zones.

With this cable, only one 25-pair cable rather than six 4-pair cables are needed, thereby decreasing installation time. Moves, adds, and changes are also simplified.

Components Used in the Demonstration

To accomplish the zone wiring physical linkage, AT&T used typical unshielded twisted pair (UTP) links built from SYSTIMAX® Structured Cabling System (SCS) HIGH-5.™ This product offering is comprised of 2061A 25-pair, enhanced category 5 UTP cable.

The cable uses AT&T's patented pair twist scheme as well as insulation made of Teflon fluoropolymer resin from DuPont. The cable ensures electrical performance so that multiple signals can be mixed in the same cable without loss of data integrity. It exceeds stringent category 5 requirements including power sum cross talk, as outlined in the EIA/TIA-T568-A standard.

Other AT&T components used were D8AU line cords, a zone box housing M100 category 5 information outlets, 110 patch cords, and connector system apparatus. Other equipment in the demo included a Bay Networks'

LattisCell® ATM switch and SBus adapter cards. These give customers the benefits of switched virtual circuit (SVC) connectivity and reduces network administration for LANs.

The LattisCell ATM switch was connected with a 100-meter link using 2061A 25-pair category 5 UTP cable to 6 Sun SPARC-2 workstations. The workstations represented an office work area. Each workstation used a Bay Networks UTP SONET STSc-3 adapter card, providing connectivity to the ATM network.

The UTP interfaces are compatible with the Letter Ballot Draft of the ATM Forum specification for running 155 Mbps SONET STSc-3 on category 5 UTP. This specification defines a two-level NRZ encoding scheme for use with category 5 cabling systems.

Video Electronics Standards Association (VESA)

At a meeting of VESA, several companies, including SONY, HP, and Samsung, put together a demo of various home electronic devices (VCRs, TVs, camcorders) that were connected using the IEEE 1394 serial bus. This was intended to demonstrate a proof of concept that 1394 is a suitable base on which to build the VESA home network. The demonstration included 100 meters of category 5 UTP in one of the segments, 50 meters of 1,000-micron plastic optical fiber, and short lengths (up to 4.5 m) of firewire, which is specified in the original 1394a specification.

National Electrical Manufacturers Association (NEMA)

The Premise Wiring Subcommittee reviewed several documents, the first of which was WC66 and high performance shielded premise cables. It includes premise wiring categories 6 and 7 to 300 MHz and 600 MHz, respectively, and is patterned after a German Deutsches Institut für Normung (DIN) specification and recent EC standards activities.

Furthermore, at a meeting of the ISO/IEC JTC1 SC25 WG3, it was suggested that if the German proposal could be developed without application support, other media (UTP and FTP) could also be enhanced and standardized without application support, thus creating a two-tier enhanced performance structure comprising Class E (UTP/FTP) and Class F (PIMF screened shielded twisted pair [SSTP]) channels. These would be based around a specification delivering positive power sum ACR at 200 MHz (category 6) and 600 MHz (category 7). This means that all 600 MHz category 6 specified cables will have to be redefined as category 7.

Category 6 Class E channels will be able to use either screened or unscreened balanced twisted pair cables and will use the existing RJ45 connector in either screened or unscreened format. Therefore, to achieve Class E channel performance, both RJ45 connector interface and cable must be specified to achieve 200 MHz performance with positive power sum ACR on all four pairs.

The channel performance will require approximately 10 percent improvement in attenuation. The pair-to-pair NEXT performance will need to be improved to provide approximately the same pair-to-pair ACR at 200 MHz as is currently required by category 5 at 100 MHz.

Category 7 Class F channels will demand individually screened twisted pair (PIMF) cables. A specific category 7 connector has not been agreed to. It will not, however, be an RJ45.

Finally, the NEMA standard (WC63.1, Twisted Pair, Premise Wiring Products) has been revised to be a procurement document for the military. Appendices were added for specific products such as category 5, 24, and 22 AWG, and patch cordage.

ICEA Standards

The Insulated Cable Engineers Association (ICEA) standards group, along with the Telecommunications Wire and Cable Standards/Technical Advisory Committee (TWCS/TAC), at their last meeting, covered several standards in progress, discussed below.

S-90-661, Revision 2, Indoor UTP Wiring Standard (Category Cables)

Discussions centered around the confusion of a plethora of Categories and a decision was reached to consolidate three categories into one. Categories 5-250, 5-275, and 5-285 were reduced to category 5-285 with an attenuation change that yields 19.9 dB/100 m @ 100 MHz. The dash number refers to the frequency at which the power sum ACR is zero or greater.

S-89-648, Aerial Service Wire

S-89-648, Aerial Service Wire is being revised to include three classes of service wire products: copper coated steel reinforced (CCSR), nonmetallic reinforced (NMR), and metallic reinforced (MR). A TWCS TAC Letter Ballot will be distributed prior to the next meeting.

The aerial service wire is intended to be self-supporting. The self-supporting properties are accomplished using copper coated steel conductors, a galvanized coated steel strength member, or an integral or multiple layer of approved compounds containing synthetic reinforcing members. There are two types of synthetic reinforcing members: Class A has decreased elongation and residual elongation allowance compared to Class B, which is beneficial for longer spans and in heavy loading areas. Class B is the standard wire used to date.

ICEA.   ICEA last met to discuss S-87-640, Optical Fiber, Outside Plant Cable standard. This standard was distributed as an ICEA Letter Ballot. In addition, S-87-640 was distributed to TIA/EIA Optical Fiber Division as well for their input. TIA/EIA has indicated that they will adopt this standard as their requirements.

A new working group to review and revise S-83-596, Fiber Optic Premises Distribution Cable Standard, continued their work on this revision. Another new working group, S-XX-696, Fiber Optic Indoor/Outdoor Cable Standard, also continued their work.

P-47-434, Pressurization Characteristics of Polyethylene-Insulated and Jacketed Telephone Cables, was authorized for reaffirmation. A TWCS TAC Letter Ballot was distributed.

BICSI

The Building Industry Consulting Services International (BICSI) is a not-for-profit telecommunications association focused on low-voltage wiring issues. The BICSI standards committee mission is to monitor telecommunications standards-making bodies and the standards they produce while influencing technical proposals on behalf of BICSI's membership in the interest of telecommunications performance. To this end the Standards Committee:

- Monitors standards-making bodies, to the best of their ability, and advises the BICSI membership of standards proposals that affect telecommunications.
- Influences standards-making bodies with proposals that serve the interest of telecommunications performance as interpreted by the experts among BICSI's membership.
- Monitors standards affecting telecommunications, to the best of their ability, and advises the membership of adopted standards [3].

BICSI's goal is the effective representation of BICSI within the telecommunications industry standards bodies for the next 2, 5, and 10 years. The goal is also to keep BICSI current with standards efforts for the next 5 and 10 years. BICSI's objectives are to:

- Gain insight of changing standards affecting BICSI (domestic/international).
- Ensure clear two-way communication of members' desires for standards recommendations.
- Ensure accurate communications between BICSI representatives, standards bodies, and the committee.
- Collaborate with the Standards Committee and the Board of Directors in the formation of BICSI standards positions in accordance with the Standards Committee Policies and Procedures.
- Work toward the effective harmonization of international standards [BICSI, 16].

BICSI's plans are to:

- Attain representation on relevant standards bodies.
- Establish and publicize use of phone mail, Web page, fax service, and MemberLetter for two-way communications of standards recommendations.
- Establish relations with higher levels within standards bodies.
- Identify subject matter experts (SMEs) and establish contact database for reference.
- Invite SMEs to BICSI general and committee meetings.
- Pursue leadership positions, where appropriate, and within budget with the approval of the committee chair and the Board of Directors.
- Promote BICSI standards liaison efforts with Rack Standards in EIA, Residential Standards, Pathway and Spaces Standards, OSP Standards, and the Installation Task Group for 568-B.
- Coordinate BICSI's responses to standards ballots by verifying intentions of member comments, compiling information, and preparing filings according to the Standards Committee Policies.
- Establish liaisons with other BICSI committees (e.g., E&M, codes, installation).
- Procure relevant published standards for file and library use.
- Author news articles and reports for publication.
- Provide technical assistance to the BICSI Institute as needed.
- Respond to standards-related BICSI member information requests.

- Prepare, coordinate, and conduct standards-related presentations to the BICSI membership and other interested groups [BICSI, 17].

GLOBAL STANDARDS

The global standards in development are as follows:

- ISO/IEC/JTC1/SC25/WG3
- Australian Standards
- CENLEC Standards
- Canadian Standards
- Japanese Standards

The current status of the global standards in development are discussed next.

ISO/IEC/JTC1/SC25/WG3

The most recent meeting of JTC1/SC25 WG3 included further work on the category 6/Class E specification, the possible selection of a category 7 connector (non-RJ45), and a presentation on the need to allow small form factor fiber optic connectors at the work area. The currently agreed-upon 4-connector channel performance specifications for category 6/Class E is shown in Table 27–2 [4].

Table 27–2 Proposed Class E Channel Performance for IS 11801 Revision

Freq	Attenuation (dB)	pr-pr NEXT (dB)	PS NEXT (dB)	pr-pr ELFEXT (dB)	PS ELFEXT (dB)	return loss (dB)	phase delay (dB)	delay skew (dB)
1	2.2	72.7	70.3	63.2	60.2	19.0	580.0	50.0
4	4.2	63.0	60.6	51.2	48.2	19.0	562.0	50.0
8	5.8	58.2	55.6	45.2	42.2	19.0	556.7	50.0
10	6.5	56.6	54.0	43.2	40.2	19.0	555.4	50.0
16	8.3	53.2	50.6	39.1	36.1	19.0	553.0	50.0
20	9.3	51.6	49.0	37.2	34.2	19.0	552.0	50.0
25	10.4	50.0	47.4	35.3	32.3	18.0	551.2	50.0
31.25	11.7	48.4	45.7	33.3	30.3	17.1	550.4	50.0
62.5	16.9	43.4	40.6	27.3	24.3	14.1	548.6	50.0

Table 27–2 (continued)

Freq	Attenuation (dB)	pr-pr NEXT (dB)	PS NEXT (dB)	pr-pr ELFEXT (dB)	PS ELFEXT (dB)	return loss (dB)	phase delay (dB)	delay skew (dB)
100	21.7	39.9	37.1	23.2	20.2	12.0	547.6	50.0
125	24.5	38.3	35.4	21.3	18.3	11.0	547.2	50.0
155.52	27.6	36.7	33.8	19.4	16.4	10.1	546.9	50.0
175	29.5	35.8	32.9	18.4	15.4	9.6	546.7	50.0
200	31.7	34.8	31.9	17.2	14.2	9.0	546.5	50.0
250	36.0	33.1	30.2	15.3	12.3	8.0	546.3	50.0

CENLEC Standards

CENELEC is the European Committee for Electrotechnical Standardization. It was set up in 1973 as a nonprofit-making organization under Belgian Law.

It has been officially recognized as the European Standards Organization in its field by the European Commission in Directive 83/189 EEC. Its members have been working together in the interests of European harmonization since the late 1950s, developing alongside the European Economic Community. CENELEC works with 50,000 technical experts from 19 EC and EFTA countries to publish standards for the European market that define access to the single market and beyond for manufacturers, producers, and suppliers of products and services. In other words, tens of thousands of technical experts have been involved in the huge effort to harmonize the European electrotechnical marketplace and to make it as international as possible. The standards discussed in the Sidebar, "The CENELEC Standards Experience," have been recently developed by the various CENELEC working groups and committees.

THE CENELEC STANDARDS EXPERIENCE

CENELEC SC46XC

SC46XC Data Cable Subcommittee recently met in Brussels and agreed to expedite the circulation of prEN50288, which includes sectional specifications for category 5 UTP cable.

CENELEC TC215/WG1

Rome Category 5E

There was inconclusive discussion regarding a proposal to include category 5 enhanced specifications.

Category 6 connectors

A major issue being discussed is backward compatibility and interoperability of different vendors' category 6 connectors.

Coupling attenuation

A report was presented highlighting the weaknesses of the coupling attenuation test method when applied to channel testing and in particular for testing of cables at multiport outlet boxes.

TC46/WG3

Coupling attenuation

Many reports were presented, with several including highlighting weaknesses in the test method. Additional enhancements were accepted, to be verified by another round robin. Progress is slow. LCL was preferred as the main test method.

EDC/Working WG2

Category 6 cable specification

An attempt was made to resolve the inconsistencies between EDC cat 6 cable specifications and the specifications in ISO and CENELEC. The PSNEXT values were aligned with those proposed in IS 11801, but the NEXT values remain 0.7 dB tighter than IS 11801.

Fire performance of cables

Agreed to support minimum requirement of IEC-332-3 for all installation, a major improvement over the currently allowed IEC-332-1.

EDC/TC

There was discussion on whether patch cords come under the EMC Directive, mainly concerning low-grade coaxial cords used for CATV, but possibly to include data patch cords.

EDC/WG5 Fiber Specifications

This WG is working toward the adoption of indoor fiber standards based either on ETSI prEN187103 (currently single mode only) or IEC 60794 specification or the present CENELEC copper sectional specifications structure using the IEC 60794 where possible. Proposals were sent to EDC/TC for consideration.

EDC/WG6 Fire Performance

A new draft CENELEC version of the Steiner Tunnel Test (called the HIFT [Horizontal Integrated Fire Test]) was put forward for consideration. There is support for higher fire performance cables.

Environmental Issues

Proposal on waste from electrical and electronic equipment 2nd draft end of life (EOL)

This draft has been recently released. Cables are now excluded as products and come under the category of components. As a measure to improve recycling, member states are required to ensure that lead, mercury, cadmium, hexavalent chromium, and halogenated flame retardants are phased out by January 2004.

Halogenated flame retardants are exempted where the relevant fire safety standards cannot be achieved through the use of other types of flame retardants.

Components containing substances (lead and halogenated flame retardants) have to be removed from any end of life electrical and electronic equipment, which is destined for land-filling incineration or recovery.

Danish ban on lead

Denmark is preparing legislation to ban lead in most of its applications. Denmark has already phased out lead stabilizers in power cables and other Nordic countries are likely to follow.

PVC

The Dutch government believes that PVC incineration may lead to emissions of dioxin, so incineration has to be prevented and PVC has to be recycled. The Dutch similarly are concerned by the use of lead as stabilizers and phtalates as softening agents [4].

Australian/New Zealand Standards

Cordless Telecommunication Version 1 (CT/1) is currently seeking interest from industry experts to participate in the following projects:

- *NWIP 9801:* Amendment to AS/NZS 3080: 1996 to reflect the changes to testing for category 5, additional category 5 parameters, and enhanced category 5.
- *NWIP 9802:* Revision of HB 27 to reflect changes to ISO/IEC Standards for field testing of category 5 UTP (including ELFEXT and return loss). This revision covers the new requirements by adopting the contents of IEC 1935-1, which reflect the need for more stringent field testing of category 5 and enhanced category 5, incorporating them into a single document with a new testing level (Level IIE).
- *NWIP 9804:* A companion to AS/NZS 3080 standardizing modular plug cord NEXT measurements, test procedures, NEXT limits, and test head connecting hardware.

- *NWIP 9808:* A liaison with international cabling standards bodies to provide a focal point to contribute to international standardization, and advice of the latest developments in the international standards process. The focus is IS 11801, however, a number of other related international, regional, and other national committees will also be monitored [4].

Canadian Standards

Canada has reaffirmed the Canadian Standard Association (CSA) T-528 Administration Standard. This is required to continue to sell the standard five years after the original publication date. Several issues have been identified that need to be addressed in the T-528 document. The plan is to work these into the revision of TIA-606 and then have CSA follow suit.

Japanese Standards

The Japanese Electronic Industry Development Association (JEIDA) hosted a seminar to introduce JEIDA Standard; JEIDA-57. The Japanese Cabling Standard is JIS X 5150, based on ISO/IEC 11801. JEIDA-57 defines each test method for cable, connecting hardware, channel and link for attenuation, NEXT, RL, characteristic impedance, and so on, for detail. JEIDA-57 includes graph, photo, and detail configuration. JEIDA-57 also suggests to use the Japanese-developed Test Calibration Kit for better accuracy and repeatability. This Test Calibration Kit was announced at BICSI in January 1998.

FROM HERE

Chapter 27 examined U.S. standards in development (TIA-T568-A Commercial Building Telecommunications Wiring Standard; TIA-569 Commercial Building Standard for Telecommunications Pathways and Spaces; TIA-570 Residential and Light Commercial Telecommunications Wiring Standard; TIA TR41.8.4 Outside Plant; TIA FO2.2 and Short Wavelength Fast Ethernet Alliance; USOC; IEEE; ATM Forum; Zone Wiring; VESA; NEMA; ICEA; and BICSI), as well as the global standards in development (ISO/IEC/JTC1/SC25/WG3; Australian Standards; CENLEC Standards; Canadian Standards; and Japanese Standards). Chapter 28 opens up Part VII, *Future Directions*, by taking a peak at the future of wireless communications: cable-less connectivity.

NOTES

[1] "EMC in the EU: What the Networking Industry Should Know About the New Emissions Directives in Europe," ITT Cannon, Systems & Services, Jays Close, Viables Estate, Basingstoke, Hampshire, England, RG22 4BW, 2000, p. 1.

[2] Mike Combs and Anne Combs, "LAN Cabling Basics," Cambridge, Massachusetts, 2000, p. 4.

[3] "Long Range Planning Report," BICSI, 8610 Hidden River Parkway, Tampa, Florida 33637-1000 USA, 2000, p. 15.

[4] "SYSTIMAX® SCS Standards Newsletter," Lucent Technologies Inc., 600 Mountain Avenue, Murray Hill NJ 07974, U.S.A., (Copyright © 2000), pp. 1–9.

[5] "Cabling Standards Documents Overview," Microtest, Inc. 4747 N. 22nd St. Phoenix, AZ 85016-4708, 2000.

Future Directions

Cableless Connectivity: The Wireless Future

Great excitement surrounds the future of wireless communications and/or cableless connectivity. Mobile Internet and Third Generation (3G) wireless multimedia products and services promise a future world of universal wireless phones, global roaming, and wireless Internet access. Yet actual customer demand, price, and performance requirements for these new products and services remains largely unknown—at least until now.

Wireless communication services have been available in the United States and elsewhere for the past 20 years or more. Fleets of police vehicles are equipped with mobile data terminals used to send and receive license plate queries as well as emergency messages (see the Sidebar, "The Future of Wireless Infrastructure and Terminals"). More recently, corporations have begun equipping their mobile sales and service forces with wireless communication capabilities. Yet when compared with the use of wireless voice, wireless data usage has been measured in terms of hundreds of thousands of users rather than in millions of users. But this is about to change.

THE FUTURE OF WIRELESS INFRASTRUCTURE AND TERMINALS

Why, over the longer term, are industry challenges not about specific RF standards? Rather, they are about adding value. Added value comes from benefits to end users—those who ultimately provide the profits that support the industry.

Added value to end users takes three forms: new services, improved services, and lower costs. New and improved services at lower costs can only be provided through an industry transition from hierarchical to distributed network architectures and hardware to software-based functionality. This is the model of the Internet. It provides infinite applications with infinite content—the solution to the carrier quest for new revenues. Distributed networks will prove as important to telecommunications as the evolution from piston to jet engines was for aviation. Given this network architecture, the radio interface becomes inconsequential.

Vendors and carriers that recognize this transition will profit. Those that continue to think in terms of hardware-based hierarchical networks will lose. Taken to its logical conclusion, the shift in network architecture implies that central switches will erode in relevance. This poses exceptional risks to infrastructure vendors that hold a central switch legacy. All are moving toward software functionality. However, they are focusing on software in their switches, not distributed to the periphery of the network.

The *old line* infrastructure providers, in particular, Alcatel, Siemens, and Lucent, are putting R&D into switches. This is the wrong place. R&D should be going into the periphery of the network.

This network evolution will take years. Only in 2009 do we see it being fully implemented. Embedded hierarchical networks will still dominate. However, new infrastructure sales will be driven by the distributed software-based architecture.

The transition to software-based networks goes beyond carriers. It implies a parallel transition in the organization of vendors as well. Efficient software engineering dictates that manufacturers adopt a common software platform across all business units—wireless infrastructure, wireless terminals, two-way radio, paging, landline infrastructure, and business systems. This, in turn, requires turning their organizational structures upside down. Operating divisions must report to a president of software engineering as well as the chief operating officer or managing director.

By the year 2004, the Internet will emerge as a key driver of demand for wireless telecommunications. This effect is already seen on wireline. Its effect on wireless will be the same. As this evolves, the distinction between wireline and wireless networks will erode. Wireless will become but one offering provided by a handful of global telecommunications carriers.

As infrastructure changes so must the terminals. Added value to end users will come from *smart* terminals, which provide instant access to the Internet, transparently and easily. Smart or intelligent terminals are not products by themselves. Rather, they depend upon the network and the functionality of the network to become *smart*. This gives a design advantage to manufacturers that produce both infrastructure and terminals.

The transition to a software-based distributed network mirrors the historical evolution of the network computing industry. This is drawing software companies such as Sun Microsystems and Microsoft into the wireless industry.

Corporate press releases are deluging readers with news of third generation, or 3G, radio interfaces. This is a spurious focus. By overinvesting in third generation radio, the wireless industry risks underinvesting in networks. This will open the door to software developers with core expertise in software-based distributed networks and the Internet. By the year 2002, they will pose pivotal competitive threats to current infrastructure vendors.

This raises an essential competitive question for both established infrastructure vendors and newcomers: cooperate or compete? New and established vendors that ally together will prosper [1].

There are a number of reasons for the limited use of wireless data communication services. First, let's look at the wireless voice model. Cellular phones were introduced into the U.S. market in 1983. As cellular phones were gaining popularity, voice-mail systems were being deployed within corporations. The combination of a cellular phone and voice mail became a powerful mobile tool for those who spent time away from their desk. Mobile workers were now able to retrieve messages and respond to them when they were away from the office without having to rely on a human point of contact.

Today, e-mail has become as important a method of communicating as voice. Today's mobile workers cannot be certain that their most important messages will arrive via their voice mail. They could just as easily appear in their e-mail. Wireless data communication provides the same type of remote access to e-mail as cellular phones provide to voice mail.

The Internet also plays a key role in why it is now time to give serious consideration to wireless data communication access. In just a few short years, the Internet has changed the way we do business, the way we obtain the very information we need to make us more competitive, and even the way we purchase goods.

Next in the *why now* list is the fact that there are data-capable wireless networks in place in both the United States and in the rest of the world. In fact, some networks have been built specifically to support wireless data communication, while some digital voice networks are capable of supporting both voice and data traffic simultaneously. Furthermore, satellite systems that provide coverage on a worldwide basis are already data-capable. The bottom line is that there are, today, many different ways of providing wireless access to data, no matter where that data is stored.

A PERCEPTION

There is a perception among many potential wireless data communication users that the networks are too slow and that their services cost too much. The term *perception* is used here because those of us who use wireless data today know that *too slow* is a relative term, and *too expensive* is not an accurate assessment.

Data speeds over today's wireless networks range from about 4 Kbps to more than 20 Kbps, depending on the network. If the type of data is matched to the wireless network, data throughput can, in fact, be perceived to be faster than over a wired connection. The reason for this is that over a wireless network, most of the data is sent and received in pure text mode. Most wireless networks are not designed for the transmission of graphics. If you think about the type of information you really need when you are away from the office, in most cases having access to text-based information—where previously you had no access—is more than sufficient.

On the issue of cost, wireless data networks have reduced the charges for using their systems to the point where they have become economical. Several of the packet-data networks are offering flat-rate, sub-$40 per month unlimited access to the Internet today. And, many corporations have been able to negotiate per-user pricing that is even lower.

The issue, then, has become one of how much value you place on having access to your data, to which you had no access in the past. You might view your current e-mail with dial-up access as virtually free, since, in most cases, the call is a local call and the e-mail is stored on your company's server. In comparison, $40 per month for wireless access to your e-mail may sound expensive. However, if some of your e-mail is mission-critical in nature, or your customers are using e-mail to communicate with you and you need e-mail access all of the time, then $40 per month is not so expensive after all. Cellular phone bills run $40 or more per month and are viewed as a legitimate expense. Yet presently, cellular service provides access to only one of the means of communicating you need when mobile.

NOW IS THE TIME

Mobile devices are available, networks capable of wireless data communication are in place or are about to be, and access to corporate information resources is now possible—all at reasonable prices. Add to this equation the user interest in wireless data communication that Microsoft has developed over the past few years or so and couple this interest with the introduction of palm-size and handheld devices that are capable of synchronizing to users' desktops or to a local area network (see the Sidebar, "The Future of Wireless Instant Messaging"). With all of these factors coming together, you can see that there are some new major revenue opportunities in the very near future.

THE FUTURE OF WIRELESS INSTANT MESSAGING

Mobile Insights (MI), recently announced that the worldwide market for instant messaging will grow to 285 million users by the year 2003. Instant messaging, sometimes referred to as online *buddy lists*, is used by over 60 million PC-based users and is now becoming available to users of hand-held computers and mobile phones.

This technology allows users to view a listing of people with whom they frequently communicate, determine if these people are currently available, and send/receive messages instantly. Instant messaging created somewhat of a cult following of savvy Internet users when it was launched three and a half years ago. It is now a mainstream Internet application with a variety of PC-based versions such as America Online's (AOL) Instant Messenger; Mirabilis' ICQ (I Seek You), recently acquired by AOL; and a host of others from the likes of Yahoo!, Microsoft, and Excite. Instant messaging is growing at a phenomenal rate. Mirabilis, pioneer in this field, grew its user base to 23 million users in less than three years and now has over 49 million users. This user community has grown primarily by word-of-mouth, and according to America Online, its Instant Messenger application and Mirabilis' ICQ have a combined user base of 74 million users sending over 860 million messages a day.

Versions of ICQ have been available for the Palm Pilot and Windows CE-based hand-held PCs, but have not been widely used because integrated wireless communications (the critical missing link for this technology) has been slow to take hold. The Palm VII is the first of many mainstream hand-held devices that will incorporate wireless data communications. Additionally, recent announcements from America Online suggest that it will work with 3Com to integrate this technology into future versions of the Palm platform. As integrated wireless communications becomes mainstream on all mobile information appliances, instant messaging will become a standard feature.

Integrated wireless communications will be the catalyst that leads to the pervasive use of mobile information appliances. Instant messaging on these wireless-handled PCs and mobile phones will become as commonplace as voice mail in only a few years.

Three years from now, the interface to most cell phones and wireless PDAs will include a buddy list. These buddy lists will transform the way people communicate and help them to avoid the necessity of making real-time two-way phone calls to handle simple communications.

Instant messaging offers a level of convenience and flexibility beyond that of traditional phone systems, which promote common problems including telephone tag and a backlog of voice-mail messages. Providing more convenience than traditional phones, mobile phones have begun to address this issue. Additionally, advances in unified messaging (providing a single number for work phone, mobile phone, and fax) have greatly reduced this telephone tag dilemma. However, neither of these communication mediums provides the ability to know someone's availability without initiating a call. Furthermore, e-mail interaction is generally a batch process and a poor medium for real-time interactions.

Instant messaging presents users with immediate feedback on a potential recipient's availability and provides a medium for short, to-the-point messaging between users. Another compelling advantage of this medium is that it uses the Internet as a delivery vehicle and can be much less expensive than a traditional phone call, especially for international communication. Instant messaging can also offer added enhancements such as the ability to update schedules, provide notification of an e-mail with the subject and sender's name, and a host of other short messaging features. As this technology is made available to the hundreds of millions of wireless telephone and wireless handheld users, instant messaging will become even more useful and pervasive. Most digital phones are already equipped with SMS (short messaging service) and there are few technical hurdles to overcome to integrate instant messaging with this feature.

Two recent announcements point to the future of wireless instant messaging: America Online's announcement of its AOL Anywhere strategy and Tegic Communications' announcement of its embedded instant messaging software for wireless phones. AOL Anywhere brings AOL content, e-mail, and instant messaging to users of mobile information appliances. A key piece of this initiative was an announcement made in late 1999 with 3Com to provide AOL e-mail to the Palm computing platform.

Tegic Communications, a company known for its T9 text input technology for hand-held PCs and smart phones, announced in 1999 that the new version of this software for wireless phones will be available with an embedded instant messaging, or "chat," application. Tegic's instant messaging technology will allow wireless subscribers to easily send instant text messages to people on their buddy lists as well as to see at a glance if individuals are online, either by wireless phone or PC—all via the subscriber's wireless phone.

The need for doing instant messaging is profound. Often, a simple one- or two-word comment is required in daily correspondence. "On my way," "Yes," "No," and "Call me" are short phrases that can easily be selected from a list included on mobile phones, pagers, or palmtops, or via a numeric keypad using Tegic's T9. In the future, as voice recognition and text-to-speech technology improves, instant messaging will be seamlessly integrated with voice messaging, leading to an exponential growth of users.

Mobile Insights believes that instant messaging will become a key element of unified messaging. Business people today may have a business phone and home phone number with voice mail, several e-mail accounts, mobile phone, fax number, and now an instant messaging number. Several companies are working to bring some or potentially all of these numbers together [2].

DRIVING WIRELESS DATA COMMUNICATIONS

We have already seen that access to e-mail drives wireless data. There are other factors coming into play. The fact that we can now synchronize information between devices when they are physically attached with a cable leads many to ask for the same capabilities when they are away from the office. There are other mission-critical types of information that we need in the field as well. Sales force automation has become a huge business. Giving a sales force instant access to inventory, billing history, and shipping information, among other things, gives mobile workers new tools to use when they are with their customers.

Having access to all of our corporate communications channels—voice, e-mail, and fax—can be an important asset to those of us who spend much of our time in the field. Today's *flat* corporate structure means that fewer of us have a person back at the office whose job it is to receive messages for us, filter them, and deliver them to us. We no longer have the luxury of having a secretary or administrative assistant there to help us when we are away. Most of us must rely completely on our mobile communications capabilities. Wireless access to our information has become more important than ever.

USERS REACH EXTENDED

Just as cellular phones have extended the reach of users by enabling them to access their voice messages, wireless data communication extends their access to e-mail, calendar, phone book, and corporate data resources. There are several types of data access, depending on the type of network used and the type of mobile device provided to the user.

Circuit-Switched Dial-Up

Perhaps the simplest of all of the access methods for wireless networks is circuit-switched dial-up. There are on the order of 55 million mobile workers today who carry notebook computers and have mastered the art of plugging them into a standard telephone line to access their e-mail and corporate data via RAS (remote access servers). The cellular and personal communications service (PCS) carriers that have deployed either global system for mobile communications (GSM) or code-division multiple access (CDMA) technologies can provide wireless circuit-switched dial-up access over their networks.

The beauty of this type of access is that the end user's experience is virtually no different from that of using a standard wired phone line. Instead of plugging the computer modem into a wired phone jack, users plug their computer into their digital wireless phone and use the same software they use for wired access. The connection is somewhat slower than a wired connection at 9.6 Kbps for GSM and 14.4 Kbps for CDMA. However, these connections are sufficient to provide access to information when wired connections are not possible.

The primary advantage of circuit-switched, dial-up wireless data access is that corporate IT managers do not have to do anything different within their own network to enable this type of access. In fact, the RAS cannot tell the difference between a circuit-switched, dial-up connection via a wireless network and a wired dial-up circuit.

The time division multiple access (TDMA) networks run by companies such as AT&T and SBC do not yet support this mode of access. However, between the GSM and CDMA carriers, there is near nationwide access available today. For carriers that have deployed GSM or CDMA technology, the ability to offer customers dial-up access results in more airtime minutes of usage, which translates directly into additional revenue for the network operator. Furthermore, if users become accustomed to this type of wireless data access, they will become more loyal customers and will be less likely to *churn* off of the system, once again translating into additional revenue.

Churn is an industry term used to describe the phenomenon of customers leaving one network and moving to another, or dropping their service all together.

Packet-Data Wireless Services

There are two *nationwide* packet-data wireless networks in place today—the American Mobile network (formerly known as ARDIS), and the BellSouth Wireless Data network (formerly known as RAM). Both of these networks offer coverage to about 93 percent of the U.S. business population and both have been designed to provide access inside buildings.

Several cellular carriers, including AT&T, Bell Atlantic Nynex, Ameritech, and GTE, also offer packet-data coverage over their cellular digital packet data (CDPD) networks. At present, CDPD networks cover about 53 percent of the U.S. business population and are better suited for street-level than in-building coverage. One advantage of CDPD networks is that they are based on the Internet protocol (IP). Thus, they do not usually require additional *middleware* in the mobile device.

Metricom's Ricochet packet-based network *looks* to the modem device like a circuit-switched network and is currently available in at least three areas—Seattle, San Jose, and Washington, D.C. [3]. At present, Ricochet should not be considered a mobile network. It is a portable wireless data network because it supports stationary connections and does not support access while in a moving vehicle.

Connecting to a packet-data network is not as straightforward as using circuit-switched dial-up, but the advantages of packet outweigh the additional effort required to make the connection. Packet-data users can stay *connected* to the network since, as with a LAN connection, the mobile device can *listen* to the channel for information without being truly connected.

OTHER SERVICES

Satellite systems are available, as are in-building wireless LANs that are useful for extending users' reach within the confines of a building or a campus. Many companies have implemented their own wireless networks that are data-capable. A number of companies are offering combined in-building and wide-area coverage using several networks. Two companies, American Mobile and BellSouth Wireless Data, offer a combination of terrestrial service for urban areas linked with satellite coverage for the more rural areas of the United States.

THE STAGE IS SET

The networks are in place, and wireless modems are now available. Wireless data access can now be provided in a variety of ways as systems are deployed.

BIG PAYOFFS

The adoption of wireless data communications by not only fleets of users such as service and sales forces, but by the more generic mobile business workers, will be accelerated during the next few years. Opportunities for both financial and productivity gains abound.

It is projected that by the year 2005 there will be more than 900 million wireless phones in use throughout the world. As wireless data becomes more easily available to mobile workers, it is believed that up to 15 percent of these people will also take advantage of wireless data capabilities. Approximately 53 percent of these 120 million projected wireless data users will be within the Americas.

THE CORPORATE INFORMATION TECHNOLOGY USERS

Because the corporate LAN is usually connected to a center, and the center is connected to a number of networks, the corporation is further protected against system obsolescence as new technologies become available. Since the connection between the corporation and the center remains constant, only the end users' wireless modem would ever need to be updated.

THE NETWORK OPERATORS

The increase in demand for wireless data should help wireless network operators whose networks support data in a number of ways. As mentioned, with the addition of wireless data, users are likely to increase the number of minutes per day they spend on the network. They are less likely to churn off of one network to another and they are accessible to the carrier that offers value-added services such as stock quotes, location services, or other information resources.

Today, the average cost of obtaining a new customer for a wireless network is in the $200–$500 range. In order for the network operator to earn a payback on this acquisition cost, it is important to increase the amount of time each user spends on the network. Offering data capabilities will drive usage minutes higher.

COMPUTER VENDORS

Computer vendors with product in the mobile space have been expressing interest in wireless data for the past few years. Unfortunately, because there has not been any way for them to provide complete end-to-end solutions for their customers, they have not been able to offer wireless-capable products. Now, many computer vendors will be using wireless data access as a way to differentiate their product offerings.

IT'S A WIN–WIN SITUATION

The time appears right for the adoption of wireless data access by mobile workers, well beyond fleets of mobile users within large corporations to individual mobile professionals and small businesses as well. It has taken the communications and computing industries a number of years to bring all of the proper pieces together and to assemble them into a solutions package. The year 1998 was a watershed year because the industries finally began working together toward a common goal—wireless data access that is easy and cost-effective.

From this point forward, as the rest of the pieces and parts for the wireless future fall into place, the adoption rate for wireless data will continue to increase dramatically, providing new revenue opportunities for those who choose to participate.

With that in mind, there are number of other mobile computing products and applications showing up on the market bundled with wireless modems and software for wireless access. Let's examine some of these and take a look into the future.

THE FUTURE OF WIRELESS COMPUTING

Wander through any airport today, and you're likely to pass dozens of fellow travelers with cell phones glued to their ears, as if growing strange space-age cloned appendages. Look into any gate area or airport lounge, and you can't miss the crowd of road warriors with laptops propped open upon briefcase or bended knee. After boarding your flight, observe the *air phone* built into your seatback or armrest. As your aircraft passes through 20,000 feet, listen to the hum of disk drives spinning up and the familiar *world of windows* jingle as passengers resume computing for the duration of your flight.

Increasingly, we live in a world obsessed with nonstop communication and computing. Once considered a luxury for upper management, laptops have become so commonplace in corporate America that the purchase of laptops is now increasing at a rate double that of desktop PCs. Cellular telephone and pager usage is growing at least as fast. The number of cellular subscribers in the United States increased from 13 to 59 million between 1993 and 1998, tracking an upward exponential curve projected to continue well into this millennium. It should come as little surprise that entrepreneurs the world over are staking their claim on the intersection between these two megatrends: wireless network computing.

The U.S. mobile data networking market boasts 3.1 million subscribers today, with a predicted annual growth rate of 47 percent per year over the next five years. What characteristics must a product possess to succeed in this emerging market?

Of course, we expect *smaller, lighter, faster, cheaper* from all evolving technologies (sounds like a NASA commercial)—and wireless network computing is no exception. But, unlike NASA, who is hampered by their cost overrunning contractors, wireless network computing will not meet the same fate. As a veteran user of leading-edge computing and communications technologies, let me suggest a few additional characteristics: reliable, integrated, ubiquitous, interoperable, and, above all, smarter. Let's now take a look at recent developments in the wireless network computing arena and consider how they fare when assessed against these basic criteria.

Luggables, Palmtops, and SmartPhones

Computers first hit the road more than a decade ago as honking big suitcase-sized *luggables*. They've shrunk considerably since that time, to 4-lb. sub-notebooks and even palmtops the size of a checkbook and weighing merely ounces (see the Sidebar, "The Wireless Future of Palm OS"). A new crop of hand-held PCs (HPCs) and personal digital assistants (PDAs) have arrived, selling for well under $800, even dropping under $300. Those running Microsoft's skinnied-down Windows CE operating system have fared well: Sharp has sold over 3 million of its Zaurus PDAs. Perhaps the biggest winner in this emerging market has been the PalmPilot from USR/3Com.

 Microsoft Windows CE is an operating system platform for a broad range of communications, entertainment, and mobile-computing devices. The Windows CE platform will make possible new categories of non-PC business and consumer devices that can communicate with each other, share information with Windows-based PCs, and connect to the Internet. Windows CE is an entirely new compact and portable operating system built from the ground up to enable the development of a broad range of business and consumer devices, including the new hand-held PCs, *wallet* PCs, wireless-communication devices such as digital information pagers and cellular smart phones, next-generation entertainment and multimedia consoles including DVD players, and purpose-built Internet access devices such as Internet TVs, digital set-top boxes, and Internet Web *phones*.

THE WIRELESS FUTURE OF PALM OS

Palm has plans for a plethora of new devices, all of which will have a common theme—wireless Internet access. According to officials of the Santa Clara, California, hand-held developer, every Palm device under development and due by year's end (year 2000) will have the ability to remotely surf the Net, through either integrated technology, add-on modems, or cell phone hook-ups. In fact, cell phones with the Palm operating system built in may hit the market as early as next year.

These two markets can be viewed as merging. Qualcomm (with its PDQ device) is a good first step, but it's bulkier than what consumers want.

Two big backers of Palm are Nokia and Motorola. Nokia will likely introduce a cell phone with a large screen and a Palm OS interface in early 2001. At the same time, Palm intends to add voice capabilities to its PDAs—for those who want Palm devices that will give them voice capability.

The modem from OmniSky that currently supports the Palm V already has voice capabilities built into it, so it's only a matter of time before people can use their Palms as cell phones. Future Palm devices also will include ports for microphones. The company expects its future success to depend on the support of third-party developers.

In addition to wide area network wireless connections, Palm has plans to support Bluetooth, an emerging standard that enables local communication between mobile devices and does not require the line of sight that Infrared does. According to Palm officials, the company will introduce an add-on accessory for Bluetooth by the end of the year 2000, but Bluetooth won't be integrated into Palm devices until 2002 or 2003 because radios for the technology are too expensive. Bluetooth will be discussed further later in the chapter.

Palm's also concentrating on expanding memory for its devices, an area in which Palm has lagged. Competing devices that support Microsoft's Pocket PC operating system include up to 32 MB of memory. Palm plans to offer a device with an expansion module similar to Compact Flash slot in the TRG Pro or the Springboard module in Handspring's Visor. Another option under consideration is Sony Corporation's memory stick technology [4].

Portable processor speed, storage, and memory have increased in parallel with desktop technology. In 1996, laptops went multimedia, shipping complete with integrated CD-ROM, speakers, and Super VGA (SVGA) video jacks. In 1997, laptops, HPCs, and palmtops went mobile: Motorola estimates that between 40 and 60 percent of all notebooks shipped in 1997 contained embedded communications devices. The remainder are equipped with a PCMCIA (PC card) slot, easily filled with one of the many after-market wireless modems selling for as little as $200. Entrants in this field include US Robotics AllPoints Wireless PC card, Motorola's Personal Messenger wireless modem, Option's PC Card modem, and Metricom's Ricochet modem.

At the other end of the spectrum, we have analog cellular phones—also getting smaller, lighter, and smarter. So smart, in fact, that they've begun to creep into data networks to support thin client applications such as e-mail and text-based browsers. The Nokia/HP OmniGo 700 is a European GSM cellular phone and personal organizer that can send e-mail and access Web pages in Tagged Text Markup Language (TTML) format. Matsushita's Pinocchio and Toshiba's Genio are two Japanese PHS (personal handy phone system) memo pads that include integrated telephones and fax/data modems. The Philips Velo is a full-fledge HPC that can be integrated with a Philips mobile phone. AT&T's PocketNet is a Cellular Digital Packet Data (CDPD) phone equipped with a small LCD screen that can be used to access e-mail, online services, and web pages in Hand-held Device Markup Language (HDML) format.

Laptops, HPCs, PDAs, and smartphones provide a hardware and operating system foundation upon which wireless data networks and applications build. These products are clearly smaller, faster, lighter, cheaper, and smarter than their predecessors, and arguably more reliable. Continued integration of voice, data, fax, and paging services is essential for products that hope to achieve large-scale market success. Nobody wants to carry around a palmtop and a cell phone and a pager. And, don't forget that other industry megatrend: multimedia. The International Telecommunications Union (ITU) is working on a variation of the H.324 standard for video conferencing systems to support wireless video phones. As for interoperability and ubiquity, we must bring our focus up a notch to look at the wireless data network services supported by these devices.

Wireless Workgroups, LANs, and Data Networks

USR's AllPoints, Motorola's Personal Messenger, Option's PC Card, and Metricom's Ricochet may all be wireless PC modems, but each of these products uses a different Physical and Link layer technology. For example, *plain old cellular*, known as advanced mobile phone service, or AMPS, can be used to support data traffic in much the same way as the *plain old telephone service* in your home can be used to access the Internet with your trusty 56 Kbps analog modem. Cellular modems like Option's PC card use modulation/demodulation to transmit circuit-switched data over radio to a mobile base station, across the public switched telephone network (PSTN), to another modem. Data loss and propagation delay over AMPS is high and variable, impeding reliability and reducing effective throughput. As the U.S. cellular market goes digital (D-AMPS), effective data transfer rates should increase due to improved resilience to RF noise and hand-off delay.

Another cellular technology, cellular digital packet data (CDPD), uses spare radio channels in the AMPS or D-AMPS spectrum to carry packetized data (IP packets) to a mobile base station at 19.2 Kbps. Packets are then routed across the good old Internet or other IP network to the destination. By using datagram packets, CDPD-based applications can better adjust to packet loss and delay than their circuit-switched cellular data counterparts. The AT&T PocketNet is based on CDPD data network access, in part because this technology is well-suited for intermittent, low-volume traffic, which does not require reliable delivery. CDPD providers charge by packet, not connect time, and utilize data encryption for security.

National wireless network providers such as ARDIS also transmit digital packet data over radio networks [5]. ARDIS uses Motorola's own wireless data network, reaching speeds between 4 and 19.2 Kbps. These wireless network providers offer store-and-forward messaging to a destination, such as an Internet/Intranet gateway or application level proxy. PC card link level drivers must be matched to the wireless network provider. For example, the USR AllPoints Wireless PC card operates over networks using a special NDIS driver. Like CDPD, these wireless network providers charge according to usage (Kbytes transferred). A variety of wireless internet service providers (see the Sidebar, "Creating the Future of Wireless Internet Communications") offer Internet access (see the Sidebar, "Seeing a Wireless Internet Access Future") over ARDIS, including GoAmerica [6], Wynd Communication, and Radiomail.

CREATING THE FUTURE OF WIRELESS INTERNET COMMUNICATIONS

Toshiba Corporation and Bellcore, announced in 1999 the creation of a joint research and development project aimed at creating the technologies necessary for the integration of wireless and Internet communications. Results of the joint research program may transform communications in the 21st century by providing users with convenient wireless access to voice, video, data, and multimedia services.

The principal focus of the Toshiba–Bellcore joint research project is the development of the middleware layers necessary to achieve an Internet protocol (IP) capable of working with all types of cellular transmission systems. The project included the development of software to enable mobility with appropriate service quality, security, network operations and management, customer care systems, and applications support.

The Toshiba–Bellcore collaboration draws on the key competencies of the two companies, Toshiba for its expertise in terminal and wireless technologies and Bellcore for its expertise in information networking software. The research project is headquartered in Morristown, New Jersey, and is staffed with engineers from Bellcore and Toshiba America Research, Incorporated (TARI), Toshiba's first U.S-based corporate-level research subsidiary.

The establishment of TARI reflects the expansion and globalization of Toshiba's R&D activities in the field of IT technologies. In 1998, Toshiba set up a Telecommunications Research Laboratory (TRL) in the U.K., which undertakes research in next-generation digital cellular phone and wireless access technologies. Both TRL and TARI work in close collaboration with Toshiba's central research labs at its corporate R&D Center in Japan.

According to Toshiba, wireless Internet and Intranet connectivity is the next frontier for the information and communications industries. But there is much work to be done before a workable system can be implemented. Toshiba officials feel confident that the combined strength of Toshiba and Bellcore engineering can solve the technological issues and lay the groundwork for what will become a multibillion-dollar market for communications hardware and network services within the next 8 years.

Through this unique relationship with Toshiba, Bellcore is looking forward to extending their capabilities in next-generation networking into the wireless domain. With their joint research initiative, they will bring IP-based voice, data and Internet services to mobile users around the world [7].

SEEING A WIRELESS INTERNET ACCESS FUTURE

Oracle has looked into its own crystal ball and seen the future: wireless Internet access. The company recently launched a new mobile subsidiary and portal that allows users to buy books on Amazon.com, bid in eBay auctions, and trade stocks on E-Trade, all through their Web-enabled pagers and cell phones.

Oracle faces stiff competition in the already-crowded yet nascent mobile field. Portal giants Yahoo, ExciteAtHome, Microsoft Network, and AOL already offer or are working on mobile portals of their own. A slew of smaller companies, such as AtMobile.com, are aggregating content to compete for the same estimated 400 million wireless subscribers worldwide. All are inking deals with wireless carriers, phone manufacturers, and each other in an incestuous market free-for-all.

Gartner Group predicts there will be more than 1 billion mobile devices in use by 2003, and Oracle expects to see wireless Internet access devices outnumber PCs by 2001. But first, more content needs to be adapted for the smaller screens and input limitations of those devices.

Oracle is one of the few firms to have a working portal that mobile customers can use now. For instance, in addition to buying from Amazon, eBay, and E-Trade, an OracleMobile customer can use the portal to look up a specific type of restaurant in a particular city, read restaurant reviews on the listings, call the restaurant, make reservations, and get driving directions, and all within nothing more than a few clicks on your phone and virtually no typing at all.

The personalized services and content at the new portal are free to any registered user. Among the 20-odd content partners of the portal, a wholly owned subsidiary of Oracle, are Astrology.com, Hollywood.com, Lottery.com, ScreamingMedia, Travelocity.com, UPS, Waiter.com, and the Weather Channel.

Motorola will be providing its wireless messaging, address book, to-do list, calendar, and voice command technologies to the Oramobile portal. The service will be voice-enabled by late 2000 so that people can use either a digital or analog phone to access the portal.

Although the portal currently is geared toward U.S. users, Oracle will offer localized content and services for users in Europe and Asia in the future. Meanwhile, Oracle is talking to mobile operators about partnering on building a branded portal customized for their subscribers [8].

Metricom is one of several emergent wireless LAN providers attempting to provide a faster, lower-cost alternative to nationwide wireless network services (see the Sidebar, "The Future of the Wireless LAN: The IEE 802.11b Standard"). Metricom uses a combination of pole top radios and wired access points, strategically located throughout a relatively small area such as a campus or urban business center. With effective throughput rates of 56 Kbps and flat-rate pricing as low as $17.95 per month for students (plus modem rental), Metricom has been successfully deployed in San Francisco, Seattle, Washington D.C., in several major airports, and many college campuses. Metricom's technology is proprietary, and requires use of Metricom's Ricochet modem. A gateway must be used to obtain Internet access through Metricom's network.

THE FUTURE OF THE WIRELESS LAN: THE IEEE 802.11B STANDARD

With the recent adoption of new standards for high-rate wireless LANs, mobile users can realize levels of performance, throughput, and availability comparable to those of traditional wired Ethernet. As a result, WLANs are on the verge of becoming a mainstream connectivity solution for a broad range of business customers.

The most critical issue slowing WLAN demand until now has been limited throughput. This sidebar very briefly describes the new IEEE 802.11b standard for wireless transmission at rates up to 11 Mbps, which promises to open new markets for WLANs. It describes 802.11 and 802.11b technology and discusses the key considerations for selecting a reliable, high-performance wireless LAN.

WHAT'S NEW IN WIRELESS LANS: THE IEEE 802.11B STANDARD

A wireless LAN (WLAN) is a data transmission system designed to provide location-independent network access between computing devices by using radio waves rather than a cable infrastructure. In the corporate enterprise, wireless LANs are usually implemented as the final link between the existing wired network and a group of client computers, giving these users wireless access to the full resources and services of the corporate network across a building or campus setting.

WLANs are on the verge of becoming a mainstream connectivity solution for a broad range of business customers. The wireless market is expanding rapidly as businesses discover the productivity benefits of going wire-free. According to Frost and Sullivan, the wireless LAN industry exceeded $300 million in 1998 and is expected to grow to around $1.6 billion in

2005. To date, wireless LANs have been primarily implemented in vertical applications such as manufacturing facilities, warehouses, and retail stores. The majority of future wireless LAN growth is expected in healthcare facilities, educational institutions, and corporate enterprise office spaces. In the corporation, conference rooms, public areas, and branch offices are likely venues for WLANs.

The widespread acceptance of WLANs depends on industry standardization to ensure product compatibility and reliability among the various manufacturers. The Institute of Electrical and Electronics Engineers (IEEE) ratified the original 802.11 specification in 1997 as the standard for wireless LANs. That version of 802.11 provides for 1 Mbps and 2 Mbps data rates and a set of fundamental signaling methods and other services.

The most critical issue affecting WLAN demand has been limited throughput. The data rates supported by the original 802.11 standard are too slow to support most general business requirements and have slowed the general adoption of WLANs. Recognizing the critical need to support higher data transmission rates, the IEEE recently ratified the 802.11b standard (also known as 802.11 high rate) for transmissions of up to 11 Mbps. Global regulatory bodies and vendor alliances have endorsed this new high-rate standard, which promises to open new markets for WLANs in large enterprise, small office, and home environments. With 802.11b, WLANs will be able to achieve wireless performance and throughput comparable to wired Ethernet.

Outside of the standards bodies, wireless industry leaders have united to form the Wireless Ethernet Compatibility Alliance (WECA). WECA's mission is to certify cross-vendor interoperability and compatibility of IEEE 802.11b wireless networking products and to promote that standard for the enterprise, the small business, and the home. Members include WLAN semiconductor manufacturers, WLAN providers, computer system vendors, and software makers—such as 3Com, Aironet, Apple, Breezecom, Cabletron, Compaq, Dell, Fujitsu, IBM, Intersil, Lucent Technologies, No Wires Needed, Nokia, Samsung, Symbol Technologies, Wayport, and Zoom.

The Competitive Advantage of Going Wireless

Today's business environment is characterized by an increasingly mobile workforce and flatter organizations. Employees are equipped with notebook computers and spend more of their time working in teams that cross functional, organizational, and geographic boundaries. Much of these workers' productivity occurs in meetings and away from their desks. Users need access to the network far beyond their personal desktops. WLANs fit well in this work environment, giving mobile workers much-needed freedom in their network access. With a wireless network, workers can access information from anywhere in the corporation—a conference room, the cafeteria, or a remote branch office. Wireless LANs provide a benefit for IT managers as well, allowing them to design, deploy, and enhance networks without regard to the availability of wiring, saving both effort and dollars.

Businesses of all sizes can benefit from deploying a WLAN system, which provides a powerful combination of wired network throughput, mobile access, and configuration flexibility.

The economic benefits can add up to as much as $16,000 per user (measured in worker productivity, organizational efficiency, revenue gain, and cost savings) over wired alternatives. Specifically, WLAN advantages include:

- Mobility that improves productivity with real-time access to information, regardless of worker location, for faster and more efficient decision making.
- Cost-effective network setup for hard-to-wire locations such as older buildings and solid-wall structures.
- Reduced cost of ownership (particularly in dynamic environments requiring frequent modifications) thanks to minimal wiring and installation costs per device and user.

WLANs liberate users from dependence on hard-wired access to the network backbone, giving them anytime/anywhere network access. This freedom to roam offers numerous user benefits for a variety of work environments, such as:

- Immediate bedside access to patient information for doctors and hospital staff.
- Easy, real-time network access for onsite consultants or auditors.
- Improved database access for roving supervisors such as production line managers, warehouse auditors, or construction engineers.
- Simplified network configuration with minimal MIS involvement for temporary setups such as trade shows or conference rooms.
- Faster access to customer information for service vendors and retailers, resulting in better service and improved customer satisfaction.
- Location-independent access for network administrators, for easier onsite troubleshooting and support.
- Real-time access to study group meetings and research links for students.

Finally, 802.11 WLANs are already commonly used in several large vertical markets. The 802.11b standard is the first standard to make WLANs usable in the general workplace by providing robust and reliable 11 Mbps performance, five times faster than the original standard. The new standard will also give WLAN customers the freedom to choose flexible, interoperable solutions from multiple vendors, since it has been endorsed by most major networking and personal computer vendors. Broad manufacturer acceptance and certifiable interoperability means users can expect to see affordable, high-speed wireless solutions proliferate throughout the large enterprise, small business, and home markets. This global wireless LAN standard opens exciting new opportunities to expand the potential of network computing [9].

The list of wireless networks services is seemingly endless. Other radio-based LAN products can be used to construct private wireless workgroups and campus networks, reaching speeds of up to 2 Mbps. Satellite networks are both available and planned to provide wireless connectivity, nationally and internationally—for example, Teledesic plans to build a global network of low-Earth-orbit satellites. Personal communication services (PCS) intends to link analog and digital cellular networks, packet data networks, and public switched telephone networks into a single, faster, reliable global network. Limited PCS deployment began in late 1996, and providers hope that consumer demand for new services (especially new data services) will drive a broad-scale PCS rollout over the next 5–10 years.

Circuit-switched cellular, CDPD, ARDIS, and Metricom wireless networks provide Physical and Data Link layer connectivity upon which wireless applications build. Most of these products crawl in comparison to 10 Mbps Ethernet LANs, and are still only half as fast as analog dial Internet access. Wireless modems used with these services are fairly small and light (PCMCIA form factor)—the inevitable battery accounts for most of the bulk and weight.

A wireless modem is just a hair more expensive than an analog PCMCIA modem, and on par with ISDN and combo LAN/WAN PCMCIA cards. But the true cost issue for most subscribers will be metered usage charges. In a corporate America obsessed with downsizing and cost-cutting, it may be difficult to budget or justify charges racked up per Kbyte of data transferred. Flat-rate pricing is a significant edge capitalized on by Metricom.

Today's wireless LAN and wireless data network services get low marks for interoperability. A notable exception is CDPD, which is based on standard network protocols. A proprietary wireless infrastructure may be cheaper or faster; weigh these against the more limited options available to you as a subscriber. If you buy a CDPD modem, you can change service providers. The same cannot be said of buying a Ricochet modem.

National wireless network providers offered ubiquitous service— almost. Wireless communication, by its very nature, is prone to service disruption as you roam about. Wireless network providers offer coverage maps—read them. Wireless LAN services are constrained to a local area and obviously do not support nationwide roaming. But then, there are many vertical applications of wireless computing that do not require nationwide roaming—campus nets, mobile workforces, restaurant order entry, hospitals, fire fighters, policemen. Even the guy at the rental car return who prints your receipt. In this case, ubiquitous should mean reliably accessible within the local area of interest.

Middleware, Custom Protocols, and Proxies

Early attempts at wireless computing used TCP/IP directly over wireless data services to offer common applications such as e-mail. The slow speeds and lengthy delays associated with wireless data transfer prevent this solution from working very effectively (or perhaps even at all). Yet, this approach may still be viable for faster, quieter wireless data services—particularly wireless LANs.

For the rest of us, several alternatives emerged. Among these were:

- Custom data transport protocols, tuned for operation over a wireless data link or network.
- Customized implementations of TCP, tweaked to improve operation over wireless IP.
- Middleware, which insulates applications from wireless network characteristics [13].

The first alternative has been evaluated for several years with minimal success. Mobile IP addresses only part of the problem—enabling mobility of IP addresses. A variety of Internet drafts defining custom transports have endured numerous incarnations without yielding a deployed standard. The enormous embedded base represented by TCP simply overwhelms the marketability of transport protocols engineered specifically for wireless.

The second alternative (custom tuning of TCP) has been implemented with some success by companies such as PADCOM. However, these products are highly customized TCP implementations. Commercial off-the-shelf TCP implementations cannot be tuned by end users to completely address the issues surrounding effective transmission over wireless. Most COTS TCP products provide only a few knobs to twiddle, even those that expose numerous configurable parameters hide complex algorithms under the covers, and (most importantly) the same tuning must be performed at both ends of a TCP connection.

These alternatives fail to provide a ubiquitous solution—one that is readily available on any wireless laptop, HPC, PDA, or smartphone and on any wireline application server that might be accessed via wireless.

The third alternative (wireless network computing middleware) addresses this concern by constraining wireless adaptation to a (smaller) set of devices, known as proxies. Wireless clients interact with proxies using a middleware protocol, which provides reliable, efficient delivery over commercial off-the-shelf UDP/IP. The hand-held device transport protocol (HDTP) used by AT&T's PocketNet and the mobile network computing protocol (MNCP) used by GoAmerica [10] and AirBoss are two examples of this approach. No ubiquitous, interoperable industry-wide solution is currently available to solve this problem. A common middleware standard is needed before robust wireless application deployment can become widespread.

Thin Clients, TTML, and HDML

AT&T's PocketNet and many other smartphones offer short ASCII text messaging services suitable for display in a relatively small window. This approach is often referred to as a thin client.

Applications involving plain text, such as integrated e-mail, voice mail, and paging, can be readily supported by this approach. Because limited data storage is available on smartphones, large volume data transfers are inappropriate. And, since the user interface (display) is so limited, display of graphics is unfeasible.

To enable Web browsing from smartphones, vendors have devised alternative *Web page* formats for use with wireless. The Nokia's Tagged Text Markup Language (TTML) and AT&T's Hand-Held Device Markup Language (HDML) both address this problem. HDML can be used to define *decks* of *cards,* which are displayed on a smartphone's display. HDML has not been mapped to HTML; this format is currently limited to use with only those Web servers that offer HDML-encoded cards.

Devices with additional computing power (laptops, HPCs, and PDAs) can use commercial off-the-shelf browsers such as Microsoft Internet Explorer or Netscape Navigator. For these devices, there is no need to limit functionality to only that provided to thin clients. These devices can access any HTML Web page using wireless services such as those provided by GoAmerica, RadioMail, and Metricom. Users may apply filters to make more effective use of wireless bandwidth. For example, the AirBrowse service offered by GoAmerica allows the user to filter by page length and graphic image.

Advanced Wireless Computing Products and Applications: UMTS and Bluetooth

Wireless communication has huge potential—that's an understatement! In a world where science fiction and reality are beginning to merge at an alarming rate, the future of wireless may be truly fantastical. We've had cellular phones for years and cellular modems for nearly as long, and now a number of companies are pushing wireless Internet access via cellular technology or PCS. But when it comes down to it, all this is just the tip of a giant, multimillion-dollar, psychedelic iceberg.

MirCorp plans to turn the Mir space station into an orbiting commercial outpost later in the year 2000. Investors were showing increasing interest in the company's plans to open the first Internet portal in space, which would be capable of relaying live images of the Earth's surface, and its plans to produce highly pure medicines and alloys.

In its current state, wireless communication is primarily used to connect remote devices (such as your Windows CE hand-held) to some larger computer or network. But what about exchanging data directly between two remote devices?

And furthermore, how about interoperability? Sure, you can exchange information between two Windows CE hand-helds using their infrared (IR) ports (which have their own limitations), but what if you need to exchange information between a Windows CE hand-held and an Apple iBook, or an Apple iBook and a Palm VII? For wireless communication to become truly pervasive, there needs to be a standard. But, like everything else in this politically charged domain, it's never that easy.

With that in mind, let's take a very brief look at a couple of advanced wireless computing products and applications: UMTS and Bluetooth.

UMTS

There are many goals yet to be achieved with wireless data. The whole data industry is moving away from X.25-based services toward TCP/IP-based services. Data transport is becoming cheaper and cheaper as economies of scale drive down the cost of routing equipment. User devices are becoming more sophisticated and smaller. The idea of e-mail and Web browsing in your pocket can be achieved today, yet it is expensive and in some cases awkward to use. But the mass market for data devices is the key to future success. Defining that mass market and the most useful services is the key. We must make the best use of the available data services to avoid excess cost. The long-term goal is the UMTS vision:

The Universal Mobile Telecommunications System, UMTS, will take the personal communications user into the Information Society of the 21st century. It will deliver advanced information directly to people and provide them with access to new and innovative services. It will offer mobile personalized communications to the mass market regardless of location, network, or terminal used [11].

What is UMTS. UMTS™ (Universal Mobile Telephone Service) is a third-generation (3G) mobile system being developed by ETSI™ within the ITU's IMT-2000 framework. It will provide data speeds of up to 2 Mbps, making portable videophones a reality.

UMTS has the support of many major telecommunications operators and manufacturers because it represents a unique opportunity to create a mass market for highly personalized and user-friendly mobile access to the information society. UMTS seeks to build on and extend the capability of today's mobile, cordless, and satellite technologies by providing increased capacity, data capability, and a far greater range of services using an innovative radio access scheme and an enhanced, evolving core network.

Spectrum for UMTS. WRC'92 identified the frequency bands 1885-2025 MHz and 2110-2200 MHz for future IMT-2000 systems. The bands 1980-2010 MHz and 2170-2200 MHz are intended for the satellite part of these future systems. See the Sidebar, "How and When."

HOW AND WHEN

For the commercial and technical success of UMTS, and to meet its 2002 launch deadline, a number of steps are being undertaken by manufacturers, standards bodies, operators, and regulators around the world:

1. Creating an adequate regulatory framework.

2. Ensuring availability of licenses.

3. Allocating adequate spectrum to operators.

4. Producing timely UMTS standards.

5. Encouraging simultaneous uptake of UMTS in several countries to stimulate uptake of services in a worldwide market.

6. Full commercial phase (2002–2005), with performance and capability enhancements, and the introduction of new, sophisticated UMTS services.

Phases Toward the Development of UMTS

Full commercial deployment will be reached through the following main steps:

1. Extension of GSM's capability with packet and high-speed data operation.

2. Pre-UMTS Trial Phase either in subsets of real GSM networks or in isolated packet-based networks.

3. Basic deployment phase in 2002, including the incorporation of UTRA base stations into *live* networks and the launch of satellite-based UMTS services [11].

Basically the implications of this are that all telecommunications networks are integrated and users really can get fast data rates of 2 Mb/s in some areas. But 2 Mb/s is only useful for the right applications and those applications need some market experience before they can be well defined. There are bound to be some winners and some losers but at least some of the battles must be fought with the existing second-generation cellular capability of up to around 64 kbits/s. The future expectation of growth in the mobile market is driven by data and multimedia. This expectation is now being realized on fixed networks, mobile networks through the enhancement on GSM, and introduction of new capabilities such as GPRS will start to build that market. UMTS is the *utopia* for meeting the market expectation; however, it needs to be technologically advanced sufficiently to meet that need.

Bluetooth

Every now and then an innovative technology is introduced to the market place that so quickly becomes a part of everyday life that you wonder, *How did I ever do without it?* Bluetooth is set to become just such a technology.

Cut to May 1998. That month, five telecommunications giants (Ericsson, IBM, Intel, Nokia, and Toshiba) joined together to form the Bluetooth Special Interest Group (SIG). The original goal of Bluetooth was to provide easier connections between mobile computers and mobile phones. In the short time since, more than 850 companies have joined the group, and the scope of the project has broadened considerably. Today, the Bluetooth specification is poised to become a global standard for wireless communication.

Bluetooth was named after the intrepid Viking who ruled Denmark in the Middle Ages. Essentially, Bluetooth uses shortwave radio to interconnect terminals (PCs, mobile phones, printers, etc.) to allow the free flow and synchronization of information. It also eradicates product compatibility problems and the need for cables.

The basic concept behind Bluetooth is simple: Provide short-range wireless communications using the 2.4-GHz RF (radio frequency) band. The group released version 1.0 of its specification in 1999, with enough information for manufacturers to develop real products in July 1999, and two amendments to the specification were put into effect in October 1999. Other amendments and modifications are expected before any products hit the market.

Although the specification is close to being finalized, nobody really expects products to be released any time soon. Like many good (and complicated) high-tech products, it'll take some time. One obstacle to Bluetooth-enabled products is that each one must be independently certified as Bluetooth-compliant. This means testing programs will have to be developed by independent labs after a final specification is published and before products are released. This was all expected to take place early this year (2000). Remember, expected is the key word here.

Bluetooth Technology.   In order to work toward a true global standard and introduce Bluetooth to the market as quickly as possible, the SIG opted to release the technical specifications (see the Sidebar, "Specifications") to any company interested in adopting the technology. As previously mentioned, this license-free and open approach has already led to more than 850 companies joining the SIG, many of whom are working to include Bluetooth in their product range.

SPECIFICATIONS

Undoubtedly technology has enriched most of our lives. But as more and better products become available, particularly in the mobile arena, technology has also added even more complications to our already complicated lives.

All of us certainly have stories about how technology has made things more difficult rather than easier. Remember, for example, that time you lost business to a competitor simply because you forgot to take the cables you needed to connect your notebook with the projector and you couldn't make your presentation? Or the time you didn't synchronize your hand-held PC's diary with that on your notebook and missed that vital customer dinner? Or how frustrating it feels having answered a whole bunch of e-mails while on a jet, only to have the hassle of finding a phone-line connection once on the ground to send them?

A new solution currently being implemented by a consortium of the world's leading technology companies is set to bring a permanent and timely halt to these frustrations. This new technology allows you to connect all your mobile items at the touch of a button, without the need for cables or even close physical proximity. Imagine being able to check your e-mails while strolling through the airport, notebook tucked safely away in your briefcase. Or being able to instantly share the information on your computer with other participants at meetings. And imagine having access to these functions anywhere in the world, regardless of how remote (see Figures 28–1 and 28–2) [12].

The enabling technology currently being implemented is called Bluetooth. It will create a new dimension in wireless communication where portable devices such as computers, phones, and hand-held PCs will all be able to talk to each other effortlessly and without interruption.

The Technology

Bluetooth uses a short-range radio link to exchange information, enabling effortless, wireless connectivity between portable devices. The Bluetooth radio will be generally available in the form of a 17 × 33 mm module and operates in the globally available 2.45 GHz ISM band for which a commercial license is not required (see Table 28–1) [12]. Each Bluetooth-enabled device can be used anywhere in the world and has a range of approximately 10 meters. A higher-power version of the radio is expected to follow, supporting connections to devices up to 100 meters away.

Any Bluetooth-equipped device can be set to establish an instant connection with another Bluetooth radio within this range. Plus, due to the sophisticated mode of transmission defined in the Bluetooth specification, data is secure and protected from interference. The technology is also very fast. In the future, users will be able to send data by means of Bluetooth at speeds up to 12 times faster than a V.90 modem.

Moreover, Bluetooth devices won't drain precious battery life. The radio chip consumes only 0.3mA in standby mode, which is less than 3 percent of the power used by a standard mobile phone, as shown in Figure 28–3 [12]. The chips also have excellent power-saving features, as they will automatically shift to a low-power mode as soon as traffic volume lessens or stops.

Bluetooth Uses

One of the main benefits of the Bluetooth technology will be the ability for Bluetooth-enabled devices to communicate with each other through a single interface, eliminating the need for numerous, bulky cables. Enabled devices will not need to remain within the line of sight, something that is necessary for devices connected via infrared, and can maintain an uninterrupted connection when in motion or even when devices are tucked away inside a pocket or briefcase (see Figure 28–4) [12].

But what does that mean for the typical business traveler? Well, as an example, if you are on a train or waiting in an airport departure lounge, you could check your e-mail even if your notebook is still in its case. By using the Bluetooth technology as soon as the computer receives an e-mail message, an alert will sound on your mobile phone. Also, by using the phones' display, you will then be able to read the e-mail. Additionally, the Bluetooth technology will enable users to surf the Internet via a completely wireless connection routed either through a mobile phone or other wireless connection point to standard communications networks such as PSTN, an ISDN line, or LAN (see Figure 28–5) [12].

For those travelers keen on using valuable time in the air to catch up on e-mail, they will be safe in the knowledge that as soon as they've landed and turned on their mobile phone, all the messages will be sent immediately. Also, a user-programmable, automatic synchronizer will keep your mobile PC and handheld PC diaries talking to each other so they will consistently match up. So no more diary foul-ups!

And finally, office-bound Bluetooth users will benefit from the technology as new wireless devices will eradicate the danger and messy appearance of cables connecting mobile computers to printers, scanners, and LANs. Users will even be able to enjoy the freedom of a wireless connection between their PC, keyboard, mouse, and other peripherals, as shown in Figure 28–6 [12].

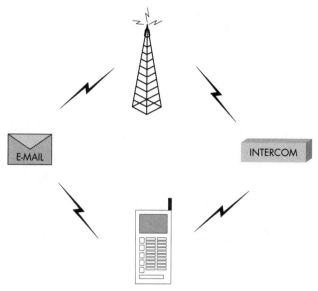

Figure 28–1   The three-in-one phone. Use the same phone wherever you are. When you're at the office, your phone functions as an intercom (no telephony charge). At home, it functions as a portable phone (fixed line charge). And when you're on the move, the phone functions as a mobile phone (cellular charge).

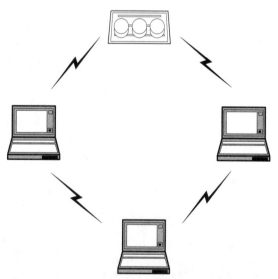

Figure 28–2   The interactive conference. Connect all participants for instant data exchange. In meetings and conferences, you can share information instantly with all participants and without any cord connections. You can also wirelessly run and control, for instance, a projector.

Table 28–1   Packet Switching Protocol Based on a Frequency Hop Scheme with 1,600 Hops/s.

Technical Facts	Specifications
Normal range	10m (0 dBm)
Optional range	100m (20 dBm)
Normal transmitting power	0 dBm (1mW)
Optional transmitting power	.30 to 20 dBm (100mW)
Receiver sensitivity	.70 dBm
Frequency band	2.45 Ghz
Gross data rate	1Mbit/s
Maximum data transfer	721 56k Bit/ 3 voice channels
Power consumption, hold/spark	$-50\mu A$
Power consumption, standby	$-300\mu A$
Power consumption, hold/max	50 mA

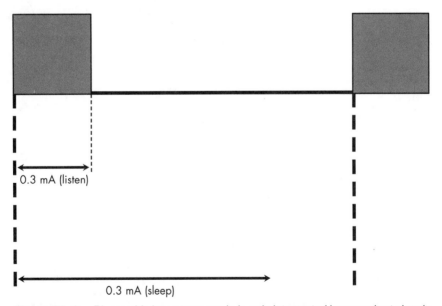

0.3 mA (listen)

0.3 mA (sleep)

Figure 28–3   Bluetooth's low-power mode is only interrupted by very short signals with the purpose of verifying an established connection.

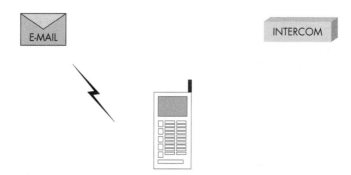

Figure 28–4   The briefcase trick. Use e-mail while your portable PC is still in the briefcase. When your portable PC receives an e-mail, you'll get an alert on your mobile phone. You can also browse all incoming e-mails and read those you select in the mobile phone's display.

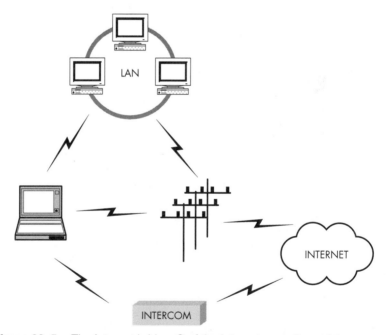

Figure 28–5   The Internet bridge. Surf the Internet regardless of the connection. Use your portable PC to surf the Internet wherever you are, and regardless of whether you're wirelessly connected through a mobile phone (cellular) or through a wire-bound connection (PSTN, ISDN, LAN, xDSL).

Figure 28–6   The wireless workplace. Connect all peripheral tools to your PC or to the LAN. Wireless connection of your desktop or portable PC to the printer, scanners, and to the LAN. Increase your sense of freedom in everyday work by wireless connection of your mouse and keyboard to your PC.

Typical User Scenarios.   Bluetooth technology has been designed so that it can be incorporated into any mobile or office product. The fact that it does so without cables, nor line-of-sight connection (Infrared), will surely kick-start a revolution in the office (and mobile office) environment.

For example, by connecting peripheral devices such as keyboards and printers to your PC using Bluetooth, valuable office space will be freed up on your desk. The business traveler, however, will feel the main benefits of Bluetooth technology. It will create a seamless link between portable PC and mobile phone, enabling the instant transfer and synchronization of information between the products.

Connecting People.   One of the most obvious benefits of Bluetooth is that information can be shared between wireless devices. In this respect, Bluetooth offers several important advantages compared to traditional IR methods. First, it has compatibility. A Bluetooth-enabled device will be able to interact with any other Bluetooth-enabled device. But that's really just a tease. IR communication requires a *line of sight* between the two devices, and also requires them to be relatively close. With Bluetooth, two people could conceivably exchange data from across the room. Imagine the benefits this could have in a conference or even a courtroom setting. And for fun's sake, think about a high school classroom. No more messy, origami-like folded notes being thrown back and forth.

Of course, this does raise some security concerns. If you can send data to someone else on the other side of the room, what's to keep some third party from intercepting that data? Fortunately, Bluetooth has this situation covered. The technology is designed to switch among 79 different channels at the rate of 1,600 hops per second (see Table 28–1). That means intercepting the data would be fairly difficult. Beyond that, the Bluetooth specification also calls for 40-bit or 64-bit data encryption. While this level of encryption can hardly be called industrial strength, it's more than adequate for the types of situations you're likely to encounter in these settings.

Finally, Bluetooth devices can automatically adjust their transmission ranges to the appropriate levels. That means that if you're communicating with another device that's 10 feet away, you can't be intercepted by a device that's, say, 15 feet away or more. In this fashion, the gamut of potential hackers is reduced significantly, while providing excellent communication means.

Fast, No-Hassle Connections.   Perhaps you've seen Internet-enabled pay phones in an airport. They look like regular pay phones, except they have a phone jack where you can plug in your modem. These things are great—until you find yourself stuck behind somebody who wants to research prices, availability, and colors for every SUV on the market.

But what if you only had to get near the Internet access point instead of actually plugging into it? With a Bluetooth-enabled Internet station at the airport, a large number of people could jack into the Net at the same time, with virtually no waiting required.

With expected data transfer rates of 1 Mbps, Bluetooth is considerably slower than the 10 Mbps of even the slowest Ethernet network. However, it's substantially faster than both wireless and standard modem connections.

This translates into less total time online at the airport or more productive use of the time at the airport. If you've used one of those home-networking packages that connects two computers through existing phone wiring, you've already experienced a 1 Mbps data connection. It's not great, but it's not horrid either.

There is the problem of people who have no idea how the phone wiring networks work.

Pay Up, Buddy.   Few people would argue with the notion that electronic cash is becoming more and more popular. There are kinks to be worked out, for sure, but the time is coming. Chief among these kinks is a viable *micropayment* solution.

Micropayment typically refers to e-transactions of $10 or less—transactions that don't make much economic sense in the current *bill my credit card* state of e-commerce. However, once a viable micropayment solution is developed, Bluetooth could become the enabling technology that makes it all come together.

For example, picture yourself in a busy downtown area. You pull into a metered parking space, but you don't have any change handy. If that happened today, you'd have to give up the space and plunk down $5 or more at a private lot. On the other hand, a year or two from now, that parking meter could be Bluetooth-enabled. All you'd have to do is whip out your Bluetooth-enabled Palm VII filled with e-cash and wirelessly *insert* some cybercoins that would give you the meter time you needed.

Industry-Wide Implications.   Over the past decade, the mobile communications industry has dominated the high-tech advance and development of the business world. The speed at which the industry has grown has been phenomenal. About 11 years ago, only a few companies were regularly using mobile phones; nowadays, those who do not are considered *behind the times* in a business era in which timing and communication is everything. Bluetooth, along with a few other select technologies (for example, wireless Internet connections), looks poised to revolutionize the mobile communications industry and unite it with the office world.

This would create a new, all-encompassing wireless office in which any product or device can quickly and easily communicate with any other. The speed at which Bluetooth is adopted is certain to rival, and probably surpass, that of mobile phones. Over the next decade, we will witness firsthand the effect it has on shaping the way we work.

It's Not the Only Game in Town.   The Bluetooth SIG isn't the only group working on ways to link us all together digitally. Recently, for example, the Massachusetts Institute of Technology unveiled a $40 million research project called Oxygen.

The Oxygen project has three major hardware components. The first is a portable unit called a Handy21 that has a high-contrast screen, a digital camera, a GPS module, and more. Handy21 can be used as a phone, a two-way radio, a television, a pager, a hand-held computer, or a pointing device— it's the ultimate PDA.

The second is Enviro21, which is the nonportable big brother of the Handy21. It can do many of the same things as the Handy21, plus it can be used for more complex tasks, such as home automation. The third hardware piece is N21, a proposed network for connecting all these Oxygen devices.

Another key component of the Oxygen project is its focus on speech technology. In the perfect Oxygen-enabled world, you talk to your Handy21, for example, just like you were talking to a human assistant. The only difference is that the Handy21 carries out your requests without ever asking for a day off or whining about raises.

Remember, though, to take all this with a grain of salt. It's cool, yes, but it's not just around the corner. Tomorrow's reality is still today's fantasy.

THE REAL FUTURE OF WIRELESS COMPUTING

Many industry experts claim that Web browsing is the *killer application* that will determine the future of wireless computing. Wireless solutions must become fast enough, reliable enough, and cheap enough to support on-demand access to Internet and corporate Intranet information servers, anywhere, anytime. Will plain-text access to HDML or TTML servers be enough to satisfy our culture's growing appetite for information?

Or will middleware evolve into smart agents, capable of searching out information we define to be of interest, aggregating it, and returning it to wireless clients in condensed form? Will the industry's current fascination with *push* technology become a presence in wireless computing as well? These approaches hold promise for both *thin* and *thick* clients, and the growth of products with these features.

Corporate acceptance of wireless computing is essential to fund market growth. The key factor will be successful integration of wireless into the corporate network. Wireless remote access must become secure and manageable. Wireless devices must offer seamless access to network operating systems (Novell's Netware, Microsoft's Windows NT, etc.) and intranet information servers and databases, and must do so without disrupting the corporate backbone network. IT managers will need proof that investment in wireless as a remote access technology is innovative and cost-effective, not frivolous or foolhardy.

It is increasingly difficult to differentiate between mobile telephony and mobile computing. This trend is expected to continue as well as the integrated wireless appliances that will fulfill every communication need: voice, data, video, and computing. The HPC or PDA is not expected to crunch spreadsheets, but it is expected to be able to search and view their contents. Users just don't want to carry a laptop around just to do that.

Smaller. Lighter. Faster. Cheaper. Reliable. Integrated. Ubiquitous. Interoperable. Smarter. We're on our way, surfing the Web over wireless. We've only caught the very beginning of this wave; just how far can we ride it?

FROM HERE

Chapter 28 opened up Part VII, "Future Directions," by taking a peek at the future of wireless communications: cableless connectivity. Chapter 29 takes a look at home networking and how to connect to your home in the future.

NOTES

[1]   "The Future of Wireless Infrastructure and Terminals, 1998-2007: The Evolution to Third Generation," Herschel Shosteck Associates, Ltd., 11160 Veirs Mill Road, Suite 709, Wheaton, MD 20902-2538, 2000.

[2]   "Wireless Instant Messaging: A 'Killer App' for the Mobile Information Appliance Market," Mobile Insights, Inc., 2001 Landings Drive, Mountain View, CA 94043, 2000.

[3]   Metricom, Inc., Headquarters, 980 University Ave., Los Gatos, CA 95032-7620, 2000.

[4]   Carmen Nobel, "Palm Shows off All-Wireless Future," Ziff-Davis UK Ltd., International House, 1 St Katharine's Way, London, E1 9UN (Palm, Inc., Corporate Headquarters, 5470 Great America Pkwy, Santa Clara, CA USA 95052), 2000.

[5]   Motient Corporation, 10802 Parkridge Blvd., Reston, Virginia 20191, 2000.

[6]   GoAmerica Communications Corp., 401 Hackensack Ave., 4th Floor, Hackensack, NJ 07601, 2000.

[7]   "Toshiba and Bellcore Team up to Create The Future Of Wireless Internet Communications," Telcordia Technologies, Inc., PYA2, 3 Corporate Place, Piscataway, NJ 08854-4157, 2000.

[8]   Ellinor Abreu, "Oracle Sees a Wireless Future," TheStandard.com, 150 E. 52nd St., 10th Floor, New York, NY 10022 (Oracle Corporation, Redwood Shores, Calif.), 2000.

[9]   "IEEE 802.11b Wireless LANs," 3Com Corporation, Santa Clara Site, 5400 Bayfront Plaza, Santa Clara, CA 95052, 2000.

[10]   GoAmerica Communications Corp., 401 Hackensack Ave., 4th Floor, Hackensack, NJ 07601, United States of America, 2000.

[11]   "UMTS (Universal Mobile Telephone Service)," Option International, NV, Corporate Headquarters, Kolonel Begaultlaan 45, B-3012 Leuven, BELGIUM, 2000.

[12]   Toshiba Europe GmbH, Geschäftsbereich Deutschland, Hammfelddamm 8, D-41460 Neuss, Germany, 2000.

[13]   Lisa A. Phifer, "Surfing the Web over Wireless," Core Competence, Inc., 344 Valley View Lane, Chester Springs, PA 19425, 2000.

The Networked House: A Brave New Home

Computer networking is being propelled from its traditional corporate base into a brave new world: the home. This chapter discusses networking from a technical perspective. The chapter explains why home networking is a viable and growing market segment, and details the benefits and market drivers behind the push. It also introduces four basic home networking technologies, compares their advantages and limitations, and outlines the reasons behind their recommended application in the home. Finally, the chapter presents factors that assist in determining the successful introduction of home networking products in the consumer marketplace.

RESOURCE SHARING, MULTIPLAYER GAMING BOOST HOME NETWORK INTEREST AND INTERNET ACCESS

The price of home computers keeps falling, while the advantages for consumers to being connected (online investing and shopping, keeping in touch with long-distance friends and relatives, enjoying multiplayer games, and tapping the vast resources of the Internet) continue to multiply. No wonder an increasing number of households own two or more PCs. Forecasters predict that more than 40 million North American households will own two or more computers by the end of 2003.

However, households are experiencing the same limitations that confronted businesses almost 20 years ago, when personal computers migrated from the basements of home hobbyists to the desktops of office workers around the world. Those limitations include the inability to share computing and peripheral resources or to share information easily between computer users. The solution to those problems then and now is networking: the ability to interconnect devices so that users can communicate with one another and share resources. Consider the four most compelling home network market drivers:

- Simultaneous high-speed Internet access using one Internet service provider (ISP) account
- Peripheral sharing
- Sharing files and applications
- Entertainment

Simultaneous High-Speed Internet Access

As the Internet becomes an essential tool in business, education, medicine, and government, as well as in our personal lives, the demand for high-speed, convenient, easily accessible Internet access is mushrooming. Cable, integrated services digital network (ISDN), and digital subscriber line (DSL) modems provide the fastest Internet connections and allow family members to talk on the phone and use the Internet simultaneously.

Peripheral Sharing

Families want to get the most out of their computer equipment investments. This can be done by sharing the same printers, modems, or other peripherals from any PC in the home.

Sharing Files and Applications

Families also want to maximize the value of their software investments by sharing applications. They also want the convenience of sharing files easily, and eliminating *sneakernet*—running from machine to machine with floppies or CDs.

Sneakernet is a very old concept and not in any major "implementation" today.

Entertainment

The new wave of multiplayer computer games, with their eye-popping graphics and exciting audio tracks, are beginning to grab consumer interest. Market analyst International Data Corporation (IDC) believes that PC games and entertainment software represent the swiftest long-term growth segment of the overall U.S. electronic gaming marketplace, and has predicted a combined unit annual growth rate of 57 percent between 2000 and 2005. The two biggest growth factors, in IDC's opinion, are the continuing price drop in home PCs (U.S. $200 PCs are already available today) and the opportunity for multiplayer gaming. PC gaming historically has trailed console gaming, especially in the important adolescent category, precisely because of the inability to play head-to-head against friends and relatives.

The Need for Bandwidth

As Figure 29–1 shows, these popular emerging applications require substantial bandwidth [1]. For a discussion of bandwidth, see the Sidebar "Speed Requirements."

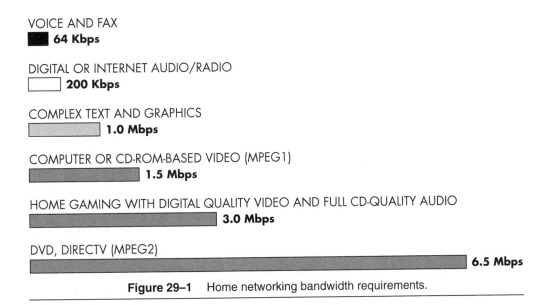

VOICE AND FAX
64 Kbps

DIGITAL OR INTERNET AUDIO/RADIO
200 Kbps

COMPLEX TEXT AND GRAPHICS
1.0 Mbps

COMPUTER OR CD-ROM-BASED VIDEO (MPEG1)
1.5 Mbps

HOME GAMING WITH DIGITAL QUALITY VIDEO AND FULL CD-QUALITY AUDIO
3.0 Mbps

DVD, DIRECTV (MPEG2)
6.5 Mbps

Figure 29–1   Home networking bandwidth requirements.

SPEED REQUIREMENTS

"Bandwidth" is a general term that can be used in different ways. One use refers to the data rate (or speed) of a network technology such as Ethernet, powerline, phoneline, or wireless. In this case, bandwidth is a function of the amount of data transmitted or received per unit of time, measured in bits per second (bps). It is used to define network performance.

The higher the bandwidth, the faster the data rate or network speed. The faster the network speed, the faster text, audio, and video data can travel from point A to point B. And, after all, time is money. Figure 29–2 shows how long a 30 MB file would take to travel from one PC to another over 1 Mbps, 10 Mbps, and 100 Mbps networks [1].

These major market drivers are spurring the demand for home networks. Industry analysts are predicting a healthy growth curve for home networking. Home networking will grow from $344 million by the end of 2000

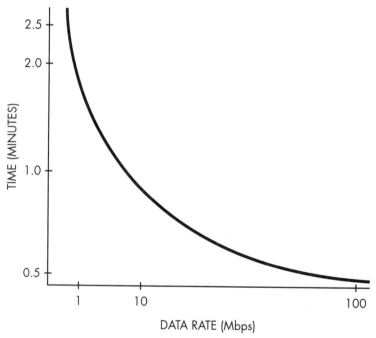

Figure 29–2   File transfer time comparison. Times shown are an average of three tests for each data rate run on a two-machine configuration. Times can vary depending on machine type, processor speed, other peripherals on the machine, and network congestion.

to over \$2.5 billion (U.S.) in annual sales by 2004. This anticipated 82 percent annual growth rate over the next five years is enticing everyone from established network vendors to brash home gaming upstarts to enter the emerging market.

However, success in the consumer market requires that home networks be inexpensive, easy to install, and easy to use. Essentially, that means the technology must be transparent to the user. To meet this requirement, networking technology is evolving to make home connectivity available to the average home computer user.

OVERCOMING THE TECHNOLOGICAL AND COMPLEXITY BARRIERS

While consumer demand has swelled, recent advances have overcome the technological and complexity barriers that once prevented networking from migrating into nontechnical environments. Component prices have dropped, available network speeds have accelerated, and signal attenuation and noise problems have been addressed using low-cost, high-performance signal processing. Consumers now have an impressive array of networking options from which to choose, depending on their application needs and how much money and effort they want to invest.

Basically, the choices are divided into wired networks and wireless networks. Wired network technologies use some form of physical cabling to connect computing devices. There are three technology choices for wired networks today: Ethernet, phoneline, and powerline. Wireless networks, on the other hand, use electromagnetic airwaves (infrared or radio) to transmit information from one point to another.

ETHERNET NETWORKS

Ethernet, the most proven network technology, is the Institute of Electrical and Electronics Engineers (IEEE) 802.3 standard technology on which the majority of business networks are built. The Ethernet protocol defines the transmission of data over copper wire at a rate of 10 Mbps. Fast Ethernet, an extension of the IEEE 802.3 standard (802.3u), defines the transmission of data over copper wire or fiber optic cable at a rate of 100 Mbps. In addition to their well-deserved reputation for reliability and security, Ethernet-based networks deliver far and away the fastest performance. At measurable rates between 10 and 100 Mbps, they are ideal for bandwidth-intensive multiplayer gaming and home office environments.

How Home Ethernet Networks Work

Ethernet is a shared network technology. Simple or small Ethernet networks typically employ a central controlling hub to which all network devices are attached (known as a star configuration). Network traffic travels through the hub to the targeted PC or peripheral.

Ethernet's carrier sense multiple access with collision detection (CSMA/CD) media access control (MAC) protocol defines the rules of access for the shared network. The protocol name itself neatly explains how the traffic control process actually works. Devices attached to the network first check, or sense, the carrier (wire) before transmitting. If the network is in use, the device waits before transmitting. Multiple access refers to the fact that many devices share the same network medium. If, by chance, two devices attempt to transmit at exactly the same time and a collision occurs, collision detection mechanisms direct both devices to wait a random interval and then retransmit. Ethernet is the most popular networking technology in use today, because the cabling and installation is comparatively inexpensive. It is also simple, secure, and requires very little overhead.

Ethernet Networking in the Home

Ethernet technology is nearly 30 years old, but there were still a few technology challenges to overcome before it was acceptable for home use. Ethernet networks are perceived as complicated, expensive to install, and somewhat administration-heavy. To overcome that perception, Ethernet home network vendors have designed networking kits (consisting of low-cost network adapters, an inexpensive nonmanaged hub, and simple configuration software) to make it easier to set up and use.

Ethernet networks do require special category 3 or 5 (preferred) unshielded twisted pair (UTP) copper wire cabling between connected devices. This type of cabling can be found in computer stores and home improvement stores, and is preinstalled in many new homes. Because of Ethernet's special cabling requirements, Ethernet networks are easiest to implement in new or remodeled homes where network cabling can be installed as part of construction. However, technically savvy home computer users can run the cable, particularly in situations where all the PCs are located in the same room, such as in a home-based office.

Figure 29–3 shows how an Ethernet network could be set up in the home [1]. Internal or external network adapters are installed in each PC. Peripheral devices without direct Ethernet connection options (such as print-

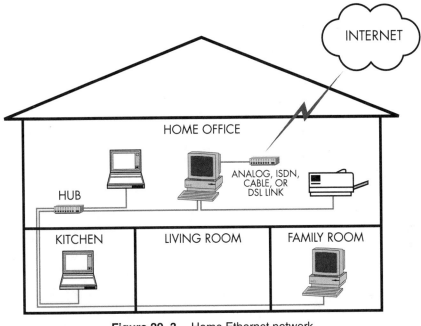

Figure 29–3   Home Ethernet network.

ers) are shared through a networked PC. Each PC is then connected to the Ethernet hub over category 3 or category 5 cabling. The hub manages the communication between the devices on the network. A single 56 Kbps analog, ISDN, cable, or DSL modem provides a shared Internet connection.

PHONELINE NETWORKS

Alternative phoneline and powerline network technologies were developed to provide a simpler way to get home users connected. Since every home already has phone and power circuits, there is no need to run new cabling to install one of these networks.

How Home Phoneline Networks Work

Phoneline networking takes advantage of unused transmission capacity to transmit data over existing telephone wires. As shown in Figure 29–4, phoneline home networks transmit information at frequencies well above that of plain old telephone service (POTS) or digital services like ISDN and DSL, so the network does not interfere with the normal use of the phone line for voice,

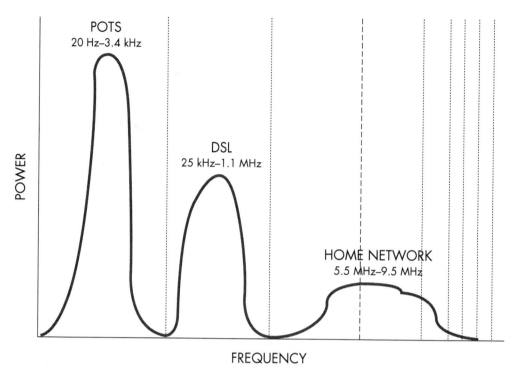

Figure 29–4 Frequency division multiplexing.

fax, or Internet services running over the same telephone circuit [1]. Nor do these other phoneline services affect network data transmission quality.

The technology used to divide up shared bandwidth is called frequency division multiplexing (FDM). This well-established technique divides up the total bandwidth into different frequency bands, called channels, using frequency-selective filters. Think of total available frequency spectrum as a freeway, with each type of traffic (power, analog voice, and digital information [including data, audio, and video]) assigned separate lanes.

The initial Home Phoneline Networking Alliance specification (Home-PNA 1.0) adopted the IEEE 802.3 media access method. It is essentially 1 Mbps Ethernet over phone lines. The recently published HomePNA 2.0 and higher specification takes advantage of digital signal processing (DSP) technology embedded in silicon to offer consistently higher performance, better adapted to poor line conditions by continuously boosting signal strength and improved filtering of noise (interference) from nearby appliances. HomePNA

2.0 and higher-based products can support transfer speeds of up to 10 Mbps, 10 times faster than HomePNA 1.0-based products.

Phoneline Networking in the Home

Figure 29–5 shows how a phoneline network could be set up in the home [1]. Internal or external network adapters are installed in each PC. Printers or other peripherals are then shared through a connected PC. Each PC is plugged into a nearby phone jack. A single 56 Kbps analog, ISDN, cable, or DSL modem provides an Internet connection that every computer on the phone circuit can use simultaneously.

Phoneline networking works best in homes where the computers are located in different rooms near phone jacks on the same circuit—that is, using the same telephone number. Once more, installation is easy because the network wiring is already in place. The network is also very secure because each home has a unique phone circuit from the telephone company's central office.

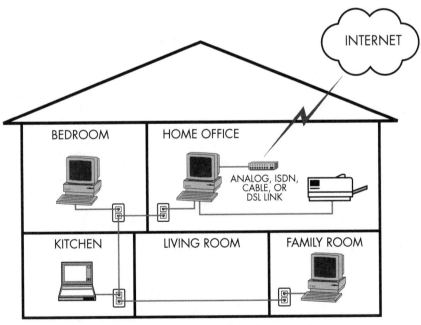

Figure 29–5   Home phoneline network.

Recent surveys indicate that 80 percent of home PCs are located near phone jacks.

POWERLINE NETWORKS

Like phoneline networking, powerline networking takes advantage of the unused bandwidth of the power cable to transmit data over existing home power cabling. A powerline network operates similarly to a phoneline network. Internal or external network adapters are installed in each PC; printers or other peripherals can be shared through a connected PC. Each PC is then plugged into a nearby power outlet. A modem provides the shared Internet connection. Powerline networking works best in homes where the computers are located in different rooms near power outlets, but on the same circuit.

How Powerline Networks Work

Powerline technologies use a variety of media access methods, from CSMA/CD and token passing to datagram sensing multiple access (DSMA) and centralized token passing (CTP). DSMA acts much like Ethernet to mediate multiple access contentions on the wire by sensing and randomly backing off if traffic is detected. In some powerline home network implementations, once a network device has gained access, it switches to a dynamic, centrally distributed, token passing scheme so that it has control of the network until it finishes transmission. This dual method reduces the incidence of transmission collisions while preserving limited bandwidth.

Powerline technology also employs a modulation technology called frequency shift keying (FSK) to send digital signals over the powerline. FSK uses two or more separate frequencies in narrowband; one is designated *1*, the other *0*, for binary transmission.

Powerline Networking Limitations

Powerline networking boasts many of the same benefits as phoneline networking. However, some powerline networks are not as fast as other networking choices. Powerlines tend to be very *noisy*, and consequently slower (compared to phonelines). Bandwidth speed using today's available technology tops at much less than 1 Mbps: rates range from 50 Kbps to 350 Kbps.

A powerline network could also have security issues due to the way power is distributed. A single power line from the utility company goes to multiple homes; a power meter at each house measures actual usage. Like an old party telephone line, anyone can potentially *listen in* on the shared bandwidth. A powerline network relies on encryption, or data scrambling, to prevent others from accessing the data running over the home network.

Because of these limitations, powerline home networking is not expected to be as viable an option as competing home networking technologies. Powerline technology will more likely be deployed in home automation and home security applications.

WIRELESS NETWORKS

As with the others, the technology for wireless networks has also been around for some time. Home networking just takes it to another level of functionality. Over the last several years, wireless networks have achieved success in a number of vertical markets, including healthcare, retail, and manufacturing.

Wireless LANs (WLANs) can now offer the same advantages to consumers: first and foremost is mobility. Consumers have the flexibility to move inside or outside their homes, and still remain connected to the Internet or to other computing devices on the network. Installation is easy because there are no wires. Wireless network components can be set up anywhere in the home. Wireless networking makes it easy to move computers and other devices without the need to reconfigure the network.

How Home Wireless Networks Work

Wireless networks use high-frequency electromagnetic waves, either infrared (IR) or radio frequency (RF), to transmit information from one point to another without relying on any physical connections. RF is expected to be of more practical use in home networking than IR because it is not limited by *line-of-sight* transmission. Radio waves travel through walls and windows. Data and voice traffic is superimposed, or modulated, onto the radio waves, or carriers, and extracted at the receiving end. Multiple radio carriers can exist in the same space at the same time without interfering with each other by transmitting at different frequencies. To extract the data, a receiver tunes in or selects one radio frequency while filtering out the others.

The home wireless RF network features an independent, peer-to-peer network that connects PCs with wireless adapters operating within one of three frequency ranges: 902 to 928 MHz, 2.400 to 2.483 GHz, and 5.725 to

5.875 GHz. Anytime two or more wireless adapters are within range of each other, they can set up an on-demand network that requires no administration.

There are a large number of different technologies that can be used in WLAN home network applications. As just one example, 3Com Corporation employs an IEEE 802.11HR-standard direct sequence spread spectrum (DSSS) technology for its home wireless network implementation [1]. DSSS generates a redundant bit pattern, called a chip or chipping code, for each transmitted bit. Error recovery mechanisms embedded in the adapter silicon can recover corrupted data without the need for retransmission. Transmission rates are surprisingly high—from 1 to 11 Mbps—and shockingly volatile!

Wireless Networking in the Home

Figure 29–6 shows how a wireless network could be set up in the home [1]. Internal or external adapters are installed on each PC. Printers or other peripherals can be shared through a connected PC. The devices then communicate using a set of reserved high-frequency radiowaves. An access point device connects to a DSL or cable modem and enables high-rate (broadband) Internet access for the entire network.

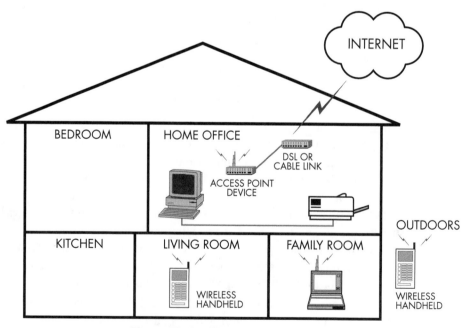

Figure 29–6   Wireless home network.

Because RF-based wireless home networking technology is not restricted by line of sight, network components do not need to be located in the same room to communicate. In a typical home, the maximum distance between devices is about 250 feet. Family members can wander from room to room or relax on the patio while surfing the Internet from their laptops.

CHOOSING THE BEST NETWORK TECHNOLOGY FOR THE HOME

Table 29–1 compares four home networking technologies [1]. It also identifies important factors to consider when selecting a home networking solution.

Table 29–1 Home Networking Technology At-A-Glance Comparison

	Phoneline	Powerline	Ethernet	Wireless
Speed (1 Mbps = 1000 Kbps)	100 Kbps– 10 Mbps	50 Kbps– 350 Kbps	10 Mbps– 100 Mbps	700 Kbps– 11 Mbps
Relative cost*	$40 –$120	$60 –$140	$65 –$190	$140 –$290
Advantages	Convenient, simple (no new wires), secure	Convenient, simple (no new wires)	Fastest, most secure and reliable	Convenient, mobile, simple (no wires), secure
Requirements	Need computers and peripherals near phone jacks on the same phoneline	Need computers and peripherals near power outlets on the same power circuit	Requires Ethernet (category 3 or 5) cabling; best in new home installations or remodels	Network components must be within a 250-foot range
Best use	Ideal for shared Internet access, file sharing, and peripheral sharing; good for home gaming	Good for low-bandwidth applications such as home security and control	Ideal for home gaming, home offices, and shared Internet access	Ideal for laptops, desktops, and hand-held connected organizers inside and outside-home or small office where mobility is required; great for shared Internet access; good for home gaming

* For comparison purposes the prices include all the necessary software and hardware required to network two PCs. Dollar amounts refer to U.S. currency.

EVALUATING HOME NETWORK SOLUTIONS

As mentioned earlier, a critical component for success in the consumer market is that the technology be transparent to the user. The home network must be simple to install, set up, and use. Consumer complaints about current home network offerings point to the importance of masking product complexity and developing solutions that are easy to use. Users should look for home network vendors that have streamlined the installation process and user interface to make the networking experience easy and understandable (or invisible) for the nontechnical consumer.

More and more products are addressing the home networking market. But it remains to be seen just how many companies really understand both the technology and consumer needs. To be successful in the consumer market, a home network solution must also be:

- Reliable and easy to expand as the home network inevitably grows.
- Compatible with other network devices, which means a standards-based solution.
- Built by reputable, experienced companies that know the complexities of networking, yet shield the consumer from that complexity.
- Secure and private; consumers are understandably concerned about the ability of hackers to tap into sensitive financial or personal communications.
- Backed by easily accessible, sound technical support. No matter how simple products are intended to be, some consumers will need assistance. The company that offers free or low-cost technical support will come out ahead through word-of-mouth recommendations [1].

Sharing high-speed Internet access. Sharing peripherals, files, and applications. Playing exciting multi-user multimedia games. The benefits of home networking are clear and consumers are more than ready to invest (an estimated $2.5 billion by 2004) in solutions that will allow them to experience a *truly connected* lifestyle.

Consumers now have an encouraging variety of networking options to choose from: Ethernet, phoneline, powerline, or wireless technologies. Each technology, with its advantages and limitations, has its optimum home application.

Vendors that are successful in this emerging market will be those that have experience and knowledge in the complexity of computer networking and that are able to provide a reliable, scalable solution that is easy for nontechnical home consumers to install, deploy, and use.

Let's now look at some of the more advanced networking technologies that are starting to invade the home to carry phone signals and television programs, link computers and peripherals, and tap into the Internet.

ADVANCED NETWORK TECHNOLOGIES FOR HOMES

Networking technologies are starting to invade the ordinary home—to carry, for example, telephone conversations; television, compact disk, digital versatile disk, and MP3 music programs; signals from surveillance cameras; commands for controlling appliances; and multimedia flows from the Internet, as shown in Figure 29–7 [2]. With home networking, it is also possible for electric utilities to remotely control the flow of electricity into individual homes and to read their meters automatically.

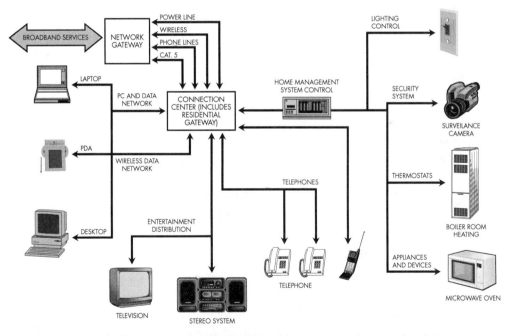

Figure 29–7   Networks in the home will distribute data and entertainment signals that are generated locally, as well as brought in from the Internet through a broadband connection. Such services could rely on input from an assortment of sources—cable modems, asymmetric digital subscriber lines, satellite broadcasts, or fixed wireless services. Information could be distributed within the home over several media, among them electric power lines, radio waves, phone lines, and category 5 twisted pairs.

For years the focus has been on the last mile (of cable to the home), but that is only half the solution. The home network (that is, about the last 100 yards) will complete the broadband access scenario.

The present foray is moving at a relaxed pace, so far mostly into relatively few multiple-dwelling units and some small businesses. But there is no doubt that the pace will accelerate in a year or two when the equipment becomes more affordable. At present, these networks fall into two main applications areas:

1. Computer interconnection—accessing the Internet and connecting multiple PCs with peripherals for communications and entertainment.
2. Controlling items like lights, appliances, climate-control systems, and surveillance cameras [2].

Prime candidates right now for home networks are homes with two or more computers, which are estimated to total some 18 million in the United States alone. The physical basis of these networks is frequently voice-grade telephone wiring or slightly more expensive category 5 twisted pairs, but electric power lines are also being used, as are wireless schemes, mainly in the 2.4 GHz unlicensed industrial, scientific, and medical (ISM) band.

To succeed, home networks will have to be based on standard products operable with any of the media just mentioned. These products include transceivers, network interface cards, gateways, small servers, sensors, and controllers, plus a widely accepted operating system. For mass market appeal, the networks will have to be inexpensive, easy to install, and the software easy to configure and operate. Homeowners, after all, cannot afford to hire information technology managers, nor should they be expected to.

The Players

Many of the players in the home networking arena are start-ups or have been in the business for only a relatively short time. Several are established and multibillion-dollar companies (including Cisco, Intel, Nortel, Motorola, Lucent, 3Com, IBM, and Panasonic) who either have bought into the fledgling concerns or have joint developments and licensing arrangements with them. Some of these heavy hitters are betting on more than one networking medium, hoping to benefit no matter which one succeeds in the marketplace.

In general, the competitors, especially the start-ups, are loath to give many details of the technologies they are deploying. Even the specifications of trade consortia are available to their members only. But some exceptions exist. There is the IEEE 802.11 specification for wireless adapted for home networking; LonWorks, an operating system for home automation developed by Echelon Corporation of Palo Alto, California, which is an open standard under EIA 709; and the Consumer Electronics Bus (CEBus) networking standard under EIA 600.

EIA stands for Electronic Industries Alliance.

The owner of another proprietary technology, X10, which controls appliances over electric power lines in the home, publishes the specifications of the transmitting devices only. Manufacturers of home appliances can design and embed X10 transmitters in them, while receiving and control devices are made by the company that owns the technology, X10 Ltd., of Hong Kong.

There are two distinct markets for home networking. One comprises computer interconnection and entertainment and requires high-speed networks. The other is control, which can be handled by slower networks. The Yankee Group, a market research firm in Boston, projects that by 2002, total annual revenue from home data and entertainment networking will hit close to U.S. $836 million. In particular, phoneline home networking will become pervasive once 10-Mb/s products are available by the end of 2000.

The biggest market right now for home networking involves control: heating, ventilating, and air-conditioning systems; lighting; pumps and sprinklers; and security. Total spending may top $3.86 billion by the end of 2001. Automation here could yield big savings because such equipment, which tends to consume large amounts of electricity, could be controlled to make its operation more efficient.

Revisiting Structured Wiring

Currently, the greatest impediment to creating a residential network is, surprisingly, a lack of useful wiring. Most existing dwellings do not have a single unused twisted wire-pair in appropriate locations, and retrofit is expensive. Also, there is no single affordable medium that meets all requirements. Consequently, the coexistence of all media will continue for quite some time to come.

Under a heavy marketing campaign by IBM Corporation, among others, some new homes, at least in the United States, are being built with home networking in mind, in particular, with the structured wiring concept introduced years ago when local area networks were first installed in offices (see Figure 29–8) [2]. With structured wiring, the networking lines come into the office at a single point (the wiring closet) and radiate out from there.

Thus, IBM, which has developed a new product line for home networking, is trying to persuade consulting and construction companies to build in

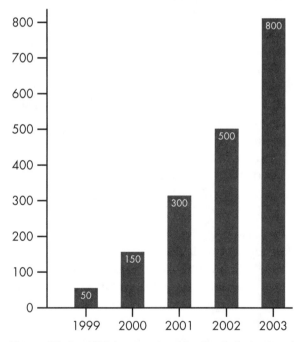

HOUSEHOLDS WITH STRUCTURED WIRING
IN THE UNITED STATES

Figure 29–8   With home networking in mind, structured wiring, a concept introduced when local area networks were first installed, is being built into some new homes. The networking lines enter at a single point—the wiring closet—and radiate out from there. The Yankee Group estimates that in the United States some 800,000 households will be outfitted with structured wiring by 2003.

such structured wiring. All lines, including category 5 twisted wire-pairs for Ethernet networks, telephone wire-pairs, power lines, and RG-6 coaxial cables for video distribution, would come in through that single point.

IBM hopes to sell the new homeowner its Home Director products, to be installed by authorized distributors. Home Director consists of a connection center that sits in the wiring closet, plus control modules and connectors. Through the center it is possible to control and manage all of the various computers and devices on the network, be they for entertainment, data, or home control. The system allows for asserting control from any point on the network and remotely, into the home, over the Internet.

The first outpost in the home is not the connection center, but a broadband gateway to the Internet (see Figure 29–7). This gateway might contain a cable modem, an asymmetric digital subscriber line (ADSL) modem, a satellite receiver, or a wireless transceiver—or combinations of these items, depending on the choice of the homeowner.

Phone Lines are in Place

Manufacturers of networking products operating over phone lines are probably the best organized to present persuasive arguments for their technology, and to standardize on product specifications, though they would not handle cable-TV signals. The Home Phoneline Networking Alliance was formed in June 1998 by 11 companies, including well-known names such as 3Com, Advanced Micro Devices, AT&T Wireless Systems, Compaq Computer, Hewlett-Packard, Intel, IBM, and Lucent Technologies. Their purpose was to draft a set of industry-wide standards. Currently, HomePNA, as it is known, has a roster of more than 110 members, a quarter of whom are from outside the United States providing for an international concern.

Home networking (that is, networking within the home) over telephone wiring should not be confused with asymmetric digital subscriber line (ADSL) technology, which is used to connect homes and offices to the Internet at speeds of up to about 6 Mb/s.

Because they are already in place in most residences, phone lines have a good shot at capturing a large share of home networks. Their devices must, of course, be simple to configure and use, secure from outside intrusion, scalable, and able to support high data rates, on the order of one to several megabits per second. Nor can the cost to the consumer be more than $110 per node, according to market analysts.

But there is a problem here. Residential phone lines, though excellent for voice signals, were not designed to carry high-speed data. Their attenuation and impedance characteristics are not well controlled. Tut Systems Incorporated, of Pleasant Hill, California, was perhaps the first company to get around these problems and develop a scheme for handling high-speed signals over such phone lines. It employs frequency-division multiplexing to create three channels, each for a different purpose: to provide ordinary telephone service (dc-3400 Hz); ADSL signals to access the Internet (25 kHz to 1.1 MHz); and for networking of entertainment programs and computer data (5.5–9.5 MHz).

In its networking channel, Tut transfers data at 1 Mb/s over a band between 5.5 and 9.5 MHz, with 7.5 MHz as the carrier frequency. Within this passband, Tut uses the well-established technology of the IEEE 802.3 carrier-sensing multiple access with collision detection (CSMA/CD), which is commonly associated with Ethernet. But, it encapsulates Ethernet frames within larger packets. To transfer packets at high speed, the company employs a patented pulse-position modulation technique to boost throughput by encoding multiple bits into each transmitted pulse, or signaling element.

Tut's 1-Mb/s technology has been adopted in the first HomePNA network specification. Transmitters and receivers have equalizing filters to improve the characteristics of the telephone lines, thereby reducing the bit error rate. To further boost reliability, received data is verified with a conventional cyclic redundancy check (CRC).

One question that arises is whether signals on a wire pair going to one apartment in a multiple-dwelling unit could electromagnetically couple into an adjacent pair going elsewhere. No significant security concerns should arise from such coupling. And, in case of concern about interference emanating from the dwelling, a filter at the network interface device (the point of entry of the Internet data into the home) would keep the signals from traveling outside. Vendors of HomePNA-compliant products include Diamond Multimedia Systems, Best Data Products, and Linksys Group. Intel makes chip sets for HomePNA and sells a complete home networking system of its own under the brand AnyPoint.

A transfer rate of 1 Mb/s is, of course, considered slow for transmitting bit streams of video programs compressed to MPEG-2 standards of 2-4 Mb/s, DVD video of 3-8 Mb/s, or high-definition TV at 19 Mb/s. But theoretically, it would be possible to transfer data at up to 100 Mb/s over home phone lines using certain portions of the 2-30 MHz band. This capability is the basis of a second release of the HomePNA specification proposed by Epigram Incorporated, in Sunnyvale, California (which was recently acquired by Broadcom Corporation, in Irvine, California), and Lucent Technologies Incorporated, of Allentown, Pennsylvania.

HomePNA would also support data rates up to 10 Mb/s while maintaining full backward compatibility with the first release. A bandwidth between 4 and 10 MHz with 7 MHz as the carrier frequency has been proposed for this purpose.

In addition, HomePNA would also employ frequency-diversity quadrature amplitude modulation (FDQAM), in which the same QAM information is repeated in two separate frequency regions to increase the robustness of data transfer in case part of the information is attenuated or corrupted. A rate-adaptive 2 bits per baud will yield data rates in the range of 4–32 Mb/s. Bell Atlantic, the giant telephone company that serves most of the eastern United States, including New York, announced recently that it will partner with Tut Systems, Lynksys, 3Com, and Diamond Multimedia in an experiment to install home networking platforms for phone lines to work with the digital subscriber-line service it already offers.

As for the international standardization of specifications for home networking over phone lines, the Geneva-based International Telecommunication Union (ITU) has a forum for receiving proposals from member countries for inclusion in its approved *Recommendation*, dubbed G.pnt (for phone network transceivers). The study group is the same one that developed the ADSL standards and is now working on standards for very high-speed digital subscriber lines (VDSLs). This should enhance the synergies between home networking using phone lines and the XDSL family of standards.

More importantly, this setup will help to address the serious concerns that exist about the risk that phone networking transceivers will interfere with VDSL and vice versa. Although the deployment of VDSL will have to wait perhaps three years or so, the problem of this interference must be addressed now. British Telecom has proposed the installation of a filter at the network interface device. But this is a costly solution, since it will require a telco technician to install the filter. With careful coordination of the respective systems, both home phone networks and VDSL can be made to share the same wire without adverse effects.

Power Line Carriers

Telephone jacks may not be available in every nook and cranny of a home, but chances are that power outlets will be. Accordingly, efforts have been under way for years to use electric wiring for communicating between different areas of a home. Since 1978, the Radio Shack chain of stores has been selling a system called X10, which consists of a control box and several modules. Each module (roughly 70 mm high, 53 mm wide, and 30 mm deep) plugs into an electrical outlet just like any other electrical appliance. The modules have two 16-step wheels so each can be assigned a distinct code. The electrical appliance such as a lamp, is then plugged into the bottom of a module.

The control box can be plugged into a wall outlet anywhere in the household, and used to control appliances plugged into any of the remote modules. The module's code may be punched on the small keypad of the controller together with the appropriate command. Control signals may also be generated in a computer, so that it is possible to remotely program the on/off sequence of devices.

Control pulses consist of 120-kHz bursts within 1-ms envelopes. A binary 1 is a burst; the absence of a burst within an envelope is a binary 0. The transmissions of the signals are synchronized by sending them as close as possible (within 200 μs) of the zero crossing point of the 60-Hz power-line frequency. Because the data packets are short, communication between X10 devices can achieve a high degree of reliability. Simple appliance modules are priced as low as $9.95, and control units are $14.95 and up, depending on their features.

Some models of the X10 appliance modules not only receive commands but can also be polled and will transmit signals back to the central controller indicating their status. This feature is helpful, for example, to remotely check on the temperature of a home or its boiler, or to turn on a surveillance camera. A Brazilian electric utility, Companhia Energética de Minas Geráis (Cemig, for short), in the state of Minas Geráis, uses this feature to help it distribute power equitably during hours of peak demand.

To gain such capability, the electric company first used a pair of 20-A circuit breakers to modify the standard 40-A panels through which many homes are supplied. It can then switch off one breaker during hours of peak demand. In order to give the householder some incentive for allowing the changeover to the 20-A breakers, the charge for using electricity during off-peak hours is lower.

Cemig is also applying X10 to automatic meter reading. Usage data is stored in the meter by the residential X10 unit, which is polled once a month by a control unit at the distribution transformer. From there, the readings from a group of homes can be downloaded to a laptop computer.

X10 Ltd., which designs its own chips for its devices, manufactures products for companies that include IBM, Thomson (GE and RCA brands), Philips (Magnavox brand), Radio Shack, Leviton, Honeywell, Stanley, Ademco, and ADT. IBM, for one, relies on X10 technology in its Home Director product. The company has shipped more than 200 million units.

Use of power lines for any data rate higher than a few bits per second, as employed in X10 technology, presents many technical problems. Among them are noise and interference, attenuation, and impedance variations as well as the reflections they cause.

Several technologies claim to surmount these problems, and protocols for such communications processes have been formalized by industry consortia. CEBus (EIA 600) is an open standard that specifies the technology and the parameters for communications using power lines, category 5 twisted wire-pair, coaxial cable, wireless, and infrared.

The media access layer (MAC) of CEBus employs carrier-sensing multiple access with collision detection and collision resolution (CSMA/CDCR). This allows any device on the network to access the medium at any time. However, a node wishing to send a data packet must first sense that no other packet is on the line at that moment, and only if the line is clear may it send its packet. This is very similar to the protocol of IEEE 802.3 local area networks.

CEBus also specifies a common application language (CAL) that enables devices to communicate among themselves and to perform certain tasks using common rules of syntax and vocabulary. Each device is defined as a *context* in CAL. A stereo player and a videocassette recorder are examples of contexts.

Each context of CAL is further divided into objects. These objects represent functions such as volume, treble, or bass. Command signals can identify contexts and activate function controls, such as raising the volume of a stereo player. Receivers attached to devices interpret the commands and act on them. Since CEBus is an open standard, a CEBus controller designed by one vendor should be able to operate with a CEBus-compatible device manufactured by any other vendor. The CEBus Industry Council [3] publishes information on CEBus and CAL. Several companies are selling CEBus products for electric line control and communications.

Spread Spectrum

Intellon Incorporated, in Ocala, Florida, achieves an impressively high data rate over electric power lines by employing a spread-spectrum carrier technology similar to the one used in wireless communications. For high data rates, Intellon employs a technology known as orthogonal frequency-division multiplexing (OFDM), which involves sending data over multiple subcarriers.

The use of OFDM technology deals with multiple reflections—a major source of interference in power-line communications. Using this multiplexing technology, it is theoretically possible to transfer data at better than 100 Mb/s, according to Intellon. Another company working with this kind of technology is Enikia Incorporated, in Piscataway, New Jersey, but it has not yet introduced products.

Intelogis Incorporated, in Draper, Utah, takes a different tack to power-line communications. It transmits data in a frequency band above the region in which most noise is found. Dubbed Plug-in PLX technology, it uses a combination of datagram-sensing multiple access (DSMA) and centralized token passing (CTP). DSMA acts in a similar fashion to the multinode contention resolution of an Ethernet network. A node, when entering the network for the first time, detects the carrier of other packets on the line, sending its own packet only if it is clear to do so.

Once all the nodes are known to each other, a dynamic, centrally distributed token-passing scheme is instituted. This avoids multinode contention and collision and thus raises the effective throughput. Intelogis claims that its technology permits simultaneous transfer of small control packets and entertainment data, say of MP3, without interfering with each other. Plug-in PLX conforms to the CEBus CAL.

Current versions of Intelogis products support a bit rate of 350 kb/s. A chip set allowing 2 Mb/s will be available to equipment manufacturers around the first part of 2001.

Another player is Itran Communications Ltd., in Beer Sheva, Israel. It designs chips for both spread spectrum and OFDM that handle data rates of 1.5 Mb/s for home networking and home office, 50 kb/s for home automation, and 7 kb/s for a secure home automation application.

While emphasis is mostly on high data rate, High Tech Horizon, of Angelholm, Sweden, has been quietly shipping its power-line communication cards for PCs. Running at a modest 2400 b/s, they can be used to send and receive messages and data files between PCs and peripherals. They also run a speech recognition program so that it is possible to *talk* to the computer from any part of the home.

In spite of vendor promises, the consumer has yet to see an affordable product capable of high-speed communication over the power line. Estimates for high-speed home networks using power lines are much lower than those using either phone lines or wireless (see Figure 29–9) [2]. And there seems to be no coherent effort to make the power-line communication products interoperable. The UK-based International Powerline Communications Forum (IPCF) is hoping to generate the momentum needed to do this.

HOME-NETWORKED HOUSEHOLDS IN THE UNITED STATES (IN THOUSANDS)
NOTE: NETWORK FOR COMMUNICATIONS AND ENTERTAINMENT

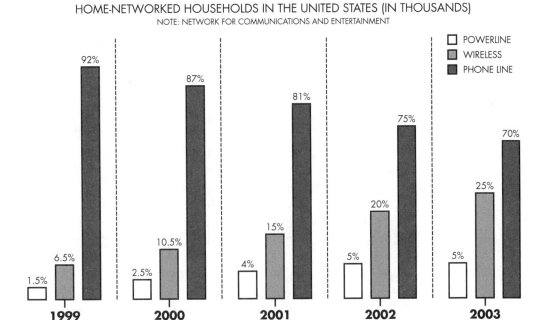

Figure 29–9   Totaling all the interconnection media that will be used, home networks for communications and entertainment will find their way into over 6 million U.S. households by 2003. Phone lines, according to this estimate, will be the dominant medium.

Wireless World

Wireless is a fast-developing technology for data and voice communications. In many situations, wireless can provide a convenient and inexpensive networking solution in a home or small/home office.

Since most homes with two or more personal computers were built before the recent explosion in telecommunications, they are probably not wired for a telephone in every room. Installing twisted wire-pairs all over the premises would be difficult. Wireless networks could prove very useful as an alternative. Unfortunately, current wireless standards are as bountiful as they are confusing. The industry needs to reach a consensus fairly soon before competing wireless home networking technologies capture significant market share.

Technologies for physical media access by wireless follow several specifications (see Table 29–2), some of which have been approved by independent standards bodies [2]. One such suite of specifications is the IEEE's 802.11. In conformity with U.S. Federal Communications Commission (FCC) requirements for the use of the unlicensed ISM band, IEEE 802.11 allows both direct-sequence (DS) and frequency-hopping (FH) spread spectrum.

The debate as to the superiority of DS versus FH is highly technical and ongoing.

The maximum data rate offered by the standard for either technique is approximately 2 Mb/s. However, a higher-speed version of IEEE 802.11 allows a data rate of up to 11 Mb/s. A drawback of the 802.11 protocol for data transfer in a home network is its high overhead. The protocol was initially developed for cellular telephony.

Products operating at 11 Mb/s as specified by IEEE 802.11 are being beta tested by Home Wireless Networks (HWN) Incorporated, of Norcross, Georgia. The final products will be ready for shipping in late 2000. The products are based on a complementary code keying technology also used in products being developed by Lucent Technologies and Apple Computer Incorporated ShareWave Incorporated, in El Dorado Hills, California (backed by Cisco Systems, Kyushu Matsushita Electric Company, and Netgear [a subsidiary of Nortel]), also plans to offer 11 Mb/s devices. To accommodate video streaming and HDTV, Home Wireless Networks is working on a new technology called layered space-time processing (LST), which promises to deliver 50-100 Mb/s over the same bandwidth as today's 11-Mb/s systems.

Eventually, but not anytime soon, the IEEE 802.11 specifications will permit data transfer rates of anywhere from 6 to 54 Mb/s using discrete multitone (DMT), as well as orthogonal frequency-division multiplexing. Most of the 11-Mb/s direct-sequence systems are designed around chip sets made by Harris Corporation, in Torrance, California. However, the FCC filed a notice of proposed rule—making for a possible discontinuation of the use of 11 Mb/s direct sequence. Hence, the future of that technology currently remains in doubt.

The next important set of specifications (one that is fairly inexpensive to deploy) has been formalized by an industry consortium known as the HomeRF Working Group and supported by many communications companies, mostly in North America. The group has produced a set of specifications known as the shared wireless access protocol (Swap). Swap uses frequency-hopping spread-spectrum technology in the 2.4 GHz band to yield a data rate of 1 Mb/s.

Table 29-2 Wireless Home-Network Technologies

Designation	Application	Characteristics	Frequency band, GHz	Modulation	Maximum data rate, Mb/s	Specifying organization	Certification agency
OpenAir	Mobile data	Small, light, low-power	2.4	Frequency hopping[1] (FH)	1.6	Wireless LAN Interoperability Forum (WLIF)	Wireless LAN Interoperability Forum (WLIF)
802.11 FH	Wireless data networking	Encryption available	2.4	FH[1]	2	IEEE[2]	WLIF
802.11 DS			2.4	Direct sequence[1] (DS)	2	IEEE[2]	WLIF
High-speed 802.11	High-speed wireless local area networks	Broadband	5	Discrete multitone/orthogonal FDM (DMT/OFDM)	6–54	IEEE[2]	Wireless Ethernet Compatibility Alliance (WECA)[3]
High-speed 802.11	High-speed wireless local area networks	Broadband	2.4	DS[1]	11	IEEE[2]	WLIF and WECA
Broadband radio access networks, or BRAN (formerly HiperLANs)[4]	High-speed multimedia	Can support voice, data, video; can coexist with 2.4 GHz; is certifiable in U.S. and Europe	5	Gaussian phase-shift keying (GPSK)	24	European Telecommunications Standards Institute (ETSI)	European Telecommunications Standards Institute (ETSI)

Table 29–2 (continued)

Designation	Application	Characteristics	Frequency band, GHz	Modulation	Maximum data rate, Mb/s	Specifying organization	Certification agency
Digital enhanced cordless telecommunications (DECT)	Voice and data for small and home offices	Integrated voice and data	1.88–1.90	Gaussian frequency-shift keying (GPSK)	1.152		
Shared wireless access protocol	Wireless communication for homes and small and home offices	Low-cost	2.4	FH[1]	2	HomeRF Working Group	HomeRF Working Group
Bluetooth	Short-range cable replacement	Low-cost, short-range, supports only voice, data	2.4	FH[1]	1	Bluetooth Consortium	Bluetooth Consortium

FDM = Frequency division multiplexing
[1] Different kinds of spread spectrum.
[2] No agency as yet certifies IEEE 802.11 products, but the WLIF is working to this end with the University of New Hampshire.
[3] WECA assesses interoperability of equipment using high speed direct-sequence spread-spectrum technology.
[4] BRAN succeeds HiperLAN as the name for an ETSI-approval set of wireless networking standards.

Swap products are being shipped by Proxim Incorporated, in Sunnyvale, California, under the brand name Symphony. There is also a move to develop a higher-speed Swap. The Home RF group petitioned the FCC to increase frequency-hopping bandwidth to 3 or 5 MHz so that it could develop 11-Mb/s frequency-hopping products. This topic is also included in the FCC's notice of proposed rulemaking. Lobbying for this ruling is strong and an official decision on the future use of spread spectrum (DS and FH) can be expected perhaps as early as the spring of 2001.

The European Telecommunications Standards Institute (ETSI) supports two wireless protocols—HiperLAN, for high-speed traffic, and digital European cordless telecommunications (DECT), which operates at lower speeds. HiperLAN, in the future to be known as BRAN (for broadband radio access networks), is a set of specifications for a network operating at 5 GHz and yielding a data rate of 24 Mb/s, which is sufficient for high-definition TV.

There is an effort to develop a North American version of HiperLAN. However, it is not clear that the United States will require HiperLAN, since the FCC has already released the unlicensed national information infrastructure (UNII) band, which occupies the spectrum between 5.7250 MHz and 5.8750 MHz.

DECT, with a data rate of 1.152 Mb/s, calls for the use of frequencies between 1,880 and 1,990 MHz. So far, equipment made to DECT specifications by European firms offer only voice communications. Nevertheless, Home Wireless Networks' research laboratory in Cambridge, England, has been able to integrate both voice and data in DECT-compliant equipment. British Telecommunications, the largest carrier in the United Kingdom, has signed contracts with Home Wireless Networks for equipment to be installed in their clients' homes.

Like Swap, and fairly inexpensive to implement, Bluetooth is the lastest wireless protocol (see Table 29–2). It is a proposed set of specifications for short-range use within the home or office. It should be possible to use Bluetooth devices to communicate with each other, without them being tethered to some network. Ericsson of Sweden, Nokia of Finland, and Intel are the primary backers of Bluetooth (see Chapter 28 for more information on Bluetooth).

Operating Systems

There is, of course, more to a communications system than the Physical and Data Link layers. Once the bits are delivered in the right order, higher layers are needed to interpret the significance of those bits and interface with application programs. The best way to undertake that interpretation depends on whether the system is carrying high-speed communications or low-speed control signals.

Aimed at control applications, LonWorks employs carrier-sense multiple-access for the Physical layer and is independent of the medium being used. That is, LonWorks can be used with phone wire-pairs, category 5 twisted wire-pairs, power lines, and wireless. Along with X10, LonWorks is one of the most widely used technologies for control purposes. There are now an estimated 5,000 developers worldwide working on hardware, software, and integrated systems for the LonWorks platform. The number of installed LonWorks devices stands at 10 million, of which 30 percent are in homes.

The LonWorks protocol is now embedded in silicon in so-called neuron chips made by Cypress Semiconductor Corporation, in San Jose, California, and Toshiba America Electronic Components Incorporated, in Irvine, California. These chips are incorporated by dozens of manufacturers into their modules for controlling household electrical equipment. For example, home appliances made by Merloni Elettrodomestici Spa, in Fabriano, Italy, are able to communicate with the utility company or the technical service desk of the manufacturer. They can be programmed so that after a power failure, they would know the order in which devices must restart in a home. In the event of a mechanical failure, service technicians can remotely access the machines.

Merloni has a joint project with the Media Laboratory of the Massachusetts Institute of Technology to develop a completely digital kitchen that will be controllable through the Internet. Not only that, the kitchen will be able to draw on recipes from Web sites on the Internet (see the Sidebar, "Wired Refrigerators and Smart Toilets").

WIRED REFRIGERATORS AND SMART TOILETS

Racing home from work, you can't remember whether the kids finished off that quart of milk or whether there's enough lettuce in the fridge for a salad. Not a problem. Just whip out your video cell phone, dial into the home network computer, and presto: an up-to-the-minute list of the refrigerator's contents. You can have access from anywhere in the world (even from the supermarket).

Japanese electronics companies may have missed out on much of the digital revolution that is transforming American households. But Silicon Valley, please take note: They are scrambling to jump back into the race. A new universe of electronic appliances linked in a home network is just what these appliance makers need to reinvigorate sales. Matsushita is working closely with Sony and other competitors to create standards that will make it easy for their machines to communicate, whether the basic operating systems are provided by

Microsoft, Sun's Microsystems, or some other software maker.

To offer a glimpse of what the future may hold, Matsushita, best known for its Panasonic-brand TVs and microwave ovens, has assembled its niftiest new gadgets in a small house south of Tokyo, wiring just about everything into a central computer. There's the delicately sculpted TV remote control that you bark orders into: Television on! Channel 5! Resume video play! The set is linked to a server containing 50 high-capacity DVD storage disks. All that content is displayed on big, beautiful flat plasma TV panels strategically installed throughout the house.

Even the toilet is wired and resembles a cross between an ejector seat and an electric chair. Once a day, first thing in the morning, the toilet sizes you up, starting with your weight. *Don't lean back. Lift your feet off the floor.* After balancing on the seat, you grab the electrodes on arms protruding from the back of the toilet, and a small electric current measures the proportion of body fat. Finally, if you are still able to perform after all that, a sensor in the bowl measures the sugar content of urine, and then sends all this vital data to the central server—or beyond to your doctor.

The sensor then retracts and cleans itself automatically.

A svelte attaché case contains electronic medical instruments (plus a tiny but powerful video camera) that can be linked directly to your doctor's office.

Viewing

Rooms in the experimental home heat, cool, light up, or darken automatically as you walk through, with each movement picked up by infrared motion detectors in the ceiling. The video phone at the entrance records the image of anyone outside the door, displays it on monitors throughout the house (or on that cute video cell phone) and then stores the images for a year. The monitors also display who is doing what all around the house, from washing clothes and watching TV to sitting on the wired toilet. The Japanese home of the future, it seems, isn't very big on privacy.

Alas, some of the gadgets aren't quite ready for prime time. Take the fridge, for example. To create the inventory, you have to call out the name of each item going in, and then somehow get it off the list when it is used up. For anyone who is that well organized, remote access is probably superfluous. Besides, older technology (phoning home and asking your significant other what to buy) still does the trick. The automatically programmable kitchen works okay, but only if you like your dinners microwaved to perfection. You'll still have to flip your pancakes manually.

The networked home won't be cheap. Installing a central server and a digital switch box will add 4 to 6 percent to the cost of a house. Is it worth it? Probably! Nevertheless, Matsushita predicts huge demand for home networks starting around 2004, when company officials expect the technology to come together. More than 200 engineers are working full time to make sure that happens. And they have full access to the bathroom.

ComEnergy Technologies Incorporated, in Marlborough, Massachusetts (a wholly owned subsidiary of NSTAR in Boston), is a systems integrator that uses LonWorks-based devices. It combines them with local area control networks to automatically read the energy consumption of individual appliances, to serve the needs of supervisory control and data acquisition in large commercial buildings. Once the detailed records of consumption are available, the client himself can program the operations of the devices or instruct the utility company to do it for him. The result, the company asserts, is a 20–40 percent reduction in electric bills.

The market for energy management in single-family residences has just started to grow. Once the cost of small control systems falls to a few hundred dollars per home, many owners will be inclined to install them not only for energy management, but also for other purposes such as surveillance.

Sentential of the Gate

When home networks are connected to the Internet, various kinds of data will enter the home over a single channel. A system is therefore needed for identifying the data and routing it to its intended destination. Coactive Networks Incorporated, in Sausalito, California, has developed a series of products that act as gateways between the Internet and a home automation network running LonWorks. Its function is to extract the LonWorks control commands from Internet transmission control protocol/Internet protocol (TCP/IP) packets and relay them to the network in the residence. Thus, it is possible for utility companies to read meters automatically and perform demand-side management chores and for service companies to check home security systems, monitor appliances remotely, or check on personal monitors carried by the elderly and disabled. Thus, the home telemetry gateway makes it possible to read and control everything from air-conditioning to security systems via the Internet.

Also of use for a home network, particularly for a home office, is a server, which could be used for such chores as file transfers and e-mail and, most important, as a firewall to keep hackers at bay. This is the reason for NetWinder, a Linux-based service introduced by Rebel.com of Ottawa, Ontario, Canada. The $906 unit is 50 mm by 240 mm by 150 mm and weighs less than a kilogram.

The freely available Linux operating system helps keep the cost down.

Currently, the unit comes with a 10 GB hard drive. The tiny server can put the Internet at every desk and permit users to share files and peripherals, host Web sites, and share e-mail. The NetWinder supports PCs, Macs, and Unix-based machines. Rebel.com is backed financially by Corel Corporation, also of Ottawa.

Finally, home area networks are here, penetrating domestic life. However, their technologies are heading in different directions, to the confusion of most users. The market will possibly grow as analysts predict. But, the model for home networking will change again if and when a new affordable and easily installed fiber optic technology appears at the garden gate.

FROM HERE

Chapter 29 took a look at home networking and how to connect to your home in the future. The final chapter concludes by making recommendations and taking a peek at the cabling industry as it continues on its way to becoming a full information service provider in the beginning of this millennium via the ever-changing cable specification process.

NOTES

[1]   "Introduction to Home Networking: Can High-Tech Migrate Successfully into the Consumer Market?," 3Com Corporation, Santa Clara Site, 5400 Bayfront Plaza, Santa Clara, CA 95052, 2000.

[2]   Amitava Dutta-Roy, "Networks for Homes," *IEEE Spectrum*, 445 Hoes Lane, Piscataway, NJ, USA 08855-1331, Vol. 36, No. 12 (December, 1999).

[3]   CEBus Industry Council, Inc., 2 Wisconsin Circle, Suite 700, Chevy Chase, MD 20815, 2000.

CHAPTER 30

Summary, Conclusions, and Recommendations

The cable industry is becoming a full service provider as it evolves its infrastructure into an all-digital superhighway. Both the telephone and computer industries are suggesting their networking models of traditional point-to-point and extended distributed local area network technology become part of the cable industry solution. Cable is creating the multimedia networking model for the next millennium as a full service provider.

This final chapter summarizes, concludes, and makes recommendations with regard to the cabling industry as it continues on its way to becoming a full information service provider in the next millennium via the ever-changing cable specification process. Recommendations about the role that optical fiber must play as the one physical medium upon which it will be possible to base national and global infrastructures that will handle the growing demands of bandwidth to the desktop in a post-2000 developed society are also discussed.

The basic areas of consideration that the cabling industry must adhere to when specifying cable are covered first. They are:

- application consideration
- basic cable type selection
- performance-level specification
- materials specification
- delivery and packaging considerations
- quality assurance considerations
- supplier specification

APPLICATION CONSIDERATION

As the cabling industry enters the next millennium, greater demands will be placed on communications media for bandwidth. It is recommended that the highest quality media practical be chosen. The scope of the cabling system to be built must also be considered.

Cabling System Scope

Add-on cabling to existing systems may be chosen simply by matching existing cable types exactly. Recently, improved versions of some older cable types have become available and it is recommended that they should be considered for expansions of existing systems.

New system design considerations are open to a full range of possibilities. The highest practical performance level should be selected for system components once the basic architecture has been determined. Also, when addressing concerns about upgradability, it is recommended that future applications be considered and the highest performance system affordable should be provided to accommodate upgrade requirements.

Present and Future Coverage of Applications

Provision for voice communications applications is a given. The basic standard wiring stem requirements mandate that at least one telecommunications media, basic unshielded twisted pair (UTP), be provided to each work location. In addition, it is strongly advised that at least one other copper media, which may be a second telecommunications media, also be installed according to EIA/TIA-T568-A, the Commercial Building Wiring Standard. In creating this standard, a complete specification for the basic telecommunications media was established. This specification may now preclude some older twisted-pair cables, but some clear transmission performance guidelines extending to higher-speed data applications have become available.

Data communications application requirements are also a given. Virtually every business employee has some form of data terminal on their desk. The most basic data communications application, data terminal equipment (DTE) service, has been covered by good telecommunications media.

There are not-as-good and maybe-even-worse telecommunications media also available, so see "Performance Level Specification," later in the chapter.

DTE was a big development, initially popularized by Digital Equipment Corporation (DEC) [1]. This development started the practice of using twisted pair for everything. Originally, data terminals were interconnected to mainframes through coax, twinax, or some other proprietary and particularly nontelecommunication-type wiring. The proprietary cables are still available, and used in large quantities, but mainly for moves, adds, and changes on older systems. Now, some kind of twisted-pair solution has been devised for virtually every terminal system on the market.

Ethernet, a Xerox development and trademark, is a fundamentally different form of data communication compared to data terminal service. Its introduction marked a critical development in computer system architecture: distributed systems. In Ethernet, it is recommended that the media accommodate broadcasting over a local area network (LAN) at much higher speeds than simple low-speed point-to-point data terminal links. To meet these requirements, the first systems used robust, thick, coaxial trunk cables, transceivers, and shielded twisted-pair drop cables. Later DEC, a codeveloper of Ethernet, created a low cost, but more practical version, Thinnet (or "cheapernet"), which is suitable for fewer nodes over a smaller area, using a thin coax in a daisy-chain wiring structure. This more limited facility has since been implemented in a 10BaseT on a UTP network. It was the establishment of the UTP specification for 10BaseT (intended to model common telecommunications UTP cables) that lead to the levels of performance for UTP cables (see "Performance Level Specification," later in the chapter).

Token ring, albeit the name for a generic LAN protocol and topology, has come to mean IBM. Seemingly in response to Ethernet, IBM introduced a cabling system based on a very ample shielded twisted pair (STP) cable design and a complete wiring system based on a logical ring (physical star) network topology. IBM followed up with a 4 Mbps token-passing LAN protocol for interconnecting computer nodes on the network, later introducing components. All of IBM's various proprietary wiring systems for their various computer and peripheral systems could also be implemented on the IBM cabling system. IBM has since upgraded the LAN system speed to 16 Mbps. This IBM cabling system was so successful that the terminology STP has become synonymous with the specific type of shielded twisted pair associated with it, as if no other form of STP could exist. As could be expected, UTP implementations of 4 Mbps and 16 Mbps token ring application have also become available, demanding a higher level of performance for UTP, beyond the UTP performance specifications established for Ethernet.

Fiber distributed data interface (FDDI), also a token-passing ring LAN protocol and topology, was conceived to run at 100 Mbps using multimode optical fiber media. Originally intended to interconnect mainframes and supercomputers in and between large data centers, by the time the standard development process was completed, FDDI became a preferred choice for interconnecting LANs within an organization to form the backbone of a comprehensive corporate-wide network. The modern replacement for the original thick coax Ethernet campus LAN is a group of separate smaller Ethernet LANs interconnected by a high-speed FDDI LAN. Given the developments in powerful workstation applications, FDDI to the individual workstation has become a practical consideration. A low-cost FDDI (LC-PMD) has been introduced, still implemented on multimode optical fiber, but at a substantial cost reduction by reducing the original 2 km FDDI maximum link requirement to 1 km. This link distance reduction permits a minor performance reduction but a major cost reduction for the transmission components. Recently, products have been introduced so that FDDI 100 Mbps protocol can be implemented on the STP IBM cabling system over 100 m links (twisted pair physical media depended [TP-PMD]) from the wiring closet to the desk. Of course, the ubiquitous UTP, in a form departing considerably from the original, has also produced a viable alternative (also TP-PMD).

Future applications will operate at considerably higher speeds, into the 1 Gbps to 2 Gbps range for backbone, introducing single-mode optical fiber into the backbone environment. Multimedia applications are expected to transcend 100 Mbps capability and will most likely transcend UTP bandwidth. Telecommunications and data communications converge at the point of transition to broadband. Digital distributed telephone switches already use single-mode optical fiber to interconnect individual equipment frames and connect into the digital telecommunications wide area network (WAN). FDDI-2 is a revision to the FDDI protocol designed to accommodate interactive voice and video. Extending Ethernet to 100 Mbps is being investigated. Fiber channel, the up-to-2 Gbps replacement for FDDI (for interconnection between mainframes and supercomputers in various distance/speed steps), uses all standard media up through single-mode optical fiber. The next LAN technology, FDDI follow-on LAN (FFOL), will accommodate the asynchronous transfer mode (ATM) protocol developed for high-speed WAN services. This will permit broadband links of at least OC-3 155.52 Mbps to be made available first near to the desk for LAN internetwork links, then all the way to the desk. Underlying the similarities in speed and hierarchical structure being developed for both WAN and LAN are the designs for their seamless interconnection.

BASIC CABLE TYPE SELECTION

The decision on the type of cable to install in a building has become more complex with the introduction of applications that operate full duplex over four cable pairs. These applications have forced infrastructure standards developers to reconsider the specifications for existing cables and add new categories of performance to the specifications. Even fiber optic cables, which were once considered to have unlimited bandwidth, are now distance limited when used with applications that operate at gigabit speeds. This has influenced the introduction of new multimode fiber optic cables onto the market to address these limitations.

When choosing media there are few fundamental engineering and design considerations:

- additional up front cost today versus future benefits
- lease or own occupied facility
- application migration plan
- criticality of network performance
- percentage of the cable installation cost versus the total LAN cost

ANSI/EIA/TIA-T568-A defines the requirements for structured wiring. This standard provides a stable platform for the installation of cabling infrastructure and provides applications developers with a model that can be used in the development of new standards for years to come. ANSI/EIA/TIA-T5686-A recognizes the following media for use in horizontal and backbone applications:

- Horizontal
  - 100 ohm unshielded twisted pair
  - 150 ohm shielded twisted pair
  - 62.5/125 multimode optical fiber
- Backbone
  - 100 ohm unshielded twisted pair
  - 150 ohm shielded twisted pair

- 62.5/125 multimode optical fiber
- single-mode optical fiber [Berk-Tek, 3–4]

In horizontal applications, the use of unshielded twisted pair cable is prevalent. Approximately 70 percent of existing buildings have category 5 UTP installed. The wide acceptance of category 5 UTP cable assures that new applications will continue to be developed to support the large installed base. The use of UTP in horizontal applications will continue until the cost of fiber optic network products drop to make them at least competitive with copper solutions.

In the backbone, 62.5/125 multimode fiber has been the preferred media. At gigabit speeds this type of fiber is very length-limited. To address the length limitations of this fiber, enhanced bandwidth 62.5/125 and 50/125 optical fibers have become available. These fibers are not included as part of the ANSI/EIA/TIA-T568-A standard but undoubtedly will be included in the next addition of the standard.

Optional Media

In addition to the recognized media, EIA/TIA-T568-A also includes in its appendices:

- optional horizontal media
  - 100 ohm shielded twisted pair
  - 100 ohm multipair shielded twisted pair (UTP) (25 pair) undercarpet cables
  - other multimode optical fiber (50/125, 100/140, etc.)
  - 75 ohm coaxial cable (CATV coax)
- optional backbone media
  - 100 ohm shielded twisted pair
  - other multimode optical fiber (50/125, 100/140, etc.)
  - single-mode optical fiber
  - 75 ohm coaxial cable (CATV coax)

Optional media are suitable for some special applications, which are outside of the scope of this chapter. Let's now look at performance-level specification considerations, particularly for UTP but also applicable to STP.

UTP PERFORMANCE SPECIFICATIONS

ANSI/EIA/TIA-T568-A includes three performance specifications for UTP cable. Although there are network applications such as 100BaseT4, which are designed to utilize category 3 cable, this cable is currently installed to support voice applications. Category 3 cable has a usable bandwidth of 16 MHz. Category 4 cable, which has a bandwidth of 20 MHz, offers little improvement over category 3 cable and is no longer available. Category 5 cable with a bandwidth of 100 MHz is widely accepted and there are many network applications that have been developed to operate over this media.

TIA is currently revising specifications for category 5 cable based on recommendations from IEEE 802.3ab (1000BaseT). Several new electrical parameters, return loss and ELFEXT, are being added to the category 5 standard. These two new parameters address requirements for full duplex operation. IEEE recommends the horizontal topology be limited to two connection points, the wall outlet and patch panel to minimize the amount of signal reflected back to the transmitted and the effects of cross talk. IEEE also recommends that existing installation must be reevaluated to these new requirements before 1000BaseT is implemented.

To increase the robustness of category 5 cable with new applications and to further address the requirements of full duplex operation over four cable pairs, TIA is also working on specifications for enhanced category 5 cable. This specification introduces the concept of power sum to horizontal cabling in addition to several other critical electrical parameters. There is little doubt that enhanced category 5 cabling still is the mainstay of new cable installations.

TIA released the specification in early 1999.

TIA and ISO are still working on solutions with greater than 100 MHz bandwidth. Proposals for category 6 cable have bandwidth up to 200 MHz, double that of category 5 cable. Category 6 offers application developers increased performance while being backward-compatible with existing category 5 installations. Category 7, currently under development by ISO, features a bandwidth of 600 MHz utilizing a cable with four individually shielded pairs. Installations that utilize this solution are not backward-compatible with existing category 5 installations and are currently proprietary in nature due to lack of a connector standard. Specifications for these new cabling solutions will be released by the year 2000 [Berk-Tek-5].

Nevertheless, with regard to the impact on limitations to bandwidth, the three most important electrical parameters for twisted-pair cables are: cross-talk attenuation impedance, characteristic impedance, and structural return loss (SRL), respectively.

Cross-Talk Attenuation Impedance

Cross talk (usually near end cross talk [NEXT] rather than far end cross talk [FEXT] is the type of greater concern) refers to the amount of signal coupled from one line or pair within a cable onto another line within the same cable. Given the preferred star network cable topology, a send and receive line will be present in all network cables. Cross talk, in this case manifested as an echo, is the primary limiting factor in most twisted-pair LAN applications. Cross talk increases at higher frequencies proportional to frequency, but does not increase for longer lengths proportional to length. For example, a typical cable with 25 dB NEXT loss at 100 feet has a NEXT loss of about 25dB at 1,000 feet. Most of the near end cross-talk coupling occurs in the near end of the cable.

NEXT cross talk between two twisted pairs is measured at the same end of the cable as the disturbing signal source.

Attenuation refers to the amount of signal loss that occurs over a distance. Attenuation increases proportionally to both frequency and length. Thus, attenuation becomes a greater consideration at both higher frequencies and longer lengths.

Characteristic Impedance

Impedance, more accurately, characteristic impedance, is a frequency-dependent characteristic of any cable. It does not directly impact system performance, except that the impedance of the cable must match the impedance baluns. Cables are designed to meet certain impedance baluns within a given range. A practical, good, nominal characteristic impedance for twisted pair is 100 ohms. IBM chose 150 ohm for their STP systems. The impedance-related influence on system performance results from deviations from the particular system impedance—either in the form of inconsistencies within the cable or mismatches to other system components. Some results of the variations are signal reflection and dispersion whereby less signal gets to the receiver, thus degrading system performance (see the Sidebar, "Managing Dispersion").

MANAGING DISPERSION

The increasing demand for bandwidth is driving most telecommunications operators toward the deployment of large-capacity transmission systems. Systems based on 10-Gb/s channel rates are being deployed, and suppliers have announced plans for channel rates as high as 40 Gb/s. Polarization mode dispersion represents a major impairment for high-bit-rate systems, producing pulse broadening and distortion, thus leading to performance degradation.

Polarization mode dispersion in optical fiber stems from the breakup of circular symmetry in the core and cladding. Ideally, this symmetry renders the fiber perfectly isotropic (nonbirefringent). The fiber's index of refraction is independent of the orientation of the electric field or, equivalently, the polarization of the light. Light propagation in single-mode fibers is governed by two orthogonally polarized fundamental modes, which, in the case of ideal fibers, are degenerate (indistinguishable).

The degeneracy can be lifted if, through a loss of the circular symmetry, any amount of anisotropy is introduced, leading to some birefringence. This is the general case of real fibers, where the loss of symmetry originates in the fiber manufacturing process from noncircular waveguide geometry (geometrical birefringence—static) or in deployed fiber from nonsymmetrically distributed mechanical stress (stress birefringence—time varying).

A single, uniformly distributed perturbation on a short section of fiber creates two orthogonally polarized modes along the directions of the stress-induced symmetry, called principal states of polarization. Polarization components simultaneously launched along these two principal states arrive at the section output at different times. This is called differential group delay.

Think of a long fiber as a series of short sections with randomly distributed, time-varying perturbations. This phenomenon is polarization mode dispersion, which is characterized for a given optical frequency by two time-dependent parameters: principal states of polarization and differential group delay. Here, principal states of polarization represent a set of two time-varying orthogonal polarization states (not necessarily linear) that do not experience differential delay at the fiber output between any of their components. Differential group delay represents the arrival time delay between both polarization states. These two parameters represent first-order polarization mode dispersion, and their frequency dependence represents higher-order dispersion.

For long fiber spans, the evolution of polarization mode dispersion with distance is fairly slow: The time-average value of the differential group delay accumulates only as the square root of the fiber length. In addition, the probability density function of the differential group delay is Maxwelltan. In particular, the probability of the delay exceeding three times its average value is only 4×10^{-5}, or 21 minutes per year.

Polarization mode dispersion actually represents three different items: the effect of polarization mode dispersion, the time-average value of a fiber's differential group delay, and the (time- and length-independent) polarization mode dispersion coefficient of the fiber (defined as the ratio of the time-average differential group delay to the square root of the fiber length).

The polarization mode dispersion-limited transmission distance on a fiber, before signal regeneration is required, decreases as R^{-2}, where R is the channel rate. The fiber's polarization mode dispersion coefficient depends primarily on the manufacturing and cabling processes.

Because polarization mode dispersion effects gained attention only with the testing of high-data-rate systems, little or no effort was made to control polarization mode dispersion coefficients until recently. Therefore, older fibers generally exhibit high coefficients, leading to serious limitations on transmission distance and/or data rates. New manufacturing and cabling processes have significantly improved dispersion values and stability. However, Bellcore's audit of the 1996 fiber cable plant, involving roughly 1,000 *installed* cabled fibers, shows that nearly 80 percent of the fibers exhibit a polarization mode dispersion coefficient lower than 0.8 ps/km$^{1/2}$, and only 25 percent lower than 0.2 ps/km$^{1/2}$.

For a 1 dB power penalty with an outage less than 30 minutes per year, this indicates that, for distances of ≥ 300 km, 20 percent of the installed fiber plant is not suitable for 10-Gb/s transmission, and 75 percent is not suitable for 40 Gb/s.

However imprecise, this observation shows that present and future transmission systems on the embedded fiber plant will greatly benefit from reducing polarization mode dispersion to upgrade capacity and expand the distance between regenerators.

Polarization mode dispersion is a difficult phenomenon to assess or counter. Whereas group velocity dispersion is deterministic, polarization mode dispersion characteristics vary in time and frequency. Reducing its impact does not necessarily cancel the effect, and actually only reduces the probability that it will cause an outage. Hence, we speak of mitigation rather than cancellation.

The effect of polarization mode dispersion is characterized by two values: a power penalty (or a bit-error ratio) and an outage probability (the probability of exceeding the power penalty value). A given pair of these values specifies a maximum tolerable value for the polarization mode dispersion, defined as the average differential group delay.

For example, for zero-chirp nonreturn-to-zero transmission (taking a 3 dB power penalty and an outage probability of 10^{-5}) the maximum tolerable value is 14 percent of the bit duration (14 ps for 10 Gb/s transmission).

The object of a polarization mode dispersion mitigation system is therefore to increase the tolerable dispersion value, given the same power penalty and outage probability values. The major requirements for such a system are adaptive operation with a tracking speed higher than the variation speed of polarization mode dispersion on the fiber line, low insertion and polarization-dependent loss values, broadband operation, and naturally low cost. The major mitigation techniques proposed over the past few years fall into two main categories: electronic equalization at the receiver and optical mitigation.

Electronic Equalization at the Receiver

One way to achieve this is through linear equalization using tapped delay lines and nonlinear cancellation using decision feedback equalization with an optimization feedback loop that contains adaptation logic. Some experimental results have proved that linear equalization can reduce polarization mode dispersion effects. Recently, a successful trial at 10 Gb/s used an integrated linear equalizer circuit based on an SiGe chip set including a four-tap voltage-controlled transversal filter and a signal-quality monitor to yield the feedback optimization parameter. Researchers are continuing to develop nonlinear equalization, which is needed for some poles of the polarization mode dispersion power penalty.

Optical Mitigation

Some proposals in this category employ a polarization controller at the input to ensure a transmission along one principal state of polarization through, for example, the use of a low-frequency modulation. These techniques are not well-adapted to real systems because the delay of the feedback signal to the transmitter can exceed the variation time of polarization mode dispersion.

More practical optical compensation systems employ a birefringent element before the receiver, preceded by a polarization controller (see Figure 30–1) [3]. A feedback loop featuring a control algorithm optimizes performance by setting the mitigator into one of two possible operating points.

The first operating point cancels differential group delay (setting the polarization controller so that the line's slow polarization state coincides with the fast polarization state of the birefringent element, and vice versa. This is valid if the birefringent element's differential group delay can vary or is roughly equal to the instantaneous differential group delay of the transmission line.

The other operating point acts on the input polarization state to ensure a transmission on a principal state of polarization of the entire path—the system (line fiber + mitigator). In this case, even if the total differential group delay is not canceled, its effect is. This will always work when the line's differential group delay is less than the birefringent element's differential group delay.

All of these considerations assume first-order polarization mode dispersion only. When accounting for higher-order dispersion for complete assessment of mitigation system performance, extensive testing with emulation of higher-order dispersion or complete numerical simulations with real dispersion statistics is required. For example, if higher-order polarization mode dispersion is taken into account, the condition for the existence of an operating point is not enough for an arbitrarily large value of differential group delay in the birefringent element.

Birefringent Elements

Optical mitigation systems have used several birefringent elements:

One Section of Polarization-Maintaining Fiber

This is the simplest implementation, requiring only one control: an input polarization controller. It requires a simple algorithm, leading to a potentially fast response if the other elements are fast enough: the polarization controller, the measurement of the feedback signal, and the control algorithm.

This configuration may seem to offer little flexibility to compensate for higher-order polarization mode dispersion and seems to be appropriate only for a very limited range of dispersion values. However, complete numerical assessment (including all orders of dispersion in a model of real fiber statistics) shows an improvement of the polarization mode dispersion tolerance of nonreturn-to-zero transmission from 14 to 33 percent of the bit time. In addition, this configuration has successfully exceeded one month of continuous operation in the field with OC-192 signals.

Several Sections of Polarization-Maintaining Fiber, Separated by Polarization Controllers

Although such a scheme would increase flexibility for first- and higher-order mitigation by adding control parameters, it dramatically increases the complexity of the optimization algorithm, reducing the overall operation speed.

One Section of Polarization-Maintaining Fiber, Twisted by Controlled Motors

This is identical to the preceding scheme, but each twisted fiber section replaces a polarization controller + fixed fiber pair.

An Integrated Polarization Controller and Birefringent Element

This is an integrated version of the two previous schemes. An implementation in Ti:LiNbO$_3$ worked in a laboratory setting. The device contained 73 TE-TM mode converters and required 246 voltages.

A Polarization Beamsplitter and a Variable Delay Line

This is a continuous version of the three previous schemes, again increasing flexibility and algorithm complexity.

Clearly, an important issue of mitigating polarization mode dispersion is a trade-off between flexibility and operation speed. High-speed operation is essential to ensure tracking of fast dispersion transients. As noted, system speed depends not only on the complexity and implementation of the control algorithm, but also on the components. For example, polarization controller speed can be a factor. So far, researchers have employed several polarization controllers (liquid crystals, fiber squeezers, LiNbO$_3$ waveguides) with a wide range of operating speeds.

The nature of the feedback parameter is also of prime importance in designing a polarization mode dispersion mitigation system. Two classes of feedback optimization signals have been used.

The first class is optical and inherently independent of bit rate. The main example assesses the degree of polarized light in the signal. This signal is well-correlated with the dispersion-related system performance and has worked in several laboratory and field experiments.

The second class is electrical, providing one or more parameters from the detected signal. The main set of parameters used is the radio frequency spectral components at $R/2^N$, where N is an integer. The power in these spectral components is well-correlated with the signal's differential group delay. There are two drawbacks to this approach: its dependence on the bit rate and its need for multiple optimization signals, used either sequentially or simultaneously to overcome a weak differential group delay dependence in some ranges.

Finally, properly assessing the system performance of a polarization mode dispersion mitigator is among the most important, but often neglected steps. First-order dispersion emulation (the generation of fixed or variable differential group delay) is not enough; it does not describe realistic statistical effect. Therefore, it is recommended that the statistics of polarization mode dispersion emulators should represent as accurately as possible the Maxwellian distribution of real fibers. Or, they should obey the following conditions: that allow reproducible dispersion conditions relate to realistic cases of installed fibers.

For these reasons, long-term field testing appears to be a crucial step. In addition, long-term laboratory conditions can poorly describe field effects, while short-period bit-error-rate testing can erroneously describe system performance. Also, it is recommended that the system must undergo fast variations in polarization mode dispersion for worst-case performance.

Furthermore, it is recommended that researchers must completely characterize polarization mode dispersion mitigators. In particular, they need to assess how mitigation will affect key characteristics: tolerance to group velocity dispersion, the performance of various modulation formats, the performance of various bit rates, and power limitations [3].

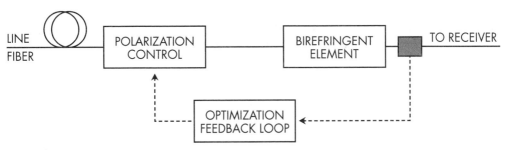

Figure 30–1   Optical methods can also help mitigate polarization mode dispersion.

Structural Return Loss

Structural return loss (SRL) is another critical parameter. It is a measurement of the difference between the sent signal and the reflected signal. The bigger the difference, the smoother the cable, the better the performance.

Combined Performance

The combined effect of these parameters can be expressed in a way that is similar to a signal-to-noise ratio. For example, given that a minimum signal-to-noise ratio for a particular system is between 10 and 15 dB, it can be seen at what frequencies a given cable may be suitable for use up to 100 meter distances.

In the above 30 MHz range, it is recommended that additional consideration must be given to being in conformance to FCC regulations for emission. Cross talk is an indication of a cable's performance in this area. Emission levels are dependent on the total systems and is impossible to predict given cable characteristics alone. But qualitatively, the better the cross-talk performance, the better the emission performance will be. If greater than 100 MHz signals are a consideration, the highest cross-talk performance cable available should be selected. Optical fiber, unlike copper media, has little or no room for variation in performance insofar as bandwidth is concerned. In the case of single-mode fiber, its inherent primary waveguide characteristic makes defining the limits of its bandwidth essentially impossible. Multimode optical fiber fabrication technology is rapidly nearing perfection. The result is that a given fiber geometry, for example 62.5/125 m with .275 NA (numerical aperture, the measure of light acceptance), has a given bandwidth unless changes are made to intentionally alter the optical characteristics. The available fiber virtually all falls within the practical allowance for deviation from the ideal. In a sense, it's all the same. There is no room for levels.

MATERIALS SPECIFICATION

Materials used in cable design and manufacture are constantly improving. Manufacturers choose materials based on application and performance requirements. Choice of materials is often best left to cable engineers who have the knowledge and experience to choose materials that best fit the application and requirements. Below is a partial list of considerations that affect the choice of materials.

- outside plant or inside installation
- robustness

- flammability requirements
- electrical requirements
- size
- weight
- compliance to applicable standards
- cost [Berk-Tek, 6]

Considerable confusion related to specifying cable materials results from misunderstandings about which part of the cable is actually being specified. The cable jacket, most accurately, is the outer plastic covering of the cable. Within the cable jacket, the individual wires are covered by a different layer of plastic—most accurately referred to as insulation or dielectric (nonconductive). These two coverings serve different purposes and can be composed of the same or entirely different plastics depending on the application. Considerations for specifying the plastic material used on a cable jacket almost always involves flammability. Further confusion occurs from the common use of plastic material types to specify a level of flammability, say plenum versus nonplenum. Based on original technology, the terms PVC and nonplenum-rated or Teflon and plenum-rated were used interchangeably. Teflon is a DuPont trademark for a fluoropolymer called fluorinated-ethylene-propylene (FEP). Permanent virtual circuit/channel (PVC)-based compounds suitable for plenum rating has essentially become mutually exclusive of the basic material types [Berk-Tek, 6].

Generally, the material most involved in carrying signals is the insulation (in this context also referred to as dielectric). Some impact to transmission performance is completely unaffected by jacket material but this effect is insignificant compared to the improvements from substituting PVC insulation with polyethylene or FEP, for nonplenum and plenum cables respectively. This is due to the latter materials having far superior high-frequency dielectric properties than PVC. Furthermore, PVC's relatively poor properties substantially deteriorate with increased temperatures, whereas the better performing dielectrics essentially do not change with temperature.

In addition to providing basic insulating properties, the plastics used for insulation have various signal-altering characteristics: dielectric constant and the dissipation factor. The dielectric constant is a function of the velocity at which energy travels through the dielectric. The dissipation factor is a function of the rate at which energy is absorbed by the dielectric. Reducing either of these factors results in improved signal transmission performance.

The plastic most commonly used for conductor insulation is PVC. Its dielectric properties are good but generally not good enough for any data communication application more demanding than basic short-distance links. PVC is normally used for power, control, instrumentation, audio, telecommunications, and applications that operate at low frequencies. High-speed data cables are normally made using polyethylene or FEP, because their dielectric properties are far superior to PVC.

There is no real disadvantage to using polyethylene compared to PVC. The cost is only slightly higher, although it is recommended that some cable design precautions must be taken to meet flammability regulations. Polyethylene is more flammable than PVC, but this is easily compensated by a flame-retardant PVC cable jacket. The only exception to the choice of polyethylene insulation is the case of plenum cables. FEP is substituted by PVC to achieve low smoke and flame-producing characteristics. The dielectric properties for FEP are slightly superior to polyethylene.

The proximity of two conductors within a cable and the dielectric constant of the insulation between the conductors determine the capacitance measured between the conductors. Capacitance is defined as the amount of electricity the dielectric between two conductors will store for a given voltage difference between the conductors. When the voltage is changing (a signal is present), a higher capacitance results in a greater resistance to the change (more attenuation at higher frequencies).

Most shielded cables use insulation with very good dielectric properties (low dielectric constant) to assure that cable capacitance are kept low when a shield is added to the cable. The addition of a shield around the two conductors introduces two very significant parasitic capacitance, those between each conductor and the shield. The conductor-to-shield capacitance combine with the conductor-to-conductor capacitance to significantly increase the overall capacitance of the pair. In order to achieve or attempt to achieve the same impedance in a shielded cable as an unshielded cable, it is recommended that insulation with a lower dielectric constant must be used and the conductor spacing must be increased. The result is that shielded cables are generally larger than unshielded ones.

It is no longer the case that plenum cables need be stiff. Originally, plenum cables constructed from fluoropolymers were inherently very rigid compared to typical nonplenum cables. The stiffness was grudgingly tolerated because of cost savings resulting from installations without conduit. Now, substantial improvements have been made to certain fluoropolymers such as giving Astochem Kynar-Flex (PVDFCP), which has near-PVC flexibility.

Although fluoropolymers as a group still hold the position of having the greatest flame retardance, it is possible to design a cable using special PVC-based compounds for jacket or insulation and still achieve a plenum rating. These special PVC-based compounds are less flexible and have lower-performing dielectric properties than ordinary PVC compounds. But on certain cable constructions they can provide definite improvements in flexibility.

DELIVERY AND PACKAGING CONSIDERATIONS

Packaging is an important consideration that may determine how easily a cable is installed. Getting the lengths of cable you need packaged the way you need them should be as simple as possible. Package design details such as cable kinking when pulled from a box varies from manufacturer to manufacturer. When approaching a possible supplier, it is advised and recommended that you consider several factors:

- What packaging options are available?
- Has the manufacturer engineered the package to minimize damage to the cable when removed from the package?
- What protection is given to the cable?
- What lengths are available?
- What does the manufacturer stock?
- How are the products labeled [Berk-Tek, 7–8]?

Available Packaging Options

Reels should of course be available. They should be sized to the length and the diameter of the cable. The end user should be wary of reels that have too small of a drum diameter, however. The manufacturer may be saving money by using an inferior reel, but if the drum is too small, it can exceed the bend radius of the cable and actually cause damage resulting in loss of signal. This is particularly true of optical fiber cables, where bending can easily cause breaks and attenuation. Boxes for most standard products should also be an option. Many end users prefer the light, disposable boxes that are easily carried, stored, and handled. There is no reel involved in the process—the cable is wound into a basket that pays off without kinking. It is recommended that boxes be used with at least a 257# proof test.

Cable Protection

It is recommended that cables be protected from dirt, damage, and moisture. Reels should be boxed, placed on skids, or wrapped with clear plastic.

Available Cable Lengths

All manufacturers of cable list standard lengths that processing attempts to meet. Most manufacturers offer optical fiber cable in standard lengths of 1.0, 1.5, and 2.0 km. Copper cables are available in standard 500 foot and 1,000 foot lengths. A reliable manufacturer should be able to run longer continuous lengths when required, or offer shorter lengths as an option. Extremely high cut charges are a sign that the manufacturer is not producing in any quantity for stock.

Manufacturer's Stock

A larger internal inventory is a sign of quick turnaround from order to shipment. Most large manufacturers offer a vast copper cable Take-From Stock internal inventory shipping program. This means that they get their products to their distributors quickly.

Labeling Products

Labeling seems like a given, but inadequate labeling can fall off, become obscured, or not contain user-friendly information. It is recommended that labels be easy to read, protected from the environment, and securely fastened to the reel or box. At the very least, information should be given on the order number, customer, internal code, and reel or box number for traceability. Desirable information includes a market description that is easily understandable by anyone associated with cable products. The description should use industry-accepted terminology for the product rather than the manufacturer's internal coding. For optical fiber cables, where mishandling can create grave problems, it is recommended that final preshipment testing information be included for each length.

QUALITY ASSURANCE CONSIDERATIONS

The quality of a cable product is invisible. It is therefore recommended that comparisons of manufacturers include an investigation of their quality assurance programs. A good program conforms to standards and is easily demonstrated.

Testing

Cable manufacturers test the final product to determine compliance to specifications. Category 5 UTP cable is typically tested at a rate of one sample every 250,000 feet of manufactured product. The sample rate varies from manufacturer to manufacturer and from product to product. Fiber optic cables are typically evaluated for fiber attenuation and dimensional requirements, while UTP cables are tested for conformance to electrical and dimensional specifications. The systematic control of in-process quality is as important as final testing to assure compliance to industry standards requirements and internal requirements. On a daily basis, it is critical that testing and quality assurance be carried out during the manufacturing process when deviations can be corrected before the product is complete. In-process testing is not only more efficient, but helps guarantee a quality end-product. Manufacturers utilize statistical process control to monitor critical aspects of the manufacturing process. An example is the control of outer insulation diameter and conductor centering in a category 5 cable.

If there is question concerning the electrical or optical performance of a specific cable, manufacturers have the ability to supply test data, which reflects the performance of the reel of cable in question [Berk-Tek, 8].

Special Testing

While most manufacturers are always trying to improve the way they handle testing for their standard products, they also have a wide range of special equipment and procedures. It is recommended that they always be prepared to conduct humidity testing, low and high temperature tests, tensile tests, cable burns, and many other standard or not-so-standard procedures.

UL Approvals/ETL Verifications

Most cabling products are used in applications requiring an Underwriter's Laboratories (UL) and/or Canadian Standard Association (CSA) rating. It is recommended that manufacturers have extensive approvals from both agencies, usually for flame ratings. Manufacturers should also have many of their products performance tested and approved by UL as proof that their cables are performing per spec. The Electrotechnical Laboratory (ETL) also verifies many cabling products.

ISO 9000

The ISO (International Standards Organization) is concerned with creating a global standard of quality assurance programs and certifications. What has become known as ISO 9000 is actually a series of five standards with 9001, 9002, and 9003 detailing specific systems for quality based on distinct functional or organizational structures.

Unlike other second-party approval agencies, ISO does not test products. Rather, it verifies that an organization is following the quality systems the organization has established. The theory behind ISO 9000 is that a manufacturer following specific quality guidelines will consistently produce higher quality, more reliable products. Companies interested in doing business on a worldwide scale are increasingly finding conformance to ISO a requirement.

SUPPLIER SPECIFICATION

Finally, the cable media you choose may make up 25 percent or more of the cost of the system. Specifying the wrong cable or buying a borderline performance cable can be a costly disaster, leading to system crashes, distorted signals, lost data, and eventual cable repulls. It is recommended that the choice you make be fully informed. Your supplier must be willing and able to provide you with the services you need, not just the right cable.

Now, if you were to make just one recommendation for the fiber-optic post-2000 developed society, what would it be? Bandwidth! Bandwidth! And more Bandwidth!

BANDWIDTH: THE FIBER-OPTIC CHALLENGE OF THE POST-2000 DEVELOPED SOCIETY

A number of individual applications today demand large bit rate per user, such as supercomputer interconnection, remote site backup for large computer centers, and digital video production and distribution, but these are isolated niches today. The best gauge of the need for the infrastructure to supply large amounts of bandwidth to individual users is probably to be found in the phenomena associated with the use of the Internet for graphics-based or multimedia applications.

Just as the use of noncommunicating computers was made much easier by the emergence of the icon- and mouse-based graphical user interface of Macintosh, Windows, and OS2, the same thing can be observed for communicating computers with the World Wide Web. The modality in which most users want to interact with distributed processing capability (measured in millions of instructions per second [MIPs]) is the same as it has always been with local MIPs: they want to point, click, and have an instant response. They will in fact want to have a response time from some remote source on any future information infrastructure that is a negligible excess over the basic propagation time between them and the remote resource. They will want the infrastructure to be not only widebanded for quick access to complex objects (which are evolving already from just still graphics to include voice and video) but also to be symmetric, so that any user can become the center of his or her own communicating community. This need for an *any-to-any* infrastructure, as contrasted to the one-way or highly asymmetrical character of most of our wideband infrastructure today (cable and broadcast), is thought by many political leaders to be the key to optimizing the use of communication technology for the public good.

Thus, a dim outline of many of the needs that the information infrastructure of the future must satisfy can be discerned in the emerging set of high-bandwidth usage modes of the Internet today, particularly the Web. The picture that emerges from examining what is happening in the Web is most instructive. Figure 30–2 shows the recent and projected growth of Web traffic per unit time

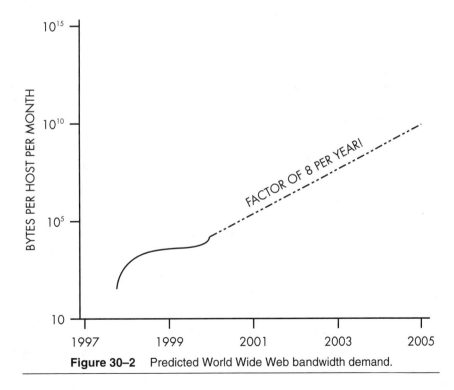

Figure 30–2   Predicted World Wide Web bandwidth demand.

per user assuming the present usage patterns, which include almost no voice, video clips, or high response speed applications such as point-and-shoot games or interactive CAD simulations [2]. As these evolve, they could exacerbate the already considerable bit rate demand per user, which Figure 30–2 shows as a factor of 8 per year. If the extrapolations in Figure 30–2 are correct, this means that in the decade to 2010, the portion of the available communication infrastructure devoted to descendants of the Web must undergo a capacity growth of about 10^9 in order to keep up with demand.

There is only one current physical transmission technology capable of supporting such growth: optical fiber. Fortunately, for the prospects of an infrastructure that will provide society what it needs, fiber has been going into the ground, on utility poles, within buildings, and under the oceans at a rapid rate. The installation rate has been over 20,000 miles per day for some years, just in the continental United States alone, so that by now over 50 million miles of installed fiber exist here. Even more fortunately, each fiber has a usable bandwidth of some 25,000 GHz, roughly 1,000 times the usable radio spectrum on planet Earth, and quite enough to handle all the phone calls in the U.S. telephone system at its busiest level. While this gigantic capacity is underused by at least a factor of 10,000 in today's practice, which is based on time division multiplexing, the technical means are rapidly evolving to open up the full fiber bandwidth. This is the all-optical networking technology, based on dense wavelength division, in which different channels travel at different *colors of light* (see the Sidebar, "Making Light Work for Transporting Heavy Data").

MAKING LIGHT WORK FOR TRANSPORTING HEAVY DATA

Industry pundits may differ on their predicted time scales, but they all agree that the volume of data traffic will far surpass the present network capacity for voice-based conversations. You only have to look at the explosive growth rate of Internet usage to understand the level of demand for high-speed data communications. The most important metric related to greatly increased data traffic is network capacity or bandwidth.

Deceptively simple in appearance, hair-thin optical fiber is the high-tech key to modern wide-bandwidth data communications. The diameter of the central core in a single fiber usually is 62.5 mm (0.0025") for multimode (MM) fiber or about 9 mm (0.00036") for singlemode (SM) fiber. Cladding of 125 mm (0.005") OD surrounds the core and serves to confine light either by reflecting it in stepped index fibers or refracting it in graded index fibers. An outer, buffering layer is added to protect the fiber from moisture and physical damage.

Both types of fiber operate in the infrared area of the spectrum and exhibit very low losses compared to coaxial or twisted-pair electrical wire. MM systems are used at 850 nm and

1,300 nm, and SM fibers run at 1,300 or 1,550 nm. These wavelengths represent the location of narrow bands of frequencies used to multiplex multiple data channels onto a single fiber.

The fiber bandwidth is divided this way into three regions to avoid operation near strong light-absorbing areas at 1,000 nm, 1,400 nm, and above 1,600 nm. Absorption at these wavelengths is caused by OH+ hydroxyl radicals that occur naturally as impurities.

For MM fiber, losses are about 3 dB/km at 850 nm and 1 dB/km at 1,300 nm. SM fiber has even lower losses: 0.4 dB/km at 1,300 nm and 0.3 dB at 1,550 km. In contrast, coaxial cable losses are so large that they are specified as a number of decibels/100 ft or dB/m.

Even very large diameter coaxial cable has losses far greater than those of optical fibers, and the coaxial losses are present at much lower frequencies. Twisted-pair characteristics are even worse than those of coaxial cables. There is no question that optical fibers are technically superior, and installed cost often can be cheaper than for copper cables.

Although only 0.0025" in diameter, MM fibers are large enough that light can travel through them on many distinct paths. Because some of the paths involve multiple reflections from the cladding, at the end, long fiber portions of the light will have traveled different distances. This results in dispersion: a pulse of light will not be as distinct when it leaves the fiber as when it entered. Uncertainty of this kind is equivalent to jitter and reduces usable bandwidth.

In contrast, the 0.00036" diameter of an SM fiber is only a few times larger than the wavelength of the light being carried. It is recommended that all the light must traverse the same path. Because only one mode of propagation is allowed, SM fibers simply don't produce the kind of dispersion seen with MM fibers.

In graded index MM fibers, the index of refraction of the core gradually decreases with radial distance from the center. Because light travels faster in glass with a low index of refraction, the portion of the light that travels farther also goes faster. Shaping the index of refraction profile in this way eliminates most of the mode-dependent dispersion effects and yields a 100x improvement in usable bandwidth over a simpler stepped-index MM fiber (see Figure 30–3) [4].

The numerical aperture (NA) of a fiber is defined by the highest angle at which light can enter the fiber. Because a MM fiber has a relatively large diameter, and because light entering at a high angle will be reflected or refracted back toward the center, a MM fiber can have a large NA value. It is easier to couple light into a fiber with a high NA, and this is one reason that MM cables are driven by LEDs. Other factors supporting the use of LEDs are cost and an LED's lower power that corresponds to the shorter distances for which MM fibers are suited.

SM fibers, being much smaller in diameter and with a different cladding design, have a lower NA figure. They also can provide long-range transmission. For these reasons, a higher-power laser is used to drive SM fibers. The increased cost of the SM fiber and laser driver is easily offset by the reduced number of repeaters required in very long haul networks.

One SM fiber may carry a few discrete wavelengths of light, typically 1,310 nm and 1,550 nm, in wavelength division multiplexing (WDM), or many frequencies (a product with 80 channels recently was announced) in dense WDM (DWDM) applications. In regard to fiber-optic networks and all-optical components on network capacity, cables will become denser with more than 800 fibers per cable to support a predicted doubling of network bandwidth requirements every six months.

Also, it is recommended that the practical bandwidth that can be provided using a single fiber of 1 Tb/s should be practical. One way to provide 1 Tb/s is to combine 400 wavelengths each modulated at a 2.5 Gb/s data rate.

One problem standing in the way of very high data rates is the imperfections of the optical fibers themselves. At the high drive powers required to achieve long transmission distances, nonlinearities can limit the extent to which DWDM can be used. An example of an improved-performance fiber is the large effective area fiber developed by Corning LEAF® optical fiber.

By designing the fiber to have two separated, concentric areas of high-refractive index, higher power can be accommodated at lower light intensity. This leads to lower distortion, especially the so-called four-wave mixing (FWM) effect in DWDM applications.

In addition to the center of the core, the outer ring of high-index material also carries significant power. Distributing the light within the core in this manner results in an effective fiber area that is typically 32 percent larger than conventional fibers (see Figure 30–4) [4].

Physical Testing

As in any data network, testing breaks down into two parts: verification of the physical layer and interpretation of the received data. Data analysis will not be discussed here because it has little to do with the fiber itself. Rather, it is a system problem that has more to do with the amount of traffic, an asynchronous transport mechanism (ATM) protocol problem, or some other high-level incompatibility. These kinds of issues are best solved using protocol analyzers, network management tools, and traffic simulators.

The most straightforward physical-layer tests are for continuity and loss. Optical power is measured with an average-reading meter that uses a silicon, germanium, or InGaAs sensor, depending on wavelength. Because the reading will be sensitive to the data duty cycle, measurements usually are made with a continuous wave (CW) or a squarewave source. When the actual data source is measured, the reading only will be repeatable if the data pattern is constant.

Tests include measurement of not just the transmitted power, but also of return loss or reflected power as low as –50 dBm or less. At the opposite extreme, community antenna television (CATV) operates with relatively high power levels up to +20 dBm to ensure a good signal-to-noise ratio (SNR). These two test examples demonstrate the need for power meters and sources with wide dynamic ranges.

A source and a meter often are combined in a convenient, hand-held tester. Generally, two testers are required, one for each end of the fiber being tested. Some manufacturers provide data download from the remote slave unit to the master unit. In this way, a single operator can set up the test and read the results from one end. It is important to run power tests from both ends of the fiber because the location of a marginal splice or connector can make a difference.

Work done by Corning demonstrates just how difficult it is to interpret test results accurately. Although 0.5 dB is an acceptable loss for an MM fiber connector, the actual loss experienced in a system depends on the transmission modes being propagated. Long fibers naturally tend to attenuate higher-order modes, which means that after a few kilometers, most of the power is concentrated in lower-order modes near the center of the fiber. This condition is termed equilibrium modal distribution (EMD). In contrast, a fully filled fiber exhibits high- and low-order modes, and all modes have equal power.

Under EMD conditions, a fiber-optic system can be up to 15 dB more efficient than the worst-case design figures would suggest. Fiber loss is about 1 dB/km less for the EMD case, and connector loss should be a few tenths of a decibel less.

Another type of test tool, the optical time domain reflectometer (OTDR), determines loss versus distance. A short pulse of light is sent down the fiber, and the reflected light caused by the fiber's backscattering properties is measured. Backscatter together with absorption are the primary loss mechanisms in fibers.

Because the backscatter coefficient varies according to the particular cable being used, OTDR displays can incorrectly show gain instead of loss if a cable with a different coefficient has been encountered. Other limitations of OTDRs are their distance resolution, the smallest distance that can be resolved, and the recovery distance required before the ambient power level is displayed again after a large signal change.

A good OTDR with modular sources to match different operating frequencies and types of cable also is relatively expensive. Regardless of these drawbacks, the OTDR is the instrument of choice for finding the location of fiber breaks or bad connectors and splices with high losses.

Bandwidth

It is possible for a fiber to pass all continuity and power-related tests and still appear to cause data errors. If the bandwidth of the transmitter or receiver is too low, single data pulses may not be correctly converted to an optical or electrical signal, respectively.

One way to check bandwidth is to attach the receive end of a fiber to an optical-to-electrical (OE) adaptor. This device allows you to view the data pattern on a digital oscilloscope as a traditional eye pattern (see Figure 30–5) [4].

On some oscilloscopes with mask-testing capabilities, you can create a test mask that is larger than the reference mask by a selectable amount. The new mask is used to determine the performance margin of the transmit/receive link above the guaranteed minimum level. If you want to see what the optical signal actually looks like, you need an OE with a much higher bandwidth than the bit rate, for example 5:1, although only 2:1 or 3:1 may be attainable at very high data rates.

The output from the receiver's photodiode sensor is a band-limited analog signal that, in turn, is converted to a digital bit stream. Band-limiting occurs because the bandwidth of a receiver is designed to be not much greater than 80 percent of the bit rate, or 8 GHz for a 10-

Gb/s system. OE converters have switchable filters built in that provide pulse response characteristics similar to those of the actual fiber receiver.

Turning on the filter allows you to view the signal as the data recovery circuitry, immediately following how the photodiode element would see it. If you want to determine the bandwidth of the fiber communications channel, turn off the filter. You need all the bandwidth you can get. Make sure the oscilloscope's bandwidth doesn't degrade your measurements.

You also may want to run a bit error rate test (BERT). The BERT is a good overall measure of fiber performance, and specialized test instruments are available to make this measurement. In regard to optical receiver elements for OC-192 (10-Gb/s) networks, BERT performs with a 0-Gb/s, 223-1 pseudorandom bit sequence. The performance of a PIN diode can also be compared to an avalanche photodiode (APD) in a receiver with 1xE-10 BER.

It is recommended that because of the APD's lower inherent noise, the optical receiver can be made about 5 dB more sensitive while achieving the same BER. The APD devices provided increased SNR, longer transmission distance, and wider dynamic range. These improvements are particularly important at 10 Gb/s, where transmission limitations (fiber dispersion, optical nonlinearities, and insertion loss) put stringent requirements on receiver performance and specifications [4].

MM STEP INDEX

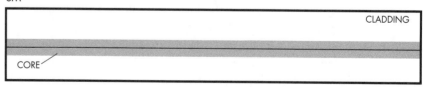

MM GRADED INDEX

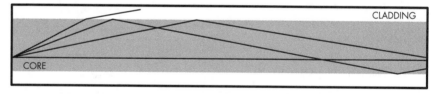

SM

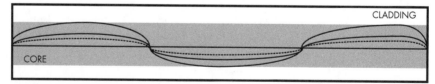

Figure 30–3   Comparison of stepped and graded index multimode fiber and single-mode fiber.

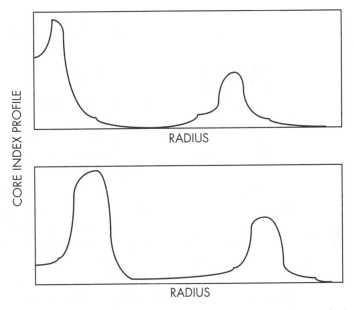

Figure 30–4 Radial variation of LEAF index of refraction in two designs.

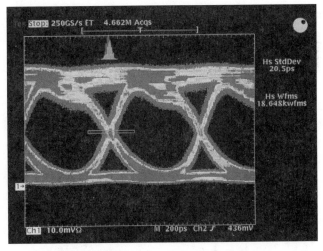

Figure 30–5 High-speed eye diagram.

Why isn't it true that the physical basis is in place over which to send the traffic of the future? Most of the answer is summarized in Figure 30–6 [2]. All the communication resources that have been installed seem to be improving in capacity by roughly 1.5 per year, totally out of scale with the 8-times-per-year growth of demand shown in Figure 30–2. The top curve of Figure 30–6 shows the capability of desktop computers to absorb and emit data into and out of the buses that connect them to the external world. The next line shows local area network capacity as it has evolved. The third one shows the evolution of high-end access to the telco backbone that allows users at one location connectivity to users elsewhere outside the local LAN environment. The capacity of this third curve has been available only to the most affluent corporations and universities, those that can afford T1, T3, or SONET connections to their premises.

While all three of these capacities are evolving at the rate of only a factor of 1.5 per year, they represent really substantial bit-rate numbers. Current Web users who can afford 10 Mb/s LANs and T-carrier connections into the backbone experience little response time frustration. However, the situation of most users is represented more accurately by the bottom curve, which shows the data rate available between our desktop and the backbone over the infamous *last mile* using telco copper connections with either modems or ISDN. There is a 10^4 performance deficiency between the connectivity avail-

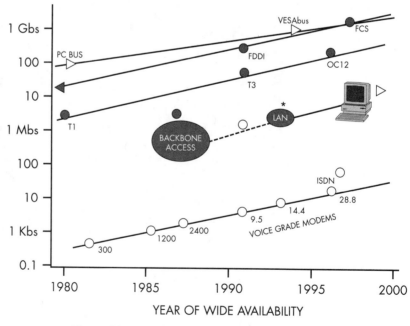

Figure 30–6   The "last mile" bandwidth bottleneck.

able between local and long-haul resources and the internal performance of both these resources. If one compares the rate of growth of Web traffic in Figure 30–2 with the data of Figure 30–6, it is clear that there is an acute need to bridge the 10^4 gap of the last mile with fiber and inevitably to increase the bandwidths of the backbone also, probably at a greater rate than the traditional factor of 1.5 per year.

As for bridging the gap between the desktop and the telco backbone, the proposed solution for years now has been *"fiber to the home,"* expressing the notion that it must pay for itself at the consumer level. The alternative of coaxial cable to the premises, while having up to a gigahertz of capacity, is proving an expensive and nonexpandable way to futureproof the last mile against the kind of bandwidth demands suggested by Figure 30–2, and the architectures used have assumed either unidirectional service or highly asymmetrical service. What is clearly needed is fiber, probably introduced first in time-division mode, and then, as demand builds up, supporting a migration to wavelength division (all-optical).

Figure 30–7 shows the rate at which fiber to the premises (*home*) has been happening in the United States [2]. The limited but rapidly growing amount of fiber that is reaching all the way to user premises today is mostly

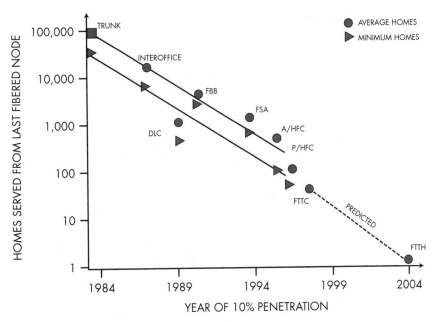

Figure 30–7   Predicted rate at which fiber reaches user premises.

to serve businesses. The overall process is seen to be quite slow; essentially nothing very widespread will happen during the next two years to serve the average citizen. However, the bandwidth demand grows daily. Meanwhile, all-optical networks are beginning to migrate off the laboratory bench and into real service in small niches.

What Figure 30–7 shows is the steady reduction of the number of homes that, on the average, lie within the area surrounding the nearest fiber end. In 1984, when fiber was used only between central offices (COs), this figure was the average number of homes or offices served by such a CO. As the carriers, cable companies, and competitive local access providers found great economies in replacing copper with fiber outward from their COs and head-ends, the number decreased. A linear extrapolation down to one residence per fiber end predicts that 10 percent of U.S. homes will be reached by fiber by about 2005, at best. In Japan, it is quite possible that a strong national effort will be launched that will leapfrog this lengthy process using large government subsidies.

During the coming decade, several things will happen, in addition to ever-increasing end-user pressure for more bandwidth to the desktop. Competition between telcos, cable companies, and competitive access providers may or may not accelerate the extrapolated trend shown in Figure 30–7. Advances in low-cost optoelectronic technology, some of them based on mass production by lithography, could also accelerate the trend. The reason for this is because analyses of costs of fiber to the home consistently show a large fraction of the cost to lie in the set-top box, splitters, powering, and, in the case of wavelength division multiplexing (WDM) approaches, ultiwavelength or wavelength-tunable sources and receivers. It is widely felt that the price of the set-top box itself will have to be below $400 for success in the marketplace. This is probably true, whether the *set-top box* is really a box sitting atop a television set or a feature card within a desktop computer. By 2005, it should become quite clear whether the TV set will be growing keyboards, hard disks, and CPUs to take over the PC, whether the PC will be growing video windows to take over the TV set, or whether both will coexist indefinitely and separately. In any case, the bottleneck to these evolutions will increasingly be the availability by means of fiber of high bit rates between the premises and the backbone, plus a backbone bandwidth growth rate that is itself probably inadequate today.

In the meantime, while we look ahead to the increasing availability of fiber paths and the customers who need them to serve their high-bandwidth needs, the all-optical networking community is hard at work trying to open up the 25,000 GHz of fiber bandwidth to convenient and economical access to end users. Already, the telcos are using four-wavelength WDM in field tests of undersea links. IBM has recently made a number of commercial installations of 20-wavelength WDM links for achieving fiber rental cost savings for some of its large customers who have remote computer site backup requirements. The rationale behind both these commercialization efforts involves not only getting more bandwidth out of existing fiber, but also making the installation *multiprotocol* or *futureproof.* This is done by taking advantage of the fact that each wavelength can carry an arbitrary bit rate and framing convention format, or even analog formats, up to some maximum speed set by the losses on the link.

These successful realizations of simple multiwavelength links represent the simplest case of the three different kinds of all-optical systems, as shown in Figure 30–8 [2]. In addition to the two-station WDM link (with multiple ports per station), the figure shows the two forms taken by full networks; structures in which there are many stations (nodes), with perhaps only one or a few ports per node.

WDM LINK

▷ = WAVELENGTH MUX/DEMUX

BROADCAST AND SELECT NETWORK

■ INCLUDES FIXED LASER AND TUNABLE RECEIVER

▷ = PASSIVE OPTICAL STAR COUPLER

WAVELENGTH ROUTING NETWORK

■ INCLUDES WAVELENGTH ROUTER

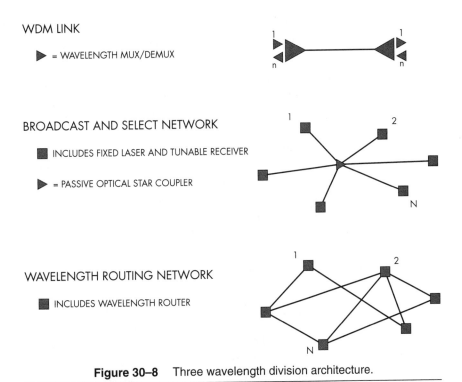

Figure 30–8   Three wavelength division architecture.

The second type, the broadcast and select network, usually works by assigning to the transmit side of each node in the network a fixed optical frequency, merging all the transmitted signals at the center of the network in an optical star coupler and then broadcasting the merge to the receive sides of all nodes. The entire inner structure, consisting of fiber strands and the star coupler, is completely passive and essentially unpowered. By means of a suitable protocol, when a node wants to talk to another (either by setting up a fixed lightpath *circuit* or by exchanging packets), the latter's receiver tunes to the former's transmit wavelength and vice versa. Broadcast and select networks have been prototyped and, while still considered not quite in the commercialization cost range, have been used in live application situations, for digital video distribution and for gigabit supercomputer interconnection at rates of 1 gigabit per second.

Aside from high cost, which is currently a problem with all WDM systems, there are two other things wrong with broadcast and select networks. The power from each transmitter, being broadcast to all receivers, is mostly wasted on receivers that do not use it. Second, the number of nodes the network can have can be no larger than the size of the wavelength pool, the number of resolvable wavelengths. Today, even though there are 25,000 GHz of fiber capacity waiting to be tapped, the wavelength resolving technology is rather crude, allowing systems with only up to about 100 wavelengths to be built, so far. The problems of both cost and number of wavelengths are gradually being solved, often by the imaginative use of the same tool that brought cost reductions to electronics two decades ago: lithography.

Clearly, a network architecture that allows only 100 nodes does not constitute a networking revolution. It is recommended that some means must be provided for achieving scalability by using each wavelength many places in the network at the same time. Wavelength routing accomplishes this, and also avoids wastage of transmitted power, by channeling the energy transmitted by each node at each wavelength along a restricted path to the receiver instead of letting it spread over the entire network, as with the broadcast and select architecture. As the name *wavelength routing* implies, at each intermediate node between the end nodes, light coming in on one port at a given wavelength gets routed out of one and only one port.

The components to build broadcast and select networks have been available on the street for nine years, but optical wavelength routers are still a reality only in the laboratory. A large step toward practical wavelength routing networks was recently demonstrated by Bellcore.

The ultimate capacity of optical networking is enormous, as shown by Figure 30–9, and is especially great with wavelength routing (Figure 30–10)

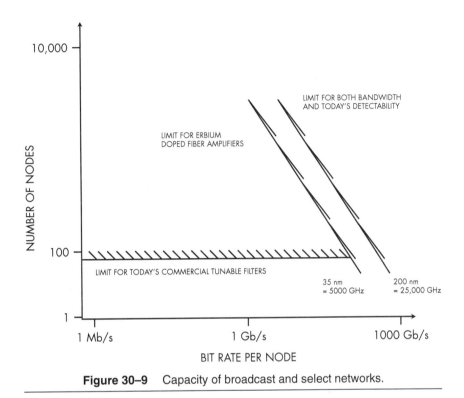

Figure 30–9 Capacity of broadcast and select networks.

[2]. Figure 30–9 shows how one might divide the 25,000 GHz into many low-bit-rate connections or a smaller number of higher-bit-rate connections. For example, in principle, one could carry 10,000 uncompressed 1 Gb/s HDTV channels on each fiber. The figure also shows that erbium amplifiers, needed for long distances, narrow down the 25,000 GHz figure to about 5,000 GHz, and also that the commercially available tunable optical receiver technology is capable of resolving no more than about 80 channels.

With broadcast and select networks, the number of supportable connections is equal to the number of available wavelengths in the pool of wavelengths. However, with wavelength routing, the number of supportable connections is the available number of wavelengths multiplied by a wavelength reuse factor that grows with the topological connectedness of the network, as shown in Figure 30–10. For example, for a 1,000-node network of nodes with a number of ports (the degree) equal to four, the reuse factor is around 50, meaning that with 100 wavelengths, there could, in principle, be five connections supportable for each of the 1,000 nodes.

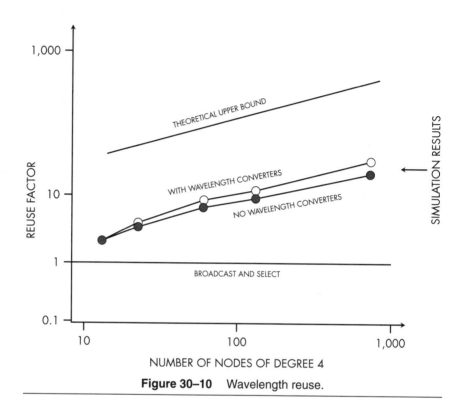

Figure 30–10   Wavelength reuse.

As far as the end user is concerned, there is sometimes a preference for circuit switching and sometimes for packet switching. The former provides protocol transparency during the data transfer interval, and the latter provides concurrency (many apparently simultaneous data flows over the same physical port, by the use of time-slicing). In both cases, very large bit rates are possible without the electronics needing to handle traffic bits from extraneous nodes other than the communicating partners.

The very real progress that has been made to date in all-optical networking owes a great deal to the foresight of government sponsors of research and development the world over. The three big players have been the Ministry of Posts and Telecommunications (MPT) in Japan, the European Economic Community (EEC), and the U.S. Advanced Research Projects Agency (ARPA). The EEC's programs, under Rationalization of Advanced Communication in Europe-1 (RACE-1) and RACE-2, have now been superseded by Advanced Communication Technology Systems (ACTS).

In 1992, ARPA initiated three consortia aimed at system-level solutions, and all three have been successful. The Optical Networking Technology Consortium, a group of some 10 organizations led by Bellcore, has demonstrated an operating wavelength routing network using acousto-optic filters as wavelength routers. The All-Optical Networking Consortium, consisting of the Massachusetts Institute of Technology, AT&T Bell Laboratories, and Digital Equipment Corporation, has installed a network that combines wavelength routing, wavelength shifting, broadcast-and-select, and electronic packet switching between Littleton, Lexington, and Cambridge, Massachusetts. With ARPA and DOE support, IBM (working with Los Alamos National Laboratory) has developed an extensive set of algorithms for distributed control of very large wavelength-routing networks, and has studied offloading of TCP/IP for supercomputer interconnection in its Rainbow-2 network.

It is fair to say that the United States now holds the lead in making all-optical networking a commercial reality, and that ARPA support was one of the important factors in this progress. At the end of 1995, ARPA kicked off a second round of 3-year consortia in the all-optical networking area, with funding roughly five times that of the earlier programs. Whether all-optical networking will be a commercially practical part of the NII depends on three factors:

1. Whether the investment will be made to continue or accelerate the installation of fiber to the premises and desktop (Figure 30–7).
2. Whether it proves feasible to reduce component costs by two to three orders of magnitude below today's values.
3. The extent to which providers offer the fiber paths in the form of *dark fiber*—that is, without any electronic conversions between path ends [2].

This last problem seems to be solving itself in metropolitan and suburban areas of many countries, simply by competition between providers, but the problems of long dark fiber paths that cross jurisdictions and require amplification have yet to be faced. In the United States, the Federal Communications Commission has viewed dark fiber as being equivalent to copper, within the meaning of the Communication Act of 1934. It is recommended that if the public interest requires making dark fiber ends available, one of the monopoly obligations implied by monopoly privileges is that the public should be offered it at a fair price.

The optoelectronic component cost issue is under active attack. Considering that there are significant efforts under way to use lithography for cost reduction of tunable and multichannel WDM transmitters and receivers, it seems possible to predict a one-order-of-magnitude decrease in price by 2005 and two orders of magnitude by 2010. This implies that the optoelectronics for each end of WDM links of 32 wavelengths should cost $10 K and $1.0 K, respectively, and that the optoelectronics in each node of a broadcast and select network of 32 to 128 nodes should cost $500 and $50, respectively. If these last numbers are correct, this means that broadcast and select MANs and LANs should be usable by desktop machines some time between 2005 and 2010, since the costs would be competitive with the several hundred dollars people typically spend year after year on each modem or LAN card for PCs.

The sources of investment in the *last fiber mile* are problematic. In the United States the telcos and the cable companies are encountering economic problems in completing the job. In several other countries with strong traditions of centralized telecommunication authority, for example, Japan and Germany, a shortcut may be taken using public money in the name of the public interest. So far in the United States, it is *pay as you go*. This has meant that only businesses can afford to rent dark fiber, and even then this has often been economical only when WDM has been available to reduce the number of strands required.

Final Words

Whether a completely laissez-faire approach to the last mile is appropriate is one of the problems governments are facing in connection with their information infrastructures. Fiber has 10 orders of magnitude more bandwidth (25,000 GHz vs. 3.5 kHz). It can also operate with 10 orders of magnitude better raw bit error rates than can voice grade copper (1015 vs. 105). And yet, on the modest base of copper, we have built the Internet, the World Wide Web, $5 telephones at the supermarket, communicating PCs and laptops, prevalent fax and answering machine resources, and other innovations. It is the vision of those working on all-optical networking that a medium with 10 orders of magnitude better bandwidth, and an error rate (less than one that gave us today's communication miracles) is unlikely to give us a future any less miraculous, once the fiber paths, the network technology, and the user understanding are all in place.

Finally, the opportunity for the cabling industry to become a full information network provider today is a reality when utilizing the technology and specification process described in this chapter and book. For over 12 years, network technologists in the computer and cable industry have been working toward this end. The time has arrived with the convergence of high-speed bandwidth technology development and societal trends to deploy interactive cable applications and services throughout communities everywhere in the coming millennium. All elements are in place, and deployment is underway to ensure that there will be a new dawn for the cabling industry well after the midnight of the next century. See you there!

NOTES

[1]   "The Seven Secrets to Specifying Cable," Cable and Wire Central, Berk-Tek, 132 White Oak Road, New Holland, PA 17557, USA, 2000, p. 2.

[2]   P.E. Green, Jr., "The Fiber-Optic Challenge of Information Infrastructures," National Academy Press, 2101 Constitution Avenue, NW, Lockbox 285, Washington, DC 20055 (IBM Thomas J. Watson Research Center, headquarters for the IBM Research Division, Located in Westchester County, New York (Hawthorne and Yorktown Heights); Corporate Offices, International Business Machines Corporation, New Orchard Road, Armonk, NY 10504), 2000.

[3]   Michel W. Chbat, "Managing Polarization Mode Dispersion," Photonics Spectra, Laurin Publishing, Berkshire Common, PO Box 4949, Pittsfield, MA 01202-4949, Vol. 34, Issue 6 (June, 2000). [Alcatel, Headquarters, 54 Rue La Boétie – 75008, Paris, France].

[4]   Tom Lecklider, "Transporting Heavy Data is Light Work," EE - Evaluation Engineering, Nelson Publishing, 2500 Tamiami Trail North, Nokomis, FL 34275, Vol. 39, No. 2 (February, 2000).

Appendices

List of Fiber Channel Products, Organizations, and High-Energy Projects and Applications

The information explosion and the need for high-performance communications for server-to-storage and server-to-server networking have been the focus of much attention during the 1990s and 2000. Performance improvements in storage, processors, and workstations, along with the move to distributed architectures such as client/server, have spawned increasingly data-intensive and high-speed networking applications. The interconnection between these systems and their input/output devices demands a new level of performance in reliability, speed, and distance. Fiber channel, a highly reliable, gigabit interconnect technology allows concurrent communications among workstations, mainframes, servers, data storage systems, and other peripherals using SCSI and IP protocols. It provides interconnect systems for multiple topologies that can scale to a total system bandwidth on the order of a terabit per second. Fiber channel delivers a new level of reliability and throughput. Switches, hubs, storage systems, storage devices, and adapters are among the products that are on the market today, providing the ability to implement a total system solution.

The following URLs are subject to change without notice!

FIBER CHANNEL PRODUCTS

- Products by manufacturer—
  http://hsi.web.cern.ch/HSI/fcs/manufac/manufac.htm
- Testers—http://hsi.web.cern.ch/HSI/fcs/testing.html
- Fabrics—http://hsi.web.cern.ch/HSI/fcs/event.html
- Interfaces—http://hsi.web.cern.ch/HSI/fcs/processing.html
- Storage devices—http://hsi.web.cern.ch/HSI/fcs/storage.html
- Routers (Ethernet, FDDI, token ring, ATM)—
  http://hsi.web.cern.ch/HSI/fcs/other/routers.htm
- Concentrators/hubs—http://hsi.web.cern.ch/HSI/fcs/other/concent.htm
- SCSI converters—http://hsi.web.cern.ch/HSI/fcs/other/scsi.htm
- Extenders—http://hsi.web.cern.ch/HSI/fcs/other/extender.htm
- Components (chips, cables, etc.)—
  http://hsi.web.cern.ch/HSI/fcs/comps.htm
- Software and services—http://hsi.web.cern.ch/HSI/fcs/sw/sw.htm

FIBER CHANNEL ORGANIZATIONS

- Fiber Channel Association (FCA)—http://www.fibrechannel.com/
- Fiber Channel Consortium (University of New Hampshire's InterOperability Lab)—http://www.iol.unh.edu/consortiums/fc/index.html

HIGH-ENERGY PHYSICS PROJECTS AND PRODUCTS

- Projects and applications—
  http://hsi.web.cern.ch/HSI/fcs/applic/applic.htm
- Readout/buffer modules—http://hsi.web.cern.ch/HSI/fcs/readout.html

List of Top Cable Installation Companies

The following statements have been taken from information contained in the descriptions at the websites listed for each of the cable installation companies listed below. The author does not personally promote or endorse any of these products or companies.

1. **Arguss Holdings, Inc.**: Installers of structured cabling systems and fiber optic installations.

   http://www.argx.com/

2. **Atlantic Netcom Limited (Atlantic Canadian IT infrastructure company)**: Supplier, installer, and manager of network and communication hardware and software components.

   http://www.atlnetcom.ca/

3. **Austin Connection, Inc.**: Installers of local area network cabling and topologies, including fiber optic, data, voice, com-gear, and cable assemblies.

   http://www.theaustinconnection.com/

4. **BF Datacom**: Designers and installers of data communications.

   http://www.bfdatacom.com/

5. **Cabling Company, The**: Installers of networking and cabling systems.

   http://www.btinternet.com/~cablingco/

6. **CCS Network Cabling**: Specializes in the proper installation of category 5+ structured cabling systems for computer networks.

   http://c-c-s.netfirms.com/netcabling.html

7. **Cedar Falls Communications**: Installers of structured cabling systems and fiber optic installations.

   http://www.frognet.net/~waddell/cedar.html

8. **Central Data Installations**: Specializes in voice and data cabling for LANs and WANs.

   http://www.cabling.co.uk/coinfo.htm

9. **Certified Cabling Company, Inc.**: Installers of all types of media cabling including voice, data, fiber optics, coax; certified technicians.

   http://www.geocities.com/SouthBeach/Boardwalk/6961/ccci.html

10. **CNS Group**: A strategic IT infrastructure consulting, systems integration, and project management company in southern Connecticut.

    http://www.cnsgroup.com/cabling.html

11. **Coastal Computer Connections, Inc.**: Installers of structured cabling; offer training, consulting, and Web page design.

    http://ccccable.com/

12. **Comlinx**: Supplier of structured cabling and equipment for business. Communication services include voice and data cable installation, network design, and consulting.

    http://www.comlinx.net/services.html

13. **Comm Plus Corporation**: Provider of outside plant cabling and splicing as well as interior LAN and voice wiring.

    http://www.comm-plus-corp.com/

14. **Communications Information Software (CIS), Inc.**: Developer of fiber optic cable utility software and integrated broadband and telephony engineering for network management in telecommunications.

    http://www.cisfocus.com/

15. **CompuNet Systems Solutions, Inc.**: Installer of LAN and MAN cabling.

    http://www.computer-networks.com/

16. **Computer Power Systems, Inc.**: Installers of structured cabling systems and fiber optic installations.

    http://www.4cps.com/

17. **Computrad Europe Ltd.**: Provides network services including installation, support, and network management.

    http://www.computrad.co.uk/srvprj.htm

18. **ComSignal Technologies, Inc.**: A full-service network cabling contractor supplying network connectivity services throughout the national capital region.

    http://www.amtech.ca/Comsignal/profile.html

19. **Comtech**: Installers of copper cabling, fiber optic, or wireless computer networking systems.

    http://www.jacktojack.com/

20. **Connectivity, Inc.**: Installers of cable for data and voice networks.

    http://www.cableme.com/

21. **Craig Communications**: Designers/consultants/installers of data/voice and fiber optic cabling; RCDD and RCDD LAN specialization.

    http://www.craigcable.com/

22. **CRC Networks & Cables, Inc.**: Installers of voice, data, and fiber optics.

    http://www.crcnet.net/

23. **Custom Cable Industries**: Installation contracting services for communications and network cabling.

    http://www.customcable.com/Install/index.htm

24. **CyberZone, Inc.**: Network cabling installation and solutions and complete solutions for workstation to server, including firewalls and security features.

    http://www.cyberzone-inc.com/services/networking.shtml

25. **DataComm Networks**: Manufacturer of custom OEM compatible cables.

    http://www.dcninc.com/redo/cabling.htm

26. **Data Link Installations**: Installers of copper and fiber optics.

    http://www.datalink.demon.co.uk/

27. **Data Technologies, Inc.**: Installers of structured cabling systems and fiber optic installations.

    http://www.dtcable.com/

28. **Dayton's Computer Networking & Custom Network Cabling Installation Providers**: Computer network cabling installation and support, Internet services, and custom programming.

    http://www.sbsr.com/

29. **DBLS**: A full-service network integration company with extensive experience in the design, installation, and maintenance of local area networks, wide area networks, Internet hosts, and WWW.

    http://www.dbls.com/landesign.htm

30. **Direct Communications Systems**: Installers of structured cabling systems and fiber optic installations.

    http://www.dircomsys.com/

31. **EastNet Communications, Inc.**: A full-service network integration company with extensive experience in the design, installation, and maintenance of local area networks, wide area networks, Internet hosts, and WWW.

    http://eastnet.com/

32. **Florida Intranet Group, Inc.**: Installers of network cable in both copper and optical fiber. Designers and installers of networks for both LANs and WANs.

    http://www.figconnect.com/

33. **Golden Communications**: Fiber optic cabling installation, telecommunications, etc.

    http://www.goldencabling.com/index.html

34. **Hess Communication Services**@: Installers of structured cabling systems and fiber optic installations.

    http://www.yahoo.com/Regional/U_S_States/New_Hampshire/
    Cities/Danville/Business/Hess_Communication_Services/

35. **IDE Ltd.**: Data, voice, fiber, and electrical installation.

    http://www.ide-ltd.co.uk/lan.htm

36. **Id Reseaux**: Installers and engineers of standardized cables compatible to all standards of networks.

    http://www.id-reseaux.com/

37. **Integrated Computer Services**: Designers and installers of SCS for data, voice, and video conferencing applications.

    http://www.intcs.com/

38. **InteliSite Group**: Installers of structured cabling systems and fiber optic installations.

  http://www.drawwire.com/

39. **ITT Cannon Network Systems & Services**: Installers of structured cabling systems and fiber optic installations.

  http://www.ittnss.com/

40. **K2 Communications, Inc.**: A network and mainframe cable installation specialist.

  http://www.k2-comm.com/serv04.htm

41. **Kelly Technical Services Ltd.**: Installers of fiber optic cable.

  http://www.kts.co.uk/

42. **LanPro Communications, Inc.**: Designers, engineers, and installers of LAN, including fiber optics, cat5, UTP, coax, and wireless.

  http://www.lpcommunications.com/

43. **Len Andrews Enterprises, Inc.**: Designers and installers of fiber optic, twisted pair, and coaxial cable systems, including maintenance and computer networking services.

  http://www.lae.mb.ca/

44. **MBC Partnership Ltd.**: Installers of cat5 and fiber networks, including hubs, routers, etc.

  http://ds.dial.pipex.com/mbc/

45. **MCA Communications, Inc.**: Involved in all phases of high technology for voice, data, and fiber, including installation, maintenance of equipment, consultation, supplier, engineering, and technical contract personnel.

  http://www.broadband-guide.com/company2/mcacom.html

46. **NetPlanner Systems, Inc.**: Installers of fiber optic and category 5 cabling systems, including certification.

  http://www.nplanner.com/

47. **Network Cabling**: Installers of structured cabling, including certification, consultation, and support.

  http://www.networkcabling.com/

48. **Network Design Systems**: A Denver-based network cable installation company.

  http://www.netdesignsys.com/begin.html

49. **OnLine-Networking**: Installers of structured wiring systems, copper and fiber, for data networking.

    http://www.online-networking.inter.net/

50. **Open Networks Engineering Ltd.**: Installers of structured cabling systems and fiber optic installations.

    http://www.one.co.uk/

51. **Optec Communications, Inc.**: Network cabling services including structured cabling installation of local and wide area networks; voice, data, audio, and video systems; fiber optics, etc.

    http://www.optec.net/company/installation.html

52. **PCCI Inc.**: Installers of computer cabling and consulting in South Florida.

    http://members.icanect.net/~igorb/

53. **Pentos Systems**: Provides network cabling and support services to commercial, industrial, and public sector organizations in a wide range of system environments, including IBM, DEC, HP, APPLE, ICL, and many others.

    http://www.pentos.co.uk/cabling.htm

54. **PerfectSite**: Designers and managers of structured cabling.

    http://www.perfectsite.com/

55. **Perry Electric**: Installers of network cabling systems, including network cabling services.

    http://www.brookings.com/perry/network.htm

56. **Pirelli Jacobson, Inc.**: Installers of worldwide submarine power and telecommunications cables.

    http://www.pjiinc.com/

57. **Powerlink Plus**: Network cabling contractor. Installation of communication cable for industry, schools, office, and home.

    http://www.powerlinkplusinc.com/

58. **Professional Network Services**: Consultants for all types of networking.

    http://www.pnsnet.com/

59. **Protocol Voice and Data Systems, Inc.**: Installers of voice, data, audio, and video systems.

    http://www.pvds.com/

60. **Quality Cable Installations**: Installers of business telephone and computer network cabling in the central Massachusetts area.

http://www.qciathol.com/

61. **S.T. Communications**: Designers and implementers of services for structured data and telecommunications cabling systems.

http://www.stcc.com/

62. **Staley, Inc.**: Data cabling and telecommunications installation company.

http://www.staleyinc.com/index.html

63. **Source Communications LLP**: Distributors, manufactures, and installers of products for organized communication and point-of-sale networks.

http://www.source-communications.com/

64. **Suttle Apparatus Corp.**: Manufacturers of on-premise voice, high-speed data connectors, and related wiring devices.

http://www.suttleapp.com/

65. **TCH**: Installers of fiber optics, networks, CAT 5, and telecommunications equipment.

http://www.cablerunners.com/homepage.html

66. **Valley Communications Inc.**: Installers of network communications, specializing in LAN, WAN, fiber optic, and copper cabling.

http://www.valleycom.com/

67. **Woods Incorporated**: Installers and designers of networks, including consulting, troubleshooting, equipment, and structured wiring.

http://www.woodsnet.com/

The preceding URLs are subject to change without notice.

List of Top Fiber Optic Cable Companies

 The following statements have been taken from information contained in the descriptions at the websites listed for each of the fiber optic cable companies listed below. The author does not personally promote or endorse any of these products or companies.

1. **Abaca Fiber Optics**: Installer of CCTV and network cabling, including electrical service and installations.

   http://www.dreamsoft.com/abaca/home.htm

2. **Abacusa Optical Mechanical**: Creator of fiber optic sensors: Fiber optic contact, pressure, impact, counter, intrusion, edge sensors.

   http://www.abacusa.com/aom/

3. **ADC Fibermux**: Installer of fiber optic cable.

   http://www.yahoo.com/Business_and_Economy/Companies/ Computers/Hardware/Components/Cables_and_Connectors/ Fiber_Optics/ADC_Fibermux/

4. **ADVA Optical Service & Solutions**: Supplier and provider of new and advanced fiber optic systems.

   http://www.advaoptical.com/

5. **Advance Fiber Optics**: Providers of optical fiber testing, documentation, and connectivity.

   http://www.advancefiber.com/

6. **Advanced Communications Technologies**: Providers of engineering services for fiber optics.

   http://www.uswi.com/actfiber.htm

7. **Advanced Custom Applications, Inc.**: Manufacturer of fiber optics splices for both mechanical and fusion splicing, along with supporting products.

   http://www.aca-inc.com/

8. **Aliant Communications**: Fiber optics installer.

   http://www.aliant.com/prodserv/fiberoptics.html

9. **Ancor Communications**: Installer of fiber optic cable.

   http://www.yahoo.com/Business_and_Economy/Companies/
   Computers/Hardware/Components/Cables_and_Connectors/
   Fiber_Optics/Ancor_Communications/

10. **APA Optics, Inc.**: Manufacturer and marketer of products for the fiber optic communications, optoelectronics, and laser industries.

    http://www.apaoptics.com/

11. **Arcade Electronics, Inc.**: Supplier of fiber optics, industrial electronics, and cable. Wide range of products supporting the fiber optic and electronics industry.

    http://www.arcade-electronics.com/

12. **Astarte Fiber Networks, Inc.**: Provider of photonic fiber optic cross-connect systems for physical level fiber management including ATM, FDDI, and SONET for test access, disaster recovery, etc.

    http://www.starswitch.com/

13. **Auriga Fibre Optics**: Provider of fiber optic online catalog and products.

    http://www.auriganet.com/

14. **Belden**: Installation and construction of fiber optic cables.

    http://www.belden.com/products/040999pr.htm

15. **Broadband Communications Products, Inc.**: Provider of fiber optic data communications equipment and high-speed fiber optic test instruments.

    http://www.iu.net/bcp/

16. **Broadband Networks, Inc.**: Provider of AM and FM fiber optic transmission equipment for interactive video and data applications.

      http://www.bnisolutions.com/

17. **Brugg Telecom AG**: Manufacturer of fiber optic cables and systems for data, utility, CATV, and telecom applications.

      http://www.brugg.com/

18. **Cable Talk Pty. Ltd.**: Distributor of fiber optic cables, custom fiber optic cable assemblies, fiber optic connectors, and all necessary tooling, test equipment, and consumables.

      http://www.fibreoptic.com.au/cabletalk/

19. **Cables of Zion**: Manufacturer of fiber optic, telecommunication, and high-voltage cable.

      http://www.coz-cables.co.il/

20. **CIENA**: Installer of fiber optic cable.

      http://www.yahoo.com/Business_and_Economy/Companies/
      Computers/Hardware/Components/Cables_and_Connectors/
      Fiber_Optics/CIENA/

21. **Communication Cable Company**: Supplier of custom cable assemblies and structured wiring components for the data communication industry.

      http://www.commcable.com/index.htm

22. **Comnet Asia Pacific Pte Ltd.**: Provider of fiber optic cable assemblies.

      http://www.comapl.com/

23. **Computer Cabling Products International, Inc.**: Distributor and installer of fiber optic supplies and cables, including reusable fiber optic connectors.

      http://www.ccpiinc.com/

24. **Computer System Products, Inc. (CSP)**: Manufacturer and supplier of fiber optic and copper cable assemblies for premise cabling applications. Also supplier of LAN/WAN hardware for Ethernet and token ring systems.

      http://www.csp.com/home.asp

25. **Condux International, Inc.**: Manufacturer of tools and equipment for fiber optic, CATV, telephone, and power cable installation. Also sup-

plier of products to telephone and power utilities, CATV companies, and contractors.

   http://www.condux.com/

26. **Data Optics**: Provider of fiber optic and telecommunication technology.

   http://www.dataoptics.co.uk/

27. **Datapac, Inc.**: Designer of telecommunications products, such as patch panels and wire managers, which meet specific product requirements.

   http://www.datapacinc.com/

28. **DESIGNet, Inc.**: Designer, engineer, and installer of communications cabling systems for all voice and data applications.

   http://www.desnet.com/

29. **Digital-Delivery Systems**: Provider of fiber optic and network installation, certification, and documentation.

   http://www.digital-delivery.com/

30. **E-Tek Dynamics, Inc.**: Provider of fiber optic passive components, active devices, test equipment, and systems.

   http://www.e-tek.com/

31. **E/O Networks**: Developer, manufacturer, and distributor of next-generation fiber access telephone networks.

   http://www.eonetworks.com/

32. **ElectroPhotonics Corporation**: Manufacturer of hardware and software products for fiber optic telecommunication and sensing industries.

   http://www.electrophotonics.com/

33. **Fiber Optic Marketplace**: Provider of fiber optic information, products, and services.

   http://fiberoptic.com/

34. **Fiber Optic Technologies, Inc.**: Provider of fiber optics technologies for fiber optic network connectivity, as well as network services and desktop support.

   http://www.teleport.com/toc/404.html

35. **Fiber Plus International**: Designer and manufacturer of fiber optic tools, components, and connection devices.

   http://www.fiberplus.com/

36. **Fiber Systems International**: Provider of mil spec fiber optic connectors for all applications.

    http://www.fibersystems.com/

37. **Fibercore Ltd.**: Manufacturer of single-mode optical fibers for special applications.

    http://www.fibercore.com/

38. **Fiberguide Industries, Inc.**: Manufacturer of specialty fiber optic products.

    http://www.fiberguide.com/

39. **FiberPlex, Inc.**: Designer and manufacturer of communications products. Also, provider of fiber optic technology used to solve security, noise, and distance problems.

    http://www.fiberguide.com/

40. **Fibertron**: Distributor and value-added reseller of fiber optic cable and components.

    http://www.fibertron.com/

41. **FiberWare, Inc.**: Manufacturer of passive fiber optic interconnect hardware for the LAN, CATV, and Telco applications.

    http://www.fiberwareinc.com/p3link.htm

42. **Fiberworks, Inc.**: Seller and installer of advanced communications systems using high-performance fiber optic technology.

    http://www.fiberworks.com/

43. **Fibre Optic Communications Ltd.**: Manufacturer of fiber optic cable assemblies, patch panels, and reseller of fiber optic connectors. Distributor for Belden fiber cable in the United Kingdom.

    http://www.fibrecomms.co.uk/

44. **Fibre-Data Group Ltd.**: Installer of fiber optic cable.

    http://www.fibredata.co.uk/

45. **FIS—Fiber Instrument Sales, Inc.**: Provider of fiber optics and technical assistance.

    http://www.fisfiber.com/

46. **Fitel-PMX@**: Installer of fiber optic cable.

    http://www.yahoo.com/Regional/Countries/Canada/Provinces_
    and_Territories/Ontario/Counties_and_Regions/Ottawa_
    Carleton_Regional_Municipality/Nepean/Business/Fitel_PMX/

47. **Focas, Inc.**: Providers of fiber optic cables, accessories, and sensors. Manufacturers of fiber optic aerial cables to be installed on transmission and distribution lines.

    http://www.focas.com/

48. **Fotec**: Providers of fiber optic training and testing products.

    http://www.std.com/fotec/dct.htm

49. **GC Technologies**: Developer, manufacturers, and sellers of fiber optic products including passive components and subassembly polishing equipment, accessories, and enclosures.

    http://www.gctechnologies.com/p_cblass.html

50. **Gibson Technical Services**: Providers of communications engineering services for fiber optics.

    http://www.gibsontech.com/

51. **Glenair, Inc.**: Fiber optic components and assemblies.

    http://www.glenair.com/brochure/page9.htm

52. **Global Fiber Optics**: Providers of fiber optics: custom patch cords, training, OTDR testing, fiber installation, fiber LANs and LAN hardware/software.

    http://www.global-fiber-optics.com/

53. **GMS Fiber Optic Cable**: Provides cable assemblies, computer cables, and custom cable assemblies.

    http://www.gmsco.com/fiber.html

54. **Hangzhou Chengfeng Electric Appliance Corporation**: Manufacturer of fiber optic cables and terminal equipment.

    http://www.chengfeng.com/

55. **Harmonic Lightwaves, Inc.**: Supplier of integrated fiber optic transmission, digital headend, and element management systems for interactive broadband networks.

    http://www.harmonic-lightwaves.com/

56. **Hitachi Cable Manchester, Inc.**: Fiber optic cable for premises applications.

    http://www.broadband-guide.com/expert/askhitachicbl1.html

57. **Integrated Optical Components Ltd. (IOC)**: Designer and manufacturer of integrated optical devices.

    http://www.intopt.com/

58. **International CableTel Incorporated**: Developer, constructor, and operator of broadband communications systems outside the United States, which provide integrated last mile telecommunications services to both business and residential customers.

    http://www.cabletel.com/

59. **International Fiberoptic Technologies, Inc.**: Producer of passive fiber optic couplers with low db loss.

    http://www.ift-info.com/

60. **J.L. Import and Export**: Dealer in fiber optic connectors, adaptors, and attenuators.

    http://www.jlfiber.com/

61. **Jerry Conn Associates**: Distributor of fiber optics, fiber optic closures, fiber optic test equipment, RF broadband, and headend.

    http://www.jerryconn.com/

62. **JM Fiber Optics, Inc.**: Provider of voice, video, and data applications as well as products, technical support, and fiber optic training.

    http://www.jmfiberoptics.com/

63. **KNS Technologies, Inc.**: Provider of fiber optic cable products.

    http://www.knstech.com/

64. **Lee Data Communications**: Manufacturer of fiber optic audio, video, and data transmission equipment.

    http://members.aol.com/johannlee/lee-data.htm

65. **Light Brigade, The**: Installer of fiber optic cable.

    http://www.lightbrigade.com/

66. **Lite-Tech**: Provider of fiber optic needs of clients across the continental United States.

    http://home.earthlink.net/~litetech/

67. **Meridian Technologies, Inc.**: Designer and manufacturer of fiber optic communication systems for video, voice, and data.

    http://www.meridian-tech.com/

68. **Metrotek Industries, Inc.**: Distributor of fiber optic stocking for connectors, adaptors, cable assemblies, etc.

    http://www.metrotek.com/

69. **Micro Electronics, Inc.**: Provider of Micro-Strip and Soft-Strip precision fiber optic stripping tools, coating strippers, jacket strippers, thermal strippers, and ribbon strippers.

    http://www.micro-strip.com/

70. **Miniflex Fibre Optic Products**: Installer and manager of fiber optic systems.

    http://www.miniflex.co.uk/

71. **Moritex U.S.A., Inc.**: Provider of fiber optics, as well as targeting markets such as industrial illumination and sensing, machine vision, cosmetic skin care imaging, pharmaceutical research, and artistic glass products.

    http://www.moritexusa.com/

72. **MRV Communications**: Installer of fiber optic cable.

    http://www.yahoo.com/Business_and_Economy/Companies/
    Computers/Hardware/Components/Cables_and_Connectors/
    Fiber_Optics/MRV_Communications/

73. **National Communications, Inc.**: Supplier of fiber optics products.
    http://www.trynci.com/cat/fiber.htm

74. **Net Optics**: Provider of fiber optic power measurement meter and fiber optic test boxes for analysis of fiber optic network systems assimilation.

    http://www.netoptics.com/

75. **Norscan**: Manufacturer of cable maintenance and monitoring systems that are used on filled copper and fiber optic cable systems.

    http://www.norscan.com/

76. **NuPower Optics**: Installer of fiber optic cable.

    http://www.nupower.com/

77. **Optelecom, Inc.**: Installer of fiber optic cable.

    http://www.yahoo.com/Business_and_Economy/Companies/
    Computers/Hardware/Components/Cables_and_Connectors/
    Fiber_Optics/Optelecom__Inc_/

78. **Optical Cable Corporation**: Installer of fiber optic cable.

    http://www.yahoo.com/Business_and_Economy/Companies/
    Computers/Hardware/Components/Cables_and_Connectors/
    Fiber_Optics/Optical_Cable_Corporation/

79. **Optical Solutions, Inc.**: Manufacturer and integrator of optical receivers, transmitters, and interface devices for broadband fiber-to-the-home networks.

    http://www.opticalsolutions.com/

80. **Optivision, Inc.**: Provider of optical switching, optical amplifiers, optical interconnects, optical computing, optical backplanes, optical signal processing, fiber optic networks, fiber optic sensing, optoelectronic systems design, and image compression.

    http://www.optivision.com/

81. **Pacific Fiberoptics, Inc.**: Installer of fiber optic cable.

    http://www.yahoo.com/Regional/U_S__States/California/Cities/Santa_Clara/Business/Computers/Pacific_Fiberoptics__Inc/

82. **Photon Technologies (Malaysia) Sdn Bhd**: Manufacturer of optical fiber and optical fiber cables.

    http://www.jaring.my/photon/

83. **Photonic Integration Research, Inc.**: Maker of integrated optical waveguide devices in silica.

    http://www.piri.com/

84. **Physical Optics Corporation**: Manufacturer and seller of fiber optic communications equipment and holographic diffusers for display screens.

    http://www.poc.com/

85. **Polycore Technologies**: Producer of high-performance fiber optic communication systems for industrial, automotive, utility, and process control applications.

    http://www.pcore.com/

86. **Princeton Optics, Inc.**: Supplier of off-the-shelf and custom-made fiber optic components to customers around the world.

    http://www.princetonoptics.com/

87. **R&M's International WebSite**: Manufacturer of copper/fiber optic distribution systems/generic cabling systems for voice, video, and data applications.

    http://www.rdm.ch/

88. **Radiant Communications Corporation**: Provider of fiber optic assemblies, connectors, couplers, patch and splice cabinets. Also, provider of video, audio, and data transmission systems for CATV and distant learning applications.

    http://www.radcom.com/

89. **Schott Fibre Optics**: Installer of fiber optic cable.

    http://www.schott.co.uk/

90. **Spectran**: Installer of fiber optic cable.

    http://www.yahoo.com/Business_and_Economy/Companies/
    Computers/Hardware/Components/Cables_and_Connectors/
    Fiber_Optics/Spectran/

91. **Spoval Company, Inc.**: Designer, engineer, and manufacturer of fiber optic interconnect panels.

    http://www.spoval.com/

92. **TC Communications, Inc.**: Manufacturer of fiber optic data and voice communication products including modems, multiplexers, LANs, mode converters, and transceivers.

    http://www.tccomm.com/

93. **Tecra Tools**: Supplier of test equipment, fiber optic cable test kit.

    http://www.tecratools.com/test/fiber.html

94. **TRITEC Developments Ltd.**: UK manufacturer of fiber optic installation equipment, including the FASE II fusion splicer and the TCII+ optical fiber cleaver.

    http://www.tritec-dev.com/

95. **TSX Corp**: Installer of fiber optic cable.

    http://www.yahoo.com/Business_and_Economy/Companies/
    Computers/Hardware/Components/Cables_and_Connectors/
    Fiber_Optics/TSX_Corp/

96. **Uniphase Corporation**: Installer of fiber optic cable.

    http://www.yahoo.com/Business_and_Economy/Companies/
    Electronics/Lasers/Uniphase_Corporation/

97. **VERSITRON**: DS3 fiber optic modems/interface extenders for high-speed applications tech specs.

    http://www.versitron.com/TDFOM5.HTML

98. **Vikimatic Sales, Inc.**: Provider of products for fiber optic cable construction.

   http://www.fibercable.com/

99. **VisionCorp**: Provider of manufacturers products that are being used to build the information superhighway through fiber optic and coax (cable TV) systems.

   http://web.iquest.net/viscorp/index.htm

The preceding URLs are subject to change without notice.

Cabling Directory

The Cabling Directory (www.wiring.com) is an interactive buyer's guide for cabling products as well as for all cabling related topics with direct links to each company's website [1]. In addition, the website is an excellent resource for informational items about today's high-speed network cabling [1]. Select a category below to view some of the sample listings:

The following contact information has been taken from information contained in the descriptions at the websites for each of the companies listed below. The author does not personally promote or endorse any of these companies or their products.

CABLE MANAGEMENT SOFTWARE

Allstar Systems, Inc.
Headquarters: Houston, TX
Phone: 713-795-2400
Geographic region: Houston, Dallas, Austin

Cablesoft, Ltd.
Headquarters: Phoenix, AZ
Phone: 602-708-2000
Geographic region: USA

Teklab
Headquarters: Torrance, CA
Phone: 310-299-1209
Geographic region: Los Angeles

CABLE ASSEMBLIES

Assembletech
Headquarters: Houston, TX
Phone: 713-430-3090
Geographic region: Texas and the southwest

Baycom
Headquarters: Hsinchu, Taiwan
Phone: 886-3-578-6178
Geographic region: North and South America

Cable Systems International
Headquarters: Phoenix, AZ
Phone: 602-233-5171
Geographic region: Worldwide

Computer Cable Connection, Inc.
Headquarters: Bellevue, NE
Phone: 402-291-9500
Geographic region: USA

Crown Electronics
Headquarters: Rockwall, TX
Phone: 972-771-4711
Geographic region: Worldwide

DataWay Design
Headquarters: San Francisco, CA
Phone: 415-882-8700
Geographic region: The San Francisco Peninsula

DV Com Systems
Headquarters: Brooklyn, NY
Phone: 718-756-9650
Geographic region: NY, NJ, CT

Electronic Imaging Materials
Headquarters: Keene, NH
Phone: 603-357-1459
Geographic region: USA

Fishel Technologies
Headquarters: Columbus, OH
Phone: 502-456-9444
Geographic region: USA

Gruber Industries
Headquarters: Phoenix, AZ
Phone: 800-658-5883
Geographic region: Worldwide

Noramco Wire & Cable
Headquarters: Burnaby, BC, Canada
Phone: 604-606-6970
Geographic region: North America

Northwest Cable and Connector Co.
Headquarters: Olympia, WA
Phone: 360-754-3606
Geographic region: USA

Peerless Electronics, Inc.
Headquarters: Lynbrook, NY
Phone: 800-285-2121
Geographic region: USA

Royal Cable Corp.
Headquarters: New York, NY
Phone: 212-293-7323
Geographic region: USA

Sequoia Diversified Products

Headquarters: Auburn Hills, MI

Phone: 810-299-4220

Geographic region: Worldwide

Shine Wire Products, Inc.

Headquarters: Adams, MA

Phone: 1-800-543-5151

Geographic region: Northeast

TEC Datawire

Headquarters: Cleveland, OH

Phone: 440-333-8300

Geographic region: USA

TEC Datawire

Headquarters: Cleveland, OH

Phone: 440-333-8300

Geographic region: USA

CABLE

Assembletech

Headquarters: Houston, TX

Phone: 713-430-3090

Geographic region: Texas and the southwest

Baycom

Headquarters: Hsinchu, Taiwan

Phone: 886-3-578-6178

Geographic region: North and South America

Cable Systems International

Headquarters: Phoenix, AZ

Phone: 602-233-5171

Geographic region: Worldwide

Electronic Imaging Materials
Headquarters: Keene, NH
Phone: 603-357-1459
Geographic region: USA

Futronix Systems Corp.
Headquarters: Houston, TX
Phone: 713-329-1100
Geographic region: Houston, TX

PMC Corporation
Headquarters: Manchester, NH
Phone: 250-480-1311
Geographic region: USA, Canada

Quabbin Wire & Cable Co., Inc.
Headquarters: Ware, MA
Phone: 413-967-3117
Geographic region: North America, Europe

CONNECTORS

AMP Netconnect
Headquarters: Harrisburg, PA
Phone: 503-650-9466
Geographic region: Oregon, SW Washington

CONNECTING HARDWARE

Ahern Communications Corporation
Headquarters: Quincy, MA
Phone: 617-471-1100
Geographic region: Worldwide

Cable Plus, Inc.
Headquarters: Deer Park, NY
Phone: 516-586-7587
Geographic region: USA

Policom Cabos E Conectores Ltda
Headquarters: Sao Paulo, Brazil
Phone: 55-11-6914-4788
Geographic region: Brazil

Specialized Engineering Services
Headquarters: Derby, Derbyshire, UK
Phone: 44-13-3238-3345
Geographic region: UK

Wandel & Goltermann
Headquarters: Research Triangle Park, NC
Phone: 847-918-9292
Geographic region: Southeast

DISTRIBUTORS

ABTECH Computer
Headquarters: Annapolis, MD
Phone: 410-295-9000
Geographic region: Mid-Atlantic

Ahern Communications Corporation
Headquarters: Quincy, MA
Phone: 617-471-1100
Geographic region: Worldwide

Asia Wiring Systems Pte Ltd.
Headquarters: Singapore
Phone: 2831445
Geographic region: Asia

Astec Hong Kong Limited
Headquarters: Central, Hong Kong
Phone: 852-2815-2425
Geographic region: Southeast Asia

Atlantic Cable International
Headquarters: Houston, Texas
Phone: 713-699-2000
Geographic region: Worldwide

Cable Plus, Inc.
Headquarters: Deer Park, NY
Phone: 516-586-7587
Geographic region: USA

CableCentral
Headquarters: Costa Mesa, CA
Phone: 714-636-5960
Geographic region: USA

Diversified Automation
Headquarters: Ringwood, NJ
Phone: 973-616-4943
Geographic region: NY, NJ, CT, PA

Electrotex, Inc.
Headquarters: Houston, TX
Phone: 713-526-3456
Geographic region: TX, OK, MS, LA, AR

Fibertron Corporation
Headquarters: Buena Park, CA
Phone: 630-978-1501
Geographic region: USA

Futronix Systems Corp.
Headquarters: Houston, TX
Phone: 713-329-1100
Geographic region: USA

H & L Enterprises, Inc.
Headquarters: Bostic, NC
Phone: 704-248-3939
Geographic region: Eastern USA

Knurr AG

Headquarters: Munich, Germany

Phone: +49(0)89/42004-0

Geographic region: Worldwide

LANequip

Headquarters: Quebec

Phone: 514-939-2163

Geographic region: Quebec, Ontario

Noramco Wire & Cable

Headquarters: Burnaby, BC, Canada

Phone: 604-606-6970

Geographic region: North America

Northwest Cable and Connector Co.

Headquarters: Olympia, WA

Phone: 360-754-3606

Geographic region: USA

Peerless Electronics, Inc.

Headquarters: Lynbrook, NY

Phone: 800-285-2121

Geographic region: USA

Policom Cabos E Conectores Ltda

Headquarters: Sao Paulo, Brazil

Phone: 55-11-6914-4788

Geographic region: Brazil

Royal Cable Corp.

Headquarters: New York, NY

Phone: 212-293-7323

Geographic region: USA

Shine Wire Products, Inc.

Headquarters: Adams, MA

Phone: 800-543-5151

Geographic region: Northeast

SPC Technologies Corporation

Headquarters: Manila, Philippine Islands

Phone: 632-551-0948

Geographic region: Southeast Asia

TEC Datawire

Headquarters: Cleveland, OH

Phone: 440-333-8300

Geographic region: USA

ENCLOSURES

BUD Industries

Headquarters: Willoughby, OH

Phone: 1-216-946-3200

Geographic region: Worldwide

Knurr AG

Headquarters: Munich, Germany

Phone: N/A

Geographic region: Worldwide

NER Data Products

Headquarters: Glassboro, NJ

Phone: 800-257-5235

Geographic region: USA

Rittal Corporation

Headquarters: Springfield, OH

Phone: 1-937-399-0500

Geographic region: Worldwide

Vero Electronics, Inc

Headquarters: Wallingford, CT

Phone: 800-242-2863

Geographic region: Worldwide

Engineering

ASD

Headquarters: Atlanta, GA

Phone: 800-CABLING

Geographic region: Worldwide

Communications Resource Group

Headquarters: Ft. Lauderdale, FL

Phone: 954-436-3900

Geographic region: International

Computel Network Services Corp.

Headquarters: Richardson, TX

Phone: 972-437-9676

Geographic region: South central USA

CPSI

Headquarters: Riverdale, CA

Phone: 909-354-7191

Geographic region: CA, OR, NV

Digital Delivery Systems

Headquarters: Fort Collins, CO

Phone: 970-221-3018

Geographic region: Rocky Mountain Region

E.R. Haskins Cable Consulting

Headquarters: Burbank, CA

Phone: 818-247-2650

Geographic region: Los Angeles and surrounding area

Fundy Engineering & Consulting Ltd.

Headquarters: Saint John, NB, Canada

Phone: 506-635-1566

Geographic region: Atlantic

GMCI NetComm, Inc.
Headquarters: Dallas, TX
Phone: 972-241-2425
Geographic region: TX

Interconnect Services, Inc.
Headquarters: Baltimore, MD
Phone: 410-687-8900
Geographic region: USA

K St. James, Inc.
Headquarters: York, PA
Phone: 717-244-0653
Geographic region: USA

Key Services, Inc.
Headquarters: Tucker, GA
Phone: 919-831-2528
Geographic region: Southeast USA

Merolan, Inc.
Headquarters: New York, NY
Phone: 914-245-4139
Geographic region: NY, NJ, CT

Micro Metrology, Inc.
Headquarters: Chatsworth, CA
Phone: 818-993-4971
Geographic region: Worldwide

NetCom Management Group
Headquarters: Phoenix, AZ
Phone: 602-470-4070
Geographic region: USA

PDS Consultants
Headquarters: Homosassa, FL
Phone: 352-621-5549
Geographic region: Southeast USA

Pinnacle Communication Services

Headquarters: Glendale, CA

Phone: 818-241-6009

Geographic region: CA, Worldwide

ProCom Technologies, Inc.

Headquarters: Twinsburg, OH

Phone: 330-425-7289

Geographic region: Northern OH

Royal Communications Consultants

Headquarters: New York, NY

Phone: 212-293-7323

Geographic region: USA

Tele-Tech Company, Inc.

Headquarters: Lexington, KY

Phone: 606-275-7503

Geographic region: USA

The State Group Ltd.

Headquarters: Etobicoke, Ontario, Canada

Phone: 416-240-0610

Geographic region: Ontario

Waldec/IKON Technology Services

Headquarters: Tampa, Florida

Phone: 813-282-4008

Geographic region: FL, PA

Waldec/IKON Technology Services

Headquarters: Tampa, FL

Phone: 813-880-7600

Geographic region: USA

Wiring Architects

Headquarters: Hurst, TX

Phone: 817-589-7483

Geographic region: TX, the south

INSTALLATION COMPANIES

1st Alliance Communications, Inc.
Headquarters: Englewood, CO
Phone: 303-766-7577
Geographic region: Worldwide

ABTECH Computer Services
Headquarters: Annapolis, MD
Phone: 410-295-9000
Geographic region: Mid-Atlantic

Allstar Systems, Inc.
Headquarters: Houston, TX
Phone: 713-795-2400
Geographic region: Houston, Dallas, Austin

ASD
Headquarters: Atlanta, GA
Phone: 800-CABLING
Geographic region: Worldwide

ASI Services Corporation
Headquarters: Atlanta, GA
Phone: 404-888-5555
Geographic region: Atlanta

BenComm
Headquarters: Gaithersburg, MD
Phone: 301-963-3257
Geographic region: Mid-Atlantic

Birnie Data Communications
Headquarters: Toronto, Ontario
Phone: 416-247-2151
Geographic region: Canada

Cable Systems Consulting

Headquarters: Houston, TX

Phone: 281-370-2172

Geographic region: Houston area

Coastal Computer Connections, Inc.

Headquarters: Pensacola, FL

Phone: 904-444-9199

Geographic region: FL, GA, AL

Communication Cabling Services

Headquarters: Corby, Northants, UK

Phone: 44-1536-443700

Geographic region: UK

ComNet Communications, Inc.

Headquarters: Danbury, CT

Phone: 203-794-8045

Geographic region: USA

CompuTeam

Headquarters: Aledo, TX

Phone: 817-244-1158

Geographic region: Aledo, TX

Computel Network Services Corp.

Headquarters: Richardson, TX

Phone: 972-437-9676

Geographic region: south central US

Computer Cable Connection, Inc.

Headquarters: Bellevue, NE

Phone: 402-291-9500

Geographic region: USA

ComputerLand Cabling Division

Headquarters: San Diego, CA

Phone: 619-492-1400

Geographic region: Southern CA

Coyote Cabling

Headquarters: Las Cruces, NM

Phone: 505-525-1422

Geographic region: AZ, NM, TX

CPSI

Headquarters: Riverdale, CA

Phone: 909-354-7191

Geographic region: CA, OR, NV

CSS

Headquarters: White Plains, MD

Phone: 301-870-3870

Geographic region: USA

Data-Tech Communications

Headquarters: Reno, NV

Phone: 702-829-9999

Geographic region: Northern Nevada, Northern California

Dataway Communications, Inc.

Headquarters: Cliffside Park, NJ

Phone: 201-313-0961

Geographic region: NJ, NY, PA, DE

DataWay Design

Headquarters: San Francisco, CA

Phone: 415-882-8700

Geographic region: The San Francisco Peninsula

Digital Delivery Systems

Headquarters: Fort Collins, CO

Phone: 970-221-3018

Geographic region: Rocky Mountain Region

Dinsmore Communications Corp.

Headquarters: Portsmouth, NH

Phone: 603-436-6344

Geographic region: New England, FL

Diversified Automation

Headquarters: Ringwood, NJ

Phone: 973-616-4943

Geographic region: NY, NJ, CT, PA

DV Com Systems

Headquarters: Brooklyn, NY

Phone: 718-756-9650

Geographic region: NY, NJ, CT

E.R. Haskins Cable Consulting

Headquarters: Burbank, CA

Phone: 818-247-2650

Geographic region: Los Angeles and surrounding area

Fishel Technologies

Headquarters: Columbus, OH

Phone: 502-456-9444

Geographic region: USA

GMCI NetComm, Inc.

Headquarters: Dallas, TX

Phone: 972-241-2425

Geographic region: TX

H & L Enterprises, Inc.

Headquarters: Bostic, NC

Phone: 704-248-3939

Geographic region: Eastern USA

H& L Telecom of Florida, Inc.

Headquarters: Pensacola, FL

Phone: 904-968-1892

Geographic region: Southeast, Southwest

Integrated Network Services

Headquarters: Marietta, GA

Phone: 770-751-8881

Geographic region: East Coast

Interconnect Services, Inc.
Headquarters: Baltimore, MD
Phone: 410-687-8900
Geographic region: USA

K St. James, Inc.
Headquarters: York, PA
Phone: 717-244-0653
Geographic region: USA

Key Services, Inc.
Headquarters: Tucker, GA
Phone: 919-831-2528
Geographic region: Southeast

LANequip
Headquarters: Quebec
Phone: 514-939-2163
Geographic region: Quebec, Ontario

M.D. Computer Link
Headquarters: Croydon, Surrey, England
Phone: 01812630252
Geographic region: UK

Merolan, Inc.
Headquarters: New York, NY
Phone: 914-245-4139
Geographic region: NY, NJ, CT

Miken Communications
Headquarters: Milwaukee, WI
Phone: 414-778-2010
Geographic region: WI, Northern IL

NetCom Management Group
Headquarters: Phoenix, AZ
Phone: 602-470-4070
Geographic region: USA

Network Century
Headquarters: Chicago, IL
Phone: 312-243-3416
Geographic region: Chicago area

Newave Communications
Headquarters: Lansing, MI
Phone: 517-226-6953
Geographic region: South MI

North America Telecommunications
Headquarters: Pittsburgh, PA
Phone: (215) 871-7674
Geographic region: Northeast USA

PDS Consultants
Headquarters: Homosassa, FL
Phone: 352-621-5549
Geographic region: Southeast USA

Pinnacle Communication Services
Headquarters: Glendale, CA
Phone: 818-241-6009
Geographic region: CA, Worldwide

ProCom Technologies, Inc.
Headquarters: Twinsburg, OH
Phone: 330-425-7289
Geographic region: Northern Ohio

Protocol Voice and Data Systems
Headquarters: Highland Park, IL
Phone: 847-831-3249
Geographic region: Chicago area

Royal Communications Consultants
Headquarters: New York, NY
Phone: 212-293-7323
Geographic region: USA

Sequoia Diversified Products
Headquarters: Auburn Hills, MI
Phone: 810-299-4220
Geographic region: Worldwide

Sequoia Diversified Products
Headquarters: Auburn Hills, MI
Phone: 248-299-4830
Geographic region: USA

SPC Technologies Corporation
Headquarters: Manila, Philippine Islands
Phone: 632-551-0948
Geographic region: Southeast Asia

Specialized Engineering Services
Headquarters: Derby, Derbyshire, UK
Phone: 44-13-3238-3345
Geographic region: UK

Symbiont, Inc.
Headquarters: Washington, D.C.
Phone: 202-887-6800
Geographic region: USA

Tele-Data Services, Inc.
Headquarters: Warminster, PA
Phone: 215-343-1499
Geographic region: Eastern PA, South NJ, North DE

Tele-Tech Company, Inc.
Headquarters: Lexington, KY
Phone: 606-275-7503
Geographic region: USA

The State Group Ltd.
Headquarters: Etobicoke, Ontario, Canada
Phone: 416-240-0610
Geographic region: Ontario

U.S. Information System
Headquarters: Nyack, NY
Phone: 1-800-358-7756 Ext. 615
Geographic region: Northeast USA

Waldec/IKON Technology Services
Headquarters: Tampa, FL
Phone: 813-282-4008
Geographic region: FL, PA

Waldec/IKON Technology Services
Headquarters: Tampa, FL
Phone: 813-880-7600
Geographic region: USA

Willow Technologies Group, Inc.
Headquarters: Norristown, PA
Phone: 610-539-2333
Geographic region: Greater Mid-Atlantic region

INSTALLATION PRODUCTS

Astec Hong Kong Limited
Headquarters: Hong Kong
Phone: 852-2815-2425
Geographic region: Southeast Asia

Atlantic Cable International
Headquarters: Houston, TX
Phone: 713-699-2000
Geographic region: Worldwide

CableCentral
Headquarters: Costa Mesa, CA
Phone: 714-636-5960
Geographic region: USA

Cablesoft, Ltd.
Headquarters: Phoenix, AZ
Phone: 602-708-2000
Geographic region: USA

Dinsmore Communications Corp.
Headquarters: Portsmouth, NH
Phone: 603-436-6344
Geographic region: New England, FL

Electrotex, Inc.
Headquarters: Houston, TX
Phone: 713-526-3456
Geographic region: TX, OK, MS, LA, AR

M.D. Computer Link
Headquarters: Croydon, Surrey, England
Phone: 01812630252
Geographic region: UK

North America Telecommunications
Headquarters: Pittsburgh, PA
Phone: (215) 871-7674
Geographic region: Northeast USA

Protocol Voice and Data Systems
Headquarters: Highland Park, IL
Phone: 847-831-3249
Geographic region: Chicago area

OPTICAL FIBER

Asia Wiring Systems Pte Ltd.
Headquarters: Singapore
Phone: 2831445
Geographic region: Asia

Birnie Data Communications
Headquarters: Toronto, Ontario
Phone: 416-247-2151
Geographic region: Canada

ComputerLand Cabling Division
Headquarters: San Diego, CA
Phone: 619-492-1400
Geographic region: Southern CA

Fibertron Corporation
Headquarters: Buena Park, CA
Phone: 630-978-1501
Geographic region: USA

Noramco Wire & Cable
Headquarters: Burnaby, BC Canada
Phone: 604-606-6970
Geographic region: North America

RW Data Ltd.
Headquarters: Northampton, UK
Phone: 44 (0) 1604-706633
Geographic region: UK

U.S. Information System
Headquarters: Nyack, NY
Phone: 1-800-358-7756 Ext. 615
Geographic region: Northeast USA

TEST EQUIPMENT

Datacom Technologies
Headquarters: Everett, WA
Phone: 206-355-0590
Geographic region: Worldwide

Micro Metrology, Inc.
Headquarters: Chatsworth, CA
Phone: 818-993-4971
Geographic region: Worldwide

Microtest, Inc.
Headquarters: Phoenix, AZ
Phone: 602-952-6484
Geographic region: Worldwide

Wandel & Goltermann
Headquarters: Research Triangle Park, NC
Phone: 847-918-9292
Geographic region: Southeast USA

TOOLS

Microtest, Inc.
Headquarters: Phoenix, AZ
Phone: 602-952-6484
Geographic region: Worldwide

TRAINING

Communications Resource Group
Headquarters: Ft. Lauderdale, FL
Phone: 954-436-3900
Geographic region: Worldwide

Coastal Computer Connections, Inc.
Headquarters: Pensacola, FL
Phone: 904-444-9199
Geographic region: FL, GA, AL

Telecom Industry Association (TIA-UK)
Headquarters: Milton, Keynes, Buckinghamshire, UK
Phone: 44 (0) 1908-645000
Geographic region: UK, Europe

The preceding contact information is subject to change without notice.

NOTE

[1]   John D. Colodny, RCDD "The Cabling Directory," C/O connect.ad, Inc., 1000 West McNab Road, Suite 236, Pompano Beach, FL 33069, 2000.

EENET Interconnect Directory

The EENet's Interconnect Directory (http://www.eenet.com/intc/index.html) is a comprehensive listing of interconnect companies in different categories. Select a category below to view the listings.

The following contact information has been taken from information contained in the descriptions at the websites for each of the interconnect companies in different categories. The author does not personally promote or endorse any of the interconnect companies in different categories or their products.

MANUFACTURERS

1. A thru C listing: http://www.eenet.com/intc/a-c.htm
2. D thru H listing: http://www.eenet.com/intc/d-h.htm
3. I thru Q listing: http://www.eenet.com/intc/i-q.htm
4. R thru Z listing: http://www.eenet.com/intc/r-z.htm

DISTRIBUTORS

1. A thru H listing: http://www.eenet.com/intc/a-hd.htm
2. I thru Q listing: http://www.eenet.com/intc/i-qd.htm
3. R thru Z listing: http://www.eenet.com/intc/r-zd.htm

MANUFACTURERS PRODUCTS

1. Back Plane: http://www.eenet.com/intc/backplan.htm
2. Card Edge: http://www.eenet.com/intc/cardedge.htm
3. D-Sub: http://www.eenet.com/intc/dsub.htm
4. Din: http://www.eenet.com/intc/din.htm
5. Header: http://www.eenet.com/intc/header.htm
6. IDC: http://www.eenet.com/intc/idc.htm
7. Metric: http://www.eenet.com/intc/metric.htm
8. Military: http://www.eenet.com/intc/mil.htm
9. Modular Jack: http://www.eenet.com/intc/modular.htm
10. PCMCIA: http://www.eenet.com/intc/pcmcia.htm
11. RF: http://www.eenet.com/intc/rf.htm
12. Ribbon: http://www.eenet.com/intc/ribbon.htm
13. Socket: http://www.eenet.com/intc/socket.htm
14. Terminal Block: http://www.eenet.com/intc/termblok.htm
15. Wire & Cable: http://www.eenet.com/intc/wirecab.htm

The preceding contact information and/or URLs are subject to change without notice.

List of Top Cable Labeling Companies

The following statements have been taken from information contained in the descriptions at the websites listed for each of the cable labeling companies below. The author does not personally promote or endorse any of these products or companies.

1. **Cabel Labels**: Manufactures a range of cable identification labels, includes software to print labels and maintain databases on cable installations.

   http://www.cabelabels.com.au/

2. **Cable Markers Co., Inc.**: Identification products, wire markers, computer printable systems, labels, tags, heat-shrink sleeving for cables and wires.

   http://www.cablemarkers.com/

3. **Computer Network Services**: Provides cable labeling and networking solutions.

   http://andcable.com/intro.htm

4. **Critchley**: Wire and cable identification products. Heat-shrink sleeves (HSI), thermal transfer printable labels, wire markers, self-laminating labels, tags, and more.

   http://www.critchley.com/

5. **Electronic Imaging Materials, Inc.**: Bar code labels for electronics manufacturing, cable labels.

   htttp://www.barcode-labels.com/cablelabels.htm

6. **Polygon Velcro Cable Management**: Manufacturer of velcro-based wire management products for telecommunications racks, desks, and computer networks.

   http://www.portal.ca/~polygon/

7. **Silver Fox**: Labeling solutions for professional engineers, the IT industry, and the oil and process industries.

   http://www.silverfox.co.uk/

The preceding contact information and/or URLs are subject to change without notice.

List of Top SCSI Companies

 The following statements have been taken from information contained in the descriptions at the websites listed for each of the SCSI companies listed below. The author does not personally promote or endorse any of these products or companies.

1. **Advanced Computer & Network Corporation**: Dedicated to the RAID (redundant array of independent disks) technology and SCSI switches, boosters, cables, extenders, and hard drives.

   http://www.acnc.com/

2. **Ancot Corporation**: Manufacturer of bus analyzers and test equipment for SCSI and Fiber Channel.

   http://www.ancot.com/

3. **APCON, Inc.**: SCSI enhancement products and high-availability network solutions.

   http://www.yahoo.com/Business_and_Economy/Companies/
   Computers/Hardware/Components/Busses/SCSI/APCON_Inc_/

4. **CS Electronics**: Manufacturer of premium grade SCSI cable interconnects.

   http://www.scsi-cables.com/

5. **Granite Digital**: Manufacturer of high performance SCSI cables and components.

   http://www.scsipro.com/

6. **Hewlett-Packard**:

   http://www.hp.com/

7. **I-TECH Corp**: Provides SCSI and Fiber Channel test equipment, software, and related accessories for manufacturers, integrators, and end users of drives and peripheral devices.

   http://www.i-tech.com/

8. **Panasonic Global**:

   http://www.panasonic.com/

9. **Paralan Corporation**: Makers of SCSI bus extenders, switches, converters.

   http://www.paralan.com/

10. **Rancho Technology, Inc.**: Provides SCSI converters, host adapters, PCMCIA cards, parallel port, and repeater products to standard and OEM companies.

    http://www.rancho.com/

11. **System Connection**: SCSI cable manufacturer.

    http://www.sconnect.com/

12. **Temp-Flex Cable, Inc.**: Designer and manufacturer of insulated wire and cable.

    http://www.tempflex.com/

The preceding URLs are subject to change without notice.

List of Wireless LAN Products and Sites

The following statements have been taken from information contained in the descriptions at the websites listed for each of the wireless LAN products, sites, and companies listed below. The author does not personally promote or endorse any of these products or companies.

WIRELESS LAN PRODUCTS AND SITES

1. **AirLAN**: AirLAN by Solectek is based on radio technology originally developed by NCR Corp., as shown in Table H–1 [1]. Except for its parallel-port wireless LAN adapter, Solectek's technology is based on OEM products from AT&T and Digital and has an advertised speed of 2 Mbps.

2. **Altair**: Motorola offers this LAN choice that operates in the 18 GHz range, which is licensed to Motorola by the FCC, as shown in Table H–1 [Wood and Jain, 2]. The Altair (http://www.mot.com/) system runs at speeds of up to 10 Mbps, and is limited by license to five channels for a 17.5-mile radius. Since Motorola controls the licenses, they can better manage the interference potential.

3. **Aironet** (http://www.ameradio.com/business_Networking_ Aironet.htm): Makes transparent wireless connectivity equipment for use under Ethernet, token ring, or Local Talk II LANs. Wireless bridge, access point (Ethernet and token ring), PCMCIA wireless LAN adapter, ISA and MCA wireless LAN client cards. Features second-generation multichannel direct sequence and frequency hopping spread spectrum technology in the 900 MHz and 2.4 GHz frequency bands. Data rates up to 11 Mbps per channel. Patented microcellular architecture for roaming and power management. Auto-detect LAN failures, diagnostics, optimization, management via Telnet, FTP, or SNMP modular design. Elements of the system operate indoors or outdoors, with point-to-point ranges up to 6 miles. No operating license required by the FCC.

4. **AIRplex Cordless Modems**: A new category of PCMCIA 28.8 modems have been developed that are similar to conventional modems but require no cord to connect to the telephone line. The idea is to permit you to use your notebook freely without being tied to your desk. They also permit multiple users in an office to easily share an analog telephone line. New wireless technology (AIRplex) is used that permits use of these modems in every room in a large building without mutual interference.

5. **BreezeCom, Inc.** (http://www.breezecom.com/): Develops and manufactures wireless access products for data and voice applications, targeted at ISPs or local exchange carriers (LECs). The products (made for indoor/outdoor wireless LAN, wireless Internet access [WIA], and IP broadband wireless local loop [IP B-WLL]), employ point to multi-point wireless packet-switching technologies, optimized for high-speed Internet and Intranet access. BreezeCom wireless LAN and access products use frequency hopping, spread spectrum radio technology and operate in the license-free 2.4 GHz ISM (industrial, scientific, and medical) band, enabling virtually any type of stationary or mobile PC device to be connected to a LAN in minutes, with reliable roaming from one access point to another. For the wireless T1/E1 applications, BreezeCom offers voice/data modem using full-duplex frequency hopping, spread spectrum technology, supporting data rates of 64 Kbps to 2.048 Mbps, in the license-free 2.4 GHz ISM band at a range of up to 20 miles; easy to install, with advanced management functions for full or fractional E1/T1 links with voice/fax channels.

6. **Proxim, Inc.** (http://www.proxim.com/): The supplier of 2.4 GHz wireless LAN technology to both OEMs and end-users worldwide. RangeLAN2TM and IEEE 802.11-compliant RangeLAN802TM product families today consist of PC card wireless LAN adapters, ISA card adapters, interchangeable antennas, access and extension points for transparent bridging to Ethernet or token ring networks, as well as micro-ISA card for OEM integration. Proxim's RangeLAN2 products are certified in more than 50 nations worldwide. Its multichannel architecture allows up to 15 independent wireless LANs to operate in the same physical space, providing roughly 24 Mbps of aggregate network bandwidth. RangeLAN2 provides mobility-centric network architecture, including such features as state-of-the-art seamless roaming, power management, advanced security, site survey diagnostics, and the IEEE-endorsed high-speed modulation technique. Proxim technology has been selected as the 2.4 GHz wireless LAN technology of choice by more than 50 suppliers of mobile computing devices, hand-held PCs and terminals, and wireless solutions providers.

7. **RangeLAN:** The RangeLAN2/PCMCIA (http://www.it.kth.se/) operates at distances of up to 500 feet in standard office environments and up to 1,000 feet in open spaces, as shown in Table H–1 [Wood and Jain, 2]. Based on frequency-hopping spread-spectrum technology in the 2.4 GHz to 2.4835 GHz bandwidth, the wireless adapter has a data rate of 1.6 Mbps. The unit's average power output is 100 mW. With the RangeLAN2/PCMCIA, as many as 15 independent wireless LANs can operate within the same physical space.

8. **RF Amplifiers (ISM Bands)** http://www.ameradio.com/business_Networking_amps.htm: Spread spectrum bidirectional amplifiers. Several models are available: 900 MHz & 2.4 GHz; output ranging from 100 mW to 25 Watts, suitable for a wide range of commercial and military applications; spread-spectrum wireless LAN applications, telemetry, wireless video, long-range wireless telephony; rugged and compact; indoor models (in-building wireless links); outdoor models (building-to-building wireless links); installation kits available—mounting hardware, cables, connectors, outdoor and indoor antennas, lightning protectors; power sources: antenna feed cable, AC adapter, battery, solar panel, vehicle's electrical system; and plug and play installations. FCC rules do not permit use of this technology with Part 15 devices in the United States. These amplifiers are available for export or military use.

9. **RoamAbout**: The RoamAbout (ftp://ftp.digital.com/pub/Digital/info/ SPD/45-71-XX.txt) PCMCIA network adapter is a PC network interface card (NIC) for wireless LANs, as shown in Table H–1 [Wood and Jain, 2]. The network adapter operates in a PC with a Type II PCMCIA slot that conforms to the PCMCIA release V2.01 specification. An antenna is externally connected via an 18" (0.5 meter) cable. The RoamAbout PCMCIA network adapter communicates with the RoamAbout PCMCIA network adapter in other portable computers, the WaveLAN NIC in stationary computers, or the RoamAbout Access Point for connectivity to the wired network.

10. **Tetherless Access Ltd. (TAL)**: TAL provides technology to allow telecommunications service providers to build high-speed, wireless TCP/IP networks, as shown in Table H–1 [Wood and Jain, 2]. TAL has developed software that leverages an open system TCP/IP networking architecture with spread-spectrum packet radio technology to deliver a scalable networking solution. With TAL's technology, communications service providers can deliver virtual private TCP/IP networking services to customers within a region or metropolitan area, over single-link distances of up to 30 Km. The raw data rate for these networks is 160 Kbps. End users will see bursts on file transfers of over 100 Kbps and enjoy average throughput of 64 Kbps.

11. **WaveLAN**: A premier spread-spectrum network system manufactured by NCR Corporation, as shown in Table H–1 [Wood and Jain, 2]. This is a 2 Mbps network system that utilizes a proprietary protocol. WaveLAN (http://www.ncr.com/) also uses a robust error-checking protocol that can detect and correct most transmission errors, and a data-encryption option that makes the network highly resistant to electronic eavesdropping.

Table H–1   Wireless LAN Products

Company	Product	Infrared/ Radio	Frequency	Advertised Speed	Advertised Distance
AT&T	WaveLAN	N/Y	902 MHz to 928 MHz	2 Mbps	800 feet
California Microwave	RadioLink	N/Y	902 MHz to 928 MHz	???	???
Digital	RoamAbout	N/Y	902 MHz to 928 MHz	2 Mbps	800 feet

Table H–1   continued

Company	Product	Infrared/ Radio	Frequency	Advertised Speed	Advertised Distance
IBM	Infrared wireless LAN adapter	Y/N	N/A	1 Mbps	17' × 17' room (integrated PC Card); 30' × 30' room (tethered transceiver)
InfraLAN Technologies	InfraLAN	Y/N	N/A	10 Mbps	90 feet
Motorola	Altair	N/Y	18 GHz*	???	???
NCR	WaveLAN	N/Y	902 MHz to 928 MHz	2 Mbps	800 feet
O'Neill Communications	LAWN	N/Y	902 MHz to 928 MHz	???	???
Photonics	Wide area and point-to-point products	Y/N	N/A	1 Mbps	20' × 20' room (integrated PC Card); 25' × 25' room (tethered transceiver)
Proxim, Inc.	RangeLAN	N/Y	902 MHz to 928 MHz	???	???
Solectek	AirLAN	N/Y	902 MHz to 928 MHz	2 Mbps	800 feet
Traveling Software and National Semiconductor	AirShare	N/Y	902 MHz to 928 MHz	No	Portable to desktop
Windata, Inc.	FreePort	N/Y	2.4 GHz & 5.8 GHz	5.7 Mbps	260 feet
Xerox	PARCTAB	Y/N	N/A	9.6Kbps, 19.2Kbps, 38.4Kbps	30' × 30' room

---

* Frequency use requires an FCC license, as shown in Table H–1.

OTHER WIRELESS-RELATED SITES

1. **Br Badrinath's ftp directory**: From Rutgers University, full of papers on mobile computing.

     ftp://paul.rutgers.edu/pub/badri/

2. **CWC**: Established in August 1992, the Centre for Wireless Communications (CWC) at the National University of Singapore is a National R&D Centre funded by the National Science and Technology Board.

     http://www.cwc.nus.sg/cwcdocs/intro.html

3. **Girish Welling's Home Page**: From Rutgers University, he's done some research in mobile computing.

     http://paul.rutgers.edu:80/~welling/

4. **Hiperlan/Netplan**: Hiperlan is a coming ETSI standard for 20 Mbps wireless LANs at 15,7 GHz. Torben Rune at Netplan was project team leader of PT41, the ETSI project team responsible for defining Hiperlan. Netplan is a Danish consulting company in the field of tele- and data-communications.

     http://www.netplan.dk/

5. **K and M Electronics, Inc.**: Since 1974, K and M has been a leader in infrared light detection electronics and wireless voice/data communication. The company has been a pioneer in diffuse (flooding) infrared communications since 1980.

     http://web2.kme.com/kme/company.htm

6. **Metricom Wireless Data**: Metricom, Inc. (Nasdaq: MCOM), founded in 1985, develops, manufactures, and markets wireless data communication networks.

     http://www.metricom.com/

7. **Mobile Computing and Personal Digital Assistants**: An informative website with topics pertaining to the use of technology, technology trends, or politics as it affects technology. Subjects include wireless networking, mobile computing, and research projects.

     http://splat.baker.com/grand-unification-theory/mobile-pda/index.html

8. **Multipoint Networks**: Multipoint Networks designs and manufactures wireless data communications systems for metropolitan area networks.

      http://www.multipoint.com/

9. **Qualcomm**: Headquartered in San Diego, CA, Qualcomm develops, manufactures, markets, licenses, and operates advanced communications systems and products based on its proprietary digital wireless technologies. The company's primary product and development areas are the OmniTRACS system (a geostationary, satellite-based, mobile communications system providing two-way data and position reporting services), code division multiple access (CDMA) wireless communications systems and products, and, in conjunction with others, the Globalstar low-earth-orbit (LEO) satellite communications system.

      http://lorien.qualcomm.com/

10. **Shiva**: http://www.shiva.com/

11. **Solectek's** (http://www.ameradio.com/business_Networking_ Solectek.htm): Line of spread spectrum wireless bridges and routers (codeveloped with Cisco Systems) provides cost-effective wireless connectivity solutions. 11 Mbps data rates combined with exclusive multipoint software design guarantees high throughput on 900 MHz and 2.4 GHz frequency bands. Typical applications: linking several remotely located rural schools into a single wireless network for cost-effective Internet access, secure communications between bank branches, telemetry transmission between sites in oil/gas exploration, and municipal government wireless internetworking systems to transfer data between public buildings (libraries, courts, record departments). Linking sites up to 25 miles apart. No recurring monthly operating fees. No license required by the FCC.

12. **Wireless, Inc.** (formerly Multipoint Networks) http://www.wire-less-inc.com/: Manufactures advanced communication network equipment for high-performance wireless transaction X.25 networks, with data rates up to 19.2 kbps @ 25 kHz of UHF radio spectrum (400-512/820-960 MHz). Transmissions to distances over 30 miles. Point-to-multipoint, point-to-point. Typical applications: wireless credit card transaction processing for multiple locations, retail POS terminals and automatic teller machine (ATM) support, branch banking, lottery, air-

line reservations, rural telephony. Transparent connections wouldn't interfere with any customer-implemented data encryption algorithms. Syncor async connections. Support for X.25, X.3, X.28, X.29, SDLC/QLLC, BSC 3270, BSC 2780/3780 protocols. Disaster recovery. Fully configured to customer-specific requirements.

12. **Wireless FAQ**: Frequently Asked Questions from the wireless newsgroup.

> http://www.cis.ohio-state.edu/~jain/cis788/wireless_lan/faq.txt

13. **Wireless LAN Group**: http://www.ecs.umass.edu/ece/wireless/

The Wireless Opportunities Coalition: The group supports the development, manufacture, and use of wireless communications and related devices that are not licensed by the FCC, but are regulated under part 15 of its rules.

> http://wireless.policy.net/wireless/wireless.html

The preceding URLs are subject to change without notice.

NOTE

[1]   Joel B. Wood and Professor Raj Jain, Department of Computer and Information Science, The Ohio State University, 2015 Neil Avenue, DL 297, Columbus, OH 43210-1277, 2000.

List of CCITT/ISO Standards

F.700:
http://cuiwww.unige.ch/OSG/info/MultimediaInfo/mmsurvey/standards.html#F.700

G.711:
http://cuiwww.unige.ch/OSG/info/MultimediaInfo/mmsurvey/standards.html#G.711

G.721:
http://cuiwww.unige.ch/OSG/info/MultimediaInfo/mmsurvey/standards.html#G.721

G.722:
http://cuiwww.unige.ch/OSG/info/MultimediaInfo/mmsurvey/standards.html#G.722

G.725:
http://cuiwww.unige.ch/OSG/info/MultimediaInfo/mmsurvey/standards.html#G.725

H.221:
http://cuiwww.unige.ch/OSG/info/MultimediaInfo/mmsurvey/standards.html#H.221

H.242:
http://cuiwww.unige.ch/OSG/info/MultimediaInfo/mmsurvey/standards.html#H.242

H.261:
http://cuiwww.unige.ch/OSG/info/MultimediaInfo/mmsurvey/standards.html#H.261

H.320:
http://cuiwww.unige.ch/OSG/info/MultimediaInfo/mmsurvey/standards.html#H.320

HyTime:
http://cuiwww.unige.ch/OSG/info/MultimediaInfo/mmsurvey/standards.html#HyTime

IIF:

http://cuiwww.unige.ch/OSG/info/MultimediaInfo/mmsurvey/standards.html#IIF

JBIG:

http://cuiwww.unige.ch/OSG/info/MultimediaInfo/mmsurvey/standards.html#JBIG

JPEG:

http://cuiwww.unige.ch/OSG/info/MultimediaInfo/mmsurvey/standards.html#JPEG

MHEG:

http://cuiwww.unige.ch/OSG/info/MultimediaInfo/mmsurvey/standards.html#MHEG

MPEG:

http://cuiwww.unige.ch/OSG/info/MultimediaInfo/mmsurvey/standards.html#MPEG

ODA:

http://cuiwww.unige.ch/OSG/info/MultimediaInfo/mmsurvey/standards.html#ODA

T.80:

http://cuiwww.unige.ch/OSG/info/MultimediaInfo/mmsurvey/standards.html#T.80

X.400:

http://cuiwww.unige.ch/OSG/info/MultimediaInfo/mmsurvey/standards.html#X.400

G.723:

http://cuiwww.unige.ch/OSG/info/MultimediaInfo/mmsurvey/standards.html#G.723

G.726:

http://cuiwww.unige.ch/OSG/info/MultimediaInfo/mmsurvey/standards.html#G.726

G.727:

http://cuiwww.unige.ch/OSG/info/MultimediaInfo/mmsurvey/standards.html#G.727

G.728:

http://cuiwww.unige.ch/OSG/info/MultimediaInfo/mmsurvey/standards.html#G.728

G.764:

http://cuiwww.unige.ch/OSG/info/MultimediaInfo/mmsurvey/standards.html#G.764

G.765:

http://cuiwww.unige.ch/OSG/info/MultimediaInfo/mmsurvey/standards.html#G.765

H.200:

http://cuiwww.unige.ch/OSG/info/MultimediaInfo/mmsurvey/standards.html#H.200

H.241:

http://cuiwww.unige.ch/OSG/info/MultimediaInfo/mmsurvey/standards.html#H.241

H.243:

http://cuiwww.unige.ch/OSG/info/MultimediaInfo/mmsurvey/standards.html#H.243

T.120:

http://cuiwww.unige.ch/OSG/info/MultimediaInfo/mmsurvey/standards.html#T.120

The preceding URLs are subject to change without notice.

Glossary

802

IEEE committee on LAN standards.

802.1

IEEE LANs and networking architecture specifications.

802.1B

IEEE network management specifications.

802.1D

IEEE committee for bridges. IEEE media-access-control-level standard for interLAN bridges linking IEEE802.3, 802.4 and 802.5 networks.

802.2

IEEE Data Link layer standards detailing logical link control (LLC).

802.3

IEEE standard for Ethernet-type systems and networks (802.3 1Base5, 802.3 10Base2, 802.3 10BaseT, and 802.3 10Broad36).

802.4

IEEE standard for token-passing system using a bus topology.

802.5

IEEE standard for token ring systems.

802.6

IEEE specifications for metropolitan area networks (MANs).

802.7

IEEE standards for broadband LANs.

802.8

IEEE specifications for fiber optic LANs.

802.9

IEEE specifications for integrating voice and digital data (isochronous traffic).

802.10

IEEE specifications for interoperable and internetwork security.

802.11

IEEE standards for wireless LANs and 802.12 high-speed LANs (100VG-AnyLAN).

3090

Large IBM mainframe (circa 1986).

3270

IBM mainframe terminal.

3270 data stream

Format for transmitting data to a 3270 terminal.

3274

IBM controllers or cluster controllers.

3770

Protocol for SNA batch transmissions.

2B+D

Describes basic ISDN service (2B+D = two bearer channels and one data channel).

4B5B Encoding

A signal modulation scheme in which groups of four bits are encoded and transmitted in five bits in order to guarantee that no more than three consecutive zeroes ever occur; used in FDDI.

8B10B Encoding

A signal modulation scheme in which eight bits are encoded in a 10-bit word to ensure that too many consecutive zeroes do not occur; used in ESCON and fiber channel.

1Base5

Specification for StarLAN at 1 Mbps data transfer rate.

10Base2

Ethernet specification for thin coaxial cable, transmits signals at 10 Mbps with a distance limit of 185 meters per segment and 10 Mbps; baseband (single channel) with a maximum of 200 m.

10Base5

Ethernet specification for thick coaxial cable, transmits signals at 10 Mbps with a distance limit of 500 meters per segment and 10 Mbps; baseband (single channel) with a maximum of 500 m.

10BaseF

Ethernet specification for fiber optic cable, transmits signals at 10 Mbps with a distance limit of 1,000 meters per segment.

10BaseT

Ethernet specification for unshielded twisted-pair cable (category 3, 4, or 5), transmits signals at 10 Mbps with a distance limit of 100 meters per segment.

10Broad36

Ethernet on broadband cable.

3COM 3+

Network operating system designed to supports PCs and Macs.

66-type Connecting Block

Used by telephone company to terminate twisted pairs. Not recommended for LAN use.

AARP

AppleTalk Address Resolution Protocol.

ABM

Asynchronous Balance Mode.

Abstract Syntax Notation One (ASN.1)

OSI method of describing data formats for application layer.

AC

Access Control.

AC alternating current

Acceptance angle; the half-angle of the cone within which incident light is totally internal, reflected by the fiber core. It is equal to sin-1 (NA).

Access method

Rules that govern how nodes on a network access the cable. Also referred to as media-access control (MAC) protocol.

Access point device

A wireless LAN device that connects to a DSL or cable modem and enables high-rate (broadband) Internet access throughout the home network.

Acknowledgment

A message indicating that data has been correctly received.

ACS

Asynchronous Communications Server.

ACSE

Association Control Service Element.

Active Open

A TCP tool for activating a connection with a node.

Active Star

Star topology with active hubs.

ACTS

Association of Cable Television Suppliers.

A/D Converter

Analog-to-digital signal converter.

AD or ADC analog-to-digital converter

A device used to convert analog signals to digital signals.

Adaptive channel allocation

Used in multiplexing signals; bandwidth is only afforded a signal by request.

Adaptive routing

Using intelligent methods for selecting routes for packet transmission.

ADC

Analog-to-digital converter.

ADCCP

ANSI's Data Link layer protocol called Advanced Data Communications Control Procedures.

Address

The unique identifier for the source or destination of a data transfer.

Addressable converter

Equipment in cable households that allows cable operators to turn on or off the converter or order pay-per-view type events.

Address Resolution Protocol (ARP)

A protocol that dynamically maps between various types of addresses (IP addresses to token ring addresses, for instance) on a local area network. Used to route data between networks through a gateway.

ADSL modem

A type of modem that connects a computer to an ADSL network, which in turn connects to the Internet. Once connected, ADSL modem users have a continuous connection to the Internet.

ADMD

Administration Management Domain.

ADSP

AppleTalk Datastream Protocol.

ADU

Asynchronous Data Unit.

Advanced Communications Function (ACP)

Official product name for all IBM SNA products (ACF/VTAM). IBM's program package (ACF) allows the sharing of computer resources through computer links. It also supports SNA.

Advanced Intelligent Network (AIN)

Developed by Bell Communications Research.

Advanced Interactive Executive (AIX)

IBM's version of UNIX.

Advanced peer-to-peer communications (APPC)

IBM system for allowing direct node-to-node interaction on networks. Nodes referred to as LU 6.2.

Advanced peer-to-peer network (APPN)

IBM's enhancement for SNA networks allowing distributed processing and other advanced features.

ADVANCENET

Hewlett Packard's network supporting OSI and SNA.

AFI

AppleTalk File Interface.

AFP

AppleTalk File Protocol; allows access to Apple shared servers.

AGC

Automatic gain control; a process or means by which gain is automatically adjusted in a specified manner as a function of input level or another specified parameter.

ALAP

AppleTalk Link Access Protocol.

Altair System

Motorola's wireless radio LAN.

Alternate Mark Inversion (AMI)

Line coding method for T-1 lines.

AM

Amplitude modulation.

AMD

Advanced micro devices.

American National Standards Institute (ANSI)

The coordinating body for voluntary standards groups within the United States. ANSI is a member of the International Organization for Standardization (ISO).

American Standard Code for Information Interchange (ASCII)

Seven-bit character data coding method for asynchronous communications.

American Telephone and Telegraph Company (AT&T)

Develops networks, among other things.

American Wire Gauge (AWG)

Used to measure the diameter of conductors in wires.

Amplitude modulation (AM)

A transmission technique in which the amplitude of the carrier is varied in accordance with the signal.

AMT

Address mapping table.

Analog

A representation of an object that resembles the original. Analog devices monitor conditions, such as movement, temperature, and sound, and convert them into analogous electronic or mechanical patterns. For example, telephones turn voice vibrations into electrical vibrations of the same shape. Analog implies continuous operation.

Analog transmission

A way of sending signals (voice, video, data) in which the transmitted signal is analogous to the original signal. In other words, if you spoke into a microphone and saw your voice on an oscilloscope and you took the same voice as it was transmitted on the phone line and threw that signal onto the oscilloscope, the two signals would look essentially the same. The only difference would be that the electrically transmitted signal would be at a higher frequency.

Angular misalignment

Loss at a connector due to fiber end face angles being misaligned.

ANTC

Advanced Network Test Center.

APAD

Asynchronous packet assembler/disassembler.

APC

Angle polished connector. A 5°–15° angle on the connector tip for the minimum possible back reflection.

APL

Average picture level; video parameter.

Apple Computer, Inc.

Pioneers of the personal computer. Manufactures Macintoshes with built-in LocalTalk ports for networking. Also developed AppleTalk protocols and AppleShare products.

AppleShare PC

Software that allows DOS-based machines to operate within an Apple-Share network.

AppleTalk

Apple Computer's network protocol originally designed to run over LocalTalk networks, but can also run on Ethernet and token ring.

Application Layer

Layer 7 of the OSI model. Defines the rules for gaining entrance into the communications system. Programs communicate with other programs through this layer.

Application Development Cycle (AD/Cycle)

SAA software from IBM to manage IS system development.

Application Development Environment (ADE)

IBM's universal application development package for SAA systems.

Applications programming interface (API)

A method of allowing an application to interact directly with certain functions of an operating system or with another application.

AR Coating

Antireflection coating; a thin, dielectric or metallic film applied to an optical surface to reduce its reflectance and thereby increase its transmittance.

ARM

Asynchronous response mode.

Armor

A protective layer, usually metal, wrapped around a cable.

AS/400

Application System/400. IBM's mid-price minicomputer.

ASCII

American standard code for information interchange. A means of encoding information.

ASCII Protocol

Simple protocol for transferring data with no error checking.

ASE

Applied service elements.

ASIC

Application-specific integrated circuit. A custom-designed integrated circuit.

ASK

Amplitude shift keying.

ASP

AppleTalk session protocol.

Asymmetric digital subscriber line (ADSL)

A popular implementation of DSL. The "asymmetric" in ADSL means that it transmits data at faster speeds downstream (from the Internet to the computer) than upstream (from the computer to the Internet). ADSL can support speeds of up to 8 Mbps downstream and up to 1 Mbps upstream. It is ideal for Internet surfing, where users typically download more information than they send.

Asynchronous

Transmission where sending and receiving devices are not synchronized. Data must carry signals to indicate data divisions.

Asynchronous Protocol

Protocol designed for asynchronous data transfers, including ASCII, TTY, Kermit, and XMODEM.

Asynchronous Transfer Mode (ATM)

A form of data transmission based on fixed-length packets, called cells, that can carry data, voice, and video at high speeds. This technology is designed to combine the benefits of switching technology (constant transmission delay, guaranteed capacity) with those of packet switching (flexibility, efficiency for intermittent traffic). ATM is defined by ITU-T ATM Forum specifications.

ATA

ARCnet Trade Association.

ATD

Asynchronous time division.

ATM

Asynchronous transfer mode; high bandwidth and low overhead networking system using something akin to packet-switching. It is the future of high-speed broadband networks.

ATM Adaptation Layer (AAL)

One of the three layers of the ATM protocol reference model. It translates incoming data into ATM cell payloads and translates outgoing cells into a format readable by the higher layers. Five AALs have been defined: AAL1 and 2 handle traffic like voice and video, which are sensitive to transmission delays, while AAL3, 4, and 5 pertain to data communications through the segmentation and reassembly of packets.

ATM DSU

A data service unit for ATM access.

ATP

AppleTalk Transaction Protocol

Attached Resources Computer network (ARCnet)

Developed by Datapoint in the late 1970s to provide data transfers at 2.5 Mbps. Very inexpensive products with great product interoperability. A token-passing bus architecture, usually on coaxial cable.

Attachment unit interface (AUI)

Transceiver for thick Ethernet systems.

Attenuation

The decrease in the power of some sort of signal.

Attenuation constant

For a particular propagation mode in an optical fiber, the real part of the axial propagation constant.

Attenuation-limited operation

The condition in a fiber optic link when operation is limited by the power of the received signal (rather than by bandwidth or distortion).

Attenuation to cross talk ration (ACR)

The difference between attenuation and cross talk measured in decibels.

Attenuator

(1) In electrical systems, a usually passive network for reducing the amplitude of a signal without appreciably distorting the waveform; (2) in optical systems, a passive device for reducing the amplitude of a signal without appreciably distorting the waveform.

AUI connector (attachment unit interface)

A 15-pin connector found on Ethernet cards that can be used for attaching coaxial, fiber optic, or twisted-pair cable.

AutoBaud rate detect (ABR)

Senses speed of incoming data.

Avalanche Photodiode (APD)

A photodiode that exhibits internal amplification of photocurrent through an avalanche multiplication of carriers in the junction region.

Average power

The average level of power in a signal that varies with time.

Axial Propagation Constant

For an optical fiber, the propagation constant evaluated along the axis of a fiber in the direction of transmission.

AXIS

The center of an optical fiber.

Backbone

A cable to which multiple nodes or workstations are attached.

Backbone cabling

Cable and connecting hardware that comprise the main and intermediate cross-connects, as well as cable runs that extend between telecommunications closets, equipment rooms, and entrance facilities.

Backscattering

The return of a portion of scattered light to the input end of a fiber; the scattering of light in the direction opposite to its original propagation.

Backup server

Device that copies applications and data into a safe place for retrieval if necessary.

Balance

An indication of signal voltage equality and phase polarity on a conductor pair. Perfect balance occurs when the signals across a twisted pair are equal in magnitude and opposite in phase with respect to the ground.

Balanced signal transmission

Two voltages, equal and opposite in phase with respect to each other, across the conductors of a twisted pair (commonly referred to as tip and ring).

BALUN (BALancedUNbalanced)

An impedance-matching device that allows conversion from one medium (like coax) to another medium (like twisted pair).

Band

Range of frequencies.

Bandwidth

The range of electrical frequencies that a device or medium can support.

Bandwidth-limited operation

The condition in a fiber optic link when bandwidth, rather than received optical power, limits performance. This condition is reached when the signal becomes distorted, principally by dispersion, beyond specified limits.

Baseband

A type of system where only digital data is carried on the transfer medium. Single-channel systems that support a single transmission at any given time.

Basic cable

The program services distributed by a cable television system to subscribers for a basic monthly fee. These may include one or more local broadcast stations, distant broadcast stations, nonpay cable networks, local-origination programming, and/or data channels.

Baud

The speed of signaling elements per second. A signaling element may represent more than one bit so bits per second and baud are not always the same.

Bayonet-Neill-Concelman (BNC)

A type of twist-locking connector used with coaxial cable.

Beacon

A special frame in token ring systems indicating a serious problem with the ring, such as a break.

Beamsplitter

An optical device, such as a partially reflecting mirror, that splits a beam of light into two or more beams. Used in fiber optics for directional couplers.

Bel (B)

The logarithm to the base 10 of a power ratio, expressed as $B = \log 10$ (P1/P2), where P1 and P2 are distinct powers. The decibel, equal to one-tenth bel, is a more commonly used unit.

Belden

A major manufacturer of network cabling.

Bonding

The permanent joining of metallic parts to form an electrically conductive path that will assure electrical continuity and the capacity to conduct safely any current likely to be imposed on it.

Bend radius
The smallest radius an optical fiber or fiber cable can bend before increased attenuation or breakage occurs.

Bell Operating Company (BOC)
One of 22 telephone service companies that used to be a part of AT&T.

BER
Basic encoding rules or bit error rate.

Berkeley Software Distribution UNIX or *Berkeley UNIX* (BSD UNIX)
UNIX system famed for having been enhanced with TCP/IP support.

Bicycling
Distribution of programming and/or commercials between systems by sending tapes by mail or messenger service. This term derives from the early practice of several movie theaters sharing the same film print and having a messenger carry the print between theaters by bicycle in time for each to show the movie as scheduled.

Bidirectional operating in both directions
Bidirectional couplers operate the same way regardless of the direction light passes through them. Bidirectional transmission sends signals in both directions, sometimes through the same fiber.

Binary
Numerical method of representing the status of bits. 1 represents an on bit and 0 is an off bit.

Bind
Assigning a physical machine address to a logical or symbolic address. Request to activate a session between a primary logical unit (PLU) and secondary logical unit (SLU).

Bindery
Novell NetWare's database for storing objects and properties. Objects are users, print servers, etc. Properties are passwords, Internet addresses, etc.

Bipolar
Transmission method that alternates between positive and negative voltages to represent bits.

Birefringent
Having a refractive index that differs for light of different polarizations.

BISDN

Broadband ISDN.

Bisync

Binary synchronous transmission. Half-duplex transmission method developed by IBM.

Bit

Binary digit in the binary numbering system. Its value can be 0 or 1. In an 8-bit character scheme, it takes 8 bits to make a byte (character) of data.

Bit error rate (BER)

The fraction of bits transmitted that are received incorrectly.

Bit-oriented protocol

A protocol in which individual bits within a byte convey information, as opposed to the whole byte only.

BITE

Built-in test equipment. Features designed into a piece of equipment that allow online diagnosis of failures and operating status.

Bits per second (BPS)

A measure of data transfer speed.

Bit stream

A continuous transfer of bits over some medium.

Bit stuffing

A method of breaking up continuous strings of 1 bits by inserting a 0 bit. The 0 bit is removed at the receiver.

BNC

Popular coax bayonet-style connector often used for baseband video.

BNC connector (Bayone-Neill-Concelman)

Standard connector used to connect 10Base2 coaxial cable.

Boundary node

An SNA device that provides protocol support for other SNA nodes.

Break test access

Method of disconnecting a circuit that has been electrically bridged to allow testing on either side of the circuit without disturbing cable terminations. Devices that provide break test access include disconnect blocks, bridge clips, plug-on protection modules, and plug-on patching devices.

BRI
ISDN basic rate interface.

Bridge
Devices that connect and pass packets between two network segments that use the same communications protocol.

Bridged tap
The multiple appearances of the same cable pair or fiber at several distribution points; also known as parallel connections.

Bridging
A means of providing through connections between conductors or pairs that are terminated on connecting blocks. These through connections are commonly provided by means of individual metallic "bridging" clips or multiple "bridging" clips that are housed in a plastic insulator.

Broadband
A system carrying many different types or channels of data by dividing the total bandwidth of the medium into smaller bandwidths (see **FDM**). Multichannel capacity equal to or greater than 45 Mbps.

Broadband Integrated Services Data Network (BISDN)
A set of standards under development by the ITU-T for services based on ATM switching and SONET/SDH (see these entries) transmission.

Broadcast
Sending data to more than one receiving device at a time.

Brouter
A device that combines the functions of a bridge and a router.

BSC
Binary synchronous transmission.

Buffer
A temporary storage place for data being received or transmitted.

Building distributor (BD)
The international term for intermediate cross-connect. A distributor in which the building backbone cable(s) terminates and at which connections to the campus backbone cable(s) may be made.

Bundled cable

An assembly of two or more cables continuously bound together to form a single unit prior to installation (sometimes referred to as loomed, speed-wrap, or whip cable constructions).

Bus network

A network topology in which all terminals are attached to a transmission medium serving as a bus.

Bus topology

A physical layout of network devices in which all devices must share a common medium to transfer data, and no two devices may transmit simultaneously.

Butt splice

A joining of two fibers without optical connectors arranged end-to-end by means of a coupling. Fusion splicing is an example.

Bypass

The ability of a station to isolate itself optically from a network while maintaining the continuity of the cable plant.

Byte

The grouping of bits making up a character. In current systems, typically eight bits.

Byte-oriented protocol

A protocol in which whole bytes represent data as opposed to single bits within the bytes, which taken by themselves are meaningless.

Cable

Transmission medium of copper wire or optical fiber wrapped in a protective cover.

Cable assembly

A cable that is connector terminated and ready for installation.

Cablecasting

Programming carried on cable television exclusive of broadcast signals. Also see **Cable origination**.

Cable converter

Equipment in the homes of cable subscribers used to convert cable signals to normal TV channels.

Cable modem

A type of modem that connects a computer to the cable (CATV) network, which in turn connects to the Internet. Once connected, cable modem users have a continuous connection to the Internet. Cable modems feature asymmetric transfer rates: around 36 Mbps downstream and from 200 Kbps to 2 Mbps upstream.

Cable origination

Programming originated by a cable operator or other nonbroadcast signals carried by a cable system.

Cable plant

The cable plant consists of all the optical elements including fiber connectors, splices, etc., between a transmitter and a receiver.

Cable system operator

The company or individual responsible for the operation of a cable television system (usually the system owner as well).

Cable Television Administration and Marketing Society (CTAM)

A professional society that deals with key management and marketing issues in the cable industry by providing a forum for idea exchange.

Cable Television Advertising Bureau (CAB)

An organization established to provide promotional and advisory services to the cable industry.

Cable system

A facility designed for the purpose of receiving multiple broadcast and/or nonbroadcast signals and distributing them via coaxial or fiber optic cable to subscribers living in unattached residences not under common ownership. Signals may be received over the air, by satellite or microwave relay, or from the system's studio or remote facilities.

Cable ready

A term that describes television sets that have circuitry built in that enables them to receive and translate cable signals without the use of separate converters. Cable-ready sets, however, usually cannot decode pay television signals that have been scrambled to prevent unauthorized reception.

Cabling

A combination of cables, wire, cords, and connecting hardware used in the telecommunications infrastructure.

Campus backbone

Cabling between buildings that share telecommunications facilities.

Campus distributor (CD)

The international term for main cross-connect. The distributor from which the campus backbone cable emanates.

Capacitance

The capacity of a wire or device to store an electrical charge.

Carrier

An electrical signal of a set frequency that can be modulated in order to carry data.

Carrier detect

Circuit that detects the presence of a carrier.

Carrier sense multiple access/collision detection (CSMA/CD)

A communication access method used by Ethernet. When a device wants to gain access to the network, it checks to see if the network is free. If it is not, it waits a random amount of time before retrying. If the network is free and two devices attempt to gain access at exactly the same time, they both back off to avoid a collision and each wait a random amount of time before retrying.

Carrier-to-noise ratio

The ratio, in decibels, of the level of the carrier to that of the noise in a receiver's IF bandwidth before any nonlinear process such as amplitude limiting and detection takes place.

Community antenna television (CATV)

A television distribution method whereby signals from distant stations are received, amplified, and then transmitted by coaxial or fiber cable or microwave links to subscribers. This term is now typically used to refer to cable TV.

Compact disk (CD)

Often used to describe high-quality audio, CD-quality audio, or short-wavelength lasers; CD laser.

CE

European compliance (this is not a certification agency, but CE is the European compliance mark).

Celsius

Measure of temperature where water freezes at 0° and boils at 100°.

Cell

The fixed-length transmission unit used by ATM. Each cell is 53 bytes long with a 5-byte header containing its connection identifier and a 48-byte payload. See **CLP, HEC, PTI, VCI/VPI**.

Cell loss priority (CLP)

A one-bit descriptor found in ATM cell headers, indicating the relative importance of a cell. If set to 0, the cell should not be discarded. If set to 1, the cell may be discarded if there is congestion in the switch. The cell content is set by the AAL.

Center wavelength

In a laser, the nominal value central operating wavelength. It is the wavelength defined by a peak mode measurement where the effective optical power resides. In an LED, the average of the two wavelengths measured at the half amplitude points of the power spectrum.

Centimeter (cm)

Approximately 0.4 inches.

Central office

A common carrier switching office in which users' lines terminate. The nerve center of a telephone system.

Certification agencies

Primarily involved in certification of products or manufacturers to standards developed by the certification agency or by others.

CGA

Color graphics adapter; a low-resolution color standard for computer monitors.

Channel

The end-to-end transmission path connecting any two points at which application-specific equipment is connected. Equipment and work area cables are included in the channel.

Channel capacity

The number of channels available for current or future use on a cable system. Capacity is determined by the capabilities of the system hardware; actual offerings are determined by the cable company based on its own marketing decisions and any requirements specified in the franchise agreement.

Character-oriented protocol

Protocol in which blocks of data are marked by special characters.

Cheapernet

Another name for thin Ethernet or 10Base2 systems.

Checkpoint

An event in a series of transactions that can be used to roll back transactions in the event of a failure. Also an HDLC error recovery mechanism.

Checksum

A value created by adding up bits in a packet. The resultant value is computed at the sender and receiver of data. Mismatches trigger error-recovery routines.

Chirp

In laser diodes, the shift of the laser's central wavelength during single-pulse durations due to laser instability.

Chromatic dispersion

All fiber has the property that the speed an optical pulse travels depends on its wavelength. This is caused by several factors including material dispersion, waveguide dispersion, and profile dispersion. The net effect is that if an optical pulse contains multiple wavelengths (colors), then the different colors will travel at different speeds and arrive at different times, smearing the received optical signal.

Churn

Turnover of cable subscribers as a result of disconnects and new customers.

Cladding

A covering of glass or plastic surrounding a fiber optic core, designed to prevent light waves from leaving the core.

Cladding mode

A mode confined to the cladding, a light ray that propagates in the cladding.

Class of Service (CoS)

A set of characteristics (such as route security, transmission priority, and bandwidth) used to construct a route between session partners. The class of service is specified by the initiator of a session.

Cleave

The process of separating an optical fiber by a controlled fracture of the glass, for the purpose of obtaining a fiber end, which is flat, smooth, and perpendicular to the fiber axis.

Client

A node on a network that requests services from a network server.

Client/server

A networking system in which one or more file servers (server) provide services, such as network management, application processing, and centralized data storage for workstations (clients).

Cluster controller

A device that handles input and output for several devices attached to it.

CMIS

Common Management Information System.

CMOS

Complementary metal oxide semiconductor; a family of IC's, particularly useful for low-speed or low-power applications.

CMOT

Common Management Information Protocol Over TCP/IP.

Coating

The material surrounding the cladding of a fiber. Generally a soft plastic material that protects the fiber from damage.

Coaxial cable

Transmission line for television and radio signals, the type most frequently used in cable television systems. Consists of two concentric tubular conductors with an insulator between. A coaxial cable is capable of carrying many TV or radio signals simultaneously.

Coder/decoder (codec)

Converts analog signals into digital signals.

Codes and standards

Installation codes and product safety, performance, and interchangeability standards.

Coherent communications

In fiber optics, a communication system where the output of a local laser oscillator is mixed optically with a received signal, and the difference frequency is detected and amplified.

Collapsed backbone

A local area network configuration wherein bridging and routing functions are located at the main cross-connect and accessed via optical fiber (usually 2 or 4). Concentrators (twisted pair to fiber) remain at the horizontal cross-connects.

Collision

When electrical signals from two or more devices sharing a common data transfer medium crash into one another. This commonly happens on Ethernet-type systems.

Color subcarrier

The 3.58 MHz signal that carries color information in a TV signal.

Common communications support (CCS)

Communication specifications used for SAA.

Common management information protocol (CMIP)

OSI protocol for network monitoring and control (ISO 9596).

Common mode transmission

A transmission scheme where voltages appear equal in magnitude and phase across a conductor pair with respect to ground. May also be referred to as longitudinal mode.

Communications controller

A specialized device for connecting several communication lines to a single computer. It is usually purchased for a specific set of protocols.

Communications satellite

A space vehicle that receives radio and television signals and transmits them back to Earth. It is located 22,300 miles above Earth in a geosynchronous orbit so that it is stationary in relationship to a fixed position on Earth. One use of the communications satellite is by the cable industry for transmitting network programming. Commonly called *bird*.

Communications server

A specialized device on a network to manage access to outside networks.

Community antenna television (CATV)
Association primarily composed of cable system operators with a small number of subscribers, usually less than 3,000.

Composite sync
A signal consisting of horizontal sync pulses, vertical sync pulses, and equalizing pulses only, with a no-signal reference level.

Composite video
A signal that consists of the luminance (black and white), chrominance (color), blanking pulses, sync pulses, and color burst.

Compression
Reducing the representation of information, but not the information itself or reducing the bandwidth or bits necessary to encode information. Full standard coding of broadcast quality television typically requires 45 to 90 Mbps. Compressed video includes signals from 3 Mbps down to 56 Kbps.

Compulsory license
The authorization enjoyed by a cable system under the Copyright Act of 1976 to retransmit programs without negotiating payments to individual copyright owners.

Concatenation
The process of connecting pieces of fiber together.

Concentrator
A device that provides a central connection point for cables from workstations, servers, and peripherals. Most concentrators contain the ability to amplify the electrical signal they receive.

Concentricity
The measurement of how well centered the core is within the cladding.

Conductor
A material that can carry an electrical signal.

Connection admission control (CAC)
The set of actions taken by the network during the connection setup phase in order to determine whether a connection-requested Quality of Service can be accepted or should be rejected. CAC is also used when routing a connection through an ATM network.

Connection-oriented

A relationship set up between sender and receiver to provide increased data transfer reliability.

Connectionless

No relationship set between sender and receiver for reliability's sake.

Connectionless network protocol (CLNP)

From OSI.

Connectionless network service (CLNS)

Also from OSI.

Connectivity

The attachment of devices on a network. The devices may be similar or dissimilar.

Connector

A mechanical or optical device that provides a demountable connection between two fibers or a fiber and a source or detector.

Connector receptacle

The fixed or stationary half of a connection that is mounted on a panel/bulkhead. Receptacles mate with plugs.

Connector variation

The maximum value in dB of the difference in insertion loss between mating optical connectors (with remating, temperature cycling, etc.). Also called optical connector variation.

CONS

Connection oriented network service.

Consolidation point (CP)

A location for interconnection between horizontal cables that extend from building pathways and horizontal cables that extend into work area pathways.

Constant bit rate (CBR)

Said of real time services/data transmissions that accept no or very little delay of the output signal. Video, for instance, may use a constant bit rate service. See **Isochronous**. Can also use VBR.

Consultative Committee for International Telegraph and Telephone (CCITT)

An international organization that develops communication standards such as Recommendation X.25. Name recently changed to ITU (International Telecommunication Union).

Contention

In reference to Ethernet-type systems, devices contend for single data channel.

Continuity

An uninterrupted pathway for electrical signals.

Controlled access unit (CAU)

Newer, more intelligent version of the token ring's multistation access unit (MAU).

Converter

A device that translates cable signals into television signals and allows the viewer to select individual channels.

Copper distributed data interface (CDDI)

The copper equivalent to fiber optic's FDDI.

Copyright Act of 1976

Bill enacted to revise 1909 copyright law in order to have a single nationwide system protecting copyrighted works. The act created the Copyright Royalty Tribunal. This act considers copyright ownership of sound recordings, television broadcasts, cable television, and phonograph records. In cable television, the law requires payment (under compulsory licensing) of royalties for retransmitting copyrighted materials by cable system. The amounts are distributed to the copyright owner by the Copyright Royalty Tribunal.

Core

The heat-conducting central portion of an optical fiber, composed of material with a higher index of refraction than the cladding. The portion of the fiber that transmits light.

Counter-rotating

An arrangement whereby two signal paths, one in each direction, exist in a ring topology.

Counter-rotating ring

Technology used in FDDI to provide fault tolerance.

Coupler

An optical device that combines or splits power from optical fibers.

Coupling ratio/loss (CR, CL)

The ratio/loss of optical power from one output port to the total output power, expressed as a percent. For a 1×2 WDM or coupler with output powers O1 and O2, and Oi representing both output powers.

CPE

Customer-provided equipment.

Critical Angle

In geometric optics, at a refractive boundary, the smallest angle of incidence at which total internal reflection occurs.

Cross-connect

A facility enabling the termination of cables as well as their interconnection or cross-connection with other cabling or equipment. Also known as a distributor.

Cross-connection

A connection scheme between cabling runs, subsystems, and equipment using patch cords or jumpers that attach to connecting hardware on each end.

Cross talk

The carryover of a signal in a wire to another wire near it. A potential problem in twisted-pair systems.

CSMA/CA

Carrier sense multiple access/collision avoidance is a network access method in which each device signals its intent to transmit before it actually does so. This prevents other devices from sending information, thus preventing collisions between signals from two or more devices. This is the access method used by LocalTalk.

CSMA/CD

Carrier sense multiple access/collision detection is a network access method in which devices that are ready to transmit data first check the channel for a carrier. If no carrier is sensed, a device can transmit. If two devices transmit at once, a collision occurs and each computer backs off and waits a random amount of time before attempting to retransmit. This is the access method used by Ethernet.

CTS

Clear to send; signal used in the RS-232 standard.

CUA

Common user access; SAA terminology.

Current

The flow of electrons through a circuit; measured in amps.

Cutback method

A technique of measuring optical fiber attenuation by measuring the optical power at two points at different distances from the test source.

Cutoff wavelength

In single-mode fiber, the wavelength below which the fiber ceases to be single mode.

Cyclic redundancy check (CRC)

An error checking technique used to ensure the accuracy of transmitting digital code over a communications channel. The transmitted messages are divided into predetermined lengths that, used as dividends, are divided by a fixed divisor. The remainder of the calculation is appended onto and sent with the message. At the receiving end, the computer recalculates the remainder. If it does not match the transmitted remainder, an error is detected.

CW

Abbreviation for continuous wave. Usually refers to the constant optical output from an optical source when it is biased (turned on) but not modulated with a signal.

D/A converter

Digital-to-analog converter.

DAC

Digital-to-analog converter.

Daisy chain

An arrangement of devices connected in a series, one after the other. Any signals transmitted to the devices go to the first device, and from the first to the second, and so on.

DAP

Data access protocol.

Dark current

The induced current that exists in a reversed biased photodiode in the absence of incident optical power. It is better understood to be caused by the shunt resistance of the photodiode. A bias voltage across the diode (and the shunt resistance) causes current to flow in the absence of light.

DAS

Dynamically assigned sockets.

DAT

Digital audio tape.

Data channels

An umbrella term for all forms of video transmission that involve electronically generated text and/or graphics rather than recorded or live action images. Generally refers to local cable channels on which alphanumeric material is displayed by character generators, although video text and teletext also fall into this category.

Data communications equipment or data circuit-terminating equipment (DCE)

Technical term for a modem. Device that establishes, maintains, and destroys a session on a network.

Datagram

A TCP/IP packet containing data and a source and destination address. It uses an unreliable delivery method.

Data Link layer

Layer 2 of the OSI model. Responsible for node-to-node validity and integrity of the transmission, it allows messages to be placed into packets and vice versa. It also controls data flow.

Data rate

The number of bits of information in a transmission system, expressed in bits per second (b/s or bps), and which may or may not be equal to the signal or baud rate.

Data service unit/channel service unit (DSU/CSU)

A communications device that connects an in-house line to an external digital circuit (T1). The DSU converts data into the required format, while the CSU terminates the line, provides signal regeneration, and remote testing. A DSU/CSU is not limited to T1; it can be used with 56K DDS and slower circuits as well.

Data set

Typically, a modem.

Data stream

A continuous flow of data from a source to a destination.

Data structure

The physical layout of data, such as fields.

Data terminal equipment (DTE)

A communications device that is the source or destination of signals on a network. It is typically a terminal or computer.

Data eXchange Interface (DXI)

Protocols used for SMDS and ATM data exchange between a router and a DSU.

DB-9

Nine-pin connector.

DB-25

Twenty-five pin connector meeting RS-232 specifications.

DDP

Datagram delivery protocol.

Decibel (dB)

A unit of relative change of power (for example, -10 dB).

Decoder

An electronic device used for converting a scrambled TV signal into a viewable picture.

Dedicated channel

A cable channel devoted to a single source for its programming.

Dedicated line

Transmission line servicing only one type of data. Pathway is permanent.

Delay skew

The difference in propagation delay between the fastest and slowest pair in a cable or cabling system.

Demarcation point (DP)

A point where operational control or ownership changes.

Demodulator

A device that removes a signal from a carrier for subsequent conversion to digital data. Modems (MOdulatorDEModulators) do this.

Demultiplexer

A module that separates two or more signals previously combined by compatible multiplexing equipment.

Detector

An opto-electric transducer used in fiber optics to convert optical power to electrical current. Usually referred to as a photodiode.

DHA

Destination hardware address.

Diameter-mismatch loss

The loss of power at a joint that occurs when the transmitting fiber has a diameter greater than the diameter of the receiving fiber. The loss occurs when coupling light from a source to fiber, from fiber to fiber, or from fiber to detector.

Dichroic filter

An optical filter that transmits light according to wavelength. Dichroic filters reflect light that they do not transmit.

DIB

Directory information base.

DID

Destination IDentification.

Dielectric

Any substance in which an electric field may be maintained with zero or near-zero power dissipation. This term usually refers to nonmetallic materials.

Differential gain

A type of distortion in a video signal that causes the brightness information to be distorted.

Differential mode transmission

A transmission scheme where voltages appear equal in magnitude and opposite in phase across a twisted pair with respect to ground. May also be referred to as balanced mode.

Differential phase

A type of distortion in a video signal that causes the color information to be distorted.

Diffraction grating

An array of fine, parallel, equally spaced reflecting or transmitting lines that mutually enhance the effects of diffraction to concentrate the diffracted light in a few directions determined by the spacing of the lines and by the wavelength of the light.

Digital

In telecommunications, in recording or in computing, digital is the use of a binary code to represent information. Recording or transmitting information digitally has two major benefits. First, the signal can be reproduced precisely. In digital transmission, the signal is first regenerated. It's put through a little *yes–no* question. Is this signal a *one* or a *zero*? The signal is reconstructed (squared off, to what it was originally). Then it is amplified and sent along its way. So digital transmission is much *cleaner* than analog transmission. The second major benefit of digital is that the electronic circuitry to handle digital is getting cheaper and more powerful.

Digital data

Information that is digital (1s and 0s) in nature.

Digital subscriber line (DSL)

A next-generation digital phone service that allows for the transmission of voice, video, and data over existing copper telephone wires at very high speeds. There are several implementations of DSL, which differ by the upstream and downstream speeds they support.

Diode

An electronic device that lets current flow in only one direction. Semiconductor diodes used in fiber optics contain a junction between regions of different doping. They include light emitters (LEDs and laser diodes) and detectors (photodiodes).

Diode laser

Synonymous with injection laser diode.

Diplexer

A device that combines two or more types of signals into a single output.

Direct broadcast satellite (DBS)

A service that transmits satellite signals directly to a home through the viewer's own earth station rather than through a cable system.

Directional coupler

A coupling device for separately sampling (through a known coupling loss) either the forward (incident) or the backward (reflected) wave in a transmission line.

Disconnects

Subscribers who have terminated cable service or whose service has been terminated for any reason.

Disconnect rate

The percentage of cable subscribers in a given area who have discontinued service in a certain time period.

Dish

A parabolic or spherical shaped antenna.

Dispersion

The temporal spreading of a light signal in an optical waveguide caused by light signals traveling at different speeds through a fiber either due to modal or chromatic effects.

Dispersion-shifted fiber

Standard single-mode fibers that exhibit optimum attenuation performance at 1,550 nm and optimum bandwidth at 1,300 nm. Dispersion-shifted fibers are made so that both attenuation and bandwidth are optimum at 1,550 nm.

Distant signal

A broadcast signal originating outside the cable system's local market as defined by the FCC under the mandatory carriage rule.

Distortion

Nonlinearities in a unit that cause harmonics and beat products to be generated.

Distortion-limited operation

Generally synonymous with bandwidth-limited operation.

Distributed feedback laser (DFB)

An injection laser diode that has a Bragg reflection grating in the active region in order to suppress multiple longitudinal modes and enhance a single longitudinal mode.

Distribution system

In a cable system, the portion of the cable system that carries signals from the headend to the subscribers' homes.

Distributor

See **Cross-connect**.

Domain

A subset of a larger network made up of endpoints and network devices. Virtual LANs are a type of autonomous domain.

Dominant mode

The mode in an optical device spectrum with the most power.

Dope

Thick liquid or paste used to prepare a surface or a varnish-like substance used for waterproofing or strengthening a material.

Double-window fiber

This term is used two ways. For multimode fibers, the term means that the fiber is optimized for 850 nm and 1,300 nm operation. For single-mode fibers, the term means that the fiber is optimized for 1,300 nm and 1,550 nm operation.

Downlink

Part of a satellite communications system by which information is carried from satellite to ground.

Drop

Coaxial cable connecting the cable in the street to the subscriber's home and television set. Also see **Cable Television System**.

DS

Directory services.

DS1/DS3

See T1/T3.

DSAP

Destination Service Access Point.

DSL modem

A type of modem that connects a computer to a DSL network, which in turn connects to the Internet. Once connected, DSL modem users have a continuous connection to the Internet.

DSU (data service unit)

Data transmission equipment used to interface to a digital circuit at the customer site. It converts the customer's datastream, such as X.21 to E1 or T1 for transmission through the CSU, which is often contained, functionally within the DSU device. DSUs can convert data to or from a native port on a router to an E1, E2, or E3 leased line, primary rate ISDN, or SMDS; DSU functionality can be built into devices such as some routers or multiplexers. In Europe a DSU can convert E1 bandwidth into RS.449, X.21, V.35 or other serial interface via a router. A DSU with an HSSI interface will deliver E2 or E3 bandwidth from the WAN to an HSSI router on a LAN.

DSx

A transmission rate in the North American digital telephone hierarchy; also called T-carrier.

DTR

Data terminal ready.

DUA

Directory user agent.

Dual attachment concentrator

A concentrator that offers two attachments to the FDDI network, which are capable of accommodating a dual (counter-rotating) ring.

Dual attachment station

A station that offers two attachments to the FDDI network, which are capable of accommodating a dual (counter-rotating) ring.

Dual ring (FDDI dual ring)

A pair of counter-rotating logical rings.

Dumb terminal

Refers to devices that are designed to communicate exclusively with a host computer. It receives all screen layouts from the host computer and sends all keyboard entry to the host. It cannot function without the host computer.

Duplex

Simultaneous two-way transmission of data; also referred to as full duplex or half duplex.

Duplex cable

A two-fiber cable suitable for duplex transmission.

Duplex transmission

Transmission in both directions, either one direction at a time (half-duplex) or both directions simultaneously (full-duplex).

Duplication

The airing of the same programs in close succession by two or more pay cable services in the same market.

Duty cycle

In a digital transmission, the fraction of time a signal is at the high level.

E1/E3

The European version of T1/T3 (see these abbreviations). E1 runs at 2.048 Mbps and E3 runs at 34 Mbps.

Earth satellite

Communications station used to send or receive electronic signals from or to a satellite (seldom both). Usually employs one of a variety of dish-type antennae used by television stations and cable operators.

EBCDIC

Extended Binary Coded Decimal Interchange Code; IBM-developed 8-bit character coding.

ECL

Emitter-coupled logic. A high-speed logic family capable of GHz rates.

Edge-emitting diode

An LED that emits light from its edge, producing more direction output than surface-emitting LEDs that emit from their top surface.

EGA

Enhanced graphics adapter; a medium-resolution color standard for computer monitors.

EIA

Electronic Industries Association. Developed the RS-232 specification.

Electromagnetic compatibility (EMC)

The ability of a system to minimize radiated emissions and maximize immunity from external noise sources.

Electromagnetic interference (EMI)

The interference in signal transmission or reception caused by electromagnetic radiation generated by other equipment or cabling.

Electromagnetic radiation (EMR)

Radiation made up of oscillating electric and magnetic fields and propagated with the speed of light. Includes gamma radiation, X-rays, ultraviolet, visible and infrared radiation, and radar and radio waves.

Electromagnetic spectrum

The range of frequencies of electromagnetic radiation from zero to infinity.

Electronic Industries Alliance (EIA)

An organization that sets standards for interfaces to ensure compatibility between data communications equipment and data terminal equipment.

Ellipticity

Describes the fact that the core or cladding may be elliptical rather than circular.

Encryption

Coding of data into indecipherable symbols.

Endoscope

A fiber optic bundle used for imaging and viewing inside the human body.

Enterprise network

A network comprising all the LANs or other networks within a single organization.

Entrance facility (EF)

An entrance to a building for both public and private network service cables (including antennae), including the entrance point at the building wall and continuing to the entrance room or space. Entrance facilities are often used to house electrical protection equipment and connecting hardware for the transition between outdoor and indoor cable.

EOT

End of transmission.

Equal level far-end cross talk (ELFEXT)

Cross talk measured at the opposite end from which the disturbing signal is transmitted, normalized by the attenuation contribution of the cable or cabling.

Equilibrium mode distribution (EMD)

The steady modal state of a multimode fiber in which the relative power distribution among modes is independent of fiber length.

Equipment cable

A cable or cable assembly used to connect telecommunications equipment to horizontal or backbone cabling systems in the telecommunications closet and equipment room. Equipment cables are considered to be outside the scope of cabling standards.

Equipment room (ER)

A centralized space for telecommunications equipment that serves the occupants of the building or multiple buildings in a campus environment. An equipment room is considered distinct from a telecommunications closet because it is considered to be a building or campus serving (as opposed to floor serving) facility and because of the nature or complexity of the equipment that it contains.

Erbium-doped fiber amplifier

Optical fibers doped with the rare earth element erbiu, which can amplify light in the 1,550 nm region when pumped by an external light source.

ESCON

Enterprise systems connection; a duplex optical connector used for computer-to-computer data exchange.

Ethernet

A network protocol invented by Xerox Corporation and developed jointly by Xerox, Intel, and Digital Equipment Corporation. Ethernet networks use CSMA/CD and run over a variety of cable types at 10 Mbps.

Evanescent wave

Light guided in the inner part of an optical fiber's cladding rather than the core.

Excess loss

In a fiber optic coupler, the optical loss from that portion of light that does not merge from the nominal operation ports of the device.

Extended Industry Standard Architecture (EISA)

A type of computer bus.

External modulation

Modulation of a light source by an external device that acts like an electronic shutter.

Extinction ratio

The ratio of the low, or OFF, optical power level (Pl) to the high, or ON optical power level (Ph).

Extrinsic loss

In a fiber interconnection, that portion of loss not intrinsic to the fiber but related to imperfect joining of a connector or splice.

Eye pattern

Also called eye diagram. The proper function of a digital system can be quantitatively described by its BER, or qualitatively by its eye pattern. The "openness" of the eye relates to the BER that can be achieved.

Fahrenheit

Measure of temperature where water freezes at 32° and boils at 212°.

Failure rate

The number of failures of a device per unit of time.

Fall time

Also called turn-off time. The time required for the trailing edge of a pulse to fall from 90% to 10% of its amplitude; the time required for a component to produce such a result. Typically measured between the 80% and 20% points or alternately the 90% and 10% points.

Faraday effect

A phenomenon that causes some materials to rotate the polarization of light in the presence of a magnetic field parallel to the direction of propagation. Also called magneto-optic effect.

Far-end cross talk (FEXT)

Cross talk measured at the opposite end from which the disturbing signal is transmitted.

Fast Ethernet

A new Ethernet standard that supports 100 Mbps using category 5 twisted-pair or fiber optic cable.

FBE

Free buffer enquiry.

FC

A threaded optical connector that originated in Japan. Good for single-mode or multimode fiber and applications requiring low back reflection.

FC/PC

See **FC**. A special curved polish on the connector for very low back reflection.

FDA

Food and Drug Administration; organization responsible for laser safety.

FDDI

Fiber Distributed Data Interface; fiber standard that uses only an iota of fiber's throughput capacity.

Federal Communications Commission (FCC)

Charged with protecting airwaves in the U.S.

Fiber distributed data interface (FDDI)

An ANSI standard for a 100 Mbps token-passing ring based on fiber optic transmission media.

Ferrule

A rigid tube that confines or holds a fiber as part of a connector assembly.

Fiber channel

An industry-standard specification that originated in Great Britain that details computer channel communications over fiber optics at transmission speeds from 132 Mb/s to 1062.5 Mb/s at distances of up to 10 kilometers.

Fiber grating

An optical fiber in which the refractive index of the core varies periodically along its length, scattering light in a way similar to a diffraction grating, and transmitting or reflecting certain wavelengths selectively.

Fiber optic attenuator

A component installed in a fiber optic transmission system that reduces the power in the optical signal. It is often used to limit the optical power received by the photodetector to within the limits of the optical receiver.

Fiber optic cable

A cable, consisting of a center glass core surrounded by layers of plastic, that transmits data using light rather than electricity. It has the ability to carry more information over much longer distances than copper cables can.

Fiber optic communication system

The transfer of modulated or unmodulated optical energy through optical fiber media, which terminates in the same or different media.

Fiber optic gyroscope

A coil of optical fiber that can detect rotation about its axis.

Fiber optic link

A transmitter, receiver, and cable assembly that can transmit information between two points.

Fiber optics

A method of transmitting signals using light waves sent through extremely thin fibers spun from glass. Fiber optic cables can carry greater amounts of information than copper wire carrying electrical signals.

Fiber optic span

An optical fiber/cable terminated at both ends that may include devices that add, subtract, or attenuate optical signals.

Fiber optic subsystem

A functional entity with defined bounds and interfaces that is part of a system. It contains solid state and/or other components and is specified as a subsystem for the purpose of trade and commerce.

Fiber optic test procedure (FOTP)

Standards developed and published by the Electronic Industries Association (EIA) under the EIA-RS-455 series of standards.

Fiber optic transmission

A communications scheme whereby electrical data is converted to light energy and transmitted through optical fibers.

Fiber-to-the-curb (FTTC)

Fiber optic service to a node connected by wires to several nearby homes, typically on a block.

Fiber-to-the-home (FTTH)

Fiber optic service to a node located inside an individual home.

Fiber-to-the-loop (FTTL)

Fiber optic service to a node that is located in a neighborhood.

File server

A computer connected to the network that contains primary files/applications and shares them as requested with the other computers on the network. If the file server is dedicated for that purpose only, it is connected to a client/server network. An example of a client/server network is Novell Netware. All the computers connected to a peer-to-peer network are capable of being the file server. Two examples of peer-to-peer networks are LANtastic and Windows for Workgroups.

Filter
A device that transmits only part of the incident energy and may thereby change the spectral distribution of energy.

Firestop
A material, device, or assembly of parts installed in a cable pathway at a fire-rated wall or floor to prevent passage of flame, smoke, or gases through the rated barrier (between cubicles or separated rooms or spaces).

FIT
Rate number of device failures in one billion device hours.

Flag
Typically a certain bit that has meaning in bit-oriented protocols.

Floor distributor (FD)
The international term for horizontal cross-connect. The distributor used to connect between the horizontal cable and other cabling subsystems or equipment.

Fluoride glasses
Materials that have the amorphous structure of glass but are made of fluoride compounds (zirconium fluoride) rather than oxide compounds (silica). Suitable for very long wavelength transmission.

FP
Fabry-Perot; generally refers to a type of laser.

Frame
A block of data in bit-oriented protocols.

Frame check sequence (FCS)
Error-detection field.

Franchise/franchise agreement
A contract between a cable television company and a local government authorizing the company to operate in the locale and defining the terms under which it may install coaxial or fiber optic cable and offer cable television service within the community.

Franchise area
The specific geographic area in which the cable television company may offer service, as defined by the franchise.

Frequency
Cycles per second; measured in Hertz (Hz).

Frequency division multiplexing

The official term for placing several different signals on a wire, each having its own unique frequencies (broadband LANs).

Frequency modulation (FM)

Used to encode data into a carrier of a set frequency. The changes in frequency represent 1s and 0s.

Fresnel reflection loss

Reflection losses at the ends of fibers caused by differences in the refractive index between glass and air. The maximum reflection caused by a perpendicular air-glass interface is about 4% or about –14 dB.

FS

Frame status.

FSK

Frequency shift keying. A method of encoding data by means of two or more tones.

FTAM

File transfer access management.

FTP

File transfer protocol.

Full duplex

Describes the simultaneous two-way flow of data.

Fused coupler

A method of making a multimode or single-mode coupler by wrapping fibers together, heating them, and pulling them to form a central unified mass so that light on any input fiber is coupled to all output fibers.

Fused fiber

A bundle of fibers fused together so they maintain a fixed alignment with respect to each other in a rigid rod.

Fusion splicer

An instrument that permanently bonds two fibers together by heating and fusing them.

FWHM

Full width half maximum; used to describe the width of a spectral emission at the 50% amplitude points.

FWHP

Full width half power; also known as FWHM.

G

Giga; one billion.

G.lite

A version of ADSL technology that does not require a POTS splitter to be installed in the customer's home. A POTS splitter separates voice from data transmission for simultaneous telephone and data access use. G.lite supports downstream data rates of up to 1.5 Mbps and upstream data rates of up to 512 Kbps.

GaALAs

Gallium aluminum arsenide; generally used for short wavelength light emitters.

GaAS

Gallium arsenide; used in light emitters.

GaInAsP

Gallium indium arsenide phosphide; generally used for long wavelength light emitters.

Gap loss

Loss resulting from the end separation of two axially aligned fibers.

Gate

(1) A device having one output channel and one or more input channels, such that the output channel state is completely determined by the input channel states, except during switching transients; (2) one of the many types of combinational logic elements having at least two inputs.

Gateway

The original term for what is now called a router or, more precisely, an IP router. A gateway connects two or more communications networks together at the Network layer. It may perform protocol conversion from one network to the other. A communications link between a local area network and a mainframe or mini-computer.

Gaussian beam

A beam pattern used to approximate the distribution of energy in a fiber core. It can also be used to describe emission patterns from surface-emitting LEDs. Most people would recognize it as the bell curve.

Gbaud

One billion bits of data per second.

Ge

Germanium; generally used in detectors. Good for most wavelengths (800–1,600 nm).

Generic flow control (GFC)

The first 4 bits of the ATM UNI 3.0 cell header; used when passing through the user-network interface (UNI).

Genlock

A process of sync generator locking. This is usually performed by introducing a composite video signal from a master source to the subject sync generator. The generator to be locked has circuits to isolate vertical drive, horizontal drive, and subcarrier. The process then involves locking the subject generator to the master subcarrier, horizontal, and vertical drives so that the result is that both sync generators are running at the same frequency and phase.

GHz

Gigahertz.

Gigabyte (GB)

One billion bytes of information; one thousand megabytes.

Global Network

A network that is global and allows access to several organizations.

GMII

Gigabit media independent interface.

GOSIP

Government OSI profile; specifies that all government agencies shall follow OSI guidelines in creating and expanding networks. Now under review.

Graded-index fiber

Optical fiber in which the refractive index of the core is in the form of a parabolic curve, decreasing toward the cladding.

GRIN

Gradient index; generally refers to the SELFOC lens often used in fiber optics.

Ground

A conducting connection, whether intentional or accidental, between an electrical circuit (telecommunications) or equipment and earth, or to some conducting body that serves in place of the earth.

Ground loop noise

Noise that results when equipment is grounded at points having different potentials, thereby creating an unintended current path. The dielectric properties of optical fiber provide electrical isolation that eliminates ground loops.

Group index

Also called group refractive index. In fiber optics, for a given mode propagating in a medium of refractive index (n), the group index (N), is the velocity of light in a vacuum (c), divided by the group velocity of the mode.

Group velocity

(1) The velocity of propagation of an envelope produced when an electromagnetic wave is modulated by, or mixed with, other waves of different frequencies; (2) for a particular mode, the reciprocal of the rate of change of the phase constant with respect to angular frequency; (3) the velocity of the modulated optical power.

Half duplex

Describes transmissions where data only travels in one direction at any given moment.

Handshaking

Signals sent by communicating devices to initiate and synchronize the communication.

Hard-clad silica fiber

An optical fiber having a silica core and a hard polymeric plastic cladding intimately bounded to the core.

HDTV

High-definition television. Television that has approximately twice the horizontal and twice the vertical emitted resolution specified by the NTSC standard.

Headend

The equipment at a cable system that receives the various program source signals, processes them, and retransmits them to subscribers.

Header Error Control (HEC)

The HEC field is an 8-bit cyclic redundancy check (CRC) computed on all fields in an ATM header and capable of detecting single-bit and certain multiple-bit errors.

Hertz (Hz)

A measure of frequency as defined in units of cycles per second.

Hewlett-Packard (HP)

Computer company often pioneering new techniques. Now implementing wireless infrared communications for transferring data from portable PCs to desktop PCs.

High-level data link control (HDLC)

A bit-oriented protocol established by the ISO.

HIPPI

High performance parallel interface as defined by ANSI X3T9.3 document.

Home Phoneline Networking Alliance (HomePNA)

A professional association of high-technology companies working to ensure the adoption of a single, unified phoneline networking standard, and to bring to market a variety of interoperable home networking solutions. 3Com is a founding member of the HomePNA.

Home-run cabling

A distribution method in which individual cables are run directly from the horizontal cross-connect to each telecommunications outlet. This configuration is also known as star topology.

Homes passed

The number of homes in which cable television service is or can be readily made available because feeder cables are in place nearby.

Horizontal cabling

The cabling between and including the telecommunications outlet and the horizontal cross-connect.

Horizontal cross-connect (HC)

A cross-connect of horizontal cabling to other cabling (horizontal, backbone, or equipment).

Host

Computer that offers services on a network.

Housedrop

The coaxial cable between the cable in the street and subscriber's television set. Also see **Cable Television System**.

Hub

A hardware device that contains multiple independent but connected modules of network and internetwork equipment. Hubs can be active (where they repeat signals sent through them) or passive (where they do not repeat but merely split signals sent through them).

Hybrid cable

An assembly of two or more cables, of the same or different types or categories, covered by one overall sheath.

Hydrogen losses

Increases in fiber attenuation that occur when hydrogen diffuses into the glass matrix and absorbs some light.

Hz

Hertz.

IC

Integrated circuits.

ICMP

Internet control message protocol.

IDF

Intermediate distribution frame. This is usually located on each floor within a building. It is tied directly to the Main Distibution Frame via 100- or 200-pair copper cables.

IDG

Interdialog gap; used in LocalTalk networks.

IDP

Internetwork datagram protocol.

IEEE 802.11 HR

The international IEEE standard for high-rate wireless networking at 11 Mbps.

IETF

Internet Engineering Task Force.

IFG

Interframe gap.

Index-matching fluid

A fluid whose index of refraction nearly equals that of the fiber's core. Used to reduce Fresnel reflection at fiber ends. See also **Index-matching gel**.

Index-matching gel

A gel whose index of refraction nearly equals that of the fiber's core. Used to reduce Fresnel reflection at fiber ends. See also **Index-matching fluid**.

Index of refraction

Also called refractive index. The ratio of the velocity of light in free space to the velocity of light in a fiber material. Symbolized by n. Always greater than or equal to one.

Industry associations

For the purpose of standardization, trade, professional development, etc.

Infrared

Electromagnetic waves whose frequency range is above that of microwaves, but below that of the visible spectrum.

Infrared fiber

Colloquially, optical fibers with best transmission at wavelengths of 2 Jim or longer, made of materials other than silica glass. See also fluoride glasses.

InGaAs

Indium gallium arsenide; generally used to make high-performance long-wavelength detectors.

InGaAsP

Indium gallium arsenide phosphide; generally used for long-wavelength light emitters.

Injection laser diode (ILD)

A laser employing a forward-biased semiconductor junction as the active medium. Stimulated emission of coherent light occurs at a pn junction where electrons and holes are driven into the junction.

Insertion loss

The loss of power that results from inserting a component, such as a connector or splice, into a previously continuous path.

Institute of Electrical and Electronics Engineers (IEEE)
Professional organization that defines some network standards, such as Ethernet.

Integrated detector/preamplifier (IDPI)
A detector package containing a PIN photodiode and transimpedance amplifier.

Integrated services digital network (ISDN)
An all-digital, circuit-switched telephone network.

Intelligent hub
A hub that performs bridging and routing functions in a collapsed backbone environment.

Intensity
The square of the electric field strength of an electromagnetic wave. Intensity is proportional to irradiance and may get used in place of the term "irradiance" when only relative values are important.

Interactive cable
Cable systems that have the technical ability to let subscribers communicate directly with a computer at the system headend from their television sets, using special converters and regular cable lines.

Interbuilding backbone
Telecommunications cable(s) that are part of the campus subsystem that connect one building to another.

Interchannel isolation
The ability to prevent undesired optical energy from appearing in one signal path as a result of coupling from another signal path. Also called cross talk.

Interconnect
Two or more cable systems distributing a commercial signal simultaneously, primarily to maximize the effectiveness of an advertising schedule by offering a multiple system buy in which only one contract need be negotiated. Interconnects can be hard, where systems are directly linked by cable, microwave relays, or by satellite, and the signal is fed to the entire interconnect by one headend; or soft, where there is no direct operational connection between the participating systems but the same commercial is run simultaneously by each of the systems.

Interconnection

A connection scheme that provides direct access to the cabling infrastructure and the ability to make cabling system changes using equipment cords.

Interferometric sensors

Fiber optic sensors that rely on interferometric detection.

Interim local management interface (ILMI)

The standard specification used to manage ATM network interfaces. The ILMI uses the SNMP protocol and an ATM UNI MIB to provide the administrator with status and configuration information.

Intermediate cross-connect (IC)

A cross-connect between first-level and second-level backbone cabling.

International Organization for Standardization (ISO)

An organization that sets international standards, founded in 1946 and headquartered in Geneva. ANSI is the U.S. member body to ISO.

International Telecom

Organization formed by 91 countries for managing global communications and satellite communications systems. COMSAT is the U.S. organization (Intelsat) member.

International Telecommunication Union (ITU)

An international organization that develops communication standards such as Recommendation X.25. Name recently changed from CCITT.

Internet

A global compendium of networks used to exchange information using the TCP/IP protocol. It allows for electronic mail and the accessing and retrieval of information from remote sources.

Internet Packet eXchange (IPX)

A Novell NetWare communications protocol that is used to route messages from one node to another. The Novell version of IP.

Internet protocol (IP)

Associated with TCP, a set of communications protocols developed to internetwork dissimilar systems. The TCP protocol controls the transfer of the data (performing at the equivalent to Layer 4 in the OSI model) and the IP protocol provides the routing mechanism (performing at the equivalent to Layer 3 in the OSI model).

Internet service provider (ISP)

A commercial organization that provides Internet access to individuals and organizations.

Internetwork

Two or more networks connected by bridges and/or routers.

Intrabuilding backbone

Telecommunications cable(s) that are part of the building subsystem that connect one closet to another.

Intrinsic losses

Splice losses arising from differences in the fibers being spliced.

Inverse address resolution protocol (INARP)

An address resolution protocol that maps hardware addresses (Ethernet, token ring) into IP addresses.

IP address

An identifier for a node's network interface, expressed as four fields separated by decimal points. The IP address is divided into a network part and a host part, site-dependent and assigned by an administrator.

IPI

Intelligent peripheral interface as defined by ANSI X3T9.3 document.

Irradiance

Power per unit area.

Isochronous

Signals that are dependent on some uniform timing or carry their own timing information embedded as part of the signal. Voice and video are isochronous signals but data transfer is generally not.

Jacket

The outer, protective covering of the cable.

Jitter

Small and rapid variations in the timing of a waveform due to noise, changes in component characteristics, supply voltages, imperfect synchronizing circuits, etc.

Jitter, data dependent (DDJ)

Also called data dependent distortion. Jitter related to the transmitted symbol sequence. DDJ is caused by the limited bandwidth characteristics, nonideal individual pulse responses, and imperfections in the optical channel components.

Jitter, duty cycle distortion (DCD)

Distortion usually caused by propagation delay differences between low-to-high and high-to-low transitions. DCD is manifested as a pulse width distortion of the nominal baud time.

Jitter, random (RJ)

Random jitter is due to thermal noise and may be modeled as a Gaussian process. The peak-to-peak value of RJ is of a probabilistic nature, and thus any specific value requires an associated probability.

JPEG

Joint photographers expert group; international standard for compressing still photography.

Jumper

A short fiber optic cable with connectors on both ends.

Jumper Wire

An assembly of twisted pairs without connectors on either end used to join telecommunications links at a cross-connect.

K

Kelvin; measure of temperature where water freezes at 273° and boils at 373°.

K

Kilo; one thousand.

KBaud

One thousand bits of data per second.

Kevlar

A very strong, very light, synthetic compound developed by DuPont that is used to strengthen optical cables.

Kg

Kilogram; approximately 2.2 pounds.

KHz

Kilohertz.

Kilobits per second (Kbps)

A measure of the speed at which data can travel. The rate of speed is measured in thousands of bits per second (approximate).

Km

Kilometer: 1km = 3,280 feet or 0.62 miles.

Lambertian emitter

An emitter that radiates according to Lambert's cosine law. This law states that the radiance of certain idealized surfaces is dependent upon the angle from which the surface is viewed. The radiant intensity of such a surface is maximum normal to the surface and decreases in proportion to the cosine of the angle from the normal.

LAN (local area network)

A network connecting computers in a relatively small area such as a building.

LAN emulation (LANE)

How an ATM network simulates a MAC layer service, such as that provided by existing LAN technology (Ethernet or token ring) to allow existing higher layer protocols and applications to be used unchanged over an ATM network.

LAP

Link access protocol.

LAPB

Link access protocol, balanced.

LAPD

Link access protocol, digital.

Large core fiber

Usually a fiber with a core of 200 μm or more.

Laser

Acronym for light amplification by stimulated emission of radiation. A light source that produces, through stimulated emission, coherent, near monochromatic light. Lasers in fiber optics are usually solid-state semiconductor types.

Laser diode

A semiconductor that emits coherent light when forward biased.

LATA

Local access and transport area.

Lateral displacement loss

The loss of power that results from lateral displacement of optimum alignment between two fibers or between a fiber and an active device.

Launch fiber

An optical fiber used to couple and condition light from an optical source into an optical fiber. Often the launch fiber is used to create an equilibrium mode distribution in multimode fiber. Also called launching fiber.

Leased channel

A channel on a cable system that the system has leased to a third party for that party's use. The leasee, not the cable system, is responsible for the programming on the channel.

LED (light emitting diode)

Semiconductor device that emits light produced by converting electrical energy. Status lights on hardware devices are typically LEDs.

LH

Long-haul; a classification of video performance under RS-25OB/C. Lower performance than medium-haul or short-haul.

L-I curve

The plot of optical output (L) as a function of current (I) that characterizes an electrical to optical converter.

Lift

The increase in basic cable penetration brought about by introduction of a new service or program.

Light

In a strict sense, the region of the electromagnetic spectrum that can be perceived by human vision, designated the visible spectrum and nominally covering the wavelength range of 0.4 µm to 0.7 µm. In the laser and optical communication fields, custom and practice have extended usage of the term to include the much broader portion of the electromagnetic spectrum that can be handled by the basic optical techniques used for the visible spectrum. This region has not been clearly defined, but, as employed by most workers in the field, may be considered to extend from the near ultra-violet region of approximately 0.3 µm, through the visible region, and into the mid-infrared region to 30 µm.

Lightguide
Synonym optical fiber.

Light piping
Use of optical fibers to illuminate.

Light wave
The path of a point on a wavefront. The direction of the light wave is generally normal to the wavefront.

Linear bus
A network topology in which each node attaches directly to a common cable.

Link
An end-to-end transmission path provided by the cabling infrastructure. Cabling links include all cables and connecting hardware that comprise the horizontal or backbone subsystems. Equipment and work area cables are not included as part of a link.

LLAP
LocalTalk link access protocol.

LLC
Logical link control.

Local area network (LAN)
A communication link between two or more points within a small geographic area, such as between buildings.

Local exchange carrier (LEC)
The local regulated provider of public-switched telecommunications services.

Local loop
Synonym for loop.

Local origination programming
Programming produced by or under the auspices of a local cable system for presentation on the system. It may also include syndicated programming acquired by the system for presentation therein.

LocalTalk
Apple Corporation proprietary protocol that uses the CSMA/CA media access scheme and supports transmissions at speeds of 230 Kbps.

Long-haul telecommunications

Long-distance telecommunications links such as cross-country or transoceanic.

Longitudinal conversion loss (LCL)

A measure (in dB) of the differential voltage induced on a conductor pair as a result of subjecting that pair to longitudinal voltage. LCL is considered to be a measure of circuit balance.

Longitudinal mode

An optical waveguide mode with boundary condition determined along the length of the optical cavity.

Loop

(1) A communication channel from a switching center or an individual message distribution point to the user terminal; (2) in telephone systems, a pair of wires from a central office to a subscribers's telephone; (3) go and return conductors of an electric circuit; a closed circuit; (4) a closed path under measurement in a resistance test; (5) a type of antenna used extensively in direction-finding equipment and in UHF reception; (6) a sequence of instructions that may be executed iteratively while a certain condition prevails.

Loss

The amount of a signal's power, expressed in dB, that is lost in connectors, splices, or fiber defects.

Loss budget

An accounting of overall attenuation in a system.

Loose-tube

A type of fiber optic cable construction where the fiber is contained within a loose tube in the cable jacket.

LSL

Link support layer.

m

Meter; 39.37".

M

Mega; one million.

MAC

Medium access control.

Macrobending

In a fiber, all macroscopic deviations of the fiber's axis from a straight line.

Main cross-connect (MC)

A cross-connect for first level backbone cables, entrance cables, and equipment cables.

MAN (metropolitan area network)

A network connecting computers over a large geographical area, such as a city or school district.

Management information base (MIB)

A collection of objects (for instance, statistics) pertaining to the general maintenance of a network that can be accessed via a network management protocol.

Mandatory carriage

Those stations whose signals must be carried by cable systems, according to FCC rules. In general, these include all local stations that request carriage, plus specialty stations and those outside stations that are significantly viewed in the community served by the cable system.

Margin

Allowance for attenuation in addition to that explicitly accounted for in system design.

Mass splicing

Simultaneous splicing of many fibers in a cable.

Master antennae television

A single antennae used to provide television service for all units in a hotel, apartment house, or housing complex.

Material dispersion

Dispersion resulting from the different velocities of each wavelength in a material.

MAU (multistation access unit)

A token ring wiring hub.

MBps

Megabytes per second.

Mbps

Megabits per second.

Mechanical splice
An optical fiber splice accomplished by fixtures or materials, rather than by thermal fusion.

Medium access control (MAC)
For local area networks, the method of determining which device has access to the transmission medium at any time (MAC protocol). The MAC sublayer is a part of the Data Link layer in the OSI model that applies a medium access method (for instance, Ethernet or token ring).

Megabits per second (Mbps)
A measure of the speed at which data can travel. The rate of speed is measured in millions of bits per second (approximate).

Message switching
A system in which the pathway for the message is determined dynamically as the data is transmitted from one holding tank to another.

Metropolitan area network (MAN)
A network covering an area larger than a local area network. A wide area network that covers a metropolitan area. Usually, an interconnection of two or more local area networks.

MF
More fragments to follow.

MH
Medium-haul; a classification of video performance under RS-25OB/C. Higher performance than long-haul and lower performance than short-haul.

MHz
MegaHertz; one million Hertz (cycles per second).

Microbending
Mechanical stress on a fiber may introduce local discontinuities called microbending. This results in light leaking from the core to the cladding by a process called mode coupling.

Micrometer
One millionth of a meter; abbreviated μm.

Microsecond
One millionth of a second; abbreviated μs.

Microwatt
One millionth of a Watt; abbreviated μW

Microwave

Refers to the part of the radio spectrum above 500 Megahertz (short-wave length) used for point-to-point communications where line-of-sight communication is not possible or necessary. Microwaves do not follow the curvature of the Earth and are not reflected by the ionosphere; they are greatly affected by obstacles.

Microwave relay system

System designed to pick up and retransmit microwave signals. Since microwaves are signals that only travel short distances, it is necessary to retransmit the signals periodically to cover distance required by some applications. The retransmission or relay stations constitute the microwave relay system. Also known as a terrestrial microwave relay.

Milhamp

One thousandth of an Amp.

Millivolt

One thousandth of a volt; abbreviated mV.

Milliwatt

One thousandth of a watt; abbreviated mW.

Misalignment loss

The loss of power resulting from angular misalignment, lateral displacement, and end separation.

mm

Millimeter; one thousandth of a meter.

Modal noise

Modal noise occurs whenever the optical power propagates through mode-selective devices. It is usually only a factor with laser light sources.

Mode

A single electromagnetic wave traveling in a fiber.

Mode coupling

The transfer of energy between modes. In a fiber, mode coupling occurs until equilibrium mode distribution (EMD) is reached.

Mode evolution

The dynamic process a multilongitudinal laser undergoes whereby the changing distribution of power among the modes creates a continuously changing envelope of the laser's spectrum.

Mode field diameter (MFD)

A measure of distribution of optical power intensity across the end face of a single-mode fiber.

Mode filter

A device that removes higher-order modes to simulate equilibrium mode distribution.

Modem (modulator/demodulator)

Devices that convert digital and analog signals. Modems allow computer data (digital) to be transmitted over voice-grade telephone lines (analog).

Mode scrambler

A device that mixes modes to uniform power distribution.

Mode stripper

A device that removes cladding modes.

Modular jack

A female telecommunications interface connector as specified in IEC 603-7 and FCC Part 68 Subpart F. Modular jacks are typically mounted in a fixed location and may have 4, 6, or 8 contact positions. Not all positions need be equipped with contacts.

Modular plug

A male telecommunications interface connector as specified in IEC 603-7 and FCC Part 68 Subpart F. Modular plugs may have 4, 6, or 8 contact positions. Not all positions need be equipped with contacts.

Modulation

The process by which the characteristic of one wave (the carrier) is modified by another wave (the signal). Examples include amplitude modulation (AM), frequency modulation (FM), and pulse-coded modulation (PCM).

Modulation index

In an intensity-based system, the modulation index is a measure of how much the modulation signal affects the light output.

Modulator

The function of a modem to encode a data signal into an analog carrier by modulating the carrier.

MonoChrome

A black and white TV signal.

Monitor

A television that receives its signal directly from a VCR, camera, or separate TV tuner for high-quality picture reproduction. Also a special type of television receiver designed for use with closed-circuit TV equipment.

MOP

Maintenance operation protocol.

MOTIS

Message-oriented text interchange systems.

Moving Pictures Experts Group (MPEG)

A group that is working to establish a standard for compressing and storing motion video and animation in digital form. The acronym can also refer to the standard under development by this group.

Motion Pictures Experts Group1 (MPEG-1)

An international standard for video and audio transmission that covers format type, data rate, and compression technique.

Motion Pictures Experts Group2 (MPEG-2)

An international standard for full-motion video that covers format type, data rate, and compression technique.

MPEG

Motion picture experts group. An international standard for compressing video that provides for high compression ratios. The standard has two recommendations: MPEG-1 compresses lower-resolution images for video conferencing and lower-quality desktop video applications and transmits at around 1.5 Mb/s. MPEG-2 was devised primarily for delivering compressed television for home entertainment and is used at CCIR resolution when bit rates exceed 5.0 Mbits per second, as in hard disk-based applications.

MPOA

Multiprotocol over ATM.

ms

Milliseconds; one thousandth of a second.

MSAU

Multistation access unit.

MTA

Message transfer agent.

MTBF

Mean time between failure. Time after which 50% of the units of interest will have failed.

Multicasting

Ability to send the same message to multiple nodes in a network. This function is connectionless. However, ATM must send the same message to various nodes by forming a multipoint connection to all nodes in the group.

Multilongitudinal mode laser (MML)

An injection laser diode that has a number of longitudinal modes.

Multimedia

(1) An application that communicates to more than one of the human sensory receptors; (2) applications that communicate information by more than one means or cabling media.

Multimode dispersion

Dispersion resulting from the different transit lengths of different propagating modes in a multimode optical fiber. Also called modal dispersion.

Multimode fiber/single-mode fiber (MMF/SMF)

A fiber cable that uses light pulses instead of electricity to carry data. In multimode cable, the light bounces off the cable's walls as it travels down, which causes the signal to weaken sooner and therefore data cannot travel as much distance as with single-mode fiber. In SMF cables, the light travels straight down the cable. The size of the cable/cladding is 62.5/125 micron for MMF and 8/125 micron for SSF.

Multimode laser diode (MMLD)

Synonym for multilongitudinal mode laser.

Multimode optical fiber

An optical fiber that will allow many bound modes to propagate. The fiber may be either a graded-index or step-index fiber. Multimode optical fibers have a much larger core than single-mode fibers.

Multiple reflection noise (MRN)

The fiber optic receiver noise resulting from the interference of delayed signals from two or more reflection points in a fiber optic span. Also known as multipath interference.

Multiple system operator

A company that owns and/or operates more than one cable system.

Multiplexer

A device that allows multiple logical signals to be transmitted simultaneously across a single physical channel.

Multiplexing

The transmission of multiple signals over a single communications line or computer channel. The two common multiplexing techniques are frequency division multiplexing, which separates signals by modulating the data onto different carrier frequencies, and time division multiplexing, which separates signals by interleaving bits one after the other.

Multipoint

A transmission channel that includes several stations.

Multipoint distribution system

A common carrier system that transmits microwave signals short distances within limited areas. It is used in business for facsimile and data transmissions; for consumer purposes, it is used to supply cable or other nonbroadcast programming services to areas not yet wired for cable.

Multi-user telecommunications outlet assembly (MuTOA)

A grouping in one location of several telecommunications/outlet connectors.

MUSE

Multiple sub-nyquist encoder; a high-definition standard developed in Europe that delivers 1,125 lines at 60 frames per second.

Must-carry

The FCC rule requiring cable systems to carry all local broadcast television signals in their markets. Also, the stations carried under the rule, commonly called *must-carries*.

NA mismatch loss

The loss of power at a joint that occurs when the transmitting half has a numerical aperture greater than the NA of the receiving half. The loss occurs when coupling light from a source to fiber, from fiber to fiber, or from fiber to detector.

Nano

One billionth; abbreviated n.

Nanoamp

One billionth of an Amp; abbreviated nA.

Nanometer

One billionth of a meter; abbreviated nm.

Nanosecond

One billionth of a second (10^{-9} seconds); abbreviated ns.

Nanowatt

One billionth of a watt; abbreviated NW.

National Cable Television Association (NCTA)

Organization of cable system owners, operators, manufacturers, and distributors.

National Electric Code (NEC)

A standard governing the use of electrical wire, cable, and fixtures installed in buildings; developed by the NEC Committee of the American National Standards Institute (ANSI), sponsored by the National Fire Protection Association (NFPA), identified by the description ANSL/NFPA 70-1990.

National Institute for Research in Computer Science and Control (INRIA)

A French public-sector scientific and technological institute under the responsibility of the Ministry for Research and the Ministry of Industry.

NBP

Name-binding protocol.

NCP

Network control program.

NCP

NetWare core protocol.

Near-end cross talk (NEXT)

Cross talk measured at the end from which the disturbing signal is transmitted.

Near infrared

The part of the infrared near the visible spectrum, typically 700 nm to 1,500 nm or 2,000 nm; it is not rigidly defined.

Network

A system of connected computers set up to share data, printers, and other devices.

Network driver interface specification (NDIS)

A Microsoft specification for writing hardware-independent drivers at the Data Link layer. The interface is between the hardware-dependent and hardware-independent parts. When transport protocols communicate to the NDIS specification, network cards with NDIS-compliant medium access control drivers can be freely interchanged.

Network interface card (NIC)

A board that provides network communication capabilities to and from a computer. Also network interface unit (NIU). It has a unique logical address for purposes of identification. It's hard-coded on a silicon chip.

Network modem

A modem connected to a local area network (LAN) that is accessible from any workstation on the network.

Network operating system (NOS)

Operating system designed to pass information and communicate between computers. Examples include AppleShare, Novell NetWare, and Windows NT Server.

Network-to-network interface (NNI)

The interface between ATM switches or an ATM switch and an entire switching system. Also called network-to-node interface.

Newtons

Measure of force generally used to specify fiber optic cable strength; abbreviated N.

Nielsen Home Video Index (NHI)

Division of Nielsen's Media Research Group responsible for syndicated and nonsyndicated measurement of cable, pay cable, VCRs, video discs, and other new television technologies.

NLM

NetWare loadable module.

NMC

Multiplexed analog components. A video standard developed by the European community. An enhanced version, HD-MAC, delivers 1,250 lines at 50 frames per second, HDTV quality.

Node

End point of a network connection. Nodes include any device attached to a network such as file servers, printers, or workstations.

Node devices

Any computer or peripheral that is connected to the network.

Noise equivalent power (NEP)

The noise of optical receivers, or of an entire transmission system, is often expressed in terms of noise equivalent optical power.

Noise

Nondata signals that can disrupt clean data communications.

NOS

Network operating system.

NRZ

Non-return to zero; data encoding method.

NRZ-I

Non-return to zero—inverted.

NRZ-L

Non-return to zero—level.

ns

Nanosecond; one billionth of a second.

NTSC

(1) National Television Systems Committee. The organization that formulated the NTSC system; (2) standard used in the U.S. that delivers 525 lines at 60 frames per second.

Numerical aperture (NA)

The light-gathering ability of a fiber; the maximum angle to the fiber axis at which light will be accepted and propagated through the fiber. The measure of the light acceptance angle of an optical fiber. NA = sin x, where x is the acceptance angle. NA is also used to describe the angular spread of light from a central axis, as in exiting a fiber, emitting from a source, or entering a detector.

NVE

Network visible entry.

NVTS

Network virtual terminal service.

OC-x

Optical carrier; a carrier rate specified in the SONET standard.

ONC

Open network computing.

Open data-link interface (ODI)

A Novell network driver standard that provides a way to load multiple protocol stacks into the memory of a computer to support multiple network protocols on one or more network interface cards. Comparable to Microsoft's NDIS.

Open standard interconnect

A seven-layer model defined by ISO for defining a communication network.

Open system interconnection (OSI)

A reference model that has been defined by ISO as a standard for worldwide communications. It defines a framework for implementing protocols in seven layers. Control is passed from one layer to the next, starting at the Application layer in one station, proceeding to the bottom layer, over the channel to the next station and back up the hierarchy.

Optical amplifier

A device that amplifies an input optical signal without converting it into electrical form. The best developed are optical fibers doped with the rare earth element erbium.

Optical BandpaSS

The range of optical wavelengths that can be transmitted through a component.

Optical carrier *n* (OC-*n*)

Optical signal standards. The *n* indicates the level where the respective data rate is exactly n times the first level OC-1. OC-1 has a data rate of 51.84 Mbps. OC-3 is 3 times that rate, or 155.52 Mbps.

Optical channel

An optical wavelength band for WDM optical communications.

Optical channel spacing

The wavelength separation between adjacent WDM channels.

Optical channel width

The optical wavelength range of a channel.

Optical continuous wave reflectometer (OCWR)

An instrument used to characterize a fiber optic link wherein an unmodulated signal is transmitted through the link, and the resulting light scattered and reflected back to the input is measured. Useful in estimating component reflectance and link optical return loss.

Optical directional coupler (ODC)

A component used to combine and separate optical power.

Optical fall time

The time interval for the falling edge of an optical pulse to transition from 90% to 10% of the pulse amplitude. Alternatively, values of 80% and 20% may be used.

Optical fiber

A glass or plastic fiber that has the ability to guide light along its axis.

Optical isolator

A component used to block out reflected and unwanted light. Used in laser modules, for example. Also called an isolator.

Optical link loss budget

The range of optical loss over which a fiber optic link will operate and meet all specifications. The loss is relative to the transmitter output power.

Optical loss test set (OLTS)

A source and power meter combined to measure attenuation.

Optical path power penalty

The additional loss budget required to account for degradations due to reflections, and the combined effects of dispersion resulting from inter-symbol interference, mode-partition noise, and laser chirp.

Optical power meter

An instrument that measures the amount of optical power present at the end of a fiber or cable.

Optical return loss (ORL)

The ratio (expressed in units of dB) of optical power reflected by a component or an assembly to the optical power incident on a component port when that component or assembly is introduced into a link or system.

Optical rise time

The time interval for the rising edge of an optical pulse to transition from 10% to 90% of the pulse amplitude. Alternatively, values of 20% and 80% may be used.

Optical time domain reflectometer (OTDR)

An instrument that locates faults in optical fibers or infers attenuation by backscattered light measurements.

Optical waveguide

Another name for optical fiber.

Outlet/connector, telecommunications

A connecting device in the work area on which horizontal cable terminates.

Outlet, telecommunications

A fixed connecting device where the horizontal cable terminates. The telecommunications outlet provides the interface to the work area cabling. Sometimes referred to as a telecommunications outlet/connector.

Overbuilds

Competing cable systems covering the same geographic area.

PAC

Data packet.

Packet

A collection of data into a form that is transmitted as a discrete unit over a network communication channel.

Packet assembler/disassembler (PAD)

Required for packet-switched networks. A hardware/software device that provides access to an X.25 network.

Packet switching

The direction of data along pathways dynamically on a packet-by-packet basis. Data is reassembled from packets at the receiver.

PAL

Phase alternation line. A composite color standard used in many parts of the world for TV broadcast. The phase alternation makes the signal relatively immune to certain distortions (compared to NTSC). Delivers 625 lines at 50 frames per second. PAL-plus is an enhanced-definition version.

PAP

Printer access protocol (packet-level procedure). A protocol for the transfer of packets between an X.25 DTE and an X.25 DCE.

PAR

Project authorization request.

Parity bit

A special bit used in error checking.

Passive branching device

A device which divides an optical input into two or more optical outputs.

Patch cord

A length of cable with connectors on one or both ends used to join telecommunications links at a cross-connect.

Patch panel

Connecting hardware that typically provides means to connect horizontal or backbone cables to an arrangement of fixed connectors that may be accessed using patch cords or equipment cords to form cross-connections or interconnections.

Pathway

A facility (conduit) for the placement and protection of telecommunications cables. Same as raceway or ducting.

Payload type identifier (PTI)

A 3-bit descriptor found in ATM cell headers, indicating what type of payload the cell contains. Payload types include user and management cells.

PC

Physical contact. Refers to an optical connector that allows the fiber ends to physically touch. Used to minimize back reflection and insertion loss.

PDN

Public data network.

PDU

Protocol data unit.

Peak cell rate (PCR)

A type of ATM traffic flow. The maximum rate at which cells can be transmitted, defined by the minimum possible space between two cells.

Peak power output

The output power averaged over that cycle of an electromagnetic wave having the maximum peak value that can occur under any combination of signals transmitted.

Peer-to-peer

Describes a network environment where there is no central server for all clients, rather, all devices may act as server or client. LANtastic is a common peer-to-peer NOS.

Peer-to-peer network

A network in which resources and files are shared without a centralized management source.

PEP

Packet exchange protocol.

Peripheral component interconnect (PCI)

A type of computer bus.

Peripheral device

A machine that performs specific tasks for a computer, such as telecommunications (a modem) or printing.

Permanent virtual circuit (PVC)

A logical (rather than physical) connection between end points, established by an administrator, which stays intact until manually torn down.

PFM

Pulse-frequency modulation. Also referred to as square wave FM.

Phase constant

The imaginary part of the axial propagation constant for a particular mode, usually expressed in radians per unit length.

Phase modulation

The encoding of data into a carrier signal by altering the carrier's phasing.

Phase noise

Rapid, short-term, random fluctuations in the phase of a wave caused by time domain instabilities in an oscillator.

Photoconductive

Losing an electrical charge on exposure to light.

Photodetector

An optoelectronic transducer such as a PIN photodiode or avalanche photodiode.

Photodiode

A semiconductor device that converts light to electrical current.

Photon

A quantum of electromagnetic energy. A particle of light.

Photonic

A term coined for devices that work using photons, analogous to "electronic" for devices working with electrons.

Photovoltaic

Providing an electric current under the influence of light or similar radiation.

Physical layer

Layer 1 of the OSI model. Defines the functional characteristics for passing data bits onto and receiving them from the connecting medium.

Physical layer (PHY)

The layer below the ATM layer in the Protocol Reference Model that passes data from the medium to the ATM layer and vice versa. Also refers to OSI Layer 1.

Physical (layer) media dependent (PMD)

Refers to the part of the NIC design that has to interface with (and is therefore dependent on) the chosen transmission medium (MMF, UTP).

Physical Topology

The physical layout of the network; how the cables are arranged; and how the computers are connected.

Pico

One trillionth; abbreviated P.

Picoamp

One trillionth of an amp; abbreviated PA.

PINFET

PIN detector plus an FET amplifier. Offers superior performance over a PIN alone.

Plain old telephone service (POTS)

The analog telephone service that runs over copper wires and is based on the original Bell telephone system.

Planer waveguide

A waveguide fabricated in a flat material such as thin film.

Pigtail

A short optical fiber permanently attached to a source, detector, or other fiber optic device.

Plastic clad silica (PCS)

Also called hard clad silica (HCS); a step-index fiber with a glass core and plastic or polymer cladding instead of glass.

Plastic fiber

An optical fiber having a plastic core and plastic cladding.

Plenum

A compartment or chamber to which one or more air ducts are connected and that forms part of the air distribution system.

Plenum cable

A cable whose flammability and smoke characteristics allow it to be routed in a plenum area without being enclosed in a conduit.

PLP

Packet level protocol.

Point-to-point

A direct link between two objects in a network.

Point-to-point transmission

Transmission between two designated stations.

Polarization

The direction of the electric field in the light wave.

Polarization maintaining fiber

Fiber that maintains the polarization of light that enters it.

Polarization mode dispersion (PMD)

Polarization mode dispersion is an inherent property of all optical media. It is caused by the difference in the propagation velocities of light in the orthogonal principal polarization states of the transmission medium. The net effect is that if an optical pulse contains both polarization components, then the different polarization components will travel at different speeds and arrive at different times, smearing the received optical signal.

Port

Hardware entity at each end of the link.

Ports

A connection point for a cable.

POTS

Plain old telephone system.

p-p

Peak-to-peak; a peak-to-peak value is the algebraic difference between extreme values of a varying quantity.

PPM

Pulse-position modulation; a method of encoding data.

Preform

The glass rod from which optical fiber is drawn.

Presentation layer

Layer 6 of the OSI model. Negotiates and manages the way data is represented and encoded.

Private branch exchange (PBX)

A private switching system usually serving an organization, such as a business, located on the customer's premises. It switches calls both inside a building or premises and outside to the telephone network, and can sometimes provide access to a computer from a data terminal.

Private network-to-network interface (P-NNI)

The interface between two ATM switches or between an ATM switch and an entire switching system in a private network.

Profile dispersion

Dispersion attributed to the variation of refractive index contrast with wavelength.

Propagation delay

The amount of time that passes between when a signal is transmitted and when it is received at the opposite end of a cable or cabling.

Protocol
A formal description of a set of rules and conventions that govern how devices on a network exchange information.

Protocol data unit (PDU)
A generic term for the format used to send information in a communications protocol, typically a packet with its headers and trailers.

Ps
Picosecond; one trillionth of a second.

Pulse
A current or voltage that changes abruptly from one value to another and back to the original value in a finite length of time. Used to describe one particular variation in a series of wave motions.

Pulse-code modulation (PCM)
A technique in which an analog signal, such as a voice, is converted into a digital signal by sampling the signal's amplitude and expressing the different amplitudes as a binary number. The sampling rate must be at least twice the highest frequency in the signal.

Pulse dispersion
The spreading out of pulses as they travel along an optical fiber.

Pulse spreading
The dispersion of an optical signal as it propagates through an optical fiber.

Punch down
A method for securing wire to a quick clip in which the insulated wire is placed in the terminal groove and pushed down with a special tool. As the wire is seated, the terminal displaces the wire insulation to make an electrical connection. The punch down operation may also trim the wire as it terminates. Also called cut down.

PW
Picowatt; one trillionth of a watt.

Quality of Service (QoS)
A set of communication characteristics required by an application such as cell loss ratio, cell transfer delay, and cell delay variations.

Quantum Efficiency

In a photodiode, the ratio of primary carriers (electron-hole pairs) created to incident photons. A quantum efficiency of 70% means 7 out of 10 incident photons create a carrier.

Quaternary signal

A digital signal having four significant conditions.

Quick clip

An electrical contact used to provide an insulation displacement connection to telecommunications cables.

Radiation-hardened fiber

An optical fiber made with core and cladding materials that are designed to recover their intrinsic value of attenuation coefficient, within an acceptable time period, after exposure to a radiation pulse.

Radiometer

An instrument, distinct from a photometer, to measure power (watts) of electromagnetic radiation.

Radiometry

The science of radiation measurement.

RAID (redundant array of inexpensive disks)

A configuration of multiple disks designed to preserve data after a disk casualty.

Rayleigh scattering

The scattering of light that results from small inhomogeneities of material density or composition.

RAYS

Lines that represent the path taken by light.

Receiver

A terminal device that includes a detector and signal-processing electronics. It functions as an optical-to-electrical converter.

Receiver overload

The maximum acceptable value of average received power for an acceptable BER or performance.

Receiver sensitivity

The minimum acceptable value of received power needed to achieve an acceptable BER or performance. It takes into account power penalties caused by use of a transmitter with worst-case values of extinction ratio, jitter, pulse rise and fall times, optical return loss, receiver connector degradations, and measurement tolerances. The receiver sensitivity does not include power penalties associated with dispersion, jitter, or reflections from the optical path; these effects are specified separately in the allocation of maximum optical path penalty. Sensitivity usually takes into account worst-case operating and end-of-life (EOL) conditions.

Recombination
Combination of an electron and a hole in a semiconductor that releases energy, sometimes leading to light emission.

Refractive index gradient
The change in refractive index with distance from the axis of an optical fiber.

Regenerative repeater
A repeater, designed for digital transmission, in which digital signals are amplified, reshaped, retimed, and retransmitted.

Regenerator
Synonym for regenerative repeater.

Repeater
A receiver and transmitter set designed to regenerate attenuated signals. Used to extend operating range.

Request for comment (RFC)
The document series, begun in 1969, which describes the Internet suite of protocols and related experiments. Not all RFCs describe Internet standards, but all Internet standards are written up as RFCs.

Residual loss
The loss of the attenuator at the minimum setting of the attenuator.

Responsivity
The ratio of a photodetector's electrical output to its optical input in Amperes/Watt (A/W).

Retraction
The changing of direction of a wavefront in passing through a boundary between two dissimilar media, or in a graded-index medium where refractive index is a continuous function of position.

Retractive index

A property of optical materials that relates to the speed of light in the material.

Retractive index profile

The description of the value of the refractive index as a function of distance from the optical axis along an optical fiber diameter.

Return loss

Return loss is a measure of the signal reflections occurring along a channel or basic link and is related to various electrical mismatches along the cabling.

Reverse address resolution protocol (RARP)

Protocol by which a TCP/IP workstation determines its own IP address.

RGB

Red, green, and blue; the basic parallel component set in which a signal is used for each primary color; or the related equipment or interconnect formats or standards.

Ribbon cables

Cables in which many fibers are embedded in a plastic material in parallel, forming a flat ribbon-like structure.

RIN

Relative intensity noise. Often used to quantify the noise characteristics of a laser.

Ring

A set of stations wherein information is passed sequentially between stations, each station in turn examining or copying the information, and finally returning it to the originating station.

Ring conductor

A telephony term used to describe one of the two conductors in a cable pair that is used to provide telephone service. This term was originally coined from its position as the second (ring) conductor of a tip-ring-sleeve switchboard plug.

Ring network

A network topology in which terminals are connected in a point-to-point serial fashion in an unbroken circular configuration.

Rise time

The time taken to make a transition from one state to another, usually measured between the 10% and 90% completion points of the transition. Alternatively, the rise time may be specified at the 20% and 80% amplitudes. Shorter or faster rise times require more bandwidth in a transmission channel.

RMON

Remote monitoring.

RMS

Root mean square; technique used to measure AC voltages.

RJ45

Standard connectors used for unshielded twisted-pair cable. Eight-pin connector used for data transmission.

Router

A device that routes information between interconnected networks. It can select the best path to route a message as well as translate information from one network to another. It is similar to a superintelligent bridge.

RSVP

Resource reservation protocol.

Rx

Receive.

RZ

Return to zero. A common means of encoding data that has two information states called "zero" and "one" in which the signal returns to a rest state during a portion of the bit period.

Satellite master antenna television (SMATV)

Whereby a single antenna is used to provide television service for all units in a hotel, apartment house, or other housing complex, except the antenna used is one for satellite signals rather than over-the-air signals.

Satellite receiver

Equipment used to obtain a specific signal.

SC

Subscription channel connector; a push–pull type of optical connector that originated in Japan. Features high packing density, low loss, low back reflection, and low cost.

Scattering

The change of direction of light rays or photons after striking small particles. It may also be regarded as the diffusion of a light beam caused by the inhomogeneity of the transmitting material.

Scrambler

An electronic device usually located in the transmitter used to change a signal so that it may not be viewed on normal television sets unless another electronic device (decoder) is attached to the subscriber's set to unscramble the picture.

Screened twisted pair (ScTP)

A balanced twisted-pair cable surrounded by metallic braid, foil (screen), or both and bound in a single cable sheath.

Segment

Refers to a section of cable on a network. In Ethernet networks, two types of segments are defined. A populated or trunk segment is a network cable that has one or more nodes attached to it. A link segment is a cable that connects a computer to an interconnecting device, such as a repeater or concentrator, or connects an interconnecting device to another interconnecting device.

Segmentation and reassembly (SAR)

Converts between the Adaptation layer and the ATM layer (AAL5 frame to ATM cells).

Server

A computer on a network that services other nodes. Also called a back end or engine.

Session layer

Layer 5 of the OSI model. Provides coordination of the communications in an orderly manner. A logical connection between two network-addressable units (NAUs).

Shielded twisted pair (STP-A)

A cable surrounded by a metallic braid, foil, or both and bound in a single plastic sheath containing balanced twisted-pair conductors that are individually shielded.

Signaling

In ATM terms, the process followed to set up virtual connections. The latest standard is UNI 3.1 signaling, which is a modified version of ITU's Q.2931 protocol.

Significantly viewed

According to the FCC definition, a station is *significantly viewed* in a given county if (1) it is a network affiliate and achieves among noncable households a share of total viewing hours of at least 3%, and a net weekly circulation of at least 25%; or (2) it is an independent station and achieves among noncable households a share of total viewing hours of at least 5%. A station that is significantly viewed becomes *local* for regulatory purposes, that is, it can demand carriage on local cable systems, and the systems are no longer required to delete the duplicate programming of a significantly viewed station at the request of a higher priority (local) station.

Signal carriage

Stations carried by a cable system, including local stations that request carriage, plus stations that are significantly viewed within the community, plus distant signals imported by the system.

Signal importation

Carriage of station signals originating outside the specified zone in which the cable community is located.

Simple network management protocol (SNMP)

A protocol used to gather activity information on a TCP/IP network for monitoring and statistical purposes.

Single-mode optical fiber

An optical fiber that will allow only one mode to propagate; this fiber is typically a step-index fiber.

Sneak current

A low-level current that is of insufficient strength to trigger electrical surge protectors and, therefore, is able to pass through them undetected. These currents may result from contact between communications lines and AC power circuits or from power induction, and may cause equipment damage unless secondary protection is used.

Sneaker net

Refers to a manual method of sharing files in which a file is copied from a computer to a floppy disk, transported to a second computer by a person physically walking (apparently wearing sneakers) to the second computer, and manually transferring the file from floppy disk to the second computer.

Society of Cable Television Engineers (SCTE)
Technical organization for engineers involved in the cable television industry.

Speed of data transfer
The rate at which information travels through a network, usually measured in megabits per second.

Star topology
LAN topology in which each node on a network is connected directly to a central network hub or concentrator.

Star-wired ring
Network topology that connects network devices (such as computers and printers) in a complete circle.

STS-*n*
Synchronous Transport Signal-*n* (see **Optical Carrier-*n***).

Subscriber
A household or business that legally receives and pays for cable and/or pay television service for its own use (not for retransmission).

Subscriber user-to-network interface (SUNI)
Name for the ATM PHY chip manufactured by PMC-Sierra.

Surge
A rapid rise in current or voltage, usually followed by a fall back to a normal level. Also referred to as transient.

Sustained cell rate (SCR)
A type of ATM traffic flow. An average of rates at which cells are transmitted over a certain period of time.

Switched multimegabit data service (SMDS)
A high-speed, packet-switched, datagram-based WAN technology.

Switched virtual circuit (SVC)
A logical (not physical) connection between endpoints established by the ATM network on demand after receiving a connection request from the source, which is transmitted using the UNI signaling protocol (See **PVC**).

Synchronous digital hierarchy (SDH)

International standard for optical digital transmission at hierarchical rates from 155 Mbps to 2.5 Gbps and beyond.

Synchronous optical network (SONET)

A U.S. standard for optical digital transmission at hierarchical rates from 155 Mbps to 2.5 Gbps and beyond.

T1/T3

T1 is a 1.544 Mbps multichannel digital transmission system for voice or data provided by long-distance carriers. T3 is similar but operates at 44.736 Mbps. Also referred to as DS1 and DS3 (data service).

TAXI

A standardized 100 Mbps fiber physical interface for ATM.

TCP

Transmission control protocol (see **IP**).

Telecommunications

Any transmission, emission, or reception of signs, signals, writings, images, sounds, or information of any nature by cable, radio, visual, optical, or other electromagnetic systems.

Telecommunications closet (TC)

An enclosed space for housing telecommunications equipment, cable terminations, and cross-connect cabling used to serve work areas located on the same floor. The telecommunications closet is the typical location of the horizontal cross-connect and is considered distinct from an equipment room because it is considered to be a floor-serving (as opposed to building- or campus-serving) facility.

Telecommunications Industry Association (TIA)

An organization that sets standards for cabling, pathways, spaces, grounding, bonding, administration, field testing, and other aspects of the telecommunications industry.

Teletext

Alphanumeric material transmitted to and displayed on television sets equipped with suitable capabilities.

Terminator

A device that provides electrical resistance at the end of a transmission line. Its function is to absorb signals on the line, thereby keeping them from bouncing back and being received again by the network.

Tiering

Supplying subscribers to a cable system with one or more programming services beyond the basic offerings at an extra charge. Each additional price increment, or the service(s) offered thereof, is called a tier.

Tip conductor

A telephony term used to describe the conductor of a pair that is grounded at the central office when the line is idle. This term was originally coined from its position as the first (tip) conductor of a tip-ring-sleeve switchboard plug.

Token

A special packet that contains data and acts as a messenger or carrier between each computer and device on a ring topology. Each computer must wait for the messenger to stop at its node before it can send data over the network.

Token ring

A network protocol developed by IBM in which computers access the network through token passing. Usually uses a star-wired ring topology.

Topology

The physical or logical layout of links and nodes in a network. These include star, ring, and bus configurations.

Transceiver (transmitter/receiver)

A device that receives and sends signals over a medium. In networks, it is generally used to allow for the connection between two different types of cable connectors, such as AUI and RJ45.

Transfer impedance

A measure (in ?) of shield effectiveness.

Transition point (TP)

A location in the horizontal cabling subsystem where flat undercarpet cabling connects to round cabling.

Transmission lines

Specifically designed cables for use in carrying radio or television signals from one point to another.

Transport layer

Layer 4 of the OSI model. Responsible for end-to-end validity and integrity of the transmission.

Tree topology

LAN topology similar to linear bus topology, except that tree networks can contain branches with multiple nodes.

Trunk

A communication line between two switching systems. The term "switching systems" typically includes equipment in a central office (the telephone company) and PBXs. A tie trunk connects PBXs. Central office trunks connect a PBX to the switching system at the central office.

Twisted pair

Network cabling that consists of four pairs of wires that are manufactured with the wires twisted to certain specifications. Available in shielded and unshielded versions.

Twisted-pair physical media dependent (TP-PMD)

Technology under review by the ANSI X3T9.5 working group that allows 100 Mb/s transmission over twisted-pair cable. Also referred to as CDDI or TPDDI.

Twisted-pair distributed data interface (TP-DDI)

Trademark of 3COM Corporation (See **Twisted-pair physical media dependent**).

Two-way cable

Cable television system capable of transmitting signals in both directions along a cable. FCC requires this capability in cable systems within major television markets that commenced operations after March 1972, in systems outside major markets that commenced after March 1977, and in all other systems by June 1986. See **Interactive**.

Tx

Transmit.

Universal test and operations physical interface for ATM (UTOPIA)

This specification defines a common hardware interface between the ATM layer performing segmentation and reassembly and the ATM Physical layer. This allows a single ATM layer to support multiple Physical layer standards such as the 100 Mbps TAXI and SONET/OC-n as well as future standards.

Unshielded twisted pair (UTP)

A cable with multiple pairs of twisted insulated copper conductors bound in a single sheath.

Unshielded twisted pair/shielded twisted pair (UTP/STP)

Two types of copper cable. STP has insulating material wrapped around the twisted wires for immunity to electrical magnetic interference. UTP does not and is subject to electrical noise and interference.

Uplink

Part of a satellite communications system from which signals are transmitted from Earth to satellite.

Upstream

Signals traveling from a subscriber's home to a primary distribution point (headend). Used in two-way communication.

User-network interface (UNI)

The interface between a user's device and an ATM switch, defined as the Physical, ATM, and higher (signaling) layer.

Variable bit rate (VBR)

A type of ATM traffic flow. As opposed to constant bit rate, VBR traffic may be bursty.

VDSL (very-high-data-rate digital subscriber line)

One of four DSL technologies. VDSL delivers 13 Mbps to 52 Mbps downstream and 1.5 Mbps to 2.3 Mbps upstream over a single twisted copper pair. The operating range of VDSL is limited to 1,000 to 4,500 feet. Compare with ADSL, HDSL, and SDSL.

Videotex

Systems for over-the-air or wired distribution of textual and/or graphical information. This term is usually used to include both teletext and view-data systems.

Viewdata

A service allowing two-way communications between home terminals and a central computer. May operate over a cable or via a telephone to provide various types of informational services to the home TV screen.

Virtual channel connection (VCC)

A concatenation of virtual channel links between two endpoints where higher layer protocols are accessed. By definition, ATM cell sequence must be preserved over a VCC.

Virtual channel identifier/virtual path identifier (VCI/VPI)

ATM addressing information. An identifying value found in the header of each ATM cell.

Virtual LAN (VLAN)

A logical collection of member endpoints and network devices grouped together in a secure, autonomous domain. Membership in a VLAN is not restricted by physical location. VLANs in ATM networks may be built on emulated LANs.

Virtual path connection (VPC)

A concatenation of virtual path links between two points. Several VCCs may be bundled into one VPC.

WAN (wide area network)

A network connecting computers within very large areas, such as states, countries, and the world.

Webbed conductors

The manufacturing process that physically binds the conductor insulation of the wire pairs of an unshielded twisted-pair cable.

Women in Cable (WIC)

Organization devoted to the interests of women in the cable industry.

Work area

The area where horizontal cabling is connected to the work area equipment by means of a telecommunication outlet. A station/desk that is served by a telecommunications outlet. Sometimes referred to as a workstation.

Work area cable

A cable assembly used to connect equipment to the telecommunications outlet in the work area. Work area cables are considered to be outside the scope of cabling standards.

Workgroup

A collection of workstations and servers on a LAN that are designated to communicate and exchange data with one another.

Workstation

A computer connected to a network at which users interact with software stored on the network.

Index

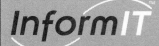

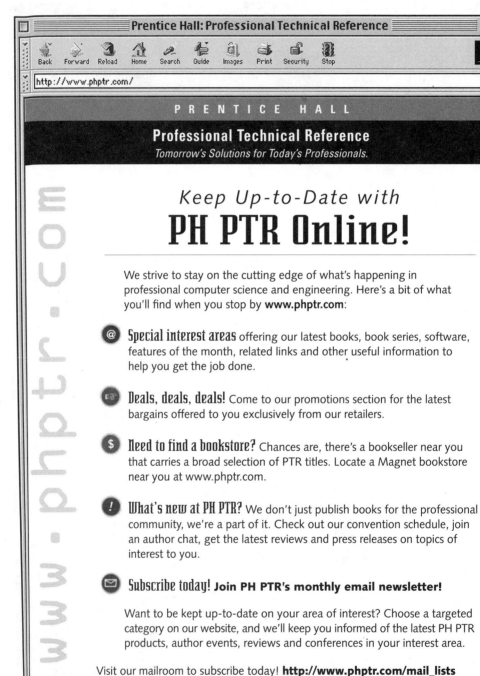